South Africa
Lesotho & Swaziland

Mary Fitzpatrick

Kate Armstrong, Becca Blond, Michael Kohn, Simon Richmond, Al Simmonds

KGALAGADI TRANSFRONTIER PARK (p537)
Revel in the Kalahari's haunting vistas and vastness

Central Kalahari Game Reserve

Tropic of Capricorn

Gobabis

WINDHOEK

BOTSWANA

Mariental

Kanye

Kgalagadi Transfrontier Park

Tshabong

NORTH-WEST PROVINCE

Kalahari

Vryburg

N14

Keetmanshoop

Rietfontein

Hotazel

NAMAQUALAND (p543)
Visit Namaqualand in springtime, when the rugged landscapes soften under an explosion of wildflowers

Noenieput

Kuruman

NAMIBIA

Fish River Canyon National Park

Richtersveld National Park

B1 B3

Augrabies Falls National Park

Upington

SOUTH AFRICA

Vaal River

Kimberley

Orange River

Alexander Bay

Noordoewer

Port Nolloth

Springbok

N10

Prieska

Orange River

N12

De Aar

ATLANTIC OCEAN

NAMAQUALAND

NORTHERN CAPE

N7

Bitterfontein

Carnarvon

Middelburg

WINELANDS (p169)
Treat yourself to fine wining and dining in the verdant valleys around Franschhoek, Paarl and Stellenbosch

Calvinia

Karoo National Park

Graaff-Reinet

St Helena Bay

Cederberg Wilderness Area

Beaufort West

Karoo Nature Reserve

Saldanha

Olifants River

Ceres

WESTERN CAPE

Uitenhage

N1

WN (p164)
...opolitan chic
...ld's most
...get pelted
...f Good
...ve

Paarl

Worcester

Montagu

Oudtshoorn

Wilderness National Park

Tsitsikamma National Park

CAPE TOWN

Stellenbosch

Swellendam

George

Knysna

Mossel Bay

Plettenberg Bay

Jeffrey's Bay

Cape St Franc

Table Mountain National Park

De Hoop Nature Reserve

N2

Cape of Good Hope

False Bay

Hermanus

Bredasdorp

Cape Agulhas

THE KAROO (p264)
Marvel in the Karoo's space and silence, or visit Graaff-Reinet, one of South Africa's most charming towns

SOUTHERN COAST (p186)
Explore South Africa's coastline, from Hermanus with its whales to the rivers and ravines of Tsitsikamma National Park

18°E   20°E   22°E   24°E

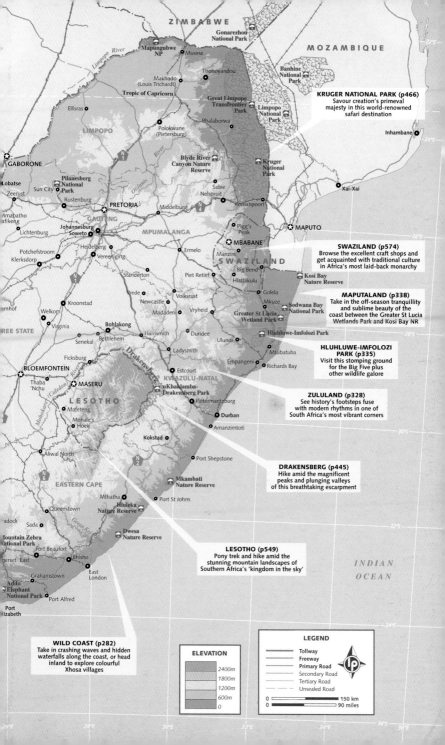

ZIMBABWE

Gonarezhou
National Park

MOZAMBIQUE

Mapungubwe
NP

Musina

Banhine
National
Park

Thohoyandou

Makhado
(Louis Trichardt)

Tropic of Capricorn

KRUGER NATIONAL PARK (p466)
Savour creation's primeval
majesty in this world-renowned
safari destination

Great Limpopo
Transfrontier
Park

Limpopo
National
Park

Bhalaborwa

Inhambane

Ellisras

LIMPOPO

Polokwane
(Pietersburg)

Blyde River
Canyon Nature
Reserve

Kruger
National
Park

GABORONE

Xai-Xai

Lobatse

Pilanesberg
National
Park

Sun City

Zeerust

Rustenburg

Sabie
Nelspruit

Komatipoort

Amabatho
afikeng

Lichtenburg

Johannesburg
Soweto

PRETORIA

Middelburg

GAUTENG

MPUMALANGA

Pigg's
Peak

MAPUTO

Potchefstroom

Heidelberg

Ermelo

MBABANE

SWAZILAND (p574)
Browse the excellent craft shops and
get acquainted with traditional culture
in Africa's most laid-back monarchy

Klerksdorp

Vereeniging

Manzini

SWAZILAND

Big Bend

Hlathikulu

Kosi Bay
Nature Reserve

Standerton

Piet Retief

Golela

MAPUTALAND (p338)
Take in the off-season tranquillity
and sublime beauty of the
coast between the Greater St Lucia
Wetlands Park and Kosi Bay NR

emhof

Welkom

Kroonstad

Vrede

Newcastle

Volksrust

Madaden

Vryheid

Mkuze

Sodwana Bay
National Park

REE STATE

Virginia

Bohlakong

Harrismith

Dundee

Greater St Lucia
Wetland Park

Senekal

Bethlehem

Ladysmith

Ulundi

Hluhluwe-Imfolozi Park

**HLUHLUWE-IMFOLOZI
PARK (p335)**
Visit this stomping ground
for the Big Five plus
other wildlife galore

BLOEMFONTEIN

Ficksburg

Estcourt

Mtubatuba

Thaba
'Nchu

MASERU

KWAZULU-NATAL

Empangeni

Richards Bay

uKhahlamba-
Drakensberg Park

ZULULAND (p328)
See history's footsteps fuse
with modern rhythms in one of
South Africa's most vibrant corners

LESOTHO

Mafeteng

Pietermaritzburg

Mohale's
Hoek

Durban

Kokstad

Amanzimtoti

Aliwal North

DRAKENSBERG (p445)
Hike amid the magnificent
peaks and plunging valleys
of this breathtaking escarpment

Port Shepstone

EASTERN CAPE

Mkambati
Nature Reserve

radock

Sada

Mthatha

Hluleka
Nature Reserve

Port St Johns

ountain Zebra
ational Park

Dwesa
Nature Reserve

LESOTHO (p549)
Pony trek and hike amid the
stunning mountain landscapes of
Southern Africa's 'kingdom in the sky'

INDIAN
OCEAN

Queenstown

merset East

Fort Beaufort

Bhisho

Grahamstown

East
London

Addo
Elephant
National Park

Port Alfred

Port
lizabeth

WILD COAST (p282)
Take in crashing waves and hidden
waterfalls along the coast, or head
inland to explore colourful
Xhosa villages

ELEVATION

2400m
1800m
1200m
600m
0

LEGEND

Tollway
Freeway
Primary Road
Secondary Road
Tertiary Road
Unsealed Road

0   150 km
0   90 miles

Destination South Africa, Lesotho & Swaziland

It's no wonder that South Africa draws more visitors than anywhere else in sub-Saharan Africa. World-class wildlife-watching, cosmopolitan cities, stunning natural panoramas and vibrant cultures make the country appealing to almost every taste and budget. Within the space of a day, you can journey from vineyard-clad hillsides in the Western Cape to the vast open spaces of the Kalahari, from Cape Town's waterfront chic to isolated Zulu villages, from elephant spotting in Kruger National Park to the pounding surf and sublime seascapes of the coast. And, unlike many other areas of the continent, it's possible to do all this while still enjoying Western amenities and, for the most part, getting by using only English. Topping off the attractions is the chance to take an easy detour to Lesotho – a hiking and pony-trekking paradise – or to nearby Swaziland, with its laid-back pace and vibrant traditional culture.

Yet, while it's easy to travel around South Africa focusing on the glitz and first-world infrastructure, you'll only get below the surface by seeking out the country's other face – most visible in the sprawling townships where far too many people live stalked by the shadows of hunger, poverty and one of the highest HIV/AIDS infection rates in the world. Behind its incredible natural beauty, South Africa is the stage for the daily drama of one of the world's greatest experiments in racial harmony. The intensity of this drama surrounds you wherever you go, and will likely be one of the most fascinating and challenging aspects of your travels. And, there's never been a better time to experience this than now, as the colours of the 'rainbow nation' finally begin to fuse.

Tradition & Culture

See local arts and crafts unmasked in Johannesburg (p415)

OTHER HIGHLIGHTS

- Watch weavers create beautiful tapestries at Teyateyaneng (p560), Lesotho
- Celebrate the rich culture of the Zulu people at a Zulu festival (p332) in KwaZulu-Natal

Witness local customs at a living cultural village (p583), Swaziland

Guests celebrate at a traditional wedding at Regina Mundi Church (p424), Soweto

Great Outdoors & Coastal Odysseys

LUKE HUNTER

Count the different shades of red at Kgalagadi Transfrontier Park (p537), Northern Cape

Look out for a kokerboom (quiver tree), Augrabies Falls National Park (p541), Northern Cape

ARIADNE VAN ZANDBERGEN

OTHER HIGHLIGHTS

- Get up close and personal with the turtles and moray eels at Sodwana Bay (p343), KwaZulu-Natal
- Marvel at the kaleidoscope of colour as daisies, perennial herbs, aloes, lilies and a host of other flowers spring to life in Namaqu National Park (p547), Northern Cape

Take advantage of the beach life along Cape Town's Atlantic Coast (p118)

NIC BOTH

DI JONES

Gaze out over spectacular landscapes of canyons, rivers and gorges in Lesotho (p550)

PAUL KENNEDY

Tame the tubes at Jeffrey's Bay (p245), Eastern Cape

Wake up to a majestic sunrise at Kruger National Park (p466)

KARL LEHMANN

Urban Contrasts

See Cape Town's impressive International Convention Centre (p155)

OTHER HIGHLIGHTS

- Visit the creatively designed Northern Cape Legislature Building (p529), with its underemphasised angles and inviting curves
- Tour the stately houses at Barberton (p462), in Mpumalanga and catch a glimpse into the town's early history

Make friends with a brightly-dressed rickshaw driver (p308) on Durban's beachfront

RICHARD I'ANSON

Learn about township life on a tour (p405) in Johannesburg

BRENT STIRTON/GETTY IMAG

Explore Cape Town's colourful Bo-Kaap area (p140)

Embrace big and brash Johannesburg (p396)

Join the locals for a late-night snack in Long Street (p109), Cape Town

Wildlife Watching

ARIADNE VAN ZANDBERGEN

Go ape over the Chacma baboons at the Cape of Good Hope Nature Reserve (p164)

OTHER HIGHLIGHTS

- See how many of the 615 bird species you can spot at Makhado (Louis Trichardt; p498), Limpopo
- Sleep under the stars on a wilderness trail in Hluhluwe-Imfolozi Park (p335), KwaZulu-Natal

TIM ROCK

Pluck up the courage and dive with the sharks in Hermanus (p189), Western Cape

CHRISTER FREDRIKSSON

Enjoy the action at Kgalagadi Transfrontier Park (p537), Northern Cape

Be charmed by the lions at Phinda Resource Reserve (p346), KwaZulu-Natal

LUKE HUNTER

Indolence & Indulgences

Dine in style in Cape Town (p147)

ARIADNE VAN ZANDBERGEN

OTHER HIGHLIGHTS

- While away a few hours browsing the boutiques and art galleries in Clarens (p387), Free State
- Lush about in five-star comfort at one of the private wildlife reserves (p485) in Kruger National Park

ARIADNE VAN ZANDBERGEN

Chill out in relaxing accommodation in Cape Town (p143)

Sip, swirl and spit your way around the wineries of Stellenbosch (p173), Western Cape

CHRISTER FREDRIKSSON

Freedom Trail

DAVE HOGAN/GETTY IMAGES

Listen as ex-prisoners share their stories on Robben Island (p107), Cape Town

OTHER HIGHLIGHTS

- Head to Pretoria's Freedom Park (p432) to remember those who sacrificed their lives in the name of freedom
- Count the bullet holes in the Regina Mundi Church (p424), Soweto – used as a community meeting place during the apartheid struggle

PAUL GILHAM/GETTY IMAGES

See where Nelson Mandela spent two decades imprisoned on Robben Island (p107), Cape Town

PER-ANDERS PETTERSSON/GETTY IMAGES

Nooses, representing political prisoners hanged during the apartheid area, at the Apartheid Museum (p404), Johannesburg

Check out the exhibits at the Apartheid Museum (p404), Johannesburg

ALEXANDER JOE/GETTY IMAGES

Contents

Regional Map Contents

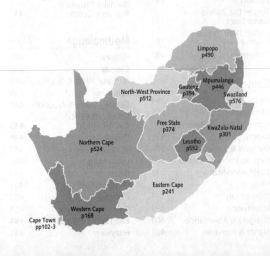

Limpopo p490
Mpumalanga p446
Gauteng p394
North-West Province p512
Swaziland p576
Free State p374
KwaZulu-Natal p301
Northern Cape p524
Lesotho p552
Eastern Cape p241
Western Cape p168
Cape Town pp102-3

The Authors

MARY FITZPATRICK   Coordinating Author

Mary first glimpsed the Johannesburg skyline over a decade ago, standing on a rise east of the city. Since then, she's returned to South Africa dozens of times, including numerous forays into Lesotho and Swaziland. Among her most cherished moments: witnessing South Africa's first multiracial elections; getting driven out of Cape of Good Hope Nature Reserve in a police paddy wagon on Christmas Eve; hiking in Lesotho; and being on the receiving end of the wonderful hospitality of residents of the region. She works as a full-time travel writer from her home base in Cairo – on the northern end of the African continent, but at least in the same time zone as South Africa.

My Favourite Trip

Time permitting, I'd try to fit as many of the following into my next Southern Africa journey: hiking at Cape of Good Hope Nature Reserve (p164); trekking around the Lesotho highlands (p564) near Oxbow; spending an afternoon perched above one of the valleys of the Golden Gate Highlands National Park (p385), taking in the silence and the scenery; a visit to Kgalagadi Transfrontier park (p537); and several weeks in KwaZulu-Natal's parks, especially Mkhuze Game Reserve (p345) and Hluhluwe-Imfolozi Park (p335). Johannesburg (p396) is my favourite city, and Swaziland (p574) the most enjoyable detour.

KATE ARMSTRONG   KwaZulu-Natal, Lesotho, Swaziland

Kate was bitten by the African bug when she lived and worked in Mozambique, and on her subsequent travels around East Africa. She jumped at the chance to explore new territory for this Lonely Planet edition. While she successfully avoided malarial mosquitoes, she was less able to escape an obsession with Zulu culture, giraffes and the overwhelming hospitality of the local people (not to mention several flat tyres along the way). When Kate's not eating, hiking and dancing her way around parts of Africa, Europe and South America, her itchy feet are grounded in Sydney where she writes travel articles and children's educational books.

LONELY PLANET AUTHORS

Why is our travel information the best in the world? It's simple: our authors are independent, dedicated travellers. They don't research using just the Internet or phone, and they don't take freebies in exchange for positive coverage. They travel widely, to all the popular spots and off the beaten track. They personally visit thousands of hotels, restaurants, cafés, bars, galleries, palaces, museums and more – and they take pride in getting all the details right, and telling it how it is. For more, see the authors section on www.lonelyplanet.com.

BECCA BLOND   Free State, North-West Province, Northern Cape

Becca fell hard for Africa while studying in Zimbabwe during her university days, and swore she'd make it back at least once every other year. With six trips to southern and eastern portions of the continent in the last eight years, including three for Lonely Planet – twice to research this guide and once to update portions of *Africa on a Shoestring* – she figures she's on target. When she's not traipsing around the globe doing the travel-writing thing, Becca lives in Boulder, Colorado with her boyfriend, Aaron, a massive bulldog named Duke and an ever-growing herd of large wooden giraffes. She contemplates packing up and moving to Cape Town often.

MICHAEL KOHN   Mpumalanga, Kruger National Park, Limpopo

Michael first visited South Africa back in 1994 during his student days. Studying, however, ended up taking a back seat to mugs of beer at the Waterfront and the chance to jump out of an airplane over Stellenbosch. He's never quite gotten his feet back on the ground and has since worked his way around the world as a journalist and travel writer. Michael has worked on half a dozen other Lonely Planet titles. When he comes to a stop it's usually back home in northern California. For this edition, Michael also wrote the Wild Coast section of the Eastern Cape chapter.

SIMON RICHMOND   Cape Town

Simon first visited Cape Town in 2001 to research Lonely Planet's *South Africa, Lesotho & Swaziland* guide and the *Cape Town* guide. He's since returned twice to work on new editions of each book. He's explored practically every corner of the city from Cape Point to Durbanville, and Clifton to Khayelitsha, staying in all kinds of accommodation from shack to penthouse. There are very few restaurants, cafés or bars that have escaped his attention and if there's an activity going, you can bet he's done it, including sandboarding and paragliding off Lion's Head. His £250 excess baggage bill after this trip suggests he took the shopping research very seriously.

AL SIMMONDS   Western Cape, Eastern Cape, Gauteng

Al Simmonds grew up in Johannesburg and lived in Cape Town before leaving South Africa in 1998 to live in London. There he worked as a travel journalist and, determined to know more about whence he had come, made sure at least one assignment a year covered South Africa. When the pull of the freelance life became overwhelming, he left to live in New York and Amsterdam, then hit Europe, the Far East and Central America, before returning to his first love, Cape Town, where he now resides. He's been everywhere in South Africa except the northern reaches of the Northern Cape. Next time…

CONTRIBUTING AUTHOR

Jane Cornwell wrote the Music Chapter (p59). Jane is an Australian-born, London-based journalist writing on music for publications including the *Evening Standard*, *Guardian*, *Songlines* and *Jazzwise*. Her articles also appear regularly in the *Australian* newspaper. She holds a postgraduate honours degree in anthropology and has worked for the Institute of Contemporary Arts; Real World Records; World of Music, Arts and Dance (Womad); and Sydney's Ignite Festival.

Getting Started

South Africa's infrastructure is well-developed, with an excellent network of tarmac roads, ready access to ATMs and the Internet, and an extensive selection of good-value, high-quality accommodation. Except during school holidays (when accommodation in popular areas is invariably booked out), it's possible to visit almost on the spur of the moment. Swaziland and (especially) Lesotho have less-developed infrastructure than South Africa. In Lesotho, for example, only a few major roads are paved, and in both countries, ATM and Internet access are only available at a handful of places in or near the capitals. Yet, both countries are so small and easily navigated that it is usually no problem to sort things out as you go. Wherever you go, however, you'll get more out of your visit with some advance planning. Tourism in all three countries is big business and a much welcomed source of revenue – resulting in a raft of informative tourist offices and a generally high level of tourism awareness throughout the region.

If travelling by public transport, allow plenty of time to wait for connections, especially away from major routes. It's quite popular and easy to journey around South Africa by private car – and this is often the only way to get around when away from the major routes. With luck and advance planning, you can sometimes find good rental deals. Car travel is also easy and reasonably priced in Lesotho and Swaziland, although – and in contrast with South Africa – public transport will take you almost everywhere you could want to go in these countries cheaply and with a minimum of hassle.

WHEN TO GO

See Climate Charts (p607) for more information.

South Africa can be visited comfortably any time. However, depending on what you plan to do, it's worth paying attention to the seasons, which are the reverse of those in the northern hemisphere. Winter (June to September) is cooler, drier and ideal for hiking and outdoor pursuits. Because vegetation is less dense, and thirsty animals congregate around rivers and other permanent water sources, winter is also the best time for wildlife-watching. In the eastern highveld, nights are often crisp and clear, with occasional frosts, so come prepared with a jacket.

Summer (late November to March) brings rain, mists and – in the lowveld, including much of eastern Swaziland – some uncomfortably hot days. Along the Indian Ocean coast, conditions are sultry and tropical, with high humidity. Spectacular summer thunderstorms are common in Swaziland and Lesotho, and in Lesotho flooding sometimes washes out sections of road.

More of a consideration than weather are school holidays. From mid-December to January, waves of vacation-hungry South Africans stream out of the cities, with visitors from Europe and North America adding to the crush. The absolute peak is from Christmas to mid-January, followed by Easter. Accommodation in tourist areas and national parks is heavily booked, and prices can more than double. If you visit Cape Town, the Garden Route or other popular areas during this time, it's essential to book accommodation in advance. On the plus side, the high summer months offer some great festivals, including the Cape Town New Year Karnaval, and Swaziland's Incwala ceremony. See p610 for more information on these, and other festivals.

Spring (mid-September to November) and autumn (April and May) are ideal almost everywhere. Spring is also the best time to see vast expanses of Northern Cape carpeted with wildflowers.

COSTS & MONEY

Travelling in South Africa is not as cheap as in many less-developed African countries. However – and despite the increasing strength of the rand – it usually works out to be less expensive than travelling in Europe or North America, and the quality of facilities and infrastructure is generally high. Among the best deals are national parks and reserves, which offer excellent and accessible wildlife-watching at significantly less cost than you would pay in parts of East Africa.

At the budget level, it's quite possible to get by on about R200 per day with a bit of effort, by camping or staying in hostels or self-catering accommodation, and using public transport.

For midrange travel – where South Africa's best value is to be found – plan on about R400 per person per day, more if you hire a vehicle and less if you stay in self-catering places (many of which are quite comfortable).

Life in the luxury lane starts at about R1500 per person per day, and can climb to more than five times this if you decide to ensconce yourself in some of the continent's top wildlife lodges.

Costs in Lesotho and Swaziland are the same as, or somewhat less than, in South Africa, with savings coming from cheaper local transport, inexpensive food and (in Lesotho) plentiful opportunities to stay with locals or camp. The unit of currency in Lesotho is the loti (plural maloti; M), which is divided into 100 liesente, while in Swaziland the lilangeni (plural emalangeni; E) is used. Both currencies are fixed at an equal value to the South African rand.

TRAVEL LITERATURE

From Jo'burg to Jozi, edited by Heidi Holland and Adam Roberts, is an eminently readable collection of short takes on this famous city by local and foreign journalists. The follow-up volume, *Soweto Inside Out*, edited by Adam Roberts and Joe Thloloe, offers more of the same, this time with the focus on South Africa's most famous township.

Although accommodation in South Africa isn't quite as full or expensive during other school holidays as during the main December–January break, prices still rise and reservations are recommended. See p612 for holiday periods.

HOW MUCH?

Bottle of wine R60-70

Car hire per day R300

Kilo of mangoes R6

Kruger National Park entry per person R120

Surfboard R1500

See also Lonely Planet Index, inside front cover.

CUTTING COSTS

In popular tourist areas, it's easy to pay much more than the averages listed under Costs & Money if you don't keep a watch on expenses. Cape Town in particular has a long history of enticing travellers, showing them a good time and emptying their wallets. However, there are also plenty of excellent-value options, both in accommodation and dining, that won't break your budget. Some ways to save include the following:

■ avoid travelling during school-holiday periods

■ always ask about midweek or weekend discounts, as well as reduced rates for children

■ take advantage of self-catering facilities and camping grounds

■ save your receipts to reclaim your value-added tax (VAT; see p615)

■ focus on just one or two areas of the country, and don't try to cover too much distance

■ use public transport, or try to travel in a group to share car-rental costs

■ book car rentals well in advance for better deals

■ book domestic air tickets online; savings can be as high as 50% of published fares

TOP TENS

Architectural Highlights

South Africa's history is written in its architecture. Hunt out these landmarks, and watch the story unfold before you.

- Regina Mundi Church in Soweto (p424)
- Cape Dutch houses along Church St in Tulbagh (p197)
- Robben Island prison, where Mandela was incarcerated (p107)
- Alayam Hindu Temple in Durban (p310)
- Owal Mosque and Cape Town's Bo-Kaap area (p104)
- Small, brightly coloured Xhosa houses in the villages inland from the Wild Coast (p282)
- Johannesburg's Constitutional Court (p404)
- Pretoria's Church Sq (p433) and Voortrekker Monument (p432)
- Linton Panel in Cape Town's South African Museum (p113)
- Freedom Park (p432)

Classic Books

The anti-apartheid struggle produced an unsurpassed collection of literature – essential reading to get into the heart of the country.

- *Long Walk to Freedom* by Nelson Mandela
- *The Marabi Dance* by Modikwe Dikobe
- *My Traitor's Heart* by Rian Malan
- *A Burning Hunger: One Family's Struggle Against Apartheid* by Lynda Schuster
- *Singing Away the Hunger: Stories of a Life in Lesotho* by Mpho 'M'atsepo Nthunya
- *The Mind of South Africa* by Allister Sparks
- *Let My People Go* by Albert Luthuli
- *The Heart of Redness* by Zakes Mda
- *Cry, The Beloved Country* by Alan Paton
- *The Lying Days* by Nadine Gordimer

Great Films

Watch some of these films for a mesmerising and often challenging introduction to South Africa.

- *Amandla! A Revolution in Four-Part Harmony* (Lee Hirsch, 2003)
- *U-Carmen eKhayalitsha* (Mark Dornford-May, 2004)
- *Drum* (Zola Maseko, 2005)
- *Zulu Love Letter* (Ramadan Suleman, 2004)
- *Sarafina!* (Darrell Roodt, 1992)
- *Boy Called Twist* (Timothy Greene, 2004)
- *Mapantsula* (Oliver Schmitz, 1988)
- *In My Country* (John Boorman, 2005)
- *A World Apart* (Chris Menges, 1988)
- *Friends* (Elaine Proctor, 1993)

DON'T LEAVE HOME WITHOUT...

■ binoculars for wildlife-watching and a zoom lens for taking great wildlife shots

■ an appetite for biltong, boerewors and mealie pap (see p92)

■ making room in your schedule to visit at least one township

■ your yellow-fever vaccination card, if you've been travelling elsewhere in Southern Africa

■ reading the Malaria section of the Health chapter (p647) in this book if you'll be travelling in malarial areas

■ a torch (flashlight) and warm, waterproof clothing for those cold, black, starry nights in the Lesotho highlands

■ a sleeping bag if you're planning on camping

■ reading a few of the books listed (opposite, or bringing one along for long bus rides.

Power Lines: Two Years on South Africa's Borders by Jason Carter chronicles a Peace Corps' volunteer's perspectives on the still-deep divisions between white and black South Africa.

While not travel literature, Nelson Mandela's superb and inspirational autobiography, *Long Walk to Freedom*, is one of the best ways to prepare for a South Africa trip. To pick up where Mandela leaves off, try the less profound but insightful *Rainbow Diary: A Journey in the New South Africa* by John Malathronas. *After the Dance: Travels in a Democratic South Africa* by David Robbins is another intriguing chronicle of travels through post-apartheid South Africa.

For a dated but still relevant perspective, look for *South from the Limpopo: Travels through South Africa*, in which inveterate Irish writer Dervla Murphy details her bicycle journey through the rainbow nation before, during and after the 1994 elections.

INTERNET RESOURCES

Government of Swaziland (www.gov.sz) The Swazi government's homepage.

Lesotho Government Online (www.lesotho.gov.ls) The Lesotho government's homepage.

Linx Africa (www.linx.co.za) Links to all things South African, including dozens of hiking and biking trails.

Lonely Planet (www.lonelyplanet.com) South Africa travel tips and the Thorn Tree bulletin board.

Mail & Guardian Online (www.mg.co.za) South Africa news.

See Lesotho (www.seelesotho.com) Background and cultural information.

South Africa Info (www.safrica.info) South Africa's info-packed official gateway.

South African National Parks (www.parks-sa.co.za) The best place to start your safari.

Times of Swaziland (www.times.co.sz) Local Swazi news.

See p618 for regional tourism websites.

Itineraries

CLASSIC ROUTES

SAFARI SPECIAL
One to Two Weeks / Johannesburg to KwaZulu-Natal

South Africa is a superb safari destination, and with as little as a week or two, it's possible to get in a good sampling. Using **Johannesburg** (p396) as a gateway, head east via **Nelspruit** (p457) to South Africa's safari showpiece, **Kruger National Park** (p466). The wildlife here and in the neighbouring **private wildlife reserves** (p485) will hold you captivated for at least several days. If time is tight, you can get a good taste of things at **Madikwe Game Reserve** (p518) or **Pilanesberg National Park** (p516), both easily reached from Johannesburg.

From Kruger, continue south into Swaziland, where you can spend a few days hiking through the grasslands and forests of **Malolotja Nature Reserve** (p590) before heading on via **Mbabane** (p578) to the wildlife-rich **Mkhaya Game Reserve** (p594), which is noted in particular for its black rhinos. From here, continue south into KwaZulu-Natal, where a collection of top-notch wildlife-watching areas awaits you. These include **Mkhuze Game Reserve** (p345) and the evocative **Hluhluwe-Imfolozi Park** (p335), with its network of walking trails. Nearby are the upmarket **Phinda Resource Reserve** (p346), and the estuaries and waterways of the **Greater St Lucia Wetlands Park** (p339).

With 10 days, you can see a good sampling of the wildlife along this 1600km-plus route. Short on time? Concentrate on just one or two parks. With three weeks or more you'll be able to get in Kruger and Swaziland plus several of KwaZulu-Natal's parks as well. Roads are good throughout, but expect some gravel and dirt roads in the parks.

CAPE & COAST   Two Weeks / Cape Town to Plettenberg Bay

Beautiful natural scenery, excellent infrastructure and an array of amenities make this the South Africa of the tourist brochures. The loop can
be done by public transport, but is better by car to take advantage of the
many possibilities for detours.

After a few days in **Cape Town** (p100), including a stay at a township
B&B, tear yourself away from this wonderful city and head to the fertile
valleys of the Winelands, with a night or two in **Stellenbosch** (p170) or
Franschhoek (p178). From here, continue east to the artists' enclave of
Montagu (p203), and then via the scenic Route 62 through the Little Karoo
to **Oudtshoorn** (p207), South Africa's ostrich capital. Possible detours along
the way include **Hermanus** (p188) for whale-watching, if the season is
right; **Cape Agulhas** (p192) for the thrill of standing at Africa's southernmost point; or **De Hoop Nature Reserve** (p193).

Oudtshoorn makes a good springboard for heading into the Karoo
via the impressive **Swartberg Pass** (p228) and on to charming **Prince Albert**
(p228), from where it's a straight shot on the N1 back to Cape Town. Alternatively, make your way south, joining the N2 along the Garden Route,
near **Knysna** (p219), with its sylvan setting, and **Plettenberg Bay** (p225), a
relaxed beachside resort town. Return to Cape Town via Oudtshoorn and
the Route 62, or directly, along the N2.

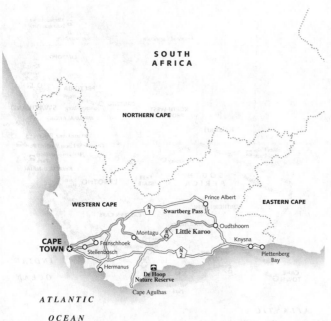

This delightful
itinerary will take
you 1000km on
good roads through
some of the most
beautiful country
in Southern Africa.
You could whizz
along in about
10 days, or relax
along the way and
stretch things out
to three weeks or
more.

GRAND CIRCUIT   Two Months / Cape Town to Cape Town

Starting in **Cape Town** (p100), head eastwards, following Route 62, the Garden Route or bits of both to Eastern Cape. If entering Eastern Cape from Prince Albert via the Karoo, don't miss **Graaff-Reinet** (p266) with its charming architecture, striking setting and the nearby **Karoo Nature Reserve** (p270). Entering Eastern Cape via the coast, recommended stops include **Tsitsikamma National Park** (p242) and **Addo Elephant National Park** (p255). Moving eastwards, **Amathole** (p273) is well worth exploration, as is the **Wild Coast** (p282), before **Durban** (p302). From here, it's in, up and over the **Sani Pass** (p565) for a Lesotho detour.

Head back to KwaZulu-Natal for as much time as possible enjoying the parks, including **Mkhuze Game Reserve** (p345), **Hluhluwe-Imfolozi Park** (p335) and the **Greater St Lucia Wetland Park** (p339). **Sodwana Bay** (p342) is an amenable spot for relaxing before moving on to **Swaziland** (p574), **Kruger National Park** (p466) and then to **Johannesburg** (p396) and **Pretoria** (p427). Possible stops en route include **Sabie** (p449) and **Pilgrim's Rest** (p451).

Time and inclination permitting, detour northwards into Limpopo, for a visit to **Mapungubwe National Park** (p500) or to the **Soutpansberg** (p497) region. Otherwise, continue from Jo'burg southwest to **Kimberley** (p526), gateway to South Africa's vast northwest, detouring to **Clarens** (p387) and the eastern **Free State** (p383) en route. Explore the **Kalahari** (p533), including **Augrabies Falls National Park** (p541), before swinging down towards **Namaqualand** (p543). Finish up by relaxing in the **Winelands** (p169) and then on to Cape Town.

Even if you can't squeeze everything in on this 5000km-plus journey, you'll undoubtedly come away with an excellent overview of South Africa, Lesotho and Swaziland. Six weeks (more via public transport) is the bare minimum, but allow at least two months to follow detours and to get into the region's pulse.

ROADS LESS TRAVELLED

THE WILD NORTHWEST   Four to Six Weeks / Cape Town to Cape Town

South Africa's northwestern reaches, with their all-pervasive sense of space, make an excellent alternative to the coast. Starting in **Cape Town** (p100), head northwards via **Citrusdal** (p236), **Clanwilliam** (p237), **Vanrhynsdorp** (p526) and the Hantam Karoo town of **Calvinia** (p548), enjoying the fine views en route. Continue to **Namaqualand** (p543) to catch the spring flowers before exploring the rugged and remote **Richtersveld National Park** (p547), with its mountainous desert landscapes, ravines and gorges. Plan on four days here to take advantage of the hiking. From Richtersveld, make your way via **Upington** (p534) to **Augrabies Falls National Park** (p541), which merits three days for hiking, rafting and canoeing. Upington itself is worth a stop, as is **Witsand Nature Reserve** (p537), where the wind sings over the dunes. Continue northwards for at least four days in **Kgalagadi Transfrontier Park** (p537). Make your way back to 'civilisation' via **Kuruman** (p534) – an unassuming but feisty frontier town – and the diamond capital of **Kimberley** (p526) with its Anglo-Boer battlefields and atmospheric pubs. From here, the route turns south along the N12 and the N1 through the Karoo, with possible stops including **Karoo National Park** (p230) and **Matjiesfontein** (p229), before entering the Winelands around **Franschhoek** (p178) and finishing in Cape Town. An alternative route from Kimberley: continue eastwards to **Bloemfontein** (p375), with its rich history and surprisingly good nightlife, and on to **Johannesburg** (p396).

After travelling about 2500km through South Africa's vast, open northwest, settling back into an urban lifestyle won't be easy. Consider a 4WD for Kgalagadi, Richtersveld and Augrabies Falls parks, and allow six weeks to include more hiking or rafting.

TRADITIONAL TRAILS   One Month / Swaziland to Johannesburg

For an introduction to traditional culture, there's no better place to start than **Swaziland** (p574). If possible, time your visit to be there for the annual **Umhlanga (Reed) Dance** (p583) or the equally colourful **Incwala** (p583), or enter the country via **Matsamo Cultural Village** (p460). Swaziland's crafts are top-notch and craft shopping is another way to step into the culture. Selection is especially good in the **Malkerns Valley** (p587) and in the **Ezulwini Valley** (p585).

From Swaziland, head south into the Zulu heartland of KwaZulu-Natal. In **Zululand** (p328), you'll find many traditional villages, and with luck will be able to catch a **Zulu festival** (p332). Continue via **Durban** (p302) to **Lesotho** (p550), where a **pony trek** (p568) or a hike through Basotho villages is an excellent way to get acquainted with local life and culture. Crafts here are also well worth seeking out. **Teyateyaneng** (p560) is the unofficial craft centre, known especially for its tapestries. Before leaving Lesotho, don't miss sampling some traditional brew – watch for the white and yellow flags hanging in villages. From Lesotho, make your way south into the areas inland from the **Wild Coast** (p282), where the rolling hills are dotted with Xhosa villages. Make your way back to Durban – perhaps enjoying some **Indian culture** (p310) en route – before finishing in **Johannesburg** (p396). A possible detour from Johannesburg: head north into Limpopo to acquaint yourself with the **Ndebele** (p492) and **Venda** (p501) people.

This 3000km-plus loop takes in some of Southern Africa's most colourful corners, and is an ideal antidote to the blandness of Western culture. It's easy to cover the distance in three weeks, but worth allowing more time. In general, the rougher the road, the more vibrant the local traditions.

TAILORED TRIPS

BODY & SOUL REJUVENATION

South Africa is one of the continent's most urbanised countries, but the rejuvenating power of the African bush is never far away. The vast **Karoo** (p227) is one of the best places to experience this, with its stark landscapes and striking light patterns. The beautiful town of **Graaff-Reinet** (p266) makes an excellent starting point. **Namaqualand's** (p543) rugged expanses are also stunning, especially in springtime when the plains are carpeted with wildflowers.

Along the coast, head to the wilds of **Maputa-land** (p338), where you'll be greeted at sunrise with bird calls echoing over the waterways. At nearby **Mkhuze Game Reserve** (p345), sit by a pan at dawn, listening to the sounds of the bush and watching the wildlife parade before you.

The magical mountain village of **Hogsback** (p274) is tamer, but no less enticing. Its relaxing setting and organic-foods–based cuisine are ideal for recharging. Want to go upscale? Book a few days at the **Santé Wellness Centre** (p183) outside **Paarl** (p182).

For something loftier, take in the scene from a perch at the edge of the Drakensberg Escarpment in the **Central Berg** (p351), listening to the wind in the ravines. Rounding out the picture is the magnificent **Kalahari** (p533), with its shifting red and white sands, unforgettable sunsets and endless expanses punctuated by prehistoric vegetation. Then journey to the **Overberg** (p186) and, to finish things up, stand at **Cape Agulhas** (p192) under spray from the crashing seas, and revel in being at Africa's southern tip.

HIKER'S CHOICE

South Africa's hiking trails – ranging from several hours to several days – are a superb way to experience the country's stunning topography. Hardcore hikers should head to the Eastern Cape, where **Tsitsikamma National Park** (p242) and the excellent **Amathole Trail** (p273) offer outstanding views and challenging terrain.

In Western Cape, the beautiful **Boesmanskloof Hiking Trail** (p201) is well worth exploration, as is **Cederberg Wilderness Area** (p235), with its sandstone formations and San rock paintings.

In the Drakensberg, try **Royal Natal National Park** (p349), with its dramatic cliffs and valleys, **Golden Gate Highlands National Park** (p385), with beautifully coloured sandstone outcrops and plenty of animals, and **Blyde River Canyon Nature Reserve** (p453), with wide vistas and sheer drop-offs. The **Giant's Cup Trail** (p356) from Sani Pass to Bushman's Nek is another highlight. In the eastern lowlands, the wilderness trails in **Kruger National Park** (p471) offer a fine opportunity to really get into the bush.

For something a bit tamer, try the Cape Peninsula, where the **Cape of Good Hope Nature Reserve** (p164) offers unsurpassed walking against a backdrop of wind-whipped sea and spray. Table Mountain itself is highly rewarding, and ideally explored on the three-day **Table Mountain Trail** (p107) over its top.

And of course there is **Lesotho** (p550) – a country seemingly created with hiking in mind – where you can set off into the hills and walk at will. Swaziland's **Malolotja Nature Reserve** (p590) is another ideal walking destination, with a wonderful wilderness atmosphere and intriguing flora and birdlife.

THE ROAD TO FREEDOM

Following in the footsteps of Nelson Mandela and other freedom fighters provides an excellent overview of recent South African history. There are far too many names and sites to list here, but an essential introduction is **Robben Island** (p107), where Mandela was incarcerated for so long, together with Walter Sisulu, Govan Mbeki and Pan Africanist Congress (PAC) founder Robert Sobukwe. Nearby in Paarl is **Victor Verster Prison** (now known as Drakenstein Prison, p183), from where Mandela walked to freedom.

The Eastern Cape was the birthplace of some of the anti-apartheid struggle's most famous figures, including Sobukwe, whose house in Graaff-Reinet's Umasizakhe township can be visited; Oliver Tambo (born in Pondoland); Govan Mbeki; Walter Sisulu; Chris Hani; and of course Mandela. Eastern Cape also has the moving **Mandela Museum** (p293); **Qunu** (Mandela's boyhood home and current residence, p292); tiny **Mveso village** (his birthplace, p292); plus the **University of Fort Hare** (p274) near Alice, where Mandela, Sobukwe, Tambo, Hani, Steve Biko and many others studied. Just outside King William's Town is Ginsberg cemetery, with **Steve Biko's gravesite** (p274).

From Eastern Cape, head to **Soweto** (p420), passing near Sharpeville, site of the Sharpeville Massacre, en route. It was in Soweto that the African National Congress (ANC) resistance to apartheid reached its fullest voice. The ANC's Freedom Charter was declared in Soweto's Kliptown (Freedom) Square, and the Soweto Uprising was ignited here (at Orlando West Secondary School on Vilikazi St). It was also to Soweto that Mandela and Sisulu returned after being released from prison, and where many other ANC activists lived. The excellent **Hector Pieterson Museum** (p423) gives a good overview of the history of the independence struggle, plus insights into life in Soweto. Nearby is **Regina Mundi Church** (p424), a central rallying point in the apartheid struggle and, later, the site of several Truth and Reconciliation Committee hearings.

In **Johannesburg** (p396), you can see the law office Mandela shared with Oliver Tambo (on Fox St, just off Ghandi Square), **City Hall** (p401), and various jails, including the notorious **Old Fort** (p404). **Museum Africa** (p401) is a worthwhile stop for its exhibit on the infamous 1956–61 Treason Trials, in which Mandela testified. It was in Pretoria's **Palace of Justice** (p433) that the Rivonia Trial was held in which Mandela, Sisulu, Govan Mbeki and five others were sentenced to life imprisonment.

Snapshot

Almost a decade and a half has passed since the official dismantling of apartheid, and South Africa is well on its way. The country's third democratic elections in 2004 passed with barely a ripple, delivering the expected massive majority to the African National Congress (ANC). The government's project for changing colonial-era place names is proceeding apace, notwithstanding vociferous objections to some of the more controversial proposals. And history is literally being rewritten as school curricula and textbooks are continually revised to include the full history of life in the region. The initial shock of apartheid-era horrors, as revealed during the 1996–98 Truth and Reconciliation Commission Hearings, has receded into the background; anti-retroviral drugs are becoming increasingly available for the country's millions of AIDS sufferers; and crime rates, while still shockingly high, are showing signs of finally beginning to fall.

Yet in many ways the real work of nation building is only now beginning. While the political violence that was threatening to engulf the country in the early 1990s has for the most part disappeared, racial and cultural divisions remain entrenched. Monuments, museums and other cultural heritage sites giving tribute to black South Africans and other previously excluded groups have been springing up across the country and filling a long vacant gap. Yet many have served to respark old tensions, and debate continues on all sides about which version of history is the 'real' one.

Perhaps the biggest attention grabber in South Africa's ongoing struggle to define itself as a nation has been Freedom Park – a multimillion dollar venture on the outskirts of Pretoria that is intended to give a sweeping overview of South African history. When finished, it will span the millennia from humankind's earliest beginnings up to the present, including a memorial to apartheid-era freedom fighters. The park, which has been lauded by President Mbeki as the country's most important national monument, is set directly opposite the Voortrekker Monument – for years an icon for most Afrikaners and a despised symbol of colonial-era injustices for many other South Africans.

What's the next step? While almost all South Africans agree that things are better than before, no one has quite been able to agree on which way forward will best balance out the diversity that is the country's greatest asset, as well as its biggest challenge. There has been talk of building a road joining Freedom Park and the Voortrekker Monument. If this road ultimately comes to be seen by those on all sides as a symbol of a united path into the future, then it will have truly captured the emerging spirit of the new South Africa and the country will be well on its way to rebuilding itself as a 'rainbow nation'.

For more on what's happening in Lesotho see p553, and in Swaziland see p577.

FAST FACTS: SOUTH AFRICA

Population: 46.9 million

Area: 1.2 million sq km

Unemployment: 26.7%

HIV/AIDS prevalence rate: 29.5%

Official languages: 11 (English, Afrikaans, Ndebele, Xhosa, Zulu, Sepedi, Sotho, Setswana, Swati, Tshivenda and Xitsonga)

Literacy rate: 86.4% (87% for males and 85.7% for females)

National flower: King Protea (Protea cynaroides)

Elephants in Kruger National Park: 12,467 (2005 census)

Age of South Africa's wine industry: almost 325 years – the oldest anywhere outside Europe

World's largest diamond: 3106.75 carats uncut, and mined in South Africa in 1905

History

The only way to begin to understand modern-day South Africa is by immersing yourself in the country's long and turbulent history. For more on the history of Lesotho see p551, and on Swaziland see p575.

THE FIRST SOUTH AFRICANS

The first people to see dawn at the southern tip of the African continent were the San – skilled hunter-gatherers who followed a nomadic lifestyle, and who left few traces other than a series of striking rock paintings. Attempts to date this rock art indicate that the San were living in what is now South Africa as early as 25,000 years ago, and possibly as early as 40,000 years ago. Small numbers still live in South Africa today, making theirs one of the world's oldest continuous cultures.

Prior to the San, the picture is murkier. A major archaeological find in 1998 at Sterkfontein near Johannesburg (Jo'burg) revealed that human-like creatures or 'hominids' were roaming and hunting across the high-veld at least three million years ago. By about one million years ago, these creatures – by then known as *Homo erectus* – had come to closely resemble modern humans, and ranged well beyond Africa, including in Europe and Asia. Somewhere around 100,000 years ago, *Homo sapiens,* or modern man, came onto the scene. Although it's still a topic of debate, fossils found near the mouth of the Klasies River in Eastern Cape indicate that our *Homo sapiens* ancestors may have been backpacking around South Africa as early as 90,000 years ago.

Beginning around 2500 years ago, some San groups acquired livestock from points further north. Gradually they abandoned their hunting-gathering traditions and became pastoralists, tending to small herds of cattle and oxen. With the livestock came concepts of personal wealth and property ownership. Community structures solidified and expanded, and chieftaincies developed. These pastoralist San, who were known as Khoekhoen ('men of men'), began to make their way south, reaching as far as the Cape coast. Over time, they established themselves along the coast, while small groups of hunter-gatherer San continued to inhabit the interior.

NEW ARRIVALS

At about this same time, Bantu-speaking peoples also began arriving in what is now South Africa. Originally from the Niger Delta area in West Africa, they had started to make their way south and eastwards about 1000 BC, reaching present-day KwaZulu-Natal by AD 500. The Bantu speakers kept livestock, farmed maize and other crops, were skilled iron workers and lived in settled villages. They arrived in Southern Africa in small waves, rather than in one cohesive migration. Some groups – the ancestors of today's Nguni peoples (Zulu, Xhosa, Swazi and Ndebele) – sought out beach-front properties and settled near the coast. Others, now known as the Sotho-Tswana peoples (Tswana, Pedi, Basotho), settled in

See www.pbs.org/wgbh /evolution/humans /humankind/o.html for an overview of human evolution in Southern Africa.

TIMELINE

c 25,000 BC	AD 100–500
The San watch the sun rise in South Africa	Bantu-speakers arrive in present-day KwaZulu-Natal

the highveld; while today's Venda, Lemba and Shangaan-Tsonga peoples made their home in the northeast of present-day South Africa.

That the Bantu-speakers and the Khoesaan mixed is certain, as evidenced by rock paintings showing the two groups interacting. The type of contact isn't known, although there's linguistic proof of integration, as several Bantu languages (notably Xhosa and Zulu) have incorporated the clicks characteristic of the earlier Khoesaan languages. Numerous Khoesaan artefacts have also been found at the sites of Bantu settlements.

EXPEDITIONING EUROPEANS

The first Europeans to reach Southern Africa were the Portuguese, who were drawn southwards in the hope of finding a sea route to India and the East. In 1487, the intrepid Bartholomeu Dias and a small band of adventurers rounded a rocky, windy cape. Dias named it Cabo da Boa Esperança (Cape of Good Hope). A decade later, in 1498, the equally intrepid Vasco da Gama rounded the same point of land, and then kept sailing northeastwards. En route, he called in at various ports along the South African and Mozambican coasts before finally reaching India.

Although the Portuguese basked in the nautical achievement of successfully negotiating the cape, they showed little interest in South Africa itself. Its fierce weather and rocky shoreline posed a threat to their ships, and many of their attempts to trade with the local Khoekhoen ended in violence. The Mozambican coast, further northeast, was altogether more to their liking, with appealing bays to use as way-stations, succulent prawns and links with the legendary gold fields of the interior.

The Portuguese had little competition in the region until the late 16th century, when the English and Dutch began to challenge them along their trade routes. Traffic around the continent's southern tip increased, and the Cape became a regular stopover for scurvy-ridden crews. In 1647 a Dutch vessel was wrecked in what is now Cape Town's Table Bay. The marooned crew – the first Europeans to attempt settlement in the area – built a fort and stayed for a year until they were rescued. Their letters back home must not have been all bad, as shortly thereafter, the Dutch East India Company (Vereenigde Oost-Indische Compagnie, or VOC) decided to establish a permanent settlement. The VOC – one of the major European trading houses sailing the spice route to the East – had no intention of colonising the area. They simply wanted to establish a secure base where passing ships could shelter, and where hungry sailors could stock up on fresh supplies of meat, fruit and vegetables. To this end, a small VOC expedition, under the command of Jan Van Riebeeck, reached Table Bay in April 1652.

THE DUTCH SETTLE IN

While the new settlement traded (out of necessity) with the neighbouring Khoekhoen people, the relationship could hardly be described as warm, and there were deliberate attempts to restrict contact. Partly as a consequence, VOC employees found themselves faced with a labour shortage. To remedy this, they released a small group of Dutch from their contracts and permitted them to establish their own farms, from which they would then supply the VOC settlement with their harvests.

As the pastoralist Khoekhoen moved south, mixing with the hunter-gatherer San, it soon became impossible to distinguish between the two groups – hence the oft-heard term 'Khoesaan'.

1487	1652
Bartholomeu Dias successfully navigates the Cape of Good Hope	First Dutch settlement, at Table Bay, Cape Town

The arrangement proved highly successful, producing abundant supplies of fruit, vegetables, wheat and wine; they later raised livestock. The small initial group of free burghers, as these farmers were known, steadily increased, and began to expand their farms further north and east into the territory of the Khoekhoen.

The majority of burghers were of Dutch descent, and members of the Calvinist Reformed Church of the Netherlands, but there were also numerous Germans. In 1688 the Dutch and the Germans were joined by French Huguenots, also Calvinists, who were fleeing religious persecution under King Louis XIV.

In addition to establishing the free burgher system, Van Riebeeck and the VOC also began to import large numbers of slaves, primarily from Madagascar and Indonesia. With this additional labour, the areas occupied by the VOC expanded further north and east where clashes with the Khoekhoen were inevitable. The beleaguered Khoekhoen were driven from their traditional lands, decimated by introduced diseases and destroyed by superior weapons when they fought back – which they did in a number of major 'wars', and with guerrilla resistance which continued into the 19th century. Most survivors were left with no option but to work for Europeans in an exploitative arrangement that hardly differed from slavery. Over time, the Khoesaan, their European overseers, and the imported slaves mixed, with the offspring of these unions forming the basis for modern South Africa's coloured population.

Among the best-known Khoekhoen groups were the Griqua, who had originally lived on the western coast between St Helena Bay and the Cederberg Range. In the late 18th century, they managed to acquire guns and horses and began trekking northeastwards. En route, they were joined by other groups of Khoesaan, coloureds and even white adventurers, and rapidly gained a reputation as a formidable military force. Ultimately, the Griquas reached the highveld around present-day Kimberley, where they carved out territory that came to be known as Griqualand.

In 1660, Jan Van Riebeeck planted a bitter-almond hedge separating the Dutch from the Khoekhoen. See sections of it in Kirstenbosch Botanical Gardens (see p119).

BURGHERS MEET THE BUSH

As the burghers, too, continued to expand into the rugged hinterlands of the north and east, many began to take up a seminomadic pastoralist lifestyle, in some ways not so far removed from that of the Khoekhoen who they were displacing. In addition to its herds, a family might have had a wagon, a tent, a Bible and a couple of guns. As they became more settled, a mud-walled cottage would be built – frequently located, by choice, days of hard travel away from the nearest European. These were the first of the Trekboers (Wandering Farmers, later shortened to Boers) – completely independent of official control, extraordinarily self-sufficient and isolated. Their harsh lifestyle produced courageous individualists, but also a backward people, whose only source of knowledge was often the Bible.

BRITS AT THE CAPE

As the 18th century drew to a close, Dutch mercantile power began to fade, and the British moved in to fill the vacuum. They seized the Cape to prevent it from falling into rival French hands, then briefly relinquished

---

A CHOSEN PEOPLE?

Boer lifestyle and culture – both real and idealised – have had a major influence on South Africa's history. While many of the early members of the Dutch VOC expedition planned to ultimately return to Europe, the Boers soon began to develop a view of themselves as a distinct community which was permanently settled in South Africa. According to their Calvinist beliefs, the Boers were God's chosen people, who had the duty to civilise their black neighbours and thereby ensure their salvation. Some scholars also say that it was Calvinism, and especially its doctrine of predestination, that spawned the Afrikaner idea of racial superiority: the separation of the races had been divinely ordained, and thus justified all efforts to preserve the purity of the white race in its promised land.

---

it to the Dutch, before finally garnering recognition of their sovereignty of the area in 1814.

Awaiting the British at the tip of the continent was a colony with 25,000 slaves, 20,000 white colonists, 15,000 Khoesaan and 1000 freed black slaves. Power was restricted to a white elite in Cape Town, and differentiation on the basis of race was deeply entrenched. Outside Cape Town and the immediate hinterland, the country was populated by isolated black and white pastoralists.

Like the Dutch before them, the British initially had little interest in the Cape Colony, other than as a strategically located port. One of their first tasks was trying to resolve a troublesome border dispute between the Boers and the Xhosa on the colony's eastern frontier. In 1820, about 5000 middle-class British immigrants – mostly traders and businesspeople – were persuaded to leave England behind and settle on tracts of land between the feuding groups with the idea of providing a buffer zone. The plan was singularly unsuccessful. By 1823, almost half of the settlers had retreated to the towns – notably Grahamstown and Port Elizabeth – to pursue the jobs they had held in Britain.

While doing nothing to resolve the border dispute, this influx of settlers solidified the British presence in the area, thus fracturing the relative unity of white South Africa. Where the Boers and their ideas had once been largely unchallenged, there were now two language groups and two cultures. A pattern soon emerged whereby English-speakers were highly urbanised, and dominated politics, trade, finance, mining and manufacturing, while the largely uneducated Boers were relegated to their farms.

The gap between the British settlers and the Boers further widened with the abolition of slavery in 1833 – a move that was generally regarded by Boers as being against the God-given ordering of the races. Meanwhile, British numbers rapidly increased in Cape Town, in the area east of the Cape Colony (present-day Eastern Cape), in Natal (present-day KwaZulu-Natal) and, after the discovery of gold and diamonds, in parts of the Transvaal (mainly around present-day Gauteng).

André Brink's novel Praying Mantis *takes an enigmatic look at life in the Cape colony in the late 18th and 19th centuries, against the backdrop of more recent apartheid-era realities.*

DIFAQANE & DESTRUCTION

Against this backdrop, the stage was being set for a time of immense upheaval and suffering among the African peoples of the region. This

---

1816	**1820**
Shaka Zulu becomes chief of the Zulu; the *difaqane* (forced migration) begins	British settlers arrive in Eastern Cape

period is known as the *difaqane* (forced migration) in Sotho, and as *mfeqane* (the crushing) in Zulu.

The roots of the *difaqane* are disputed, although certain events stand out. One of the most significant was the rise of the powerful Zulu kingdom. In the early 19th century, Nguni tribes in what is now KwaZulu-Natal began to shift from loosely organised collections of kingdoms into a centralised, militaristic state under Shaka Zulu, son of the chief of the small Zulu clan. After building large armies, Shaka set out on a massive programme of conquest and terror. Those who stood in his way were either enslaved or decimated.

Not surprisingly, tribes in the path of Shaka's armies turned on their heels and fled, in turn becoming aggressors against their neighbours. This wave of disruption and terror spread throughout Southern Africa and beyond, leaving death and destruction in its wake. It also accelerated the formation of several states, notably those of the Sotho (present-day Lesotho; see p551) and Swazi (now Swaziland; see p575).

In 1828, Shaka met his untimely end when he was killed by his half-brothers Dingaan and Umhlanga. The weaker and less-skilled Dingaan became king and attempted to establish relations with British traders on the Natal coast, but events were unfolding that were to see the demise of Zulu independence.

Natal was named by Vasco da Gama, who, sighting its coast on Christmas Day 1497, named it for the natal day of Christ.

THE GREAT TREK

Meanwhile, the Boers were growing increasingly dissatisfied with British rule in the Cape Colony. The British proclamation of equality of the races was a particularly sharp thorn in their side. Beginning in 1836, several groups of Boers, together with large numbers of Khoekhoen and black servants, decided to trek off into the interior in search of greater independence. North and east of the Orange River (which formed the Cape Colony's frontier) these Boers, or Voortrekkers (Pioneers), found vast tracts of apparently uninhabited grazing lands. They had entered, so it seemed, their promised land, with space enough for their cattle to graze, and for their culture of antiurban independence to flourish. Little did they know that what they found – deserted pasture lands, disorganised bands of refugees and tales of brutality – were the result of the *difaqane*, rather than the normal state of affairs.

With the exception of the more powerful Ndebele, the Voortrekkers encountered little resistance among the scattered peoples of the plains. They had been dispersed by the *difaqane* and lacked horses and firearms. Their weakened condition also solidified the Boers' belief that European occupation meant the coming of civilisation to a savage land.

However, the mountains (where King Moshoeshoe I was forging the Basotho nation that was later to become Lesotho) and the wooded valleys of Zululand were a more difficult proposition. Resistance here was strong, and the Boer incursions set off a series of skirmishes, squabbles and flimsy treaties that were to litter the next 50 years of increasing white domination.

A RIVER RUNS RED

The Great Trek's first halt was at Thaba 'Nchu, near present-day Bloemfontein, where a republic was established. Following disagreements among their leadership, the various Voortrekker groups split, with most crossing the Drakensberg into Natal to try and establish a republic there. As this was Zulu territory, the Voortrekker leader Piet Retief paid a visit to King Dingaan, and was promptly massacred by the suspicious Zulu. This massacre triggered others, as well as a revenge attack by the Boers. The culmination came in December 1838 at the Ncome River in Natal. Several Boers were injured, while several thousand Zulus were killed, reportedly causing the Ncome's waters to run red.

After this victory (the result of superior weapons), the Boers felt that their expansion really did have that long-suspected stamp of divine approval. Yet their hopes for establishing a Natal republic were short-lived. The British annexed the area in 1843, and founded their new Natal colony at present-day Durban. Most of the Boers headed north, with yet another grievance against the British.

The British set about establishing large sugar plantations in Natal, and looked to India to resolve their labour shortage. From 1860 into the early 20th century, a stream of over 150,000 indentured Indians arrived, as well as numerous free 'passenger Indians', building the base for what was to become one of the largest Indian communities outside India.

Until 1994, 16 December was celebrated by whites as the Day of the Vow, before being renamed the Day of Reconciliation.

THE BOER REPUBLICS

The Boers meanwhile pressed on with their search for land and freedom, ultimately establishing themselves at Transvaal (encompassing parts of Gauteng, Limpopo, North-West and Mpumalanga provinces) and the Orange Free State. Then the Boers' world was turned on its head in 1869 with the discovery of diamonds near Kimberley. The diamonds were found on land belonging to the Griqua, but to which both the Transvaal and Orange Free State laid claim. Britain quickly stepped in and resolved the issue by annexing the area for itself.

The discovery of the Kimberley diamond mines unleashed a flood of European and black labourers to the area. Towns sprang up in which the 'proper' separation of whites and blacks was ignored, and the Boers were angry that their impoverished republics were missing out on the economic benefits of the mines.

THE ANGLO-BOER WARS

Long-standing Boer resentment turned into full-blown rebellion in the Transvaal, and the first Anglo-Boer War broke out in 1880 (it was known by Afrikaners, as the descendants of the early Boers became known – see the boxed text on p52 – as the War of Independence). It was over almost as soon as it began, with a crushing Boer victory at the Battle of Majuba Hill in early 1881. The republic regained its independence as the Zuid-Afrikaansche Republiek (ZAR; South African Republic). Paul Kruger, one of the leaders of the uprising, became president of the ZAR in 1883.

Meanwhile, the British, who viewed their defeat at Majuba as an aberration, forged ahead with their desire to federate the Southern African colonies and republics.

In 1879, Zululand came under British control. Then in 1886, gold was discovered on the Witwatersrand (the area around Jo'burg), accelerating the federation process and dealing the Boers yet another blow. Jo'burg's

1860	1869
MS Truro arrives in Durban with over 300 Indians for indentured service	Diamonds found near Kimberley

population exploded to about 100,000 by the mid-1890s, and the ZAR suddenly found itself hosting thousands of uitlanders (foreigners), both black and white, with the Boers squeezed to the sidelines. The influx of black labour was particularly disturbing for the Boers, many of whom were going through hard times and resented the black wage-earners.

The situation peaked in 1899, when the British demanded voting rights for the 60,000 foreign whites on the Witwatersrand (until this point, Kruger's government had excluded all foreigners from the franchise). Kruger refused, calling for British troops to be withdrawn from the ZAR's borders. When the British resisted, Kruger declared war. This second Anglo-Boer War was more protracted and the British were better prepared than at Majuba Hill. By mid-1900, Pretoria, the last of the major Boer towns, had surrendered. Yet resistance by Boer *bittereinders* (bitter enders) continued for two more years with guerrilla-style battles, which in turn were met by scorched-earth tactics by the British. By 1902, 26,000 people had died of disease and neglect. In May 1902, the Treaty of Vereeniging brought a superficial peace. Under its terms, the Boer republics acknowledged British sovereignty, while the British committed themselves to reconstruction of the areas under their control.

The Witwatersrand contains the world's largest gold deposit, thus far yielding roughly one-third of all the gold ever mined on earth.

PEACE & UNITY?

During the immediate postwar years, the British focused their attention on rebuilding the country, in particular the mining industry. By 1907, the mines of the Witwatersrand were producing almost one-third of the world's gold. But the peace brought by the treaty was fragile, and challenged on all sides. The Afrikaners found themselves in the position of being poor farmers in a country where big mining ventures and foreign capital rendered them irrelevant. They were particularly incensed by Britain's unsuccessful attempts to anglicise them, and to impose English as the official language in schools and the workplace. Partly as a backlash to this, Afrikaans came to be seen as the *volkstaal* (people's language) and a symbol of Afrikaner nationhood, and several nationalistic organisations sprang up.

Blacks and coloureds were completely marginalised. Harsh taxes were imposed, wages were reduced and the British caretaker administrator encouraged the immigration of thousands of Chinese to undercut any resistance. Resentment was given full vent in the Bambatha Rebellion of 1906, in which 4000 Zulu lost their lives after protesting onerous tax legislation.

The British, meanwhile, moved ahead with their plans for union. After several years of negotiation, the 1910 Act of Union was signed, bringing the republics of Cape Colony, Natal, Transvaal and Orange Free State together as the Union of South Africa. Under the provisions of the act, the Union was still a British territory, with home-rule for Afrikaners. The British High Commission Territories of Basotholand (now Lesotho), Bechuanaland (now Botswana), Swaziland and Rhodesia (now Zimbabwe) continued to be ruled directly by Britain.

English and Dutch were made the official languages. (Afrikaans was not recognised as an official language until 1925.) Despite a major campaign by blacks and coloureds, the voter franchise remained as it was in

1879	1881
Zululand comes under British control	First Anglo-Boer War ends; Transvaal becomes the South African Republic

the pre-Union republics and colonies, and only whites could be elected to parliament.

REPRESSION, RESISTANCE & RACISM

The first government of the new Union was headed by General Louis Botha, with General Jan Smuts as his deputy. Their South African National Party (later known as the South African Party or SAP) followed a generally pro-British, white-unity line. More radical Boers split away under the leadership of General Barry Hertzog, forming the National Party (NP) in 1914. The NP championed Afrikaner interests, advocating separate development for the two white groups and independence from Britain.

There was no place in the new Union for blacks, even though they constituted over 75% of the population. Under the Act of Union, they were denied voting rights in the Transvaal and Orange Free State areas, and in Cape Colony were granted the vote only if they met a property ownership qualification. Coming on the heels of British wartime propaganda promising freedom from 'Boer slavery', the failure to grant the franchise was regarded by blacks as a blatant betrayal. It wasn't long before a barrage of oppressive legislation was passed, making it illegal for black workers to strike, reserving skilled jobs for whites, barring blacks from military service and instituting restrictive pass laws. In 1913, the Natives Land Act was enacted, setting aside 8% of South Africa's land for black occupancy. Whites, who made up 20% of the population, were given over 90% of the land. Black Africans were not allowed to buy, rent or even be sharecroppers outside their designated area. Thousands of squatters were evicted from farms and forced into increasingly overcrowded and impoverished reserves, or into the cities. Those who remained were reduced to the status of landless labourers.

Black and coloured opposition began to coalesce, and leading figures such as John Jabavu, Walter Rubusana and Abdullah Abdurahman laid the foundations for new nontribal black political groups. Most significantly, a Columbia University-educated attorney, Pixley ka Isaka Seme, called together representatives of the various African tribes to form a unified national organisation to represent the interests of blacks, and to ensure that they had an effective voice in the new Union. Thus was born the South African Native National Congress, known from 1923 onwards as the African National Congress (ANC).

See www.anc.org.za for more on the ANC and South African history.

Parallel to this, Mohandas (Mahatma) Gandhi had been working with the Indian populations of Natal and the Transvaal to fight against the ever-increasing encroachments on their rights (see p40).

In 1924 the NP, under Hertzog, came to power in a coalition government, and Afrikaner nationalism gained a greater hold. Dutch was replaced by Afrikaans (previously only regarded as a low-class dialect of Dutch) as an official language of the Union, and the so-called *swart gevaar* (black threat) was made the dominant issue of the 1929 election. Hertzog joined briefly in a coalition with the more moderate Jan Smuts in the mid-1930s, after which Smuts took the reins and, amid much controversy, led South Africa into WWII on the side of the Allies. However, any hopes of turning the tide of Afrikaner nationalism were dashed when Daniel François (DF) Malan led a radical breakaway movement,

1886	1893
Gold discovered on the Witwatersrand	Mahatma Gandhi sets sail for South Africa

MAHATMA GANDHI

In 1893 Mohandas (Mahatma) Gandhi, a young Indian solicitor, set sail for Durban, South Africa, to take on a one-year legal contract in South Africa. Anti-Indian sentiment in Natal was high, and upon his arrival he was thrown out of a 1st-class train wagon at Pietermaritzburg because of his race.

The incident had a profound effect on Gandhi. He began schooling himself in methods of nonviolent resistance, and became increasingly involved with the local Indian community, working with them to safeguard their political rights. Within a short period, Gandhi had not only established himself as a successful attorney, but also as the leading spokesperson for Indian interests in South Africa.

In 1896, and again in 1901, Gandhi returned briefly to India where he lobbied extensively to bring attention to the plight of Indians in South Africa. Back in South Africa, Gandhi developed the thinking that was to guide his political activity for the rest of his life. He gave up the trappings of a successful attorney, began washing his own clothes, committed himself to a life of celibacy and nonpossession, and devoted himself fully to service. He also developed his defining philosophy of satyagraha (meaning, very loosely, truth through nonviolence).

In 1907, the Transvaal government passed the Asiatic Registration Act requiring all Indians to register with the Registrar of Asiatics, and to carry a certificate of registration. Gandhi called on the Indian community to defy the act, and to offer no resistance if they should be arrested. Over the next seven years, numerous similar discriminatory incidents followed, including a court decision nullifying all Hindu and Muslim marriages, which Gandhi and his followers also peacefully defied. In response, Gandhi – along with thousands of other Indians who had joined him in his satyagraha struggle – was repeatedly arrested.

Gandhi finally returned to India in 1914 – over 20 years after he first arrived in South Africa for a year-long stay. Apart from the profound global influence of Gandhi's life, his tactics in South Africa resulted in the 1914 passage of the Indian Relief Bill, which among other concessions restored recognition of Hindu and Muslim marriages.

the Purified National Party, to the central position in Afrikaner political life. The Afrikaner Broederbond, a secret Afrikaner brotherhood that had been formed in 1918 to protect Afrikaner culture, soon became an extraordinarily influential force behind both the NP and other organisations designed to promote the *volk* ('people', the Afrikaners).

Due to the booming wartime economy, black labour became increasingly important to the mining and manufacturing industries, and the black urban population nearly doubled. Enormous squatter camps grew up on the outskirts of Jo'burg and, to a lesser extent, outside the other major cities. Conditions in the townships were appalling, but poverty was not only the province of blacks; wartime surveys found that 40% of white schoolchildren were malnourished.

THE WALLS OF APARTHEID GO UP

In the run-up to the 1948 elections, the NP campaigned on its policy of segregation, or 'apartheid' (an Afrikaans term for the state of being apart). It was voted in, in coalition with the Afrikaner Party (AP), and under the leadership of DF Malan.

Apartheid, long a reality of life, became institutionalised under Malan. Within short order, legislation was passed prohibiting mixed marriages,

1902	1910
Treaty of Vereeniging ends the second Anglo-Boer War	Union of South Africa created, with no voting rights for blacks; Lesotho and Swaziland remain British protectorate

making interracial sex illegal, classifying every individual by race and establishing a classification board to rule in questionable cases. The noxious Group Areas Act of 1950 set aside desirable city properties for whites, while banishing nonwhites into the townships. The Separate Amenities Act created, among other things, separate beaches, buses, hospitals, schools and even park benches.

The existing pass laws were further strengthened: blacks and coloureds were compelled to carry identity documents at all times and were prohibited from remaining in towns, or even visiting them, without specific permission. Couples were not allowed to live together (or even visit each other) in the town where only one of them worked, and children had to remain in rural areas.

In 1960, tensions came to a head in the Sharpeville massacre (see below). Soon thereafter, Prime Minister Hendrik Verwoerd, whose rabid racism earned him the unofficial title of 'architect of apartheid', announced a referendum on whether the country should become a republic. The change was passed by a slim majority of voters. Verwoerd withdrew South Africa from the Commonwealth, and in May 1961 the Republic of South Africa came into existence.

ACTION & ACTIVISM

These developments pushed the hitherto relatively conservative ANC into action. In 1949 it developed an agenda that for the first time advocated open resistance in the form of strikes, acts of public disobedience and protest marches. Resistance continued throughout the 1950s, and resulted in occasional violent clashes. In June 1955, at a congress held at Kliptown near Jo'burg, a number of organisations, including the Indian Congress and the ANC, adopted a Freedom Charter. This articulated a vision of a nonracial democratic state, and is still central to the ANC's vision of a new South Africa.

In 1959, a group of disenchanted ANC members, seeking to sever all links with white government, broke away to form the more militant Pan African Congress. First on the PAC's agenda was a series of nationwide demonstrations against the hated pass laws. On 21 March 1960, police opened fire on demonstrators surrounding a police station in Sharpeville, a township near Vereeniging. At least 67 people were killed, and 186 wounded; most of those were shot in the back.

To many domestic and international onlookers, the struggle had crossed a crucial line at Sharpeville, and there could no longer be any doubts about the nature of the white regime. In the wake of the shooting, a massive stay-away from work was organised, and demonstrations continued. Verwoerd declared a state of emergency, giving security forces the right to detain people without trial. Over 18,000 demonstrators were arrested, including much of the ANC and PAC leadership, and both organisations were banned.

As black activists continued to be arrested, the ANC and PAC began a campaign of sabotage through the armed wings of their organisations, Umkhonto we Sizwe (Spear of the Nation, MK) and Poqo ('Pure' or 'Alone'), respectively. In July 1963, 17 members of the ANC underground movement were arrested. Together with ANC leader Nelson Mandela,

Nelson Mandela's autobiographical *Long Walk to Freedom* offers an unparalleled recounting of the days of resistance, and of the years that followed.

1912	1914
South African Native National Congress established; forerunner to the African National Congress (ANC)	Indian Relief Bill is passed, restoring recognition of Hindu and Muslim marriages

For more on Nelson Man-
dela, read the exhaustive
*Mandela: the Authorised
Biography* by Anthony
Sampson.

who had already been arrested on other charges, they were tried for
treason at the widely publicised Rivonia Trial. In June 1964, Mandela
and seven others were sentenced to life imprisonment. Oliver Tambo,
another member of the ANC leadership, managed to escape South Africa
and lead the ANC in exile.

> I have fought against White domination and I have fought against
> Black domination. I have cherished the ideal of a democratic and free
> society in which all persons live together in harmony and with equal
> opportunities. It is an ideal which I hope to live for and to achieve.
> But if needs be, it is an ideal for which I am prepared to die.
>
> *Nelson Mandela, 20 April 1964, Rivonia Trial*

DECADES OF DARKNESS

With the ANC banned, and Mandela and most of the rest of its leadership in jail or exile, South Africa moved into some of its darkest times.
Apartheid legislation was enforced with increasing gusto, and the walls
between the races were built ever higher. Most odious was the creation
of separate 'homelands' for blacks (see the boxed text on p521). In 1966,
Verwoerd was stabbed to death, but his policies continued under BJ
Vorster and, later, PW Botha.

During the 1970s, resistance again gained force, first channelled
through trade unions and strikes, and then spearheaded by the South
African Students' Organisation, under the leadership of the charismatic
Steve Biko. Biko, a medical student, was the main force behind the growth
of South Africa's Black Consciousness Movement, which stressed the
need for psychological liberation, black pride and nonviolent opposition
to apartheid.

Things culminated in 1976, when the Soweto Students' Representative
Council organised protests against the use of Afrikaans (regarded as the
language of the oppressor) in black schools. On 16 June police opened fire
on a student march, beginning a round of nationwide demonstrations,
strikes, mass arrests, riots and violence that, over the next 12 months,
took over 1000 lives.

In September 1977, Steve Biko was killed (see p274). Unidentified
security police bashed him until he lapsed into a coma; he went without
medical treatment for three days and finally died in Pretoria. At the subsequent inquest, the magistrate found that no one was to blame, although
the South African Medical Association eventually took action against the
doctors who failed to treat Biko. South Africa would never be the same
again. A generation of young blacks committed themselves to a revolu-
tionary struggle against apartheid ('Liberation before Education' was the
catch-cry) and the black communities were politicised.

*A Burning Hunger:
One Family's Struggle
Against Apartheid* by
Lynda Schuster is an
extraordinary recounting
of a black family's fight
against apartheid, from
the Soweto uprisings in
1976 until liberation in
the early 1990s.

SOUTH AFRICA UNDER SIEGE

By 1980 South Africa was the only country in Africa with a white government and a constitution discriminating against the majority of its
citizens. As international opinion turned decisively against the white
regime, the government (and most of the white population) increasingly
saw the country as a bastion besieged by communism, atheism and black

1932	1948
World-famous singer Miriam Makeba (Mama Africa) is born in Johannesburg	National Party gains control of the government; apartheid is institutionalised

THE 'HOME'LANDS

In 1962 – two years before Nelson Mandela was sentenced to life imprisonment – the Transkei was born. It was the first of 10 so-called 'Bantustans' or 'homelands' that were intended to provide a home for all black South Africans. On these lands – so went the white South African propaganda – blacks would be self-sufficient, self-governing citizens, living together with others of their own tribe.

The realities were much different. The homeland areas had no infrastructure or industry, and were incapable of producing sufficient food for the burgeoning black population. They were also completely disproportionate in size to the numbers of people they were supposed to host. All the homelands together constituted only 14% of South Africa's land, while blacks made up close to 80% of the country's population. Tribal divisions were made arbitrarily, and once a person had been assigned to a homeland, they could not leave without a pass and permission. The resulting suffering was intense and widespread. Overpopulated farming lands were rapidly exhausted, and families were divided as men were forced to return alone to urban areas as guest workers without rights.

Following creation of the homelands, blacks flooded to the cities seeking work: while life in urban squatter camps was bad, life in the homelands was worse. To stop this, the government banned blacks from being employed as shop assistants, receptionists, typists and clerks. The construction of housing in the black 'locations' (dormitory suburbs for black workers) was halted, and enormous single-sex hostels were built instead.

The situation in the homelands was further worsened by internal political strife. In an effort to garner more power for themselves, some homeland leaders became collaborators with the government, accepting 'independence' while crushing all resistance to their control and to the South African government.

Although the homelands came to an end with the demise of apartheid, their legacies – including completely insufficient infrastructure and distorted population concentrations in the homeland areas – continue to scar South Africa today.

anarchy. Considerable effort was put into circumventing sanctions, and the government even developed nuclear weapons (which have since been destroyed).

Negotiating majority rule with the ANC was not considered an option (publicly, at least), which left the government to defend the country against external and internal threats through sheer military might. A siege mentality developed among whites, and although many realised that a civil war against the black majority could not be won, they preferred this to 'giving in' to political reform. Brutal police and military actions seemed entirely justifiable. Paradoxically, the international sanctions that cut whites off from the rest of the world enabled black leaders to develop sophisticated political skills, as those in exile forged ties with regional and world leaders.

From 1978 to 1988 the South African Defence Force (SADF; now the South African National Defence Force, or SANDF) made a number of major attacks inside Angola, Mozambique, Zimbabwe, Botswana and Lesotho. All white males were liable for national service, and thousands fled into exile to avoid conscription. Many more were scarred mentally and physically by their participation in vicious struggles in the region, or in the townships of South Africa.

Soweto Blues: Jazz and Politics in South Africa by Gwen Ansell takes a fascinating look at the interaction of jazz and politics in apartheid-era South Africa.

1960	1961
Sharpeville massacre; ANC and Pan African Congress (PAC) banned	South Africa leaves the Commonwealth and becomes a republic

WINDS OF CHANGE

In the early 1980s, a fresh wind began to blow across South Africa. Whites constituted only 16% of the total population, in comparison with 20% 50 years earlier, and the number was continuing to fall. Recognising the inevitability of change, PW Botha told white South Africans to 'adapt or die'. Numerous reforms were instituted, including repeal of the pass laws. But Botha stopped well short of full reform, and many blacks (as well as the international community) felt the changes were only cosmetic. Protests and resistance continued at full force, as South Africa became increasingly polarised and fragmented, and unrest was widespread. A white backlash also arose, giving rise to a number of neo-Nazi paramilitary groups, notably the Afrikaner Weerstandsbeweging (AWB), led by Eugène Terre'Blanche. The opposition United Democratic Front (UDF) was also formed at this time. With a broad coalition of members, led by Archbishop Desmond Tutu and the Reverend Allan Boesak, it called for the government to abandon its proposed reforms, and instead to abolish apartheid and eliminate the homelands.

International pressures also increased, as economic sanctions began to dig in harder, and the value of the rand collapsed. In 1985, the government declared a state of emergency, which was to stay in effect for five years. The media was censored and, by 1988, 30,000 people had been detained without trial, with thousands tortured.

Beyond the Miracle: Inside the New South Africa by Allister Sparks is a realistic yet optimistic analysis of South Africa as it steps into the future, written by one of South Africa's most respected journalists.

STALKED BY A SHADOW

Amid this turmoil, a perhaps even darker shadow had started to move across South Africa. In 1982, the first recorded death from AIDS occurred in the country. Within a decade, the number of recorded AIDS cases had risen to over 1000, and by the mid-1990s, it had reached 10,000. Yet these officially recorded cases were only the tip of the iceberg, with some estimates placing the actual number of HIV-positive cases at close to one million in 1995. Fuelled by the entrenched migrant labour system at South Africa's mines, AIDS is estimated to have been spreading at the explosive rate of over 500 new cases per day.

In the late 1980s, the South African Chamber of Mines began an education campaign to try and stem the rise of cases. But without a change in the underlying conditions of mine workers, success could hardly be expected. Long periods away from home under bleak conditions, and a few days leave a month were the apartheid-induced realities of life under which thousands of miners and other labourers worked. Compounding the problem was the fact that, as of the mid-1990s, many health officials were still focused more on the incidence of tuberculosis than of AIDS.

As South Africa began to take its first tenuous steps to dismantle the walls of apartheid, AIDS lay waiting to explode like a ticking time bomb.

THE WALLS BEGIN TO FALL

In 1986, President Botha announced to parliament that South Africa had 'outgrown' apartheid. The government started making a series of minor reforms in the direction of racial equality, while maintaining an iron grip on the media and on all anti-apartheid demonstrations.

In late 1989, a physically ailing Botha was succeeded by FW de Klerk. At his opening address to the parliament in February 1990, de Klerk announced that he would repeal discriminatory laws and legalise the ANC, the PAC and the Communist Party. Media restrictions were lifted, and de Klerk released political prisoners not guilty of common-law crimes. On 11 February 1990, 27 years after he had first been incarcerated, Nelson Mandela walked out of the grounds of Victor Verster prison a free man.

From 1990 to 1991 the legal apparatus of apartheid was abolished. A referendum – the last of the whites-only vote held in South Africa – overwhelmingly gave the government authority to negotiate a new constitution with the ANC and other groups.

FREE ELECTIONS

In December 1991 the Convention for a Democratic South Africa (Codesa) began negotiations on the formation of a multiracial transitional government and a new constitution extending political rights to all groups. Months of wrangling finally produced a compromise and an election date, although at considerable human cost. Political violence exploded across the country during this time, particularly in the wake of the assassination of Chris Hani, the popular leader of the South African Communist Party. It's now known that elements within the police and army contributed to this violence. There have also been claims that high-ranking government officials and politicians ordered, or at least condoned, massacres.

In 1993, a draft constitution was published guaranteeing freedom of speech and religion, access to adequate housing and numerous other benefits, and explicitly prohibiting discrimination on almost any grounds. Finally, at midnight on 26–27 April 1994, the old national anthem 'Die Stem' (The Call) was sung and the old flag was lowered, followed by the raising of the new rainbow flag and singing of the new anthem, 'Nkosi Sikelele Afrika' (God Bless Africa). The election went off peacefully, amid a palpable feeling of goodwill throughout the country.

The ANC won 62.7% of the vote, less than the 66.7% that would have enabled it to rewrite the constitution. As well as deciding the national

VRYE WEEKBLAD

In 1988, renegade Afrikaner journalist Max du Preez, together with a handful of other white anti-apartheid activists, founded *Vrye Weekblad*, South Africa's first Afrikaans-language anti-apartheid newspaper. From the start, the newspaper drew the wrath of the state. Its offices were bombed, du Preez received numerous threats and the newspaper was sued for defamation by then-president PW Botha. Yet, during its short life, it was ground-breaking for its commitment to free speech, its tireless campaigning against oppression and its exposés of corruption and brutality on all sides of the political spectrum. After just over five years of cutting-edge investigative reporting, *Vrye Weekblad* was forced to close down shortly before the 1994 elections. Du Preez later went on to work as producer for SABC's TV coverage of the Truth & Reconciliation hearings, and today continues to work as a highly respected journalist. For a fascinating account of the paper's history, look for a copy of du Preez's book, *Oranje Blanje Blues*.

1977	1982
Steve Biko murdered	The first recorded AIDS death in South Africa

government, the election decided the provincial governments, and the ANC won in all but two provinces. The NP captured most of the white and coloured vote and became the official opposition party.

REWRITING HISTORY

Following the elections, focus turned to the Truth & Reconciliation Commission (1994–99), which worked to expose crimes of the apartheid era under the dictum of Archbishop Desmond Tutu: 'Without forgiveness there is no future, but without confession there can be no forgiveness'. Many stories of horrific brutality and injustice were heard by the commission, offering some catharsis to people and communities shattered by their past.

NELSON MANDELA

Nelson Rolihlahla Mandela is without doubt one of the global leaders of the millennium. Once vilified by South Africa's ruling whites and sentenced to life imprisonment, he emerged from 27 years of incarceration calling for reconciliation and forgiveness, and was able to rally together all South Africans at the most crucial of times.

Mandela, son of a Xhosa chief, was born on 18 July 1918 in the small village of Mveso on the Mbashe River. When he was young the family moved to Qunu, south of Mthatha in what is now Eastern Cape. Here he grew up living in a kraal (rural housing compound) such as those that still dot this landscape, living a typical rural life, while at the same time being groomed for a future position in the tribal leadership. After attending school at the University College of Fort Hare, Mandela headed to Jo'burg, where he soon became immersed in politics. He also finished his law degree and, together with Oliver Tambo, opened South Africa's first black law firm. Meanwhile, in 1944, together with Tambo and Walter Sisulu, Mandela formed the Youth League of the African National Congress (ANC), which worked to turn the ANC into a nationwide grass-roots movement. During the 1950s, Mandela was at the forefront of the ANC's civil disobedience campaigns, for which he was first arrested in 1952, tried and acquitted. Various arrests and detention followed. After the ANC was banned in the wake of the Sharpeville massacre, Mandela advocated establishing its underground military wing, Umkhonto we Sizwe. In 1964, while serving time for an earlier arrest, Mandela was brought to stand trial for sabotage and fomenting revolution in the widely publicised Rivonia Trial. After brilliantly arguing his own defence, he was sentenced to life imprisonment, and spent the next 18 years in the infamous Robben Island prison, before being moved to Pollsmoor Prison on the mainland, and later to Victor Verster prison near Paarl, from which he was eventually released.

Throughout his incarceration, Mandela repeatedly refused to compromise his political beliefs in exchange for freedom, saying that only free men can negotiate. Among other things, he rejected offers of release in exchange for recognising the independence of the Transkei (and thereby giving tacit approval of the legitimacy of the apartheid regime).

On 18 February 1990, Mandela was released and in 1991 he was elected president of the ANC. From this position, he continued the negotiations (which had started secretly while he was in prison) to demolish apartheid and bring an end to minority rule. In 1993, Mandela shared the Nobel peace prize with FW de Klerk and, in the first free elections the following year, was elected president of South Africa. In his much-quoted speech, 'Free at Last!', made after winning the 1994 elections, he focused the nation's attention firmly on the future, declaring, 'This is the time to heal the old wounds and build a new South Africa'.

In 1997, Mandela – or Madiba, his traditional Xhosa name – stepped down as ANC president, although he continues to be actively involved in politics as an elder statesman.

1990	1994
Nelson Mandela freed	First democratic elections; Nelson Mandela elected president

---

SOUTH AFRICA'S GOVERNMENT

In 1996, after much negotiation and debate, South Africa's parliament approved a revised version of the 1993 constitution that established the structure of the country's new, democratic government. Today, the national government consists of a 400-member National Assembly, a 90-member National Council of Provinces and a head of state (the president), who is elected by the National Assembly. In addition, there are nine provincial governments, each headed by a premier and a 10-person executive council. The provinces (and their capitals) are: Western Cape (Cape Town), Eastern Cape (Bisho), Northern Cape (Kimberley), KwaZulu-Natal (Pietermaritzburg), Mpumalanga (Nelspruit), Gauteng (Jo'burg), Free State (Bloemfontein), North-West Province (Mafikeng) and Limpopo (Polokwane, or Pietersburg). Cape Town is the national legislative capital, Pretoria the country's administrative capital and Bloemfontein the judicial capital.

A South African president has more in common with a Westminster-style prime minister than a US president, although as head of state the South African president has some executive powers denied to most prime ministers. The constitution stands at the centre of the legal system, and is most notable for its expansive Bill of Rights.

Operating parallel to these Western-style institutions is a system of traditional leadership, under which all legislation pertaining to indigenous law, tradition or custom must be referred to the Council of Traditional Leaders. Although the council cannot veto or amend legislation, it can delay its passage.

National elections are held every five years, and are next due in 2009.

The commission operated by allowing victims to tell their stories and perpetrators to confess their guilt, with amnesty on offer to those who made a clean breast of it. Those who chose not to appear before the commission would face criminal prosecution if their guilt could be proven. Yet, while some soldiers, police and 'ordinary' citizens have confessed their crimes, it seems unlikely that the human-rights criminals who gave the orders and dictated the policies will present themselves (PW Botha is one famous no-show), and it has proven difficult to gather evidence against them.

FREE ELECTIONS – ROUND TWO

In 1999, South Africa held its second democratic elections. In 1997 Mandela had handed over ANC leadership to his deputy, Thabo Mbeki, and there was speculation that the ANC vote might therefore drop. In fact, it increased to put the party within one seat of the two-thirds majority that would allow it to alter the constitution.

The NP, restyled as the New National Party (NNP), lost two-thirds of its seats, as well as official opposition status to the Democratic Party (DP) – traditionally a stronghold of liberal whites, with new force from conservatives disenchanted with the NP, and from some middle-class blacks. Coming in just behind the DP was the KwaZulu-Natal–based Inkatha Freedom Party (IFP), historically the voice of Zulu nationalism. While the IFP lost some support, its leader, Chief Mangosouthu Buthelezi, held onto power as the national Home Affairs Minister.

SOUTH AFRICA TODAY

Despite the scars of the past and the enormous problems ahead, South Africa today is an immeasurably more optimistic and relaxed country

1997	1999
Nelson Mandela retires as ANC president, succeeded by Thabo Mbeki	ANC wins landslide victory in second democratic elections

According to some stud-
ies, almost three-quarters
of deaths of South African
children under five years
old are from AIDS-related
illnesses.

than it was a decade ago. While Mbeki is viewed with far less affection by
the ANC grass-roots than the beloved 'Madiba' (Mandela), he has proven
himself a shrewd politician, maintaining his political pre-eminence by
isolating or coopting opposition parties. The 2004 national elections
were won decisively by the ANC with 70% of the votes, with Mbeki at the
helm, and today continues its dominance in daily political life.

Yet it has not been all clear sailing. In the early days of his presidency,
Mbeki's effective denial of the HIV/AIDS crisis invited global criticism,
and his conspicuous failure to condemn the forced reclamation of white-
owned farms in neighbouring Zimbabwe unnerved both South African
landowners and foreign investors.

In the coming years – in addition to choosing a successor for Mbeki,
who has announced that he will step down in 2009 – attention is likely
to focus overwhelmingly on crime, economic inequality, overhauling
the education system and, especially, HIV/AIDS. With an estimated
4.5 million South Africans affected – more than in any other country in
the world – this scourge threatens to eclipse all of South Africa's other
problems.

For more on AIDS in
South Africa, including
what's being done,
see www.avert.org
/aidssouthafrica.htm.

In recent years, efforts by AIDS activists and NGOs (nongovernment
organisations) have focused on urging the government to make anti-
retroviral drugs available for treatment for all AIDS sufferers, and on
reducing the major social stigma associated with infection. While huge
strides have been made – with many provinces now providing widespread
access to treatment – there is still a long way to go, both in ensuring treatment reaches all those who need it (especially children), and in lowering
the still alarmingly high infection rate.

2003	2006
South African government approves provision of free anti-retroviral drugs in public hospitals	Close to five million South Africans are living with HIV/AIDS

The Culture

THE NATIONAL PSYCHE

More than a decade has passed since South Africa's first democratic elections, and the country is still finding its way. While the streets pulsate with the same determination and optimism that fuelled the liberation struggle, the beat is tempered by the sobering social realities that are the legacy of apartheid's long years of oppression and bloodshed. Freedom has brought with it a whole new set of challenges.

Unemployment, crime and HIV/AIDS are the top concerns of most South Africans today, and the nation is fast becoming a society divided by class rather than colour. The gap between rich and poor is vast – one of the highest in the world, according to World Bank statistics. Manicured suburbs rub shoulders with squalid townships where clean drinking water is a scarce commodity and palatial residences overlook cramped tin-roofed shanties. Violent crime has stabilised at unacceptably high levels, and a generation that saw almost daily brutality and uncertainty during its formative years is now coming of age. Although the formal racial divisions of apartheid have dissolved, shadows and old ways of interacting remain, and suspicions and distrust still run high.

While crime continues to grab headlines and undermine South Africa's reputation as a tourism destination, it's important to keep it in perspective. The slowly and often fitfully emerging new South Africa is a unique and refreshing place to visit, and one of the most inspiring and hope-filled places that you'll find anywhere on the continent. Its political history is so fresh that those who lived through it are still there to guide you and grass-roots activism is high; visiting provides a rare chance to experience a nation that is rebuilding itself after profound change. As a backdrop to all this is the stunning natural magnificence, and the remarkably deep bond – perhaps best expressed in the country's literature (see p55) – that most South Africans feel for their land.

HIV/AIDS is the leading cause of death in South Africa, accounting for about 30% of deaths nationwide (versus about 6% of deaths from homicide and violence).

LIFESTYLE

It's difficult to present a unified picture of everyday life in South Africa. Many middle-class and wealthy families live in heavily secured homes and spend their leisure time in equally fortified shopping centres. Visit an upmarket shopping mall and you'll see people dining alfresco-style, under umbrellas at cafés that are actually indoors. Guards patrol the walkways and shops to keep criminals at bay, there's still a lingering sense of fear and loss connected with the passing of the old regime, and conversations are peppered with gloomy predictions about the government and the future.

Life is very different for the millions of South Africans who are still living in poverty. Tiny matchbox houses are home to large extended families, clean drinking water remains a luxury in some areas, and health facilities are not uniformly available.

Yet, township life is vibrant and informal. People gather on street corners and in local bars known as *shebeens*. Weddings are big events, and frequently spill onto the streets with plenty of dancing. If you're passing by, don't be surprised if you're encouraged to join in.

Unfortunately, funerals are becoming one of the most common gatherings in South Africa, as well as in Lesotho and Swaziland, and on weekends, cemeteries are routinely crowded with mourners. Many of those who are dying are youths, and people spend their time attending the funerals of one relative after the next. Many women have even formed burial societies to save money to cover the increasing costs.

According to one survey, South Africans spend more time attending funerals than shopping, going to braais (barbecues) or having their hair cut.

Thousands of households in South Africa, Lesotho and Swaziland are now headed by children whose parents have died from AIDS. Sometimes the only survivors from an entire family are the eldest children, who were born before their parents became infected. A large number of grandparents who have nursed and lost their adult offspring to AIDS are also looking after their orphaned grandchildren, many of whom are also HIV-positive.

Despite its prevalence, there's still a heavy stigma attached to HIV/AIDS. Many people are ashamed to admit that a relative died of AIDS, and family members will often tell you that their loved one passed away from tuberculosis or the flu.

POPULATION & PEOPLE

South Africa, Lesotho and Swaziland together form a beautiful and rich tapestry of cultures and ethnic groups – see the boxed text, p52.

In addition to their cultural roots, the three countries also have fascinatingly complex and interlocking socioeconomic compositions. South Africa's Gauteng province, which includes Johannesburg (Jo' burg) and Pretoria, is the economic engine of the country, generating more than half of South Africa's wealth. It's also the most densely populated and urbanised province. At the other end of the scale is the rural and underdeveloped Eastern Cape, where up to 20% of adults have never received any formal schooling.

Millions of immigrants from across the continent make their way to South Africa to take advantage of the country's powerhouse economy. While some arrive legally, many others take their chances – for example, jumping out of the windows of moving trains as they are being deported. Many of these illegal immigrants live in Jo'burg's impoverished inner city, causing resentment among some South Africans who accuse the outsiders of taking jobs and creating crime.

Swaziland's socioeconomic scene is almost completely wrapped up in that of its larger neighbour. Almost three-quarters of Swazi exports go to South Africa and even more goods and services are imported. Up to 70% of Swazis live in rural areas and many rely on farming for survival. Swazi culture is very strong and quite distinct from that of South Africa. The monarchy influences many aspects of life, from cultural ceremonies to politics. While some Swazis are proud of the royal traditions and suspicious of those who call for greater democracy, there's a small but growing number of human rights and opposition activists who believe power should be transferred from the king to the people.

Lesotho's main link with South Africa has been the mining industry. In the 1990s, at least 120,000 Basotho men were employed by South African mines, and up to one third of Lesotho's household incomes were from wages earned by the miners. When the mining industry was restructured though, tens of thousands of jobs were lost. Today, many former miners have returned home to Lesotho to join the ranks of the unemployed.

Beyond economics, different racial groups have complicated links. While much of the focus in South Africa has been on black and white relations, there is also friction and distrust between blacks, coloureds and South Africans of Indian descent. Yet, sometimes locals are surprisingly open when they talk about the stereotypes and prejudices that exist between various groups. Ask a Zulu what he or she thinks about Xhosas or quiz English-speaking whites about their views on Afrikaners.

WOMEN

In some respects, South African women have enjoyed a uniquely high profile during the country's turbulent history. Women were at the centre of the anti-pass law demonstrations and bus boycotts of the 1950s, protesting under the slogan 'You strike the woman and you strike the rock', and women are also strongly represented in South Africa's parliament. One-third of parliamentarians, as well as one-third of government ministers, are female, including the speaker of the National Assembly – a ranking that puts South Africa among the top 11 countries in the world for representation of women in government. Women's rights are also guaranteed in the constitution, and the ANC has a quota system for the party.

However, the daily reality for many South African women is very different, with poverty, sexual violence and HIV overshadowing other gains. Sexual violence statistics are particularly sobering. South Africa has the highest incidence of reported rape in the world, with approximately 52,000 cases of rape reported to the police annually, and a woman assaulted in the country every 26 to 60 seconds on average. Some women's groups say the real figures are much worse, because many women are too afraid to report the crime. Even more saddening is the fact that at least 20% – some place the figure closer to 40% – of reported rapes and attempted rapes are of girls below 18 years of age.

Women are statistically more likely than men to be infected with HIV, and many women become infected at an early age because they are having sex with older men. Worsening the situation is the threat of sexual violence, which often undermines the ability of young women to ensure their partner is wearing a condom.

In Swaziland, women have long held the legal status of minors – unable to own property in their own name, enter into contracts or secure bank loans without the sponsorship of a male relative. As recently as 2003, widows were disqualified from voting in elections, and were ordered to stay at home in accordance with the traditional Swazi belief that a widowed woman is 'unclean' because she still carries the spirit of her dead husband. A new constitution approved in 2005 guarantees women equal political, economic and social rights, reserves one-third of parliamentary seats for women and states that 'a woman shall not be compelled to undergo or uphold any custom to which she is in conscience opposed'. It's not yet clear how much of an actual gain this represents, as some of these provisions may be negated if traditional law is given precedence in the courts. Ironically, against this backdrop, a government survey has found that more than 70% of small businesses in Swaziland are operated by women.

In Lesotho, women shouldered a big share of economic, social and family responsibilities while their husbands and male relatives went to work in the mines in South Africa. Many of the mining jobs have now disappeared and – despite some bumps in recent years – the textile industry has become an important part of Lesotho's economy, with up to 90% of the new jobs going to women. Contrary to the trend elsewhere in the region, Basotho women are often better educated than their male counterparts, as many boys in rural areas are forced to tend cattle (or head off to South Africa to work), instead of spending time in the classroom.

South Africa has the world's largest HIV-positive population, and Swaziland its highest HIV-infection rate (38.8%), with Lesotho just a few steps behind.

The Zulu word for grandmother is *gogo*. The *gogo* plays a vital role in many families and her monthly pension is often the only regular source of income for the extended family.

SPORT

South Africans are sports fanatics, and after decades of being shut out of international competition, the national teams are now hungry for glory.

SOUTHERN AFRICA'S SLOWLY MELTING POPULATION POT

There are few countries where racial and ethnic conflicts have been as turbulent, protracted and high-profile as in South Africa. The country's heart pulses with the blood of groups with a diversity that covers the ancient San and Khoekhoen, 17th-century Dutch settlers, 19th-century British traders, Bantu-speaking African peoples, Indians, Jews, Portuguese and more. Yet it is only since 1994, with the commitment of the African National Congress (ANC) to build a nonracial 'rainbow nation', that there has been any significant degree of collaboration and peace between the various groups.

During the apartheid era, the government attempted to categorise everyone into one of four major groups – easily enough said, perhaps, but disastrous to implement. The classifications – African (at various times also called 'native' and 'Bantu', and sometimes now also 'black'), coloured, Asian or white – were often arbitrary and highly contentious. They were used to regulate where and how people could live and work, and became the basis for institutionalised inequality and intolerance.

Today, these times are slowly fading into history, although now discrimination based on wealth is threatening to replace racial discrimination. Yet the apartheid-era classification terms continue to be used. While we've also used these terms throughout this book, they work only to a certain extent, and within each of the four major categories are dozens of subgroups that are even more subjective and less clearly defined.

Lesotho and Swaziland were never subject to racial categorisation. This, plus the fact that both countries were for the most part formed around a single tribal group (the Basotho in Lesotho, and the Swazi in Swaziland), means that the constant awareness of racism that you'll encounter while travelling in South Africa is largely absent from these societies.

African

The vast majority of South Africans – about 77% – are Africans. Although subdivided into dozens of smaller groups, all ultimately trace their ancestry to the Bantu-speakers who migrated to Southern Africa in the early part of the 1st millennium AD. Due to the destruction and dispersal of the *difaqane* (forced migration), and to the forced dislocations and distortions of the apartheid era, tribal affiliation tends to be much weaker in South Africa than in other areas of the continent.

Today, discussions generally focus on ethno-linguistic groupings. With the new constitution's elevation of 11 languages to the status of 'official' language, the concept of ethnicity is also gaining a second wind. The largest ethno-linguistic group is the Nguni, which includes Zulu, Swazi, Xhosa and Ndebele peoples. Other major groups are the Sotho-Tswana, the Tsonga-Shangaan and the Venda.

The Zulu have maintained the highest profile ethnic identity over the years, centred in recent times around Chief Mangosouthu Buthelezi's Inkatha Freedom Party and its calls for an autonomous Zulu state. About 23% of South Africans speak Zulu as a first language. The second-largest group after the Zulu are the Xhosa, who have been extremely influential in politics. Nelson Mandela is Xhosa, as were numerous other figures in the apartheid struggle, and Xhosa have traditionally formed the heart of the black professional class. About 18% of South Africa's population uses Xhosa as a first language. Other major groups include the Basotho (who live primarily in and around Lesotho and South Africa's Free State), the Swazi (most of whom are in Swaziland) and the Tswana (who live primarily in Limpopo and North-West Province, and in Botswana). The Ndebele and Venda peoples are fewer in number, but have maintained very distinct cultures. These and other groups are profiled in the regional chapters throughout this book.

Coloured

During apartheid, 'coloured' was generally used as a catch-all term for anyone who didn't fit into one of the other racial categories. Despite this, a distinct coloured cultural identity has developed over the years – forged at least in part by whites' refusal to accept coloureds as equals and coloureds' own refusal to be grouped socially with blacks.

Among the diverse ancestors of today's coloured population are Afrikaners and others of European descent, West African slaves, political prisoners and exiles from the Dutch East Indies, and some of South Africa's original Khoesaan peoples. One of the largest subgroups of coloureds is the Griqua (p33), most of whom are members of the Dutch Reformed Church. Another major subgroup is the Cape Malays, with roots in places as widely dispersed as India, Indonesia and parts of East Africa. Most Cape Malays are Muslims and have managed to preserve their culture – especially evident today in Cape Town's Bo-Kaap district, in the *karamats* (tombs of Muslim saints) circling the city, and at the end of Ramadan, when you can see thousands of Muslims praying on Cape Town's Sea Point promenade.

Today, most coloureds live in Northern Cape and Western Cape, with significant populations also in KwaZulu-Natal. About 20% speak English as their first language. The vast majority – about 80% – are Afrikaans-speakers, and one of the oldest documents in Afrikaans is a Quran transcribed using Arabic script.

The most vibrant expression of Cape coloured culture is the riotous Cape Town New Year Karnaval (p610).

White

Most of South Africa's approximately 5.5 million whites (about 12% of South Africans) are either Afrikaans-speaking descendents of the early Dutch settlers or English-speakers. The Afrikaners, who mix German, French, British and other blood with their Dutch ancestry, constitute only about 7% of the country's total population. Yet they have had a disproportionate influence on South Africa's history. Rural areas of the country, with the exception of Eastern Cape, KwaZulu-Natal and the former homelands, continue to be dominated by Afrikaners, who are united by the Afrikaans language and by membership in the Dutch Reformed Church – the focal point of life in country towns.

While some Afrikaners still dream of a *volkstaat* (an independent, racially pure Boer state), the urbanised middle class tends to be considerably more moderate. Interestingly, the further the distance between the horrors of the apartheid era and the 'new South Africa', seemingly the more room there is for Afrikaners to be proud of their heritage. One expression of this is the growing popularity of the Absa Klein Karoo National Arts Festival (p611).

Important Afrikaner cultural organisations include the secret Afrikaner Broederbond, which is highly influential in National Party politics; the Federasie van Afrikaanse Kultuurvereniginge (FAK), which coordinates cultural events and movements; and the Voortrekkers, an Afrikaner youth organisation based on the scouting movement.

About two-thirds of South Africa's white English-speakers trace their roots to the English immigrants who began arriving in South Africa in the 1820s, although they are far less cohesive as a group than the Afrikaners. Other white South Africans include about 100,000 Jews, many of whom immigrated from Eastern Europe, or fled Nazi Germany during the 1930s and 1940s; a sizable Greek population; and about 50,000 Portuguese, most of whom came over from Mozambique during the 1970s.

Asian

About 98% of South Africa's roughly one million Asians are Indians. Many are descended from the indentured labourers brought to KwaZulu-Natal in the second half of the 19th century, while most of the others trace their ancestry to the free 'passenger Indians' who came to South Africa during the same time as merchants and business people. During apartheid, Indians were discriminated against by whites, but were frequently seen as white collaborators by some blacks.

Today's South African Indian population is primarily Hindu, with about 20% Muslims, and small numbers of Christians. Close to 90% live in Durban and other urban areas of KwaZulu-Natal, where Hindu temples, curries and Eastern spices are common parts of everyday life. Most speak English as a first language; Tamil or Hindi and Afrikaans are also spoken.

In addition to the Indians, there are about 25,000 Chinese, concentrated primarily in Jo'burg, and small numbers of other East Asians.

South Africa's national football team is called Bafana Bafana ('Boys Boys' in Zulu). The women's team is called Banyana Banyana (Girls Girls).

Football, followed by rugby and cricket, is the most popular spectator sport. The majority of football fans are black, while cricket and rugby attract predominately white crowds, although this is slowly changing.

South African rugby, in particular, is still struggling to shake its reputation as a whites-only domain, despite the inclusion of black players and officials. Development programmes are nurturing talent across the colour divides, and both rugby and cricket are now played regularly in Soweto and in some other townships. Victory in the 1995 Rugby World Cup was a turning point, and the image of President Nelson Mandela celebrating while wearing a Springboks jersey became a symbol of reconciliation. South African fans adore their beloved 'Boks' and Springbok-fever runs high in the lead up to international rugby tournaments.

In 2010, South Africa will host the football World Cup. The big local match is the Soweto Derby, pitting Jo'burg's 'Orlando Pirates' and 'Kaizer Chiefs' teams against each other. Wherever you are in the country, if a local invites you to a game, don't miss it. And if you're in the townships, watch for football stars cruising the streets in their expensive cars. Many of the top players are flamboyant and enjoy pop-star status among their fans.

MEDIA

After decades of restrictions and repression, South Africa's media is in a state of transition. The national broadcaster, SABC, is an important source of news for millions of South Africans, and is adjusting to its role as an independent voice. Discussion invariably centres around sport, business and crime, and investigative and political journalism are slowly evolving. SABC currently has 18 radio stations and several TV channels.

Privately owned e-tv, which was launched about a decade ago, has a younger, funkier style and smooth presentation.

Minibus taxis have been named after former Olympic distance runner Zola Budd because of their reputation for being fast and reliable.

Surf the radio airwaves and you'll get a sense of South Africa's diversity, with specialist stations broadcasting in all of the 11 official languages. Jo'burg's Y-FM (www.yfm.co.za) – a youth station that broadcasts in a mixture of English and township slang – has been one of the biggest success stories.

The media industry, mirroring political developments, has been the site of significant black empowerment deals, as stations and publications have changed hands. Previously white-dominated radio station Jacaranda-FM, for example, is now one of the top-rated black stations.

South Africa's best-selling English daily newspaper is the *Sowetan*. Although catering primarily to a poorly educated audience, it has a more sophisticated political and social outlook than most of the major white papers.

RELIGION

'When the missionaries came to Africa they had the Bible and we had the land. They said, "Let us pray." We closed our eyes. When we opened them we had the Bible and they had the land.' (Archbishop Desmond Tutu)

Religion plays a central role in the lives of most people in South Africa, Lesotho and Swaziland. Christianity is dominant in all three countries, with more than 75% of South Africans, about 90% of Lesotho's population, and around 60% of Swazis identifying themselves as Christians. Major South African denominations include the Nederduitse Gereformeerde (NG) or Dutch Reformed Churches, which have a national congregation of more than 3.5 million people and more than 1200 churches across the country, and the considerably more flamboyant Zion Christian Church (ZCC), with an estimated four million followers, plus many more in Swaziland. Every year more than one million ZCC members gather at Zion city near Polokwane in Limpopo Province during festivals at Easter and in September. Across all denominations, church attendance is generally high. On Sunday mornings in Lesotho, for example, you'll see families walking long distances through the mountains to go to church on even the most bitter winter days.

Despite their disproportionately large social influence, Muslims, Hindus and Jews combined make up less than 6% of South Africans. The rest of the population are atheist and agnostic, with a small number of people following traditional African beliefs.

Up to two-thirds of South Africa's Indians have retained their Hindu faith, and today most of the country's Hindus are of Indian descent. Islam has a small but growing following, particularly in the Cape. The Jewish community is estimated to be around 100,000, mostly in Jo'burg.

African traditional believers are a small group, although their traditions and practices have a significant influence on the cultural fabric and life of the region. The use of *muti*, or traditional medicine, is widespread, even among those who practise Christianity – just stop by the Museum of Man & Science shop on Diagonal St in central Jo'burg, or walk near the entrance to Chris Hani Baragwanagth Hospital in Soweto, where you'll see hawkers selling all sorts of herbs, powders and liquid concoctions.

Muti comes from the Zulu word *umuthi*, meaning 'tree'. *Muti* is derived from many different sources, including plants and animal parts.

ARTS
Cinema
Much of the history of South African cinema since its beginnings in the late-19th century has been one of exclusion and fragmentation. With the collapse of apartheid, the walls hemming in and dividing the industry began to fall as well. Ramadan Suleman's *Fools* (1998) was the first major feature film directed by a black South African. Since this release, the industry has given rise to a host of new talents, including Zola Maseko *(Drum)*, Zulfah Otto-Sallies *(Raya)*, who is also noted for her work on TV, and many others. For more film titles, see the boxed text, p22.

Literature
South Africa has an extraordinarily rich literary history, and there's no better way to get a sense of where the country has come from, and where it is heading, than delving into local literature.

Many of the first black South African writers were missionary-educated, including Solomon Tshekisho Plaatje, who was also the first Secretary-General of the African National Congress (ANC). In 1930, his epic romance, *Mhudi*, became one of the first books published in English by a black South African. (The first was RR Dhlomo's *An African Tragedy*, published in 1928.)

In 1948, South Africa moved onto the world literary stage with Alan Paton's international bestseller, *Cry, the Beloved Country*. Today, this beautifully crafted, lyrical tale of a black priest who comes to Jo'burg to find his son is still one of the country's most widely recognised titles. Other Paton classics include *Too Late the Phalarope*, which looks at the Afrikaner psyche and the inhumanity of apartheid, and *Ah, But Your Land is Beautiful*, another poignant look at the human toll of the apartheid system.

During the 1950s, *Drum* magazine became the focal point of lively satire, fiction and comment, and routinely drew attention as a major anti-apartheid mouthpiece. It gave a popular voice to urban black culture, telling the stories of those who were trying to live their lives despite oppression, and launched the careers of numerous prominent journalists and authors. Among these were Can Themba, known in particular for his short stories, and journalist Moses 'Casey' Motsisi.

Drum: The Making of a Magazine, by Anthony Sampson, tells the story of *Drum* as it moved into its 1950s heyday, becoming a mouthpiece for the anti-apartheid movement, and featuring some of the era's most prominent literary figures.

Age of Iron, by JM Coetzee, is the tale of a lone elderly woman who is confronted by unexpected bloodshed. Coetzee's writing is exquisite and gives a sense of the violence and isolation of apartheid South Africa.

In the 1960s, future Nobel laureate Nadine Gordimer began publishing her first books, including *Not for Publication and Other Stories* (1965) and the widely acclaimed *A Guest of Honour* (1970). Her most famous novel, *July's People,* was released in 1981, and depicts the collapse of white rule.

It was also in the 1960s and into the '70s that Afrikaner writers began to gain prominence as powerful voices for the opposition. Breyten Breytenbach – a poet and novelist who spent much of the '60s in self-imposed exile – was later jailed for becoming involved with the liberation movement, while André Brink was the first Afrikaner writer to be banned by the apartheid government. Brink's classic novel, *A Dry White Season,* portrays the lonely struggles of a white South African who discovered the truth about a black friend who died in police custody. Other Brink titles include *The Rights of Desire* – a tale of post-apartheid South Africa – and the recently published *Praying Mantis.*

The '70s also gave rise to several influential black poets, including Mongane Wally Serote, a veteran of the liberation struggle. His work, including the moving epic poem 'No Baby Must Weep', served as a rallying force for those living under apartheid, and today continues to give insights into the lives of black South Africans during the worst years of oppression.

John Maxwell (JM) Coetzee was also published in the 1970s, although it wasn't until two decades later that he gained international acclaim. His novel *Disgrace* – a powerful, brittle and complex look at South African social realities – was released in 1999 and won Coetzee his second Booker Prize. Coetzee won the Nobel Prize for Literature in 2003.

One of the most prominent contemporary authors is Zakes Mda, who – with the publication of *Ways of Dying* in 1995 – made a successful transition from poetry and plays to become an acclaimed novelist. His most recent book, *The Whale Caller* (2005), takes a somewhat sceptical look at the optimism surrounding the new South Africa.

For more literary highlights see the boxed text, p22.

Architecture

Among the highlights of Southern African indigenous architecture are the 'beehive huts' that you'll see dotted throughout the region, as well as in Swaziland and in rural parts of KwaZulu-Natal. These structures consist of a frame made of wooden sticks or poles, bent and lashed together to form a dome, and then covered with grass mats and thatching. A typical homestead or *umuzi,* as it's known in Zulu, consists of a group of these dwellings arranged in a circle around a cattle kraal, and surrounded by a fence made of stones or bush. Traditionally the huts were set on an eastward-facing slope, with the hut of the chief at the highest point.

Beehive huts are also found in Xhosa areas, where they are used primarily in initiation rites, though the more common residential variant is the thatched, round, straight-walled huts that you'll see throughout rural parts of Eastern Cape. While mud bricks or other materials are now often used, traditionally, the sides of these huts were constructed with a mixture of clay and cattle dung spread over a circular frame topped with thatching. Xhosa huts are typically seen scattered over the hillsides, rather than arranged in the kraals characteristic of Zulu areas.

Elaborately painted Ndebele houses – a relatively recent tradition – are another highlight. Their exteriors sport brightly coloured geometric motifs or more elaborate artwork that may depict anything from airplanes to double-storey dwellings and street lamps.

Basotho homes are also often brightly painted, and feature geometric and often highly symbolic mural art known as *litema*. The tradition began

Tune into Y-FM 99.2 for a taste of the local version of hip-hop, known as Kwaito music.

Reporters Without Borders ranks South Africa 31st in the world in terms of press freedoms, equal with Australia, and before the USA (which is ranked 44th).

with women painting symbols on their houses as a form of supplication for rain and good fortune. Beginning during the anti-apartheid struggles, some Basotho women also used *litema* as a political statement, painting their houses in the gold, black and green colours of the ANC. Today, *litema* is used particularly around special celebrations and holidays, such as births, weddings and religious feasts.

The colonial era also left a rich architectural legacy. One of its most attractive building styles is that of the graceful and gabled Cape Dutch house so typical of the Western Cape. Pretoria is another showpiece of colonial-era architecture, with an impressive collection of conservative and stately creations, including the famous Union Buildings (p434), designed by English architect Sir Herbert Baker.

Jo'burg grew quickly after the discovery of gold in 1886 and those who were making money were eager to show off their wealth with palatial homes and grand offices. In Durban, the designs were more playful. Beginning in the 1930s, flamboyant buildings with Art Deco influences gave the city its own style. Take a stroll along Victoria Embankment, or up Broad or Aliwal Sts for a sampling. Cape Town's building boom in the 1930s also left a wealth of impressive Art Deco designs, especially around Greenmarket Square. Many of the highlights are included in the walking tour, p138.

The dour days of apartheid delivered many bland office blocks and public buildings, and much of contemporary architecture is now centred on overcoming this heritage. The white-dominated industry is gradually attracting more black professionals, but it's a slow process and South Africa is still finding a sense of style that reflects the nation. Security is a major consideration for contemporary architects, as the country's crime rate means that high walls, electric fences, boom gates and guard houses are a required part of many building plans.

One of the most noteworthy examples of new South African architecture is the Constitutional Court in Jo'burg (p403). Inaugurated in 2004, it was built on the site of the old Jo'burg Fort where many famous anti-apartheid activists were jailed during the liberation struggle. Another is the new Northern Cape Legislature Building in Kimberley (p529), which is notable for its lack of columns, and minimisation of angles and straight lines.

For some more architectural highlights, see the boxed text, p22.

Visual Arts

South African art had its beginnings with the San, who left their distinctive designs on rock faces and cave walls throughout the region. When European painters arrived, many of their early works centred on depictions of Africa for colonial enthusiasts back home, although with time, a more South Africa–centred focus developed.

Black artists were sidelined for many decades. Gerard Sekoto was one of the first to break through the barriers, and is viewed today as one of the major figures in the development of South African contemporary art. Before departing South Africa for France in 1947, he lived in Sophiatown and Kliptown, and much of his early work depicts the colour and vibrancy of township life. One of Sekoto's most famous paintings from this time was *Yellow Houses* (1940), which became the first work by a black painter to be bought by the Jo'burg Art Gallery.

At about the same time that Sekoto was gaining prominence, a Sophiatown neighbour, John Koenakeefe Mohl, began spearheading artistic instruction and schooling for young black artists. In 1960, he was one of

The beautifully photographed *Shack Chic*, by Craig Fraser, is a captivating portrayal of the strength and spirit of those living in South Africa's townships.

See www.artthrob.co.za for the latest on South Africa's contemporary visual arts scene.

Artists Under the Sun (www.artistsunder thesun.org) was founded during the apartheid era to promote visual arts regardless of colour. It's still going, with a free exhibition on the first weekend of each month at Zoo Lake in Parktown, Johannesburg.

the founding members of the Artists' Market Association, which was set up to provide a showcase for young talent – today continued in Artists Under the Sun.

Throughout the apartheid era, racism, oppression and violence were common themes on canvas. Many black artists who were unable to afford materials adopted cheaper alternatives, including lino prints. Artists also played an important role in designing the logos for T-shirts, banners and posters during the liberation struggle.

In more recent times, a lack of public funds for the arts sector has meant that it has become more reliant on corporate collectors and the tourism industry. Contemporary art ranges from vibrant crafts sold on the side of the road to high-priced paintings that hang in trendy galleries. Innovative artists are using anything from telephone wire, safety pins, beads and plastic bags to tin cans to create their works.

Local sculpture is also diverse. Artists including Jackson Hlungwane, known for his highly symbolic, religiously oriented woodcarvings, and Helen Martins, whose concrete sculptures can be seen at her Owl House in Nieu Bethesda (see p271), have experimented with a range of styles and materials.

Theatre & Dance

During the colonial era, South African theatre was dominated by European and American plays staged for local audiences. But home-grown playwrights, performers and directors gradually emerged, particularly in the 1930s, when theatre began to gain popularity in the townships. One of the first black South African writers to have his work published in English was Herbert Dhlomo, who won acclaim for his 1936 drama *The Girl Who Killed to Save*. Jo'burg's old Sophiatown neighbourhood was a particularly prolific font for new artists and pieces. Yet, the apartheid regime's National Theatre Fund didn't provide support to black theatre companies and development was marked by a constant struggle for resources.

A major turning point came with the arrival on the scene of writer and director Athol Fugard. Fugard, who played a crucial role in developing and nurturing black theatrical talent, established several troupes in Port Elizabeth and Jo'burg during the 1950s. By the 1960s and '70s, theatre and politics were inextricably intertwined. Several artists were arrested and charged for their role in the fight against apartheid and others had their work banned. The innovative two-man show *Woza Albert!*, which portrayed Jesus Christ arriving in apartheid-era South Africa, won rave reviews and international acclaim.

In 1974, run-down buildings at Jo'burg's old 'Indian' fruit market were converted to become the Market Theatre, with patrons and performers defying the apartheid government's notorious Group Areas Act to ensure that it became an all-race venue. Today, the Market Theatre is still one of the best-known performance spaces in the country (p415).

While the end of apartheid took with it the powerful themes of racism and oppression that had spawned decades of local creative output, South Africa's performing arts scene is now enjoying a renaissance and beginning to explore new topics.

African Footprint (www.africanfootprintonline.com), which had its world premiere in 2000, has been a highly successful showcase of young South African dancers. Another highlight is the First National Bank Dance Umbrella – an annual festival of dance and choreography that brings together local and international artists and provides a stage for new work.

Music Jane Cornwell

Nelson Mandela once declared that music would be the salvation of his people. Just as music fuelled the resistance to apartheid, it continues to sing out for freedom and justice, providing a soundtrack to everyday lives. Music is everywhere in South Africa, coming through every available medium, communicating in every imaginable style. Want a 'typical' South African sound? Forget it: South Africa has the greatest range of musical styles on the African continent, and more than any country of similar size anywhere in the world. A nation of record collectors, the people of South Africa love their music. Rock, jazz, classical, gospel, rap, reggae, maskanda, mbaqanga, kwaito…and much more. Here centuries-old traditions jostle with new genres sprung from old ones. Western styles are given an idiosyncratic stamp. The country's gargantuan recording industry (with its new, small-but-determined crop of independent black-owned labels) watches, ready to pounce.

Pascale Lamche's *Sophiatown* (2003) looks at Jo'burg's bustling Sophiatown, the Harlem of South Africa. Home to many artists and musicians, it was flattened for redevelopment in the 1950s. Archive footage and interviews with Nelson Mandela, Hugh Masekela and Dorothy Masuka make for compulsive viewing.

The sounds of South Africa have an inevitable influence on its smaller neighbours Lesotho and Swaziland. Vocal choirs are popular in Lesotho, as is Afropop, jazz, reggae and especially kwaito. Traditional musical instruments such as the *lekolulo* flute and the *setolo-tolo* mouth bow continue to be played by the Sotho. Swaziland, too, has its traditional music, which is used as accompaniment for harvests, weddings, births and other events. It also has local choral music, jazz, Afropop, rock, a burgeoning hip-hop scene and, above all else, gospel.

In South Africa, over a decade's worth of freedom has proved that a recovering country can still produce sophisticated talent to the highest international standards. The Rainbow Nation continues to address social concerns, express sadness and bring joy. No one sound will ever identify South Africa, which can only be a good thing (the annual South African Music Awards is a multicategory, multitextured and very long ceremony as a result). Part of what makes South Africa so astonishing is its range. What follows is a by-no-means definitive look at the major genres, with their major players. So get humming, swing your hips and dive in.

A POTTED HISTORY OF SOUTH AFRICAN MUSIC

The Zulu, Xhosa and Sotho people have been singing and dancing for thousands of years – this is the music that attracted Paul Simon before he recorded his 1988 album *Graceland* – just as the Venda (and in Lesotho, the Basotho) have been playing their *mbiras* (thumb pianos) and reed pipes. There are eight distinct 'tribal' traditions in South Africa, and democracy has seen a resurgence in traditional musicians making very traditional music. But from the earliest colonial times to the present day, South Africa's music has created and reinvented itself from a mixture of older local and imported styles. Most of the popular ones use either Zulu a-capella singing or harmonic mbaqanga as a vocal base, ensuring that whatever the instrument – and the banjo, violin, concertina and electric guitar have all had a profound influence – the sound stays proudly, resolutely African.

In the Time of Cannibals: The Word Music of South Africa's Basotho Migrants (1994) is a legendary tome by ethnomusicologist David B Coplan, who focuses on the sung oral poetry of the workers who migrate from Lesotho to the mines and cities of South Africa.

Ever wondered why the chord sequences of many South African songs seem familiar? Blame the church: the Protestant missionaries of the 19th century developed a choral tradition that, in tandem with the country's first formal music education, South African composers would blend with traditional harmonic patterns: Enoch Sontonga's 1897 hymn 'Nkosi

Sikelel, i Afrika' (God Bless Africa), originally written in Xhosa, is now the country's national anthem. Today the gospel movement is the major industry player. Gloria Bosman, Sibongile Khumalo, Pinise Saul and other top black South African artists now working across a range of genres – classical, jazz, gospel, opera – started singing in mission-school choirs or in church. Others, such as redoubtable gospel superstar Rebecca (who has dropped her surname, Malope), crossed over from the shiny world of pop. Swaziland's biggest gospel star is Shongwe, a former gold miner.

INTERVIEW WITH HUGH MASEKELA

After almost three decades away, one of South Africa's most renowned musicians in exile during the apartheid era, Hugh Masekela, has reclaimed his place in the national music terrain. Since his return in 1990, Masekela's drive, musicality and business acumen have provided a much needed spark for the explosion in South Africa's recorded music scene. It hasn't been easy, he shrugs. But he's glad to be back, just the same.

'I am like a pig in dirty mud,' he says with a grin. 'I have been very fortunate to be able to reimmerse myself in the things that I missed when I was away. People like myself, Miriam (Makeba) and Abdullah (Ibrahim) were always living overseas reluctantly. To tell you the truth, until I came back here, which I never thought I would, my career never really started.'

Masekela's 21st-century success – with albums like Sixty, Black to the Future and Time – is hugely satisfying for an individual who began playing music some 50 years ago. 'Creatively I get my energy from this place,' he says. 'I always have. Now the time has come to give back.' Beyond his solo work, which also provides a platform for a slew of talented musicians (such as Zwai Bela, former member of kwaito group TKZee), Masekela is committed to rebuilding the country. There is his initiative MAAPSA (Musicians and Artists Programme of South Africa), which implements drug rehabilitation projects in the creative community (Masekela is a former addict himself). There is his record company, Chissa, which has expanded to include music events, theatre productions, opera and films.

'Chissa is the first African-owned independent record company. It has been a hell of a fight to get where we are because everything that is entertainment-oriented in Africa was always owned by the old, colonial-era order,' says the unapologetically political Masekela, eyes flashing. 'There is resistance, because they know that in the end we will kick them out. So this is the new fight. The new revolution. The government would like to help, but because they're politicians they don't know how to.'

He isn't alone, he adds. Masekela and his colleagues aim to establish the same sort of music distribution network that exists in, say, India, Japan and Brazil – even in America or Europe. 'But to do that we have to own it. So that's what we're going through now. It's the kind of legacy a few of us would like to leave: the ownership and reclaiming of our culture. That is what will bring our self-esteem back. Apartheid basically killed our culture – and for us to re-energise and revive it we have to own the audio-visual industry.'

It's been a long personal road. The Witbank, Jo'burg, boy was moved to pick up a trumpet after watching Kirk Douglas playing Bix Beiderbecke in the movie Young Man With A Horn ('He had the finest clothes, he stood in front of the band, he always got the girl'). He co-founded The Jazz Epistles, the first black South African jazz band to make a long-playing record, and left his fractured homeland for Great Britain and then the US ('Miles, Dizzy and Louis all said to me, "Put some of that South African flavour in your music and everyone will sit up and take notice"') and elsewhere in Africa. He married (and divorced) Miriam Makeba, impressed Nelson Mandela, and befriended the likes of Harry Belafonte, Paul Simon and Fela Kuti. Most of all, he used his profile to remind his people and the world of what they were, and what was going on.

Masekela is now back where he belongs. 'To rebuild a nation that has been repressed and kicked around is very rough. People look at us as this amazing miracle "Rainbow Nation", but the after-effects don't go away the day after you stand in line to vote, you know.' Hugh Masekela pauses, smiles. 'We'll get there, slowly,' he says. 'But we need to work together.'

Zulu music's veteran exponents Ladysmith Black Mambazo – wrongly considered 'typical' South African music by many Westerners, thanks to their rapid-fire album releases and relentless international touring schedule – exemplify the way indigenous harmonies were neatly mixed with the sounds of European and African church choirs (a vocal style known as *mbube*). In the same way that much contemporary South African art was born from oppression, Ladysmith's 'tiptoe' *isicathamiya* music, with its high-kicking, soft-stepping dance, has its origins in all-male miner's hostels in Natal province in the 1930s, with workers at pains not to wake their bosses. *Isicathamiya* choirs still appear in weekly competitions in Johannesburg (Jo'burg) and Durban; such choirs, or versions thereof, often busk South African city streets.

Kwela music, like most modern South African styles, came out of the townships. Kwela, meaning 'jump up', was the instruction given to those about to be thrown into police vans during raids. Once-infamous areas like Soweto, Sharpeville, District Six and Sophiatown gave rise to urban, pan-tribal genres, mostly inspired by music coming in (or back) from America such as jazz, swing, jive and soul. Black South Africans added an urban spin: kwela, with its penny whistles (an instrument evolved from the reed flutes of indigenous cattle herders) and one-string bass became sax-jive, or mbaqanga. Marabi soul took off in the 1970s. Bubblegum pop dominated the 1980s. Kwaito, South Africa's very own hip hop, exploded in the 1990s and remains, apart from gospel and a burgeoning R&B scene, the country's most popular genre. Kwaito superstar and former township heavy Zola even has his own TV show.

America and Europe were the inspiration for white South African artists. Sixties phenomenon Four Jacks and a Jill were pure Western pop. British punk inspired 1970s working-class outfits a la Wild Youth. The 1980s saw a crossover of black and white musicians: Johnny Clegg and Juluka (now Savuka) used a fusion of white rock and pop with traditional Zulu music to challenge racist restrictions and set a precedent for others. Grunge helped shape the likes of Scooters Union, the Springbok Nude Girls and other 1990s guitar bands. The likes of Seether, the Parlotones and former Springbok frontman Arno Carstens means that rock continues to, well, rock the country today. Afrikaans music – through Anna Davel, Chris Chameleon, Lize Beekman and Theuns Jordaan – continues its renaissance. And then there's the huge cutting edge dance scene: house, techno, acid jazz, R&B, dancehall and all grooves in between, often with live elements thrown in.

The effects of apartheid on lives and culture are still sorely felt; musicians such as jazz legend and former exile Hugh Masekela stress the need for continued vigilance. (Look out, too, for the multitalented protest singer, Vusi Mahlasela.) The creation of a black-owned, black-run music industry and distribution network is still a long way off (resistance by moguls in the old white biz has been fierce), but is vital nonetheless. South African music still needs to be Africanised. In the meantime, the music of the resistance has maintained its fire by changing its focus: other scourges – such as HIV/AIDS, poverty, the abuse of women and children – are being written about, talked about and sung about. Opportunities abound in the current climate of cultural and artistic expression.

In Swaziland, where the enthusiastically polygamous King Mswati allegedly had his teenage daughter and her friends whipped in 2005 for refusing to turn down the music at a party, and where the ancient but controversial Reed Dance ceremony sees thousands of bare-breasted virgins

Paul Simon's *Graceland* album has sold 7 million copies worldwide and – despite the controversy over the breaking of sanctions – was vital in alerting the rest of the world to the music of South Africa.

The 2006 Oscar-winning township drama *Tsotsi* features a soundtrack composed by kwaito star Zola (who also plays local gang boss Fela), as well as haunting tracks by singer-songwriter Vusi Mahlasela (*Music From the Motion Picture Tsotsi*, Milan Records).

The Morija Arts and Cultural Festival is a five-day celebration of Basotho culture and Lesotho heritage that takes place in Morija (40km from Lesotho's capital, Maseru) at the end of September each year.

dance for the absolute monarch, things aren't quite so liberal. Mswati, who has his own 'electronic' praise singer, Quawe Mamba (who runs the king's TV studio as well as a private TV channel), has long hosted fundraising concerts that feature both international stars (Eric Clapton, Erykah Badu) and local acts. Music, he has said, 'is a healing weapon for a depressed soul as well as an expression of joy'. And indeed, music pulses strongly in Swaziland, courtesy of everyone from kwaito DJ Kwephe and reggae outfit Black Roses to fast-rising singer Fanaza Tsabedze.

Up in Lesotho, the hills and valleys are alive with the sound of music. The Basotho people love their songs and instruments: children in villages harmonise their hearts out in choirs; shepherd boys play their *lekolulo* flutes and sing in pure, pitch-perfect voices; women play the stringed *thomo;* and men the *setolo-tolo,* a sort of extended Jew's Harp played using the mouth.

In South Africa, however, boundaries are down. Styles are cross-pollinating. Many genres, especially jazz, are booming (venues, however, need to follow suit). Democracy, so bitterly won, has never sounded so sweet.

SOUTH AFRICAN MUSICAL STYLES
Marabi

In the early 1900s travelling African-American minstrel shows, vaudeville acts, ragtime piano players and gospel groups impressed local audiences in the growing cities of Cape Town and Jo'burg. Urbanisation had a domino effect on musical styles: visiting American jazz artists and records by the likes of Louis Armstrong and Duke Ellington kick-started what would later become the South African jazz scene. By the 1920s and 1930s the urban ghettos were singing and swinging to a defining, dangerous (in Sotho it means 'gangster') small band sound: marabi.

Played on cheap pedal organs and keyboards with accompaniment from pebble-filled cans, marabi flooded illegal township shebeens (unlicensed bars) and dancehalls. Its siren call got people in and drinking, but it also offered some dignity and consolation to the oppressed working-class areas where it was played. Marabi's trancelike rhythms and cyclical harmonies had links to American Dixieland and ragtime; subsequent decades saw the addition of penny whistle, drums, banjo and a big-band swing, even bebop aesthetic.

Marabi made its way into the jazz-dance bands that produced the first generation of professional black musicians: the Jazz Maniacs, Merry Blackbirds and Jazz Revellers. Often referred to, simply (and not always correctly) as 'African jazz' or 'jive', marabi went on to spawn other styles. One of these was kwela.

Kwela

Kwela was the first popular South African style to make the world sit up and take notice. Initially played on acoustic guitar, banjo, one-string bass

---

A SLEEPING GIANT

In 1939 Zulu migrant worker Solomon Linda recorded a song called 'Mbube' (Lion) for Gallo; retitled 'Wimoweh/The Lion Sleeps Tonight' it made big bucks for everyone from Pete Seeger to Disney, who used it in 1994's *The Lion King.* Linda had signed away his rights to his song (which has made an estimated US$15 million), but in 2006 a loophole was discovered in South African law that brought the rights back to Linda's family.

and, most importantly, the penny whistle, kwela was taken up by kids with no access to horns and pianos but keen to put their own spin on American swing. Groups of tin-flautists would gather to play on street corners in white areas, with the danger of arrest (for creating a 'public disturbance') upping the music's appeal and attracting rebellious white kids known as 'ducktails'. Many such groups were also lookouts for the *shebeens*.

Kwela combos gained a live following but little recording took place until 1954, when Spokes Mashinyane's Ace Blues became the smash African hit of the year and sent white producers scurrying into the black market. Artists such as Sparks Nyembe and Jerry Mlotshwa became popular; the hit 'Tom Lark' by Elias Lerole and His Zig-Zag Flutes even crossed over to Britain, where – probably because of its similarity to skiffle – it stayed in the charts for 14 weeks.

In the early 1960s Mashinyane introduced the saxophone to kwela with his song 'Big Joe Special', ending the penny-whistle boom and creating sax-jive. Sax-jive quickly became mbaqanga.

Mbaqanga

The saxophone became vital to jazz music, which, much to the dismay of white kwela fans, was now limited to performances in the townships. Mbaqanga ('easy money') had its innovators: Joseph Makwela and Marks Mankwane of celebrated session players the Makhona Tshole Band added electric guitars to the cascading rhythms – notably a funky, muscular bass – while sax player/producer West Nkosi set the pace. This hugely popular electric sound backed singers whose vocal style was later christened 'mqashiyo' (after a dance style), even though it was really no different from mbaqanga.

Mbaqanga's idiosyncratic vocals echoed 1950s groups such as the Manhattan Brothers and Miriam Makeba's Skylarks, groups who copied African-American do-wop outfits but used Africanised five-part harmonies instead of four. In the 1960s Aaron Lerole of Black Mambazo added his groaning vocals to the mix, but it was the growling bass of Simon 'Mahlathini' Nkabinde and his sweet-voiced Mahotella Queens (backed by the Makhona Tshole Band) who would inspire a generation, including Izintombi Zeze Manje Manje and the Boyoyo Boys who would be sampled by British producer/chancer Malcolm McLaren on the 1981 British number one, 'Double Dutch'. The Mahotella Queens – sans Mahlathini – are still going strong.

Mbaqanga remains a dominant force in South African music, its influence apparent in everything from soul and reggae to R&B, kwaito and, of course, jazz.

Jazz

Structurally, harmonically and melodically distinctive, the force that is South African jazz started as an underground movement and became a statement of protest and identity. In the hands of such exiled stars as singer Miriam Makeba, pianist Abdullah Ibrahim (formerly Dollar Brand) and trumpeter Hugh Masekela, it was famously an expatriate music that represented the suffering of a people. Legendary outfit the Blue Notes – led by Chris McGregor and featuring saxophonist Dudu Pukwana – helped change the face of European jazz after relocating to the UK. Jazzers who stayed behind kept a low profile while developing new sounds and followings with, variously, jazz-rock fusion, Latin and even Malay crossovers.

South African Music Week takes place every August in Cape Town.

South African Music (www.music.org.za) has links to local artists, performances and music news.

ESSENTIAL LISTENING

▪ marabi – *From Marabi to Disco*, Various Artists (Gallo, South Africa)

▪ kwela – *Spokes Mashiyane*, King Kwela (Gallo, South Africa)

▪ mbaqanga – *Soul Brothers*, Kuze Kuse (Gallo, South Africa)

▪ jazz – *Sheer Jazz*, Various Artists (Sheer Sound, South Africa)

▪ gospel – *Tales of Gospel S.A.* (Sheer Sound, South Africa)

▪ neotraditional music – *Sthandwa*, Phuzekhemisi (Gallo, South Africa)

▪ soul and reggae – *Respect*, Lucky Dube (Gallo, South Africa)

▪ bubblegum, kwaito and current trends – *New Construction*, Bongo Maffin (Gallo, South Africa)

Featuring music and interviews by Abdullah Ibrahim, Hugh Masekela and Miriam Makeba among others, Lee Hirsch's *Amandla! A Revolution in Four-Part Harmony* (2003) explores the role of music in the fight against apartheid. Made over nine years, this is a deeply affecting film.

World-renowned exiles who returned home after the end of the anti-apartheid cultural boycott had to work hard to win back local audiences. Most now enjoy healthy followings – Masekela remains his country's most enduring musical ambassador – in what is a thriving (if occasionally backbiting) mainstream scene. Frequent festivals, often featuring top overseas acts, are providing platforms (among the best is the Cape Town International Jazz Festival each April) and the South African media is lending its support.

Well known locals are moving jazz forward, working with DJs, artists, poets and dance companies. Coltrane-esque saxophonist Zim Ngqawana (who led a group of 100 drummers, singers and dancers at Nelson Mandela's inauguration in 1994) is drawing on folk and rural traditions as well as Indian, avant garde and classical music. His former sideman, pianist Andile Yenana, combines the traditional and experimental with Monk-ish flair. Guitarist Jimmy Dludlu, a sort of African George Benson, takes time out to work with music school graduates. Lesotho-born Tsopo 'The Village Pope' Tshola has made an astounding comeback. Female vocalists Gloria Bosman, Sibongile Khumalo, Judith Sephumo and myriad others are making their mark. Many are enjoying success in another genre with common roots: gospel.

Gospel

The music industry's biggest market – bolstered by the country's 80% Christian black population – South Africa's gospel is an amalgam of European choral music, American influences, Zulu a-cappella singing and other African traditions incorporated within the church (Zionist, Ethiopian, Pentecostal and Apostolic). All joy, colour and exuberance, rhythm, passion and soul, gospel choirs perform throughout South Africa, lifting the roofs off big, formal venues and community halls alike. The 24-piece ensemble and overseas success story, Soweto Gospel Choir (check out their new album, *Blessed*), like many big choirs features a band with drummers and dancers.

This vast genre is divided into both traditional gospel – as personified by the heavyweight Pentecostal Church Choir (IPCC) and others such as Solly Moholo, Lusanda Spiritual Group and Jabu Hlongwane – and contemporary gospel. Beacons of the latter include tiny diva Rebecca (who also sings in the traditional style), multiplatinum KwaMashu Deborah 'Debs' Fraser, Reverend Benjamin Dube ('the Gospel Maestro') and classical ensemble Soweto String Quartet. Former gold miner Shongwe – who created his gospel songs while working underground and hummed them until his shift was over – is Lesotho's biggest star.

Gospel also comprises much of the oeuvre of Ladysmith Black Mambazo (whose 2006 album *Long Walk To Freedom* finds them collaborating with Western artists including Emmylou Harris and Natalie Merchant). Their Zulu *isicathimiya* music is a prime example of the way traditional South African music has appropriated Western sounds to produce unique musical styles.

Neotraditional Music

Away from the urban life of the townships and the cities' recording studios, traditional musicians from the Sotho, Zulu, Pedi and Shangaan regions were creating dynamic social music. By the 1930s many were mixing call-and-response singing with the dreamy 10-button concertina, an instrument that has made a comeback in Zulu pop. The Sotho took up the accordion (accordion players and groups still abound in Lesotho); the Pedi the German autoharp; and the Zulu embraced the guitar.

Maskanda (or maskandi) is a form of rhythmic and repetitive guitar picking born through the Zulu experience of labour migration. Many made do with an *igogogo*, an instrument fashioned from an oil can; maskanda stalwart Shiyani Ngcobo still uses the *igogogo* in his live sets. Today's top-selling maskanda acts include Bhekumuzi Luthuli, Inkunzi Emdaka, Thokozani and Phuzekhemisi, whose shows often include dozens of singers, dancers and instrumentalists.

The upbeat and vaguely Latin-sounding Tsonga (formerly Shangaan) music tends to feature a male leader backed by, variously, a female chorus, guitars, synths, percussion and an unabashed disco beat. Best known acts include Doctor Sithole, George Maluleke, Matshwa Bemuda & Magenge Sisters and Thomas Gezane Mzamani.

Young Xhosa artist Lungiswa is one of the few female South African musicians to play the *mbira* in her traditional/urban crossovers. Veteran singer Busi Mhlongo (like Tsepo Tsola, now addiction-free after support from Hugh Masekela's MAAPSA drug rehabilitation programme) fuses the traditional Zulu sound with hip hop and kwaito.

In Lesotho, a group of shepherds known as Sotho Sounds play instruments made from rubbish: one-string fiddle *(qwadinyana),* guitars *(katara)* and drums fashioned out of disused oil cans, car tyres, twigs and a kitchen sink. Having played WOMAD UK in 2003 they have returned to their base in Malealea, where they continue to compose and rehearse (they perform for guests of Malealea Lodge every second night).

But again, it's in South Africa that roots are being mixed with every sound imaginable, from country, blues, rap (check out Hip Hop Pantsula, H2O, Tuks Senganga) and house (see DJs Fresh, Oskido, Christos) to rock, reggae and soul.

Soul & Reggae

The American-led soul music of the 1960s had a huge impact on township teenagers. The local industry tried various cheap imitations; the few South African 'soul' groups that made it did so on the back of a blend of soul and marabi, like the Movers, or soul and electric bass mbaqanga, like the Soul Brothers, a band who spawned dozens of imitators and are still going strong today. Contemporary South African soul is often filed under mbaqanga: the genre from which evergreen reggae star Lucky Dube sprang (in 1984) into another style of music entirely. Dube's legacy aside, in South Africa reggae is often subsumed into other genres like ragga and

Rage (www.rage.co.za) is an online magazine with music news, reviews and fashion.

One World (www.one world.co.za) is an independent music cyberstore selling South African music and a limited range of books and videos.

kwaito: the redoubtable Bongo Maffin (the Fugees of South Africa) throw kwaito, house, reggae, ragga, gospel and hip hop into the pot.

Homegrown R&B has also surged ahead: hugely popular female singer Lebo Mathosa fuses traditional and dance music, funk and R&B. Big-voiced belter Pebbles cites Mariah and Whitney as inspirations. The hunky Camagu mixes his smooth voice with electronic beats, while the wonderful Thandiswa (Bongo Maffin's Lauryn Hill) makes nods in the R&B direction on her latest release, *Zabalaza*.

Bubblegum, Kwaito & Current Trends

The disco that surfaced during the 1970s came back – slick, poppy and Africanised – in the 1980s as 'bubblegum'. Vocally led and aimed squarely at the young, this electronic dance style owed a debt to mbaqanga as well as America. What the Soul Brothers started, superstars like Brenda Fassie, Sello 'Cicco' Twala and Yvonne Chaka Chaka refined. (The sudden death of the outrageous and brilliant Fassie in May 2004 left South Africa reeling.) Bubblegum's popularity waned in the 1990s, and in its place exploded kwaito (kwi-to, meaning 'hot').

The music of young, black, urban South Africa, kwaito is a rowdy mix of everything from bubblegum, hip hop, R&B and ragga to mbaqanga, traditional, jazz, and British and American house music. It is also a fashion statement, a state of mind and a lifestyle. Chanted or sung in a mixture of English, Zulu, Sesotho and the street slang Isicamtho (usually over programmed beats and backing tapes), kwaito's lyrics range from the anodyne to the fiercely political. A unique fusion, kwaito has caught the imagination of post-apartheid South Africa. Acts such as Zola, Boom Shala, TK Zee and Arthur remain major players, while the current crop includes Brickz, Brown Dash, Spikiri and Prokid – though he is also considered a rapper. (The rap versus kwaito debate is a noisy one.)

Freedom of expression used to be a luxury for black youth living in a country torn apart by apartheid. Not any more. The first place this freedom became visible was the music scene – a scene that is thriving, creating and reinventing itself in ways too numerous to mention here.

Environment

THE LAND

South Africa spreads over 1,233,404 sq km – five times the size of the UK – at the tip of the African continent. On three sides, it's edged by a windswept and stunningly beautiful coastline, winding down the Atlantic seaboard in the west, and up into the warmer Indian Ocean waters to the east.

Much of the country consists of a vast plateau averaging 1500m in height, and known as the highveld. To the east is a narrow coastal plain (the lowveld), while to the northwest is the low-lying Kalahari basin. The dramatic Drakensberg escarpment marks the point where the highveld plummets down towards the eastern lowlands.

Tiny Lesotho is completely surrounded by South Africa. It sits entirely above 1000m, perched on a 30,350 sq km patch of highland plateau and rugged peaks. Swaziland is almost half Lesotho's size, measuring only 17,363 sq km. Yet within its borders it encompasses diverse ecological zones, ranging from rainforest in the northwest to savanna scrub in the east.

Lesotho has the highest lowest point of any country in the world:1380m, in southern Lesotho's Senqu (Orange) River valley.

WILDLIFE

Southern Africa contains some of the most accessible and varied wildlife-watching found anywhere on the continent.

Animals

SOUTH AFRICA

South Africa is home to an unparalleled diversity of wildlife. It boasts the world's largest land mammal (the African elephant), as well as the second largest (white rhino) and the third largest (hippopotamus). It's also home to the tallest (giraffe), the fastest (cheetah) and the smallest (pygmy shrew). You probably have a better chance of seeing the Big Five – the black rhino, Cape buffalo, elephant, leopard and lion – in South Africa than anywhere else. There's also a lesser-known 'Little Five' – the rhinoceros beetle, buffalo weaver, elephant shrew, leopard tortoise and ant lion – if you're looking for a challenge. See the colour Wildlife Guide (p69) for a glimpse of some of these and other animals.

Good safari companions: Field Guide to Mammals of Southern Africa and A Field Guide to the Tracks and Signs of Southern and East African Wildlife both by Chris and Tilde Stuart, and The Safari Companion: A Guide to Watching African Mammals by Richard Estes.

RESPONSIBLE TRAVEL

Tourism is a big industry in Southern Africa. Following are a few guidelines for minimising strain on the local environment:

- ask permission before photographing people
- don't give money, sweets or pens to children; donations to recognised projects or local charitable organisations are a better option
- support local enterprise
- avoid buying items made from ivory, skin, shells etc
- carry a Sassi wallet card (see p94) if you enjoy dining at seafood restaurants
- use water and other natural resources prudently
- inform yourself of South Africa's history, and be sensitive to it in your travels

Also check the website of Fair Trade in Tourism South Africa (www.fairtourismsa.org.za).

The best time for wildlife-watching is the cooler, dry winter (June to September) when foliage is less dense, and animals congregate at waterholes, making spotting easier. Summer (late November to March) is rainy and hot, with the animals more widely dispersed and often difficult to see. However, the landscape turns beautiful shades of green around this time and birdlife is abundant.

South Africa hosts over 800 bird species, including the world's largest bird (the ostrich), its heaviest flying bird (Kori bustard), and vividly coloured sunbirds and flamingos. Also here in abundance are weavers, who share their huge city-like nests with pygmy falcons, the world's smallest raptors.

Bird-watching is good year-round, with spring (August to November) and summer the best.

Endangered Species

The black rhino is the highest profile entry on South Africa's threatened species list (good places to spot these include Mkhuze Game Reserve, p345 and Hluhluwe-Imfolozi Park, p335). The riverine rabbit is the country's most endangered mammal (the only place in the world it is found is near rivers in the central Karoo). The wild dog (seen with luck in Hluhluwe-Imfolozi Park) is also endangered, as is the roan antelope.

Endangered bird species include the graceful wattled crane and the blue swallow. The African penguin and the Cape vulture are considered threatened.

LESOTHO

Thanks primarily to its altitude, Lesotho is home to fewer animals than many Southern African countries. Those you may encounter include rheboks, jackals, mongooses, meerkats and elands.

Close to 300 species of birds have been recorded in Lesotho, notably bearded vultures, lammergeiers and bald ibises.

SWAZILAND

Tiny Swaziland boasts about 120 species of mammals – one-third of Southern Africa's nonmarine mammal species. Many (including elephants, rhinos and lions) have been introduced, and larger animals are restricted to nature reserves and private wildlife farms. Mongooses and large-spotted genets are common, and hyenas and jackals are found in the reserves. Leopards are present, but rarely seen.

Swaziland's varied terrain supports abundant birdlife, including the blue crane, ground woodpecker and lappet-faced vulture.

Plants

Over 20,000 plant species sprout from South Africa's soil – an amazing 10% of the world's total, although the country constitutes only 1% of the earth's land surface.

Dozens of flowers that are domesticated elsewhere grow wild here, including gladiolus, proteas, birds of paradise and African lilies. South Africa is also the only country with one of the world's six floral kingdoms within its borders (see p85).

In the drier northwest, there are succulents (dominated by euphorbias and aloes), and annuals, which flower brilliantly after the spring rains, and are one of Northern Cape's major tourist attractions (see p543).

Among the most comprehensive field guides covering South Africa, Lesotho and Swaziland are Newman's *Birds of Southern Africa* by Kenneth Newman, and *Birds of Southern Africa* by Ian Sinclair et al.

The Johannesburg-based Endangered Wildlife Trust (www.ewt.org.za) is the best source of information on South Africa's endangered species.

Among Lesotho's earliest wild inhabitants were dinosaurs, including the small, fast-running Lesothosaurus, which was named after the country.

(Continued on page 85)

Wildlife Guide

Mention Africa, and the first thing many people think of is the wildlife. South Africa – home to one of the most magnificent groupings of wildlife on the planet – is no exception. On even just a short visit to the country's parks you are almost guaranteed to see dozens of hoofed, tusked, winged and other creatures, and the chance to spot the fabled big cats and great herd animals is one of the region's prime attractions.

Thanks to its varied terrain, which ranges from woodland and savanna to dry shrub land and coastal marshes, South Africa hosts an amazing diversity of species, plus a full range of experiences – from the epic seasonal migrations of huge zebra herds, to the skittish antics of a troop of vervet monkeys to the drama of lions closing in on a kill. Another attraction is that the local wildlife is eminently viewable – the animals in many areas are used to the presence of human beings (in vehicles), and visitors can enjoy up-close encounters of the sort normally limited to researchers and specialists.

Most significant wildlife populations in South Africa are enclosed within fences, intended to minimise conflict with their human neighbours. Yet, due to the vast spaces, you'll generally only see the fences when you drive through the park gates – the wildlife itself is satisfyingly and completely wild.

When on safari, it's worth remembering that wildlife tourism is one of the main sources of revenue for conservation efforts in South Africa (as well as in neighbouring Swaziland). The money you spend in national parks and reserves is ploughed back into these areas, thus ensuring that future visitors will be able to collect their own unforgettable memories.

Chacma Baboon in front of *fynbos* vegetation, Cape of Good Hope Nature Reserve, Western Cape.
PHOTO BY KARL LEHMANN

Both bushbaby species are often found in family groups of up to six or seven individuals.
PHOTO BY MITCH REARDON

PRIMATES

BUSHBABIES
GREATER BUSHBABY

Otolemur crassicaudatus (pictured);
lesser Bushbaby Galago moholi

Named for their plaintive wailing call, bushbabies are actually primitive primates. They have small heads, large rounded ears, thick bushy tails and the enormous eyes that are typical of nocturnal primates. The greater bushbaby has dark-brown fur, while the tiny lesser bushbaby is very light grey with yellowish colouring on its legs. Tree sap and fruit are the mainstay of their diet, supplemented by insects as well as, in the case of the greater bushbaby, lizards, nestlings and eggs.

Size: Greater bushbaby length 80cm, including a 45cm tail; weight up to 1.5kg; lesser bushbaby length 40cm; weight 150g to 200g. **Distribution:** Greater bushbaby is restricted to far northeast of region; lesser bushbaby to north of Limpopo. **Status:** Common but strictly nocturnal.

The male vervet monkey has a distinctive bright blue scrotum, an important signal of status in the troop.
PHOTO BY ADRIAN BAILEY

VERVET MONKEY

Cercopithecus aethiops

The most common monkey of the woodland-savanna, the vervet is easily recognisable by its speckled grey hair and black face fringed with white. Troops may number up to 30. The vervet monkey is diurnal and forages for fruits, seeds, leaves, flowers, invertebrates and the occasional lizard or nestling. It rapidly learns where easy pickings can be found around lodges and camp sites, but becomes a pest when it becomes habituated to being fed. Most park authorities destroy such individuals, so please avoid feeding them.

Size: Length up to 130cm, including a 65cm tail; weight 3.5kg to 8kg; male larger than female. **Distribution:** Widespread in woodland-savanna throughout much of the east and north of the region; absent from deserts, except along rivers. **Status:** Very common and easy to see.

The chacma baboon lives in troops of up to 150 animals, and there is no single dominant male.
PHOTO BY LUKE HUNTER

CHACMA BABOON

Papio ursinus

The snout of the chacma baboon gives it a more aggressive appearance than other primates, which have more humanlike facial features. However, when you see the interactions within a troop, it's difficult not to make anthropomorphic comparisons. It is strictly diurnal and forages for grasses, fruits, insects and small vertebrates. The chacma baboon is a notorious opportunist and may become a pest in camp sites, which it visits for hand-outs. Such individuals can be dangerous and are destroyed by park officials: don't feed them.

Size: Shoulder height 75cm; length up to 160cm, including a 70cm tail; weight up to 45kg; male larger than female and twice as heavy. **Distribution:** Throughout the region, except for the heart of deserts. **Status:** Common in many areas and active during the day.

RODENTS

SPRINGHARE
Pedetes capensis

In spite of its name and large ears, the springhare is not a hare but a very unusual rodent with no close relatives. With its powerful, out-sized hind feet and small forelegs, it most resembles a small kangaroo and shares a similar energy-efficient hopping motion. The springhare digs extensive burrows, from which it emerges at night to feed on grass and grass roots. Reflections of spotlights in its large, bright eyes often give it away on night safaris.

Size: Length 80cm, including a 40cm tail; weight 3kg to 4kg. **Distribution:** Widespread in the centre and north of the region; favours grassland habitats with sandy soils. **Status:** Common but strictly nocturnal.

Although swift and able to leap several metres in a single bound, the springhare is preyed upon by everything from jackals to lions.
PHOTO BY ANTHONY BANNISTER/ABPL

CAPE PORCUPINE
Hystrix africaeaustralis

The Cape porcupine is the largest rodent native to Southern Africa. Its spread of long black-and-white banded quills from the shoulders to the tail makes it unmistakable. For shelter, it either occupies caves or excavates its own burrows. The porcupine's diet consists mainly of bark, tubers, seeds and a variety of plant and ground-level foliage. The young are born during the hot summer months, in litters of between one and four.

Size: Length 70cm to 100cm, including a 15cm tail; weight 10kg to 25kg. **Distribution:** Throughout the region. **Status:** Nocturnal but occasionally active on cooler days; difficult to see.

If attacked, a porcupine drives its rump into the predator – the quills are easily detached from their owner but can remain embedded in the victim, causing serious injury or death.
PHOTO BY DAVE HAMMAN

CAPE GROUND SQUIRREL
Xerus inauris

The Cape ground squirrel is a sociable rodent that lives in a colonial burrow system, usually containing up to a dozen individuals but sometimes as many as 30. It feeds on grass, roots, seeds and insects, but readily takes hand-outs from people in tourist camps. The ground squirrel is well adapted to dry surroundings: it does not need to drink, extracting all the moisture it requires from its food. It often stands on its hind legs to scan its surroundings, and erects its elegant fan-like tail when danger threatens. The tail is also used as a sunshade.

Size: Length 45cm, including a 20cm tail; weight up to 1kg. **Distribution:** North-central South Africa. **Status:** Common; active throughout the day.

The burrows of the ground squirrel are often shared with meerkats.
PHOTO BY MITCH REARDON

The jackal is persecuted by farmers but is very resilient and can be readily seen on farms.
PHOTO BY ANDREW MACCOLL

CARNIVORES

JACKALS
BLACK-BACKED JACKAL
Canis mesomelas (pictured);
side-striped jackal Canis adustus

This jackal relies heavily on scavenging but is also an efficient hunter, taking insects, birds, rodents and even the occasional small antelope. It also frequents human settlements and takes domestic stock. Pairs of black-backed jackals form long-term bonds, and each pair occupies an area varying from 3 to 21.5 sq km. Litters contain one to six pups; they are often looked after by older siblings as well as by their parents. The less-common side-striped jackal is grey in colour with a distinctive white-tipped tail.

Size: Shoulder height 35cm to 50cm; length 95cm to 120cm, including 30cm to 35cm tail; weight 12kg. **Distribution:** Black-backed throughout region; side-striped only in northeast. **Status:** Black-backed common, active night and day; side-striped less abundant, active night and early morning.

The huge ears of this little fox detect the faint sounds of invertebrates below ground, before it unearths them in a burst of frantic digging.
PHOTO BY DAVE HAMMAN

BAT-EARED FOX
Otocyon megalotis

The bat-eared fox eats mainly insects, especially termites, but also wild fruit and small vertebrates. It is monogamous and is often seen in groups comprising a mated pair and offspring. Natural enemies include large birds of prey, spotted hyenas, caracals and larger cats. It will bravely attempt to rescue a family member caught by a predator by using distraction techniques and harassment, which extends to nipping larger enemies on the ankles.

Size: Shoulder height 35cm; length 75cm to 90cm, including a 30cm tail; weight 3kg to 5kg. **Distribution:** Throughout western half of South Africa and open parts of Limpopo. **Status:** Common, especially in national parks; mainly nocturnal but often seen in the late afternoon and early morning.

The wild dog requires enormous areas of habitat and is one of the most endangered large carnivores in Africa.
PHOTO BY MITCH REARDON

WILD DOG
Lycaon pictus

The wild dog's blotched black, yellow and white coat, and its large, round ears, make it unmistakable. It is highly sociable, living in packs of up to 40, although 12 to 20 is typical. Great endurance hunters, the pack chases prey to the point of exhaustion, then cooperates to pull down the quarry. The wild dog is reviled for killing prey by eating it alive, but this is probably as fast as any of the 'cleaner' methods used by other carnivores. Mid-sized antelopes are the preferred prey, but it can kill animals as large as buffaloes.

Size: Shoulder height 65cm to 80cm; length 100cm to 150cm, including a 35cm tail; weight 20kg to 35kg. **Distribution:** Restricted to major parks of the extreme northeast. **Status:** Highly threatened, with numbers declining severely from a naturally low density.

HONEY BADGER
Mellivora capensis

Africa's equivalent of the European badger, the honey badger (also known as the ratel) has a reputation for a vile temper and ferocity. Mostly nocturnal, it is omnivorous, feeding on small animals, carrion, berries, roots, eggs, honey and especially on social insects (ants, termites and bees) and their larvae. Its

While stories of it attacking animals the size of buffaloes are probably folklore, the honey badger is pugnacious and very powerful for its size.
PHOTO BY LORNA STANTON/ABPL

thick, loose skin is an excellent defence against predators, bee stings and snake bites. In some parks, honey badgers habitually scavenge from bins, presenting the best opportunity for viewing this animal.
Size: Shoulder height 30cm; length 95cm, including a 20cm tail; weight up to 15kg. **Distribution:** Widespread, although absent from central South Africa and from Lesotho. **Status:** Generally occurs in low densities; mainly nocturnal.

GENETS
SMALL-SPOTTED GENET
Genetta genetta; large-spotted genet
Genetta tigrina (pictured)

Relatives of mongooses, genets resemble long, slender domestic cats and have pointed foxlike faces. The two species in the region are very similar, but can be differentiated by the tail tips (white in the small-spotted genet, black in the large-spotted genet). They are solitary

Like many other mammals, genets deposit their droppings in latrines, usually in open or conspicuous sites.
PHOTO BY ARIADNE VAN ZANDBERGEN

animals, sleeping by day in burrows, rock crevices or hollow trees and emerging at night to forage. Very agile, they hunt well on land or in trees, feeding on rodents, birds, reptiles, nestlings, eggs, insects and fruits.
Size: Shoulder height 18cm; length 85cm to 110cm, including a 45cm tail; weight 1.5kg to 3kg.
Distribution: Small-spotted genet is widespread in South Africa, but absent from the central east; large-spotted is common in eastern and southern coastal regions. **Status:** Very common but strictly nocturnal.

MONGOOSE

Although common, most mongooses are solitary and are usually seen only fleetingly. The slender mongoose (*Galerella sanguinea*; pictured) is recognisable by its black-tipped tail, which it holds aloft like a flag when running. A few species, such as the dwarf mongoose (*Helogale parvula*), the banded mongoose (*Mungos mungo*)

Social behaviour helps the mongoose when confronting a threat: collectively, they can intimidate much larger enemies.
PHOTO BY DAVE HAMMAN

and the meerkat (*Suricata suricatta*), are intensely sociable. Family groups are better than loners at spotting danger and raising kittens. Insects and other invertebrates are their most important prey.
Size: Ranges from 40cm and 400g (dwarf mongoose) to 120cm and 5.5g (white-tailed mongoose). **Distribution:** At least two or three species in most of region; the greatest diversity is in northeast. **Status:** Common where they occur; sociable species are diurnal, solitary species are nocturnal.

The male aardwolf assists the female in raising the cubs, mostly by baby-sitting at the den while the mother forages.
PHOTO BY MITCH REARDON

AARDWOLF
Proteles cristatus

The smallest of the hyena family, the aardwolf subsists almost entirely on harvester termites (which are generally ignored by other termite eaters because they are so noxious), licking over 200,000 from the ground each night. Unlike other hyaenids, it does not form clans; instead, it forages alone, and mates form only loose associations with each other. The aardwolf is persecuted in the mistaken belief that it kills stock, and may suffer huge population crashes following spraying for locusts (the spraying also kills termites).

Size: Shoulder height 40cm to 50cm; length 80cm to 100cm, including a 25cm tail; weight 8kg to 12kg. **Distribution:** Throughout the region, except for southern and western coasts. **Status:** Uncommon; nocturnal but occasionally seen at dawn and dusk.

Female spotted hyena are larger than, and dominant to, males and have male physical characteristics, the most remarkable of which is an erectile clitoris (which renders the sexes virtually indistinguishable).
PHOTO BY ARIADNE VAN ZANDBERGEN

SPOTTED HYENA
Crocuta crocuta

Widely reviled as a scavenger, the spotted hyena is actually a highly efficient predator with a fascinating social system. Clans, which can contain dozens of individuals, are led by females. The spotted hyena is massively built and appears distinctly canine, although it's more closely related to cats than to dogs. It can reach speeds of up to 60km/h and a pack can easily dispatch adult wildebeests and zebras. Lions are its main natural enemy.

Size: Shoulder height 85cm; length 120cm to 180cm, including a 30cm tail; weight 55kg to 80kg. **Distribution:** Occurs only in the northeast of the region. **Status:** Common where there is suitable food; mainly nocturnal but also seen during the day.

The caracal's long back legs power a prodigious ability to leap – it even takes birds in flight.
PHOTO BY JANE SWEENEY

CARACAL
Felis caracal

Sometimes also called the African lynx due to its long tufted ears, the caracal is a robust, powerful cat that preys predominantly on small antelopes, birds and rodents but is capable of taking down animals many times larger than itself. Like most cats, it is largely solitary. Females give birth to one to three kittens and raise them alone. The caracal is territorial, marking its home range with urine sprays and faeces. It occupies a range of habitats but prefers semiarid regions, dry savannas and hilly country; it is absent from dense forest.

Size: Shoulder height 40cm to 50cm; length 95cm to 120cm; weight 7kg to 18kg; male slightly larger. **Distribution:** Throughout the region except for much of KwaZulu-Natal and the western and southern coasts. **Status:** Fairly common but largely nocturnal and difficult to see.

LEOPARD
Panthera pardus

The leopard is the supreme ambush hunter, using infinite patience to stalk within metres of its prey before attacking in an explosive rush. It eats everything from insects to zebras, but antelopes are its primary prey. It is a solitary animal, except during the mating season when the male and female stay in close association for the female's week-long oestrus. A litter of up to three cubs is born after a gestation of three months and the females raise them without any assistance from the males.

The leopard is highly agile and hoists its kills into trees to avoid losing them to lions and hyenas.
PHOTO BY ADRIAN BAILEY

Size: Shoulder height 50cm to 75cm; length 160cm to 210cm, including a 70cm to 110cm tail; weight up to 90kg. **Distribution:** Absent from most of region except northeast and mountainous areas of south and east. **Status:** Common, but being mainly nocturnal they are the most difficult of the large cats to see.

LION
Panthera leo

The lion lives in prides of up to about 30, the core comprising four to 12 related females, which remain in the pride for life. Males form coalitions and defend the female groups from foreign males. The lion is strictly territorial, defending ranges of between 50 to 400 sq km. Young males are ousted from the pride at the age of two or three, entering a period of nomadism that ends at around five years old when they are able to take over their own pride. The lion hunts virtually anything, but wildebeests, zebras and buffaloes are the mainstay of its diet.

The lion spends much of the night hunting, patrolling territories and playing.
PHOTO BY LUKE HUNTER

Size: Shoulder height 120cm; length 250cm to 300cm, including a 100cm tail; weight up to 260kg (male), 180kg (female). **Distribution:** Restricted to major reserves of South Africa's northeast. **Status:** Common where it occurs; mainly nocturnal but easy to see during the day.

CHEETAH
Acinonyx jubatus

The world's fastest land mammal, the cheetah can reach speeds of at least 105km/h. The cheetah preys on antelopes weighing up to 60kg, as well as hares and young wildebeests and zebras. Litters may be as large as nine, but in open savanna habitats most cubs are killed by other predators, particularly lions. Young cheetahs disperse from the mother when aged around 18 months. The males form coalitions; females remain solitary for life.

The cheetah usually stalks prey to within 60m before unleashing its tremendous acceleration, as it becomes exhausted after a few hundred metres.
PHOTO BY ANDREW VAN SMEERDIJK

Size: Shoulder height 85cm; length 180cm to 220cm, including a 70cm tail; weight up to 65kg. **Distribution:** Kgalagadi Transfrontier Park, parts of Limpopo and reserves of South Africa's northeast. **Status:** Uncommon, with individuals moving over large areas; active by day.

The aardvark digs deep, complex burrows for shelter, which are also used by many other animals such as warthogs and mongooses.
PHOTO BY PHOTO BY ANTHONY BANNISTER/ABPL

UNGULATES (HOOFED ANIMALS)

AARDVARK
Orycteropus afer

Vaguely pig-like (its Afrikaans name translates as 'earth-pig') with a long tubular snout, powerful kangaroo-like tail and large rabbitlike ears, the aardvark is unique and has no close relatives. Protected by thick wrinkled pink-grey skin, aardvarks forage at night by sniffing for termite and ant nests, which they rip open with their astonishingly powerful front legs and large spadelike nails. Normally nocturnal, they occasionally spend cold winter mornings basking in the sun before retiring underground.

Size: Shoulder height 60cm; length 140cm to 180cm, including a 55cm tail; weight 40kg to 80kg. **Distribution:** Widely distributed throughout nearly the entire region. **Status:** Uncommon; nocturnal and rarely seen.

An adult African elephant's average daily food intake is about 250kg of grass, leaves, bark and other vegetation.
PHOTO BY ALEX DISSANAYAKE

AFRICAN ELEPHANT
Loxodonta africana

The African elephant usually lives in small family groups of between 10 and 20, which frequently congregate in much larger herds at a common water hole or food resource. Its society is matriarchal and herds are dominated by old females. Bulls live alone or in bachelor groups, joining the herds when females are in season. A cow may mate with many bulls during her oestrus. An elephant's life span is about 60 to 70 years, though some individuals may reach 100 or more.

Size: Shoulder height up to 4m (male), 3.5m (female); weight 5 to 6.5 tonnes (male), 3 to 3.5 tonnes (female). **Distribution:** Restricted to a few reserves in South Africa's northeast, east and south. **Status:** Very common in some parks.

Despite its resemblance to a large guinea pig, the dassie is actually related to the elephant.
PHOTO BY LUKE HUNTER

ROCK DASSIE
Procavia capensis

The rock dassie (also known as the hyrax) occurs practically everywhere there are mountains or rocky outcrops. It is sociable, living in colonies of up to 60 individuals. It feeds on vegetation, but spends much of the day basking on rocks or chasing other rock dassies in play. Where it's habituated to humans it is often quite tame, but otherwise it dashes into rock crevices when alarmed, uttering shrill screams. Rocks streaked white by dassies' urine are often a conspicuous indicator of a colony's presence.

Size: Length 40cm to 60cm; weight up to 5.5kg. **Distribution:** Throughout the region except the central eastern coast; absent from dense forest. **Status:** Common and easy to see, especially where they have become habituated to humans.

ZEBRAS
BURCHELL'S ZEBRA
Equus burchellii (pictured);
mountain zebra Equus zebra

Burchell's zebra has shadow lines between its black stripes, whereas the mountain zebra lacks shadows and has a gridiron pattern of black stripes just above its tail. Both species are grazers but occasionally browse on leaves and scrub. Stallions may hold a harem for as long as 15 years, but they often lose single mares to younger males, which gradually build up their own harems. Both types of zebras are preyed upon by all the large carnivores, with lions being their main predators.

The zebra social system centres around small groups of related mares over which stallions fight fiercely.

PHOTO BY MANFRED GOTTSCHALK

Size: Shoulder height 140cm to 160cm; weight up to 390kg; mountain zebra smaller than Burchell's zebra; female of both species smaller than male. **Distribution:** Burchell's zebras in northeast of region; mountain zebras in a few reserves in Southern Africa. **Status**: Burchell's zebra common; mountain zebra less common.

RHINOCEROSES
WHITE RHINOCEROS
Ceratotherium simum (pictured);
black rhinoceros Diceros bicornis

The white rhino is a grazer, preferring open plains, while the black rhino is a browser, living in scrubby country. The black rhino is prone to charging when alarmed – its eyesight is extremely poor and it has been known to charge trains or elephant carcasses. The white rhino is generally docile, and the more sociable species, forming cow-calf groups numbering up to 10. The black rhino is solitary and territorial, only socialising during the mating season.

Aggressive poaching for rhino horn has made rhinos Africa's most endangered large mammals.

PHOTO BY CAROL POLICH

Size: White rhino shoulder height 180cm; weight 2100kg to 1500kg; black rhino shoulder height 160cm; weight 800kg to 1200kg. **Distribution:** Restricted to protected areas, occurs naturally only in some reserves of KwaZulu-Natal. **Status:** White rhino threatened but well protected; black rhino endangered.

WARTHOG
Phacochoerus aethiopicus

The warthog's social organisation is variable, but groups usually consist of one to three sows with their young. Males form bachelor groups or are solitary, only associating with the female groups when a female is in season. The warthog feeds mainly on grass, but also eats fruit and bark. In hard times, it will burrow with its snout for roots and bulbs. It rests and gives birth in abandoned burrows or in excavated cavities of abandoned termite mounds.

The distinctive facial warts can be used to determine the sex of warthogs – females have a single pair of warts under the eyes whereas males have a second set further down the snout.

PHOTO BY ADRIAN BAILEY

Size: Shoulder height 70cm; weight up to 105kg, but averages 50kg to 60kg; male larger than female. **Distribution:** Restricted to the region's northeast. **Status:** Common and easy to see.

The hippo is extremely dangerous on land and kills many people each year, usually when someone inadvertently blocks the animal's retreat to the water.
PHOTO BY DAVID WALL

HIPPOPOTAMUS
Hippopotamus amphibius

The hippo is found close to fresh water, and spends the majority of its day submerged in water before emerging at night to graze on land. It can consume around 40kg of vegetable matter each evening. The hippo lives in large herds, tolerating close contact in the water but prefering to forage alone when on land. Adult bulls aggressively defend territories against each other, and most males bear the scars of conflicts (providing a convenient method of sexing hippos). Cows with calves are aggressive towards other individuals.

Size: Shoulder height 150cm; weight 1 to 2 tonnes; male larger than female. **Distribution:** Restricted to the region's northeast. **Status:** Common in major watercourses.

Despite the giraffe's incredibly long neck, it still has only seven cervical vertebrae – the same number as all mammals, including humans.
PHOTO BY JOHN HAY

GIRAFFE
Giraffa camelopardalis

The name 'giraffe' is derived from the Arabic word zarafah (the one who walks quickly). Both sexes have 'horns' – they are actually short projections of skin-covered bone. The giraffe browses on trees, exploiting a zone of foliage inaccessible to all other herbivores except elephants. Juveniles are prone to predation and a lion will even take down fully grown adults. The giraffe is at its most vulnerable at water holes and always appears hesitant when drinking.

Size: Height 4m to 5.2m (male), 3.5m to 4.5m (female); weight 900kg to 1400kg (male), 700kg to 1000kg (female). **Distribution:** Restricted to the region's northeast. **Status:** Common where it occurs and easy to see.

During the dry season the nyala is active only in the morning and evening, but during the rains they more often feed at night.
PHOTO BY LUKE HUNTER

NYALA
Tragelaphus angasii

The nyala is one of Africa's rarest and most beautiful antelopes. Males are grey with a mane and long hair under the throat and hind legs; they also have vertical stripes down the back and long, lyre-shaped horns with white tips. Females are a ruddy colour with vertical white stripes and have no horns. The nyala browses on trees and bushes. Female nyala and their young live in small groups. The young may be taken by baboons and birds of prey.

Size: Shoulder height 115cm (male), 100cm (female); weight 100kg to 140kg (male), 60kg to 90kg (female); horns up to 85cm long. **Distribution:** Restricted to the region's northeast. **Status:** Common where it occurs, but well camouflaged.

BUSHBUCK
Tragelaphus scriptus
A shy and solitary animal, the bushbuck inhabits thick bush close to permanent water and browses on leaves at night. It is chestnut to dark brown in colour and has a variable number of white vertical stripes on its body between the neck and rump, as well as a number of white spots on the upper thigh

When startled, the bushbuck bolts and crashes loudly through the undergrowth.
PHOTO BY MITCH REARDON

and a white splash on the neck. Normally only males grow horns, which are straight with gentle spirals and average about 30cm in length. It can be aggressive and dangerous when cornered.
Size: Shoulder height 80cm; weight up to 80kg; horns up to 55cm long; male larger than female.
Distribution: Throughout the region's northeast and eastern and southern coastal areas. **Status:** Common, but difficult to see in the dense vegetation of their habitat.

GREATER KUDU
Tragelaphus strepsiceros
The greater kudu is Africa's second-tallest antelope and the males carry massive spiralling horns much sought after by trophy hunters. It is light grey in colour with between six and 10 white stripes down the sides and a white chevron between the eyes. The kudu lives in small herds comprising females and their

A strong jumper, the greater kudu readily clears barriers more than 2m high.
PHOTO BY LUKE HUNTER

young, periodically joined by the normally solitary males during the breeding season. It is primarily a browser and can eat a variety of leaves, but finds its preferred diet in woodland-savanna with fairly dense bush cover.
Size: Shoulder height up to 150cm; weight 200kg to 300kg (male), 120kg to 220kg (female); horns up to 180cm long. **Distribution:** Throughout much of region's north, and with populations in central and southern South Africa. **Status:** Common.

ELAND
Taurotragus oryx
Africa's largest antelope, the eland is massive. Both sexes have horns averaging about 65cm long that spiral at the base and sweep straight back. The male has a distinctive hairy tuft on the head, and stouter horns than the female. The eland prefers savanna scrub, feeding on grass and leaves in the early morn-

The eland normally drinks daily, but can go for over a month without water.
PHOTO BY DAVID WALL

ing and from late afternoon into the night. It usually lives in groups of around six to 12, generally comprising several females and one male. Larger aggregations (up to a thousand) sometimes form at 'flushes' of new grass.
Size: Shoulder height 124cm to 180cm; weight 300kg to 950kg; horns up to 100cm long.
Distribution: Small parts of north-central and northeastern South Africa and the Drakensberg.
Status: Naturally low density, but relatively common in their habitat and easy to see.

The common duiker is capable of going without water for long periods, but it will drink whenever water is available.
PHOTO BY MITCH REARDON

COMMON (OR GREY) DUIKER
Sylvicapra grimmia
One of the most common small antelopes, the common duiker is usually solitary, but is sometimes seen in pairs. It is greyish light brown in colour, with a white belly and a dark-brown stripe down its face. Only males have horns, which are straight and pointed, and rarely grow longer than 15cm. This duiker is predominantly a browser, often feeding on agricultural crops. This habit leads to it being persecuted outside conservation areas, though it is resilient to hunting.
Size: Shoulder height 50cm; weight 10kg to 20kg; horns up to 18cm long; female slightly larger than male. **Distribution:** Very widespread throughout the region. **Status:** Common; active throughout the day, except where disturbance is common.

The waterbuck's oily hair has a strong musky odour – especially with mature males, potent enough that even humans can smell them.
PHOTO BY DAVID WALL

WATERBUCK
Kobus ellipsiprymnus
The waterbuck has a bull's-eye ring around its rump, and white markings on the face and throat. It's a solid animal with a thick, shaggy, dark-brown coat. Only males have horns, which curve gradually out before shooting straight up to a length averaging about 75cm. The small herds consist of cows, calves and one mature bull; younger bulls live in bachelor groups. This grazer never strays far from water and is a good swimmer, readily entering water to escape predators.
Size: Shoulder height 130cm; weight 200kg to 300kg (male), 150kg to 200kg (female); horns up to 100cm long. **Distribution:** Wet areas in northeastern South Africa. **Status:** Common and easy to see.

The whistling call of the reedbuck is often repeated when advertising territories, and is also given in alarm.
PHOTO BY ANDREW VAN SMEERDIJK

REEDBUCKS
COMMON REEDBUCK
Redunca arundinum (pictured);
mountain reedbuck Redunca fulvorufula
The common reedbuck is found in wetlands and riverine areas. The rarer mountain reedbuck inhabits hill country and is the smaller, but is otherwise physically similar, with the underbelly, inside of the thighs, throat and underside of the tail white, and with males having distinctive forward-curving horns. However, their social systems differ: common reedbucks live in pairs on territories; female mountain reedbucks form small groups, the range of each encompassing the territories of several males.
Size: Common reedbuck shoulder height 90cm; weight 50kg to 90kg; mountain reedbuck shoulder height 70cm; weight 20kg to 40kg; male bigger in both species. **Distribution:** Common reedbucks in north and east of region; mountain reedbucks in region's east. **Status:** Common and easy to see.

ROAN ANTELOPE
Hippotragus equinus

The roan antelope is one of Southern Africa's rarest antelopes, and one of Africa's largest. A grazer, it prefers tall grasses and sites with ample shade and water. Its coat varies from reddish fawn to dark rufous, with white underparts and a conspicuous mane of stiff, black-tipped hairs from the nape to the shoulders. Its face is distinctively patterned black and white and its long, pointed ears are tipped with a brown tassel. Herds of normally less than 20 females and young are led by a single adult bull; other males form bachelor groups.

Both sexes of roan antelope have long backward-curving horns.
PHOTO BY JASON EDWARDS

Size: Shoulder height 140cm; weight 200kg to 300kg; horns up to 100cm long. **Distribution:** Can be seen in Kruger NP. **Status:** One of the less common antelopes; although numbers are declining, they are not difficult to see where they occur.

SABLE ANTELOPE
Hippotragus niger

The sable antelope is slightly smaller than the roan antelope, but more solidly built. It is dark brown to black, with a white belly and face markings. Both sexes have backward-sweeping horns, often over 1m long; those of the male are longer and more curved. It occurs in habitat similar to, but slightly more wooded than, that of the roan antelope. Females and young live in herds, mostly of 10 to 30. Mature males establish territories that overlap the ranges of female herds; other males form bachelor groups.

Both the roan and sable antelopes are fierce fighters, even known to kill attacking lions.
PHOTO BY DENNIS JONES

Size: Shoulder height 135cm; weight 180kg to 270kg; horns up to 130cm long. **Distribution:** Restricted to extreme northeastern South Africa. **Status:** Common and easy to see.

GEMSBOK
Oryx gazella

The gemsbok (or oryx) can tolerate arid areas uninhabitable to most antelopes. It can survive for long periods without drinking (obtaining water from its food) and tolerates extreme heat. A powerful animal with long, straight horns present in both sexes, it's well equipped to defend itself and sometimes kills attacking lions. Herds usually contain five to 40 individuals but aggregations of several hundred can occur. The gemsbok is principally a grazer, but also browses on thorny shrubs unpalatable to many species.

As a means of conserving water, the gemsbok can let its body temperature climb to levels that would kill most mammals.
PHOTO BY ANDREW MACCOLL

Size: Shoulder height 120cm; weight 180kg to 240kg; horns up to 120cm long; male more solid than female and with thicker horns. **Distribution:** North-central South Africa. **Status:** Common where it occurs, but often shy, fleeing from humans.

Bontebok and blesbok often stand about in groups facing into the sun with their heads bowed.

PHOTO BY LUKE HUNTER

BONTEBOK & BLESBOK
Damaliscus dorcas dorcas &
Damaliscus dorcas phillipsi

Closely related subspecies, the bontebok and the blesbok are close relatives of the tsessebe. The best way to tell them apart is to look at their colour – the blesbok has a dullish appearance and lacks the rich, deep brown-purple tinge of the bontebok. Both species graze on short grass, and both sexes have horns. As with many antelope, males are territorial, while females form small herds. The bontebok was once virtually exterminated and numbers have recovered to only a few thousand.

Size: Shoulder height 90cm; weight 55kg to 80kg; horns up to 50cm long. Female smaller than male.
Distribution: Endemic to South Africa; bontebok confined to southwest; blesbok widespread in central region. **Status:** Bontebok rare but easy to see where they occur; blesbok is common.

The tsessebe is a grazer, and although it can live on dry grasses, it prefers flood plains and moist areas that support lush pasture.

PHOTO BY ARIADNE VAN ZANDBERGEN

TSESSEBE
Damaliscus lunatus

The tsessebe is dark reddish-brown, with glossy violet-brown patches on the rear thighs, front legs and face. The horns, carried by both sexes, curve gently up, out and back. A highly gregarious antelope, it lives in herds and frequently mingles with other grazers. During the mating season, bulls select a well-defined patch, which they defend against rivals, while females wander from one patch to another. It is capable of surviving long periods without water as long as sufficient grass is available.

Size: Shoulder height 120cm; weight 120kg to 150kg (male), 75kg to 150kg (female); horns up to 45cm long. **Distribution:** Found in parts of northeastern South Africa. **Status:** Common where they occur.

The wildebeest is a grazer, and moves constantly in search of good pasture and water.

PHOTO BY LUKE HUNTER

BLUE WILDEBEEST
Connochaetes taurinus

The blue wildebeest is gregarious, forming herds of up to tens of thousands in some parts of Africa, often in association with zebras and other herbivores. In Southern Africa, numbers are much reduced and huge herds are a rarity. Males are territorial and attempt to herd groups of females into their territory. Because it prefers to drink daily and can survive only five days without water, the wildebeest will migrate large distances to find it. During the rainy season it grazes haphazardly, but in the dry season it congregates around water holes.

Size: Shoulder height 140cm; weight 200kg to 300kg (male), 140kg to 230kg (female); horns up to 85cm long. **Distribution:** The region's central eastern coast, northeast and central north. **Status:** Very common but mostly restricted to protected areas.

KLIPSPRINGER
Oreotragus oreotragus

A small, sturdy antelope, the klip-springer is easily recognised by its curious tip-toe stance – its hooves are well adapted for balance and grip on rocky surfaces. The widely spaced short horns are present only on the male of the species. The klipspringer normally inhabits rocky outcrops; it also sometimes ventures into adjacent grasslands, but always retreats to the rocks when alarmed. This amazingly agile and sure-footed creature is capable of bounding up impossibly rough rock faces.

Male and female klipspringers form long-lasting pair bonds and occupy a territory together.
PHOTO BY LUKE HUNTER

Size: Shoulder height 55cm; weight 9kg to 15kg; horns up to 15cm long; female larger than male.
Distribution: On rocky outcrops and mountainous areas throughout the region; absent from dense forests. **Status:** Common.

STEENBOK
Raphicerus campestris

The steenbok is a very pretty and slender small antelope; its back and hindquarters range from light reddish-brown to dark brown with pale underpart markings. The upper surface of its nose bears a black, wedge-shaped 'blaze' use-ful for identification. Males have small, straight and widely separated horns. Although steenboks are usually seen alone it appears likely that they share a small territory with a mate, but only occasionally does the pair come together. The steenbok is active in the morning and evening.

If a potential predator approaches, the steenbok lies flat with neck outstretched, zigzagging away only at the last moment.
PHOTO BY ARIADNE VAN ZANDBERGEN

Size: Shoulder height 50cm; weight up to 10kg to 16kg; horns up to 19cm long. **Distribution:** Apart from a large area of the central east and eastern coast, steenbok are widely distributed throughout the region in all habitats, except desert areas. **Status:** Common where it occurs.

SUNI
Neotragus moschatus

This tiny antelope, which vies with the blue duiker for the title of small-est in the region, is best looked for from observation hides at water holes. It is often given away by the constant side-to-side flicking of its tail (blue duikers wag their tails up and down). Suni are probably mon-ogamous, living in pairs on their small territories, and use secretions from a large scent gland in front of their eye to mark their territories. They nibble selectively on leaves and fallen fruit.

When surprised the suni will freeze, sometimes for prolonged periods, before bounding away with a barking alarm call.
PHOTO BY RICHARD I'ANSON

Size: Shoulder height 35cm; weight 4kg to 6kg; horns up to 14cm long. **Distribution:** Wooded areas of the region's extreme northeast; can be seen in Kruger National Park and False Bay Park. **Status:** Difficult to see because it is small, shy and lives in thickets; active in the early morning and late afternoon.

The impala is known for its speed and its ability to leap – it can spring as far as 10m in one bound, and 3m into the air.
PHOTO BY ADRIAN BAILEY

IMPALA
Aepyceros melampus

Although it is often dismissed by tourists because it is so abundant, the graceful impala is a unique antelope that has no close relatives. Males have long, lyre-shaped horns averaging 75cm in length. The impala is a gregarious animal, and forms herds of up to 100 or so. Males defend female herds during the oestrus, but outside the breeding season they congregate in bachelor groups. It is the common prey of lions, leopards, cheetahs, wild dogs and spotted hyenas.

Size: Shoulder height 90cm; weight 40kg to 70kg; horns up to 80cm long; male larger than female. **Distribution:** Widespread in the northeast of the region. **Status:** Very common and easy to see.

The springbok is extremely common in arid areas, usually in herds of up to 100, whose social structure varies considerably.
PHOTO BY ARIADNE VAN ZANDBERGEN

SPRINGBOK
Antidorcas marsupialis

The springbok is one of the fastest antelopes (up to 88km/h) and has a distinctive stiff-legged, arched-backed bounding gait called 'pronking', which is commonly displayed when it sees predators. When pronking, it raises a white crest along the back (normally hidden within a skin fold) and the white hairs of the rump. It can survive for long periods without drinking, but may move large distances to find new grazing, sometimes congregating in herds of thousands when doing so. Both sexes have ridged, lyre-shaped horns.

Size: Shoulder height 75cm; weight 25kg to 55kg; horns up to 50cm long; male larger than female. **Distribution:** Northwestern and central-northern South Africa. **Status:** Very common and easy to see.

Although it is generally docile, the buffalo can be very dangerous and should be treated with caution.
PHOTO BY LUKE HUNTER

AFRICAN BUFFALO
Syncerus caffer

The African buffalo is the only native wild cow of Africa. Both sexes have distinctive curving horns that broaden at the base and meet over the forehead in a massive 'boss'; those of the female are usually smaller. It has a fairly wide habitat tolerance, but requires areas with abundant grass, water and cover. The African buffalo is gregarious and may form herds numbering thousands. Group composition is fluid and smaller herds often break away, sometimes rejoining the original herd later.

Size: Shoulder height 160cm; weight 400kg to 900kg; horns up to 125cm long; female somewhat smaller than male. **Distribution:** Restricted to some reserves of the region's northeast and east. **Status:** Common; can be approachable where they are protected.

(Continued from page 68)

In contrast to this floral wealth, South Africa has few natural forests. They were never extensive, and today only remnants remain. Temperate forests occur on the southern coastal strip between George and Humansdorp, in the KwaZulu-Natal Drakensberg and in Mpumalanga. Subtropical forests are found northeast of Port Elizabeth in the areas just inland from the Wild Coast, and in KwaZulu-Natal.

In the north are large areas of savanna, dotted with acacias and thorn trees.

Lesotho is notable for its high-altitude flora, including Cape alpine flowers and the spiral aloe (*Aloe polyphylla*).

Swaziland's grasslands, forests, savannas and wetlands host about 3500 plant species – or about 14% of Southern Africa's recorded plant life.

More bird species have been sighted in Swaziland than in the larger Kruger National Park.

NATIONAL PARKS & RESERVES
South Africa

South Africa has close to 600 national parks and reserves, collectively boasting spectacular scenery, impressive fauna and flora, excellent facilities and reasonable prices. They'll likely be the highlight of your visit. The most famous feature wildlife, while others are primarily wilderness sanctuaries or hiking areas. The table on p88 lists some of the best, though all are well-worth exploring.

The majority of the larger wildlife parks are under the jurisdiction of the **South African National (SAN) Parks Board** (☎ 012-428 9111; www.sanparks .org), except for those in KwaZulu-Natal, which are run by **KZN Wildlife** (☎ 033-845 1000; www.kznwildlife.com). Several other provinces also have conservation bodies that oversee smaller conservation areas within their boundaries. **Komatiland Eco-Tourism** (☎ 013-754 2724; www.komatiecotourism.co.za) oversees forest areas, promotes ecotourism and manages several hiking trails around Mpumalanga. Other useful contacts include **Cape Nature Conservation** (☎ 021-426 0723; www.capenature.org.za) and the **Eastern Cape Tourism Board** (☎ 043-701 9600; www.ectb.co.za).

The spiral aloe is Lesotho's national flower. Look for its left- and right-handed (clockwise and anticlockwise) varieties on the slopes of the Maluti Mountains.

All South African national parks charge a daily entry ('conservation') fee. Amounts vary; see individual park listings for details. If you are a South African resident or a national of a South African Development Community (SADC) country (this includes many of South Africa's neighbours), you are entitled to reduced rates. Another way to save is to consider purchasing a 'Wild Card' from SAN Parks. There are different

---

THE CAPE FLORAL KINGDOM

The tiny Cape Floral Kingdom – parts of which are now a Unesco World Heritage site – is the smallest of the world's six floral kingdoms, but unquestionably the most diverse. Here you'll find an incredible 1300 species per 10,000 sq km, some 900 more species than are found in the South American rainforests.

The Cape Floral Kingdom extends roughly from Cape Point east to Grahamstown and north to the Olifants River. Today, most of the remaining indigenous vegetation is found only in protected areas, such as Table Mountain and the Cape Peninsula.

The dominant vegetation is *fynbos* (fine bush), with small, narrow leaves and stems. The *fynbos* environment hosts nearly 8500 plant species, most of which are unique to the area.

Some members of the main *fynbos* families – heaths, proteas and reeds – have been domesticated elsewhere, but many species have a remarkably small range: clearing an area the size of a house can mean extinction.

versions of the card, including one for foreign tourists which gives you 10 days entry into any one park for R795 (R1395 per couple, R1795 per family). This isn't much of a saving for some of the less expensive parks, but if you're planning at least five days in Kruger National Park (where the daily entry fee is R120), it's worth buying. They also have cards targeted at different park clusters, depending where in the country you'll be travelling, and various loyalty programs. For details on acquiring a Wild Card, see www.wildinafrica.com.

James Stevenson Hamilton's classic, *A South African Eden*, chronicles South Africa's early wildlife conservation efforts and the creation of Kruger National Park.

In addition to its national parks, South Africa is also party to several transfrontier parks joining conservation areas across international borders. These include Kgalagadi Transfrontier Park, combining Northern Cape's old Kalahari Gemsbok National Park with Botswana's Gemsbok National Park; and the ambitious Great Limpopo Transfrontier Park, which spreads nearly 100,000 sq km (larger than Portugal) across the borders of South Africa, Mozambique and Zimbabwe (see p467). Private wildlife reserves also abound.

In total, just under 7% of South African land has been given protected status. The government has started teaming up with private landowners to bring private conservation land under government protection, with the goal of ultimately increasing the total amount of conservation land to over 10%.

Lesotho

Rhinos aren't named for their colour, but for their lip shape: 'white' comes from *wijde* (wide) – the Boers' term for the fatter-lipped white rhino.

In part because of a land tenure system that allows communal access rights to natural resources, less than 1% of Lesotho's area is protected – the lowest protected area coverage of any nation in Africa. Remote Sehlabathebe National Park (p572) is the main conservation area, known for its isolated wilderness setting. Others include Ts'ehlanyane National Park (p563) and Bokong Nature Reserve (p567). Also see p554.

Swaziland

About 4% of Swaziland is protected, and its conservation areas are particularly good value for money. They are also quite low-key, with fewer visitors than many of their counterparts in South Africa. Among the best are the easily accessed Mlilwane Wildlife Sanctuary (p586), Mkhaya Game Reserve (p594) and the beautiful Malolotja Nature Reserve (p590), which is used primarily for hiking.

SAFARIS

The best and cheapest (especially if you're in a group) way to visit the parks is usually with a hired car. A 2WD is perfectly adequate in most parks, but during winter when the grass is high, a 4WD or other high-

---

SOUTH AFRICA'S UNESCO WORLD HERITAGE SITES

- Greater St Lucia Wetland Park (p339)
- Robben Island (p107)
- Hominid fossil sites of Sterkfontein and Kromdraai (p427)
- uKhahlamba-Drakensberg Park (p346)
- Mapungubwe Cultural Landscape (p500)
- Cape Floral Region Protected Areas (p85)
- Vredefort Dome (p383)

DON'T GET CHARGED

One of South Africa's major attractions is the chance to go on safari and to get 'up close and personal' with the wildlife. Remember, however, that the animals aren't tame and their actions are often unpredictable. Some tips to avoid getting charged (and to avoid other less dramatic perils of the bush):

- heed the warnings of safari guides
- don't move in too close to an animal – for good photos, invest in a telephoto lens
- never get between a mother and her young, or between a hippo and the water
- don't feed animals; baboons' canine teeth are sometimes larger than those of a lion
- watch out for black rhinos, which will charge just about anything
- brush up on your tree-climbing skills
- avoid snake bites by wearing boots, socks and long trousers when walking through undergrowth, and taking care around holes, crevices and when collecting firewood
- avoid ticks by wearing insect repellent when hiking; check your body and clothes if you've been walking through tick-infested areas (ie any scrubland, even in cities) or sitting under camel thorn trees (a favoured haunt for ticks)

clearance vehicle will enable you to see more. Organised safaris are readily arranged with all major tour operators and with backpacker-oriented outfits, most of which advertise at hostels.

Several major parks (including Kruger, Hluhluwe-Imfolozi and Pilanesberg) offer guided wilderness walks accompanied by armed rangers. These are highly worthwhile, as the subtleties of the bush can be much better experienced on foot than in a vehicle. They should be booked well in advance with the relevant park authority (see contacts listed earlier in this section, and in the individual park listings in the regional chapters). Shorter morning and afternoon walks are also possible at many wildlife parks, and can generally be booked the day before. For overnight walks, it's necessary to get a permit in advance from the relevant park authority, and you'll generally be restricted to overnighting in official camp sites or huts.

Throughout South Africa, park infrastructure is of high quality. You can often get by without a guide, although you'll almost certainly see and learn more with one. All national parks have rest camps offering good-value accommodation, ranging from self-catering cottages to camp sites. Most have restaurants, shops and petrol pumps. Advance bookings for camping and cottages are essential during holiday periods. Otherwise, it's generally possible to get accommodation at short notice.

Most park and reserve entrances close around sunset.

ENVIRONMENTAL ISSUES
South Africa

South Africa is the world's third most biologically diverse country. It's also one of Africa's most urbanised, with approximately 60% of the population living in towns and cities. Major challenges for the government include managing increasing urbanisation and population growth while protecting the environment. The picture is complicated by a distorted rural-urban settlement pattern – a grim legacy of the apartheid era (p40) – with huge population concentrations in townships that generally lack adequate utilities and infrastructure.

For a wide selection of links on environmental issues in South Africa, see www-sul.stanford.edu/depts/ssrg/africa/southafrica/rsaenviro.html and www.environment.gov.za/Enviro-Info/env/salinks.htm.

See the World Wide Fund for Nature (WWF) South Africa website (www.panda.org.za) for an overview of conservation efforts in the country.

Land degradation is one of the most serious problems, with about one-quarter of South Africa's land considered to be severely degraded. In former homeland areas (see p43), years of overgrazing and overcropping have resulted in massive soil depletion. This, plus poor overall conditions, is pushing people to the cities, further increasing urban pressures.

Water is another issue. South Africa receives an average of only 500mm of rainfall annually, and droughts are common. To meet demand, all major South African rivers have been dammed or modified. While this has improved water supplies to many areas, it has also disrupted local ecosystems and caused increased silting.

South Africa has long been at the forefront among African countries in conservation of its fauna. However, funding is tight, and will likely

TOP PARKS & RESERVES

Location	Park	Features	Activities	Best Time to Visit	Page
Cape Peninsula	Table Mountain National Park	rocky headlands, seascapes; water birds, bonteboks, elands, African penguins	hiking, mountain biking	year-round	p107
Western Cape	Cederberg Wilderness Area	mountainous and rugged; San rock paintings, bizarre sandstone formations, abundant plant life	hiking	year-round	p235
Mpumalanga/ Limpopo	Kruger National Park	savanna, woodlands, thornveld; the Big Five and many more	vehicle safaris, guided wildlife walks	Jun-Oct	p466
	Blyde River Canyon Nature Reserve	canyon, caves, river; stunning vistas	hiking, kloofing	year-round	p453
Northern Cape	Augrabies Falls National Park	desert, river, waterfalls; klipspringers, rock dassies; striking scenery	hiking, canoeing, rafting	Apr-Sep	p541
	Richtersveld National Park	mountainous desert; haunting beauty; klipspringers, jackals, zebras, plants, birds	hiking	Apr-Sep	p547
Eastern Cape	Addo Elephant National Park	dense bush, coastal grasslands, forested kloofs; elephants, black rhinos, buffaloes	vehicle safaris, walking trails, horse-riding	year-round	p255
	Tsitsikamma National Park	coast, cliffs, rivers, ravines, forests; Cape clawless otters, baboons, monkeys, rich birdlife	hiking	year-round	p242

remain so as long as many South Africans still lack access to basic amenities. Potential solutions include public-private sector conservation partnerships, and increased contributions from private donors and international conservation bodies such as World Wide Fund for Nature (WWF).

THE GREAT IVORY DEBATE

In 1990, following a massive campaign by various conservation organisations, the UN Convention on International Trade in Endangered Species (Cites) banned ivory trading in an effort to protect Africa's then-declining elephant populations. This promoted recovery of elephant populations in areas where they had previously been ravaged. Yet in South Africa – where

Location	Park	Features	Activities	Best Time to Visit	Page
KwaZulu-Natal	Hluhluwe-Imfolozi Park	lush, subtropical vegetation, rolling savanna; rhinos, giraffes, lions, elephants, lots of birds	wilderness walks, wildlife-watching	May-Oct	p335
	Greater St Lucia Wetland Park	wetlands, coastal grasslands; elephants, birds, hippos	wilderness walks, vehicle/boat safaris	Mar-Nov	p339
	Mkhuze Game Reserve	savanna, woodlands, swamp; rhinos and almost everything else; hundreds of bird species	guided walks, bird walks, vehicle safaris	year-round	p345
	uKhahlamba-Drakensberg Park	awe-inspiring Drakensberg escarpment; fantastic scenery and wilderness areas	hiking	year-round	p346
Free State	Golden Gate Highlands National Park	spectacular sandstone cliffs and outcrops; zebras, jackals, rheboks, elands, birds	hiking	year-round	p385
Lesotho	Sehlabathebe National Park	mountain wilderness; bearded vultures, rheboks, baboons; wonderful isolation	hiking	Mar-Nov	p572
Swaziland	Malolotja Nature Reserve	mountains, streams, waterfalls, grasslands, forests; rich bird and plant life, impalas, klipspringers	hiking	year-round	p590

Earthlife Africa (www
.earthlife.org.za) is one of
South Africa's most active
environmental groups,
and a good contact for
anyone wanting to get
involved.

elephants had long been protected – the elephant populations continued to grow, leading to widespread habitat destruction.

Solutions to the problem of elephant overpopulation have included creating transfrontier parks to allow animals to migrate over larger areas; relocating animals; small-scale elephant contraception efforts; and, most controversially, culling.

As a result of culling, South Africa has amassed significant ivory stockpiles. In 2002, after much pressure, Cites relaxed its worldwide ivory trading ban to allow ivory from legally culled elephants to be sold, with the idea that earnings could go towards conservation projects. However, the decision has been disputed by several other governments on the (quite plausible) grounds that resuming trade will increase demand for ivory, and thus encourage poaching.

Under the current plan, Cites will monitor things to see whether poaching does indeed increase after the ban is relaxed (early signs suggest that it will). Meanwhile, ivory's popularity is growing. In China – one of the main markets for the illegal ivory trade – ivory is now the rage in mobile phone ornamentation.

Lesotho

Environmental discussion in Lesotho centres on the controversial Highlands Water Project (see p566). Among the concerns are disruption of traditional communities, flooding of agricultural lands and possible adverse ecological impact on the Senqu (Orange) River.

Other environmental issues include animal population pressure (resulting in overgrazing) and soil erosion. About 18 to 20 tonnes of topsoil per hectare is lost annually, with sobering predictions that there will be no cultivatable land left by 2040.

On a brighter note, Lesotho and South Africa recently combined forces in the Maluti-Drakensberg Transfrontier Conservation and Development Project to protect the alpine ecosystem of the Maluti and Drakensberg mountains.

THE KUYASA PROJECT

Although South Africa is only responsible for between 1% and 1.5% of the total global warming effect, it releases more greenhouse gases than any other country in sub-Saharan Africa, and is ranked in the top 15 worldwide contributors to greenhouse warming. With about 90% of the country's electricity coming from coal firing plants, electricity generation is the main culprit in the production of greenhouse gases.

The Kuyasa Project is a small but widely lauded step towards minimising greenhouse gas emissions through the use of alternative energy sources. It began in 2003, when 10 low-income houses in Cape Town's Khayelitsha township were retrofitted with renewable energy technologies such as solar water heaters, energy efficient lighting and insulated ceilings. In addition to promoting impressive energy savings – averaging about 40% per household – the project also created jobs and offered other sustainable development benefits.

The project – which was spearheaded by SouthSouthNorth, a nonprofit development organisation – gained international recognition when it qualified for the World Wide Fund for Nature's (WWF) Clean Development Mechanism Gold Standard for its design and its contributions to sustainable development. It is now slated for replication elsewhere in Khayelitsha, and in other areas of the country.

In another impressive initiative, the GreenHouse Project's (www.greenhouse.org.za) People's Environmental Centre holds regular workshops in Johannesburg to raise awareness about energy efficiency and promote the use of renewable energy sources.

LYNEDOCH ECO-VILLAGE

About 15km south of Stellenbosch in the centre of the Cape Winelands is the site of South Africa's first ecologically designed and socially mixed community. Utopic, perhaps, but Lynedoch Eco-Village is well on its way to becoming a reality, with a preschool, a primary school, a community hall and a home owners association already in existence. Houses as well as community buildings will all be energy efficient – outfitted with solar panels and other energy-saving devices – and the emphasis will be on recycling and on making the community self-sufficient. The idea is that the development of this and other similar communities will ultimately save Stellenbosch and surrounding areas from uncontrolled urbanisation or semi-urbanisation, while at the same time protecting the local environment and economy. For more, see www.sustainabilityinstitute.net.

Swaziland

Three of Swaziland's major waterways (the Komati, Lomati and Usutu Rivers) arise in South Africa, and Swaziland has been closely involved in South Africa's river control efforts. Drought is a recurring problem in eastern lowveld areas.

Other concerns include lack of community participation in conservation efforts, and insufficient government support.

Food & Drink

Check out *The South African Illustrated Cookbook* by Lehla Eldridge for a collection of recipes highlighting the many faces of South African cuisine.

It's only since the dismantling of apartheid that anyone has talked of 'South African cuisine' as a unified whole. Earlier, the Africans had their mealie pap, the Afrikaners their boerewors, and the Indians and Cape Malays their curries. Today, along with divisions in other aspects of life, the culinary barriers are starting to fall.

Awaiting the visiting gastronome is a fusion of influences: hearty meat and vegetable stews that resulted when the Dutch encountered the bush; the seemingly endless variety of maize dishes that have been at the centre of African family-life for centuries (and also feature throughout Lesotho and Swaziland); a sprinkling of *piri-piri* (hot pepper) from Mozambique; and scents of curry and coriander that have wafted over the Indian Ocean from Asia.

It can take some work to discover this diversity, and not get overwhelmed by the fast-food chains and homogenised, over-sauced dishes that are easy to find anywhere. But if you're willing to forage a bit for your food, South Africa, Lesotho and Swaziland offer a delectably rich culinary heritage that's just waiting to be discovered.

STAPLES & SPECIALITIES

What you'll be served at mealtimes is likely to be completely different, depending on where you are. Afrikaners have developed breakfast into an art form – albeit unbelievably calorie-rich – featuring lots of meat, eggs and sugar. It's easier to keep the figure trim travelling in Swaziland and Lesotho, or among South Africa's African population, where you'll be treated to bowls of piping hot maize or sorghum porridge, sometimes sweetened, sometimes slightly fermented and sour. Breakfast buffets at many hotels keep up their loyalty to the queen, with classic British breakfasts of eggs, limp toast and grilled tomatoes. In Cape Town's Bo-Kaap area, or among Durban's Indian population, you're just as likely to be served a spicy curry or *atchar* (pickled fruits and vegetables).

In *Flavours of South Africa,* South African culinary guru Peter Veldsman traces the history of South African cuisine, with lots of information on ingredients and local specialities.

Biltong & Boerewors

Traditional Afrikaner cuisine traces its roots back to the early days of Dutch settlement. Your first introduction is likely to be biltong (dried meat, called *umncweba* in Swaziland). Rusks (dried bread) are another common item, as are spicy boerewors (farmer's sausages). If you're having trouble getting used to boerewors, it could be that you're eating *braaiwors* (barbecue sausages), an inferior grade. *Potjiekos* (pot food) kept Boer families well fed as their wagons rolled into the horizon. It traditionally featured stewed meat and vegetables that bubbled away for hours in a three-legged pot over hot coals.

Perhaps more than anything else, it's the braai (barbecue) – an Afrikaner institution that has broken across race lines – that defines South African cuisine. It's as much a social event as a form of cooking, with the essential elements boerewors and beer.

Real boerewors must be 90% meat, of which 30% can be fat. We can only imagine what goes into unregulated *braaiwors*…

Cape Cuisine

Often referred to as Cape Malay cuisine, Cape cuisine has its roots in the mixing of the 'Malay' slaves (many of whom were from Madagascar and Indonesia) with the Dutch settlers. Often stodgy and overly sweet, it's nonetheless well worth trying, as is its close cousin, Afrikaner cuisine. The central feature is a mixture of Asian spices and local produce. Dishes to watch for include *bobotie, waterblommetjie bredie* and *malva* (all described on p96). True Cape cuisine, which is strongly associated with the Muslim community, contains no alcohol.

Curries

Along with Mahatma Gandhi, India's other great export to South Africa has been the curry. Durban is the place to go for the spiciest curries. Curries are also popular in Cape cuisine, though they're usually not as spicy.

Mealie Pap

Mealie pap (maize porridge) is the most widely eaten food in South Africa, as well as in Swaziland and Lesotho. It's thinner or stiffer (depending on where you eat it), bland and something of an acquired taste. However, it's ideal if you want something filling and economical, and can be quite satisfying served with a good sauce or stew.

Meat

There are few areas in the world where meat could be considered a 'staple', but certain parts of South Africa would certainly be among them. Anything that can be grilled is – with ostrich, crocodile, warthog and kudu only a few of the variants you'll find, along with the more traditional beef and lamb. Steaks in particular tend to be excellent value.

Seafood

Considering the fact that it's surrounded by two oceans, South Africa has a remarkably modest reputation as a seafood-lover's destination. Yet Cape Town, the west coast and the Garden Route have some delicious fish dishes. Among the highlights: lightly spiced fish stews, *snoekbraai* (grilled snoek), mussels, oysters and even lobster. Pickled fish is popular in Cape cuisine, while in Swaziland prawns are a common feature on restaurant menus, courtesy of nearby Mozambique.

DRINKS
Beer

Beer is the national beverage. There are numerous reasonable brands, including Castle, Black Label and Namibia's all-natural Windhoek. In the Cape provinces try Mitchell's and Birkenhead's. Lager-style beer comes in cans or dumpies (small bottles) for around R8. Bars serve long toms (750mL bottles) from around R10. Draught beers are uncommon.

Water

Tap water is generally safe in South Africa's cities. However, in rural areas (or anywhere that local conditions indicate that water sources may be contaminated), as well as throughout Swaziland and Lesotho, stick to bottled water and purify stream water.

Wine

South African wine debuted in 1659. Since then, it's had time to age to perfection, and is both of a high standard and reasonably priced. Dry whites are particularly good – try Sauvignon Blanc, Riesling, Colombard and Chenin Blanc – while popular reds include Cabernet Sauvignon, pinotage (a local cross of Pinot and Cinsaut, which was known as Hermitage), Shiraz and Pinot Noir. No wine may use any estate, vintage or origin declaration on its label without being certified. In addition,

Hungry for a quick bite? Try a roasted mealie (cob of corn) or Durban's filling *bunny chow* (curry-to-go: half a loaf of bread, scooped out and filled with curry).

In Lesotho, look for *motoho* – a fermented sorghum porridge. Swazi variants include *sishwala* (maize and bean porridge, usually eaten with meat or vegetables) and *incwancwa* (slightly fermented maize porridge).

no South African sparkling wine may be called champagne, although a number of producers use Chardonnay and Pinot Noir blends and the *méthode champenoise*.

Wine prices average from around R60 in a restaurant or bottle store. Most restaurants stock a few varieties in dinkies (250mL bottles).

In Lesotho, watch for white or yellow flags hung in villages to advertise home-brew – yellow for maize beer and white for sorghum beer or *joala*.

WHERE TO EAT & DRINK

If you're after fine dining in cosy surroundings, head to the Winelands (p169. Along the Western Cape coast, open-air beachside eateries serve fish braais under the stars. A highlight of visiting a township is experiencing family-style cooking in a B&B. In addition to speciality restaurants, every larger town has several places offering homogenised Western fare at homogenised prices (from about R50). Most restaurants are licensed, but some allow you to bring your own wine for a minimal or no corkage charge.

Larger towns have cafés, where you can enjoy a cappuccino and sandwich or other light fare. In rural areas, 'café' usually refers to a small corner shop selling soft drinks, chips and meat pies. Most places are open from about 8am to 5pm.

In the old days most South African pubs had a *kroeg* (bar) where white men would drink; a ladies' bar and lounge for white couples; and a hole in the wall where bottles would be sold to blacks and coloureds. Unofficial segregation is still the norm, and bars are heavily male-dominated. Johannesburg, Durban, Cape Town and Kimberley have the best selection of pubs. Reasonable but soulless franchised bars proliferate in urban areas, and most smaller towns have at least one hotel. In townships, things centre around *shebeens* – informal drinking establishments that were once illegal but are now merely unlicensed. Throughout South Africa, and in major towns in Lesotho and Swaziland, you can also buy alcoholic drinks at bottle stores and supermarkets.

VEGETARIANS & VEGANS

South Africa is a meat-loving society, but it's easy enough to find vegetarian offerings in larger towns, and to make do in rural areas by self-catering. In tourist areas and student towns, such as Grahamstown, you'll even find the occasional vegetarian restaurant. Otherwise, there's little that's specifically vegetarian. Cafés are good bets, as many will make veggie food to order. Indian and Italian restaurants are also good,

---

SOUTHERN AFRICAN SUSTAINABLE SEAFOOD INITIATIVE

South Africa's oceans abound with fish, but supplies are not unlimited. While populations of many fish – including snoek, hake and yellowtail – are considered to be at healthy levels, overfishing and use of inappropriate fishing methods means that those of others (eg white mussel crackers and steenbras) are dangerously low.

To address this situation, South Africa's WWF (World Wide Fund for Nature) marine programmes office began the Southern African Sustainable Seafood Initiative (SASSI) to spread information about the situation in the seas, and to promote seafood enjoyment that's also healthy for the environment. To learn more about the initiative, check www.panda.org.za/sassi. The site also has a free downloadable 'Consumer's Seafood Pocket Guide' wallet card with colour-coded listings of the conservation status of popular fish species (red – no; yellow – maybe; green – yes), so that you can make an informed, pro-environment choice the next time you sit down to dinner at a seafood restaurant. As the WWF notes, giving exploited species a break allows their populations to recover, and saying 'no' to illegally caught or sold species helps to fight unsustainable environmental practices.

although many pasta sauces contain animal fat. Major cities have health food stores selling tofu, soy milk and other staples, and can point you towards vegetarian-friendly venues.

Eating vegan is difficult: most nonmeat dishes contain cheese, and eggs and milk are common ingredients. Health-food shops are your best bet, though most are closed in the evenings and on weekends.

In Lesotho and Swaziland, while you'll find plenty of bean, peanut and other legume dishes, it's more challenging to keep variety in a vegetarian diet.

EATING WITH KIDS
Children are well catered for in South Africa, and most restaurants are very family-friendly. Many have special children's meals, and it's easy to find menu items that are suitable for young diners. Highchairs are readily available at restaurants in tourist areas. Apart from curries and other spicy dishes, there isn't anything in particular to avoid. Although tap water is fine to drink, if you've been giving your child bottled water at home or elsewhere on your travels, it's probably best to continue to do so here. Child-size boxes of fresh juice and beverages, such as carbonated apple juice, make good snacks. For more on travelling with children, see p605.

HABITS & CUSTOMS
In tourist areas, dining etiquette and customs are very Westernised. However, eating and snacking on the street is much less common than it is in Europe and the US.

For those who can afford it, three meals per day is the norm. Dinner is the main event, although lunch may be more filling in rural areas. Portions are usually large. For something light in restaurants, a soup and salad (which often comes with cheese) should more than suffice. The most popular snack is roasted mealies, sold along roadsides throughout all three countries covered in this book.

In rural areas you may also have the chance to try eating with your fingers. It's a bit of an acquired art: use your right hand only, work to ball up the staple (pap) with your fingers, dip it in the sauce or stew, and then eat it, ideally without dripping sauce down your elbow or having your ball of staple break up in the communal stew pot.

Braais are the main food-centred social event. If you're invited to one, dress is casual and the atmosphere relaxed.

A little-advertised treat of South Africa travel is the country's wide variety of excellent natural fruit juices, including passion fruit and *nartjie* (tangerine).

COOKING COURSES
Cape Town, a gourmet's paradise, is the best place for cooking courses. A few to try:

Andulela (☎ 021-790 2592; www.andulela.com) A tour company offering both a half-day Cape Malay cookery course in the Bo-Kaap every Saturday (R295) and an African cooking safari (R295) in the township of Kayamandi near Stellenbosch where you can learn to prepare traditional Xhosa foods.
Cape Gourmet Adventure Tours (☎ 083-693 1151; http://gourmet.cape-town.info) Another tour company offering upmarket custom-designed cooking classes in Cape Town, plus restaurant tours to sample the local cuisine.
Cooking with Conrad Gallagher (☎ 021-794 0111; www.conradgallagherfood.com; Bramasole House, 31 Alphen Dr, Constantia) Two-day gourmet cooking courses (R1850) run by Michelin Star chef Conrad Gallagher, and covering everything from breakfasts to braais plus table dressings and flower arrangements. His 'Desperate Housewives' one-day course (R1000) for 'ladies of leisure' is on the first and last Saturday of the month.
Kopanong (☎ 021-361 2084; kopanong@xsinet.co.za) Thope Lekau offers a half-day cook up (R150) at this Khayelitsha-based B&B (p165) where you can learn to cook African style.

EAT YOUR WORDS

Want to know *phutu* from *umphokoqo*? A boerewor from a *braaiwor*? Get behind the cuisine scene by getting to know the language. For pronunciation guidelines see p651.

Menu Decoder

It's unlikely that you'll see all of these items on the same menu, but they provide an insight into the diversity of South African cuisine.

FOOD
Meat Dishes

bobotie – a curried-mince pie topped with egg custard, usually served on a bed of rice with a dab of chutney

boerewors – spicy sausage, traditionally made of beef and pork plus seasonings and plenty of fat; an essential ingredient at any braai and often sold like hot dogs by street vendors

braaiwors – inferior grade boerewor

bredie – hearty Afrikaner pot stew, traditionally made with lamb and vegetables

eisbein – pork knuckles

frikkadel – fried meatball

potjiekos – meat and vegetables cooked for hours on a three-legged pot over a fire

russian – a large red sausage, fried but often served cold

smilies – slang term for boiled and roasted sheep heads, often sold in rural areas

sosatie – lamb cubes, marinated with garlic, tamarind juice and curry powder, then skewered with onions and apricots, and grilled; originally Muslim, but now often made with pork fat

venison – if you see this on a menu it's bound to be some form of antelope, usually springbok

vienna – a smaller version of the russian

waterblommetjie bredie – Cape Malay stew mixing lamb with water-hyacinth flowers and white wine

Curries, Condiments & Spices

atchar – a Cape Malay dish of pickled fruits and vegetables, flavoured with garlic, onion and curry

bunny chow – South Africa's answer to Indian fast food: half a loaf of bread, scooped out and filled with curry; best eaten in Durban

chakalaka sauce – a spicy tomato-based sauce seasoned with onions, *piri-piri*, green peppers and curry, and used to liven up pap and other dishes

curry – just as good as in India; head to Durban if you like your curry spicy, and to Cape Town (Bo-Kaap) for a milder version

monkey gland sauce – a sauce made from tomato and Worcester sauces and chutney; often offered with steaks

Mrs Balls' Chutney – most famous brand of this sweet-sour condiment

piri-piri – hot pepper

samosa – spicy Indian pastry

slaphakskeentjies – a Cape Malay dish of onions poached in a milk and mustard sauce

Breads & Sweets

fetkoeks – literally, 'fat cakes'; deep-fried bread dough with a rich fruit or mince-meat filling

koeksesters – small doughnuts dripping in honey, which are very gooey and figure-enhancing

konfyt – fruit preserve

malva – delicious sponge dessert; sometimes called vinegar pudding, since it's traditionally made with apricot jam and vinegar

melktart – a rich, custard-like tart made with milk, eggs, flour and cinnamon

rooster koek – griddle cake traditionally cooked on the braai

rusk – twice-cooked biscuit, usually served for breakfast or as a snack and much better than those given to teething babies

vetkoek – deep-fried dough ball sometimes stuffed with mince; called *amagwinya* in Xhosa

Grains, Legumes & Vegetables

amadumbe – yam-like potato; a favourite staple in KwaZulu-Natal

imbasha – a Swazi fried delicacy of roasted maize and nuts

imifino – Xhosa dish of mealie meal and vegetables

mashonzha – mopane worms, fried, grilled or served with *dhofi* (peanut sauce); common in Venda areas

mealie – cob of corn, popular grilled as a snack

mealie meal – finely ground maize

mealie pap – maize porridge; a Southern African staple, best eaten with sauce or stew

mopane worms – caterpillars found on mopane trees; dried and served in spicy sauce as a crunchy snack

morogo – leafy greens, boiled, seasoned and served with pap; called *imifino* in Xhosa

pap & sous – maize porridge with a tomato and onion sauce

phutu – a Zulu dish of crumbly maize porridge, often eaten with soured milk; called *umphokoqo* in Xhosa

rystafel – Dutch/Afrikaner version of an Indonesian meal consisting of rice with many accompanying dishes

samp – mix of maize and beans; see *umngqusho*

tincheki – boiled pumpkin cubes with sugar, common in Swaziland

ting – sorghum porridge, popular among the Tswana

umngqusho – samp (dried and crushed maize kernels), boiled, then mixed with beans, salt and oil, and simmered; a Xhosa delicacy (called *nyekoe* in Sotho)

umvubo – sour milk and mealie meal

Fish

kingklip – an excellent firm-fleshed fish, usually served fried; South Africa's favourite fish

line fish – catch of the day

snoek – a firm-fleshed migratory fish that appears off the Cape in June and July; served smoked, salted or curried

DRINKS

Don Pedro – an alcoholic milkshake traditionally made with whiskey and ice cream, but also commonly available with other liquors

mampoer – home-distilled brandy made from peaches and prickly pear

rooibos – literally, 'red bush' (Afrikaans); herbal tea that reputedly has therapeutic qualities

spook & diesel – rum and cola

springbok – a cocktail featuring créme de menthe topped with Amarula Cream (a South African version of Baileys Irish Cream)

steen – Chenin Blanc; most common variety of white wine

sundowner – any drink, but typically alcohol, drunk at sunset

umnqombothi – Xhosa for rough-and-ready, home-brewed beer; *umqombotsi* or *tjwala* in Swaziland

witblitz – 60-proof 'white lightning'; a traditional Boer spirit distilled from fruit

Food & Drinks Glossary

Following are a few more terms – mostly in Afrikaans, except as noted – to help you make your way around.

FOOD

biefstuk	steak
biltong	dried, salted meat
brood	bread
dipadi	toasted maize with salt and sometimes sugar (Sotho)
groente	vegetables
ho seal	mealie meal (Sotho)

hoender	chicken
incwancwa	fermented maize porridge (Swati, Zulu)
ingubela	pumpkin porridge (Xhosa)
isijingi	mashed pumpkin and ground maize (Zulu)
kaas	cheese
lipolokoe	steamed bread
motoho	fermented sorghum porridge (Sotho)
ntswanatsike	fermented barley porridge (Sotho)
sishwala	pap, usually served with meat or vegetables (Swati)
tinkhobe	boiled, whole maize (Swati)
umncweba	biltong (Swati)
varkvlies	pork
vis	fish
vleis	meat
vrugte	fruit

DRINKS

amasi	sour milk (Xhosa)
bier	beer
cool drink	canned soft drink
dinkies	250mL bottles of wine
dumpies	small bottles of beer
glas melk	glass of milk
ijinja	local ginger brew (Xhosa)
joala	local sorghum brew
koppie koffie	cup of coffee
long toms	750mL bottles of beer
moqopothi	local sorghum brew (Zulu)
tee	tea
wyn	wine

OTHER

braai	open-air barbecue; from *braaivleis* (grilled meat)
kroeg	bar
padkos	picnic
shebeen	unlicensed bar

South Africa

JANE SWEENEY

Cape Town

Good-looking, fun-loving, sporty and laid-back. If Cape Town was in the dating game that's how her profile would read. And – for once – it's all true. The Mother City occupies one of the world's most stunning locations, with an iconic mountain slap-bang in its centre. As beautiful as the surrounding beaches and vineyards can be, it's the rugged wilderness of Table Mountain, coated in a unique flora, that is the focus of attention.

Complementing this natural beauty is Cape Town's eye-catching way with design and colour – in everything from the brightly painted façades of the Bo-Kaap and the Victorian bathing chalets of Muizenberg, to the contemporary Afro-chic décor of the many excellent guesthouses, restaurants and bars. The city's multiethnic population is proof of South Africa's 'rainbow nation'.

It's a place of extremes, with the wealth of Camps Bay and Constantia side by side with the poverty of townships such as Khayelitsa. Even in the townships and the deprived coloured areas of the city – home to the vast majority of Capetonians – there are huge differences in lifestyle and many great examples of civic pride and optimism to balance against the shocking crime and HIV/AIDS statistics. Discovering the Mother City's true diversity and spirit is all part of getting the most out of a visit here.

It has great eating and drinking establishments, a lively cultural scene, particularly when it comes to music, and scores of adrenaline pumping outdoor activities. Now don't you think it time you made a date with Cape Town?

HIGHLIGHTS

- Sailing out to the infamous prison **Robben Island** (p107), and pondering the country's past and present

- Taking the cable car to the top of magnificent **Table Mountain** (p107) and looking down on the city

- Exploring the **City Bowl** (p108), where you'll find museums, the Company's Gardens and wonderful Art Deco and Victorian architecture

- Heading to the **Cape of Good Hope Nature Reserve** (p164) for wide open spaces, wildlife, empty beaches and the dramatic scenery of the peninsula's rugged tip

- Browsing the fish market, antique shops and convivial cafés at **Kalk Bay** (p160)

Robben Island ★

★ City Bowl
★ Table Mountain

★ Kalk Bay

★ Cape of Good Hope Nature Reserve

■ POPULATION: 3.1 MILLION   ■ AREA: 2487 SQ KM

HISTORY

Long before the Dutch East India Company (Vereenigde Oost-Indische Compagnie; VOC; see p33) established a base here in 1652, the Cape Town area was settled by the San and Khoekhoen nomadic tribes, collectively known as the Khoesaan. The indigenous people shunned the Dutch, so the VOC was forced to import slaves from Madagascar, India, Ceylon, Malaya and Indonesia to deal with the colony's chronic labour shortage. Women were in even shorter supply, so the Europeans exploited the female slaves and the local Khoesaan for both labour and sex. In time the slaves also intermixed with the Khoesaan. The offspring of these unions formed the basis of sections of today's coloured population and also helps explain the unique character of the city's Cape Muslim population (see p104).

Under the 150-odd years of Dutch rule, Kaapstad, as the Cape settlement became known, thrived and gained a wider reputation as the 'Tavern of the Seas', a riotous port used by every sailor travelling between Europe and the East. But by the end of the 18th century the VOC was practically bankrupt, making Cape Town an easy target for British imperial interests in the region. Following the British defeat of the Dutch in 1806 at Bloubergstrand, 25km north of Cape Town, the colony was ceded to the Crown on 13 August 1814. The slave trade was abolished in 1808, and all slaves were emancipated in 1833.

The discovery and exploitation of diamonds and gold in the centre of South Africa in the 1870s and 1880s led to rapid changes. Cape Town was soon no longer the single dominant metropolis in the country, but as a major port it too was a beneficiary of the mineral wealth that laid the foundations for an industrial society. The same wealth led to imperialist dreams of grandeur on the part of Cecil John Rhodes (premier of the Cape Colony in 1890), who had made his millions at the head of De Beers Consolidated Mines (see p527).

An outbreak of bubonic plague in 1901 was blamed on the black African workers (although it actually came on boats from Argentina) and gave the government an excuse to introduce racial segregation: blacks were moved to two locations, one near the docks and the other at Ndabeni on the western flank of Table Mountain. This was the start of what would later develop into the townships of the Cape Flats.

In 1948 the National Party stood for election on its policy of apartheid and narrowly won. In a series of bitter court and constitutional battles, the limited rights of blacks and coloureds to vote in the Cape were removed and the insane apparatus of apartheid was erected. This resulted in whole communities, such as District Six (see p112), being uprooted and cast out to the bleak Cape Flats.

The government tried for decades to eradicate squatter towns, such as Crossroads, which were focal points for black resistance to the apartheid regime. In its last attempt between May and June 1986, an estimated 70,000 people were driven from their homes and hundreds were killed. Even this brutal attack was unsuccessful in eradicating the towns, and the government accepted the inevitable and began to upgrade conditions.

Hours after being released from prison on 11 February 1990, Nelson Mandela made his first public speech in decades from the balcony of Cape Town's City Hall, heralding the beginning of a new era for South Africa. Much has improved in Cape Town since – property prices keep booming and the city centre is a safer and more pleasant place to shop, work and live, with the development of ritzy loft-style apartments in grand old structures such as Mutual Heights (p113).

Full integration of Cape Town's mixed population, however, remains a long way off, if it's achievable at all. The vast majority of Capetonians who live in the Cape Flats remain split along race lines and suffer horrendous economic, social and health problems, not least of which are the HIV/AIDs pandemic and high levels of drug-related crime. At the most recent local elections in March 2006, among the issues that helped the Democratic Alliance receive a higher percentage of the vote than the ruling African National Congress (ANC) were local government corruption, the rolling power outages in the city and lack of funds for the overstretched fire brigade.

CLIMATE

Great extremes of temperature are unknown in Cape Town, although it can be relatively

CAPE TOWN & THE PENINSULA

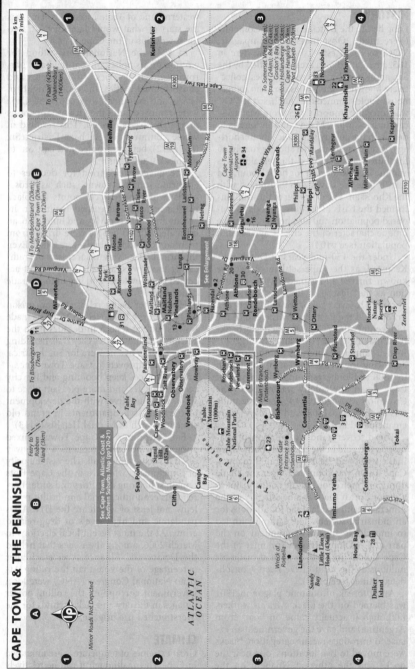

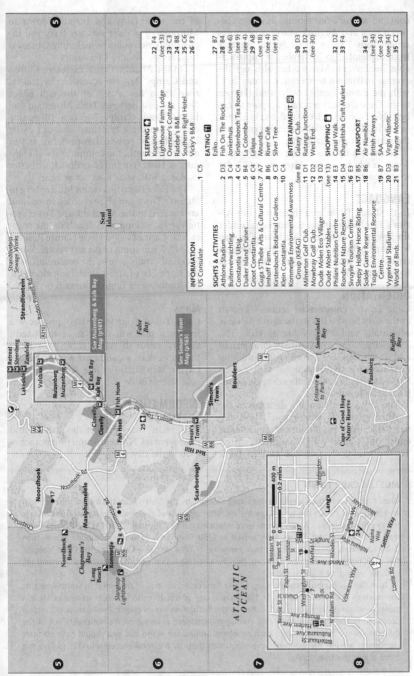

INFORMATION

US Consulate 1 C5

SIGHTS & ACTIVITIES

Athlone Stadium 2 D3
Buitenverwachting 3 C4
Constantia Uitsig 4 C4
Duiker Island Cruises 5 B4
Groot Constantia 6 C4
Guga S'Thebe Arts & Cultural Centre. 7 A7
Imhoff Farm 8 B6
Kirstenbosch Botanical Gardens. 9 C3
Klein Constantia 10 C4
Kommetjie Environmental Awareness
   Group (KEAG) .... (see 8)
Milnerton Golf Club 11 D1
Mowbray Golf Club 12 D2
Oude Molen Eco Village 13 D2
Oude Molen Stables .... (see 13)
Philani Nutrition Centre 14 E3
Rondevlei Nature Reserve 15 D4
Siuoyle Tourism Centre 16 E3
Sleepy Hollow Horse Riding .. 17 B5
Solole Game Reserve 18 B6
Tsoga Environmental Resource
   Centre 19 B7
Vygerkraal Stadium 20 D3
World of Birds 21 B3

SLEEPING

Kopanong 22 F4
Lighthouse Farm Lodge ...... (see 13)
Overseer's Cottage 23 C3
Radebe's B&B 24 B8
Southern Right Hotel 25 C6
Vicky's B&B 26 F3

EATING

Eziko 27 B7
Fish On The Rocks 28 B4
Jonkerhuis .... (see 6)
Kirstenbosch Tea Room ...... (see 9)
La Colombe .... (see 4)
Lelapa 29 A8
Mnandis .... (see 18)
River Café .... (see 4)
Silver Tree .... (see 9)

ENTERTAINMENT

Galaxy Club 30 D3
Ratanga Junction 31 D2
West End .... (see 30)

SHOPPING

Canal Walk 32 D2
Khayelitsha Craft Market 33 F4

TRANSPORT

Air Namibia 34 E3
British Airways .... (see 34)
SAA .... (see 34)
Virgin Atlantic .... (see 34)
Wayne Motors 35 C2

cold and wet for a few months in winter (between June and August) when temperatures range from 7°C to 18°C. Spring weather from September to November is unpredictable. December to March is hot, although the average maximum temperature is only 26°C with the strong southeasterly wind (known as the Cape Doctor) generally keeping things bearable. From March to April, and to a lesser extent in May, the weather remains good and the wind is at its most gentle.

For hourly updates on the weather, check www.weathersa.co.za. Also see p607 for more information.

LANGUAGE

In the Cape Town area three of South Africa's 11 official languages (all equal under the law) are prominent: Afrikaans (spoken by many whites and coloureds), English (spoken by nearly everyone) and Xhosa (spoken mainly by blacks).

ORIENTATION

Cape Town's commercial centre – known as the City Bowl – lies to the north of Table Mountain and east of Signal Hill. The inner-city suburbs of Gardens, Oranjezicht and Tamboerskloof are all within walking distance of it. Nearby Signal Hill, Green Point and Sea Point are other densely populated seaside suburbs.

The city sprawls quite a distance to the northeast (this is where you'll find the beachside district of Bloubergstrand and the enormous Canal Walk shopping centre). To the south, skirting the eastern flank of the mountains and running down to Muizenberg at False Bay, are leafy and increasingly rich suburbs including Observatory, Newlands and Constantia.

On the Atlantic Coast, exclusive Clifton and Camps Bay are accessible by coastal road from Sea Point or through Kloof Nek, the pass between Table Mountain and Lion's Head. Camps Bay is a 10-minute drive from the city centre and can easily be reached by public transport, but as you go further south, the communities of Llandudno, Hout Bay and Noordhoek are better explored with your own car or bike.

The False Bay towns from Muizenberg to Simon's Town can all be reached by rail and are covered in the Around Cape Town section (p160), along with details on the spectacular Cape of Good Hope Nature Reserve (p164), 70km south of the city centre. You'll also find details here of the communities in the Cape Flats (p165), stretching along the N2 southeast of Table Mountain.

Maps

Cape Town Tourism (p106) produces a free map that will serve most short-term visitors' needs. If you're staying for more than a week or so, and have a car, consider buying Map Studio's *Cape Town & Peninsula Street Guide*.

INFORMATION
Bookshops

The main mass-market bookshop and newsagent is CNA, with numerous branches around the city.

MUSLIM CAPE TOWN

Islam first came to the Cape with the slaves brought by the Dutch from the Indian subcontinent and Indonesia (hence the term Cape Malays, although few of them actually hailed from what is today called Malaysia). Among them were educated political dissidents such as the exiled Islamic leader Tuan Guru from Tidore, who arrived in 1780. During his 13 years on Robben Island, Tuan Guru accurately copied the Quran from memory. In 1794 he helped establish the Owal Mosque, the city's first mosque, in the Bo-Kaap, thus making this area the heart of the Islamic community in Cape Town that it still is today.

Tuan Guru is buried in the Bo-Kaap's Tana Baru cemetery, one of the oldest in South Africa, at the western end of Longmarket St. His grave is one of the 20 or so *karamats* (tombs of Muslim saints) encircling Cape Town and visited by the faithful on a mini pilgrimage. Islam is still widely practiced in the city, predominantly among the coloured community. It's noticeably not of the militant variety that has caused such problems around the world and you should have no fears wandering around the Bo-Kaap, where you can drop by the local museum (p112) to find out more about the community.

CAPE TOWN IN...

Two Days

Start with a trip up **Table Mountain** (p107). After admiring the view return to the city and wander through the **Company's Gardens** (p109), nipping into the **SA National Gallery** (p113) to sample the best of the country's art. Get a taste of African cuisine at **Café African Image** (p147), then go souvenir shopping at **Greenmarket Sq** (p156) and along **Long St** (p109).

Kick off day two by exploring the southern end of the Cape Peninsula and the False Bay coast. The obvious destination is magnificent **Cape Point** (p164), where you could easily spend the whole day. However, it would be a shame to miss out on charming **Simon's Town** (p162), the cute penguin colony at **Boulders** (p163), and the antique shops and picturesque fishing harbour at **Kalk Bay** (p160). A good option for lunch is Kalk Bay's **Olympia Café & Deli** (p162). Return to the city via the Atlantic Coast and **Chapman's Peak Drive** (p118), pausing at **Camps Bay** (p118) for a sundowner cocktail.

Four Days

Start day three with a half-day **township tour** (p141). These generally include the **District Six Museum** (p108). Sail out to **Robben Island** (p107) in the afternoon; then either hang out at the **Waterfront** (p378) in the evening, or head over to the **Waterkant** to dine (p149) and dance (p153) the night away with the gorgeous guys and girls.

On day four explore the Southern Suburbs, dropping by the **Irma Stern Museum** (p119) or leafy **Constantia** (p119) for a spot of wine tasting. An afternoon stroll around **Kirstenbosch Botanical Gardens** (p119) is recommended. You could have afternoon tea here or at the tearoom beside the nearby **Rhodes Memorial** (p122), with its sweeping view across the Cape Flats. Cap off your trip with dinner back in the city, say at **Africa Café** (p148) or **Madame Zingara & Cara Lazuli** (p148).

Clarke's Bookshop (Map pp110–11; ☎ 021-423 5739; www.clarkesbooks.co.za; 211 Long St, City Bowl) Stocks an unsurpassed range of books on South Africa and the continent, and has a great secondhand and antiquarian section.

Exclusive Books Waterfront (Map pp116–17; ☎ 021-419 0905; Victoria Wharf); Cavendish Sq Mall (Map pp120–1; Claremont); Lifestyles on Kloof (Map p114) Has an excellent range, including some books in French.

Travellers Bookshop (Map pp116–17; ☎ 021-425 6880; Victoria Wharf, Waterfront)

Emergency

In an emergency call ☎ 107, or ☎ 112 if using a mobile phone. Other useful phone numbers:

Ambulance (☎ 10177)
Fire brigade (☎ 021-535 1100)
Mountain Rescue Services (☎ 021-948 9900)
Police (☎ 10111)
Sea Rescue (☎ 021-405 3500)

Internet Access

Cape Town is one of the most wired cities in Africa. Most hotels and hostels have Internet facilities and you'll seldom have to hunt far for an Internet café. Rates are pretty uniform at R10 per hour.

Catwalk TV (Map pp110–11; ☎ 021-423 8999; www.catwalk.co.za; 16 Burg St, City Bowl; ☯ 24 hr) Central and handy.

Media

Cape Town's morning newspaper, the **Cape Times** (www.capetimes.co.za), and the afternoon **Cape Argus** (www.capeargus.co.za), print practically the same news. The weekly *Mail & Guardian*, published Friday, has a good arts review supplement with details of what's going on in Cape Town. **Cape Etc** (www.capeetc.com) is a decent bimonthly arts and listings magazine dedicated to what's going on around town.

Medical Services

Medical services are of a high standard in Cape Town. Many doctors make house calls; they're listed under 'Medical' in the phone book, and hotels and most other accomodation places can arrange a visit.

Christian Barnard Memorial Hospital (Map pp110–11; ☎ 021-480 6111; www.netcare.co.za; 181 Longmarket

St, City Bowl) The best private hospital; reception is on the 8th floor.

Groote Schuur Hospital (Map pp120–1; ☎ 021-404 9111; capegateway.gov.za/gsh; Main Rd, Observatory) In an emergency, you can go directly to the casualty department.

SAA-Netcare Travel Clinic (Map pp110–11; ☎ 021-419 3172; 11th fl, Picbal Arcade, 58 Strand St, City Bowl; ☺ 8am-5pm Mon-Fri, 9am-1pm Sat) For vaccinations and travel health.

Money

Money can be changed at the airport, most commercial banks and at Cape Town Tourism (below). Rennies Travel (right) is the local agent for Thomas Cook and also has foreign-exchange offices.

There are ATMs all over town; see p614 for information on ATM scams.

American Express City Bowl (Map pp110-11; ☎ 021-425 7991; Thibault Sq); Waterfront (Map pp116-17; ☎ 021-419 3917; V&A Hotel Mall, Waterfront)

Post

General post office (Map pp110-11; ☎ 021-464 1700; Parliament St, City Bowl; ☺ 8am-4.30pm Mon-Fri, 8am-noon Sat) Has a poste restante counter.

Telephone

At phone boxes a phonecard is useful; you can buy one at Cape Town Tourism, newsagents and general stores.

You can rent mobile phones or get a pay-as-you-go SIM card from the MTM and Vodacom desks at the airport or in town, where you'll also find Cell-C shops. Top-up cards are available all over town.

Tourist Information

Cape Town Tourism (www.tourismcapetown.co.za) City Centre (Map pp110-11; ☎ 021-487 6800; cnr Castle

& Burg Sts, City Bowl; ☺ 8am-6pm Mon-Fri, 8.30am-2pm Sat, 9am-1pm Sun Oct-Mar, 8am-5.30pm Mon-Fri, 8.30am-1pm Sat, 9am-1pm Sun Apr-Sep); Waterfront (Map pp116-17; ☎ 021-405 4500; Clock Tower Centre; ☺ 9am-9pm) At this impressive and well-run centre, you'll find advisers who can book accommodation, tours and rental cars. At the City Centre branch you can also get advice on Cape Nature Conservation Parks (☎ 021-426 0723) and the National Parks & Reserves (☎ 021-423 8005). There's also an Internet café and a foreign-exchange booth. The Waterfront office is a scaled-down version of the main city-centre office.

Travel Agencies

Africa Travel Centre (Map p114; ☎ 021-423 5555; www.backpackers.co.za; the Backpack, 74 New Church St, Tamboerskloof) Books all sorts of tours and activities, including day trips, hire cars and extended truck tours of Africa.

Atlantic Tourist Information Centre (Map pp120–1; ☎ 021-434 2382; www.arokan.co.za; 242 Main Rd, Three Anchor Bay) Gay-run tour company and travel agent.

Flight Centre (Map p114; www.flightcentre.co.za; ☎ 021-461 8658; Gardens Centre, Mill St, Gardens)

Rennies Travel (www.renniestravel.co.za) City Bowl (Map pp110–11; ☎ 021-423 7154; 101 St George's Mall); Sea Point (Map pp120–1; ☎ 021-439 7529; 182 Main Rd); Waterfront (Map pp116–17; ☎ 021-418 3744; Victoria Wharf Shopping Centre) Handles international and domestic bookings and is the agent for Thomas Cook travellers cheques. It can arrange visas for neighbouring countries for a moderate charge.

STA Travel (Map pp120–1; ☎ 021-686 6800; 14 Main Rd, Rondebosch)

Wanderwomen (☎ 021-788 9988; www.wanderwomen .co.za) Travel agent and tour company run by women.

Visa Extensions

Department of Home Affairs (Map pp110-11; ☎ 021-465 0333; www.samigrationservices.co.za; 56 Barrack St, City Bowl; ☺ 8am-3.15pm Mon-Fri)

CAPE TOWN PASS

If you want to pack in a lot of sightseeing in Cape Town (and we do mean a lot!), consider investing in the **Cape Town Pass** (☎ 021-886 7080; www.thecapetownpass.co.za). The pass, which is valid for one, two, three or six consecutive days (adult R275/425/495/750, child R180/285/350/550), covers entry to some 70-odd Cape Peninsula and Winelands attractions; the only main exceptions are the Table Mountain cable car and Robben Island. You'll have to work pretty hard to get the full value from the one- or two-day cards, but the three- and six-day ones can work out a good deal. The pass also offers discounts at many places around town as well as free cell phone rental and a local SIM card from Vodashop-Cellucity. It's available at Cape Town Tourism's main City Bowl and Waterfront offices, or you can buy it online and have it delivered to wherever you'll be staying.

HOERIKWAGGO TRAILS

As with Uluru (Ayres Rock) in Australia, we will all have to get used to knowing Table Mountain by its indigenous Khoesaan name Hoerikwaggo (meaning 'mountain in the sea'). In 2005 Table Mountain National Park launched the first of its planned suit of three **Hoerikwaggo Trails** (www .hoerikwaggotrails.co.za) designed to allow visitors, for the first time, to sleep on the mountain, and eventually to hike 80km or so from the City Bowl to Cape Point.

The three-day Table Mountain Trail is a fully guided hike starting at the Waterfront and proceeding through the City Bowl. Hikers then spend the night at a well-appointed lodge at the historic Platteklip Wash House (Map p114) in Vredehoek, on the lower northern slopes of the mountain. On day two the hike continues up to the cableway and then to the summit and across the mountaintop, and hikers spend the night on the Back Table at the Overseers Cottage (Map pp102–3). On the final day hikers explore the Back Table and descend via the eastern slopes of the mountain to Kirstenbosch Botanical Gardens (p119). The trail costs R1900 per person (based on double occupancy of a room), which includes all meals, portering of luggage and accommodation of a very high standard. There's a maximum of 16 people on a hike.

By the start of 2007 the less-pampered Tip to Top Trail should be up and running. This six-day, five-night hike beginning at Cape Point will involve carrying your own food, gear and sleeping bag and camping at fixed spots in the national park. By the end of 2007 a luxury version, running in the opposite direction (Top to Tip), and sleeping in comfortable huts, should be available.

DANGERS & ANNOYANCES

Cape Town remains one of the most relaxed cities in Africa, which can instil a false sense of security. Thefts are most likely to happen when visitors do something stupid like leaving their gear on a beach while they go swimming.

Paranoia is not required, but common sense is. There is tremendous poverty on the peninsula and the 'informal redistribution of wealth' is reasonably common. The townships on the Cape Flats have an appalling crime rate and unless you have a trustworthy guide or are on a tour they are not places for a casual stroll.

Stick to the roads when you walk around the city, and always listen to local advice. There is safety in numbers.

Swimming at any of the Cape beaches is potentially hazardous, especially for those inexperienced in surf. Check for warning signs about rips and rocks and only swim in patrolled areas.

For safety tips while walking in Table Mountain National Park, see p137.

SIGHTS
Table Mountain National Park

Covering some three quarters of the peninsula, **Table Mountain National Park** (www.tmnp .co.za) stretches from flat-topped Table Mountain to Cape Point (see p164). For the vast majority of visitors the main attraction is

the 1086m-high mountain itself, the top of which can easily be accessed by the **cableway** (Map pp120-1; ☎ 021-424 5148; www.tablemountain.net; adult one way/return R57.50/115, child R30/60; ☺ 8.30am-7pm Feb-Nov, 8am-10pm Dec & Jan), which runs every 10/20 minutes in high/low season.

The views from the revolving cable car and on the summit are phenomenal. Once you're at the top there are souvenir shops, a café and some easy walks to follow. The cableway doesn't operate when it's dangerously windy, and there's little point going up if you are simply going to be wrapped in the cloud known as the 'tablecloth'. Call in advance to see if they're operating. The best visibility and conditions are likely to be first thing in the morning or in the evening. For information about climbing the mountain see p124.

If you don't have your own transport, Rikkis (p159) will drop you at the cable car from the city centre for R16; a nonshared taxi will cost around R50.

Robben Island & Nelson Mandela Gateway

Prisoners were incarcerated on **Robben Island** (☎ 413 4220; www.robben-island.org.za; adult/child R150/ 75; ☺ hourly ferries 9am-3pm, sunset tour 5pm Dec-Jan) from the early days of the VOC right up until 1996. Now a museum and UN World Heritage Site, it is one of the most popular destinations in all of Cape Town.

While we heartily recommend going to Robben Island, a visit here is not without its drawbacks. Most likely you will have to endure crowds and being hustled around on a guided tour that at a maximum of two hours on the island (plus a 30-minute boat ride in both directions) is woefully short. You will learn much of what happened to Mandela and others like him, since one of the former inmates will lead you around the prison. It seems a perverse form of torture to have these guys recount their harrowing time as prisoners here, but the best of the guides rise above this to embody the true spirit of reconciliation.

The standard tours, which have set departure and return times when you buy your ticket, include a walk through the old prison (with the obligatory peek into Mandela's cell), as well as a 45-minute bus ride around the island with commentary on the various places of note, such as the lime quarry in which Mandela and many others slaved, and the church used during the island's stint as a leper colony. If you're lucky, you'll have about 10 minutes to wander around on your own. The guides will suggest checking out the jackass penguin colony near the landing jetty, but we recommend heading straight to the prison's A-section to view the remarkable and very moving exhibition *Cell Stories*. In each of 40 isolation cells is an artefact and story from a former political prisoner.

Tours depart from the **Nelson Mandela Gateway** (Map pp116-17; admission free; 9am-8.30pm) beside the Clock Tower at the Waterfront. Even if you don't plan a visit to the island, it's worth dropping by the museum here, with its focus on the struggle for freedom. For island tours an advance booking is recommended; at holiday times all tours can be booked up for days. Make bookings at the Nelson Mandela Gateway departure point or at Cape Town Tourism (see p106) in the city.

City Bowl

City Bowl, the commercial heart of Cape Town, is squeezed between Table Mountain, Signal Hill and the harbour. Immediately to the west is the Bo-Kaap and the Waterkant, and to the east is Zonnebloem (once known as District Six). One of the best ways to see the many sights here is on a walking tour; see p140 for some recommended tour companies, or follow our self-guided tour (p138).

DISTRICT SIX MUSEUM

If you see only one museum in Cape Town make it the **District Six Museum** (Map pp110-11; ☎ 021-466 7200; www.districtsix.co.za; 25A Buitenkant St; adult/child R15/10; 9am-3pm Mon, 9am-4pm Tue-Sat). Note that almost all township tours stop here first to explain the history of the pass laws. This emotionally moving museum is as much for the people of the now-vanished District Six as it is about them. Displays include a floor map of District Six on which former residents have labelled where their demolished homes and features of their neighbourhood once stood; reconstructions of home interiors; and faded photographs and recordings. Many of the staff, practically all displaced residents themselves, have heartbreaking stories to tell (see the boxed text, p112).

You can also arrange a **walking tour** (☎ 021-466 7208; per person R50, 10 people minimum) of the old District Six.

CASTLE OF GOOD HOPE

Many visitors are surprised to find a **castle** (Map pp110-11; ☎ 021-787 1249; www.castleofgoodhope.co.za; Mon-Sat adult/child R20/10, Sun R10/5; 9am-4pm, tours 11am, noon & 2pm Mon-Sat) in Cape Town. Built between 1666 and 1679 to defend Cape Town, this stone-walled pentagonal structure is commonly touted as the city's oldest building. It's worth coming for one of the tours (the noon tour on weekdays coincides with the changing of the guard, since the castle is still the headquarters for the Western Cape military command), although you can quite easily find your own way around. A key ceremony at the castle gate – when the keys to the gate are handed over in an orchestrated ceremony – is held at 10am Monday to Friday. There are extensive displays of militaria and some interesting ones on the castle's archaeology and the reconstruction of the so-called Dolphin Pool. The highlight is the bulk of the William Fehr Collection (open 9.30am to 4pm), including some fabulous bits of Cape Dutch furniture, such as a table seating 100, and paintings by John Thomas Baines.

The entrance is on Buitenkant St.

COMPANY'S GARDENS
These shady green **gardens** (Map p114; ⏱ 7am-7pm) in the heart of the city are a lovely place to relax during the heat of the day. The surviving six hectares of what started as the vegetable patch for the Dutch East India Company are found around Government Ave, with gates next to the National Library of South Africa and off both Museum and Queen Victoria Sts. As the VOC's sources of supply diversified, the grounds became a superb pleasure garden, planted with a fine collection of botanical specimens from South Africa and the rest of the world, including frangipani and African flame trees, aloes and roses.

The squirrels that scamper here were imported to Cape Town from North America by Cecil Rhodes, whose statue stands in the centre of the gardens. A craft market is held next to the café in the centre of the garden once or twice a month; enquire at the garden's information centre for details.

HOUSES OF PARLIAMENT
Although it sounds unlikely, visiting South Africa's **parliament** (Map pp110-11; ☎ 021-403 2266; www.parliament.gov.za; Parliament St; admission free; tours by appointment Mon-Fri) can make for a fascinating tour, especially if you're interested in the country's modern history. Opened in 1885, the hallowed halls have seen some pretty momentous events; this is where British prime minister Harold Macmillan made his 'Wind of Change' speech in 1960, and where president Hendrik Verwoerd, architect of apartheid, was stabbed to death in 1966. Enthusiastic tour guides will fill you in on the mechanisms and political make-up of their new democracy. You must present your passport to gain entry.

MICHAELIS COLLECTION & GREENMARKET SQUARE
Donated by Sir Max Michaelis in 1914, the impressive **Michaelis Collection** (Map pp110-11; ☎ 021-481 3933; www.museums.org.za/michaelis; Greenmarket Sq; admission by donation; ⏱ 10am-5pm Mon-Fri, 10am-4pm Sat) is found in the superbly restored Old Townhouse, which used to be the City Hall. Masterworks from the collection of 16th- and 17th-century art (including works by Rembrandt, Frans Hals and Anthony Van Dyck) hang beside contemporary pieces.

Outside, browse the lively souvenir market in cobbled **Greenmarket Square** (p156) and inspect the striking Art Deco façades of the buildings around the square.

LONG STREET
Whether you come to browse the antique shops, secondhand bookstores and streetwear boutiques, or to party at the host of bars and clubs that crank up at night, a stroll along Long St (Map pp110-11) is an essential part of a Cape Town visit. The most attractive section, lined with Victorian-era buildings with wrought-iron balconies, runs from the junction with Buitensingle St north to around the Strand. Long St once formed the border of the Muslim Bo-Kaap so you'll find several old mosques along the street, including the **Noor el Hamedia Mosque** (1884), on the corner of Dorp St, and the **Palm Tree Mosque** at 185 Long St, dating from 1780. For information about Long St Baths see p138.

SIGNAL HILL & NOON GUN
Once also known as Lion's Rump, as it's attached to Lion's Head by a 'spine' of hills, **Signal Hill** (Map pp110-11) separates Sea Point from the City Bowl. There are magnificent views from the 350m-high summit, especially at night. Head up Kloof Nek Rd from the city and take the first turn-off to the right at the top of the hill.

At noon Monday to Saturday, a cannon known as the **Noon Gun** (Map pp110-11) is fired from the lower slopes of Signal Hill. You can hear it all over town. Traditionally this allowed the burghers in the town below to check their watches. It's a stiff walk up here through the Bo-Kaap. Take Longmarket St and keep going until it ends. The Noon Gun Tearoom & Restaurant (p148) is a good place to catch your breath.

SLAVE LODGE
One of the oldest buildings in South Africa, dating back to 1660, **Slave Lodge** (Map pp110-11; ☎ 021-460 8240; www.museums.org.za/slavelodge; 49 Adderley St; adult/child R10/5; ⏱ 10am-4.30pm Mon-Sat) has a fascinating history. Until 1811 the building was home, if you could call it that, to as many as 1000 slaves, who lived in damp, insanitary, crowded conditions. Up to 20% died each year. The slaves were bought and sold just around the corner on Spin St.

CITY BOWL & BO-KAAP

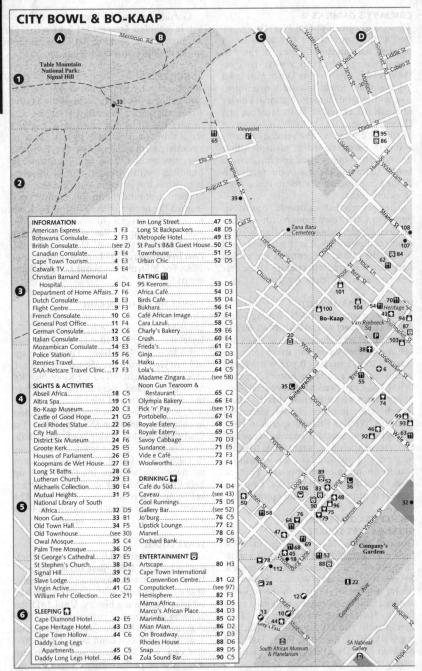

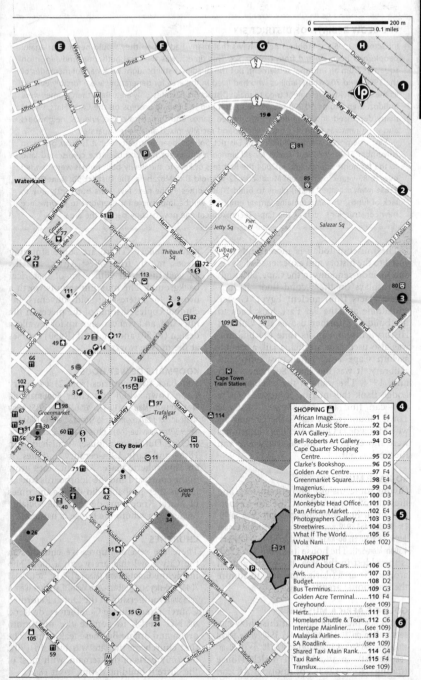

CAPE TOWN

THE SLOW REBIRTH OF DISTRICT SIX

In October 2005 Capetonians heard news that many had hoped they would never hear again: people had been evicted from District Six. This time it was the local authorities moving in on squatters from an informal settlement, but the headlines still brought back painful memories of the 1960s and 70s when families who had lived in the area for generations were forcibly evicted as the apartheid government tried to make District Six a whites-only area. Back then, homes were bulldozed and some 50,000 people were dumped in bleak townships on the Cape Flats, where many depressed and dispirited youths joined gangs and turned to crime. Friends, neighbours and even relatives from this once vibrant and racially-mixed area were separated.

Since democracy, the rebuilding of District Six has been a priority but it is slow going. In November 2000 President Thabo Mbeki signed a document handing back the confiscated land to the former residents, and in 2004 the first sets of keys to the newly-built homes were handed over to 87-year-old Ebrahiem Murat and 82-year-old Dan Mdzabela. The **District Six Beneficiary Trust** (www.d6bentrust.org.za) plans to build 2000 homes in the next few years but, partly due to lack of funds, the area remains largely empty. It will be impossible for everyone to return since new constructions such as the Cape Technikon college now occupy part of the area.

The museum today is increasingly devoted to the history and experience of slaves and their descendants in the Cape, although the displays on the second floor, including artefacts from ancient Egypt, Greece and Rome and the Far East, hark back to the building's former use as the Cultural History Museum. In its time the building was also used as a brothel, a jail, a mental asylum, Cape Town's first post office and a library. It was the Cape Supreme Court until 1914. The walls of the original Slave Lodge flank the interior courtyard, where you can find the tombstones of Cape Town's founder, Jan van Riebeeck, and his wife Maria de la Queillerie. The tombstones were moved here from Jakarta where van Riebeeck is buried.

BO-KAAP MUSEUM

Giving some insight into the history and lifestyle of the people of the Bo-Kaap is this small but engaging **museum** (Map pp110-11; ☎ 021-481 3939; www.museums.org.za/bokaap/index .html; 71 Wale St, Bo-Kaap; adult/child R5/2; ☒ 9.30am-4.30pm Mon-Sat). The house itself, built in 1763, is the oldest in the area. It's worth a stroll around the area (during the day) to admire the traditional architecture.

GOLD OF AFRICA MUSEUM

You'll see plenty of bling in this glitzy **museum** (Map pp110-11; ☎ 021-405 1540; www.goldof africa.com; 96 Strand St; adult/child R20/10; ☒ 9.30am-5pm Mon-Sat), in the Martin Melck House (dating from 1783), promoting African gold jewellery. There are some stunning pieces, mostly from West Africa, and it's all well displayed with a lot of historical background. The museum shop is worth a browse for interesting gold souvenirs, including copies of some of the pieces in the museum, and you can sign up for jewellery design (R650) and gold leaf (R450) courses at the on-site workshop.

KOOPMANS DE WET HOUSE

Step back two centuries from 21st-century Cape Town when you enter **Koopmans de Wet House** (Map pp110-11; ☎ 021-481 3935; www .museums.org.za/koopmans; 35 Strand St; adult/child R5/2; ☒ 9.30am-4pm Tue-Thu). This classic example of a Cape Dutch townhouse, furnished with 18th- and early 19th-century antiques, is an atmospheric place. Ancient vines grow in the courtyard and the floorboards squeak just as they probably did during the times of Marie Koopmans de Wet, the socialite owner after whom the house is named.

CHURCHES

There are several impressive churches in the City Bowl that are worth a look. Nip inside the **Groote Kerk** (Map pp110-11; ☎ 021-461 7044; Adderley St; ☒ 10am-2pm Mon-Fri, services 10am & 7pm Sun), mothership of the Dutch Reformed Church (Nederduitse Gereformeerde Kerk, or NG Kerk), to admire the mammoth organ and ornate Burmese teak pulpit. The first church on the site was built in 1704, but only parts of this remain, with most of the current building dating from 1841.

Converted from a barn in 1780, the first **Lutheran Church** (Map pp110-11; ☎ 021-421 5854; 98 Strand St; ⊙ 10am-2pm Mon-Fri) in the Cape has a striking pulpit, perhaps the best created by the master German sculptor Anton Anreith, whose work can also be seen in Groote Kerk and at Groot Constantia (p119).

The Anglican **St George's Cathedral** (Map pp110-11; ☎ 021-24 7360; www.stgeorgescathedral.com; 1 Wale St) is where Archibishop Desmond Tutu once preached. Check the website for details of orchestral concerts held here, usually on the last Sunday of the month.

Gardens & Around

Rising up Table Mountain's slopes are the ritzy suburbs of Gardens, Tamboerskloof, Oranjezicht and Vredehoek. Most of the major sights here are clustered around the Company's Gardens (p109).

SA NATIONAL GALLERY

South Africa's premier **gallery** (Map p114; ☎ 021-467 4660; www.museums.org.za/sang; Government Ave, Gardens; adult/child R10/5, Sat by donation; ⊙ 10am-5pm Tue-Sun) is a must for art lovers. The permanent collection harks back to Dutch times and includes some extraordinary pieces, but it's often contemporary works, such as the *Butcher Boys* sculpture by Jane Alexander, that stand out the most. Also check out the remarkable teak door

in the courtyard, carved with scenes representing the global wanderings of the Jews. There's a pleasant café and a shop with some interesting books and gifts.

SOUTH AFRICAN MUSEUM & PLANETARIUM

Although there has been some reorganisation in recent years and a few new exhibits, South Africa's oldest **museum** (Map p114; ☎ 021-481 3330; www.museums.org.za/sam; 25 Queen Victoria St, Gardens; adult/child R10/5, Sat by donation; ⊙ 10am-5pm) is showing its age. Although not a must-see, it does contain a wide and often intriguing series of exhibitions, many on the country's natural history. The best galleries are the newest, showcasing the art and culture of the area's first peoples, the Khoekhoen and San, and including the famous Linton Panel, an amazing example of San rock art. There's an extraordinary delicacy to the paintings, particularly the ones of graceful eland.

Attached to the museum is the **planetarium** (☎ 021-481 3900; www.museums.org.za/plane tarium; 25 Queen Victoria St, Gardens; adult/child R20/6; ⊙ 10am-5pm). The displays and star shows here unravel the mysteries of the southern hemisphere's night sky. Shows using images caught by the Southern African Large Telescope in the Karoo are held at 2pm, Monday to Friday, 2.30pm Saturday and Sunday, and 8pm Tuesday. Childrens'

REINVENTING THE OLD MUTUAL

Cape Town experienced a building boom in the 1930s, resulting in the many Art Deco buildings that dot the City Bowl today. The most impressive is Mutual Heights (Map pp110–11) on the corner of Parliament and Darling Sts. Commissioned by the Old Mutual financial company, this once was not only the tallest structure in Africa bar the Pyramids, but also the most expensive. It was clad in rose- and gold-veined black marble and decorated with one of the longest continuous stone friezes in the world (designed by Ivan Mitford-Barberton and chiselled by master stonemasons the Lorenzi brothers).

Unfortunately the building's completion in 1939 was eclipsed by the start of WWII. Additionally, its prime position on the foreshore was immediately quashed when the city decided to extend land 2km further into the bay. Old Mutual began moving its business out of the building to the suburbs in the 1950s. If it hadn't been awarded protected heritage status, it's likely the building would have been demolished. Thankfully, the Old Mutual's fortunes changed in 2004 when it was converted into apartments. The units sold out in a matter of weeks, thus kicking off a frenzy among developers to convert similarly long-neglected and empty city centre office blocks.

Much of the building's original detail and decoration has been left intact, including the impressive central banking hall – a space fit for a grand MGM musical – which is in the process of being converted into a retail showcase for the **Cape Craft and Design Institute** (www.capecraftanddesign .org.za). If you want a taste of the high life it's possible to rent out the building's stunning four-bedroom **penthouse** (☎ 794 3140; simonhudson@mweb.co.za; apt for 4 people R5000).

GARDENS, ORANJEZICHT & ZONNEBLOEM

0 _____ 300 m
0 _____ 0.2 miles

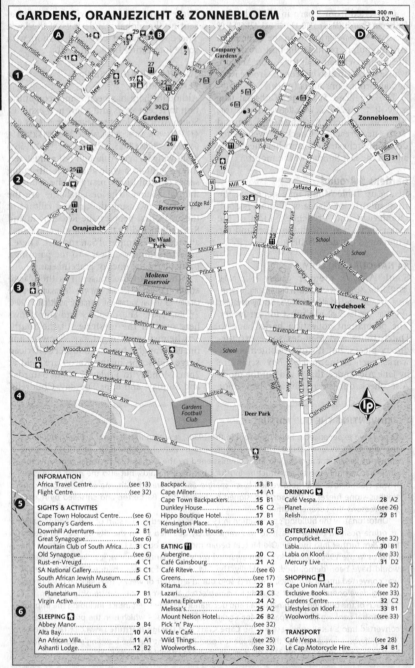

shows are at noon and 1pm on Saturday and Sunday.

SOUTH AFRICAN JEWISH MUSEUM & CAPE TOWN HOLOCAUST CENTRE

The **South African Jewish Museum** (Map p114; ☎ 021-465 1546; www.sajewishmuseum.co.za; 88 Hatfield St, Gardens; adult/child R35/15; ✆ 10am-5pm Sun-Thu, 10am-2pm Fri) is one of the most imaginatively designed and interesting of the city's museums. Entry is through the beautifully restored Old Synagogue (1862), from where a wooden gangplank leads to state-of-the-art galleries with displays on the vibrant history of the nation's Jewish community, which today numbers around 90,000.

In the same complex you'll also find the **Cape Town Holocaust Centre** (☎ 021-462 5553; www.museums.org.za/ctholocaust; admission free; ✆ 10am-5pm Sun-Thu, 10am-1pm Fri). Although small, the centre packs a lot in with a considerable emotional punch. The history of anti-Semitism is set in a South African context with parallels drawn to the local struggle for freedom. In the auditorium beneath the centre take time to watch the 20-minute documentary *A Righteous Man*, about Nelson Mandela's connection with the South African Jewish community.

While here you can also browse the gift shop, eat at the kosher Café Riteve and visit the beautifully decorated **Great Synagogue** (guided tours free; ✆ 10am-4pm Sun-Thu). Dating from 1905, this is one of a handful of buildings in Cape Town built in the Neo-Egyptian style.

RUST-EN-VREUGD

The delightful 18th-century mansion **Rust-en-Vreugd** (Map p114; ☎ 021-464 3280; www.museums .org.za/rustvreugd; 78 Buitenkant St, City Bowl; admission by donation; ✆ 8.30am-4.30pm Mon-Fri) was once the home of the state prosecutor. It now houses part of the William Fehr collection of paintings and furniture (the major part is in the Castle of Good Hope, p108).

Paintings by John Thomas Baines show early scenes from colonial Cape Town, while the sketches of Cape Dutch architecture by Alys Fane Trotter are some of the best you'll see. There's also a pleasant garden.

Green Point & Waterfront

Cape Town's prime Atlantic Coast suburbs start at the Waterfront, from where you'll depart for Robben Island (p107). Near here you'll also find Green Point, which has lately seen some development such as the Portside shopping and dining complex on Main Rd.

VICTORIA & ALBERT WATERFRONT

Commonly referred to as just the **Waterfront** (www.waterfront.co.za), this tourist-orientated precinct offers masses of shops, restaurants, bars, cinemas and other attractions, including cruises of the harbour (p123). Its success is partly down to the fact that it remains a working harbour. The Alfred and Victoria Basins date from 1860 and are named after Queen Victoria and her son Alfred. Although these wharves are too small for modern container vessels and tankers, the Victoria Basin is still used by tugs, harbour vessels of various kinds, and fishing boats. In the Alfred Basin you'll see ships under repair, and there are always seals splashing around or lazing on the giant tyres that line the docks.

Recent developments at the Waterfront include the millionaire's playground of the **V & A Marina** with some 600 apartments and 200 boat moorings, and the construction of **Nobel Square** (Map pp116-17; Dock Rd). Claudette Schreuders designed the larger than life statues of South Africa's four Nobel Prize winners: Nkosi Albert Luthuli, Archbishop Desmond Tutu, and former presidents FW De Klerk and Nelson Mandela. It's fast become a visitors' favourite, not least for the chance to be photographed standing shoulder to shoulder with Madiba.

TWO OCEANS AQUARIUM

Always a hit with the kids, this excellent **aquarium** (Map pp116-17; ☎ 021-418 3823; www.aqua rium.co.za; Dock Rd, Waterfront; adult/child R65/30; ✆ 9.30am-6pm) features denizens of the deep from both the cold and the warm oceans that border the Cape Peninsula, including ragged tooth sharks. There are seals, penguins, turtles, an astounding kelp forest open to the sky, and pools in which you can touch sea creatures. If that isn't good enough, if you're a qualified diver you can actually get into one of the tanks for an up-close meeting with the sharks, a 150kg short-tailed stingray, other predatory fish and a turtle. The cost is R400 including hire of diving gear.

GREEN POINT, WATERKANT & WATERFRONT

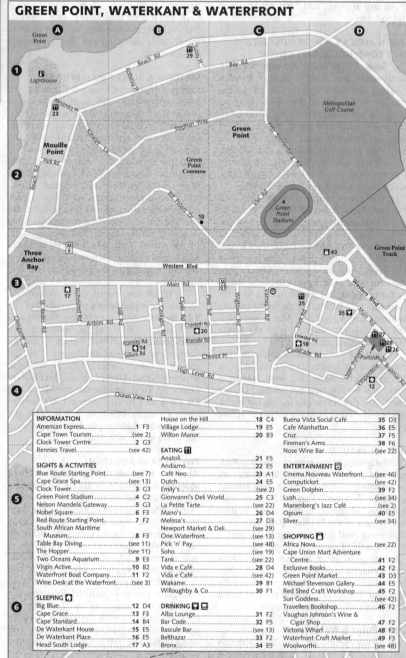

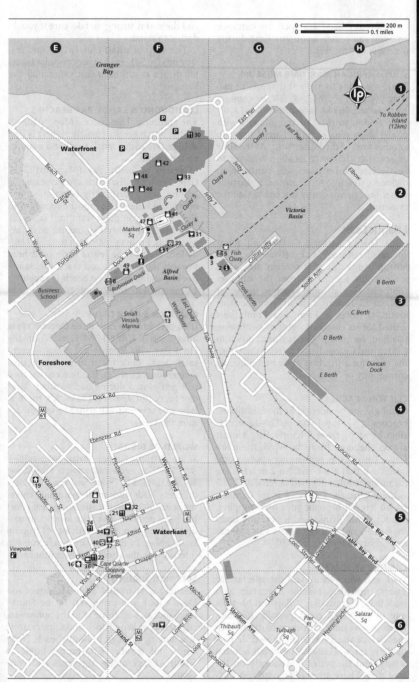

Have your hand stamped on entrance and you can return again any time during the same day for free.

SOUTH AFRICAN MARITIME MUSEUM

There are plans to move this specialist **museum** (Map pp116-17; ☎ 021-405 2880; www.museums .org.za/maritime; Dock Rd, Waterfront; adult/child R10/5; ☯ 10am-5pm), stocked to the gunnels with model ships plus some full-sized ones, to another area of the Waterfront. At the time of research the exact location was yet to be decided. Admission will continue to include entry to SAS *Somerset*, a wartime vessel now permanently docked beside the museum.

Atlantic Coast

Cape Town's Atlantic Coast is all about spectacular scenery and soft-sand beaches. Strong winds can be a downer and while it's possible to shelter from the summer southeasterlies at some beaches, the water at them all, flowing straight from the Antarctic, is freezing. From Sea Point (best visited for its excellent outdoor swimming pavilion; see p138), you can head down to Clifton and Camps Bay. The road then hugs the coast for a thrilling drive to the fishing community of Hout Bay.

CLIFTON BEACHES

Giant granite boulders split the four linked beaches at Clifton (Map pp120-1), accessible by steps from Victoria Rd. Almost always sheltered from the wind, these are Cape Town's top sunbathing spots. Local lore has it that No 1 and No 2 beaches are for models and confirmed narcissists, No 3 is the gay beach, and No 4 is for families. If you haven't brought your own supplies, vendors hawk drinks and ice creams along the beach, and you can rent a sun lounger and umbrella for around R50.

CAMPS BAY BEACH

With soft white sand, and the spectacular Twelve Apostles of Table Mountain as a backdrop, Camps Bay (Map pp120-1) is one of the city's most popular beaches. Because it is only a 15-minute drive from the city centre it can get crowded, particularly on weekends. The beach is often windy, and the water is decidedly on the cool side. There are no lifeguards on duty

and the surf is strong, so take care if you do decide to swim.

The strip of smart bars (p152) and restaurants (p150) here are very popular places for drinks at sunset or just general all-day lounging.

LLANDUDNO & SANDY BAY BEACHES

The surfing at Llandudno (Map pp102-3) on the beach breaks (mostly rights) is best at high tide with a small swell and a southeasterly wind.

Nearby is Sandy Bay (Map pp102-3), Cape Town's nudist beach and gay stamping ground. It's a particularly beautiful stretch of sand and there's no pressure to take your clothes off if you don't want to. Like many such beaches, Sandy Bay has no direct access roads. From the M6, turn towards Llandudno, keep to the left at forks, and head towards the sea until you reach the Sunset Rocks parking area. The beach is roughly a 15-minute walk to the south.

CHAPMAN'S PEAK DRIVE

It's a breathtaking ride along **Chapman's Peak Drive** (Map pp102-3; ☎ 021-790 9163; toll R22), linking Hout Bay with Noordhoek. Despite recent safety work undertaken to protect against dangerous rock slides, the 5km coastal road still gets closed during bad weather. Most day tours to Cape Point take this route at least one way and will pause to let you admire the views.

WORLD OF BIRDS

South Africa's largest **aviary** (Map pp102-3; ☎ 021-790 2730; www.worldofbirds.org.za; Valley Rd, Hout Bay; adult/child R50/32; ☯ 9am-5pm) has over 3000 different birds and small mammals covering some 400 different species. A real effort has been made to make the aviaries as natural looking as possible with lots of tropical landscaping. In the monkey jungle you can interact with the cheeky squirrel monkeys.

Southern Suburbs

Heading west around Table Mountain and Devil's Peak will bring you to the Southern Suburbs, beginning with the bohemian, edgy areas of Woodstock and Observatory, and moving through to Rondebosch, Newlands and wealthy Constantia, home to South Africa's oldest vineyards and wine estates.

KIRSTENBOSCH BOTANICAL GARDENS

Location and unique flora combine to make Cape Town's **botanical gardens** (Map pp102-3; ☎ 021-799 8783 Mon-Fri, 021-761 4916 Sat & Sun; www .sanbi.org; Rhodes Dr, Newlands; adult/child R25/5; ☯ 8am-7pm Sep-Mar, 8am-6pm Apr-Aug) among the most beautiful in the world. The 36-hectare landscaped section seems to merge almost imperceptibly with the 492 hectares of *fynbos* (fine bush) vegetation cloaking the mountain slopes.

The main entrance at the Newlands end of the gardens is where you'll find plenty of parking, the information centre, an excellent souvenir shop and the conservatory (open 9am to 5pm). Further along Rhodes Dr is the Ryecroft Gate entrance, the first you'll come to if you approach the gardens from Constantia. Call to find out about free guided walks, or hire the My Guide electronic gizmo (R35) to receive recorded information about the various plants you'll pass on the three signposted circular walks.

Apart from the almond hedge, some magnificent oaks, and the Moreton Bay fig and camphor trees planted by Cecil John Rhodes, the gardens are devoted almost exclusively to indigenous plants. About 9000 of Southern Africa's 22,000 plant species are grown here. You'll find a fragrance garden that has been elevated so you can more easily sample the scents of the plants, a Braille Trail, a kopje (hill) that has been planted with pelargoniums, a sculpture garden and a section for plants used for *muti* (traditional medicine) by *sangomas* (traditional healers).

There is always something flowering but the gardens are at their best between mid-August and mid-October. The Sunday afternoon concerts (p143) are a Cape Town institution.

You can hire a Rikki (p159) to get you here or hop on the City Sightseeing Cape Town bus (p140). If you're driving from the city centre, the turn-off to the gardens is on the right at the intersection of Union Ave (the M3) and Rhodes Dr (the M63).

GROOT CONSTANTIA

A superb example of Cape Dutch architecture, **Groot Constantia** (Map pp102-3; ☎ 021-794 5128; www.grootconstantia.co.za; Groot Constantia Rd, High Constantia; tastings incl glass R25; ☯ 9am-6pm Dec-Apr, 9am-5pm May-Nov) is set in beautiful grounds. Not surprisingly, it can become busy with tour groups, but the estate is big enough for you to escape the crowds, if need be.

In the 18th century, Constantia wines were exported around the world and were highly acclaimed; today you should try its Sauvignon Blanc, riesling and pinotage. The beautifully restored homestead is now a **museum** (☎ 021-795 5140; www.museums .org.za/grootcon; adult/child R8/2; ☯ 10am-5pm) and appropriately furnished; take a look at the tiny slave quarters beneath the main building. The Cloete Cellar, the estate's original wine cellar, now houses old carriages and a display of storage vessels. Book for tours of the modern cellar, which run every hour in summer. It's a lovely spot to bring a picnic, although there are also a couple of restaurants on the estate (see p151).

OTHER WINERIES

Of Constantia's other wineries, one of the best ones to visit is **Buitenverwachting** (Map pp102-3; ☎ 021-794 5190; www.buitenverwachting .co.za; Klein Constantia Rd; tastings free; ☯ 9am-5pm Mon-Fri, 9am-1pm Sat). Buitenverwachting means 'beyond expectations' – certainly the feeling one gets on visiting this lovely estate, where the employees are known to have good living and working conditions. For R90 you can enjoy a picnic lunch (bookings ☎ 083-257 6083) in front of the 1786 manor house.

Another outstanding winery is **Klein Constantia** (Map pp102-3; ☎ 021-794 5188; www .kleinconstantia.com; Klein Constantia Rd; tastings free; ☯ 9am-5pm Mon-Fri, 9am-1pm Sat). Part of the original Constantia estate, it's famous for its Vin de Constance, a deliciously sweet muscat wine, and a favourite tipple of both Napoleon and Jane Austen. It has an excellent tasting room and informative displays. At the estate's entrance, pause to look at the *karamat* (saint's tomb) of Sheik Abdurachman Matebe Shah; he was buried in 1661.

Another winery in the area is **Constantia Uitsig** (☎ 021-794 1810; www.uitsig.co.za; Spaanschemat River Rd; tastings free; ☯ 9am-4.30pm Mon-Fri, 10am-3.30pm Sat & Sun) which is best known for its hotel (p147) and restaurants (p151).

IRMA STERN MUSEUM

The most enjoyable **museum** (Map pp120-1; ☎ 021-685 5686; www.irmastern.co.za; Cecil Rd, Rosebank;

CAPE TOWN

CAPE TOWN, ATLANTIC COAST & SOUTHERN SUBURBS

A · **B** · **C** · **D**

INFORMATION
Atlantic Tourist Information
  Centre.....................................1 D1
Flight Centre................................2 C5
Groot Schuur Hospital..............3 H4
Rennies Travel............................4 D1
STA Travel...................................5 H5

SIGHTS & ACTIVITIES
Angsana Spa............................(see 29)
City Rock.....................................6 H3
Graaff's Pool...............................7 C2
Groote Schuur.............................8 H5
Irma Stern Museum.....................9 H5
Milton's Pool.............................10 C2
Newlands Cricket Ground.......11 H6
Newlands Rugby Stadium........12 H6
Pro Divers.................................13 D1
Rhodes Memorial......................14 H5
Rugby Museum.........................15 H6
Sanctuary Spa...........................16 B5
Sea Point Pavilion....................17 C2
Sports Science Institute of
  South Africa..........................(see 15)

SLEEPING
Aardvark Backpackers...............18 D2
Bay Hotel...................................19 C4
Camps Bay Retreat...................20 C4
Cape Town Backpackers
  Sea Point................................21 D1
Deco Lodge...............................22 G3
Green Elephant.........................23 H3
Huijs Haerlem...........................24 D2
Lion's Head Lodge................(see 18)
O on Kloof................................25 C2
Primi Royal...............................26 C5
Primi Seacastle.........................27 C4
Twenty Nine.............................28 C4
Vineyard Hotel & Spa...............29 H6
Winchester Mansions Hotel......30 C1

EATING
Ari's Souvlaki.............................31 C2
Café Ganesh..............................32 F6
Cedar...33 D2
Gardener's Cottage...................34 H6
La Perla.....................................35 C2
Melissa's................................(see 42)
New York Bagels.......................36 C2
Paranga.....................................37 C4
Sandbar.....................................38 C4
Saul's...39 C2
Sea Point Gardens....................40 C2
Vida e Café............................(see 54)

DRINKING
A Touch of Madness..................41 F6
Asylumn.................................(see 40)
Barristers...................................42 H6
Café Caprice..............................43 C4
Café Carte Blanche...................44 F6
Cool Runnings..........................45 F6
Ignite..46 C5
La Med......................................47 B4
La Vie..48 C2

ENTERTAINMENT
Adelphi Centre..........................49 D1
Baxter Theatre..........................50 H5
Cavendish Nouveau...............(see 54)
Computicket...........................(see 49)
Independent Armchair Theatre...51 F6
Obz Café...................................52 F6
Sobhar......................................53 H6

SHOPPING
Cavendish Square.....................54 H6
Exclusive Books......................(see 54)
Montebello.............................(see 34)
Woolworths...............................55 C2
Woolworths............................(see 54)
Young Designers Emporium...(see 54)

TRANSPORT
Air Mauritius..........................(see 58)
KLM..56 H6
Same Garage............................57 D2
Singapore Airlines.....................58 H6

Mouille
Point

Green
Point

ATLANTIC
OCEAN

Rocklands
Beach

Western Blvd

Three
Anchor
Bay High Level Rd

Sea
Point

Schotsche
Kloof

Queens
Beach

Sea Point

Fresnaye

Saunders
Rocks

Tamboerskloof

Bantry
Bay

Clifton

Lion's
Head
(669m)

Kloof Nek Rd

Gardens

Kloof Rd

Mocke
Reservoir

Lower
Cableway
Station

Whale
Rocks

Camps Bay

Upper
Cableway
Station

Table
Mountain
(1073m)

Bakoven

Table Mountain
National Park

Kasteelpoort

Camps Bay Drive

Back
Table

Woodhead
Reservoir

Twelve Apostles

CAPE TOWN

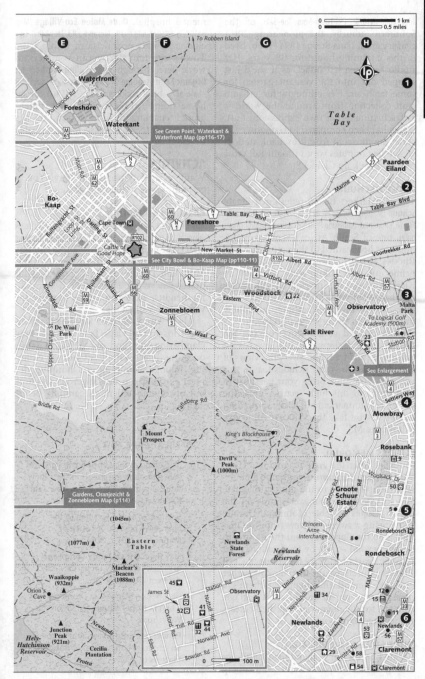

0   1 km
0   0.5 miles

To Robben Island

Table Bay

See Green Point, Waterkant & Waterfront Map (pp116–17)

Waterfront
Foreshore
Waterkant
Beach Rd
Portswood Rd

Paarden Eiland
Marine Dr
Table Bay Blvd

Bo-Kaap
Main Rd
Buitengracht St
Loop St
Long St
Darling St

Cape Town
Castle of Good Hope

Foreshore
Table Bay Blvd
New Market St
Church St
Voortrekker Rd

See City Bowl & Bo-Kaap Map (pp110–11)

Albert Rd
Albert Rd

Woodstock
Victoria Rd
Eastern Blvd
Durham Ave

Observatory
Malta Park
To Logical Golf Academy (500m)

Zonnebloem
De Waal Cr

Salt River

Annandale Rd
Government Ave
Upper Orange St
Buitenkant St
Roeland St
De Waal Park

Bridle Rd

Gardens, Oranjezicht & Zonnebloem Map (p114)

Tafelberg Rd

Mount Prospect

King's Blockhouse

Devil's Peak (1000m)

See Enlargement

Settlers Way

Mowbray

Rosebank
Woolsack Dr

Groote Schuur Estate
Rhodes Dr

Princess Anne Interchange

Rondebosch

(1045m)

(1077m)   Eastern Table

Newlands State Forest

Newlands Reservoir

Union Ave
Newlands Ave

Waaikoppie (932m)
Orion's Cave

Maclear's Beacon (1088m)

Hely-Hutchinson Reservoir

Junction Peak (921m)

Cecilia Plantation

Protea

45
James St
51
52
Oxford Rd
Trill Rd
32
41
44
Nuttall Rd
Station Rd
Norwich Ave
Bowden Rd
Eden Rd

Observatory

0   100 m

Newlands
Liesbeek Rd
Protea Rd

Claremont

34

42
29
53
58
54
56
11
12
15
Main Rd
Claremont

adult/child R10/5; ☉ 10am-5pm Tue-Sat) of the Southern Suburbs, the pioneering 20th-century artist Irma Stern (1894–1966) lived in this charming house for 38 years. Her studio has been left intact, as if she'd just stepped out into the verdant garden for some fresh air. Her ethnographic art and craft collection from around the world is as fascinating as her own expressionist art, which has been compared to Gauguin's. To reach the museum from Rosebank station, walk a few minutes west to Main Rd, cross over and walk up Chapel St.

GROOTE SCHUUR
The Sir Herbert Baker–redesigned **Groote Schuur** (Map pp120-1; ☎ 021-686 9100; Groote Schuur Estate, Klipper Rd; admission R60; ☉ tours by appointment only), one of South Africa's seminal buildings, was bequeathed to the nation by Cecil Rhodes. It was the home of a succession of prime ministers culminating with FW de Klerk. The restored interior, all teak panels and heavy colonial furniture, antiques and tapestries of the finest calibre, is suitably imposing. But its most beautiful feature is the colonnaded veranda overlooking the formal gardens sloping uphill towards an avenue of pine trees and sweeping views of Devil's Peak. The tour includes tea on this veranda. You must bring your passport to gain entry to this high security area; the entrance is unmarked but easily spotted on the left as you take the Princess Anne Ave exit off the M3.

RHODES MEMORIAL
Modelled after the arch at London's Hyde Park Corner, the impressive granite memorial (Map pp120-1) to the mining magnate and former prime minister stands on the eastern slopes of Table Mountain. Despite there being a sweeping view from the memorial to the Cape Flats and the mountain ranges beyond – and, by implication, right into the heart of Africa – the statue of Cecil Rhodes himself has the man looking rather grumpy. Behind the memorial there's a pleasant tearoom in an old stone cottage. The exit for the memorial is at the Princess Anne Interchange on the M3.

OUDE MOLEN ECO VILLAGE
Located in the once-abandoned buildings and grounds of part of the Valkenberg mental hospital, **Oude Molen Eco Village** (Map pp102-3; ☎ 021-448 6419; Alexandra Rd, Mowbray) includes the only organic farm within Cape Town's city limits. You can volunteer to work here through the **Willing Workers on Organic Farms scheme** (www.wwoof.org) as well as stay at a backpackers lodge (p146), or go horse riding (p137). A large government grant is enabling the folks who run the site to turn it into a showcase for sustainable development.

ACTIVITIES
Want an activity-packed holiday? You've certainly come to the right place.

Abseiling & Kloofing
Abseil Africa (Map pp110-11; ☎ 021-424 4760; www .abseilafrica.co.za; 1 Vredenburg Ln, City Bowl; abseiling R295) is the one to see if you want to shimmy 112m down a rope off the top of Table Mountain. Don't even think of tackling this unless you've got a head (and a stomach) for heights. Take your time, because the views are breathtaking.

Abseil Africa also offer kloofing (canyoning) trips around Cape Town. The sport of clambering into and out of kloofs (cliffs or gorges) also entails abseiling, climbing, hiking, swimming and jumping. It's great fun, but can be dangerous so check out operators' credentials carefully before signing up.

OFFBEAT CAPE TOWN

- Clap along as the Cape Minstrel groups dance through the streets in their shiny satin suits in the **Cape Town New Year Karnaval** (p142).

- Spend an evening listening to the open-mike poets at **A Touch of Madness** (p153) in Observatory.

- Stay the night at **Daddy Long Legs** (p143), where every room is a wildly different art installation.

- Give Nelson Mandela or Desmond Tutu a hug at **Nobel Square** (p115) on the Waterfront.

- Ponder our close connection to apes on a tour with the guides of **Baboon Matters** (p165).

Another reliable operator is Day Trippers (see p141).

Amusement Parks

The big African-themed amusement park, **Ratanga Junction** (Map pp102-3; ☎ 021-550 8504; www.ratanga.co.za; Century City, Milnerton; adult/child R95/45; ⏱ 10am-5pm Fri-Sun, daily school holidays) is next to Canal Walk shopping centre, around 5km north of the city centre along the N1. It's only open from the end of November to the beginning of May. The entry fee covers all rides, including various roller coasters and stomach churners.

Cruises

DUIKER ISLAND CRUISES

From Hout Bay's harbour you can catch regular daily cruises to Duiker Island, also known as Seal Island because of its colony of Cape fur seals. Three companies run these cruises daily, usually with guaranteed sailings in the mornings. The cheapest, with a none-too-spectacular glass-bottom boat, is **Circe Launches** (☎ 021-790 1040; www .circelaunches; adult/child R35/10); the others are **Drumbeat Charters** (☎ 021-791 4441; adult/child R50/20) and **Nauticat Charters** (☎ 021-790 7278; www.nauticatcharters.co.za; adult/child R50/20). All are based at the harbour (Map pp102–3).

HARBOUR CRUISES

If only to take in the panoramic view of Table Mountain from the water, a cruise into Table Bay should not be missed. **Waterfront Boat Company** (Map pp116-17; ☎ 021-418 5806; www .waterfrontboats.co.za; Shop 7, Quay 5, Waterfront) offers a variety of cruises, including the highly recommended 1½-hour sunset cruises (R180) on its handsome wood- and brass-fitted schooners *Spirit of Victoria* and *Esperance*. A jet-boat ride is R250 per hour.

See www.waterfront.co.za/play/leisure for details of other cruise operators at the Waterfront.

Cycling

Thrill-miesters will enjoy the variety of cycling trips and adventures offered by **Downhill Adventures** (Map p114; ☎ 021-422 0388; www .downhilladventures.com; cnr Orange & Kloof Sts, Gardens). Try a mountain-bike ride down from the lower cable car station on Table Mountain (R350), or ride through the Constantia winelands and the Cape of Good Hope

(R500). You can also rent bikes (R100 per day).

Also see the listing for Day Trippers (p141); some of its tours include cycling, including trips to Cape Point.

Diving

Cape Town offers a number of excellent shore and boat dives, although it's the shark-cage diving in Gansbaai, some 150km southeast of city, that is the big draw; see p189 for details of reliable operators. Alternatively, if you want to get up close and personal with a shark, the Two Oceans Aquarium (p115) offers a decent alternative.

A couple of good local dive operators: **Pro Divers** (Map pp120-1; ☎ 021-433 0472; www.prodiverssa.co.za; 88B Main Rd, Sea Point) **Table Bay Diving** (Map pp116-17; ☎ 021-419 8822; www.tablebaydiving.com; Shop 7, Quay 5, Waterfront)

Flying & Paragliding

The are several legal ways to get high in Cape Town and all are guaranteed to give you a fantastic buzz. Paragliding is amazing but if you want to do this, it's essential to make an inquiry on your first day in Cape Town. The weather conditions have to be just right and arranging flights at short notice is difficult, particularly if you want to fly off Lion's Head.

Ian Willis at **Air Team** (☎ 082-727 6584; www .tandemparagliding.co.za; flights from R750) is part of a collective of paragliding instructors and enthusiasts offering tandem flights in and around Cape Town. As well as launches off Lion's Head, Air Team also offers options to fly from Silvermine over False Bay and from the mountains overlooking Hermanus.

With the **Hopper** (Map pp116-17; ☎ 021-419 8951; www.thehopper.co.za; Shop 6, Quay 5, Waterfront), R400 gets you a 15-minute helicopter flight over either Sandy Bay or out to the Twelve Apostles at 4pm daily. A 30-minute flight to see both oceans is R900.

For more information on aerial pursuits, see p600.

Golf

Golf is a big deal on the Cape, with some 55 courses dotted around the city. Some are superb and many welcome visitors (but you should book). Contact the **Western Province Golf Union** (☎ 021-686 1668; www.wpgu.co.za) for more details of fees etc.

Logical Golf Academy (☎ 021-448 6358; www.logical golf.co.za; the River Club, Observatory Rd, Observatory) Driving range and golf school where you can practise your swing to perfection. A 30-minute lesson is R150.

Milnerton Golf Club (Map pp102-3; ☎ 021-434 7808; www.milnertongolfclub.co.za; Tanglewood Cres, Milnerton) Around 12km north of the City Bowl along Rte 27, Milnerton has a magnificent position overlooking Table Bay with great views of Table Mountain. Wind can be a problem, though.

Mowbray Golf Club (☎ 021-685 3018; www.mowbray golfclub.co.za; Raapenberg Rd, Mowbray) Considered by some as the best in-town course for its rural setting and birdlife.

Gyms

Virgin Active (www.virginactive.co.za; admission per day/ month R80/435; Green Point Map pp116-17; ☎ 434 0750; Bill Peters Drive; Foreshore Map pp110-11; ☎ 421 5857; Lower Long St; Gardens Map pp114; ☎ 462 6239, Wembley Sq, Glynn St), South Africa's largest chain of gyms, has several well-equipped branches around Cape Town.

Health & Day Spas

Head to Cape Town's top-end hotels to find the most luxurious spas. All offer the usual range of facial and body treatments including various forms of massage and day-long packages. Women should also check out the massage at Long St Baths (see p138).

Altira Spa (Map pp110–11; ☎ 021-412 8200; www .altiraspa.com; Arabella Sheraton Grand Hotel, Convention Sq, Lower Long St, Foreshore; ☺ 8am-8pm) Swim laps looking out at the Waterfront, relax in the Jacuzzi while gazing up at Table Mountain. There's also a full gym, a sauna, a steam room and foot baths.

Angsana Spa (Map pp120–1; ☎ 021-674 5005; www .angsanaspa.com; Vineyard Hotel, Colinton Rd, Newlands; ☺ 10am-8pm) Cape Town's most stylish spa offers Balinese-style techniques in a lush, luxurious environment.

Cape Grace Spa (Map pp116–17; ☎ 021-410 7140; www.capegrace.com/spa; Cape Grace, West Quay, Waterfront; ☺ 8am-8pm) There's both an African and a spice route theme going on here with some massages incorporating traditional San methods. The treatment rooms overlook Table Mountain.

Sanctuary Spa (Map pp120–1; ☎ 021-437 9000; www.12apostleshotel.com/spa.htm; Twelve Apostles Hotel, Victoria Rd, Camps Bay; ☺ 8am-8pm) Occupying a mock cave that could be the set from a James Bond movie, a feeling that is compounded by the state-of-the-art contraptions in the treatment rooms. It has Cape Town's only Rasul chamber (a Middle Eastern sauna) as well as a flotation pool.

Hiking & Rock Climbing

The mountainous spine of the Cape Peninsula is a hiker's and rock climber's paradise, but it's not without its dangers, chief of which is the capricious weather conditions (see the boxed text, p137). Numerous books and maps give details, including Mike Lundy's *Best Walks in the Cape Peninsula*, but to get the best out of the mountains hire a local guide. Also see p107 for details of the Table Mountain National Park's guided hikes.

City Rock (Map pp120–1; ☎ 021-447 1326; www.city rock.co.za; cnr Collingwood & Anson Sts, Observatory; ☺ 11am-9pm Mon-Thu, 10am-6pm Fri-Sun) Popular indoor climbing gym offering climbing courses. It also rents and sells climbing gear. A day pass for the climbing wall is R55.

Kabbo African Adventures (☎ 021-701 0867, 072-024 6537; www.kabboadventures.com) This operation has put together its own version of the Hoerikwaggo Trail (see p107), making use of the Mountain Club's hut on the Back Table as well as backpacker and camping sites close to the City Bowl to Cape Point route. An overnight trip to the mountain costs R725, while a summit hike or sunrise/sunset walk is R320.

Mountain Club of South Africa (Map p114; ☎ 021-465 3412; www.mcsa.org.za; 97 Hatfield St, Gardens) Serious climbers can contact the club, which can recommend guides. It has a climbing wall (R5) which is open 10am to 2pm Monday to Friday, 6pm to 9pm Tuesday and Wednesday.

Venture Forth (☎ 021-556 4150; www.ventureforth.co .za) Enthusiastic guides will tailor a hike or climb to your requirements and get you off the beaten track. The fee of R400 includes all refreshments and city centre transfers.

CLIMBING TABLE MOUNTAIN

Over 300 routes up and down the mountain have been identified, perhaps indicating how easy it is to get lost. Bear in mind that the mountain is over 1000m high and conditions can become treacherous quickly. Thick mists can make the paths invisible, and you'll just have to wait until they lift. Unprepared and foolhardy hikers die here ever year; read our dos and don'ts (p137) before setting off.

None of the routes is easy but the **Platteklip Gorge** walk on the City Bowl side is at least straightforward. Unless you're fit, try walking down before you attempt the walk up. It takes about 2½ hours from the upper cableway station to the lower, taking it fairly easy. Be warned that the route is exposed to the sun and, for much of the way, a vertical slog.

(Continued on page 137)

BRENT STIRTON/GETTY IMAGES

Bar on Long Street (p109), Cape Town

Young busker, Cape Town (p100)

RICHARD I'ANSON

CAROL POLICH

Table Mountain (p107), Cape Town

Long Street (p109), Cape Town, at night

BRENT STIRTON/GETTY IMAGES

BRENT STIRTON/GETTY IMAGES

Antique and collectables shop, Kalk Bay (p160), Cape Town

BRENT STIRTON/GETTY IMAGES

Fisherman, Kalk Bay (p160), Cape Town

Dutch café, Waterkant (p149), Cape Town

ARIADNE VAN ZANDBERGEN

Gospel singers, Cape Town (p100)

RICHARD I'ANSON

BRENT STIRTON/GETTY IMAGES

Cape Point, Cape of Good Hope Nature Reserve (p164), Cape Town

Karoo National Park (p230), Western Cape

ADRIAN BAILEY

PAUL KENNEDY

Surfing 'the Kom' – Kommetjie (p138), Cape Town

Boy in field of wildflowers, Ceres (p198), Western Cape

NIC BOTHMA

ARIADNE VAN ZANDBERGEN

Robberg Nature & Marine Reserve (p227),
Western Cape

Dutch Reformed Church, Western Cape
(p167)

RICHARD I'ANSON

RICHARD I'ANSON

African penguins at Boulders Beach (p163),
Cape Town

Cape gannets at Lambert's Bay (p234), Western Cape
ANDREW PARKINSON

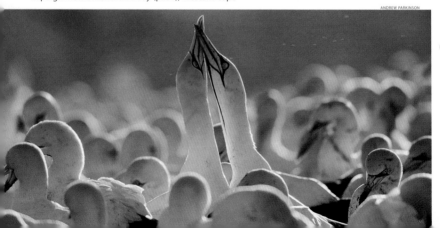

RICHARD I'ANSON

Edward Protea Hotel (p253), Port Elizabeth,
Eastern Cape

Sand boarding at Jeffrey's Bay (p245),
Eastern Cape

PAUL KENNEDY

TIM ROCK

Tsitsikamma National Park (p242), Eastern Cape

Xhosa architecture (p56), Eastern Cape

DENNIS JONES

RICHARD I'ANSON

Windsurfer at Port Elizabeth (p252), Eastern Cape

Addo Elephant National Park (p255), Eastern Cape

CAROL POLICH

ERIC L WHEATER

Family from the township of Cradock (p264), Eastern Cape

Surfer, Jeffrey's Bay (p245), Eastern Cape

PAUL KENNEDY

Zulu man preparing for a performance, Zululand (p328), KwaZulu-Natal

Zulu woman carrying water, Dumazulu Cultural Village (p335), KwaZulu-Natal

Rock art, Monk's Cowl (p352), KwaZulu-Natal

Zulu village chief, Dumazulu Cultural Village (p335), KwaZulu-Natal

132

Lion at sunset, Hluhluwe-Imfolozi Park (p335), KwaZulu-Natal

Loggerhead turtle hatchlings (p342) being released after marking, KwaZulu-Natal

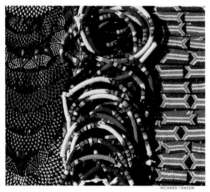

Beadwork for sale on Durban's promenade (p308), KwaZulu-Natal

Scenic route to Southern Berg (p353), KwaZulu-Natal

Guest at a traditional wedding, Regina Mundi
Church (p424), Soweto

Souvenir mask, Bruma Lake Market World
(p415), Johannesburg

Woman making wooden souvenirs (p415),
Johannesburg

Man outside decorated Ndebele house (p56), Pretoria

BRENT STIRTON/GETTY IMAGES

Security at a Melville nightspot (p413),
Johannesburg

Nightclub (p414), Johannesburg

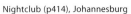

BRENT STIRTON/GETTY IMAGES

BRENT STIRTON/GETTY IMAGES

Bar at the Market Theatre (p415), Johannesburg

Newtown cultural district (p401), Johannesburg

BRENT STIRTON/GETTY IMAGES

Young children, Soweto (p420)

Devotee of the Shembe religion (p332)

Soweto township (p420)

Woman with a colourful load, Soweto

Firecracker wildflowers in the Blyde River Canyon Nature Reserve (p453), Mpumalanga

RICHARD I'ANSON

Bourke's Luck Potholes (p453), Blyde River Canyon, Mpumalanga

ARIADNE VAN ZANDBE

CAROL POLICH

Ndebele woman, Mpumalanga (p492)

Lone Creek Falls (p449), Mpumalanga

CAROL

(Continued from page 124)

Another option, far trickier and recommended for experienced climbers only, is the **Indian Windows** route that starts from directly behind the lower cableway station and heads straight up. The hikers you see from the cable car, perched like mountain goats on apparently sheer cliffs, are taking this route.

The **Pipe Track** is a less steep route that runs along the west side of the mountain towards the Twelve Apostles. There are also two popular routes up the mountain from Kirstenbosch Botanical Gardens along either the **Skeleton Gorge** (which involves negotiating some sections with chains) or **Nursery Ravine**. These can be covered in three hours by someone of moderate fitness. The trails are well marked, and steep in places, but the way to the gardens from the cableway and vice versa is not signposted.

LION'S HEAD
The 2.2km hike from Kloof Nek to the peak of Lion's Head (Map pp120–1) is one of the best you can do in Cape Town and is highly recommended on a full-moon night when many people gather at the summit to watch the sun go down. The moonlight aids the walk back down, although you should always bring a torch (flashlight) and go with company. The track's start is clearly marked at the top of Kloof Nek Rd; it involves a little climbing but there are chains on the rocks.

CAPE OF GOOD HOPE
You'll need to book to walk the two-day/one-night Cape of Good Hope Trail, which traces a spectacular 33.8km circular route through the reserve (p164). The cost is R88 (not including the Cape Point entry fee) with accommodation at the basic Protea and Restio huts at the southern end of the reserve. Contact the reserve's **Buffelfontein Visitors Centre** (☎ 021-780 9204) for further details.

Horse Riding
Oude Molen Stables (Map pp102–3; ☎ 072-199 7395; Violet Bldg, Oude Molen Eco Village, Alexandria Rd, Mowbray; per hr R100) Contact Kendre about horse riding at this eco-village where you'll also find a number of other interesting operations (see p122).

Sleepy Hollow Horse Riding (Map pp102–3; ☎ 021-789 2341, 083-261 0104; Noordhoek) Reliable operation which can arrange horse riding along wide and sandy Noordhoek beach as well as in the mountainous hinterland.

Kayaking
Real Cape Adventures (☎ 021-790 5611, 082-556 2520; www.seakayak.co.za) Runs a variety of kayaking trips around the Cape and further afield for paddlers of all levels. The half-day Hout Bay paddle, good for novice kayakers, kicks off at R200.

Sea Kayak Simon's Town (Map p163; ☎ 082 501 8930; www.kayakcapetown.co.za; Wharf Rd, Simon's Town) Paddle out to the penguins at Boulders (R200) with this Simon's Town-based operation. They also offer a variety of other tours including to Cape Point (R650), whale watching from kayaks off Glencairne and overnight kayaking safaris.

Skydiving
Cape Town is one of the cheapest places for you to learn to skydive or do a tandem dive. The view over Table Bay and the peninsula alone makes it worthwhile.

Skydive Cape Town (☎ 082-800 6290; www.sky divecapetown.za.net; skydives per person R1200) is an experienced, local outfit based approximately 20km north of the city centre in Melkboshstrand.

For more information, see p123.

Surfing & Sandboarding

The Cape Peninsula has plenty of fantastic surfing possibilities, from gentle shore breaks ideal for beginners to 3m-plus monsters for experts only. In general, the best surf is along the Atlantic side, with most breaks working best in southeasterly conditions. Water temperatures as low as 8°C mean a steamer wet suit and booties are required.

Kommetjie (Map pp102–3), pronounced Kommi-kee, is the Cape's surf mecca, offering an assortment of reefs that hold a very big swell. Outer Kommetjie is a left point cut from the lighthouse. Inner Kommetjie is a more protected smaller left with lots of kelp (only at high tide). They both work best with a southeasterly or southwesterly wind.

On False Bay (Map p161), head to **Muizenberg** and **Kalk Bay**. The waves here tend to be less demanding in terms of size and temperature (up to 20°C), and work best in northwesterlies. For the daily surf report call ☎ 082-234 6353 or check www.wavescape.co.za.

And if you don't want to get wet there's always sandboarding, which is just like snowboarding except on sand dunes.

Downhill Adventures (Map p114; ☎ 021-422 0388; www.downhilladventures.com; cnr Orange & Kloof Sts, Gardens) offer an introductory surfing course for R350. A sandboarding trip to Atlantis, north of the city centre, is R500.

At **Gary's Surf School** (Map p161; ☎ 021-788 9839; www.garysurf.co.za; Surfer's Corner, Muizenberg; ☺ 8.30am-5pm), if you don't get up on the surfboard, you don't pay for the two-hour lesson (R380). Gary's shop, a focus of Muizenberg's surf scene, rents out boards and wetsuits for R100 each per day. The school also runs sandboarding trips (R250) to the dunes at Kommetjie.

Sunscene Outdoor Adventures (☎ 021-783 0203, 083-517 9383; www.sunscene.co.za) offer a two-hour sandboarding lesson (R250), held in sheltered Fishhoek sand dunes, with expert guides and refreshments (essential!) included. They also offer traditional surfing lessons and trips, fishing trips from Kalk Bay and a host of other adrenalin-pumping activities.

Swimming

If you are looking for a real swimming work-out, there are a couple of stand-out institutions. The **Sea Point Pavilion** (Map pp120-1; ☎ 021-434 3341; Beach Rd, Sea Point; adult/child R9.50/6; ☺ 7am-6.50pm Oct-Apr, 8.30am-5pm May-Sep) is a huge outdoor pool complex with some lovely Art Deco decoration. The pools are always at least 10°C warmer than the ocean.

Long St Baths (Map pp110-11; ☎ 021-400 3302; cnr Long & Buitensingel Sts; pool only adult/child R8/5; ☺ 7am-7pm Mon-Sat, 7am-6pm Sun) are a city centre institution. The pool is heated and very popular with the local community. The separate Turkish steam baths (R52) are a great way to sweat away some time, especially during the cooler months. Women are admitted 8.30am to 7.30pm Monday and Thursday, 9am to 6pm Saturday; men 1pm to 7.30pm Tuesday, 9am to 7.30pm Wednesday and Friday, and 8am to noon Sunday. Massages are available for women (R39 massage only, R73 massage and Turkish steam bath).

If you want to swim safely in the sea, Sea Point also has a couple of rock pools: at the north end, **Graaff's Pool** (Map pp120–1) is for men only and is generally favoured by nudists; just south of here is **Milton's Pool** (Map pp120–1), which also has a stretch of beach. Be warned though that the water here will be freezing.

Windsurfing & Kiteboarding

With all that summer wind it's hardly surprising that the Cape coast is a top spot for windsurfers and kiteboarders. Bloubergstrand, 25km north of the City Bowl on the Atlantic Coast, is a popular location and is where you'll find **Windswept** (☎ 082-961 3070; www.windswept.co.za), offering a three-hour beginners course for R450, or if you know the ropes you can hire a board from R250. Packages including accommodation are available.

Another key place for these sports is Langebaan (see p232); contact **Cape Sport Centre** (☎ 022-772 1114; www.capesport.co.za) for details of its windsurfing and kiteboarding rates.

WALKING TOUR

Cape Town's turbulent history is revealed in the many buildings, statues and street names that grace the City Bowl and Bo-Kaap. This walk will give you an insight into the forces and personalities that have shaped the city you see today.

South Africa's oldest European fortification, the **Castle of Good Hope (1**; p108) is an appropriate place to start. Immediately west is **Grand Parade (2)**, the former military-parade and public-execution ground, which is now home to a lively market every Wednesday and Saturday. Jan van Riebeeck's original, mud-walled fort was here, too, and you can see its position outlined in red at the Plein St end of the Parade. The balcony of the impressive **Old Town Hall (3)** on the southwest side of the parade is where Nelson Mandela gave his first public speech in 27 years following his release from prison in February 1990.

Walk up Buitenkant St to the **District Six Museum (4**; **p108)** to learn about the history of this demolished inner-city area, a victim of apartheid's laws. From the museum turn right onto Albertus St, then turn right again at Corporation St to reach Mostert St and its continuation, Spin St. On the traffic island beside Church Square, look down to see a circular plaque marking the location of the old **slave tree (5)**, under which slaves were sold until emancipation in 1834.

WALK FACTS
Start Castle of Good Hope
Finish Heritage Square
Distance 3km
Duration 2 hours minimum

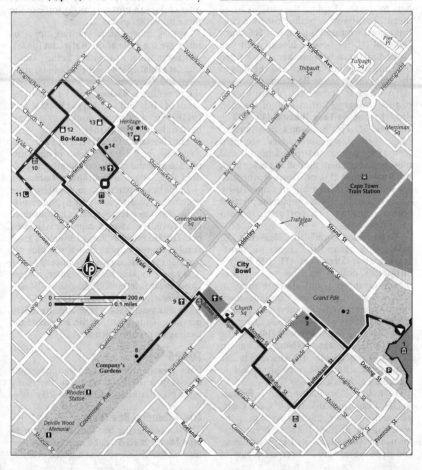

In front of you is the **Groote Kerk** (**6**; **p112**), mother church for the Dutch Reformed Church. Across the road is the old **Slave Lodge** (**7**; **p109**), now a museum; at the back of the lodge on Parliament St look up at the sculpted relief on the pediment of an exhausted-looking lion and unicorn, a satirical comment by the stone mason on the Empire following the Napoleonic Wars.

Spin St leads into Adderley St, named after the politician Charles Adderley who barracked successfully in London for Cape Town not to be turned into a penal colony. Prior to the mid-19th century, Adderley St was called the Heerengracht (Gentleman's Canal) after the waterway that once ran from the **Company's Gardens** (**8**; **p109**) down here to the sea. Explore the gardens by all means, but if you're pushed for time continue northwest up Wale St, past **St George's Cathedral** (**9**), for several blocks until you cross Buitengracht (another canal filled over and made into a road) and the start of the area known as the Bo-Kaap.

To discover something of the history of this strongly Muslim area of the city, drop by the **Bo-Kaap Museum** (**10**; p112), on Wale St. The Bo-Kaap's steep streets, some of which are still cobbled, are lined with 18th-century, flat-roofed houses and mosques; you'll hear the call to prayer from the **Owal Mosque** (**11**), on Dorp St, the oldest such place of worship in Cape Town. Chiappini and Rose Sts contain the prettiest houses, many of which sport bright modern paint jobs.

Along Rose St you'll find **Monkeybiz** (**12**; **p156**), while around the corner on Shortmarket St is **Streetwires** (**13**; p157), two businesses doing their bit to empower the disadvantaged and alleviate some of the city's social problems. Continue down Shortmarket St to the junction with Buitengracht St, across which you'll see a large car park covering **Van Riebeeck Sq (14)**. On the Bree St side is **St Stephen's Church (15)**, built in 1799; it was originally the African Theatre and later a school for freed slaves before becoming a church in 1839.

Adjacent to Van Riebeeck Sq is **Heritage Sq (16)**, a beautiful collection of Cape Georgian and Victorian buildings saved from the wrecking ball in 1996. It's since been transformed into one of the city's smartest dining and drinking enclaves. There are plenty of places to grab something to eat in Heritage Square, including the wine bar **Caveau** (**17**; p152). Alternatively take a right turn along Bree St and head to the junction with Church St, where you'll find **Birds Café** (**18**; p147), one of the city's most delightful cafés.

CAPE TOWN FOR CHILDREN

Cape Town, with its fun family attractions such as the **Two Oceans Aquarium** (p115), **Solole Game Reserve** (p164) and **Ratanga Junction** amusement park (p123), is a great place to bring the kids. South Africans tend to be family oriented, so most places can cope with childrens' needs. 'Family' restaurants, such as the Spur chain (www.spur.co.za; you'll find branches all over Cape Town), offer children's portions, as do some of the more upmarket places.

Among other animal-spotting opportunities are the seals at the **Waterfront** (p378), which can usually be seen at Bertie's Landing; **Cape Point** (p164), with its zebras, antelope and baboons; those crowd pleasers the penguins at **Boulders** (p163); and thousands of birds and monkeys at **World of Birds** (p118). For a ride on a donkey or a camel head to **Imhoff Farm** (p164).

The **Planetarium** (p113) screens a kids' star show daily, and there are plenty of other displays to grab the attention of inquisitive children at the attached **South African Museum**.

At the beach, parents should watch out for rough surf (not to mention hypothermia-inducing water temperatures!); **Muizenberg beach** (p160) on a warm, calm day is the best bet. The **Sea Point Pavilion** (p138) has a great family swimming pool that is significantly warmer than the surrounding ocean.

If you're looking for a babysitter, contact either **Childminders** (☎ 021-788 6788, 083-254 4683; www.childminders.co.za) or **Super Sitters** (☎ 021-439 4985; www.supersitters.net), who charge from R30 per hour (minimum of three hours), excluding transport expenses.

TOURS

Cape Town Tourism (p106) should be your first stop to find out about all the many tours on offer in and around the city.

City & General Bus Tours

The double-decker bus tour **City Sightseeing Cape Town** (☎ 021-511 1784; www.hyltonross.co.za; adult/child R90/40) is good for a quick orientation on a fine day. The Red Route circular tour (taking just over two hours), starting at the Waterfront, heads into the city centre, up to the cable car, down to Camps Bay and back along Sea Point promenade. The Blue Route also starts from the Waterfront but goes via Kirstenbosch and Hout Bay. They're hop-on, hop-off services and run at roughly half-hourly intervals between 9.30am and 3.30pm with extra services in peak season.

For organised walking tours, try one of the following:

Cape Town on Foot (☎ 021-487 6800; tours R100; 🕑 11am Mon-Fri) Led by experienced guide Ursula Stevens, the tour leaves from Cape Town Tourism's office on Burg St.

Day Trippers (☎ 021-511 4766; www.daytrippers .co.za) Has an excellent reputation. Many of the tours include the chance to go cycling, if you so choose. Most tours cost around R385 and include Cape Point, the Winelands and whale-watching (in season).

Footsteps to Freedom (☎ 021-426 4260, 083-452 1112; www.footstepstofreedom.co.za; tours R100) City walks also depart from Cape Town Tourism.

Special-Interest Tours

Organised tours cater to a number of interests, including wine, nature and sports.

Plenty of companies offer day trips to the Winelands, but unless you're tight for time it's better to stay overnight closer by, say in Stellenbosch, and take a tour there. See p174 for details of a couple of operators.

Some recommendations:

Birdwatch Cape (☎ 021-762 5059; www.birdwatch .co.za; half-day tour R270) Offers informative tours pointing out the many unique species of the Cape bird kingdom.

Cape Wine Tours (☎ 021-462 1121, 083-659 8434; capewinetours@telkomsa.net; R365) Recommended day tour of the Winelands ticking off several wineries in Stellenbosch, Franschhoek and Paarl.

Ferdinand's Tours & Adventures (☎ 021-913 8800, 072-132 2482; ferdinand@telkomsa.net; tours R335) This winery-focused Winelands tour takes in at least four wineries and includes lunch. Things can get pretty raucous.

Gateway to Newlands (☎ 021-686 2151, 021-686 2150; www.newlandstours.co.za) Sports fans may be interested to take these tours of Cape Town's main cricket and rugby stadiums and the Sports Science Institute of South Africa (Map pp120–1). Whistle-stop tours kick off at adult/child R35/22, while longer ones including the tiny Rugby Museum (Map pp120–1) cost R60/36.

Imvubu Nature Tours (☎ 021-706 0842; www.im vubu.co.za; tours adult/child R30/15) Based at the Rondevlei Nature Reserve (p160). Take a tour around the reserve and you might be lucky enough to see the elusive hippos. Increase your chances by arranging to stay at the island bush camp. Boat trips (per person R30), for a minimum of four people, are held between August and February.

Sunpath (☎ 072-417 6800; www.sunpath.co.za; tours R100-325) Offers a series of fascinating tours and hikes around the peninsula. Discover the ancient sunpaths thought to have been used by the indigenous people of the Cape.

Wine Desk at the Waterfront (Map pp116-17; ☎ 021-405 4550; www.winedeskwaterfront.co.za; Clocktower, Waterfront; tours R490) Daily wine tours take in a different selection of wineries each day. The Saturday morning wine club visits two or three wineries, ending with a meal on one of the farms.

Township & Cultural Tours

Lots of operators offer township tours. The half-day tours are sufficient – the full-day tours tack on a trip to Robben Island that is best done separately and for which you don't need a guide. Consider asking the tour operator how much of what you spend actually goes to help people in the townships, since not all tours are run by Cape Flats residents.

Adventure Kalk Bay (☎ 021-788 5113, 0783-211 4508; arcadia@49er.co.za) Community-based tourism project offering guided walks around Kalk Bay and harbour explaining the fishing culture of the village (R30, including lunch R100). The half-day fishing trip (R120) starts before dawn, so consider arranging a homestay with one of the local families (R220 full board).

Andulela (☎ 021-790 2592; www.andulela.com) Offering cookery-focused tours of both the Bo-Kaap and the township of Kayamandi in Stellenbosch, this innovative company can arrange a number of other offbeat adventures.

Cape Capers Tours (☎ 083-358 0193; www.tour capers.co.za) Award-winning guide Faizel Gangat leads a band of informative guides to the townships, with tours concentrating either on Langa (R280) or the Cape Care Route (R460), highlighting some of the city's standout community and environmental projects. They also have a half-day tour of the Bo-Kaap and former District Six area.

Charlotte's Walking Tours (☎ 083-982 5692; nomthunzie@webmail.co.za) The ebullient Charlotte Swatbooi will take you on a walking tour of the township of Masiphumelele, on the way to Kommetjie. It's a good alternative to the standard bus tour around the Cape Flats townships.

JOIN THE MERRY MINSTRELS

The Mother City's equivalent of Rio's Mardi Gras parade is the **Cape Town New Year Karnaval**. It's a noisy, joyous and disorganised affair with practically every colour of satin, sequin and glitter used in the costumes of the marching troupes, which can number as many as 1000-plus members!

Dating back to the early 19th century when slaves enjoyed a day of freedom over the New Year period, today's carnival was inspired by visiting American minstrels in the early 20th century, hence the face make-up, colourful costumes and ribald song-and-dance routines. The vast majority of participants come from the coloured community (although you will notice a few black and even fewer white faces among the troupe participants).

The main parades are on 31 December and 2 January, kicking off from Darling St in front of Old City Hall and culminating at Green Point Stadium (Map pp116–17). However, the actual Cape Minstrel competition, when troupes are judged on variety of criteria, including costume, singing and dancing, runs throughout January and into early February each Saturday night. If you miss the main parade, there are chances to catch the minstrels in action on these nights at Green Point, Athlone Stadium (Map pp102–3) and Vygerkraal Stadium (Map pp102–3) – it makes for a really unique Capetonian experience! Note that late-night traffic in the city centre (particularly around Whale and Adderly Sts) on these nights can be chaotic as the competition participants parade back to their buses.

Coffee Beans Routes (☎ 021-448 8080, 084-762 4944; www.coffeebeans.co.za; tours R390) Head up to Kalkfontein, a township north of the city, in the company of local poet Jethro Louw. Or take the highly recommend Cape Town Jazz Safari (Monday from 7pm) where you'll meet jazz musicians and catch a jam session. On Friday it runs a trip to Marcus Garvey, a Rastafarian settlement in Philippi, for a night of Jamaican food and, after midnight, reggae at a dance hall.

Grassroute Tours (☎ 021-706 1006; www.grass routetours.co.za) One of the most experienced operators of townships tours (half/full day R290/450). Its programme includes evening tours (R340 including dinner) with a visit to a *shebeen* (drinking establishment) and a ride on a donkey cart, as well as a walking tour of the Bo-Kaap (R260).

One City Tours (☎ 021-555 1468, 082-970 0564) Sam Ntimba's half-day trip (R250) includes visits to a dormitory and *shebeen* in Langa and a crèche project in Khayelitsha. His Sunday tours to see a gospel choir in a Baptist church in Langa are popular.

Pure Pondo Adventures (☎ 072-302 9489; www.purepondo.co.za/cape_town_tours.htm) White *sangoma* (traditional healer) Chris Ntombemhlophea leads tours into the townships using local transport and visiting a traditional herbalist shop and other *sangomas*. He also leads a medicinal-plants tour through Kirstenbosch.

Township Tours SA (☎ 083-719 4870; suedafrika .net/imizamoyethu) Afrika Moni guides you on a two-hour walking tour (R85) of the Hout Bay township Imizamo Yethu, including a visit to a *sangoma*, a drink of homebrew at a *shebeen* and a look at some art projects. Tours run daily at 10.30am, 1pm and 4pm; bookings essential.

FESTIVALS & EVENTS

Events and celebrations are a regular part of Cape Town life. For a full run-down check with **Cape Town Tourism** (www.tourismcapetown.co .za). Also see p610 for more festival listings.

JANUARY & FEBRUARY
Cape Town New Year Karnaval (☎ 021-696 9538) The main parades are held on 31 December and 2 January; see the boxed text, above, for more details.

Opening of Parliament A grand parade with military marching bands brings Adderley and Parliament Sts to a halt when parliament opens in early February.

Cape Town Pride (☎ 083-274 3579; www.capetown pride.co.za) A 10-day gay and lesbian event in February where the Mother City flies its rainbow colours with pride.

MARCH & APRIL
Cape Town Festival (☎ 021-465 9042; www.cape townfestival.co.za) This three-week arts festival, beginning early March, takes place throughout the City Bowl and at the Waterfront. It includes comedy, drama, debates and a short-film festival.

Cape Town International Jazz Festival (☎ 021-4122 5651; www.capetowninternationaljazzfestival.com) Cape Town's biggest jazz event, attracting all the big names from both South Africa and overseas, is usually held at the Cape Town International Convention Centre (Map pp110–11) at the end of March. It includes a free concert in Greenmarket Sq.

Old Mutual Two Oceans Marathon (☎ 021-671 9407; www.twooceansmarathon.org.za) Mid-April sees this tough yet scenic marathon cover a 56km route around the peninsula.

MAY & JULY

Cape Gourmet Festival (☎ 021-797 4500; www .gourmetsa.com) For two weeks from early May, Cape Town celebrates with various food-focused events.

Vodacom Comedy Festival (☎ 021-680 3988; www.computicket.com) Catch some of South Africa's top comedians at this festival, held at various venues across town for three weeks in July.

Nokia Cape Town Fashion Week (☎ 021-422 0390; www.capetownfashionweek.co.za) Fashion in Cape Town is hot and this event held in July is the place to catch the hottest of designers' work.

SEPTEMBER

Penguin Festival (☎ 021-786 1758) Come celebrate those cute black-and-white birds with the folks down at Boulders near Simon's Town over a mid-September weekend.

Gun Run (☎ 021-511 7130) Starting from Beach Rd in Mouile Point, this popular half-marathon is the only time that the Noon Gun on Signal Hill gets fired on a Sunday – competitors try to finish the race before the gun goes off. It's generally held at the end of September.

NOVEMBER & DECEMBER

Mother City Queer Project (☎ 082-885 0018; www.mcqp.co.za) Massive, must-attend gay dance party held in early December. Run yourself up a fabulous costume – they won't let you in unless you're dressed according to the theme.

Kirstenbosch Summer Sunset Concerts
(☎ 021-799 8782; www.nbi.ac.za; adult/child incl entry to the gardens R35/10; ☻ 5.30pm Nov-Apr) Bring a blanket, a bottle of wine and a picnic and join the crowds enjoying anything from an aria performed by local divas to a funky jazz combo at these Sunday afternoon concerts. There's always a special concert for New Year's Eve, too.

SLEEPING

Whether you're into lively hostels, char-acterful guesthouses or unfettered luxury, Cape Town has it. Remember, location is everything here. If beaches are your thing, then suburbs along the Atlantic or False Bay Coast make better sense than, say, Gardens or City Bowl. If you have transport, then anywhere is OK, but remember to inquire about the parking options when making a booking and check whether there's a charge (anything from R20 to R50 per day for city-centre hotels).

Advance booking is recommended, es-pecially during school holidays from mid-December to the end of January, and at Easter – prices can double and many places are fully booked. We quote high-season rates following, which cover the peak Christmas and New Year period. Un-less otherwise mentioned rates also include breakfast. A 1% tourism promotion levy is usually added to the bill, but some places, particularly the budget ones, include this in the room rates. Budget places are ones with a double room for R400 or under; midrange places charge R400 to R2000; and top-end ones are R2000 and over.

City Bowl
BUDGET

Inn Long Street (Map pp110-11; ☎ 021-424 1660; innlongstreet@ataris.co.za; 230 Long St; dm R75, d without/ with bathroom R240/290; P 🖳) There's a calm vibe at this backpackers with it being in the thick of Long St. There's a wrap-around balcony that all rooms access, and a recent paint job and funky lights give it some style. Parking is R20 per day.

Long St Backpackers (Map pp110-11; ☎ 021-423 0615; www.longstreetbackpackers.co.za; 209 Long St; dm/ s/d R80/120/160) Backpackers dot the length of Long St, but this one remains the best. In a block of 14 small flats, with four beds and a bathroom in each, accommodation is arranged around a leafy, quiet courtyard decorated with funky mosaics.

St Paul's B&B Guest House (Map pp110-11; ☎ /fax 021-423 4420; stpaul@absamail.co.za; 182 Bree St; s/d R150/250; P) A quiet alternative to a back-packers. The simply furnished and spacious rooms have high ceilings and there's a vine-shaded courtyard where you can relax or take breakfast.

MIDRANGE

Cape Diamond Hotel (Map pp110-11; ☎ 021-461 2519; www.capediamondhotel.co.za; cnr Longmarket & Parlia-ment Sts; s/d from R370/530; P 🖳) Great-value new hotel that has kept features of its Art Deco building such as the wood panelled floors. It's short on natural light but there's a rooftop Jacuzzi with a view to Table Mountain. Breakfast is R45 extra and park-ing is R45 per day.

Townhouse (Map pp110-11; ☎ 021-465 7050; www .townhouse.co.za; 60 Corporation St; s/d from R572/1045; P 🗴 🖳 🖳) The cheaper old-style rooms are fine at this popular hotel, but it's worth paying slightly more for the smartly reno-vated deluxe ones (and ask for one with a view of the mountain). Parking is R35 per day.

Metropole Hotel (Map pp110-11; ☎ 021-424 7247; www.metropolehotel.co.za; 38 Long St; s/d/ste from R600/1200/1650; P ✗ ☐) The trendy Metropole is all minimalist lines and soothing colours. Go for the larger superior rooms with their ostrich-leather trimmed bedsteads. Its stylish restaurant and bar remain deservedly popular. Parking is R50 per day.

Cape Town Hollow (Map pp110-11; ☎ 021-423 1260; www.capetownhollow.co.za; 88 Queen Victoria St; s/d R745/1060; P ✗ ☐ ☎) Overlooking the Company's Gardens, this good-value hotel has pleasant rooms and decent facilities, including a tiny pool, small gym, business centre and restaurant with leafy aspect. Parking is R30 per day.

Daddy Long Legs (Map pp110-11; ☎ 021-422 3074; www.daddylonglegs.co.za; 134 Long Street; r R750; ☐) This boutique hotel/art installation is what you get when artists are given free reign to design the boudoirs of their dreams. The results range from bohemian garret to a hospital ward. Favourites include the karaoke room (with a mike in the shower), and the room designed by pop group Freshly Ground. There's nowhere to put your luggage – hey, these are artists, not hoteliers! – but a stay here is anything but boring. They also offer super-stylish apartments (same price) at 263 Long St, an ideal choice if you crave hotel-suite luxury and want to self-cater.

Cape Heritage Hotel (Map pp110-11; ☎ 021-424 4646; www.capeheritage.co.za; 90 Bree St; s/d from R825/1190, ste s/d R1325/1950; P ✗ ☐) Gracious service matches the Cape Dutch style of this elegant boutique hotel that's part of the Heritage Square redevelopment of 18th-century buildings. Parking is R25 per day.

Urban Chic (Map pp110-11; ☎ 021-423 2086; www.urbanchic.co.za; cnr Long & Pepper Sts; r R1242; P ✗ ☐) Rooms with fabulous floor-to-ceiling views towards Table Mountain feature at this stylish new boutique hotel. The ground floor Gallery Bar (p151) is currently a very hip watering hole. Parking is R40 per day.

Gardens & Around
BUDGET
Ashanti Lodge (Map p114; ☎ 021-423 8721; www.ashanti.co.za; 11 Hof St, Gardens; camp sites R50, dm/d with shared bathroom R90/250, guesthouse d R370; P ☐ ☎) One of Cape Town's premier party hostels,

with much of the action focused on its lively bar and deck overlooking Table Mountain. For something quieter, opt for the excellent en-suite rooms in two separate heritage-listed houses around the corner.

Backpack (Map p114; ☎ 021-423 4530; www.backpackers.co.za; 74 New Church St, Tamboerskloof; dm/s/d with shared bathroom R90/250/300, s/d R300/360; P ☐ ☎) Cape Town's longest running backpackers remains a relaxed and comfortable place with something for everyone, be it a lively time at the Thursday night African drumming sessions or just chilling out in the chic en-suite rooms. They've also recently got Fair Trade in Tourism accreditation. Parking is R20 per day.

Cape Town Backpackers (Map p114; ☎ /fax 021-426 0200; www.capetownbackpackers.com; 81 New Church St, Tamboerskloof; dm/s/d with shared bathroom R90/180/220, guesthouse s/d R275/320; P ☐) The backpacker hostel grows up at this stylish place that offers both pleasant dorms, and a chic guesthouse with en-suite rooms on neighbouring Kohling St. There's an equally appealing Sea Point branch (see p146).

MIDRANGE
An African Villa (Map p114; ☎ 021-423 2164; www.capetowncity.co.za/villa; 19 Carstens St, Tamboerskloof; s/d from R640/800; ☐ ☎) There's a sophisticated and colourful 'African-Zen' look at this appealing guesthouse, sheltering behind the façade of three 19th-century terrace houses.

Dunkley House (Map p114; ☎ 021-462 7650; www.dunkleyhouse.com; 3B Gordon St, Gardens; d/ste from R700/990; ☐ ☎) Ultra-stylish guesthouse tucked away on a quiet street. The rooms are decorated in neutral tones, all with CD players and satellite TV, and there's a plunge pool in the courtyard.

Hippo Boutique Hotel (Map p114; ☎ 021-423 2500; www.hippotique.co.za; 5-9 Park Lane, Gardens; s/d R800/1200; P ✗ ☐ ☎) This appealing boutique property offers spacious, stylish rooms with a small kitchen for self-catering. Gadget lovers will also be pleased with the DVD player and music system.

Abbey Manor (Map p114; ☎ 021-462 2935; www.abbey.co.za; 3 Montrose Ave, Oranjezicht; s/d from R995/1290; P ✗ ☐ ☎) A luxurious guesthouse occupying a grand home built in 1905 for a shipping magnate. Fine linens, antique furnishings, a decent-sized pool and courteous staff enhance the experience.

Cape Milner (Map p114; ☎ 021-426 1101; www .threecities.co.za; 2A Milner Rd, Tamboerskloof; s/d/ste R995/1300/2140; P ✄ 🖳 🐾) Silks and velvets add quite a sophisticated touch to the contemporary-styled rooms here. Friendly service, views of Table Mountain and a spacious pool deck are also pluses. Parking is R25 per day.

TOP END

Alta Bay (Map p114; ☎ 021-487 8800; www.altabay .com; 12 Invermark Crescent, Higgoval; d R2100; P ✄ 🖳 🐾) Cascading down the hillside, Alta Bay is a haven of tranquillity as well as de-signer heaven. The six luxury rooms are adorable, mixing locally handcrafted fur-nishings (including huge king size beds) with European artworks.

Kensington Place (Map p114; ☎ 021-424 4744; www.kensingtonplace.co.za; 38 Kensington Cres, Higgovale; d with breakfast R2550; P ✄ 🖳 🐾) One of Cape Town's finest boutique properties, Kensing-ton Place offers eight spacious and tastefully decorated rooms, all with balconies and beautifully tiled bathrooms. There's also free Internet access, fresh fruit and flowers, a small pool and faultless service.

Waterkant
MIDRANGE

De Waterkant House Map pp116-17; ☎ 021-409 2500; www.dewaterkant.com; cnr Napier & Waterkant Sts, Water-kant; s/d R470/720; 🖳 🐾) Property company Village and Life (www.villageandlife.com) run this pleasant B&B in the heart of the gay village, with a plunge pool and rooms with glossy magazine-style furnishings. They also have a wide range of apartments in the area kicking off at s/d R650/950, as well as their popular budget-level 'crash pads' (s/d R280/400) which are not nearly as shabby as they sound.

De Waterkant Place (Map pp116-17; ☎ 021-419 2476; www.dewaterkantplace.com; 35 Dixon St; s/d from R500/600; 🖳) This appealing guesthouse with five antique decorated rooms offers good value. Guests are free to use the kitchen and there's a lovely view from the roof.

Village Lodge (Map pp116-17; ☎ /fax 021-421 1106; www.thevillagelodge.com; 49 Napier St; s/d R750/1220; ✄ 🖳 🐾) Rooms at this chic guesthouse are smart if somewhat cramped. The rooftop pool is a prime spot for guests to check each other out, as is the lodge's good Thai res-taurant, Soho.

Atlantic Coast
GREEN POINT & WATERFRONT
Budget

Big Blue (Map pp116-17; ☎ 021-439 0807; www.bigblue backpackers.hostel.com; 7 Vesperdene Rd, Green Point; dm/ s/d with shared bathroom R85/220/270, d R320; 🖳 🐾) This brightly painted hostel remains a lead-ing light of the Capetonian backpacking scene – come and enjoy its grand hallway, Zen garden and friendly atmosphere.

House on the Hill (Map pp116-17; ☎ 021-439 3902; www.houseonthehillct.co.za; 25 Leinster Rd, Green Point; d/tr with shared bathroom R260/315, d/tr R265/385) This self-catering house is a fine alternative to the bigger hostels. Book ahead for the five rooms which are very pleasantly furnished in African style, with the added bonus of a TV and CD player.

Midrange

Wilton Manor (Map pp116-17; ☎ 021-434 7869; www .wiltonmanor.co.za; 15 Croxteth Rd, Green Point; s/d from R550/600; P 🖳 🐾) A stylish guesthouse where each of the seven rooms are indi-vidually decorated. Guests are free to use the kitchen. The owners also run the more con-temporary Wilton Place higher up Signal Hill, and Altona Lodge, a budget guesthouse also on Croxteth Rd – check the website for further details.

Head South Lodge Map pp116-17; (☎ 021-434 8777; www.headsouth.co.za; 215 Main Rd, Green Point; s/d with breakfast R650/750; P ✄ 🖳 🐾) A fabulous homage to the 1950s with its retro furnish-ings and collection of Tretchikoff prints hung en masse in the bar. The 15 rooms are spacious and there's a tiny plunge pool in the front garden.

Cape Standard (Map pp116-17; ☎ 021-430 3060; www.capestandard.co.za; 3 Romney Rd, Green Point; s/d R750/990; P 🖳 🐾) This secluded boutique hotel, one of Cape Town's nicest, offers whitewashed beach-house chic rooms downstairs, or more edgy, contemporary rooms upstairs. The showers are big enough to dance in.

Top End

Cape Grace (Map pp116-17; ☎ 021-410 7100; www .capegrace.com; West Quay, Waterfront; s/d from R4360/ 4490; P ✄ 🖳 🐾) This luxurious hotel op-erates like an exclusive but very welcoming club. The best rooms face Table Mountain. Also here you'll find the excellent One. Waterfront restaurant (p150), the convivial

Bascule whisky bar and the relaxing Cape Grace Spa (p124).

SEA POINT
Budget
Cape Town Backpackers Sea Point (Map pp120-1; ☎ /fax 021-426 0200; www.capetownbackpackers.com; 1 Rocklands Rd; dm/d R90/400; ☐ ☎) Easily the best budget option in Sea Point, steps away from the sea front. There's a six-bed dorm and three en-suite double rooms with giant rain showers as well as a spacious communal kitchen, all presided over by the convivial Mama Fefe.

Lion's Head Lodge (Map pp120-1; ☎ 021-434 4163; www.lions-head-lodge.co.za; 319 Main Rd; d R398; P ☒ ☎) An old-fashioned budget hotel offering lower rates for stays longer than one night. It has a reasonable-sized pool and a bar. Sharing the hotel's facilities is the even more run-down Aardvark Backpackers (☎ 021-434 4172; dorm/double R100/398), which has its dorms in converted flats. HI members get a 10% discount.

Midrange
Huijs Haerlem (Map pp120-1 ☎ 021-434 6434; www.huijshaerlem.co.za; 25 Main Dr; s/d R680/980; P ☒ ☐ ☎) Up one of the steeper slopes of Sea Point, this excellent gay-friendly (but not exclusively gay) guesthouse comprises of two houses decorated in top-quality antiques and joined by delightful gardens.

Winchester Mansions Hotel (Map pp120-1; ☎ 021-434 2351; www.winchester.co.za; 221 Beach Rd; s/d from R1150/1500; P ☒ ☐ ☎) Choose between classic and modern-style rooms at this Cape Dutch-style beauty with a prime position along the Sea Point promenade. The pool is a good size and the lovely courtyard fountain restaurant is popular for its Sunday brunch with live jazz (R145; open 11am to 2pm) for which you should book ahead.

O on Kloof (Map pp120-1; ☎ 021-439 2081; www.oonkloof.co.za; 92 Kloof Rd, Bantry Bay; d from R1500; P ☒ ☐ ☎) A gorgeous contemporary guesthouse with six spacious rooms. The cheapest rooms don't have full sea views but the good facilities, including a big indoor pool and gym, are ample compensation.

CAMPS BAY
Midrange
Camps Bay Retreat (Map pp120-1; ☎ 021-437 0485; www.campsbayretreat.com; 7 Chilworth Rd, The Glen; s/d from R1200/1500; P ☒ ☐ ☎) Based in the grand Earl's Dyke Manor, this is a splendid option with a choice of 16 rooms in either the main house or the contemporary Deck House, reached by a rope bridge over a ravine. There's also a couple of decent, self-catering rooms (per person R380) next to the tennis court, one of the cheapest deals you'll get in Camps Bay.

Primi Royal (Map pp120-1; ☎ 021-438 2741; www.primi-royal.com; 23 Camps Bay Dr; d from R1500; P ☒ ☐ ☎) All 10 rooms are individually decorated at this comfortable, sleek boutique hotel that overlooks Camps Bay. Rose petals scattered across the bed linen on welcome is a romantic touch. The owners also run the equally appealing Primi Seacastle at the opposite end of the Camps Bay.

Twenty Nine (Map pp120-1; ☎ 021-438 3800; www.twentynine.net; 29 Atholl Rd; d/ste R2000/2600; P ☐ ☎) Utterly gorgeous gay-friendly retreat high above Camps Bay. There are five rooms, all so tastefully decorated you could die happy, listening to a CD from their collection of 600 or watching one of 400 DVDs on the Bang & Olufsen equipment.

Top End
Bay Hotel (Map pp120-1 ☎ 021-438 4444; www.thebay.co.za; 69 Victoria Rd; d from R2450; P ☒ ☐ ☎) This hang-out for the well heeled is a stone's toss from the beach. The spacious rooms in white and earth tones are soothing; the ones with sea views are pricier (R3660). There's also a good-size pool.

Southern Suburbs
BUDGET
Lighthouse Farm Lodge (Map pp102-3; ☎ /fax 021-447 9177; msm@mweb.co.za; Violet Bldg, Oude Molen Village, Alexandria Rd, Mowbray; dm/d with shared bathroom R60/150; P) A simple and relaxed hostel that is the better of the two on the grounds of Oude Molen Eco Village (see p122). You can pay your way by working on the organic farm. It's within walking distance of Pinelands train station.

Deco Lodge (Map pp120-1; ☎ 021-447 4216; www.capetowndeco.com; 22 Roodebloem Rd, Woodstock; dm/d R80/220; P ☐ ☎) This huge purple Art Deco house is a great alternative for the independent-minded traveller who doesn't mind being a suburb or two removed from Long St. The garden is lush with a cooling pool, and rooms are colourfully decorated.

Green Elephant (Map pp120-1; ☎ 021-448 6359; greenele@iafrica.com; 57 Milton Rd, Observatory; dm/s/d with shared bathroom R85/180/280, d R310) The famous tree-climbing dog here is getting on, but this long-running backpackers, split between two houses, remains a popular alternative to the city-centre hostels.

TOP END

Vineyard Hotel & Spa (Map pp120-1; ☎ 021-657 4500; www.vineyard.co.za; Colinton Rd, Newlands; s/d/ste from R990/1392/2880; Ⓟ ⊠ ⌨ ⓡ) The core of this excellent hotel is the 1799 house built for Lady Anne Barnard. A recent upgrade has given it a fresh, contemporary look, as well as brand new rooms attached to a fabulous spa (see p124). It is all surrounded by lush gardens with great views onto the mountain.

Constantia Uitsig (Map pp102-3; ☎ 021-794 6500; www.uitsig.co.za; Spaanschemat River Rd, Constantia; s/d from R1600/2400; Ⓟ ⊠ ⌨ ⓡ) Set within the vineyard of the same name, this hotel offers appealing, chintzy Victorian-styled rooms, all florals and checks. There are beautiful gardens and three top-notch restaurants to choose from.

EATING

Dining in the Mother City is a pleasure. There are places to suit practically everyone's taste and budget, with a particularly strong selection of cafés and delis. With both the sea and fruitful farmlands on hand, you can be pretty much assured of fresh, top-quality ingredients wherever you eat. Don't miss the opportunity to sample some traditional Cape Malay food, and there are several good African restaurants in Cape Town, too.

Most restaurants are licensed but some allow you to bring your own wine for little or no corkage charge. Call ahead to check the restaurant's policy. Several bars and pubs serve good food too; see p151.

There are many great places in the city to buy the provisions you'll need for a picnic or to self-cater. Stock up at the major supermarkets Pick 'n' Pay and Woolworths; there are branches all over the city including at Victoria Wharf (Map pp116–17) and Gardens Centre (Map p114). For specialist products there are excellent delis, such as Gionvanni's Deli World (p150) and Melissa's (p150).

Cafés and restaurants generally open daily, the former serving food from 7.30am to around 5pm. A few places (more usually in the City Bowl) will be closed on Sunday or occasionally Monday. If a restaurant opens for lunch it will generally be from 11.30am to 3pm, with dinner usually kicking off around 7pm with last orders at 10pm. Variations of more than half an hour from these times are listed in the reviews.

City Bowl & Bo-Kaap

Long St has many great places to eat, plus fantastic street life. Head to the Bo-Kaap to sample authentic Cape Malay dishes in unpretentious surroundings.

CAFÉS & QUICK EATS

Crush (Map pp110-11; ☎ 021-422 5533; 100 St George's Mall, City Bowl; mains R20-30) One on the most pleasant and interesting places to eat on St George's Mall, Crush offers freshly squeezed juices, smoothies and tasty wraps, proving healthy eating need not be boring.

Lola's (Map pp110-11; ☎ 021-423 0885; 228 Long St, City Bowl; mains R20-30; ☺ 8am-midnight) Whether you come for breakfast or a late night coffee or beer, a visit to pastel painted Lola's is a right of passage on Long St. Grab a street table and watch the passing parade.

Portobello (Map pp110-11; ☎ 021-426 1418; 111 Long St, City Bowl; mains R20-30) This rustic and peaceful veggie café serves a great range of all-day breakfasts, toasties and freshly made sandwiches. The lunch buffet is R30 for three hot or cold servings, R40 for four serves.

Frieda's (Map pp110-11; ☎ 021-421 2404; 15 Bree St, City Bowl; mains R30-40; ☺ 8am-4pm Mon-Fri) Jumblesale chic is the look at this cavernous and highly convivial café in the louche but up-and-coming area at the base of Bree St. They do a fine line in sandwiches, wraps, salads and comfort food such as lasagne.

Café African Image (Map pp110-11; ☎ 021-426 1857; 48 Church St, City Bowl; mains R30-45; ☺ 8am-6pm Mon-Fri, 8am-3pm Sat) Easily Cape Town's most colourful café, sporting groovy African-print cushions and table cloths and a fabulous chandelier made of recycled plastic. Sample Tanzanian fish curry, African village stew or a range of healthy salads.

Birds Café (Map pp110-11; ☎ 021-426 2534; 127 Bree St, City Bowl; mains R40) This delightful café takes birds as its theme. The sophisticatedly rustic style – think milk-bottle crate seats in a grand old Dutch building, and handmade crockery – matches the artisan food including delicious homemade pies, strudles and chunky scones.

Also worth checking out are **Sundance** (Map pp110-11; ☎ 021-465 9990; 21 Adderley St, City Bowl; sandwiches R30-40; ☺ 6.30am-9.30pm) for its coffee, and **Charly's Bakery** (Map pp110-11; ☎ 021-461 5181; 20 Roeland St, City Bowl; ☺ 7.30am-4pm Mon-Fri) for the amazing cupcakes (R10) and pies.

RESTAURANTS

95 Keerom (Map pp110-11; ☎ 021-422 0765; 95 Keerom St, City Bowl; mains R50-100; ☺ 12.30-2pm Mon-Fri, 7-11pm Mon-Sat) Bookings are essential for this super-stylish Italian restaurant round the back of Rhodes House (p155). Given the quality of food the prices are very reasonable, particularly for the handmade pastas.

Africa Café (Map pp110-11; ☎ 021-422 0221; www .africacafé.co.za; 108 Shortmarket St, City Bowl; set banquet R160; ☺ 6.30-11pm) Age hasn't withered the Africa Café's appeal as the best place to sample African food. Come with a hearty appetite as the set feast comprises some 15 dishes from across the continent. The décor and friendly staff, who dance and sing through the restaurant, are equally fantastic.

Madame Zingara & Cara Lazuli (Map pp110-11; ☎ 021-426 2458; 192 Loop St, City Bowl; mains R70; ☺ 7-11pm Mon-Sat) Every night is party night at this bohemian, crowd-pleasing restaurant with two sections. Unless you're a committed carnivore we'd advise against its infamous whopper stack of beef fillets doused in chilli-chocolate sauce. Magic tricks, tarot-card readings, belly dancing and dressing up in silly hats is all part of the fun.

Ginja (Map pp110-11; ☎ 021-426 2368; 121 Castle St, Bo-Kaap; 1/2/3 courses R95/175/195; ☺ 7-10pm Mon-Sat) Book well ahead for this dining gem. Chef Mike Basset conjures up inventive fusion dishes such as the amazing skewers of salt and pepper prawns dipped in coriander foam and sprayed with coriander perfume. Upstairs is the more casual Shoga bar and brasserie.

Haiku (Map pp110-11; ☎ 021-424 7000; 33 Church St, City Bowl; mains R35-70; ☺ noon-2.30pm & 6-10.30pm Mon-Fri, 6-10.30pm Sat) Run by the owners of long-established Indian restaurant Bukhara (which is upstairs), this is a sophisticated Asian brasserie. The 'Asian tapas' menu

promiscuously plunders dishes from Japan, China and Southeast Asia and the quality is good. Booking for dinner, when the minimum spend is R132, is recommended.

Royale Eatery (Map pp110-11; ☎ 021-422 4536; 279 Long St, City Bowl; mains R60; ☺ noon-midnight Mon-Sat) Our favourite gourmet burger bar keeps growing, opening a cute satellite branch around the corner on Vredenburg Lane which is worth trying when it's full here (always). For something different try the Big Bird ostrich burger.

Savoy Cabbage (Map pp110-11; ☎ 021-424 2626; 101 Hout Lane, City Bowl; mains R70-90) The standard bearer of the city's contemporary dining scene remains a great place for inventive cooking, offering the chance to try local game meats such as zebra and wildebeest. The tomato tart is legendary as are the stuffed cabbage rolls.

Noon Gun Tearoom & Restaurant (Map pp110-11; ☎ 021-424 0529; 273 Longmarket St, Bo-Kaap; mains R50-70; ☺ 10am-10pm Mon-Sat) There's a fantastic view of Table Mountain and the bay from this family-run restaurant high on Signal Hill. The Cape Malay dishes such as bobotie (curried mince pie topped with egg custard) and curries are excellent.

Gardens & Around

Kloof St offers the best dining selection in Gardens. Both the Lifestyles on Kloof and Gardens Centre malls have pleasant cafés, too.

CAFÉS & QUICK EATS

Mount Nelson Hotel (Map p114; ☎ 021-483 1000; www.mountnelsonhotel.orient-express.com; 76 Orange St; afternoon tea R120; ☺ 2.30-5.30pm) If you can't afford to stay at the pink-painted 'Nelly', there's always their splendid afternoon tea, including local delicacies such as samosas (fried savoury pastry parcels), as well the usual finger sandwiches, cakes and scones.

Lazari (Map p114; ☎ 021-461 9895; cnr Upper Maynard St & Vredehoek Ave, Vredehoek; mains R30-40; ☺ 7.30am-6pm Mon-Fri, 8am-3pm Sat, 9am-3pm Sun) A metrosexual air hangs over this buzzy café, great for brunch or an indulgent moment over coffee and cake.

Wild Things (Map p114; ☎ 021-424 3445; 96 Kloof St, Tamboerskloof; mains R30; ☺ 7am-7pm Mon-Fri, 7.30am-7pm Sat, 8am-5pm Sun) Specialising in game meats, this deli-café prepares its own biltong (dried meat), bakes its own pies and offers a range of tempting preserves. Try the traditional venison *bobotie* with rice (R28) or venison sandwich (R24.50).

Vida e Café (Map p114; ☎ 021-426 0627; www.caffe .co.za; 34 Kloof St, Gardens; mains R20; ✆ 7.30am-5pm Mon-Fri) Capetonians have taken this home-grown chain's freshly brewed coffee, orange juice, Portuguese-style pastries and filled rolls to their hearts. It's ideal for breakfast or a fast lunch. There are also branches at the Waterfront (Map pp116–17), Thibault Square (Map pp110–11), Cavendish Centre (Map pp120–1) and at Green Point's Port-side complex (Map pp116–17).

RESTAURANTS

Aubergine (Map p114; ☎ 021-465 4909; www.aubergine .co.za; 39 Barnet St, Gardens; mains R65-125; ✆ 7-10pm Mon-Sat, noon-3pm Thu) At some Cape Town restaurants it's all about the wild party at-mosphere. Here, it's about the food, which is world class. Harald Bresselschmidt's in-novative dishes, such as worthog confit or salmon trout ice-cream, are on the à la carte menu, but we recommend indulging in the degustation menu (three/four/five courses R220/260/295) of old favourites such as prawn and fish sate on vegetable spaghetti or a sweet pumpkin soufflé. A sommelier is on hand to advise on wine and service is uniformly excellent.

Manna Epicure (Map p114; ☎ 021-426 2413; 151 Kloof St, Tamboerskloof; ✆ 8am-7pm Tue-Sat, 8am-3pm Sun) Join the style set for a deliciously simple breakfast or lunch at this trendy café, or come for late afternoon cocktails and tapas on their streetfront veranda.

Café Gainsbourg (Map p114; ☎ 021-422 1780; 64 Kloof St, Gardens; mains R40-50) This minimalist-decorated café has expanded its dining area and menu range. It's a great spot for any of the day's meals, with the lamb shank, burg-ers and salads especially recommended.

Greens (Map p114; ☎ 021-422 4415; 5 Park Lane, Gardens; ✆ 8am-5pm Mon, 8am-11pm Tue-Sun) This relaxed brasserie, with a spacious outdoor seating area, specialises in wood-fired pizza with Californian (topped with fresh greens), classic or gourmet toppings. There is also a good selection of wines served by the glass.

Kitama (Map p114; ☎ 021-422 1633; Rheede Street Mall, Gardens; mains R60; ✆ 6am-11pm Mon-Sat) The menu at this hip 'Eastern eatery' rambles around the Orient but the food on the

whole is tasty, beautifully presented and comes in giant portions.

Waterkant
The Cape Quarter continues to be the nexus around which this trendy, compact neighbourhood revolves.

CAFÉS & QUICK EATS
La Petite Tarte (Map pp116-17; ☎ 021-425 9077; Shop A11, Cape Quarter, 72 Waterkant St; mains R30-40; ✆ 8am-3pm Mon-Fri, 8am-2pm Sat) Fancy teas and delicious homemade savoury and sweet French-style tarts are served at this ador-able café on the Dixon St side of the Cape Quarter – it's a great spot for a pick-me-up or light meal.

Dutch (Map pp116-17; ☎ 021-425 0157; 34 Napier St; mains R30; ✆ 8am-5pm Mon-Fri, 8am-3pm Sat) A Euro vibe lingers over this popular, orange-coloured Waterkant café. People watch from their terrace while sipping a cappuc-cino or tucking into a toasted ciabatta.

RESTAURANTS
Anatoli (Map pp116-17; ☎ 021-419 2501; 24 Napier St, Green Point; dishes R60; ✆ 6.30pm-11.30pm Mon-Sat) This little piece of Istanbul in Cape Town has been serving its tasty meze (R15 to R28 a dish) both hot and cold for around 20 years. It remains a popular party spot, and on the weekends you might even be treated to a belly dance.

Andiamo (Map pp116-17; ☎ 021-421 3687; Shop C2, Cape Quarter, Waterkant St; mains R60; ✆ 8am-11pm) Andiamo's tables have colonised a large chunk of the Cape Quarter since our last visit, confirming its popularlity as one of the best casual eateries in the area. Their well-stocked deli is also worth a browse.

Tank (Map pp116-17 ☎ 021-419 0007; Shop B15, Cape Quarter, Waterkant St; mains R80-100; ✆ noon-3pm & 6-11pm Tue-Sun) A luminous bar, giant fish tank and sushi bar create the ideal envir-onment for the chic set. If you don't fancy the sushi, which isn't too bad, then there are some appealing Pacific Rim–style dishes, such as seared tuna.

Green Point & Waterfront
It's natural that you'll want to dine with an ocean view while in Cape Town. The Waterfront's plethora of restaurants and cafés fit the bill nicely although it's es-sentially a giant tourist trap. Better value

CAPE TOWN

and a less touristy dining experience is on offer a short walk away in Green Point and Mouille Point.

CAFÉS & QUICK EATS

Café Neo (Map pp116-17; ☎ 021-433 0849; South Seas, 129 Beach Rd, Mouille Point; mains R30-40; ☻ 7am-7pm) Our favourite seaside café has a relaxed vibe and a pleasingly contemporary design. Order your food and drinks at the counter before taking a seat on the deck overlooking the red-and-white painted lighthouse.

Gionvanni's Deli World (Map pp116-17; ☎ 021-434 6983; 103 Main Rd, Green Point; mains R20-30; ☻ 8.30am-9pm) Giovanni's can make up any sandwich you fancy – ideal for a picnic if you're on your way to the beach. The pavement café is a popular hangout; try the original Red Expresso, a shot of rooibos tea prepared like a regular expresso.

Melissa's (Map pp116-17; www.melissas.co.za; 1 Portside, cnr Upper Portswood & Main Rds, Green Point; mains R30; ☻ 7.30am-8pm Mon-Fri, 8am-8pm Sat & Sun) We love the latest in Melissa's chain of distinguished deli and café emporiums on the corner of the trendy Portside complex. Pay by the kilogram for the delicious buffets then browse the grocery shelves for picnic fare or gourmet gifts. Other branches are on the corner of Kildare and Main Rds, Newlands (Map pp120–1) and 94 Kloof St (Map p114).

RESTAURANTS

One.Waterfront (Map pp116-17; ☎ 021-418 0520; Cape Grace Hotel, West Quay, Waterfront; mains R70-100) Bruce Robertson is an accomplished chef and although it's the daring combinations of ingredients that catch the eye on the menu, the best dishes are those that keep it simple, such as the lovely fishcakes. The inventive vegetarian options are welcome, too.

Wakame (Map pp116-17; ☎ 021-433 2377; www.wakame.co.za; cnr Beach Rd & Surrey Place, Moullie Point; mains R70; ☻ noon-10pm) Tucking into Wakame's salt and pepper squid or sushi platter while gazing at the glorious coastal view is a wonderful way to pass an afternoon. Book for a balcony spot for sunset drinks. Downstairs is the Newport Market & Deli, another of Cape Town's cool deli-cafés.

Mano's (Map pp116-17; ☎ 021-434 1090; 39 Main Rd, Green Point; mains R40-80; ☻ noon-3pm Mon-Fri, 7-11pm Mon-Sat) A simple menu including Greek salad, fillet steak, egg and chips, and

chicken schnitzel might not set your mouth drooling, but the crowds that regularly dine here would beg to differ, proving you don't need to be fancy to be successful.

Willoughby & Co (Map pp116-17; ☎ 021-418 6115; Shop 6132 Victoria Wharf, Waterfront; mains R60-70; ☻ restaurant 11.30am-10.45pm, deli 9am-8.30pm) Huge servings of sushi are the standout from a good value fish-based menu at this casual eatery and deli, on the ground floor of Victoria Wharf. Commonly acknowledged as one of the better places to eat at the Waterfront.

Emily's (Map pp116-17; ☎ 021-421 1133; Shop 202, Clock Tower Centre, Waterfront; mains R80) Flamboyant is a word that could have been coined for Emily's, both for its décor and its approach to cooking, which can seem wildly reckless in its mixture of ingredients. Everything is beautifully presented and there's an epic wine list. The owners also run the café in the historic Clock Tower outside – a nice spot for a sundowner or snack.

Atlantic Coast

Along Sea Point's Main Rd and Regent St you can cruise a range of budget dining spots, such as **Ari's Souvlaki** (Map pp120-1; ☎ 021-439 6683; 83A Regent St), a honest Greek joint, or the 24-hour **Saul's** (Map pp120-1; ☎ 021-434 5404; 152 Main Rd), famed for its gut-busting burgers. In Camps Bay, a playground of the rich and beautiful, making a booking is essential if you wish to get a prime spot for sunset drinks and nibbles. Further south in Hout Bay try **Fish on the Rocks** (Map pp102-3; ☎ 021-790 0001; Harbour Rd; ☻ 10.30am-8.15pm) for cheap, tasty fish 'n' chips.

CAFÉS & QUICK EATS

Cedar (Map pp120-1; ☎ 021-433 2546; 100 Main Rd, Sea Point; mains R40; ☻ 11.30am-9.30pm) It's nothing fancy, but this family-run operation rates highly for its tasty range of meze and Middle Eastern dishes.

New York Bagels (Map pp120-1; ☎ 021-439 7523; 51 Regent Rd, Sea Point; mains R30-40; ☻ 7am-11pm) At this Sea Point institution you can browse the well-stocked deli or tempting food court. Put together a mix 'n' match meal of, say, a hot-beef-on-rye sandwich followed by freshly made waffles and fruit salad.

Sandbar (Map pp120-1; ☎ 021-438 8336; 31 Victoria Rd, Camps Bay; mains R30; ☻ 9.30am-10pm) One of Camps Bay's better value options is this less self-consciously fashionable café with street tables, serving good sandwiches and light meals.

RESTAURANTS

La Perla (Map pp120-1; ☎ 021-439 9538; cnr Church & Beach Rds; mains R70; ⊙ noon-11.30pm) Retro stylish La Perla has been a permanent fixture on the Sea Point promenade for decades. Enjoy something from the long menu of pasta, fish and meat dishes on the terrace shaded by stout palms, or retreat to the intimate bar.

Paranga (Map pp120-1; ☎ 021-438 0404; Shop 1, The Promenade, Victoria Rd, Camps Bay; mains R90) Paranga's success means it now sells its own chill-out CDs and branded range of clothing alongside its seafood, salads, burgers and sushi. The soft, cream-coloured furnishings and terrace make it one of the most pleasant places to dine on a very competitive strip.

Sea Point Gardens (Map pp120-1; ☎ 021-439 2820; 78 Regents Rd, Sea Point; 2/3 courses R99/129; ⊙ noon-10.30pm) Dine on dishes such as tuna carpaccio and sole with béarnaise sauce in the romantic courtyard garden of this 1919 villa that once was the official residence of Cape Town's mayor. After, head upstairs to their slinky cocktail lounge Asylumn (open 5pm to 2am).

Southern Suburbs

At Lower Main Rd in Observatory the menus are slanted towards the tastes and budgets of the resident student population. More upmarket restaurants can be found in and around Constantia's wineries. Kirstenbosch also has decent cafés in case you forget to pack your picnic basket.

CAFÉS & QUICK EATS

Gardener's Cottage (Map pp120-1; ☎ 021-689 3158; Montebello Craft Studios, 31 Newlands Ave, Newlands; mains R40; ⊙ 8am-4.30pm Tue-Sun) This cute café and tea garden in the grounds of the craft studios is worth visiting in its own right for the relaxed atmosphere and simple, hearty meals.

Kirstenbosch Tea Room (Map pp102-3; ☎ 021-797 4883; Kirstenbosch Botanical Gardens, Rhodes Dr, Newlands; mains R20-30) Fresh breads and cakes baked on the premises are available at this popular café at the top entrance to the gardens. For a more fancy meal on a crisp white table

cloth try the Silver Tree (☎ 021-762 9585) near the garden's main gate.

Café Ganesh (☎ 021-448 3435; 38B Trill Rd, Observatory; mains R30-40; ⊙ 6-11.30pm Mon-Sat) Sample pap and veg, grilled spingbok or lamb curry at this funky hang-out, where junkyard décor and matchbox label wallpaper create that chic-shack look.

RESTAURANTS

La Colombe (Map pp102-3; ☎ 021-794 2390; Constantia Uitsig, Spaanschemat River Rd; mains R90) Bookings are essential at this highlight of the Constantia dining scene. The shady garden setting is one of Cape Town's nicest and the service excellent, but its chef Franck Dangereux's fine touch on his Provençal-style dishes that really impresses at this hugely decadent restaurant.

River Café (Map pp102-3; ☎ 021-794 3010; Constantia Uitsig, Spaanschemat River Rd; mains R60) At the entrance to the Constantia Uitsig estate, this delightful and popular café serves big portions of food made with organic and free-range products. A booking is essential, especially for weekend brunch.

Jonkerhuis (Map pp102-3; ☎ 021-794 4255; Groot Constantia, Constantia; mains R80; ⊙ 10am-10pm Mon-Fri, 9am-10pm Sat, 9am-4pm Sun) A change of management has led to a more casual brasserie style at this atmospheric restaurant with its pleasant vine-shaded courtyard. Sample cured meats with a glass or two of the local wines or satisfy your sweet tooth with the desserts.

DRINKING

Cape Town didn't become known as the 'Tavern of the Seven Seas' for nothing. Head out on a Friday or Saturday night to Long St, the Waterkant or Camps Bay for an eye-opening experience of how the locals like to party. There are plenty of quieter places for a drink, too. Most bars open around 3pm and close after midnight, and much later Friday and Saturday. Alternative opening times are listed in the reviews following.

City Bowl & Waterkant

Marvel (Map pp110-11; ☎ 021-426 5880; 236 Long St, City Bowl; ⊙ 1pm-4am Mon-Sat) Stuffed as a sardine can, Marvel is a fantastic bar where cool kids of all colours rub shoulders (not to mention practically everything else). If you can, grab one of the cosy booths at the front, or linger on the pavement and enjoy the foot-tapping grooves from the DJ.

Gallery Bar (Map pp110-11; ☎ 021-423 2086; cnr Long & Pepper Sts, City Bowl) The chic urban black set gather beneath the Urban Chic Hotel at this sophisticated bar, with windows opening onto Long St and a nice line in cocktails.

Orchard Bank (Map pp110-11; www.orchardbank.co .za; 229B Long St, City Bowl) One of Long St's more interesting and laid-back venues, with a roster of events including stand-up comedy. The comfy sofas are a good place to put a dent into the jugs of cocktail mixes.

Nose Wine Bar (Map pp116-17; ☎ 021-425 2200; www.thenose.co.za; Cape Quarter, Dixon St, Waterkant) A first-class wine bar where you can sip your way around 38 of the Cape's best wines, with 12 changing on a monthly basis. It also serves excellent food and runs wine-tasting courses.

Caveau (Map pp110-11; ☎ 021-422 1367; www .caveau.co.za; Heritage Square, 92 Bree St; ☺ 7am-11.30pm Mon-Sat) A welcome addition to the handsome Heritage Square. It has a goodly selection of local drops, and the tapas dishes are tasty.

Café du Süd (Map pp110-11; ☎ 021-422 0500; 107-109 Loop St, City Bowl; ☺ 10am-11pm Mon-Sat) With its quirky retro furnishings (all for sale), Café du Süd is a mecca for the style set. The food is unmemorable but the drinks divine – great for afternoon tea or late-night cocktails.

Also worth trying are the old-style pub **Fireman's Arms** (☎ 021-419 1513; 25 Mechau St, City Bowl), and two stand-bys on Long St: **Jo'burg** (☎ 021-422 0142; 218 Long St, City Bowl), and **Cool Runnings** (☎ 021-426 6584; 227 Long St), which also has a branch in **Observatory** (☎ 021-448 7656; 96 Station St).

Gardens & Around

Relish (Map p114; ☎ 021-422 3584; 70 New Church St, Tamboerskloof; ☺ noon-2am Mon-Fri, 5pm-2am Sat & Sun) You'll get panoramic views off Table Mountain and Lion's Head from this trendy place, rising up three glass-fronted floors and with a wide outdoor deck. The food is good and during happy hour (6pm to 7pm) cocktails are only R12.

Café Vespa (Map p114; ☎ 021-426 5042; www.café vespa.com; 108 Kloof St, Tamboerskloof; ☺ 9am-midnight) As well as renting out Vespas (see p158), this hipsters' hangout does a mean line in

cocktails, coffee and tapas, all of which can be enjoyed on the terrace with a grandstand view of Table Mountain.

Planet (Map p114; ☎ 021-483 1000; Mount Nelson Hotel, 76 Orange St, Gardens) Cocktails and champers at the Mount Nelson's deliciously chic bar – who could resist?

Green Point & Waterfront

Alba Lounge (Map pp116-17; ☎ 021-425 3385; 1st fl Hildegards, Pierhead, Waterfront) Easily the most stylish place for cocktails at the Waterfront. The view across the harbour is seductive, the drinks inventive and there's a roaring fire in winter to add to that inner alcoholic glow.

Belthazar (Map pp116-17; ☎ 021-421 3753; Shop 153, Victoria Mall, Waterfront) Offering 600 different South African wines, 170-odd of which you can get by the (Riedel) glass! The restaurant specializes in top-class Karan beef and it also does plenty of seafood dishes.

Mitchell's Scottish Ale House & Brewery (Map pp116-17; ☎ 021-419 5074; www.mitchellsbreweries .co.za; East Pier Rd, Waterfront; ☺ 11am-2am) Check all airs and graces at the door of this traditional pub serving a variety of freshly brewed beers and good-value meals.

Buena Vista Social Café (Map pp116-17; ☎ 021-433 0611; Exhibition Bldg, 81 Main Rd, Green Point) They mix a nice mojito at this Cuban-themed bar and restaurant, taking its inspiration from the famous CD. Book a seat on the airy balcony and come on Sunday if you want to salsa dance.

Atlantic Coast

Café Caprice (Map pp120-1; ☎ 021-438 8315; 37 Victoria Rd, Camps Bay; ☺ 9am-2am) The bronzed and beautiful gather at this café-bar, which is as popular for breakfast as it is for sundowners. Grab a pavement table for the best view.

Ignite (Map pp120-1; ☎ 021-438 7717; 2nd fl, The Promenade, Victoria Rd, Camps Bay) New name and a slight makeover for this slick venue, with a broad terrace and dress circle views of the beach.

La Med (Map pp120-1; ☎ 021-438 5600; Glen Country Club, Victoria Rd, Clifton) This eternal al-fresco bar gets its cred from the killer view down the length of the Twelve Apostles. Sinking a sundowner here is a Cape Town ritual. Keep an eye out for the easily missed turn-off, on the way to Clifton from Camps Bay.

GAY & LESBIAN CAPE TOWN

Gay-friendly destinations hardly get more glam than Cape Town, and there are enough bars and clubs in the city's self-proclaimed gay village, the **Waterkant** (Map pp116–17), to please even the fussiest of queens. Apart from the Waterkant, a few venues along Sea Point's Main Rd (Map pp120–1) fly the rainbow flag. The beaches to head for are **Clifton No 3** (Map pp120–1) and **Sandy Bay** (Map pp102–3), the clothing-optional stretch of sand discreetly located near Llandudno Bay.

Check your travel calendar for the city's two main gay events – the Cape Town Pride Festival in February and the Mother City Queer Project dance event every December; see p142 for more details.

Most places of interest are clustered in a tight grid of streets in the Waterkant. **Cafe Manhattan** (Map pp116–17; ☎ 021-421 6666; 74 Waterkant St), generally credited with getting the Waterkant's gay scene up and running, is a friendly place to kick off your night. **Cruz** (Map pp116–17; ☎ 021-421 5401; www.cruzcapetown.co.za; 21B Somerset Rd) is the hot, glamour bar of the moment, although the less-glitzy **Bronx** (Map pp116–17; ☎ 021-419 9219; www.bronx.co.za; 35 Somerset Rd, Waterkant) remains popular and attracts a lively mixed crowd. Next door is the top dance club **Sliver** (Map pp116–17; ☎ 021-421 4798; www.sliver.co.za; 27 Somerset Rd, Waterkant; cover R20), a spacious, fun venue with a fairy-light festooned courtyard and rooftop chill out areas. If you're into leather and latex, head to **Bar Code** (Map pp116–17; ☎ 021-421 5305; www.leatherbar.co.za; 18 Cobern St).

Cape Town's lesbian scene is pretty low-profile, although there is a regular lesbian venue in the Waterkant now, **Lipstick Lounge** (☎ Map pp116–17; 082-738 3612; www.lipstickcapetown.co.za; 2 Lelie Lane, Waterkant) and the biweekly club **Lush** (Map pp116–17; ☎ 082-565 6174; www.lushcapetown .co.za) is held at Sliver (see above).

A new, larger venue for the cabaret and supper club **On Broadway** (p156) means it's more popular than ever – the resident artists are dynamic drag duo Mince.

The **Triangle Project** (☎ 021-448 3812; www.triangle.org.za) is the city's and South Africa's leading gay, lesbian and transgender resources centre. Their website has a host of useful info. For the latest on what's hot also check the *Pink Map*, updated annually; local listings magazine *Cape Etc*; and the website www.gaynetcapetown.co.za.

La Vie (Map pp120–1; ☎ 021-439 2061; 205 Beach Rd, Sea Point; ☼ 7.30am-midnight) One of the very few places where you can have anything from breakfast to late-night cocktails within sight of Sea Point promenade.

Southern Suburbs

Barristers (Map pp120–1; ☎ 021-674 1792; cnr Kildare Rd & Main St, Newlands; mains R70; ☼ 9.30am-10.30pm) Upmarket Newlands' favourite watering hole offers up a series of cosy rooms hung with an eye-catching assortment of items in ye-olde country pub style. Has a very decent menu, too.

Café Carte Blanche (Map pp120–1; ☎ 021-447 8717; 42 Trill Rd, Observatory) Candles, cosy nooks and crannies and avant-garde music set the scene at this tiny café-bar, a favourite with the Obs alternative set.

A Touch of Madness (Map pp120–1; ☎ 021-448 2266; www.caféatom.co.za; 12 Nuttal Rd, Observatory; ☼ noon-late Mon-Sat, 7pm-late Sun) This long-running bar and restaurant offers an ec-

lectic art-house atmosphere, dressed up in purple with lace trimmings. Wannabe poets should check out the Monday night open-mike poetry fests.

ENTERTAINMENT

There are cinemas and theatres aplenty in Cape Town, while live music spans the gamut from classical to rock via jazz and marimba. Check the weekly arts guide in the **Mail & Guardian** (www.chico.mweb.co.za/art /daily/menu-guide.htm) to find out what's going on, and the Tonight section in the **Cape Argus** (tonight.co.za). The bimonthly magazine **Cape etc** (www.capeetc.com) is also good for listings.

You can book seats for practically anything with **Computicket** (☎ 083-915 8000; www .computicket.com). There are outlets in the Golden Acre Centre (Map pp110–11), in the Gardens Centre (Map p114), in Sea Point's Adelphi Centre (Map pp120–1) and at the Waterfront (Map pp116–17).

Cinemas

Cape Town's cinemas show all the latest international releases. The big multiplexes can be found in Victoria Wharf at the Waterfront (Map pp116–17), Cavendish Sq (Map pp120–1) and Canal Walk (Map pp102–3).

Labia (Map p114; ☎ 021-424 5927; www.labia.co.za; 68 Orange St, Gardens; tickets R25) Together with the two-screen Labia on Kloof (Map p114; ☎ 021-424 5727) around the corner, Labia is the best cinema for 'mainstream alternative' films. It's named after the old Italian ambassador and local philanthropist Count Labia. Their African Screen programme is one of the rare opportunities you'll have to see locally made films.

Cavendish Nouveau (Map pp120–1; ☎ 0861-300 444; Cavendish Sq, Claremont; tickets Tue R18, Wed-Mon R35) With its sibling Cinema Nouveau Waterfront (Map pp116–17), this is a classy multiplex showcasing the best of independent and art-house movies. The facilities are good, but check first whether the same movies are playing at the Labia since tickets are much cheaper there.

Live Music

CLASSICAL

The incredibly active **Cape Town Philharmonic** (www.cpo.org.za) leads the way on the Mother City's classical music scene, performing concerts mainly at **City Hall** (Map pp110–11; ☎ 021-410 9809; Darling St, City Bowl) as well as at Artscape, the Waterfront and elsewhere around the Cape. It also teams up with **Cape Town Opera** (www.capetownopera.co.za) and **Cape Town City Ballet** (www.capetowncityballet .org.za), both of whom usually perform at Artscape.

Artscape (Map pp110–11; ☎ 021-410 9800; www.art scape.co.za; 1-10 DF Malan St, Foreshore) Consisting of three different-sized auditoria, this performing-arts complex is the hub of classical and theatrical performances in Cape Town. Walking around this area at night is not recommended; book ahead for a non-shared taxi since there are none to be found on the streets. There's plenty of secure parking.

JAZZ

Green Dolphin (Map pp116–17; ☎ 021-421 7471; www .greendolphin.co.za; Waterfront; cover R25) There's a consistently good line-up of artists at this upmarket jazz venue and restaurant (serving decent food). Shows kick off at 8.15pm daily – if you don't mind an obstructed view, the cover charge is R20.

Manenberg's Jazz Café (Map pp116–17; ☎ 021-421 5639; Clock Tower Centre, Waterfront; cover R30-80) Swing to jazz and African jive at this famed jazz club that seems to have survived its move to the Waterfront. On Friday and Saturday it's free to see the bands playing the sundowner set from 5pm to 7pm, but a cover charge kicks in later.

Marimba (Map pp110–11; ☎ 021-418 3366; www .marimbasa.com; Cape Town International Convention Centre, City Bowl; diners R20, nondiners R30) Yes, they do have a marimba band playing occasionally at this slick Afro-chic venue that's part of the Cape Town International Convention Centre, as well as a packed schedule of other jazz artists. The food is good and the music sets start at 8pm.

West End (Map pp102–3; ☎ 021-637 9132; Cine 400 Bldg, College Rd, Ryelands Estate, Athlone; cover R30; ☺ 8pm-late Fri & Sat) Mainstream jazz is the name of the game here. This is one of Cape Town's top venues, attracting a well-heeled clientele and top performers. There's plenty of security, if you drive.

ROCK/AFRICAN

Mercury Live (Map p114; ☎ 021-465 2106; www.mer curyl.co.za; 43 De Villiers St, Zonnebloem; cover R20-40) Cape Town's premier rock venue plays host to top South African bands and overseas visitors. The sound quality is good and if you don't like the band, there's always the DJ bar Mercury Lounge below and the Shack bar next door.

Drum Café (☎ 021-462 1064; www.thedrumcafe .com) At the time of research this café had yet to confirm its new venue. Check the website or call for details.

For African bands head to these long-running restaurants:

Mama Africa (Map pp110–11; ☎ 021-426 1017; 178 Long St, City Bowl; diners R10 nondiners R15; ☺ 7pm-2am Mon-Sat)

Marco's African Place (Map pp110–11; ☎ 021-423 5412; 15 Rose Lane, Bo-Kaap; cover R10; ☺ noon-11pm)

Nightclubs

The major nightclubs are concentrated in the City Bowl around Long St and in the Waterkant. The big nights are Wednesday, Friday and Saturday.

Club Galaxy (Map pp102-3; ☎ 021-637 9132; College Rd, Ryelands Estate, Athlone; cover R30) Long-time Cape Flats dance venue where you can get down to R&B, hip-hop and live bands with a black and coloured crowd. The equally legendary West End jazz venue is next door.

Hemisphere (Map pp110-11; ☎ 021-421 0581; www .hemisphere.org.za; 31st fl, ABSA Centre, Riebeeck St, City Bowl; cover R50; ☷ 9pm-3am Tue-Sat) Twinkling views of the city are part of the deal at this super-stylish club atop the ABSA Centre. It's real velvet rope and glamour model stuff, so dress to the nines and pack that shoulder chip of attitude.

Mian Mian (Map pp110-11; ☎ 021-422 5823; 196½ Long St, City Bowl; cover R30) Lofty palms, twinkling fairy lights and a spacious bar and dance space are hidden down a narrow alley. Very hip, even though the wannabe crowd aren't always as cool as they think they are.

Opium (Map pp116-17; ☎ 021-425 4010; www .opium.co.za; 6 Dixon St, Waterkant; cover R40) With three dance floors, big bars, plush décor and a too-cool-for-school attitude it's no surprise that Opium scores highly on the Capetonian clubbing scene. Come to see model types practice their catwalk strut and pout.

Rhodes House (Map pp110-11; ☎ 021-424 8844; www.rhodeshouse.com; 60 Queen Victoria St, City Bowl; cover R50) Not so hot as it once was, this luxurious venue spread over a grand old house can still provide a good dance night out. Thursday is R&B night.

Snap (Map pp110-11; ☎ 083-940 3983; 6 Pepper St, City Bowl; cover R20) The Cape Flats comes to the city at this urban African club with a welcoming, predominantly black audience. Dance to music from across Africa.

Zula Sound Bar (Map pp110-11; ☎ 021-424 2442; 194 Long St, City Bowl; cover R20) Hosts an interesting range of events including live bands, DJs and even open-mike poetry sessions. Their long balcony is the place to watch Long St go by.

Sports

CRICKET

Newlands Cricket Ground (Map pp120-1; ☎ 021-657 3300, ticket hotline 021-657 2099; Camp Ground Rd, Newlands) Venue for all international matches. The season runs from September to March with the day/night matches drawing the biggest crowds. Grab a spot on the grass bank to soak up the festive atmosphere. Tickets cost around R50 for local matches and up to R200 for internationals.

FOOTBALL

With tickets costing just R20, attending the footy in Cape Town is not only cheap but also a hugely fun and loud night out, with Capetonian supporters taking every opportunity to blow their plastic trumpets. The season runs from August to May. Ajax Cape Town, affiliated with the Dutch club Ajax Amsterdam, sometimes plays matches at Newlands Rugby Stadium (below). Matches are also played at Green Point Stadium (Map pp116–17) off Beach Rd in Green Point, and Athlone Stadium (Map pp102–3), home to the team Santos, off Klipfontein Rd in Athlone. Tickets can be purchased through **Computicket** (☎ 021-918 8910; www.computicket.com).

RUGBY

Newlands Rugby Stadium (Map pp120-1; ☎ 021-659 4600; www.wprugby.com; Boundary Rd, Newlands) This hallowed ground of South African rugby is home to the Stormers. Tickets for Super 12 games cost at least R85, for international matches around R325.

Theatre, Cabaret & Comedy

What Cape Town's theatre scene lacks in size it certainly makes up for in ambition. There's often something interesting to catch beyond the blockbusters that check into Artscape (opposite), and the **Cape Town International Convention Centre** (Map pp110-11; ☎ 410 5000; www.cticc.co.za; Convention Sq, 1 Lower Long St, Foreshore). There isn't a dedicated venue for comedy in town at present but there are plenty of good comedians and shows do regularly happen at places such as On Broadway, the Obz Café and **Sobhar** (Map pp120-1; ☎ 021-674 3377; www.sobhar.co.za; 1 Letterstedt House, Main Rd, Newlands).

Baxter Theatre (Map pp120-1; ☎ 021-685 7880; www.baxter.co.za; Main Rd, Rondebosch) The three venues at this landmark theatre in the Southern Suburbs cover everything from kids' shows to Zulu dance spectaculars.

Obz Café (Map pp120-1; ☎ 021-448 5555; www .obzcafé.co.za; 115 Lower Main Rd, Observatory; cover R20-50) As if the human theatre of Lower Main Rd wasn't enough, inside this spacious café-bar is a separate performance space where you can catch all manner of shows, including comedy and cabaret.

On Broadway (Map pp110-11; ☎ 424 0250; www .onbroadway.co.za; 88 Shortmarket St, City Bowl; tickets R70-75; ◯ 8.30pm) This is a hugely popular cabaret and supper venue, so book ahead, especially for resident drag and comedy duo, Mince, who strut their glamourous stuff Sunday and Monday nights.

Independent Armchair Theatre (Map pp120-1; ☎ 021-447 1514; www.armchairtheatre.co.za; 135 Lower Main Rd, Observatory) Theatre-cum-lounge bar with an eclectic range of events, including comedy, short dramas and band gigs. On Monday night see a movie and eat pizza for R30; doors open 8pm, movie starts 9pm.

SHOPPING

Bring an empty bag because chances are that you'll be leaving Cape Town laden with local booty. Shops in the city centre and the Waterfront stock most things you'll need, but if you hunger for a suburban mall, visit one of the following:

Canal Walk (Map pp102-3; ☎ 0860-101 165; www .canalwalk.co.za; Century Blvd, Century City, Milnerton; ◯ 9am-9pm) The largest mall on the continent, about 5km north of the city centre.

Cavendish Sq (Map pp120-1; ☎ 021-671 8042; www.cavendish.co.za; Cavendish St, Claremont; ◯ 9am-6pm Mon-Thu, 9am-9pm Fri, 9am-6pm Sat, 10am-4pm Sun) A stylish mall.

Gardens Centre (Map p114; Mill St, Gardens) Another handy central shopping complex.

The city centre is bursting with interesting galleries (see opposite) and antique shops: head to Long St and Church St, where a small antiques market happens along the pedestrianised section from 9am to 4pm Monday to Saturday. For crafts and souvenirs browse the markets:

Green Point Stadium (Map pp116-17; Western Blvd, Green Point; ◯ 8.30am-6pm Sun) Outside the stadium.

Greenmarket Sq (p109; cnr Shortmarket & Burg Sts, City Bowl; ◯ 9am-4pm Mon-Sat)

Hout Bay (Map pp102-3; Baviaanskloof Rd, Hout Bay; ◯ 10am-5pm Sun)

Khayelitsha Craft Market (p165; ☎ 021-361 2904; www.stmichaels.org.za; St Michael's Church, Ncumo Rd, Harare, Khayelitsha; ◯ 9am-4pm Mon-Sat) A great place to look for interesting souvenirs.

Waterfront Craft Market (☎ 021-408 7842; Dock Rd, Waterfront) Also known as the Blue Shed.

Crafts

There are craft shops scattered all over town but few of the traditional African items come from the Cape Town area itself. Great buys include the local township-produced items, such as beadwork dolls, toys made from recycled tin cans and wire sculptures.

Africa Nova (Map pp110-11; ☎ 021-425 5123; Cape Quarter, 72 Waterkant St, Waterkant) A stylish collection of contemporary African textiles, art and craft (including printed fabrics), jewellery and pottery.

African Image (Map pp110-11; ☎ 021-423 8385; www.african-image.co.za; cnr Church & Burg Sts, City Bowl) Fab range of ancient African artefacts and a lot of township crafts here, as well as wildly patterned shirts.

Imagenius (Map pp110-11 ☎ 021-423 7870; www .imagenius.co.za; 117 Long St, City Bowl) A treasure trove of modern African design offering an eclectic range, including ceramics, beachware, jewellery and super-cute buckskin baby booties. There's stylish gift cards, boxes and wrapping paper too.

Monkeybiz (Map pp110-11; ☎ 021-426 0145; www .monkeybiz.co.za; 65 Rose St, Bo-Kaap) Brilliant beaded products, including long-legged dolls, animals and bags, all made by women in the townships, with the profits going to a HIV/AIDS clinic (held upstairs every Friday).

Montebello (Map pp120-1; ☎ 021-685 6445; www .montebello.co.za; 31 Newlands Ave, Newlands) Worthy development project promoting good local design and creating jobs in the craft industry. On Monday to Friday you can visit the artists studios.

Pan African Market (Map pp110-11; ☎ 021-426 4478; www.panafrican.co.za; 76 Long St, City Bowl) A microcosm of the continent with a bewildering range of art and craft as well as a cheap café and music store packed into its three floors. On the 3rd floor you'll find Wola Nani (☎ 021-423 7385; www.wola nani.co.za), a nongovernment organisation addressing the needs of those infected with HIV/AIDS. Buy one of the colourful label-covered papier-mâché bowls or photo frames.

Red Shed Craft Workshop (Map pp116-17; ☎ 021-408 7847; Victoria Wharf, Waterfront; ◯ 9am-9pm Mon-Sat, 10am-9pm Sun) This permanent market focuses on local crafts including ceramics and textiles. Look for the delicate jewel-

---

GALLERY CRAWL

There are some talented artists at work in Cape Town and a day spent exploring the following centrally located galleries is a rewarding experience. Unless otherwise mentioned, opening hours are 10am to 5pm Monday to Friday and 10am to 3pm Saturday.

AVA Gallery (Map pp110-11; ☎ 021-424 7436; www.ava.co.za; 35 Church St, City Bowl) Exhibition space for the nonprofit Association for Visual Arts (AVA), which shows some interesting work by local artists.

Bell-Roberts Art Gallery (Map pp110-11; ☎ 021-422 1100; www.bell-roberts.com; 89 Bree St, City Bowl) A move to larger, light-filled premises has allowed this gallery and art-book publisher wider scope for its exhibitions.

Michael Stevenson Gallery (Map pp116-17; ☎ 021-421 2575; www.michaelstevenson.com; Hill House, De Smidt St, Waterkant) One of the city's best exhibitions spaces. The catalogues, art books and posters are a good buy if you can't afford the art itself.

Photographers Gallery (Map pp110-11; ☎ 021-422 2762; www.erdmanncontemporary.co.za; 63 Short-market St, City Bowl; ☜ 10am-5pm Tue-Fri, 10am-1pm Sat) As well as the fine work of many top South African photographers, you'll also find pieces here by graphic artists Lien Botha and Conrad Botes.

What If The World (Map pp110-11; ☎ 021-461 2573; www.whatiftheworld.com; 11 Hope St, City Bowl; ☜ 10am-6pm Mon-Sat) Edgy little gallery and design collective that has exhibitions by emerging artists, and quirky events.

---

lery of Get Wired and the colourful textile products of Ikamva Labantu.

Streetwires (Map pp110-11; ☎ 021-426 2475; www.streetwires.co.za; 77/79 Shortmarket St, Bo-Kaap) Watch wire sculpture artists at work at this social upliftment project for young blacks and coloureds. Stocks an amazing range, including working radios and artier products such as the lovely beaded Nguni Cow sculptures.

Fashion & Outdoor Gear

Cape Union Mart Adventure Centre (Map pp116-17; ☎ 021-425 4559; www.capeunionmart.co.za; Quay 4, Waterfront) Set yourself up for everything from a hike up Table Mountain to a Cape-to-Cairo safari at this impressive outdoors shop. There are many other branches around the city, including at the Gardens Centre.

Sun Goddess (Map pp116-17; ☎ 021-421 7620; www.sungoddess.co.za; Shop 230, Victoria Wharf, Waterfront) Fun and contemporary clothes inspired by traditional African culture, using daring design combinations with modern fabrics and embellishments.

Young Designers Emporium (Map pp120-1; ☎ 021-683 6177; Shop F50, Cavendish Sq, Cavendish St, Claremont) A bit of a jumble, but you'll most likely find something groovy for both him and her among the street clothes and accessories by new South African designers.

Other

African Music Store (Map pp110-11; ☎ 021-426 0857; 134 Long St, City Bowl) The prices are higher than in the chain CD shops, but the range of local music, including all top jazz, kwaito and dance and trance recordings, can't be surpassed, and staff are knowledgeable about the music scene.

Vaughan Johnson's Wine & Cigar Shop (Map pp116-17; ☎ 021-419 2121; www.vaughanjohnson.com; Dock Rd, Waterfront) Selling practically every South African wine you could wish to buy (plus a few more from other countries). They're open on Sunday, unlike most wine sellers.

GETTING THERE & AWAY
Air

Cape Town International Airport (Map pp102-3; ☎ 021-937 1200; www.airports.co.za) is 20km east of the city centre, approximately 20 minutes' drive depending on traffic. There is a tourist information office and Internet access at both the international and domestic terminals.

For domestic flights it's always cheaper to book and pay on the Internet. Apart from **South African Airways** (SAA; ☎ 0860-359 722; www.flysaa.com) there are two budget airlines operating out of Cape Town: **Kulula.com** (☎ 0861-585 852; www.kulula.com) and **1time** (☎ 0861-345 345; www.1time.co.za). All three fly to the major South African cities. The following are the cheapest one-way fares you might pay from Cape Town to Durban (R502); East London (R593); Jo'burg (R694); Port Elizabeth (R718); and Upington (R712). For details on other airlines, see p622.

International airlines with offices in Cape Town:

Air Mauritius (Map pp120–1; ☎ 021-671 5225; www.airmauritius.com; Sanclare Bldg, 21 Dreyer St, Claremont)

Air Namibia (Map pp102–3; ☎ 021-936 2755; www.airnamibia.com.na; Cape Town International Airport)

KLM (Map pp120–1; ☎ 086-024 7747; www.klm.co.za; Slade House, Boundary Terraces, 1 Mariendahl Lane, Newlands)

Lufthansa (Map pp102–3; ☎ 086-184 2538; Cape Town International Airport)

Malaysia Airlines (Map pp110–11; ☎ 021-419 8010; fax 419 7017; 8th fl, Safmarine House, 22 Riebeeck St, City Bowl)

Singapore Airlines (Map pp120–1; ☎ 021-674 0601; 3rd fl, Sanclaire, 21 Dreyer St, Claremont)

South African Airways (SAA; Map pp102–3; ☎ 021-936 1111; www.flysaa.com; Cape Town International Airport)

Virgin Atlantic (Map pp102–3; ☎ 021-934 9000; Cape Town International Airport)

Bus

Four major long-distance bus lines operate out of Cape Town. Their booking offices and main arrival and departure points are at the Merriman Sq end of Cape Town train station (City Bowl).

Greyhound (☎ 021-505 6363; www.greyhound.co.za)

Intercape Mainliner (☎ 021-380 4400; www.intercape.co.za)

SA Roadlink (☎ 021-425 0203; www.saroadlink.co.za).

Translux (☎ 021-449 3333; www.translux.co.za)

For more information on bus routes and fares, and the Baz Bus, see p633.

Car & Motorcycle

Cape Town has an excellent road and freeway system that, outside the late-afternoon rush hour (starting at around 4pm), carries surprisingly little traffic. The only downside is getting used to the sometimes erratic breaking of road rules by fellow drivers.

Major local and international car and motorcycle hire companies in Cape Town:

Around About Cars (Map pp110–11; ☎ 021-422 4022; www.aroundaboutcars.com; 20 Bloem St, City Bowl)

Avis (Map pp110–11; ☎ 086-102 1111; www.avis.co.za; 123 Strand St, City Bowl)

Budget (Map pp110–11; ☎ 086-001 6622; www.budget.co.za; 120 Strand St, City Bowl)

Café Vespa (Map p114; ☎ 083-448 2626, 083-646 6616; www.cafévespa.com; 108 Kloof St, Tamboerskloof; ⏱ 9am-midnight) New 150cc Vespas from R110 a day.

Hertz (Map pp110–11; ☎ 021-400 9650; www.hertz.co.za; cnr Loop & Strand Sts, City Bowl)

Le Cap Motorcycle Hire (Map p114; ☎ 021-423 0823; www.lecapmotorcyclehire.co.za; 43 New Church St, Tamboerskloof; ⏱ 9am- 5pm Mon-Fri, 10am-1pm Sat)

Minibus Taxi

Most long-distance minibus taxis start picking up passengers in townships, especially Langa and Nyanga, perhaps also making a trip into Cape Town train station if they need more people. The townships are not great places to be wandering around in the early hours of the morning so *do not* go into them without good local knowledge; it's preferable to go with a reliable local guide. Langa is relatively safe and long-distance taxis leave from the Langa shopping centre early in the morning. A local-area minibus taxi from Cape Town train station to Langa costs about R5.

The price difference these days with regular buses is negligible, and given that a minibus taxi journey will take longer, is more uncomfortable and far more potentially dangerous (because of driver fatigue), we don't recommend them for long-distance journeys.

Train

All trains leave from the main Cape Town train station. It can take a long time to get to the front of the queue at the **booking office** (☎ 021-449 4596; ⏱ 7.30am-4.55pm Mon-Fri, 7.30-10.30am Sat).

For detailed information about train routes and fares, see p643.

GETTING AROUND
To/From the Airport

Both **Backpacker Bus** (☎ 021-447 4991, 082-809 9185; www.backpackerbus.co.za) and **Homeland Shuttle & Tours** (Map pp110-11; ☎ 021-426 0294, 083-265 6661; www.homeland.co.za; 305 Long St, City Bowl) pick up from accommodation in the city and offer airport transfers for R90 per person (R120 between 5pm and 8am).

Expect to pay around R200 for a non-share taxi; the officially authorised airport taxi company is **Touch Down Taxis** (☎ 021-919 4659). If there are four of you, consider making a booking with Rikkis (opposite) which charges R125 for hire of the minivan cabs.

All the major hire car companies (see left) have desks at the airport. Driving along the N2 into the city centre from the airport usually takes 15 to 20 minutes, although during rush hours (7am to 9am and 4.30pm to 6.30pm) this can extend up to an hour. There is a petrol station just outside the airport, handy for refilling the tank before drop-off.

Bicycle & Scooter

The Cape Peninsula is a great place to explore by bicycle, but there are many hills, and distances can be long – it's nearly 70km from the centre to Cape Point. Unfortunately, you aren't supposed to take bicycles on suburban trains. For bicycle hire, try Downhill Adventures (p123), Atlantic Tourist Information Centre (p106) or Homeland Shuttle & Tours (opposite).

Bus

For local bus services the main station is the **Golden Acre Terminal** (Map pp110-11; Grand Parade, City Bowl). From here **Golden Arrow** (☎ 0800-656 463; www.gabs.co.za) buses run, with most services stopping early in the evening. Buses are most useful for getting along the Atlantic Coast from the city centre to Hout Bay (trains service the suburbs to the east of Table Mountain). When travelling short distances, most people wait at the bus stop and take either a bus or a shared taxi, whichever arrives first. A tourist-friendly alternative is the City Sightseeing Cape Town bus service (p140).

Destinations and off-peak fares (applicable from 8am to 4pm) from the city include the Waterfront (R3), Sea Point (R3), Kloof Nek (R3), Camps Bay (R4.50) and Hout Bay (R7). Peak fares are about 30% higher. If you're using a particular bus regularly, it's worth buying 'clipcards', with 10 discounted trips.

Minibus Taxi

Minibus taxis cover most of the city with an informal network of routes and are a cheap way of getting around. Useful routes are from Adderley St (opposite the Golden Acre Centre) to Sea Point along Main Rd (R3) and up Long St to Kloof Nek (R2).

The main stop is on the upper deck of the main train station, accessible from a walkway in the Golden Acre Centre or from stairways on Strand St. It's well organised, and finding the right stop is easy. Anywhere else, you just hail minibus taxis from the side of the road and ask the driver where they're going. For minibus taxi etiquette, see p640.

Rikki

A cross between a taxi and a shared taxi are the tiny minivans of **Rikkis** (☎ 021-418 6713; www.rikkis.co.za; ☷ 7am-7pm Mon-Fri, 8am-4pm Sat). They can be booked or hailed on the street and travel within a 5km radius of the city centre. A trip from the main train station to Tamboerskloof costs R10; to Camps Bay is R15. A Rikki from the City Bowl to Kirstenbosch Botanical Gardens or Hout Bay costs R70 for the first four people. Rikkis also operate out of Simon's Town (☎ 021-786 2136); they meet all trains to Simon's Town and go to Boulders.

Although cheap, Rikkis may not be the quickest way to get around, as there is usually a certain amount of meandering as passengers are dropped off, and they are notoriously slow to turn up to a booking.

Taxi

It's worth considering taking a nonshared taxi late at night or if you're in a group. Rates are about R10 per km. There's a taxi rank at the Adderley St end of the Grand Parade in the city, or call **Marine Taxi** (☎ 021-434 0434), **SA Cab** (☎ 0861-172 222; www.sacab.co.za) or **Unicab Taxis** (☎ 021-447 4402).

Train

Metro commuter trains are a handy way to get around, although there are few (or no) trains after 6pm Monday to Friday and after noon on Saturday. For information contact **Cape Metro Rail** (☎ 0800-656 463; www.capemetrorail.co.za).

Metro trains have 1st- and economy-class carriages only. The difference in price and comfort is negligible, although you'll find the 1st-class compartments to be safer on the whole.

The most important line for visitors is the Simon's Town line, which runs through Observatory and then around the back of Table Mountain through upper-income white suburbs, such as Newlands, down to Muizenberg and along the False Bay coast. These trains run at least every hour from around 5am to 7.30pm Monday to Friday (to 6pm on Saturday), and from 7.30am to

6.30pm on Sunday. (Rikkis meet all trains and go to Boulders.) On some of these trains you'll find Biggsy's, a restaurant carriage and rolling wine bar. There's a small extra charge to use it.

Metro trains run some way out of Cape Town, to Strand on the eastern side of False Bay, and into the Winelands to Stellenbosch and Paarl. They are the cheapest and easiest means of transport to these areas; security is best at peak times.

Some economy/first-class fares include Observatory (R4.2/5.50), Muizenberg (R5.50/8.50), Simon's Town (R7.30/12), Paarl (R8.50/14.50) and Stellenbosch (R7.50/12).

AROUND CAPE TOWN

The communities hugging the coastal strip of the Cape Peninsula around False Bay – Muizenberg, Kalk Bay and Simon's Town – are villages compared to Cape Town proper. Here you'll also find the natural wonders of the Rondevlei Nature Reserve at Zeekoevlei; the penguins at Boulders; the Solole Game Reserve and Imhoff Farm near Kommetjie on the Atlantic Coast of the southern peninsula; and the dramatic expanses of the Cape of Good Hope, part of the Table Mountain National Park (p107).

The townships of the Cape Flats, spreading east from Table Mountain, are best visited on a day trip from Cape Town, although we'd recommend you stay at one of the B&Bs there to experience the full extent of *ubuntu* (Xhosa hospitality).

RONDEVLEI NATURE RESERVE

This small **nature reserve** (Map pp102-3; ☎ 021-706 2404; Fisherman's Walk Rd, Zeekoevlei; adult/child R10/5; ☺ 7.30am-5pm Mar-Nov, 7.30am-7pm Mon-Fri, 7.30am-7pm Sat & Sun Dec-Feb) covers a picturesque wetlands with native marsh and dune vegetation. Hippos were reintroduced to the reserve in 1981 and there are now eight of them, but it is very unlikely you will spot them unless you stay overnight – for details contact Imvubu Nature Tours (p141) which is based at the reserve. Guided walks are available and you can spot some 230 species of birds from the waterside trail, two viewing towers and hides. You will need a car to get here; follow the M5 from the Foreshore.

MUIZENBERG & KALK BAY

A popular holiday resort in the early-20th century, **Muizenberg**, 25km south of the City Bowl, is on the up again after a period in the economic doldrums. Properties are being renovated and new cafés and restaurants are opening. Muizenberg's broad white beach is popular with surfers – hire boards or get lessons from Gary's Surf School (p138). The beach – along which you'll see the colourfully painted and much-photographed Victorian bathing huts – shelves gently and the sea is generally safer (and warmer) here than elsewhere along the peninsula. There's plenty of parking, and a pleasant **coastal walk** from the handsome train station to the neighbouring suburb of **St James**, where you'll find a tidal pool that's good for splashing in with the kids.

Next along the coast is **Kalk Bay**, where the attractive fishing harbour is at its most picturesque in the late morning when the community's few remaining fishing boats pitch up with their daily catch, and a lively quayside market ensues. For an insight into the lives of the Kalk Bay's fisher folk sign up for a local walking tour (p141).

For more information go to **Cape Town Tourism Muizenberg** (☎ 021-788 6176; the Pavilion, Beach Rd, Muizenberg; ☺ 8am-5.30pm Mon-Fri, 9am-1pm Sat & Sun Oct-Mar, 8.30am-5pm Mon-Fri, 9am-noon Apr-Sep).

Sights
JOAN ST LEGER LINDBERGH ARTS CENTRE
The great granddaughter of the founder of the *Cape Times*, Joan St Leger was an artist and poet. She bequeathed her Sir Herbert Baker–designed home and the adjoining properties to the **Joan St Leger Lindbergh Arts Foundation** (☎ 021-788 2795; www.muizenberg.info/jsllaf.asp; 18 Beach Rd, Muizenberg; ☺ 8.30am-4.30pm Mon-Fri). There are art displays, a café, a wonderful reference library and a gallery of photos of how Muizenberg once looked. Concerts are regularly held on the Thursday morning at the start of the month (R40) and Wednesday evening at the end of the month (R90 to R110).

RHODES COTTAGE MUSEUM
Cecil Rhodes' pretty cottage is now the engaging **Rhodes Cottage Museum** (☎ 021-788 1816;

246 Main Rd, St James; admission by donation; 🕙 10am-4pm) where you can find out all about the founder of De Beers, who died here in 1902; for more on Rhodes, see p527. Yet another of Sir Herbert Baker's designs, the cottage has particularly pleasant gardens, which are a lovely spot to rest and to spot whales from during the season.

NATALE LABIA MUSEUM

Call ahead to see whether anything is showing at this charming Venetian-style **mansion** (☎ 021-788 4106; www.museums.org.za/natale; 192 Main Rd, Muizenberg; admission R3; 🕙 Mon by appointment only), a satellite of the South African National Gallery. The house still belongs to the family of the Italian Count Natale Labia

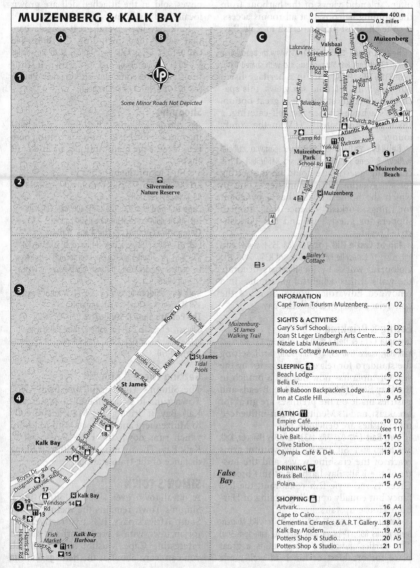

MUIZENBERG & KALK BAY

0 — 400 m
0 — 0.2 miles

Some Minor Roads Not Depicted

Silvermine Nature Reserve

Muizenberg Beach

Bailey's Cottage

Muizenberg-St James Walking Trail

St James Tidal Pools

St James

Kalk Bay

False Bay

Fish Market

Kalk Bay Harbour

who had it built in 1930 when it served as the Italian Legation.

Sleeping

Blue Baboon Backpackers Lodge (☎ 021-788 3645, 083-641 6808; 136 Main Rd, Kalk Bay; s/d with shared bathroom R120/220) Above the Olympia Bakery & Deli, this simply furnished budget lodge offers splendid views of the harbour from the running balcony that all rooms access. It's the cheapest place to crash in Kalk Bay, so book ahead.

Beach Lodge (☎ 021-788 1771; www.thebeachlodge .co.za; 13-19 York Rd, Muizenberg; s/d with shared bathroom R150/260; P   🖳) Set in a heritage-listed building with splendid sea views, this spacious budget guesthouse is a great option. There's a huge kitchen for self-catering, a small gym and satellite TV in the comfy lounge.

Bella Ev (☎ 021-788 1293; www.capestay.co.za/bella %2Dev/; 8 Camp Rd, Muizenberg; s/d R480/580) This charming guesthouse could be the setting for an Agatha Christie mystery, one in which the home's owner has a penchant for things Turkish – hence the Ottoman slippers for guests' use and the Turkish-style breakfast.

Inn at Castle Hill (☎ 021-788 2554; www.castle hill.co.za; 37 Gatesville Rd, Kalk Bay; s/d R350/640; P) Colourful works by local artists decorate the walls at this delightful guesthouse in a renovated Edwardian home. Some of the convivial rooms overlook the bay.

Eating & Drinking

Olympia Café & Deli (☎ 021-788 6396; 134 Main Rd, Kalk Bay; mains R40-75; ⏰ 7am-9pm) Still setting the standard for relaxed rustic cafés by the sea, Olympia has now opened a branch in the City Bowl (Map pp110–11). Breads and pastries made on the premises are great for breakfast, and its Mediterranean-influenced main dishes are delicious, too.

Live Bait (☎ 021-788 4133; Kalk Bay Harbour, Kalk Bay; mains R60) Sit practically within arms reach of the crashing waves and the bustle of the Kalk Bay harbour at this breezy, Greek-island-style fish restaurant, the less fancy but equally appealing sibling of Harbour House upstairs.

Empire Café (☎ 021-788 1250; 11 York Rd, Muizenberg; mains R50; ⏰ 7am-4pm Mon-Sat, 8am-4pm Sun) The surfies' favourite hang-out is a great place for breakfast or lunch of well-made

pasta dishes and salads. Local art exhibitions enliven the walls. Call to see if it's open for dinner on Thursday and Saturdays.

Olive Station (☎ 021-788 3264; 165 Main Rd, Muizenberg; mains R40-50; ⏰ 8am-5pm Mon-Wed, Fri & Sat, 8am-9pm Thu, 9am-5pm Sun) Dine on Lebanese dishes at the relaxed café overlooking the sea or a wind-sheltered courtyard. The olives sold in the attached deli are grown locally and cured in wooden barrels.

Kalk Bay has several great seaside bars that serve food including the **Brass Bell** (☎ 021-788 5455; Kalk Bay Station, Main Rd; mains R50-80; ⏰ 11am-10pm), a Cape Town institution, and the convivial and trendy **Polana** (☎ 021-788 7162; Kalk Bay Harbour).

Shopping

Apart from Kalk Bay's harbour and its fishing market, the best reason for visiting here is to browse the many antique, art and craft shops.

Our pick of the bunch:

Artvark (☎ 021-788 5584; www.artvark.org; 48 Main Rd, Kalk Bay) For crafts.

Cape to Cairo (☎ 021-788 4571; 100 Main Rd, Kalk Bay) An Aladdin's cave of interior-design goods.

Clementina Ceramics & The A.R.T. Gallery (☎ 021-788 8718; www.clementina.co.za; 20 Main Rd, Kalk Bay; ⏰ 10am-5pm Tue-Sun) For the full selection of Clementina van der Walt's distinctive tableware as well as one-off pieces.

Kalk Bay Modern (☎ 021-788 6571; Windsor House, 150 Main Rd, Kalk Bay) For arts and crafts.

The Potter's Shop & Studio (☎ 021-788 7030; 6 Rouxville Rd, Kalk Bay) For pottery. There's also a branch in Muizenberg (☎ 021-788 8737; 9 Atlantic Rd; ⏰ 9am-4pm Mon-Fri)

Getting There & Around

The Simon's Town train line from Cape Town runs to Muizenberg, St James and Kalk Bay. If driving, the M4 leads directly to Muizenberg and connects with Main Rd which runs down the False Bay coast to Kalk Bay. The sights are all within walking distance of the train stations.

SIMON'S TOWN

A naval town ever since colonial times, Simon's Town remains the main base for South Africa's navy. It's an attractive, Victorian town with a pretty harbour and an interesting Cape Muslim history, which you can learn about at the **Heritage Museum**

(☎ 021-786 2302; Almay House, King George Way; adult/child R3/2; ☽ 11am-4pm Tue-Fri, Sat & Sun by appointment only).

There are two other mildly diverting museums – the **Simon's Town museum** (☎ 021-786 3046; Court Rd; donation R5; ☽ 9am-4pm Mon-Fri, 10am-1pm Sat, 11am-3pm Sun), covering the town's general history; and the self-explanatory **South African Naval Museum** (☎ 021-787 4635; St George's St; admission free; ☽ 10am-4pm). But the main reason most people head down this way is to visit the penguin colony at Boulders Beach (right).

Among the several boat tour operators in Simon's Town is **Southern Right** (☎ 083-257 7760, 021-786 2136; Simon's Town Harbour Jetty; harbour cruise R30), which runs the popular *Spirit of Just Nuisance* cruise around the harbour. Speed-boat trips to Cape Point and Seal Island are R250 and during the whale-watching season they also offer cruises that allow you to get up close to these magnificent animals.

It's possible to kayak in the harbour and down the coast towards Cape Point (see p137).

For tourist information go to **Cape Town Tourism Simon's Town** (☎ 021-786 5798; 111 St George's St, Simon's Town; ☽ 8am-6pm Mon-Fri, 10am-5pm Sat & Sun Oct-Mar, 9am-5pm Mon-Fri, 10am-3pm Sat Apr-Sep).

Boulders Beach

Famous for being home to a colony of 3000 African penguins, **Boulders Beach** (☎ 021-701 8692; www.tmnp.co.za; adult/child R20/5; ☽ 7am-7.30pm Dec-Jan, 8am-6.30pm Feb-May & Sep-Nov, 8am-5pm Jun-Aug) is some 3km south of Simon's Town. Delightful as they are, the penguins are also pretty stinky, which may put you off spending too long paddling with them.

There are two entrances to the penguins' protected area, which is part of Table Mountain National Park. The first, as you come along Queens Rd (the continuation of St George's St) from Simon's Town, is at the end of Seaforth Rd; the second is at Bellevue Rd. You can observe the penguins from the boardwalk at Foxy Beach, but at Boulders Beach you can get in the water with them. The sea is calm and shallow in the coves, so Boulders is popular with families

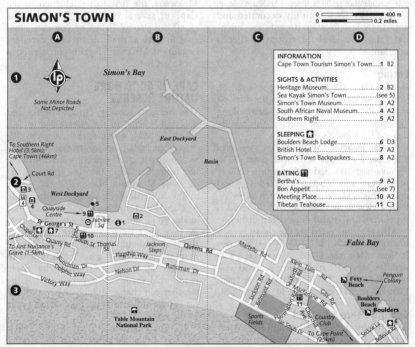

SIMON'S TOWN

0 ——— 400 m
0 ——— 0.2 miles

INFORMATION	
Cape Town Tourism Simon's Town....**1** B2	

SIGHTS & ACTIVITIES	
Heritage Museum..................................**2** B2	
Sea Kayak Simon's Town................(see 5)	
Simon's Town Museum.......................**3** A2	
South African Naval Museum..........**4** A2	
Southern Right.....................................**5** A2	

SLEEPING	
Boulders Beach Lodge........................**6** D3	
British Hotel...**7** A2	
Simon's Town Backpackers...............**8** A2	

EATING	
Bertha's..**9** A2	
Bon Appetit.....................................(see 7)	
Meeting Place...................................**10** A2	
Tibetan Teahouse.............................**11** C3	

Simon's Bay

Some Minor Roads Not Depicted

To Southern Right Hotel (3.5km); Cape Town (46km)

Court Rd

West Dockyard

East Dockyard

Basin

Quayside Centre

St George's St

Jubilee Sq

Chapel St

Quarry Rd

Smith St

St Thomas St

To Just Nuisance's Grave (1.5km)

Jackson Steps

Flagship Way

Runciman Dr

Dolphin Way

Nelson Dr

Victory Way

Runciman Dr

Queens Rd

Martello Rd

Jackson Rd

Belmont Rd

Klein Tuin Rd

Seaforth Rd

Macrdacrane Rd

Cay Rd

Harrington Rd

Church Rd

Jan Smuts Dr

Seacole La

Bellevue Rd

Table Mountain National Park

Sports Fields

Country Club

To Cape Point (25km)

False Bay

Foxy Beach

Penguin Colony

Boulders Beach

Boulders

CAPE TOWN

and can get extremely crowded, especially on holidays and at weekends.

Sleeping

Simon's Town Backpackers (☎ 021-786 1964; www .capepax.co.za; 66 St George's St, Simon's Town; dm/d R70/200; ⌨) The spacious rooms are brightly painted at this relaxed backpackers overlooking Simon's Town's harbour.

Southern Right Hotel (☎ 021-782 0314; www .southernright.info; 12-14 Glen Rd, Glencairn; s/d R375/590; Ⓟ) A couple of kilometres before Simon's Town is this historic inn run by the Boulders Beach Lodge people. The rooms are simply but appealingly furnished with lots of candles adding a romantic ambiance. There's also a restaurant, deli and wine shop.

Boulders Beach Lodge (☎ 021-786 1758; www .bouldersbeach.co.za; 4 Boulders Pl, Boulders Beach; s/d R450/790, apt R1500; ⌨ Ⓟ) Share the beach with the penguins after the day-tripper crowds have gone home at this smart guesthouse with rooms decorated in wicker and wood. There are also self-catering units and a pleasant café.

British Hotel (☎ /fax 021-786 2214; www.british hotelapartments.co.za; 90 St George's St, Simon's Town; apt from R1400) These quirkily decorated and amazingly spacious apartments are splendid value and ideal for groups of friends or a family.

Eating

Meeting Place (☎ 021-786 1986; 98 St George's St, Simon's Town; mains R40; ☽ 9am-4pm Mon, 9am-9pm Tue-Sun) Relax on the balcony overlooking Simon's Town's main street at this trendy deli-café, a foodie's delight.

Tibetan Teahouse (☎ 021-786 1544; www.sophea gallery.com; 2 Harrington Rd, Seaforth; mains R30-40; ☽ 10am-5pm) Attached to the Sophea Gallery of Tibetan and Tibetan inspired arts and crafts, this is a lovely café in which to revive, with a view across the bay. All the food is vegetarian and it also does vegan dishes.

Also recommended are the classy French bistro **Bon Appetit** (☎ 021-786 2412; 90 St George's St, Simon's Town; mains R80-90; ☽ noon-2pm & 6.30-10pm Tue-Sun) and harbourside seafood restaurant **Bertha's** (☎ 021-786 2138; Quayside Centre, 1 Wharf Rd, Simon's Town; mains R55-90; ☽ 7am-10pm).

Getting There & Around

See p162 for details on the train from Muizenberg. Rikkis (p159) meet all trains arriving at Simon's Town and go to Boulders and Cape Point.

IMHOFF FARM

There is a great deal to see and do at this historic and attractive **farmstead** (Map pp102-3; ☎ 021-783 4545; www.imhofffarm.co.za; Kommetjie Rd; admission free; ☽ 10am-5pm Tue-Sun) just outside Kommetjie. Craft shops and studios, a café, the Kommetjie Environmental Awareness Group (KEAG), a snake and reptile park, a farmyard stocked with animals, and camel and donkey rides are among the many attractions. The best way to get here is by car.

SOLOLE GAME RESERVE

The cheeky irreverence of this **game reserve** (Map pp102-3; ☎ 021-785 3248; www.solole.co.za; 6 Wood Rd, Sunnydale; ☽ 9.30am-5.30pm Mon-Fri, 9am-5pm Sat & Sun), covering 350 hectares on the way to Kommetjie, has to be admired. For example, a 45-minute game drive costs R30 unless you're an 'ill-disciplined brat' and then its R5000! View nine different species of buck, buffalo and the lone black rhino Mokwena, the first to be returned to the Cape in several centuries. Guided walks (R90) are also available, or you can game spot for free at the hide by their excellent restaurant Mnandis. Again, you'll need a car to get here.

CAPE OF GOOD HOPE NATURE RESERVE

The awesome scenery, fantastic walks and deserted beaches of the **reserve** (Map pp102-3; ☎ 021-780 9204; www.tmnp.co.za; admission R45; ☽ 6am-6pm Oct-Mar, 7am-5pm Apr-Sep) can easily swallow up a day. If you come on one of the day tours that whip into the reserve (part of Table Mountain National Park), pause at the Buffelsfontein Visitor Centre, walk to Cape Point and back, and then zip out again, you'll not even have seen the half of it. Take your time to explore the reserve the way it should be: on foot. Pick up a map at the entrance gate if you intend to go walking, but bear in mind that there is minimal shade in the park and that the weather can change quickly. Also see p137 for details of the two-day hike you can take in the reserve.

It's not a hard walk, but if you're feeling lazy a **funicular railway** (adult one way/return

R32/24, child R16/12; ☻ 10am-5pm) runs up from beside the restaurant to the souvenir kiosk next to the old lighthouse (1860). The old lighthouse was too often obscured by mist and fog, so a new lighthouse was built at Dias Point in 1919 – take the thrilling walkway along the rocks here to avoid the crowds.

Numerous tour companies include Cape Point on their itineraries (see p140). The only public transport to the Cape is with Rikkis, which run from Simon's Town train station (p159). The best option is to hire a car for the day, so you can explore the rest of the peninsula.

CAPE FLATS

For the majority of Capetonians, home is in one of the poverty-stricken townships sprawling across the shifting sands of the Cape Flats. Taking a tour – the only way of safely travelling here besides making friends with and being accompanied by a resident – is one of the most illuminating and life-affirming things you can do while in Cape Town. You'll learn a lot about South African history and the cultures of black South Africans.

Although there are trains and buses into the townships, for safety reasons we don't recommend taking them unless you're in the company of a local. Better are the township tours (p221). The half-day itineraries of most tours are similar, usually including a visit to the District Six Museum (p108), then being driven to the Cape Flats to visit some or all of the following townships: Langa, Guguletu, Crossroads and Khayelitsha. Tour guides are generally flexible in where they go, and respond to the wishes of the group.

Places you'll visit will most likely include the brilliantly decorated **Guga S'Thebe Arts and Cultural Centre** (Map pp102-3; ☎ 021-695 3493; cnr Washington & Church Sts, Langa); the **Tsoga Environmental Resource Centre** (Map pp102-3; ☎ 021-694 0004; Washington St, Langa); the **Sivuyile Tourism Centre** (Map pp102-3; ☎ 021-637 8449) in Guguletu, which has an interesting photographic display on the townships, artists at work, and a good gift shop; the **Philani Nutrition & Development Project** (Map pp102-3; ☎ 021-387 5124; www.philani.org.za) in Crossroads and Khayelitsha; and the **Khayelitsha Craft Market** (Map pp102-3; ☎ 021-361 2904; www

BABOON MATTERS

The signs at Cape Point warning you not to feed the baboons are there for a reason. After years of interacting with tourists, the baboons will quite happily grab food from your hands or climb in the open doors and windows of your car to get at it. *Never* challenge them as they will turn aggressive. The damage inflicted might end up being far more serious than baboon crap over your car seats, so keep an eye open, and your food carefully hidden away.

Showing a much gentler side of baboon life is the project **Baboon Matters** (☎ 021-783 3882; www.baboonmatters.org.za; adult/child R200/100). On a two- to three-hour guided hike you'll get to spend time observing a baboon troop at very close quarters – it's an amazing experience. The project was started to help preserve the Chacma baboon population, estimated at 247 and dangerously close to extinction on the Cape. Monitors have been employed to keep the baboons out of the villages where they come into conflict with humans; 25% of tour fees go towards the project.

.stmichaels.org.za; St Michael's Church, Ncumo Rd, Harare, Khayelitsha; ☻ 9am-4pm Mon-Sat), a great place to look for interesting souvenirs, where you can be sure that your money goes directly to the people who need it most. Usually a marimba band is playing and you can buy their CDs.

Sleeping

Vicky's B&B (Map pp102-3; ☎ 021-387 7104, 082-225 2986; www.vickysbandb.com; Site C 685A Kiyane St, Khayelitsha; s/d with breakfast & shared bathroom R190/380; ▯) Vicky Ntozini's unique selling point is that she lives in a shack. Given her success she could well afford not to, but she and her extended family love it here and guests clearly enjoy the experience. There are two compact, comfy guest rooms and (rare for a shack) an inside bathroom with toilet and shower.

Radebe's B&B (Map pp102-3; ☎ 021-695 0508, 082-393 3117; radebes@ananzi.co.za; 23 Mama Way, Settlers Place, Langa; s/d R200/360; ▯ P) Minah Radebe brings her confident Sowetan style to the best of Langa's B&B's. One of her three delightfully decorated guest rooms has an en-suite bathroom and there's the attached Coffee Shack restaurant, where breakfast and other meals are served.

Kopanong (Map pp102-3; ☎ 021-361 2084, 082-476 1278; kopanong@xsinet.co.za; Site C-329 Velani Cres, Khayelitsha; s/d with breakfast R290/480; Ⓟ ▯) Thope Lekau runs Khayelitsha's best B&B, with her equally ebullient daughter, Mpho. Her substantial brick home offers two stylishly decorated guest rooms, each with their own bathrooms. She also runs a cookery course (R150) on request.

Eating

Arrange with a tour company (see p140) or private guide to visit the following places.

Eziko (Map pp102-3; ☎ 021-694 0434; cnr Washington St & Jungle Walk, Langa; mains R30-40; ☺ 9am-6pm Mon-Fri, 9am-10pm Sat) Offers simple, good food in a pleasant setting; try the chef's special fried chicken or the breakfast.

Lelapa (Map pp102-3; ☎ 021-694 2681; 49 Harlem Ave, Langa; buffet R85) Sheila has been so successful with her delicious African-style buffets that she's taken over the neighbours, extending the once cosy home restaurant into a space for big tour groups.

Western Cape

As the image of Table Mountain begins to fade, the Western Cape comes into focus, proving there's much, much more to this part of the yard than that famous chunk of rock and the city that clutches to it. One of the world's premier destinations, it's hard to describe without using clichés or superlatives. Here you can dive with sharks, jump out of an aeroplane, surf some of Southern Africa's best breaks, cruise with whales, eat fresh crayfish at a beachside barbecue, stand at the southernmost tip of Africa and sample some of the world's finest wines.

The uniqueness of this part of the country has many Westerners calling it 'not really Africa'. This seems to be a reference to its First World amenities – classy hotels, top-notch restaurants, designer stores and modern shopping malls – or the distinct lack of chaos and cholera. Either way, it's an insult to both the continent and to a province in whose history are centuries of mixing between indigenous Khoesaan, migrating Bantu tribes, colonising Europeans and 'imported' Indonesian slaves. Indeed, this is Africa in all its forms, and amid the tourism-brochure beauty it's easy to forget a major portion of the population still lives in abject poverty.

This is the country's most visited province, particularly along the Garden Route, but it's still a magical place, with ample opportunities to flee the crowds. Try heading up the desolate West Coast, cruising the sun-drenched Karoo, or hiking through a mountain pass in the Cederberg. Whichever way you go, however, in the Western Cape there's no escaping the splendour.

HIGHLIGHTS

- Soaring in a hot-air balloon above the dramatic mountain ranges and centuries-old vineyards of the **Cape Winelands** (p184)

- Getting a tan or an adrenaline rush on the bold, beautiful **Garden Route** (p211)

- Hiking past bizarre sandstone formations with San rock art in the rugged and desolate **Cederberg Wilderness Area** (p235)

- Enjoying scenery to soothe the soul in the **Overberg** (p186) – a wonderful area to spot whales

- Marvelling in the silence, space and hospitality of the **Karoo** (p227), at the semidesert oasis **Oudtshoorn** (p207), at quaint **Prince Albert** (p228) or along the remarkable **Swartberg Pass** (p228)

- Having a beachside lobster braai (open barbecue) or viewing flower-carpeted hills along the **West Coast** (p231)

POPULATION: 5.2 MILLION	AREA: 129,370 SQ KM

WESTERN CAPE

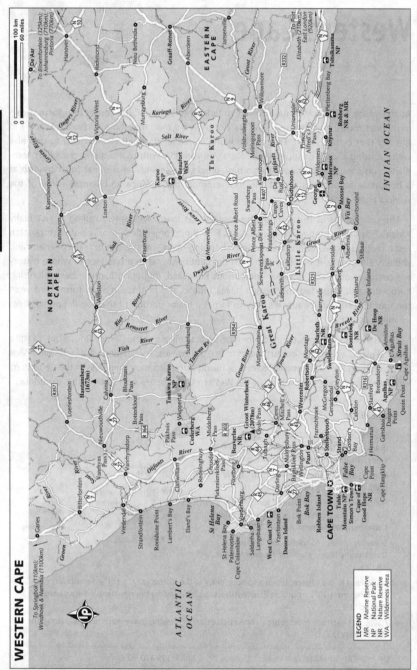

HISTORY

The Khoesaan peoples populated the area long before the arrival of Bantu Africans and Europeans. Today very few have survived, and their traditional cultures and languages have been almost completely lost. There is a large population of so-called 'coloureds', though, with origins as diverse as Khoesaan (indigenous) and Indonesian (slavery); the majority are Christian and Afrikaans-speaking. In the last couple of centuries, many blacks (in particular the Xhosa from the Eastern Cape) have gravitated here in search of work.

CLIMATE

The Western Cape has dry, sunny summers (October to March) where average temperatures are warm to hot but in some regions can reach 38°C. It is often windy, however, and the southeasterly 'Cape Doctor', which buffets the Cape, can reach gale force and cool things down. Winters (June to August) can be cold, with average minimum temperatures around 5°C, and maximums around 17°C. There is occasional snow on the higher peaks. The coast north from the Cape becomes progressively drier and hotter. Along the southern coast the weather is temperate.

NATIONAL PARKS & RESERVES

The Western Cape parks do not offer Big Five wildlife-viewing opportunities, but nevertheless they are wonderful wilderness retreats. The West Coast National Park (p232) protects wetlands of international significance and is an important home to seabird breeding colonies.

The Cederberg Wilderness Area (p235) is rugged and mountainous, offering excellent opportunities for hiking and wildlife-spotting including baboons, rheboks, klipspringers and grysboks, and predators such as caracals, Cape foxes, honey badgers and leopards.

Covering 36,000 hectares on land and 5km out to sea, De Hoop Nature Reserve (p193) is one of **Cape Nature Conservation's** (☎ 021-426 0723; www.capenature.org.za) best reserves. It includes a scenic coastline with stretches of beach, dunes and rocky cliffs, plus a freshwater lake and Potberg Mountain.

Bontebok National Park (p196) is home to the endangered bontebok, and is known for its wildflowers in late winter and early spring.

The Karoo National Park (p230) covers 33,000 hectares of impressive Karoo landscapes and representative flora. The plains carry a variety of short shrubs with well-wooded dry watercourses and mountain grasslands at higher elevations.

Wilderness National Park (p219) is bordered by the ocean to the south and the Outeniqua Range to the north and covers a unique system of lakes, rivers, wetlands and estuaries. There are opportunities for canoeing, fishing and hiking.

LANGUAGE

The Western Cape is one of only two provinces in South Africa (the other is the Northern Cape) where the majority of the population (55%) is classified as coloured. Most coloureds speak Afrikaans as a first language, the most widely spoken of the province. English is spoken and/or understood everywhere.

GETTING THERE & AROUND

The Western Cape is easily accessible by bus, plane and car. From Johannesburg (Jo'burg) there are daily bus services and flights to Cape Town, where you can pick up public transport around the province or hire a vehicle. The province is easy to negotiate – roads are good and distances are not too long. **Baz Bus** (☎ 021-439 2323; www.bazbus .com) offers a hop-on/hop-off shuttle service (with no time limit) through most of the province (R810), or you can book a direct ticket (R300 to R350). The exception is the west coast, where public transport is almost nonexistent.

WINELANDS

The Boland, stretching inland and upwards from Cape Town, is not the only wine-growing region in South Africa, but it's certainly the most famous. Its name means 'Upland', a reference to the dramatic mountain ranges that shoot up to more than 1500m, on whose fertile slopes the vineyards form a patchwork. The Franschhoek and Bainskloof Passes that crisscross the region are among the country's most spectacular.

CAPE WINERIES Simon Richmond

It was Stellenbosch in the 1970s that first promoted a 'wine route', an idea that has since been enthusiastically taken up by 16 other parts of the country. Stellenbosch's wine route remains the largest, covering around 100 wineries; if you lump in the nearby areas of Franschhoek, Helderberg and Paarl, you're looking at more than 200 wineries within a day's drive of Cape Town.

Several wineries are capitalising on the industry's popularity by adding on restaurants, accommodation and other attractions. Of these, we've selected some of the more notable ones, as well as vineyards that are renowned for their fine wines; you'll find them listed in the sections on Cape Town (p119), Stellenbosch (p173), Franschhoek (p179), Paarl (p184), Tulbagh (p197) and Robertson (p200). For more information, the annual John Platter's *South African Wine Guide* is the place to look.

History

Today, praise be the Lord, wine was pressed for the first time from Cape grapes.

Jan Van Riebeeck, 2 February 1659

Although the founder of the Cape Colony, Jan Van Riebeeck, had planted vines and made wine himself, it was not until the arrival of Governor Simon Van Der Stel in 1679 that wine making began in earnest. Van Der Stel created Groot Constantia (p119), the superb estate on the flanks of Table Mountain, and passed on his wine-making skills to the burghers settling around Stellenbosch.

Between 1688 and 1690, some 200 Huguenots arrived in the country. They were granted land in the region, particularly around Franschhoek, and although only a few had wine-making experience, they gave the nascent industry impetus.

For a long time, Cape wines other than those produced at Groot Constantia were not in great demand and most grapes ended up in brandy. But the industry received a boost in the early 19th century as war between Britain and France meant more South African wine was imported into the UK.

Apartheid-era sanctions and the power of the Kooperatiewe Wijnbouwers Vereeniging (KWV; the cooperative formed in 1918 to control minimum prices, production areas and quota limits) didn't exactly encourage innovation, and hampered the industry. However, since 1992 KWV, now a private company, has lost much of its former influence.

Many new and progressive wine makers are leading South Africa's re-emergence onto the world market. New wine-producing areas are being established away from the hotter inland areas, in particular in the cooler coastal areas east of Cape Town around Mossel Bay, Walker Bay and Elgin.

With its centuries-long history of colonial settlement, there's a distinctly European feel to the Boland, particularly in French-themed culinary hotspot Franschhoek ('French corner'). Lively student-town Stellenbosch offers the most activities, while Paarl is a busy commercial centre with excellent estates.

It is possible to see these towns on day trips from Cape Town. Stellenbosch and Paarl are accessible by train, and Franschhoek is the easiest to get around if you don't have a car. To do justice to the region and to visit the many wineries, you'll need to stay over and get yourself some wheels – bicycle wheels will do, if you're not too ambitious, but if you plan to pack in a lot of wineries, a car is essential.

STELLENBOSCH & AROUND

☎ 021 / pop 220,000

South Africa's second-oldest European settlement, established on the banks of the Eerste River by Governor van der Stel in 1679, Stellenbosch wears many faces. At times it's a rowdy joint, as Stellenbosch University students celebrate one or other form of freedom in a series of music festivals (the Afrikaans-language University of Stellenbosch, established in 1918, continues to play an important role in Afrikaner politics and culture). At others it's a stately monument to colonial splendour, its quiet oak-lined streets featuring some of the world's finest examples of Cape Dutch, Georgian and Victorian architecture. But most times it's just plain busy, as Capetonians, wine-farm workers

Black empowerment in the wine industry is happening too. **Thabani** (☎ 021-882 8790; www .thabani.co.za) in Stellenbosch is South Africa's first wholly black-owned wine company, although it's not open to the public. It hit the big time in the USA when promoted by talk-show host Oprah Winfrey, and students of the wine-maker Jabulani Ntshangase are now being hired by big vineyards, including KWV.

The **Fair Valley Workers Association** (Map p181; ☎ 021-863 2450) is a 17-hectare workers' farm next to Fairview estate near Paarl. It's still developing its own vineyards but has already produced six seasons of Chenin Blanc (sold through the UK wine chain Oddbins) made with grapes bought in from Fairview, as well as a Sauvignon Blanc and a pinotage (a cross between Pinot Noir and Hermitage or Shiraz, which produces a very bold wine).

Also worth checking out is **Thandi** (☎ 844 0605; www.cluver.co.za; ☉ 9am-5pm Mon-Sat) from the Elgin area, available at Tesco in the UK.

All this has to be balanced against the facts of a black and coloured workforce of some 350,000 toiling for minimum wages in vineyards owned by 4500 whites. The infamous dop system, whereby the wages of labourers were paid partly in wine, is now officially illegal, but its social and physiological consequences have been disastrous.

Wines

The most common white cultivar is Chenin Blanc, or steen. In the last decade or so, more fashionable varieties such as Chardonnay and Sauvignon Blanc have been planted on a wide scale. Table whites, especially Chardonnay, once tended to be heavily oaked and high in alcohol, but lighter, fruitier whites are now in the ascendancy. For good Sauvignon Blancs look to wineries in the cooler wine-growing regions of Constantia, Elgin and Hermanus.

Older, more-robust red varieties such as Shiraz, Cabernet Sauvignon and the Cape's own pinotage are being challenged by lighter blends of Cabernet Sauvignon, Merlot, Shiraz and Cabernet Franc, making a style closer to Bordeaux styles.

The Worcester region is the country's leading producer of fortified wines, including port, brandy and South Africa's own hanepoot. This dessert wine is made from the Mediterranean grape variety known as muscat of Alexandria to produce a strong, sweet and suitably high-alcohol tipple for the domestic market. In Worcester you'll also find the KWV Brandy Cellar, the largest in the world and the final stop on the Brandy Route, which runs from Van Ryn Brandy Cellar (p174) at Vlottenburg, 8km southwest of Stellenbosch. For more information contact the **South African Brandy Foundation** (☎ 021-886 6381; www.sabrandy.co.za).

and tourists descend on its interesting museums, buzzing markets, quality hotels and varied eating and nightlife options.

Orientation

The train station is a short walk west of the centre. The train line effectively forms the western boundary of the town and the Eerste River the southern. Dorp St, which runs roughly parallel to the river, is the old town's main street. The commercial centre lies between Dorp St and the university to the east of the Braak, the old town square.

Information

Ex Libris (Map p172; ☎ 021-886 6871; 18 Andringa St) Offers a solid collection of titles, including rarer South African publications.

Fandangos Internet Café (Map p172; per hr R30) Mill St (☎ 021-887 4628); Drostdy Centre (☎ 021-887 7501; Bird St)

Java Café (Map p172; ☎ 021-887 6261; cnr Church & Andringa Sts; per hr R18) Stellenbosch's cheapest Internet access.

Rennies Travel (Map p172; Mill St) A block from Dorp St, with a Thomas Cook foreign-exchange office.

Stellenbosch Publicity Association (Map p172; ☎ 021-883 3584; www.tourismstellenbosch.co.za; 36 Market St; ☉ 8am-6pm Mon-Fri, 9am-5pm Sat, 9am-4pm Sun) The staff here are extremely helpful. Pick up the excellent brochure Discover Stellenbosch on Foot (R3), with a walking-tour map and information on many of the historic buildings (also available in French and German). Also useful is the free brochure Stellenbosch Wine Routes, which gives information about opening times and tastings at many nearby wineries.

WESTERN CAPE

STELLENBOSCH

0 ——————— 400 m
0 ——————— 0.2 miles

Ⓐ   **Ⓑ**   **Ⓒ**   **Ⓓ**

INFORMATION	
Ex Libris	**1** C5
Fandangos Internet Café	**2** C5
Fandangos Internet Café	(see 33)
Java Café	(see 25)
Rennies Travel	**3** C5
Stellenbosch Publicity Association	**4** B5

SIGHTS & ACTIVITIES	
Braak	**5** C5
Easy Rider Wine Tours	(see 17)
Fick House	**6** B5
Grosvenor House	**7** D5
St Mary's on the Braak Church	**8** C5
Sasol Art Museum	**9** C4
Toy & Miniature Museum	**10** B5
Village Museum	**11** D5
VOC Kruithuis	**12** B5

SLEEPING 🏠	
De Goue Druif	**13** B5
De Oude Meul	**14** C5
D'Ouwe Werf	**15** C5
Stellenbosch Hotel	**16** C5
Stumble Inn	**17** B5
Wild Mushroom	**18** C5

EATING 🍴	
Beads	(see 27)
De Oewer	**19** A6
De Soete Inval	**20** C5
De Volkskombuis	**21** A6
Decameron	**22** D5
Fishmonger	**23** D5
Greengate	**24** C4
Java Café	**25** B5
L'Olive Deli & Café	**26** C5
Voila!	**27** C5
Wijnhuis	**28** C5

DRINKING 🍷	
Binelli's	**29** A6
Bohemia	**30** C4
De Akker	**31** B6
De Kelder	**32** B6
Dros	**33** B4
Fandangos Internet Café	(see 33)
Mystic Boer	**34** C4
Nu Bar	**35** C5
Terrace	(see 33)
Tollies	(see 33)

SHOPPING 🛍	
Craft Market	**36** C5
Green Sleeves	**37** C4
Oom Samie se Winkel	**38** B6
Simonsberg Cheese Factory	**39** A3

TRANSPORT	
Minibus Taxis	**40** C4

①

②

To Paarl (30km)

③

Jan Cilliers

Hammanshand

Muller

To Franschhoek (29km)

Molteno

Borcherd

Bird

Stoffel Smit St

Paul Kruger

Dennesig

Banghoek

Joubert

Hospital

De Beer

Latsky

Merriman St

④

Merriman St

Van der Stel Sports Club

George Blake

Plankenburg Creek

R44

40

37

Crozier

Andringa St

Ryneveld St

University of Stellenbosch

Victoria St

To Lanzerac (4km); Jonkershoek Forest Reserve (8km)

Du Toit

Drostdy Centre

R304

33

Beyers St

30 34

9

24

Neethling

⑤

Adam Tas

Papegaai

Stellenbosch

Alexander

6

8

5

12

Plein St

36

Bloem

3

2

Church (Kerk) St

35

1

26 15

28

25

16

23 22

18

27

11

Van Riebeeck

7

20

Dorp St

Drostdy St

The Avenue

Herold

Herte

(Mark) St

Market

To Oude Libertas Amphitheatre (1km); Van Ryn Brandy Cellar (6km); Cape Town (46km)

10

13

14

17

29

38 31

32

Krige

Hannah

Piet Retief

Louw

Heldenberg

Suidwal

⑥

R44

Eerste River

To 96 Winery Rd (12km); Vergelegen (16km)

39

Sights & Activities

If you've had all the wine you can take, Stellenbosch's many museums are worth a visit. If you need to sober up first, explore the town yourself or take a **guided walk** (R50 per person), with a minimum of three people, from the Stellenbosch Publicity Association, daily at 10am and 3pm.

VILLAGE MUSEUM

A group of exquisitely restored and period-furnished houses dating from 1709 to 1850 make up this **museum** (Map p172; ☎ 021-887 2902; 18 Ryneveld St; adult/child R15/10; ◷ 9.30am-5pm Mon-Sat, 2-5pm Sun), which occupies the entire city block bounded by Ryneveld, Plein, Drostdy and Church Sts and is a must-see. Also included are charming gardens and, on the other side of Drostdy St, stately **Grosvenor House**.

SASOL ART MUSEUM

Featuring one of the country's best selections of local art, both famous and emerging, this **museum** (Map p172; ☎ 021-808 3693; 52 Ryneveld St; adult/child R9/5; ◷ 9am-4.30pm Tue-Fri, 9am-4pm Sat) also contains an irreplaceable collection of African anthropological treasures, housed here as part of an assemblage by the Anthropology section of the University of Stellenbosch. The exhibition displays at once the different ecological, social and cultural contexts of the human experience in Africa, and is not to be missed.

TOY & MINIATURE MUSEUM

This delightfully surprising **museum** (Map p172; ☎ 021-887 9433; 116 Dorp St; adult/child R10/5; ◷ 9.30am-5pm Mon-Sat, 2-5pm Sun), based in Voorgelegen House, features a remarkable collection of amazingly detailed toys ranging from railway sets to doll's houses – ask a guide to point out some of the best pieces.

BRAAK

At the north end of the **Braak** (Map p172; Town Sq), an open stretch of grass, you'll find the neo-Gothic **St Mary's on the Braak Church**, completed in 1852. To the west is the **VOC Kruithuis** (Powder House; admission free; ◷ 9.30am-1pm Mon-Fri), which was built in 1777 to store the town's weapons and gunpowder and now houses a small military museum. On the northwest corner is **Fick House**, also known as the Burgerhuis, a fine example of Cape Dutch style from the late 18th century. Most

of this building is now occupied by Historical Homes of South Africa, established to preserve important architecture.

JONKERSHOEK FOREST RESERVE

This small **forest reserve** (Map p175; ☎ 021-866 1560; admission car/bicycle R110/5) is around 8km southeast of town along the WR4 and set within a timber plantation. Here you'll find walking and biking trails.

WINERIES

There are too many good wineries in the Stellenbosch area to list all of them, so it's sometimes best to drive around and stop on a whim. We do, however, recommend a visit to **Blaauwklippen** (Map p175; ☎ 021-880 0133; www .blaauwklippen.com; tastings R25; ◷ 9am-5pm Mon-Sat, 9am-4pm Sun), a rustic 300-year-old estate with several fine Cape Dutch buildings, known for its red wines, particularly its Cabernet Sauvignon and Zinfandel.

Try to make it to **Neethlingshof** (Map p175; ☎ 021-883 8988; www.neethlingshof.co.za; tastings R20; ◷ 9am-5pm Mon-Fri, 10am-6pm Sat & Sun), where a beautiful tree-lined approach leads to a charming estate with a rose garden and tea room. There are cellar and vineyard tours, and their pinotage (a cross between Pinot Noir and Hermitage or Shiraz) and Cabernet Sauvignon have won several awards.

Also unmissable is **Delaire** (Map p175; ☎ 021-885 1756; www.delairewinery.co.za; tastings R10; ◷ 10am-5pm), known as the 'vineyard in the sky' because of its high-altitude location at the top of the Helshoogte Pass on Rte 310 towards Franschhoek. Naturally, the views are stunning and it's a friendly place with wheelchair access to the restaurant and picnics available from October to April (bookings essential). Try its Cabernet Sauvignon and Merlot, the latter well cultivated at **Hartenberg** (Map p175; ☎ 021-882 2541; www.hartenbergestate .com; tastings free; ◷ 9am-5pm Mon-Fri, 9am-3pm Sat), thanks to a favourable microclimate. It also produces a top Cabernet and Shiraz. Lunch is available from noon to 2pm (bookings essential).

There are some old stalwarts. **Lanzerac** (Map p175; ☎ 021-886 5641; www.lanzeracwines.co.za; Jonkershoek Valley; tastings R16; ◷ 9am-4.30pm Mon-Thu, 9am-4pm Fri, 10am-2pm Sat, 11am-3pm Sun) produces a very good Merlot and quaffable Cabernet Sauvignon and Chardonnay, and you'll also find Stellenbosch's most luxurious hotel (see p176) here. **L'Avenir** (Map p175; ☎ 021-889 5001; www.lavenir.co.za; tastings R10-20; ⏲ 10am-5pm Mon-Fri, 10am-4pm Sat), where a visit is not about facilities (there is no restaurant) but about the simply splendid wine: the Chenin Blanc is divine and its pinotage has won more awards for this cultivar than any other in the country.

Back towards Cape Town is the magnificent setting of **Spier** (Map p175; ☎ 021-809 1100; www.spier.co.za; tastings R12; ⏲ 9am-5pm), which has something for everyone. This mega-estate offers steam-train trips from Cape Town (call ☎ 419 5222 for information), horse riding, a cheetah centre, performing-arts centres, beautifully restored Cape Dutch buildings and several restaurants, including the spectacular Moyo (see p177). The wines produced here are nothing to shout about, but in the tasting you can try lots of other vineyards' wines. Check out the annual **arts festival** that runs from January to March – it's as good a reason as any for coming here. If you want to stay over there's a good Cape Malay–style hotel, the Village at Spier (see p176).

For lovers of the burnt stuff, there's **Van Ryn Brandy Cellar** (Map p175; ☎ 021-881 3875; www.distell.co.za; Vlottenburg; tastings R15; ⏲ 8am-5pm Mon-Fri, 9am-1.30pm Sat) on the **Western Cape Brandy Route** (www.sabrandy.co.za). It generally runs three tours a day, including a tasting. In its boardroom you can view fine South African art.

HELDERBERG

This area around Somerset West, 20km south of Stellenbosch, has some 20 wineries, including **Vergelegen** (Map p175; ☎ 021-847 1334; www.vergelegen.co.za; Lourensford Rd, Somerset West; admission R10, tastings R2.50-10; ⏲ 9.30am-4pm), arguably the most beautiful estate in the Cape. Simon van der Stel's son Willem first planted vines here in 1700. The buildings and elegant grounds have ravishing mountain views and a 'stately home' feel to them. On the dining front you can choose from the casual Rose Terrace overlooking the Rose Garden, the upmarket Lady Phillips Restaurant, or a picnic hamper (R110 per person) – bookings are essential for the last two options, and they are not available between April and September.

Tours

Easy Rider Wine Tours (Map p172; ☎ 021-886 4651; www.jump.to/stumble; 12 Market St) is a popular, long-established company offering good value for a full-day trip at R250 including lunch and all tastings. The wineries it visits sometimes change, but on the schedule at the time of research were Boschendal, Delaire, Fairview and Simonsig.

Wine Walks' (Map p175; ☎ 083-631 5944; www.winewalks.co.za) local expert Annelee Steyn takes visitors on an 8km walking tour of wineries in the Simonsberg area. The walk (R395) includes a picnic lunch and tastings; phone for bookings, and to ask about group discounts.

Festivals & Events

Oude Libertas Amphitheatre (Map p175; ☎ 021-809 7380; www.oudelibertas.co.za) and the Spier wine estate (see left) both hold **performing-arts festivals** between January and March.

Rag Week If you're into live music, try to catch early February's Rag Week where local band members vie for the attention of freshmen here to celebrate their recent student status.

Wine Festival (www.wineroute.co.za) This event in early August offers visitors the chance to sample up to 400 different drops in one spot as well as attend talks and tutorials on wine.

Stellenbosch Festival (www.stellenboschfestival.co.za) Runs for two weeks at the end of September, celebrates music and the arts in various events around the town including a street carnival.

Van der Stel Festival Held at the end of September and early October, this festival combines with the Stellenbosch and Wine Festivals.

Sleeping

There's plenty of accommodation in Stellenbosch; contact the Stellenbosch Publicity Association if you find the recommendations listed here are booked up.

BUDGET

Stumble Inn (Map p172; ☎ 021-887 4049; www.jump.to/stumble; 12 Market St; camp sites per person R40, dm R60, d with shared bathroom R160; 🖳 🏊) With a lively and welcoming atmosphere, this place is split over two old houses, one with a small pool and the other with a pleasant garden, which now offers self-catering apartments for R250. The owners, travellers and wine-lovers themselves, are a good source of information and offer wine discounts for longer stayers. They also run Easy Rider Wine Tours and rent bicycles for R50 per day.

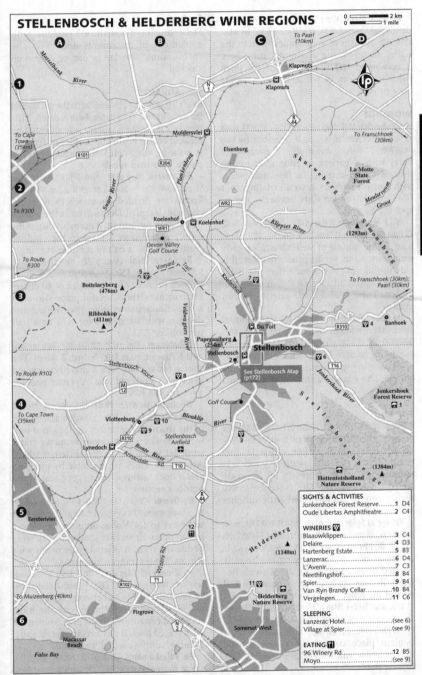

STELLENBOSCH & HELDERBERG WINE REGIONS

WESTERN CAPE

SIGHTS & ACTIVITIES
Jonkershoek Forest Reserve................**1** D4	
Oude Libertas Amphitheatre..............**2** C4	

WINERIES 🍷
Blaauwklippen.....................................**3** C4	
Delaire...**4** D3	
Hartenberg Estate..............................**5** B3	
Lanzerac..**6** D4	
L'Avenir..**7** C3	
Neethlingshof.....................................**8** B4	
Spier..**9** B4	
Van Ryn Brandy Cellar.......................**10** B4	
Vergelegen..**11** C6	

SLEEPING
Lanzerac Hotel..............................(see 6)	
Village at Spier.............................(see 9)	

EATING 🍴
96 Winery Rd...................................**12** B5	
Moyo...(see 9)	

De Oude Meul (Map p172; ☎ 021-887 7085; www
.deoudemeul.snowball.co.za; 10A Mill St; s/d incl breakfast
R375/550; ❄) Above an antiques shop in the
centre of town, the accommodation here
is very good and reasonable for the price
(which is lower in winter). Some rooms
have balconies.

MIDRANGE

Stellenbosch Hotel (Map p172; ☎ 021-887 3644; www
.stellenbosch.co.za/hotel; 162 Dorp St; s/d incl breakfast from
R425/700; ❄) A comfortable country-style
hotel with a variety of rooms, including
those with self-catering facilities and others
with four-poster beds. A section dating from
1743 houses the Jan Cats Brasserie, a good
spot for a drink.

Wild Mushroom (Map p172; ☎ 021-886 9880;
15 Ryneveld St; s/d incl breakfast R450/780; ❄) Slap-
bang in the middle of Stellenbosch's trendy
restaurant zone, yet surprisingly quiet, this
chic multilevel guesthouse offers plush accommodation, all in very stylish shades of
brown. There is also a self-catering option
available.

De Goue Druif (Map p172; ☎ 021-883 3555; http://
gouedruif.hypermart.net; 110 Dorp St; s/d incl breakfast
R650/700; ❄ ▯ ❄) In a Cape Dutch build-
ing dating back to 1792, this 'Golden Grape'
is a charming guesthouse run by a Belgian
couple. There is also a small gym and sauna
on offer.

TOP END

D'Ouwe Werf (Map p172; ☎ 021-887 4608; www
.ouwewerf.com; 30 Church St; s/d incl breakfast R900/990;
❄ ❄) This is an appealing, old-style hotel
(dating back to 1802) with a good restaurant. It's worth dropping by its shady
courtyard for lunch. The more expensive
luxury rooms are furnished with antiques
and brass beds.

Village at Spier (Map p175; ☎ 021-809 1100; www
.spier.co.za; Vlottenburg; d/ste incl breakfast R1450/2500;
❄ ▯ ❄) Forgo the usual Cape Dutch style
in favour of a design copying the brightly
painted houses found in Cape Town's Bo-
Kaap. Rooms are large, well appointed and
part of the Spier wine estate.

Lanzerac Hotel (Map p175; ☎ 021-887 1132; www
.lanzerac.co.za; Jonkershoek Valley; s/d/ste incl breakfast
R1700/2960/4140; ❄ ▯ ❄) This unashamedly
opulent place consists of a 300-year-old
manor house and winery. Some suites have
private pools.

Eating

Stellenbosch is a *bon vivant's* paradise, with
a plethora of restaurants and bars. The
surrounding winelands are equally well
stocked.

RESTAURANTS

Beads (Map p172; ☎ 021-886 8734; cnr Church & Ryneveld
Sts; mains R30-80; ❤ breakfast, lunch & dinner) This
trendy à la carte restaurant is frequented by
Stellenbosch's beautiful people. In front of
it is the bustling deli Voila!, where you can
create your own meal.

Decameron (Map p172; ☎ 021-883 3331; 50 Plein
St; mains R40-60; ❤ lunch & dinner Mon-Sat, lunch Sun)
Locals are divided about whether or not
cheesily designed Decameron is the town's
best Italian restaurant. Arguments are commonly settled over a pizza in the outdoor
seating area on a balmy summer evening.

De Soete Inval (Map p172; ☎ 021-886 4842;
5 Ryneveld St; mains R50; ❤ breakfast, lunch & dinner)
Known primarily for its choice of 40 different pancakes, this cheerful place also does
a fine Indonesian *rijstafel* (rice with many
dishes), with six dishes for R75 or a half
portion for R50.

Fishmonger (Map p172; ☎ 021-887 7835; cnr Ryneveld & Plein Sts; mains R50; ❤ lunch & dinner) The
choice for seafood. It's a snazzily designed
place with a relaxed vibe. A platter goes for
a reasonable R79.

Wijnhuis (Map p172; ☎ 021-887 5844; cnr Church &
Andringa Sts; mains R50-100; ❤ lunch & dinner) One
of the town's more pricey options, but well
worth it. There's an extensive menu and a
wine list stretching to 350 different labels.
Around 20 wines are available by the glass
and it does tastings. Try to get a seat in the
outdoor section.

De Oewer (Map p172; ☎ 021-886 5431; Aan de
Wagenweg; mains R70; ❤ lunch & dinner Mon-Sat, lunch
Sun) Next to De Volkskombuis, De Oewer
has an open-air section shaded by oak trees
beside the river. It offers lighter meals with
a more Mediterranean emphasis.

96 Winery Rd (Map p175; ☎ 021-842 2945; Zand-
berg Farm, Winery Rd; mains R70; ❤ lunch & dinner Mon-
Sat, lunch Sun) Off Rte 44 between Stellenbosch
and Somerset West, this is one the most
respected restaurants in the area, known for
its dry aged beef. It has a relaxed style and a
belief in simply cooked, real food.

De Volkskombuis (Map p172; ☎ 021-887 2121;
Aan de Wagenweg; mains R75; ❤ lunch & dinner Mon-

Sat, lunch Sun) A local favourite that's open 365 days a year, this no-frills, atmospheric place specialises in traditional Cape Malay cuisine and features a terrace with views of the Stellenbosch mountain range. Booking is advisable.

Moyo (Map p175; ☎ 021-809 1100; Spier Estate, Vlottenburg; buffet R180; ⊗ lunch & dinner) The mandatory face painting is a bit much, but this tourist-pleasing place brings a fantasy vision of Africa to the middle of the Spier wine estate, and guests love it. It's a lot of fun, with roving musicians and dancers and alfresco dining in tents and up in the trees (you're given a blanket in winter).

CAFÉS & QUICK EATS

Java Café (Map p172; ☎ 021-887 6261; cnr Church & Andringa Sts; snacks from R15; ⊗ 8.30am-11pm) A good range of drinks and snacks are available at this stylish café with pavement tables. It also offers Stellenbosch's cheapest Internet access (R18 per hour) and is a wi-fi hotspot.

Greengate (Map p172; ☎ 021-886 6111; 44 Ryneveld St; snacks from R20; ⊗ 8am-5pm Mon-Fri, 8am-noon Sat) An organic and farm-food deli that looks good and smells terrific. It sells nuts, fruits and organic vegetables, offers a pay-by-weight buffet at R90/kg and a daily changing menu.

L'Olive Deli & Café (Map p172; ☎ 021-887 8985; Shop 1, Oude Hoek, Andringa St; snacks from R25; ⊗ 8am-6pm Mon-Sat) This is a stylish deli offering a range of delicious snacks built around the eponymous fruit, of which it offers several varieties.

Drinking

Stellenbosch's nightlife scene is geared largely towards the interests of the university students, but there are alternatives if you ask around. It's safe to walk around the centre at night, so a pub crawl could certainly be on the cards (if you're staying at the Stumble Inn one will probably be organised for you).

Nu Bar (Map p172; ☎ 021-886 8998; 51 Plein St) This place has a nightclub feel, with a small dance floor beyond the long bar where the DJ pumps out hip-hop and house.

Mystic Boer (Map p172; ☎ 021-886 8870; 3 Victoria St) Cool Afrikaans kids hang out here in surroundings perhaps best described as post-transformation era retro-Boer chic.

Fandangos Internet café (Map p172; ☎ 021-887 7501; Drostdy Centre, Bird St) If you're looking for a slightly more sophisticated option try this cocktail bar and Internet café in the Drostdy Centre.

Binelli's (Map p172; ☎ 021-886 9009; Black Horse Centre, cnr Dorp & Market Sts) Binelli's represents more than any other place the changing face of Stellenbosch: it's a supremely slick, New York–styled 'event bar', offering a selection of coffees, tapas and cocktails using only high-grade ingredients.

Classic student watering holes:

Bohemia (Map p172; ☎ 021-882 8375; cnr Andringa & Victoria Sts) Offers live music every Tuesday, Thursday and Sunday and hubbly-bubblies (R25) with a range of different tobaccos.

De Akker (Map p172; ☎ 021-883 3512; 90 Dorp St) Pub meals from under R30 and an upstairs cellar for live music.

De Kelder (Map p172; ☎ 021-883 3797; 63 Dorp St) A reasonably pleasant restaurant, bar and beer garden popular with German backpackers.

Dros (☎ 021-886 4856), the **Terrace** (☎ 021-887 194) and Tollies, clustered together in the Drostdy Centre complex (Map p172), just off Bird St and north of the Braak, are among the liveliest bars; you can eat at all of them, but that's not what most patrons have in mind.

Shopping

Oom Samie se Winkel (Uncle Sammy's Shop; Map p172; ☎ 021-887 0797; 84 Dorp St; ⊗ 8.30am-6pm Mon-Fri, 9am-5pm Sat & Sun) This place was on the Stellenbosch map before Stellenbosch was on the map. It's an unashamedly touristy general dealer but still worth visiting for its curious range of goods – from high kitsch to genuine antiques and everything in between.

Green Sleeves (Map p172; ☎ 021-883 8374; 2 Crozier St; ⊗ 9am-5pm Mon-Fri, 9am-noon Sat) Green Sleeves features a charming selection of retro, funky and vintage clothing; next door is a sister shop offering similar styles in furniture and homeware.

The town offers other excellent shopping opportunities, from the **craft market** (Map p172; ⊗ 9am-5pm) near the Braak, to the **Simonsberg Cheese Factory** (Map p172; ☎ 021-809 1017; 9 Stoffel Smit St; ⊗ 9am-5pm Mon-Fri, 9am-12.30pm Sat), which has free tastings and inexpensive cheese.

Getting There & Away

BUS

Long-distance bus services charge high prices for the short sector to Cape Town and do not take bookings. You're better off using **Backpacker Bus** (☎ 021-447 4991; www.back packerbus.co.za), which charges R140 to R220 one way and will pick you up from where you are staying.

MINIBUS TAXI

A minibus taxi ride to Paarl is about R30 (45 minutes), but you may have to change taxis en route at Pniel. They leave from the stand on Bird St.

TRAIN

Metro trains run the 46km between Cape Town and Stellenbosch (1st/economy class R12/7.50, about one hour). Note there are no 2nd-class tickets. For inquiries, call **Metrorail** (☎ 0800 656 463). To be safe, travel in the middle of the day.

Getting Around

Stellenbosch is navigable on foot and, being largely flat, this is good cycling territory. Bicycles can be hired from the Stumble Inn (p174), the Publicity Association (p171) and Fandangos (p171) in the Drostdy Centre for R20 per hour or R90 for the day.

For local trips in a private taxi call **Daksi Cab** (☎ 082-854 1541).

FRANSCHHOEK

☎ 021 / pop 13,000

Franschhoek bills itself as the country's gastronomic capital. The toughest decision you'll face in Franschhoek is where to eat. And with a clutch of art galleries, wine farms and stylish guesthouses thrown in, there's a sense here that this is all too good to be true. It certainly has one of the loveliest settings in the Cape, and if it all feels a bit too much like a theme park this a good base from which to visit both Stellenbosch and Paarl, as long as you have transport.

Orientation & Information

The town is clustered around Huguenot St. At the southern end it reaches a T-junction at Huguenot Memorial Park. Continue northeast along Rte 45 for the spectacular Franschhoek Pass.

Franschhoek Photolab (Map p179; ☎ 021-876 4911; Huguenot St; per hr R30) There's Internet access here.

Franschhoek Wine Valley Tourism (Map p179; ☎ 021-876 3603; www.franschhoek.org.za; Huguenot St; ⊙ 9am-6pm Mon-Fri, 9am-5pm Sat, 9am-4pm Sun) This office is to the left on the main street shortly after you enter the town. Staff here can provide you with a map of the area's scenic walks and issue permits (R10) for walks in nearby forestry areas, as well as book accommodation.

Sights & Activities

HUGUENOT MEMORIAL MUSEUM

This engrossing **museum** (Map p179; ☎ 021-876 2532; Lambrecht St; adult/child R5/2; ⊙ 9am-5pm Mon-Sat, 2-5pm Sun) celebrates South Africa's Huguenots and houses the genealogical records of their descendants. Some of the names of the original settlers, such as Malan, de Villiers, Malherbe and Roux, are among the most famous Afrikaner dynasties in the country. Behind the main complex is a pleasant café, in front is the **Huguenot Monument** (adult/child R5/1; ⊙ 9am-5pm), opened in 1948, and across the road is the **annexe**, which offers displays on the Anglo-Boer War and natural history, and a souvenir shop.

MONT ROCHELLE EQUESTRIAN CENTRE

For details about a horseback tour of the wine estates around town contact the **equestrian centre** (☎ 083-300 4368; fax 021-876 2363; per hr R90). It's based in the Mont Rochelle Wine Estate.

ARTS & CRAFTS

Franschhoek boasts many fine galleries, most along Huguenot St. You can watch David Walters, one of South Africa's most distinguished potters, at work at the **Roubaix House Gallery** (Map p179; ☎ 021-876 4304; 24 Dirkie Uys St; ⊙ 10am-6pm), in the beautifully restored home of Franschhoek's first teacher behind the tourist info office. There are also exhibits of work by other artists.

HUGUENOT FINE CHOCOLATES

An empowerment programme helped give the two local coloured guys who run this Belgian-style **chocolate shop** (Map p179 ☎ 021-876 4096; 62 Huguenot St) a leg up and now people are raving about their confections. Call them a day in advance to arrange a tour and chocolate-making demonstration including tasting of samples (R12).

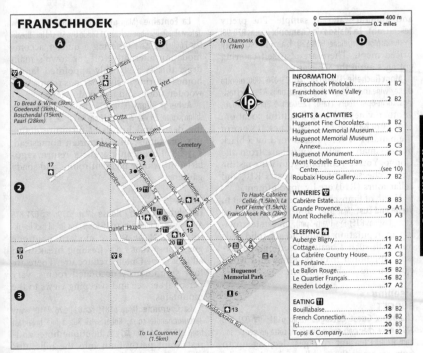

FRANSCHHOEK

0 — 400 m
0 — 0.2 miles

To Chamonix (1km)

To Bread & Wine (3km);
Goederust (3km);
Boschendal (15km);
Paarl (28km)

Cemetery

To Haute Cabrière
Cellar (1.5km); La
Petit Ferme (1.5km);
Franschhoek Pass (2km)

Huguenot
Memorial Park

To La Couronne
(1.5km)

WESTERN CAPE

WINERIES

Many of Franschhoek's wineries are within walking distance of the town centre, but you'll need transport to reach famous **Boschendal** (Map p181; ☎ 021-870 4210; www.boschendal.com; Pniel Rd; ☼ 8.30am-4.30pm), the classic Winelands estate, with lovely architecture, food and wine. The vineyard and cellar tours (R20 per person) are well worth it; booking is essential. Note the Taphuis wine-tasting area (where tastings cost R15 or R22 for a formal tasting with a guide) is at the opposite end of the estate from the **Groote Drakenstein manor house** (admission R10) and restaurants. The blow-out buffet lunch (R195) in the main restaurant is mainly a group affair; far nicer, especially in fine weather, is **Le Café** (☎ 021-870 4274), where you can have a snack or something more substantial. Also very popular are 'Le Pique Nique' hampers (R95 per person), served under parasols on the lawn from mid-October to the end of April. There's a minimum of two people and you'll need to book. Its reds, including Cabernet Sauvignon and Merlot, get top marks.

Back in town, **Cabrière Estate** (Map p179; ☎ 021-876 8500; www.cabriere.co.za; Berg St; tastings with/without cellar tour R25/20; ☼ 9.30am-4.30pm Mon-Fri, 10.30am-3.30pm Sat, tours 11am & 3pm Mon-Fri, 11am Sat) offers tastings that include a couple of sparkling wines and one of the vineyard's excellent range of white, red and dessert wines and brandies. No wonder it's so popular. At the Saturday session, stand by for the proprietor's party trick of slicing open a bottle of bubbly with a sabre.

Off Main Rd is **Grande Provence** (Map p179; ☎ 021-876 8600; www.grandeprovence.co.za; Main Rd; tastings free; ☼ 10am-6pm), a beautifully revamped, 18th-century manor house that is home to a stylish restaurant and a splendid gallery showcasing the best local artists. In the tasting room you can try its very easy-drinking Angel's Tears blends or the more upmarket Grande Provence wines.

Up the hill to the west of town is **Chamonix** (Map p181; ☎ 021-876 2494; www.chamonix.co.za; Uitkyk St; tastings R15; ☼ 9.30am-4.30pm), which has cellar tours at 11am and 3pm by appointment. The tasting room is in a converted blacksmith's; there's also a range of schnapps

WESTERN CAPE

and mineral water to sample. The pretty restaurant, **La Maison de Chamonix** (mains R70-90; (Y) lunch Mon-Sun, dinner Fri & Sat), has a reasonably priced menu. There are also self-catering cottages amid the vineyards.

Mont Rochelle (Map p179; ☎ 021-876 3000; montrochelle@wine.co.za; Daniel Hugo St; tastings R15; (Y) tastings 10am-6pm, tours 11am, 12.30pm & 3pm Mon-Fri), another vineyard in a beautiful location, Mont Rochelle offers great wines. It's one of the handful of vineyards owned by a black businessman – Miko Rwayibare from the Congo. You can combine your wine tasting with a cheese tasting for an extra R10, and cellar tours (R10) are by appointment.

North of Franschhoek, it's worth a visit to **Vrede and Lust** (Map p181; ☎ 021-874 1611; www.vnl.co.za; tastings R15; (Y) 10am-5pm), an estate growing in reputation thanks to its solid reds but, with such a beautiful setting and lavishly appointed main building, you won't care too much about the vino.

Sleeping
BUDGET

Chamonix Guest Cottages (Map p181; ☎ 021-876 2494; www.chamonix.co.za; Uitkyk St; cottages per person from R200) Pleasant cottages sleeping up to four are set in the middle of the vineyards, a 10-minute walk uphill north of Huguenot St. There are considerable winter discounts (May to October).

Cottage (Map p179; ☎ 021-876 2392; thecottage55@iafrica.com; 55 Huguenot St; s/d R260/350) There is just one cottage sleeping two, or four at a pinch, but it's a beauty. It's private, quiet, just a few minutes' walk from the village centre and now has self-catering facilities.

Reeden Lodge (Map p179 ☎ 021-876 3174; www.reedenlodge.co.za; off Cabrière St; cottages from R400; (🖳 🐾) A terrific option for families, with well-equipped, self-catering cottages sleeping up to eight people, situated on a farm about 10 minutes' walk from town. Parents will love the peace and quiet and their kids the sheep, tree house and open space.

MIDRANGE

Le Ballon Rouge (Map p179; ☎ 021-876 2651; www.ballon-rouge.co.za; 7 Reservoir St East; s/d incl breakfast R500/650; (❄ 🖳 🐾) A small guesthouse with good-quality rooms and stylish suites (with underfloor heating and stunning bathrooms) all opening on to a patio. It also has a popular restaurant.

La Fontaine (Map p179; ☎ 021-876 2112; www.lafontainefranschhoek.co.za; 21 Dirkie Uys St; s/d incl breakfast R600/750; 🐾) Offering a quieter accommodation alternative off the town's main drag, this is a stylishly appointed family home featuring twelve spacious rooms with wooden floors and mountain views.

Auberge Bligny (Map p179; ☎ 021-876 3767; www.bligny.co.za; 28 Van Wyk St; d from R650; 🐾) Charming décor and heavy-set furniture define this guesthouse in a Victorian homestead. Largely European travellers return regularly for its nine pleasant rooms and shady garden.

TOP END

La Cabrière Country House (Map p179; ☎ 021-876 4780; www.lacabriere.co.za; Middagkrans Rd; d incl breakfast R1050; (❄ 🖳 🐾) A modern boutique guesthouse that's a refreshing break from all that Cape Dutch architecture. There are four sumptuously decorated rooms, very personal service and sweeping views to the mountains.

La Couronne (Map p181; ☎ 021-876 2110; www.lacouronnehotel.co.za; Robertsvlei Rd; d incl breakfast from R1970; (❄ 🖳 🐾) A boutique hotel-and-restaurant partly built into the hills, this place offers gilt-edged luxury and magnificent views across the valley.

Le Quartier Français (Map p179; ☎ 021-876 2151; www.lequartier.co.za; 16 Huguenot St; d from R2350; (❄ 🖳 🐾) This is one of the best places to stay in the Winelands. Set around a leafy courtyard and pool, guest rooms are very large with fireplaces, huge beds and stylish décor. There's also a fine restaurant, called Ici, here.

Eating

Franschhoek's compactness means it's possible to stroll around and let your nose tell you where to eat. The following places are well established, however, so advance booking is best.

Goederust (Map p181; ☎ 021-876 3687; Main Rd, La Motte; mains R30-40; (Y) breakfast & lunch) A new take on Cape farm-kitchen food is served in this charming old-fashioned farm-restaurant set in a pleasant garden. The spicy calamari salad (R40) is a knockout, as are the filled pancakes. Come on Sunday for a spit-lamb buffet (bookings essential).

French Connection (Map p179; ☎ 021-876 4056; 48 Huguenot St; mains R50; (Y) lunch & dinner)

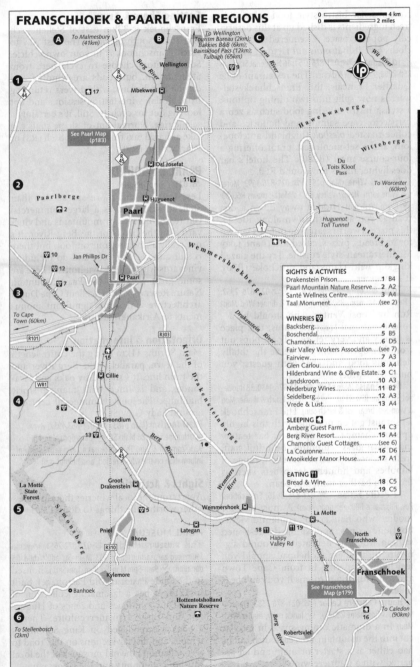

FRANSCHHOEK & PAARL WINE REGIONS

0 —————— 4 km
0 —————— 2 miles

To Malmesbury (41km)

To Wellington Tourism Bureau (2km); Bakkies B&B (6km); Bainskloof Pass (12km); Tulbagh (65km)

Wellington

Mbekweni

Berg River

Leeu River

Wit River

Hawekwaberge

Witteberge

Paarlberge

Dal Josefat

Huguenot

Paarl

Du Toits Kloof Pass

To Worcester (60km)

Huguenot Toll Tunnel

Duitoitsberge

Jan Phillips Dr

Suid-Agter-Paarl Rd

Wemmershoekberge

To Cape Town (60km)

Drakenstein River

Klein Drakensteinberge

Simondium

Berg River

La Motte State Forest

Simonsberg

Groot Drakenstein

Pniel

Rhone

Kylemore

Banhoek

Wemmers River

Lategan

Wemmershoek

Happy Valley Rd

La Motte

Robertsvlei Rd

North Franschhoek

Franschhoek

See Franschhoek Map (p179)

Hottentotsholland Nature Reserve

To Caledon (90km)

Berg River

Robertsvlei

To Stellenbosch (2km)

WESTERN CAPE

See Paarl Map (p183)

SIGHTS & ACTIVITIES	
Drakenstein Prison	**1** B4
Paarl Mountain Nature Reserve	**2** A2
Santé Wellness Centre	**3** A4
Taal Monument	(see 2)

WINERIES	
Backsberg	**4** A4
Boschendal	**5** B5
Chamonix	**6** D5
Fair Valley Workers Association	(see 7)
Fairview	**7** A3
Glen Carlou	**8** A4
Hildenbrand Wine & Olive Estate	**9** C1
Landskroon	**10** A3
Nederburg Wines	**11** B2
Seidelberg	**12** A3
Vrede & Lust	**13** A4

SLEEPING	
Amberg Guest Farm	**14** C3
Berg River Resort	**15** A4
Chamonix Guest Cottages	(see 6)
La Couronne	**16** D6
Mooikelder Manor House	**17** A1

EATING	
Bread & Wine	**18** C5
Goederust	**19** C5

No-nonsense bistro-style food using only fresh ingredients is dished up at this deservedly popular place. Chequered red tablecloths give it that *mais oui* factor.

Ici (Map p179; ☎ 021-876 2151; 16 Huguenot St; mains R50-R280; ☻ lunch & dinner) The restaurant of Le Quartier Français, this Franschhoek stalwart is now split into two dining options: a stylish bistro offering food such as zebra carpaccio, cape salmon and liquorice and coffee-roasted *blesbok* (highland antelope) loin; and a set-meal restaurant offering a four-course meal (R280). The hotel's bar does lighter meals for around R60.

Bread & Wine (Map p181; ☎ 021-876 3692; Môreson Wine Farm, Happy Valley Rd, La Motte; mains R60-80; ☻ lunch Wed-Sun) Hidden away down a dirt road as you approach town along Rte 45, this place is worth searching out. It's known for its breads, pizzas, cured meats and tasty Mediterranean-style cuisine. Try the glazed kingklip with clams and artichoke (R70). It's a winner.

Topsi & Company (Map p179; ☎ 021-876 2952; 7 Reservoir St; mains R60-85; ☻ lunch & dinner Wed-Mon) Run by Topsi Venter, who should be accorded national-treasure status, this place is quirky and very relaxed. Topsi pops out from her open kitchen to serve the totally delicious food and chat with guests; you must BYO wine.

Bouillabaise (Map p179; ☎ 021-876 4430; 38 Huguenot St; mains R70-R110; ☻ breakfast, lunch & dinner Mon & Wed-Sat, breakfast & lunch Sun) The Franschhoek jet set just got an upgrade, with this highly opulent champagne-and-oyster bar featuring blown-glass sculptures, beautiful staff, fresh seafood dishes, an excellent range of bubblies and homemade sorbets such as lime and basil or mint and pear.

La Petite Ferme (☎ 021-876 3016; Franschhoek Pass Rd; mains R80; ☻ noon-4pm) A must-visit for foodies who hanker for romantic views, boutique wines and smoked, de-boned salmon trout, its delicately flavoured signature dish. There's a helipad should you feel like choppering in from Cape Town and some luxurious rooms if you can't bear to leave.

Haute Cabrière Cellar (☎ 021-876 3688; Franschhoek Pass Rd; mains R80-90; ☻ lunch daily, dinner Wed-Mon) In a dramatic dining space in a cellar cut into the mountain side, each dish can be had either as a starter or main and all are paired with a Cabrière wine.

Getting There & Away

Franschhoek is 32km east of Stellenbosch and 25km south of Paarl. The best way to reach Franschhoek is in your own vehicle. Some visitors choose to cycle here from Stellenbosch, but roads are winding and can be treacherous, with drivers returning from all-day wine-tasting sessions and not looking out for cyclists. Still, it's certainly a scenic ride. Normal out-of-shape souls can take a shared taxi from Stellenbosch (R8) or Paarl station (R9).

PAARL & AROUND
☎ 021 / pop 165,000

Less touristy and more spread out than Stellenbosch, Paarl is a large commercial centre, surrounded by mountains and vineyards, on the banks of the Berg River. It's not really a town to tour on foot, but there is still quite a lot to see and do including vineyards within the town limits. There are some great walks in the Paarl Mountain Nature Reserve, some excellent Cape Dutch architecture and some significant monuments to Afrikaner culture.

Orientation & Information

Main St runs 11km along the entire length of the town, parallel to the Berg River and the train line. It's shaded by oaks and jacarandas and is lined with many historic buildings. The busy commercial centre is around Lady Grey St.

Paarl Tourism (Map p183; ☎ 021-863 4937; www .paarlonline.com; 86 Main St; ☻ 8am-6pm Mon-Fri, 9am-2pm Sat & Sun) This office has an excellent supply of information on the whole region, and helpful staff.

Sights & Activities

Apart from the local wineries there are a few other worthwhile things to do in Paarl.

PAARL MUSEUM

This **museum** (Map p183 ☎ 021-872 2651; www.museums.org.za/paarlmuseum; 303 Main St; adult/child R5 donation; ☻ 9am-5pm Mon-Fri, 9am-1pm Sat) is housed in the Oude Pastorie (Old Parsonage), built in 1714. It has a fascinating collection of Cape Dutch antiques and relics of Huguenot and early Afrikaner culture. There's a bookcase modelled on King Solomon's temple, and display sections on the 'road to reconciliation', the old mosques of the local Muslim community and the Khoesaan.

AFRIKAANS LANGUAGE MUSEUM

Paarl is considered the wellspring of the Afrikaans language, a fact covered by this interesting **museum** (Map p183; ☎ 021-872 3441; www.taalmuseum.co.za; 11 Pastorie Ave; adult/child R10/2; ۞ 9am-4pm Mon-Fri, 9am-1pm Sat). It also shows, thanks to a multimedia exhibition, how three continents contributed to the formation of what is a fascinating and often beautiful language. Follow up a visit here with a visit to the somewhat phallic Taal Monument.

PAARL MOUNTAIN NATURE RESERVE

The three giant granite domes that dominate this popular reserve (Map p181) and loom over the western side of town apparently glisten like pearls if they are caught by the sun after a fall of rain – hence the name 'Paarl'. The reserve has mountain *fynbos* (literally 'fine bush'; primarily proteas, heaths and ericas), a cultivated wildflower garden in the middle that's a nice spot for a picnic, and numerous walks with excellent views over the valley.

Access is from the 11km-long Jan Phillips Dr, which skirts the eastern edge of the reserve. The picnic ground is about 4km from Main St. A map showing walking trails is available from Paarl Tourism.

While up this way you could also visit the **Taal Monument** (Map p181; adult/child R10/5; ۞ 8.15am-5pm), a giant needlelike edifice that commemorates the Afrikaans language (*taal* is Afrikaans for 'language'). On a clear day there are stunning views from here as far as Cape Town. There's also an adjoining restaurant and curio shop.

DRAKENSTEIN PRISON

On 11 February 1990, when Nelson Mandela walked free from incarceration for the first time in more than 27 years, the jail in question was not Robben Island, but here. Then called the Victor Verster, this prison (Map p181) was where Mandela spent his last two years of captivity in the relative comfort of the warders cottage, negotiating the end of apartheid. It's still a working prison so there are no tours, but there is a pretty good à la carte restaurant.

SANTÉ WELLNESS CENTRE

The chief selling point of this luxurious **spa** (Map p181; ☎ 021-875 8100; www.santewellness.co.za; Klapmuts), around 7km southwest of Paarl,

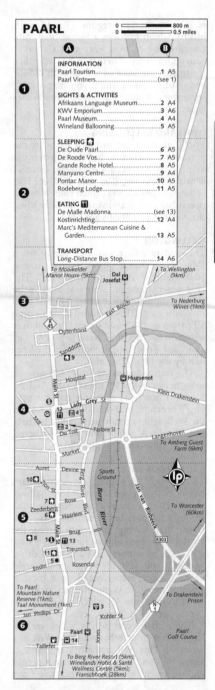

PAARL

0 — 800 m
0 — 0.5 miles

INFORMATION
Paarl Tourism......................................1 A5
Paarl Vintners..............................(see 1)

SIGHTS & ACTIVITIES
Afrikaans Language Museum..........2 A4
KWV Emporium...................................3 A6
Paarl Museum.....................................4 A4
Wineland Ballooning.......................5 A5

SLEEPING
De Oude Paarl....................................6 A5
De Roode Vos.....................................7 A5
Grande Roche Hotel.........................8 A5
Manyano Centre................................9 A4
Pontac Manor..................................10 A5
Rodeberg Lodge..............................11 A5

EATING
De Malle Madonna........................(see 13)
Kostinrichting..................................12 A4
Marc's Mediterranean Cuisine &
    Garden..13 A5

TRANSPORT
Long-Distance Bus Stop.................14 A6

is its vinotherapy regime (R1645 with lunch), which includes a Shiraz body rub, Chardonnay cocoon wrap and Cabernet Sauvignon bath! There are lots of other treatments available as well as both indoor and outdoor pools, and if you simply can't leave you can stay at the sumptuous Winelands Hotel.

WINELAND BALLOONING

You'll need to get up very early in the morning, but a hot-air balloon trip over the Winelands will be unforgettable. Contact **Wineland Ballooning** (Map p183; ☎ 021-863 3192; 64 Main St; per person R1500), which runs trips between November and April but only when the weather conditions are right.

WELLINGTON

This sedate and reasonably pretty town (Map p181) has a population of around 50,000 and is 10km north of Paarl. The landowner whose property was used by the railway stipulated that all trains must stop in Wellington. This included King George VI's train in 1947, and today Wellington is a stop on the Metrorail route between Paarl and Cape Town and accounts for the brief halt by the *Blue Train* also.

The **Tourism Bureau** (☎ 021-873 4604; www.visit wellington.com; 104 Main St) is next to the Andrew Murray Church. The friendly staff can provide a brochure and map of the wineries in the Wellington area, which are less touristy than Paarl's. A popular one is Hildenbrand Wine & Olive Estate (opposite).

BAINSKLOOF PASS

This is one of the country's great mountain passes, with a superb caravan park halfway along. Thomas Bain developed the road through the pass between 1848 and 1852. Other than having its surface tarred, the road has not been altered since, and is now a national monument. It's a magical drive, which, if you have the lungs for it, would be even better experienced on a bicycle. Rte 303 runs from Wellington across Bainskloof to meet Rte 43, which runs south to Worcester and north to Ceres.

There are several nearby walks, including the five-hour **Bobbejaans River Walk** to a waterfall. This walk actually starts back at Eerste Tol and you need to buy a permit (R30), which is available from the Cape

Nature Conservation desk at Cape Town Tourism (see p106).

WINERIES

For information about wineries in the area, contact **Paarl Vintners** (☎ 021-863 4886; 86 Main St).

The first stop on your Paarl wine exploration should probably be **KWV Emporium** (Map p183; ☎ 021-807 3007; www.kwv-international.com; Kohler St; tastings R20; ⏱ 9am-4pm Mon-Sat), one of the country's best-known wineries because its products are mostly sold overseas. Some KWV port and sherry is available inside South Africa, and its fortified wines, in particular, are among the world's best. Cellar tours are at its complex near the train line. Call for times of cellar tours (R20), which are worth taking if only to see the enormous Cathedral Cellar built in 1930.

Another hugely popular estate on the Suid-Agter-Paarl Rd, off Rte 101 6km south of Paarl, is **Fairview** (Map p181; ☎ 021-863 2450; www.fairview.co.za; tastings R10; ⏱ 8.30am-5pm Mon-Fri, 8.30am-1pm Sat), a wonderful winery but not the place to come for a calm wine tasting. Peacocks and goats in a tower (apparently goats love to climb) greet you on arrival, and tastings are great value since they cover some 23 wines *and* a wide range of goat's- and cow's-milk cheeses. You can sample and buy the pinotage and Chenin Blanc of the **Fair Valley Workers Association** (Map p181; ☎ 021-863 2450) here too; see p170 for more information.

If you've made it to Fairview, don't miss **Seidelberg** (Map p181; ☎ 021-863 3495; www.seidel berg.co.za; tastings with/without cellar tour R18/12; ⏱ 9am-6pm Mon-Fri, 10am-6pm Sat & Sun), next door. Seidelberg offers an escape from the Bacchanalian hordes and, uniquely, features tours and demonstrations of onsite bronze-casting and glassblowing. Its selection of reds is nothing to be ashamed of either.

Next along is **Landskroon** (Map p181; ☎ 021-863 1039; tastings R10; ⏱ 8.30am-5pm Mon-Fri, 9am-1pm Sat), an estate representing five generations of the De Villiers family, who have been perfecting their wine-making skills on this pleasant estate. There's a nice terrace overlooking the vines on which you can quaff its impressive Cinsaut and celebrated *jerepigo* (dessert wine).

Further south **Glen Carlou** (Map p181; ☎ 021-875 5528; www.glencarlou.co.za; Simondium Rd, Klapmuts; tastings free; ⏱ 9am-4.45pm Mon-Fri, 9am-1pm Sun) has a new gallery and tasting room with panoramic view of Tortoise Hill. Its Shiraz is made with a small percentage of viognier and mourvèdre grapes.

To the northeast, **Hildenbrand Wine & Olive Estate** (☎ 021-873 4115; www.wine-estate-hildenbrand .co.za; tastings R15; s/d incl breakfast R370/560; ☺ winery 10am-4pm; ☝) has a restaurant and good accommodation. You can also taste locally grown olives and buy freshly-pressed olive oil. The estate is in the centre of a large loop road east of Wellington. Follow the signposting off Rte 303 as you approach Wellington from Paarl.

A visit to **Nederburg Wines** (Map p181; ☎ 021-862 3104; www.nederburg.co.za; tastings R10; ☺ 8.30am-5pm Mon-Fri year-round, plus 10am-2pm Sat & Sun Dec-Mar) is a must. This is one of South Africa's most well-known labels, a big but professional and welcoming operation featuring a vast range of wines and informative food and wine tasting (R20) that teaches you how best to match wine with food flavours. The picnic lunches cost R90 per person (December to March only, bookings essential) and are very popular. Nederburg is off the N1, 7km east of Paarl.

Further down the road, check out **Backsberg** (Map p181; ☎ 021-875 5141; www.backsberg.co.za; tastings R15; ☺ 8.30am-5pm Mon-Fri, 9am-2pm Sat, 11am-3pm Sun), an immensely popular estate thanks to its reliable label and lavish outdoor lunches. Backsberg is around 12km southwest of Paarl along the WR1. Its white wines have won awards, but along with L'Avenir (p174) this is one of the country's best examples of the homegrown pinotage cultivar. The estate is closed in July and August.

Sleeping

BUDGET

Manyano Centre (Map p183; ☎ 021-872 2537; man yano@eject.co.za; Sanddrift St; dm with full board R110) An enormous YMCA-style accommodation complex with spartan three-bed dorms; you'll need to bring a sleeping bag. Call in advance, especially on weekends when it fills up with groups. Huguenot train station is closer than the main Paarl station.

De Roode Vos (Map p183; ☎ /fax 021-872 5912; 152 Main St; s/d R150/240) This unspectacular guesthouse has clean lodgings and is about as cheap as you'll get in central Paarl.

Berg River Resort (Map p181; ☎ 021-863 1650; bergr@mweb.co.za; camp sites R155, d chalets R520; ☝) An attractive municipal campground beside the Berg River, 5km from Paarl on the N45 towards Franschhoek. Facilities include canoes, trampolines and a café.

Bakkies B&B (Map p181; ☎ 021-873 5161; www .bakkiesbb.co.za; Bainskloof Rd; s/d R170/280; ☒ ☐ ☝) This place, out on the Bainskloof Rd past Wellington, offers good-value, well-equipped rooms and is an excellent budget base for exploring the area. Lunch and dinner are by arrangement, and a daily breakfast (R40) is offered.

MIDRANGE

Rodeberg Lodge (Map p183; ☎ 021-863 3202; www .rodeberglodge.co.za; 74 Main St; s/d incl breakfast R290/460; ☒) Good rooms (some with air-con and TV) are sensibly located away from the busy main road, and there's a family room (R200 per person) in the attic. The hosts are friendly and breakfast is taken in the conservatory, opening onto a leafy garden.

Amberg Guest Farm (Map p181; ☎ 021-862 0982; amberg@mweb.co.za; Rte 101; s/d incl breakfast R330/500; ☝) Accommodation is in cottages (one of which is self-catering for R360) with spectacular views. The amiable hosts also run the Swiss-style Amberg Country Kitchen, serving Swiss specialities. It's along Du Toits Kloof Pass.

Mooikelder Manor House (Map p181; ☎ 021-869 8787; www.capestay.co.za/mooikelder; Main St, Noorder Paarl; s/d incl breakfast R350/650; ☐ ☝) Around 5km north of the town centre in an elegant homestead once occupied by British empire-builder and former Governor of the Cape Colony Cecil John Rhodes, this is a lovely, quiet spot amid citrus orchards and with plenty of antique atmosphere in the rooms.

TOP END

De Oude Paarl (Map p183; ☎ 021-872 1002; www.de oudepaarl.com; 132 Main St; s/d incl breakfast R650/930; ☒ ☐ ☝) This is a new boutique-style hotel; the rooms have antique touches and there's a secluded courtyard at the back. Attached are shops selling a good selection of wine and delectable but pricey Belgian chocolates.

Pontac Manor (Map p183; ☎ 021-872 0445; www .pontac.com; 16 Zion St; s/d incl breakfast R1090/1400; ☒ ☝) A small, stylish, Victorian-era hotel that commands a good view of the valley. The rooms are comfortable, there's one self-catering cottage and a restaurant, which is recommended.

Grande Roche Hotel (Map p183; ☎ 021-863 2727; www.granderoche.co.za; Plantasie St; d from R2420; 🅿 🖥 🍴 🕭) An unashamedly opulent hotel set in a Cape Dutch manor house, offering mountain views, a heated swimming pool and the award-winning Bosman's Restaurant (mains R140), whose wine list runs to over 50 pages! Various set menus start at R320 for three courses.

Winelands Hotel (ste incl breakfast R2670; 🅿 🖥 🍴) This place at the Santé Wellness Centre offers king-sized beds, the latest in audiovisual equipment and decadent bathrooms.

Eating

Several of the local wineries have restaurants or do picnic lunches and they are among the best places to eat.

Kostinrichting (Map p183; ☎ 021-871 1353; 19 Pastorie Ave; mains R30; 🕒 lunch Mon-Sat) This place is ideal if you are looking for a pleasant central café. It's in a Victorian building that once was a school, and has an attached crafts shop.

De Malle Madonna (Map p183; ☎ 021-863 3925; 127 Main St; mains R40-65; 🕒 breakfast & lunch Wed-Sun, dinner Wed & Sun) Marc Chagall is the inspiration for this breezy café-bistro, whose emphasis is on 'Mediterranean comfort food'. There's a sunny patio with views of the mountains, and the *biltong* (dried meat) and glazed-beetroot salad (R41) is a winner.

Marc's Mediterranean Cuisine & Garden (Map p183 ☎ 021-863 3980; 129 Main St; mains R60-75; 🕒 lunch Tue-Sun, dinner Mon-Sat) The current favourite of restaurant reviewers, and with good reason. Patron Marc Friedrich has created a light and bright place with food to match and a Provence-style garden to dine in.

Getting There & Away
BUS

All the major long-distance bus companies offer services going through Paarl, so it's easy to build it into your itinerary. The bus segment between Paarl and Cape Town is R110, so consider taking the cheaper train to Paarl and then linking up with the buses.

The long-distance bus stop (Map p183) is opposite the Engen petrol station on Main St as you enter the town from the N1.

TRAIN

Metro trains run roughly every hour between Cape Town and Paarl (1st/economy class R14.50/8.50, 1¼ hours, Monday to Friday). Note there is no 2nd class. The services are less frequent on weekends. Take care to travel on trains during the busy part of the day, as robberies have been reported.

You can travel by train from Paarl to Stellenbosch; take a Cape Town–bound train and change at Muldersvlei.

Getting Around

If you don't have your own transport, your only option for getting around Paarl, apart from walking and cycling, is to call a taxi; try **Paarl Radio Taxis** (☎ 021-872 5671).

THE OVERBERG

All roads heading east from Cape Town suddenly and unforgivably come against a mountainous barrier, forcing you to hit the lower gears. Once you're up and over the top, you're 'over the mountain', the literal meaning of Overberg.

Roughly the region south and west of the Franschhoek Range, and south of the Wemmershoek and Riviersonderend Ranges, which form a natural barrier with the Breede River Valley, the Overberg is reached from Cape Town via the N2 (quicker) or via Rte 44 from Strand, towards Hermanus around Cape Hangklip.

The latter is a breathtaking coastal drive, in the same class as the Chapman's Peak Dr in Cape Town, and with no toll. The first major stop is Hermanus, a seaside resort famous for the whales that frequent its shores (although it's so famous now that you might choose to do your whale-watching at a less crowded location along the coast).

If you're looking for somewhere quiet to hang out, the miraculously undeveloped fishing village of Gansbaai will fit the bill, as will Arniston and the De Hoop Nature Reserve a little further on. The best all-round base for the area is Swellendam, a historic and attractive town beneath the impressive Langeberg Mountains.

This region's wealth of *fynbos* is unmatched; most species flower somewhere in the period between autumn and spring. The climate basically follows the same

WATCHING WHALES

Between June and November, southern right whales *(Eubalaena australis)* come to Walker Bay to calve. There can be up to 70 whales in the bay at once. South Africa was a whaling nation until 1976 – this species was hunted to the verge of extinction but its numbers are now recovering. Humpback whales *(Megaptera novaeangliae)* are also sometimes seen.

Whales often come very close to shore and there are some excellent vantage points from the cliff paths that run from one end of Hermanus to the other. The best places are Castle Rock, Kraal Rock and Sievers Point. There's a telescope on the cliff top above the old harbour.

It's only recently that the people of Hermanus bothered to tell the outside world the whales were regular visitors. They took them for granted. Now, however, the tourism potential has been recognised and just about every business in town has adopted a whale logo. There's a **whale crier** (☎ 073-214 6949), who walks around town blowing on a kelp horn and carrying a blackboard that shows where whales have been recently sighted. A whale festival (p188) is held in September.

Despite all this hoopla, boat-viewing of whales is strictly regulated. No boat-viewing is allowed in the bay and jet skis are banned. There are only two boat-viewing outfits licensed to operate in the seas outside the bay: **Southern Right Charters** (☎ 082-353 0550) and **Hermanus Whale Cruises** (☎ 028-313 2722). They charge around R400 for a one- to two-hour trip.

Although Hermanus is the best-known whale-watching site, whales can be seen all the way from False Bay (Cape Town) to Plettenberg Bay and beyond. The west coast also gets its share.

For those with private transport, there is a large whale-watching car park in a terrific elevated location near the Old Harbour. On windier days, you can watch the whales from the comfort of your vehicle!

---

pattern as Cape Town – a temperate Mediterranean climate with relatively mild winters and warm summers. Rain falls throughout the year but peaks in August, and it can be very windy in any season.

KOGEL BAY
☎ 024

The best bit of the drive along Rte 44 from Cape Town is between Gordon's Bay and Kleinmond. The views are stunning. At times it feels as if the road is going to disappear into the sea. On one side is blue-green water, on the other rock-strewn cliffs. The **Kogel Bay Pleasure Resort** (☎ 024-856 1286; fax 024-856 4741; Rte 44; day visitors per person R8, per vehicle R15; camp sites R70) has camp sites and reasonable facilities on a fantastic beach (although it's unsafe for swimming and sometimes windy). Bring all your own food. It's popular with South Africans during school holidays.

BETTY'S BAY
☎ 028

The small, scattered holiday village of Betty's Bay, just to the east of Cape Hangklip, is the next place worth a pause on Rte 44. Here you'll find the **Harold Porter National Botanical Gardens** (☎ 028-272 9311; adult/child R8/4; ⏱ 8am-4.30pm Mon-Fri, 8am-5pm Sat & Sun, 8am-7pm Dec-Jan), definitely worth visiting. There are paths exploring the indigenous plant life in the area and, at the entrance, tearooms and a formal garden where you can picnic. Try the Leopard Kloof Trail, which leads through fern forests and up to a waterfall. It's a 3km round trip, and you'll need to pay a key deposit (R30) and get your key and permit (from the main ticket office) before 2pm. Coming from Cape Town, look for the turn-off to the gardens after driving through Betty's Bay. Another worthwhile stop is at **Stony Point**, on Rte 44 coming from Cape Town before you reach Betty's Bay. Take a short stroll to the lookout point for a colony of **African penguins**. It's very picturesque with crashing waves and a sea of black-and-white birds.

KLEINMOND
☎ 028

Close to a wild and beautiful beach, Kleinmond (on Rte 44) is, thanks to a recent revival, now rather chic. It's a great place to spend an afternoon, eat some fresh seafood and browse through the art gallery and little shops. The area also has some reliable swells for surfers and some good walking. There is no tourist info here; just ask the friendly residents for assistance.

OVERBERG & ROUTE 62

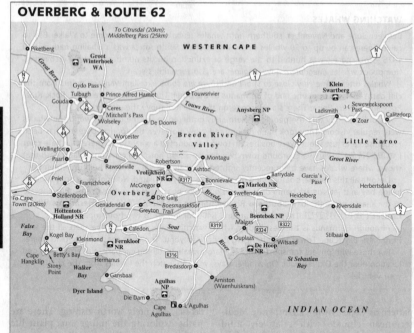

Sleeping & Eating

Most eating options are on Harbour Rd; just head in the direction of the sea.

Palmiet Caravan Park (☎ 028-271 4050; camp sites from R80) Beside the beach on the western side of town, where you can hear the waves breaking from your tent. Follow the signs from Rte 44.

Fifth Avenue Guesthouse (☎ 028-271 4254; 5thae guesthouse@telkomsa.net; 171 Fifth Ave; s & d from R250; cottages from R750; 🐾) It's a bit away from the main drag but offers clean and comfortable rooms at sensible prices. It's also just four blocks from the Kogelberg Nature Reserve, with pleasant walks and bird-watching, but no real facilities.

Roxy's Pizza Tavern & Pub (☎ 028-271 5378; 18 Harbour Rd; mains R30-50; 🍽 lunch & dinner) It isn't pretty, but this local favourite does exactly what it says on the tin and, with parties stretching into the wee hours, is Kleinmond's only late-night option.

Sandpiper (☎ 028-271 5368; 17 Harbour Rd; mains R30-70; 🍽 lunch & dinner Tue-Sun) A busy place with a Mediterranean-themed menu offering well-cooked food from a beach-facing terrace.

Alive Alive-O (☎ 028-271 3774; 35 Harbour Rd; mains R35-150; 🍽 lunch Mon-Sat) An outdoor beach-shack shellfish-bar claiming to be the only restaurant in the country allowed to serve the endangered abalone. The shellfish, known for their aphrodisiac qualities, are fried in garlic butter and served in a wine cream sauce (R140 for 200g).

HERMANUS

☎ 028 / pop 24,700

Hermanus (pronounced hair-maan-es) was founded as a fishing village, and while it retains vestiges of its heritage, its proximity to Cape Town (122km) has made it a day-tripper's paradise, in part thanks to the fact that it is considered the best land-based whale watching destination in the world.

The town centre, 2km east of the new harbour, is easily negotiated on foot and is well endowed with restaurants and shops, but the town's recent success means it has become highly commercialised and crowded, particularly during the **Hermanus Whale Festival** (www.whalefestival.co.za) in September and during school holidays in December and January.

LEGEND
NP   National Park
NR   Nature Reserve
WA   Wilderness Area

WESTERN CAPE

There is respite to be found at the appealing beaches, most east of the town centre, and the surrounding rocky hills, vaguely reminiscent of Scotland, offer good walks and a nature reserve protecting some of the prolific *fynbos*.

Orientation & Information
Route 43 leads you into Hermanus along dead-straight Main Rd, which itself leads southeast towards the town centre clustered just north of the Old Harbour.

Hermanus Tourism (☎ 028-312 2629; www.hermanus .co.za; Old Station Bldg, Mitchell St; ☼ 9am-5pm Mon-Sat, noon-5pm Sun) East of the town centre, this office has a large supply of information about the area, including walks and drives in the surrounding hills, and can book accommodation.

Internet City (☎ 028-312 4683; Waterkant Bldg, Main Rd; per hr R20; ☼ 8am-8pm) Offers reliable and speedy Internet connections.

Sights & Activities
There is no shortage of outdoor activities in Hermanus, and most places to sleep can arrange anything from sea kayaking to shark-diving to local wine tastings. Those looking for handicrafts can check out the small **daily market** (Lemm's Corner, Market Sq) off Main Rd; on Saturday there's a craft market held there, too.

SHARK-DIVING
Many operators in Hermanus heavily promote this, but most boats actually depart from Gansbaai (see p192), some 53km along the coast (all companies transport you there). There's no doubting the activity's popularity, but it doesn't come without controversy. Operators use bait to attract the sharks to the cage, which means that these killer fish are being trained to associate humans with food. It's not a pleasant scenario, especially if you're a surfer – attacks on whom have increased of late.

With the majority of operators, an internationally recognised diving qualification is required in order to take part in the dive, although some allow snorkellers into the cage. The most highly recommended operators are **Brian McFarlane** (☎ 028-312 2766; www.sharkcagediving.net; trips R800) and **Shark Lady Adventures** (☎ 028-313 3287; www.sharklady.co.za; 61 Marine Dr; trips R1000). Ask here about the spherical 'crystal cage' dive (R1700), which gets you even closer to the fish, and is strictly for divers only. Tours generally include breakfast, lunch and diving gear.

WALKING
The **Cliff Path Walking Trail** meanders from town along the sea to Grotto Beach, a long, narrow surf beach with excellent facilities. The walk takes about 1½ hours and along the way you'll pass Kraaiwater, a good whale-watching lookout, and Langbaai and Voelklip Beaches. The 1400-hectare **Fernkloof Nature Reserve** (Map pp188-9; ☎ 028-313 8100; Fir Ave; admission free; ☼ 9am-5pm) is worth a visit if you're interested in *fynbos*. Researchers have identified 1100 species so far. There's a 60km network of hiking trails for all fitness levels.

SEA KAYAKING
Walker Bay Adventures (☎ 028-314 0925; Prawn Flats; kayaking R250, canoeing R350, paragliding R750, boat-based whale-watching adult/child R400/150) runs sea-kayaking tours that give you the opportunity to see whales up close and personal. The company also does lagoon cruises and rents kayaks and boats.

WESTERN CAPE

OLD HARBOUR

The old harbour clings to the cliffs in front of the town centre; here you'll find a small, drab **museum** (☎ 028-312 1475; adult/child R2/1; ⏰ 9am-1pm & 2-5pm Mon-Sat, noon-4pm Sun) and a display of old fishing boats. The museum's annexe, in the old schoolhouse on the market square, displays some evocative old photographs of the town and its fishermen.

Sleeping

Despite a recent mushrooming of accommodation options in Hermanus, you might still find yourself searching in vain for a bed in the holiday season, so take care to book ahead. Hermanus Tourism will help

you or put you on to the many accommodation agencies. Below are some recommended establishments, but by no means all of them.

BUDGET

Hermanus Backpackers (☎ 028-312 4293; moobag@mweb.co.za; 26 Flower St; dm R75, d with shared bathroom R210; 💻 🍺) This is a smashing place with clued-up staff, and great décor and facilities, including a reed-roof bar. Free breakfast is served in the morning.

Moby's Traveller's Lodge (☎ 028-313 2361; www.mobys.co.za; 9 Mitchell St; dm R85, s/d with shared bathroom R200/260; 🍺) Travellers give this place rave reviews, and we can see why – it's a whole lot of fun. You can party the night

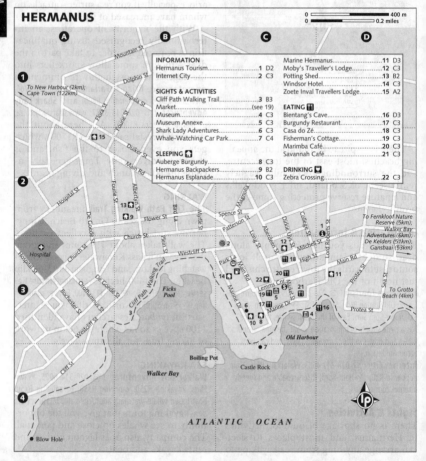

HERMANUS

0 — 400 m
0 — 0.2 miles

To New Harbour (2km); Cape Town (122km)

To Fernkloof Nature Reserve (5km); Walker Bay Adventures (6km); De Kelders (51km); Gansbaai (53km)

To Grotto Beach (4km)

INFORMATION
Hermanus Tourism.............................1 D2
Internet City.......................................2 C3

SIGHTS & ACTIVITIES
Cliff Path Walking Trail......................3 B3
Market...(see 19)
Museum...4 C3
Museum Annexe.................................5 C3
Shark Lady Adventures.......................6 C3
Whale-Watching Car Park..................7 C4

SLEEPING 🏠
Auberge Burgundy.............................8 C3
Hermanus Backpackers.......................9 B2
Hermanus Esplanade.........................10 C3

Marine Hermanus.............................11 D3
Moby's Traveller's Lodge...................12 D3
Potting Shed....................................13 B2
Windsor Hotel...................................14 C3
Zoete Inval Travellers Lodge.............15 A2

EATING 🍴
Bientang's Cave................................16 D3
Burgundy Restaurant........................17 C3
Casa do Zé.......................................18 C3
Fisherman's Cottage.........................19 C3
Marimba Café...................................20 C3
Savannah Café..................................21 C3

DRINKING 🍷
Zebra Crossing..................................22 C3

Ficks Pool

Old Harbour

Boiling Pot

Castle Rock

Walker Bay

ATLANTIC OCEAN

Blow Hole

away at the big bar or chill out in the awesome rock pool with its own waterfall. There's a daily pub lunch on offer and an Internet café (R30 per hour).

Zoete Inval Travellers Lodge (☎ 028-312 1242; www.zoeteinval.co.za; 23 Main Rd; dm R85, d with shared bathroom & breakfast R340) More a guesthouse than a hostel, this is a quiet place with good amenities (including a Jacuzzi) and neatly furnished rooms. Heavy smokers and drinkers should look elsewhere; families are accommodated in four-person doubles.

MIDRANGE

Hermanus Esplanade (☎ 028-312 3610; info@hermanus.com; 63 Marine Dr; flats from R250) Some of these cheery, self-catering apartments with colourful furniture overlook the sea; the lowest rates on offer actually cover the whale-watching season from May to October.

Potting Shed (☎ 028-312 1712; www.thepottingshedguesthouse.co.za; 28 Albertyn St; s/d incl breakfast from R300/440; P ☒ ☒) An excellent-value guesthouse that's drawn glowing reader reviews. The neat rooms are comfortable, but the bathrooms are shower-only. There is wheelchair access to all rooms and the pool area.

Windsor Hotel (☎ 028-312 3727; www.windsorhotel.co.za; 49 Marine Dr; s/d incl breakfast from R650/900) An old stalwart situated on an oceanside cliff; naturally you'll want one of the more expensive sea-facing rooms that give you the opportunity to view whales without leaving your bed.

Auberge Burgundy (☎ 028-313 1202; www.hermanus.co.za/accom/auberge; 16 Harbour Rd; s/d incl breakfast R735/980; ☒) This is a wonderful place, built in the style of a Provençal villa, with fine facilities, wrought-iron balconies and unique art on the walls.

TOP END

Marine Hermanus (☎ 028-313 1000; www.marine-hermanus.co.za; Marine Dr; s/d incl breakfast from R1700/2800; ☒ ☒ ☒) Right on the sea with immaculate grounds and amenities, this place is as posh as a five-star hotel should be. The staff are very friendly and will work with what you're looking for – sea views or rooms with balconies. The hotel has two restaurants, both sea-facing. One serves nouveau South African cuisine (two/three courses R155/195) and the other light seafood lunches (R95) with a view.

Eating & Drinking

There's no shortage of places to eat in Hermanus; many of which offer views within whale range.

Fisherman's Cottage (☎ 028-312 3642; Lemm's Cnr; mains R22-75; ☺ lunch & dinner) The emphasis is on good-value seafood at this restaurant in a whitewashed cottage draped with fishing nets.

Zebra Crossing (☎ 028-312 3906; 121 Main Rd; mains R35; ☺ lunch & dinner) This cheesy DJ bar with a funky zebra theme is, we're told, *the* late-night party spot on weekends, and popular with backpackers. At other times there's an open fire and pool tables.

Savannah Café (☎ 028-312 4259; Village Theatres Bldg, Marine Dr; mains from R40; ☺ breakfast & lunch) Enjoy a 'Whale of a Breakfast' – eggs, juice, coffee, bacon, chips, mushrooms and *boerewors* (spicy traditional sausage), or a sweet pastry while staring at the sea. There's also a decent selection for vegetarians, vegans and diabetics.

Marimba Café (☎ 028-312 2148; 9 Royal Lane off Main Rd; mains R45-85; ☺ dinner) The lively atmosphere matches the eclectic menu at this rather unkempt but recommended restaurant and bar, where you can eat traditional African dishes from around the continent.

Bientang's Cave (☎ 028-312 3454; Marine Dr; mains R55; ☺ lunch & dinner) Nestled in the cliffs beside the water, this really *is* a seaside cave, a remarkable setting that obscures the fact that the restaurant is only so-so. Access is only via a steep flight of cliffside stairs.

Casa do Zé (☎ 028-313 0377; 12 Mitchell St; mains R60; ☺ lunch & dinner Mon-Sat) A quaint Portuguese restaurant specialising in fresh grilled fish and the famous LM (Lourenço Marques) prawns. Try the imported Mozambiquan beer.

Burgundy Restaurant (☎ 028-312 2800; Marine Dr; mains R60-95; ☺ lunch & dinner) Booking is essential at this eatery, one of the most acclaimed and popular in the area. It's in the oldest buildings in town (1875), with a garden and sea views. The menu is mostly seafood with a different vegetarian dish each day.

Getting There & Away

Trevis Tours (☎ 072-608 9213) offers daily shuttles to Gansbaai (R50, 30 minutes) and Cape Town (R150, 1½ hours).

All three hostels run a shuttle service (R30 one way, 30 minutes) to the Baz Bus drop-off point in Botrivier, 50km west of town. Otherwise, there are no regular bus services to Hermanus from Cape Town.

GANSBAAI
☎ 028 / pop 12,000

Rustic, blissfully undeveloped Gansbaai's star has risen in recent years thanks to shark-diving, but there's more to the town than the fierce marine predators who frequent its shores. It boasts a sparkling unspoilt coastline perfect for those wishing to explore more out-of-the-way Overberg nature spots.

Orientation & Information

The road from Hermanus leads you 53km past the village of De Kelders straight into Main Rd, which runs parallel to the coastline. Kleinbaai, 7km further east along the coast, is where you'll find most activity. First follow the signs along Main Rd to efficient **Gansbaai Tourism** (☎ 028-384 1439; www.danger-point-peninsula.co.za; cnr Main & Berg Rds; ☹ 9am-5pm Mon-Fri, 9am-2pm Sat).

Sights & Activities

Gansbaai is the nexus of the Danger Point Peninsula area, which includes Kleinbaai. It's here where you'll find most amenities and activities.

Naturally, **whale-watching** and **shark-diving** are big draws here, but most tour operators are based in Hermanus (see p189). Good places to start asking around Gansbaai are Gansbaai Backpackers or the Great White House.

Danger Point Lighthouse (☎ 021-449 2400), dating from 1895, is worth a visit, as is the **Walker Bay Reserve** (☎ 028-384 0111). This offers excellent walks, such as the Duiwelgat and Fynbos Hiking Trails, and bird-watching, along with the Klipgat Caves, site of a recent archaeological discovery of Khoesaan artefacts.

Contact **iKhaya Laba Thembu** (☎ 072-218 0742) for a trip through the booming township community of Masakhane. Handmade products are on sale and traditional Xhosa food can be ordered and eaten in the shade of milkwood trees.

Sleeping & Eating

The tourism office has a comprehensive list of places to stay and eat in De Kelders and the Danger Point area.

Gansbaai Backpackers (☎ 028-384 0641; gansbaai backpackers@yahoo.com; 6 Strand St; dm R75, s/d with shared bathroom R140/220) Efficient and friendly, this is a great place to start for either budget accommodation or tour and activity bookings.

Aire del Mar (☎ 028-384 2848; info@airedelmar .co.za; 77 Van Dyk St, Kleinbaai; r R200, s/d incl breakfast R350/580; ☐) Offers a good range of prices, including basic self-catering units for backpackers and stylish rooms with panoramic sea views out to Dyer Island. It also serves a filling breakfast (R45).

Great White House (☎ 028-384 3273; 5 Geelbek St, Kleinbaai; mains R35-70; ☹ breakfast, lunch & dinner Mon-Sun Aug-Sep & Dec-Feb). A multifarious place that dishes up fresh seafood, clothing and curios, helps with tour information and offers three-star accommodation.

Die Buitesteen (☎ 028-384 0601; 3 Dover St, De Kelders; mains R40; ☹ 10am-2am Mon-Sun) This is a pub, its walls bedecked with *perlemoen* (abalone) shells, that captures the laidback ethos of Gansbaai. Thus it's a perennial favourite with backpackers and local fishermen alike.

Getting There & Away

Entry and exit to the town is largely limited to private vehicles. When we were there, construction was well under way on a new sealed road between Gansbaai and Elim, part of the exciting Fynbos Rd project that will link Danger Point Peninsula with Cape Agulhas.

Trevis Tours (☎ 072-608 9213) has daily shuttles to Hermanus (R50, 30 minutes) and Cape Town (R180, two hours).

L'AGULHAS
☎ 028

Once described, somewhat cruelly, as 'nothing more than a seagull and a mussel', the settlement of L'Agulhas does unfortunately offer little for the visitor in and of itself, but **Cape Agulhas**, just south of town, is the southernmost point of Africa.

On a stormy day the low, shattered rocks and crashing seas can be atmospheric. Otherwise, there's no real reason to linger longer than it takes to snap a photo and peek at the nearby **lighthouse** (☎ 028-435 6222; adult/child R6/3; ☹ 9am-4.15pm Mon-Sat, 9am-2pm Sun). Built in 1848, this is the second-oldest lighthouse in South Africa. If you are peckish, the **tearoom** (☎ 028-435 7506) here isn't bad, serving reasonably priced meals and snacks.

L'Agulhas can be reached by car, or if you don't have wheels, several companies out of Swellendam offer day tours. For more information see p194.

ARNISTON (WAENHUISKRANS)

☎ 028

One of the Western Cape's gems, Arniston is a charming village in a dramatic, wind-swept setting. It has a bit of an identity crisis – it's named after *both* the vessel wrecked off its treacherous coast in 1815 and the large sea cave capable of housing several ox wagons (Waenhuiskrans means 'ox-wagon crag').

Colourful boats, warm blue-green waters and the backdrop of **Kassiesbaai**, the 200-year-old hamlet of whitewashed cottages that forms the core of the town, make for a pretty picture. South of Kassiesbaai is **Roman Beach** with white sand and gentle waves. It's a good place to bring the children as there are caves, coves and rock pools filled with sea urchins and colourful anemones at both ends. Be careful not to touch the sea urchins, though, as they can cause nasty cuts.

The village has no centralised area nor any real street signs, so finding your away around can sometimes be a challenge. Look for signs leading to the various eating and sleeping establishments.

Sleeping & Eating

Southwinds (☎ 028-445 9303; southwinds@arniston -info.co.za; 12 First Ave; d incl breakfast R550) Just 200m from the sea, this unique place puts rough, whitewashed walls and wooden ceilings together and throws in interesting angles for good measure. All have separate entrances, and there are seaside cottages around the corner. Ask owners Allister and Jane about local tours.

Die Herberg & South of Africa Backpackers' Resort (☎ 028-445 9240; www.southofafrica.co.za; s/d R279/390, with shared bathroom R130/210; ⚡) This backpackers is in a rather bizarre location, next to a military test site signposted off Rte 316, 2km outside Arniston. It's a modern place with tons of amenities, including a conference centre, gym, large pool, sauna and two full-sized billiard tables. There are

two classes of rooms – cheaper backpacker doubles and more expensive en suite rooms, all with TV. The attached Castaway Restaurant (mains R20 to R50) has something for everyone, including the kids.

Arniston Hotel (☎ 028-445 9000; www.arniston hotel.com; s/d incl breakfast R720/1790; ⚡) The Arniston is a breezy luxury hotel facing the sea, with a shipwreck theme – framed descriptions of events surrounding the boat wrecks and items salvaged from the boats themselves make up the décor. Sea-facing rooms have floor-to-ceiling windows. The classy ocean-view restaurant serves lunch (R40) and dinner (R45 to R115) and has an extensive wine list.

Die Waenhuis (☎ 028-445 9797; Dupreez St; mains from R40) The only restaurant in town not attached to a hotel, this one is full of character – the walls are covered in graffiti and candles grace the tables. It serves a good range of dishes and is tucked behind the Arniston Centre general store.

DE HOOP NATURE RESERVE

Covering 36,000 hectares, plus 5km out to sea, is **De Hoop Nature Reserve** (☎ 028-425 5020; bredasdorp@capenature.org.za; admission R20; camp sites R95, 4-person cottages from R325; ⏱ 7am-6pm). This is one of Cape Nature Conservation's best reserves, including a scenic coastline with stretches of beach, dunes and rocky cliffs, plus a freshwater lake and Potberg Mountain. Visitors come here to see both mountain and lowveld *fynbos* and a diverse cross section of coastal ecosystems. Fauna includes the Cape mountain zebra, the bontebok and a wealth of birdlife. The coast is an important breeding area for the southern right whale.

Although there are numerous day walks, an overnight mountain-bike trail and good snorkelling along the coast, the reserve's most interesting feature is the five-day **Whale Route** (R700 per person). Covering 55km, it offers excellent opportunities to see whales between June and December. Accommodation is in modern, fully equipped self-catering cottages. The trail needs to be booked in advance, and only group bookings are accepted. You'll need a minimum of six and a maximum of 12 people. The fee includes a shuttle service back to your car at the end of the trip. If you don't feel like carrying your own bags, your group can pay an extra R1200 (for six people) to have your belongings transported every morning to that night's overnight cottage.

Those just looking to spend the night in the reserve can choose from a variety of sleeping options, including camping (R95) basic cottages (from R325) and a 10-person beach house. Accommodation prices include entrance fees into the reserve.

The reserve is about 260km from Cape Town, and the final 50km from either Bredasdorp or Swellendam is along gravel roads. The only access to the reserve is via Wydgeleë on the Bredasdorp to Malgas road. At Malgas a manually operated *pont* (river ferry) on the Breede River still operates (between dawn and dusk). The village of **Ouplaas**, 15km away, is the nearest place to buy fuel and supplies. If you don't have your own car you can reach the reserve by joining a tour (see right).

SWELLENDAM

☎ 028 / pop 30,000

Rapidly growing Swellendam, dating back to 1776, offers an unbeatable combination of location, beauty and history that makes it an unmissable destination. Its a disarming town, dotted with old oaks and surrounded by rolling wheat country and mountains, that makes a great base for exploring the Overberg and the Little Karoo. It's also a handy stopover between Cape Town and the Garden Route, and even if you don't have wheels there's the chance to walk in indigenous forest near town.

The town backs up against a spectacular ridge, part of the 1600m Langeberg Range, and is particularly impressive on a cloudy day when the mist rolls in over the mountains. Like Franschhoek, it is becoming a favoured destination of European expats settling in South Africa.

Information

IT Solutions (☎ 028-514 3688; Voortrek St; per hr R40; ☯ 8am-5pm Mon-Fri, 8.30am-1pm Sat) The cheapest Internet connection.

Swellendam Tourism Bureau (☎ 028-514 2770; Voortrek St; ☯ 9am-5pm Mon-Fri, 9am-12.30pm Sat) In the old mission, or Oefeninghuis, on the main street. Note the twin clocks, one of which is permanently set at 12.15pm. This was the time for the daily service; the illiterate townspeople only had to match the working clock with the painted one to know when their presence was required.

Sights

The main sight in town is the excellent **Drostdy Museum** (☎ 028-514 1138; 18 Swellengrebel St; adult/child R12/2; ☯ 9am-4.45pm Mon-Fri, 10am-3.45pm Sat & Sun). The centrepiece is the beautiful *drostdy* (residence of an official) itself, which dates from 1746. The museum ticket also covers entrance to the nearby **Old Gaol**, where you'll find part of the original administrative buildings; the **Gaoler's Cottage** and a watermill; and **Mayville**, another residence dating back to 1853, with a formal Victorian garden. Onsite there's an excellent restaurant and shop selling stylish African curios.

Take a picture of the **Dutch Reformed Church** (Voortrek St) in the centre of town; Swellendam residents swear it's the third-most-photographed sight in the Southern Hemisphere!

Activities

Swellendam has adventures for all ages, budgets and tastes. A good place to sort yourself out is at **Bontebok Tours & Travel** (☎ 028-514-3650; info@bontebok.co.za; 23 Swellengrebel St; ☯ 9am-6pm Mon-Sat, 10am-6pm Sun), which seems to arrange just about anything.

Popular day trips include Cape Agulhas (R295), where you will have the option of quad biking for one hour (R200), De Hoop Nature Reserve (R295), day wine trails around Barrydale, Montagu, Ashton and Bonnievale (R295), and mountain-bike hire (R90 per day).

The company also arranges activities near **Buffeljachts Dam**. These include sunset cruises on a double-decker wooden raft on the lake (R60) and abseiling (R200).

For day permits (R15) to walk in **Marloth Nature Reserve** in the Langeberg Range, 3km north of town, contact the **Nature Conservation Department** (☎ 028-514 1410) at the entrance to the reserve.

Two Feathers Horse Trails (☎ 082-494 8279; per hr R100) caters to inexperienced as well as experienced riders (but doesn't offer hard hats). Overnight rides into the Langeberg Range cost R1000. Two Feathers is located at the edge of the Marloth Nature Reserve. Advanced booking is essential.

Give **Zephyr Travel** (☎ 082-771 2765) a call (there's no office) for individualised tours that use Swellendam as their base but explore the entire Overberg and beyond.

Sleeping

There are now more than 100 accommodation options in and around Swellendam. We recommend those listed below, but ask for help at the tourism office.

BUDGET

Swellendam Backpackers Adventure Lodge (☎ 028-514 2648; backpack@telkomsa.net; 5 Lichtenstein St; camp sites per person R40, dm R70, d with shared bathroom R170) Set on a huge plot of land with its own river, 15 horses and Marloth Nature Reserve a stone's throw away, this is an excellent hostel with enthusiastic management. Don't skip one of the homemade dinners (around R40); they are mouthwatering and gigantic. The Baz Bus will drop you right outside.

MIDRANGE

Cypress Cottage (☎ 028-514 3296; www.cypresscottage.info; 3 Voortrek St; s/d R250/500; ✕ ⟳) There are five individually decorated rooms in this 200-year-old house with a gorgeous garden and a refreshing saltwater pool. Try an African-themed room complete with mosquito nets.

Roosje Van de Kaap (☎ 028-514 3001; www.roosjevandekaap.com; 5 Drostdy St; s/d R320/440; ⟳) Take a swim with a mountain view. This Cape-country inn has 10 cosy rooms and an excellent restaurant (mains R70-R80) serving Cape Malay dishes and wood-fired pizzas; it's open to the public, but booking is essential.

Braeside B&B (☎ 028-5143325; www.braeside.co.za; 13 Van Oudtshoorn Rd; s/d incl breakfast R350/500; ✕) This quiet, gracious Cape Edwardian home boasts a beautiful garden, fantastic views and knowledgeable, friendly hosts.

Old Mill Guest Cottages (☎ 028-514 2790; www.oldmill.co.za; 241 Voortrek St; d incl breakfast from R460) This cute whitewashed cottage complex is behind the antiques/craft shop and has a pleasant café of the same name. Guests choose from a variety of tidy cottages.

TOP END

Bloomestate (☎ 028-514 2984; www.bloomestate.co.za; 276 Voortrek St; s/d incl breakfast R550/1100; Ⓟ ✕ ▯ ⟳) A purpose-built, modern guesthouse set on a beautiful 2.5-hectare property, which offers tremendous privacy to go

WESTERN CAPE

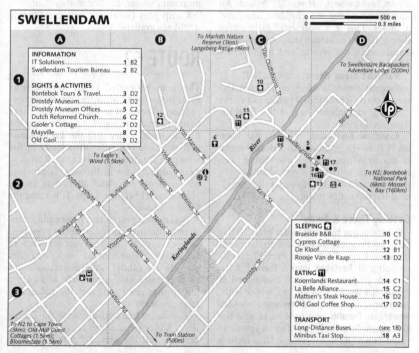

SWELLENDAM

0 — 500 m
0 — 0.3 miles

To Marloth Nature
Reserve (3km);
Langeberg Range (4km)

To Swellendam Backpackers
Adventure Lodge (200m)

INFORMATION	
IT Solutions	1 B2
Swellendam Tourism Bureau	2 B2

SIGHTS & ACTIVITIES	
Bontebok Tours & Travel	3 D2
Drostdy Museum	4 D2
Drostdy Museum Offices	5 C2
Dutch Reformed Church	6 D2
Gaoler's Cottage	7 D2
Mayville	8 C2
Old Gaol	9 D2

To Eagle's
Wind (T, 5km)

To N2; Bontebok
National Park
(6km); Mossel
Bay (160km)

SLEEPING 🏠	
Braeside B&B	10 C1
Cypress Cottage	11 C1
De Kloof	12 B1
Roosje Van de Kaap	13 D2

EATING 🍴	
Koornlands Restaurant	14 C1
La Belle Alliance	15 C2
Mattsen's Steak House	16 D2
Old Gaol Coffee Shop	17 D2

TRANSPORT	
Long-Distance Buses	(see 18)
Minibus Taxi Stop	18 A3

To N2 to Cape Town
(3km); Old Mill Guest
Cottages (1.5km);
Bloomestate (1.5km)

To Train Station
(500m)

with the luxury you'd expect. It's a refreshing change from the cottage-cutesy décor more commonly favoured in these parts. All rooms have wireless broadband Internet access.

De Kloof (☎ 028-514 1303; www.dekloof.co.za; 8 Weltevrede St; s/d incl breakfast R900/1500; P 🌀 🖳 🖳) One of Swellendam's swankiest options, a supremely stylish guesthouse with a surprisingly personal touch. Set in an estate dating back to 1801, it offers a library, cigar room and wonderful views. Honeymooners can head straight to the double-storey suite with waterbed and Jacuzzi, other guests should probably try the free daily wine tastings beforehand.

Eating

La Belle Alliance (☎ 028-514 2252; 1 Swellengrebel St; mains R20-50; 🕒 breakfast & lunch) This appealing tearoom had the honour of serving Nelson Mandela in 1999. In an old Masonic lodge with shaded outdoor tables beside the Koringlands River, it's a good spot for lunch.

Old Gaol Coffee Shop (☎ 028-514 3847; Old Gaol Complex, Swellengrebel St; light meals R30; 🕒 lunch) All staff members are shareholders here, and it shows. This is a wonderful little coffee shop, offering delicious snacks, traditional breads, excellent service and high-quality African curios.

Mattsen's Steak House (☎ 028-514 2715; 25 Swellengrebel St; mains R30-60; 🕒 lunch & dinner) The pizzas are delicious and, if you're not starving, large enough for two, at this English-style country inn.

Koornlands Restaurant (☎ 028-514 3567; 5 Voortrek St; mains R75; 🕒 dinner) An eclectic menu of mostly African meat – everything from crocodile to ostrich – is served in an intimate candlelit setting. It's generally considered the top eat in town.

Getting There & Away

All three major bus companies plus the Baz Bus pass through Swellendam on their runs between Cape Town and Port Elizabeth, stopping at **Bontebok Tours & Travel** (☎ 028-514-3650; info@bontebok.co.za; 23 Swellengrebel St; 🕒 9am-6pm Mon-Sat, 10am-6pm Sun), which is the Intercape, SA Roadlink, **Greyhound** (www.greyhound.co.za), **Translux** (www.translux.co.za) and Baz Bus agent. Bontebok also offers a shuttle to Cape Town (R140). Intercape fares include

Cape Town (R95, 2½ hours, twice daily) and Mossel Bay (R90, two hours).

Minibus taxis depart from Station Rd by the Caltex petrol station. Services include Cape Town (R100, 2½ hours, daily) and Mossel Bay (R80, two hours).

The weekly *Southern Cross* train that runs between Cape Town and Oudtshoorn stops in Swellendam.

BONTEBOK NATIONAL PARK

Some 6km south of Swellendam is **Bontebok National Park** (☎ 028-514 2735; adult/child R60/30; 🕒 7am-7pm Oct-Apr, 7am-6pm May-Sep), set aside to ensure the preservation of the endangered bontebok, the unusually marked antelope that once roamed the region in large numbers.

The park falls within the coastal *fynbos* area and is on the banks of the Breede River, where swimming is possible. It boasts nearly 500 grasses and other plant species; in the late winter and early spring, the veld (grassland) is covered with flowers. In addition to the bonteboks, there are rheboks, grysboks, duikers, red hartebeests and mountain zebras. Birdlife is abundant.

Camp sites (R75) and cottages (double R200) are available.

ROUTE 62

This area, promoted as the longest wine route in the world while technically encompassing all sorts of topography (and more than one route marker), takes in both the Breede River Valley and the Little Karoo and stretches from the Winelands in the west past Uniondale, in the Little Karoo, to near Humansdorp in the east. It provides an excellent hinterland alternative to the N2 for travel between Cape Town and the Garden Route.

Breathtaking mountain passes and intensively cultivated valleys, perfectly preserved 18th-century towns and vast stretches of semi-arid plains dotted with ostriches provide eye candy, while delectable wine, country cafés, charming B&Bs and even a hot-springs resort enchant the palate and relax the body.

Europeans had settled most of the Breede River Valley by the beginning of the 18th century, but the area did not really take off until passes were pushed through the mountains a century later. The headwaters of the Breede River (sometimes called the Breë), in the beautiful mountain-ringed Ceres Basin, escape via Mitchell's Pass and flow southeast for 310km before meeting the Indian Ocean at Witsand. Many tributaries join the Breede, and by the time it reaches Robertson it has been transformed from a mountain stream to a substantial river.

The Klein (Little) Karoo is east of the Breede River Valley and bordered in the south by the Outeniqua and Langkloof Ranges and by the Swartberg Range in the north. It is more fertile and better watered than the harsher Great Karoo to the north.

The towns in this region are presented in the order they would be reached driving the route from Cape Town.

TULBAGH
☎ 023 / pop 18,000

Easy on the eye and ringed by the dramatic Witzenberg Range, Tulbagh – first settled in 1699 – is one of the most complete examples of an 18th- and 19th-century Cape Dutch village in South Africa. Many buildings were substantially rebuilt after an earthquake in 1969, but it doesn't feel in the least bit fake thanks to painstaking restoration. A meander down Church St, lined with trees and flowering bushes, provides a unique brand of stress relief.

Orientation & Information
Church St, the famous street in which every building has been declared a national monument, runs parallel to the town's main thoroughfare, Van der Stel St.

Tourist information centre (☎ 023-230 1348; www.tourismtulbagh.co.za; 4 Church St; 9am-5pm Mon-Fri, 10am-4pm Sat, 11am-4pm Sun) Provides information and maps about the area, including the Tulbagh Wine Route.

Sights & Activities
Wandering down Church St is a pleasant way to spend an afternoon. When you finish, take in a few wine tastings or visit the town's museum.

OUDE KERK VOLKSMUSEUM
The **Old Church Folk Museum** (☎ 023-230 1041; 1 Church St; adult/child R7/2; 9am-5pm Mon-Fri, 9am-4pm Sat, 11am-4pm Sun) is a mildly interesting

museum made up of three buildings. Start at No 4, which has a photographic history of Church St, covering the earthquake and reconstruction; visit the beautiful Oude Kerk itself (1743); then go on to No 22, a reconstructed town dwelling from the 18th century.

WINERIES
The Tulbagh Valley produces a variety of wines and has a number of cellars to visit, all of which are well signposted. Three standouts are **Twee Jonge Gezellen** (☎ 023-230 0680; tastings free; 9am-4pm Mon-Fri, 10am-2pm Sat), the second-oldest family-owned wine estate in South Africa and the first to introduce night harvesting, with classic views and buildings along with friendly informed staff; **Drostdy Wines** (☎ 023-230 0203; Van der Stel St; museum admission & tastings R12; 10am-5pm Mon-Fri, 10am-2pm Sat), built in 1806 and almost destroyed in the 1969 earthquake but completely restored; and **Rijk's Private Cellar** (☎ 023-230 1622; www.rijks.co.za; Van der Stel St; tastings R5; 9am-6pm Mon-Fri, 10am-4pm Sat), which has won several awards for its Sauvignon Blanc, Shiraz and pinotage wines. It is in a lovely location 2km north of town, and there's also a hotel here.

Sleeping
There are very good sleeping and eating options in Tulbagh. Couples looking for a romantic destination won't be disappointed.

Tulbagh Country House (☎ 023-230 1171; 24 Church St; s/d incl breakfast R350/550;) Built in 1809, this authentic Cape Dutch manor house retains the original wood ceilings and a lived-in feel, and its rooms are huge. The owner is a wealth of information about the surrounding region. There are two self-catering cottages from R175 per person.

De Oude Herberg (☎ 023-230 0260; www.deoudeherberg.co.za; 6 Church St; s/d incl breakfast R375/550;) A guesthouse since 1885 (although not continuously), this is a very friendly place with traditional country furniture and a lovely patio. Its restaurant (mains R90), which is open to nonguests, boasts a good wine list and an inventive menu; booking ahead for dinner is essential.

Rijk's Country Hotel (☎ 023-230 1006; www.rijks.co.za; Van der Stel St; s/d R700/950;) If you yearn to stay on a classy wine estate, this is the hotel for you. Located on the same property

WESTERN CAPE

as the Rijk's Private Cellar, this place is picturesque, romantic and overlooks a lake. There's a restaurant on the premises. The hotel is 2km north of the town centre.

Eating

Reader's Restaurant (☎ 023-230 0087; 12 Church St; mains R25-60; ☯ lunch & dinner) As its name suggests, this is a good place for literature (and feline) lovers, with books, cards and cat sculptures everywhere. The menu changes daily, but you can expect food as varied as tuna with wasabi and ginger butter and the Cape Malay dish, *bobotie* (curried mince with a topping of savoury egg custard, usually served on turmeric-flavoured rice).

Forties (☎ 023-230 0940; 40 Church St; mains R40-60; ☯ dinner Wed-Sun) The hip industrial feel – think exposed walls and peeling plaster – at this lively pub comes in part from authentic earthquake damage. It's an excellent drinking choice and also serves pizza, pasta and steak.

Plum (☎ 023-230 8005; 10 Church St; mains R45-60; ☯ breakfast & lunch Wed-Sun) Light lunches and local delicacies such as springbok sausage are served up in this pleasant garden overlooking Church St.

Paddagang Restaurant (☎ 023-230 0242; 23 Church St; mains R50-60; ☯ breakfast, lunch & dinner) The town's best-known restaurant, in a beautiful old homestead with a vine-shaded courtyard, also serves snacks and light meals (R20 to R40). For dinner try one of the steaks followed by a mouth-watering dessert. There's a good wine list, but little for vegetarians.

Getting There & Away

Tulbagh is reached either via Rte 44 from the Bainskloof Pass or off Rte 60 via Worcester, a more scenic route.

Keep going along Van der Stel St (parallel to Church St) past the Old Drostdy Museum and you'll come to a dead end at the head of the valley (overlooked by the rugged mountains of the Groot Winterhoek Wilderness Area).

To get back to Rte 46 (from where you can head east to Ceres or west onto Rte 44 to Piketberg, which is on the N7), go in the opposite direction down Van der Stel St. Halfway up the hill leading away from the town, turn right. There's a small, faded sign to Kaapstad (Cape Town) and Gouda on Rte 46.

CERES & AROUND

☎ 023 / pop 68,000

Sometimes referred to as the Switzerland of South Africa, Ceres, the most important deciduous fruit- and juice-producing district in South Africa, is set in majestic scenery.

The valley has a very high rainfall, mostly between June and September, and four well-defined seasons. It can get very cold in winter, with temperatures dropping below zero (snow on the mountains) and hot in summer (36°C). It is most beautiful in spring and particularly in autumn, when the fruit trees change colour. The town is perhaps best for a lunch stop in between spending the morning and afternoon exploring the exciting regional mountain passes.

Orientation & Information

Coming off Mitchell's Pass you'll enter the town along the central Voortrekker St.

The friendly **tourism bureau office** (☎ 023-316 1287; www.ceres.org.za; cnr Owen & Voortrekker Sts; ☯ 9am-5pm Mon-Fri, 9am-noon Sat) is in the library. It has information on accommodation, tours and activities in the area.

Sights & Activities

Ceres was once a famous centre for making horse-drawn vehicles. Consequently, the **Togryers' Museum** (Transport Riders' Museum; ☎ 023-312 2045; 8 Oranje St; adult/child R3/1; ☯ 8.30am-1pm & 2-5pm Mon-Fri year-round, plus 9am-noon Sat Dec & Jan) has an interesting collection of original buggies, wagons and carriages. Oranje St is one street north of and parallel to Voortrekker St.

For some stupendous scenery don't miss a drive through the **Middelberg** and **Gydo Passes**. The reds, ochres and purples of the rocky mountains, the blue of the sky, the blossom of the orchards, fresh green pastures, wildflowers, dams and wading birds combine to create a beautiful sight.

About 20km from Ceres you hit a sealed road. If you're coming into Ceres from Citrusdal in the north, you feel as if you've lost altitude, so when you come out on the 1000m Gydo Pass overlooking the Ceres Valley, the world seems to drop away at your feet.

To experience a little history of the region take a drive over the magnificent **Mitchell's Pass**. Completed in 1848, it became the main route onto the South African plateau to the north, remaining so until the Hex River Pass was opened in 1875.

Sleeping & Eating

The tourism bureau will help you find quality accommodation and eating options that don't fall under the what-you-see-is-what-you-get franchisee banner.

Farm Backpackers (☎ 023-231 1415; White Bridge Farm, cnr Rte 46 & Rte 43; camp sites R25, dm R50, d with shared bathroom R150; ⊋) A rowdy place that markets itself as 'a true South African experience', and we can't argue. Accommodation is on a converted farm, and activities organised here include cooking classes, river tubing, San rock-art visits and everything in between. It even offers a work-exchange programme. It's located 10km south of Ceres on the road to Wolseley, and you can call ahead to be picked up for free from Wolseley train station.

Die Herberg (☎ 023-312 2325; 125 Voortrekker St; s/d R200/300) Rooms are simple and clean and come with TV at this comfortable, yet somewhat old-fashioned place. There is a café (meals R15 to R20) serving light meals, while adjoining Witherley's Restaurant (mains R30 to R60) serves reliable fare covering all tastes.

Four Seasons (☎ 023-312 1918; 1 Staff St; s/d incl breakfast R290/400; ⊋) A comfortable B&B with a personal touch: each room is cool and comfortable, and cleverly designed to reflect each season; we liked 'winter' best. There is a self-catering option, which knocks R40 off the per person price.

Getting There & Away

Ceres is on Rte 46, 53km north of Wellington. It's on the western side of a green and fertile bowl that is ringed by the rugged Skurweberg Range, and the passes into the valley are particularly spectacular. As with many destinations, having your own vehicle is best, but there are minibus taxis running between Voortrekker St and Worcester (R20, 35 minutes).

WORCESTER

☎ 023 / pop 107,000

A service centre for the rich farmland of the Breede River Valley, Worcester is a large and fairly nondescript place that needn't detain you longer than it takes to visit its farm museum and botanic gardens.

Most of the town lies south of the N1. There are some impressive old buildings near and around the edge of Church Sq (off High St). For local information, visit **Breede Valley Tourism** (☎ 023-348 2795; 23 Baring St; ☯ 8am-4.30pm Mon-Fri, 8.30am-12.30pm Sat), on the east side of Church Sq.

Sights & Activities

KLEINPLASIE FARM MUSEUM

This **farm museum** (☎ 023-342 2225; adult/child R12/5; ☯ 9am-4.30pm Mon-Sat, 10.30am-4.30pm Sun) is one of South Africa's best museums, and takes you from a Trekboer's hut to a complete, functioning 18th-century farm complex. It's a 'live' museum, meaning there are people wandering around in period clothes and rolling tobacco, making soap, operating a smithy, milling wheat, spinning wool and so on.

At the museum shop you can sample and buy various flavours of toe-curling *witblitz* (white lightning), a traditional Boer spirit distilled from fruit. To get the full taste, first inhale, then sip and roll the liquor around your mouth before swallowing and exhaling. Next door is the **Kleinplasie Winery**, where you can sample less potent libations.

KAROO NATIONAL BOTANIC GARDEN

This outstanding **garden** (☎ 023-347 0785; adult/child R12/6; ☯ 8am-4pm) takes in 140 hectares of semidesert vegetation – with Karoo and *fynbos* elements – and 10 hectares of landscaped garden, where many of the plants have been labelled. This is an ideal opportunity to identify some of the extraordinary indigenous plants. Your entrance ticket is valid for the whole season you're in.

KWV CELLAR

Not as famous as its counterpart in Paarl (see p184), this cellar and **brandy distillery** (☎ 023-342 0255; cnr Church & Smith Sts; tours adult/child R20/13; ☯ 8am-4.30pm Mon-Fri) is the largest of its kind in the world under one roof. A must-see for brandy enthusiasts looking to sample the product; hour-long tours in English are held at 2pm.

Sleeping

Nekkies (☎ 023-343 2909; fax 343 2911; chalets from R250) These are smart wooden chalets with good facilities, overlooking the dam. Bikes are available for hire. Nekkies is 4.5km from Worcester at the Brandvlei Dam.

Wykeham Lodge B&B (☎ 023-347 3467; wykeham lodge@telkomsa.net; 168 Church St; s/d incl breakfast R360/460) This fine guesthouse is in a thatched-roof building dating from 1835. Rooms with wooden beams and floors face onto a quiet courtyard and there's also a large garden.

Kleinplasie Country Chalets (☎ 023-347 0091; Kleinplasie Farm Museum; self-catering cottages from R400) These four-person chalets attached to the Kleinplasie Farm Museum are simple yet comfortable enough for a night's stay.

Eating

Dros (☎ 023-347 5131; 29 Baring St; mains R40; ☺ break-fast, lunch & dinner) This reliable chain steakhouse is worth a mention thanks to its handy location near the tourist office. The faux cellar interior and smoky scent promise much and deliver; the wines are good and steaks well cooked.

Kleinplasie Restaurant (☎ 023-347 5118; Klein-plasie Farm Museum; mains R40-50; ☺ breakfast & lunch Mon-Sat, lunch Sun) Attached to the Kleinplasie Farm Museum, this place offers traditional Cape Malay/Afrikaner dishes such as bo-botie and chicken pie; outdoor seating is available.

St Geran (☎ 023-342 2800; 48 Church St; mains R55-70; ☺ lunch & dinner) This popular steakhouse in the town centre also does some seafood and chicken dishes, although there is little for vegetarians. There's a kid's menu and large wine list.

Getting There & Away

All **Translux** (☎ 021-449 3333; www.translux.co.za), **SA Roadlink** (☎ 021-425 0203; www.saroadlink.co.za), **Greyhound** (☎ 021-505 6363; www.greyhound.co.za) and **Intercape** (☎ 0861-287 287; www.intercape .co.za) buses stop at the Shell Ultra City petrol station in town. Fares include Cape Town (R140, two hours, daily) and Jo'burg (R375, 17 hours, daily). The corner of Durban and Grey Sts is a good place to look for minibus taxis. Rates include Cape Town (R65, two hours, daily).

The daily *Trans Karoo* train between Cape Town and Jo'burg stops in Worcester; the *Southern Cross* between Cape Town and Oudtshoorn stops at Worcester on Friday evening when heading east, early Monday morning when heading west. The extremely circuitous *Trans Oranje* to Durban also stops there. For bookings call ☎ 023-348 2203.

ROBERTSON

☎ 023 / pop 43,500

At the centre of one of the largest wine-growing areas in the country, and also famous for its horse studs, prosperous and unpretentious Robertson offers wonderful surrounding vineyards and more outdoor activities – including hiking, white-water rafting and horse riding – than its better-known Route 62 neighbours.

The helpful **Robertson Tourism Bureau** (☎ 023-626 4437; www.robertsonr62.com; cnr Reitz & Voortrekker Sts; ☺ 8am-5pm Mon-Fri, 9am-4pm Sat, 10am-2pm Sun) can give you loads of information about the wine region, Route 62 and hiking trails that lead you into the mountains above the town.

Sights & Activities

WINERIES

The Robertson Wine Valley is worth a visit for its 43 wineries (*all* of which offer free tastings!), its scenery and the general absence of tourist buses. Ask the Tourism Bureau for a map.

Van Loveren (☎ 023-615 1505; www.vanloveren.co .za; ☺ 8.30am-5pm Mon-Fri, 9.30am-1pm Sat) is one of the Cape's best wine-tasting experiences, taking place in a garden surrounded by trees planted for historical events – good and bad – such as the day of Mandela's release or the Pearl Harbour invasion. Besides spectacular grounds this place has a different take on tastings. You'll pick what wines you want to try and be brought the entire bottle. You can choose as many bottles and pour as much as you like. The wine is good, too – try the Colombard/Chardonnay.

Tastings at **Graham Beck** (☎ 023-626 1214; www .grahambeckwines.co.za; ☺ 9am-5pm Mon-Fri, 10am-3pm Sat) are in a striking orange aircraft hangar–like building with huge plate-glass windows overlooking a long pool. The winery comes as a breath of fresh air after all those Cape Dutch estates – as do its eminently drinkable products. Its fizzy wines give French champagne a run for its money and the muscatel is heaven in a glass.

Robertson Winery (☎ 023-628 8817; www.robert sonwinery.co.za; Voortrekker St; ☺ 8am-5pm Mon-Thu, 8am-5.30pm Fri, 9am-3pm Sat, 9am-3pm Sun) is more commercial and lacking in views, but is the region's oldest cellar. It's in a boring modern building smack in the middle of town but produces some decent products. The Sauvignon Blanc, Wide River Cabernet Sauvignon Reserve and semisweet wines are the ones to go for.

SOEKERSHOF WALKABOUT

Tired of checking out wineries? Take a break and stretch your legs in these fabulous **gardens** (☎ 023-626 4134; Klaas Voogds West; adult/child R40/20; ☺ 8am-4pm Wed-Sun Aug-Jun), where you can wander through numerous mazes filled with indigenous plants and hedges as well as more than 1700 different species of succulents. Guided tours (adult/child R90/20) last about two hours, and there are also full-moon tours (R60). Soekershof is 8km past Robertson on Rte 60 heading towards Ashton. Turn left at the turn-off for Klaas Voogds West.

Sleeping & Eating

Robertson Backpackers (☎ 023-626 1280; www.rob ertsonbackpackers.co.za; 4 Dordrecht Ave; camp sites per person R40, dm R60, d with shared bathroom R160, cottage from R200; ☐) A terrific place to lay your hat, with spacious dorms and doubles and a cosy Bohemian vibe. There's a big grassy backyard with a fire pit for chilling out at night, and wine and activity tours can be arranged.

Grand Hotel (☎ 023-626 3272; fax 626 1158; 68 Barry St; s/d R250/400; ☒) The rooms, a couple with balconies, are of better quality than the foyer would suggest, and there's also an adjoining lodge at R125 per person. The reasonably priced, if old-fashioned, Simone's Grill Room & Restaurant (mains R55) serves a range of chicken, seafood and steak dishes.

Ballinderry (☎ 023-626 5365; info@ballinderryguest house.com; 8 Le Roux St; s/d incl breakfast R465/780; ☐ ☒) A smart family home has, thanks to the care of hosts Luc and Hilde, been transformed into an impeccably designed luxury guesthouse. A champagne breakfast is served, as is dinner on request, and Dutch, French and German are spoken. Try to get either the downstairs double with garden views, or the separate 'African Room' in the garden.

Branewynsdraai (☎ 023-626 3202; 1 Kromhout St; mains R40; ☺ lunch & dinner Mon-Sat) With a pleas-

ant tea garden and more formal dining room, this restaurant specialises in meaty local dishes, full-bodied wines and kiddies' specials.

Bourbon Street (☎ 023-626 5934; 22 Voortrekker Rd; mains R40-70; ☺ breakfast, lunch & dinner) A firm favourite with overseas visitors, this stylish deli-restaurant impresses with its fusion cuisine including fresh oysters and tapas. It is divided into casual and formal sections, with accompanying menus.

Getting There & Away

SA Roadlink (☎ 021-425 0203; www.saroadlink.co.za) and **Translux** (☎ 021-449 3333; www.translux.co.za) buses stop at the train station. Routes include Oudtshoorn (R110, three hours, daily), Knysna (R125, five hours), Cape Town (R120, three hours, daily) and Port Elizabeth (R165, 6½ hours, daily).

Minibus taxis running between Cape Town (R45, three hours), Oudtshoorn (R120, three hours) and Montagu (R27, 30 minutes) stop at the **Shell petrol station** (cnr Voortrekker & John Sts). Theoretically there is daily service, but when the buses actually show up is anyone's guess.

MCGREGOR

☎ 023 / pop 1500

McGregor feels like it fell asleep in another time – the mid-19th century to be precise, from when most of the buildings along its one major thoroughfare, Voortrekker St, date – and never woke up. Many of the vineyards, orchards and vegetable gardens surrounding the town's whitewashed thatched-roof cottages have been turned into B&Bs and self-catering units to cope with growing visitor numbers. The village nonetheless remains a place of retreat, and, with the magnificent Riviersonderend Mountains on its doorstep, a base for hiking. It is one end of the highly recommended Boesmanskloof Trail (below) to Greyton.

The **tourism bureau** (☎ 023-625 1954; www.tour ismmcgregor.co.za; Voortrekker St; ☺ 9am-1pm & 2-4.30pm Mon-Fri, 9am-1pm Sat & Sun) is about halfway along Voortrekker St (there are no street numbers).

Activities

Some argue the best reason for coming to McGregor is to hike the **Boesmanskloof Trail**

(1-day tour adult/child R20/10, 2-day tour R60/46) to Greyton, roughly 14km through the spectacular *fynbos*-clad Riviersonderend Mountains. The trail actually starts at Die Galg, about 15km south of McGregor; you'll need your own transport to get here. Many people then hike back to Die Galg. The McGregor to Greyton direction is easier. You must book in advance at all times, but especially for weekends and during the holidays, since only 50 people per day are allowed on the trail.

If you don't fancy the full hike, it's quite possible to do a six-hour round trip to the lovely **Oak Falls** (1-day permit adult/child R20/10), roughly 6km from Die Galg, where you can cool off with a swim in the tannin-stained waters.

The **Vrolijkheid Nature Reserve**, near the Cape Nature Conservation offices on the McGregor Rd, offers day hikes in rugged and strikingly scenic landscapes. There are numerous succulents, dwarf trees and shrubs, as well as animal and bird species. You can choose from a number of trails. Fees (R18) are paid into an honesty box at the entrance to the reserve.

Both the Boesmanskloof Trail and the Vrolijkheid Nature Reserve are administered by **Cape Nature** (☎ 028-435 5020; www.cape nature.org.za; ⏰ 7.30am-4pm Mon-Fri), which has offices about 15km south of Robertson on the McGregor Rd. On weekends you'll have to get a permit from the tourism bureau.

The self-styled 'McGregor Wine Experience' can't compete with the wine routes of its neighbours, but does offer a half-dozen or so decent estates. Start at environmentally friendly **McGregor Wines** (☎ 023-625 1741; www.mcgregorwinery.co.za; ⏰ 8am-5pm Mon-Fri, 9am-2pm Sat) and explore from there.

Sleeping & Eating

The tourism bureau has a full list of accommodation around the village but doesn't take bookings. Eating options in McGregor are almost limited to where you sleep.

Whipstock Farm (☎ 023-625 1733; www.whipstock .za.net; s/d R295/590) Working fireplaces, amiable dogs, a serene location and fresh farmstall produce combine to wonderful effect at this guesthouse set in a series of historic buildings. The friendly hosts make breakfast and dinner on request, and can organise transfers to and from the Boesmanskloof

Trail. Follow Voortrekker Rd towards the mountains until it becomes a dirt road; Whipstock is 7km down this road.

Temenos Retreat (☎ 023-625 1871; temenos@lando .co.za; cnr Bree St & Voortrekker Rd; s/d R330/495; 🖭) These unique cottages set in spacious gardens are open to all (except children under 12), not just those on retreat. It's a peaceful place, with a decent lap pool, health treatments, nooks for contemplation and a coffee shop. Three-course dinner costs R90.

McGregor Country Cottages (☎ 023-625 1816; Voortrekker Rd; d R375; ♿) Located beside an apricot orchard at the north end of the village is this complex of seven whitewashed, thatched-roofed self-catering cottages, each with its own fireplace. Three of the cottages are wheelchair accessible. The entire place has a quaint farmlike feel with a cosy bar and sitting room and sociable hosts.

Trossachs (☎ 023-612 1881; www.trossachs.co.za; s/d incl breakfast R850/1100; 🖭) This is one of the province's most popular wedding venues, where guests stay in thatched, stone cottages with a distinctly Scottish theme – each has its own clan name and accompanying tartan – and splendid views. Look out for the turn-off 10km before McGregor.

Villagers Coffee Shop (☎ 023-625 1787; Voortrekker Rd; mains R20; ⏰ breakfast & lunch Mon-Sat) A convivial country store offering light meals and a refreshing range of homemade fruit juices.

Getting There & Away

Apart from hiking in from Greyton, there's only one road in and out of McGregor (the road to Robertson), and you're going to need your own transport.

GREYTON

☎ 028

Although officially part of the Overberg region, we've included Greyton and the neighbouring village of Genadendal here because of their link to McGregor along the Boesmanskloof Trail.

Much more twee and polished than McGregor, even locals admit that the whitewashed, thatched-roof cottages of Greyton are a bit artificial. As pleasant as the village is, it needs to be seen in conjunction with the old Moravian Mission of neighbouring Genadendal, with its well-preserved historic buildings that couldn't be more authentic.

Information

Tourist information office (☎ 028-254 9414; info@
greyton.net; ☼ 10am-noon & 2.30-4.30pm Mon-Sat)
There's a small but helpful tourist office on the village's
main road.

Sights & Activities

GENADENDAL MISSION STATION

Some 7km west of Greyton is **Genadendal**,
the oldest mission station in South Africa,
founded in 1738 and for a brief time the
largest settlement in the colony after Cape
Town. Entering the village from Rte 406,
head down Main Rd until you arrive at
the cluster of national monuments around
Church Sq.

The Moravian Church is a handsome,
simply decorated building. Opposite you'll
find the village's **tourist information centre**
(☎ 028-251 8291; ☼ 8.30am-5pm Mon-Fri, 10am-1pm
Sat). There's a café here selling homemade
bread and souvenirs, including pottery.

The village's fascinating history is documented in the excellent **Mission Museum**
(☎ 028-251 8582; adult/child R8/4; ☼ 9am-1pm & 2-5pm
Mon-Thu, 9am-3.30pm Fri, 9am-1pm Sat), which is in
what was South Africa's first teacher-training
college. Elsewhere in this historic precinct is
one of the oldest printing presses in the country, still in operation, and a water mill.

GENADENDAL TRAIL

Greyton comes into its own as a base for
hiking in the Riviersonderend Mountains,
which rise up in Gothic majesty immediately to the village's north. Apart from
the Boesmanskloof Trail there are several
shorter walks, as well as the two-day Genadendal Trail for the serious hiker. This
is a 25.3km circular route that begins and
ends at Genadendal's Moravian Church;
for more details pick up the Cape Nature
Conservation leaflet at the Greyton tourist
information office.

Sleeping & Eating

For its size, Greyton has a wide range of
accommodation and places to eat.

Guinea Fowl (☎ 028-254 9550; jpagencies@telkomsa
.net; cnr DS Botha & Oak Sts; s/d incl breakfast from R350/500;
☒) Comfortable and quiet, this guesthouse
has a pool for summer, log fire for winter
and good breakfasts year-round.

Post House (☎ 028-254 9995; fax 254 9920; 24 Main
Rd; d incl breakfast from R400) Based in the town's

historic former post house and set around a
pretty garden, rooms are named after Bea-
trix Potter characters (we told you Greyton
was a twee place). Its English-style pub, the
Ball & Bass, is a wonderfully atmospheric
spot for a drink or meal.

Greyton Lodge (☎ 028-254 9800; www.greyton
lodge.com; 46 Main Rd; s/d incl breakfast R500/700; ☒)
An upmarket, gay-friendly hotel in the old
police station. Catch the live crooners in
the garden terrace from 5pm on Fridays.
There's a pool and a reasonably priced but
unadventurous bistro.

High Hopes B&B (☎ /fax 028-254 9898; 89 Main Rd;
d incl breakfast from R580) Readers love this place,
and it's easy to see why: tastefully furnished
rooms, lovely gardens with a beautiful koi
(carp) pond and a well-stocked library.
There's now also a Healing Energy Centre
offering massages and other treatments to
get you back on track. Convenient for hikers, it's the closest B&B to the start of the
Boesmanskloof Trail.

Rosie's Restaurant (☎ 028-254 9640; 9 High St;
mains from R40; ☼ dinner) The house specialities
at this unpretentious place are wood-fired
pizzas (which are delicious and huge) and
steaks.

Oak & Vigne Café (☎ 028-254 9037; DS Botha St;
mains R50; ☼ breakfast & lunch) Evidence of the
gentrification of Greyton is this trendy
deli-art gallery-café, which is a fine place to
grab a snack, chill out and watch the world
go by.

Getting There & Away

If you're not hiking in from McGregor, the
only way to Greyton is by your own transport. From Cape Town follow the N2 to
just before Caledon and then take Rte 406.
From Robertson take Rte 317 south to the
N2 at Stormsvlei, then head west to Riviersonderend to connect with Rte 406.

MONTAGU

☎ 023 / pop 9500

Populated by artists, dreamers and other
escapees, country hospitality is spread thick
in picturesque, invigorating Montagu.

Founded in 1851, it's the first town up
the pass from the Breede River Valley –
once you pop through the Cogmanskloof
near Robertson you are suddenly in a very
different world. It's a good place to go if
you want to escape the 21st century and

get a brief taste of the Little Karoo, making it the perfect retreat for couples looking for some space; backpackers looking for a party might be happier elsewhere.

There are some 24 restored national monuments, including fine examples of Art Deco architecture, but it's Montagu's splendid range of activities – including hot springs, permit-free meanders and hikes, hearty meals in old-world buildings – that have turned it into such a popular Route 62 destination.

Orientation & Information

The town is small, so it's easy to get around on foot. Most activity and accommodation is centred on Bath St.

Printmor (70 Bath St; per hr R40; 7.30am-5.30pm Mon-Fri, 8am-1pm Sat) Internet access is available at this place at the Succulent Café.

Tourism bureau (☎ 023-614 2471; www.tourism montagu.co.za; 24 Bath St; 8am-6pm Mon-Fri, 9am-5pm Sat, 9.30am-12.30pm & 3-5pm Sun) This office is extremely efficient and helpful. It can provide information on accommodation (including a good range of B&Bs and self-catering cottages), hikes and other activities.

Opening hours are slightly shorter between May and October.

Sights & Activities

Don't be fooled by its size; Montagu has enough to keep you entertained for at least a few days.

HOT SPRINGS & LOVER'S WALK TRAIL

Water from the **hot mineral springs** (☎ 023-614 1150; admission R25; 8am-11pm; P) finds its way into the concrete pools of the Avalon Springs Hotel, about 3km from town. Heated to 43°C, energising and renowned for their healing properties, the pools are a lively place on weekends, when many local families come for a soak.

A great way to get here is to hike along the 2.2km Lover's Walk Trail, which starts at the car park at the end of Barry St. Pick up the *Hiking Trails* leaflet from the tourism bureau. The route leads past Montagu's top rock-climbing spots and can get tricky (and wet). For guidance on climbing and hiking in the area contact **De Bos** (☎ 023-614 2532; sdbrown@mweb.co.za).

MONTAGU

0 — 300 m
0 — 0.2 miles

INFORMATION		
Printmor	1	D3
Tourism Bureau	2	B3

SIGHTS & ACTIVITIES		
Cottage Café & Bike Hire	(see 13)	
Joubert House	3	B3
Montagu Museum	4	C3

SLEEPING		
7 Church Street	5	B3
Airlies Guest House	6	B3
De Bos	7	A3
Kingna Lodge	8	B3
Mimosa Lodge	9	B3
Montagu Caravan Park	10	A3
Montagu Country Hotel	11	C2
Olive House	12	B3

EATING		
Cottage Café	13	D3
Docks	(see 13)	
Jessica's	14	C2
Josephine's	15	B3
Preston's	16	C3
Succulent Café	17	B3

TRANSPORT		
Local Minibus Taxis	18	C3

To Carpark; Bloupunt & Kogmanskloof Trails

To Hot Mineral Springs (50m); Avalon Springs Hotel (200m)

To Avalon Springs Hotel (1.5km); Montagu Springs Holiday Resort (1.5km); Die Stal (7km); Tractor-Trailer Rides (29km); Protea Farm (29km)

R318

Meul St
Tanner St
Lover's Walk Trail
Joubert St
Piet Retief St
River
Kerste
Rose St
Barry St
Church St
Bath St
Kohler St
Du Toit St
Market St
Cross St
Long St
Kingna River
Van Riebeeck St

To Ashton (9km); Cape Town (180km)

To Barrydale (66km); Oudtshoorn (210km)

R 62

TRACTOR-TRAILER RIDES

Niel Burger, owner of the Protea Farm at the top of the Langeberg Range, 29km from Montagu, takes fun **tractor-trailer rides** (☎ 023-614 2471; adult/child R60/30; ☼ tours 10am & 2pm Wed & Sat) to the farm, from where you can look way down into the Breede River Valley. Even locals enjoy the three-hour trip, so it must be something special. You can have a delicious lunch of *potjiekos* (traditional pot stew) with homemade bread for R40/10 per adult/child, and stay on at the farm accommodation (four-person cottages R350).

MONTAGU MUSEUM & JOUBERT HOUSE

Interesting displays and some good examples of antique furniture can be found at the **Montagu Museum** (☎ 023-614 1950; 41 Long St; adult/child R3/1; ☼ 9am-1pm & 2-5pm Mon-Fri, 10.30am-12.30pm Sat & Sun) in the old mission church.

Joubert House (☎ 023-614 1774; 25 Long St; adult/ child R3/1; ☼ 9am-1pm & 2-4.30pm Mon-Fri, 10.30am-12.30pm Sat, 10am-noon Sun), a short walk away, is the oldest house in Montagu (built in 1853) and has been restored to its Victorian finery.

HIKING

The **Bloupunt Trail** is 15.6km long and can be walked in six to eight hours; it traverses ravines and mountain streams, and climbs to 1000m. The flora includes proteas, ericas, aloes, gladioli and watsonias. The **Cogmanskloof Trail** is 12.1km and can be completed in four to six hours; it's not as steep as the Bloupunt Trail. Both trails start from the car park at the end of Tanner St. To hike either trail costs R18 per person. The tourist bureau handles bookings for overnight cabins near the start of the trails. The huts (per person R60) are fairly basic (wood stoves, showers and toilet facilities), but they are cheap.

MOUNTAIN BIKING

Biking is a great way to see the surrounding countryside. To rent a mountain bike, call Ron Brunings or visit him at the **Cottage Café & Bike Hire** (☎ /fax 023-614 1932; 78 Bath St; per hr R20). Ron also runs **Dusty Sprocket Trails** (brunings@lando.co.za), offering 11 guided mountain-bike trails in the area for all skill levels; trails range from 12km to 43km.

Sleeping

In town there are some lovely guesthouses, but there are also fine dining and accommodation on the outskirts, particularly in the vicinity of the hot springs.

BUDGET

De Bos (☎ 023-614 2532; www.debos.co.za; Bath St; camp sites per person R30, dm R45; s/d R120/170; ☒) A genuine farm-stay for backpackers – there's a river, chickens and pecan-nut trees in this 7-hectare property, where colourful old workers' cottages have been converted into self-catering cottages (R200). On weekends there is a two-night minimum stay, except for camping.

Montagu Caravan Park (☎ 023-614 3034; Bath St; camp sites per person R40, 4-person cabins/chalets R180/240) This park is in a pleasant location with apricot trees and lots of shade and grass. The chalets come with cooking equipment and TVs, though bedding (R40) is optional. The park is at the far west end of Bath St.

MIDRANGE

Olive House (☎ 023-614 1095; www.theolivehouse .co.za; Bath St; r from R300; ☒) A refreshing change from so much traditional country décor: whitewashed minimalism and stylish artistic flourishes that shouldn't work within this 1854 national monument, but do. Food is served at the adjacent Succulent Café and the whole place can be hired for weddings. Sheer sophistication.

Montagu Springs Holiday Resort (☎ 023-614 1050; www.montagusprings.co.za; Warmbronne Hot Springs; 4-person chalets from R380) These self-catering chalets are the cheaper option at the hot-springs resort. Those interested in waterfowl, pigeons and chickens should check out the 'feathered friends' sanctuary where more than 160 types of bird are on display. There are daily feedings.

Airlies Guest House (☎ 023-614 2943; www.airlies .co.za; Bath St; s/d incl breakfast R390/590; ☒) Quaint accommodation in a roomy, thatched-roof house with spacious wood-floored rooms looking out on the mountains. The hosts are very obliging and the breakfast is excellent.

TOP END

Kingna Lodge (☎ 023-614 1066; www.kingnalodge .co.za; 11 Bath St; s/d R400/600; ☒) Tastefully restrained Victoriana is the design choice at this elegant guesthouse, where the five-course dinners (R150) draw rave reviews. Each room is uniquely decorated and named after a different grape cultivar, but all come with marble bathrooms and fireplaces. Former presidents Nelson Mandela and FW De Klerk each stayed here in 1995. Karoo hospitality exemplified.

7 Church Street (☎ 023-614 1186; www.7church street.co.za; 7 Church St; s/d incl breakfast R400/600; 🐾) A luxury guesthouse in a charming Karoo building with traditional wrought-iron *broekie-lace* (panty-lace) filigree and a manicured garden. The plush interior doubles as a gallery of the owner's personal art collection.

Montagu Country Hotel (☎ 023-614 3125; www .montagucountryhotel.co.za; 27 Bath St; s/d R480/800; 🍴 🐾) In a large pink building with stunning Art Deco finishes, this pleasant hotel with reasonably decorated rooms offers all the usual facilities, and has a streetside courtyard, pool, smart restaurant and bar. There is an à la carte lunch from R35.

Mimosa Lodge (☎ 023-614 2351; www.mimosa .co.za; Church St; s/d incl breakfast R580/850; 🐾) An upper-crust lodge in a restored Edwardian landmark building with manicured gardens, an artful pool complete with a thatched-roof gazebo for shade and a small waterfall. The dinners (R155) are open to nonguests, and are a highlight.

Avalon Springs Hotel (☎ 023-614 1150; www.ava lonsprings.co.za; Warmbronne Hot Springs; s/d from R625/ 1050) This old-fashioned hotel and timeshare complex draws good reviews, despite the eerie, period horror-movie décor and its mercenary policy of jacking up prices by 25% on weekends (when there's a two-night minimum stay) and at holiday times. As well as the outdoor hot-spring pools, massages, a gym and a 24-hour café are available. Plenty for the kids to do, too.

Eating

As well as meals in the Montagu Country Hotel, Mimosa Lodge and Kingna Lodge (for these last two you must book in advance), there are a few other options.

Cottage Café (☎ 023-614 1932; 78 Bath St; mains R10-30; 🕐 breakfast & lunch Mon-Sat) Light lunches are served in a grassy garden. The daily specials are usually tasty and good value. Those with a sweet tooth will enjoy the ice cream.

Docks (☎ 023-614 3360; 80 Bath St; mains R20-55; 🕐 dinner Tue-Fri, breakfast, lunch & dinner Sat & Sun) The perfect place for a post-boozing stomach filler. No-nonsense, good-value food served indoors or on benches around a swimming pool.

Succulent Café (20 Bath St; mains R20-60; 🕐 breakfast, lunch & dinner) Streamlined design, quality coffee, a solid vegetarian menu and fresh ingredients characterise this breezy café loved by local artists, with large pictures of succulents on the walls and breakfast dishes equally juicy. The table layout is cleverly switched according to mealtimes, and there's Internet access (per hour R42), too. It's closed on Monday nights.

Die Stal (☎ 082-324 4318; Touwsrivier Rd, off Rte 318; mains R35-65; 🕐 breakfast & lunch Tue-Sun) A countryside dining experience just 7km north of town on a working citrus farm, this place serves up the creations of local chefs. The menu changes daily, but large country breakfasts are always on offer.

Preston's (☎ 023-614 3013; 17 Bath St; breakfast R30, mains R40-70; 🕐 breakfast, lunch & dinner) There's a variety of steak and seafood as well as some veg options served in a lovely garden. Those looking for just a drink can head to the attached Thomas Bain Pub.

Jessica's (☎ 023-614 1805; 47 Bath St; mains R60-90; 🕐 dinner) Named after the family dog, Jessica's serves up inventive bistro dishes, such as butternut ravioli and pan-fried springbok strips, in a cosy atmosphere.

Josephine's (☎ 023-614 3939; 63 Bath St; mains R60-90; 🕐 lunch & dinner Mon-Fri, dinner Sat) A local favourite, with seasonal menus and plenty of fresh fish specials. We love the burgundy and pumpkin colour theme.

Getting There & Around

Translux (☎ 021-449 3333; www.translux.co.za) buses stop at Ashton, 9km from Montagu, on the run between Cape Town (R120, 2½ hours, daily) and Port Elizabeth (R170, six hours, daily).

Most accommodation establishments offer (prebooked) shuttles from Ashton to Montagu, but you can also jump in one of the minibus taxis (R8) that ply this route. If you're arriving after hours, you may need to hire a car from one of the companies at the bus depot.

JJ's Transport (☎ 023-614 3975; per person R30) runs a taxi service between town and the hot springs. The price includes a glass of wine. Call for bookings.

Munnik's (☎ 021-637 1850; per person R70; ☷ Wed, Fri, Sat & Sun) runs a shuttle between Montagu and Cape Town. It'll also take you on to the hot springs for an extra R10.

Local minibus taxis leave from the **OK Supermarket** (Bath St) near the corner of Market St and run to Cape Town (R110, 3½ hours) and Oudtshoorn (R40, 2½ hours).

CALITZDORP

☎ 044 / pop 9000

Lovers of either port or unexpectedly charming towns shouldn't join the majority of motorists who judge Calitzdorp by its nondescript main street and zoom past on their way to more-fashionable places. Apart from the vineyards, there's a **museum** (cnr Van Riebeeck & Geyser Sts; admission free; ☷ 9am-noon & 2-5pm Mon-Fri, 9am-noon Sat) housing Calitzdorp memorabilia. There's also a **Dutch Reformed Church**, which is a national monument.

The **information centre** (☎ 044-213 3312; cnr Voortrek & Barry Sts; ☷ 9am-noon & 2-5pm Mon-Fri, 9am-noon Sat), tucked in behind the Shell petrol station, can provide details on accommodation and the local wineries.

The best winery is generally considered to be **Boplaas** (☎ 044-213 3326; www.boplaas.co.za; Zaayman St; tastings wine/wine & port R15/35; ☷ 8am-5pm Mon-Fri, 9am-3pm Sat), with several international awards under its belt. Follow the signs from Andries Pretorius St off Voortrekker Rd, and call ahead to book a cellar tour. There's also a general **port festival** held in July every odd-numbered year.

If it's too late, or you're too drunk, to leave town, opposite Boplaas is the **Port-Wine Guest House** (☎ 044-213 3131; portwine@mweb.co.za; 7 Queen St; s/d incl breakfast R400/760; ☐ ☒ ☒ ☒), in a beautifully appointed, thatched Cape cottage. It's perfect for a romantic weekend – there are no TVs in the bedrooms (but there are four-poster beds).

There are seven restaurants and 27 other guesthouses in town, all of similar quality, so it's best to ask at the information centre where to stay and eat.

OUDTSHOORN

☎ 044 / pop 85,000

If you're an ostrich, this is the place to come for work. Otherwise, there's much, much more to the sedate tourist capital of the Little Karoo than these feckless feathered friends (despite their appearance in some form or another on just about every piece of publicity).

Certainly, that it bills itself as the ostrich capital of the world is no overstatement. These birds have been bred hereabouts since the 1870s, and at the turn of the 20th century fortunes were made from the fashion for ostrich feathers. Oudtshoorn boomed, and the so-called 'feather barons' built the grand houses that lend the town its distinctive atmosphere today.

The town still turns a pretty penny from breeding the birds for meat and leather, and the ostriches also pay their way with tourists – you can buy ostrich eggs, feathers and *biltong* all over town – but more importantly Oudtshoorn is a great base for exploring the different environments of the Little Karoo, the Garden Route (it's 55km to George along the N12) and the Great Karoo.

The nearby Swartberg and Seweweekspoort Passes – two of South Africa's scenic highlights – are geological, floral and engineering masterpieces. Oudtshoorn has a strong Afrikaans feel, tree-lined streets, interesting shops and top-class restaurants.

Orientation & Information

Oudtshoorn itself is navigable on foot, but as many attractions are some distance from one another, your own transport, or a willingness to take a tour, is recommended. The main commercial street is High (Hoog) St, to the east of Baron van Rheede St, where you'll find most of the restaurants.

If you need to check your email, there's Internet access at Oasis Shanti hostel. **Oudtshoorn Tourism Bureau** (☎ 044-279 2532; www.oudtshoorn.com; Baron van Rheede St; ☷ 7am-5pm Mon-Fri, 9am-1pm Sat & Sun) This helpful bureau is next to the CP Nel Museum. Ask here about the numerous B&Bs in town and about tours of the local sights.

Sights & Activities

Many of Oudtshoorn's sights are outside of the town limits. Some hostels and B&Bs offer discounts on attractions if you stay the night.

CP NEL MUSEUM & LE ROUX TOWNHOUSE

Extensive displays about ostriches, as well as Karoo history, make up this large and interesting **museum** (☎ 044-272 7306; 3 Baron van Rheede

St; adult/child R10/3; 9am-5pm Mon-Sat), housed in a striking sandstone building completed in 1906 at the height of ostrich fever. It also features some impressive reconstructed Victorian shops and the interior of an 1896 synagogue transferred here when its original home was demolished.

Included in the ticket price is admission to the **Le Roux Townhouse** (044-272 3676; cnr Loop & High Sts; 9am-1pm & 2-5pm Mon-Fri). This place is decorated in authentic period furniture and is as good an example of a 'feather palace' as you're likely to see.

CANGO WILDLIFE RANCH & CHEETAHLAND

If you're all ostriched out, head to this **ranch** (044-272 5593; adult/child R60/45; 8am-4.30pm).

It's got a bit of a zoolike feel but has a good collection of wildlife and big cats (in rather small enclosures), including cheetahs, which you may pat for an extra R30 (funds go to the Cheetah Conservation Foundation). The ranch is 3km from town on the road out to Prince Albert. Other big cats here include lion, pumas and Bengal white tigers, and there are also crocodiles, alligators and other wild animals.

MEERKAT MAGIC CONSERVATION PROJECT

Everyone loves a meerkat, but none with as much devotion as Grant McIlrath, the so-called Meerkat Man of Oudtshoorn. On his unique **meerkat experience** (082-413

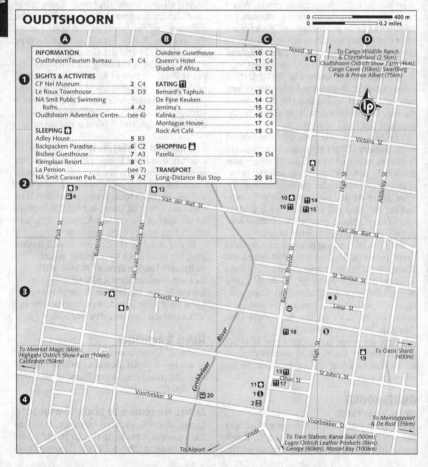

OUDTSHOORN

INFORMATION	
Oudtshoorn Tourism Bureau	1 C4

SIGHTS & ACTIVITIES	
CP Nel Museum	2 C4
Le Roux Townhouse	3 D3
NA Smit Public Swimming Baths	4 A2
Oudtshoorn Adventure Centre	(see 6)

SLEEPING	
Adley House	5 B3
Backpackers Paradise	6 C2
Bisibee Guesthouse	7 A3
Kleinplaas Resort	8 C1
La Pension	(see 7)
NA Smit Caravan Park	9 A2

Oakdene Gusethouse	10 C2
Queen's Hotel	11 C4
Shades of Africa	12 B2

EATING	
Bernard's Taphuis	13 C4
De Fijne Keuken	14 C2
Jemima's	15 C2
Kalinka	16 C2
Montague House	17 C4
Rock Art Café	18 C3

SHOPPING	
Pasella	19 D4

TRANSPORT	
Long-Distance Bus Stop	20 B4

0 ___ 400 m
0 ___ 0.2 miles

To Cango Wildlife Ranch & Cheetahland (2.5km); Oudtshoorn Ostrich Show Farm (4km); Cango Caves (30km); Swartberg Pass & Prince Albert (75km)

Noord St

Victoria St

Van der Riet St

Van der Riet St

St Saviour St

Church St

Loop St

River

To Meerkat Magic (6km); Highgate Ostrich Show Farm (10km); Calitzdorp (50km)

St John's St

Oliver St

Voortrekker St

Vrede

To Oasis Shanti (400m)

To Meiringspoort & De Rust (35km)

To Train Station; Karoo Soul (500m); Lugro Ostrich Leather Products (8km); George (60km); Mossel Bay (100km)

To Airport

WESTERN CAPE

6895; www.meerkatmagic.com; minimum donation R400; ☿ sunset & sunrise Oct-Apr, sunrise May-Sep), a pioneering conservation project, you will get to see up close how these curious, highly intelligent creatures communicate and live. It's truly unique in that the subjects, thanks to Grant's many years of building trust with them, are entirely unaffected by your presence while allowing you to enter their environment. If you have only one wildlife encounter in the Western Cape, make it this one. The natural meerkat burrows are at various locations a few kilometres west of Oudtshoorn along Rte 328, but meet-ups and collections are in town. Ask about farm accommodation near the burrows.

OSTRICH FARMS

There are *four* show farms in town, which offer guided tours of 45 minutes to one hour. There's little to choose between them; we found the staff at the **Oudtshoorn Ostrich Show Farm** (☎ 044-279 1861; Cango Caves Rd; adult/child R40/20; ☿ 8am-5pm) very informative. The **Highgate Ostrich Show Farm** (☎ 044-272 7115; www.highgate.co.za; adult/child R40/20; ☿ 8am-5pm) also gets good reviews. It's 10km from Oudtshoorn en route to Mossel Bay.

TWO PASSES ROUTE

If you're going to one of the ostrich farms north of town or to the Cango Caves, carry on driving and take the **Swartberg Pass** all the way to Prince Albert, then return to Oudtshoorn via the **Meiringspoort Pass**. Both are engineering masterpieces, and halfway down the latter there is a waterfall and small visitor centre. The road will take you past the town of De Rust and back home – it is a great day's excursion. Ask your accommodation or at the local tourist office for a route map.

CANGO CAVES

Named after the Khoesaan word for 'a wet place', the **Cango Caves** (☎ 044-272 7410; www.cangocaves.co.za; admission from R50; ☿ 9am-4pm) are heavily commercialised but impressive. There's a choice of tours on offer. The halfhour tour gives you just a glimpse – it's better to choose a longer tour. The longest tour is the most fun, but involves crawling through tight and damp places so is not recommended for the claustrophobic or unfit. The caves are 30km north of Oudtshoorn.

MOUNTAIN-BIKE RIDES

If you're looking for a little exercise and a lot of thrill then hop on a mountain bike and ride from the top of Swartberg Pass down into Oudtshoorn. The **Oudtshoorn Adventure Centre** (☎ 044-272 3436; www.backpackers paradise.hostel.com; 148 Baron van Rheede St; tours from R120) at Backpackers Paradise hostel (see below) runs these trips, which depart daily at 8.30am. You'll be driven up and then cycle back to town. Be warned, it's not all downhill and it's a long ride.

SWIMMING

It's not uncommon for the mercury to hit upwards of 40°C (104°F) in summer. Escape the swelter at the **NA Smit Public Swimming Baths** (☎ 044-203 3119; Park St; adult/child R5/2.65; ☿ 9.30am-6.30pm Mon-Sat, 2-5pm Sun).

Festivals & Events

Early each April, the enthralling **Klein Karoo Nationale Kunstfees** (Little Karoo National Arts Festival; www.kknk.co.za; cnr Church & Baron van Rheede Sts) dedicates itself to the 'renaissance of Afrikaans' and showcases indigenous artists, poets, thespians and musicians in a riotous week-long festival of creativity. It's South Africa's best-attended festival of its kind.

Sleeping

BUDGET

Oasis Shanti (☎ 044-279 1163; oasis@mailbox.co.za; 3 Church St; camp sites per person R35, dm R60, d with shared bathroom from R180; ☒) Friendly and well run, this recently refurbished hostel is in a large house with a spacious braai and swimming pool area, and shady camping spots. The lounge has a roaring fireplace to take the chill out of cold nights and there are the requisite ostrich braais.

Backpackers Paradise (☎ 044-272 3436; www.back packersparadise.hostel.com; 148 Baron van Rheede St; camp sites per person R40, dm R65, r from R180, d with bathroom R250; ☐ ☒) In a large old house, this excellent hostel has a separate dorm-bed annexe, bar, ostrich braais and free ostrich-egg breakfasts (in season, you'll be given an egg – cook it any way you please). It also offers curios at knock-down prices, discounts to area attractions and an adventure centre that can set you up with a host of activities.

Karoo Soul (☎ 044-272 0330; www.karoosoul.com; 170 Langenhoven Rd; camp sites per person R40, dm incl breakfast R80, d with shared bathroom & breakfast R250; 🖳 🖾) The lack of atmosphere and small kitchen may show this newish place is still finding its feet, but its luxury linens, quietude and comfort are proof that the backpacker has come of age. It's also the only place offering a view of Oudtshoorn. Try to get one of the west-facing doubles for a romantic sundowner from your bed, or ask about the en suite garden cottage (R300).

NA Smit Caravan Park (☎ 044-272 2313; fax 279 1915; Park St; camp sites R89, rondavels R200; 🖾) There's not much shade or grass, but facilities are decent. The kids will love the playground.

Kleinplaas Resort (☎ 044-2725811; kleinpls@mweb .co.za; 171 Baron van Rheede St; camp sites R120, 4-person chalets R380; 🖾) A terrific caravan park, with a restaurant and a big pool.

MIDRANGE

Bisibee Guesthouse (☎ 044-2724784; bisibee@hotmail .com; 171 Church St; s/d incl breakfast R280/500; 🖾 🖾) One of the first guesthouses in town, this is a spotless but somewhat old-fashioned building once used as a place for departing soldiers to bid adieu to their loved ones.

La Pension (☎ 044-279 2445; www.lapension.co.za; 169 Church St; s/d incl breakfast R350/500; 🖾) A reliable choice with a plainly designed range of rooms, La Pension includes some self-catering units with TV, plus a good-sized pool, sauna and a large, immaculate garden.

Oakdene Guesthouse (☎ 044-272 3018; www.oak dene.co.za; 99 Baron van Rheede St; s/d R395/620; 🖾 🖾) Elegant cottage furniture, wooden floors, ostrich eggs, linens with high thread counts and an earthy-coloured paint job make each room special. The lush gardens and excellent pool add to the charm. Electric blankets are provided in winter.

Shades of Africa (☎ 044-272 6430; shades@mweb .co.za; 238 Jan van Riebeeck Rd; s/d incl breakfast R400/650; 🖾) Colourful Afro-chic touches make this contemporary-styled guesthouse, with a small pool, a charming place to stay.

Adley House (☎ 044-272 4533; www.adleyhouse.co .za; 209 Jan van Riebeeck Rd; s/d incl breakfast R515/700; 🖾 🖾) Rooms, all with private entrance, in the 1905 'Feather Palace' have bags of charm, though the separate add-on ones less so. There's a couple of pools and a beautiful outdoor braai and bar area.

Queen's Hotel (☎ 044-272 2101; www.queenshotel .co.za; 11 Baron van Rheede St; s/d R680/950; 🖾 🖾)

This attractive old-style country hotel with spacious, understated rooms is refreshingly cool inside. It's an expansive place with ivy on the exterior walls and a faux marble entrance hall, yet it has an inviting appeal.

Eating

As you'd expect, most places serve ostrich in one form or another, but dining options are in general remarkably good.

Rock Art Café (☎ 044-279 1927; 62 Baron van Rheede St; breakfast from R20, mains R30-65; 🕑 lunch & dinner Mon-Sat, dinner Sun) Grab an outdoor bench and choose from a wide range of simple dishes at this often-busy bar, which has live music on Friday or Saturday.

Montague House (☎ 044-272 3208; cnr Baron van Rheede & Olivier Sts; mains R30; 🕑 breakfast, lunch & dinner) Breakfast is served until 2.30pm and there is a huge number of choices. Otherwise dine on pasta, salads or sandwiches under umbrellas in the large flower garden.

Bernard's Taphuis (☎ 044-272 3208; cnr Olivier & Montague Sts; mains R45-80; 🕑 lunch & dinner) This place has a European flair, multiple selections for vegetarians and lots of ostrich dishes.

Jemima's (☎ 044-272 0808; 94 Baron van Rheede St; mains from R50; 🕑 dinner Mon-Sun, lunch & dinner Fri) Recognised as one of the country's finest restaurants, Jemima's delights both the palate and the eyes. It's the small touches that make this place so delightful, but the food that ultimately takes centre stage. The Cape Malay dishes are legendary. After your meal try a *swepie*, a mix of brandy and *jerepigo* (dessert wine).

De Fijne Keuken (☎ 044-272 6403; 114 Baron van Rheede St; mains R50-70; 🕑 lunch & dinner) The funky atmosphere – bright-coloured walls plastered with old maps of the continent – is just another good mark for this highly recommended restaurant. There's loads of outdoor seating, and the varied menu includes ostrich cooked every way imaginable, and a large selection of pastas.

Kalinka (☎ 044-279 2596; 93 Baron van Rheede St; mains R60-85; 🕑 lunch & dinner Mon-Sun, breakfast Sat & Sun only) A stylish bistro with an imaginative menu interspersed with Russian delights thanks to skilful chef Olga's love for Muscovite ingredients. Try the Russian tomato salad (R32).

Shopping

There's plenty for the shopper in Oudts-hoorn, with Baron van Rheede St providing most outlets. Ostrich goods are naturally in demand, particularly ostrich leather. The leather is very pricey because of the low hide yield per bird, so it's worth shopping around here, including at show ranches and in hotels.

Lugro Ostrich Leather Products (☎ 044-272 7012; Off George Rd; ☿ 9am-5pm Mon-Sat) Considered one of the best-value ostrich-leather purveyors in town, Lugro is independent of local ranches, so offers a shopping experience that avoids the tacky tourist vibe usually accompanying the search for ostrich goods.

Pasella (☎ 044-272 6690; 100 Adderley St; ☿ 9am-5pm Mon-Fri, 9am-1pm Sat) For an alternate shopping experience, make time to get to Pasella, where you'll find a magnificent collection of old-school South African curios, second-hand furniture, bric-a-brac and 'high-class junk'.

Getting There & Around

Intercape (☎ 0861-287 287; www.intercape.co.za) has service to Jo'burg (R320, 14½ hours, daily). Otherwise you can take a **Translux bus** (☎ 021-449 3333; www.translux.co.za) to Mossel Bay (R50, one hour, daily) and from there you can get to multiple destinations (see p216). Buses stop in the Riverside Centre off Voortrekker St.

The Baz Bus stops at George, from where you can arrange a transfer to Oudtshoorn with Backpackers Paradise (R35).

Every Saturday the *Southern Cross* train leaves for Cape Town at 5pm.

Taxis aren't easy to find – try Union St near the Spar supermarket or check with the tourism bureau.

GARDEN ROUTE

The Garden Route is perhaps the most internationally renowned South African destination after Cape Town and the Kruger National Park, and with good reason. Within a few hundred kilometres, the range of topography, vegetation, wildlife and outdoor activity is breathtaking.

Roughly encompassing the coastline from Mossel Bay in the west to just beyond Plettenberg Bay in the east, it caters to all kinds of travellers. Backpackers are taken care of with plenty of hostels, and midrange and top-end folks will be pleased with the range of swanky hotels and charming guesthouses.

You can hike in old-growth forests, quad bike through wildlife reserves, commune with monkeys, chill out on the beach and canoe in the series of extensive lagoons that run behind a barrier of sand dunes and superb white beaches that make up the Garden Route's outer fringes. Inland, the Outeniqua and Tsitsikamma Ranges, which are between 1000m and 1700m high and crossed by some spectacular road passes, split the coast from the semidesert Karoo. The Garden Route also has some of the most significant tracts of indigenous forest in the country, including giant yellow-wood trees and many wildflowers. The climate is mild and noticeably wetter than elsewhere; the highest chance of rainfall and grey days is from August to October. The towns most commonly used as bases are Knysna and Plettenberg Bay, though we prefer less crowded Wilderness and Buffalo Bay.

It's worth mentioning that the region's celebrated status has been a mixed blessing. Its popularity has driven up competition, so facilities from restaurants to hotels to activity centres are uniformly top-notch. But in recent years development has spiralled seemingly out of control, and at times you might feel like you're a cog in a huge tourist machine. During the summer and South African school holidays prices soar and places quickly fill up, so it's best to book ahead. All in all, the Garden Route is great, but if you leave South Africa without having seen it, it isn't a disaster. If you leave having seen nothing else, it might be.

MOSSEL BAY

☎ 044 / pop 78,000

Once one of the jewels of the Garden Route, Mossel Bay was marred by rampant industrial sprawl in the 1980s, in particular that of the gas/petrol-conversion refinery on its outskirts. Following a clean-up (and an aggressive marketing campaign), the town is enjoying a revival, thanks in large part to its historic and sandstone buildings, excellent places to stay, plenty of activities, the only north-facing beach in the country and some top surf spots (see p215). Just ignore the town's approach, still showing the scars of its 'boom'.

The first European to visit the bay was the Portuguese explorer Bartholomeu Dias in 1488. Vasco de Gama followed him in 1497. From then on many ships stopped to take on fresh water, and to barter for provisions with the Gouriqua Khoekhoen who lived in the region. A large milkwood tree beside the spring was used as a postal collection point – expeditions heading east would leave mail to be picked up by ships returning home. The spring and the tree still exist, and you can post letters (they receive a special postmark) from a letterbox on the site.

Orientation & Information

The town lies on the northern slopes of Cape St Blaize. The museum complex, which overlooks the bay, is the best place to start your exploration. Marsh St, which runs through town, has a large concentration of restaurants and pubs. The Point is the place to head for a late-afternoon drink and to watch the surfers try their luck on the breaks. Santos Beach is the town's swimming beach.

Tourism bureau (☎ 044-691 2202; Market St; ☽ 8am-6pm Mon-Fri, 9am-1pm Sat & Sun) This office is very friendly and can help with accommodation bookings.

Sights

BARTHOLOMEU DIAS MARITIME MUSEUM

The highlight of the **museum complex** (☎ 044-691 1067; Market St; admission R6; ☽ Maritime, History & Shell Museums 8.30am-4.45pm Mon-Fri, 9am-3.45pm Sat & Sun) includes the **spring** where Dias watered the **postal tree**, the 1786 VOC **granary**, a **shell museum** (with some interesting aquarium tanks) and a local **history museum**. The highlight is the replica of the vessel that Dias used on his 1488 voyage of discovery. Its small size brings home the extraordinary skill and courage of the early explorers. The replica was built in Portugal and sailed to Mossel Bay in 1988 to commemorate the 500th anniversary of Dias' trip.

BOTLIERSKOP GAME FARM

This **farm** (☎ 044-696 6055; Little Brak River; admission from R360; s/d with dinner & breakfast R2685/3580; ☽ 9am-noon & 3-6pm) offers the chance to stay on a ranch and view a vast range of wildlife, including lion, elephant, rhino, buffalo, giraffe and blue wildebeest. These are bred for sale to other parks and although they are free to roam, the chances of spotting most breeds are high. The most popular activity is the quad-bike rides (R550), which include a buffet serving South African dishes. There are also three-hour game drives (R360) including a buffet meal. The farm is around 20km east of Mossel Bay along the N2 (take the Little Brak River turn-off and follow the signs towards Sorgfontein). Booking ahead is recommended.

GARDEN ROUTE

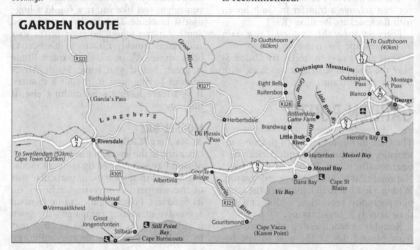

WESTERN CAPE

Activities

Mossel Bay is chock full of activities. There are regular boat trips on both the **Romonza** (☎ 044-690 3101) and the **Seven Seas** (☎ 044-691 3371) to view the seal colony, birds, dolphins and whales that frequent the waters around Seal Island. The trips last one hour and cost around R60. In late winter and spring the *Romonza* also runs special whale-watching trips (R400, two hours).

Electrodive (☎ 082-561 1259; George St; gear hire per day R100, shore-/boat-based dives R60-130) is a family-run operation offering a number of diving and snorkelling options. In addition to PADI/NAUI courses, it does an introduction to diving, charter dives, rubber ducking and snorkelling trips. The instructors are top-notch and very patient with beginners. While diving in Mossel Bay offers the opportunity to see quite a lot of coral, fish and other sea creatures, remember these aren't tropical waters and you're not going to have the top-notch visibility.

Shark Africa (☎ 044-691 3796; sharkafrica@mweb .co.za; Ochrebaan Sq, Market St; R1200) organises cage dives and snorkelling to view great white sharks.

Face Adrenalin (☎ 044-697 7001; www.faceadre nalin.com; R170; ☧ 9am-5pm) offers bungee jumping off Gourits Bridge 35km west of Mossel Bay. Ask about transfers at one of the hostels.

Skydivers can experience awesome views and possibly a beach landing when they jump with **Tandem Sky Dive** (☎ 082-824 8599; Mossel Bay Airfield; R1500).

Hikers should tackle the **Oystercatcher Trail** (☎ 044-699 1204; forban@mweb.co.za), a three- or five-day trail from Mossel Bay to Dana Bay via Cape St Blaize, including an encounter with wildlife such as the endangered Black Oystercatcher. While at Cape St Blaize, it's worth a stop at the **Lighthouse** and the adjoining **Khoi Village** (☎ 044-691 1031).

If you're interested in seeing how the other three-quarters live, contact **Meet the People** (☎ 083-262 2307; 4-hr tour R400), which offers home visits with traditional meals in nearby Tarka and KwaNonqaba townships – immensely preferable to the zoolike township tours offered in larger cities.

Sleeping

BUDGET

Mossel Bay Backpackers (☎ 044-691 3182; www.gar denrouteadventures.com; 1 Marsh St; camp sites per person R55, dm R80, d with shared bathroom R220; ☐ ☒ ☒) Close by the beach at the Point and the bars on Marsh St, this long-established place is reliable and well run. It offers a pool and bar and an impressive new fully equipped kitchen for aspirant chefs.

Garden Route Backpackers (☎ 044-690 4640; info@gardenroutebackpackers.co.za; 38 Marsh St; dm with/without linen R75/60) There are only dorms and no kitchen at this clean, airy backpackers, but with the downstairs restaurant (mains R40 to R80), you won't go hungry. It serves Cuban meals and has a cigar lounge.

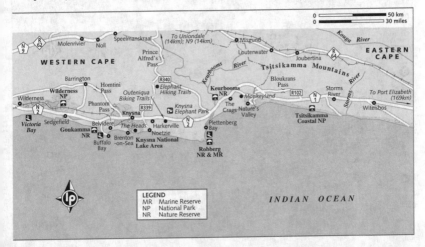

WESTERN CAPE

Park House Lodge & Travel Centre (☎ 044-691 1937; www.park-house.co.za; 121 High St; dm R90, d with shared bathroom from R220; 🖳) This place in an 1860s stone mansion is friendly, smartly decorated and has beautiful pond-filled gardens. Doubles are hardly quiet, largely thanks to the shared bathrooms being *between* the rooms, but are clean and comfortable.

Santos Express (☎ 044-691 1995; www.santosexpress .co.za; Santos Beach; dm R75, s/d with shared bathroom & breakfast R105/210) The position of this converted train, right beside the beach, can't be beaten, but the compartments are undeniably cramped. You can choose between cars sleeping two or four. There's an attached bar-restaurant (mains R40 to R60) with a very large menu, overlooking the water.

There are three municipal **caravan parks** (☎ 044-691 2915; camp sites from R55, chalets from R160) in town. Bakke and Santos are next to each other on pretty Santos Beach. The Punt is on the Point and very close to the surf. Prices rise in the high season. All offer sea views.

MIDRANGE

Huis te Marquette (☎ 044-691 3182; marquette@pixie .co.za; 1 Marsh St; s/d from R360/600; 🐾 ♿) This classy, long-running guesthouse, near the Point, has its more-expensive rooms facing the pool. These come with spa baths. The place is attached to Mossel Bay Backpackers and has a good bar.

Point Hotel (☎ 044-691 3512; www.pointhotel.co .za; Point Rd; s/d R550/700) The building is an

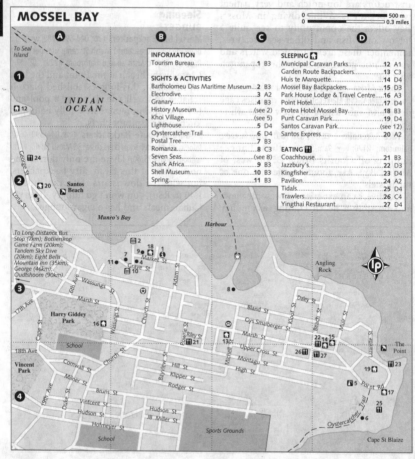

MOSSEL BAY

```
0          500 m
0         0.3 miles
```

INFORMATION
Tourism Bureau.................................1 B3

SIGHTS & ACTIVITIES
Bartholomeu Dias Maritime Museum...2 B3
Electrodive....................................3 A2
Granary...4 B3
History Museum.........................(see 2)
Khoi Village................................(see 5)
Lighthouse......................................5 D4
Oystercatcher Trail..........................6 D4
Postal Tree.....................................7 B3
Romanza..8 C3
Seven Seas.................................(see 8)
Shark Africa....................................9 B3
Shell Museum................................10 B3
Spring..11 B3

SLEEPING
Municipal Caravan Parks....................12 A1
Garden Route Backpackers................13 C3
Huis te Marquette...........................14 D4
Mossel Bay Backpackers...................15 D3
Park House Lodge & Travel Centre.....16 A3
Point Hotel....................................17 D4
Protea Hotel Mossel Bay..................18 B3
Punt Caravan Park..........................19 D4
Santos Caravan Park...................(see 12)
Santos Express...............................20 A2

EATING
Coachhouse...................................21 B3
Jazzbury's.....................................22 D3
Kingfisher.....................................23 D4
Pavilion..24 A2
Tidals...25 D4
Trawlers.......................................26 C4
Yingthai Restaurant........................27 D4

SURFING ALONG THE GARDEN ROUTE *David Malherbe & Nic Vorster*

As you travel up from Cape Town, the water gets a lot warmer. A spring suit or baggies in summer and autumn, and a good 3/2mm full suit in winter, is all you need. Local surfers are friendly and helpful if you show them the necessary respect. Tidal variations and changing wind directions are extremely important when it comes to the quality of the waves you'll find. There is a fantastic variety of waves.

Recommended breaks are at **Still Point Bay**, a right-point break, best at pushing tide, with sections and lots of cutting back into the juice. It doesn't hold a big swell, 1.5m to 2m is good, otherwise a strong rip; southwesterly wind is perfect offshore. Check out also the right-breaking waves of **Groot Jongensfontein**, 11km west of Stilbaai, and the five excellent, consistent-quality reef and point breaks of the **Mossel Bay Peninsula**. The main spots are Inner & Outer Pool, and Dingdang Reef, a left and right reef that works well on a big southwesterly or easterly direction swell. All these spots work on a west to southwest wind.

One of the rare spots that works on a northeasterly wind is **Herold's Bay**, great for those small onshore days. There is usually a left wedge, coming off the left-hand corner. Another beautiful small bay with a great right-hand break is **Victoria Bay**, the home break of Springbok surfers Leonard Giles, David Pfaff and Sean Holmes. It's worth finding out what's happening at **Buffalo Bay**, as the point can get good waves and works on a southwesterly wind, and **Plettenberg Bay** also offers some rare breaks, but is very fickle. Combine east or west swells with rare northwesterly or northerly winds and you'll surf some classic beach breaks. If you're starting out, ask your accommodation about board and/or wetsuit hire and lessons. Most will have connections with local surf shop and agencies, or have their own equipment.

---

eyesore but boasts a spectacular location, right above the wave-pounded rocks at the Point. There's a decent restaurant (mains R50 to R70) and the spacious rooms have balconies with ocean views.

TOP END

Protea Hotel Mossel Bay (☎ 044-691 3738; www .proteahotels.com/mosselbay; Market St; s/d from R690/900; 🖭) One of the more individual of the Protea chain's hotels, this is a characterful refurbishment of the old post-office building. Its restaurant (breakfast/lunch/dinner R40/45/80) has a large seafood, meat and pizza menu. Locals call this the best eat in town. For a sea-facing sunset cocktail try the attached Blue Oyster Bar.

Eight Bells Mountain Inn (☎ 044-631 0000; www .eightbells.co.za; s/d R730/1100; 🖭) This place is 35km north of Mossel Bay on Rte 328. It's in a lovely mountain setting at the foot of the Robinson Pass. Rooms are small but tastefully decorated with TVs and safes. There's a tea garden, restaurant and opportunity to hike and ride horses (R90 per hour) on the property.

Eating

Marsh St is the party strip in Mossel Bay, take a cruise and see what tickles your fancy.

Trawlers (☎ 044-691 3073; 18 Marsh St; mains R25-50; 🕒 lunch & dinner) Fish-net décor and maritime murals dominate this place. It serves inexpensive seafood-combo baskets, burgers and steaks. Looking for just a drink? Check out the long wooden bar. There's also a kids' menu.

Yingthai Restaurant (☎ 044-690 8238; 12 Marsh St; mains R40-60; 🕒 lunch & dinner) The rich scent of fusion Asian cuisine bombards your nostrils when you enter. If it's all too much, sit outside on the front porch and try the pork wheels with honey mustard potatoes (R65), the chef's favourite. Ask about the homemade truffles.

Pavilion (☎ 044-690 4567; Santos Beach; mains R40-60; 🕒 lunch & dinner) In a 19th-century bathing pavilion (hence the name), this is a fine choice for a beachside meal. The menu offers just about everything.

Jazzbury's (☎ 044-691 1923; 11 Marsh St; mains R40-70; 🕒 dinner) Under new management, Jazzbury's has beefed up its traditional African dishes, so now you can try *mopani* worms and Cape Malay food as well as the more common ostrich, beef and seafood creations.

Kingfisher (☎ 044-690 6390; Point Rd; mains R45-100; 🕒 lunch & dinner) Locals love the seafood dishes and ocean views dished up here. You

WESTERN CAPE

can choose between sushi, seafood platters, fish and salads.

Coachhouse (☎ 044-691 1177; cnr Riley & Powrie Sts; mains R60; ✆ lunch & dinner) The Coachhouse gives friendly service, and serves a range of dishes, including interesting salads and pastas. Eat either indoors or in the candlelit courtyard.

Tidals (☎ 044-691 3777; Point Rd) This is a good spot for a sunset drink. It's right on the rocks at The Point, often has live music and draws a young crowd.

Getting There & Away

Mossel Bay is off the highway, so long-distance buses don't come into town; they drop you at the Voorbaai Shell petrol station, 7km away. The hostels can usually collect you if you give notice, but private taxis (R25) are often waiting for bus passengers who need onward travel. If none is there you can book ahead (☎ 082-673 7314) or during the day take a minibus taxi (R4). The Baz Bus will drop you in town.

Translux (☎ 021-449 3333; www.translux.co.za), **Greyhound** (☎ 021-505 6363; www.greyhound.co.za) and **Intercape** (☎ 0861-287 287; www.intercape.co.za) buses stop here on their Cape Town to Port Elizabeth services. Intercape fares from Mossel Bay include Knysna (R110, 1¾ hours, twice daily), Plettenberg Bay (R115, 2½ hours, twice daily), Cape Town (R125, 7¾ hours, twice daily) and Port Elizabeth (R110, 5½ hours, twice daily).

GEORGE

☎ 044 / pop 170,000

George, founded in 1811, is the largest town on the Garden Route yet remains little more than an important commercial centre with little to keep visitors for long. It has some attractive old buildings, including the tiny St Mark's Cathedral and the more imposing Dutch Reformed Mother Church, but it's 8km from the coast and for most people its chief draw is the *Outeniqua Choo-Tjoe* steam train (see below). Golf enthusiasts, however, may be drawn to stay and take on the world-famous Fancourt Links, 10km outside town.

Orientation & Information

The N2 turn-off leads into town from the south on York St, a long four-lane avenue, terminating at a T-junction with Courtenay St – head west for Oudtshoorn, east for Wilderness. The main commercial area is on the eastern side of York St around Hibernia and Market Sts.

George Tourism (☎ 044-801 9295; www.tourism george.co.za; 124 York St; ✆ 8am-5pm Mon-Fri, 9am-1pm Sat) Has a wealth of information and maps for George and the surrounding area.

Sights

The starting point and terminus for journeys on the *Outeniqua Choo-Tjoe* steam train is the **Steam Train Museum** (☎ 044-801 8295; admission by donation; ✆ 7.30am-6pm Mon-Sat), just off Courtenay St. It's worth visiting in its own right, especially if you're interested in trains. Some 11 locomotives and 15 carriages, as well as many detailed models, have found a retirement home here, including a carriage used by the British royal family in the 1940s.

Sleeping & Eating

French Lodge International (☎ 044-874 0345; www .frenchlodge.co.za; 29 York St; s/d incl breakfast R500/800; ✆ ✆) French style meets bush-lodge chic at this friendly hotel – possibly the best deal in town. Rooms are in thatched-roof

---

OUTENIQUA CHOO-TJOE

The **Outeniqua Choo-Tjoe** (☎ in George 044-801 8264, in Knysna 044-382 1361; www.onlinesources.co.za /chootjoe/booking.htm; adult/child to Knysna return R80/60, one way R70/50), in operation since 1928, chugs at a leisurely pace along the coast and through the country from George to Knysna. It's a fantastic ride with some amazing scenery. Two trains run daily, departing from George at 9.30am and 2pm and leaving Knysna at 9.45am and 2.15pm. Reservations are recommended. You can also pick up the service in Wilderness.

The return trip from George is 7½ hours, so if you have to return to collect your car, consider taking the 9.30am train to Sedgefield (arriving 10.53am), then hopping across the platform onto the waiting train from Knysna (departing 10.58am) to return to George at 12.30pm. You'll still see some beautiful scenery on this section.

rondavels with satellite TV and a bathroom with a six-jet Jacuzzi. Décor is African safari motif – giant wooden giraffes stare at you while you sit on hand-carved chairs.

Fancourt Hotel (☎ 044-804 0000; www.fancourt .com; Montagu St, Blanco; d from R2700; 🌐 🏊) This is the area's most luxurious place, about 10km from the town centre, and has four 18-hole golf courses (two designed by Gary Player). In 2003 the Links Golf Course was the site of the President's Cup. The hotel and country club has a range of top-notch accommodation options, a health spa and a few restaurants.

Het Vijfde Seizoen (☎ 044-870 7320; 3 Maitland St, Blanco; mains R50-70; 🕑 breakfast, lunch & dinner) Continental European and traditional South African cuisine combine for buffet breakfasts, lunches on the terrace and atmospheric candlelit dinners at this well-appointed eatery just outside George.

Reel n' Rustic (☎ 044-884 0707; Courtenay St; mains from R55; 🕑 lunch & dinner) Specialising in Creole and Cajun steaks and seafood, this is one of the best restaurants hereabouts, with another popular branch in nearby Wilderness. It gets busy on weekends, so bookings are advised.

Getting There & Away

Kulula (www.kulula.com) and **Nationwide Airlines** (☎ 0861-737 737; www.flynationwide.co.za) fly to **George airport** (☎ 8044-76 9310), which is about 15km west of town.

Bus services stop in George on their route between Cape Town and Port Elizabeth and on their runs between Jo'burg and the Garden Route. **Greyhound** (☎ 021-505 6363; www.greyhound.co.za) services stop in St Mark's Sq behind the Geronimo Spur steakhouse on the main street, while **Translux** (☎ 021-449 3333; www.translux.co.za), and **Intercape** (☎ 0861-287 287; www.intercape.co.za) stop at the train station 2km south of the tourism office. Intercape fares include Knysna (R95, one hour, twice daily), Mossel Bay (R100, 45 minutes, twice daily), Plettenberg Bay (R95, 1½ hours, twice daily), Port Elizabeth (R125, five hours, twice daily), Cape Town (R110, 6½ hours, twice daily), Bloemfontein (R280, 10 hours, daily) and Jo'burg (R370, 16 hours, daily).

The Baz Bus drops off in town and you can call the hostels in Oudtshoorn for shuttle services there.

The weekly *Southern Cross* train between Cape Town and Oudtshoorn stops here.

AROUND GEORGE

There are a number of drives around George that make good day trips.

Montagu & Outeniqua Passes

Leaving George, the Montagu Pass is a quiet dirt road that winds its way through the mountains; it was opened in 1847 and is now a national monument. Take a picnic, because there are some great picnic sites and beautiful *fynbos* to admire along the way, then head back on the Outeniqua Pass, where views are even better, but because it's a main road, it's more difficult to stop when you want to.

Seven Passes Road

This used to be the main road link, and it's easy to imagine how difficult and dangerous it must have been for the pioneers and their ox wagons. The road is still unsurfaced for quite a way and, thanks to the timber trucks, some parts are rough, so the trip will take two hours. It's a pleasant enough route but most of the countryside is now dominated by pine, gum trees and alien vegetation such as the Port Jackson wattle, leaving only small patches of *fynbos* – if you want spectacular views, stick to the N2.

Outeniqua Country Hop

The name refers as much to the peripatetic nature of this organised tour as it does to a visit to a farm where the hop is farmed – George is beer country. The route heads up Montagu Pass and past a collection of tourist experiences in the heart of the Outeniqua Mountains, stopping at a series of agricultural and art destinations including strawberry picking and cheese tasting. Contact George Tourism (opposite) for booking information.

Herold's Bay

☎ 044

On a beautiful stretch of beach that provides consistent swells for surfers (see p215) is the sleepy village of Herold's Bay. It's generally quiet, although it can become very crowded on summer weekends. The town is 16km southwest of George. If you fancy staying the night try **Dutton's Cove**

WESTERN CAPE

(☎ 044-851 0155; www.duttonscove.co.za; 21 Rooidraai Ave; s/d incl breakfast R495/790; 🏊)), which provides lovely upmarket accommodation and a restaurant (mains from R50) with a large wine list, or **Dolphin View** (☎ 044-851 0110; www.garden route.co.za/dolphin; 51 Rooidraai Ave; 2-bedroom cottages from R460), stylishly appointed self-catering apartments on a quiet, scenic patch 1km from the beach.

Victoria Bay
☎ 044

Victoria Bay is tiny and picturesque, and sits at the foot of steep cliffs, around 8km south of George. It's also a popular surf spot (see p215). If you're set on staying the night, try either the **caravan park** (☎ /fax 044-889 0081; camp sites R70) or the self-catering **Sea Breeze Holiday Cottages** (☎ 044-889 0098; seabreeze@pixie .co.za; cottages from R150).

WILDERNESS
☎ 044

The name says it all: dense old-growth forests and steep hills run down to a beautiful stretch of coastline of rolling breakers, miles of white sand, bird-rich estuaries and sheltered lagoons. All this has made Wilderness very popular but thankfully it doesn't show – the town does not come across as overproduced. The myriad of holiday homes blend into the verdant green hills, and the town centre is compact and unobtrusive. The only drawback is everything is quite widely scattered, making life very difficult if you don't have a vehicle.

Information
Internet café (☎ 044-877 0951; 5 Wilderness Centre; per hr R60; ⏰ 8am-5pm)
Wilderness Tourism Bureau (☎ 044-877 0045; Milkwood Village, George Rd; ⏰ 8am-6pm Mon-Fri, 8am-1pm Sat, 3-5pm Sun) This office is just off the N2 as you pull into the village. It makes accommodation bookings and takes reservations for the *Outeniqua Choo-Tjoe* steam train (see p216).

Activities
Wilderness is jam-packed with activities. You can try **Eden Adventures** (☎ 044-877 0179; www.eden.co.za; Wilderness National Park) if you're looking to rent a canoe (R110 per day) or try your hand at abseiling (R235), kloofing (ravine climbing) and canyoning (R235). The company also organises tours of the area.

If you're a beach bum, the beach here is beautiful, but be warned: a strong riptide means swimming is not advised.

Sleeping & Eating
Fairy Knowe Backpackers (☎ 044-877 1285; www.red card.co.uk/fairyknowe; Dumbleton Rd; camp sites per person R60, dm R80, d with shared bathroom R240; 💻) Set in spacious, leafy grounds overlooking the Touws River, this 1874 farmhouse was the first in the area; it has yellowwood floors and some original fittings. The bar and café are in another pretty little building some distance away, so boozers won't keep you awake. It's a great place to relax, but numbers are limited so book ahead. The Baz Bus comes to the door and the steam train stops just along the lane. If you're driving, head into Wilderness town and follow the main road for 2km to the Fairy Knowe turn-off.

Village B&B (☎ 044-877 1187; George Rd; s/d incl breakfast R175/300) Without a doubt the best value B&B in town. Host Hester Stassen goes out of her way to ensure guests are looked after. All rooms are three minutes from the beach, and have décor best described as 'African cute'.

Interlaken (☎ 044-877 1374; www.interlaken.co.za; 713 North St; d with/without breakfast R520/440; 🅿) Rave reviews from readers, and we can't argue: this is a well-run guesthouse offering a choice between B&B doubles or self-catering units, all with magnificent lagoon views. Delicious dinners are served.

Palms Wilderness Guest House (☎ 044-877 1420; www.palms-wilderness.com; George Rd; s/d incl breakfast R900/980; 🏊) This is a very good bet, and blends into the surrounding landscape perfectly. Rooms are luxurious, it's a two-minute walk from the beach and there is a black-marble swimming pool. Its restaurant (mains R80) has a fusion menu and comes highly recommended.

Wilderness Grille (☎ 044-877 0808; George Rd; mains R25-65; ⏰ lunch & dinner) Sit outside among the trees and murals in the garden area. There is an interesting selection of steaks, from blackened sirloin to Cajun, as well as decent pizzas.

Pomodoro (☎ 044-877 0808; George Rd; mains R30-70; ⏰ breakfast, lunch & dinner) There's nothing particularly authentic about the Italian food here, but it's tasty and filling and the staff are eager to please. The breakfast paninis are a good start to any day.

WILDERNESS NATIONAL PARK

This **national park** (☎ 044-877 1197; adult/child R60/30; ☺ 8am-5pm Jan-Nov, 8am-7pm Dec) encompasses the area from Wilderness and the Touws River in the west to Sedgefield and the Goukamma Nature Reserve in the east. The southern boundary is the ocean and the northern boundary is the Outeniqua Range. It covers a unique system of lakes, rivers, wetlands and estuaries that are vital for the survival of many species.

There are three types of lake in the park: drowned river valleys (eg Swartvlei); drowned low-lying areas among the dune system (eg Langvlei); and drowned basins that have been formed by wind action (eg Rondevlei). The rich birdlife includes the beautiful Knysna lourie and many species of kingfisher.

There are several nature trails taking in the lakes, the beach and the indigenous forest. The **Kingfisher Trail** is a day walk that traverses the region and includes a boardwalk across the intertidal zone of the Touws River. The lakes offer anglers, canoeists, windsurfers and sailors an ideal venue. Pedal boats and canoes can be hired at Ebb & Flow South camp, where there is also a small shop.

There are two similar **camps** (camp sites R150, d rondavels with shared bathroom R205, d forest cabins R350) in the park, Ebb & Flow North and Ebb & Flow South. The park is signposted from the N2. It's possible to walk there from Wilderness.

BUFFALO BAY

☎ 044

Buffalo Bay, 17km west of Knysna, is distinctly un–Garden Route: a long, almost deserted surf beach, only a tiny enclave of holiday homes, a beach-shack backpackers and a nature reserve. That's about it, and it's more than enough.

Wild Side Backpackers (☎ 044-383 0609; dm R70, d with shared bathroom R180) is one of the best hostels in the country. You won't find a lot of luxury here – it's right on the beach and there's a constant battle to keep the sand out – but there's tons of atmosphere and attitude. Partake in one of their legendary parties or just chill out in the lounge overlooking the ocean. Surf lessons and sunset beach horse rides can be arranged. Meals are available for between R30 and R50.

You can also explore the **Goukamma Nature Reserve** (☎ 044-383 0042; admission R15; ☺ 9am-5pm), which is accessible from the Buffalo Bay road, and protects 14km of rocky coastline, sandstone cliffs, dunes covered with coastal *fynbos* and forest, and Groenvlei, a large freshwater lake. Accommodation options are camp sites (R55) or four-person rondavels (R270).

KNYSNA

☎ 044 / pop 54,000

Perched on the edge of a serene lagoon and surrounded by forests, Knysna (pronounced ny-znah) began as a timber port and shipbuilding centre, thanks to the lagoon and the rich indigenous forests of the area. Continuing the legacy of the timber industry are a number of excellent woodwork and furniture shops and a thriving artistic community.

With its sylvan setting, gay-friendly vibe, good places to stay, eat and drink, and wide range of activities, Knysna has plenty going for it. But if you're after something quiet and undeveloped, you might like to look elsewhere, particularly in season, when the numbers of visitors threaten to overwhelm it and getting around can be hell.

There's an **arts festival** in late September and early October and an **oyster festival** in July, while in May the town confirms its gay-friendly credentials with the **Pink Loerie Festival** (www.pinkloerie.com).

Orientation & Information

Almost everything of importance is on Main St, which is effectively the N2, or at the bustling Waterfront area.

Adventure Café (Map p220; ☎ 044-382 4959; 1 Gray St; per hr R40; ☺ 9am-7pm) High-speed Internet access.

Knysna Tourism (Map p220; ☎ 044-382 5510; www .tourismknysna.co.za; 40 Main St; ☺ 8am-5pm Mon-Fri, 8.30am-1pm Sat year-round, plus 8.30am-1pm Sun Dec-Jan & Jul) This is an excellent information office, with very knowledgeable staff. You can't miss the place – there's an enormous elephant skeleton in the storefront.

Sights & Activities
KNYSNA LAGOON

Although regulated by **SAN Parks** (Map p224; ☎ 044-382 2095; www.sanparks.org; Long St, Thesen's Island), Knysna Lagoon, covering 13 sq km, is not a national park or wilderness area. Much

WESTERN CAPE

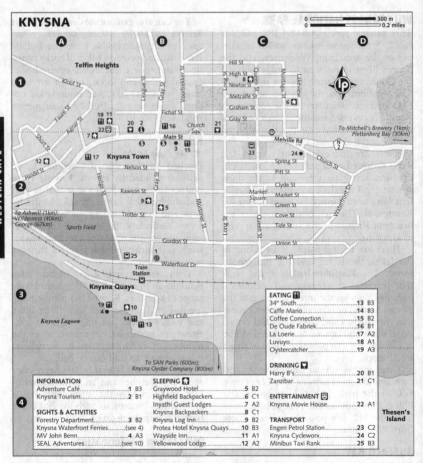

KNYSNA

0 .... 300 m
0 .... 0.2 miles

INFORMATION
Adventure Café.....................**1** B3
Knysna Tourism.....................**2** B1

SIGHTS & ACTIVITIES
Forestry Department...............**3** B2
Knysna Waterfront Ferries........(see 4)
MV John Benn......................**4** A3
SEAL Adventures..................(see 10)

SLEEPING 🏠
Graywood Hotel....................**5** B2
Highfield Backpackers.............**6** C1
Inyathi Guest Lodges..............**7** A2
Knysna Backpackers................**8** C1
Knysna Log Inn....................**9** B2
Protea Hotel Knysna Quays.......**10** B3
Wayside Inn.......................**11** A1
Yellowwood Lodge.................**12** A2

EATING 🍴
34° South..........................**13** B3
Caffe Mario.......................**14** B3
Coffee Connection.................**15** B2
De Oude Fabriek...................**16** B1
La Loerie.........................**17** A2
Luvuyo............................**18** A1
Oystercatcher.....................**19** A3

DRINKING 🍷
Harry B's.........................**20** B1
Zanzibar..........................**21** C1

ENTERTAINMENT 🎭
Knysna Movie House...............**22** A1

TRANSPORT
Engen Petrol Station..............**23** C2
Knysna Cycleworx.................**24** C2
Minibus Taxi Rank.................**25** B3

Thesen's
Island

is still privately owned, and the lagoon is used by industry and for recreation. The protected area starts just to the east of Buffalo Bay and follows the coastline to the mouth of the Noetzie River. The lagoon opens up between two sandstone cliffs, known as the Heads – once proclaimed by the British Royal Navy the most dangerous harbour entrance in the world. There are good views from a lookout on the eastern head, and a private nature trail on the western head.

The best way to appreciate the lagoon is to take a cruise. The **MV John Benn** (Map p220; ☎ 044-382 1697; www.featherbed.co.za; Waterfront; adult/ child R80/35, with lunch R250/110; ☒ departs 10am, 11.30am & 12.30pm) riverboat offers the recommended Featherbed cruise, a four-hour affair that includes lunch and takes you to the privately owned **Featherbed Nature Reserve** (Map p224), where you'll be driven around. The company also runs cheaper, shorter cruises.

Those searching for romance can take a 2½-hour sunset cruise that includes champagne and oysters. Contact **Knysna Waterfront Ferries** (Map p220; ☎ 044-382 5520; www.knysnaferries .co.za; Waterfront; tickets R250; ☒ departs 5pm).

MITCHELL'S BREWERY
Drop by **Mitchell's Brewery** (Map p224; ☎ 044-382 4685; Arend St; tastings R20, tours R30; ☒ tours 10.30am Mon-Fri) to the east of town. The beers, which include a draught lager, a bitter, a stout and an ale, can be found all over Western Cape.

TOWNSHIP TOURS & HOMESTAYS

Follow Gray St uphill and eventually you'll leave town and emerge on the wooded slopes of the hills behind. On top is the sprawling township of Concordia, best visited on an excellent tour (R200) run by **Eco Afrika Tours** (☎ 082-925 0716) or **The Heads Adventure Centre** (Map p224; ☎ 044-384 0831; the Heads) for R250. Knysna's townships have a different look from others in South Africa: homes are built mostly with timber from the nearby forests. The two-hour tours are led by local guides and take you through the usual township sites – schools, a visit to a tribal witch doctor and a *shebeen* (unlicensed bar) – but then add a twist. You'll also get to visit the Grass Routes neighbourhood, the largest community of Rastafarians in the country.

If you want to stay overnight in either the Rastafarian community or in the township, contact Glendyrr at Knysna Tourism. It just might be the highlight of your Garden Route experience.

KNYSNA FOREST TRAILS

There are excellent hikes in the Knysna forests, and you can book walking trails and collect maps and information at the regional office of **SAN Parks** (Map p224; ☎ 044-382 2095; www.sanparks.org; Long St, Thesen's Island). Overnight hikes cost R45 per day including the use of trail huts.

The **Knysna Forestry Department** (Map p220; ☎ 044-302 5606; Main St; 8am-1pm & 1.45pm-4pm Mon-Fri), above Wimpy restaurant, administers the **Harkerville Coastal Trail** (☎ 044-302 5606; per day R80), which is a two-day hike that leads on to the popular Outeniqua Trail. To reach the coastal trail, exit the N2 at Harkerville.

The **Outeniqua Trail** takes a week to walk, although you can also do two- or three-day sections. The trail costs R45 per night to stay in a basic hut. You will need your own bedding.

Outeniqua Biking Trails (Map pp212-13; ☎ 044-532 7644) rents bikes (R95 per day) and will give you a map to the surrounding trails. It also can arrange guided trips – to find it exit the N2 at Harkerville.

Other trails through the forests include the four **Elephant Trails**. These day walks cost R20. There are three elephants in the forest, but spotting one is so rare it's become mythical.

OTHER ACTIVITIES

There are plenty of other activities on offer in the area; start by making inquiries at **The Heads Adventure Centre** (Map p224; ☎ 044-384 0831; the Heads). Among the possibilities are boat and short-entry scuba dives (R80 to R120) to some of South Africa's best spots. Snorkelling equipment can be rented for R90. Ask the guides to point out the good snorkelling trails. They may even go with you.

Quad-biking trips in the Featherbed Nature Reserve are available with **SEAL Adventures** (Map p220; ☎ 044-382 5599; Shop 1, Protea Hotel Knysna Quays; 2½hr trip R280; ✆ departs 11am & 3.30pm). The company also runs an Awesome Foursome adventure trip – quad biking, abseiling, canoeing and cliff-jumping for R400.

There are also bike trails around the area; for more information on biking, and for bike rentals and maps, head to Knysna Cycleworx (p223).

Sleeping

Low-season competition between the several backpackers and many guesthouses in town keeps prices down, but in high season expect steep rate hikes (except at the backpackers) and book ahead.

BUDGET

Knysna Backpackers (Map p220; ☎ 044-382 2554; knybpack@netactive.co.za; 42 Queen St; dm R70, d with shared bathroom from R180) You'll find mainly dorm beds at this large and spruce Victorian house on the hill a few blocks up from the main street. It tends to be quieter and more relaxing than other places.

Highfield Backpackers (Map p220; ☎ 044-382 6266; www.highfieldsbackpackers.co.za; 2 Graham St; dm R70, d with/without shared bathroom from R300/200) In a spacious old house, Highfield feels like a B&B. Its focus is on doubles decorated with hardwood floors, brass beds and nice linens. *Potjiekos* (pot stew) dinners are often served.

Woodbourne Resort (Map p224; ☎ 044-384 0316; w48@mweb.co.za; George Rex Dr; camp sites R120, chalets from R330) Here you'll find spacious, shaded camping and simple chalets with TVs. It's a quiet place a little way out of town. Rates go up 10% during high season and holidays. Follow the signs to the Heads.

Ashwill (Map p224; ☎ 044-382 5920; knyacc@polka .co.za; 146 Old Cape Rd; d with/without shared bathroom from

R250/200) This extremely comfortable, serene backpackers is a bit out of town (20-minute walk) but is neatly tucked in next to a couple of restaurants and an almost private stretch of lagoon. There are no dorms.

MIDRANGE

Wayside Inn (Map p220; ☎ 044-382 6011; www.way sideinn.co.za; Pledge Sq; s/d R265/420) Intimate and well managed, the Wayside Inn has nicely decorated rooms and is in a handy location just off Main St by the cinema.

Yellowwood Lodge (Map p220; ☎ 044-382 5906; www.yellowwoodlodge.co.za; 18 Handel St; s/d from R400/800; ⚡ ♨) A traditional and sumptuously decorated guesthouse, Yellowwood boasts a lovely garden setting and views of the lagoon. See if you can grab the one room with air-con.

Inyathi Guest Lodges (Map p220; ☎ 044-382 7768; www.inyathi-sa.com; 52 Main St; s/d from R435/570) This is the most imaginatively designed guesthouse in Knysna, with a real African flair that avoids the kitsch. Accommodation is in uniquely decorated timber lodges – some with Victorian bathtubs, others with stained-glass windows. Excellent value for money and worth a stay.

Graywood Hotel (Map p220; ☎ 044-382 5850; reservations@thegraywood.co.za; cnr Gray & Trotter Sts; s/d R475/630; ⚡ ♨ ♿) The recently rebranded Graywood can't escape its past, the former Caboose Hotel has rooms about the same size as sleeping compartments. Still, the upgrading is impressive and the furnishings top-notch. Watch out for high-season price hikes.

TOP END

Knysna Log Inn (Map p220; ☎ 044-382 5835; www.kli .co.za; 16 Gray St; s/d R855/1040; ⚡ ♨) The Knysna Log Inn is said to be the largest log structure in the southern hemisphere. The rooms are comfortable enough, and there's a pool, but the whole place resembles a Disneyland exhibit a little too much.

Protea Hotel Knysna Quays (Map p220; ☎ 044-382 5005; www.proteahotels.com; Waterfront Dr; s/d R1276/1600; ⚡ ♨) Rooms are tastefully decorated at this stylish, posh hotel, which is a better option than the other Protea on Main St. It has a very inviting pool and is just moments away from shopping and eating options at the Waterfront. Lagoon-facing rooms cost more.

Under Milk Wood (Map p224; ☎ 044-384 0745; www.proteahotels.com; Waterfront Dr; cottages from R1820; ⚡) Named for a nature-loving quote from the Dylan Thomas play of the same name, this is a series of highly impressive self-catering log cabins on the shores of Knysna Lagoon. There are B&B tariffs if you don't feel like cooking, and prices vary according to cabin location.

Phantom Forest Eco-Reserve (☎ 044-386 0046; www.phantomforest.com; s/d R2000/2400; ⚡ ♨) This 137-hectare private ecoreserve, 6km west of Knysna along the Phantom Pass road, overlooks the lagoon and comprises 14 cleverly designed and elegantly decorated tree houses. Various activities, including conducted nature walks, are available. If nothing else, visit for the award-winning six-course Pan-African dinner (R225) served from 6.30pm to 8.30pm daily; booking is essential.

Eating

Oystercatcher (Map p220; ☎ 044-382 9995; Knysna Quays; tapas R35; ⏱ lunch & dinner) The Oystercatcher is a relaxed place serving four sizes of farmed oyster, and other seafood tapas dishes in a great waterside setting.

Knysna Oyster Company (Map p224; ☎ 044-382 6941; www.mbendi.co.za/koyster; Thesen's Island; mains from R40; ⏱ lunch & dinner) This company, opened in 1949, grows its own oysters out in the lagoon; you can take a tour of the processing plant and have a tasting of a cultivated and wild oyster for R20 at its restaurant afterwards. It's touristy, but for good reason.

Paquita's (Map p224; ☎ 044-384 0408; the Heads; mains from R40; ⏱ lunch & dinner) Seafood, steaks, pizza and pasta are available at this ideally located restaurant and bar next to the Heads right on the water. If you're lucky you may spot whales frolicking only metres away. There's also a Sunday carvery.

East Head Caffé (Map p224; ☎ 044-384 0933; the Heads; mains R40-50; ⏱ breakfast & lunch) Our favourite breakfast spot. There's an outdoor deck overlooking the lagoon and ocean, and the smoked salmon, eggs and cream cheese breakfast (R38) is scrumptious.

34° South (Map p220; ☎ 044-382 7268; Waterfront; mains R40-90; ⏱ lunch & dinner) Wildly varying reports on this place made us give it a good going over, and all seemed in order. What can't be denied are its outdoor tables overlooking the water, lavish salads, deli produce and seafood pâtés. And the wine selection is the best in town.

De Oude Fabriek (Map p220; ☎ 044-382 5723; cnr Main & Gray Sts; mains R45-80; ⌣ lunch & dinner) Despite its shopping-centre setting, this restaurant is a convivial spot to sample some interesting South African dishes – game meat, crocodile and Knysna oysters are all on the menu.

Luvuyo (Map p220; ☎ 044-382 1662; Cinema Complex, 50 Main St; mains R60; ⌣ dinner Mon-Sat) A gay haunt popular with heteros thanks to its efficient service, good food and regular cabaret acts. It also has the largest vegetarian selection in Knysna.

La Loerie (Map p220; ☎ 044-382 1616; 57 Main St; mains R60-80; ⌣ dinner) Booking is essential at this deservedly popular but small place with copper pots hanging from the ceiling, linen napkins and a French flavour to its menu.

There are plenty of good snack and coffee places along Main St, including the excellent **Coffee Connection** (Map p220; ☎ 044-382 2845; ⌣ breakfast & lunch), serving 36 types of coffee. In the Knysna Quays centre, the best coffee and snack option is **Caffé Mario** (Map p220; ☎ 044-382 7250; ⌣ breakfast, lunch & dinner).

Drinking

Head along Main St and check out the local bars, many of which are seasonal.

Zanzibar (Map p220; ☎ 382 0386; Main St) This place offers a relaxed vibe, a balcony area for lounging and a theatre where shows are held occasionally.

Harry B's (Map p220; ☎ 382 5065; 42 Main St; mains R70-90) Knysna's first residence (1863) now houses a popular restaurant and bar.

Entertainment

Knysna Movie House (Map p220; ☎ 382 7813; 50 Main St; movies R20) If you fancy catching a flick, try this theatre on Main St.

Getting There & Away
BUS

The major bus companies, **Translux** (☎ 021-449 3333; www.translux.co.za), **Greyhound** (☎ 021-505 6363; www.greyhound.co.za) and **Intercape** (☎ 0861 287 287; www.intercape.co.za), all stop at the **Engen petrol station** (Map p220; Main St); Baz Bus will take you where you want. For travel between nearby towns on the Garden Route, you're better off looking for a minibus taxi

than travelling with the major bus lines, which are very expensive on short sectors.

Intercape destinations include George (R95, one hour, twice daily), Mossel Bay (R110, 1¾ hours, twice daily), Port Elizabeth (R80, 3¾ hours, twice daily), Cape Town (R150, eight hours, twice daily) and Jo'burg (R385, 17 hours, daily).

MINIBUS TAXI

The main minibus taxi stop (Map p220) is on the corner of Hedge St and Waterfront Dr near Knysna Quays. Routes include Plettenberg Bay (R20, 30 minutes, daily) and Cape Town (R150, 7½ hours, daily). Contact **Georgina Booi** (☎ 044-384 9717), local transport expert and woman-about-town, to find out about route and door-to-door pick-ups.

TRAIN

The historic *Outeniqua Choo-Tjoe* steam train runs between Knysna and George daily except Saturday and public holidays. See p216 for details.

Getting Around

In Knysna there are several car-hire companies dotted along Main Rd. Even if you have a car, the summer traffic jams on the main street (much worse than anything you'll find in Cape Town) will make you look for alternative transport.

Knysna Cycleworx (☎ 044-343 1710; 3A Church St; per day R115) is one of several places selling and renting good bicycles.

AROUND KNYSNA
Prince Alfred's Pass

The Knysna–Avontour road climbs through the Outeniqua Range via the beautiful Prince Alfred's Pass, regarded by some as better than the Swartberg Pass. Be warned that the road is a bit rough and it's slow going.

Outside Knysna, the road passes pine and eucalypt plantations and indigenous forest (the home of Knysna's elephants). There are few really steep sections but the pass reaches a height of over 1000m, and there are great views to the north before the road winds into the Langkloof Valley.

Belvidere & Brenton-on-Sea

Belvidere, 10km from Knysna, is so immaculate it's positively creepy. But it's worth a quick look for the beautiful Norman-style

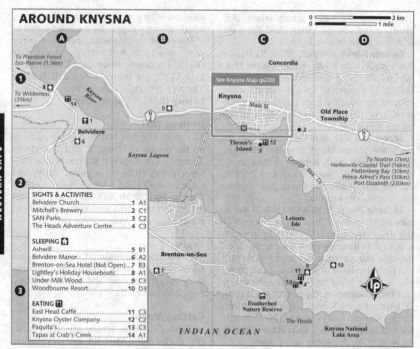

AROUND KNYSNA

0 ———— 2 km
0 ———— 1 mile

SIGHTS & ACTIVITIES
Belvidere Church	1 A1
Mitchell's Brewery	2 C1
SAN Parks	3 C2
The Heads Adventure Centre	4 C3

SLEEPING
Ashwill	5 B1
Belvidere Manor	6 A2
Brenton-on-Sea Hotel (Not Open)	7 B3
Lightley's Holiday Houseboats	8 A1
Under Milk Wood	9 C3
Woodbourne Resort	10 D3

EATING
East Head Caffé	11 C3
Knysna Oyster Company	12 C2
Paquita's	13 C3
Tapas at Crab's Creek	14 A1

church (Map p224) built in the 1850s by home-sick English expats.

Belvidere Manor (Map p224; ☎ 044-387 1055; www.belvidere.co.za; Duthie Dr; d incl breakfast R1240) is an undoubtedly impressive collection of luxury guest cottages, some with lagoon views, in a garden setting. There is also a restaurant (mains R90) serving regional dishes such as locally produced cheese, Karoo lamb and ostrich.

For a very different night's sleep check out **Lightley's Holiday Houseboats** (Map p224; ☎ 044-386 0007; www.houseboats.co.za; off the N2; 4-berth boats from R800), on the western side of the bridge over the Knysna River, which offers fully equipped houseboats. You can navigate up to 20km upriver from the Heads, but you have to pay extra for fuel. Rates vary drastically depending on the boat and the season.

Tapas at Crab's Creek (Map p224; ☎ 044-386-0011; off the N2; mains R40; ☥ lunch & dinner) is a local favourite watering hole, in a chilled-out setting right on the lagoon. There are often afternoon drink specials. Try the very tasty cold seafood meze platter for two (R89).

Another 10km on, the *fynbos*-covered hills drop to Brenton-on-Sea, overlooking a magnificent 8km beach, stretching from the western head of Knysna Lagoon to Buffalo Bay. The famous **Brenton-on-Sea Hotel** (Map p224; ☎ 044-381 0081) had recently burnt down when we were here; its wonderful sea views alone make it worth calling to check out the rebuilding status. Further on is the Featherbed Nature Reserve (p220).

Knysna to Plettenberg Bay

Not to be outdone by Belvidere, another romantic English family built holiday homes in a mock-castle style at **Noetzie**, reached by a turn-off along the N2, 10km east of Knysna. The homes are still privately owned, and are not as bad as you might imagine. Noetzie has a lovely surf beach (spacious but dangerous) and a sheltered lagoon running through a forested gorge. It's a steep trail between the car park and the beach.

Knysna Castles (☎ 044-375 0100; www.knysnacastles.com; d from R1300) is a four-bedroom home. If you're looking for a romantic getaway, renting one of these cosily decorated Noetzie castles right beside the beach might be just the ticket.

It's extremely unlikely that you will see the last remaining wild elephants that live in Knysna's forests, but you are sure to see them at either **Elephant Sanctuary** (☎ 044-534 8145; www.elephantsanctuary.co.za; tours R40; ☺ 8am-6pm), 15km east of Knysna, or **Knysna Elephant Park** (☎ 044-532 7732; www.knysnaelephantpark.co.za; tours R50; ☺ 8.30am-4.30pm), 22km east of Knysna on the N2. Here, small groups of visitors go on walking tours with the elephants. The tours are hardly authentic wildlife encounters, but kids love them.

Next to the Elephant Sanctuary is the equally fake but highly popular **Monkeyland** (☎ 044-534 8906; www.monkeyland.co.za; adult/child R70/35; ☺ 8am-6pm). Home to more than 200 primates from 14 different species, this 12-hectare sanctuary helps rehabilitate wild monkeys that have been in zoos or private homes. As the critters run free here, you'll soon see why they have a reputation for mischief. The walking safari through a dense forest and across a 120m-long rope bridge is a brilliant way to find out more about them.

PLETTENBERG BAY

☎ 044 / pop 34,000

Plettenberg Bay, or 'Plett' as it's more commonly known, is a resort town through and through, with mountains, white sand and crystal-blue water making it one of the country's top local tourist spots. As a result, things can get very busy and somewhat overpriced, but the town retains a relaxed, friendly atmosphere and does have very good-value hostels. The scenery to the east in particular is superb, with some of the best coast and indigenous forest in South Africa.

Orientation & Information

Plettenberg Bay is deceptively large and sprawling. The town centre is on a high promontory overlooking the Keurbooms River lagoon and Beacon Island.

Computer Shop & Internet Café (☎ 044-533-6007; First National Bank Bldg, Main St; per hr R30; ☺ 8.30am-6.30pm Mon-Fri, 9am-6pm Sat, 9am-4pm Sun) Internet access.

Plett Tourism (☎ 044-533 4065; www.plettenberg bay.co.za; Mellville's Corner Shopping Centre, Main St; ☺ 8.30am-5pm Mon-Fri Nov-Mar year-round, plus 9am-1pm Sat April-Oct) This office has a great deal of useful information, ranging from accommodation to a craft trail and walks in the surrounding hills and reserves.

Activities

Apart from lounging on the beaches or hiking on the Robberg Peninsula (p227) there's a lot to do in Plett; check with Albergo for Backpackers as it can organise most things, often at a discount.

Boat trips to view dolphins and whales in season are available with **Ocean Blue Adventures** (☎ 044-533 5083; www.oceanadventures.co.za; Milkwood Centre, Hopewood St) and **Ocean Safaris** (☎ 044-533 4963; Milkwood Centre, Hopewood St). Trips cost about R290 for 2½ hours on 12-person boats.

Equitrailing (☎ 044-533 0599), 11km east of Plett on the N2, offers horse riding through the forest for R110 per hour. **Dolphin Adventures** (☎ 072-751 1798) has sea kayaking (R250, 2½ hours). It doesn't have an office in town, so just phone for a booking.

For skydiving try the recommended **Sky Dive Plettenberg Bay** (☎ 044-533 9048; Plettenberg Airport; tandem jump R1250), which offers outstanding views on the way down. Those wanting to try surfing can take a lesson through the **International Surf School** (☎ 082-636 8431; 3½hr lesson R300), which caters to all levels of surfers. It doesn't have an office, so just phone.

Sleeping

There is a great deal of holiday accommodation in town and nearby – in low season there are bargains to be found. The tourism bureau has a full list and can tell you about the many camping options, all out of town.

BUDGET

Albergo for Backpackers (☎ 044-533 4434; www.alber go.co.za; 8 Church St; camp sites per person R50; dm R75; d with shared bathroom R220; 🖳) Well run and friendly, Albergo encourages activities in town and in the area and can organise just about anything. Try for the upstairs dorm with huge windows and stellar ocean views from the balcony.

Nothando Backpackers Hostel (☎ 044-533 0220; info@nothando.co.za; 5 Wilder St; dm R75, d with/without shared bathroom R230/210) Our choice for best budget option in town, this spotless and spacious, YHA-affiliated, award-winning

WESTERN CAPE

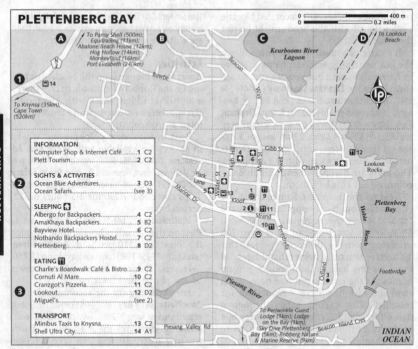

PLETTENBERG BAY

0 _____ 400 m
0 _____ 0.2 miles

To Pansy Shell (500m);
Equitrailing (11km);
Abalone Beach House (12km);
Hog Hollow (14km);
Monkeyland (16km);
Port Elizabeth (240km)

To Knysna (35km);
Cape Town
(520km)

Keurbooms River
Lagoon

To Lookout
Beach

Lookout
Rocks

Plettenberg
Bay

Robbie
Beach

Footbridge

To Periwinkle Guest
Lodge (1km); Lodge
on the Bay (1km);
Sky Dive Plettenberg
Bay (5km); Robberg Nature
& Marine Reserve (9km)

Piesang Valley Rd

Piesang River

INDIAN
OCEAN

hostel is owner-run and it shows. There's a happening bar area with satellite TV, yet you can still find peace and quiet in the large grounds.

AmaKhaya Backpackers (☎ 044-533 4010; amaka yabackpackers.com; 1 Park Lane; dm R80, s/d with shared bathroom R100/200) The new budget kid on the block. A double-storey family home has been converted into a clean, if somewhat characterless, hostel. The dorms are cramped and military-style, but the private rooms are large and airy. There is one en suite double room (R260).

Abalone Beach House (☎ 044-535 9602; beach house@global.co.za; 50 Ifafi Properties, Keurboomstrand; d with shared bathroom R180; 🖳) It's a hop to the beach from this great hostel run by friendly people. And what a beach! Surf and boogie boards can be hired (R10). To reach the beach house follow the Keurboomstrand signs from the N2 (about 6km east of Plett), then turn into El Remo/Ifafi.

MIDRANGE

Bayview Hotel (☎ 044-533 1961; fax 533 2059; cnr Main & Gibb Sts; d 760; 🍴) Right in the town centre,

this is a small, serviceable and modern three-star hotel with a range of rather plain rooms but a pleasant balcony.

Periwinkle Guest Lodge (☎ 044-533 1345; www .periwinkle.co.za; 75 Beachy Head Dr; d incl breakfast from R1150) This bright, colourful beachfront guesthouse offers individually decorated rooms, all with great views – you might even be able to spot whales and dolphins.

TOP END

Plett has some shamefully luxurious options. Get out the wallet and take your pick.

Hog Hollow (☎ 044-534 8879; www.hog-hollow .com; s/d incl breakfast R1320/1850) Hog Hollow, 18km east of Plett along the N2, provides delightful accommodation in African art–decorated units, which are around an old farmhouse overlooking the forest. Each unit comes with a private wooden deck and hammock. It's possible to walk to Monkeyland (p225) from here. A four-course dinner costs R175.

Plettenberg (☎ 044-533 2030; www.plettenberg .com; 40 Church St; s/d from R1600/2650; 🍴 🖳 🐾) The (heated) pool here alone is worth the stay – it's one that gives the illusion of ending in the sea. Built on a rocky headland with breathtaking vistas, this five-star palace is pure decadence, with fantastic rooms, a spa and a top-class restaurant. Romantics can dine in the Wine Cellar surrounded by vintage bottles.

Lodge on the Bay (☎ 044-533 4724; www.thelodge .co.za; 77 Beachy Head Dr; d from R3165; 🖭 🖳) The highly sophisticated and ultramodern Lodge has just six rooms and very personal service. There's a Japanese day spa on the premises. The place is worth splashing out on.

Eating

There are very good restaurants in most of the top-end hotels. Otherwise you can choose from quite a few places in town.

Charlie's Boardwalk Café & Bistro (☎ 044-533 1420; 6 Yellowoods Bldg, Main St; mains R15-50; 🕑 breakfast, lunch & dinner) A hang-out for local surfies as well as visitors, this pleasant café offers plenty of snacks and meals at reasonable prices.

Miguel's (☎ 044-533 5056; Mellville Corner Shopping Centre, Main St; breakfast/dinner R30/80; 🕑 breakfast, lunch & dinner) A modern place with an eclectic menu, it's bright and airy with floor-to-ceiling windows and patio seating. It's a good option any time of day.

Lookout (☎ 044-533 1379; Lookout Rocks; mains R40; 🕑 breakfast, lunch & dinner) With a deck overlooking the beach, this is a great place for a simple meal and perhaps views of dolphins surfing the waves.

Cranzgot's Pizzeria (☎ 044-533 1660; 9 Main St; mains R40-60; 🕑 breakfast, lunch & dinner) This perennial Plett favourite, established in 1973, serves mouthwatering pizzas, pastas and char-grilled steaks. You might have to wait for a table in the evenings, but there is also a bar. You can take the kids here.

Cornuti Al Mare (☎ 044-533 1277; 1 Perestrella St; mains R50-70; 🕑 lunch & dinner) A stylishly decked out Italian oyster bar with hearty pizzas and refreshing cocktails served on a sun terrace. Try the homemade spinach and cream cheese ravioli (R45).

Pansy Shell (☎ 044-533 6016; Old Nick Shopping Centre; mains R60; 🕑 dinner) This formal restaurant gets rave reviews for its steaks, seafood and overall ambience.

Getting There & Away

All the major buses stop at the Shell Ultra City on the N2; the Baz Bus will come into town. **Intercape** (☎ 0861-287 287; www.[...] .za) destinations from Plett include [...] (R95, 1½ hours, three times daily), [...] Elizabeth (R80, three hours, twice dai[...] Cape Town (R160, eight hours, twice daily[...] Jo'burg (R385, 18 hours, daily), Graaff-Reinet (R195, 5½ hours, daily) and Bloemfontein (R300, 12 hours, daily).

If you're heading to Knysna (R20, 30 minutes) you're better off taking a minibus taxi – services leave from the corner of Kloof and High Sts. Most other long-distance taxis stop at the Shell Ultra City on the highway.

ROBBERG NATURE & MARINE RESERVE

This **reserve** (☎ 044-533 2125; admission R20; 🕑 7am-5pm Feb-Nov, 7am-8pm Dec-Jan), 9km southeast of Plettenberg Bay, protects a 4km-long peninsula with a rugged coastline of cliffs and rocks. There's a great circular walk approximately 11km long, with rich intertidal marine life and coastal-dune *fynbos*, but it's very rocky and not for the aged or anyone with knee problems! The peninsula acts as a sort of marine speed bump to larger sea life, with mammals and fish spending time here before moving on. To get to the reserve head along Robberg Rd, off Piesang Valley Rd, until you see the signs.

CENTRAL KAROO

The Karoo is pure magic. It's a vast semi-arid plateau (its name is a Khoesaan word meaning 'land of thirst') that promises stunning sunsets and starscapes and delivers. Here you'll feel simultaneously dry at the mouth (for the mercury can hit 45°C in summer), slack at the jaw (the landscape is spare, violent and beautiful) and *tiny* – the horizons have been known to send agoraphobics scrambling for the nearest conurbation.

Perhaps the best thing about the Karoo, though, is the way life moves slowly, and how off the main highways you can drive for hours without seeing another car. If you've had your fill of the Garden Route, head over the Swartberg Pass and unwind here.

The Karoo covers almost one-third of South Africa's total area and is demarcated in the south and west by the coastal mountain ranges, and to the east and north by

WESTERN CAPE

...Thomas Bain, between 1881 and 1888, the Swartberg Pass is arguably ...the country. It's 24km long and reaches nearly 1600m in height.

...as and other *fynbos* are prolific. After the summit (Die Top) – where there are ...ws over the bleak Karoo and, on the other side, the greenery of the Little Karoo – ...meanders down into a fantastic geology of twisted sedimentary layers. The best picnic ...es are on the northern side; the gorge narrows and in spring is full of pelargoniums. There are some quiet spots where you can sunbathe or swim.

Don't be put off by the warning signs at each end of the pass. It's a fairly easy drive as long as you take it very slowly. The road is narrow, there are very long drops and many of the corners are blind.

The hostels in Oudtshoorn will drive you and a bicycle to the top and you can ride back down. This is a huge buzz (although take along plenty of water), but the real beauty of the pass is deeper in, towards Prince Albert.

the mighty Senqu (Orange) River. It's often split into the Great Karoo (north) and the Little Karoo (south), but it doesn't respect provincial boundaries and sprawls into three provinces, so for our purposes it's the Central Karoo here, Eastern Karoo in the Eastern Cape chapter and Upper Karoo in the Northern Cape.

PRINCE ALBERT & AROUND
☎ 023 / pop 2500

To many urban South Africans, Prince Albert – a charming village dating back to 1762 and dozing at the foot of the Swartberg Pass – represents an idyllic life in the Karoo. If you have your own transport, you can easily visit on a day trip from Oudtshoorn or even from the coast. Alternatively, stay in Prince Albert and make a day trip to Oudtshoorn via the spectacular Swartberg Pass and Meiringspoort, or – if the weather isn't too hot – consider going on a hike.

Despite being surrounded by very harsh country, the town is green and fertile (producing peaches, apricots, grapes and olives), thanks to the run-off from the mountain springs. A system of original water channels runs through town and most houses have a sluice gate, which they are entitled to open for a set period each week.

Contact the helpful **tourist information office** (☎ 023-541 1366; www.patourism.co.za; Church St; ⏰ 9am-5pm Mon-Fri, 9am-noon Sat) for more information.

Sights & Activities
Prince Albert's best attractions are actually outside town. It's a good base for explor-

ing the Karoo and hiking on the more than 100km of trails in the Swartberg Nature Reserve. Overnight walks have to be booked through **Cape Nature** (☎ 044-279 1739; Queen's Mall, Baron van Rheede St, Oudtshoorn). For guides, contact the Prince Albert of Saxe-Coburg Lodge.

There's a good drive east to **Klaarstroom**, a tiny *dorp* (small town) along the foot of the mountains. The road runs along a valley, beneath the Groot Swartberg Range, which is cut by dramatic gullies, clefts and waterfalls. On Rte 407 between Prince Albert (40km) and Klaarstroom (10km), **Remhoogte Hiking Trail** can be walked in about five hours but there is a camping place on the trail.

Meiringspoort, south of Klaarstroom, on the N12 route between Beaufort West and Oudtshoorn, is an extraordinary place, following a river that cuts right through the Swartberg Range. It's not quite in the same class as Swartberg Pass, partly because it's a main road and partly because it's not as deep or as narrow.

On the road up to Prince Albert Road station and at the station itself, keep an eye out for the work of local celebrity **Outa Lappies**, a septuagenarian artist and philosopher who makes 'something out of nothing'. His old homestead is on Rte 407, while his new cottage is opposite the station – it's the one with the tin toy windmills on the fence and a front yard full of junk creations.

Sleeping & Eating
Prince Albert of Saxe-Coburg Lodge (☎ 023-541 1267; www.saxecoburg.co.za; 60 Church St; s/d from R180/360; ✖ ⛱) This place offers quality accommodation, and its owners are a great

source of information and offer guided hikes in the area, including a three-day trip to Die Hel that's free as long as you stay at the lodge. Rooms come with satellite TVs and mosquito nets, and are lovely.

Karoo Lodge (☎ 023-541 1647; www.karoolodge .com; 66 Church St; s/d from R225/450; 🚫 🏊) This lodge is an owner-run guesthouse with a large garden and beautiful antique furniture. Hosts George and Elsabe are terrific, and very knowledgeable about the area.

Swartberg Hotel (☎ 023-541 1332; www.swartberg .co.za; 70 Church St; s/d incl breakfast R380/553; 🖥 🏊) Swartberg is three-star country inn; you can choose from thatched-roof huts or rooms in the main hotel. There are amazing gardens to relax in and the hotel organises area activities. The attached coffee shop (mains R18 to R35) looks out on the main road and is a popular spot for lunch or a home-made dessert. Also attached is the Swartberg Arms (mains R30), popular with locals for an evening pint. It has a large menu of pizzas and burgers as well as a kiddie menu.

Sampie se Plaasstal (Church St; 🕙 9am-5pm) This is a simple but good farm-produce stall selling a range of snacks and refreshing home-made ginger beer.

Karoo Kombuis (☎ 023-541 1110; Karoo Kitchen; 18 Deurdrift St; mains R60; 🕙 dinner Mon-Sat) As good a reason to come to Prince Albert as any, this excellent restaurant serves traditional home-cooked dishes with panache. It offers either a three-course dinner (R95) or an à la carte menu. Bring your own drinks.

Getting There & Away

Most people visit by driving over one of the area's passes from Oudtshoorn, or from the N1 between Cape Town and Jo'burg. However, if you've come for hiking there's no reason not to take a train, which is cheaper than the buses. There is no direct bus or train service to Prince Albert; the closest drop-off point is at the train station on Prince Albert Rd, 45km northwest of Prince Albert, which also serves as the long-distance bus stop. Private taxis cost R50, but most places to stay will pick you up from the train station.

DIE HEL

In a narrow valley in the Swartberg Range is Die Hel, or Gamkaskloof. The first citizens of Die Hel were early Trekboers, who developed their own dialect. There was no road into Die Hel until the 1960s, and donkeys carried in the few goods the self-sufficient community needed from Prince Albert. Maybe it's a coincidence, but within 30 years of the roads being built all the farmers had left.

Now the area is part of a nature reserve where there is self-catering **accommodation** (☎ 023-541 1107; www.diehel.com; Gamkaskloof; caravan sites R60, camp sites R70, farmhouse R120). You might want to avoid the campsite; it's beautiful but has suffered from human intervention. When we visited it was crawling with tiny cockroaches (hell indeed!). The owners are aware of this, so it may be a temporary problem.

The dirt road to Die Hel turns off the Swartberg Pass road about 20km from Prince Albert and extends for another 60km or so before hitting a dead end.

MATJIESFONTEIN
☎ 023

One of the most curious and fascinating places in the Karoo, Matjiesfontein (pronounced mikeys-fontein) is an almost entirely privately-owned railway siding around a grand hotel that has remained virtually unchanged for 100 years. In its heyday it entertained the likes of Cecil John Rhodes, Lord Randolph Churchill and the Sultan of Zanzibar no less!

The developer of the hotel and surrounding hamlet was one Jimmy Logan, a Scot whose rise through Cape society was so swift that by the age of 36 he not only was a member of parliament, but also ran every railway refreshment room between the Cape and Bulawayo (Zimbabwe). Matjiesfontein was his home base, and the hotel and other accommodation, together with the climate (the crisp air is likened to dry champagne), attracted wealthy people as a health resort.

As well as the attractive old buildings, including a church, courthouse and post office/general store, there's a fascinating **museum** (admission R3; 🕙 8am-5pm Tue, Thu, Sat & Sun, 8.30am-5.30pm Mon, Wed & Fri) in the train station that's a right old jumble sale, containing everything from trophy heads to a collection of commodes.

If you decide to stay, check out the **Lord Milner Hotel** (☎ 023-551 3011; www.matjiesfontein .com; s/d from R310/480; 🏊), a classic period

WESTERN CAPE

piece with bags of old-world charm. There is a range of comfortable rooms and an atmospheric reception area. Surprisingly, meals in the hotel's dining room (mains R40), with waitresses in lace bobble caps, are reasonably priced and there is silver service to boot. At night have a drink in the Laird's Arms bar.

Matjiesfontein is just off the N1, 240km from Cape Town and 198km from Beaufort West. A night in the hotel would be worth a stopover on the *Trans Karoo* train trip between Jo'burg and Cape Town, though 24 hours here might be a bit long unless you have a good book. Alternatively, take the train from Cape Town (arriving at 2.46pm), stay the night and catch the 8.25am train back again the next day; it's a 5½-hour trip. The *Blue Train* also pauses here for an hour, with travellers being given a tour of town on the double-decker London bus that stands outside the station.

BEAUFORT WEST

☎ 023 / pop 35,400

A transit town if ever there were one, Beaufort West is not a place to linger but none-theless has a strange faded charm about it if you know where to look. Established in 1818, it's the oldest and largest town in the Karoo and in summer becomes a sluice gate for the torrent of South Africans heading for the coast – accommodation is booked out and prices rise. The town also serves as a gateway for the nearby Karoo National Park.

Tourist information (☎ 023-415 1488; cnr Donkin & Church Sts; ◷ 8am-4pm Mon-Fri) is on the main street in the old town hall opposite the church with the tall white spire. Next door is the **museum** (☎ 023-415 2308; Donkin St; adult/child R5/1; ◷ 8.30am-4.45pm Mon-Fri, 9am-noon Sat), which has displays on local-lad-made-good Dr Christiaan Barnard, who performed the world's first human heart transplant.

Given the plethora of accommodation options established to shore up all the through traffic (and the fly-by-night na-ture of many of them), any accommodation listing for Beaufort West has become an exercise in futility.

Inquire at the tourist office or visit the Beaufort West website (www.beaufortwestsa.co.za) for more information. On the other hand, if you have tents and transport, go to the Karoo National Park.

Getting There & Away

Beaufort West is a junction for many bus services. **Translux** (☎ 021-449 3333; www.translux.co.za), **Greyhound** (☎ 021-505 6363; www.greyhound.co.za) and **Intercape** (☎ 0861-287 287; www.intercape.co.za) stop at the **Total petrol station** (Donkin St) in the centre of town. Minibuses stop at the **BP petrol station** (Donkin St). Destinations in-clude Jo'burg (R240, 12 hours, daily), Cape Town (R225, seven hours, daily) and Bloem-fontein (R210, six hours, daily). From these cities you can then connect with buses to other parts of the country.

The *Trans Karoo* stops at the station on Church St on its daily journey between Cape Town and Jo'burg.

KAROO NATIONAL PARK

Just 5km north of Beaufort West, the **Karoo National Park** (☎ 023-415 2828/9; www.sanparks.org; adult/child R60/30; ◷ 5am-10pm), proclaimed in 1979, covers 33,000 hectares of impressive Karoo landscapes and representative flora and is run by SAN Parks. The plains carry a variety of short shrubs, with well-wooded dry watercourses and mountain grasslands at higher elevations.

The park has 61 species of mammal, the most common of which are dassies (agile, rodent-like mammals, also called hyraxes) and bat-eared foxes. The antelope popula-tion is small but some species have been reintroduced and their numbers are grow-ing. These include springboks, kudus, gemsboks, reedbucks, red hartebeests and rheboks. Mountain zebras have also been reintroduced, as has the odd black rhino. There are a great many reptiles and birds.

Facilities include a shop and restaurant. There are two short nature trails and an 11km day walk. There are also vehicle routes and day or overnight 4WD guided trails.

Accommodation is either at pleasant camp sites (R100) or in Cape Dutch–style cottages (R410 per double). The cottages are fully equipped with kitchens, towels and bedding. Two of the cottages have disabled access.

Public transport will take you to Beaufort West (see left), from where you will need to either hike in or catch a taxi from town; however the rest camp is 10km further into the park.

WEST COAST & SWARTLAND

If you're keen to do the Western Cape the way locals do it, head north of Cape Town and explore the jagged coastline, rugged, desolate mountains and windswept hills of the West Coast and Swartland, a peaceful and undeveloped getaway. You'll come across quiet, whitewashed fishing villages, beautiful lagoons, hidden camping spots in dramatic valleys and a country town serving up a big dish of South African cabaret, all within a few hours from the Cape Peninsula.

To the west is an angler's and surfer's paradise: an untamed coastline of duned beaches and rocky promontories, resort towns and the West Coast National Park, where bird-lovers flock. The coastal area is particularly spectacular in late winter and early spring when the dunes are carpeted with a stupendous array of wildflowers. Moving inland and east, the Cederberg Wilderness Area is tailor-made for hikers, who use this remote area to get lost for a few days. In between the two, and roughly following the N7 north to south, is the Sandveld, an arid, sandy tract of huge moonrises and creeping sunsets and, adjacent, the Swartland (Black Land), an agricultural area of rolling plains whose rich soil enables farmers to produce more than 20% of South Africa's wheat, as well as high-quality wine. Here you'll find the country town of Darling, home of South African entertainment icon Tannie Evita Bezuidenhout.

Most public transport through this area travels from Cape Town north along the N7, either going all the way to Springbok and Namibia or leaving the N7 and heading through Calvinia to Upington. Getting to the coastal towns west of the N7 isn't easy if you don't have a car.

DARLING

☎ 022

A quiet country town, Darling was best known for its good-quality milk until the actor and satirist Pieter-Dirk Uys, along with his alter ego Evita Bezuidenhout, set up stall here.

It might be best to head first to **tourist information** (☎ 022-492 3361; cnr Hill Rd & Pastorie St; ⏱ 9am-1pm & 2-4pm Mon-Thu, 9am-1pm & 2pm-3.30pm Fri, 10am-3pm Sat & Sun), but as most Capetonians who make the 70km trek north do so to catch the uniquely South African cabaret at **Evita se Perron** (Evita's Platform; ☎ 022-492 2851; www.evita.co.za; tickets R80; ⏱ performances 2pm & 8pm Sat, 2pm Sun), this is as good a place as any to start. The shows, featuring Pieter-Dirk Uys' characters, touch on everything from South African politics to history to ecology. Nothing is off limits – including the country's racially charged past. Although the shows include a fair smattering of Afrikaans, there's much for English-speaking audiences to enjoy, and they are often hilarious and thought-provoking.

The splendidly kitsch **restaurant** (mains R20-40; ⏱ lunch Tue-Sun) serves traditional Afrikaans food including *bobotie*.

Don't forget to ask tourist information or your guesthouse about the underrated **Darling Wine Experience**, the collective name for the four estates in the vicinity.

Sleeping & Eating

Darling is so close to Cape Town that there's no pressing need to stay overnight, but for lingerers or those heading onward, there are some nice guesthouses.

Trinity (☎ 022-492 3430; 19 Long St; s/d incl breakfast from R270/500; 🖳) A painstakingly renovated Victorian homestead with cosy country-style bedrooms where you can sample a selection of homemade toiletries. There's also a country-cuisine restaurant (mains R50) that's been voted one of the country's top 100.

Granary (☎ 022-492 3155; 5 Long St; s/d incl breakfast from R300/440) A neat guesthouse with lots of light and windows to make the big rooms feel especially spacious. Breakfasts are enough to fill you up for the day. The place welcomes children, though the rooms are up steep wooden steps, so are not for the frail or old.

Darling Guest Lodge (☎ 022-492 3062; 22 Pastorie St; s/d incl breakfast R360/540; 🖳) An elegant and imaginatively decorated place, one of the first in the area.

Marmalade Cat (☎ 022-492 2858; 19 Main Rd; breakfast R30) For an afternoon coffee or all-day breakfast, don't miss this arty café with an Internet connection (R40 per hour). It also serves sandwiches, delicious cheeses and homemade sweet treats.

Getting There & Away

Tannie Evita has taken over the old train station, so to get to Darling, it is best to have your own transport. Drive up Rte 27 from Cape Town and look out for the signs. An alternate route back to Cape Town, which is much more scenic and not nearly as busy as Rte 27, is to head east out of the town and turn south down Rte 307. Turn right just before the town of Mamre to rejoin Rte 27. Do not follow Rte 304 past Atlantis.

WEST COAST NATIONAL PARK

Encompassing the clear, blue waters of the Langebaan Lagoon and home to an enormous number of migratory wading birds is the **West Coast National Park** (☎ 022-772 2144; admission Aug-Oct R30, Nov-Jul R20; ☽ 7am-7.30pm Apr-Sep, 6am-8pm Oct-Mar). The park covers around 18,000 hectares and is made up of a peculiar mix of semi-independent zones, some of which are only leased by the national park authorities.

The park protects wetlands of international significance and important seabird breeding colonies. Wading birds flock here by the thousands in summer. The most numerically dominant species is the curlew sandpiper, which migrates north from the sub-Antarctic in huge flocks. The offshore islands are home to colonies of jackass penguins.

The vegetation is predominantly stunted bushes, sedges and many flowering annuals and succulents. There is some coastal *fynbos* vegetation in the east, and the park is famous for its wildflower display, which is usually between August and October. Several animal species can be seen in the part of the park known as the Postberg section, which is open from August to September.

The park is only about 120km from Cape Town, 7km south of Langebaan. The return trip from Langebaan to the northern end of the Postberg section is more than 80km; allow yourself plenty of time. The rainy season is between May and August.

LANGEBAAN

☎ 022

A rather unusual and beautiful location overlooking the Langebaan Lagoon has made this seaside resort a favourite holiday destination with locals. If you're looking for untouched you might be happier elsewhere, but the town does support an excellent hotel, open-air seafood restaurants, phenomenal sunset views, superb sailing and windsurfing on the lagoon and a few good beaches, the best of which is **Langebaan Beach**, in town, a favourite with swimmers. The town is also a good base for exploring the West Coast National Park.

The **Tourist Information Centre** (☎ 022-772 1515; www.langebaaninfo.com; Bree St; ☽ 9am-5pm Mon-Fri, 9am-1pm Sat & Sun) has information about the area.

Sights & Activities

WEST COAST FOSSIL PARK

The first bear discovered south of the Sahara, lion-sized sabre-toothed cats, three-toed horses and short-necked giraffes are all on display at this **fossil park** (☎ 022-766 1606; www.museums.org.za/wcfp; admission adult/child/pensioner/family R60/12/18/25; ☽ 9am-4pm Mon-Fri, 10am-12pm Sat & Sun) on Rte 45 about 16km outside Langebaan. Tours depart daily at 11.30am and take you to the excavation sites. Children can sieve for their own fossils in a special display area.

HORSE RIDING

At the **Oliphantskop Farm Inn** (☎ 022-772 2326; per hr R90) you can ride along the beach. The Inn is about 3km from Langebaan on the main road. Follow the signs.

Sleeping & Eating

Many of the sleeping options double as restaurants.

Farmhouse (☎ 022-772 2062; www.thefarmhouselangebaan.co.za; 5 Egret St; s/d incl breakfast R575/850; ☒) This is by far Langebaan's best hotel, on a hill overlooking the bay with lovely sunset views. Rooms are large, with country décor and their own fireplaces. For such a classy place the restaurant is reasonably priced with a creative menu (mains R50 to R80); and a rustic, intimate dining room.

Oliphantskop Farm Inn (☎ /fax 022-772 2326; Main Rd; s/d R180/300; ℗ ☒) An attractive place around 3km from town, across the road from the Mykonos resort complex, Oliphantskop's restaurant has a good reputation with nice ambience – cool and dark with rough, white walls and a wooden ceiling. The menu (mains R50) is meat and seafood oriented and offers no vegetarian options.

Club Mykonos (☎ 0800 226 770; theretha@club mykonos.co.za; 4-person cabins R1550; P 🏊 🖥 🍸) This is a major resort geared towards families, as there is plenty here to entertain the kids, but its Greek-themed, pseudo-Mediterranean architecture and crowds mean you'll either love it or hate it. There are no fewer than six outdoor swimming pools, a casino, restaurants and an arcade.

Die Strandloper (☎ 022-772 2490; buffet R140; 🕑 lunch & dinner) The West Coast life exemplified – a *10*-course outdoor fish and seafood braai right on the beach. All food is delicious, but our favourites are the snoek (firm-fleshed migratory fish) and the mussels cooked in white wine. There's also freshly made bread, bottomless *moerkoffie* (freshly ground coffee) and a local crooner who plays West Coast ballads at your table. You can BYO or get drinks from the rustic bar, whose view is sensational. Bookings essential; call for availability out of season.

Getting There & Away

Langebaan is an hour's drive north of Cape Town, but no public transport runs here. There are minibus taxi services from the commercial hub of Vredenburg (R17, 30 minutes).

SALDANHA & HOEDJIES BAY

Dominated by an enormous iron-ore pier, navy yards and fish-processing factories, **Saldanha** is at the northern end of the same lagoon as Langebaan. Despite this, the town's bays are pleasant and, because they are sheltered, much warmer than the ocean. **Hoedjies Bay**, near the town centre, is the most popular for swimming. There are some decent accommodation options in town; call the **tourist office** (☎ 022-714 2088; www.capewestcoast.org; Van Riebeeck St; 🕑 8.30am-4.30pm Mon-Fri, 9am-noon Sat) for information.

Schaafsma Charters (☎ 022-714 4235; www.sail boats.co.za) does boat trips to the harbour and to offshore islands. For those entering their yachtsman stage, they also offer a two-week all-inclusive boat trip (R6000).

PATERNOSTER
☎ 022
Until relatively recently, Paternoster was the West Coast's last traditional fishing village,

little more than a clutch of simple white-washed homes with green roofs up against the blue sea. Then wealthy Capetonians and foreigners became captivated by its charms and property is now a hot commodity – there are 'sold' signs left and right and new guesthouses are opening every day.

Still, it remains a lovely town to visit, and the surrounding countryside – rolling hills scattered with strange granite outcrops – is attractive. Further north along the coast is the similar village of **St Helena Bay**, with a lovely sheltered stretch of water, but no real beach. Paternoster is 15km from the missable inland town of Vredenburg.

Sleeping & Eating
Paternoster is rather lacking in street signs; instead look out for individual guesthouse signs. There are many B&Bs, so it may be worth checking out a few places first. During crayfish season (15 November to late December) you will see the tasty crustaceans for sale on the side of the road for between R50 and R70.

Camping & Caravan Park (Tietiesbaai; ☎ 022-752 1718; camp sites R30) Beyond Cape Columbine is this superbly located but windy park.

Paternoster Hotel (☎ 022-752 2703; paternoster hotel@wol.co.za; s/d R220/440) This rough-edged, lively, quirky country hotel is a popular venue for those interested in fishing. Its graffiti-covered walls and fish and crayfish braais are famous. We warn you, the bar is a feminist's nightmare.

Cape Columbine (☎ 021-449 2400; salato@npa .co.za; cottages from R525) Three kilometres past the town, you can stay in neat self-catering cottages next to the lighthouse (admission R12) in the Cape Columbine Nature Reserve, which protects 263 hectares of coastal *fynbos*.

Paternoster Lodge (☎ 022-752 2023; paterlodge@ telkomsa.net; s/d R560/700) A slick enterprise, with seven neat minimalist rooms and a breezy restaurant (mains R50 to R70) that's open all day. From the sun deck you can watch the fishermen bringing in their catch.

Voorstrandt Restaurant (☎ 022-752 2038; Strand-loperweg; mains R40-95; 🕑 breakfast, lunch & dinner) You can hop from this designer red-and-green-painted beach shack right onto the sand. Specialising in seafood, this is also an excellent spot to watch the sunset over a beer.

WESTERN CAPE

ELAND'S BAY & AROUND
☎ 022

From excellent surf to serene country getaways, the Eland's Bay area is quickly becoming the top West Coast getaway. The town itself is rather nondescript, but its setting couldn't be better: mountains run to the sea past a large lagoon frequented by waterbirds – this is a bird-lover's mecca.

The **Eland Hotel** (☎ 022-972 1640; Hunter St; s/d incl breakfast R250/460) is practically city hall here, acting as meeting point, accommodation and general tourist information for everyone.

Further inland, it's worth a visit to the up-and-coming hamlet of **Redelinghuys**, and further south a stay at **Sandveld Country Cottages** (☎ 022-962 1609; cwykeham@mweb.co.za; Rte 366; cottages per person R100; P ☺), undoubtedly the best accommodation in the region. Here you have your own cottage, garden and view of an exquisite valley. Look for the turn-off 12km south of Redelinghuys along the Aurora road; head 9km down this road.

LAMBERT'S BAY
☎ 027

The refreshing sea breezes of Lambert's Bay offer respite from the West Coast sun, but the ubiquitous fish-processing factories mean you'd be advised to stay upwind.

The helpful **information centre** (☎ 027-432 1000; Main Rd; ☺ 9am-1pm & 2-5pm Mon-Fri, 9am-12.30pm Sat) can tell you about area attractions, but the **Lambert's Bay Hotel** (☎ 027-432 1126; Voortrekker St; s/d incl breakfast from R395/500; ☺) is probably a better base as it can organise other accommodation and tours.

Lambert's Bay is also known for its large **gannet rookery**, but when we visited the birds had upped and left following an ongoing fight with colonising seals. If you are a gannetophile, call ahead to find out if they are back.

From July to January you might also spot some humpback whales off the coast, and Lambert's Bay is home to the heaviside dolphin, an endemic species. Indeed, many tour groups are attracted to the town just for a glimpse of these unusual and exquisite creatures. For boat trips contact **Lambert's Bay Boat Charter** (☎ 082-922 4334). This is also **quad biking** (☎ 083-306 6684; per person R180) country.

GOOFY-FOOTER

Eland's Bay is a goofy-footer's (surfing with the right foot at the front of the board) paradise, with extremely fast left-point waves working at a range of swell sizes. The bay can hold a very big wave. The main left-point break is virtually in front of the hotel, towards the crayfish factory – it breaks along a rocky shelf in thick kelp, after southwesterly winds on a low and incoming tide. There's a right-beach break and more lefts on Baboon Point, along the gravel road past the crayfish factory.

In March, the **Crayfish Festival** means cheap seafood and plenty of entertainment, but if you can't wait till then, try a seafood buffet at one of the two open-air restaurants just outside town. There's not much to choose between **Muisbosskerm** (☎ 027-432 1017; meals R120, crayfish R150) and **Bosduifklip** (☎ 027-432 2735; meals R110); call ahead as opening times vary and bookings are essential.

OLIFANTS RIVER VALLEY

The scenery changes dramatically at the Piekenierskloof Pass; coming north on the N7 you suddenly overlook the intensively cultivated Olifants River Valley. The elephants that explorer Jan Danckaert came upon in 1660, and which gave their name to the area, are long gone.

Today the river provides irrigation for hectares of grapevines and orange trees, which are beautifully maintained by a huge labour force. The comfortable bungalows of the white farmers are surrounded by green and leafy gardens, masking them from the shanties.

On the valley floor are some acclaimed wineries and co-ops, which specialise in white wine – you can get details of wine routes at tourist information centres. The eastern side is largely bounded by the spectacular Cederberg Range, which is protected by the extensive Cederberg Wilderness Area. Citrusdal and Clanwilliam, to the southwest and northwest of the wilderness area, are the two main towns in the region.

As an alternative to the N7, there's a spectacular partly tarred road (Rte 303) between Citrusdal and Ceres, a great drive through the Cederberg Wilderness Area from Citrusdal to Clanwilliam, and another memorable route (Rte 364) running between Clanwilliam and Calvinia (in Northern Cape to the northeast).

CEDERBERG WILDERNESS AREA

Bizarre-shaped, weathered-sandstone formations, San rock art, craggy and rugged mountains and green valleys all make the desolate Cederberg a must-see. The peaks and valleys extend roughly north–south for 100km, between Citrusdal and Vanrhynsdorp. A good proportion is protected by the 71,000-hectare Cederberg Wilderness Area, which is administered by the Porterville offices of **Cape Nature** (☎ 022-931 2088; www.capenature.org.za). The highest peaks are Sneeuberg (2027m) and Tafelberg (1969m). San rock-art paintings (see p237) can be found on the rocks and in some of the area's caves.

The region is famous for its plant life, which is predominantly mountain *fynbos*. Spring is the best time to see the wildflowers, although there's plenty of interest at other times of the year. The vegetation varies with altitude but includes the Clanwilliam cedar (which gives the region its name) and the rare snowball protea. The Clanwilliam cedar survives only in relatively small numbers, growing between 1000m and 1500m, and the snowball protea (now limited to isolated pockets) grows only above the snow line.

There are small populations of baboons, rheboks, klipspringers and grysboks; and predators such as caracals, Cape foxes, honey badgers and the elusive leopard.

Orientation & Information

The Cederberg is divided into three excellent hiking areas of around 24,000 hectares. Each area has a network of trails. However, this is a genuine wilderness area with a genuine wilderness ethos. You are *encouraged* to leave the trails, and little information is available on suggested routes. It's up to you to survive on your own. Similarly, you probably won't be given directions to the area's rock art. Work out for yourself where the Khoesaan were likely to have lived.

There is a buffer zone of conserved land between the wilderness area and the farmland, and here more-intrusive activities such as mountain biking are allowed.

There's no real season for walking; from May to the end of September expect rain and possibly snow. From December to April there's likely to be very little water.

A Cape Nature permit (adult/child R20/ 10) is required if you want to walk, and the number of visitors per hiking area is limited to 50 people. The maximum group size is 12 and, for safety, the minimum is two adults. To be certain you'll get a permit, apply well in advance. Outside school holidays and weekends you may be able to get one on the spot, but you should definitely phone before arriving to make sure.

The entrance to the Algeria camping ground closes at 4.30pm (9pm on Friday). You won't be allowed in if you arrive late. You can only collect your permit (if you haven't already organised it in Cape Town or had it posted to you) during office hours, so if you're arriving on Friday evening you'll need to make arrangements.

ROOIBOS TEA

Rooibos, literally 'red bush', is a red-coloured tea with a distinctive aroma. It's made from the leaves of the *Aspalathus linearis* plant, grown in the Cederberg region of Western Cape.

Malay slaves first discovered that the plant could be used to make a beverage, although it was not until the 20th century that a Russian immigrant Benjamin Ginsberg introduced it to the wider community, and it didn't become a cash crop until the 1930s. Despite this, some brands feature trek wagons and other icons of old South Africa.

The drink contains no caffeine and much less tannin than normal tea. This is probably its major health benefit, although it's claimed to have others, due to minute amounts of minerals such as iron, copper and magnesium. It's also a great thirst quencher, drunk straight or with lemon or milk.

Tours of one of the main packing plants, **Rooibos Ltd** (☎ 027-482 2155; www.rooibosltd.co.za), just outside Clanwilliam, are available at 10am, 11.30am, 2pm and 3.30pm Monday to Friday.

There are no eating places in the area so you will need to bring your own food.

Sleeping

Kleinkliphuis (☎ 027-482 2564; camp sites R25, dm R50, cottages per person R100) One option is this charming place near the Pakhuis Pass on Rte 364, about 15km northeast of Clanwilliam. It's a small country home in attractive grounds, with excellent self-catering huts. From here you can explore the surrounding countryside with ease.

Algeria (☎ 027-482 2404; 6-person camp sites R95, d cottages R380) This is the main camping spot in the area, with exceptional grounds in a beautiful, shaded site alongside the Rondegat River, the headwaters of the Olifants River. There are swimming holes and lovely spots to picnic. For those not interested in camping there are fully equipped stone cottages. Rates do not include the park entry fee. If Algeria is full, you can call Cape Nature (☎ 022-931 2088) for other camping areas.

See both Citrusdal and Clanwilliam for places to stay outside the Cederberg Wilderness Area.

Getting There & Away

The Cederberg Range is about 200km from Cape Town, accessible from Citrusdal, Clanwilliam and the N7.

There are several roads into Algeria camping ground, and they all offer magnificent views. It takes about 45 minutes to get here from Clanwilliam by car, much longer if you give in to normal human emotion and stop every now and again. Algeria is not signposted from Clanwilliam, but you just follow the road above the dam to the south. Algeria *is* signposted from the N7 and it's only 20 minutes from the main road; there's an amazing collection of plants, including proteas, along the side of the road.

There are some dusty but interesting back roads that run southeast through the hamlet of Cederberg on Rte 303, and on to Ceres. There's a good but tough walk from the camping ground up to the Wolfsberg Crack, a well-known rock formation. Allow at least seven hours to complete the return trip.

Unfortunately, public transport into Algeria is nonexistent.

CITRUSDAL & AROUND

☎ 022 / pop 9000

The small town of Citrusdal is a good base for exploring the Cederberg. August to September is wildflower season, and the displays can be spectacular. This is also one of the best times for hiking. Although the town itself is quaint, some of the most interesting and beautiful places to stay are in the surrounding mountains. Make sure to explore beyond the town limits – the scenery is stupendous.

The **tourism bureau** (☎ 022-921 3210; www .citrusdal.info; 39 Voortrekker St; ☼ 8.30am-5pm Mon-Fri, 9am-1pm Sat) can help you find accommodation in the area and provide information on mountain biking and hiking trails.

Sleeping

Beaverlac (☎ 022-931 2945; Beaverlac Nature Reserve; camp sites R30) Hard to reach but impossible to forget, this is one of the country's best camping spots. A valley hidden beneath pine trees is the base, and there are rock pools for swimming and fascinating terrain for exploring. There's a shop for all basic necessities. Head down Rte 44 south of Citrusdal until the signs to Dasklipspas, 5km north of Porterville. Follow the road for 20km up a magnificent pass and down a poor dirt road, until you see the signs to Beaverlac Nature Reserve. No car radios or parties allowed!

Gekko Backpackers Lodge (☎ 022-921 3721; http://home.mweb.co.za/vi/vism; camp sites per person R40, dm R65, d with shared bathroom R170) A friendly low-key place on a large citrus farm, 17.5km from Citrusdal on the N7 towards Clanwilliam. Activities here include tubing on the adjacent river or hiking through the mountains and caves on the enormous property – there are even San rock-art trails on the grounds. Bring your own food, as there is no restaurant, just an honesty bar.

Baths (☎ 022-921 8026/7; www.thebaths.co.za; camp sites per person R55, d from R335; ⛲) In a glorious location thick with trees and right up against the craggy peaks is this health spa with two outdoor pools. It's a good place to relax for a couple of days. The pools have superb views and are family-friendly. Day visitors (adult/child R45/22.50) are welcome. Prices jump on the weekends. There's also a swanky new restaurant and stylish Victorian-styled four-sleeper chalets

(R550). The place is about 18km from Citrusdal on the same road as the Elephant Leisure Resort. It is well signposted. Booking ahead is essential, and note that in summer (November to February) it can be scorchingly hot here.

Staalwater (☎ 022-921 3337; cottage per person R150) A twisty dirt road leading off Rte 303 to Citrusdal climbs past groves of citrus trees and flowering bushes before ending at the whitewashed farm buildings of Staalwater. The self-catering cottage sleeps eight. The property is large, and there are decent walks on the grounds. Staalwater is 12km from town on the way to the Baths.

Tree Tops (☎ 022-921 3626; www.citrusdal.info/kardouw; huts R240) In a poplar forest by the Olifants River, 12km further on from the Baths, the wooden chalets here are on stilts. It's a great place, but you'll need to bring everything with you and book well ahead. Prices go up on weekends.

Cedarberg Lodge (☎ 022-921 2221; www.cedarberglodge.co.za; Voortrekker St; s/d R250/340; breakfast R40; ☒ ☜) A friendly hotel with large rooms with TVs and an attached restaurant (mains R50) that focuses on meat and seafood.

Elephant Leisure Resort (☎ 022-921 2884; d R475; ☒ ☜) There is a private Jacuzzi on the porch of every chalet at this serene spot 9km outside Citrusdal amid the trees and rocks. Accommodation is in either two- or four-person self-catering chalets with tiled floors, cheery walls and spotless bathrooms. There's a hot-springs swimming pool behind the main building.

Eating

Uitspan Café (☎ 022-921 3273; 39 Voortrekker St; mains from R30; ☒ breakfast & lunch) This extremely friendly, bright café located next to the tourism bureau does tasty sandwiches, salads and cakes.

Patrick's Restaurant (☎ 022-921 3062; 77 Voortrekker St; mains from R50; ☒ noon-2.30pm Tue-Fri, 7-11pm Mon-Thu, 7pm-midnight Fri & Sat) This is the best, and practically the only, place for dinner in town. It does good steaks and, curiously in a town famed for its oranges, pizza with banana topping.

Getting There & Around

Intercape (☎ 0861-287 287; www.intercape.co.za) buses stop at the petrol station on the N7 highway outside town. Destinations include Cape Town (R135, three hours) and Springbok (R145, five hours).

There's an excellent scenic road (Rte 303) over Middelburg Pass into the Koue (Cold) Bokkeveld and a beautiful valley on the other side, which is only topped by the Gydo Pass and the view over the Ceres Valley. The back road into the wilderness area is also excellent.

CLANWILLIAM & AROUND
☎ 027 / pop 37,000

The adjacent dam and some adventurous dirt roads into the Cederberg make the compact town of Clanwilliam a popular weekend resort. Well-preserved examples of Cape Dutch architecture and trees line the main street. The dam is a favourite with water skiers.

The **information centre** (☎ 027-482 2024; ☒ 8.30am-5pm Mon-Sat, 8.30am-12.30pm Sun) is at the top end of the main street, across from the old *tronk* (jail in Afrikaans), dating from 1808, which doubles as the town's museum.

While up here, if you have the time, travel out to **Wuppertal** (☎ 027-492 3410). This

---

SAN ROCK-ART SITES

The nomadic San, South Africa's indigenous people, inhabited the area north of Clanwilliam for millennia. While as a people they have been decimated and/or assimilated, thankfully the area is still home to some of the finest examples of their rock art in the country. Indeed, archaeologists consider some of the sites the most well-preserved of their kind in the world. It can make for a fascinating exploration and has recently risen to prominence.

Unsurprisingly, several tour operators have sprung up, but they can be pricey. So if you're interested in learning more or visiting sites, contact the highly reputable **Living Landscape Project** (☎ 027-482 1911; chap@lando.co.za; 18 Park St, Clanwilliam; tours R40), which hosts art site visits and runs a community development programme. If you'd like to use other organised tour operators, contact the Clanwilliam information centre (above).

One of the best places to stay north of Clanwilliam (while still visiting rock-art sites) is Oudrif (p238).

Moravian mission station, 74km southeast of Clanwilliam, dates back to 1830 and is reached along a gravel road. The original church and the workshops – where hand-made leather shoes (called *velskoene*) are still made – are worth seeing.

Sleeping & Eating

Clanwilliam Dam Municipal Caravan Park & Chalets (☎ 027-482 8012; camp sites with/without electricity R85/62, 6-person chalets R535) This caravan park overlooks the water-skiing action on the other side of the dam from the N7. Travellers arriving here after weeks in Namibia will be pleased to pitch their tents on the grassy sites, though the water is disappointingly a bit of a diesel-fume and duck-dropping soup. The chalets are very nice but you need to book ahead for school holidays and weekends.

Strassberger's Hotel (☎ 027-482 1101; strassberger@lando.co.za; Main St; s/d R260/460; ☒) This comfortable and popular three-star hotel is basically a converted pub with acceptable rooms. Prices go up in flower season (August to September). Dinner is available from R100.

Saint du Barrys (☎ 027-482 1537; 13 Augsburg Dr; s/d incl breakfast R300/500; ☒ ☒) A 120-year-old banyan tree looms over this pleasant thatch-roofed guesthouse with six en suite, good-sized rooms and a charming garden.

Bushman's Kloof (☎ 027-482 2627; www.bushmanskloof.co.za; s/d R3000/3900; ☒ ☒) This is an upmarket private reserve, 46km east of Clanwilliam along the Pakhuis Pass, known for its excellent San rock-art sites and extensive animal and birdlife. If you've got the cash, staff can also arrange fly-in safaris from Cape Town.

Reinhold's (☎ 027-482 1101; Main St; mains from R50; ☽ dinner Tue-Sat) This à la carte restaurant is run by the Strassberger's Hotel across the road. It specialises in fish and grills and is the most popular place in town for dinner, so book ahead.

Olifantshuis (☎ 027-482 2301; cnr Augsburg Dr & Main St; mains from R40; ☽ dinner) A delightful garden with a cherub fountain makes this pub-restaurant in a big house a nice place for a drink on a hot night. There is also decent accommodation.

Oudrif (☎ 027-482 2397; moondance@49er.co.za; per person with full board week/weekends R375/495) A piece of paradise alongside the Doring River in the foothills of the Cederberg around 60km north of Clanwilliam, here you can really unwind, with an abundance of outdoor activities including river paddling. Accommodation is in stylish straw-bale cottages. It's a great place to stay if you want to see San rock-art sites (p237).

Getting There & Away

All the buses that go through Citrusdal also go through Clanwilliam. It's about 45 minutes between the two. Minibus taxis running between Springbok (R110, five hours) and Cape Town (R90, three hours) go through Clanwilliam, stopping at the post office.

Eastern Cape

Entry into the Eastern Cape is likely to be along the N2 from Cape Town, where you'll be struck by the beauty of the Tsitsikamma National Park, before the landscape flattens out past Cape St Francis and Jeffrey's Bay, through Port Elizabeth and on to East London. Inland to the north are the rolling hills of Grahamstown and surrounding 'settler country', which soon gives way to the majesty of the semiarid Karoo, dotted with intriguing towns such as Graaff-Reinet. Beyond East London lies the subtropical Wild Coast, and to the north the mountain ranges of the North-Eastern Highlands. You get the picture: for its relative size, the province has a remarkable range of differing climates, topographies and vegetation.

It has a complex history, too, one of settlement, migration, tragedy and conflict. In the 19th century, Trekboers clashed with the Xhosa eight times along the Great Kei River, and just about everywhere in a guerrilla conflict with the British. Later the area became a wellspring of resistance heroes including Thabo Mbeki, Nelson Mandela, Steve Biko, Robert Mangaliso Sobukwe, Chris Hani and Oliver Tambo.

Xhosa culture dominates the former apartheid 'homelands' of Transkei (the Wild Coast) and Ciskei, nominally independent republics that were used as dumping grounds for 'undesirables'. Today these regions celebrate their heritage with institutions such as the Nelson Mandela Museum in Mthatha. If you prefer the less complicated culture of animals, the province has excellent wildlife parks offering a viable safari alternative to parks such as the Kruger.

EASTERN CAPE

HIGHLIGHTS

- Hiking or riding the spectacular **Wild Coast** (p282) with its crashing waves, shipwrecks, spectacular gorges and hidden waterfalls

- Hitting the breaks at **Jeffrey's Bay** (p245), a world surfing centre

- Putting your head in the clouds at magical **Rhodes** (p295), South Africa's only ski spot

- Admiring the 360-degree views or meditating in the forest glades of **Hogsback** (p274)

- Spending tranquil hours by a waterhole with the elephants of **Addo Elephant National Park** (p255)

- Strolling down the well-kept streets of exquisite **Graaff-Reinet** (p266) and artistic village **Nieu Bethesda** (p271)

- Searching for the elusive Cape clawless otter in the magnificent **Tsitsikamma National Park** (p242)

- Visiting the **Nelson Mandela Museum** (p293) in Mthatha, a celebration of the struggle for freedom

■ POPULATION: 7.3 MILLION	■ AREA: 169,580 SQ KM

Climate

The rainfall and climate of Eastern Cape reflects the region's geographic variation, with a moderate climate on the coast, heavy rainfall (including snow in winter) in the mountains and low rainfall on the fringes of the Karoo. Average temperatures in East London and Port Elizabeth range from 26°C in summer to 18°C in the winter months of June to August, while further inland in the Karoo, temperature variations are far more extreme, with the thermometer plunging to around 6°C in winter, and rising as high as 40°C in summer.

National Parks & Reserves

The Eastern Cape is scattered with national parks and private reserves, wildly varying in quality and facilities. Flora and fauna are just as varied – from the pachyderms at Addo Elephant National Park (p255) and the rare Cape mountain zebra at Mountain Zebra National Park (p266) near Cradock to the subtler attraction of rare plants – and beach-loving wildebeest – in remote Dwesa Nature Reserve (p286).

Language

Start practising those tongue clicks – Xhosa is the predominant language in the Eastern Cape. Whites here speak either English or Afrikaans.

Getting There & Around

Travelling around the western side of the Eastern Cape isn't too hard – numerous bus services ply the route between Cape Town, Port Elizabeth and East London (which also both have international airports), stopping at major towns on the way and continuing to Durban, Johannesburg (Jo'burg) and Pretoria.

Further off the beaten track, notably on the Wild Coast and in the Eastern Highlands, users of public transport will have to take to the minibus taxis to find their way into more obscure spots. Some places in the highlands and on the Wild Coast are only accessible on foot or horseback.

Even if you have your own car, travel isn't always simple – in many parts of the Wild Coast, for instance, there are no reliable maps and no signposts, but there are lots of stray cows, food-seeking pigs and errant children wandering the roads.

WESTERN REGION

The western region includes the self-designated 'Sunshine Coast', which encompasses the coastline running from Nature's Valley to Port Alfred. Further inland is Grahamstown, at the heart of an Anglo-centric area originally home to the '1820 Settlers' (see p260). Also in this region are the recently extended Addo Elephant National Park and the exclusive, internationally renowned Shamwari Game Reserve.

NATURE'S VALLEY

☎ 044

Nature's Valley is a small village nestled in yellowwood forest (*outeniqua* or 'they who bear honey'; thought to be derived from the name of a Khoesaan group once resident in the forest) next to a magnificent beach in the west of Tsitsikamma National Park. This is where the Otter Trail ends and the Tsitsikamma Trail begins (see p242), but if you don't want to walk for that long, there are plenty of shorter hikes in the area.

Nature's Valley Trading Store & Information Centre (☎ /fax 044-531 6835; Beach Rd) is the hub of the village, incorporating a pub-restaurant and a small shop. Staff here can help with pamphlets on the surrounding area.

One of the most popular places to stay is **Nature's Valley Rest Camp** (☎ 042-281 1607, bookings 012-428 9111; www.sanparks.org; 1-2 person camp sites R100, forest huts d R260), the national park camp site, east of town and a 2km walk from the beach. It's a lovely spot at the edge of a river with clean ablutions and shared kitchens and laundry. Keep food well stored; there are pesky primates everywhere.

Another good option is **Hikers Haven** (☎ 044-531 6805; patbond@mweb.co.za; 411 St Patrick's Ave; dm R70, d with breakfast R250), a large and very comfortable home near the beach, with an attic dorm for backpackers and hikers. It's deservedly popular with Otter Trail groups, so bookings are essential. The guesthouse can arrange transport to the start of the Otter Trail (see p242).

Getting There & Away

There's no public transport to Nature's Valley, although the **Baz Bus** (☎ 021-439 2323; www.bazbus.com) will drop off or pick up here on request.

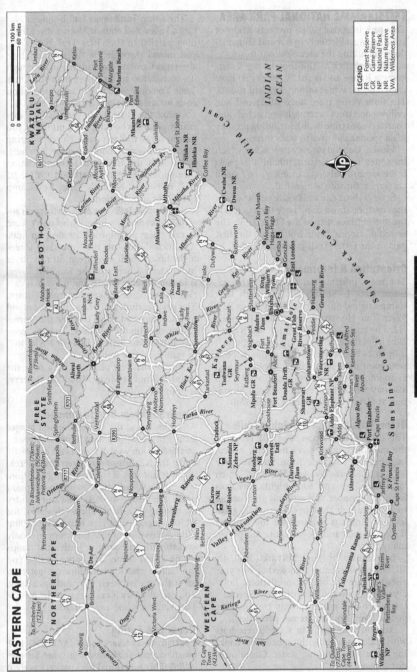

EASTERN CAPE

TSITSIKAMMA NATIONAL PARK AREA

This **park** (adult/child R80/40) protects 82km of coast between Plettenberg Bay and Humansdorp, including the area 5km out to sea.

The park lies at the foot of the Tsitsikamma Range and is cut by rivers that have carved deep ravines into the ancient forests. The flora varies from huge stinkwood and yellowwood trees to ferns, lilies, orchids and coastal *fynbos* (fine bush), including proteas. It's a spectacular area to walk through.

Elusive Cape clawless otters, after which the Otter Trail is named, inhabit this park; there are also baboons, monkeys and small antelopes. Birdlife is plentiful.

Several short day walks give you a taste of the coastline if you don't have time to tackle the longer hikes such as the Otter Trail. The waterfall circuit (four hours) on the first part of the Otter Trail is recommended.

Orientation & Information

The main information centre for the national park is Storms River Mouth Rest Camp (right), 68km from Plettenberg Bay, 99km from Humansdorp and 8km from the N2. The park gate is 6km from the N2. It's 2km from the gate to the main camp, which is open 24 hours and has accommodation, a restaurant and a shop selling supplies, as well as an information/reception centre. You can also pay park entrance fees and get information at Nature's Valley Rest Camp (p240).

Otter, Tsitsikamma & Dolphin Trails

The 42km **Otter Trail** (per person R500) is one of the most acclaimed hikes in South Africa, hugging the coastline from Storms River Mouth to Nature's Valley. The walk, which lasts five days and four nights, involves fording a number of rivers and gives access to some superb stretches of coast. A good level of fitness is required for the walk, as it goes uphill and down quite steeply in many places.

Book the trail through **SAN Parks** (☎ 012-426 5111). The trail is usually booked up one year ahead. There are often cancellations, however, so it's always worth trying, especially if you are in a group of only two or three people (single hikers are not permitted).

Accommodation is in six-bed rest huts with mattresses but without bedding, cooking utensils or running water. Camping is not allowed.

The 64km **Tsitsikamma Trail** begins at Nature's Valley and ends at Storms River, running parallel to the Otter Trail but taking you inland through the forests. This hike also takes five days and four nights, although it's considered to be easier than the Otter Trail. You only need to pay accommodation costs for the **hiking huts** (per person per night R70).

Unlike the Otter Trail, there is little difficulty getting a booking, and midweek you may have the trail to yourself, except during school holidays. Accommodation is in huts. Book both the trail and accommodation through the **Forestry Department** (☎ 042-281 1712), or contact Nature's Valley Rest Camp (p240) for information.

The **Dolphin Trail** (www.dolphintrail.co.za; per person R2700) is ideal for hikers who don't want to carry heavy equipment or sleep in huts. Accommodation on this four-day, three-night hike, which runs from Storms River Mouth to the banks of the Sanddrif River, is in comfortable hotels, and luggage is carried on vehicles between overnight stops. The price includes all accommodation and meals, guides and a boat trip into the Storms River Gorge on the way back. To book, contact **Tsitsikamma National Park** (☎ 042-281 1607) or visit the trail's website.

One of the best places to stay near the Dolphin Trail is Misty Mountain Reserve; see opposite.

Bloukrans River Bridge Bungee

At 216m, this is the world's highest **bungee jump** (☎ 042-281 1458; www.faceadrenalin.com; jump R580), 21km west of Storms River directly under the N2. Jumps run seven days a week; if you're not sure if you have the gumption, you can walk out to the jumping-off point under the bridge for R50. You can also try the Flying Fox *foefie*-slide (zipslide), for R150, under the bridge, a hair-raising 200m slide across the gorge. Bookings are only available to large groups; individual jumps are on a first-come, first-served basis. You can call to check availability or just turn up at the site between 9am and 5pm daily. You can also buy local curios at the on-site Tsitsikamma Khoesaan Village.

Sleeping & Eating

Bloukrans Backpackers Lodge (☎ 042-281 1450; www.tsitsikamma.org.za; dm/d with shared bathroom R90/180) This functional backpackers is right next to the bungee jump site and near the start of some shorter walking trails, and includes a decent bar. You can also stay at the adjoining Bloukrans Chalets (four/six people R480/680).

Storms River Mouth Rest Camp (☎ 012-428 9111; www.sanparks.org; camp sites/forest huts/family cottages R140/230/730) This camp offers forest huts, chalets, cottages and 'oceanettes'; all except the forest huts are equipped with kitchens (including utensils), bedding and bathrooms. When booking, it's worth asking if there are any winter (May to August) discounts on offer. When we asked SAN Parks, there weren't any, but some readers have told us about a 10% discount on forest huts and a 35% discount on camping (May to November).

Tsitsikamma Falls Adventure Park (☎ 042-280 3770; www.tsitsikammaadventure.co.za; Witelsbos; s/d with breakfast from R180/360) A family-run guesthouse about halfway between Nature's Valley and Jeffrey's Bay, and near a beautiful waterfall where you can abseil or take a *foefie*-slide across the falls. There's a range of accommodation to choose from according to your budget.

Misty Mountain Reserve (☎ 042-280 3699; www .misty-sa.co.za; chalets per person R400, 4-person cottage R1000). This is a great place to stay if you want to hike the Dolphin Trail (opposite). Accommodation is in luxury wooden cottages or chalets with wonderful views and full amenities. There's a restaurant (mains R50) if you don't feel like cooking. To get to the reserve look out for the Bluelilybush turn-off on the N2 6km east of Storms River Village; head 6.5km down this road.

Storms River Restaurant (☎ 042-281 1190; mains R70; ⏰ breakfast, lunch & dinner) At the reception complex to Tsistikamma National Park, this place has great views of the coast and reasonable prices. There's also a small shop and an outdoor terrace with a boardwalk over the rocks to the river mouth.

For information on Nature's Valley Rest Camp, see p240.

Getting There & Away

There is no public transport to either Nature's Valley or Storms River Mouth Rest Camps. Greyhound, Intercape and Translux buses run along the N2 (see p158 for contact details in Cape Town, and p254 for details in Port Elizabeth), from where it's an 8km walk to Storms River Mouth. The **Baz Bus** (☎ 021-439 2323) stops at Nature's Valley on request.

STORMS RIVER
☎ 042
Don't be confused between Storms River and Storms River Mouth in Tsitsikamma National Park. From the N2 the Storms River signpost points to this village that lies outside the national park. The turn-off is 4km east of the turn-off to the national park, which is signed as Storms River Mouth (or Stormsriviermond in Afrikaans).

Storms River is an odd little hamlet with tree-shaded lanes, a few places to stay and an outdoor centre. **Tsitsikamma Tourism Information Office** (☎ 042-280 3561; www.tsitsikamma .net) at the PetroPort petrol station, 4km east on the N2, provides information.

East of the village on the N2 is the **Big Tree**, a huge, 36m-high yellowwood, and a forest with many fine examples of candlewood, stinkwood and assegai. The 4.2km **Ratel Trail** (admission R4) begins here, with signs describing the trees in this forest, one of the best-preserved in South Africa.

Activities
Most activities on offer are organised by **Storms River Adventures** (☎ 042-281 1836; www .stormsriver.com; Darnell St, Storms River). These include a tree canopy slide (R395), a 'woodcutter's journey' forest tractor ride (R90) and an overnight bush experience (all equipment provided) at the Konga Bush Eco-Camp (R350).

Sleeping & Eating
BUDGET
Tube 'n Axe (☎ 042-281 1757; tube-n-axe@telkomsa .net; cnr Darnell & Saffron Sts; camp sites R50, dm/d with shared bathroom R70/200; 💻) If you are after a post-bungee rest, try the elevated two-person tented accommodation (R160) away from the main house. Otherwise, the dorms are close enough to the bar for you to hear adrenaline junkies reliving their experiences over the pool table while quaffing the hostel's own-brand beer. The hostel rents out mountain bikes (R80 per day) and organises a *foefie*-slide tour (R250) of the nearby Witelsbos Falls.

Storms River Rainbow Lodge (☎ 042-281 1530; rainbowl@lantic.net; 72 Darnell St; dm/d with shared

EASTERN CAPE

bathroom R70/200; ⬛) This is a comfortable, quiet and homely backpackers, with lovely gardens at the back. There's one self-catering cottage (R250) sleeping up to four or five people, and some rooms with private bathrooms inside the house. A healthy breakfast costs R25.

MIDRANGE

Ploughman's Rest (☎ 042-281 1726; www.ploughmansrest.co.za; 31 Formosa St; s/d with breakfast R210/390) This friendly B&B is just off the eastern side of the road before you enter Storms River. Accommodation has a log-cabin feel, and there are two terrific new timber-and-brick self-catering family units (R200 per person) designed to offer privacy for each generation. Ask about their reduced winter prices.

Tsitsikamma Village Inn (☎ 042-281 1711; www.village-inn.co.za; d from R295; ❌ ⬛ ♿) This is an extremely attractive three-star hotel, offering rooms, each with a four-poster bed and individual décor, set around a lawn. There's a restaurant and bar, which are popular with tour groups.

Armagh Country Guest House (☎ 042-281 1557; www.thearmagh.com; d R350; ⬛) This homely guesthouse has a relaxed feel to it. The Rafters restaurant (meals R100) serves hearty five-course dinners of home-cooked South African fare.

TOP END

Tsitsikamma Lodge (☎ 042-250 3802; www.tsitsikamma.com; d low/high season R385/425, ste low/high season R405/445; ⬛) This lodge, 8km east of Storms River, is a group of log cabins set close together around a very tidy garden. The deluxe rooms have an open fireplace, spa bath and CD player. But it's too close to the road to have a wilderness feel, and it's all slightly tacky, particularly the coy 'striptease river trail'. Low season runs from April to October, and high season from November to March.

Getting There & Away

The **Baz Bus** (☎ 021-439 2323) stops at Storms River, but there's no other public transport to the village. Buses and minibus taxis running along the N2 could drop you off at Bloukrans River Bridge or Tsitsikamma Lodge, both right next to the road, from where it's a 2km walk.

CAPE ST FRANCIS
☎ 042

Cape St Francis, 22km south of Humansdorp, is a small and unpretentious town chiefly famous for the Seal Point and Bruce's Beauties surf breaks. If the surf's not up or you prefer land-based activities, you can walk up the **lighthouse** (admission R10), built in 1888 and the tallest masonry tower on the South African coast, or enjoy a late-afternoon drink at the so-called 'Sunset Rocks'. Whales can be seen offshore between July and November.

St Francis Bay (☎ 042-294 0076) is an ever-growing upmarket resort 10km north of Cape St Francis, partially constructed around a network of canals. Visiting off-season, when many of the holiday homes are deserted, the town has a rather bleak and surreal air to it. It does, however, come to life in the high season, when it's jam-packed with sun-seeking yuppies zooming around the canals on speedboats or swimming off the beach.

There is some evidence to suggest that the scale of development around St Francis Bay is starting to impact on the supply of windblown sand to beaches in the area, an environmentally damaging phenomenon known as 'sand starvation'.

Sleeping & Eating

Cape St Francis Resort (☎ 042-298 0054; www.capestfrancis.co.za; Da Gama Way; camp sites/d R65/215, Christmas season R250/400; ⬛) The various chalets and units at this well-run resort are big, clean and attractive, many with TV and outside kitchen. There's a restaurant, a small shop and a bar on site.

Seal Point Lodge & Backpackers (☎ 042-298 0284; www.seals.co.za; Da Gama Way; dm/d R75/220; ⬛) This well-located lodge is just 200m from the legendary Seal Point. Dorms are clean, and the spacious doubles in self-catering units are good value. Downstairs you'll find the lively Full Stop Pub (mains R15 to R25), which also does food. Boards and wetsuits can be hired, and hiking, fishing and kite surfing arranged.

Lyngenfjord House (☎ 042-298 0444; www.lyngenfjord.co.za; 7 Lyngenfjord Rd; s/d with breakfast R470/720; ⬛) A classy but friendly B&B, exquisitely furnished and surrounded by panoramic views. Dinner is available and includes local specialities such as blesbok and calamari.

EASTERN CAPE

SURFING IN THE EASTERN CAPE   Chester Mackley & David Malherbe

The Eastern Cape coast is one of the greatest and most consistent surfing regions in the world. Head the Kombi anywhere between Jeffrey's Bay and Port Edward for excellent, uncrowded surf, and meet some of the friendliest locals in the country.

Jeffrey's Bay is world famous and those with the slightest interest in the motion of the waves will have heard of Supertubes. In July it hosts the Billabong Pro and in August the Pro Junior competition – partying, bands and a few hangovers are commonplace. Keep your eye on the low-pressure systems – anything below 970 millibars and you will be in heaven.

Heading north, **Port Elizabeth** is at its best with an unusual easterly swell or a big south swell and a southwesterly wind. With the right conditions, excellent waves can be found, particularly at the Fence, a hollow wedging left on the south side of the harbour wall.

Rock on to **Port Alfred** where there are excellent right-handers from the eastern pier of this sleepy fishing town.

Then on to **East London**, home of the legendary Nahoon Reef, a world-class right-hander known to be one of the most consistent waves in the country. This thick, juicy wave rises from deep water and thumps down on a boulder reef. If you find yourself stuck in the bowl, this wave will rattle your bones. Nahoon Beach and the Corner are the nursery for East London grommets and ideal for debutantes wanting to learn to surf. Buy the dudes at Buccaneers pub a beer and they'll let you in on Graveyards, Yellow Sands and Igoda.

Further north is **Wacky Point**, a great barrelling right-hander on a big swell. Then finally there's the **Wild Coast**, which boasts some of the most spectacular (and dangerous) coastline you will ever see and point breaks reputed to be as good as Supertubes, some known and many others as yet unnamed and yet to be surfed.

Some rooms have private balconies; try to get one facing the sea. Prices go up slightly in high season (December to April).

Getting There & Away

There's no public transport to Cape St Francis, but the Seal Point Lodge & Backpackers (opposite) will pick up from the **Baz Bus** (☎ 021-439 2323) drop-off at Humansdorp.

JEFFREY'S BAY

☎ 042 / pop 25,000

A far cry from its origins as a sleepy seaside town frequented by young families, 'J-Bay' takes its place as one of the world's top surfing destinations. It is certainly South Africa's foremost centre of surfing and surf culture. Boardies from all over the planet flock here to ride waves such as the famous Supertubes, once described as 'the most perfect wave in the world'. June to September are the best months for experienced surfers, but novices can learn at any time of the year.

Development is raging at a furious pace, with shopping in the myriad clothing stores almost overtaking surfing as the main leisure activity, but so far the local board-waxing vibe has been retained. The biggest surf crowd comes to town every July for the Billabong Pro championship.

Information

Most ATMs are in Da Gama Rd, the main thoroughfare.

Atlantic Internet Café (☎ 042-293 2399; Da Gama Rd; per min R0.40; ☼ 8am-7pm Mon-Fri, 8am-5pm Sat, 10am-3pm Sun) Also puts digital photos onto CD and provides free tea and coffee.

Jeffrey's Bay Tourism (☎ 042-293 2923; jbaytourism@telkomsa.net; Da Gama Rd; ☼ 9am-5pm Mon-Fri, 9am-noon Sat) Friendly and helpful, and can make bookings for accommodation.

Sights & Activities

The **Shell Museum** (☎ 042-293 1111, ext 286; Drommedaris St; admission by donation; ☼ 9am-4pm Mon-Sat, 9am-1pm Sun), next to the information office, contains over 350 deep-water and rare shells. They look beautiful but rather sad in glass boxes out of the sea.

For nonsurfers, there is **windsurfing** and great **bird-watching** at Kabeljous Beach, **dolphin- and whale-watching** from many of the surrounding beaches or **sand boarding** on nearby dunes. Sand boarding is just like snowboarding, with sand dunes replacing the snow. At **Aloe Afrika Sandboarding**

EASTERN CAPE

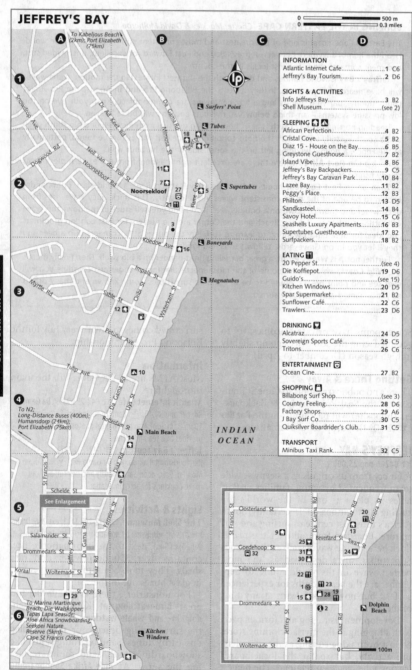

JEFFREY'S BAY

0	500 m
0	0.3 miles

INFORMATION
Atlantic Internet Cafe.....................1 C6
Jeffrey's Bay Tourism.....................2 D6

SIGHTS & ACTIVITIES
Info Jeffreys Bay...........................3 B2
Shell Museum...........................(see 2)

SLEEPING
African Perfection.........................4 B2
Cristal Cove................................5 B2
Diaz 15 - House on the Bay...............6 B5
Greystone Guesthouse....................7 B2
Island Vibe.................................8 B6
Jeffrey's Bay Backpackers.................9 C5
Jeffrey's Bay Caravan Park...............10 B4
Lazee Bay.................................11 B2
Peggy's Place.............................12 B3
Philton....................................13 D5
Sandkasteel...............................14 B4
Savoy Hotel...............................15 C6
Seashells Luxury Apartments..............16 B3
Supertubes Guesthouse...................17 B2
Surfpackers...............................18 B2

EATING
20 Pepper St...........................(see 4)
Die Koffiepot.............................19 D6
Guido's................................(see 15)
Kitchen Windows..........................20 D5
Spar Supermarket.........................21 B2
Sunflower Café............................22 C6
Trawlers..................................23 D6

DRINKING
Alcatraz...................................24 D5
Sovereign Sports Café.....................25 C5
Tritons....................................26 C6

ENTERTAINMENT
Ocean Cine................................27 B2

SHOPPING
Billabong Surf Shop.....................(see 3)
Country Feeling...........................28 D6
Factory Shops.............................29 A6
J Bay Surf Co..............................30 C5
Quiksilver Boardrider's Club..............31 C5

TRANSPORT
Minibus Taxi Rank........................32 C5

(☎ 082-576 4259; aloe@agnet.co.za; Marina Martinique; 2hr sessions R200), punters can try their luck on the slopes with instruction, while care is taken to minimise the impact on the environment.

Tours

Info Jeffrey's Bay (☎ 042-296 2563; www.infojeffreys bay.com; Spar Centre, Da Gama Rd) is a private information office that can organise a range of tours and activities in the region, including horse-riding, mountain biking, sand boarding, and township tours with local guides.

Sleeping

Like many places in this part of Eastern Cape, J-Bay is choc-a-block with holiday-makers between mid-December and mid-January, so you'll have to book way ahead for accommodation at this time. There's a good range of B&Bs and backpackers but no really upmarket hotels.

BUDGET

Peggy's Place (☎ 042-293 2160; pegjbay@yahoo.com; 8a Oribi St; camp sites/dm/d R35/50/200) A wonderfully rustic, friendly place in a comfortable old house on the outskirts of town, near the surf area and justifiably loved by readers. A self-catering flat is available for R200/350 in the low/high season.

Island Vibe (☎ 042-293 1625; ivibe@lantic.net; 10 Dageraad St; camp sites/dm/d R40/70/180) The most popular backpackers in town, Island Vibe is 500m south of the city centre but the attendant raft of surfies attests to its prime location. Activities on offer include surf lessons (R180), drumming, horse-riding and kite surfing, plus of course plenty of drinking and partying. For those wanting a quieter time, the new, beautifully decorated beach house has double rooms (R250) only and a separate kitchen. Breakfast and dinner are on offer in the open-air restaurant.

Cristal Cove (☎ 042-293 2101; www.cristalcove.co .za; 49 Flame Cres; dm R60, d from R150; 🖳) Offering a choice of either neat rooms within self-catering flats or new en-suite, sea-facing doubles, Cristal Cove is a chilled-out backpackers with a personal touch. It's also a stone's throw from Supertubes. Free pickups can be arranged from the buses at Humansdorp.

Jeffrey's Bay Backpackers (☎ 042-293 1379; back pac@netactive.co.za; 12 Jeffrey St; dm/d R60/150; 🖳) A

colourful house conveniently located near the centre of town and offering lots of local information. There are bicycles and surfboards for hire, surf lessons and a free shuttle to Supertubes when the surf's up.

Surfpackers (☎ 042-293 2671; 1 Pepper St; dm/d with shared bathroom R70/150) A new kid on the block, right opposite the chi-chi accommodation near Supertubes. Rooms are very clean and very blue, and the large grounds mean there's plenty of space to chill and hang your wetsuit out to dry.

Jeffrey's Bay Caravan Park (☎ 042-200 2241; fax 293 1114; Da Gama Rd; camp sites low/high season R75/135) Somewhat exposed but well located near the sea midway between the town centre and the surf, and offering plenty of plush lawn.

MIDRANGE

Jeffrey's Bay Tourism can put you in touch with a good selection of B&Bs and self-catering establishments.

Lazee Bay (☎ 042-296 2090; lazeebay@worldonline .co.za; 25 Mimosa St; d with breakfast R300; 🖳) One of J-Bay's best guesthouses, noticeable up on a hill above Da Gama Rd thanks to its bright blue frontage and memorable for its warm welcome, funky décor and great sea views. There's a pool deck, a braai (barbecue) area and a bar.

Savoy Hotel (☎ 042-293 1106; savoy@lantic.co.za; 16 Da Gama Rd; s/d with breakfast R320/560; 🔀 🖳) One of the town's first buildings and still its only hotel, the Savoy won't win awards for atmosphere but recalls a more innocent age thanks in part to cheesy Italian murals and a bingo hall. Rooms are drab but clean.

Supertubes Guesthouse (☎ 042-293 2957; super tubes@agnet.co.za; 10/12 Pepper St; s/d with breakfast R350/500, s/d luxury rooms with breakfast R550/800; 🔀 🖳) A stalwart of J-Bay accommodation, this is right in the prime surfing spot and provides luxurious accommodation with very smart bedrooms, sharing a kitchen. Surf lessons can be arranged.

Sandkasteel (☎ 042-293 1585; www.sandkasteel .co.za; 3 Diaz Rd; 2-/3-bedroom flats R350/610) Good-value, no-frills flats loved by recent graduates of colleges, universities and surf schools.

Greystone Guesthouse (☎ 042-296 0616; grey stone@telkomsa.net; 11 Mimosa St; d with breakfast low/high season R360/500; 🖳 🖳) A large, airy house with a range of neat sea-themed rooms and studios. Many have a corner bath, fridge or kitchenette, and there's a sizzling hot outdoor Jacuzzi and a pool table. There are also two self-catering units.

Philton (☎ /fax 042-293 1287; 25 Diaz Rd; 2-/3-bedroom flats R400/500) This doesn't look like much from afar, but its combination of beachside location, good-sized self-catering units with balconies and fantastic sea views make it excellent value.

African Perfection (☎ 042-293 1401; www.africanperfection.com; 20 Pepper St; s/d with breakfast R450/800; ☒) A massive circular wooden staircase is the centrepiece of this impressive luxury option, with all rooms offering stunning sea views in earthy tones and textures. There's also a four-sleeper self-catering loft (R1500) and a separate restaurant in the basement (see right).

Seashells Luxury Apartments (☎ 042-293 1104; www.seashell.co.za; 125 Da Gama Rd; 2-/3-bedroom flats R630/840; ☒) The apartments are rather nondescript but are serviced, spacious and well located directly in front of Magnatubes.

Diaz 15 – House on the Bay (☎ 042-293 1779; www.diaz15.co.za; 15 Diaz Rd; 2-bedroom flats with breakfast from R1350; ☒) This place has luxury apartments with tiled floors, leather sofas, and patio doors opening onto well-kept lawns. There's an infinity pool right on the ocean's doorstep.

Eating

Trawlers (☎ 042-293 1353; 19 Da Gama Rd; meals R15-30; ☒ breakfast, lunch & dinner) A greasy takeaway serving hamburgers, chips and calamari.

Die Koffiepot (☎ 042-293 2590; Dolphin Beach; snacks R20; ☒ breakfast & lunch) You don't need to speak Afrikaans to figure out that this place offers a solid caffeine and pastry fix while staring out at the big blue.

Guido's (☎ 042-293 2288; 36 Da Gama Rd; pizzas R20-30; ☒ lunch & dinner) Guido's is part of a chain of neo-Italian restaurants that are very popular throughout the Eastern Cape. The interior features lots of plaster columns and fake Roman statues, and the menu consists mostly of passable pizzas and a variety of pasta dishes.

Kitchen Windows (☎ 042-293 4230; Diaz Rd; mains R36-50; ☒ lunch & dinner Tue-Sun) Bookings are essential at this, one of the town's more upmarket eateries. A great view of the sea complements splendidly cooked fresh fish and a good selection of salads for lunch. Enter on Diaz Rd.

Sunflower Café (☎ 042-293 1682; 20 Da Gama Rd; mains R40; ☒ breakfast, lunch & dinner Tue-Sat, breakfast & lunch Sun & Mon) This bright, cheerful and friendly café does some healthy and vegetarian options.

20 Pepper St (☎ 042-293 1728; 20 Pepper St; mains R50-80; ☒ breakfast, lunch & dinner) Savour sushi, sashimi and Thai-style calamari in this classy, well-styled tile-and-bamboo eatery below African Perfection guesthouse. There's a decent wine selection, too.

Tapas Lapa Seaside (☎ 042-292 0119; Marina Martinique; mains R50-85; ☒ dinner) Tapas Lapa is just across the car park from the seashore, so the sand on the floor has to be shovelled in! Meals feature decent seafood, and there's a bar next door.

Die Walskipper (☎ 082-800 9478; Marina Martinique; seafood platters R120; ☒ lunch & dinner Tue-Sat, lunch Sun) This alfresco restaurant is just metres from the lapping sea at the Marina Martinique beach. It specialises in seafood, plus crocodile and ostrich steaks. At weekends, the long trestle tables are packed with locals enjoying giant platters of oysters, calamari, crab and langoustine.

For self-caterers, **Spar supermarket** (Da Gama Rd) offers a decent selection of food.

Drinking & Entertainment

Tritons (☎ 042-293 3893; 12 Da Gama Rd) A traditional pub with a TV for sports, Triton's is a popular drinking spot. It also offers big breakfasts and traditional South African *potjiekos* (meat and vegetables cooked in a cast-iron pot over an open fire). A move was imminent when we were there, so ask ahead if it's still in this location.

Sovereign Sports Café (☎ 042-293 2311; Da Gama Rd) A cavernous and popular drinking spot with the requisite big-screen TV. Hot dogs and burgers are available to sop up all that beer.

Alcatraz (☎ 042-293 1801; Time Out Bldg, Ferreira St) Dishes up all the same ingredients as the other two – plus games machines and pool tables – but dispenses with food altogether.

Ocean Cine (☎ 042-296 2702; Wavecrest Centre, Da Gama Rd; admission R20) Near the Spar supermarket; screens current movies.

Shopping

The clothing industry has really taken off in J-Bay, with much of the stuff on sale made and designed in the town itself.

Billabong Surf Shop (☎ 042-296 1797; Da Gama Rd)
Hires boards for R15 per hour and wetsuits
for R10 an hour, and stocks a big range of
new and used boards.

Quiksilver Boardrider's Club (☎ 042-293 2203;
Da Gama Rd) This shop also has a good selection of boards and baggies, a coffee shop
and a quaint Surfing Museum upstairs.

Clothing emporia in the town centre in-
clude **Country Feeling** (☎ 042-200 2611; Da Gama Rd)
and **J-Bay Surf Co** (☎ 042-200 2617; cnr Da Gama Rd
& Goedehoop St), which sells surfboards for
R2800 to R3000.

Check the various factory shops at the
lower end of Jeffrey St for the best bargains,
as well as the local independent stores dotted around the high street.

Getting There & Away

The **Baz Bus** (☎ 021-439 2323) stops daily at
hostels in both directions. A fare from Jeffrey's Bay to Cape Town costs R380 and
takes 12 hours; Port Elizabeth to Jeffrey's
Bay costs R70 and takes two hours. The
Sunshine Express (☎ 293 2221) runs door-to-
door between Port Elizabeth and Jeffrey's
Bay (R100, one hour).

Minibus taxis depart from the **Friendly
Grocer** (Goedehoop St); it's R12 to Humansdorp
(30 minutes) and R35 to Port Elizabeth
(one hour).

Long-distance buses (Greyhound only)
plying the Cape Town–Port Elizabeth–
Durban route arrive at and depart from the
stand at the Pick 'n Pay centre on St Francis
St (Map p246).

PORT ELIZABETH

☎ 041 / pop 1.5m

Port Elizabeth, the Eastern Cape's biggest
town and its major transport hub, seems
to have something of an identity crisis. It
is known by South Africans as 'PE', by the
locals as the 'friendly city', by marketeers
as part of the 'Sunshine Coast' and by the
local government as the core of 'Nelson
Mandela Bay' – an area incorporating the
city centre, the nearby industrial area of
Uitenhage and the huge, sprawling townships that surround both. In keeping with
this, its buildings are a hodgepodge of
styles and have a dishevelled charm: monuments at once to its growth period (the
1880s) and to its boycott-era stagnation
(the 1970s).

While many consider Port Elizabeth no
more than a charmless, convenient place
to stop for a rest and stock up on supplies
before moving onward, it does offer some
of the Eastern Cape's best bathing beaches.
If you do end up here for a few days, take a
look at the interesting South End and Port
Elizabeth museums or explore the vibrant
shebeen (drinking establishment) scene of
the surrounding townships.

Orientation

The train station is just to the northwest
of the city, which is circled by a ghastly
freeway. The beachfront runs between
Humewood and Summerstrand, a couple
of kilometres southeast of the centre. Shops
and businesses are concentrated in the big
malls: the Boardwalk at Summerstrand, and
Greenacres, just west of the town centre
on Rte 102.

Information

INTERNET ACCESS

Boardwalk Internet Café (☎ 041-583 4725; the
Boardwalk, Marine Dr, Summerstrand; per hr R40;
🕑 9.30am-8.30pm Mon-Sat, 10am-6pm Sun)

MONEY

There are branches of all the major banks
along Govan Mbeki Avenue, located in the
city centre.

Amex (☎ 041-583 2025; the Boardwalk, Marine Dr,
Summerstrand; 🕑 8am-10pm Mon-Fri, 10am-2pm
Sat & Sun)

Rennies Foreign Exchange (☎ 041-368 5890;
Walmer Park Shopping Centre; 🕑 9am-5pm Mon-Fri,
9am-noon Sat) About 3km from the town centre.

TOURIST INFORMATION

Nelson Mandela Bay Tourism (☎ 041-585 8884,
041-583 2030; www.nmbt.co.za; Donkin Reserve;
🕑 8am-4.30pm Mon-Fri, 9.30am-3.30pm Sat & Sun) Has
an excellent supply of information and maps, including of
the Donkin Heritage Trail (R18), which details a two-hour
self-guided walk around the city's historic buildings. It's in
the lighthouse building in Donkin Reserve and its handy
visitors' guide includes details of disabled-friendly sights
and accommodation.

Dangers & Annoyances

The city centre can be dangerous at night –
take a taxi if you're going out. The main
beachfront, however, is considered one of
the safest in the country.

PORT ELIZABETH

EASTERN CAPE

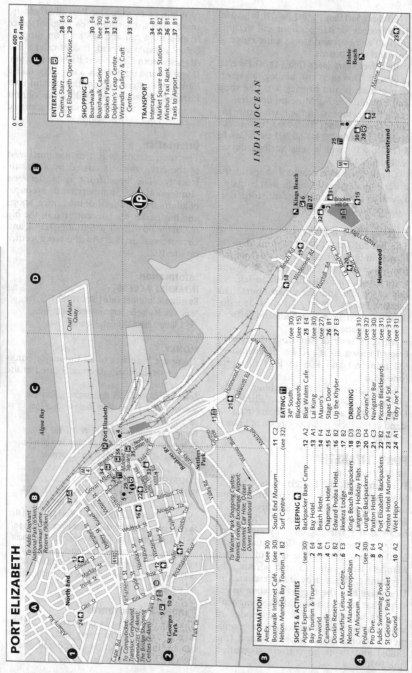

0	600 m
0	0.4 miles

INFORMATION

AmEx	(see 30)	
Boardwalk Internet Café	(see 30)	
Nelson Mandela Bay Tourism	1	B2

SIGHTS & ACTIVITIES

Apple Express	(see 30)	
Bay Tourism & Tours	2	E4
Bayworld	3	E4
Campanile	4	C1
Donkin Reserve	5	B2
MacArthur Leisure Centre	6	E3
Nelson Mandela Metropolitan Art Museum	7	A2
Polani	8	B2
Pro Dive	9	A2
Public Swimming Pool	10	A2
St George's Park Cricket Ground		
South End Museum	11	C2
Surf Centre	(see 32)	

SLEEPING

Backpacker Base Camp	12	A2
Bay Hotel	13	A1
Beach Hotel	14	F4
Chapman Hotel	15	E4
Edward Protea Hotel	16	B2
Jikeleza Lodge	17	B2
Kings Beach Backpackers	18	D3
Langerry Holiday Flats	19	D3
Lungile Backpackers	20	D4
Paxton Hotel	21	C3
Port Elizabeth Backpackers	22	B2
Protea Hotel Marine	23	F4
Wet Hippo	24	A1

EATING

34° South	(see 30)	
Blackbeards	(see 15)	
Blue Waters Cafe	25	E4
Lai Kung	(see 30)	
Mauro's	(see 27)	
Stage Door	26	B1
Up the Khyber	27	E3

DRINKING

Dros	(see 31)	
Giovani's	(see 32)	
Navigator Bar	(see 30)	
Piccolo Blackbeards	(see 31)	
Tapas Al Sol	(see 31)	
Toby Joe's	(see 31)	

ENTERTAINMENT

Cinema Starz	28	E4
Port Elizabeth Opera House	29	B2

SHOPPING

Boardwalk	30	E4
Boardwalk Casino	(see 30)	
Brookes Pavilion	31	E4
Dolphin's Leap Centre	32	E4
Wezandla Gallery & Craft Centre	33	B2

TRANSPORT

Intercape	34	B1
Market Square Bus Station	35	B2
Minibus Taxi Rank	36	B1
Taxis to Airport	37	B1

INDIAN OCEAN

Sights

SOUTH END MUSEUM

This small but fascinating **museum** (☎ 041-582 3325; admin@semuseum.co.za; cnr Walmer Blvd & Humewood Rd; admission free; 9am-4pm Mon-Fri, 10am-3pm Sat & Sun) records multicultural Port Elizabeth, a vibrant district once known as South End. The apartheid bulldozers put an end to the neighbourhood during forced removals between 1965 and 1975 under the infamous Group Areas Act. The inhabitants, which included blacks, coloureds, Asians and whites, were relocated to parts of the city designated by race.

BAYWORLD

One of the best and largest museum complexes in the country, **Bayworld** (☎ 041-584 0650; www.bayworld.co.za; Beach Rd; adult/child R31/15; 9am-12.45pm & 1.45-4.30pm) incorporates the Port Elizabeth Museum, an oceanarium and a snake park. Alongside the many stuffed and pickled marine mammals in the museum is some beautiful Xhosa beadwork incorporating modern materials, and a replica of the Algoasaurus dinosaur.

At the oceanarium, trained dolphins and seals perform at 11am and 3pm daily. It's old-fashioned, tacky and exploitative, but still has the kids in raptures and carries a strong educational message about pollution and marine conservation.

NELSON MANDELA METROPOLITAN ART MUSEUM

Port Elizabeth's **art museum** (☎ 041-586 1030; www.artmuseum.co.za; 1 Park Dr, St George's Park; admission free; 9am-5pm Mon & Wed-Fri, 2-5pm Tue, Sat & Sun) is housed in two rather handsome buildings at the entrance to St George's Park. It has a permanent collection of paintings and sculpture by contemporary South African artists, some older British and Eastern works, plus regular rolling exhibitions and graduate shows.

CAMPANILE

This **bell tower** (☎ 041-506 3293; Strand St, 9am-12.30pm Tue-Sat, 2-4pm Sun & Mon), visible from the city centre, was erected to commemorate the landing of the 1820 British Settlers. Unfortunately, it's located near the entrance to the harbour and railway station, a bit of a dodgy area. If you're keen to climb the 53.5m structure via 204 steps to view the largest carillon of bells in the country, do so in a group if possible.

DONKIN RESERVE

The Donkin Reserve is immediately behind the town centre and has good views over the bay. It's a handy point for getting your bearings. The **pyramid** on the reserve is a memorial to Elizabeth Donkin, the beloved wife of Sir Rufane Donkin, once the governor of Cape Province. A plaque on the pyramid pays tribute to: 'One of the most perfect human beings, who has given her name to the town below'.

Also on the reserve is the **Port Elizabeth Opera House**, the oldest in the country (see p254).

STEAM TRAIN

The **Apple Express** (bookings through Eas'capism ☎ 041-583 2030; www.apple-express.co.za; the Boardwalk, Marine Dr, Summerstrand; adult/child R120/60; alternating Sat Jan-Aug, every Sat Sep-Dec) tourist steam train runs a day trip to Thornhill and back, with a two-hour stop for a braai. It crosses over the highest narrow-gauge bridge in the world.

Activities

The wide sandy beaches to the south of central Port Elizabeth make the town a major watersports venue. Kings Beach stretches from the harbour breakwater to Humewood Beach; both beaches are sheltered. Catamaran sailors and surfers make for Hobie Beach, which is 5km from the city centre.

If you prefer calmer waters, there's a rather beautiful **public swimming pool** (☎ 041-585 7751; St George's Park; adult/child R4/2.50; 7am-6pm Mon-Fri, 9am-6pm Sat, 10.30am-6pm Sun) in among the trees and lawns of St George's Park.

Just up the road is **St George's Park Cricket Ground** (☎ 041-585 1646), the home of Eastern Province Cricket and famous for its band-playing supporters who turn one-day internationals into tub-thumping affairs.

There's a bigger pool complex with a whale-viewing jetty at **MacArthur Leisure Centre** (☎ 041-582 2285; Kings Beach Promenade; adult/child R30/15; 8.30am-6pm Sep-Apr). The MacArthur complex includes a pool bar and two restaurants, with direct access to the beach.

Good **diving sites** around Port Elizabeth include some wrecks and the St Croix

Islands, a marine reserve. Contact either **Ocean Divers International** (☎ 041-581 5121; www .odipe.co.za; 10 Albert Rd, Walmer) or **Pro Dive** (☎ 041-583 5316; www.prodive.co.za; Shark Rock Pier, Beach Rd, Summerstrand; per dive R275); both of these offer PADI and NAUI diving courses, starting at around R900.

The **Surf Centre** (☎ 083-656 8429; Marine Dr, Humewood; surfboards/body boards per day R100/30) sells and hires surfboards and body boards. Its surf school will teach you how to use them for R150 per day.

Port Elizabeth's blustery climate also makes it a popular **windsurfing** destination, with many private tour operators around town. Contact Nelson Mandela Bay Tourism (p249) for a list of reputable companies.

Tours

Bay Tourism & Tours (☎ 041-584 0622; www.baytours .co.za; Beach Rd; ☾ 9am-5pm) runs local tours, including trips to Addo Elephant National Park (R550) and city/townships (R250).

There are several cross-cultural township tours, which give the opportunity to visit squatter camps, *shebeens* and *abakhwetha* (initiation camps for boys). The guides are locals who are proud of the Port Elizabeth townships' part in the antiapartheid struggle, and highlight places of historical and political interest along the way. The cost is from R200 to R250 per person for a half-day tour and includes a light lunch or dinner at a *shebeen*. Contact **Calabash Tours** (☎ 041-585 6162; calabash@iafrica.com), **Tanaqua Tours** (☎ 041-452 7692) or **Molo Tours** (☎ 082-970 4037).

Raggy Charters (☎ 073-152 2277) offers cruises led by a qualified marine biologist to St Croix, Jahleel and Benton Islands. You can see penguins, Cape fur seals, dolphins and whales on its half-day tour, which departs at 8am daily (R450).

For a sunset yacht cruise, including a fish barbeque, contact **Polani** (☎ 041-583 2141; the Boardwalk, Marine Dr, Summerstrand). Boats go towards Cape Recife, and there's a good chance of seeing dolphins en route. The R120 price tag doesn't include drinks.

Sleeping

As you might imagine, Port Elizabeth is well provided with accommodation, mostly of a very good standard. The tourist office in Donkin Reserve can help with lists of B&Bs. Most of Port Elizabeth's fairly unex-

citing hotel choices are lined up along the beachfront.

BUDGET

Lungile Backpackers (☎ 041-582 2042; lungile@hi-active.co.za; 12 La Roche Dr, Humewood; camp sites/dm/ tw/d with shared bathroom R40/65/160/175; 🖳 🖳) Port Elizabeth's most popular and busy backpackers is contained in an airy Swiss-style home minutes from the beachfront. The large entertaining area rocks most nights, and the dorms and tiny camp site can get full when the Baz Bus arrives, so book ahead. There are also some handsome stone-flagged doubles with their own bathrooms (R195). The hostel does pick-ups from the airport and city-centre bus stops.

Jikeleza Lodge (☎ 041-586 3721; winteam@hinet .co.za; 44 Cuyler St; camp sites/dm/s/d with shared bathroom R55/70/135/170; 🖳) Jikeleza Lodge is small and clean rather than especially charming, but there's a big garden and braai area, and it's a good place to organise township visits and other local tours.

Backpackers Base Camp (☎ 041-582 3285; pebase camp@yahoo.com; 58 Western Rd; dm/s/d with shared bathroom R60/120/160; 🖳) Its entrance is far from welcoming, but this is a neat back-packers near St George's Park. Rooms have plush futons, there's a bar with pool table and a lounge with an open fireplace, plus an indoor braai.

Wet Hippo (☎ 041-533 6260; www.wethippo.com; 14 Glen St, Richmond Hill; dm/d with shared bathroom R60/ 160; 🖳) Port Elizabeth's newest backpackers is pretty smart, with a sunny kitchen, a big pool and a pretty garden, all set in a leafy suburban street far from the hustle of the beachfront.

Kings Beach Backpackers (☎ 041-585 8113; king sb@agnet.co.za; 41 Windermere Rd, Humewood; dm/d with shared bathroom R65/160; 🖳) A quieter, more intimate backpackers, with some so-so cottage rooms and comfortable en-suite doubles (R190). High-speed Internet (R30 per hour) and satellite TV keep you connected to the world, and the staff can help organise tours in the area.

Port Elizabeth Backpackers (☎ 041-586 0697; pebakpak@global.co.za; 7 Prospect Hill; dm/d with shared bathroom R75/180; 🖳) This friendly, laid-back hostel is in a 100-year-old building within walking distance of the city and places to eat and drink up on the headland. It's quieter and less ritzy than Lungile, but still very comfortable, with a braai area and a garden. Breakfast costs R20 – try the homemade bread! The hostel organises transport for the Owl House Backpackers in Nieu Bethesda (see p272).

MIDRANGE

Bay Hotel (☎ 041-585 1558; info@bayberry.co.za; 7 Lutman St; s/d with breakfast R250/375) An upmarket place that feels more like a B&B than a hotel, with very reasonable rates for elegant rooms with plenty of character. It also has an attractive restaurant (mains R40) and bar attached.

Edward Protea Hotel (☎ 041-586 2056; edward@ pehotels.co.za; Belmont Tce; s/d R410/550) The Edward Protea Hotel, in the heart of the city, is a gracious, old-style Edwardian hotel with comfortable rooms and charming colonial décor. It's a superior member of the Protea chain. A full English breakfast in the palm-filled courtyard restaurant costs R68.

Chapman Hotel (☎ 041-584 0678; www.chapman .co.za; 1 Lady Bea Cres, Brookes Hill, Summerstrand; s/d with breakfast R460/550; 🞨 🖳 🛋) The family-run Chapman, overlooking the sea south of the city centre, is an upmarket choice with a waterfall horizon pool. Modern rooms have private balconies with sea views.

Paxton Hotel (☎ 041-585 9655; www.paxton.co.za; Carnarvon Pl, Humerail; s/d R555/680; 🞨 🖳 🛋 🚱) This is a fairly characterless corporate hotel in a concrete tower halfway between the beach and the city centre. There are some wheelchair-adapted rooms available.

In addition to the places already mentioned, there are dozens of self-catering flats along the beachfront. If you're looking for a clean, no-frills apartment, head for **Langerry Holiday Flats** (☎ 041-585 2654; langerry@icon.co.za; 31 Beach Rd; 1-/2-bedroom flats R180/350). All flats have TV, telephone and kitchen, and the two-bedroom ones have a microwave. The same company also has other blocks in the area.

TOP END

Neither of Port Elizabeth's top-end hotels is much to write home about, but they both have good views of the sea.

Beach Hotel (☎ 041-583 2161; resbeach@pehotels.co .za; Marine Dr, Summerstrand; s/d with sea view R850/860, without sea view R695/860; 🞨 🖳 🛋) The four-star Beach Hotel is part of the Protea chain. The terracotta and mint-green rooms are austere but have all the trimmings, and it's

well positioned opposite Hobie Beach and next to the Boardwalk. There is a dining room, sea-facing terrace for light meals, a bar and a coffee shop.

Protea Hotel Marine (☎ 041-583 2101; www.pe hotels.co.za; Marine Dr, Summerstrand; s/d R770/970; 🞨 🖳 🛋 🚱) The Protea Marine is one of the most expensive hotels in Port Elizabeth, so you'd think they could have increased the size of the swimming pool a bit – it's tiny, and right next to the road. Inside, things improve slightly, with a jazzy bar, a gym and comfortable, if characterless rooms with a bathroom and personal safe.

Eating

Most of Port Elizabeth's best cafés are in the Boardwalk Casino Complex in Summerstrand, at the far end of Beach Rd. The atmosphere is a bit artificial, but you can at least sip a cappuccino in peace away from the plastic fast-food joints of the beachfront. Try Dulce's Continental Diner or Tarantino's for lunch.

Blue Waters Café (☎ 041-583 4110; Marine Dr, Summerstrand; mains R30-90; 🕒 lunch & dinner Mon-Sat, dinner Sun) A bright, lively café-restaurant with an imaginative menu – lots of seafood platters, salads and pasta, and a good black-mushroom vegetarian dish. It's quite popular, so book ahead.

Stage Door (☎ 041-586 3553; Phoenix Hotel, 5 Chapel St; mains R35; 🕒 lunch & dinner) The Stage Door has won awards for good-value pub grub, but the surroundings are a bit grungy and the area can be dodgy at night. It's popular with students and middle-aged rockers.

Lai Kung (☎ 041-583 1123; the Boardwalk, Marine Dr, Summerstrand; mains R40-60; 🕒 lunch & dinner) It's undeniably theme-park-ish across a lantern-adorned bridge in the Boardwalk shopping centre, but this is Chinese-run and Chinese-supported, so they must be doing something right. The Sichuan duck (R56) is tops.

34° South (☎ 041-583 1085; the Boardwalk, Marine Dr, Summerstrand; dinner R45-100; 🕒 lunch & dinner) We've heard both very good and very bad things about this place, but what we liked most was the fact that you can pick your own ingredients from the goodies served up at its counter or select fine foods from all around the world on offer in the shop. If you'd prefer to be served, there's a large bistro-style seafood menu and an extensive wine list.

EASTERN CAPE

Up the Khyber (☎ 041-582 2200; Beach Rd; mains R46-64; ☺ lunch & dinner) Next door to Mauro's, this is one of two fairly classy beachfront options within the MacArthur Leisure Centre. Indian food has recently taken a back seat to the usual steaks and burgers, but there are a couple of vegetarian (and one vegan) curries on the menu.

Mauro's (☎ 041-582 2700; Beach Rd; mains R52-79; ☺ lunch & dinner Mon-Sat, lunch Sun) Mauro's is something of an anomaly among the bucket-and-spade kitsch of the beachfront – a Californian-style bistro with very good interior décor and trendy black-clad waiting staff. It's within the MacArthur Leisure Centre complex, and has some outside tables looking over the beach.

Blackbeard's (☎ 041-584 0678; Chapman Hotel, 1 Lady Bea Cres, Brookes Hill, Summerstrand; mains R70-90; ☺ breakfast & dinner) Blackbeard's, and its sister restaurant Piccolo Blackbeard's at Brookes Pavilion, Beach Rd in Humewood, specialise in seafood platters – you can pick the ingredients to create your own platter.

Drinking & Entertainment

Wednesday seems to be the biggest night in the pubs and clubs, although Friday and Saturday are popular as well.

Toby Joe's (☎ 041-584 0082; Brookes Pavilion, Beach Rd, Humewood; ☺ Tue-Sun) Port Elizabeth's current hotspot for the young and student crowd is this cavernous pub, filled to bursting every night with surfer types, glamorous girls and the requisite scowling bouncers. There are live DJs at weekends, karaoke on Thursday, and Sunday deck parties on the wooden terrace. A 'smart casual' dress policy means guys can expect to be turned away if they're wearing flip-flops.

Giovani's (☎ 041-586 3189; Dolphin's Leap Centre) A buzzy, trendy bar-diner with a fairly young crowd but a tad more sophistication than Toby Joe's. There's a big-screen TV, a long cocktail menu, loud music and American diner-style booths to cosy up in. It's busiest after 10pm on Friday.

Dros (☎ 041-585 1021; Brookes Pavilion, Beach Rd, Humewood) Part of the fast-growing South African chain, Dros is a favourite spot to quaff down a beer while watching the rugby. There's a pub grub menu and a good selection of wines, too.

Tapas Al Sol (☎ 041-586 2159; Brookes Pavilion, Beach Rd, Humewood) No tapas here, but live bands play most nights and the Sunday afternoon deck party is legendary.

Navigator Bar (☎ 041-507 7777; the Boardwalk, Marine Dr, Summerstrand) A swanky bar next to the casino, with plenty of chinos and high heels. Cocktails (from R20) are worth a try.

Boardwalk Casino (☎ 041-507 7777; the Boardwalk, Marine Dr, Summerstrand; ☺ 24hr) Try your luck on the slot machines or sample the dubious cabaret, but not before you've stashed your firearm in the special gun cloakroom near the entrance.

Port Elizabeth Opera House (☎ 041-586 3177; White's Rd) Port Elizabeth's opera house is the oldest in South Africa, with a beautiful 19th-century interior. It shows a lively programme of concerts, ballets, plays and jazz recitals – drop into the box office for the latest.

Cinema Starz (☎ 041-583 2000; the Boardwalk, Marine Dr, Summerstrand; admission R20) Shows five screens of blockbusters.

Shopping

Wezandla Gallery & Craft Centre (☎ 041-585 1185; 27 Baakens St) This brightly coloured arts and crafts centre has a good selection of artefacts made by local groups and a small coffee shop. Staff can also help with tourist information.

There's also the Brookes Pavillion, Dolphin's Leap Centre, and Boardwalk shopping malls in Humewood.

Getting There & Away

AIR

SAA (☎ 041-507 1111) has daily flights between Jo'burg (R1300 return), Durban (R1100), Cape Town (R1200) and Port Elizabeth. **SA Airlink** (☎ 0861-359 722) flies daily from Port Elizabeth to East London (around R750), Durban (R900) and Cape Town (R900). **Kulula** (☎ 0861-585 852; www.kulula.com) flies daily to Jo'burg. Return fares start at around R900.

BUS

Greyhound (☎ 041-363 4555; www.greyhound.co.za) buses depart from opposite Checkers at Greenacres Shopping Centre, around 3km from Humewood. Phone a private taxi or take a bus from the city centre – see opposite for details. Reservations can also be made at **Computicket** (☎ 083-915 8000; Greenacres Shopping Centre). **Translux** (☎ 041-392 1333; www.translux.co.za; Ernst & Young Bldg, Greenacres Shopping Centre,

Ring Rd) also operates out of the Greenacres Shopping Centre. **Intercape** (☎ 041-586 0055; www.intercape.co.za) only accepts telephone bookings; the buses depart from the **bus stop** (cnr Fleming & North Union Sts) behind the old post office.

To Cape Town

Translux has a daily bus to and from Cape Town (R180, 12½ hours) via the Garden Route.

Intercape also has two daily Garden Route services linking Cape Town and Port Elizabeth (R270, 12 hours).

Greyhound stops in Port Elizabeth daily on the journey between Durban (R325, 15 hours) and Cape Town (R270, 12 hours).

The **Baz Bus** (☎ 021-439 2323) runs daily from Port Elizabeth to Cape Town (R810 one-way – hop-on, hop-off).

To Johannesburg

Greyhound has nightly buses from Port Elizabeth to Jo'burg (R335, 15 hours) via East London. Translux has daily services from Port Elizabeth to Jo'burg (R350, 14½ hours) via Bloemfontein (R240, 10 hours) and Graaff-Reinet (R315, 11 hours). From February to September, Intercape has daily services from Port Elizabeth to Jo'burg (R310, 15 hours) via Graaff-Reinet (R180, four hours).

To Durban & East London

Translux runs to Durban daily (R280, 15 hours) via Grahamstown (R75, 2½ hours), East London (R125, five hours), Mthatha (R170, nine hours) and Port Shepstone (R240, 13 hours). Greyhound runs to Durban daily (R300, 15 hours). Intercape runs between Port Elizabeth and East London daily (R120, six hours).

The **Baz Bus** (☎ 021-439 2323) runs Monday, Tuesday, Thursday, Friday and Sunday from Port Elizabeth to Durban, and returns on Monday, Wednesday Thursday, Saturday and Sunday; it's R720 for a one-way hop-on, hop-off ticket.

CAR

All the big car-rental operators have offices in Port Elizabeth or at the airport, including **Avis** (☎ 041-581 4291), **Budget** (☎ 041-581 4242) and **Imperial** (☎ 5041-81 1268). Also try **Economic Car Hire** (☎ 041-581 5826; 104 Heugh Rd, Walmer).

MINIBUS TAXI

J-Bay Sunshine Express (☎ 042-293 2221) minibus taxis run between Jeffrey's Bay, Port Elizabeth and other coastal areas.

Most minibus taxis leave from the large townships surrounding Port Elizabeth and can be difficult to find. The **minibus taxi rank** (Strand St), a few blocks north of the bell tower, services the local area.

TRAIN

The **Shosholoza Meyl** (☎ 0860-008 888; www.spoor net.co.za) runs overnight to Jo'burg (1st/2nd class R365/245, 18 hours) via Bloemfontein.

Getting Around

The **airport** (Allister Miller Rd, Walmer) is about 5km from the city centre. You can catch a minibus taxi (R4) from the minibus taxi rank terminus near Port Elizabeth station. This will drop you off on Third St, Walmer, from where the airport is a 10 minute walk. Taxis and hire cars are available at the airport. For a private taxi (around R65), call **Hurter Cabs** (☎ 041-585 5500) or catch one from the taxi rank on Strand St.

For information about bus services, contact **Algoa Bus Company** (☎ 041-404 1200), which runs scheduled central city services departing from the Market Sq bus station on Strand St.

ADDO ELEPHANT NATIONAL PARK

This **national park** (☎ 042-223 0556; www.sanparks .org; adult/child R80/40; ⏱ 7am-7pm) is 72km north of Port Elizabeth, near the Zuurberg Range in the Sundays River Valley. Following a recent expansion, Addo now encompasses around 120,000 hectares of malaria-free wildlife viewing.

The park protects the remnants of the huge elephant herds that once roamed Eastern Cape. When farmers started to develop the area at the beginning of the 20th century, they found themselves in conflict with the elephants. A man named Major Pretorius was commissioned to deal with the 'menace', and until he was stopped by a public outcry, he seemed likely to succeed. When Addo was proclaimed a national park in 1931, there were only 11 elephants left.

Today there are more than 300 elephants in the park, and you'd be unlucky not to see some. A day or two at Addo is a highlight of any visit to this part of the Eastern Cape, not only for the elephants but for the zebras, elands, kudus, warthogs, myriad birds and even lions and hyenas, relatively new introductions to the park.

Information

The park's dirt roads can become impassable in the wet, so the park is closed if there has been heavy rain – if in doubt, call ahead. There is a well-stocked **shop** (☺ 8am-7pm) at the park headquarters, 7km from the village of Addo on Rte 335. It offers food, curios and a respite from the heat, which in midsummer can be intolerable.

The elephants of Addo were once addicted to the oranges and grapefruits fed to them during droughts, and took to mobbing vehicles containing citrus fruit. For this reason, no citrus fruits of any kind are allowed in the park boundaries. Do *not* get out of your car except at designated climbout points, and if you're lucky enough to get close to the elephants, treat them with respect, however docile they may seem.

During the summer it's best to arrive at the park by midmorning and to stake out one of the waterholes where the elephants tend to gather during the heat of the day. In the winter, early mornings are the best time to see animals. For optimum wildlife-spotting, pick up one of the **'hop-on rangers'** (R50) at the gate, who can give you advice on where to go and explain what you're looking at in interesting detail. The park's own **vehicle** (2hr drive per person R150) can also be used for elephant-spotting drives.

Horse trails (2hr ride per person R100) are available twice a day – they go through the Zuurberg section of the park, which doesn't contain the lions.

Sleeping & Eating

Park accommodation can get very booked up at busy periods, so always reserve in advance if possible.

Meals are available at the park's restaurant (mains R30), which is presided over by the stuffed head of the legendary bull, Hapoor. If you've brought your own grub, the rest camp's shady picnic area has a fine view of the waterhole.

Several B&B places have sprung up around the tiny town of Addo, just a few kilometres from the park gate.

Homestead B&B (☎ 042-233 0354; homestead@ webmail.co.za; camp sites R25, backpackers s/d R100/180, B&B s/d 250/500; ☒) Homestead is cheaper than others, and has a few backpackers' rooms and self-catering units, as well as camping, alongside the normal B&B accommodation.

Addo Rest Camp (bookings ☎ 042-223 0556; www .sanparks.org; camp sites/safari tents/forest cabins with shared bathroom R105/260/350, 4-person chalets R390) Addo's main camp site is at the main park headquarters. It's a great spot with a picnic area, and some of the accommodation overlooks a waterhole where elephants come to drink. Various accommodation options are available sleeping anything from two to six people, most of which are very well decorated and excellent value for money. Addo also has a bush camp (one to four people R440) and bungalows (one to four people R120) in the northern section of the park, which have to be booked in their entirety. Inquire at the park headquarters for details.

Chrislin (☎ 042-233 0022; www.africanhuts-addo.co .za; s/d with breakfast R450/700; ☒) This place has friendly owners and very pretty African-style huts on a working citrus farm. A big braai dinner can be provided for R100 per person.

Valley View (☎ 042-233 0349; www.valleyview.co .za; s/d with breakfast R400/500; ☒) This B&B has big, spacious twin and double rooms, full of character, in a 100-year-old farmhouse.

Getting There & Away

The park is signposted from the N2. Alternatively you can travel via Uitenhage on Rte 75; there are attractive citrus farms along the banks of the Sundays River from Uitenhage to Kirkwood.

SHAMWARI GAME RESERVE

Undoubtedly the most high-powered of the Eastern Cape's many private wildlife reserves, **Shamwari** (☎ 042-203 1111; www.shamwari .com; d all inclusive May-Sep R5900, Oct-Apr R9800; ☒ ☐ ☒), 30km east of Addo Elephant National Park, is an internationally renowned reserve dedicated to restocking large tracts of reclaimed land with animals that were common in the region before the advent of the farmers and big-game hunters. All of the Big Five (elephant, rhino, lion, leopard and buffalo) are present, and well-managed wildlife drives mean that you'll have a very good chance of seeing at least four of them during the course of a couple of days' stay.

The **Wilderness Trail** (per person per night R950) is also available in the 3000 hectares of the reserve that have been set aside as an untouched Wilderness Area. Here you have the option of two-night camping trip, or four-night trip with the first and last days' accommodation at the base camp.

Room rates vary from lodge to lodge, and many are discounted by as much as 50% during April, May and June. Rates are all inclusive, but call ahead to check as some discounts apply only to South African residents.

Shamwari's volunteer programme, **African Global Academy** (☎ 046-624 5449; www.african globalacademy.co.za), offers the chance to do hands-on conservation work at the various wildlife reserves in the Eastern Cape.

The reserve can only be reached if you have your own car (and at these prices, you probably will). If you're coming from Port Elizabeth, travel along the N2 towards Grahamstown for about 65km, take the Paterson turnoff (Rte 342), continue for a further 7km, then turn right at the Shamwari sign.

GRAHAMSTOWN
☎ 046 / pop 100,000
Grahamstown is the capital of Settler Country. The town's genteel conservatism and English-style prettiness belie a bloody history. The town centre has some fine examples of Victorian and early Edwardian building styles, with beautiful powder-blue and lemon-yellow shop fronts.

Of course, the British weren't the only people to settle in Grahamstown. Visit the nearby townships for a glimpse into the culture of the Xhosa – once rulers of the region, they were defeated by British and Boer forces after a fierce struggle.

Socially, the students from Rhodes University, who are to be found packing out the pubs and bars during term time, dominate the town. But as established artists settle here and the population ages, a new side of Grahamstown is developing, as evidenced by a sudden breed of beautiful people fraternising a raft of newly opened, trendy restaurants and chic bars.

Information
Go Sure Travel (☎ 046-622 2235; marianl.gbstravel@ galileosa.co.za; Pepper Grove Mall, cnr African & Allen Sts) Handles bookings for all local travel; it is also the agent for most car rental companies and cashes travellers cheques (no commission charged).

Makana Tourism (☎ 046-622 3241; www.grahams town.co.za; 63 High St; ☺ 8.30am-5pm Mon-Fri, 9am-1pm Sat) This office, in a small building next to the Standard Bank, is efficient and friendly. It is an agent for Translux buses and also has Internet access (per hr R30).

Pick 'n Pay centre (African St) A pleasant, open-air place north of the city centre that will handle your banking, telecommunication and grocery needs.

Post office (High St)

Standard Bank (Church Sq)

Sights & Activities
Grahamstown is rightly proud of its museums, four of which are administered by the **Albany Museum Group** (☎ 046-622 4450; www .ru.ac.za/albany-museum). The most interesting is the wonderfully eccentric **Observatory Museum** (Bathurst St; adult/child R8/5; ☺ 9am-1pm & 2-5pm Mon-Fri, 9am-1pm Sat). In this old house you'll find rare Victorian memorabilia, the Meridian Room (which shows that Grahamstown is 14 minutes behind South African time!), and the truly wonderful *camera obscura*. Built in 1882 and the only one of its kind in the world outside the UK, this is a series of lenses, a bit like a periscope, which reflect a perfect panoramic image of the town onto a flat white disc hidden in a tower in the roof. It's like watching a live, high-resolution movie of the city around you.

Also under the Albany aegis is the **Albany History Museum** (Somerset St; admission R5; ☺ 9am-1pm & 2-5pm Mon-Fri, 9am-1pm Sat), which details the history and art of the peoples of the Eastern Cape including the Xhosa and the 1820 settlers. The art exhibitions in its gallery change regularly.

There's also the **National English Literary Museum** (Beaufort St; admission free; ☎ 8.30am-1pm & 2-5pm Mon-Fri), which contains the first editions of just about every work by famous South African writers.

Considerably less exciting, but worth half an hour on a rainy afternoon, is the **Albany Natural Science Museum** (Somerset St; admission R5; ☺ 9am-1pm & 2-5pm Mon-Fri, 9am-1pm Sat), which depicts early human history and has some interesting artefacts, including a traditional Xhosa hut.

EASTERN CAPE

EASTERN CAPE

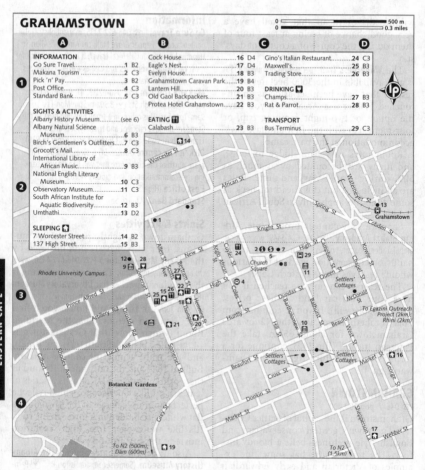

GRAHAMSTOWN

0	500 m
0	0.3 miles

INFORMATION
Go Sure Travel..........................**1** B2
Makana Tourism **2** C3
Pick 'n' Pay.............................**3** B2
Post Office...............................**4** C3
Standard Bank..........................**5** C3

SIGHTS & ACTIVITIES
Albany History Museum............(see 6)
Albany Natural Science
Museum.................................**6** B3
Birch's Gentlemen's Outfitters....**7** C3
Grocott's Mail..........................**8** C3
International Library of
African Music..........................**9** B3
National English Literary
Museum...............................**10** C3
Observatory Museum................**11** C3
South African Institute for
Aquatic Biodiversity..............**12** B3
Umthathi................................**13** D2

SLEEPING
7 Worcester Street....................**14** B2
137 High Street........................**15** B3

Cock House.............................**16** D4
Eagle's Nest............................**17** D4
Evelyn House...........................**18** B3
Grahamstown Caravan Park......**19** B4
Lantern Hill............................**20** B3
Old Gaol Backpackers..............**21** B3
Protea Hotel Grahamstown.......**22** B3

EATING
Calabash................................**23** B3

Gino's Italian Restaurant..........**24** C3
Maxwell's...............................**25** B3
Trading Store...........................**26** B3

DRINKING
Champs..................................**27** B3
Rat & Parrot............................**28** B3

TRANSPORT
Bus Terminus..........................**29** C3

The second coelacanth (a marine fish with limblike pectoral fins) ever caught is exhibited in the **South African Institute for Aquatic Biodiversity** (☎ 046-603 5800; www.jlbsmith .ru.ac.za; Prince Alfred St, Rhodes University; admission free; ⏱ 8am-1pm & 2-5pm Mon-Fri), formerly the more lavishly titled JLB Smith Institute of Ichthyology. Until 1938 this primitive fish was thought to have been extinct.

On the Rhodes University campus is the **International Library of African Music** (ILAM; ☎ 046-603 8557; http://ilam.ru.ac.za; Prince Alfred St, Rhodes University; ⏱ 8.30am-12.45pm & 2-5pm Mon-Fri), a treasure trove of instruments and recordings – call ahead for an appointment. You can examine one of the 200 or so instruments, listen to field recordings and then

try and emulate what you have heard on *nyanga* pipes from Mozambique, a *kora* (stringed instrument) from West Africa or a Ugandan *kalimba* (thumb piano).

The best examples of preserved Victorian and Edwardian storefronts are **Grocott's Mail** (Church Sq), still a working newspaper office, and **Birch's Gentlemen's Outfitters** (Church Sq). The latter still has a marvellously old-fashioned 'slider', a pulley system that sends money and change across the ceiling to and from the central till. Staff will demonstrate if you ask them nicely.

For a taste of local student life, head to the **Dam** up Grey St on the way out of town. It's a place to chill out and have a swim, and on Fridays there are drumming sessions.

The surrounding area offers many outdoor activities including excursions to the Fish River and Addo Elephant National Park, and skydiving. Contact Makana Tourism for more information.

Tours

There are plenty of opportunities to meet local Xhosa in the safe and friendly townships around Grahamstown. **Umthathi** (☎ 046-622 4450; www.umthathi.co.za; Station Bldg, High St), with an office in the old train station building, organises township visits including a traditional Xhosa meal (R50), and visits to a herbal nursery in Rhini township. **Egazini Outreach Project** (☎ 083-428 9424; per group of 1-4 people R300) runs two-hour tours that allow you to relive the battle of Grahamstown through the eyes of young Xhosa historians. There is no office in town; just call.

Alan Weyer, a well-known local historian, conducts the **Spirits of the Past** (☎ 046-622 7896; www.spiritsofthepast.co.za; half-/full-day tours R475/775) tour through the so-called 'Frontier Country' around Grahamstown. Some include a visit to the Valley of the Ancient Voices, a pristine valley filled with rock art, relics and stone-age artefacts and all include a lavish picnic lunch with wine and beer. Again, no office in town, so call Alan directly.

Festivals & Events

Grahamstown bills itself as 'Africa's Festival Capital', with events of various kinds happening several times a year. The biggest is the hugely popular **National Arts Festival** (☎ 046-603 1103; www.nafest.co.za) and its associated Fringe Festival. The Fringe alone has more than 200 events. The festival runs for 10 days at the beginning of July, but re-

---

CITY OF SAINTS?

Grahamstown's nickname is 'City of Saints', an appellation that is generally thought to refer to the town's 40 churches. But another, more interesting theory comes from a message reportedly sent during one of the region's frontier wars. In reply to a requisition for carpentry tools, including a steel vice, the quartermaster wrote, 'We regret no vice in Grahamstown'. The reply from headquarters read: 'Then I believe, sir, you must all be saints'.

---

member two things: check ahead, as accommodation at this time can be booked out a year in advance, and nights can be freezing so bring something warm.

The **National Festival of Science, Engineering & Technology** (☎ 046-603 1106), held in late March, aims to promote 'a culture of science in a festive way', and features interactive exhibits, laser shows and inventors vying for innovation awards.

Growing in popularity is the **Makana Freedom Festival** (☎ 082-932 1304), held in late April. It's a festival of song and dance, with live bands playing in various venues in the townships around Grahamstown.

Sleeping

With more than 100 accommodation options in the area, including a dozen or so in the surrounding townships, we recommend checking in with Makana Tourism for a full list.

BUDGET

Umso Township Homestays (☎ 046-637 1632, 083-245 0496) Mrs Thabisa Xonxa arranges overnight homestays in good standard rooms in Grahamstown's townships. Ask Makana Tourism for more details.

Grahamstown Caravan Park (☎ 046-603 6072; Grey St; camp sites/4-bed rondavels/5-bed chalets R45/120/250) The park is a wooded, hilly spot off the N2, although it's a bit of a walk from the town centre. Bedding is not supplied for the rondavels.

Old Gaol Backpackers (☎ 046-636 1001; Somerset St; dm/s/d with shared bathroom R70/100/170) Built in 1824 and used right up until 1976, this former jail – now a national monument – offers the chance to feel like an inmate, complete with fingerprinting upon registration, a barred door and eerie 19th-century graffiti. The cells are all considerably more comfortable than in their previous incarnation, though you'll probably spend most of your time in the atmospheric bar anyway.

MIDRANGE

Eagle's Nest (☎ 046-622 7189, 082-657 0359; www.grahamstown.co.za/eaglesnest; cnr Webber St & Shepperson Lane; s/d with breakfast R175/340; ☒) This good-value B&B has two studio flats sleeping two to four people, with a kitchenette and an outside terrace.

EASTERN CAPE

Lantern Hill (☎ 046-622 8782; www.lanternhill .co.za; 2 Thompson St; s/d R275/380; ♿) Superbly refurbished recently, this friendly B&B has cosy and comfy wooden-floored rooms with TV and safe. Some of the rooms also have wheelchair ramps and bath rails. Owners Danny and Sterna Biermann speak German.

137 High Street (☎ 046-622 3242; 137highstr@xsinet .co.za; 137 High St; s/d with breakfast R295/470; ✖ 🖳) Well-situated within walking distance of museums and shops, this guesthouse in a charming Georgian cottage also has a private courtyard for functions and a restaurant locals claim makes the best cappuccino in town.

Cock House (☎ 046-636 1287; www.cockhouse.co .za; 10 Market St; s/d with breakfast R390/660) Lest you snigger, this was named after William Cock, one of the 1820 settlers, and was once home to author André Brink. Today it's a National Monument and a hugely popular guesthouse, with chintzy, comfortable rooms in converted stables and a pretty garden. The rustic restaurant (three-course menu R115) is very highly regarded and often booked out.

TOP END

Protea Hotel Grahamstown (☎ 046-622 2324; www .albanyhotels.co.za; 123 High St; s/d with breakfast R470/ 590; 🍸) This hotel, in a characterless building in the centre of town, has modern but tasteful and fairly luxurious rooms with TV. There's a bar and a carvery.

7 Worcester Street (☎ 046-622 2843; www.wor cesterstreet.co.za; 7 Worcester St; s/d with breakfast R550/ 1100; ✖ 🍸) This luxurious guesthouse is filled with sumptuous period furniture and priceless artworks. The house was built in 1888 and once served as a student hostel – these days it provides accommodation to parents visiting their little darlings at Grahamstown's private boarding schools. Three-course dinner is available for R120.

Evelyn House (☎ 046-622 2324; www.albanyhotels .co.za; High St; s/d with breakfast R560/770; 🍸) An annexe of the Protea Hotel Grahamstown and just across the road, this is quieter and more upmarket, with a small pool of its own.

Eating & Drinking

Grahamstown's eating out scene and nightlife is now starkly divided between places serving the trendy and/or affluent, a plethora of pubs and fast-food joints dotted around the town centre for students drinking hard and eating cheap, and swanky eateries for when their wealthy foreign parents come to town to check up on them.

Trading Store (☎ 046-622 9987; 131 High St; mains R35; 🕙 breakfast & lunch Mon-Sun, dinner Wed, Fri & Sat) If any evidence were needed that Grahamstown is evolving, this is it: a supremely stylish New York–style café that's causing controversy among some city stalwarts seemingly threatened by its very existence. Garish floral wallpaper, bistro food (try the warm pear and chick pea salad, R30), 1970s chic, live jazz and an outdoor cocktail bar

---

A(NOTHER) GREEN AND PLEASANT LAND

In 1820 British settlers, duped by their government into believing they were going to a peaceful land of plenty, arrived at Algoa Bay. In reality, they were arriving in a heavily contested border region, where Boers on one side of the Great Fish River and Xhosa on the other battled interminably over the cattle-rich country known as the Zuurveld.

Grahamstown was at the centre of the maelstrom. In 1819, in the Fifth Frontier War, 9000 Xhosa under the leader Makana attacked Grahamstown and very nearly defeated the garrison. The story goes that Makana would have succeeded had he not observed the Xhosa war code and given free passage to a woman who carried a hidden keg of gunpowder to the defenders.

It was not long before the thousand immigrant families found farming untenable. The odds were stacked against them: inexperience, hostile neighbours, labour shortages, floods, droughts and crop diseases all played a role.

By 1823 nearly half the settlers had retreated to the towns to pursue the trades and businesses they had followed in England. Grahamstown developed into a trading and manufacturing centre, where axes, knives and blankets were exchanged for ivory and skins. Tradespeople among the settlers produced metal implements, wagons and clothes. Port Elizabeth and Port Alfred initially developed to service what had quickly become the second-largest city in the Cape Colony.

combine to great effect in this historical building.

Maxwell's (☎ 046-622 5119; cnr Somerset St & High St; mains R70-110; ☽ lunch & dinner Tue-Sun) Offering excellent service and hearty lunches of self-styled 'colonialised' food, Maxwell's is gaining a reputation as the perfect place to avoid returning to work on a Friday afternoon, which means booking on weekend nights is a must.

Calabash (☎ 046-622 2366; 123 High St; mains R50-70; ☽ breakfast, lunch & dinner) Calabash offers traditional South African food in a warm, reed-ceilinged dining room. Xhosa hotpots and *pap en wors* (maize meal and sausage) are a speciality, and there are some spicy veggie options even meat-lovers would like. Still, the menu does offer the standard breaded calamari/T-bone steak fare as well.

Gino's Italian Restaurant (☎ 046-622 7208; 8 New St; mains R25-35; ☽ lunch & dinner) Grahamstown's most popular student restaurant is a very average pizza and pasta joint with an attached bar. The thick dough pizza special on Mondays wins undiscerning local plaudits. Entrance via Hill St.

Rat & Parrot (☎ 046-622 5002; 59 New St; mains R20-30; ☽ lunch & dinner) A pseudo-British drinking den and another popular student haunt, with surprisingly decent pub grub, loud music, a big-screen TV and a beer garden. It's closed on Sundays out of term time.

Champs (Scotts Ave) A laddish sports bar with pool tables and, later on, plenty of beer goggles.

Getting There & Away

Buses depart from the **terminus** (cnr High & Bathurst Sts). The **Bee Bus** (☎ 082-652 0798) runs to Port Elizabeth and Port Alfred from Sunday to Friday, and **Mini Lux** (☎ 043-741 3107) runs to East London and Port Elizabeth from Sunday to Friday. Check with the tourist office for prices and times.

Intercape (☎ 046-622 2235; www.intercape.co.za) stops in Grahamstown on its daily run between Cape Town (R240, nine hours) and East London (R110, 2½ hours).

Translux (☎ 046-622 3241; www.translux.co.za) buses stop at the bus terminus on the daily run between Cape Town (R230, 15 hours), Port Elizabeth (R75, two hours) and Durban (R280, 12 hours), via East London and Mthatha.

Greyhound (☎ 046-622 2235; www.greyhound.co.za) buses also stop at the terminus on their way to Durban (R270, 13 hours) and Port Elizabeth (R70, two hours).

You'll find minibus taxis on Raglan St, but most leave from Rhini township. Destinations include Fort Beaufort (R25, two hours), King William's Town (R35, three hours), Port Elizabeth (R35, 2½ hours) and East London (R35, four hours).

BATHURST
☎ 046

From the thick vegetation along the road between Port Alfred and Grahamstown, this charming but scattered village of narrow lanes and neat hedges seems to appear out of nowhere. It's a famous Eastern Cape drinking spot, particularly during the annual December **Ox Braai**, a huge party that takes place around New Year's Eve every year. Open-air drinking and the barbecuing of vast quantities of meat are the main activities.

Near the turn-off to Bathurst (look for the Protea Hotel sign) is **Summerhill Farm** (☎ 046-625 0833; off Rte 67; tours adult/child R30/15; ☽ 9am-5pm Mon-Fri), which has the dubious honour of being home to the world's biggest pineapple – a rip-off of the Big Pineapple on the Sunshine Coast in Queensland, Australia. Standing 16.7m high, it is a mere 70cm taller than the original (and no, it's not real). There's also a reconstructed Xhosa village where you can buy handicrafts; meals are available from the Protea Hotel restaurant. Tours in a tractor include pineapple tasting and take place at 10am, noon and 3pm daily.

Watersmeeting Nature Reserve (☎ 046-425 0876; admission per vehicle R10, plus per person R5; ☽ 7am-5pm), just outside town, protects the start of the Kowie River, where fresh and tidal waters meet. There's bird-watching in the forests here, plus a nice view of the horseshoe bend in the river. The road down to the river is steep and shouldn't be attempted after rain.

A good budget sleep option in town is the recently refurbished **Bathurst Arms 1820 Tavern** (☎ 046-625 0738; High St; dm R60), which offers clean, no-nonsense board and lodging above an English-style pub. This is the only place to get a meal after 9pm.

The **Pig & Whistle Hotel** (☎ 6046-25 0673; Kowie Rd; s/d R350/550; ☽ lunch & dinner) could be in England, which is not at all surprising considering it was built in 1832 in the centre of Settler Country and claims to be the country's oldest pub. It's a popular stopping point on the Port Alfred–Grahamstown road for good-value lunches and Thai food on Friday and Saturday evening. It can also help out with information about canoe and hiking trails in the area. Try to get a room in the main house if you're staying – they have much more character than the newer ones in the garden.

PORT ALFRED

☎ 046 / pop 32,500

Port Alfred is an odd little place that's one part unkempt seaside town and the other part upmarket holiday resort, making it at once an exemplar of the province's lack of funds and an island of style and serenity. Which face it wears depends largely on the season: off-peak it's staid and quiet except on weekends, when students from Grahamstown come to lounge on the beach and drink in the pubs. In season (mid-December to January) the place bustles with life as people arrive from other parts of the province to soak up the holiday atmosphere, and prices surge.

Information

Palms Video (☎ 046-624 2182; Heritage Mall, Main St; per min R0.50; ☽ 9am-8pm) Internet access.
Tourism Port Alfred (☎ 046-624 1235; www.port alfred.net; Causeway Rd; ☽ 8am-4.30pm Mon-Fri, 8.30am-noon Sat) This office near the municipal offices on the western bank of the Kowie River has brochures detailing accommodation, walks and canoe trails.

Activities

Lovers of **horse riding** frequent the Port Alfred area. If you're into equestrian endeavours, contact **Fish River Horse Safaris** (☎ 046-675 1271; www.fishriverhorsesafaris.co.za; 2½ hr trails R180, 5hr trails R500), which offers daily horse rides on the beach or through bushland. Experienced riders can do the longer ride, which covers both terrains.

For **surfers**, there are good right- and left-hand breaks at the river mouth; for golfers, there is the beautiful **Royal Port Alfred Golf Course** (☎ 046-624 4796; St Andrews Rd; 18-hole round R200), one of the four 'Royals' in South Africa. There's also an 8km **walking trail** through the Kowie Nature Reserve –

maps (R6.50) are available from the tourist office. For the fit, **Rufanes River Trails** (☎ 041-624 1469) has mountain bike trails.

The two-day **Kowie Canoe Trail** (☎ 041-624 2230; per person R80) is a fairly easy 18km canoe trip upriver from Port Alfred, with an overnight stay in a hut at Horseshoe Bend Nature Reserve. Mattresses, water and wood are provided, but you'll need your own food and bedding.

Keryn's Dive School & Maximum Exposure (☎ 046-624 4432; keryn@compushop.co.za; NAUI scuba-diving course R1485, advanced diver course R1100) offers diving courses and various other adventure activities. Diving is between May and August. Visibility is not outstanding (5m to 8m) but there are plenty of big fish, soft corals and raggy sharks. The same company rents out sandboards (per two hours R50) and canoes with a map of the river route (per half day R70). Waterskiing costs R320 per hour per boat (three people). Keryn's is located in the small boat harbour of the Royal Alfred Marina.

Sleeping

Tourism Port Alfred lists the town's numerous B&Bs. Given the town's drastically different tourist seasons, most places bump their rates up during the busier times of the year, which are December to January and over Easter.

BUDGET

Willows Caravan Park (☎ /fax 046-624 5201; off Albany Rd; camp sites low/high season R30/100) Next to the river, the Willows has powered camp sites and an elderly clientele.

Station Backpackers (☎ 046-624 5869; off Pascoe Cres; dm/d R70/180) More care seems to have been placed in the adjoining sports bar than in the hostel, housed in the town's old train station. The result is you'll probably spend more time there than in the hostel's dark, musty rooms and grotty kitchen.

Medolino Caravan Park (☎ 046-624 1651; www .caravanparks.co.za/medolino; 23 Stewart Rd; camp sites R100, 2-/4-bedroom chalets R320/425) This park, in town off Princes Ave, is near both Kowie River and Kelly's Beach. The chalet rates double in high season.

Bretton Beach Crest (☎ 046-624 1606; www.brett onbeach.co.za; Freshwater Rd; self-catering cottages from R235) A charming collection of self-contained beach cottages 3km from the Kowie River mouth with wonderful sea views and neat rooms 100m from the beach. Prices rise sharply in high season.

MIDRANGE

Residency (☎ 046-624 5382; www.theresidency.co.za; 11 Vroom Rd; s/d with breakfast R260/460) The Residency is a gracious B&B in a magnificently restored Victorian house built in 1898. Its lovely rooms have freestanding enamel baths, wooden walls and sprigged cotton bedspreads. A big breakfast is served on the wide veranda every morning. Rates go up in high season.

Villa de Mer (☎ 046-624 2315; www.villademer.co .za; 22 West Beach Dr; s/d with breakfast from R295/590; 🐾 🗷) A large, bright, ultramodern four-star B&B right on the beachfront. All of the smart rooms have their own fridge.

Royal St Andrews Lodge (☎ 046-624 1379; www .compushop.co.za/standrew; 19 St Andrews Rd; s/d with breakfast R320/550; 🐾 🗷) This old-fashioned, mock-Scottish pub and inn opposite the golf course has some quaint Victorian-style rooms in the original building, plus more modern self-catering units in the garden.

Its restaurant, Highlander (p264), rates a mention.

Halyards Hotel (☎ 046-604 3300; www.riverhotels .co.za; Royal Alfred Marina, Albany Rd; s/d with breakfast R515/655; 🐾 🗷 🕭) This comfy waterfront hotel with attractive Cape Cod–style architecture has large well-equipped rooms overlooking the harbour. The interior is light and airy, with wicker furniture and black-and-white tiled floors.

Eating & Drinking

Butler's (☎ 046-624 3464; 25 Van der Riet St; mains R45-95; 🕑 lunch & dinner Wed-Mon) As one of the country's best restaurants, it's no surprise Butler's is Port Alfred's top dining experience. The imaginative, oft-changing menu always features a terrific fish and seafood selection (including the legendary Kowie African Dream, fish grilled in fruit sauce), but the food-loving chefs will whip up practically any dish you desire.

Guido's Restaurant (☎ 046-624 5264; West Beach Dr; mains R20-45; 🕑 lunch & dinner) Guido's is a trendy pizza-and-pasta restaurant on the beach. It has got slow service but a lively

EASTERN CAPE

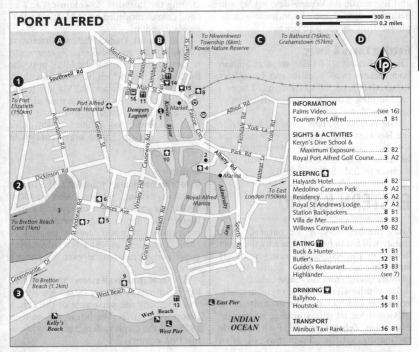

PORT ALFRED

0 ___ 300 m
0 ___ 0.2 miles

To Nkwenkwezi Township (6km); Kowie Nature Reserve

To Bathurst (16km); Grahamstown (57km)

Southwell Rd

To Port Elizabeth (150km)

Port Alfred General Hospital

Dempers Lagoon

Kowie River

Market

Pascoe Cres

Alfred Rd

Ferndale Rd

York La

York Rd

Park Rd

Albany Rd

Marina

Haldsact La

To East London (150km)

Dickinson Rd

Atherstone Rd

George Rd

Causeway Rd

Wesley Hill

Princes Ave

Muller Dr

St Andrews Rd

Grand St

Beach Rd

Royal Alfred Marina

Admiralty Way

Sports Rd

To Bretton Beach Crest (1km)

Greenmantle Dr

To Bretton Beach (1.2km)

West Beach Dr

Kelly's Beach

West Beach

West Pier

East Pier

INDIAN OCEAN

INFORMATION	
Palms Video	(see 16)
Tourism Port Alfred	1 B1

SIGHTS & ACTIVITIES	
Keryn's Dive School & Maximum Exposure	2 B2
Royal Port Alfred Golf Course	3 A2

SLEEPING 🛏	
Halyards Hotel	4 B2
Medolino Caravan Park	5 A2
Residency	6 A2
Royal St Andrews Lodge	7 A2
Station Backpackers	8 B1
Villa de Mer	9 B2
Willows Caravan Park	10 B2

EATING 🍴	
Buck & Hunter	11 B1
Butler's	12 B1
Guido's Restaurant	13 B3
Highlander	(see 7)

DRINKING 🍷	
Ballyhoo	14 B1
Houtstok	15 B1

TRANSPORT	
Minibus Taxi Rank	16 B1

ambience, especially on Saturday and Sunday when it fills up with students visiting from Grahamstown.

Buck & Hunter (☎ 046-624 5960; Main St; mains R35-55; ☺ lunch & dinner, closed Sun Feb-Nov except Easter) The Buck & Hunter is a down-to-earth pub-restaurant serving game dishes such as kudu and ostrich to a macho clientele. It also offers no fewer than 35 pizzas, including six vegetarian options.

Highlander (☎ 046-624 1379; 19 St Andrews Rd; mains R40-65; ☺ lunch & dinner) The pub-restaurant at the Royal St Andrews Lodge has a cosy, British feel to it and serves good-quality food, including an excellent king prawn platter. There's live music on Thursday and Saturday nights.

Houtstok (☎ 073-143 7541; cnr Wharf & Main Sts) Its name is Afrikaans for 'Woodstock', but this is no hippy refuge. Upon entry, you are welcomed by one-armed bandits, a chalkboard declaring current unpaid bar tabs and a price list that promises drinking well into the night.

Ballyhoo (☎ 046-624 9062; 33 Van der Riet St) With outdoor seating by the Kowie River and live music on Wednesday, Friday and Saturday, this is one of the more atmospheric drinking spots in town.

Getting There & Away

The **Baz Bus** (☎ 021-439 2323) stops at Station Backpackers (p262) on its run from Port Elizabeth (1½ hours) to Durban (12 hours) on Monday, Tuesday, Wednesday, Friday and Saturday.

The **minibus taxi rank** (Biscay Rd) is outside the Heritage Mall. There are daily services to Port Elizabeth (R50), Grahamstown (R22) and East London (R65). Local daily services include Bathurst (R9).

EASTERN KAROO

Only the heartless or the naturally very thirsty will fail to be bewitched by the quiet beauty of the Karoo, the vast semidesert stretching across the great South African plateau inland from the Cape coast.

Its southeastern extension is in Eastern Cape and includes the exquisite town of Graaff-Reinet, the stunning scenery of Mountain Zebra National Park and the fascinating artistic community of Nieu Bethesda. It's one of the region's most intriguing areas, with an overwhelming sense of space and peace that stands in sharp contrast to the cheery, sometimes overdeveloped coastline.

Between December and February, temperatures in Karoo towns can reach 45°C, and things barely cool down in March and April. June and July see the thermometer plummet to -5°C, with snow in the mountain passes and hard frosts. September to November are the best times to visit if you want to experience a moderate climate.

See p227 for more information about the central section of the Karoo, and p525 for more about the northern sections of the Karoo.

CRADOCK
☎ 048 / pop 40,000

A busy agricultural and commercial centre for the farming district along the Great Fish River, Cradock, established as a military outpost in 1813, appears rather shabby at first. But a closer look will reveal its fine collection of beautiful old buildings including the *tuishuise* (townhouses) and an 1867 church modelled on St Martin-in-the-Fields, London.

The helpful **Cradock Publicity Association** (☎ 048-881 2383; www.cradock.co.za; Stockenstroom St) is located in the town hall building opposite the Spar Centre, which has an ABSA Bank ATM. Other banks and ATMs are found mainly on Adderley St. At the time of writing, all Internet cafés in town had gone out of business. Ask at the tourism office if anyone has since been brave enough to open another.

Sights

Olive Schreiner House (☎ 048-881 5251; 9 Cross St; admission by donation; ☺ 8.30am-12.45pm & 2-4.30pm Mon-Fri) is a good example of a typical Karoo house. Shreiner is best remembered for her provocative novel *Story of an African Farm*, published in 1883 but advocating views considered radical even by today's standards.

The **Great Fish River Museum** (☎ 048-881 4509; High St; admission by donation; ☺ 8am-4pm Mon-Fri) was originally the parsonage of the Dutch Reformed Church. The house was built in 1825 and the displays depict pioneer life in the 19th century.

Sleeping

Aureyana B&B (☎ 048-881 3853; 59 Sprigg St; s/d with breakfast R140/280) Cradock's most inexpensive B&B offers a warm welcome and big, clean rooms, some with TV. We've received good reader feedback on this place, too.

Victoria Manor (☎ 048-881 1650; cnr Market & Voortrekker Sts; s/d R220/400) This very elegant 1840s inn feels like a Victorian museum, with heavy furniture and atmospheric wood-panelled rooms. Breakfast costs R45. Cheaper rooms in the annexe (single/double R120/220) are also available.

Heritage House B&B (☎ /fax 048-881 3210; 45 Bree St; s/d with breakfast R220/350; 🖳) The homely Heritage House offers comfortable, rustic rooms and old-fashioned hospitality. Try to get the cottage in the pleasant garden, where you'll meet several zany dogs and a playful springbok named Bendy.

Tuishuise Guesthouses (☎ 048-881 1322; www.tuishuise.co.za; 36 Market St; cottages with breakfast per person R300) In one of Cradock's old streets, 18 cottages have been beautifully restored. The cottages have various numbers of bedrooms, but all have a sitting room with fireplace, self-catering kitchen and garden. There are also smaller and more modest one-bedroom garden cottages (R90 per person). Breakfast is served at Victoria Manor.

Eating & Drinking

Cradock eating tends towards fast food, so eating at your accommodation might be best. Following are some alternatives.

Buffalo Dan's (☎ 048-881 4321; Engen petrol station, Rte 61; mains R35; 🕒 dinner Mon-Fri, lunch Sat) It has a strange name and an even stranger location (next to a petrol station) but locals swear this modest steakhouse is Cradock's best restaurant. It's found on the way out of town towards Mountain Zebra National Park.

Kaffee en Kie (☎ 048-881 3779; Stockenstroom St; 🕒 breakfast & lunch Mon-Sat) This café serves up delicious breakfasts and a solid cup of coffee.

Schreiner Tea Room (☎ 072-381 3422; 49 Market St; 🕒 breakfast & lunch Mon-Fri, breakfast Sat) Just about the only other coffee fix in town, this charming spot near the *tuishuise* is a good place to escape the heat after checking out the local architecture.

Sportsman's Bar (☎ 048-881 2431; cnr Stockenstroom & Durban Sts) A great place to drink up the atmosphere with some of the more eccentric locals.

Getting There & Away

Translux (www.translux.co.za) runs daily to Cape Town (R225, 10 hours) via Graaff-Reinet (R100, two hours).

The **Shosholoza Meyl** (☎ 0860-008 888) train stops here en route between Port Elizabeth (six-/four-bed sleeper R90/115, 4½ hours) and Jo'burg (six-/four-bed sleeper R210/295, 16 hours).

Most minibus taxis leave from the nearby township; ask at the petrol stations in town.

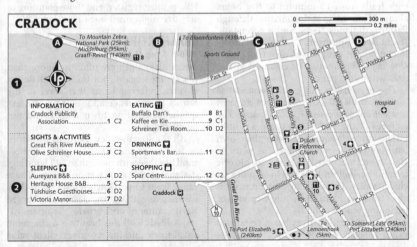

MOUNTAIN ZEBRA NATIONAL PARK

This **national park** (☎ 048-881 2427; adult/child R60/30; ☻ 7am-7pm Oct-Apr, 7am-6pm May-Sep), 26km west of Cradock, is on the northern slopes of the Bankberg Range (2000m) and has superb views over the Karoo. The park protects one of the rarest animals in the world: the mountain zebra *(Equus zebra)*. Mountain zebras are distinguished from other zebra species by their small stature, reddish-brown nose and dewlap (a loose fold of skin hanging beneath the throat).

Among the silence and wide-open spaces, thick patches of sweet thorn and wild olive are interspersed with rolling grasslands and succulents. The park also supports many antelope species. The largest predator is the caracal, and there are several species of small cats, genets, bat-eared foxes and black-backed jackals. Some 200 bird species have been recorded. The entrance gate is well signposted off Rte 61. It's quite feasible to get a taste of the park in a half-day excursion from Cradock. You'll find a shop and restaurant in the main camp. The park runs guided three-night **trails** within the park on Monday and Thursday only – four people are needed for the trail to run, and no children under 12 are accepted. There's also a guided four-hour trail (R50). Various self-guided trails are also possible – ask at parks reception for details. A sunset guided **wildlife drive** costs R100 per adult.

The park, largely comprised of unsealed roads, is also famed for its **mountain biking**, with trails from 15 minutes to five hours along 37km of gravel coursing through Eastern Midlands Nama Karoo vegetation. If you're coming from Cradock or Graaff-Reinet, ask at your hostel about bike hire. **Abseiling** (R200) can also be arranged at two sites within the park.

The park has a range of **accommodation** (bookings ☎ 048-881 2427; camp sites/4-bed family cottages/6-bed guesthouses R75/350/650; ☒). The cottages at the park's rest camp are utilitarian but well-equipped, with their own bathrooms. The most interesting place to stay is at Doornhoek, a restored historic farmhouse, built in 1836 and hidden in a secluded valley. There is a 10% discount available from early June to mid-September, excluding school holidays.

The park headquarters has a restaurant called **Jabulani** (mains R40), with a decent se-

lection of pasta, salad, steaks and burgers. There's no public transport to the park so the only option is to bring your own car. One of the tour agencies in Graaff-Reinet (see p268) should be able to organise a day trip.

SOMERSET EAST

☎ 042 / pop 20,000

This attractive old town at the foot of the Bosberg Range (1600m) is sometimes referred to as the 'oasis of the Karoo', since the surrounding mountains mean that it receives a soaking 600mm of rainfall annually. After the dry country to the north and south, the rich forest on the mountain slopes is a surprise. There's no public transport to Somerset East, so you'll most likely only visit if you're passing in your own car and need a refresher.

The **Somerset East Tourist Office** (☎ 042-243 1333; Nojoli St; www.somerseteast.co.za; ☻ 7.45am-1pm & 1.45-4.30pm Mon-Fri) can help with local information.

Thirty-three kilometres from Somerset East is **Bosberg Nature Reserve**, covering 2000 hectares of thickly wooded ravines, dense grassland and Karoo shrubs. Most prominent of the larger animal species are mountain zebras and bushbucks. More than 83 bird species have been identified. There are several hiking trails in the park, including the circular 15km-long **Bosberg Hiking Trail** (bookings ☎ 042-243 1333; per person R35), which has a 10-bed rest hut with toilet facilities. Hikers must register, and those planning to stay overnight must book in advance.

GRAAFF-REINET

☎ 049 / pop 43,300

Town nicknames are often no more than marketing slogans, but that Graaff-Reinet is often referred to as the 'jewel of the Karoo' is no exaggeration – it's a safe, exquisite, fascinating town that should not be missed.

It's the fourth-oldest European town in South Africa, and it has a superb architectural heritage with more than 220 buildings designated as national monuments. These range from Cape Dutch houses, with their distinctive gables, to classic flat-roofed Karoo cottages and ornate Victorian villas. Added to all this beauty is a charming small-town quirkiness, some excellent-value accommodation and a variety of eccentric local characters who add to the benignly surreal feel of the whole place.

The wild and beautiful Karoo Nature Reserve is within walking distance of Graaff-Reinet.

History

The interior of the Cape in the 18th century was a wild and dangerous place, with Boers clashing frequently with the Khoesaan in the Sneeuberg and the Xhosa to the east around the Great Fish River. The settlement, named after former provincial Governor van der Graaff and his wife Reinet, became an outpost in a harsh countryside and was the fourth district in the Cape Colony to be granted a Drostdy, or seat of local government. This came about through an attempt by the British to establish a bit of law and order. The idea failed and the town's citizens promptly threw out the Landdrost (magistrate) and established an independent republic. The British regained a semblance of control soon afterwards, but were constantly harried by both disgruntled

Boers and a joint force of Khoesaan and Xhosa warriors.

In the early to mid-19th century, Boers seeking to escape the control of the Cape Town administration began their legendary Great Trek, and Graaff-Reinet became an important stepping stone for Voortrekkers heading north.

Orientation & Information

Graaff-Reinet is built in a cleft in the magnificent Sneeuberg Range on a bend of the Sundays River. The centre of town is compact and safe, so getting around on foot is not only possible but also highly recommended.

ABSA bank (Church St) Near the Dutch Reformed Church.

Graaff-Reinet Publicity Association (☎ 049-892 4248; www.graaffreinet.co.za; Church St; ☼ 8am-5pm Mon-Fri, 9am-noon Sat & Sun) This helpful office has an abundance of maps and information about accommodation in the area.

Karoo Connections (☎ 049-892 3978; www.karoo tours.co.za; Church St) Internet access next to the publicity association.

Standard Bank (Caledon St)

EASTERN CAPE

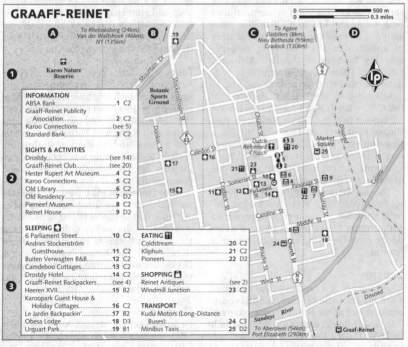

GRAAFF-REINET

0   500 m
0   0.3 miles

To Rheboksberg (24km);
Van der Waltshoek (46km);
N1 (135km)

To Agave
Distillers (8km);
Nieu Bethesda (55km);
Cradock (130km)

Karoo Nature Reserve

Botanic Sports Ground

INFORMATION	
ABSA Bank	1 C2
Graaff-Reinet Publicity Association	2 C2
Karoo Connections	(see 5)
Standard Bank	3 C2

SIGHTS & ACTIVITIES	
Drostdy	(see 14)
Graaff-Reinet Club	(see 20)
Hester Rupert Art Museum	4 C2
Karoo Connections	5 C2
Old Library	6 C2
Old Residency	7 D2
Pierneef Museum	8 C2
Reinet House	9 D2

SLEEPING	
6 Parliament Street	10 C2
Andries Stockenström Guesthouse	11 C2
Buiten Verwagten B&B	12 C2
Camdeboo Cottages	13 C2
Drostdy Hotel	14 C2
Graaff-Reinet Backpackers	(see 4)
Heeren XVII	15 B2
Karoopark Guest House & Holiday Cottages	16 C2
Le Jardin Backpackin'	17 B2
Obesa Lodge	18 D3
Urquart Park	19 B1

EATING	
Coldstream	20 C2
Kliphuis	21 C2
Pioneers	22 D2

SHOPPING	
Reinet Antiques	(see 2)
Windmill Junction	23 C2

TRANSPORT	
Kudu Motors (Long-Distance Buses)	24 C3
Minibus Taxis	25 D2

Mountain Dr

Stockenstroom St

Donkin St

Caledon St

Dutch Reformed Church

Market Square

Somerset St

Parliament St

Caroline St

Middle St

Bourke St

Church St

Murray St

Parsonage St

Cypress Ave

West St

Sundays River

To Aberdeen (54km);
Port Elizabeth (290km)

Graaf-Reinet

Sights

MUSEUMS

You can buy a combined **pass** (☎ 049-892 3801; pass R16) that gives access to any four of the town's museums. It's not valid on Sunday.

The **Hester Rupert Art Museum** (☎ 049-892 2121; Church St; adult/child R5/3; ☺ 9am-12.30pm & 2-5pm Mon-Fri, 9am-noon Sat & Sun) was originally a Dutch Reformed Mission church, consecrated in 1821. The beautiful interior space and permanent collection of paintings and sculptures are refreshingly contemporary after all the Victoriana at the town's other museums.

Pierneef Museum (☎ 049-892 6107; Middle St; admission free; ☺ 9am-12.30pm & 2-5pm Mon-Fri) is another very interesting contemporary art museum housing a set of panels by South African artist Jacob Hendrik Pierneef. Among the almost Japanese-looking paintings is one stunning rendition of the Valley of Desolation near Graaff-Reinet.

The **Old Library** (☎ 049-892 3801; cnr Church & Somerset Sts; adult/child R5/4; ☺ 8am-12.30pm & 2-5pm Mon-Fri, 9am-3pm Sat, 9am-4pm Sun) houses a collection of historical clothing, rock paintings and fossils from the Karoo (including some nasty-looking skulls of 'mammal-like, flesh-eating reptiles' from 230 million years ago) and an exhibition telling the life story of Robert Mangaliso Sobukwe, the pipe-smoking founder of the Pan Africanist Congress. There's also the impressive William Roe photographic collection.

Reinet House (☎ 049-892 3801; Murray St; adult/child R7/2; ☺ 8am-12.30pm & 2-5pm Mon-Fri, 9am-3pm Sat, 9am-4pm Sun), the Dutch Reformed parsonage built between 1806 and 1812, is a beautiful example of Cape Dutch architecture. The cobblestone rear courtyard has a grapevine planted in 1870 that is now one of the largest in the world.

The **Old Residency** (☎ 049-892 3801; Parsonage St; adult/child R5/2; ☺ 8am-noon & 2-5pm Mon-Fri, 9am-noon Sat) is another well-preserved 19th-century house with creaking wooden floors, now displaying a large collection of firearms.

DROSTDY

The residence of a Landdrost was known as a *drostdy* and included his office and courtroom as well as his family's living quarters. The Graaff-Reinet **drostdy** (Church St) was built in 1806. Have a look at the old slave bell, which was restored and then, in an awful piece of irony, unveiled by apartheid-era prime minister BJ Vorster. The *drostdy* is now a hotel (see opposite).

GRAAFF-REINET CLUB

For something a little different, go along to the **Graaff-Reinet Club** (Church St). This one-time 'men's only' club, the second oldest in South Africa, has walls and halls adorned with numerous hunting trophies, including a giant pair of elephant feet that, unbelievably, someone saw fit to turn into wine coolers! Terrence and Nita Gush from Le Jardin Backpackin' (see opposite) can get you an invitation.

AGAVE DISTILLERS

Some 8km north of town just off the N9 to Middelburg you'll notice an imposing building resembling a military facility, dotted with cactuslike *garingbome*. It is in fact the world's only **agave spirit distillery** (☎ 049-891 8145; Middelburg Rd; tasting tours R20) outside of Mexico, open by appointment only. While the drink produced cannot legally be called tequila, it's identical to that famous drink and, unlike most tequilas, which contain cane spirit, the 100 per cent agave drink produced here is so pure you can actually sip it. Bottles (R70 to R85) can be purchased onsite.

Tours

Several readers have recommended the tours offered by Xolile Speelman, a lifelong township resident and owner of **Irhafu Tours** (☎ 082-844 2890). A three-hour township tour giving an insight into both Xhosa culture and history and modern township life costs R75. Xolile, who was brought up in the area, can also organise homestays and group meals.

Karoo Connections (☎ 049-892 3978; www.karoo tours.co.za; Church St) operates tours to the Valley of Desolation at sunset (R180; sundowners on request – the preferred drop is gin and tonic), Nieu Bethesda and the Owl House (R225) and the Karoo Nature Reserve (R145). It can also arrange township walks, wildlife drives, microlighting, nature walks and city tours.

Sleeping

Graaff-Reinet is blessed with an overwhelming range of accommodation, most of it seriously good value compared to other towns in the Eastern Cape. The Publicity Association can help with bookings.

BUDGET

Graaff-Reinet Backpackers (☎ 049-892 5334; cnr Church & Parsonage Sts; dm R85, d/tr/q with shared bathroom R200/270/340; 🖳) This newer backpackers benefits from its location but is still second best in the budget stakes thanks to its relative inexperience and subdued atmosphere. The latter is helped by the fact that it is in the historical 'Colonial Trust Corporation' building, and rooms are airy and bright.

Le Jardin Backpackin' (☎ 049-892 5890, 082-644 4938; cnr Donkin & Caledon Sts; s/d with shared bathroom R90/180; 😂) A firm favourite with weary backpackers in need of a bit of pampering, Le Jardin provides homely rooms and a large garden for excellent prices. Hosts Terrence and Nita Gush go out of their way to make their guests welcome and are both mines of information about the area's attractions. Booking is highly advisable.

MIDRANGE

Urquart Park (☎ /fax 049-892 2136; Stockenstroom St; camp sites/rondavels/bungalows/chalets R50/100/120/300) To the north of town near the Van Ryneveld Dam, Urquart has pretty views towards the Karoo National Park. The good-quality chalets have their own kitchens.

Obesa Lodge (☎ 082-588 5900; www.graaffreinet .co.za; 64 Murray St; s/d without breakfast R140/230, 2-bedroom cottages R350; 😂 😂) Something very different from Graaff-Reinet's olde-worlde accommodation options – Obesa is a whole street of psychedelically coloured cottages with names like Moody Blues and Bad Mama. All are cheerfully designed and have self-catering and braai facilities. Opposite the lodge is the owner's Cactus Garden, which features an enormous collection of cacti and succulents from all over the world. Some reportedly have hallucinogenic qualities.

Karoopark Guest House & Holiday Cottages (☎ 049-892 2557; www.karoopark.co.za; 81 Caledon St; s/d R180/250; 😂) The friendly Karoopark has adequate self-contained cottages as well as comfortable but *very* chintzy rooms in its guesthouse. There's an à la carte restaurant for dinner, and breakfast is R40.

6 Parliament Street (☎ 049-892 6059; 6 Parliament St; r R250) This very stylishly done up period

cottage is ideal for a group of six people – the three bedrooms share two bathrooms. The wooden floors and antique furniture give the interior the same kind of feel as Reinet House or the Old Residency, but the old-fashioned look is offset by some contemporary touches such as a satellite TV and a sound system. Booking (and breakfast if required) is through Pioneers on Parsonage St (see p270).

Buiten Verwagten B&B (☎ 049-892 4504; www .buitenverwagten.co.za; 58 Bourke St; s/d with breakfast from R340/480; 🖳 😂) The beautiful Buiten Verwagten, surrounded by a lovely garden, has charming rooms, some with self-catering facilities. Each is very different in décor and furnishings.

Camdeboo Cottages (☎ 049-892 3180; www.karoo park.co.za; 16 Parliament St; 4-bed cottages R420; 😂) The modest but charming self-catering Camdeboo Cottages are restored Karoo cottages, some featuring reed ceilings and yellowwood floors. There's a pool and a braai area. *Camdeboo* is the Khoekhoen word for 'green valleys' and is used to describe the hills around Graaff-Reinet.

TOP END

Heeren XVII (☎ 049-891 0404; www.heerenxvii.co.za; 104 Somerset St; s/d with breakfast R325/650; 😂) With its centrepiece a house built in 1817 by Thomas Perry, the area's first district surgeon, Heeren XVII is a series of extremely elegant cottages set in a large garden. The luxurious cottages (which can sleep up to six) are not designed for self-catering, but with the sumptuous alfresco breakfasts served up you'll see no need to cook.

Drostdy Hotel (☎ 049-892 2161; www.drostdy .co.za; 30 Church St; s/d R410/640; 😂) The main part of this beautiful old hotel is in Graaff-Reinet's restored *drostdy*. The courtyard café is particularly enchanting, surrounded by fruit trees and the scent of flowers from the stunning gardens. The reception and the hotel restaurant are in the *drostdy*, while guests stay in restored mid-19th-century cottages, originally built for freed slaves along Stretch's Crt.

Andries Stockenström Guesthouse (☎ 049-892 4575; 100 Cradock St; s/d with breakfast R730/960; 😂 😂) A very upmarket B&B with all the trimmings, famed in particular for its superb restaurant. The Karoo-style haute cuisine is available to guests only, so you'll have to book in if you want to sample the award-winning menu. There are no dinners on Sundays.

Eating

Pioneers (☎ 049-892 6059; 3 Parsonage St; light meals R10-30, mains R60; ✆ breakfast, lunch & dinner) This café-restaurant serves so-so sandwiches but delicious cakes and big cooked breakfasts. There's streetside seating, tourist info, an Internet café and a small curio shop.

Kliphuis (☎ 049-892 2345; 46 Bourke St; mains R40-65; ✆ breakfast, lunch & dinner Tue-Sat, lunch & dinner Sun) Kliphuis is one of Graaff-Reinet's most popular eating spots, with the Sunday carvery of Karoo lamb or venison a speciality. The rest of the menu is refreshingly grease-free, with dishes such as moussaka and quiche. There's a good selection of wines, and some accommodation too if you pick a very drinkable one.

Coldstream (☎ 049-891 1181; 3 Church St; mains R45-60; ✆ breakfast, lunch & dinner Mon-Sat) An excellent restaurant in a converted family home near the Dutch Reformed Church specialising in local variations on old favourites, such as the blue cheese and biltong quiche, and the beloved 'trio' platter of beef, ostrich and kudu or springbok.

Shopping

Graaff-Reinet has a wonderful selection of shops selling everything from Karoo crafts to designer clothing.

Windmill Junction (☎ 049-892 4504; www.windmilljunction.co.za; Somerset St) Check out this store for local goods including artwork, deli foods and handmade soaps.

Reinet Antiques (☎ 049-892 4221; Church St) A massive collection of high-class antiques can be found here.

Getting There & Away

BUS

Long-distance buses stop at **Kudu Motors** (Church St). The Publicity Association office acts as the Translux agent. Translux stops here on the run from Cape Town (R250, 8½ hours) to Queenstown (R140, three hours) via Cradock (R120, 1½ hours) and on the way to Port Elizabeth (R200, three hours).

Intercape (www.intercape.co.za) passes through Graaff-Reinet daily on its run to Jo'burg (R310, 11 hours).

MINIBUS TAXIS

Minibus taxis leave from Market Sq. Major destinations are Port Elizabeth (R100), Cape Town (R220) and Jo'burg (R320).

AROUND GRAAFF-REINET

Farm Trails

Several farmers of the Camdeboo region have developed walks and activities on their beautiful properties.

The friendly **Rheboksberg** (☎ 049-891 8004; s/d with breakfast R110/220) farm, 24km northwest of Graaff-Reinet, is highly recommended. Dinner is available for an extra R40.

Some 46km northwest of Graaff-Reinet, **Van Der Waltshoek** (☎ 049-845 9007; s/d with breakfast R130/160) is a historical farm with great walking all around. Dinner is R50.

KAROO NATURE RESERVE

A donation in 2005 from the World Wildlife Fund has meant the Karoo Nature Reserve is to become a national park under the auspices of SAN Parks. This means the former reserve, which virtually surrounds Graaff-Reinet and protects 16,000 hectares of mountainous veld typical of the Karoo, will give the park access to the international marketing network of SAN Parks as well as Wild Card (see p85) eligibility. What it will be called, to avoid confusion with the Karoo National Park near Beaufort West, remains to be seen.

There are plenty of animals, but the real draw is the spectacular rock formations and great views overlooking the town of Graaff-Reinet and the plains. The park is subdivided into three main sections: the wildlife-viewing area to the north of the dam, the western section with the Valley of Desolation and the eastern section with the overnight hiking trail. Plans are to one day merge the park with Mountain Zebra National Park, creating a unique African Karoo experience.

In the **wildlife-viewing area** (admission free; ✆ 7am-dusk) there are buffaloes, elands, kudus, hartebeests, wildebeests, springboks, the rare Cape mountain zebra and a host of smaller mammals. Bird species include black eagles, blue cranes and kori bustards. Visitors must stay in their vehicles.

The **Valley of Desolation** (admission free; ✆ 24hr) is the nature reserve's most popular sight. It's a hauntingly beautiful valley with an

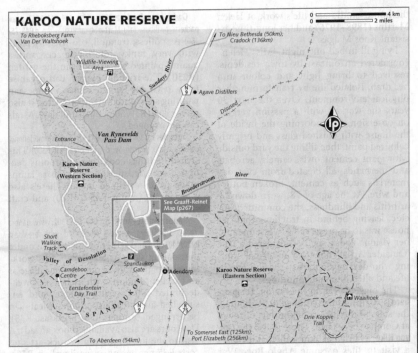

KAROO NATURE RESERVE

0 --- 4 km
0 --- 2 miles

To Rheboksberg Farm;
Van Der Waltshoek

Wildlife-Viewing
Area

Sundays River

To Nieu Bethesda (50km);
Cradock (136km)

R63

Gate

N9 ● Agave Distillers

Disused

Entrance

Van Rynevelds
Pass Dam

Karoo Nature
Reserve
(Western Section)

Broederstroom

River

See Graaff-Reinet
Map (p267)

Short
Walking
Track

Valley of Desolation

Camdeboo
Centre

Spandaukop
Gate

● Adendorp

Eerstefontein
Day Trail

S P A N D A U K O P

N9

R75

Karoo Nature Reserve
(Eastern Section)

Waaihoek

Drie Koppie
Trail

To Aberdeen (54km)

To Somerset East (125km);
Port Elizabeth (256km)

outstanding view – the rugged, piled dolorite columns of the valley are set against the backdrop of the endless Karoo plains. The town is also visible, nestled in a bend of the Sundays River. The valley can be reached by car on a steep but sealed road, and there's a 1.5km circuit walk. It's the sort of place that makes you wish you were an eagle. The best times to come are at sunrise or sunset.

The **Eerstefontein Day Trail** is also in the western section and has three trail options: 5km, 11km and 14km long. The information office supplies a map. Free permits are available from a self-help permit box at the Spandaukop gate. A longer, overnight trail in the eastern section, the **Drie Koppie Trail**, costs R15 per person and can be booked with the **Nature Reserve office** (☎ 049-892 3453) or by contacting Karoo Connections (p268) in Graaff-Reinet.

You'll need to have your own car to get around the reserve, or contact Karoo Connections in Graaff-Reinet for a tour. Accommodation (except on the overnight trail) is only available in Graaff-Reinet.

NIEU BETHESDA
☎ 049

The tiny, isolated village of Nieu Bethesda, once one of the most obscure places in South Africa, has achieved worldwide fame as the home of the extraordinary Owl House. These days Nieu Bethesda has become a minor artistic colony attracting scores of wealthy Europeans. With its dirt roads, brewery, fine accommodation, a couple of pretty cafés and endless stars, it's a great place to kick back for a few days and contemplate life.

Nieu Bethesda is 55km from Graaff-Reinet. The drive here is very scenic with the Sneeuberg Range dominating the region as you approach; there are several turn-offs onto unsealed roads from the N9 between Graaff-Reinet and Middelburg. Note that petrol is not available in Nieu Bethesda.

Sights & Activities
It was the **Owl House** (☎ 049-841 1603; adult/child & student R15/8; ☷ 8am-6pm Nov-Apr, 9am-5pm May-Oct) that put Nieu Bethesda on the map, and it's easy to see why. This fascinating place was

the home, studio and life's work of Helen Martins (1898–1976) and her long-time assistant Koos Malgas.

Lying ill in bed one night, 'Miss Helen', considered an outcast by town residents, resolved to bring light and colour into her drab, isolated life by transforming her physical environment. Over the next 30 years she worked with a passion verging on obsession, first adorning the inside of the house with crushed glass and brightly coloured paint, then filling the yard outside with giant cement owls, camels, acrobats and mermaids, all created from everyday materials such as cement, broken bottles and wire. At the age of 78, worn down by arthritis and blindness, she committed suicide, leaving behind instructions that her house was to be preserved as a testament to her vision. Today she is considered a true 'Outsider Artist', one with no formal training who develops an artistic vision late in life and alters their surroundings.

The biggest peak in the region, **Compassberg** (2502m), can be climbed in 2½ hours – the start of the hike is 35km out of town, at Compassberg farm. There is also the **Canyon Hike**, a fairly flat 3km walk that includes a visit to sites of some Anglo-Boer War engravings. Ask in the village for directions to the trail.

Don't miss a visit to the **Sneeuwitjie Creche** (☎ 049-841 1656, 072-449 0662; sneeuwitjie@adsactive.com; Hudson St). A community initiative, this gives you the chance to see the other side of Nieu Bethesda life. Local women have formed an adopt-a-child programme involving interventions, education, guidance and meals. The creche relies largely on external support, and the best way to give this is by having a meal in the **restaurant** (mains R55; ☽ dinner). It's the only place in town that serves dinner every night, and creche supervisor Dorah Oliphant will make sure, like the kids under her charge, that no-one goes home hungry. Fresh karoo lamb with homemade bread and ginger beer is a common meal, but it does cater for vegetarians. Ask Dorah about meeting local township residents.

Sleeping

The **Accommodation Booking Agency** (☎ 049-841 1623; Main Rd) arranges accommodation in guesthouses in and around Nieu Bethesda.

Owl House Backpackers (☎ 049-841 1642; backpackers@owlhouse.info; Martin St; camp sites/dm/d R45/75/180) A spotless, tranquil, eco-friendly place with very funky interior spaces and a quaint, painted tower room in the garden (R250). The friendly owners can organise trips to Graaff-Reinet, visits to Khoesaan painting sites, and donkey cart rides. It also hires bikes (R30/50 per half/full day). Meals can be arranged.

Outsiders B&B (☎ 049-841 1642; accommodation@owlhouse.info; Martin St; d with breakfast R300) This stylish B&B has cool, spacious rooms decorated with artistic touches such as lamps made from reclaimed metal. There's also a restaurant (mains R45 to R70) and craft shop here.

Ganora Guest Farm (☎ 049-841 1302; www.ganora.co.za; 3-bedroom cottages R630, s/d with breakfast R220/440) If you'd rather be out of town for the soaring skies of the Karoo, this working sheep farm 7km out of the village is an excellent option, with a choice of well-decorated self-catering cottages and en-suite bed-and-breakfast doubles. Meals can be arranged (dinner R50, breakfast R35). Day tours are also available (book ahead). A visit to the fossil museum or rock-art sites costs R35 per person; a fossil walk is R55.

Eating

Egbert's Place (☎ 049-841 1716; Main Rd; ☽ breakfast & lunch) A restaurant and bookshop, both with a good selection. There's a great range of new and second-hand books, plus tasty, wholesome meals. The food menu has no prices, so customers simply put whatever payment they think fit into an old red kettle!

Village Inn Coffee Shop (☎ 049-841 1635; mains R50; ☽ breakfast & lunch Tue-Sun) This small coffee shop just down from the Owl House serves light lunches, sandwiches and cakes. There's also a small second-hand bookshop here. Dinner is available if you order in advance.

Two Goats Deli & Brewery (☎ 049-841 1602; Pienaar St; ☽ lunch Wed-Sun) Across a bridge from the main part of the village is this excellent place to buy goat's milk cheeses, have a cold meat lunch or simply quaff lots of homemade Two Goats beer! Dinner is available in high season, but generally opening times are irregular, so booking ahead is advised.

Another great dinner option is the creche (left).

Getting There & Away

There is no public transport to Nieu Bethesda. Owl House Backpackers (opposite) will organise a local to do a pick-up/drop off (one-way/return R30/50) to Graaff-Reinet. Le Jardin Backpackin' (p269) in Graaff-Reinet also organises transport.

AMATHOLE

The stretch of coast and hinterland known as Amathole (pronounced 'ama-tawl-eh', from Xhosa for 'calves') extends from the Great Fish River to the Great Kei River on the so-called Shipwreck Coast, and inland as far as Queenstown. It includes the surfside city of East London, the enchanting mountain village of Hogsback, and the little-visited and wild government wildlife reserves of Mpofu, Double Drift and Tsolwana. Much of this area was the former Xhosa homeland of Ciskei.

KING WILLIAM'S TOWN
☎ 043

Established by the London Missionary Society in 1826, King William's Town (known as 'King') was a colonial capital and an important military base in the interminable struggle with the Xhosa. The main reason for a visit is the excellent **Amathole Museum** (☎ 043-642 4506; 3 Albert Rd; admission R5; ⏰ 9am-4.30pm Mon-Fri, 10am-1pm Sat), one of the finest in the region, with an excellent **Xhosa Gallery** featuring in-depth explanations of Xhosa culture, mysticism and history. There are some wonderful examples of beadwork, plus wire cars made by local artists.

Pride of place in the natural history section is given to the stuffed corpse of Huberta, a hippo that became famous between 1928 and 1931 when she wandered down the coast from St Lucia in Natal – more than 1000km away – to the vicinity of King William's Town. The King of England declared she was to be left in peace, but she was shot by local farmers, causing a national outcry.

There are a limited number of sleeping options in King, and many are overpriced, so it's probably better to stay in East London and visit for the day. The town **library** (☎ 043-642 3391; Ayliff St; ⏰ 9am-5.30pm Mon-Fri, 9am-1pm Sat) can provide a list of guesthouses and B&Bs.

Nearby King is **Steve Biko's grave** (see p274), and the beginning of the Amathole Trail (see below).

Getting There & Away

Buses arrive at and depart from the Engen petrol station on Cathcart St. **Intercape** (www .intercape.co.za) buses stop in King on their daily run between Cape Town (R220, eight hours) and East London (R90, one hour). **Translux** (www.translux.co.za) buses run to Cape Town (R360, 18 hours).

Greyhound (www.greyhound.co.za) also stops in town on its daily run between Jo'burg/Pretoria (R300, 12 hours) and East London (R95, one hour) via Bloemfontein (R215, six hours).

Minibus taxis run from King to Bhisho (R10, 20 minutes).

BHISHO
☎ 040 / pop 171,000

Bhisho, once capital of Ciskei, is now the administrative capital of Eastern Cape. The centre of Bhisho was built to house Ciskei's bureaucrats and politicians, so there is a compact bunch of suitably grandiose and ugly public buildings, which are now in the service of the new provincial bureaucracy.

Regular minibuses run from the King William's Town train station to Bhisho.

AMATHOLE & KATBERG MOUNTAINS

The area north and west of King William's Town is partly degraded grazing land and partly rugged mountains with remnant indigenous forest. There are some good walks. When the mists are down on the Amathole Mountains, the forests take on an eerie silence.

The easiest way into this area is via King William's Town or Queenstown. Daily **City to City** (☎ 011-773 2762) buses stop in Katberg, Seymour and Alice on the Jo'burg–King William's Town run. There are occasional minibus taxis too.

Amathole Trail

The 121km, six-day **Amathole Trail** (per person R180) begins at the Maden Dam, 23km north of King William's Town, and ends at the Tyumie River near Hogsback. Accommodation is in huts.

It ranks as one of South Africa's top mountain walks, but is pretty tough and

STEVE BIKO

Steve Biko (1946–77) is buried in the Ginsberg cemetery just outside King William's Town. His insistence that people must begin by changing their own attitudes and feelings of inferiority – a process he called Black Consciousness – created a movement that is credited with playing a huge part in the downfall of apartheid.

This former medical student from the University of Natal refused to be silenced by the persecution of the apartheid government, and was eventually put under house arrest and banned from speaking in public. In 1977 he was detained in Port Elizabeth for 26 days under the Terrorism Act. He died in police custody after a series of brutal assaults.

To reach Biko's grave, follow Cathcart St south of the town and turn left down a dirt track that is signposted to the cemetery.

should only be attempted if you are reasonably experienced and fit. Walkers are rewarded with great views, although about a third of the walk goes through dense forest and numerous streams with waterfalls and swimming holes. Shorter sections of the hike are available outside school holidays. Guides can also be arranged.

The trail must be booked with the **Department of Water Affairs & Forestry** (☎ 043-604 5433; www.dwaf.co.za; 9 Chamberlain St, King William's Town).

Alice & Around

☎ 040 / pop 9800

Alice is a busy little town with little for the tourist other than the **University of Fort Hare**, which was established in 1916 and has played an important role in the development of Southern Africa. Former students include Steve Biko, Nelson Mandela and, ahem, Robert Mugabe. Parts of the original Fort Hare are also preserved in the grounds.

Within the campus, the excellent **De Beers Centenary Art Gallery** (☎ 040-602 2277; admission free; 7.30am-4.30pm Mon-Fri) has some very important work by contemporary South African artists, plus archive material on Steve Biko, Black Consciousness and the African National Congress.

Frequent minibus taxis run from King William's Town to the main gates of the university and to Alice; they cost R15. From Alice to Fort Beaufort is R5. A minibus taxi to Hogsback will cost about R25, but you'll probably have to change taxis en route.

Fort Beaufort

☎ 046 / pop 26,400

In 1846 a Xhosa man called Tsili stole an axe from a shop in Fort Beaufort. In a masterly display of overreaction, a British force invaded the Xhosa province of Queen Adelaide, beginning the Seventh Frontier War, known as the War of the Axe (1846–47). Today, Fort Beaufort has left such drama long behind and is a quiet, attractive and unassuming little town, but you can still learn about its past (and about its current attractions) at the **Historical Museum** (☎ 046-645 1555; fbmus eum@procomp.co.za; 44 Durban St; adult/child R2/0.50; 8.30am-5pm Mon-Fri, 8.30am-12.45pm Sat) in the old officers' mess. It's bursting with memorabilia from firearms to fossils, and offers tourist advice.

If you're staying over, the fairly decent **Savoy Hotel** (☎ 046-645 1146; 53 Durban St; s/d R215/350;) opposite the museum has uninspiring but clean rooms with TV. There's a pretty garden and an à la carte restaurant (mains R50). Look out for newspaper clippings in the lobby relating to a UFO sighting in the town in 1972!

The only public transport to Fort Beaufort is by minibus taxis, which leave several times a day from Alice (R7, 30 minutes).

Hogsback

☎ 045 / pop 1500

For years now South Africa's worst-kept secret, magical Hogsback is unlike any destination in the country. Located improbably 1300m up in the beautiful Amathole Mountains, about 100km northwest of Bhisho, the small village has enjoyed a recent renaissance and is supposedly a favourite getaway among politicians and celebrities. Yet with its English climate (four distinctive seasons), quietude, organic food, environmentally conscious population and mind-boggling views of mountains and forested valleys in all directions, this is an eco-destination *par excellence*. Even a one-night stopover will feel like you're being transported to another time and place, particularly one reminiscent of *The Hobbit*. Locals make much of the fact that JRR Tolkien was inspired by Hogsback, but in reality he lived in Bloemfontein and remembered the place from childhood holidays. Still, it's certainly easy to imagine a scene from one of his books happening here.

The steepest slopes around Hogsback are still covered in beautiful rainforest: yellow-wood, assegai and tree fuchsia are all present. There are also, sadly, extensive pine plantations on land that was once indigenous forest. The peaks of the hills are high and bare, with 'bristles' known in geological circles as a 'hogsback' – hence the town's name.

The hogs made of mud that you'll see being sold along the road (R10 to R15) are not fired; when they get wet they make a hell of a mess.

INFORMATION

There's an ATM in the Hogsback Inn, just off the main road.

Community Tourism Info Centre (☎ 045-962 1026; www.hogsbackinfo.co.za; ✆ 9am-5pm Mon-Fri) On the main road.

SIGHTS & ACTIVITIES

On one side of the village is the mystical **ecoshrine** (adult/child R10/free; ✆ 10am-5.30pm Wed, Sat & Sun), a cement sculpture and garden that celebrates the forces of nature. The town's climate and history of green-fingered Englishmen who settled here mean it is blessed with gorgeous (though seasonal) market garden estates. Flower lovers should definitely contact the **Garden Club** (☎ 045-962 1259; tours R15), whose aim is to turn Hogsback into a 'botanical paradise'.

There are some great walks, bike rides and drives in the area. Some of the best roads are unsealed, so check locally before trying anything ambitious, and definitely think twice if it's been snowing (snow falls in 11 months out of 12, but it is rare that falls are heavy). Be prepared for rain at any time, and in winter for temperatures that can drop to -1°C.

SLEEPING & EATING

Don't be fooled by excessive signposting on your way into town; there are only a few genuinely worthy, well established places to stay, as listed below. In general, it's best to ask at the info centre for those establishments who've been around a long time.

Away with the Fairies (☎ 045-962 1031; hogsback1@iafrica.com; Hydrangea Lane; camp sites/dm/d with shared bathroom R40/70/170; ✆) A wonderful backpackers, where care and attention to detail (along with terrific views) have paid dividends. The interiors are painted with fantastical designs featuring nubile fairies, and there's a log fire in the lounge that crackles cosily on cold evenings. The most popular spot for those deep and meaningful conversations is the tree house, perched in the forest among parrots and monkeys. The Hog & Hobbit bar is the spot to sink a few beers in the evenings. There are hearty meals (dinner R40), mountain bikes (R50 per day) for hire, lots of rock climbing, and horse trails (three-hour trails R150) on offer.

Edge (☎ 045-962 1159; info@theedge_hogsback.co.za; Bluff End; self-catering cottages from R350; ✆) This is a collection of 12 stunningly decorated self-catering cottages strung out along the mountain's edge. The cottages all have one big bedroom (there's one twin and one family unit) with a log fire and TV, plus separate bathroom and kitchen. The more expensive ones (up to R750) have heart-stopping views too. The vibe here is peace, quiet and relaxation rather than raucous partying. It's an unbeatable place for a healthy rest – or a romantic weekend. The star of the onsite restaurant, Tea Thyme (mains R40 to R75), has risen now that it is run by the Edge. Have a health breakfast here before visiting the mystical labyrinth reminiscent of the patterns formed by crop circles. To find the Edge, follow the signs from the main road (look for the pink triangle).

Granny Mouse House (☎ 045-962 1259; ingi@iafrica.com; 1 Nutwoods Dr; s/d with breakfast R250/500; ✆) This is a charming guesthouse with rooms in an old wattle and daub house, plus a self-catering cottage in the garden. Have a breakfast here and you'll lustily taste the difference between organic and mass-produced food. Guests can also include dinner (often including wild mushroom soup) in their booking for an extra R100. The very friendly owner speaks German.

Arminel Hotel (☎ 045-962 1005; www.katleisure.co.za; Main Rd; s/d with breakfast R475/1000; ✆) A fair amount of tom has been splashed out to give this historic old place a new lease of life, and it's paid off. It's the only hotel in town (it's a three-star), but its neat thatched building, charming interior design and peaceful setting make it feel more like a very large guesthouse.

Nina's (☎ 045-962 1326; Main Rd; mains R25-40; ☺ breakfast, lunch & dinner) Next to the info centre is this popular restaurant and deli in a quaint A-frame house. Locals love the pizzas (try the FBR: fig, bacon and roquefort!) and visitors love the local produce on sale.

GETTING THERE & AWAY

If you can, try to arrive in Hogsback by day, as the road in can be frequented by itinerant livestock. Unless you have a 4WD, only come here via Rte 63 or Rte 67. Do not take the roads via Seymour or Cathcart. To be absolutely sure about road conditions, call ahead from Queenstown. The easiest way to get to Hogsback without a car is by shuttle bus from the Sugarshack Backpackers (p280) in East London, Buccaneer's Backpackers (p284) in Cintsa (Chintsa), or Old Gaol Backpackers (p259) in Grahamstown to Away with the Fairies on Monday, Tuesday, Thursday, Friday and Sunday (R45 one way). Beware of trying to come to Hogsback for a single night – you'll regret it!

EASTERN CAPE WILDLIFE RESERVES
☎ 040

With over a million hectares of malaria-free game viewing, the Eastern Cape's reserves are a major drawcard. There are three main wildlife reserves administered by the **Eastern Cape Tourism Board** (☎ 043-701 9600; www.ectourism.co.za; cnr Longfellow & Aquarium Rds, Quigney, East London). All reserves organise wildlife viewing, and many have multiday walking trails available. You'll need to be self-sufficient with food and water to visit the reserves.

Tsolwana Game Reserve (☎ 040-635 2115; adult/child R6/3, plus per car R20; ☺ 8am-6pm) is 57km southwest of Queenstown. The park is managed in conjunction with the local Tsolwana people, who benefit directly from the jobs and revenue produced. It protects some rugged Karoo landscape south of the spectacular **Tafelberg** (1965m) and adjoining the Swart Kei River. The reserve's rolling plains are interspersed with valleys, cliffs, waterfalls, caves and gullies. There is a diverse range of animals including large herds of antelopes, rhinos, giraffes and mountain zebras. Wildlife viewing is possible in the park's vehicle (up to four people R160).

Double Drift Game Reserve, 42km south of Fort Beaufort, has been combined with the Sam Knott Nature Reserve and the Andries Vosloo Kudu Reserve to form the **Great Fish River Reserve** (☎ 040-653 8010; ectbdd@icon.co.za; adult/child R6/3, plus per car R20; ☺ 8am-5pm). There is much large wildlife to be seen in this area of thick bushveld, which is sandwiched between the Great Fish and Keiskamma Rivers.

To the north of Fort Beaufort is **Mpofu Game Reserve** (☎ 040-864 9450; adult/child R6/3, plus per car R20; ☺ 8am-5pm), where you are likely to see *mpofu* (eland), a large antelope. The grassland and valley bushveld make the region ideal for wildlife viewing. The 60km, three-day **Katberg Trail** begins here and ends at the Katberg Forest Station, just below the Katberg Pass. When we visited, the trail was closed for revamping; call the **Department of Water Affairs & Forestry** (☎ 043-604 5433; www.dwaf.co.za; 9 Chamberlain St, King William's Town) to check on the status.

Sleeping

Tsolwana Game Reserve has three comfortable **farmhouses** (up to 4 people R650, extra person R170). There are also two trail huts here, Phumlani and Fundani. Double Drift and Mpofu Game Reserves have comfortable **lodge accommodation** (4-person r R650).

Getting There & Away

You'll need your own vehicle to visit all these reserves. Some are remote and hard to find – phone Eastern Cape Tourism or the lodges for directions and leave plenty of time to get there.

EAST LONDON
☎ 043 / pop 980,000

The country's only river port, with a good surf beach and a spectacular bay that curves round to huge sand hills. Few cities in the world with this many inhabitants are as dour as East London, yet a strange, inescapable malaise hangs over the town. Unless you're a surfer (or a shark), there isn't really much to keep you here, though it can be a good base for moving on to holiday spots along the Sunshine or Wild Coasts.

Its Khoesaan name means 'Place of the Buffalos', and the whole area has been named 'Buffalo City' by the tourism authorities.

Orientation

The main street in the centre is Oxford St, with the city centre extending from about Argyle St south to Fleet St. Fleet St runs east, and eventually, after a few corners and name changes, meets the Esplanade, where all the beachfront hotels and restaurants are situated. To the west, around Buffalo St, is a run-down and slightly edgy area dominated by the minibus taxi ranks.

Orient Beach, which is east of the river mouth, is popular with families and has a tidal pool. Eastern Beach is the long main beach fronting the Esplanade, but Nahoon Reef on the northern headland is better for surfing.

The massive and sprawling township of Mdantsane, 15 km from town, is the second-largest township in South Africa (Soweto being the largest).

Information

INTERNET ACCESS

Cyber Lounge (☎ 083-375 9040; 58 Beach Rd, Nahoon; per hour R40; ☼ 8.30am-7.30pm Mon-Thu, 8.30am-6.30pm Fri, 10am-6pm Sat, 3-6pm Sun)

Guido's (043-743 4441; Esplanade) Has a fairly slow connection.

MONEY

There are ATMs for all the major banks on Oxford St. For safety, only use ATMs during the day; better still, use one of the ATMs in the **Vincent Park shopping centre** (Devereux Ave) instead.

POST

Main post office (Oxford St) Halfway up Oxford St; with a row of Telkom telephone boxes nearby.

TOURIST INFORMATION

There are two tourist offices in East London, both in **King's Tourist Centre** (cnr Longfellow & Aquarium Rds) on the beachfront and both seemingly down on their luck. Staff try their best but don't achieve it – you'll end up with a handful of colourful brochures and a few fairly useful maps.

Eastern Cape Tourism Board (☎ 043-701 9600; www.ectourism.co.za; ☼ 8am-4.30pm Mon-Fri) Covers the wider area.

Tourism Buffalo City (☎ 043-042-722 6015; www.visitbuffalocity.co.za; ☼ 8am-4.30pm Mon-Fri, 9am-2pm Sat, 9am-1pm Sun) Deals with matters relating to the city and neighbouring townships.

TRAVEL AGENCIES

Wild Coast Holiday Reservations (☎ 043-743 6181; www.wildcoastholidays.co.za; King's Tourist Centre, cnr Longfellow & Aquarium Rds) Books accommodation and hiking trails on the Wild Coast.

Dangers & Annoyances

The eastern end of Eastern Beach and the area around Nahoon River mouth are not considered safe to walk on. Take care on the Esplanade and get a taxi home from anywhere in East London after dark. Watch out for pickpockets if you end up in the area around Buffalo St and the minibus taxi ranks.

Sights & Activities

The **East London Museum** (☎ 043-743 0686; Dawson Rd; admission R5; ☼ 9.30am-5pm Mon-Fri, 2-5pm Sat, 11am-4pm Sun) shot to fame in 1938 when the young curator, Marjorie Latimer, discovered a strange-looking fish on a vessel in East London harbour. It turned out to be a coelancanth, a type of fish thought to have become extinct over 50 million years ago. To find it still in existence was the marine equivalent of stumbling upon a living dinosaur. The fish was named *Latimeria chalumnae* in honour of its finder, and over 5000 people came to the museum on the first day it was exhibited. Coelacanths have since been discovered all over the world, but the stuffed original is still on display at the museum. Other exhibits at the museum include trace-fossil human footprints and a living beehive.

The **Ann Bryant Art Gallery** (☎ 043-722 4044; St Marks Rd; admission free; ☼ 9am-5pm Mon-Fri, 9.30am-noon Sat), south of the museum, is in an old mansion featuring an eclectic collection of paintings and sculptures, mostly by South African artists. There's also a small coffee shop here.

Gately House (☎ 043-722 2141; 1 Park Gates Rd; adult/child R1/free; ☼ 10am-1pm Tue-Thu, 2-5pm Fri, 10am-1pm Sat, 3-5pm Sun) was the residence of the first mayor of East London, John Gately, and still contains all his original furniture. It's near the entrance to Queen's Park, but it's easiest to access the house by walking up from the zoo.

EASTERN CAPE

EAST LONDON

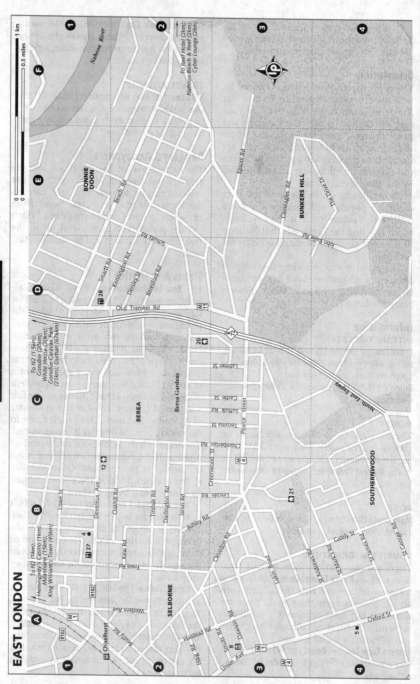

0   0.5 miles
0   1 km

A R102
To N2 (1km);
Hemingway's Casino (1km);
Mdantsane (15km);
King William's Town (45km)

B

C
To N2 (1.5km);
Gonubie (20km);
White House (20km);
Gonubie Caravan Park
(21km); Durban (676km)

D

E
BONNIE
DOON

F
Nahoon River

To Reef Hotel (2km);
Nahoon Beach & Reef (2km);
Cyber Lounge (2km)

BUNKERS HILL

SOUTHERNWOOD

SELBORNE

BEREA

Chiselhurst

Berea Gardens

Old Transkei Rd

North East Expwy

Oxford St

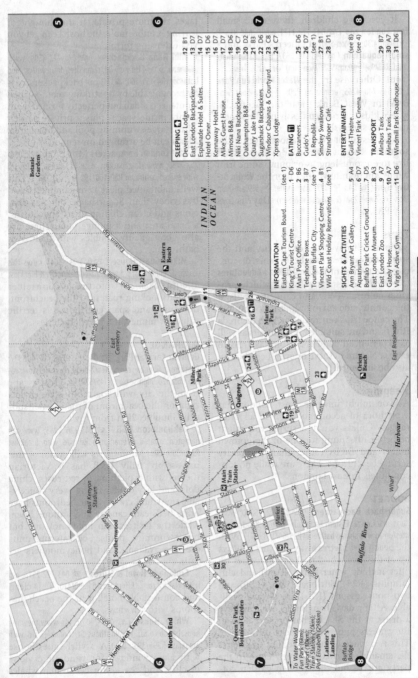

SLEEPING
Devereux Lodge......................12	B1
East London Backpackers..........13	D7
Esplanade Hotel & Suites..........14	D7
Hotel Osner............................15	D6
Kennaway Hotel......................16	D7
Mike's Guest House.................17	D7
Mimosa B&B...........................18	D6
Niki Nana Backpackers..............19	C7
Oakhampton B&B.....................20	D2
Quarry Lake Inn.......................21	B3
Sugarshack Backpackers............22	D6
Windsor Cabanas & Courtyard....23	C8
Xpress Lodge...........................24	C7

EATING
Buccaneers............................25	D6
Guido's.................................26	D7
Le Republik............................27	B1
Smokey Swallows.............(see 1)	
Strandloper Café.....................28	D1

ENTERTAINMENT
Guild Theatre..................(see 8)	
Vincent Park Cinema..........(see 4)	

TRANSPORT
Minibus Taxis..........................29	B7
Minibus Taxis..........................30	A7
Windmill Park Roadhouse..........31	D6

INFORMATION
Eastern Cape Tourism Board........(see 1)	
King's Tourist Centre.................1	D6
Main Post Office......................2	B6
Telephone Boxes......................3	B7
Tourism Buffalo City............(see 1)	
Vincent Park Shopping Centre....4	B1
Wild Coast Holiday Reservations..(see 1)	

SIGHTS & ACTIVITIES
Ann Bryant Art Gallery..............5	A4
Aquarium...............................6	D7
Buffalo Park Cricket Ground........7	D5
East London Museum.................8	A3
East London Zoo......................9	A7
Gately House..........................10	A7
Virgin Active Gym....................11	D6

If you have children, there's the small **East London zoo** (☎ 043-722 1171; adult/child R15/9; ☺ 9am-4.30pm Mon-Sun) at Queen's Park, and a small **aquarium** (☎ 043-705 2637; Esplanade; adult/child R15/9; ☺ 9am-5pm Mon-Sun) on the beachfront. Otherwise try the **Water World Fun Park** (☎ 043-748 4265; admission R20; ☺ 9am-5pm Sep-Easter) in West Bank (near the racetrack), where kids can ride endlessly on the supertube and speed slides.

The best **surfing** is at Nahoon Reef at the southern end of Nahoon Beach. If you'd like to do some lengths or pump some iron while you're in town, head for the **Virgin Active Gym** (☎ 043-743 3777; Esplanade; ☺ 5.30am-8pm Mon-Fri, 7am-12pm & 4-7pm Sat & Sun). Day visitors pay R85.

Tours

Various half-day tours of the city and the surrounding area can be organised; contact the tourist office or **Off Road Adventures** (☎ 082-783 1288; 4wd@mweb.co.za), which provides cultural, 4WD and canoeing trails in the countryside surrounding East London. The canoe trips centre on the Fish or Breda Rivers and are suitable for beginners as well as experienced paddlers. Multiday trips to Dwesa Nature Reserve or even Lesotho can also be arranged.

Sleeping

As you might imagine, East London has a plethora of accommodation in all price ranges. Unless you're a surfer you might be better off opting for one of the uptown hotels and B&Bs rather than the pretty scruffy beachfront. There are really no top-end hotels in East London.

BUDGET

Sugarshack Backpackers (☎ 043-722 8240; www .sugarshack.co.za; Eastern Esplanade, Eastern Beach; camp sites/dm/d with shared bathroom R35/65/160; ☐) With the beach just metres away, the surf's always up at this lively backpackers. Activities on offer include waterskiing (R160) and cliff jumping (R25). Surfboard hire (R50) and two-hour lessons (R75) are always available. After a day's hanging 10, you can have a drink at the Shack's bar or next door at Buccaneers pub, which rocks until dawn. This is a place to cut loose, not to sleep – the smallish dorms are pretty close to the party area – but the wooden garden cot-

tages are more private. If the thought of leaving is unbearable, the hostel can get you visa extension forms.

Niki Nana Backpackers (☎ 043-722 8509; www .nikinana.co.za; 4 Hillview Rd; camp sites/dm/d with shared bathroom R45/65/160; ☒) This backpackers, easily recognisable by its striking zebra-striped frontage, is small but perfectly formed, with comfy inside spaces plus a private garden with a large swimming pool and braai area. Meals can be arranged on request.

East London Backpackers (☎ 043-781 1122, 084-782 7780; www.elbackpackers.co.za; 11 Quanza St; dm/s/d with shared bathroom R60/100/150, d R180; ☒) This well-maintained place is much quieter and less vibey than Sugarshack, but has spacious and clean chilling areas and dorms, a braai area and a plunge pool. There are also good-quality doubles with their own bathroom.

Mike's Guest House (☎ 043-743 3647; mikes@his .co.za; 22 Clifford St; s/d with shared bathroom & breakfast R120/180, s/d R200/270) Unfortunately up a rather dubious looking road near the beachfront, this spick and span guesthouse is terrific value for money, if a bit characterless.

MIDRANGE

Gonubie Caravan Park (☎ 043-705 9748; fax 740 5937; Beachfront, Gonubie; camp sites/2-bedroom chalets low season R65/320, high season R145/520) A great escape from the city, with log cabin–style chalets right on the beachfront of rustic outer suburb Gonubie, 2km from town.

Oakhampton B&B (☎ 043-726 9963; www.oak hampton.co.za; 8 Okehampton Rd; s/d with breakfast R250/380; ☒) Minimalists will swoon – this impossibly frilly B&B has a Victorian theme, with a plethora of red roses, china dolls and lacy doilies filling every conceivable nook and cranny. The bedrooms have brass bedstead, canopy and antique linen, while the lush garden holds not one but two swimming pools. Self-catering units are also available, and honeymooners get satin sheets.

Esplanade Hotel & Suites (☎ 043-722 2518; esp hotel@iafrica.com; Clifford St; s/d R290/410) This clean and comfortable hotel, near the beach, has rooms with sea views.

White House (☎ 043-740 0344; www.thewhite housebandb.co.za; 10 Whitthaus St, Gonubie; s/d with breakfast R295/395; ☒) A stylish guesthouse with glass windows for panoramic views of cliffs and sea – you can watch whales and dolphins passing by while you're having breakfast! There's a helipad too, should you need one.

Devereux Lodge (☎ 043-726 9459; coastdev@iafrica .com; 7A Devereux Ave; s/d with breakfast R400/550; ⓟ ⚎) Another very comfortable and upmarket guesthouse, mainly aimed at visiting businessmen, that lets you choose between Victorian and Tuscan surroundings. The huge rooms have TV and fridge.

Quarry Lake Inn (☎ 043-707 5400; www.quarry lakeinn.co.za; Quartzite Dr, Selbourne; s/d with breakfast R650/880; ⚎) This is one of East London's most upmarket hotels, built next to a tranquil artificial lake. The rooms are elegant and comfortable with modern facilities, including a microwave, bar fridge and private balconies.

One organisation, **Kat Leisure** (☎ 0800-422 433; www.katleisure.co.za), which runs the following places to stay, has a virtual monopoly of the hotels and apartments in East London. Places that include breakfast provide a prepacked airline-style continental affair.

Hotel Osner (Court Cres; s/d/family R360/420/700) Breezy rooms that are ideal for families.

Kennaway Hotel (Esplanade; d R520) Over-the-top colonial-style rooms, heavy on the velour furnishings but quite luxurious.

Mimosa B&B (Marine Tce; s/d with breakfast R270/380) Good-value units with kitchenette; often booked out.

Reef Hotel (18 Harewood Dr, Nahoon; s/d with breakfast R270/330) Near the river in Nahoon, this place has bright, comfortable rooms.

Windsor Cabanas & Courtyard (Marine Tce; s/d with breakfast R550/730) A fairly upmarket Mediterranean-style place with cheaper rooms (R305/400) in the courtyard.

Xpress Lodge (Fitzpatrick St; s/d R175/255) Rooms here include a kitchenette with fridge and microwave.

Eating
Most beachfront hotels have restaurants. You can also try the following midrange places.

Buccaneers (☎ 043-743 5171; Eastern Esplanade; mains R15-40; ⓨ lunch & dinner) Next to Sugarshack Backpackers, this down-to-earth pub serves steaks, toasted sandwiches and pizzas to soak up the alcohol.

Guido's (☎ 043-743 4441; Esplanade; mains R20-40; ⓨ lunch & dinner) This Italian chain, complete with faux-Grecian columns and a water feature, is a good standby for pizza and pasta.

Le Republik (☎ 043-722 0076; King's Tourist Centre, cnr Longfellow & Aquarium Rds; mains R40-60; ⓨ breakfast, lunch & dinner) This bright, noisy diner above the tourist office offers good hearty food and elevated seaside views. A central heater warms the place nicely on winter nights.

Strandloper Café (☎ 043-735 4570; 95 Old Transkei Rd; mains R60-90; ⓨ dinner Mon-Sat) This very elegant, simple and classy restaurant specialises in seafood, with dishes such as chilli and coriander prawns, paella and Cajun fish of the day. There's a good wine list and a couple of veggie options, too.

Smokey Swallows (☎ 043-727 1349; Devereux Ave; mains R60-100; ⓨ lunch & dinner) A perfect cross-section of East London life, frequented by everyone from the emerging black middle class to Jazz aficionados disappearing in a fog of pipe smoke, this is one of the city's trendiest venues. It's a lounge bar-restaurant (with a bistro menu including such delights as peppered ostrich fillet and hand-rolled sushi) with frequent live acts.

Entertainment
For bookings at general-release cinemas contact **Ster-Kinekor** (central bookings ☎ 082-16789; www.sterkinekor.co.za); for live shows including sporting events contact **Computicket** (☎ 011-915 8000; www.computicket.com).

Vincent Park Cinemas (☎ 043-726 8122; Vincent Park Shopping Centre, Devereux Ave; admission R15) Has six cinemas showing the latest movies.

Guild Theatre (☎ 043-743 0704; Dawson Rd) This is East London's main theatre. Everything from ballet performances to beauty contests take place here.

Hemingway's Casino (☎ 043-707 8000; Western Ave) Featuring gambling halls, restaurants and a cinema, this is the best place in town to squander your spondulicks.

Getting There & Away
AIR
The airport is 10km from the centre. **South African Airways** (SAA; ☎ 043-706 0203) has an office at the airport and flies from East London daily to Port Elizabeth (around R700), Durban (around R1100) and Cape Town (around R1650).

BUS
Translux, Greyhound and SA Connection stop at the **Windmill Park Roadhouse** (Moore St). Intercape buses stop at the **main train station** (Station St) and at the airport.

EASTERN CAPE

Translux (☎ 043-700 1999; www.translux.co.za) has daily buses to Mthatha (R125, four hours), Port Elizabeth (R155, four hours), Durban (R195, 10 hours), Cape Town (R300, 15 hours) and Jo'burg/Pretoria (R280, 14 hours).

Greyhound (☎ 043-743 9284; www.greyhound.co.za) has a daily bus between Durban (R200, 10 hours) and Cape Town (R340, 16 hours) via Port Elizabeth (R145, 5½ hours).

Intercape (☎ 043-743 9284; www.intercape.co.za) has daily buses from East London to Cape Town (R320, 7½ hours) and Port Elizabeth (R125, five hours).

SA Connection (☎ 086-110 2426) has buses weekly to Jo'burg (R325) and a twice-weekly connection to Cape Town (R350).

The **Baz Bus** (☎ 021-439 2323) runs from Port Elizabeth to Durban via East London Monday, Tuesday, Wednesday Friday and Saturday. It runs in the other direction Monday, Tuesday, Thursday, Friday and Sunday. It picks up from hostels.

MINIBUS TAXI

On the corner of Buffalo and Argyle Sts are long-distance minibus taxis to destinations north of East London. Nearby on the corner of Caxton and Gillwell Sts are minibus taxis for King William's Town, Bhisho and the local area. The following are sample fares: King William's Town (R15, one hour), Butterworth (R35, three hours), Mthatha (R70, five hours), Port Elizabeth (R80, six hours), Jo'burg (R220, 15 hours) and Cape Town (R240, 18 hours).

TRAIN

The overnight **Shosholoza Meyl** (☎ 0860-008 888) *Amathole* from East London to Jo'burg (1st/2nd class R335/235, 18 hours) departs daily via Bloemfontein.

Getting Around

Most city buses stop at the **city hall** (Oxford St). For information on times and routes, contact **Buffalo City Municipal Buses** (☎ 043-705 2666).

For private taxis, contact **Border Taxis** (☎ 043-722 3946).

SHIPWRECK COAST

The coast between the Great Fish River and East London is also known as the Shipwreck Coast, as it is the graveyard for many ships. The 64km **Shipwreck Hiking Trail**

(per person per night R40) leads from the Great Fish River to the Ncera River, but it is possible to do any section as there are several easy entry and exit points. This is one of the few walking areas in South Africa where hikers can set their own pace and camp more or less where they choose. They are rewarded with wild, unspoilt sections of surf beach, rich coastal vegetation and beautiful estuaries. The trail must be booked through **Wild Coast Reservations** (☎ 043-743 6181) in East London.

WILD COAST

With its rugged cliffs plunging into the sea, remote coves sheltering sandy beaches and a history of shipwrecks and stranded sailors, the aptly named Wild Coast is a place for adventure and intrigue.

The Wild Coast stretches for 350km from East London to Port Edward. Dotted along its shore are tiny Xhosa settlements and the occasional holiday resort or backpacker hostel.

You may hear some people refer to the area as the 'Transkei', which was the name of the apartheid-era homeland that once covered this part of the country. 'Transkei', however, stills bears the stigma of an area once feared for its crime rate and its extreme poverty. Today, 'the Wild Coast' is increasingly used to refer not just to the shoreline, but to the nearby inland areas as well.

Whatever the name for the region, the Xhosa people are some of the friendliest you'll meet anywhere in South Africa, and chances are you'll be invited inside a few of their brightly painted homes which dot the landscape.

Access to the coast from the N2 (which connects East London and Port St Johns via Mthatha) is limited by the rugged terrain and exploring the area inevitably leads travellers down more than one bone-jarring road. This is the place to forego the bus or your car for a while and make use of the walking paths that connect the coastal villages. The five-day walk between Port St Johns and Coffee Bay is the most popular route.

If you plan to hike or drive around inland on the Wild Coast, always ask permission before camping. Don't drive after dark, and remember that most of the roads here don't appear on maps, and signposts are few and far between. It's also important to watch out for animals and people in the middle of the roads. Unsealed roads can be impassable after rain.

TOURS

Even if guided tours aren't your usual style, the following outfits can help immeasurably in understanding the rich and complex culture of the Xhosa and Mpondo peoples who live on the Wild Coast. To make booking all along the coast, check www.wild coastbookings.com.

African Heartland Journeys (☎ 043-734 3012, 082-327 3944; www.africanheartland.co.za) is a very well-regarded tour company that runs small-group adventure tours into the area across the Great Kei River from their base at Buccaneer's Backpackers (p284) in Cintsa (Chintsa). Tours encompass travel by Land Rover, canoe, horse or mountain bike. Tents and camping equipment are provided. Overseas travellers are encouraged to offer their skills and sign on for

volunteer programmes; check the website for details.

The **Wild Coast Trails** (☎ 039-305 6455; www .wildcoast.org.za) project runs horse-riding, hiking and canoeing routes of different lengths up and down the coast. Guides and hosts are drawn from local Mpondo and Diba communities, supported by local hotels and private companies. Accommodation is in tented camps, guesthouses or local homes, and the trails go through nature reserves, along beaches and into rural villages.

EAST LONDON TO KEI MOUTH

The East Coast Resorts turn-off from the N2 will get you to most of the resorts closest to East London, the most attractive of which is Cintsa (Chintsa). The excellent Strandloper Trails (see p285) are the best introduction to this part of the coastline.

Cintsa (Chintsa)
☎ 043 / pop 2000

Heading up the N2, the sea spray starts to hit your face at an unspoilt stretch of white-sand beach called Cintsa, 38km from East

EASTERN CAPE

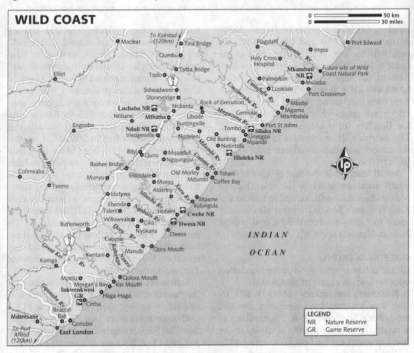

WILD COAST

0 — 50 km
0 — 30 miles

LEGEND
NR   Nature Reserve
GR   Game Reserve

THE XHOSA

Travelling along the southwestern Wild Coast is an excellent way to get to know Xhosa culture. You may hear the term 'red people', which refers to the red clay and red clothes worn by many adults.

Clothing, colours and beaded jewellery all indicate a Xhosa's subgroup. The Tembu and Bomvana, for example, favour red and orange ochres in the dyeing of their clothing, while the Pondo and Mpondomise use light blue. The isi-danga – a long turquoise necklace that identifies the wearer to their ancestors – is also still seen today.

Belief in witches (male and female) among the Xhosa is strong, and witch burning is not unknown. Most witchcraft is considered evil, with possession by depraved spirits a major fear. A main source of evil are *tokoloshe*, mythical manlike creatures who live in water but are also kept by witches. One reason that many Xhosa keep their beds raised high off the ground is to avoid being caught in their sleep by the tiny *tokoloshe*.

The *igqirha* (spiritual healer) is empowered to deal with both the forces of nature and the trouble caused by witches, and so holds an important place in traditional society. The *ixhwele* (herbalist) performs some magic but is more concerned with health. Both of these healers are often referred to as *sangomas*.

Many Xhosa have the top of their left little finger removed during childhood to prevent misfortune. Puberty and marriage rituals also play a central role. Boys must not be seen by women during the three-month initiation period following circumcision; during this time the boys disguise themselves with white clay, or in intricate costumes made of dried palm leaves. In the female puberty ritual, a girl is confined in a darkened hut while her friends tour the area singing for gifts. Unmarried girls wear short skirts, which are worn longer as marriage approaches. Married women wear long skirts and cover their breasts. They often put white clay on their faces, wear large, turban-like cloth hats and may smoke long-stemmed pipes.

London. Cintsa comprises two small, pretty villages, Cintsa East and Cintsa West. It's definitely the best place on this part of the coast to hang out for a few days (or weeks). Also in the area is the private, upmarket **Inkenkwesi Game Reserve** (☎ 043-734 3234; www .inkwenkwezi.com; morning/afternoon game drive R495/ 395; ☿ 8am-4pm), which contains four of the Big Five (only elephants are missing). The morning drive includes lunch. Any of the accommodation listed can help organise activities.

Imonti Tours (☎ 043-745 3884; 26 Venice Rd, Morningside) organises tours to the townships of Mdantsane and Zwelitsha, and to Bhisho and King William's Town. There are also full-day tours to Qunu on the Wild Coast, where Nelson Mandela spent his childhood.

SLEEPING & EATING

Cintsa offers several good accommodation options and an excellent restaurant.

Buccaneer's Backpackers (☎ 043-734 3012, 734 3749; www.cintsa.com; Cintsa West; camp sites/dm/d with bathroom R45/75/180; ☐ ☎) Something of a rarity, 'Bucks' is a sort of all-inclusive holiday resort for backpackers. Among the many activities on offer are free canoes and surfboards, a surf school, horse riding, booze cruises and school visits (the nearby Belugha school is supported partially by donations from guests). There is also a volleyball court, climbing wall, and a 'beauty bungalow' where you can get a massage. Meals (breakfast R15 to R40, mains R30 R65) are available and on Sunday, the owners prepare a free breakfast for guests. Buccaneer's is also the base of the excellent African Heartland Tours (see p283), which offers single and multiday trips into the interior. Sleeping arrangements are in comfortable dorms and rooms, as well as safari tents (R160) and cottages (R280) with their own bathrooms and private sundecks. To get to Buccaneer's, follow the Cintsa West turn-off for about 200m until you reach the entrance; the main buildings are a further 2km along the dirt road.

Crawfords Lodge & Cabins (☎ 043-738 5000; www .crawfordscabins.co.za; Cintsa East; s/d with breakfast R300/550, self-catering cottages R450; ☒ ☐ ☎) This midrange miniresort has 23 cottages plus three B&B apartments. It's close to the pool, has good beach access and tennis courts.

Dolphin View (☎ 738 5432; dabeat@mweb.co.za; 18 Dolphin Dr, Cintsa East; s/d with breakfast R195/390; 🖳) Far more modest but very charming, this little B&B has just one guest room, with TV, microwave, radio and CD player.

Michaela's of Cintsa (☎ 043-738 5139; Steenbras Dr, Cintsa East; meals R49-69; 🕒 lunch & dinner Wed-Mon) Michaela's offers fusion-style food with South African ingredients. Book early for Sunday lunches. Wooden stairs lead diners up through a mini rainforest to the restaurant; for the less fit there is always the air-conditioned funicular!

Country Bumpkin Restaurant (☎ 043-738 5226; Heron Loop Dr, Cintsa East; meals R30-40; 🕒 4pm-midnight Tue-Sat, noon-5pm Sun) Perched in the hills above Cintsa East, this flashy restaurant serves up panini, salads, pots of mussels, calamari and pasta among other delights.

GETTING THERE & AWAY
To reach Cintsa from East London, take Exit 26 (East Coast Resorts) off the N2. Go over the overpass and follow the road for 1km to the Cintsa East turn-off. The Cintsa West turn-off is another 16km further on.

Morgan's Bay & Kei Mouth
☎ 043 / pop 2200
Along the coast from Cintsa, and reached by turning off the N2 onto Rte 349, is the village of Morgan's Bay, a good place for some peace and quiet and for beachcombing and surfing. Prices skyrocket and places get booked solid between mid-December and mid-January.

Just after Morgan's Bay and slightly more developed, **Kei Mouth** (www.keimouth.co.za) is the last resort before the beginning of the Wild Coast, which is reached by taking the **pont**

(vehicle ferry; per car R45; 🕒 7am-6pm) across the Great Kei River.

Yellowwood Park (☎ 043-841 1598, 043-841 1319; camp sites R45 plus R10 per person; hut shelters s/d R55/90), located about 1km from Morgan's Bay, is a very tranquil and eco-friendly camp site, surrounded by indigenous forest and frequented by birds and monkeys. Lifts can be arranged from East London or Mooiplaas on the N2.

Mitford Lodge (☎ 043-841 1510; 14 Beach Rd, Morgan's Bay; dm/d/tr R65/200/350) is a clean budget hotel with rustic décor and restaurant. Alternatively, the **Morgan Bay Hotel** (☎ 043-841 1062; www.morganbay.co.za; Beach Rd, Morgans Bay; r with breakfast & dinner R315-365; 🖳 🍴) is a light and airy family hotel with a Mediterranean feel and a bar serving pub grub. It rents mountain bikes (R150 per half day) and canoes (R25 per hour) There's also a **camp site** (camp sites R60-215) next door.

Strandloper Trails
The 60km, five-day **Strandloper Hiking Trail** and the one-night **Strandloper Canoe Trail** (bookings ☎ 043-841 1046; www.strandlopertrails.org.za; trail R220) run between Kei Mouth and Gonubie, just outside East London. The hiking trail is fairly easy, but good fitness is required. The Strandlopers (meaning 'Beach Walkers') were a Khoesaan tribe who lived on the coast but disappeared as a distinct group after white settlement. You'll need a copy of the tide tables published in the *Daily Dispatch* newspaper in East London, as there are several estuaries to cross.

There are four overnight huts and the cost of staying in these is included in the booking fee. Camping on the beach is prohibited, but most of the coastal hotels have camp sites.

THE XHOSA CATTLE KILLING

In 1856 a young Xhosa girl named Nongqawuse went down to the banks of the Gxarha stream, just east of the Great Kei River, to help keep birds away from her uncle's fields. When she returned, she announced that she had met with the spirits of dead ancestors, who told her that the Xhosa must slaughter all their vast herds of cattle and cease to cultivate their fields. When this was done, all the ancestors would return from the dead, bringing with them herds of fat, glossy cattle, and drive the white men into the sea.

To the Xhosa, their cattle dying en masse from European diseases and their chiefs reeling in the wake of a succession of frontier wars with the land-hungry Boers, it was a vision of hope. In the aftermath of the prophecy, over 100,000 Xhosa slaughtered their own cattle and slowly starved to death. The British governor of the province, Sir George Grey, rounded up the survivors to be used as slave labour and gave their abandoned lands to white settlers.

GREAT KEI RIVER TO COFFEE BAY

There are a number of hotels and resorts along the stretch of coast from the Great Kei River to Coffee Bay. Most can be booked through **Wild Coast Holiday Reservations** (☎ 043-743 6181; www.wildcoastholidays.co.za; King's Tourist Centre, cnr Longfellow & Aquarium Rds, East London). Most places cater to fishermen and South African families; prices rise sharply around Christmas and Easter. Locals take share taxis to get around the area, but the best way to get around the area is with your own vehicle.

Following is just a selection of the sleeping options available, listed from south to north.

About 16km north of the pont (ferry), **Trennery's Hotel** (☎ 043-498 0004; www.trennerys .co.za; s/d with full board R350/700; ☎) has attractive thatched bungalows, a bit run-down on the inside but still comfortable. There's a basic restaurant, a lovely beach, gardens and a pool.

The wooden deck at the smart **Wavecrest Resort Hotel** (☎ 047-498 0022; www.wavecrest.co.za; s/d with full board R390/780; ☎) has some amazing views over sand dunes at the mouth of the Nxaxo River. There are plenty of activities to keep you occupied here, including fishing, boat rides and horse trips. It's reached from Butterworth via Kentani; turn left at Kentani.

This family **Kob Inn** (☎ 047-499 0011; www.kob inn.co.za; s/d with full board R360/720) can be reached by car from Idutywa via Willowvale. There are some good hiking trails in the area.

Haven (☎ 047-576 8904/8906; fax 047-576 8905; s/d with full board R265/530) is a good base for exploring Cwebe Nature Reserve, close to the mouth of the Mbashe River. Coming from the south, you can reach it via Elliotdale; turn off at the village of Qunu, 31km south of Mthatha. It is about 70km from Qunu to the hotel and the road is unsealed from Elliotdale. If you're coming from the north, turn off at Viedgesville, 20km south of Mthatha.

Bulungula Backpackers (☎ 047-577 8900, 083-391 5525; www.bulungula.com; camp sites per person/dm/ d with shared bathroom R30/60/150; ☐) has only been around a few years but has already gained legendary status on the Wild Coast for its stunning location, community-based activities and eco-friendly ethos. It's 40% owned by the local Xhosa community who run all the tours including horse riding, hiking and canoeing trips. Guests are invited to help with community activities, including farming and teaching projects. At times the divide between the locals and guests is blurred – there are no fences or locked doors so local friends and neighbours are always stopping by for a chat. There's an overall mellow vibe about the place, but it does get raucous when a beach party is organised. (These are well away from the main camp so noise is not a problem for those who want to sleep.) Xhosa-style rondavels – painted in creative, sometimes psychedelic, colour schemes – serve as guest quarters. Ablution blocks include eco-friendly compost loos and 'rocket showers'.

The brain child behind Bulungula is Dave Martin, a South African who spent years searching the continent for the perfect place to set up a backpackers, and wound up right back in his own country.

Reaching this little slice of paradise requires some effort. (If you can get here on local transport you get to stay the first night free – there's a challenge!) Bulungula is 4km north of the Xora river mouth and around two hours drive from Coffee Bay. If you are coming in your own car it's essential to contact Bulungula in advance to get directions. Pick-ups can also be arranged.

Dwesa & Cwebe Nature Reserves

Nature lovers and ornithologists will appreciate both of these small reserves, which together take in about 6000 hectares of coastal land. Both have tracts of forest as well as good beaches and hiking trails. Some 290 species of birds have been identified. The reserves are separated by the Mbashe River. The only way to get to either reserve is with your own vehicle.

Dwesa Nature Reserve (bookings ☎ 047-499 0073; day visitors R10; ☺ 6am-6pm) is one of the most remote and beautiful reserves in South Africa, bounded by the Mbashe River in the north and the Nqabara River in the south. You may see the herd of eland come down to the beach near the Kobole estuary in the late afternoon. Other species present include buffalos and white rhinos. If you want to hike, you must take a ranger (R40 per day) with you.

To get to Dwesa, go to Willowvale and ask for directions there – the road has many junctions, very few of which are signposted.

In **Cwebe Nature Reserve** (bookings ☎ 047-576 9443; day visitors R10; ☉ 6am-6pm), you can walk to the Mbanyana Falls or to the lagoon, where if you are lucky, you may see Cape clawless otters in the late afternoon. On the southern edge of the reserve near the Mbashe is a small cluster of white mangroves where crabs and mudskippers are found near the stems.

To get to Cwebe, take the Elliotdale (Xhora) turn-off from the N2 (about 40km southwest of Mthatha), then follow signs to the Haven hotel.

There is **self-catering accommodation** (2-bedroom bungalows R150) at Dwesa, and **camping** (camp sites R30) at both Cwebe and Dwesa.

COFFEE BAY
☎ 047 / pop 600

No one is sure how tiny Coffee Bay got its name, but there is a theory that a ship wrecked here in 1863 deposited its cargo of coffee beans on the beach. These days, this once remote hamlet is a backpacker's mecca, with two busy hostels and a couple of more upmarket hotels jostling for space in the village centre. In between, a few hopeful locals hover, trying to sell *dagga* (marijuana), curios and day trips.

Coffee Bay itself is a fairly scruffy place, but the surrounding scenery is dramatic, with a beautiful kilometre-long beach set in front of towering cliffs. The two backpacker hostels, Bomvu Paradise and the Coffee Shack, run all sorts of day trips, including **horse riding** (2hr treks about R150), **guided hikes** (from R50), **cultural visits** (from R60) and **surfing trips** (R60).

Sleeping & Eating
Competition is fierce for backpacker bucks in Coffee Bay. Since you've come all this way you might as well take a look at a couple of places before settling down. You can buy mussels, crayfish and other seafood from locals and there's a well-stocked grocery store.

Bomvu Paradise (☎ 047-575 2073; www.bomvu backpackers.com; camp sites/dm/d with shared bathroom R30/65/160) This is the more hippified of the two backpackers in Coffee Bay. It's a soulful place, with yoga instruction, organic meals and drum sessions – it even has its own am-

phitheatre for locals and guests to convene for late-night jam sessions. If you don't have a drum, not to worry, the owner will show you how to make one. The dorms and rooms are rustic, comfortable and funky and the staff very efficient and friendly.

Coffee Shack (☎ 047-575 2048; www.coffeeshack .co.za; camp sites/dm/d with shared bathroom R40/70/200; 🖳) Just across the road from Bomvu, the Coffee Shack has a definite party vibe, with regular live local music in the evenings. This is an excellent place to learn to surf – owner David Malherbe was a surfing champion. There are dorms in the main block but the rondavels across the river offer a little more privacy. The ablutions on both sides are very good. Three-course dinners are available for R35, with free *potjiekos* on Sunday night. If you're coming from elsewhere on the Wild Coast, the hostel offers a shuttle service – the first pick-up is free.

Ocean View Hotel (☎ 047-575 2005; www.ocean view.co.za; s/d with half board R405/600, without sea views R351/520; ✖ 🖳 🖵) Ocean View has good-quality, bungalow-style rooms, with a deck overlooking the ocean. There is a restaurant (R80 set dinner) and seafood snacks are served in the bar in the evenings. Prices go up in high season.

Getting There & Away
If you're driving to Coffee Bay, take the sealed road that leaves the N2 at Viedgesville. When you reach Coffee Bay, you'll see the Coffee Bay Hotel on the right. A little further on is the backpackers' enclave. A minibus taxi from Mthatha to Coffee Bay costs R22 and takes one hour. The backpacker hostels meet the **Baz Bus** (☎ 021-439 2323) at the Shell Ultra City, 4km south of Mthatha.

AROUND COFFEE BAY
The walking around Coffee Bay is spectacular – one of the best walks is to the **Hole in the Wall**, a rock formation featuring an impressive natural hole that has been carved through the cliffs by the pounding of the ocean. The signposted turn-off to the Hole in the Wall is about 20km before Coffee Bay. There is also a direct unsealed road from Coffee Bay (about 8km).

Mdumbi Backpackers (☎ 047-575 0437, 073-810 7246; www.mdumbi.co.za; camp sites/dm/d with shared bathroom R30/55/110) is a great place to get away from it all. It's a rural backpackers in the grounds of a mission set in rolling hills next to a secluded beach. There are lots of water-based activities (the surf can be phenomenal here) and lots of opportunities to meet the local Xhosa people in a genuine setting. To get here, turn off the Coffee Bay road to Mdumbi and follow the signs.

About 8km south of Coffee Bay, the fenced-in **Hole in the Wall Hotel** (☎ 047-575 0009; http://home.intekom.com/holeinthewall; s/d with half board R265/530; 🖵 🔊) has plain rooms and good-value, well-decorated self-catering cottages (R300 for a two-bedroom unit). The landmark after which the hotel is named is a 2km walk away. Prices go up sharply in the high season, when the hotel gets very busy with holidaying families. There's an unsealed road here from Coffee Bay.

The no-nonsense **Hole in the Wall Backpackers** (☎ 083-317 8786; holeitwh@iafrica.com; camp sites/dm/d with shared bathroom R40/70/180; 🔊) is located in the Hole in the Wall Hotel complex, giving you access to all the amenities here. Facilities include use of the hotel's swimming pool and volleyball court, plus horse riding (R50 per hour). Meals are available at the hotel (breakfast R30, dinner R60).

COFFEE BAY TO PORT ST JOHNS

The route between Coffee Bay and Port St Johns takes in the **Hluleka and Silaka Nature Reserves** (☎ 043-742 4450; http://reserves.wildcoast.org.za/rs/10.xml), as well as Mpande village, home of the well-known Kraal Backpackers (below). It's a great route to walk, but there have been reports of ambushes and muggings along the way, so it may be best to take a local guide. See p283 for details.

Kraal Backpackers (☎ 082-871 4964; www.the-kraal-backpackers.co.za; camp sites/dm with shared bathroom R50/80) is a down-to-earth, eco-friendly backpackers that gets rave reviews from travellers. There is no electricity, no TV and no telephone – just peace, a friendly vibe and spectacular scenery on all sides. Nearby villagers look upon it as an extension of their community and come to sell fish and vegetables; visitors are welcome to go with them to their *shebeens* or visit the local *sangoma*. Hiking, horse riding, surfing and kayaking are all on offer. Meals (dinner R35 to R60) are available.

The turn-off to the Kraal is 70km from Mthatha and 20km from Port St Johns at Tombo Stores. From here it's signposted all the way. It is a 30- to 40-minute drive on a rough road from the turn-off to Mpande, where the Kraal is situated. To get here by public transport, get to the Shell Ultra City in Mthatha, then take a minibus taxi (R30) from there – just say you want to go to the Kraal. It's best to ring ahead before turning up. The **Back 2 Back shuttle bus** (☎ 082-400 3335; back2back@absamail.co.za) from Port St Johns (p290) will also get you here.

Umngazi River Bungalows (☎ 047-564 1115; www.umngazi.co.za; s/d with full board R530/1060; 🔊) This very popular and relaxed resort is at the mouth of the Umngazi River, about 21km south of Port St Johns. Lots of activities are on offer, including canoeing through mangroves, fishing, mountain biking and hiking. There's no public transport to Umngazi. To get there in your own car from Port St Johns, take the Mthatha road for 10km to the Umngazi turn-off. Turn left, and travel 11km to the hotel.

Accommodation with locals is also possible at Mpande. Readers recommend **Mpande Huts** (per person R60), located about 300m past Kraal Backpackers. There is no sign outside, but they have accommodation in rondavels with separate toilet and shower block.

Accommodation in Hluleka Nature Reserve is in self-catering wooden chalets (R230) for up to six people. In Silaka, you can stay in thatched bungalows (R200). To book either, call the **Eastern Cape Tourism Board** (☎ 040-635 2115) in Bhisho. Bring all your own provisions. Silaka also has 15 comfortable huts (R316).

Hluleka Nature Reserve

The crashing of the ocean and the wind whipping through the evergreen forest make for soulful sounds in **Hluleka Nature Reserve** (☎ 047-575 0410; admission R10; ☀ 8am-5pm), located midway between Coffee Bay and Port St Johns. The reserve combines rocky seashore, lagoons, forestland and spectacular ocean views. Burchell's zebras, blesboks and blue wildebeests have all been introduced.

Accommodation in Hluleka Nature Reserve is in self-catering wooden chalets (R230) for up to six people. To book, call the **Eastern Cape Tourism Board** (☎ 040-635 2115) in Bhisho. Bring all your own provisions.

To get to the reserve, take the road from Mthatha to Port St Johns and turn right at Libode, about 30km from Mthatha. The reserve is about 90km further on.

Silaka Nature Reserve

Silaka (☎ 047-564 1177; admission R5; ⏰ 6am-6pm) shows off its grace with the subtle and sublime detail of its tide pools and rocky shoreline. This small reserve, 6.5km south of Port St Johns, runs from Second Beach to Sugarloaf Rock. Near the estuary, where the Gxwaleni flows into the sea, aloes grow down almost to the water. Clawless otters are often seen on the beach and white-breasted cormorants clamber up onto Bird Island. It's a magical place.

Accommodation in Silaka is in thatched bungalows (R200) or 15 comfortable huts (R316). As with Mthatha accommodation, call the **Eastern Cape Tourism Board** (☎ 040-635 2115) to book, and bring all your own provisions.

PORT ST JOHNS

☎ 047 / pop 2100

The deliciously laid-back Port St Johns is a magnet for hippy types both young and old. This idyllic little town on the coast at the mouth of the Umzimvubu River has tropical vegetation, dramatic cliffs, great beaches, no traffic jams and absolutely no stress. Many travellers, lulled by the clinking of wind chimes and the sound of the waves, succumb to the famous 'Pondo Fever' and stay for months.

Information

Island Backpackers Lodge (☎ 047-564 1958; www.theislandbackpackers.co.za; 4 Berea Rd; per min R1) Internet access.

Tourist office (☎ 047-564 1206; www.portstjohns .org.za/tourism.htm) Located at the top of the roundabout when you enter Port St Johns.

Sights

A favourite sunset spot is **Mt Thesiger**, a hill with one of the most spectacular views on the Wild Coast. On its top is a disused airstrip that nowadays makes a good place for a sundowner. It's on the banks of the Umzimvubu River, just west of the town centre.

Sleeping

The emphasis in Port St Johns is on back-packers' accommodation, but there are a few more upmarket options too.

Amapondo Backpackers (☎ 047-564 1344, 083-315 3103; www.amapondo.co.za; Second Beach Rd; camp sites/dm/d with shared bathroom R45/75/180) Four kilometres from the town centre, this is a beautiful hostel with a great view of Port St Johns' idyllic Second Beach. The peaceful atmosphere is complemented by genuinely helpful staff, beautiful rooms and

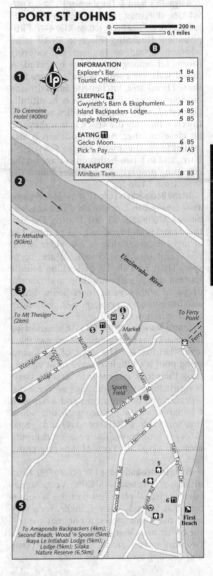

PORT ST JOHNS

0 ——— 200 m
0 ——— 0.1 miles

INFORMATION
Explorer's Bar................................1 B4
Tourist Office................................2 B3

SLEEPING 🏠
Gwyneth's Barn & Ekuphumleni.......3 B5
Island Backpackers Lodge...............4 B5
Jungle Monkey...............................5 B5

EATING 🍴
Gecko Moon...................................6 B5
Pick 'n Pay....................................7 A3

TRANSPORT
Minibus Taxis................................8 B3

To Cremorne Hotel (400m)

To Mthatha (90km)

To Mt Thesiger (2km)

Umzimvubu River

Market

To Ferry Point

Ferry

Westgate St

Victoria St

North St

Bridge St

Sports Field

Main St

Church St

Beach Rd

Hermes St

Second Beach Rd

Berea Rd

Shell Taylor Dr

First Beach

To Amapondo Backpackers (4km);
Second Beach; Wood 'n Spoon (5km);
Ikaya Le Intlabati Lodge (5km);
Lodge (5km); Silaka
Nature Reserve (6.5km)

EASTERN CAPE

holistic massage treatments. Activities at Amapondo include horse riding (R180 per day), boat trips, dive charters, canoeing and surfing – plus plenty of lying around in hammocks. Meals (breakfast R20 to R35, dinner R25 to R50) are available and the relaxed bar gets lively with locals and travellers at night.

Gwyneth's Barn & Ekuphumleni (☎/fax 047-564 1506; off Pussfoot Lane, First Beach; d with shared bathroom R220, 2-bedroom cottage R350-440) Ekuphumleni (meaning 'Place to Rest') is an adorable group of wooden self-catering rooms set among indigenous bushland. A raised walkway connects the cottages to a shared braai area, kitchenette and a dreamy outdoor shower. Each room is beautifully decorated, with scented candles and fluffy towels – the only drawback is that they're a bit close together. Accommodation is also available in the main house, Gwyneth's Barn, and in a two-bedroom cottage on the adjoining property. To get there follow the signs from Main St.

Island Backpackers Lodge (☎ 047-564 1958; www .theislandbackpackers.co.za; 4 Berea Rd; dm/d/tr with shared bathroom R70/180/225; 🖳 🖾) During the day this hostel is an island in a sea of calm, but at night it comes alive as a popular Israeli restaurant (dishes R35 to R50) and night spot. There's an all-day deli selling Middle Eastern delights like hummus and falafels, prepared with organic ingredients. Island also has laundry service, movies, book swap and a splash pool.

Jungle Monkey (☎ 047-564 1517; junglemonkey@ iafrica.com; 2 Berea Rd; camp sites/dm/d with shared bathroom R40/65/160; 🖾) The sight of the swimming pool is enough to make most visitors drop their bags and move in straight away. It sports hippy-chic paintings on the walls, a garden full of hammocks and a bar with a billiards table in the garage. It offers hiking, horse riding (R150 per day) and special rates for long stays. There's a big camping area and a typically Port St Johns arty-crafty feel.

Ikaya Le Intlabati Lodge (☎ 047-569 1266; ikaya@ telkomsa.net; Second Beach; s/d R140/180) A cute, somewhat neglected place just past the Wood 'n Spoon at Second Beach. It makes for a very quiet retreat and is good for animal lovers – the owner has a feisty crow named Jane, plus two boas and an iguana. Good quality crafts and clothing are also made here.

Lodge (☎ 564 1171, 076-134 7232; thelodge@ananzi .co.za; Second Beach; r with breakfast R400) Tucked behind Second Beach, the Lodge is a midrange option with well-appointed rooms and a very laid back atmosphere. You can order meals here, or eat at the nearby Wood 'n Spoon.

Cremorne Hotel (☎ 047-564 1113; www.cremorne .co.za; camp sites R50, cabins without bedding per person R90, s/d with breakfast R480/720; 🖾) Clean, comfortable rooms and rustic fishermans' cabins are on offer at this friendly, family hotel, in a spectacular location over the ferry from town on the banks of the Umzimvubu River. There's a cosy pub and a restaurant. Four-bedroom self-catering cottages are also available (R480).

Eating

Most of the eating options are within the hostels and hotels themselves. For self-caterers there is a **Pick 'n Pay** (cnr Westgate & Main Sts), outside of which is a small street market where you might be able to buy fresh seafood – mussels, crayfish and fish – to cook your own meal.

Gecko Moon (☎ 047-564 8354; Stan Taylor Dr; mains R35-65; lunch & dinner) This snazzy and popular restaurant serves about 20 types of pizza, plus pan fried mussels, shrimp and grilled chicken. It also has a few rooms (s/d with breakfast R295/480) behind it. They're very funkily decorated, but a little hot in summer. There's a craft studio here, too.

Wood 'n Spoon (☎ 047-564 8202; Second Beach; mains R35-80; 🕒 lunch & dinner Thu-Tue) This is a wonderfully rustic and laid-back restaurant in a fantastic location right by Second Beach, around 5km from town. The funky 'salvage' décor perfectly complements the friendly service and imaginative menu, which includes a few Swiss specialities such as alpe macaroni and cheese fondue, plus lots of fresh seafood.

Getting There & Away

Most backpacker places will pick you up from the Shell Ultra City, 4km south of Mthatha (where the Baz Bus stops) for around R45, but it's essential to book ahead (and turn up when you've booked). There are also regular minibus taxis to Port St Johns from here (R30, two hours) that drop you at the roundabout.

The **Back 2 Back Shuttle** (☎ 082-400 3335; this andthat@telkomsa.net) is a private transportation service catering primarily to hikers who need drop-offs and pick-ups. They also have a handy airport shuttle that makes runs to the airports in Mthatha and East London. Back 2 Back also has guided tours around the Port St Johns area; these include horse rides, canoe trips, village tours and meals with local families.

If you're driving from Port Edward, there is a good sealed road to Lusikisiki and then 17km of dirt road; watch out for maniacal drivers on blind corners. The road from Mthatha to Port St Johns is sealed.

PONDOLAND

On the 110km stretch of coast between Port St Johns and the Umtamvuna River lies some of the biologically richest landscape in the whole region. It's the future site of the Wild Coast National Park and possible mining interests (see below).

North of the Kokstad corridor is an isolated tract of Eastern Cape created by apartheid area land policies, with Umzimkulu as its main centre.

Mkambati Nature Reserve (☎ 039-306 9000; http://reserves.wildcoast.org.za/rs; admission R10; ⏲ 6am-6pm) encompasses expanses of grassland, dotted with forest and flanked by the Msikaba and Mtentu River Gorges. In future years, environmentalists hope that it will be the centrepiece of the 'Wild Coast National Park', if that project gets off the ground.

Mkambati's great scenery is a haven for a spectacular variety of birds, including trumpeter hornbills and African fish eagles. Animal species include elands and red hartebeests.

There are canoe and walking trails, or you can hire the park's own open vehicle and guide for a wildlife drive. A shop sells basic food. **Self-catering units** (☎ 039-727 3124; 10-bed lodges R550, cottages per person R70) are available. You get there from Flagstaff, which is 65km south of the N2. Take the turn-off just north of Flagstaff to Holy Cross Hospital.

THE BATTLE FOR PONDOLAND

In September 2005 the government of South Africa approved long-standing plans to create a national park in Pondoland. If and when the park opens it will save rainforest, sensitive animal habitat and important archaeology sites. The heart of the 'Wild Coast National Park' will rest on what is currently the Mkambati Nature Reserve. The decision, however, is not without controversy.

While environmentalists can claim a victory over the establishment of a new national park, many allege that the government is merely trying to throw them a bone while it allows investors to swarm around the park boundaries, laying toll roads and mining the coastal sand dunes. Even when the decision to create the park was announced, government officials could not reply when asked about the boundaries of the park, leading many to believe that the 'Wild Coast National Park' is merely a smokescreen and that the best parts of Pondoland will be sold off piecemeal.

The major attraction for investors is the mineral-heavy sand-dune mine at Xolobeni, eyed by Australian mining company Mineral Commodities (MRC). Of course, MRC would also need a road to haul out the sand to its proposed smelter in Coega.

With or without the mine, the government still wants a road built through Pondoland. The proposed highway is part of a major scheme to upgrade and change the course of the N2. The new N2 toll road between Durban and East London will shave 80km off the route, but carries a R6 billion price tag, offset by tolls topping R150 per vehicle.

The future of the road is still under heavy debate between local assemblies and interest groups, but if the government wins approval the N2 will alter the face of the Wild Coast. The section most affected would be Pondoland, which would need a new highway cutting through virgin landscape. Three huge suspension bridges are planned to span the breathtaking gorges – the one across the Mtetu gorge will be the longest in the world.

Environmentalists warn that the road will lead to high impact tourism that will destroy the last tract of untouched wilderness on South Africa's Indian Ocean coast. Instead they propose a 'biosphere' around the new national park that will be available for low-intensity agriculture.

For now, Pondoland sits undisturbed, its rushing waterfalls still flowing towards the sea and its wildlife still roaming without hindrance. But if you have any plans to visit the area, better make it sooner rather than later.

There are also buses running from Port St Johns to Msikaba, on the southern edge of the reserve.

The only hotel in this area is the glitzy and over-the-top **Wild Coast Sun Casino & Country Club** (☎ 039-305 9111; www.casinocity.co.za/wildcoast/sawild; r from R1400; ☒). It's reached from the Kokstad region via Bizana on Rte 61. If coming from Durban, turn off the N2 at Port Shepstone and follow Rte 61 (there are numerous signs along the way).

If this isn't really your style, you could opt for a tented camp or a village homestay on one of the trips operated by Wild Coast Trails (see p283).

MTHATHA

☎ 047 / pop 79,000

After dulling your senses on some idyllic stretch of the Wild Coast, chaotic Mthatha might come as a shock to the system. It's a scruffy, lively place with a fearsome but probably exaggerated reputation for crime. Commonsense precautions apply – don't carry your valuables in obvious places, and stay out of the city centre after dark.

The town was originally founded in 1871, when Europeans settled on the Mthatha River at the request of the Thembu tribe to act as a buffer against Pondo raiders. During the apartheid era it became the capital of the Transkei, the largest of the black 'homelands'.

The area around Mthatha is now famed as the early childhood home of Nelson Mandela. The first president of free South Africa was born in the village of **Mveso** on the Mbashe River, but he spent most of his childhood at **Qunu**, 31km south of Mthatha. A museum that incorporates both these areas has been built to commemorate the man who became the symbol of freedom and reconciliation for the new South Africa (see opposite).

Information

Dot Com Solutions (☎ 5047-32 2572; 45 Nelson Mandela Dr; per hr R25; ☒ 7.30am-6pm Mon-Fri, 8am-1pm Sat) Internet access.

Eastern Cape Tourism (☎ 047-531 5290/2; www.ectourism.co.za; 64 Owen St; ☒ 8am-4.30pm Mon-Fri) Provides maps and basic travel info.

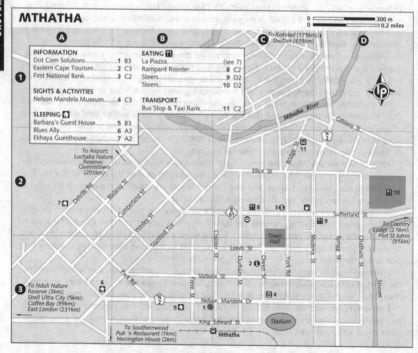

MTHATHA

| 0 | 300 m |
| 0 | 0.2 miles |

INFORMATION
Dot Com Solutions...................1 B3
Eastern Cape Tourism.............2 C3
First National Bank..................3 C2

SIGHTS & ACTIVITIES
Nelson Mandela Museum.......4 C3

SLEEPING 🛏
Barbara's Guest House............5 B3
Blues Ally..............................6 A3
Ekhaya Guesthouse...............7 A2

EATING 🍴
La Piazza................................(see 7)
Rampant Rooster....................8 C2
Steers....................................9 D2
Steers...................................10 D2

TRANSPORT
Bus Stop & Taxi Rank............11 C2

To Kokstad (175km);
Durban (439km)

Mthatha River

Callaway St

Bridge St

Elliot St

Sutherland St

To Country
Lodge (2.5km);
Port St Johns
(97km)

Madeira St

Durham St

Sprigg St

Delville Rd

Balaray St

Cumberland St

Wesley St

Stanford Tce

Cloister St

Leeds St

Durban St

Owen St

York Rd

Park Rd

Frere St

Victoria St

Town
Hall

To Airport;
Luchaba Nature
Reserve;
Queenstown
(251km)

To Nduli Nature
Reserve (3km);
Shell Ultra City (5km);
Coffee Bay (99km);
East London (231km)

Nelson Mandela Dr

King Edward St

Stadium

To Southernwood
Pub 'n Restaurant (1km);
Herrington House (2km)

Mthatha

MANDELA'S LEGACY

The Nelson Mandela Museum project, located in the heart of the Transkei where he grew up, was opened officially 10 years to the day after he was released from prison in February 1990. With characteristic humility, Mandela insisted that the museum not simply be a celebration of his own achievements but that it serve the whole community. The museum thus has three components – the Mandela Museum in Mthatha, a cultural and youth centre in Qunu, the village where he grew up, and a memorial near the remains of his family homestead in Mveso. It's the first museum ever to be built to a living person.

The **Nelson Mandela Museum** (☎ 047-532 5110; www.mandelamuseum.org.za; Bunga Bldg, Owen St, Mthatha; admission free; ⏰ 9am-4pm Mon-Fri, 9am-12.30pm Sat) contains the honours and gifts given to the former president, from schoolchildrens' artwork to presents from world leaders and celebrities. There's also a multimedia exhibition that encapsulates Mandela's role in the liberation of South Africa.

The **Nelson Mandela Youth Heritage Centre** is in Qunu, 34km away, close to the ex-president's own house (modelled on the bungalow in Victor Verster prison in which he spent his last few weeks of imprisonment). Cultural displays and workshops are held at this venue – ask at the museum in Mthatha for the latest events.

The **Nelson Mandela Monument**, the final component of the museum, is well off the beaten track in the small village of Mveso. It's a simple concrete structure adorned with photographs of Mandela. Follow the signposted route off the N2 between East London and Mthatha.

For more information about Nelson Mandela and his part in the reconciliation of the South African nation, see p46.

First National Bank (cnr Sutherland St & York Rd) Has an ATM.

Sights

The highlight of any trip to Mthatha is the **Nelson Mandela Museum** (☎ 047-532 5110; www .mandelamuseum.org.za; Bunga Bldg, Owen St; admission free; ⏰ 9am-4pm Mon-Fri, 9am-12.30pm Sat), which charts the inspirational life of South Africa's former president.

Nduli Nature Reserve (☎ 047-531 1191) is in a valley 3km south of Mthatha, while **Luchaba Nature Reserve** (☎ 047-531 1191) is on the Mthatha Dam, next to the water-sports area. Both reserves have zebras, wildebeest and antelope species, as well as many species of wetland birds.

Sleeping

There's a complete dearth of decent budget accommodation in Mthatha, so if you find yourself needing to stay the night here, be prepared to fork out.

Blues Ally (☎ 047-531 5047, 073-496 8496; stellah@ telkomsa.net; 80 Stanford Terrace; r per person R350; 🏊) This new kid on the block offers immaculate rooms with TV, an attached bathroom and a nice backyard with a swimming pool and braai. It's near the junction of Stanford Tce and Nelson Mandela Dr.

Herrington House (☎ 047-532 5692; herrington@tel komsa.net; 46 Vukutu St; s/d with half board R390/420) This is a good option 2km from the centre – a smart B&B with a big restaurant and bar, and satellite TV in every room. Ring ahead and staff will pick you up from the bus at Ultra City.

Ekhaya Guesthouse (☎ 072-432 7244; fax 532 4007; 36 Delville Rd; s/d with breakfast R475/627) This is a smart new place on the edge of the golf course. There's a pretty garden with a braai area and modern rooms with TV.

Barbara's Guest House (☎ 047-531 1751; barbp@ cybertrade.co.za; 55 Nelson Mandela Dr; s/d with half board R400/570) This motel style place is faded and fairly depressing-looking, but it's conveniently easy to find and the meals are surprisingly good.

Country Lodge (☎ 047-532 5730, 047-501 2812; clodge@wildcoast.co.biz; Port St Johns Rd; s/d R332/504) Situated just 2.5km out of town on the Port St Johns road, this lodge is a great relief after Mthatha's urban hustle, with chickens and guinea fowl pecking peacefully around in the shady garden. Breakfast (R40) and dinner (à la carte) are available.

Eating

La Piazza (☎ 5047-31 0795; 36 Delville Rd; mains R22-32; ⏰ lunch & dinner Mon-Sat) This no-nonsense restaurant in the Mthatha Country Club serves a decent range of pizza, pasta, salads and chops. It does room service for the Ekhaya Guesthouse.

Southernwood Pub 'n Restaurant (☎ 047-532 6336; Pick 'n Pay Complex, Southernwood; mains R20-60; ☙ lunch & dinner Mon-Sat) Another reasonable option is this straightforward pizza and seafood joint. It is just outside the town centre.

Rampant Rooster (☎ 047-531 0311; 92 Sutherland St; ☙ breakfast, lunch & dinner) Downtown choices are limited but you could try a plate of chicken at this place, located on the western end of Sutherland St.

There are two branches of Steers on Sutherland St.

Getting There & Away

AIR
Mthatha's Mantanzima airport is 17km from the city. SA Airlink (☎ 047-536 0024) has daily services to Jo'burg (R1600).

BUS
Translux (www.translux.co.za) offers a daily service from Cape Town (R350, 17 hours) to Mthatha.

Greyhound (☎ 047-531 0603; www.greyhound.co.za) stops in Mthatha on its daily run between Durban (R210, six hours) and Cape Town (R410, 20 hours). Local bus company DMJ Transport is reputedly much faster and cheaper than either of the above (Mthatha to Cape Town R220, 13 hours) – inquire at the downtown bus stop and taxi rank.

The **Baz Bus** (☎ 021-439 2323) passes through Mthatha on its Port Elizabeth–Durban run Monday, Tuesday, Wednesday, Friday and Saturday; it runs in the other direction Monday, Tuesday, Thursday, Friday and Sunday.

Translux, Greyhound and the Baz Bus stop at the Shell Ultra City, which is the pick-up point for backpacker shuttles heading to the coast.

MINIBUS TAXI
Minibus taxis in Mthatha depart from both Shell Ultra City and the main bus stop and taxi rank near Bridge St. Destinations include Port St Johns or the Kraal backpackers (R35), Coffee Bay (R30) and East London (R80).

NORTH-EASTERN HIGHLANDS

Roughly comprising the out-of-the-way area that stretches from the lush valleys of the Wild Coast to the sharply ascending peaks of Lesotho, the North-Eastern Highlands area enjoys the best of both worlds: stunning scenery and tourist scarcity. Summer brings excellent hiking and fishing, while snowfalls in winter provide the opportunity to ski (albeit on mostly artificial pistes). Watch out for harsh weather conditions in the high passes at all times of the year. In the more remote parts, you'll need your own vehicle.

QUEENSTOWN
☎ 045 / pop 80,000
Queenstown acts largely as a commercial centre and base for exploring the surrounding area. The town itself, nondescript and rather dull, was established in 1847 and laid out in the shape of a hexagon for defence purposes. This pattern enabled defenders to shoot down the streets from a central point.

The **Chris Hani Area Regional Tourism Office** (☎ 045-839 2265; sarto@eci.co.za; Shop 14, the Mall; ☙ 9am-4pm Mon-Fri, 9am-12pm Sat) is in the Pick 'n Pay complex.

Sleeping & Eating
Alisa Cottage (☎ /fax 045-839 2761; 37 Haig Ave; s/d with breakfast R140/220; 🔊) The best place to stay in town is the extremely good-value Alisa Cottage. Each room is a flat, with a sitting area, small kitchen and TV.

Conifer Place (☎ 082-926 6584; 42 Livingston Rd; s/d with breakfast R220/310) This relatively new guesthouse offers five neat en-suite rooms, all with separate entrances.

De Oude Werf (☎ 045-838 5702; 65 Berry St; s/d R265/350) A charming old-style Karoo cottage is the setting for this quiet and cosy guesthouse. There's a hearty optional country breakfast for R35.

Black Swan (☎ 045-839 7475; cnr Grey St & Ebden Sts; mains R30-50; ☙ lunch & dinner Mon-Sat) Still one of the best eating spots in town, this restaurant has a nicely decorated interior and a good menu featuring fish, pasta and a few vegetarian dishes.

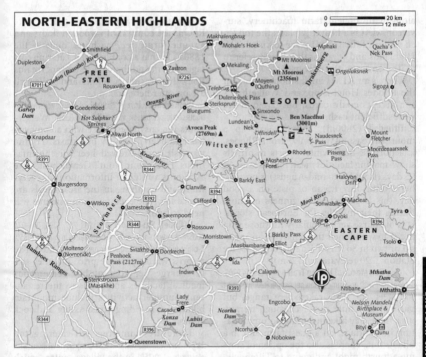

NORTH-EASTERN HIGHLANDS

0   20 km
0   12 miles

Getting There & Away

Queenstown is the hub for all transport in and out of the Highlands.

Greyhound (www.greyhound.co.za) passes through Queenstown on the Jo'burg/Pretoria to Port Elizabeth run (Port Elizabeth R150, 5½ hours; Jo'burg R260, 9½ hours). All buses stop at the Shell Ultra City (Cathcart St) petrol station. Greyhound buses also run from Queenstown to Aliwal North (R110, two hours). **Translux** (www.translux.co.za) runs daily to Cape Town (R230, 13 hours).

City to City (☎ 011-773 2762) buses have daily services to Jo'burg/Pretoria (R100). Another daily City to City bus runs from Jo'burg to Idutywa via Queenstown (R90).

From the **minibus taxi rank** (cnr Victoria & Komani Sts) you can travel to Cathcart (R15), Stutterheim (R20), King William's Town (R40) and East London (R80).

ELLIOT

☎ 045 / pop 17,500

Elliot marks the start of the Maloti Route, which takes in a particularly scenic region southeast of Barkly East. Otherwise, the town is rather derelict so there's nothing to keep you hanging around, particularly at night.

On Denorbin farm, near Barkly Pass between Barkly East and Elliot, are some well-preserved examples of **San rock art**. At 32m in length, this is the longest gallery of San paintings in South Africa. It depicts shamans entering a trancelike state while dancing. The rock paintings can be viewed by prior arrangement. Call **Gavin Small** (☎ 045-971 9052).

If you arrive late and need to overnight it, head to the **Merino Hotel** (☎ 045-931 2987; greg@imaginet.co.za; Maclear Rd; s/d with breakfast R200/320). It looks forbidding from the outside, but the managers are friendly and will either check you in or recommend other accommodation.

RHODES

☎ 045

Grassy, gorgeous Rhodes began life as a *nagmaal* (communion) town, where churchgoers from the surrounding area would regularly convene. Their original homes, along with ancient farm machinery, survive in what is a heavenly place: the top (in all senses of the world) place to visit in the Highlands and what locals jokingly refer to as 'the centre of the universe'.

There's an ATM (small amounts only) at the Rhodes Hotel shop, and Walkerbouts Inn accepts credit cards, but try to arrive with sufficient cash.

Tiffindell (2800m), about 23km up a mountain pass (4WD only) from Rhodes, is a purpose-built winter sports resort. Its snow-making facilities mean that a season of 95 days (late May to mid-August) is possible here. With only 1.5km of piste on a good day, this is perfect for beginners or those flexing their muscles for European slopes. It is of course very popular with those who prefer to spend their time enjoying an après-ski or two in South Africa's highest pub, Ice Station 2720 (elevation: 2720m).

The **Ben Macdhui Hiking Trail** (☎ 045-974 9305; 3-night trail with accommodation per person R200) is not too steep for the Drakensberg range, but parts of the route run over rough terrain; it's a three-day hike including accommodation in a cottage, on a guest farm and in a hiker's hut. There is also the option of staying a fourth night and going to Tiffendell.

This is considered one of South Africa's best hikes (especially at these prices), climbing all the way to the Ben Macdhui peak – at 3001m it's the highest point in the Western and Eastern Cape. Inquire at the Rhodes Hotel for more details. Mountain bikers arrive every October for the 84km **Rhodes Mountain Bike Challenge** (☎ 045-974 9290), while crazy joggers converge in July for the **Rhodes Ultra Marathon**, 52km of scenic torture up Naude's Nek. If you're into fishing, visit the **Linecasters Flyshop** (☎ 045-974 9298), where expert fly fisherman Fred Steynberg will set you up with equipment for fishing in summer and hunting in winter.

Sleeping & Eating

Rhodes Campsite & Caravan Park (☎ 045-974 9290; camp sites R40) The village camp site is in a great spot under shady trees right in the middle of the village. Inquire at Walkerbouts Inn for the key.

Rhodes Hotel (☎ 045-974 9305; www.rhodesvillage .co.za; s/d with full board R330/660, self-catering cottages per person from R105) Rhodes' only hotel is a charming establishment that looks

very much as it would have a century ago. Rooms are comfy, with wooden floors and antique furniture. The hotel, built in the 1880s, also has a couple of self-catering cottages to rent and there's a restaurant (mains R50). Horse riding, tennis and volleyball are on offer here, too.

Walkerbouts Inn (☎ 9045-74 9290; www.walker bouts.co.za; per person with full board R350) Walkerbouts is a cosy guesthouse with a convivial bar and hearty country breakfasts. Try the moreish home-brewed beer, or the infamous 'Fall About Stout'. Genial host Dave Walker is a mine of information on everything and anything in the area. Meals are available in the evenings; nonresidents will need to book.

Tiffindell Ski Resort (☎ 011-787 9090, 045-974 9005/4/8; www.snow.co.za; 4-bed chalets in summer R350, 3-night winter ski packages per person from R2000) The resort's winter package price includes skilift charges, equipment hire, emergency medical facilities and meals in the restaurant. Summer activities include mountain biking, horse riding, grass skiing and rock climbing.

There are numerous self-catering **cottages** (www.highlandsinfo.co.za; per person without/with electricity R120/150) in the village centre, which can be rented through the Walkerbouts Inn. Book early in high season, and wrap up warm in winter – some of the cottages have only gas stoves. There are three brief high seasons throughout the year: from 1 December to 15 January; 15 March to 30 April; and 25 May to 31 August.

Getting There & Away

The road to Rhodes from Barkly East, through the exquisite Mosheshes Ford, is rough but fine for 2WD cars (60km, 1½ hours), but don't attempt the route from Maclear unless you have a 4WD, and ring ahead to check weather conditions. The road to Tiffindell is now 2WD friendly, but Walkerbouts Inn does organise a shuttle (R115 return) – call for details.

BARKLY EAST

☎ 045 / pop 7500

On Rte 58, this town with its scenic and mountainous location bills itself as the 'Switzerland of South Africa'. In reality, however, it has little magic in comparison with Rhodes, a tiring but worthwhile 60km away. The **Magic Moments** (☎ 082-499 2388; 5 Molteno St; ☯ 9am-4.30pm Mon-Sat) craft shop can help with tourist information and occasionally has Internet access. For more information on activities in the area, visit www.wartrail.co.za.

The **trout fishing** near Barkly East is reputedly some of the best in the country. Anglers should contact the **Wild Trout Association** (☎ 045-974 9290; www.wildtrout.co.za).

Barkly East Caravan Park (☎ 045-971 0123/0299; Victoria Park; camp sites per tent R40) has clean toilets and pleasant sites. Follow the signs from Cole St, the main street running through town.

On the edge of the town near the road to Lady Grey, the olde-worlde **Old Mill Inn** (☎ 045-971 0277; fax 045-971 0972; cnr White & De Smidt Sts; s/d R190/350) has charming, good-value Victorian-style rooms, a bar and a restaurant (mains R30 to R80). It can also help with tourist info.

LADY GREY
☎ 051

A tree-lined road leads you into the village of Lady Grey, a sleepy town whose setup is nondescript but whose setting, the dramatic Witteberge mountain range, is anything but. Stop for a waffle and discover what the town has to offer at the **At Home Coffee Shop** (☎ 051-603 0176; Martin St; ☯ breakfast, lunch & dinner Mon-Sat), which provides tourist information.

There's excellent fishing, bird-watching and hiking in the area, and each Easter local thespians put on a three-day **Passion Play**, the largest of its kind in Africa.

Late November sees the annual **Sky Run**, an extreme mountain-top run all the way to Tiffendell. The run starts at the friendly **Mountain View Country Inn** (☎ 051-603 0421; mountainview@ladygrey.co.za; 36 Botha St; s/d with breakfast R250/460); call for entry details.

The private nature reserve **Lammergeier Adventure Trails** (☎ 051-603 1114; www.adventure trails.co.za; cottages per person R155, with full board R400), halfway between Lady Grey and Barkly East, features spectacular scenery and a range of ways to enjoy it, from quad biking to 4WD safaris to fly-fishing. There are also several multiday circular hiking trails to choose from.

Baggers & Packers (☎ 051-603 0346; 35 Heut St; joh andp@telkomsa.net; camp sites/dm/d with shared bathroom R45/60/140) is a hikers' guesthouse in a

former mission church. It's charmingly crumbling and a bit eccentric, with higgledy-piggledy rooms in various outhouses in the garden.

The very pretty and well-kept **Comfrey Cottage** (☎ 051-603 0407; www.comfreycottage.co.za; 51-59 Stephenson St; s/d R195/380, with half board R320/640) is actually a set of cottages situated around a parklike garden right at the foot of the mountains. Ask here about the geological and botanical tours of the area conducted by local expert George Freeme.

City to City (☎ 011-773 2762) buses leave Jo'burg travelling to Lady Grey (R80) on Monday, Wednesday and Friday at 8am; there is also a Friday service at 7pm.

ALIWAL NORTH
☎ 051 / pop 28,500

Aliwal North, on the border between the Free State and Eastern Cape, was in the early 20th century a major tourist drawcard, as visitors flocked here to enjoy its thermal spa. Evidence of this heyday remains somewhat circumstantial, and Aliwal North is today an obscure and somewhat tatty (if rather friendly) town. The original **spa complex** (admission R15; ☯ 6am-10pm) has dwindled to a few grubby swimming pools, but the countryside around the town is still ravishing. Contact the **Eastern Cape Tourism Board** (☎ 051-633 3567; www.ectourism.co.za; 97 Somerset St) for information.

At the southern end of town is a **Boer Concentration Camp Memorial** dedicated to the 700-plus Afrikaners who died in the British-run camp.

Sleeping & Eating

There are plenty of places to stay near the spa, but the best options are outside the (poorly signposted) town centre.

Conville (☎ 051-633 2203; www.conville-farm .com; s/d with breakfast R180/320) This exquisite, stately 1906 farmhouse designed by famed architect Sir Herbert Baker is like a living museum. It sits in stunning gardens overlooking a lake just outside town, and inside it's all rather grand, with brass beds and antique furniture.

Toll Inn (☎ 051-634 1541; tolherberg@xsinet.co.za; Rte 58, off Lady Grey St; s/d with breakfast R305/480, self-catering units s/d R260/390) A shame it's so near the road, but this former government toll station still makes a charming B&B, with smart rooms with TV and kitchenette in converted stables. Self-catering units are also available. Look out for signposting off Rte 58; the entrance is via the historic Sauer Bridge.

Queen's Terrace (☎ 082-262 0131; nff@xsinet.co.za; cnr Smith St & Queen's Tce; s/d with breakfast R300/400) One of the town centre's best B&B options, with stylishly appointed rooms each with its own theme. Try to get a room off the main road. There is a also a family room that sleeps four (R600).

Riverside Pub 'n Grill (☎ 051-633 3282; 1 Aliwal St; mains R40-50; ⏱ lunch & dinner) Located on the banks of the Senqu (Orange) River; the terrace at this restaurant is a good place for evening drinks.

Welgemoed Chalets (☎ 051-633 2692; cnr Duncan & Dirkie Uys Sts; 4-/6-person chalets R220/260) This

place is the best of the options near the spa, with self-catering chalets and a communal braai area.

Pink Lady Steakhouse (☎ 051-684 2189; 14 Dan Pienaar Ave; mains R45-55; ⏱ dinner Mon-Sat) A local favourite, offering no-nonsense meals.

Getting There & Away

A daily **City to City** (☎ 011-773 2762) bus stops here on the Jo'burg–Idutywa (via Queenstown) run.

Translux (www.translux.co.za), **Greyhound** (www .greyhound.co.za) and **Intercape** (www.intercape.co.za) services stop at Nobby's Restaurant (on the N6), near the junction with the Rte 58. City to City buses stop at the Balmoral Hotel.

The **minibus taxi rank** (Grey St) is near the corner of Somerset St.

KwaZulu-Natal

Rough and ready, smart and sophisticated, rural and rustic, KwaZulu-Natal is as eclectic as its cultures, people and landscapes. It's a region where glassy malls touch shabby suburbs, action-packed adventurers ooze adrenaline, while laid-back beach bods drip with suntan lotion. Mountainous landscapes contrast with flat dry savannas while the towns' downtown streets, teeming with African life, markets and noise, are in stark contrast to the sedate tribal settlements in rural areas. Throw in the wildlife, from the Big Five to rare marine species, the historic intrigue of the old Battlefields, and the sand, sea, surf and sun of the coast's glossy resort towns, and you get a tantalising taste of local heritage and authentic African highlights. Little wonder then that this is on the tourist 'must-do' list.

KwaZulu-Natal has its metropolitan heart in the port of Durban and its nearby historic capital, Pietermaritzburg. The beaches along this coast attract local holiday-makers and visitors wishing to soak up the four 'S's. Head north and you enter Zululand and the Elephant Coast, home to some of Africa's most evocative traditional settlements and cultural sites, where Zulu culture and heritage are proudly displayed. The region also boasts alluring national parks and isolated, wild, coastal reserves. Head northwest of Durban, around the towns of Ladysmith and Dundee, and you enter another realm: the historic heartland where the history of the province was thrashed out on the Battlefields during the Anglo-Zulu and Anglo-Boer Wars. The province's border in the far west, the heritage-listed uKhahlamba-Drakensberg mountain range, features awesome peaks, unforgettable vistas and excellent hiking opportunities. KwaZulu-Natal stimulates your senses.

KWAZULU-NATAL

HIGHLIGHTS

- Wildlife-spotting through the Big Five stomping ground of **Hluhluwe-Imfolozi Park** (p335) or sitting near a pan at dawn at **Mkhuze Game Reserve** (p345)
- Visiting five distinct ecosystems in one day in the **Greater St Lucia Wetland Park** (p339)
- Hiking the peaks of the Drakensberg's magnificent Amphitheatre in **Royal Natal National Park** (p349)
- Driving through the clouds over the **Sani Pass** (p356) to Lesotho
- Reliving the timeless clashes of the Anglo-Zulu War at **Isandlwana** and **Rorke's Drift** (p370)
- Enjoying the museums and restaurants of the capital, **Durban** (p302)

| ▪ POPULATION: 9.3 MILLION | ▪ AREA: 92,100 SQ KM |

HISTORY

Battled over by Boers, Brits and Zulus, Natal was named by Portuguese explorer Vasco da Gama, who sighted the coastline on Christmas Day 1497, and named it for the natal day of Jesus. It took the British Empire more than 300 years to set its sights on the region, proclaiming it a colony in 1843. Briefly linked to the Cape Colony in 1845, Natal again became a separate colony in 1856, when its European population numbered less than 5000.

The introduction of Indian indentured labour in the 1860s – sections of the province still retain a subcontinental feel – and the subsequent development of commercial agriculture (mainly sugar) boosted development, and the colony thrived from 1895, when train lines linked Durban's port (dredged to accommodate big ships) with the booming Witwatersrand.

The recorded history of the province up until the Union of South Africa is full of conflict: the *mfeqane* (the 'forced migration' of South African tribes; the 'crushing' in Zulu) the Boer-Zulu and the Anglo-Zulu Wars, which saw the Zulu kingdom subjugated; and the two wars between the British and the Boers. See p35 for more details about the origin and development of the *mfeqane*.

Just after the 1994 elections, Natal Province was renamed KwaZulu-Natal, in recognition of the fact that the Zulu homeland of KwaZulu comprises a large part of the province. From that time, Ulundi (the former KwaZulu capital), and Pietermaritzburg (the former Natal homeland capital) enjoyed joint status as capital of the KwaZulu-Natal until 2005, when Pietermaritzburg was named the province's official capital.

CLIMATE

The weather (and the water, thanks to the Agulhas current) stays warm year-round along much of the coast, with Durban lapping up a heady 230 sunny days a year. In summer, the heat and humidity, combined with the crowds that flood to the coast to enjoy it, can be exhausting, with temperatures regularly in the mid-thirties (Celsius). Most of the interior enjoys similarly balmy conditions, but sudden and explosive electrical thunderstorms, especially in the uKhahlamba-Drakensberg mountains and northern KwaZulu-Natal, often roll in during the afternoon. Winter even brings a dusting of snow to the higher peaks.

NATIONAL PARKS & RESERVES

KwaZulu-Natal (KZN) Wildlife (Map p359; ☎ 033-845 1000; www.kznwildlife.com; Queen Elizabeth Park, Duncan McKenzie Dr, Pietermaritzburg) is an essential first stop for those planning to spend time in the province's excellent parks and reserves. Accommodation within the parks ranges from humble camp sites to luxurious lodges; the free *Fees & Charges* booklet lists accommodation options and prices, as well as entrance charges, for all KZN Wildlife reserves. Maps to the parks are also available here.

Except where expressly stated, all accommodation must be booked in advance through either the Pietermaritzburg office, or the **KZN Wildlife booking office** (Map pp306-7; ☎ in Durban 031-304 4934, in Pietermaritzburg 033-845 1000; Tourist Junction, 1st fl, cnr 160 Pine St & Soldiers Way, Durban). You can book in person, by phone or via email. Last-minute bookings (ie those within 48 hours) must be made direct with the camp site (and are subject to availability).

Officially, the gate entry times of all parks are 5am to 7pm (1 October to 31 March: summer) and 6am to 6pm (1 April to 30 September: winter). These tend to change, although not substantially. We have listed the summer hours promoted by the individual parks at the time of research.

While many of the parks are a must-see for animal lovers and outdoorsy types, their camp sites are also excellent for those touring South Africa on a budget.

If you only have time to visit one or two reserves, highlights include the Royal Natal National Park (p349) for uKhahlamba-Drakensberg vistas, Hluhluwe-Imfolozi (p335) for the wildlife, Ithala (p337) and Mkhuze (p345) for stunning African atmosphere, and Kosi Bay (p344) and the Greater St Lucia Wetland Park (p339) for classic coastal scenery.

LANGUAGE

Eleven official languages are spoken in South Africa, but English, Zulu, Xhosa and Afrikaans are most widely used in KwaZulu-Natal. Also see p651.

KWAZULU-NATAL

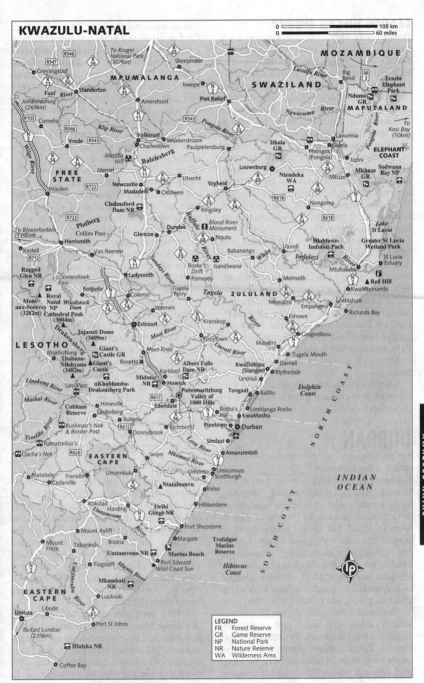

0 ——————— 100 km
0 ——————— 60 miles

MOZAMBIQUE

To Kruger
National Park
(307km)

Sheepmoor

MPUMALANGA

Iswepe

Piet Retief

SWAZILAND

Lusutfu River

Big
Bend

Tembe
Elephant
Park

Greylingstad

R547

R546

Standerton

Amersfoort

Pongola River

Ndumo
GR

MAPUTALAND

Johannesburg
(269km)

Vaal River

Wakkerstroom

Paulpietersburg

Ngwavuma River

Lavumisa

Golela

To
Kosi Bay
(10km)

Cornelia

Klip River

Volksrust
Charlestown

Ithala
GR

Phongolo
(Pongola)

Jozini

ELEPHANT
COAST

Vrede

R543

Majuba
Hill

Balelesberg

Louwsburg

Ntendeka
WA

Mkuze

Mkhuze
GR

Sodwana
Bay NP

FREE
STATE

Warden

Memel

Newcastle
Madadeni
Osizweni

Utrecht

Vryheid

Nongoma

Lake
St Lucia

To
Bloemfontein
(339km)

Chelmsford
Dam NR

Kingsley

Babanango

Uiundi

Hluhluwe-
Imfolozi Park

Greater St Lucia
Wetland Park

Kestell

Platberg

Collins Pass

Dundee

Nqutu

Imfolozi

St Lucia
Estuary

Harrismith

Glencoe

Blood River
Monument

Isandlwana

White River

Red Hill

Rugged
Glen NR

Van Reenen

Rorke's
Drift

Melmoth

Mtubatuba

KwaMbonambi

Olivieshoek
Pass

Bergville

Ladysmith

Colenso

Pomeroy

Nikwalini

ZULULAND

Nikwalini

Empangeni

uMhlatuze

Royal
Natal
NP

Woodstock
Dam

Cathedral Peak
(3004m)

Weenen

Tugela
Ferry

Tugela River

Eshowe

Gingindlovu

Richards Bay

Mont-
aux-Sources
(3282m)

Estcourt

Kranskop

Mooi River

Mandini

Tugela Mouth

LESOTHO

Injasuti Dome
(3409m)

Giant's
Castle GR

Mooi River

Greytown

Mvoti River

Darnall

Mokhotlong

Thabana-
Ntlenyana
(3482m)

Giant's
Castle

Rosetta

Karkloof

Albert Falls
Dam NR

KwaDukuza
(Stanger)

Blythedale

Umhlali

Dolphin
Coast

Linakeng River

uKhahlamba-
Drakensberg Park

Midmar
NR

Howick

Tongaat

Ballito

Mashai River

Sani Pass

Himeville

Pietermaritzburg
Valley of
1000 Hills

Umhlanga Rocks

Cobham
Reserve

Underberg

Edendale

Botha's
Hill

KwaMashu

Tsoelike River

Bushman's Nek
& Border Post

Bulwer

Richmond

Pinetown

Durban

Ramatseliso's

Donnybrook

Umlazi

Qacha's Nek

EASTERN
CAPE

Ixopo

Mkomazi River

Amanzimtoti

Matatiele

Franklin
Cedarville

Umzimkulu

Umzinto

Umkomaas
Scottburgh

INDIAN
OCEAN

Ntatabomvu

Kelso

Kokstad
Harding

Hibberdene

Mount Ayliff

Umtamvuna
River

Oribi
Gorge NR

Port Shepstone

Mount
Frere

Tabankulu

Bizana

Margate

Trafalgar
Marine
Reserve

Umtamvuna NR

Marina Beach

Flagstaff

Mzintu River

Port Edward
Wild Coast Sun

Hibiscus
Coast

Mkambati
NR

Umzimkulu River

Lusikisiki

EASTERN
CAPE

Umtata

Libode

Port St Johns

To East London
(235km)

Hluleka NR

Coffee Bay

NORTH COAST

SOUTH COAST

KWAZULU-NATAL

DURBAN

GETTING THERE & AROUND

Durban, with flights, buses and trains to destinations across the country, is KwaZulu-Natal's undisputed transport hub, and at least nationally, the city is well connected. Getting around the province itself, however, is a different story. While long-distance buses run to Port Shepstone, Margate and Kokstad in the south, Richards Bay, Empangeni and Vryheid in the north and a string of towns including Estcourt, Ladysmith and Newcastle in the west, many of the more remote locations are a headache to get to on public transport. Minibus taxis provide a useful back-up, but distances are large and relying on them as your sole means of getting about will mean many long hours in the back of a cramped van.

If you want to explore the region's true highlights (Drakensberg, the national parks and reserves and the Battlefields), you are better off hiring a car. Durban has a reasonable choice of operators, although they are not as competitive as those in its sister cities. Most roads are good, but a few locations – the Sani Pass (to which you can easily take a tour from Underberg), Tembe Elephant Park and Kosi Bay require a 4WD.

The Baz Bus links most of the province's hostels.

See p318 and Getting There & Away sections in this chapter for more details on transport.

DURBAN

☎ 031 / pop 3.5 million

Durban is like a maturing adolescent: sophisticated, sinful and ever-changing. Stretching along a swathe of butter-yellow sand, South Africa's third-largest city (known as eThekweni in Zulu) has always been known as one of the country's great escapes, offering a lively, if slightly tacky, prepackaged seaside holiday. But this has changed over the past few years. More recently, Durban is frequented as much for its stylish cafés, good shopping and cultural offerings.

The beachfront, with its multikilometre stretch of high-rise hotels and snack bars, remains a city trademark. Traditionally Durban was the silly-season stomping ground of white tourists from Johannesburg (Jo'burg) and Pretoria, who relished the beaches and

central metropolitan hub. Today, however, Durban caters to a more cosmopolitan market of all colours and creed. The city centre, peppered with some grandiose colonial buildings and fascinating Art Deco architecture, throbs to a distinctly African beat. Home to the largest concentration of people of Indian descent in the country, Durban also boasts a distinctive Asian twang, with the marketplaces and streets of the Indian area teeming with the sights, sounds and scents of the subcontinent.

Much of Durban's seafront looks the worse for wear and the centre's streets have lost some shimmer, especially when the sun goes in. Many international offices have relocated to the suburbs and, despite tax incentives introduced in 2004 to encourage investment in central buildings, plus ongoing development around the Point, areas of the city are like the visitors at the end of their stay – a little tired.

While the beachfront is still a favourite spot (the popular uShaka Marine World, casino and the Point developments have added some safer beach zones to those that were previously no-go areas), many visitors, wary of the city's increasing reputation for crime, and seeking more than surf, sun, sea and sand, base themselves at the more sedate suburbs such as Greyville, Morningside and Berea. These are chock-a-block with accommodation options, shopping malls, funky bars, stylish eateries and upper-echelon Durbanites. They also feature excellent museums and galleries.

HISTORY

It took some time for Durban to be established. Natal Bay, on which the city is centred, provided refuge for seafarers at least as early as 1685, and it's thought that Vasco da Gama anchored here in 1497. Though the Dutch bought a large area of land around the bay from a local chief in 1690, their ships didn't make it across the sand bar at the entrance to the bay until 1705, by which time the chief had died, and his son refused to acknowledge the deal.

With a good port established at Delagoa Bay (now Maputo in Mozambique), Natal Bay attracted little attention from Europeans until 1824, when Henry Fynn and Francis Farewell set up a base here to trade for ivory with the Zulu. Shaka, a powerful Zulu

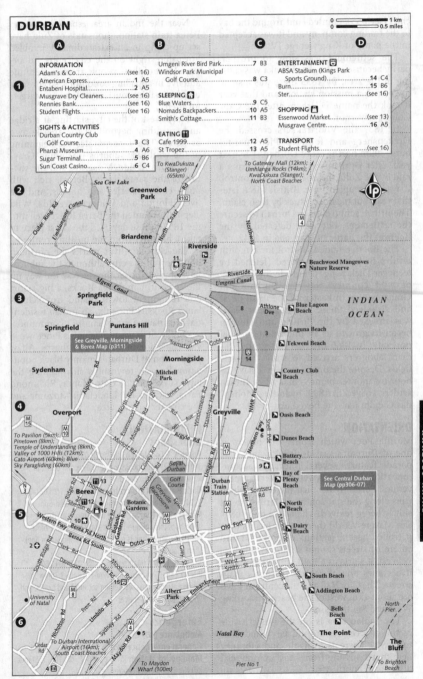

DURBAN

0 ——— 1 km
0 ——— 0.5 miles

INFORMATION
Adam's & Co.....................................(see 16)
American Express.................................1 A5
Entabeni Hospital................................2 A5
Musgrave Dry Cleaners.......................(see 16)
Rennies Bank....................................(see 16)
Student Flights..................................(see 16)

SIGHTS & ACTIVITIES
Durban Country Club
  Golf Course.......................................3 C3
Phanzi Museum.....................................4 A6
Sugar Terminal.....................................5 B6
Sun Coast Casino..................................6 C4

Umgeni River Bird Park...........................7 B3
Windsor Park Municipal
  Golf Course......................................8 C3

SLEEPING
Blue Waters..9 C5
Nomads Backpackers............................10 A5
Smith's Cottage..................................11 B3

EATING
Cafe 1999...12 A5
St Tropez..13 A5

ENTERTAINMENT
ABSA Stadium (Kings Park
  Sports Ground)................................14 C4
Burn...15 B6
Ster..(see 16)

SHOPPING
Essenwood Market.............................(see 13)
Musgrave Centre.................................16 A5

TRANSPORT
Student Flights..................................(see 16)

KWAZULU-NATAL

chief (see p35), granted land around the bay to the trading company and it was accepted in the name of King George IV.

The settlement was slow to prosper, partly because of the chaos Shaka was causing in the area. By 1835 there was a small town with a mission station, and that year it took the name D'Urban, after the Cape Colony governor.

In 1837 the Voortrekkers crossed the Drakensberg and founded Pietermaritzburg, 80km northwest of Durban. The next year, after Durban was evacuated during a raid by the Zulu, the Boers claimed control. It was reoccupied by a British force later that year, but the Boers stuck by their claim. The British sent troops to Durban to secure the settlement, but were defeated by the Boers at the Battle of Congella in 1842.

The Boers retained control for a month until a British frigate arrived (fetched by teenager Dick King, who rode the 1000km of wild country between Durban and Grahamstown in Eastern Cape in 10 days) and dislodged them. The next year Natal was annexed by the British, and Durban began its growth as an important colonial port city. In 1860 the first indentured Indian labourers arrived to work the cane fields. Despite the unjust system – slave labour by another name – many free Indian settlers arrived in 1893, including Mohandas Gandhi (see the boxed text, p40).

ORIENTATION

Marine Pde, which fronts the beach, is one of Durban's seaside focal points. The parade features several midrange accommodation options, as well as entertainment venues. Formerly derelict, the Point, which runs along the spit south of Marine Pde, is slowly being revived. The area's huge uShaka Marine World theme park has its own patrolled beach; sections of Point Rd and adjoining streets should still be avoided.

West St starts as a mall, but further west it becomes one of central Durban's main streets. The City Hall and the centre of town are about 1km west of the beach, straddling West and Smith Sts.

The Indian area is on the western side of the city centre, around Grey and Victoria Sts. There is a bustle and vibrancy here that's missing from most commercial districts in South Africa.

Near the Indian area, especially around Berea train station, thousands of Zulu have set up camp in an extraordinarily jumbled 'township' right on the city centre's doorstep. Most of these people are near-destitute and live in appalling conditions, so conspicuously wealthy tourists are obvious targets for theft.

Northwest of the city, starting at a ridge and spreading beyond, is the area known as Berea. This incorporates the beginning of the wealthier suburbs (including Greyville, Morningside, Musgrave and the suburb of the same name, Berea), rich with pubs, clubs, eateries and hostels, and the lively Florida and Windermere Rds. Wild elephants roamed the Berea Ridge well into the 1850s; these days, it's the safest place to take a breather from the bustling centre.

The Umgeni River marks the northern boundary of the city, although the suburbs have sprawled over the river all the way up the coast to Umhlanga Rocks, a big resort and retirement town. Inland from Umhlanga Rocks is Phoenix, an Indian residential area named after Gandhi's commune.

On the city's western fringe is Pinetown, a vast collection of dormitory suburbs. A fair proportion of Durban's mainly black population lives in townships surrounding the city. These include Cato Manor, Richmond Farm, KwaMashu, Lindelani, Ntuzuma and the Greater Inanda area.

INFORMATION
Bookshops

Adam's & Co (Map pp306-7; ☎ 031-304 8571; 341 West St) Good bookshop with a second outlet at the Musgrave Centre in Berea.

Ike's Books & Collectables (Map p311; ☎ 031-303 9214; 48a Florida Rd, Morningside; ☽ 10am-5pm Mon-Fri, 9am-2pm Sat) More like a museum than a bookshop, this antique-filled delight is chock-a-block with 1st editions and is everything an antiquarian bookshop should be.

Steve & Toni's (Map pp306-7; ☎ 031-301 2801; 7 Mark Lane; ☽ 8am-5pm Mon-Fri, 8am-3.30pm Sat) A labyrinthine bookshop selling second-hand books, and with an exchange service.

Emergency

Ambulance (☎ 10177)
General emergency (☎ 031-361 0000)
Main police station (Map pp306-7; ☎ 10111; Stanger Rd) North of the city centre.

Police office (Map pp306-7; ☎ 031-368 3399; Marine Pde) Near Funworld on the beach.

Internet Access

Most hostels offer Internet access. Charges start at about R40 per hour. Other options:
Internet café (Map pp306-7; ☎ 031-305 6998; 1st fl, Workshop, Aliwal St; per hr R25; ☯ 8.30am-7pm Mon-Fri, 8.30am-6pm Sat & Sun) In the city centre.
Internet café (Map p311; ☎ 031-202 7733; Musgrave Centre, Photoworld, Shop 323; per hr R34; ☯ 9am-6pm)

Laundry

McKleens (Map pp306-7; ☎ 031-337 5722; Palmer St; ☯ 8am-5pm)
Musgrave Dry Cleaners & Laundry Services (Map p303; ☎ 031-201 1936; 2nd fl, Shop 242, Musgrave Centre, Musgrave Rd; ☯ 7am-5pm Mon-Fri, 7am-2pm Sat)

Medical Services

Entabeni Hospital (Map p303; ☎ 031-204 1200, 24hr trauma centre 031-204 1377; 148 South Ridge Rd, Berea) The trauma centre charges R600 per consultation, the balance of which is refunded if the full amount is not utilised.
Travel Doctor (Map pp306-7; ☎ 031-360 1122; durban@traveldoctor.co.za; International Convention Centre, 45 Ordnance Rd; ☯ 8am-4pm Mon-Fri, 8am-noon Sat) For travel-related advice.

Money

There are banks with ATMs and change facilities across the city. These include Standard Bank, FNB and Nedbank.
American Express Central Durban (Map pp306-7; ☎ 031-301 5541; 11th fl, Nedbank Bldg, Durban Club Place; ☯ 8.30am-4.30pm Mon-Fri, 9-11am Sat); Musgrave Centre (Map p303; ☎ 031-202 8733; FNB House, 151 Musgrave Rd, Musgrave) The central Durban branch is accessed from the lane leading from Smith St to the Durban Manor Hotel.
Rennies Bank Central Durban (Map pp306-7; ☎ 031-305 5722; ground fl, 333 Smith St); Musgrave Centre (Map p303; ☎ 031-202 7833; Shop 311, Level 3, Musgrave Centre; ☯ 8.30am-4.30pm Mon-Fri, 8.30-11.30am Sat)

Post

Branch post office (Map pp306-7; Sea View St; ☯ 8am-4.30pm Mon-Fri, 8.30am-4.40pm Wed, 8am-noon Sat)
Main post office (Map pp306-7; cnr West & Gardiner Sts; ☯ 8am-4.30pm Mon-Fri, 8am-noon Sat) Has a poste restante service.

Tourist Information

You can pick up a free copy of the bimonthly *What's On in Durban* pamphlet at Tourist Junction. The monthly *Durban for All Seasons* is available from most hotels.
Durban Africa Tourist Junction (Map pp306-7; ☎ 031-304 4934; www.durbanexperience.co.za; 1st fl, Tourist Junction) Covers Durban; Airport (☎ 031-408 1000; ☯ 7am-9pm) In the arrivals hall; Marine Pde (Map pp306-7; ☎ 031-332 2595; ☯ 8am-5pm Mon-Fri, 8am-4pm Sat & Sun) Next to Joe Kool's; uShaka Marine World (Map pp306-7; ☎ 031-337 8099; ☯ 9am-6pm).
KwaZulu-Natal Tourism Authority Information Office (Map pp306-7; ☎ 031-366 7516/7; www.zulu.org.za; ground fl, Tourist Junction) Deals with the whole province and offers a smorgasbord of reference and promotional brochures.
Tourist Junction (Map pp306-7; ☎ 031-304 4934; 160 Pine St, cnr Soldiers Way; ☯ 8am-4.30pm Mon-Fri, 9am-2pm Sat) The main tourist information centre is in the old train station (built in 1894).

There are various booking agencies in the Tourist Junction complex:
KZN Wildlife (Map pp306-7; ☎ 031-304 4934; www.kznwildlife.com; 1st fl, Tourist Junction) Here you can reserve accommodation in KZN Wildlife parks and reserves.
South African Parks Reservations (Map pp306-7; ☎ 031-304 4934; www.sanparks.org; 1st fl, Tourist Junction) Takes accommodation bookings for national parks across the country.

Travel Agencies

Student Flights (Map p303; ☎ 031-202 5995; www.studentflights.co.za; Shop 324, Musgrave Centre, Musgrave Rd; ☯ 9am-5.30pm Mon-Fri, 9am-4pm Sat) Specialises in discounted student and backpacker flights.

DANGERS & ANNOYANCES

Crime against tourists and locals alike is a stark reality in Durban. Muggings and pickpockets are a problem around the beach esplanade and some central areas. Particular care should be taken around Point Rd and the area behind the esplanade. Avoid South Beach and areas around the Wheel Shopping Centre. Extra care should also be taken around the train station and the informal settlements nearby.

Many areas including the centre and beachfront are potentially dangerous (especially at night) and central Durban becomes a ghost town as people head to the suburbs for entertainment. Always catch a cab to nightspots (and with a group) if possible.

KWAZULU-NATAL

CENTRAL DURBAN

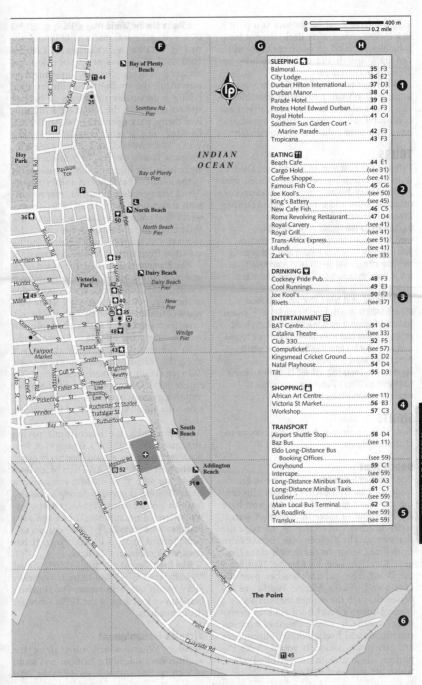

KWAZULU-NATAL

If you have a car, make sure you park it in a locked garage after dark. Do not leave valuables exposed on your car seats while driving – 'smash and grabs' have been increasing occurrences.

Wherever you are, do not make yourself a target: don't carry or flaunt valuables of any kind and wherever you are, if you are confronted by muggers, never resist and hand over your valuables – immediately.

TOURS

Perhaps the best way to experience Durban is in the company of a professional tour guide. Many hostels arrange backpacker-oriented tours and activities in the Durban area and around KwaZulu-Natal.

Durban Africa (Map pp306-7; ☎ 304 4934; www.durbanexperience.co.za; 1st fl, Tourist Junction) Runs interesting three-hour walking tours of the oriental and historical regions of the city (adult/child R50/25), as well as township tours. It can also provide a list of tour guides.

Sharks Board boat trip (☎ in Umhlanga Rocks 031-566 0400; Durban Harbour; 2hr trip R150; ☺ departs 6.30am) A fascinating trip is to accompany Sharks Board personnel in their boat when they tag and release trapped sharks and other fish from the shark nets that protect Durban's beachfront (see p326).

Tekweni Eco-Tours (☎ 031-463 2576; www.tekweni ecotours.co.za) Offers a Durban City Explorer tour to museums, markets and townships.

SIGHTS

Note that a tour may be the best way to see Durban's sights.

Beachfront

You'll either love or hate the Durban beachfront and sandy beaches. If you dip into the city's summer surf and sun, you have a playground of more than 6km of warm-water beaches (protected by the requisite shark nets). The 'Golden Mile' Beaches run from Blue Lagoon (at the mouth of the Umgeni River) to uShaka Marine World on the Point. The 'private' beaches near the casino and uShaka Marine World are accessed through the venues themselves.

But Durban's beachfront ain't for everyone. To some, its smorgasbord of bars and restaurants and hectic holiday atmosphere are garish and tacky. If you do take the plunge, always swim in patrolled areas, which are indicated by flags.

uShaka Marine World (Map pp306-7; ☎ 031-368 6675; www.ushakamarineworld.co.za; Addington Beach, the Point; Wet'n'Wild adult/child/senior R60/45/45, Sea World R85/55/75; ☺ 9am-6pm high season, 10am-5pm low season) is a massive new investment in improving the southern beachfront area. Filling a previously run-down 16-hectare site on the Point, the showcase R700-million theme park opened on 30 April 2004. Divided into several areas (Sea World, Wet'n'Wild World and uShaka Beach), the park boasts one of the world's largest aquariums, the biggest collection of sharks in the southern hemisphere, a seal stadium, Africa's largest dolphinarium, marine animals and exhibits, a mock-up 1940s steamer wreck featuring two classy restaurants, a shopping centre, enough freshwater rides to make you seasick, and a beach featuring activities from surfing lessons to kayaking.

The **Promenade** is the pedestrianised tourist superhighway running up the beach from Smith St north of uShaka. On the other side of the road, particularly along Marine Pde, you will find the canyon of high-rise hotels, bars, restaurants and nightclubs typical of seaside cities from Florida to Queensland.

In summer, rickshaws ply their trade along the beachfront, many sporting exotic Zulu regalia. In 1904 there were about 2000 registered rickshaw pullers, and it was an important means of transport. A 15-minute ride costs about R25 (plus R10 for a happy snap).

After uShaka, the beachfront's paying attractions are a bit of a letdown. A few, however, make for a good afternoon out.

The glitzy, nouveau Art Deco of **Sun Coast Casino** (Map p303; ☎ 031-328 3000; www.suncoastcas ino.co.za; Snell Pde) is popular among locals and features slot machines, cinemas and some well-attended restaurants. The casino's **Sun Coast Beach** (admission R5; ☺ 8.30am-5pm) is a safe and pleasant spot to lie and bake. It has lawn, deck chairs and brollies.

Mini Town (Map pp306-7; ☎ 031-337 7892; 114 Snell Pde; adult/child R12/6; ☺ 9.30am-4.30pm) is a typically tacky model city with replicas of Durban's best-known buildings of the 1970s – best for the mini adults.

Victoria Embankment

Maydon Wharf, which runs along the southwestern side of the harbour and south of Victoria Embankment, contains the **Sugar**

Terminal (Map p303; ☎ 031-365 8153; 51 Maydon Rd; adult/concession R13/6; tours 8.30am, 10am, 11.30am & 2pm Mon-Thu, 8.30am, 10am & 11am Fri), which offers an insight into the former importance of the sugar trade.

A little further north, **Wilson's Wharf** (Map pp306-7; www.wilsonswharf.co.za) is a reasonably hip waterside development, with a clutch of decent eateries (p315), boat-charter outfits (p312), shops and a theatre. Enter by car opposite Fenton St.

Dick King Statue (Map pp306-7; Victoria Embankment), near Gardiner St, commemorates the historic ride of this teenager in 1842 to fetch a British frigate, after the Boers took control of Durban.

The **Port Natal Maritime Museum** (Map pp306-7; ☎ 031-311 2230; Maritime Dr; adult/child R3/1.50; ⊗ 8am-3.45pm Mon-Sat, 11am-3.45pm Sun) is on a service road running parallel to Victoria Embankment. You can explore two former steam tugs and see the huge wicker basket once used for hoisting passengers onto ocean liners.

BAT Centre (Map pp306-7; Maritime Pl) is a colourful bohemian arts centre started in 1995 as a job-creation and training project. It houses upmarket art and craft shops, artists' studios (explore a bit to find them), occasional live music, and a bar-restaurant (Trans-African Express), all cut through with a lively trans-Africa theme. Free activities, such as regular drum circles, are on offer.

The **Vasco da Gama Clock** (Map pp306-7), a florid Victorian monument on the Embankment just east of Stanger St, was presented by the Portuguese government in 1897, the 400th anniversary of Vasco da Gama's sighting of Natal.

Durban's **harbour** is the busiest in Southern Africa (and the ninth busiest in the world). A pleasant place to view the activity is from Wilson's Wharf or the balcony at the BAT centre. At the southern end of the beachfront, the Point is an old area on a spit of land between the harbour and the ocean. From the restaurants at the end of the Point you can watch ships coming through the narrow heads into the harbour. These eateries will be relocated in the future; there are plans to widen the channel mouth by a further 100m in 2007. Point Rd, leading down to the Point, runs through a notoriously dodgy area and is definitely unsafe at night.

City Centre

Dominating the city centre is the opulent 1910 Edwardian neobaroque **City Hall** (Map pp306-7; ☎ 031-311 2137; Smith St). In front of the hall is Francis Farewell Sq, where Fynn and Farewell made their camp in 1824.

The **Art Gallery** (Map pp306-7; ☎ 031-311 2264; City Hall; admission free; ⊗ 8.30am-4pm Mon-Sat, 11am-4pm Sun) houses an outstanding collection of contemporary South African works, especially Zulu arts and crafts – both temporary and rotating exhibitions (look out for the collection of baskets from Hlabisa, finely woven from a variety of grasses and incorporating striking natural colours).

The **Natural Science Museum** (Map pp306-7; ☎ 031-311 2256; City Hall; admission free; ⊗ 8.30am-4pm Mon-Sat, 11am-4pm Sun) boasts an impressive display of stuffed birds and insects, plus African animals. Check out the cockroach and dung beetle displays, the reconstructed dodo and the life-sized dinosaur model.

The **municipal library** (Map pp306-7; ☎ 031-311 2117; ⊗ 8.30am-5pm Mon-Fri, 8.30am-1pm Sat) is also in the City Hall complex.

The **Old Courthouse Museum** (Map pp306-7; ☎ 031-311 2229; 77 Aliwal St; admission free; ⊗ 8.30am-4pm Mon-Sat, 11am-4pm Sun) is in the beautiful 1863 courthouse behind the City Hall. It offers a worthwhile insight into the highs and lows of colonial living and houses an interesting sugar-mill exhibit.

The excellent **KwaMuhle Museum** (Map pp306-7; ☎ 031-311 2237; 130 Ordinance Rd; admission free; ⊗ 8.30am-4pm Mon-Sat, 11am-4pm Sun) is a must-see for those interested in understanding South Africa. This was formerly Bantu Administration headquarters, where Durban's colonial authorities formulated the structures of urban racial segregation (the 'Durban System'), the blueprints of South Africa's apartheid policy. There are powerful displays on urban Durban as it was, plus another on Cato Manor, Durban's contemporary informal settlement and the site of the new South Africa's ambitious urban-renewal programme.

On the eastern side of the main post office on West St is **Church Sq** (Map pp306-7), with its old vicarage and the 1909 **St Paul's Church**.

The **Old House Museum** (Map pp306-7; ☎ 031-311 2261; 31 St Andrews St; admission free; ⊗ 8.30am-4pm Mon-Sat, 11am-4pm Sun) is the restored home of Natal's first prime minister.

KWAZULU-NATAL

Indian Area

The big **Juma Mosque** (Map pp306-7; ☎ 031-306 0026; cnr Queen & Grey Sts; �9am-4pm Mon-Fri, 9am-11am Sat) is the largest in the southern hemisphere; call ahead for a guided tour. **Madrassa Arcade** is next to the mosque between Grey St and Cathedral Rd near the Catholic Emmanuel Cathedral.

Alayam Hindu Temple (Map pp306-7; Somtseu Rd; ☎7am-6pm) is the oldest and biggest in South Africa. It's away from the main Indian area, on Somtseu Rd, which runs between Stanger St and NMR Ave.

See p318 for information on the popular Victoria St Market.

Greyville, Morningside & Berea

The **Campbell Collections** (Map p311; ☎ 031-207 3432; 220 Marriott Rd, cnr Essenwood Rd; admission R15; ☎by appointment only) are well worth seeing. Muckleneuk, a superb house designed by Sir Herbert Baker, holds the documents and artefacts collected by Dr Killie Campbell and her father Sir Marshall Campbell (KwaMashu township is named after him), which are extremely important records of early Natal and Zulu culture.

Killie Campbell began collecting works by black artists 60 years before the Durban Gallery did so, and she was the first patron of Barbara Tyrrell. Tyrrell recorded the traditional costumes of the indigenous peoples; her paintings beautifully convey clothing and decoration, and the grace of the people wearing them.

The **Phanzi Museum** (Map p303; ☎ 031-206 1591; 41 Cedar Rd, Glenwood, cnr Frere Rd; admission R30; ☎by appointment) houses a private collection of Southern African tribal artefacts, displayed in the basement of a Victorian home. Owner-collector Paul Mikula has amassed outstanding examples of contemporary sculptures, beadwork of KwaZulu-Natal, carved statues, and artefacts from pipes to fertility dolls.

The **Botanic Gardens** (Map p303; ☎ 031-309 1170; Sydenham Rd; admission free; ☎7.30am-5.15pm 16 Apr-15 Sep, 7.30am-5.45pm 16 Sep-15 Apr) is a 20-hectare garden with one of the rarest cycads, *Encephalartos woodii*, as well as many species of bromeliad and is a pleasant place to wander. On weekends local bridal parties galore pose with their petals for the photographers. The gardens play host to an annual concert series featuring the KZN Philharmonic

Orchestra and other musicians (adults/children/students R35/free/25).

North & West Durban

Umgeni River Bird Park (Map p303; ☎ 031-579 4600; Riverside Rd; adult/child R20/15; ☎9am-5pm) on the Umgeni River makes for a relaxing escape from the throng. You can see many African bird species in lush vegetation and aviaries. Look out for the chicks in the 'baby room'.

Temple of Understanding (☎ 031-403 3328; Bhaktieedanta Sami Rd; ☎10am-1pm & 4-8pm), situated 8km west of Durban, is the biggest Hare Krishna temple in the southern hemisphere. This unusual building also houses a vegetarian restaurant. Follow the N3 towards Pietermaritzburg and then branch off to the N2 south. Take the Chatsworth turn-off and turn right towards the centre of Chatsworth.

ACTIVITIES

With a temperate climate and excellent facilities, Durbanites are passionate about their nature, outdoor and adrenaline-inducing activities. Durban offers heaps of fun for outdoor types.

Bird-Watching

Avian EcoTours (☎ 031-262 8984; www.avianeco.co.za; activities from R350) offers birding walks and excursions around Durban and elsewhere. Guide Terry Walls is also passionate about wildlife conservation.

Canoeing

Trips on nearby rivers can be organised through **180° Adventures** (☎ 031-566 4955; www.180.co.za). Keen paddlers can try their luck by fronting up to one of the canoeing clubs at Blue Lagoon Beach on Umgeni River.

Cycling

Durban Mountain Bike Club (☎ 031-312 9076) runs informal Saturday-afternoon rides. Give it a call and find out where riders meet.

Diving & Fishing

Underwater World (Map pp306-7; ☎ 031-332 5820; www.underwaterworld.co.za; 251 Point Rd) runs open-water courses from R1850 and organises dives to sites around Durban over the weekend (from R140).

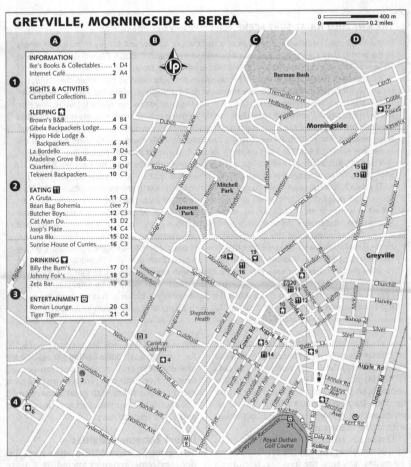

GREYVILLE, MORNINGSIDE & BEREA

INFORMATION
Ike's Books & Collectables......1 D4
Internet Café..........................2 A4

SIGHTS & ACTIVITIES
Campbell Collections.............3 B3

SLEEPING
Brown's B&B.........................4 B4
Gibela Backpackers Lodge.....5 C3
Hippo Hide Lodge &
  Backpackers.......................6 A4
La Bordello...........................7 D4
Madeline Grove B&B.............8 C3
Quarters..............................9 D4
Tekweni Backpackers............10 C3

EATING
A Gruta...............................11 C3
Bean Bag Bohemia............(see 7)
Butcher Boys.......................12 C3
Cat Man Du.........................13 D2
Joop's Place........................14 C4
Luna Blu.............................15 D2
Sunrise House of Curries.......16 C3

DRINKING
Billy the Bum's....................17 D1
Johnny Fox's.......................18 C3
Zeta Bar.............................19 C3

ENTERTAINMENT
Roman Lounge.....................20 C3
Tiger Tiger..........................21 C4

Dozens of outfits offer sport-fishing charters across Durban. The following include food, drinks and a day's fishing (maximum four to six people) in their prices.
Cool Runnings (Map pp306-7; ☎ 084-701 6912; 49 Milne St; per day from R3000) Kevin from the bar, Cool Runnings, offers a laid-back, distinctly Jamaican-style experience.
Lynski Fishing Charters (☎ 539 3338; www.lynski .com; Durban Harbour; per day 1-6 people from R3800) Ask how the boat got its name.

Golf

Durban has an array of decent golf courses. **Windsor Park Municipal Golf Course** (Map p303; ☎ 031-312 2245; fax 303 2479; NMR Ave; per person from R50; ☺ visitors welcome 9am-1pm Sat, 8-11am Sun) is one of South Africa's most popular courses.

On another par is the **Durban Country Club** (Map p303; ☎ 031-313 1777; Walter Gilbert Rd; per person from R425), considered by some to be the best golf course in South Africa.

Paragliding & Skydiving

Blue Sky Paragliding (☎ 031-765 1318; www.blusky .co.za) provides tandem flights from R350 and introductory courses from R950. It is at Cato Airport, 60km out of Durban. **Skydive Durban** (☎ 072-214 6040; www.skydivedurban .co.za; tandem jump R1250) offers a seagull's view of Durban.

Surfing, Sailing & Kite-surfing

For surfers, Durban has a multitude of good surfing beaches with any number of breaks

KWAZULU-NATAL

THE KWAZULU-NATAL SURF SCENE *Patrick Moroney & David Malherbe*

Durban and the KwaZulu-Natal coast have a surf culture, quality and history to match anywhere in the world. They are the home of true legends such as Shaun Tomson, Frankie Oberholzer (also known as The Search), Travis Logie, David Weare and Jordy Smith.

Durban itself has a range of quality breaks, given the right swell, all best when the sou'wester blows. South Beach and Addington are normally the best beginner spots, but with the right swell they can throw some gaping barrels. Dairy Pier has the best left-hander of the lot while New Pier, North Beach, Bay of Plenty and Snake Park can be long and hollow, often with great right-handers breaking off the piers. If the town starts getting a little too crowded, then head for the northern town beaches, Battery and Tekweni, which can produce quality waves with fewer people in the water. Joe Kool's (see p317), right on North Beach, is the most popular postsurfing *jol* (party).

The Bluff, just south of Durban, has some good spots, with the infamous Cave Rock being its showpiece. Often compared with Hawaii's Backdoor, the Rock is for experienced surfers only.

The KwaZulu-Natal coast really comes into its own on the north and south coasts, which offer a selection of world-class point breaks and the chance to get away from the city crowds. The coast is best in winter, from April to August, before 10am or 11am, when you're basically guaranteed a northwest land breeze. When solid groundswells roll in from the south, you are assured solid waves. On the north coast the best-known spots are Westbrook (arguably the hollowest wave around), Ballito Bay and Zinkwazi Beach. The south coast offers Greenpoint, Scottburgh, Happy Wanderers, St Michaels and the Spot (all right-handers). Each produces incredibly rideable 1m to 2.5m-plus grinders over rock and sand bottom, with the occasional ride that is a couple of hundred metres. Plenty of barrels are around, but check with locals to be safe. Lucien Beach, near Margate, is the place to check when the northeasterly is blowing. Further south are more right-hand points along the Wild Coast (p282), with plenty of quality waves between.

(see above). **Surf Zone** (Map pp306-7; ☎ 031-368 5818; Ocean Sports Centre, North Beach; ☼ 9am-5pm Mon-Sat, 8am-5pm Sat & Sun) rents out boards (R70/100 per half/full day) and offers lessons (R180 per hour). Upstairs, you'll find the **Time-Warp Surf Museum** (☎ 031-368 5842; admission donation; ☼ 10am-4pm), which is packed with surfie memorabilia.

Durban is an excellent place to learn to sail. **Ocean Sailing Academy** (☎ 031-301 5726; www .oceansailing.co.za) runs the five-day, beginner's ASA 101 course for R2995.

Kite-surfing is available through **Windsports** (Map pp306-7; ☎ 031-337 4069; www.windsports .co.za; 71 Pine St). A full course (three two-hour lessons, covering everything from safety to surfing) costs R900. Gear hire is available for R300 per day.

White-Water Rafting

The Umkomaas River and mighty Tugela River (uThukela in Zulu, meaning 'the Startling One') are *the* rafting places in KwaZulu-Natal. The Umkomaas offers some of the best white-water rafting, especially from November to April, when you can rip through Grade II–IV rapids. **180° Adventures** (☎ 031-566 4955; www.180.co.za) organises rafting on both

rivers (from R625 for Tugela and from R350 for Umkomaas). **Umko Rafting** (☎ 083-2700 403; www.umkorafting.co.za) runs an action-packed four- to five-hour trip plus a more lazy river ride of about 18km with great scenery and a few rapids to keep you alert and busy (R495 and R400 respectively).

Indoor Extreme Activities

The giant Gateway Mall houses some indoor extreme activities including a wave house, the first of its kind in the world, and the highest free-standing indoor climbing rock in the world.

Cruises

The luxury yacht **African Queen** (Map pp306-7; ☎ 032-943 1118; Durban Yacht Harbour; R150; ☼ depart 10am & 1pm) cruises dolphin waters for three hours. Several other boat and charter trips can be arranged from Wilson's Wharf.

FESTIVALS

Kavadi Festival This major Hindu festival is held twice a year (January/February and April/May). It honours the god Muruga, who heals and dispels misfortune and, as a sign of devotion, much self-inflicted pain accompanies the ceremony.

Draupadi Festival An 18-day festival in April/May, in honour of the goddess Draupadi, culminates in fire-walking.

Mariamman For 10 days during July/August the Mariam-man, or Porridge Festival, is celebrated.

Diwali The three-day Diwali in December is also known as the Festival of Lights.

Ratha Yatra The colourful, five-day Hare Krishna festival Ratha Yatra, held in December, is also known as the Festival of Chariots.

SLEEPING

Durban Africa's accommodation website www.bookabedahead.co.za allows you to browse and book online. **Durban Africa** (Map pp306-7; ☎ 031-304 4934; www.durbanexperience.co .za; 1st fl, Tourist Junction) can also help you out, whatever your budget, but it's best not to front up here on arrival with your luggage as you could become an easy target for theft.

Despite what you think when you see the hotel-lined beachfront promenade, much of Durban's accommodation is also in the western and northwestern suburbs, mainly in the form of upmarket B&Bs and hostels for the budget traveller. Unless you are in Durban for the sun and sand alone, accommodation in the suburbs is better value than the beachfront options. Some hostels will collect you from the airport and many arrange trips to the beach and other places of interest. Many top-end options are in

MARATHON EFFORTS

Three annual sporting events dominate the Durban calendar.

Each January canoeists compete in the popular **Dusi Marathon**, a three-day, 80km event along the Dusi and Umgeni Rivers from Pietermaritzburg to Durban.

The **Comrades Marathon** started in 1921 when 34 runners left Pietermaritzburg for Durban to commemorate their comrades who fell during the Great War. Nowadays, each 16 June, more than 13,000 runners participate in the race, which runs between Pietermaritzburg–Durban ('down run') or vice versa ('up run'), a varying distance which covers around 89km.

Each November thousands of cyclists compete in the **Amashoshova Cycling Race** from Pietermaritzburg to Durban.

the suburbs and towards Umhlanga Rocks, with a few in and around the city centre.

Beachfront
MIDRANGE
Parade Hotel (Map pp306-7; ☎ 031-337 4565; www .paradehotel.co.za; 191 Marine Pde; s/d incl breakfast R323/435; ⊠) The Parade Hotel is a bit old, with a slightly dowdy array of 1970s sales-room furniture and saggy mattresses, but its charming Art Deco dining room resembles a 1950s ballroom. Request a sea-facing room.

Tropicana (Map pp306-7; ☎ 031-337 4222; www .goodersonleisure.com; 85 Marine Pde; s/d R515/780; P ⊠) The bright and breezy Tropicana is another beachfront tower with an '80s feel, with spacious rooms boasting air-con and TV.

Blue Waters (Map p303; ☎ 031-368 3877; www.blue watershotel.co.za; 175 Snell Pde; s/d incl breakfast R650/ 720; P ⊠) At the northern end of the beach-front away from the madding Promenade crowd, Blue Waters is a classic hotel. The quilted bedheads, velvet chairs and pleasant rooms, all of which are front-facing with balconies, are the type your Aunty Dot would love.

TOP END
Ask about special rates at top-end hotels.

Southern Sun Garden Court – Marine Parade (Map pp306-7; ☎ 031-337 3341; www.southernsun.com; 167 Marine Pde; s/d incl breakfast R704/850; P ⊠ ▢ ▨) One of Southern Sun's four beachfront offerings, this comes from the steel-and-glass school of architecture, with modernish décor and uncluttered rooms.

Protea Hotel Edward Durban (Map pp306-7; ☎ 031-337 3681; www.proteahotels.com/edwarddurban; 149 Marine Pde; s/d R792/922; P ⊠ ▢ ▨) King of the seafront hotels, this is classic and comfortable, with fresh-polish smells and full-on décor with piped music to match.

Balmoral (Map pp306-7; ☎ 031-368 5940; www .raya-hotels.com; 125 Marine Pde; s/d incl breakfast R940/1260; P ⊠) Making the odd concession to colonial-era splendour, this beachfront place has lashings of understated style and plenty of plush rooms.

Victoria Embankment
Durban Manor (Map pp306-7; ☎ 031-366 0700; fax 031-366 0701; 93-96 Victoria Embankment; s/d incl breakfast R385/570; P ⊠) Housed in the former Durban

Club, one of the city's finest and most opulent colonial-era landmarks, Durban Manor is an impressive jumble of Victorian and Edwardian architectural elements. It has lost some of the Club's former glory (there's no sign of the billiard table) but the large recently renovated rooms ensure a comfortable stay.

City Centre

City Lodge (Map pp306-7; ☎ 031-332 1447; www.city lodge.co.za; cnr Brickhill & Old Fort Rds; s/d R555/690; ﾟ ﾟ) This secure place offers motel styling and slick service. It doesn't ooze charm, but it does have everything you would want for the price. Ask about the 'spouse-on-house' special.

Royal Hotel (Map pp306-7; ☎ 031-333 6000; www .theroyal.co.za; 267 Smith St; s/d incl breakfast R1620/2160; ﾟ ﾟ ﾟ) Overlooking the City Hall, the Royal is one book you shouldn't judge by its modernish cover. This five-star institution is one of the city's most historical and swankiest offerings and has hosted royalty and Nelson Mandela. There is a special floor assigned to female clients.

Durban Hilton International (Map pp306-7; ☎ 031-336 8100; www.hilton.com; 12 Walnut St; r incl breakfast R1805; ﾟ ﾟ ﾟ ﾟ) Glitzy and chic, this slick, modern behemoth is arguably Durban's most exclusive hotel, with crowds of business travellers and local movers-and-shakers filling the downstairs bar. Some excellent deals take rooms down to R1275.

Greyville, Morningside & Berea

BUDGET

Nomads Backpackers (Map p303; ☎ 031-202 9709; www.durban.co.za/nomads; 70 Essenwood Rd, Berea; dm R60, d with/without bathroom R200/160; ﾟ ﾟ ﾟ) An organised and neat, yet relaxed kind of joint (for those who like relaxing joints), and one that likes to party. If it's too cool in the pool, or the chilled-out crowd at the hostel's 'Bambooza' bar is not your 'thang', then you're a jump away from the cinemas and cappuccino bars of the Musgrave Centre.

Hippo Hide Lodge & Backpackers (Map p311; ☎ 031-207 4366; www.hippohide.co.za; 2 Jesmond Rd, Berea; dm/s/d with shared bathroom R75/120/180; ﾟ ﾟ ﾟ) There's not much room to swing a hippo in this cosy hide, but it pulls in the punters with its friendly, informal style and high standards. It's out on a limb in

terms of location but the staff will help you organise outings. You can always enjoy a wallow in the 'mock rock' pool or kick back in the TV room.

Tekweni Backpackers (Map p311; ☎ 031-303 1433; www.tekwenibackpackers.co.za; 169 Ninth Ave, Morningside; dm with shared bathroom R80, s with shared bathroom R140-160, d with shared bathroom R225-240; ﾟ ﾟ) This place looks as hung over as the travellers who stay here. It has a reputation as one of the party hostels, and this is the place for those wanting raucous, gregarious surrounds. Its friendly staff are in the 'nightlife know', and you're just off Florida Rd for social snacks.

Gibela Backpackers Lodge (Map p311; ☎ 031-303 6291; www.gibela.co.za; 119 Ninth Ave, Morningside; dm/s/d with shared bathroom & breakfast R90/175/240; ﾟ ﾟ) Housed in a stylish terracotta-coloured 1950s building with a Tuscan feel, this place takes a lot of beating. It has tasteful ethnic décor throughout, shower heads the size of dinner plates, bathroom floors you could eat off, and a friendly, personable feel in a secure location, close to Florida Rd. If you want to know about South Africa, the former tour-guide-now-hostel-owner is your man. Oh, and did we say anything about the delicious breakfasts?

MIDRANGE

Madeline Grove Bed & Breakfast (Map p311; ☎ 031-303 5425; www.madeline.co.za; 116 Madeline Rd, Morningside; s/d incl breakfast R295/450; ﾟ ﾟ) This large mansion is configured into various comfortable self-contained apartments both upstairs and down. The separate poolside room is popular among waterbabies. Speaking of which, it's child-friendly.

La Bordello (Map p311; ☎ 031-309 6019; www.bean bagbohemia.co.za; 47/49 Campbell Ave, Morningside; s/d R400/600; ﾟ) In former times, this boutique hotel was a house of ill-repute. Nowadays it's owned by the Bean Bag Bohemia team, who does good trade with the beautiful people who enjoy its plush Moroccan interiors, aroma oils and breakfast in its small fountain court. It's off Windermere Rd.

Brown's Bed & Breakfast (Map p311; ☎ 031-208 7630; brownb@iafrica.com; 132 Marriott Rd, Essenwood; s/d R440/660; ﾟ ﾟ) The communal living area of this smart establishment is decked out with chic interiors, ornaments and guests to match. These elegant suites are good value.

TOP END

Quarters (Map p311; ☎ 031-303 5246; ceres@threecities .co.za; 101 Florida Rd; s/d R825/1170; P 🐾) Right in the throbbing heart of Durban's most fashionable eating and drinking quarter, this attractive boutique hotel balances colonial glamour with small-scale home comforts. The cosy rooms have tasteful soft furnishings and balconies, and the restaurant is one of the best in the area.

Umgeni Heights

Smith's Cottage (Map p303; ☎ 031-564 6313; www .smithscottage.8m.com; 5 Mount Argus Rd, Umgeni Heights; dm/d incl breakfast R70/170, self-catering cottage R450; P 🖳) Travellers frequently praise this comfortable 'home away from home'. Super-helpful owner Pat has it 'down pat', offering accommodation in all shapes and sizes in a friendly, laid-back atmosphere. It's a bit further out, though within chirping distance from the Umgeni River Bird Park, and the hostel's shuttle transport ensures you're not cooped up for long.

EATING

Finding a decent bite to eat in Durban is rarely difficult; the ingredients are fresh and the helpings plentiful, although variety is a little harder to come by. Without doubt, your best bet for a good feed is in the suburbs. Many of the following eateries double as bars once the plates have been cleared.

Beachfront & The Point

While the beachfront is chock-a-block with cheap and cheerful diners, you'll be hard-pressed to find much more than the usual spread of burgers, pizza and candy floss. Several of the beachfront hotels house some passable restaurants. There is a clutch of decent seafood places around the Point (King's Battery), but it's safer to drive there. At the time of research, there was talk of restaurants on the Point being relocated due to the port expansion.

Beach Cafe (Map pp306-7; ☎ 082-762 9223; Bay of Plenty Beach; mains R26-45; ⏱ breakfast, lunch & dinner) Durbs's hot new beach hang-out. Soak up the sun in a deck chair or sun lounge (R15/25 hire per day), or chill out with a cocktail on the restaurant deck, overlooking the beach and life guards. Seafood BBQs and music on Sundays are planned for the future.

Joe Kool's (Map pp306-7; ☎ 031-332 9697; Lower Marine Pde, North Beach; mains R30-48; ⏱ breakfast, lunch & dinner) This popular nightspot's own claim to fame is as 'the world's worst restaurant' – a statement that is not too far from the truth come midnight on a Saturday – but it does serve a great Sunday morning fry-up.

Cargo Hold (Map pp306-7; ☎ 031-328 8065; mains R45-190; ⏱ lunch & dinner) A seafood encounter of the most novel kind. On the Phantom Ship in uShaka Marina, your dining companions are fish with very large teeth – the glass tank forms one of the walls to a shark aquarium. Well-known for casting some high-quality fish dishes with international flavours.

Famous Fish Co (Map pp306-7; ☎ 031-368 1060; King's Battery, the Point; mains R75-190; ⏱ lunch & dinner; 🐾) Something of a Durban institution, with a dreamy sea view (and the cargo ships are so close, they're almost on your plate) this reliable fish restaurant has fed such luminaries as Danny Glover, Jimmy Carter and the Springboks.

Victoria Embankment

The new Wilson's Wharf development on Victoria Embankment has a good choice of seaside eats.

Zack's (Map pp306-7; ☎ 031-305 1677; Wilson's Wharf, Victoria Embankment; mains R27-75; ⏱ breakfast, lunch & dinner; 🐾) Offering café-style dining, this stylish (chain) eatery serves good bistro fare washed down with a blast of fresh sea air.

Trans-Africa Express (Map pp306-7; ☎ 031-332 0804; 1st fl, BAT Centre, Victoria Embankment; mains R28-95; ⏱ lunch & dinner) Upstairs at the Bat Centre, with terrace views over the docks, this restaurant serves taste-tempting meals from Madagascar to Morocco. Try the Congo crocodile curry (R95).

New Cafe Fish (Map pp306-7; ☎ 031-305 5062; 31 Yacht Mole, Victoria Embankment; mains R45-200; ⏱ lunch & dinner) This distinctive green and blue construction was designed to look like an upside-down ship. Its seafood dishes are as appealing as its views of the city and surrounding moored yachts. The best catch is the good-value set menu.

City Centre

Takeaway places around Victoria St Market (p318) have good Indian snacks including *bunny chow* (a thick slice of Durban history!), which is a half or quarter loaf of bread hollowed out and filled with beans, traditionally, or curry stew. For daytime munchies and a cheap lunch, follow your nose to near the main post office where there's usually someone with a braai (barbecue) cooking sausages, or try one of the fast food chains at the Workshop (p318).

Roma Revolving Restaurant (Map pp306-7; ☎ 031-332 3337; 32nd fl, John Ross House, Victoria Embankment; mains R50-95; ☒ lunch & dinner; ☒ ☒) One of only 37 revolving restaurants worldwide, and one of the few central restaurants surviving in Durban, this reasonably priced Italian eatery offers stunning views over Durban in its own leaning House of John Ross.

The **Royal Hotel** (Map pp306-7; ☎ 031-333 6000; www.theroyal.co.za; 267 Smith St) has several renowned restaurants (closed Sundays): the **Coffee Shoppe** (mains 28-40) is great for a luncheon snack or relaxing cuppa; **Ulundi** (mains R36-60) is the place to sample a Bombay fish curry or a lamb dish; and the **Royal Carvery** (buffet R125) has a buffet for both lunch and dinner.

Greyville, Morningside & Berea

Durban's more affluent suburbs are filled with adventurous and not-so-adventurous eateries. Most whip up the same staple spread of pasta, steak and pizza, usually pepped up with a selection of Indian and African specialities. Prices are generally fair and standards reliable. The adjoining arteries of Florida and Windermere Rds are the best places to start.

St Tropez (Map p303; ☎ 031-201 9175; 199 Essenwood Rd; ☒ breakfast, lunch & dinner) Housed in a former power station, this pleasant sidewalk café-cum-bistro gives a pleasant shock – it has good coffee! Great for a Saturday brunch recharge (it's next to the Essenwood market on Berea Park), it has jazz on Sunday afternoons.

Sunrise House of Curries (Map p311; ☎ 031-303 6076; 275 Florida Rd; mains R12-45; ☒ 10am-9pm Mon-Thu & Sat, 10am-10pm Fri) You don't come here for the vinyl tablecloths, but for the food – this tiny place serves the cheapest and most satisfying *bunny chows*, roti wraps and curries. The chip chows will cure the hottest of hangovers.

Luna Blu (Map p311; ☎ 031-312 4665; 427 Windermere Rd; mains R28-68; ☒ lunch & dinner) Small restaurant, big aromas. Offering a range of gourmet toppings (Thai chicken, gorgonzola, roast lamb), this is the ideal place to order that special takeaway pizza (free delivery).

Cat Man Du (Map p311; ☎ 031-312 7893; 411 Windermere Rd; mains R30-100; ☒ lunch & dinner) This groovy diner-cum-cocktail bar serves international fusion-style tucker (and Cuban cigars) in barlike surrounds. Carnivores might like the kudu fillet in red wine (R85) and vegos are extremely well catered for.

Bean Bag Bohemia (Map p311; ☎ 031-309 6019; 18 Windermere Rd; mains R31-77; ☒ breakfast, lunch & dinner) The food and flavours are as creative as the mosaics, chandeliers and gothic décor of the artistically hip restaurant (upstairs) and downstairs café-bar. Temporary art exhibitions complement the theme. Don't miss the burnt-chocolate ice cream (R20).

A Gruta (Map p311; ☎ 031-312 8675; 200C Florida Rd; mains R43-130; ☒ lunch & dinner; ☒) If you're not heading on to Mozambique (or Portugal for that matter), this is a great place to sample the flavours of Iberia. It fills up at night, making for a nearly authentic Mediterranean-style ambience.

Cafe 1999 (Map p303; ☎ 031-202 3406; Silvervause Centre, Silverton Rd, Berea; mains R45-100; ☒ lunch & dinner) *The* place to eat for trendy Durbanites. This buzzing restaurant serves creative fusion food which comes in 'bitparts' – 'titbit' and 'bigbit'. Try the crispy roast duck on vanilla-seed risotto (R51/81).

Joop's Place (Map p311; ☎ 031-312 9135; Avonmore Centre, Ninth Ave, Morningside; mains R50-90; ☒ dinner) In a most unlikely location at the back of a shopping centre, Durbanites flock to this unpretentious place for its high-quality steaks. Rare indeed.

Butcher Boys (Map p311; ☎ 031-312 8248; 170 Florida Rd; mains R60-90; ☒ lunch & dinner; ☒) This stylish joint's catchphrase 'Grill by design' refers as much to its clientele as to its menu. The 'steak as you like it' is popular with business people and the 'it' market.

DRINKING

While there are basic drinking and dancing dens along the beachfront (watch what you wander into), the best options are found in the suburbs.

Zeta Bar (Map p311; ☎ 031-312 9436; 258 Florida Rd) Voluptuous red-plush seats and curvy soft lines provide the backdrop for this lounge lizard's favourite. Sip your cocktail and watch the beautiful people – or just have a cold beer on the terrace.

Billy the Bum's (Map p311; ☎ 031-303 1988; 504 Windermere Rd, Morningside) Attracting a crowd of Durban's upwardly mobile (even the sign above the bar says 'elegantly wasted'), this suburban cocktail bar is reliably raucous.

Cool Runnings (Map pp306-7; ☎ 031-368 5604; 49 Milne St) Ten years on (it recently had its anniversary) this (in)famous place is still true to its name – it has a truly Rasta bohemian feel and it stays open until 6am. Come late as it fills up after 11pm and catch a cab – this is *not* an area to walk around.

Joe Kool's (Map pp306-7; ☎ 031-332 9697; Lower Marine Pde, North Beach) The inevitable finish line for any day on the beach, this venerable nightspot cooks up a cocktail of cold beer, big-screen TV, dance music and feisty crowds. Sunday night is party night.

Johnny Fox's (Map p311; ☎ 031-303 5404; 295 Florida Rd) This no-nonsense Irish bar, set in a plush colonial villa, serves up a passable pint of Guinness, a massive TV sports screen and a fair dose of *craic* (good times).

Rivets (Map pp306-7; ☎ 031-336 8100; Durban Hilton, 12 Walnut St) As glossy as you'd expect a bar in the guts of the Hilton to be, Rivets boasts Thursday jazz nights, chichi décor, a contingent of the beautiful set and pricey cocktails.

Cockney Pride Pub (Map pp306-7; ☎ 031-337 5511; cnr Marine Pde & West St) This little slice of East London features all the authentic features of a true English boozer: pub tucker, caricatures of the regulars on the walls, billows of smoke and stained carpets.

ENTERTAINMENT

Durban is a lively city with a vibrant cultural scene. Many events, from the Natal Sharks games to Shakespeare performances, can be booked through **Computicket** (Map pp306-7; ☎ 083-915 8000; 1st fl, the Workshop, Commercial Rd; ☉ 9am-5pm Mon-Fri, 9am-1pm Sat).

Cinemas

There are cinemas in all of the major malls: **Imax** (☎ 031-566 4415; Gateway Mall, Umhlanga Ridge) Big-screen action in the Gateway Mall.

Ster Gateway Mall (☎ 031-566 3222; Gateway Mall, Umhlanga Ridge); Musgrave Centre (Map p303; ☎ 0860-300 222; www.sterkinekor.com; Musgrave Centre, Musgrave Rd)

Gay & Lesbian Venues

Durban is a bit short on gay and lesbian venues. However, new on the scene is **Bent** (www.bent.co.za), which organises monthly parties (not on set nights) at roaming, classy venues in Durb's 'burbs. Parties range from between 200 to 600 patrons – both guys and gals – although they're more popular among the 'wymyn' (their spelling, not ours). International guests are welcome.

Roman Lounge (Map p311; ☎ 031-303 9023; 202 Florida Rd, Morningside) Right in the heart of the bar district, this is a good place to hook up and caters to both men and women.

Live Music

KwaZulu-Natal Philharmonic Orchestra (☎ 031-369 9438; www.kznpo.co.za) The orchestra has an interesting spring concert programme with weekly performances in the City Hall (see p309). It also performs in the Botanic Gardens Music at the Lake concert series.

BAT Centre (Map pp306-7; ☎ 031-332 0451; www.batcentre.co.za; 45 Maritime Pl, Victoria Embankment) One of Durban's more interesting haunts, this fun venue features everything from DJs on Friday and Sunday evenings to a regular drum circle. It also plays host to regular performances by some excellent jazz musicians.

Rainbow Restaurant & Jazz Club (☎ 031-702 9161; 23 Stanfield Lane) In Pinetown, 8km west of the centre, this was the first place in Natal to cater to blacks in a so-called 'white area' in the 1980s. With a reputation as the centre of the jazz scene and still the preferred local haunt, it features concerts and headline acts on the first or last Sunday of the month.

Nightclubs

Tilt (Map pp306-7; ☎ 031-306 9356; 11 Walnut Rd) This place shares DJs with the Hilton's Rivets bar. Friday is often the big one, with quality music ranging from deep house to chunky bass.

Club 330 (Map pp306-7; www.330.co.za; 330 Point Rd) Clubbing in a point-blank sense. In-your-face full-on rave scene and throb city, depending what level you're on. This is not an area to walk around – taxis are obligatory.

Other recommendations:

Burn (Map p303; ☎ 082-325 9746; 112 Umbilo Rd) Heavy rock to sizzle on the dance floor.

Tiger Tiger (Map p311; ☎ 031-303 7681; 15 Mitchell Cres, Greyville) A mature, trendy disco scene.

KWAZULU-NATAL

Sport

Soccer and rugby are played in KwaZulu-Natal. Professional teams such as AmaZulu and Manning Rangers play in town, and international teams also visit.

ABSA Stadium (King's Park Sports Ground) (Map p303; ☎ 031-312 5022; Jackson Dr) With 60,000 seats, King's Park is home to the Natal Sharks (www.sharksrugby.co.za) rugby team.

Sahara Stadium (Kingsmead Cricket Ground; Map pp306-7; ☎ 031-335 4200; 2 Kingsmead Close) Cricket fever is cured here, where the international knockabouts are hosted.

Theatre

Natal Playhouse (Map pp306-7; ☎ 031-369 9444; www.playhousecompany.com; Smith St) Opposite the City Hall, Durban's central theatre has dance, drama and music most nights.

Other venues:

Barnyard Theatre (☎ 031-566 3945; www.barnyard theatre.co.za; Gateway Mall, Umhlanga Ridge)

Catalina Theatre (Map pp306-7; ☎ 031-305 6889; Wilson's Wharf, Victoria Embankment)

SHOPPING

Victoria St Market (Map pp306-7; ☎ 031-306 4021, Victoria St; ☼ 6am-6pm Mon-Sat, 6am-4pm Sun) At the western end of Victoria St, this is the hub of the Indian community and offers a typically rip-roaring, subcontinental shopping experience, with more than 160 stalls selling wares from across Asia. It's the main tourist attraction in the area, but watch your wallet. Grey St, between Victoria and West Sts, is the main shopping area. Prices are low and you can bargain. Most Muslim shops close between noon and 2pm on Friday.

Essenwood Market (Map p303; ☎ 031-306 7744; Berea Park, Essenwood; ☼ 9am-2pm Sat) Sells a good range of handicrafts, homemade wares and clothes.

African Art Centre (Map pp306-7; ☎ 031-301 2717; www.afriart.org.za; 160 Pine St; ☼ 8.30am-5pm Mon-Fri, 9am-1pm Sat) In the same building as Tourist Junction, this not-for-profit gallery is not a curio shop, but has an excellent selection of work by rural craftspeople and artists.

Car boot & second-hand clothing flea market (Map pp306-7; ☼ 7am-noon Sun) This Sunday market, behind Greyville Racecourse and opposite Standard Bank, is a regular event for some Durbanites who buy and sell the second-hand items, which are sublime and ridiculous.

Gateway Mall (☎ 031-5662332;www.gatewayworld .co.za; 1 Palm Blvd, Umhlanga Ridge; ☼ 9am-7pm Mon-Thu, 9am-9pm Fri & Sat, 9am-6pm Sun) The mother of all shopping malls, it's north of central Durban and popular among locals living in the area.

Musgrave Centre (Map p303; ☎ 031-201 5129; Musgrave St, Musgrave) is another shopping mall with all the necessities, while **Pavilion** (☎ 031-265 0558; ☼ 9am-6pm Mon-Fri, 9am-5pm Sat, 10am-5pm Sun) is similar to the Musgrave Centre and is on the city's outskirts in Westville, just a quick drive from the centre on the N3 towards Pietermaritzburg.

The city centre's shopping mall, **Workshop** (Map pp306-7; ☎ 031-304 9894; 99 Aliwal St; ☼ 8.30am-5pm Mon-Fri, 9am-5pm Sat, 10am-5pm Sun), is housed in a former train shed.

GETTING THERE & AWAY

Air

Durban International Airport (☎ 031-451 6666) is off the N2, 16km south of the city. **Student Flights** (Map p303; ☎ 031-202 5995; www.studentflights .co.za; Shop 324, Musgrave Centre, Musgrave Rd; ☼ 9am-5.30pm Mon-Fri, 9am-4pm Sat) is a good first stop for flights.

Several airlines link Durban with South Africa's other main centres. Prices quoted (Internet fares) are for the cheapest available one-way fares at the time of research and may cost less than prices quoted by travel agents.

1time (☎ 0861-345 345; www.1time.co.za) A no-frills airline offering some great deals to Jo'burg (R299).

Kulula (☎ 0861-585 852; www.kulula.com) A no-frills competitor to 1time, it links Durban with Jo'burg (R499), Cape Town (R569) and Port Elizabeth (R429).

Nationwide Air (☎ 0861-737 737; www.nationwideair .co.za) Flies at least once daily to Jo'burg (R450), Cape Town (R600) and Port Elizabeth (R429).

South African Airlink (SAAirlink; ☎ 011-978 1111; www.saairlink.co.za) Flies daily to Port Elizabeth (R421), Bloemfontein (R1490) and Nelspruit (R1930).

South African Airways (SAA; ☎ 031-978 1111; www .flysaa.com) Flies at least once daily to Jo'burg (R763), Port Elizabeth (R888), East London (R888), Cape Town (R968), George (R1500) and Nelspruit (R1420).

Bus

The popular and useful **Baz Bus** (Map pp306-7; ☎ 031-304 9099; www.bazbus.com; 1st fl, Tourist Junction; ☼ 8.30am-4.30pm Mon-Fri, 8.30am-noon Sat) has an office next to Durban Africa. You can hop-on/-off as often as you like along the Baz Bus route for a given price and are picked up and dropped off at selected hostels. The seven-/14-day (R850/1600) passes allow you to travel in any direction and as often as you like within the time period.

Long-distance buses leave from the bus stations near the Durban train station (Map pp306–7). It's safest to enter from NMR Ave, not Umgeni Rd. The following long-distance bus companies have their offices here.

Eldo Coaches (Map pp306-7; ☎ 031-307 3363) has three buses daily to Jo'burg (R130 to R170, eight hours).

Greyhound (Map pp306-7; ☎ 083-915 9000; www .greyhound.co.za) has daily buses to Richards Bay (R100, 2½ hours), Jo'burg (R195 to R220, eight hours), Cape Town (R465, 22 to 27 hours), Port Elizabeth (R330, 15 hours) and Port Shepstone (R120, 1¾ hours).

Buses also run daily to Pietermaritzburg (R80 to R100, one hour), Estcourt (R95 to R100, 2½ hours), Ladysmith (R160, four hours) and Newcastle (R170, 5½ hours), as well as to Vryheid (R100 to R200, six hours) and Paulpietersburg (R190, 6½ hours).

Intercape (Map pp306-7; ☎ 0861-287 287; www.in tercape.co.za) has several daily buses to Jo'burg (R195 to R220, eight hours), Cape Town (R490, 23 hours), Gaborone (via Jo'burg; R345, 15½ hours) and Maputo (via Jo'burg; R230, 15 hours).

Luxliner (Map pp306-7; ☎ 031-305 9090; www.inter city.co.za) operates daily services from Durban to Margate (R85, 2½ hours), Jo'burg International Airport and Park Station (R180 to R190, 8½ hours) and Pretoria (R180 to R190, nine hours).

SA Roadlink (Map pp306-7; ☎ 031-307 5424; www .saroadlink.co.za) has double-decker buses to Cape Town (via Bloemfontein; R449, 23 hours), Jo'burg (R195, 6½ hours) and Port Elizabeth (via Mthatha and East London; R299, 15 hours).

Translux (Map pp306-7; ☎ 031-308 8111; www .translux.co.za) runs daily buses to Jo'burg (R200 to R210, eight hours) and Cape Town (R465, 27 hours). City to City buses, operated in partnership with Translux, go to destinations across the country.

You can also book at the Greyhound office for the **Margate Mini Coach** (☎ 039-312 1406), which links Durban and Margate three times a day (R80, 2½ hours).

Car

Hiring a car is pricey in KZN but it's one of the best ways of getting around. Be aware that few car-rental companies cover damage to tyres and undercarriage.

Around-about Cars (☎ 021-422 4022; www.around aboutcars.com) This is a Capetown-based agent for National Alamo in Durban. Its rates are more competitive than most and it has options with unlimited mileage and full insurance; but dealing with two organisations can be confusing if there are problems.

Comet Car Rental (☎ 031-903 4994; www.cometcar .co.za) Has some reasonable deals.

Most major car-rental companies also have offices at the airport:

Avis (☎ 031-304 1741, 086-102 111)
Budget (☎ 086-101 6622)
Imperial (☎ 031-337 3731)

Hitching

Although we *don't* recommend it, if you do choose to hitch, and are heading south, hitch from the traffic lights at the Victoria Embankment or catch a cab to the airport and try your luck from the car park's exit access to the south coast.

Minibus Taxi

Some long-distance minibus taxis leave from stops in the streets opposite the Umgeni Rd entrance to the train station (Map pp306–7). Others running mainly to the south coast and the Wild Coast region of Eastern Cape leave from around the Berea train station (Map pp306–7) – minibus taxis to Swaziland leave from the corner of Fynn and May Sts. To Jo'burg it costs R130 and to Swaziland Manzini it about R120. The areas in and around the minibus taxi ranks are unsafe and extreme care should be taken if entering them. Travellers are probably better off paying slightly more and taking the buses.

Train

Durban train station (Map pp306-7; ☎ 0860-008 888) is huge. Use the NMR Ave entrance, 1st level. The local inner-city or suburban trains are not recommended for travellers; even hardy travellers report feeling unsafe.

Long-distance services are another matter – they are efficient and arranged into separate male and female sleeper compartments (double-, four- or six-sleeper). Bookings are highly recommended. Trains include the *Trans Natal*, which leaves Durban daily (except Tuesday and Saturday) for Jo'burg (1st-/2nd-class R250/165, 12½ hours), and the *Trans Oranje*, which makes a weekly run (phone the station for the departure day) to Cape Town (R645/435, 38 hours).

The **Rovos** (www.rovosrail.co.za) is a luxury steam train on which, for a mere R8500 starting price, you can enjoy old-world luxury on a three-day choof from Durban to Pretoria via Swaziland and Kruger National Park.

GETTING AROUND
To/From the Airport
Some hostels run their own taxi shuttle services for clients at competitive prices. By taxi, the same trip should cost about R150. The **Airport Shuttle Bus** (☎ 031-465 1660) departs the airport regularly for the beach and city centre's major hotels (R30). Buses return to the airport on the hour between 5am to 10pm from the corner of Aliwal and Smith Sts (Map pp306–7).

Bus
The main bus terminal and information centre for inner-city and metropolitan buses is on Commercial Rd across from the Workshop (Map pp306–7).

Durban Transport (☎ 031-309 5942) runs the bus services Mynah and Aqualine. Mynah covers most of the beachfront and central residential areas. Trips cost around R3 and you get a slight discount if you prebuy 10 tickets. Routes are as follows: North Beach, South Beach, Musgrave Rd/Mitchell Park Circle, the Ridge/Vause, Botanic Gardens, Kensington/Mathias Rd. The larger Aqualine buses run through the outer-lying Durban metropolitan area. Timetables are also available from the **Tourist Junction** (Map pp306–7; 160 Pine St, cnr Soldiers Way).

Taxi
A taxi between the beach and Florida Rd, Morningside usually costs about R30. **Mozzie Cabs** (☎ 0860-669 943) runs a reliable 24-hour service.

WEST OF DURBAN
VALLEY OF 1000 HILLS
☎ 031
A very pleasant and hassle-free (if slightly kitsch) getaway from the steamy streets of Durban, the Valley of 1000 Hills runs from the city's western outskirts to Nagle Dam, east of Pietermaritzburg. The area abounds in touristy craft shops and eateries, but the rolling hills, sleepy villages and traditional Zulu communities make for an interesting visit. You can drive on Rte 103, which begins in Hillcrest, off the M13 freeway, or head to Hillcrest from the N3 between Durban and Pietermaritzburg. If you want to see more of the valley, head north from this road, which just skirts the southern edge.

Information
Thousand Hills Tourism (☎ 031-777 1874; www
.1000hills.kzn.org.za; Old Main Rd, Botha's Hill; ❧ 7.45am-4.15pm Mon-Fri, 10.30am-1.30pm Sat & Sun) is strangely situated in the middle of the 1000 Hills trail. It offers the useful *1000 Hills Experience* brochure, listing six routes through the region and stacks of places to stay and eat.

Sights & Activities
Shongweni Resource Reserve (☎ 031-769 1283; fax 769 1175; adult/child R20/10; ❧ 5am-7pm Oct-Mar, 6am-6pm Apr-Sep), about halfway between Durban and Pietermaritzburg off the N3, is Route 5 & 6 of the 1000 Hills experience. Part of a beautiful river valley and grassland area, it has a number of mammals and birds. Canoeing is available (R65/85 half/full day). Accommodation is in **safari tents** (per person R110-160) erected on wooden platforms peeking over the edge of the lake and complete with braai, mosquito net.

Surprisingly, Route 2 of the 1000 Hills experience is one of the region's best-kept secrets. The 600-hectare **Krantzkloof Nature Reserve** (adult/child R10/5; ❧ 6am-6pm year-round) has a variety of stunning gorge, wetland and grassland walks of between one and six hours' duration. There are also picnic sites available. Ask where you can get the best views of the gorge. Maps of self-guided trails are available from the security guard for R5.

KWAZULU-NATAL

PheZulu Safari Park (☎ 031-777 1000; www.phe zulusafaripark.co.za; Old Main Rd, Botha's Hill; adult/child R60/30; ☺ shows 10am, 11.30am, 2pm & 3.30pm) is a reptile park, and small and touristy traditional Zulu village, complete with cultural displays.

The **Umgeni Steam Railway** (☎ 031-764 6706; adult/child R70/40) operates out of the old Kloof station (now home of the Stoker's Arms Tavern). The 1000 Hills choo-choo service departs on the first and last Sundays of every month at 8.45am and 12.30pm and huffs and puffs its way through the area for about an hour.

Tekweni Eco-Tours (☎ in Durban 031-463 2576; www.tekweniecotours.co.za) organises tours (R380) to a Zulu village in the region, where you meet traditional healers. For an extra R150 or so, you can stay overnight in a local house.

Sleeping & Eating

Valley Trust (☎ 031-716 6800; www.thevalleytrust.org .za; s/d with shared bathroom R80/160) Home of the Simunye Handicraft Project, which promotes traditional handicrafts to raise funds for local development projects, this place off Old Main Rd in Nyuswa offers cheap, clean beds in basic rooms.

Longacre B&B (☎ 031-777 1335; www.longacre 1000hills.co.za; 160 Old Main Rd, Botha's Hill; s/d self-catering R150/300, incl breakfast R200/400; P ☺) The views over the valley from the pool and garden are the most appealing aspects of this pleasantly decked-out B&B. The thatched studio in the front is the pick of the bunch.

Chantecler (☎ 031-765 2613; chantecler@mweb.co .za; 27 Clement Stott Rd, Botha's Hill; s/d incl breakfast R350/600; ☺) Known for its living birdlife (as opposed to Chaucer's dead rooster), this thatched place oozes high-country class, with pleasant gardens, water features aplenty and old-meets-new styling.

Pot & Kettle (☎ 031-777 1312; 168 Old Main Rd, Botha's Hill; mains R38-68) A casual restaurant with a kitsch gift shop as an entrance, but a delightful outdoor terrace overlooking the valley.

The Chantecler has a restaurant, as does Rob Roy (signposted on the main road), which is great for tea and scones. Several train stations in the area, such as Botha's Hill and Kloof, have been renovated as English-style pubs and tea gardens.

SOUTH COAST

The South Coast is a 160km-long string of seaside resorts and suburbs running from Durban to Port Edward, near the Eastern Cape border. There's a bit of a Ground Hog Day feel about this mass of the shoulder-to-shoulder getaways along the N2 and Rte 102, albeit a pleasant one. The coastal region's sandy beaches are interspersed with some pretty gardens and grassy areas. The region is a surfers' and divers' delight (the latter because of the Aliwal Shoal), and in summer there ain't much room to swing a brolly. Inland, the sugar cane, bananas and palms provide a pleasant, lush, green contrast to the beach culture. The stunning Oribi Gorge Nature Reserve, close to Port Shepstone, provides beautiful forest walks, eating and accommodation options.

The South Coast's first official town is Amanzimtoti, a huge resort and residential area about 10km from Durban International Airport. Further south, other major centres are Umkomaas, Scottburgh, Park Rynie and Hibberdene. The area from Hibberdene to Trafalgar is called the Hibiscus Coast. Information is available from **Hibiscus Coast Tourism** (☎ 039-312 2322; www.hibiscuscoast.kzn.org .za; Panorama Pde, Main Beach, Margate; ☺ 8am-5pm Mon-Fri, 8am-1pm Sat, 9am-1pm Sun). Its useful *Southern Explorer* brochure is a must-have for any visitor.

Port Shepstone is the South Coast's industrial administrative centre, but has some pleasant surrounding areas, while 10km south, frantic Margate is the claustrophobic holiday hub. Port Edward is the last main centre in the region.

AMANZIMTOTI & KINGSBURGH
☎ 031

Called 'Toti' for short, Amanzimtoti (Sweet Waters) is a high-rise jungle of apartment blocks. Warner Beach, at the southern end of Amanzimtoti, is less built-up and more relaxed. From here Amanzimtoti merges into Kingsburgh, which has a number of beaches, to the south. Some might prefer to base themselves here, rather than in 'Durbs'.

The **Amanzimtoti information office** (☎ 031-903 7498; fax 903 7493; 95-97 Beach Rd; ☺ 8am-12.30pm & 1-4pm Mon-Sat) is not far from the Inyoni Rocks.

KWAZULU-NATAL

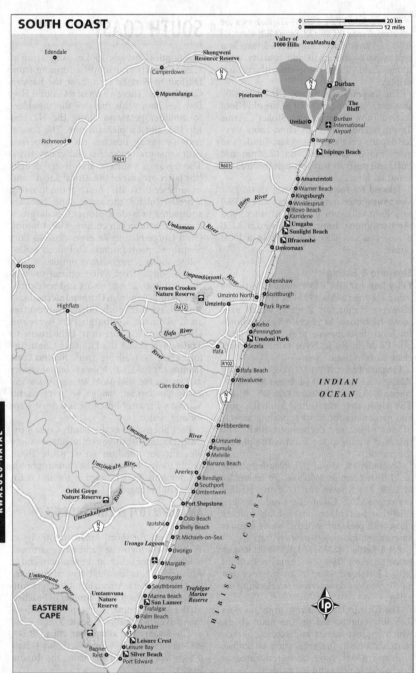

SOUTH COAST

0 ——————— 20 km
0 ——————— 12 miles

Edendale

Shongweni
Resource Reserve

Valley of
1000 Hills

KwaMashu

Camperdown

Durban

Mpumalanga

Pinetown

The
Bluff

Richmond

R624

R603

Umlazi

Durban
International
Airport

Isipingo

Isipingo Beach

Illovo River

Amanzimtoti

Warner Beach

Kingsburgh

Winklespruit

Illovo Beach

Karridene

Umgaba

Sunlight Beach

Ilfracombe

Umkomaas

Umkomaas River

Ixopo

Umpambinyoni River

Renishaw

Vernon Crookes
Nature Reserve

Umzinto North

Scottburgh

Highflats

R612

Umzinto

Park Rynie

Umtwalume River

Ifafa River

Kelso

Pennington

Umdoni Park

Ifafa

Sezela

R102

Ifafa Beach

Glen Echo

Mtwalume

INDIAN
OCEAN

Umzumbe

River

Hibberdene

Umzumbe

Pumula

Umzimkulu River

Melville

Banana Beach

Anerley

Bendigo

Oribi Gorge
Nature Reserve

Southport

Umtentweni

Umzimkulwana River

Port Shepstone

Izotsha

Oslo Beach

Shelly Beach

Uvongo Lagoon

St Michaels-on-Sea

Uvongo

Margate

Umtamvuna River

Ramsgate

Southbroom

Trafalgar
Marine
Reserve

Umtamvuna
Nature Reserve

Marina Beach

San Lamer

EASTERN
CAPE

Trafalgar

Palm Beach

R
61

Munster

Leisure Crest

Leisure Bay

Banner
Rest

Silver Beach

Port Edward

HIBISCUS COAST

KWAZULU-NATAL

Sleeping

There are plenty of B&Bs, apartments and holiday homes – visit the Amanzimtoti Information Office for details.

Blue Sky Mining (☎ 031-916 5394; bsml@mweb.co.za; 5 Nelson Palmer Rd, Warner Beach; camp sites per person R45, dm/d R80/200; 🖳 🐾) Rev into this designer-recycler's delight where you can sleep in a converted F250, spin out at the funky psychedelics and chill by the pool. Seriously revitalising.

Angle Rock Backpackers (☎ 031-916 7007; angle rock@mweb.co.za; 5 Ellcock Rd, Warner Beach; camp sites R50, dm R80, d with shared bathroom from R180) This chilled hang-out is a pebble's throw from the beach and offers free use of surfboards and bikes. Management does free pick-ups from Durban. Take Exit 133 (Kingsburgh) off the N2.

Protea Hotel Karridene (☎ 031-916 7228; www.proteahotels.com/karridene; Old Coast Rd, Illovo Beach; s/d R935/1000; 🏖 🐾) A monolithic cityscape-meets-seascape with rooms and timeshare units.

UMKOMAAS TO MTWALUME
☎ 039

The main towns on this strip are Umkomaas, Scottburgh, Park Rynie, Kelso and Pennington. You can get tourist information from the **Blue Marlin hotel** (☎ 039-978 3361; www.bluemarlin.co.za; 180 Scott St) in Scottburgh. There are plenty of little eateries on offer to satisfy tummy grumbles.

Sleeping

There are plenty of B&Bs around the area. Out of season you may be able to negotiate some cheaper deals.

Aliwal Dive Lodge (☎ 039-973 2233; www.aliwalshoal.co.za; dm R100, d R400-450) At the time of research, the crew from Aliwal Dive Charters was renovating a large mansion into a pleasant dive lodge, a snorkel's breath from its office in Umkomaas.

La La Manzi (☎ 039-973 0161; www.lalamanzi.co.za; s incl breakfast R150-260, d R300-520) La La Manzi, meaning 'Sleeping Waters', also draws the divers to Umkomaas. Decked out with a massive balcony and African paraphernalia, this is as colourful and fun as the Southern Coast shoals.

Blue Marlin (☎ 039-978 3361; www.bluemarlin.co.za, 180 Scott St, Scottburgh; d incl breakfast R590; 🐾) Lifted straight out of the English Riviera but with a nautical feel, the Blue Marlin is fresh, airy and unpretentious.

VERNON CROOKES NATURE RESERVE
☎ 033

Inland from Park Rynie, off Rte 612 past Umzinto, this **reserve** (☎ 033-845 1000; www.kznwildlife.com; adult/child R10/5; ⏱ 5am-7pm) has abundant mammal and bird species and some indigenous forest. If you walk through the reserve, beware of ticks.

Accommodation is offered by **KZN Wildlife** (☎ 033-845 1000; 2-bed huts per person R95).

KWAZULU-NATAL

SOUTH COAST DIVING

The highlight of this strip is the **Aliwal Shoal**, touted as one of the best 10 dive sites in the world. The shoal was created from dune rock around 30,000 years ago. A mere 6500 years ago, the sea level rose, thereby creating a reef. It was named after the wrecked ship, the *Aliwal*, which ran aground in 1849. Other ships have since met a similar fate here. Today, the shoal's ledges, caves and pinnacles are home to everything from wrecks, rays, turtles, 'raggies' (ragged-mouth sharks), tropical fish and soft corals.

Numerous operators along the South Coast offer dive charters and PADI courses and accommodation packages. Most have four-day courses with dives, equipment hire and air-tank refills. Rates range from R1700 to R1900.

Aliwal Dive Charters (☎ 039-973 2542; www.aliwalshoalscubadiving.co.za; Umkomaas) On the main road past the village.

La La Manzi Dive Charters (☎ 039-973 1345; www.divealiwal.co.za; Umkomaas) On the main road past the village.

Quo Vadis (☎ 039-978 1112; www.raggiecave.com; Scottburgh) Based at the Cutty Sark Hotel, and recommended for its charters.

Sea Fever Dive Centre (☎ 039-973 1328; www.seafever.co.za; Umkomaas) Towards the front of the village facing the sea.

PORT SHEPSTONE & AROUND

☎ 039 / pop 29,000

The industrial town of Port Shepstone is of little interest to tourists. However, it does have the **Banana Express** (☎ 039-682 4821), a steam-powered train which, when it's got puff in the holiday season, runs daily (R60; Thursday and Saturday out of season), to Izotsha, the site of a craft school. The train departs at 10am from the station next to the Sharks Den Family Restaurant on the beachfront.

Sleeping & Eating

There are plenty of hotels in Port Shepstone, but two backpackers on the strip of coast north of Port Shepstone are well worth a stopover.

Mantis & Moon Backpacker Lodge (☎ 039-684 6256; travelsa@saol.com; 7/178 Station Rd, Umzumbe; camp sites R50, dm R70, d R180-220; 🏊) 'A' for atmosphere. The new owner has done justice to this jungle oasis with its range of quality accommodation options. Guests can bubble away in the Jacuzzi, wallow in the rock pool or chill under the stars in an open-air bath.

Spot Backpackers (☎ 039-695 1318; spotbackpackers@netactive.co.za; Ambleside Rd, Umtentweni; camp sites R50, dm/d with shared bathroom R70/180) Closer to Port Shepstone, this is spot-on for position, (right on the beach), and is another well-regarded place. Clean, basic and ideal for the four 'S's of sand, sun, sea and surf.

Saffron on 3rd Avenue (☎ 039-695 1295; Third Ave, Umtentweni; ⏰ 8.30am-late) Close to Spot Backpackers, this new eatery has funky chairs, lights, décor and marble table tops in a tasteful indoor/outdoor setting. Creative main meals are R34 to R70.

Getting There & Away

Greyhound (☎ 083-915 9000; www.greyhound.co.za) has daily buses between Port Shepstone and Durban (R120, 1¾ hours). If you are staying at one of the backpackers, ask the driver to drop you in Umzumbe or Umtentweni.

ORIBI GORGE NATURE RESERVE

☎ 039

This **nature reserve** (☎ 039-679 1644; www.kzn wildlife.com; admission R10,, camp sites R30, 2-bed huts R108; ⏰ 6am-6pm) is inland from Port Shepstone, off the N2. The spectacular gorge, on the Umzimkulwana River, is one of the

highlights of the South Coast with beautiful scenery, animals and birds. The reception office is accessed via the N2.

Oribi Gorge Hotel (☎ 039-687 0253; www.oribi gorge.co.za; s/d incl breakfast R430/660; 🏊) is a large pine place (with the foyer incorporating a jacaranda tree). If you can ignore the piped 'Jingle Bell Rock' music in the foyer, for rocks of a more natural variety in the nearby gorge (R10 for the viewpoint), then there's fun to be had.

Wild 5 Extreme Adventures (☎ 082-566 7424) is based at the Oribi Gorge Hotel. It offers a 100m Gorge Swing (read bungee jump) off Lehr's Falls (R300), abseiling (R200) and white-water rafting (R350). It is 11km off the N2 along the Oribi Flats Rd.

MARGATE & AROUND

☎ 039 / pop 34,000

The south coast's tourist mecca is loud and lively, with a string of bars and clubs pumping up the volume, and a knot of hotels putting up the visitors. This claustrophobic concrete jungle's string of chain restaurants and shops ensures that it's not a 'glamour' resort, but it's fun if you're into the bump-and-grind brand of beach life. Nearby Ramsgate is a quieter version of Margate, with a nice little beach.

Ocean Safaris (☎ 082-960 7682; www.oceansafaris.co.za; Shelly Beach; adult/child R200/160) runs whale-watching tours (best between June and November) and the sardine run from the Ski Boat Club on Shelly Beach, north of Margate.

Sleeping & Eating

A decent night's sleep in Margate can come at a premium during the high season.

Wailana Beach Lodge (☎ 039-314 4606; www.wailana.co.za; 436 Ashmead Dr, Ramsgate; s incl breakfast from R430, d incl breakfast per person from R350; 🏊🏊) This svelte guesthouse, 200m from the sea in nearby Ramsgate, has five 'designer' bedrooms with contemporary, individual styling and private sun decks, leafy gardens and a bar.

Sunlawns Hotel (☎ /fax 039-312 1078; Uplands Rd, Margate; r per person incl breakfast R210; 🏊🏊) This long-established hotel has delightful old-English charm. There is a 'Ladies Lounge' and pub, as well as a good-sized pool.

Margate Hotel (☎ 039-312 1410; info@margatehotel.co.za; Marine Dr, Margate; s incl breakfast R495, d incl breakfast per person from R325; ⊠) This place is a little plain, but it is in a top location (if you want to be in the heart of things) on the main drag.

Keg & Galleon (☎ 039-312 2575; Marine Dr, Margate; mains R20-55; ⏲ breakfast, lunch & dinner) This busy boozer is typical of Margate's eating and drinking options. Icy beer and decent pub grub – especially the pies – draw the tourists, who flock here to be amply fed and watered.

La Capannina (☎ 039-317 1078; Marine Dr, Ramsgate North; mains R45-90; ⏲ lunch & dinner Tue-Sat) Locals recommend this authentic Italian restaurant, with all the pasta, seafood and meat favourites that Mama used to make, including lamb shanks with rosemary and red wine.

Getting There & Away

SA Airlink (☎ 031-250 1111; www.saairlink.co.za) flies daily between Margate and Jo'burg (R1020).

The **Margate Mini Coach** (☎ 031-312 1406; www .margate.co.za/minicoach) links Durban and Margate twice daily (R80 one way, R110 for a same-day return). Book through **Hibiscus Coast Tourism** (☎ 039-312 2322; www.hibiscuscoast .kzn.org.za; Panorama Pde, Main Beach, Margate; ⏲ 8am-5pm Mon-Fri, 8am-1pm Sat, 9am-1pm Sun).

Luxliner (☎ 039-317 4628; www.luxliner.co.za) has an office in Hibiscus Coast Tourism, and runs regular buses between Margate and Jo'burg (R250, 10 hours).

PORT EDWARD & AROUND
☎ 039

The little village of Port Edward and its surrounds are as sedate as their pleasant lush environs; they make a pleasant escape from the concrete jungle.

The **tourist office** (☎ 039-311 1211; ⏲ 9am-4.30pm Mon-Fri) is in Ilva's Craft Shop, 2.5km north of Port Edward on Rte 61.

Umtamvuna Nature Reserve (☎ 039-311 2383; admission R10; ⏲ 6am-6pm) is on a gorge on the Umtamvuna River (which forms part of the border with Eastern Cape). This beautiful dense forest has great nature walks, with wildflowers in spring, plus mammals and many species of birds. To get to the reserve from Port Edward, follow the signs off Rte 61 to Izingolweni and continue for a few kilometres.

The **Umtamvuna Mountain Bike Trail** (☎ 039-311 1130; www.clearwatertrails.co.za; per trail/guided trails R30/190) operates out of Clearwater Trails Chalets and rents out bikes for use on a network of trails above the gorge.

There are a couple of small restaurants and a supermarket in Port Edward, but it's best to bring some of your own food if you are staying at the hostels.

Sleeping

Clearwater Trails Chalets (☎ 039-311 1130; clearwa ter@venturenet.co.za; s/d with shared bathroom R135/190) Your own two-in-one 'chalets' and separate (private) doll-house kitchen and bathroom are set in a stunning location above the gorge. From Port Edward, cross Rte 61 and follow signs to Izingolweni Rd and continue 5.5km (past Old Pont Rd and Beaver Creek Coffee Estate). Turn left at the T-Junction and follow the Clearwater Trails sign.

Ku-Boboyi River Lodge Backpackers (☎ 039-319 1371; www.kuboboyi.co.za; Old Main Rd, Leisure Bay; camp sites per person R60, s/d with shared bathroom R170/250, d with private bathroom R350; P ⊠) This hilltop lodge has a chilled African feel with a French twist (the brekky crepes are *delicieux*), plus great inland and sea views. It is 4km north of Port Edward and just off Rte 61. Take the Leisure Bay South turn and follow the signs.

NORTH COAST

The stretch of coast from Umhlanga Rocks north to the Tugela River is a profusion of upmarket timeshare apartments and retirement villages with some pleasant beaches. The section from Zimbali, slightly north of Umhlanga, to the Tugela is known as the Dolphin Coast. The coast gets its name from the bottlenose dolphins that favour the area, attracted by the continental shelf and warm water conditions.

Dolphin Coast Publicity (☎ 032-946 1997; www .dolphincoast.co.za; Ballito Dr; ⏲ 8.30am-4.30pm Mon-Fri, 8.30am-noon Sat) is near the BP petrol station, just where you leave the N2 to enter Ballito. It books B&Bs and lists other accommodation.

The North Coast is home to a fascinating mix of peoples: descendants of former colonialists, Indians, French Mauritian sugar-cane growers and indentured labourers from the Indian subcontinent, plus colourful Zulu cultures.

KWAZULU-NATAL

King Shaka is said to have established a military camp on the coast; Royal handmaidens gathered salt from tidal pools, since immortalised in the name Salt Rock. A memorial to King Shaka can be found at KwaDukuza (Stanger), slightly inland.

Metropolitan buses run between Durban and Umhlanga Rocks, and buses and minibus taxis also run between Durban and KwaDukuza (Stanger) and other inland towns. The latter can get very crowded, so are possible havens for petty thieves.

UMHLANGA ROCKS
☎ 031

The buckle of Durban's chichi commuter belt, Umhlanga is a cosmopolitan mix of upmarket beach resort, moneyed suburbia and small malls. Umhlanga means 'Place of Reeds' (the 'h' is pronounced something like 'sh').

At the time of research, **Umhlanga Tourism Information Centre** (☎ 031-561 4257; www.umhlanga-rocks.com) was temporarily housed on the 1st floor of the Lighthouse Mall, Chartwell Dr.

NORTH COAST

0   5 km
0   3 miles

To Pietermaritzburg (50km)
Umvoti River
Damall
Zinkwazi River
R74
Zinkwazi Beach
KwaDukuza (Stanger)
Blythedale
Umhlali River
Tinley Manor Beach
Sheffield Beach
Umhlali
Umhlali Beach
To Pietermaritzburg (50km)
Salt Rock
Shaka's Rock
COAST
Tongaat
Ballito
Hambanati
Westbrook Beach
R102
INDIAN OCEAN
DOLPHIN
To Durban (16km)
La Mercy
uMdloti Beach
Gateway Mall
Umhlanga Rocks
Umhlanga Lagoon Nature Reserve
Natal Sharks Board
R27

KWAZULU-NATAL

Sights & Activities
NATAL SHARKS BOARD

A research institute, the **Natal Sharks Board** (☎ 031-566 0400; www.shark.co.za; 1A Herrwood Dr; audiovisual & dissection adult/child R20/12; ☿ 8am-4pm Mon-Fri, noon-6pm Sun) is dedicated to studying sharks, specifically in relation to their danger to humans. With the great white shark – a big shark with a fearsome, but largely undeserved reputation for attacks on humans – frequenting the KwaZulu-Natal coast, this is more than an academic interest. There are audiovisual presentations and shark dissections at 9am and 2pm Tuesday to Thursday. The public can accompany the Sharks Board personnel on their boat trips (see p308).

The Natal Sharks Board is signposted; it is about 2km out of town, up the steep Umhlanga Rocks Dr (the M12 leading to the N3).

UMHLANGA LAGOON NATURE RESERVE

This **nature reserve** (admission free; ☿ 6am-6pm) is on a river mouth just north of town. Despite its small size (26 hectares) there are many bird species. The trails lead through stunning dune forest, across the lagoon and onto the beach.

Sleeping & Eating

Umhlanga is crowded with holiday apartments, most of which are close to the beach. A two-bedroom serviced apartment in low/high season starts at about R400/600 per night (a minimum number of nights often applies); contact **Umhlanga Accommodation** (☎ 031-561 2012; www.umhlangaaccommodation.co.za; Protea Mall, Chartwell Dr; ☿ 8.30am-4.30pm Mon-Fri, 8.30-11.30am Sat) for help. There are also plenty of B&Bs around the area. Hotel prices are seasonal and vary enormously; expect a 10% fluctuation either way in low or high season.

There's a huge choice of eating options for breakfasts, lunches and dinners and many pleasant pavement cafés.

Oyster Box (☎ 031-561 2233; www.oysterbox.co.za; 2 Lighthouse Rd; s incl breakfast R530-795, d per person R430-625; ☒ ▯ ▨) In the shadow of Umhlanga's lighthouse, this spot exudes colonial-era grace (is that a straw pith helmet on the doorman's head?), with an old-school atmosphere that offers an antidote to Umhlanga's trademark concrete towers.

Beverley Hills Sun Intercontinental (☎ 031-561 2211; www.southernsun.com; Lighthouse Rd; s & d R2750; ❌ 🖥 🏊) They didn't pull out the stops on the exterior, but this top-notch classic is deliciously stylish on the inside. It's the perfect place for a platinum-card splurge.

Ile Maurice (☎ 031-561 7609; 9 McCausland Cres; mains R79-95; ☯ lunch & dinner Tue-Sun) For a special seaside splurge with a Gallic touch, try this chic eatery; it's much *bon gout*, not to mention having a reputation among Durban's connoisseurs as *la* place-to-eat-by-*la-mer*.

Sugar Club (☎ 031-561 2211; Lighthouse Rd; mains R90-365; ☯ lunch & dinner) This award-winning eatery is at the Beverley Hills Sun Intercontinental.

Getting There & Away

Metro buses 716 and 706 run between Umhlanga and Durban.

TONGAAT

A big, sedate sugar town with some fine old buildings, Tongaat is on the train line running north from Durban. With a large Indian population, it is home to a handful of temples including the small but fascinating **Shri Jagganath Puri Temple**.

BALLITO TO SHEFFIELD BEACH

☎ 032

Ballito, Shaka's Rock, Salt Rock, Umhlali and Sheffield Beach lack Zulu flavour; they form a continuous, strip of seaside suburbia, luxury guesthouses and multistorey condos, most with pleasant beaches at their doorstep. They are connected by the old coast road, so you don't have to jump back and forth on the N2 to travel between them.

Dolphin Coast Publicity Association (☎ 946 1997; www.thedolphincoast.co.za; cnr Link Rd & Ballito Dr; ☯ 8.30am-5pm Mon-Fri, 9am-1pm Sat & Sun) is near the BP petrol station.

Much of the accommodation is in apartments, and in the high season most are let by the week. A good rental agency in Ballito is **Realty 1** (☎ 031-946 2140; www.realty1parsons .co.za; Ballito Business Centre, Ballito Dr).

Secret Spot (☎ 082-495 9811; www.secretspot.co.za; Main Rd, Shaka's Rock; dm R75, d with shared bathroom R180) Carve your way to this surfers' (and landlubbers') paradise, nestled above Shaka's Rock beach and boost yourself with surf lessons. For serious surf rats, there's a board shaping bay. The quality cabins or dorms are a great place to hang ten. Best to ring for directions. Surfing packages available.

Dolphin Holiday Resort (☎ 031-946 2187; www .dolphinholidayresort.co.za; Dolphin Cres, Ballito; camp sites R300, r R660) This resort has camp sites in lush surrounds and some pleasant cottages. Rates are much cheaper out of season.

KWADUKUZA (STANGER)

☎ 032 / pop 36,700

In July 1825, Shaka established KwaDukuza as his capital and royal residence. It was here that he was killed in 1828 by his half-brothers Mhlangane and Dingaan; Dingaan then took power (see the boxed text, p334). Also known as Stanger, KwaDukuza is a busy, rough-and-ready town with a large Indian population and an African buzz. The town has no accommodation, but it's an important stop for those undertaking a Shaka pilgrimage or interested in Zulu culture.

The **Dukuza Interpretive Centre** (☎ 032-552 7210; 5 King Shaka Rd; admission by donation; ☯ 8am-4pm Mon-Fri, 9am-4pm Sat & Sun) is worth visiting for limited, but clear, historical and chronological information on Shaka and his kingdom. It also hands out a brochure with other places of (some) interest relating to Shaka and colonialists.

Dukuza Museum (☎ 032-437 5075; King Shaka Rd; admission by donation; ☯ 8.30am-4pm Mon-Fri), opposite the interpretive centre, has related historical exhibits.

Head to Cooper St to visit the **Shaka Memorial Gardens**, where a memorial stone was erected in 1932 over Shaka's burial chamber, originally a grain pit. There is a rock featuring a well-worn groove where it's believed Shaka sharpened his spears. Each year Zulus, donned in their traditional gear, gather in the gardens for Shaka Day (also known as Heritage Day) celebrations (see p332).

Minibus taxis link KwaDukuza with Durban (R25, one hour) and towns along the coast.

BLYTHEDALE

☎ 032

Blythedale is a quiet seaside village with a sandy (shark-net) beach and crashing surf.

Mini Villas (☎ 032-551 1277; www.minivillas.co.za; Umvoti Dr; r R229) is a bit like a series of bowling green clubs, offering excellent-value self-catering villas with sea views. **La Mouette Caravan Park** (☎ 032-551 2547; www.caravanparks .co.za/lamouette; 1 Umvoti Dr; camp sites R60) is a clean, suburban-style place right on the beach, with braais and tarred roads. Prices sky-rocket in summer. There are a few simple eateries in town.

Occasional minibus taxis run between Blythedale and KwaDukuza (R10, 15 minutes), 7km away.

ZULULAND

Evoking images of wild landscapes and tribal rhythms, this beautiful swathe of KwaZulu-Natal offers a different face of South Africa, where fine coastline, mist-clad hills and traditional settlements are in contrast to the ordered suburban developments around Durban. Dominated by the Zulu tribal group, the region offers a fascinating historical and contemporary insight into one of the country's most enigmatic, and best-known, cultures. However, while the name Zulu (which means Heaven) aptly describes the rolling expanses that dominate the landscape here, it doesn't tell the whole story. Intense poverty and all the social problems that come with it are still commonplace, and much of the population struggles in a hand-to-mouth existence. Head off the main roads and this becomes glaringly obvious.

Zululand extends roughly from the mouth of the Tugela River up to St Lucia and inland west of the N2 to Vryheid. The region is most visited for the spectacular Hluhluwe-Imfolozi Park and its many traditional Zulu villages. Here, you can learn about Zulu history and the legendary King Shaka (see p334).

TUGELA MOUTH
☎ 032

The sprawl of resort towns on the north coast comes to an end with Blythedale, giving way to a wilder landscape at the mouth of the mighty Tugela River. With one of the most unspoilt sweeps of sand in the region (beware, there are a lot of sharks here – you're advised not to swim), the small town of Tugela Mouth, which sits on the north bank of the Tugela estuary

and on the very boundary of Zululand, is a soporific, undeveloped alternative to the gloss and glitz of the tried-and-tested holiday centres. Fantastic fishing and a remote atmosphere only bolster the appeal.

Emolweni (☎ 032-458 4133; w2wog@lantic.net; s/d R100/200; ☐) is a rustic, no-frills hotchpotch of several self-catering cottages with heaps of bohemian and sand-dune charisma.

You can take the **Baz Bus** (☎ in Durban 031-304 9099; www.bazbus.com) to Eshowe and phone ahead to be collected.

GINGINDLOVU
☎ 035

Crowds and dust are Gingindlovu's trademarks, but there are two fine accommodation options in the area, making it a good pit stop on the route north. The town was once one of King Cetshwayo's strongholds and two battles of the Anglo-Zulu War of 1879 were fought in the vicinity.

Mine Own Country House (☎ 035-337 1262; fax 337 1025; s/d incl breakfast R500/700), in an opulent villa, is surrounded by sugar plantations and has lashings of colonial-era nostalgia. It's 4km north of Gingindlovu, off Rte 102.

At rustic **Inyezane** (☎ 082-704 4766; inyezane@ ethniczulu.com; camp sites R50, dm/d with shared bathroom R80/200), the open-air herbal and (very natural) mud baths need a thorough detox themselves, but hopefully the new owners will revitalise this colourful and alternative experience in the heart of sugar-cane Zululand. Go 1.5km north of Gingindlovu on Rte 66 (to Eshowe), turn left onto a gravel road at the large school building and follow the signs.

MTUNZINI
☎ 035

A little oasis of neatly tended lawns surrounded by the wild, rolling hills of Zululand, Mtunzini screams 'Europe' in the heart of Africa. But there is more to this pretty village than herbaceous borders. Sitting above a lush sweep of rare Raffia palms, and bordering the Umlalazi Nature Reserve, Mtunzini makes an excellent base for exploring this beautiful slice of Zululand.

The town had a colourful beginning. John Dunn, the first European to settle in the area, was granted land by King Cetshwayo.

He became something of a chief himself, took 49 wives and sired 117 children. He held court here under a tree, hence the town's name (*mtunzini* is Zulu for 'a place in the shade'). After the British defeated Cetshwayo and divided the kingdom, Dunn was one of the chiefs granted power.

The town was declared a Conservancy in 1995. Visitors can enjoy its network of nature trails, as well as some antelope and bird species.

Information

ABSA (Hely Hutchinson Rd) Has an ATM.

Fat Cat Coffee Shop (☎ 035-340 2897; 2 Station Rd; ☼ 8am-4.30pm Mon-Fri, 8am-1pm Sat) Tourist information is available from the gift shop here.

Sights & Activities

Near the mouth of the Mlalazi River, there is lush tropical forest where you'll find the **Raffia Palm Monument** (admission free; ☼ 24hr). *Raphia Australis* were first planted here in 1916 from seeds sent to the local magistrate by the Director of Prisons in Pretoria. The idea was to use the palms' fibres to make brooms for the prison service, but as the fibres were too short the commercial enterprise soon ended. The palms flourished, however, and by 1942 had been declared a National Monument. The palms are home to the palmnut vulture (*Gypohierax angolensis*), South Africa's rarest breeding bird-of-prey.

The entrance to **Umlalazi Nature Reserve** (☎ 035-340 1836; www.kznwildlife.com; admission R10;

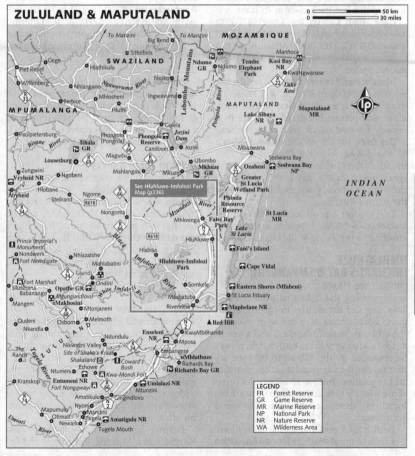

ZULULAND & MAPUTALAND

KWAZULU-NATAL

(☾ 5am-10pm) is 1.5km east of town, on the coast. It has trails through the dune and forested ecosystems and is great for birders. Visit the Indaba Tree, where John Dunn held his court gatherings, and the remains of John Dunn's Pool, which he built so his wives could swim safely away from hippos and crocs.

Sleeping & Eating

Nature's Way Backpackers (☎ 082-936 2370; nway@ zini.co.za; 1 Nature's Way, Mtunzini; dm R70, s/d R80/150) On the edge of coastal reserves, with dune forest, wetlands, lagoons and access to beaches, this place is seriously in tune with nature. The open-air showers, basic tented facilities and chilled bar are all you'll need – the natural surroundings do the rest. Even a zebra has adopted this laid-back place as its home.

Trade Winds Country Inn (☎ 035-340 2533; trade winds@microweb.co.za; Hely Hutchinson Rd; s/d incl breakfast R305/465) This motel-styled place is a reliable, if slightly carpet-stained and over-priced, option.

Mtunzini Forest Lodge (☎ 035-340 1953; fax 035-340 1955; 4-/5-bed chalets R720/750; ⚐) These attractive and spacious chalets – with pool, a bar and private beach access – are in a densely forested nature reserve by the sea.

Clay Oven (☎ 035-340 1262; 32 Hely Hutchinson Rd; mains R34-45; ☾ lunch & dinner Tue-Sun) This friendly diner whips up excellent pizzas (yes, cooked in the clay oven) and serves them on the breezy wooden terrace or in the refined interior.

You can get a good feed at **Tides Inn restaurant** (mains R30-70; ☾ breakfast, lunch & dinner), attached to the Trade Winds Country Inn.

UMHLATHUZE (RICHARDS BAY & EMPANGENI)
☎ 035 / pop 115,000

Incorporating the industrial port of Richards Bay and the nearby town of Empangeni, uMhlathuze is a mass of modern suburbia, aluminium smelters and a web of roads linking very little. Bird-watchers may be rewarded by the 350 or so bird species that favour the surrounding lakes, marshes and vegetation, but for most visitors (even those who fly here direct to access northern locations), there are better places to spend your time.

Both Empangeni and Richards Bay have a branch of the **uMhlathuze Tourism Association**

(☎ 035-907 5018; www.tourismassociation.org.za; 5 Mark Strasse St, Richards Bay; ☾ 8am-4pm Mon-Fri, 10am-2pm alternate Sat).

BirdLife South Africa (☎ 035-753 5644; www.bird life.org.za; Imvubu Log Cabins, cnr Hibberd & Davidson Lane, Meerensee; ☾ 7.30am-4pm Mon-Fri, 7.30am-noon Sat & Sun) may be sponsored by a major industrial company, but this excellent organisation offers guides, birding routes and tours for keen birders around KZN. At the traffic lights in front of Meerensee Mall turn right into Krewekring Rd and left at the next stop street (500m).

Empangeni Arts & Crafts Centre (☎ 035-907 5405; cmi@richemp.org.za; Turnbull St; ☾ 8am-4pm Mon-Fri, 9am-noon Sat) is worth a browse.

Sleeping

Woodpecker Inn (☎ 035-786 1230; fax 786 1243; Pelican Pde, Richards Bay; s/d R280/340; ⚐ ⚐) Offering thatched, lodge-style country comforts in a garden setting, this popular place has a bar and swish rooms with en suite. It's close to the airport.

Harbour Lights (☎ 035-796 6239; www.harbour lights.co.za; per camp site R120, plus per person R5, s/d 190/290) A decent range of affordable accommodation for tight budgets. Formerly a sugar plantation, this resort is off the N3, between Richards Bay and Empangeni.

Getting There & Away

Greyhound buses stop at the Empangeni branch of the uMhlathuze Tourism Association, where you can also get tickets and information; and by McDonald's, next to the Bay Hospital in Richards Bay. Buses run daily to Durban (R100, 2½ hours) and Jo'burg (R220, eight hours). Most of the surrounding towns can be reached from here by minibus taxi.

ESHOWE
☎ 035 / pop 14,700

Situated around a beautiful indigenous forest and surrounded by green rolling hills, Eshowe is in idiosyncratic Zululand. The centre has a rural, rough-and-tumble atmosphere, but the suburbs are leafy and quiet. It is well placed for exploring the wider region and there are many decent attractions and accommodation options on offer.

Eshowe has been home to four Zulu Kings (Shaka, Mpande, Cetshwayo and Dinizulu). It was Cetshwayo's stronghold before he moved to Ondini and, like Ondini, it was destroyed during the Anglo-Zulu War. The British occupied the site and built Fort Nongqayi in 1883, establishing Eshowe as the administrative centre of their newly captured territory.

Information

ABSA (Miku Bldg, Osborne Rd) Changes money and has an ATM.

Eshowe Computers (☎ 035-474 5441; Osborne Rd; per hr R40; ☺ 8am-4.30pm Mon-Fri, 8-10am Sat) Internet access.

Umlalazi Municipality Publicity & Tourism Office (☎ 035-474 1141; www.umlalazi.org.za; cnr Hutchinson & Osborne Rds; ☺ 7.15am-4pm Mon-Thu, 7.30am-3pm Fri) For information on the area.

Sights & Activities

The **Fort Nongqayi Museum Village** (☎ 035-474 1141; zhm@umlalazi.org.za; Nongqayi Rd; adult/child R20/4; ☺ 7.30am-4pm Mon-Fri, 9am-4pm Sat & Sun) is based around the three-turreted, mud-and-brick Fort Nongqayi. The entrance fee includes access to the Zululand Historical Museum, with artefacts and Victoriana; the excellent Vukani Zulu Basketry Collection; the Zululand Missionary Museum; and the Museum Crafter's Market, where local crafts are sold.

From the museum you can also walk to **Mpushini Falls** (40 minutes return), but note that bilharzia has been reported here in the past.

When war approached, King Shaka is said to have hidden his wives in the thick swathe of forest that now makes up the 200-hectare **Dlinza Forest Reserve** (☎ 035-474 4029; www.zbr .co.za/boardwalk; admission free; ☺ 6am-6pm Sep-Apr, 8am-5pm May-Aug). There is prolific birdlife – look out for crowned eagles (*Stephanoaetus coronatus*) – as well as some walking trails, some of which are believed to have been made by British soldiers stationed here after the Anglo-Zulu War.

The 100m-long **Dlinza Forest Aerial Boardwalk** (www.zbr.co.za/boardwalk; adult/child R25/5) offers some great views of the canopy and birdlife. This is the start of the Prince Dabulamanzi Trail, a three-day circuit through nature reserves and rivers. **Entumeni Nature Reserve** (☎ 035-474 5084; admission free; ☺ 6am-6pm) is larger than Dlinza, and preserves indigenous mist-belt forest in a sugar-cane

region. It's 16km west of town, off the road to Entumeni and Nkandla.

Sleeping & Eating

Amble Inn (☎ 035-474 1300; ambleinn@corpdial.co.za; 116 Main St; s/d incl breakfast R225/315) Filling the guts of an old British Army brothel, this place offers slightly shabby but spacious backpacker charm, complete with a giant gargoyle.

George Hotel & Zululand Backpackers (☎ 035-474 4919; www.eshowe.com; 38 Main St; s/d incl breakfast R245/345; ☐ ☒) March into this attractive, whitewashed building with rooms that ooze colonial-era pretensions. Troops let down their guard on a Friday night for Eshowe's party of the week. The separate backpackers (camp sites R55, dorm/single/double with shared bathroom R75/130/180) in this Zululand institution is hung-over, but the George's microbrewery and 101 activities (also on tap) distract any thoughts of deserting.

Adam's Outpost (☎ 035-474 1787; mains R25-60; ☺ lunch) Find refuge in the garden café and cosy, corrugated-iron restaurant, complete with real fireplaces and candles. This little gem is the victor in Eshowe's culinary roll call.

Getting There & Away

Minibus taxis leave from the bus and taxi rank (downhill from KFC near the Osborne/ Main Sts roundabout – go across the bridge and to the right) to Empangeni, (R30, one hour), Gingindlovu (R7) and Melmoth (R20, 45 minutes), the best place to catch taxis deeper into Zululand.

Washesha Buses (☎ 035-477 4504) runs services in the area, including a scenic but rough run on dirt roads through forest areas to Nkandla (R30, two hours), where you can get a taxi to Melmoth.

NIKWALINI VALLEY

Shaka's kraal (fortified village), KwaBulawayo, once loomed over this beautiful valley but today Nikwalini is regimented with citrus orchards and cane fields rather than Zulu warriors. From Eshowe head north for 6km on Rte 66, and turn right onto Rte 230 (a dirt road that will eventually get you to Rte 34).

Across the road from the KwaBulawayo marker is **Coward's Bush**, now just another

KWAZULU-NATAL

marker, where warriors who returned from battle without their spears, or who had received wounds in the back, were executed.

Further west, a few kilometres before Rte 230 meets Rte 66, the **Mandwe Cross** was erected in the 1930s, against the wishes of the Zulu. There are excellent views from the hill.

Shakaland & Simunye
☎ 035

There are several Zulu-village cultural experiences in this area. Created as a set for the telemovie *Shaka Zulu*, the Protea-managed **Shakaland** (☎ 035-460 0912; www.shakaland.com; Nandi Experience R195; ⊙ display 11am) beats up a touristy, but entertaining, blend of perma-grin performance and informative authenticity. The Nandi Experience (Nandi was Shaka's mother) is a display of Zulu culture and customs (including lunch); the Zulu dance performance is said to be the best in the country. You can also stay overnight at the four-star **hotel** (s/d with Nandi Experience & full board R1150/980).

Shakaland is at Norman Hurst Farm, Nikwalini, 3km off Rte 66 and 14km north of Eshowe.

Simunye Zulu Lodge (☎ 035-450 3111; s/d with full board R1365/2050) is owned by renowned 'white Zulu' Barry Leitch. The Simunye experience gives you a chance to move with the rhythm of Zulu life. Located between Melmoth and Eshowe, and nestled at the bottom of cliffs on the banks of the Mfuli, Simunye Lodge – cottages, beehive huts or rondavels – is accessed by horse, donkey cart or ox (4WD for the less hardy), as arranged by your hosts. Guests meet local Zulus and learn about their traditional and contemporary culture. This authentic experience doesn't come cheap but you'll be richer for it.

MELMOTH
☎ 035 / pop 3800
Named after the first resident commissioner of Zululand, Melmoth is a small but pretty town dozing in the hills.

Golf View Lodge B&B (☎ 035-450 2476; 33 AF Leitch Dr; s/d incl breakfast R260/520) Behind a lovely

---

ZULU FESTIVALS

Throughout the year there are a few major festivals that celebrate the rich culture of the Zulu people. These peaceful and joyous occasions involve colourful displays of traditional singing and dancing and are not to be missed. See www.kzn.org.za for a sneak preview, and for further details contact Graham Chennells of Zululand Eco-Adventures at the **George Hotel & Zululand Backpackers** (☎ 035-474 4919; www.eshowe.com) in Eshowe.

King Shaka Day Celebration
On the last Saturday in September, thousands of Zulus converge on KwaDukuza (formerly Stanger) for the King Shaka Day Celebration. The annual event, attended by the current Zulu king, pays homage to the Zulu hero.

Reed Dance
Every year thousands of young bare-breasted Zulu 'maidens' gather before their king, honouring the ancient tradition of the Reed Dance. In days long gone, the king would select a new bride from the mass of beautiful young maidens before him. The dance takes place around the second weekend of September before the King Shaka Day Festival at King Nyonkeni's Palace, which lies between Nongoma and Ulundi.

Shembe Festival
During the month of October, more than 30,000 Zulus gather at Judea, 15km east of Eshowe, for the annual Shembe Festival. This eye-opening festival celebrates the Shembe, the Church of the Holy Nazareth Baptists – an unofficial religion that somehow manages to combine Zulu traditions with Christianity. Presiding over the festivities is the church's saviour, Prophet Mbusi Vimbeni Shembe. Throughout the festival the emphasis is on celebration, with much dancing and singing and the blowing of the horns of Jericho.

old homestead, these comfortable rooms live up to their tag line: 'Your leisure – our pleasure'.

From here, you can catch minibus taxis to Eshowe (R20, 45 minutes) and Ulundi (R20, 30 minutes).

ULUNDI
☎ 035 / pop 15,200

Once the hub of the powerful Zulu empire and until recently joint capital of KZN (with Pietermaritzburg, which gained pre-eminence), Ulundi has lost much of its heart. Brightly coloured box houses have replaced the traditional huts of old and its small centre (cum-shopping mall) has a temporary feel. It's merely a functional place that sprawls across the surrounding hills. For Zulu fanatics, however, there are still plenty of historic sites to explore in the immediate area.

Information
There are plenty of banks, with ATMs, in town.

Ulundi Tourism (☎ 035-870 0034; Princess Magogo St; ☯ 7.30am-4.30pm Mon-Thu, 7.30am-3pm Fri) Has an office in the municipal building.

Zululand Tourism (☎ 035-870 0812; www.zululand .org.za; Princess Magogo St; ☯ 7.30am-5pm Mon-Fri) Also in the municipal building, offers information on the whole of Zululand.

Sights
ONDINI
Established as Cetshwayo's capital in 1873, **Ondini** (High Place; ☎ 035-870 2050; admission R15; ☯ 8am-4pm Mon-Fri, 9am-4pm Sat & Sun) was razed by British troops after the Battle of Ulundi (July 1879), the final engagement of the 1879 Anglo-Zulu War.

It took the British nearly six months to defeat the Zulu army, but the Battle of Ulundi went the same way as most of the campaign, with 10 to 15 times more Zulus killed than British. Part of the reason for the British victory at Ulundi was the adoption of the Boer laager tactic, with troops forming a hollow square to protect the cavalry, which attacked only after the Zulu army had exhausted itself trying to penetrate the walls.

The royal kraal section of the Ondini site has been rebuilt and you can see where archaeological digs have uncovered the floors

of identifiable buildings. The floors, of mud and cow dung, were preserved by the heat of the fires, which destroyed the huts above. The huge area is enclosed in a defensive perimeter of gnarled branches.

Also at Ondini is the **KwaZulu Cultural-Historical Museum** (included in Ondini admission; ☯ 8am-4pm Mon-Fri, 9am-4pm Sat & Sun), with good exhibits on Zulu history and culture and an excellent audiovisual show. It also has one of the country's best collections of beadwork on display. An excellent collection of books is for sale.

To get to Ondini, take the 'Cultural Museum' turn-off from the highway just south of Ulundi centre and keep going for about 5km. Minibus taxis occasionally pass Ondini. This road continues on to Hluhluwe-Imfolozi Park (tarred for 30km).

En route to Ondini, you will also pass the **Ulundi Battlefield** (admission free; ☯ 24hr), where there is a small memorial.

CITY CENTRE
The former **KwaZulu Legislative Assembly** is just north of the train line, and has some unique tapestries charting a course through Zulu history. You can request permission from the guards at the gate to enter; at the time of research, the official guide had left.

Opposite the Legislative Assembly is the site of King Mpande's *iKhanda* (palace), **kwaNodwengu**. Mpande won control from Dingaan after the disaster at Blood River (see p371). He seized power with assistance from the Boers but Zululand declined during his reign. The king's grave is there, but there's little else to see.

AROUND ULUNDI
Emakhosini Ophathe Heritage Park (Valley of the Kings; admission free; ☯ 8am-4pm) is of great significance to the Zulu. The great *makhosi* (chiefs) Nkhosinkulu, Senzangakhona (father of Shaka, Dingaan and Mpande) and Dinizulu are buried here. A monument, the **Spirit of eMakhosni**, sits on a hill (go up Rte 34 for about 30km, beyond the junction with Rte 66 to Ulundi). This comprises a massive bronze Zulu beer pot, surrounded by seven large horns symbolising the seven kings buried in the valley. The park produces an excellent brochure outlining the many historic sites in the park, including graves and battlefields.

LEGENDARY KING SHAKA

Despite all that is written about him, King Shaka is an enigmatic and controversial figure. Whether fact or mythology, Shaka is frequently portrayed as either a vicious and bloodthirsty tyrant or a military genius.

Shaka was the illegitimate son of Nandi with whom he was very close. By the 1820s he had created one of the most powerful kingdoms in the subcontinent. Violence was one of his weapons, both against his enemy and his own warriors. (On the death of his mother it is said that he killed many Zulus who he believed weren't grieving enough.)

He is probably best known for his fighting tactics: he devised the ingenious 'bull formation' where groups of warriors – the 'head and chest' – penetrated the enemy front on, while the 'horns' encircled the enemy from behind. He shortened the throwing spear to a short-shafted, close-range stabbing spear and lengthened the shield.

In 1828 Shaka's life came to an unpleasant end – he was murdered by his half-brothers Dingaan and Mhlangane (who was later toppled by Dingaan). Contemporary Zulus are incredibly proud of their Warrior King. Shaka Day is celebrated annually on 24 September at the Shaka Memorial Gardens in KwaDukuza (see p327). Thousands of Zulus wearing traditional dress and carrying shields, spears and dancing sticks descend upon the gardens. The current king and Chief Minister Dr Buthelezi usually lead the celebration.

Opathe Game Reserve (☎ 870 5000; www.kzn wildlife.com; adult/child R10/5; ☼ 7am-6pm), 10km from Ulundi on Rte 66 towards Melmoth, has a good menagerie of animals, including black and white rhinos.

Sleeping

uMuzi Bushcamp (☎ 035-450 2531; d incl breakfast R395) Inside the Ondini complex is this privately run group of traditional beehive huts. The owners seemed to have capitalised on the location; the price stings for what you get.

Holiday Inn Garden Court (☎ 035-870 1012; fax 035-870 1220; Princess Magogo St; s/d R699/750; ☒ ☐ ☒) Catering to passing dignitaries and bureaucrats, this offers the predictably safe comforts of a chain hotel. Ask about the weekend specials.

Getting There & Away

The minibus taxi park is opposite the Holiday Inn, with services to destinations including Vryheid (R45, 1½ hours) and Eshowe (R45, 1½ hours).

MGUNGUNDLOVU

This was Dingaan's capital from 1829 to 1838, and it was here that Pieter Retief and the other Voortrekkers were killed by their host in 1838, the event that precipitated the Boer-Zulu War. (There are several variations of the spelling of Mgungundlovu, including Ungungundhlovu.) There's a small **interpretative centre** (admission R15; ☼ 8am-4pm) outlin-

ing the life history of Dingaan, and artefacts (note the sweat scraper used by the British troops) and a monument to the Voortrekkers nearby. In 1990 excavations revealed the site of Dingaan's *indlu* (great hut).

The site is 5km off Rte 34, running between Melmoth and Vryheid. Turn off to the left (west) about 5km northeast of the intersection with Rte 66 to Ulundi.

KWAMBONAMBI
☎ 035

KwaMbonambi (often called Kwambo) is a tiny town off the N2, between Empangeni and Mtubatuba. Some believe that KwaMbonambi means 'Place of the Gathering of Kings', while others believe it means 'Place of the Blacksmith', as Shaka's spears were made here. Nowadays it's a place where very little happens, although it's close to the wildlife parks.

Cuckoos Nest (☎ 035-580 1001; www.cuck-nest .com; 28 Albizia St; dm/d with shared bathroom R70/170; ☒), especially the tree house (R160), has lost some of its perkiness since the former owners moved on, but it's spacious and friendly and with its lush garden, is a pleasant stopover if stuck.

MTUBATUBA & AROUND
☎ 035

The name Mtubatuba comes from a local chief, Mthubuthubu, meaning 'He who was Pummelled Out', referring to his difficult birth. After a stroll through the chaotic centre you may feel much the same.

The main reason to visit is that minibus taxis run through here on their way south to Durban (R70, two hours) north to Phongolo (R80 to R100, two hours; via Hluhluwe and Mkuze) and west into Zululand. Coming from those destinations, Mtubatuba is the stop for St Lucia (St Lucia Estuary is 25km east; take Rte 8 by minibus taxi).

On the southern side of Mtubatuba is Riverview, a neat town with a sugar mill. Here, **Wendy's B&B Country Lodge** (☎ 035-550 0407; www.wendybnb.co.za; 3 Riverview Rd, Riverview; r incl breakfast R560; 🖭) drips with soft furnishings and old-fashioned homey charm. It provides a warm welcome and an inhouse restaurant and pub.

HLUHLUWE & AROUND
☎ 035 / pop 3200

Hluhluwe village (roughly pronounced shloo-shloo-wee) is northeast of Hluhluwe-Imfolozi Park. Here, next to the Engen petrol station on the main road through town, you will find the **Hluhluwe Tourism Association** (☎ 035-562 0353; www.hluhluwe.net; Bush Rd; 🕑 8am-5pm Mon-Fri, 9am-4pm Sat & Sun), which has useful advice on accommodation and transport in the area.

You can also indulge in some local retail therapy at **Ilala Weavers** (☎ 035-562 0630; www.ilala.co.za; 🕑 8am-5pm Mon-Fri, 9am-4pm Sat & Sat), where there's an excellent selection of Zulu handicrafts and aims to make local women more self-sufficient. Some 2000 Zulus now contribute to the works on offer.

Dumazulu means 'thundering Zulu', although it's the tourists who crash through the 'living museum' of **Dumazulu Cultural Village** (☎ 035-562 2260; www.goodersonleisure.com; admission R95; 🕑 shows 8.15am, 11am & 3.15pm). This popular Zulu cultural experience features spear-throwing, basket-weaving exhibitions and dancing. It's 14km south of Hluhluwe and east of the N2.

Sleeping
Isinkwe Backpackers Lodge (☎ 035-562 2258; www.isinkwe.co.za; camp sites per person R65; dm/d with shared bathroom R85/200, d R280; 🖳 💷 🖭) This well-managed place, in a sweep of virgin bush 14km south of Hluhluwe, is as close as you can get to a bona fide bush-lodge backpackers. There's a list of activities as tall

---

> **WARNING**
>
> There is malaria in the low-lying areas of coastal Zululand and parts of the Elephant Coast (especially Maputaland). It also exists in the north of KwaZulu-Natal, especially as you get close to the Mozambique and eastern Swaziland borders. There is the risk of bilharzia in some waterways and dams, especially those below 1200m above sea level. See p647 for more information.

as a giraffe, and you can exchange hippo-adventure stories at the bar-deck by the pool. Ring for directions.

Hluhluwe Hotel (☎ 035-562 0251; www.hluhluwehotel.co.za; 104 Bush Rd; s/d incl breakfast R570/840; 🖭 🖭) This monolithic, central and sanitised motel-with-a-thatched-roof caters for the mass-tourist market.

Zululand Tree Lodge (☎ 035-562 1020; s/d with full board R2100/2800; 🖭) Seven kilometres outside Hluhluwe, and set in the Ubizane reserve amid fever trees, this romantic spot offers dreamy, thatched tree houses, and some self-catering, four-bed safari lodges (R690). Tours are included in the price; it has excellent specials.

HLUHLUWE-IMFOLOZI PARK
☎ 035

Hluhluwe-Imfolozi Park (☎ 035-550 8476; www.kznwildlife.com; adult/child R70/35; 🕑 5am-7pm Nov-Feb, 6am-6pm Mar-Oct) is one of South Africa's best-known and most evocative parks. Covering 96,000 hectares, the park is best visited in winter as the animals then range widely without congregating at water sources, although the lush vegetation sometimes makes viewing difficult. However, summer visits can also be very rewarding, especially at Imfolozi where there is more-open savanna country.

The park has lion, elephant, rhino (black and white), leopard, giraffes and wild dogs. The land is quite hilly except on the river flats: the White Imfolozi River flows through Imfolozi, and the Black Imfolozi forms the northern border of the park; the Hluhluwe River bisects Hluhluwe, and the dam on it attracts wildlife.

The **Centenary Centre** (🕑 8am-4pm), a wildlife-holding centre with an attached museum and information centre, is in the eastern section of Imfolozi. It incorporates rhino enclosures and antelope pens (open 9am to 3pm), and was established to allow visitors to view animals in transit to their new homes.

The wildlife drives here are very popular. **Hilltop Camp** (☎ 035-562 0848) offers morning and night drives, while Mpila Camp does night drives only. The drives are open to resort residents only and cost R150 per person.

Bear in mind that the reserves are in a (low-risk) malarial area and there are lots of mosquitoes – come prepared.

Wilderness Trails

One of Imfolozi's main attractions is its trail system, in a special 24,000-hectare wilderness area (note: these are seasonal). The **Base Trail** (3 nights/4 days, R2700) is, as the name suggests, at a base camp. Trailists carry daypacks on the daily outings.

The **Short Wilderness Trail** (2 nights/3 days, R1500) is at satellite camps with no amenities (bucket shower), yet are fully catered. Similar is the **Extended Wilderness Trail**

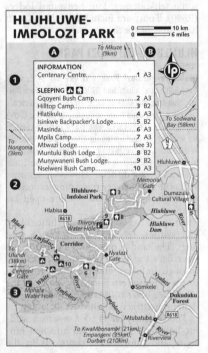

HLUHLUWE-IMFOLOZI PARK

0 — 10 km
0 — 6 miles

INFORMATION
Centenary Centre.....................1 A3

SLEEPING 🏕️ 🏠
Gqoyeni Bush Camp.................2 A3
Hilltop Camp............................3 B2
Hlatikulu................................4 A3
Isinkwe Backpacker's Lodge.....5 B2
Masinda..................................6 A3
Mpila Camp.............................7 A3
Mtwazi Lodge......................(see 3)
Muntulu Bush Lodge................8 B2
Munywaneni Bush Lodge..........9 B2
Nselweni Bush Camp..............10 A3

To Mkuze (9km)

To Sodwana Bay (58km)

Hluhluwe

To Nongoma (3km)

Hluhluwe-Imfolozi Park

Memorial Gate

Dumazulu Cultural Village

Hlabisa

R618

Thiyeni Water Hole

Hluhluwe River

Hluhluwe Dam

Black Imfolozi

To Ulundi (38km)

Corridor

Nyalazi Gate

White Imfolozi River

Cengeni Gate

Mphafa Water Hole

Somkele

Nyalazi River

Dukuduku Forest

Mtubatuba

R618

To KwaMbonambi (21km); Empangeni (95km); Durban (210km)

Riverview

(3 nights/4 days, R2250) but guests must carry their gear for 7km into camp. On the **Primitive Trail** (4 nights/5 days, R1800), you carry equipment, help prepare the food (provided) and sleep under the stars. Some consider this trail to be more fun as you get to participate more (for example, hikers must sit up in 1½-hour watches during the night).

Bushveld Trail (2 nights/3 days, R1600) is a softer experience; the base camp has amenities (including fridge) and guests have walks and summer siestas.

Tours

Most of the accommodation options, including hostels, offer day trips to Hluhluwe-Imfolozi. If you've got time, a good option is to hire a car and travel at your own pace through the park.

Tekweni Eco-Tours (☎ in Durban 031-463 2576; www.tekweniecotours.co.za) offers tours from Durban.

Sleeping & Eating

You must book accommodation in advance through **KZN Wildlife** (☎ 033-845 1000; www.kznwildlife.com) in Pietermaritzburg or at Durban's **Tourist Junction** (☎ 035-304 4934; 160 Pine St, cnr Soldiers Way; ⏰ 8am-4.30pm Mon-Fri, 9am-2pm Sat). Last-minute bookings – those made 48 hours ahead – should be made direct with the camp site.

Hilltop Camp (☎ 035-562 0848; rest huts/chalets per person R230/466, 2-bed units with full board per person R466) is the signature resort on the Hluhluwe side, with stupendous views, a restaurant and a much-needed bar (it gets very hot here). The drawback is that it's the most popular destination for tour buses and is generally quite busy. If you want peace and quiet, try one of the smaller and more sedate accommodation centres in Imfolozi.

Muntulu Bush Lodge (8-bed bush lodges per person R515) is perched high above the Hluhluwe River; and **Munywaneni Bush Lodge** (8-bed bush lodges per person R468, minimum R3090) is secluded and self-contained. There's also a fully hosted and catered nine-bed lodge at **Mtwazi Lodge** (per person incl wildlife drives & walks price on application).

The main accommodation centre on the Imfolozi side is spectacular **Mpila Camp** (4-bed rest huts per person R213, 2-bed safari camps per person R242) in the centre of the reserve. **Masinda**

(9-bed lodge per person incl wildlife drives & walks R1800), near the Centenary Centre, is fully hosted and catered. There is also accommodation available at **Nselweni Bush Camp** (8-bed bush camps per person R319), **Gqoyeni Bush Camp** (8-bed bush camps per person R515) and **Hlatikulu** (8-bed bush camps per person R515).

Be warned: all accommodation options are billed per person but are subject to a minimum charge. Additionally, if you are self-catering, remember to bring your own food!

Getting There & Away

You can access the park via three gates. The main entrance, Memorial Gate, is about 15km west of the N2, about 50km north of Mtubatuba. The second entrance, the Nyalazi Gate, is accessed by turning left off the N2 onto Rte 618 just after Mtubatuba to Nongoma. The third, Cengeni Gate, on Imfolozi's western side, is accessible by road (tarred for 30km) from Ulundi.

Petrol is available at Mpila Camp in Imfolozi and at Hilltop Camp in Hluhluwe, where you can also get diesel.

PHONGOLO (PONGOLA)

☎ 034

Back on the N2, Phongolo (also known as Pongola) is a small town in a sugar-growing district near the Mpumalanga and Swaziland borders. There's an ATM, and petrol is available 24 hours. There's not a lot here, unless you stop en route to the **Phongolo Reserve** (☎ 034-435 1012; www.kznwildlife.com; adult/child/vehicle R18/9/20; ◷ 6am-6pm), a lovely area southeast of Phongolo, backed by the Lebombo Range and encompassing a large lake, on which you can go boating.

KZN Wildlife (☎ 034-033-845 1000; www.kznwildlife.com; camp sites per person R45) has (unfenced) camp sites in Phongolo Reserve. Minimum charges apply.

Pongola Country Lodge (☎ 034-413 1352; fax 413 1353; 14 Jan Mielie St; s/d R350/400) Modern, comfortable and central, this is a good bet for an overnight stay in Phongolo.

ITHALA GAME RESERVE

KZN Wildlife's **Ithala Game Reserve** (☎ 033-845 1000, 034-983 2540; www.kznwildlife.com; adult/child/vehicle R35/18/30; ◷ 5am-7pm) has all the trappings of a private wildlife reserve but much lower prices. It also doesn't get the crowds that flock into Hluhluwe-Imfolozi, as it's

slightly off the main routes, but is equally as captivating.

Most of the 30,000 hectares are taken up by the steep valleys of six rivers (tributaries of the Phongolo), with some open grassland on the heights, rugged outcrops and bushveld. Some of the world's oldest rock formations are found here, as are Stone Age spear and axe heads.

Animals include black and white rhino, elephant, tsessebes, buffalo and giraffes (the park's emblem as they are believed to be indigenous to Ithala) and rare bird species.

Guided walks (R65 per person) and wildlife and night drives (R86 per person) are available.

Sleeping

There are camp sites available at **Mhlangeni** (☎ 033-845 1000; www.kznwildlife.com; camp sites per person R40), and bush camps at **Thalu** (R275) and **Mbizo** (R275). Minimum charges apply.

Ntshondwe (☎ 033-845 1000; www.kznwildlife.com; self-catering 2-bed chalets per person R352, 2-bed non-self-catering units per person R319; 🏊) This is the main centre, with superb views of the reserve below. Facilities include a restaurant, shop and swimming pool. There's a full-board option for the units, on request (R440).

Getting There & Away

Ithala is reached from Louwsburg, about 55km northeast of Vryheid on Rte 69, and about the same distance southwest of Phongolo via Rtes 66 and 69. Louwsburg is much smaller than many maps indicate.

VRYHEID

☎ 034 / pop 63,600

Vryheid (Liberty) is the largest town in northern Zululand. Today it is an agricultural, timber and mining centre but in 1884 it was the capital of the Nieuwe Republiek, which was absorbed into the Zuid-Afrikaansche Republiek (South African Republic) four years later. After the Anglo-Boer War, the area was transferred to Natal. There's still a strong Afrikaner presence here.

The helpful **Vryheid information office** (☎ 034-982 2133; www.vryheid.co.za; cnr Market & High Sts) can provide information on the surrounding area, and on tours of the Battlefields.

The interesting **Nieuwe Republiek Museum** (☎ 034-982 2133; 119 Landdrost St; admission free;

KWAZULU-NATAL

BLURRED BORDERS

Historically and traditionally, the region of Zululand ran from the Tugela River all the way to the Mozambique border, and west as far as Vryheid. The northeastern section of this region was known as Maputaland. Over the years, the increase in tourism has led to an explosion of promotional activity. A more recent branding exercise by tourist authorities has created (or blurred) borders, by renaming the eastern coast the Elephant Coast. References to 'Maputaland' are being phased out, although it still exists on many maps, and in this book.

⌚ 7.30am-4pm Mon-Fri, by appointment Sat & Sun), in the former Parliament building, is devoted to the shortlived Nieuwe Republiek. The **Lucas Meijer Museum** (☎ 034-982 2133; cnr Landdrost & Mark Sts; ⌚ 7.30am-4pm Mon-Fri, by appointment Sat & Sun) is a small local-history museum in the old Lucas Meijer House (Meijer was the only president of the Nieuwe Republiek).

Sleeping

With the exception of Mountain View, accommodation in Vryheid is generally overpriced for what you get.

Vryheid Lodge (☎ 034-981 5201; fax 034-981 5467; 200 Kerk St; s/d R130/190) Resembling 1950s-style university accommodation, these digs are frugal on every front. They're above a pub; single females may not feel comfortable here.

Mountain View (☎ 034-980 1199; mountainview@ vryheid.co.za; 90 Smal St; s/d R250/350; ℗) This is a welcome addition to the town's B&B market. The rooms are as welcoming and generous as the owner, and have a tasteful touch of ethnic design.

Villa Prince Imperial (☎ 034-983 2610; www.prince imperial.com; 136 Bree St; s/d incl breakfast R410/620; ℗ 🅇 🅖) Vryheid's most upmarket home-cum-hotel offers a splash of frontier-town French luxury, if with a touch of stale-smoke syndrome (despite the no-smoking signs).

Getting There & Away

Greyhound (☎ in Durban 031-334 9700; www.grey hound.co.za) runs daily buses between Durban and Vryheid (R190, six hours) and Jo'burg and Vryheid (R200, 6½ hours).

The well-organised minibus taxi park is near the former train station. Vryheid is the centre for minibus taxis in this part of KwaZulu-Natal. Services from Vryheid include Ulundi (R45, 1½ hours), Dundee (R25, 1¼ hours), Phongolo (R45, two hours), Durban (R100, four hours; via Melmoth) and Jo'burg (R100, five hours).

THE ELEPHANT COAST

Up there on the podium with the world's great ecotourist destinations, and not far from the top of the scribbled list marked 'Places I Must See In South Africa', the tourism-authority labelled Elephant Coast (which incorporates the northern region known as Maputaland) is a phenomenal stretch of natural beauty, with a fabulously diverse mix of environments and wildlife. The Elephant Coast is bound in the south by the Umfolozi River just below the St Lucia Estuary, and to the northwest by the Lebombo Mountains. (Note, some tourist literature can be confusing, with both the Elephant Coast and Zululand promotions claiming parks, such as Hluhluwe-Imfolozi, to be their own.)

This large stretch of coastline includes some of the country's true highlights, including the wonderfully diverse and perennially photogenic Greater St Lucia Wetland Park and the coffee table–book vistas of Kosi Bay Nature Reserve. Sparsely populated and uncompromisingly untamed, this region, away from the scattered resort towns, offers a glimpse of the wild heart of Africa. The climate becomes steadily hotter as you go north and, thanks to the warm Indian Ocean, summers are steamy and almost tropical. The humid coastal air causes frequent dense mists on the inland hills, reducing visibility to a few metres. If driving, be careful of pedestrians and animals suddenly appearing around a corner.

There is a good network of minibus taxis and local-bus companies covering this area. The **Baz Bus** (☎ in Durban 031-304 9099; www.bazbus.com) also goes up the coast, on the run between Durban and Jo'burg via Swaziland.

GREATER ST LUCIA WETLAND PARK
☎ 035

The Greater St Lucia Wetland Park, a Unesco World Heritage site, stretches for 280 glorious kilometres, from the Mozambique border near Kosi Bay in the north of Maputaland, to Maphelana, at the southern end of Lake St Lucia. With the Indian Ocean on one side, and a series of lakes on the other (including Lake St Lucia), the 328,000-hectare area is made up of a jumbled jigsaw of different reserves (with separate accesses) and protects five distinct ecosystems, offering everything from offshore reefs and beaches, to lakes, wetlands, woodlands and coastal forests. Loggerhead and leatherback turtles nest along the park's shores. The ocean beaches pull big crowds during the holiday season.

Lake St Lucia itself is Africa's largest estuary. Despite its past healthy water levels, it is currently at its lowest level for 50 years, due to a severe drought. Controversy surrounds a long-term solution to the management of the lake, with both animal and plant species being affected by the changing ecological factors (see the boxed text, p341).

At the time of research, the Greater St Lucia Wetland Park was about to relaunch its ecodestination image. Part of this included granting concessions to 'responsible' ecotour operators as well as renaming the park to better reflect the merging (several years ago) of the jigsaw of reserves and parks down the eastern seaboard.

In any case, your best bet is to spend a night in St Lucia Estuary to visit the KZN Wildlife office for information on parks and reserves and get your head around the activities and destinations on offer.

Remember that unless specified, all KZN Wildlife accommodation must be booked at **KZN Wildlife** (☎ in Pietermaritzburg 033-845 1000, in Durban 031-304 4934) with 48 hours' notice. Within 48 hours, try your luck directly with the lodges and camp sites.

Activities & Tours

Numerous fascinating day and night tours are on offer. Most of the hostels run or can organise tours through tour operators. Tour companies are being granted 'concessions', which identify them as the region's ecoresponsible operators. Many of these

> **WARNING**
>
> Although St Lucia Estuary has itself been declared malaria-free following a hefty spraying program, the area outside the Greater St Lucia Wetland Park, especially towards Kosi Bay, is a malarial area and there are lots of mosquitoes. Ticks and leeches can be a problem. Also beware of crocs and hippos: both can be deadly. Be careful at night, as this is when hippos roam. In more remote areas hippos might be encountered on shore during the day – maintain your distance and retreat quietly. Sharks sometimes venture up near the St Lucia Estuary.

have offices based in St Lucia Estuary and are useful first stops for information.

BIRDING
Zululand Birding Route (☎ 033-753 5644)

BOAT TOURS
Advantage Tours (☎ 035-590 1259)
Born Free and Fannas (☎ 035-590 1047)
Santa Lucia (☎ 035-590 1340)

CANOEING
Muzi Pan Adventures (☎ 073-161 8189)
St Lucia Kayak Safaris (☎ 035-590 1233)

DIVING & SNORKELLING
Amoray (☎ 083-252 9448)
Coral Divers (☎ 033-345 6531)
Rocktail Bay Lodge (☎ 011 807 1800)
Thonga Beach Lodge (☎ 035-474 1473)

HIKING
Hiking is awesome around the region. The main trails are all in the Eastern Shores (Mfabeni) area and are guided walks. For more information, see p341. There are also day walks, detailed in the scant KZN Wildlife literature at St Lucia Estuary office.

HORSE RIDING
Bhangazi Horse Safaris (☎ 035-550 4898)
Exodus Adventures (☎ 083-349 8575)

TURTLE TOURS
David Ngubane (☎ 072-847 7057) & **Richard Mathenjwa** (☎ 082-968 3766) Both are community guides.
EuroZulu Safaris (☎ 035-590 2173)

KWAZULU-NATAL

Rocktail Bay Lodge (☎ 011 807 1800)
Shaka Barker Tours (☎ 035-590 1162)
Sodwana Bay Lodge (☎ 035-571 0117)
Thonga Beach Lodge (☎ 035-474 1473)

WHALE-WATCHING
Advantage Tours (☎ 035-590 1259)

WILDLIFE DRIVES
Leisure EcoTours (☎ 035-590 4059)
Shaka Barker Tours (☎ 035-590 1162)

St Lucia Estuary
St Lucia Estuary, the park's main resort town and the region's gateway, is a good place in which to get your bearings for the region. In high season, this pleasant village is a hotbed of activity as the population swells from 600 to the thousands. But outside the silly season, you're guaranteed a comfortable bed, a cold beer and a good feed. The main drag, MacKenzie St (a former hippo pathway), is packed with restaurants, lively hostels and bars, but the quieter avenues behind offer a touch more hush and a good selection of midrange B&Bs. Hippos sometimes amble down the town's quieter streets (beware, these are not cute).

INFORMATION
First National Bank (MacKenzie St) Has an ATM.
Internet café (☎ 035-590 1056; 310 MacKenzie St; per hr R30; ☼ 7am-10pm) At BiB's International Backpackers.
KZN Wildlife (☎ 035-590 1340; fax 035-590 1343; Pelican Rd; ☼ 8am-12.30pm & 2-4.30pm) Offers information on the reserves.
St Lucia Tours & Charters (☎ 035-590 1259; www .advantagetours.co.za; cnr MacKenzie St & Katonkel Rd; ☼ 6.30am-6pm) Offers plenty of information and tour bookings. There is another office on the corner of Mac Kenzie St and Rte 618.
Standard Bank (MacKenzie St) Has an ATM.

SIGHTS
About 1km north of St Lucia, on the road to Cape Vidal, is the KZN **Crocodile Centre** (☎ 035-590 1386; croc-centre@kznwildlife.com; adult/ child R30/25; ☼ 8.30am-4.30pm Mon-Fri, 8.30am-5pm Sat, 9am-4pm Sun), where a fine array of crocs can be seen in their not-so-natural habitat.

SLEEPING
There is rarely a shortage of places to stay, but it is worth booking ahead during the summer months.

In St Lucia Estuary itself, you can camp at three sites run by **KZN Wildlife** (☎ 033-845 1000, 590 1340; www.kznwildlife.com; Pelican St). The pretty **Sugarloaf** (per person R52) is on the estuary, as are **Eden Park** (per person R65), near the KZN Wildlife office, and **Iphiva** (per person R52), off MacKenzie St.

BiB's International Backpackers (☎ 035-590 1056; www.bibs.co.za; 310 MacKenzie St; camp sites R45, dm/d with shared bathroom R70/150, d R200; P 🖳 🖳) Occupying a series of sprawling buildings, the tarnished rooms in this happening place are as tired as its guests after their day of activities. But the atmosphere makes up for it: BiB's offers all the backpacker staples – a busy bar, a huge (serviced) kitchen for cooking, and organised fun.

Hornbill House (☎ 035-590 1071; 43 Hornbill St; s/d incl breakfast R245/390; 🖳 🖳) A pleasant place to nest, with homey B&B comforts, plus pool and deck. That is, if you're not flitting about on one of the many ecofriendly trips or activities offered by the knowledgeable owner, also a tour-company operator.

Santa Lucia Guest House (☎ 035-590 1151; www .santalucia.co.za; 30 Pelican St; s/d incl breakfast R290/580; 🖳 🖳) This highly acclaimed B&B adds some old-fashioned luxury to the usual standard fare. It's chock-a-block with décor and hotel trimmings and the friendly, hospitable owners ensure a pleasant hippo-free stay.

Hippo Hideaway (☎ 035-590 1025; www.hippohide away.co.za; 70 MacKenzie St; s/d R500/560; 🖳 🖳) The new hippo in the hide, this smart place caters to the better-heeled traveller: the small complex of self-catering apartments is spanking new, sparkling clean, and decked out in the inevitable ethnic (hippo-themed) décor.

EATING
St Pizza (☎ 035-590 1048; MacKenzie St; mains R18-62; ☼ lunch & dinner) Pizza with a South African spin (they'll even put biltong – strips of meat dried and cured in the sun – on top) is on the menu at this down-to-earth place with a buzzy, beer-garden atmosphere.

Quarterdeck (☎ 035-590 1116; MacKenzie St; mains R25-75; ☼ breakfast, lunch & dinner) With a slightly tacky maritime theme, this lively place serves up mountainous portions and plenty of atmosphere. Steaks and seafood top the billing, but come nightfall, the outside terrace takes on a bustling, bar-style buzz.

KWAZULU-NATAL

POSING PROBLEMS – THE ST LUCIA ESTUARY

Lake St Lucia, Africa's largest estuary, is part of the Greater St Lucia Wetland Park, which covers 320,000 hectares, features five ecosystems and was declared a World Heritage Site in 1999.

But not all is going swimmingly. The lake – and estuarine system of 35,000 hectares – is the centre of an ecological conundrum. Scientists and others are at loggerheads over the best way of dealing with a complicated combination of drought, a former river diversion and expanded water usage (through population increases, crop irrigation, farm dams and timber plantations), all of which have resulted in a severe drop in the lake's water levels – currently 80cm below mean sea level. This not only has major ecological repercussions, but tourist numbers in the area are said to have decreased due to a resulting decline in fish populations and a ban on beach driving. (That said, the nature of the tourist has changed from fishermen, who have decreased in numbers, to more ecodestination-driven visitors, whose numbers are increasing.)

Part of this complex problem is the Umfolozi River which, diverted from the estuary mouth in 1951 to become a separate entity, is being prevented – with the construction of artificial sand barriers – from breaking into the estuary. The mouth of the Umfolozi is moving north towards the estuary due to erosion and force of currents. (Five other rivers enter the lake, but the Umfolozi River has a runoff that is larger than all these combined.)

The main issue is whether or not the estuary mouth should be opened or remain closed. The pro-closure camp believes that if the river enters the estuary, it may cause the closed estuary mouth to break open. This would result in millions of tonnes of sea water surging into the estuary, as well as massive deposits of salt from the sea and sediment from both the sea and river – causing permanent ecological damage. They believe that the healthy animal life including hippo, crocs, pelicans and waders, thrive on the rich feeding.

The anti-closure camp says that the current dry conditions are a threat to the future of the lake. They are concerned that St Lucia is in danger of turning into a freshwater lake, with freshwater species invading a traditional estuarine area. The lake is a nursery and rich feeding ground for many fish species, prawns and crabs which, unable to spawn at sea, are now facing decline.

The Wetland Authority has sought research funding from the Global Environment Facility, which assists developing countries in finding solutions to environmental problems. It is looking at a holistic approach to water-management issues in the catchment system. A possible suggestion includes restoring a number of surrounding sugar farms to swampland (acting as a sediment filter for water flowing into the lake).

Alfredo's Italian Restaurant (☎ 035-590 1150; MacKenzie St; mains R40-58; ☻ lunch & dinner) Don't let the tartan tablecloths mislead – the pizza, pasta and salads at this smart place bring Little Italy to town.

GETTING THERE & AWAY
The **Baz Bus** (☎ in Durban 031-304 9099; www.bazbus .com) drops backpackers several times a week. If you're not doing tours out of St Lucia Estuary, the only way of getting around is to have your own wheels.

Eastern Shores (Mfabeni) Reserve
☎ 035
Two kilometres north of St Lucia Estuary, on the eastern side of the lake, is the boom gate for the **Eastern Shores (Mfabeni) Reserve** (☎ 035-590 9002; www.kznwildlife.com; adult/child/ vehicle R20/15/35; ☻ 5am-7pm), which has the sea

on its eastern flank. This section of the park has an excellent selection of wildlife, and a variety of ecosystems from rocky shore and swamp to open grassland. Fourteen kilometres north of the boom gate are the **Mission Rocks**, where you will find the **ranger station** (☎ 035-590 9002) for the hiking trails. At low tide, the Mission Rocks are covered in rock pools containing a fabulous array of sea life.

HIKING TRAILS
You can drive through the reserve on a day trip, but by far the best way to see this section of the park is to take one of the trails offered by KZN Wildlife.

The **Mziki Trail** (☎ 035-90 9002; per person per night R70) is a guided, three-day trail of about 40km. In fact, the route is made up of three, distinct one-day trails, which span out

KWAZULU-NATAL

from the Mount Tabor Base Camp, where accommodation is in a basic, eight-bed hut. Reservations should be made on the listed phone number and you should check in at the Mission Rocks ranger station between 2pm and 4pm on the first day. You must bring your own food.

The **Emoyeni Trail** (☎ 035-590 9002; per person R55) is a guided, five-day excursion. The trail is 65km long and you stay each of the four nights in a different camp. The trail offers an indepth insight into the ecosystems and history of the area – there used to be a WWII British radar observation post on Mt Tabor. Reservations should be made on the listed phone number and you should check in at the Mission Rocks ranger station before noon on the first day. You must bring your own food, cooking equipment, sleeping bag and tent.

See KZN Wildlife for the latest information on unguided trails.

Cape Vidal
☎ 035
This beautiful **coastal camp** (☎ 033-845 1000, 590 9024; www.kznwildlife.com; adult/child/vehicle R20/15/35; ☽ 6am-6pm) takes in the land between the lake and the ocean, north of Cape Vidal itself. Some of the forested sand dunes are 150m high and the beaches are excellent for swimming.

There is KZN Wildlife accommodation at the **Bhangazi Complex** (☎ 033-845 1000; www .kznwildlife.com; camp sites R72, 5–8-bed log cabins per person R222, 8-bed bush lodge R350), near Lake Bhangazi. Minimum charges apply.

From St Lucia Estuary head north, past the Crocodile Centre and through the entrance gates. Cape Vidal is approximately 35km further on.

Fani's Island & False Bay Park
Both Fani's Island and False Bay Park desperately need the rainbird to sing; it hasn't for many years. Due to the drought, there is no water in the lake and the area has been closed for several years. It will reopen as soon as there is sufficient rainfall. Check with KZN Wildlife – there are two excellent camps.

Sodwana Bay
☎ 035
Spectacular Sodwana Bay, a sheltered recess at the very northern tip of the Greater St Lucia Wetland Park, isn't a whole lot more than sand, sea and silence. And that's its appeal. The spread-out village of Sodwana Bay is also here, but the two nearby parks – Sodwana Bay National Park and Ozabeni – provide most of the highlights.

Isolated and peaceful (outside the holidays, – when 4WDs take to the sands and scuba-diving groups gather), this little slice of paradise offers stunning coastal scenery, guided walking trails and some serious deep-sea game fishing (note: self-guided walks are no longer available due to robberies). It's possibly best known on the tourist trail for its scuba diving and its diversity of underwater seascapes and marine flora and fauna.

Tourist information is best obtained from the KZN Wildlife office at the camp site reception. (This is further on from the first log cabin labelled 'tourist office', which has extremely limited information.)

Sodwana Bay National Park (☎ 035-571 0051; www.kznwildlife.com; adult/child R20/15; ☽ 6am-6pm) is on the coast, east of Mkuze. There are some animals, and the dunes, swamps and offshore coral reefs are well worth visiting,

---

MARINE TURTLES

Five species of turtle live off the South African coast but only two actually nest on the coast: the leatherback turtle (Dermochelys coriacea) and the loggerhead turtle (Caretta caretta). The nesting areas of the leatherback extend from the St Lucia mouth north into Mozambique, but the loggerhead only nests in the Maputaland Marine Reserve.

Both species nest at night in summer. The female moves above the high-tide mark, finds a suitable site and lays her eggs. The loggerheads' breeding area is more varied as they clamber over rocks in the intertidal zone; leatherbacks will only nest on sandy beaches.

About 70 days later, the hatchlings scramble out of the nest at night and make a dash for the sea. Only one or two of each thousand hatchlings will survive until maturity. The females return 12 to 15 years later to the very same beach to nest.

SNORKELLING & DIVING

The coastline near Sodwana Bay, which includes the southernmost coral reefs in Africa, is a diver's paradise. Schools of fish glide through the beautiful coral, turtles swim by, and moray eels peer inquisitively from rock crevices. Predominantly soft coral over hard, the reef has one of the world's highest recorded numbers of tropical-fish species. All of these wonders can be seen using scuba or snorkelling equipment, and excellent visibility and warm winter waters allow for diving year-round.

Popular snorkelling spots are Cape Vidal, Two-Mile Reef off Sodwana Bay, Mabibi and the Kosi Mouth with its famous 'aquarium', so named because of the diversity of fish. Scuba divers should head for Tenedos Shoal, between the Mlalazi River and Port Durnford, and Five-Mile, Seven-Mile and Nine-Mile Reefs. Courses are held at Two-Mile Reef.

but the area can become very congested during holidays. Between November and February there are turtle-viewing tours (R150 per person).

If you opt for accommodation in the park's massive camp-site area (some of the lodges are also here), you pay a one-off charge of R45 at reception; day visitors pay R5.

For a more peaceful look at a similar ecosystem, head south to the adjoining **Ozabeni** (☎ 035-571 0268; www.kznwildlife.com; adult/child/vehicle R20/10/15; ☺ 6am-6pm), which runs all the way down to Lake St Lucia. Bird-watchers are in for a treat here, as more than 330 species have been recorded. Visitors are free to walk through the reserve.

Orca Launches (☎ 035-571 5000, 083-654 7204; www.orcasafaris.co.za; ☺ 8.30am-4.30pm Mon-Fri, 8.30am-noon Sat) is in the artistic-looking store on the main street of the village and organises a host of activities from snorkelling to turtle tours (activities from R150 per person). Nearby, **Off Road Fun** (☎ 082-785 7704) offers quad-bike tours (R180).

The nearest ATM is in Mbazwana, 14km west.

SLEEPING & EATING

KZN Wildlife (☎ 033-845 1000; www.kznwildlife.com; Ozabeni camp sites per person R30, Sodwana Bay National Park camp sites/5-bed cabins per person R140/220) Offers camping at Ozabeni, and hundreds of camp sites and cabins at Sodwana Bay National Park. Minimum charges apply.

Coral Divers (☎ 033-345 6531; www.coraldivers.co.za; Sodwana Bay National Park; s/d with shared bathroom from R165/300; ☐ ☒) Some readers have reported feeling like a small tadpole in a big pond at this Professional Association of Diving Instructors (PADI) resort (others

feel like sharks). While it's a factory-style operation, it has cabins in a lovely setting, satellite TV, a pool and a bar, plus a shoal of other activities. Standard dive packages with three nights' accommodation and five dives starts at around R1300. For R150, staff will pick you up from Hluhluwe.

Sodwana Bay Lodge (☎ 035-571 0095; www.sodwanadiving.co.za; s/d with half board R738/1210) This slick resort, with neat boardwalks, banana palms and thatched roofs, caters to high-life divers, offering combinations of dive packages (from R1410 per person sharing). It's on the main road through the village.

Mseni Lodge (☎ 035-571 0284; www.mseni.co.za; Sodwana Bay National Park; s/d with half board R905/1190) Nestled in lush dune forest, these luxury cabins are worth diving into your wallet for. The lodge also offers dive courses through **Amoray Diving** (☎ 083-252 9448; www.amoraydiving.com), which cost between R750 and R2,500.

Also recommended for accommodation with diving, tours and other activities:

Da Blu Juice (☎ 082-924 7757, 082-681 5459; www.dabluejuice.co.za; dm per person R120, cabins from R200)

Natural Moments Bush Lodge & Diving (☎ 035-571 0167; naturalmoments@planetblue.co.za; bungalows per person from R100)

GETTING THERE & AWAY

There are two road routes from the N2. The northern route leaves the highway about 8km north of Mkuze and runs up into the Lebombo Mountains to the small town of Jozini. After Jozini it's a dirt road running through flat country. The southern route is sealed the whole way and leaves the N2 north of the turn-off for Hluhluwe village. Both routes converge at the village of Mbazwana, from where it's about 20km to the park.

Minibus taxis run from the N2 up to Jozini. From there to Sodwana Bay you shouldn't have trouble finding transport (taxis) as it's a fairly densely populated region. There are far fewer taxis on the southern route but there is a fair amount of tourist traffic, so hitching should be fairly easy.

LAKE SIBAYA NATURE RESERVE

Protecting the largest freshwater lake in South Africa, **Lake Sibaya Nature Reserve** (www .kznwildlife.com; adult/child/vehicle R20/10/35; ⊙ 6am-6pm) covers between 60 and 70 sq km, depending on the water level. It lies very close to the coast, and between the eastern shore and the sea is a range of sand dunes up to 165m high. There are hippo, some crocs and a large range of birdlife (more than 280 species have been recorded). The lake is popular for fishing; you can hire boats (complete with skipper) for fishing trips.

There is currently no accommodation in the reserve. The main route to the reserve is via the village of Mbazwana, south of the lake, either from Mkuze or from Mhlosinga, off Rte 22.

KOSI BAY NATURE RESERVE
☎ 033

The jewel of the Elephant Coast, **Kosi Bay Nature Reserve** (☎ 033-845 1000, 035-592 0234; www .kznwildlife.com; adult/child/vehicle R20/10/15; ⊙ 6am-6pm) features a string of four lakes, Nhlange, Mpungwini, Sifungwe and Amanzimnyama, that tip down the hillside into an estuary lined with some of the most beautiful (and quietest) beaches in South Africa. Fig, mangrove and raffia-palm forests provide the greenery, while a coral reef offers excellent snorkelling just offshore.

There are antelope species in the drier country and hippo, Zambezi sharks and some crocs in the lake system. More than 250 bird species have been identified here, including the rare palmnut vulture.

The 44km **Kosi Bay Trail** (4 days per person for group of 10 R350, minimum charge R3500) is a self-catered, guided hike around the Kosi estuarine system, stopping each night in remote camps, which focus on different aspects of the reserve. This trail includes a walk to the estuary at Kosi Mouth.

There are camp sites and basic cabins in the reserve, but very little else. **KwaNgwanase** is the nearest service centre, some 10km west of the reserve, and you will find shops and an ATM here. There are two entrances to the reserve – Kosi Bay Camp (7km north of KwaNgwanase) and Kosi Bay Mouth (19km north of KwaNgwanase). The access roads to both can get very bad, and you may need a 4WD. The Total petrol station, on the main road through KwaNgwanase, is a good place to ask about the state of the roads (ask for Jan, the owner) and the best spot to try and hitch into the reserve with a passing 4WD.

Sleeping & Eating

Most lodge accommodation is dispersed around the region's sandy dunes several kilometres from KwaNgwanase and often away from the water. In many cases 4WDs are needed to negotiate the sandy tracks.

Utshwayelo Campsite (☎ 033-592 9626, 073-134 3318; camp sites per person R60) This quiet, community-run camp site offers camping right by the parks-board office on the Kosi Bay Mouth access road. From here, you can walk to one of the country's best beaches in 20 minutes.

KZN Wildlife (☎ 033-845 1000; www.kznwildlife .com; camp sites per person R65, 2- & 4-bed cabins per person R236) Offers camping and cabin accommodation on the western shore of Nhlange – minimum charges apply.

I Gwala Gwala Lodge (☎ 084-588 0564; camp sites R50, s/d R150/300) Around 1km from the parks-board office on the Kosi Bay Camp access road, this excellent place offers transfers to all beaches, picks up from Mkuze and organises snorkelling, dolphin swims, boat trips and diving. Accommodation is in basic chalets.

Maputaland (☎ 033-592 0654; maputaland@polka .co.za; Posbus 757, KwaNgwanase; s/d incl breakfast R345/590) These 10 modern chalets in KwaNgwanase have all the mod cons including DSTV, bar and restaurant, plus the 'mother' of mozzie nets hanging from ropes. Great for those who want to base themselves in a creature-free zone, but close enough to explore the reserve with transport.

Getting There & Away

You need your own transport to get to Kosi Bay. Take the Jozini turn-off from the N2 and head towards Tembe Game Reserve. If heading from Sodwana Bay continue north up the major Rte 22. Note, Kosi Bay Mouth and Kosi Bay Camp are two different places in the reserve, each serviced by a different access road north of KwaNgwanase. The first road (7km north) leads to Kosi Bay Camp and the second (19km north) leads to Kosi Bay Mouth. Both may require a 4WD to access.

TEMBE ELEPHANT PARK
☎ 035

Heading back to the N2 from Kosi Bay, South Africa's last free-ranging elephants are protected in the sandveld (dry, sandy belt) forests of **Tembe Elephant Park** (☎ 035-592 0001; www.tembe.co.za; adult/child/vehicle R30/15/35; ⏰ 6am-6pm) on the Mozambique border. There are now about 160 elephants in the area, many of them the last remnants of elephant herds from the Maputo Elephant Reserve, saved from Mozambique's civil war. The park boasts the Big Five (lion, leopard, buffalo, elephant and rhino).

Although this is a KZN Wildlife park, the accommodation is privately run.

Tembe Lodge (☎ 035-592 0545; www.tembe.co.za; r with full board & activities from R1600; 🏊) offers accommodation in secluded safari tents built on wooden platforms. In the centre of the camp there is a large dining area, a shaded pool and braai facilities.

There's a sealed road all the way to the park entrance, but only 4WD vehicles are allowed to drive through the park itself.

NDUMO GAME RESERVE
☎ 033

A little further west, the **Ndumo Game Reserve** (☎ 033-845 1000, 035-591 0004; www.kznwildlife.com; adult/child/vehicle R35/18/35; ⏰ 5am-7pm) is beside the Mozambique border and close to the Swaziland border, about 100km north of Mkuze. On some 10,000 hectares, there are black and white rhino, hippo, crocodiles and antelope species but it is the birdlife on the Phongolo and Usutu Rivers, and their flood plains and pans, which attracts visitors. It is known locally as a 'mini Okavango'.

Wildlife-viewing and bird-watching guided walks (R45) and vehicle tours (R100) are available. This is the southernmost limit of the range of many bird species and the reserve is a favourite with bird-watchers, with more than 400 species recorded.

Fuel and limited supplies are usually available 2km outside the park gate. Camping and rest huts are offered by **KZN Wildlife Accommodation** (☎ 033-845 1000; www.kznwildlife.com; camp sites per person R55, 2-bed rest huts per person R200) – minimum charges apply.

MKHUZE GAME RESERVE & AROUND
☎ 035

A possible trip highlight is the **Mkhuze Game Reserve** (☎ 031-845 1000, 573 9001; www.kznwildlife.com; adult/child/vehicle R35/18/35; ⏰ 6am-6pm). Established in 1912, this reserve, covering some 36,000 spectacular hectares, is a well-kept 'secret'. It lacks lions, but just about every other sought-after animal is represented, as well as more than 400 species of birds, including the rare Pel's fishing owl (*Scotopelia peli*).

Better still, the reserve has hides at water holes, which offer some of the best wildlife viewing in the country. Morning is the best time. It's 15km from Mkuze (18km from Bayla if heading north). Wildlife drives (R90) are available.

KZN Wildlife (☎ 033-845 1000; www.kznwildlife.com; Nhlonhlela bush lodge R199, Mantuma rest huts/2- & 4-bed safari camps & chalets per person R99/244) offers a bush lodge at Nhlonhlela, and a variety of accommodation at Mantuma. Minimum charges apply.

The best route is via the north from Mkuze town (from the south, you turn off the N2 around 35km north of Hluhluwe village but it's on dirt road).

The town of Mkuze is west of the Lebombo Range on the N2. **Ghost Mountain**, south of the town, was an important burial place for the Ndwandwe tribe and has a reputation for eerie occurrences, usually confined to strange lights and noises. Occasionally human bones, which date from a big battle between rival Zulu factions in 1884, are found near Ghost Mountain.

Ghost Mountain Inn (☎ 035-573 1025; www.ghostmountaininn.co.za; s/d incl breakfast R515/930; 🚗 🏊) is an old-school colonial place with a modern (and luxurious) touch. A massive indoor-outdoor lounge area with an *Out of Africa* feel, blooming gardens, tennis courts and drives to the Mkhuze Game Reserve all add to the appeal.

PHINDA RESOURCE RESERVE

This 17,500-hectare reserve, to the northwest of Lake St Lucia, is an 'ecotourism' showpiece of the Conservation Corporation, a private-reserve chain.

There are seven different habitats in the park, from sand forests and riverine woodland to natural pans and savanna grasslands. This attracts more than 380 species of birds and promotes a diverse range of plant life. Prolific animal life includes the Big Five, and lion and cheetah kills can occasionally be spotted (even leopard are occasionally seen during wildlife drives). In addition to these, there are also accompanied walks, canoeing and river-boat cruises on offer.

But 'ecoluxury' adventures don't come cheap: doubles with full board and activities start at R2605. Bookings can be made through **Conservation Corporation Africa** (☎ 011-809 4300; www.ccafrica.com).

To get there, take the Phinda/Southern Maputaland turn-off from the N2 and follow the signs.

UKHAHLAMBA-DRAKENSBERG

The tabletop peaks of the uKhahlamba-Drakensberg Range, which form the boundary between South Africa and the mountain kingdom of Lesotho, offer some of the country's most awe-inspiring landscapes. They provided the backdrop for the films *Zulu* (1964) and *Yesterday* (2004) and the setting for Alan Paton's novel *Cry The Beloved Country,* and are and the inspiration for a million picture postcards.

This vast 243,000-hectare sweep of basalt summits and buttresses was formally granted World Heritage status in November 2000, when it was renamed uKhahlamba-Drakensberg Park. Today, some of the vistas, particularly the unforgettable curve of the Amphitheatre in the Royal Natal National Park, are so recognisably South African that they have become tourist-brochure clichés. But that doesn't make them any less magnificent. If any landscape lives up to its airbrushed, publicity-shot alter ego, it is the jagged, green sweep of the Drakensberg.

Drakensberg means 'Dragon Mountains'; the Zulu named it Quathlamba, meaning 'Battlement of Spears'. The Zulu word is a more accurate description of the sheer escarpment but the Afrikaans name captures something of the Drakensberg's otherworldly atmosphere. People have lived here for thousands of years – this is evidenced by the many San rock-art sites – yet many of its peaks were first climbed little more than 50 years ago.

The San, already under pressure from the tribes that had moved into the Drakensberg foothills, were finally destroyed with the coming of white settlers. Some moved to Lesotho, where they were absorbed into the Basotho population, but many were killed or simply starved when their hunting grounds were occupied by others. Khoesaan cattle raids annoyed the white settlers to the extent that the settlers forced several black tribes to relocate into the Drakensberg foothills to act as a buffer between the whites and the Khoesaan. These early 'Bantu locations' meant there was little development in the area, which later allowed the creation of a chain of parks and reserves.

Be aware that the Drakensbergs are deceptive – it's not easy to 'do' the whole 'Berg. There is no single road linking all the main areas of interest – you have to enter and exit and re-enter each region from the N3 or Rte 103. You are better off to select one (or only a few) places of interest and enjoy what each area has to offer – from hiking to bird-watching – rather than spend most of your time behind a wheel in search of sites and sights.

Orientation

The uKhahlamba-Drakensberg Park, which is actually several spectacular parks in and around the Drakensberg Range, is usually divided into three sections, although the distinctions aren't strict. The Northern Berg runs from the Golden Gate Highlands National Park in Free State (see p385) to the Royal Natal National Park. Harrismith and Bergville are sizable towns in this area.

The Central Berg's main feature is Giant's Castle Game Reserve, the largest reserve in the area. North of Giant's Castle is Cathedral Peak and two wilderness areas. Estcourt and Winterton are towns adjacent to the central Berg.

The Southern Berg runs down to the Wild Coast area of Eastern Cape. There's a huge wilderness area here and the Sani Pass route into southern Lesotho. Pietermaritzburg to the east and Kokstad to the south are the main access points to the southern Drakensberg and in the hills are some pleasant towns, notably Underberg and Himeville.

David Bristow's books *Guide to the Drakensberg* and *Best Walks of the Drakensberg* are useful references for those planning to explore the region. KZN Wildlife sells six 1:50,000 topographic maps, which detail hiking trails, camp sites etc, for around R40 each. They're available from KZN Wildlife's headquarters in Pietermaritzburg, the various park offices and some shops in the area.

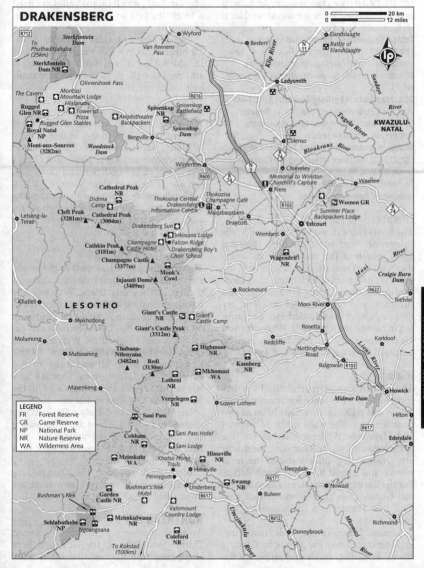

DRAKENSBERG

0 — 20 km
0 — 12 miles

KWAZULU-NATAL

Information

KZN Wildlife (☎ 033-845 1000; www.kznwildlife.com) in Pietermaritzburg can provide information on the various parks and accommodation options. In general, you must book all KZN Wildlife accommodation (except camping) in advance through either the Pietermaritzburg or Durban **KZN Wildlife** (☎ 031-304 4934; www.kznwildlife.com; 1st fl, Tourist Junction) branches. There are also several local information offices:

Central Drakensberg Information Centre (☎ 036-488 1207; www.cdic.co.za; Thokozisa; ☺ 9am-6pm) Based in the Thokozisa complex, 13km outside Winterton on Rte 600, this private enterprise is extremely helpful.

Okhahlamba Drakensberg Tourism (☎ 036-448 1557; www.drakensberg.org.za; Tatham Rd, Bergville; ☺ 9am-4.30pm Mon-Fri, 9am-1pm Sat) Covers the northern and central Drakensberg.

Southern Drakensberg Escape Tourism Centre (☎ 033-701 1471; www.drakensberg.org; Clocktower Centre, Old Main Rd, Underberg; ☺ 9am-4.30pm Mon-Fri, 9am-12.30pm Sat) Covers the southern region from Underberg, Himeville and Sani Pass.

Climate

The frosts come in winter, but the rain falls in summer, and snow has been recorded every month of the year. While the summer weather forecasts, posted in each of the KZN Wildlife park offices, often make bleak reading for those hoping for blue skies and sunshine, you can often bet on clear, dry mornings, with the thunderheads only rolling in during the afternoon. Whenever you visit, always carry wet-weather gear, and be prepared for icy conditions and snowfalls.

Hiking

The uKhahlamba-Drakensberg Park has some superb walks and hikes, ranging from gentle day walks to strenuous hikes of two or more days. The trails in the Mkhomazi and Mzimkulu Wilderness Areas, and the Mzimkulwana Nature Reserve, in the southern Drakensberg, offer some of the most remote and rugged hiking in South Africa. For the less experienced there's also the five-day Giant's Cup Trail, running from near Sani Pass Hotel down to Bushman's Nek (p354).

Summer hiking can be made frustrating, and sometimes even dangerous, by flooding rivers; in winter, frosts and snow are the main hazards. April and May are the best months for hiking.

Make sure you get the relevant maps (see p347) that show trails and have essential information for hikers.

Permits are needed on most of the hikes; get them from KZN Wildlife offices at the various trailheads. Trail accommodation is often in huts (which means you don't need a tent). It's best to book accommodation in advance.

Due to serious incidents involving single hikers KZN Wildlife warns that walkers should *not* go alone (even on day walks) and must sign the register. Guides are available for hire.

Sleeping

The perfect way to see the uKhahlamba-Drakensberg Park is to stay at one of KZN Wildlife's excellent reserves. The biggest and most popular are Royal Natal and Giant's Castle, but accommodation and camp sites can also be found in other reserves.

Usually more expensive than the parks board's accommodation are the private resorts, which dot the foothills near Royal Natal and Giant's Castle.

Getting There & Around

There is little public transport in the northern and central Drakensberg, although there is a lot of tourist traffic. With so many resorts all needing staff there are some minibus taxis. The main jumping-off points are on or near the N3; for more information, see Estcourt, Mooi River, Winterton and Bergville. The **Baz Bus** (☎ in Durban 031-304 9099; www.bazbus.com) drops off and picks up at a couple of hostels in the area. Through hostels in Durban you can arrange a lift to the hostels near Sani Pass and Himeville.

Sani Pass is the best-known Drakensberg route into Lesotho. There are other passes over the escarpment but most don't connect with anything in Lesotho larger than a walking track (if that).

Many back roads in the Drakensberg area are unsealed and after rain some are impassable – stick to the main routes.

NORTHERN BERG

An ideal stopover on the journey between Durban and Jo'burg, the Northern Berg is crowned with the beautiful Royal Natal

National Park and some wonderfully empty spaces.

Royal Natal National Park
☎ 036

Spanning out from some of the range's loftiest summits, the 8000-hectare **Royal Natal Park** (☎ 036-438 6310; www.kznwildlife.com; adult/child R25/15; ☼ 5am-7pm) has a presence that far outstrips its relatively meagre size, with many of the surrounding peaks rising as high into the air as the park stretches across. With some of the Drakensberg's most dramatic and accessible scenery, the park is crowned by the sublime Amphitheatre, an 8km wall of cliff and canyon, which is spectacular from below and even more so from up on high. Here the Tugela Falls drop 850m in five stages (the top one often freezes in winter). Looming up behind is Mont-aux-Sources (3282m), so called because the Tugela, Elands and Western Khubedu Rivers rise here; the latter eventually becomes the Senqu (Orange) River and flows all the way to the Atlantic.

Other notable peaks in the area are Devil's Tooth, the Eastern Buttress and the Sentinel. Rugged Glen Nature Reserve adjoins the park on the northeastern side.

The park's **visitors centre** (☼ 8am-12.30pm & 2-4.30pm) is about 1km in from the main gate. There's also a shop selling basic provisions. Fuel is available in the park. Look out for the latest copy of *Royal Natal Walks & Climbs*.

WILDLIFE
With plentiful water, a range of more than 1500m in altitude and distinct areas such as plateaus, cliffs and valleys, it isn't surprising that the park's flora is extremely varied. Broadly speaking, much of the park is covered in grassland, with protea savanna at lower altitudes. This grassland depends on fire for reproduction and to discourage other vegetation. In areas that escape the park's periodic fires, scrub takes over. At lower levels, but confined to valleys, are small yellowwood forests. At higher altitudes grass yields to heath and scrub.

Royal Natal is not as rich in wildlife as Giant's Castle and other sections of the Drakensberg but there is still quite a lot to be seen. Of the six species of antelope, the most common is the mountain reedbuck. Hyraxes are everywhere, as are hares.

Royal Natal also has a large population of baboons, the feeding of which by tourists and visitors has become a growing problem as the baboons hang around camp sites and steal food.

If you have your own tackle, there is also good trout fishing here. Permits are available from the visitors centre.

ROCK ART
There are several San rock-art sites, although Royal Natal's are fewer and not as well preserved as those at Giant's Castle; the latter has many more rock shelters and caves, and has suffered less from vandalism. The notable sites are Sigubudu Shelter, north of the road just past the main gate, and Cannibal Caves, on Surprise Ridge, outside the park's northern boundary.

HIKING TRAILS
Except for the **Amphitheatre-to-Cathedral** (62km, four to five days) and the **Mont-aux-Sources** (20km, 10 hours) hikes, most of the 25-odd walks in Royal Natal are day walks. Only 50 day visitors and 50 overnighters are allowed on Mont-aux-Sources each day. The hike to the summit starts from the Mahai camp site and takes you up to Basotho Gate. Note that the Nek is closed

---

PROTECTING THE SAN PAINTINGS

There are thousands of San paintings in caves and rockscapes around KZN. More are being discovered all the time. Sadly, many of these have already suffered from ignorant visitors: many have been defaced with graffiti, while visitors have even splashed water on some to make the colours appear brighter. Some artwork has been destroyed altogether. Travellers should be aware of taking appropriate measures to ensure the ongoing preservation of these precious cultural treasures.

KZN currently has an agreement with Amafa, the provincial cultural and heritage conservation body, to build preservation practices into its management plans. This includes ensuring that guides accompany visitors to the sites and educating visitors not to touch the sites or do anything to cause harm when a guide is not in attendance.

KWAZULU-NATAL

and it's necessary to walk to the Sentinel car park. Or, you can drive to the Sentinel car park on the road from Phuthaditjhaba in QwaQwa (p386).

If you plan to camp on the mountain, you should book with the **QwaQwa tourist officer** (☎ 058-713 4415). Otherwise there's a basic hut on the escarpment near Tugela Falls. Unlike other KZN Wildlife accommodation, you don't need to book (except for registering before walking here) and there's no fee for the hut, but an overnight hiking permit costs R30.

Guides to see the San paintings can be booked through the visitors centre.

HORSE RIDING

Just outside the park gates, **Rugged Glen Stables** (☎ 036-438 6422) organises a wide range of horse-riding activities, including two-day trails.

CLIMBING

Some of the peaks and faces were first climbed by mountaineers just over 50 years ago, and the park has become a mecca for climbers. You must apply for a permit from the KZN Wildlife office before you attempt a climb; unless you are experienced, it may not be granted. If you plan to venture into Lesotho, take your passport.

SLEEPING & EATING

Thendele (☎ 033-845 1000; chalets per person R320-350) The park's main camp has a variety of accommodation, including some reasonable two-bed chalets – minimum charges apply.

You can also camp at **Mahai** (☎ 033-845 1000, 438 6303; fax 033-438 6231; camp sites per person R60) inside the park, or in the nearby **Rugged Glen Nature Reserve** (☎ 033-845 1000, 438 6303; fax 438 6231; camp sites per person R60).

The following places are all outside the park.

Amphitheatre Backpackers (☎ 036-438 6675; www.amphibackpackers.co.za; camp sites R45; dm/d 75/200) Facing out over the Amphitheatre, this is an in-your-face experience. The key to this recently relocated backpackers are the tours to Lesotho (R265) and activities galore (but there are no locks on the dorm room doors). A rock-climbing wall is being constructed, plus there's a bar where you can restore aching limbs. It's 21km north of Bergville on R74.

Hlalanathi (☎ 036-438 6308; www.hlalanathi.za.net; camp sites per person R50, 2-/4-bed chalets R390/690; 🔋) With a location lifted straight from an African chocolate-box lid, this pretty resort offers camping and excellent accommodation on a finger of land overlooking the Tugela River. Go for a site facing the river and mountains.

Cavern (☎ 036-438 6270; www.cavernberg.co.za; s/d with full board R690/920) North of Royal Natal, this award-winning resort offers family-friendly service in lush forest surrounds. There's even babysitting available.

Montusi Mountain Lodge (☎ 036-438 6243; www.montusi.za.net; s/d with half board R1030/1560; 🔋 🖳 🔋) With oodles of bush-lodge exclusivity, this opulent place blends a thatch-and-fireplace homeliness with plenty of five-star comforts, including 4WD trails, trout fishing and some very swish chalets. The turn-off is just after the Tower of Pizza; follow the signs from there.

Tower of Pizza (☎ 036-438 6480; http://towerofpizza.co.za; mains R27-50; 🕑 lunch & dinner; 🖳) Yep, there really is a tower, where very good oven-fired pizza is prepared. It also offers comfortable cottages (doubles per person, including breakfast, R370) and Internet access.

GETTING THERE & AWAY

The road into Royal Natal runs off Rte 74, about 30km northwest of Bergville and about 5km from Oliviershoek Pass.

Bergville
☎ 036

Small and a little rough around the edges, Bergville is nevertheless a useful stock-up and jumping-off point for the northern Drakensberg.

ABSA (Tatham Rd) Has an ATM.

Okhahlamba Drakensberg Tourism (☎ 036-448 1557; www.drakensberg.org.za; Tatham Rd; 🕑 9am-4.30pm Mon-Fri, 9am-1pm Sat)

SLEEPING & EATING

Bergville Caravan Park (☎ 036-448 1273; bergcarav@xsinet.co.za; camp sites R60, rondavels R80, caravans R120, 2-bed chalets R280; 🔋) This park is a bit like Bergville itself – pleasant, but a little gritty. But it's a reasonable budget option and has some pleasant spots by the water. It's south of town on Rte 74 – turn off 500m before the Tugela River bridge.

NATURE AREAS

The use of 'Nature Reserve' and 'Game Reserve' is now being phased out in the uKhahlamba-Drakensberg region to more accurately reflect its amalgamation as one large protected wilderness area. You will increasingly see signs, maps and texts without these terms.

Drakensberg Inn (☎ 036-448 2946; www.drakens berginn.com; 3 Tatham Rd; s/d incl breakfast R230/420) A terrace restaurant, real fires and a comfortable communal lounge all help to spice up this slightly plain, small town inn.

Sanford Park Resort (☎ 036-448 1001; sanfordpark lodge@mweb.co.za; s/d with half board R520/830; ℗ ⊠) Bergville's swankier option, the Sanford offers cosy rooms in thatched rondavels or in a creaking, 150-year-old farmhouse with memorabilia-filled bar. Head a few kilometres out of Bergville, off the road to Ladysmith (Rte 616).

GETTING THERE & AWAY

None of the long-distance bus lines runs very close to Bergville. You'll have to get to Ladysmith and take a minibus taxi from there (R20, 45 minutes). A daily Greyhound bus stops at Estcourt and Ladysmith.

The minibus taxi park is behind the tourist office. Taxis run into the Royal Natal National Park area for about R10 but few run all the way to the park entrance.

CENTRAL BERG

Crowned with some of the Drakensberg's most formidable peaks – Giant's Castle Peak (3312m), the Monk's Cowl (3234m) and Champagne Castle (3377m) are found here – the Central Berg is a big hit with climbers. But with dramatic scenery aplenty, this beautiful region is just as popular with those who prefer to admire their mountains from a safe distance.

Just off Dragon Peaks road are South Africa's singing ambassadors, the **Drakensberg Boys' Choir School** (☎ 036-468 1012; www.dbchoir.co .za). There are public performances at 3.30pm on Wednesday during school term. Seven kms from the Drakensberg Sun turn-off is **Falcon Ridge** (☎ 082-774 6398; adult/child R30/10; talks 10.30am), with awesome falcon-, kites- and eagle-flying demonstrations and talks.

Thokozisa (☎ 036-488 1273; thokozisa@futurest .co.za), 13km out of Winterton on Rte 600, is a creative village in every respect, housing the **Central Drakensberg Information Centre** (☎ 036-488 1207; www.cdic.co.za; 9am-6pm), which has Internet access, a clutch of crafts shops and an excellent restaurant.

Winterton
☎ 036

Quaint and sedate, this peaceful little town is the gateway to the Central Drakensberg and makes a pleasant stopover. **Winterton Museum** (☎ 036-488 1885; Kerk St; admission by donation; 9am-3pm Mon-Fri, 9am-noon Sat) offers an excellent insight into San rock art, Zulu history and the Spioenkop battle (see the boxed text, p366). There are ATMs in the main street.

SLEEPING & EATING

Bridge Lodge (☎ 036-488 1554; thebridge@futurenet .co.za; Main Rd; s/d R160/260) Doubling as the town's favoured nightspot (Friday's the big one), this has a pleasant thatched restaurant and dowdy rooms.

Lilac Lodge (☎ 036-488 1025; www.wheretostay.co .za/lilaclodge; Springfield Rd; s/d incl breakfast R180/360) Yes, there's a purple house, but this deceptive place is actually a string of cottages and units, set on an expanse of lawn with braais and a trampoline. The impersonal owners are clearly used to groups.

Thokozisa Restaurant (☎ 036-488 1827; mains R36-70; lunch & dinner) In the Thokozisa crafts village, this lively little place serves a delicious range of steaks, wraps and salads (including vegetarian options) in courtyard surrounds. Try the Drakensburger (R33).

GETTING THERE & AWAY

There are minibus taxis to Cathedral Peak (R8, 30 minutes), Bergville (R6, 15 minutes) and Estcourt (R12, 45 minutes).

Cathedral Peak Nature Reserve
☎ 036

In the shadow of the ramparts of Cathedral Peak, **Cathedral Peak Nature Reserve** (☎ 036-488 8000; www.kznwildlife.com; adult/child R25/13; 6am-6pm) backs up against a colossal escarpment of peaks between Royal Natal National Park and Giant's Castle, west of Winterton. With the Bell (2930m), the Horns (3005m) and Cleft Peak (3281m) on the horizon, this is a

KWAZULU-NATAL

beautifully photogenic park. Cathedral Peak is a long day's climb (10km, seven hours return) but other than being physically fit, no special ability or equipment is required (ask at the park office for trail details).

The **Didima San Art Centre** (☎ 036-488 1332; adult/child R40/20; ⏱ 8am-4pm), 1km into the park, offers an excellent, multimedia insight into San rock art.

The **park office** (☎ 036-488 8000; www.kznwild life.com), in Didima Camp, sells permits for the scenic drive (4WD only) up Mike's Pass (R15/35 per person/vehicle) and arranges guides.

SLEEPING & EATING
Didima Camp (☎ 033-845 1000; www.kznwildlife.com; camp sites per person R45, chalets per person R330-360; ⊠ 🛆) One of KZN Wildlife's swankiest offerings, this upmarket, thatched lodge boasts huge views, a restaurant, tennis courts, lashings of elegant style and a range of excellent two- and four-bed self-catering chalets (full-board options are also available on request). Minimum charges apply.

There is also camping available near the main gate.

Monk's Cowl
☎ 036

Monk's Cowl (☎ 036-468 1103; www.kznwildlife.com; adult/child R20/10; ⏱ 6am-6pm), another stunning slice of the Drakensberg range, offers superb hiking and rock climbing. Within Monk's Cowl are the two peaks Monk's Cowl and Champagne Castle.

The **park office** (☎ 036-468 1103; camp sites per person R70) is 3km beyond Champagne Castle Hotel, which is at the end of Rte 600 running southwest from Winterton. The office takes bookings for camping and overnight hiking (R30 per person).

SLEEPING & EATING
As well as camping in the reserve, there are some other accommodation options in the area.

Inkosana Lodge (☎ 036-468 1202; www.inkosana .co.za; dm/d with shared bathroom R85/250, thatched rondavels with/without en suite R165/125; 🛆) When a sign on a bunk says 'This bed is ready' you know you have one hell-of-an-organised owner. This Drakensberg delight's indigenous garden, rock-pool view and clean rooms make it one of the best backpackers

in KZN. Excellent cuisine (make sure you put your name down) and heaps of activities and walks are on offer. It's on Rte 600, en route to Champagne Castle.

Champagne Castle Hotel (☎ 036-468 1063; www .champagnecastle.co.za; s/d with full board R680/1160; 🛆) The ever-reliable, predictably 'nice' Champagne Castle is one of the best-known resorts, conveniently in the mountains at the end of the road to Champagne Castle Peak, off Rte 600. Staff will collect you from Estcourt (R120) and Durban (R400).

Drakensberg Sun (☎ 036-468 1000; www.southern sun.com; d with half board R1149; 🛆) This chain-style place with a ski-resort feel is just before Champagne Castle Hotel en route to Champagne Castle Peak. It sometimes quotes for family rooms, meaning that up to two children can stay in the room for free. Standards are predictably high.

Giant's Castle Game Reserve
☎ 036

Rising up to Injisuthi Dome (3409m), South Africa's highest peak, **Giant's Castle Game Reserve** (☎ 033-845 1000, 353 3718; www.kzn wildlife.com; adult/child R25/13; ⏱ 5am-7pm) is one of the Drakensberg's loftiest – even its lowest point sits at 1300m above sea level. It was established in 1904, mainly to protect the eland, and it is a rugged, remote and popular destination, with huge forest reserves to the north and south, and Lesotho's barren plateau over the escarpment to the west.

Limited supplies (including fuel) are available at Giant's Castle Camp (opposite) and there's a kiosk selling provisions.

WILDLIFE
The reserve is mainly grassland, wooded gorges and high basalt cliffs with small forests in the valleys. There's also some protea savanna and, during spring, swathes of wildflowers.

The reserve is home to several species of antelope, with relatively large numbers of elands, mountain reedbucks, grey rhebok and oribis. The rarest antelope is the klipspringer, which is sometimes spotted on the higher slopes. The rarest species is a small, short-tailed rodent called the ice rat, which lives in the boulders near the mountain summits. Altogether there are thought to be about 60 mammal species.

The rare lammergeier, or bearded vulture (*Gypaetus barbatus*), which is found only in the Drakensberg, nests in the reserve. Reserve staff sometimes give guests bones to put out to encourage the birds to feed here. The **Lammergeier Hide** (☎ 036-353 3718; giants@kznwildlife.com; per person R150, minimum R480; ☽ May-Sep) has been built nearby, and is the best place to see the vultures. The hide is extremely popular so it's necessary to book in advance.

ROCK ART
Giant's Castle Game Reserve is rich in San rock art, with at least 50 sites. It is thought that the last San lived here at the beginning of the 20th century.

You can see the paintings at **Main Cave** (adult/child R25/5; ☽ 9am-4pm), 2km south of Giant's Camp (a 30-minute walk), which must be visited as part of a tour that departs from Giant's Camp every hour, on the hour, during the cave's opening times.

Battle Cave (admission R25) is near Injisuthi and must be visited on a self-guided tour. It's an 8km walk each way; there's a good chance of seeing wildlife en route. The cave's name reflects the paintings here, which record a clash between San groups.

HIKING
Trails begin at Giant's Camp and lead to Meander Hut (5.5km, two hours), on a cliff above the Meander Valley; Giant's Hut (10.5km, four hours), under Giant's Castle itself; and Bannerman's Hut (11km, 4½ hours), close to the escarpment near Bannerman's Pass.

Hikers can stay at mountain huts (R30) for which you'll need sleeping bags and cooking utensils. The fee for the huts is a one-off 'hiking fee'. If you're planning to walk between huts rather than return to Giant's Camp, you have to arrange to collect keys. Unless you've booked the entire hut, you must share it with other hikers.

There are other trails. The booklet *Giant's Castle Day Walks* (R5), available at Giant's Castle Camp, gives details and has a basic map of the trails (distances not stated). Before setting out on a long walk you must fill in the rescue register.

Don't confuse trails around here with the Giant's Cup Trail (p356), further south in the Drakensberg.

SLEEPING
There are several accommodation centres inside the reserve, as well as trail huts and caves for hikers. Note that hikers are not allowed to light fires, so you'll need to bring a stove. There's a small shop at reception with basic supplies only.

Giant's Castle Camp (☎ 033-845 1000; www.kzn wildlife.com; mountain huts per person R30, chalet per person R315-346) The main camp has two-, four- and six-bed chalets and four- and eight-bed mountain huts. Book through KZN Wildlife in Pietermaritzburg or Durban.

Injisuthi Hutted Camp (☎ 033-845 1000, 036-431 7849; camp sites per person R48) This secluded and pleasant spot on the northern side of the reserve has camp sites. It is accessed from Loskop, northwest of Estcourt. Turn south 4km west of Loskop or 6km east of Rte 600; the road is signposted. Minimum charges apply.

There are several places outside the reserve, on and around Rte 600, which runs southwest from Winterton towards Cathkin Peak and Champagne Castle.

GETTING THERE & AWAY
The roads from both Mooi River and Estcourt are sealed – do not take the unsealed back roads as they can become impassable and in the past, robberies have been reported.

Infrequent minibus taxis run from Estcourt to villages near the main entrance (KwaDlamini, Mahlutshini and Kwa-Mankonjane), but these are still several kilometres from Giant's Camp.

SOUTHERN BERG
Best accessed from the pleasant towns of Himeville and Underberg, the Southern Berg boasts one of the region's highlights: the journey up to Lesotho over the Sani Pass. It is also renowned as a serious hiking area and as well as some great walks, including the fabulous Giant's Cup Trail, the region also offers a smorgasbord of wilderness areas.

Southern Drakensberg Wilderness Areas
Four reserves, Highmoor, Mkhomazi, Cobham and Garden Castle, all run south from Giant's Castle to beyond Bushman's Nek, to meet Lesotho's Sehlabathebe National Park at the top of the escarpment.

The wilderness areas are near the escarpment and to the east are Kamberg, Lotheni, Vergelegen and Mzimkulwana Nature Reserves.

These areas are administered by KZN Wildlife. The costs for overnight-hiking permits is dependent on what you do. You must sign the hiking registers.

COBHAM NATURE RESERVE
The Mzimkulu Wilderness Area and the Mzimkulwana Nature Reserve are in **Cobham Nature Reserve** (☎ 033-702 0831; www.kznwildlife.com; adult/child R20/10; ☼ 6am-6pm). The park office is about 15km from Himeville on the D7; it's a good place to get information on the many hiking trails in the reserve, some with trail huts (R60 per person). Basic camp sites (R40 per person) are available.

GARDEN CASTLE & BUSHMAN'S NEK
The park office of **Garden Castle** (☎ 033-701 1823; www.kznwildlife.com; adult/child R20/10; camp sites per person R40, huts per person R60; ☼ 6am-6pm) is 30km west of Underberg – carry along the road past Khotso Horse Trails (opposite).

This reserve incorporates beautiful **Bushman's Nek Valley**, dominated by the 3051m Rhino Peak. The area has many sandstone buttresses and rock-art sites and a good (long) day walk.

Overnight hikers can use trail huts, camp sites or even caves.

HIGHMOOR NATURE RESERVE
The park office of **Highmoor Nature Reserve** (☎ 033-845 1000, 033-263 7240; www.kznwildlife.com; adult/child R20/10; camp sites per person R40; ☼ 6am-6pm) is off the road from Rosetta to Giant's Castle and Kamberg. Turn off to the south just past the sign to Kamberg, 31km from Rosetta.

Camp sites are available.

KAMBERG NATURE RESERVE
Southeast of Giant's Castle and a little away from the main escarpment area, **Kamberg Nature Reserve** (☎ 033-267 7251; www.kznwildlife.com; adult/child R20/10; 2-bed huts R200; ☼ 6am-6pm) has a number of antelope species and guided rock-art walks.

You can get there from Rosetta, off the N3 south of Mooi River, travelling via either Nottingham Road or Redcliffe.

Other sleeping options in the area include the **Spotted Horse Country Inn** (☎ 033-267 7194;

karene@mjvn.co.za; dm/f with shared bathroom per person R95/150, d R195), 32km west of Rosetta along Rte 103. This is the new foal in the herd. Trot on in for the choice of a thoroughbred 'stable' and 'tack' rooms with 'mare' and 'stallion' bathrooms. Choice feed available for R35. Horse trips are its speciality in case you hadn't realised.

LOTHENI NATURE RESERVE
Lotheni (☎ 033-702 0540; www.kznwildlife.com; adult/child R20/10; ☼ 6am-6pm) has a Settlers' Museum and some very good day walks.

KZN Wildlife (☎ 033-845 1000; camp sites R50, 3-bed chalets per person R164) offers camp sites and chalets.

The access road runs from Lower Lotheni, about 30km northeast of Himeville or 65km southwest of Nottingham Road (off Mooi River). The roads aren't great and heavy rain can close them. They are, however, some of the most scenic in South Africa, with the Drakensberg as a backdrop and picturesque Zulu villages in the area.

MKHOMAZI WILDERNESS AREA & VERGELEGEN NATURE RESERVE
The **Mkhomazi Wilderness Area** (033-266 6444; www.kznwildlife.com; adult/child R20/10; ☼ 6am-6pm) is one of the few places where you can hike for days without seeing anyone else. The **Vergelegen Nature Reserve** (☎ 033-702 0712; www.kznwildlife.com; adult/child R15/10; ☼ 6am-6pm) has trout fishing. There are no established camp sites in the area, but you can camp on hikes (R30). The turn-off is 44km from Nottingham Road, off the Lower Lotheni to Sani Pass road, at the Mzinga River. From there the area is another 2km.

Underberg
☎ 033 / pop 1500
Clustered in the foothills of the southern Drakensberg, this small farming town fills up in summer, when Durbanites head to the peaks for a breath of the fresh stuff. It has good infrastructure, and is the place to go for money, shopping and to organise activities in the region. The more sedate Himeville, just down the road, is also a pleasant place to stay.

INFORMATION
First National Bank (Old Main Rd) Has an ATM. Close to NUD Entertainment.

NUD Entertainment (☎ 033-701 1317; Old Main Rd; per hr R60; ⓨ 10am-6pm) Internet access, next to Spar.
Sani Pass Tours (☎ 033-701 1064; www.sanipasstours .com; Clocktower Centre, Old Main Rd; day tours per person R280; ⓨ 9am-5pm Mon-Fri, 9am-2pm Sat & Sun) Offers day tours up the Sani Pass, as well as packages tailored to more specialist interests. It also takes bookings for the Sani Top Chalet in Lesotho (p565). Several other companies around town also offer similar tours.
Southern Drakensberg Escape Information Office
(☎ 033-701 1471; www.drakensberg.org; Clocktower Centre, Old Main Rd; ⓨ 9am-4.30pm Mon-Fri, 9am-1pm Sat & Sun) Publishes the *Sani Saunter* map and booklet (free) listing hotels, hostels, restaurants and tour guides.
WC Books (☎ 033-701 2059; Clocktower Centre, Old Main Rd; ⓨ 9am-5pm Mon-Fri, 9am-2pm Sat & Sun) Sells a wide range of local maps.

ACTIVITIES
Khotso Horse Trails (☎ 033-701 1502; www.khotso trails.co.za) offers rides and treks in the area. (Owner Steve is described by readers as 'South Africa's Crocodile Dundee'.) It's about 7km northwest of Underberg. Nearby, **Pennygum** (☎ 033-701 1023) rents out rafts for (relatively) gentle, river drifting.

FESTIVALS
The annual Easter weekend features the **Splashy Fen Festival**, a long-running music festival of gentle, alternative styles. It's held 20km from Underberg, on the road to Drakensberg Gardens.

SLEEPING & EATING
Underberg Hotel (☎ 033-701 1412; Old Main Rd; dm/ s/d incl breakfast R70/190/320) Old-world-meets-spit-and-sawdust. Underberg's inn has seen better days, but the bar's good for a tipple and the rooms are fine after a nightcap.
   Valemount Country Lodge (☎ 033-701 1686; www .valemountafrica.com; s/d incl breakfast R385/680) This cosy, thatched farmhouse B&B oozes graceful charm, with roaring fires in winter and 48 hectares of grounds to explore when things heat up again. It's 8km from Underberg on the Kokstad road.
   Lemon Tree Bistro (☎ 033-701 1589; Clocktower Centre, Main Rd; ⓨ breakfast & lunch) This friendly place serves up zesty pastas, burgers and pancakes, and it has filter coffee (R7).

GETTING THERE & AWAY
Sani Pass Carriers (☎ 033-701 1017; spc@y.co.za) runs minibuses to Underberg from Kokstad

(R125, 1½ hours) on Monday and Thursday, and daily except Sunday to Pietermaritzburg (R115, two hours), from where you can catch buses to Durban. You must book these services. Return fares are slightly cheaper than buying two one-way tickets.
   There is a new shuttle from Durban to Underberg, and from Underberg to Durban (R200 one-way, three hours) organised by **Gibela Backpackers** (☎ 031-303 6291). The shuttle runs any day on demand (minimum two people), picking you up from central hostels in Berea and the city, and dropping you off at the Underberg Inn, from where you can arrange to be collected by your accommodation.
   Minibus taxis run to Himeville (R5, 10 minutes) and Pietermaritzburg (R30, 1½ hours) and you might find one running to the Sani Pass Hotel (p356).

Himeville
☎ 033
A skip and a jump from Underberg, Himeville is a prettier, more-sedate jumping-off point for the southern Drakensberg.
   The **Himeville Museum** (☎ 033-702 1184; admission by donation; ⓨ 9am-12.30pm) is one of the best rural museums in the country. Housed in the last laager built in South Africa (c 1896), the museum now contains an incredible array of bric-a-brac, from the Union Jack flown at the siege of Ladysmith to a map of El Alamein signed by Montgomery. Mike, the man-at-the-desk is the man-in-the-know.

SLEEPING & EATING
See above for information on a couple of hostels near Himeville, on the road to Sani Pass.
   Himeville Arms (☎ 033-702 1305; www.himeville hotel.co.za; Main Rd; dm R95, s R270-290, d R480-520) Quaint Middle England meets modern(ish) Himeville at this homey inn, with cosy bar, comfy rooms and lashings of rustic, village-green atmosphere.
   Robin's Nest (☎ 702 1039; 11 Thomas St; s/d incl breakfast R190/380) As English as they come: this is your old-world B&B with oak furniture, florals and stupendous garden views.
   Moorcroft Manor (☎ 033-702 1967; info@moorcroft .co.za; s/d incl breakfast R660/1100) Designer Africa hits Himeville. For those who can't afford such luxury, dust the frock off and enjoy a

meal at a starched table setting. On Sunday there's a R75 luncheon. Bookings are obligatory (children under 12 aren't permitted).

GETTING THERE & AWAY

About the only regular transport from Himeville is minibus taxis to Underberg (R5, 10 minutes).

See Sani Pass (below) for details on transport into Lesotho.

The road from Himeville to Nottingham Road is well worth driving. The distance between the two towns is 92km, with 60km on a dirt road that winds through some spectacular country. The section between Himeville and Lower Lotheni is well gravelled, but check on its condition before you leave. The section between Lower Lotheni and the sealed road that runs to Nottingham Road could require 4WD after heavy rain.

Sani Pass
☎ 033

The drive up the Sani Pass is a trip to the roof of South Africa: a spectacular ride around hairpin bends into the clouds to the kingdom of Lesotho. At 2865m, this is the highest pass in the country and the vistas (on a clear day!) are magical, offering stunning views out across the Umkhomazana River to the north and looming cliffs, almost directly above, to the south. There are hikes in almost every direction and inexpensive horse rides are available. Amazingly, this is also the only road link between Lesotho and KwaZulu-Natal.

At the top of the pass, just beyond the Lesotho border crossing, is the Sani Top Chalet (p565). Various operators run 4WD trips up to the chalet.

Daily minibus taxis bring people from Mokhotlong (Lesotho; R65 between Mokhotlong and Underberg) to South Africa for shopping; if there's a spare seat going back, this would be the cheapest option, and you would get to a town, not just the isolated lodge at the top of the pass. Ask around in Himeville. You need a passport to cross into Lesotho. The border is open daily from 8am to 4pm on the South African side (until 5pm on the Lesotho side).

SLEEPING

The following places are all at the bottom of the pass.

Sani Lodge (☎ 033-702 0330; www.sani-lodge .co.za; camp sites R45, dm/d with shared bathroom R65/80, 2-bed rondavels R220) Owned by Russell Suchet, the author of *A Backpacker's Guide to Lesotho*, Sani Lodge tops the pops in the local-knowledge stakes, offering a range of fabulous tours and activities and insider tips about the region through its company, Drakensberg Adventures. It's about 10km from Himeville on the Sani Pass road.

Sani Pass Hotel (☎ 033-702 1320; www.sani passhotel.co.za; r with half board R1100) This tidy, three-star hotel, complete with guards and razor-wire fence, is on the Sani Pass road, 14km from Himeville. Not great reports about the food.

Giant's Cup Trail

If you are planning to stretch your legs anywhere in South Africa, this is the place to do it. Without doubt, the Giant's Cup Trail (68km, five days and five nights), running from Sani Pass to Bushman's Nek, is one of the nation's great walks. Any reasonably fit person can walk it, so it's very popular. Early booking (up to nine months ahead), through KZN Wildlife (☎ in Pietermaritzburg 033-845 1000) is advisable. Weather-wise, the usual precautions for the Drakensberg apply – expect severe cold snaps at any time of the year. Fees are based on the composition of the hiking party.

The stages are: day one, 14km; day two, 9km; day three, 12km; day four, 13km; and day five, 12km (note, it's not a circuit walk). Highlights include the Bathplug Cave with San rock paintings and the breathtaking mountain scenery on day four. You can make the trail more challenging by doing two days in one, and you can do side trips from the huts if the weather is fine. Maps are sold at Sani Lodge for R45.

Camping is not permitted on this trail, so accommodation is in limited shared huts (adult/child per trail R65/50), hence the need to book ahead. No firewood is available so you'll need a stove and fuel. Sani Lodge (above) is almost at the head of the trail; arrange for the lodge to pick you up from Himeville or Underberg.

Bushman's Nek
☎ 033

This is a South Africa–Lesotho border post (no vehicles!). From here there are hiking trails up into the escarpment, including to Lesotho's Sehlabathebe National Park. You can trot through the border and into Lesotho on horseback (see Khotso Horse Trails, p355).

Accommodation options include the **Bushman's Nek Hotel** (☎ in Pinetown 031-701 9999; r with half board R300), about 2km east of the border post, and the **Silverstreams Caravan Park** (☎ 033-701 1249; www.silverstreams.co.za; camp sites per person R90), which has camp sites right next to the border.

EAST GRIQUALAND

Recently classified as the Southern Drakensbergs, the region of East Griqualand has a fascinating history. The Voortrekkers had been moving into the Griqua territory between the Vaal and Senqu (Orange) Rivers, around Philippolis, since the 1820s. The Griqua chief, Adam Kok III, realising that there would soon be no land left, encouraged his people to sell off their remaining titles and move elsewhere.

In 1861 Kok's entire community of 2000, along with about 20,000 cattle, began its epic, two-year journey over the rugged mountains of Lesotho to Nomansland, a region on the far side of the Drakensberg. When they reached the southern slopes of Mt Currie, they set up camp. Later, in 1869, they moved to the present site of Kokstad. Nomansland was called East Griqualand after it was annexed by the Cape in 1874. Kok died the following year when he was thrown from his cart.

Kokstad & Around
☎ 039 / pop 25,100

Kokstad is named in honour of Adam Kok III. It lies 1280m above sea level in the Umzimhlava River Valley, between Mt Currie and the Ngele Mountains. Today it's a bustling little place with some solid buildings and excellent transport connections.

The Avis office next to the Mount Currie Inn also doubles as a **tourist office** (☎ 039-727 2178; exploreeg@futurenet.co.za; ⏰ 8am-4.30pm).

The **East Griqualand Museum** (Main St; admission by donation; ⏰ 9am-4pm Mon-Fri, 9am-noon Sat) has some interesting information on the history of the Griquas, as well as the usual small-town relics.

A few kilometres north of Kokstad, off Rte 626 to Franklin, is KZN Wildlife's **Mount**

Currie Nature Reserve (☎ 039-727 3844; www.kzn wildlife.com; adult/child Mon-Fri R10/5, Sat & Sun R9; ⏰ 6am-6pm). There are walking trails, fishing and bird-watching in this 1800-hectare reserve. A memorial marks the site of Adam Kok's first laager. You can camp (R45 per person) or stay in a two-bed hut (R95 per person) – for this, you must book direct.

SLEEPING & EATING
Mount Currie Inn (☎ 039-727 2178; fax 039-727 2196; s/d R440/580) This hotel, on the outskirts of town on the main road leading to the N2, is the best place to stay in Kokstad. The hotch-potch of petrol stations and fast-food joints out the front is deceptive: it's actually a pleasant hotel with a good bar and Cassandra's restaurant (mains R35 to R70).

GETTING THERE & AWAY
Shoprite's 'Money Market' kiosk sells tickets for Translux and Cityliner buses, which stop at Wimpy (near Mount Currie Inn), a little way out of town on the Durban–Mthatha road, and run daily to destinations including Durban (R120, four hours), Port Elizabeth (R230, 11 hours), Cape Town (R420, 23 hours) and Jo'burg (R230, nine hours).

The minibus taxi park is on the corner of Groom and Main Sts, and regular taxis or buses go to Pietermaritzburg (R45, 4½ hours) and Durban (R45, 4½ hours).

THE MIDLANDS

The Midlands run northwest from Durban to Estcourt, skirting Zululand to the northeast. This is mainly farming country with little to interest visitors. The main town is Pietermaritzburg – KwaZulu-Natal's joint capital along with Ulundi.

West of Pietermaritzburg is picturesque, hilly country, with horse studs and plenty of European trees. It was originally settled by English farmers.

Today, the region is as highly promoted as the Midlands Meander ('registered trade mark') – a slightly contrived concoction of craft shops, artistic endeavours, tea shops and B&Bs – winding along Rte 103 west of the N3, northwest of Pietermaritzburg. While the meander beyond Pietermaritzburg is a relaxing jaunt, don't amble too long in lieu of more interesting nature-based locations. The informative *Midlands Meander* brochure is available from tourist offices and contains a detailed colour-coded map of the area.

PIETERMARITZBURG

☎ 033 / pop 457,000

Billed as the heritage city, and KZN's administrative and legislative capital (previously shared with Ulundi), Pietermaritzburg's grand historic buildings hark back to an age of pith helmets and midday martinis. Today, these stand proudly as house museums and refurbished hotels. By day, the city is vibrant: its large Zulu community sets a colourful flavour and the Indian community brings echoes of the subcontinent to its busy streets. A large student population adds to the city's vitality. While the centre is appealingly scruffy, the outer suburbs are leafy and sedate. Unfortunately, Pietermaritzburg suffers from smog, thanks to its location in a 'basin'.

History

After defeating the Zulu at the decisive Battle of Blood River (see p371), the Voortrekkers began to establish their republic of Natal. Pietermaritzburg (usually known as PMB) was named in honour of leader Pieter Mauritz Retief, and was founded in 1838 as the capital (later the 'u' was dropped and, in 1938, it was decreed that Voortrekker leader Gert Maritz be remembered in the title). In 1841 the Boers built their Church of the Vow here to honour the Blood River promise. The British annexed Natal in 1843 but they retained Pietermaritzburg – well positioned and less humid than Durban, and already a neat little town – as the capital.

Orientation

The central grid of Pietermaritzburg contains most places of interest to travellers, including the museums, and is easy to get around on foot. Southeast of the centre is the University of Natal, to the west lie the Botanical Gardens and to the north is a fairly recent development, the Liberty Midlands Mall.

The northeastern end of the city, beyond Retief St, is a largely Indian commercial district. Along much of the city centre

it shuts down at night and is the most unsafe part of the city centre. North of here is the Indian residential area of Northdale (with suburbs such as Bombay Heights and Mysore Ridge). To the southwest of the city are Pine and West Sts – do not walk around here at night. Further in this direction is Edendale, the black dormitory suburb. To the northwest, beyond Queen Elizabeth Park, is the leafier, more upmarket residential area, including Hilton about 10km further on. If it's rainy (or smoggy) in Pietermaritzburg, then Hilton will probably be in the clouds.

Information

BOOKSHOPS

Adams (☎ 033-394 6830; 230 Church St; ☾ 8.30am-4.30pm Mon-Fri, 8am-1pm Sat) Has a wide selection of books and maps.

EMERGENCY

Police station (☎ 845 2421, 10111; Loop St)

INTERNET ACCESS

IDS Computers (☎ 342 7135; Victoria Centre, 157 Victoria Rd; per hr R20)

LAUNDRY

Wash Tub (☎ 033-345 7458; Shop 2, Park Lane Centre, cnr Greyling & Commercial Rds; per 5kg R27; ☾ 7am-5.30pm Mon-Fri, 7am-4pm Sat, 8am-2pm Sun)

MEDICAL SERVICES

St Anne's Hospital (☎ 033-897 5000; Loop St)

MONEY

There are several banks across town.
ABSA (cnr Longmarket & Buchanan Sts) Has an ATM and change facilities.
American Express Bureau de Change (Victoria Centre, 157 Victoria Rd)
First National Bank (Church St)

POST

Main post office (Longmarket St)

TOURIST INFORMATION

KZN Wildlife Headquarters (☎ 033-845 1000; www .kznwildlife.com; Queen Elizabeth Park, Duncan McKenzie Dr; ☾ 8am-5pm Mon-Fri, 8am-noon Sat) Provides information and accommodation bookings for all KZN Wildlife parks and reserves. To get to the office, head out to Howick Rd (from Commercial Rd) and after some kms you'll come to a roundabout – don't go straight ahead (to Hilton) but take the road veering to the right. This road has a very small sign directing you to 'QE Park', which is 2km further on. Some minibus taxis running to Hilton pass this roundabout.

Pietermaritzburg Tourism (☎ 033-345 1348; www .pmbtourism.co.za; 117 Commercial Rd; ☿ 8am-5pm Mon-Fri, 8am-1pm Sat) Has excellent information on the city and surrounds. Ask for a copy of the 'mini-guide', which has a good walking tour of the city.

Sights & Activities

In keeping with Pietermaritzburg's self-styled role as the 'heritage city', one of its finest sights is the **Tatham Art Gallery** (☎ 033-342 1804; fax 394 9831; Commercial Rd; admission free; ☿ 10am-6pm Tue-Sun), which was started in 1903 by Mrs Ada Tatham. Housed in the beautiful Old Supreme Court, it contains a

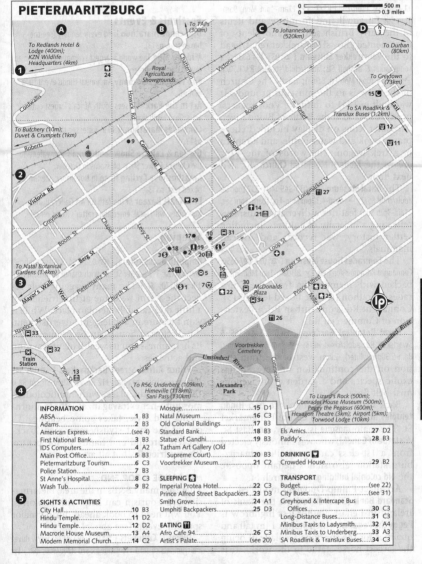

INFORMATION		Mosque	15	D1
ABSA	1 B3	Natal Museum	16	C3
Adams	2 B3	Old Colonial Buildings	17	B3
American Express	(see 4)	Standard Bank	18	B3
First National Bank	3 B3	Statue of Gandhi	19	B3
IDS Computers	4 A2	Tatham Art Gallery (Old		
Main Post Office	5 B3	Supreme Court)	20	B3
Pietermaritzburg Tourism	6 C3	Voortrekker Museum	21	C2
Police Station	7 B3			
St Anne's Hospital	8 C3	**SLEEPING** 🏠		
Wash Tub	9 B2	Imperial Protea Hotel	22	C3
		Prince Alfred Street Backpackers	23	D3
SIGHTS & ACTIVITIES		Smith Grove	24	A1
		Umphiti Backpackers	25	D3
City Hall	10 B3			
Hindu Temple	11 D2	**EATING** 🍴		
Hindu Temple	12 D2	Afro Cafe 94	26	B3
Macrorie House Museum	13 A4	Artist's Palate	(see 20)	
Modern Memorial Church	14 C2			

Els Amics	27	D2
Paddy's	28	B3
DRINKING 🍷		
Crowded House	29	B2
TRANSPORT		
Budget	(see 22)	
City Buses	(see 31)	
Greyhound & Intercape Bus		
Offices	30	C3
Long-Distance Buses	31	C3
Minibus Taxis to Ladysmith	32	A4
Minibus Taxis to Underberg	33	A3
SA Roadlink & Translux Buses	34	C3

KWAZULU-NATAL

fine collection of French and English 19th- and early-20th-century works. Every 15 minutes, little figurines appear out of the building's treasured ormolu clock to chime the bells. The nearby, colonial-era **City Hall** (cnr Church St & Commercial Rd) is the largest load-bearing red-brick building in the southern hemisphere.

At **Macrorie House Museum** (☎ 033-394 2161; 11 Loop St; adult/child R5/2; 🕙 11am-4pm Mon, 9am-1pm Tue-Fri) you'll find furniture and items of the early British settlers, and plenty of documented ghosts! For trekker relics, head to the **Voortrekker Museum** (☎ 033-394 6834; cnr Longmarket & Boshoff Sts; adult/child/student R3/1.50/1; 🕙 8am-4.30pm Mon-Fri, 8am-1pm Sat). The Church of the Vow is in the museum grounds. It was built in 1841 to fulfil the Voortrekkers' promise to God at the Battle of Blood River. Afrikaner icons on display include Retief's prayer book and water bottle, and a replica of a trek wagon. The words of the Vow are in the **Modern Memorial Church**, located next door.

The **Natal Museum** (☎ 033-345 1404; 237 Loop St; adult/child R5/2; 🕙 9am-4.30pm Mon-Fri, 10am-4pm Sat, 11am-3pm Sun) features a diversity of displays reflecting a diversity of cultures, including settler history, war records and African mammals.

The **Comrades House Museum** (☎ 033-897 8650; Connaught Rd; admission free; 🕙 8.30am-1pm Mon-Fri) is packed with memorabilia from the Comrades Marathon (see the boxed text, p313). Connaught Rd is off Durban Rd, an extension of Commercial Rd.

Natal Botanical Gardens (☎ 033-344 3585; 5 Swartskop Rd; adult/child R8/3; 🕙 8am-6pm summer, 8am-5.30pm winter), 2km west of the train station on the continuation of Berg St, has exotic species and a garden of indigenous mist-belt flora.

Back in the centre, there are two **Hindu temples** at the northern end of Longmarket St. The main **mosque** is nearby, on East St. A **statue of Gandhi**, who was famously ejected from a 1st-class carriage at Pietermaritzburg station, also stands defiant opposite the **old colonial buildings** on Church St.

Architect Phillip Dudgeon modelled the **Standard Bank** (Church St Mall) on the Bank of Ireland in Belfast. Rather less highbrow is **Peggy the Pegasus**, which stands 14m tall and qualifies for the spurious accolade of being the largest horse statue in the world. It is at the entrance to the **Golden Horse Casino** (☎ 033-395 8136; 45 New England Rd).

Tours

Pietermaritzburg Tourism (☎ 033-345 1348; www .pmbtourism.co.za; 117 Commercial Rd; 🕙 8am-5pm Mon-Fri, 8am-1pm Sat) organises city walking (R80 per person) and driving (R150 per person) tours.

Festivals & Events

Dusi canoe marathon Held every January (see the boxed text, p313).

Midmar Mile The world's largest swimming event on an inland dam in February.

Fire walking ceremony An annual Hindu event held in April.

Art in the Park May sees South Africa's largest outdoor art-selling exhibition.

Comrades Marathon Held in June; see the boxed text, p313.

Garden & Leisure Show South Africa's 'equivalent' to the Chelsea Flower Show blossoms in October.

Amashoshova Cycling Race In November; see the boxed text, p313.

Echo Craft Bazaar At the Tatham Art Gallery during November, with local, emerging crafter's items on sale.

Sleeping

BUDGET

Umphiti Backpackers (☎ 033-394 3490; umphiti@ mweb.co.za; 317 Bulwer St; dm with shared bathroom R75, d from R170; 🐾) The many wagging tails reflect the warm welcome at this friendly, if a little dog-eared, bohemian place. While it won't feature in a detergent advertisement, this Victorian house can be promoted for its helpfulness and its wealth of information and activities.

Prince Alfred Street Backpackers (☎ 033-345 7045, www.chauncey.co.za; 312 Prince Alfred St; s/d R85/170) This bright place, with multicoloured mosquito-net extravaganzas, ethnic adornments and style, takes some beating. It's one of the most stylish renovated 'backpackers' around and handy to the centre. It's gay-friendly, but all are welcome.

MIDRANGE & TOP END

There are many B&Bs in the area; Pietermaritzburg Tourism can help with bookings. You will need to book ahead during major sporting events (see above).

Duvet & Crumpets (☎ 033-394 4133; www.duvet andcrumpets.co.za; 1 Freelands Pl; s/d R200/300; 🐾) In a quiet, leafy location, this place offers a combo of unpretentious, clean rooms and self-catering units (great for a roll in bed with honey). If you prefer, you can lay back by the pool. Breakfast is extra.

Smith Grove (☎ 033-345 3963; www.smithgrove .co.za; 37 Howick Rd; s/d R250/400) This renovated Victorian home offers English-style B&B comforts with decorated, individually styled rooms, each in a different colour.

Torwood Lodge (☎ 033-390 1072; www.torwood .co.za; tw R420; ☲) With a quaint rural setting, lungfuls of fresh air and a landscaped rock pool, this excellent out-of-town option is great for those seeking city days and rustic nights. It's 10km out of town (ring ahead or see the website for directions). Owners are happy to pick you up or lead the way.

Redlands Hotel & Lodge (☎ 033-394 3333; www .guestnet.co.za; cnr Howick Rd & George McFarlane Lane; s R545-770, d R675-880; ☒ ☲) Swish and stately, this elegant place offers contrived but tasteful colonial-style surrounds and personal service. The spacious grounds add to the escape-from-it-all ambience. It's north of the centre off Howick Rd, past the Royal Agricultural Showgrounds.

Imperial Protea Hotel (☎ 033-342 6551; www .proteahotels.com/imperial; 224 Loop St; s/d incl breakfast R825/930; ☒) With more history than most, this was the spot the French Prince Imperial rode out from prior to coming to a sticky end during the 1879 Anglo-Zulu War. A few of the old fixtures and fittings survive and the plush rooms are good value if you catch a special (as low as R500).

Eating & Drinking

Paddy's (☎ 033-345 4835; 22 Timber St; mains R10-30; ☽ lunch & dinner) Greasy spoon meets Tudor tearoom serving some of the cheapest eats around.

Artist's Palate (☎ 033-342 8327; Commercial Rd; lunch R25-35; ☽ breakfast & lunch) Upstairs at the Tatham Gallery, this arty little café whips up a range of creative and fresh, healthy fare. It's open during gallery hours.

TAPs (☎ 033-342 9658; Chatterton Rd; mains R17.50-35; ☽ lunch & dinner; ☒) Numerous drinkable draughts, a massive deck and an enormous sports screen are here for those who want a big 'pubby' night out. There's a grill to appease hearty appetites.

Afro Cafe 94 (☎ 033-345 0773; 266 Prince Alfred St; mains R25-80; ☽ lunch & dinner) Less patriotic carnivores can get their mouths around 'world African cuisine': from Hluhluwe Impala salad to springbok loin and Cuban oxtail. This friendly African eatery is handy to several sleeping options.

Els Amics (☎ 033-345 6524; 380 Longmarket St; mains R40-95; ☽ lunch & dinner Tue-Fri, dinner Sat) The city's fine-dining option is in a cosy Victorian house with a series of rooms and a classy Spanish-influenced menu. Bookings essential.

Butchery (☎ 033-342 5239; www.thebutchery.co.za; 101 Roberts Rd; mains R46-70; ☽ noon-late) There are no prizes for guessing the menu here. Ladies (200g) and gents (300g) steaks of every type, racks of drying biltong, wall-to-wall wine racks and a packed deck of eaters make for a sizzling night out. Vegetarians are also catered for. Bookings essential.

Another recommendation is **Lizard's Rock** (☎ 033-345 7745; Durban Rd; mains R25-50; ☽ lunch & dinner; ☒) cocktail bar and seafood restaurant southeast of the centre.

Entertainment

Crowded House (☎ 033-345 5977; 99 Commercial Rd; ☽ 8pm-late Tue-Sat) Late-night boozers head here, where 'Pigs Night' means you can down as many drinks as you can stomach in two hours for only R30.

There are several theatres including the **Hexagon** (☎ 033-260 5537; Golf Rd), which is part of Natal University. It's about 3km south of the centre, off Durban Rd. For all other entertainment bookings, call **Computicket** (☎ 083-915 8000).

Getting There & Away

AIR

SAAirlink (☎ 033-386 92861), with an office at the airport, flies to Jo'burg daily (R845 high season).

BUS

Most bus companies' head offices are in Berger St, or directly opposite in McDonalds Plaza. **Greyhound/Cityliner** (☎ 083-915 9000; www.greyhound.co.za), **Translux** (☎ 031-308 8111; www .translux.co.za), **SA Roadlink** (☎ 345 6890; www.saroad link.co), **Luxliner** (☎ 011-914 4321; www.luxliner.co.za) and **Intercape** (☎ 0861 287 287; www.intercape.co.za) offer similar prices depending on the level of onboard services. City to City (see Translux) and Cityliner (see Greyhound) have the cheapest no-frills deals. Offices are generally

KWAZULU-NATAL

open 7am or 8am until 11pm. Checkers/
Shoprite also sells tickets for some major
bus routes. Destinations offered by the listed
companies from Pietermaritzburg include
Jo'burg (R125 to R200, six to seven hours),
Pretoria (R195, seven to eight hours), Cape
Town (R400 to R480, 22 hours), Port Eliza-
beth (R310, 15 hours) and Durban (R50 to
R180, 1½ hours).

Cheetah Coaches (☎ 033-342 4444) runs daily
between Durban, Pietermaritzburg and
Durban International Airport. The fare to
Durban is R60.

Sani Pass Carriers (☎ 033-701 1017; spc@y.co.za)
runs buses up into the Southern Drakensberg. See p355 for more details.

The **Baz Bus** (☎ in Durban 031-304 9099; www
.bazbus.com) travels between Durban and Pietermaritzburg twice a week.

Another option is to arrange 'transfers'
through a tour operator to destinations including Estcourt (R100), Ladysmith (R140),
Jo'burg (R200), Pretoria (R200) and Durban (R100). Call **African Link Travel** (☎ 033-
345 3175) for further information.

CAR

Most of the major car-rental companies
have agents here. **Budget** (☎ 033-342 8433; 224
Loop St; ◷ 8am-5pm Mon-Fri, 8am-noon Sat) is in the
Imperial Protea Hotel.

HITCHING

Lonely Planet does not recommend hitch-
ing. However, if you are hitching on the
N3, the safest places to get off are Exit 82
(Sanctuary/Armitage Rds) from Durban or
Exit 83 (Chatterton Rd) from Jo'burg.

MINIBUS TAXI

Minibus taxis generally congregate in
Church St in front of the train station. Destinations from Pietermaritzburg include:
Durban (R30, one hour), Estcourt (R40,
1¾ hours), Ladysmith (R55, 2½ hours),
Underberg (R40, 2½ hours), Newcastle
(R80, 3½ hours) and Jo'burg (R120, eight
hours). Other taxis depart from Market Sq
(behind Pietermaritzburg Tourism).

TRAIN

Pietermaritzburg is serviced by the *Trans
Natal*, which runs daily (except Tuesday
and Saturday) to Jo'burg (1st/2nd class
R215/145, 10 hours) and Durban (R50/35,

2½ hours); and the *Trans Oranje*, which
heads to Cape Town (1st/2nd class R610/415,
36 hours) on Wednesday, returning on
a Monday. There is a **train information line**
(☎ 0860-008 888).

Getting Around

The main rank for city-area buses is on
the road running behind Pietermaritzburg
Tourism.

If you're after a taxi, phone **Yellow Cabs**
(☎ 033-397 1910).

HOWICK & AROUND
☎ 033

In the town of Howick, about 25km northwest of Pietermaritzburg on the N3, are the
popular 95m **Howick Falls**, which you can
abseil down – call **Over The Top Adventures**
(☎ 082-736 3651; www.overthetop.co.za). Just before
the falls there is the small **Howick Museum**
(admission free; ◷ 9am-noon & 2-3.30pm Tue-Fri, 10am-
1pm Sat, 10am-3pm Sun), an unabashedly paro-
chial celebration of the town.

Umgeni Valley Nature Reserve (☎ 033-330 3931;
www.wildlifesociety.org.za/umgeni.htm; 1 Karkloof Rd;
adult/child R10/6; ◷ 8am-4.30pm) is nearby, with
giraffes, zebras, antelopes and six walking
trails. Around 260 bird species have been
recorded here.

Midmar Nature Reserve (☎ 033-330 2067; www
.kznwildlife.com; admission R15; ◷ 6am-6pm) is 7km
from Howick off the Greytown Rd. Although there are some animals in the reserve, it is mainly a recreation area, and has
water sports on the dam.

END OF FREEDOM

One of the most significant events in South
Africa's apartheid history occurred in the
KwaZulu-Natal Midlands.

In August 1962 it was just outside Howick that Nelson Mandela's days of freedom ended and his lengthy incarceration
began.

Mandela had been driving to Johannesburg along the Old Howick Rd with
Umkhonto we Sizwe (Spear of the Nation,
MK) member Cecil Williams, when their
car was stopped by police. The place of his
arrest on Rte103 is now marked by a
memorial, which Mandela unveiled himself in 1996.

In Karkloof, 14km north of Howick, **Karkloof Canopy Tours** (☎ 033-330 3415; www .karkloofcanopytour.co.za; groups up to 6 R395; ☻ 8am-3pm) conducts three-hour tours through the canopy of Karkloof forest. Do not attempt this if you have vertigo; book ahead.

Sleeping

Midmar Nature Reserve (☎ 033-845 1000; www.kzn wildlife.com; Munro Bay; camp sites R45, chalets R190) You can camp or take a chalet at Munro Bay in the reserve.

Windermere Guest House (☎ 033-330 8284; windermeregh@yebo.co.za; 11 Windermere Pl; s/d incl breakfast R280/500; 🖳) One of the best-value places (for its calibre), this Cape Dutch–style home has luxurious old-world rooms with designer-style décor. The enthusiastic, well-travelled owner is keen on the local war history.

MOOI RIVER

☎ 033 / pop 10,000

The early Voortrekkers probably had high hopes for Mooi River, as *mooi* means 'beautiful'. The Zulu were more matter of fact, calling it Mpofana, 'Place of the Eland'. Today, it's a town on the verge of going to seed. The surrounding countryside to the west is, however, horse-stud country on rolling hills dotted with old European trees.

Mooi River is closer to Giant's Castle than Estcourt and, while there are fewer minibus taxis, the town is right on the N3 so hitching to and from Mooi River may be easier. If you do find yourself here, a good sleeping option is **Gleneagles Guest House**

(☎ 033-263 2883; www.gleneagles.co.za; Claughton Tce; s/d incl breakfast R250/500). Just off the Giant's Castle Rd, this restored manor offers spacious 1950s-style floral rooms, plus some fake flowers inside and real ones outside. It's child-friendly.

There are some excellent country guesthouses in the surrounding area – for details, see below.

Greyhound buses running between Durban (R100, two hours) and Jo'burg/Pretoria (R175, eight/nine hours) stop at the Engen petrol station on the Rosetta road near the N3, 1km from the centre.

Minibus taxis aren't frequent and run mainly to nearby villages.

NOTTINGHAM ROAD & AROUND

☎ 033

The quaint little town of Nottingham Road was so-named to honour the Nottinghamshire Regiment of the British Army, which was garrisoned here. After the Cape Winelands, this is probably the most gentrified rural area in the country (it falls under the Midlands Meander); there are some excellent guesthouses, and most have extensive gardens.

Stillwaters Guest House (☎ 033-267 7280; still waters@futurenet.co.za; s/d R190/380) The owner is as down-to-earth and pleasant as her homely cottage in a delightful cottage-garden setting. There are plans afoot to build a backpackers within the grounds, overlooking a small lake. It's 500m along the Kamberg Rd from Rosetta.

Granny Mouse Country House (☎ 033-234 4071; www.grannymouse.co.za; Old Main Rd; s/d incl breakfast from R395/790) This deceptively named award-winning country house near the village of Balgowan, south of Mooi River, is not one abode, but rather a range of neat, thatched, luxurious cottages, complete with a chapel. It's off Rte 103, a scenic road running parallel to the N3 between Howick and Mooi River. There are also midweek specials on offer.

Hartford House (☎ 033-263 2713; www.hartford .co.za; s incl breakfast R610-1120, d per person R470-1015; 🗶 🖳) Worthy of dignitaries, this posh place was the home of a former Natal prime minister. It's now one of the country's top luxury lodges, with prices to show for it – it's South African interior design at its opulent best.

BATTLEFIELDS

Big wildlife, big mountains and big waves may top the agenda for many visitors to the province, but the history of KwaZulu-Natal is intrinsically linked to its Battlefields, the stage on which many of the country's bloodiest chapters were played out. KwaZulu-Natal is where the British Empire was crushed by a Zulu army at Isandlwana. Here they subsequently staged the heroic defence of Rorke's Drift, where the Boers and the Brits slogged it out at Ladysmith and Spioenkop, and where fewer than 600 Voortrekkers avenged the murder of their leader Piet Retief by defeating a force of 12,000 Zulu at Blood River.

Roughly following the N11 and Rte 33 roads and occupying an area that stretches north from Estcourt to the Free State and Mpumalanga borders, the Battlefields are a crusade to get to without a car. Even with a car, they are isolated and can be a challenge to find. Having a guide is the best suggestion for tackling this area – you won't feel as though you're traipsing through a string of empty fields. With a knowledgeable person at hand, and with a bit of swatting up beforehand, the so-called Battlefields Route can be extremely rewarding.

Less satisfying are the towns of Mooi River, Estcourt and Colenso – they look like they've been in more recent wars, and in a way they have. With the construction (in the 1980s and 1990s) of the N3, which bypassed these destinations, and the subsequent closure of the towns' factories, many local people left for the cities; these once-thriving towns appear to have been marginalised.

If you want to do some advance planning, visit www.battlefields.kzn.org.za or pick up KZN Tourism's *Battlefields Route* brochure – available at Durban's **Tourist Junction** (☎ in Durban 031-304 4934) or from tourist offices across the region.

ESTCOURT & AROUND
☎ 036

Once a thriving town, the Estcourt of today has a quieter and more rough-and-tumble feel, although it's surrounded by pleasant farming communities. It's connected on the Durban to Jo'burg/Pretoria bus route, and an excellent wildlife reserve and an interesting museum are both nearby.

Bushman's River Tourism Association (☎ 036-352 6253; Old Civic Bldg, Upper Harding St; ☉ 8am-4pm Mon-Fri) can help with accommodation. **Makarios Reservations** (☎ 036-352 5187; makarios res@absamail.co.za; ☉ 8am-4pm Mon-Fri), in the same building, can also book Battlefields tours and transport.

Fort Durnford (☎ 036-352 3000; admission by donation; ☉ 9am-noon & 1-4pm), now a museum, was built in 1874 to protect Estcourt from Zulu attack. In 1914 it was a reformatory for 20 'naughty girls'. There are interesting displays and a reconstructed Zulu village at the gate.

Around 25km northeast of Estcourt is the 5000-hectare undulating thornveld of the **Weenen Game Reserve** (☎ 036-354 7013; www.kzn wildlife.com; adult/child/vehicle R12/12/15; ☉ 6am-6pm), which has black and white rhinos, giraffes and several antelope species, including the rare roan. There is a hide and water hole, picnic sites and guided trails. The two self-guided trails are iMpofu (2km), and Beacon View (3km). The reserve also has **camp sites** (per person R45) and a **five-bed cottage** (per person R108) – minimum charges apply.

Almost at the point where Rte 103 meets Rte 74, 16km north of Estcourt, is the site where the young Winston Churchill was captured by the Boers in 1899 when they derailed the armoured train he was travelling in; there is a cairn and **plaque** just off the road. Beware: it's isolated here.

Sleeping
Summer Place Backpackers Lodge (☎ 083-561 8996; dm with/without breakfast R150/175, with half board R220) The name of the backpacker's cottage is 'Ekhumphumuleni' or 'a place to chill out', and indeed this nine-bed cottage 'dorm' is a pleasant place to be stranded. It backs onto the New Formosa Nature Reserve, in New Formosa near Estcourt. Turn left from Rte 103 at the sign to the reserve.

Ashtonville Terraces (☎ 036-352 7770; dlsa@tel komsa.net; 76 Albert St; s/d incl breakfast R260/390; ☒) Owned by the chairman of the local tourism association – most handy if you need information – this homey place is in a lovely colonial villa, ringed by tropical gardens and boasting plenty of slick extras such as Victorian baths and massive breakfasts.

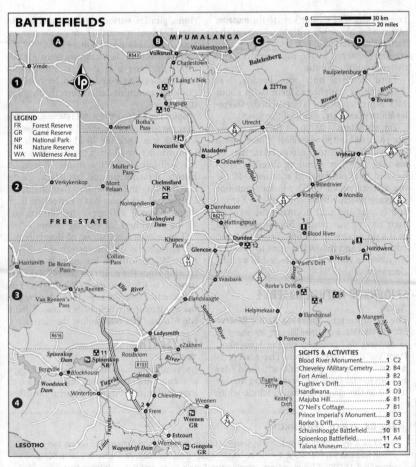

BATTLEFIELDS

LEGEND
FR   Forest Reserve
GR   Game Reserve
NP   National Park
NR   Nature Reserve
WA   Wilderness Area

SIGHTS & ACTIVITIES

Blood River Monument	1 C2
Chieveley Military Cemetry	2 B4
Fort Amiel	3 B2
Fugitive's Drift	4 D3
Isandlwana	5 D3
Majuba Hill	6 B1
O'Neil's Cottage	7 B1
Prince Imperial's Monument	8 D3
Rorke's Drift	9 C3
Schuinshoogte Battlefield	10 B1
Spioenkop Battlefield	11 A4
Talana Museum	12 C3

Getting There & Away

BUS

Greyhound (☎ 031-334 9720; www.greyhound.co.za) buses stop outside the Bushman's River Tourism Association office, on Upper Harding St – you also book tickets here. They run daily to Durban (R100, 2½ hours) and Jo'burg (R175, 7½ hours).

MINIBUS TAXI

The main minibus taxi rank is at the bottom of Phillips St, in the town centre, downhill from the post office. Fares from Estcourt include Winterton (R12, 40 minutes), Ladysmith (R18, one hour), Pietermaritzburg (R45, 1¾ hours), Durban (R55, 2½ hours) and Jo'burg (R95, eight hours).

COLENSO

☎ 036

Some might say that the best thing about Colenso is the view over your shoulder as you head out of town. This sad and crumbling, frontier-style town was once the British base during the Relief of Ladysmith. Those who are likely to dally here are die-hard battlefield beavers. As well as Spioenkop, there are several other Anglo-Boer War battlefields near here, most examples of the triumph of Boer guerrilla tactics over British imperial discipline.

There is a quaint museum and some memorial sites relating to the Battle of Colenso (December 1899) – another disaster for the hapless General Buller at the hands of

KWAZULU-NATAL

Louis Botha. The elusive keys to the **museum** (admission free) are either with Mrs Louw at the **Battlefields Hotel** (☎ 036-422 2242), at the police station (adjacent to the museum) or with the enthusiastic curator.

Lord Roberts' only son, Freddy, was among those slaughtered here (with about 1100 other British); he is buried in the **Chieveley Military Cemetery**, south of the town.

Zingela Safaris (☎ 036-354 7005; www.zingela safaris.co.za; full board per person R550), a bush camp in a glorious setting, offers relaxation or loads of activities including abseiling, fishing and river rafting (add another R150 for the activity package). The indoor-outdoor units are tasteful designer numbers of stone and canvas and built to make the most of their natural surrounds. Bookings advised as it's popular with groups. From Colenso take Rte 74 and follow the signs to Weenen from where you will be collected in a high-clearance vehicle.

SPIOENKOP NATURE RESERVE
☎ 036

The 6000-hectare **Spioenkop Nature Reserve** (☎ 036-488 1578; www.kznwildlife.com; admission R15; ☽ 6am-6pm; ☒) is based on the Spioenkop Dam on the Tugela River. The reserve is handy for most of the area's battlefield sites and not too far from the Drakensberg for day trips into the range. Animals include white rhino, giraffes, various antelope species and over 270 bird species. There's a swimming pool, horse riding and vulture hide.

iPika (camp sites/bush camp per person R50/146) inside the reserve in a valley, offers camp sites and one four-bed tented bush camp. Book all accommodation directly through the reserve.

Spion Kop Lodge (☎ 036-488 1404; www.spionkop .co.za; r per person with full board R890, 4-/6-person cottages R890/990) was once the headquarters of the Commander-in-Chief of the British Forces. It's well known for the owner, Raymond Heron, a raconteur and battlefield guide. Overlooking the Spioenkop Battlefield, his luxury 'barracks' also has a converted barn dining room, a well-appointed library, and all the trimmings for visiting 'troops'.

The reserve is northeast of Bergville but the entrance is on the eastern side, 13km from Winterton off Rte 600. If you are coming from the south on the N3, take the turn-off to Rte 74 to get to Winterton. You will need a car to get here. If coming by car, the Spioenkop Battlefield is accessed from Rte 616 (not Rte 600; follow the signs).

LADYSMITH
☎ 036

Ladysmith was named after the wife of Cape governor Sir Harry Smith, but it could well have had a much more colourful moniker;

THE BATTLE OF SPIOENKOP

On 23 January 1900 the British, led by General Buller, made a second attempt to relieve Ladysmith, which had been under siege by the Boers since late October 1899. At Trichardt's Drift, 500 Boers prevented 15,000 of his men from crossing the Tugela River, and Buller decided that he needed to take Spioenkop – the flat-topped hill would make a good gun emplacement from which to clear the annoying Boers from their trenches.

During the night, 1700 British troops climbed the hill and chased off the few Boers guarding it. They dug a trench and waited for morning. Meanwhile the Boer commander, Louis Botha, heard of the raid. He ordered his field guns to be trained onto Spioenkop and positioned some of his men on nearby hills. A further 400 soldiers began to climb Spioenkop as the misty dawn broke.

The British might have beaten off the 400, but the mist finally lifted, and was immediately replaced by a hail of bullets and shells. The British retreated to their trench and, by midafternoon, continuous shellfire caused many to surrender. By now, reinforcements were on hand and the Boers could not overrun the trench. A bloody stalemate was developing.

After sunset, the British evacuated the hill; so did the Boers. Both retreats were accomplished so smoothly that neither side was aware that the other had left. That night Spioenkop was held by the dead.

It was not until the next morning that the Boers again climbed up Spioenkop and found that it was theirs. The Boers had killed or wounded 1340 British – Gandhi's stretcher-bearer unit performed with distinction at this battle. Buller relieved Ladysmith a month later on 28 February.

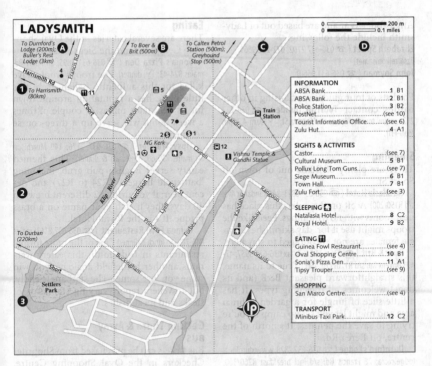

LADYSMITH

0 — 200 m
0 — 0.1 miles

INFORMATION
ABSA Bank...1 B1
ABSA Bank...2 B1
Police Station.....................................3 B2
PostNet..(see 10)
Tourist Information Office..........(see 6)
Zulu Hut...4 A1

SIGHTS & ACTIVITIES
Castor..(see 7)
Cultural Museum...............................5 B1
Pollux Long Tom Guns.................(see 7)
Siege Museum....................................6 B1
Town Hall...7 B1
Zulu Fort...(see 3)

SLEEPING
Natalasia Hotel.................................8 C2
Royal Hotel..9 B2

EATING
Guinea Fowl Restaurant.............(see 4)
Oval Shopping Centre......................10 B1
Sonia's Pizza Den............................11 A1
Tipsy Trouper................................(see 9)

SHOPPING
San Marco Centre.........................(see 4)

TRANSPORT
Minibus Taxi Park...........................12 C2

KWAZULU-NATAL

her actual name was Lady Juana Maria de los Dolores de Leon Smith.

The town achieved fame during the 1899–1902 Anglo-Boer War, when it was besieged by Boer forces for 118 days. Recently, it has made world headlines as the home of the group, Ladysmith Black Mambazo. Apart from the historical aspect – several buildings were here during the siege – Ladysmith is a nice place to walk around.

Information

ABSA (cnr Queen & Murchison Sts) Has two branches on the same crossroads, one with an ATM.

Police station (☎ 036-638 3309; King St) By the NG Kerk.

Tourist information office (☎ 036-637 2992; www .ladysmith.co.za; Murchison St; ☼ 9am-4pm Mon-Fri, 9am-1pm Sat) In the Siege Museum. Ask here about guided tours of the Battlefields.

Zulu Hut (☎ 036-631 4413; San Marco Centre, 3 Francis Rd; per hr R40; ☼ 8am-5pm Mon-Sat, 8am-1pm Sun) Internet access.

Sights & Activities

The excellent **Siege Museum** (☎ 036-637 2231; adult/child R2/1; ☼ 9am-4pm Mon-Fri, 9am-1pm Sat),

next to the town hall in the Market House (built in 1884), was used to store rations during the siege. You can pick up a guide to Ladysmith here.

There's also the small **Cultural Museum** (☎ 036-637 2231; 25 Keate St; adult/child R2/1; ☼ 9am-4pm Mon-Fri), with some dusty displays including a room dedicated to Ladysmith Black Mambazo.

Outside the **town hall** are two guns, **Castor** and **Pollux**, used by the British in defence of Ladysmith. Nearby is a replica of **Long Tom**, a Boer gun capable of heaving a shell 10km. Long Tom was put out of action by a British raiding party during the siege, but not before it had caused a great deal of damage.

On King St (opposite Settlers Dr) is a wall with loopholes from the original **Zulu Fort**, built as a refuge from Zulu attack. The wall is now part of the police station.

Tours

The only way to do justice to the Battlefields is to hire a guide for the day. Sites can be isolated and signage poor. Highly recommended guides who specialise in the

Anglo-Boer War and are based out of Lady-smith include the following:

Elizabeth Spiret (☎ 036-637 7702, 072-262 9669; lizs@telkomsa.net)

John Snyman (☎ 036-631 0660)

For lists of tour guides specialising in other battles contact **Tourism Dundee** (☎ 034-212 2121; www.tourdundee.co.za; Victoria St; ☺ 9am-4.30pm Mon-Fri).

Sleeping

There are plenty of B&Bs out of town off Short St.

Natalasia Hotel (☎ 036-637 6821; 342 Kandahar Ave; s/d R150/200) A bit on the outer, this place has neat rooms with no trimmings. Feels like the troops might use it for 'day skirmishes'. Single females are not encouraged to stay here.

Boer & Brit (☎ 036-631 2184; fax 036-637 3957; 47-49 Convent Rd; s/d R170/220; ☒) True to its name, this straightforward pleasant B&B (and its dogs) welcomes all travelling types. It has a little slice of jungle for a garden, a braai area and might let you set up camp if you're trying to save the pennies. It's north of the centre, off Berea Rd.

Durnford's Lodge (☎ 036-637 2828; www.durnfords lodge.co.za; 28 Francis Rd; s/d incl breakfast R260/360; ☒ ☒) The rooms at this siege-proof place may be cell-like in size, but they're pleasant in nature. Freedom comes in the form of the spacious African-style, indoor-outdoor lounge, garden and pool.

Buller's Rest Lodge (☎ 036-637 6154; www.bullers restlodge.co.za; 61 Cove Cres; s/d incl breakfast R325/440; ☒ ☒) You'll want to dig in long-term at this smart thatched abode. There's the snug 'Boer War' pub complete with Battlefields artefacts (if you're lucky, you might make it to Andy's cellar), scrumptious home cooking, and views of the Drakensbergs from the sundeck. It's popular with the local business crowd and fills up on weekdays. Turn right at Francis Rd off Harrismith (Port) Rd and follow the signs.

Royal Hotel (☎ 036-637 2176; royalhotel@intekom .co.za; 140 Murchison St; s/d incl breakfast R335/575; ☒ ☒) Enjoy these historical digs, which combine predictable old-style grandeur (floral borders) with some 1980s renovations (shag-pile carpet). You can discuss tactics at the hotel's pub before engaging in the tourist onslaught of the surrounding streets.

Eating

There are several eateries in the Oval Shopping Centre behind the Siege Museum.

Sonia's Pizza Den (☎ 036-631 2895; 28 Poort Rd; mains R24-43; ☺ dinner) The troops would have killed for this authentic Italian grub; this little place has a reputation around town for its delectable pizzas. A couple of times a week Sonia will serve up a three-course set menu.

Tipsy Trouper (☎ 036-637 2176; 140 Murchison St; mains R30-60; ☺ lunch & dinner) This themed eatery serves English pub grub, including 'battlefield burgers' (R24 to R27) and decent beer; if you drink 32 different brews in 40 days, they'll etch your name on a brass plaque. It's in the Royal Hotel.

Guinea Fowl Restaurant (☎ 036-637 8163; mains R40-70; ☺ lunch & dinner) One of the more formal restaurants in Ladysmith, this eatery warrants another battlefield analogy: 'you win some you lose some'. The staff are friendly, but travellers report varying standards of steaks and meat dishes.

Getting There & Away

BUS

Bus tickets can be purchased from Shoprite/Checkers in the Oval Shopping Centre. Buses depart from the Caltex petrol station on Murchison Rd, and connect Ladysmith with Durban (R160, four hours), Jo'burg (R195, six hours), Pretoria (R195, seven hours) and Cape Town (R390, 19 hours).

MINIBUS TAXI

The main taxi rank is east of the town centre near the corner of Queen and Lyell Sts. Taxis bound for Jo'burg are nearby on Alexandra St. Some destinations are Newcastle (R35, one hour), Durban (R75, 2½ hours) and Jo'burg (R110, five hours).

TRAIN

The *Trans Oranje* (Durban to Cape Town) and the daily *Trans Natal* (Durban to Jo'burg/Pretoria) both stop here, but at inconvenient times. For more details about train schedules see p643.

NEWCASTLE & AROUND
☎ 034

Now twinned with its UK namesake, Newcastle (population 309,000) lacks the big-city feel of its English counterpart. As a coal-mining and steel-producing centre, however, it does share the same no-nonsense atmosphere.

The **tourist information office** (☎ 034-315 3318; www.tourismnewcastle.co.za; Scott St; ☸ 9am-4pm Mon-Fri, 9.30-10.30am Sat) is in the colonial-era town hall.

There's an Anglo-Boer War museum in **Fort Amiel** (☎ 034-328 7621; admission R5; ☸ 9am-1pm Tue-Thu, 11am-4pm Fri, 9am-1pm Sat), which was established in 1876 when the British anticipated conflict with the Zulu.

The turn-off to **Chelmsford Nature Reserve** (☎ 034-351 1753; www.kznwildlife.com; admission R10; ☸ 6am-7pm) is off the N11 (turn-off 7km to the gate) and 25km south of Newcastle. As well as fishing and spring wildflowers, there's a beautiful wildlife reserve with the highest concentration of the endangered oribi species in South Africa. Accommodation is available.

Sleeping & Eating

KZN Wildlife (☎ 033-845 1000; www.kznwildlife.com; camp sites/5-bed chalets per person R55/117) Offers camp sites and chalets with good facilities in the pleasant Chelmsford Nature Reserve.

Cannon Lodge (☎ 034-315 2307; fax 315 2308; 96 Allen St; s/d incl breakfast R260/350) In a red-brick, colonial-style building, this B&B combines clean, motel-style rooms with a vibrant, English-style pub serving lunches and dinners (mains R30 to R68).

Newcastle Inn (☎ 034-312 8151; fax 034-312 4142; cnr Hunter & Victoria Rds; s/d R325/395; ☒ ☒) Predictable and reliable, this is a decent, business-style offering. You'll need your own transport as it's slightly out of the city centre.

Getting There & Away

Shoprite Hyper and Checkers Hyper in town and at Amajuba Mall (opposite the Newcastle Inn) sell Greyhound tickets. Buses run daily to Jo'burg (R175, five hours) and Durban (R170, 5½ hours) from the Shell petrol station on Allen St.

Car-rental companies with agents in Newcastle include **Imperial** (☎ 034-312 2806), which is based at the Engen petrol station on Murchison St, east of Allen St.

MAJUBA HILL

The first Anglo-Boer War ended abruptly with the British defeat at Majuba Hill, 40km north of Newcastle, in early 1881. The **site**

(adult/vehicle R3.50/10; ☸ 7am-5pm) is off the N11. A rudimentary map is available. The more remote Laing's Nek battlefield is signposted and Schuinshoogte battlefield is also in the vicinity.

Peace negotiations took place at **O'Neill's Cottage** at the foothills near Majuba. The cottage, used as a hospital during the battle, has a photographic display.

UTRECHT

☎ 034 / pop 3500

Utrecht was once the capital of one of the original Voortrekker republics, measuring just 30km by 65km, and then the British headquarters during the Anglo-Zulu War. By 2000, several decades after the closure of the mines in the 1960s and 1970s and the town's subsequent demise, Utrecht was almost a ghost town. To attract tourism to the area, residents came up with the wild idea of rebranding it 'a town within a game park'. Over 3500 hectares of land – including the town – was fenced in so that introduced wildlife could roam freely. While you can be lucky to spot an animal in the street during the day, you can see other interesting monuments and buildings in this compact place.

The **Utrecht Information Bureau** (☎ 034-331 3613; www.utrecht.co.za; 1 Voor St; ☸ 7.30am-4pm Mon-Fri) is near the town's *lapa* (circular, thatch-roofed building used for cooking and parties) entrance. The **Old Parsonage Museum** (admission R5; Loop St; ☸ 9am-4pm Mon-Fri) displays local history.

For guaranteed wildlife sightings head to the pretty **Balele Community Game Park** (per pedestrian/car load R11/50; camp sites/4-bed cottages/4-bed rondavels/4-bed safari tents R90/179/221/400) at the far end of town. It's on a dam and boasts a huge range of sleeping options.

Mangosuthu Art & Craft Village & Backpackers (upuba@worldonline.co.za; 1 Voor St; r with shared bathroom R90) has great-value accommodation in rondavels.

DUNDEE

☎ 034 / pop 29,000

Coal mines pepper the surrounds, but Dundee is another planned swathe of middle-class, South African suburbia. There's not much to do, but it's a decent base for exploring the region's history.

Tourism Dundee (☎ 034-212 2121; www.tourdundee.co.za; Victoria St; ☸ 9am-4.30pm Mon-Fri), by the gardens in the centre, can put you in touch with Battlefields guides, who charge between R300 and R500 for a one-day tour of sites including Rorke's Drift and Isandlwana.

On the Vryheid road, 1.5km out of town, is the fascinating **Talana Museum** (☎ 034-212 2654; www.talana.co.za; adult/child R15/2; ☻ 8am-4.30pm Mon-Fri, 10am-4.30pm Sat & Sun). Talana means 'the shelf where precious items are stored', strangely appropriate for this excellent museum and its surrounds, which have memorials, cairns and several historic buildings relating to the 1899 Anglo-Boer Battle of Talana. There are comprehensive displays on the Anglo-Zulu and the Anglo-Boer Wars (including a photograph of Mahatma Gandhi during his stretcher-bearing days), local history, exquisite Zulu beading, and a glassworks and coal-mining display. Curator Pam McFadden is the guru on all things Talana. Allow time to spend here.

East of Dundee, 52km away via Rtes 33 and 66, is the regional centre of Nqutu, an important trading hub for the surrounding Zulu community. A further 30km north of Nqutu, near Nondweni, is the memorial to the Prince Imperial Louis Napoleon, the last of the Bonaparte dynasty, who was killed here on 1 June 1879. Both places are isolated and poorly signposted; it's not recommended to go without a guide.

Sleeping

Royal Country Inn (☎ 034-212 2147; www.royalcountry inn.com; Victoria St; backpackers & d R175, s/d incl breakfast R335/460) With oodles of late-19th-century charm, an English-style pub and courtyard fit for a spot of post-Rorke's Drift R'n'R and cosy rooms named after the battle's Victoria Cross recipients, this is a great little place to stay during a tour of the Battlefields.

Penny Farthing Country House (☎ 034-642 1925; www.pennyf.co.za; s/d with half board R440/1050; ☒) In the midst of a 3000-hectare beef and wildlife farm, this homey Victoriana-filled place offers snug accommodation, big spaces and a sociable atmosphere. It's 30km south of Dundee on Rte 33 towards Greytown and well placed for visits to Rorke's Drift and Isandlwana. The owner, Foy Vermaak, is also a tour guide (R600 for four people with own transport).

Kwa Rie (☎ 034-212 2333; www.caravanparks.co.za; Tandy Rd; camp sites R55, s/d R100/200; ☒) With *Flintstones*-style mock-rock chalets, a lake,

garden and mock-rock pool, this relaxing place is an excellent budget option. It's 1.5km southwest of the centre – head down Victoria St.

Also recommended is **Battlefields Backpackers** (☎ 034-212 4040; battlepackers@telkomsa.net; dm from R80, d R200), which is run by registered Battlefields guide Evan Jones and his wife. This friendly place offers welcoming drinks and Battlefields tours, just to scratch the surface.

Getting There & Away

There is very little transport to Dundee. You can arrange a pick-up with **PMB Heritage Tours** (☎ 034-212 4040), from the Greyhound bus drop-off at Fort Mistake (R80 one-way, 70km), and from the **Baz Bus** (☎ in Durban 031-304 9099; www.bazbus.com) at Winterton (R180, 250km).

ISANDLWANA & RORKE'S DRIFT
☎ 034

If you have seen *Zulu*, the film that made Michael Caine a star, you will have doubtless heard of Rorke's Drift, a victory of the misty-eyed variety, where on 22–23 January 1879, 139 British soldiers successfully defended a small mission station from around 4000 Zulu warriors. A propaganda-minded Queen Victoria lavished 11 Victoria Crosses on the survivors and the battle was assured its dramatic place in British military history.

For the full picture, however, you must travel 15km across the plain to Isandlwana, the precursor of Rorke's Drift, where only hours earlier the Zulus dealt the Empire one of its great Battlefields disasters by annihilating the main body of the British force in devastating style. Tellingly, *Zulu Dawn* (1979), the film made about Isandlwana, never became the cult classic *Zulu* (1964) is now. Victories sell better than defeats.

Ideally, the two battlefields should be visited together. Start at the **Isandlwana Visitors Centre** (☎ 034-271 8165; adult/child R15/5; ☻ 8am-4pm), where there is a small museum. The battlefield itself is extremely evocative. Spread out from the base of Isandlwana hill, white cairns and memorials mark the spot where each British soldier fell – the hillside is peppered with them.

If you have seen *Zulu*, which was filmed in the Drakensberg, the scenery around Rorke's

THE BATTLE OF ISANDLWANA

It hardly bears thinking about. When a soldier from one of the five British armies sent to invade Zululand peered over a ridge on 22 January 1879, he was confronted not with an empty stretch of savanna, but with 25,000 Zulu warriors, crouching in the grass less than 1km away. They had intended to delay their attack until the following day, the day after the full moon, but once discovered moved into battle formation – two enclosing horns on the flanks and the main force in the centre – and fell on the British, catching them off guard and unprepared. By the end of the day, the British column had been annihilated and the Anglo-Zulu War, for the invaders at least, had got off to a very bad start.

Meanwhile, the small British contingent that had remained at Rorke's Drift (where the army had crossed into Zululand) to guard supplies, heard of the disaster and fortified their camp. They were attacked by about 4000 Zulus but the defenders, numbering fewer than 100 fit soldiers, held on through the night until a relief column arrived. Victoria Crosses were lavished on the defenders – 11 in all – and another couple went to the two officers who died defending the Queen's Colours at Fugitive's Drift, about 10km south of Rorke's Drift.

Drift may come as a bit of a disappointment. The landscape is still beautifully rugged, however, and the **Rorke's Drift Orientation Centre** (☎ 034-642 1687; adult/child R15/5; ☷ 8am-4pm Mon-Fri, 9am-4pm Sat & Sun), on the site of the original mission station, is excellent. The Zulu know this site as Shiyane, their name for the hill at the back of the village. The *Rorke's Drift-Shiyane Self-Guided Trail* brochure (R3) is helpful for understanding the close nature of the fighting in this battle.

Next to the museum, there's the **Evangelical Lutheran Church Art & Craft Centre** (☎ 034-642 1627; admission by donation; ☷ 8am-4.30pm Mon-Fri, 10am-3pm Sat & Sun), one of the few places to offer artistic training to black artists during apartheid. It still has a workshop, although does not always stick to its opening hours.

About 10km from Rorke's Drift is **Fugitive's Drift**. Two British soldiers were killed here while attempting to rescue the Queen's Colours.

Sleeping

Rorke's Drift Lodge (☎ 034-642 1805; www.rorkes driftlodge.co.za; Rorke's Drift; s/d with half board R285/570; ☒ ☐) With wonderful views over the Battlefields, this hospitable place promotes an 'eat well, sleep well' policy. It's 5km up a rough track from the Rorke's Drift Orientation Centre – turn left out of the museum and you will see the sign on the right. Call ahead to check on road conditions and for pick-ups from Ladysmith and Dundee. It organises tours of the battlefields.

Fugitives' Drift Lodge (☎ 034-642 1843; www .fugitives-drift-lodge.com; Fugitives' Drift; s/d with half board

R2880/4360; ☒ ☐ ☒) Run by Battlefields authority David Rattray (tours R700), this opulent private wildlife reserve is dripping in colonial-style class and military memorabilia. There are rooms in a slightly less glamorous guesthouse (R1550/2200 singles/doubles). Low-season rates are reduced. It is by Fugitives' Drift, about 10km from Rorke's Drift.

Getting There & Away

The battle sites are southeast of Dundee. Isandlwana is about 70km from Dundee, off Rte 66; Rorke's Drift is 42km from Dundee, accessible from Rte 66 or Rte 33 (the Rte 33 turn-off is 13km south of Dundee). The roads to both battlefields can be dusty and rough. A dirt road connects Isandlwana and Rorke's Drift.

BLOOD RIVER MONUMENT
☎ 034

On 16 December 1838 a small force of Voortrekkers avenged the massacre of Piet Retief's diplomatic party by crushing an army of 12,000 Zulu. More than 3000 Zulu died – the river ran red with their blood – while the Voortrekkers sustained barely a few casualties. The battle became a seminal event in Afrikaner history. The victory came to be seen as the fulfilment of God's side of the bargain and seemed to prove that the Boers had a divine mandate to conquer and 'civilise' Southern Africa, and that they were in fact a chosen people.

However, Afrikaner nationalism and the significance attached to Blood River grew in strength simultaneously and it has been argued (by Leach in *The Afrikaners – Their Last Great Trek* and others) that the importance of Blood River was deliberately heightened and manipulated for political ends. The standard interpretation of the victory meshed with the former apartheid regime's world view: hordes of untrustworthy black savages were beaten by Boers who were on an Old Testament–style mission from God. Afrikaners still visit the site on 16 December, but the former 'Day of the Vow' is now the 'Day of Reconciliation'.

The battle site is marked by a full-scale bronze re-creation of the 64-wagon laager. The cairn of stones was built by the Boers after the battle to mark the centre of their laager. The monument and the nearby **Blood River Museum** (☎ 034-632 1695; adult/child R15/5; ☽ 8am-4.30pm) are 20km southeast of Rte33; the turn-off is 27km from Dundee and 45km from Vryheid.

The **Ncome Museum** (☎ 034-271 8121; admission by donation; ☽ 8am-4.30pm), on the other side of the river, offers the Zulu perspective of events.

Free State

Nelson Mandela once said that when he visited the Free State, he felt nothing could shut him in, and his thoughts could roam as far as the horizons. If you spend enough time in this land of golden light and pistachio grasses you'll start to catch his drift. This is a place where farmers in floppy hats and overalls drive rusty *baackies* full of sheep over bumpy roads; where giant fields of sunflowers languish by brightly painted Sotho houses. Golden Gate Highlands National Park is heavenly in late afternoon, while artsy Clarens is surprisingly hip for a middle-of-nowhere town, bursting with eclectic galleries and charming guesthouses.

It's true that Free State doesn't hold any trump cards when it comes to South Africa's not-to-be-missed attractions. But if you travel to dig beneath the surface, to immerse yourself in the ideologies and idiosyncrasies of places you visit, we'd encourage you to linger. A journey through the Free State can be a mind-opening experience. In this staunchly Afrikaans region it often seems the clock stopped ticking in the early 1990s. The line between the colours is stark, and dreams of an Afrikaner Arcadia live on. It's not the easiest pill to swallow, but to grasp this country's complex social dynamics it's imperative to see the picture from every angle. And while there's no question that Free State has a long way to travel on the road to racial harmony, progress is happening. Today, even in the smallest rural villages, the once-impenetrable barrier between black and white is beginning to break apart.

HIGHLIGHTS

- Shopping for art in surprisingly sophisticated little **Clarens** (p387)
- Visiting **Golden Gate Highlands National Park** (p385) at sunset when the pistachio grasslands and sandstone formations glow golden
- Traversing the **Sentinel Hiking Trail** (p386), which leads up over the dizzying heights of the Drakensberg plateau
- Following the Tolkein trail in **Bloemfontein** (p375), a town full of college kids and judicial bigwigs that's also home to funky old pubs
- Hanging in beautiful **Rustlers Valley** (p389), where you'll find stunning views and two ultra-cool guesthouses

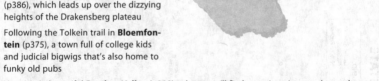

- POPULATION: 2.7 MILLION
- AREA: 129,480 SQ KM

FREE STATE

LEGEND
GR Game Reserve
NP National Park
NR Nature Reserve

100 km
60 miles

MPUMALANGA

KWAZULU-NATAL

EASTERN CAPE

NORTH-WEST PROVINCE

NORTHERN CAPE

LESOTHO

FREE STATE

Maluti Mountains

Drakensberg

To Swaziland (120km)
To Ermelo
To Durban (80km)
To Johannesburg (40km)
To Cape Town (750km)

Newcastle, Dundee, Glencoe, Ladysmith, Van Reenen, Harrismith, Collins Pass, Memel, Warden, Mullers Pass, Moolen River Pass, Chelmsford Dam, Estcourt, Greytown, Pietermaritzburg, Umzinto, Umzimkulu River, Umsinduzi River

Standerton, Volksrust, Vrede, Cornelia, Villiers, Frankfort, Tweeling, Reitz, Petrus Steyn, Arlington, Bethlehem, Kestell, Phuthaditjhaba, Golden Gate Highlands NP, Sterkfontein Dam, Woodstock Dam, Mokhotlong, Orange River

Balfour, Vereeniging, Vanderbijlpark, Sasolburg, Heilbron, Koppies, Kroonstad, Lindley, Senekal, Marquard, Clocolan, Ficksburg, Fouriesburg, Clarens, Kgubetswana, Paul Roux, Rosendal

Potchefstroom, Viljoenskroon, Vredefort, Parys, Vierfontein, Odendaalsrus, Virginia, Welkom, Ventersburg, Winburg, Theunissen, Brandfort, Soutpan

Klerksdorp, Bothaville, Wesselsbron, Hoopstad, Bultfontein, Dealesville, Boshof, Hertzogville

Wolmaransstad, Bloemhof Dam, Bloemhof, Sandveld NR, Warrenton, Kimberley, Ritchie, Jacobsdal, Koffiefontein, Fauresmith, Jagersfontein, Philippolis, Donkerpoort, Trompsburg, Springfontein, Bethulie, Gariep Dam, Gariep Dam NR, Colesberg, De Aar, Strydenburg, Hopetown, Britstown, Carnarvon, Prieska

Vryburg, Wigdol, Delareyville, Kuruman, Danielskuil, Hotazel, Koegelbeen Caves, Griekwastad (Griquatown), Postmasburg

Wonderwerk Caves, Vaalbos NP, Modder River, Riet River, Orange River, Vaal River, Harts River

Bloemfontein, Botshabelo, Dewetsdorp, Wepener, Zastron, Rouxville, Aliwal North, Smithfield, Reddersburg, Edenburg, Caledon River

Thaba Nchu, Tweespruit, Ladybrand, Excelsior, Tsejane, Maseru, Mafeteng, Maria Maroka NP, Hobhouse, Welbedacht Dam

Van Rooyens Gate, Mohale's Hoek, Makhaleng Bridge, Sepharo's Gate, Aasvoelberg (Vulture Mountain), Tussen-die-Riviere Farm, Tweespruit

Vaal Dam NR, Vaal Dam, Vaal River, Wilge River, Klip River, Rhenoster River, Liebenberg, Vresbergbaken, Willem Pretorius GR, Erfenis Dam, Sand River, Soetdoring NR, Petrusburg, Kalkfontein Dam NR

Drakensberg, Lesotho, Maletsunyane, Makheng, Katse Dam, Maluti Bridge, Teyateyaneng, Peka Bridge, Ficksburg Bridge, Caledonspoort, Golden Gate Highlands NP, Rustler's Valley, Visierskerf Peak

HISTORY
The Free State's borders reflect the prominent role it has played in the power struggles of South Africa's history. To the east,
across the Caledon River, is Lesotho, where
forbidding mountains combined with
the strategic warfare of the Sotho king
Moshoeshoe the Great halted the tide of
Boer expansion. To the southeast, however, Free State spills across the river as the
mountains dwindle into flat grassland –
this area proved harder for Moshoeshoe
to defend.

The Voortrekkers established their first
settlement near modern-day Thaba 'Nchu,
and various embryonic republics then came
and went, in addition to a period of British sovereignty after the 1899–1902 Anglo-
Boer War.

The 'Orange Free State' was created in
1854, with Bloemfontein as the capital. The
'Orange' part of the province's title was
dropped in 1994, following South Africa's
first democratic elections.

CLIMATE
The Free State experiences a dry, sunny climate from June to August, with showers,
thunderstorms and hail between October
and April. Snow falls quite thickly each
winter around the foothills of the Maluti
Mountains, near the Golden Gate Highlands National Park in the eastern highlands.

LANGUAGE
Sotho is the dominant tongue in the
Free State, followed by Afrikaans, Xhosa,
Tswana, Zulu and English (just 2% of the
Free State's inhabitants speak English as a
first language).

GETTING THERE & AROUND
Bloemfontein is well served by public transport, with trains and buses stopping here
on their way to and from Johannesburg
(Jo'burg) and Pretoria and southern parts
of the country. Likewise, it's easy to get to
and from Lesotho – taxis and buses leave
Thaba 'Nchu and Bloemfontein daily for
the border.

Elsewhere in the province, you'll need
to take your own vehicle, or rely on the
sporadic minibus taxis.

BLOEMFONTEIN

☎ 051 / pop 480,499
Whether you're coming from Jo'burg or
Cape Town, Kimberly or Lesotho, Bloemfontein's location, smack in the middle of
the country at the intersection of a few
major highways, makes it an ideal place to
crash. Easy and safe to navigate, there are
sophisticated restaurants and more than a
few great pubs to drown the memory of a
hard day's drive with icy pints of lager.

As the provincial capital of the Free State
and South Africa's judicial capital, tourism
in Bloem (as the locals call it) is generally
business oriented. But it's also a university
town, so when school's in session, nightlife is raging. There's no real reason to go
out of your way to visit Bloem, although
it has a few interesting sights if you are
in the neighbourhood. It's definitely more
of a jumping off point than anything else.
However, if you've got some time to kill
within city limits this relaxed place boasts a
few interesting attractions, including one of
South Africa's most striking galleries.

HISTORY
Originally called Manguang (Place of Cheetahs) by the Tswana people who inhabited
it, today the Afrikaans name translates to
'Fountain of Flowers.' Bloemfontein became
the capital of the newly minted Orange Free
State in 1854. At the time it was a struggling frontier village in constant danger of
being wiped out by the soldiers of Sotho king
Moshoeshoe. By the end of Johannes Brand's
25-year term as president, however, Bloem
had grown into a wealthy city with imposing
buildings and rail links to the coast.

ORIENTATION
There are endless sprawling suburbs in
Bloemfontein but the central area is laid
out on a grid and is easy to navigate. Hoffman Sq is the centre of the downtown area.
Botshabelo, on the Thaba 'Nchu road, is one
of the largest townships in the country.

INFORMATION
Internet Access
Connix Internet (☎ 051-448 5648; Loch Logan Waterfront; per hr R30) A flash place in the Waterfront shopping
centre, with fast connections and prices to match.

FREE STATE

LORD OF BLOEMFONTEIN

JRR Tolkein, author of *Lord of the Rings*, was born in Bloemfontein in 1892. Although he moved to England when he was five, his recollection of the Bloemfontein district as 'hot, dry and barren' is considered a sign by Bloem's residents that his years here inspired him to create the legendary kingdom of Mordor. Or perhaps, as some graffiti in a Cape Town pub once said, 'Tolkein was just another Bloemfontein boy on acid'...

Regardless, if you're interested in learning more about the local Tolkein scene, head over to the **Hobbit Boutique Hotel** (p379), home of the local Tolkein literary society. They can direct you towards the house where Tolkein was born, the cathedral he was baptised in, and to the grave where his father is buried. Although the town had high hopes of cashing in on the *Lord of the Rings* movie craze a few years ago (a provincial tourism official was once quoted as saying 'Tolkein is Bloemfontein's best kept secret') its 'Tolkein Trail' hasn't quite taken flight as quickly as town promoters had hoped. Still, if you're in the area, and fascinated with all things JRR Tolkein, it is definitely worth strolling over to the Hobbit for a cosy fireside chat – ask to speak with manager Jake Uys.

Money

There are banks with ATMs in the town centre and handy ATMs at the tourist centre and at the Waterfront.

ABSA In the Pick 'n' Pay Centre opposite the western side of the Mimosa Mall (with bureau de change).

Amex (Mimosa Mall)

Post

Main post office (Groenendal St) Near Hoffman Sq.

Tourist Information

Free State Department of Environmental Affairs & Tourism (☎ 051-405 4062; fax 051-403 3778; PO Box 264, Bloemfontein 9300) For information about national parks and reserves in the area, phone or write.

Information centre (☎ 051-405 8489; www.bloem fontein.co.za; 60 Park Rd; ⏱ 8am-4.15pm Mon-Fri; 8am-noon Sat) Pick up a walking-tour map here and a *Bloemfontein Art Route* brochure for galleries, museums and handicraft outlets.

Tourist centre (Park Rd) Long-distance buses arrive here, and there are ticket counters for all major bus companies.

SIGHTS & ACTIVITIES

Surprisingly, Bloem has quite a few noteworthy attractions.

Oliewenhuis Art Museum

One of South Africa's most striking art galleries, the **Oliewenhuis Art Museum** (☎ 051-447 9609; oliewen@nasmus.co.za; 16 Harry Smith St; admission by donation; ⏱ 8am-5pm Mon-Fri, 10am-5pm Sat, 1-5pm Sun) is housed in an exquisite 1935 mansion. The gallery's name comes from the wild olive trees growing in the beautiful gardens that surround it. It holds a collection of

works by South African artists, including Thomas Baines. There's also a strong contemporary collection.

Many an hour can be spent lazing at one of the tables in the museum's café, the Terrace at Oliewenhuis, which has breakfast and lunch mains for R20 to R35 (it's closed on Monday).

National Women's Memorial & Anglo-Boer War Museum

Commemorating the 26,000 women and children who died in British concentration camps during the 1899–1902 Anglo-Boer War (see p378), the National Women's Memorial is the creation of well-known South African sculptor Anton von Wouw. The sandstone obelisk depicts a bearded Afrikaner, setting off on his pony to fight the British, bidding a last farewell to his wife and baby, who are to perish in one of the camps. It's a powerful image and one still buried in the psyche of many Afrikaners.

The memorial is in front of the **Anglo-Boer War Museum** (☎ 051-447 3447; Monument Rd; admission R5; ⏱ 8am-4.30pm Mon-Fri, 10am-5pm Sat, 2-5pm Sun), which has some interesting displays, including photos from concentrations camps set up not only in South Africa, but also in Bermuda, India and Portugal.

Manguang

You can hang out in the *shebeens* (unlicensed bars) or eat a simple meal at a local dive with people you're unlikely to meet on a trip to the Waterfront or the Mystic Boer (p379) in the vibrant Manguang township.

BLOEMFONTEIN

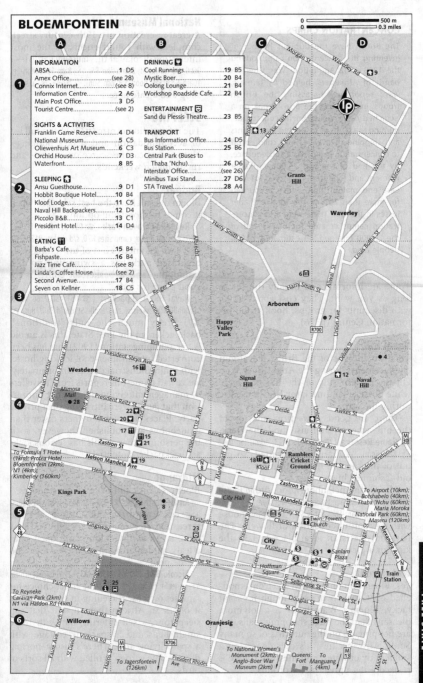

INFORMATION		
ABSA	1	D5
Amex Office	(see 28)	
Connix Internet	(see 8)	
Information Centre	2	A6
Main Post Office	3	D5
Tourist Centre	(see 2)	

SIGHTS & ACTIVITIES		
Franklin Game Reserve	4	D4
National Museum	5	C5
Oliewenhuis Art Museum	6	C3
Orchid House	7	D3
Waterfront	8	B5

SLEEPING		
Ansu Guesthouse	9	D1
Hobbit Boutique Hotel	10	B4
Kloof Lodge	11	C5
Naval Hill Backpackers	12	D4
Piccolo B&B	13	C1
President Hotel	14	D4

EATING		
Barba's Cafe	15	B4
Fishpaste	16	B4
Jazz Time Café	(see 8)	
Linda's Coffee House	(see 2)	
Second Avenue	17	B4
Seven on Kellner	18	C5

DRINKING		
Cool Runnings	19	B5
Mystic Boer	20	B4
Oolong Lounge	21	B4
Workshop Roadside Cafe	22	B4

ENTERTAINMENT		
Sand du Plessis Theatre	23	B5

TRANSPORT		
Bus Information Office	24	D5
Bus Station	25	B6
Central Park (Buses to Thaba 'Nchu)	26	D6
Interstate Office	(see 26)	
Minibus Taxi Stand	27	D6
STA Travel	28	A4

FREE STATE

CONCENTRATION CAMPS

The British have the dubious honour of inventing the concentration camp, during the 1899–1902 Anglo-Boer War. Guerrilla bands of Afrikaners, helped by farmers, were reportedly harassing the British troops. In response the British took on a 'scorched earth' policy in the countryside, burning the farms of suspected combatants and shipping their wives and children off to concentration camps. As a consequence, by the end of the war 26,000 Afrikaner women and children had died of disease and malnutrition, which accounted for more than 70% of the total Afrikaner losses in the war. There were also concentration camps created for blacks and of the 80,000 interned, an estimated 14,000 people died.

Tours are informal and usually run for as long as you want. They cost about R200, with discounts for groups. Book at the Information Centre (p376).

Naval Hill

This was the site of the British naval-gun emplacements during the Anglo-Boer War. On the eastern side of the hill is a large white horse, a landmark for British cavalry during the war.

There are good views from the top of the hill, where you'll also find the **Franklin Game Reserve** (☎ 051-405 8124; admission free; ☼ 8am-5pm). Walking is permitted, so get out of the car and hit the trail for a good old-fashioned bush romp.

Also in the neighbourhood, **Orchid House** (☎ 051-405 8488; admission free; Union Ave; ☼ 10am-6pm Mon-Fri, 10am-5pm Sat & Sun) is a glasshouse with a beautiful collection of flowers. The park outside is an ideal place to take the kids for a picnic.

Waterfront

Yes, Bloemfontein has a Waterfront, modelled on Cape Town's. Although it's a bit tacky, Bloem's Waterfront is a lot more pleasant than the huge shopping malls that are popping up on the outskirts of so many South African cities. It's outside, set on a small body of water, and the atmosphere is relaxed – it's a great place for kids.

National Museum

A great re-creation of a 19th-century street, complete with sound effects, is the most interesting display at this **museum** (☎ 051-447 9609; 36 Aliwal St; admission R5; ☼ 8am-5pm Mon-Fri, 10am-5pm Sat, noon-5.30pm Sun). There is also a shop and a café here.

SLEEPING

The information centre (p376) has a full list of accommodation and makes bookings. Note rooms can be scarce on cricket- and rugby-match weekends.

Budget

Bloem doesn't have the best selection when it comes to shoestring options.

Reyneke Caravan Park (☎ 051-523 3888; fax 523 3887; Petrusburg Rd; camp sites R70, s/d chalets R180/220; ☒) Two kilometres out of town, this well-organised park has a swimming pool, a trampoline and a basketball court. It's a good place for kids.

Naval Hill Backpackers (☎ 051-430 7266; www .navalhillbackpackers.co.za; Delville St; dm/d R80/180; P ☐) Pretty much the only 'traditional' backpackers in the Free State, this is an old water-pumping station (1902) that has been converted into an über-cool looking hostel with funky industrial décor. Unfortunately, we've had numerous reports from travellers of management giving the distinct impression that guests were intruding on a private party. Places can switch owners faster than guidebooks are published, however, so if the personnel change this has serious kick-ass backpacker potential.

Midrange

Bloem is chock-full of small guesthouses.

Ansu Guesthouse (☎ 051-436 4654; www.ansuguesthouse.com; 80 Waverley Rd; s/d R220/260; P ☒) The three modern rooms here are light and airy, done up in earthy colours and open onto a leafy garden area where there's a gazebo by the pool.

Piccolo B&B (☎ 051-436 1483; kay@imaginet.co.za; 4 Prophet St; r from R250; P) A perfect choice for families or those travelling in small groups, it offers an African-themed unit that can sleep four, a self-catering flat with three single beds and a spacious cottage with a spare living area. There's also a normal double. The garden is filled with all sorts of birds.

FREE STATE

Formula 1 Hotel (☎ 051-444 3523; cnr Nelson Mandela Ave & Kriega St; r R299; P 🚭) This cut-price hotel west of Kings Park is a bit claustrophobic but cheap and spotless. Rooms sleep up to three people (in a double bed and a bunk).

Kloof Lodge (☎ 051-447 7603; kloof@global.co.za; 7 Kellner St; s/d R300/400; P ✕ 🚭) This rambling place is nothing fancy, but perfectly comfortable for a night. There's a cosy bar and lounge and you'll find a very good restaurant, Seven on Kellner (right), just next door. Prices include a full breakfast (think eggs, sausages etc). Ask for the luxury room – it's huge, boasts cooler furniture and costs the same.

Top End

Bloem has a few luxurious options.

President Hotel (☎ 051-430 1111; 1 Union Ave; s/d R485/560; P 🚭 🖳 🍽) The President is very modern and shiny looking with lots of gold trim and offers all the amenities of a well-managed business-class hotel – slightly bland but comfortable rooms with soft sheets and fluffy towels, TVs with more than one channel and the requisite pub and restaurant.

Hobbit Boutique Hotel (☎ 051-447 0663; www .hobbit.co.za; 19 President Steyn Ave; s/d with breakfast R600/800; P 🚭 🖳 🍽) This charming old-world hotel, comprising two 1921 houses, is the winner of numerous awards for service and décor. The cottage-style bedrooms have sprigged counterpanes and painted bathtubs, plus a couple of teddy bears apiece. There's a great view from the outdoor patio. The reading room has a chess table and the local Tolkein society meets here to talk about all things JRR. The hotel is popular with visiting dignitaries, but also perfect for literati and romantic types.

Protea Hotel Bloemfontein (☎ 051-444 4321; bloemf@iafrica.com; 202 Nelson Mandela Ave, Brandweg; s/d R645/960; P 🖳 🍽) This place is smart and glossy and part of the Protea Luxury Collection. The upscale all-white rooms are Asian-inspired minimalist and quite calming to sleep in. You can order drinks on the terrace by the long, skinny pool in summer or check out the year-round onsite gourmet restaurant and cocktail bar with a fireplace.

EATING

Many of the hotels and guesthouses do their own meals in the evenings, but there are a few good restaurants in Bloem, along with the usual fast-food joints in the Waterfront and Mimosa Mall shopping centres.

Fishpaste (☎ 051-430 2662; 31 President Steyn Ave; mains R30-50; 🕑 lunch & dinner Mon-Fri, dinner Sat) Fishpaste is a rare thing – a Free State restaurant with a trendy, funky interior and an interesting modern fusion menu. Choose from blackened Canadian salmon with green-bean salad, Vietnamese prawn rolls or rolled pork fillet. The fashionably black-clad staff are super-friendly, the bar is buzzy and the prices extremely reasonable.

Seven on Kellner (☎ 051-447 7928; 7 Kellner St; mains R50-80; 🕑 lunch & dinner) An eclectic restaurant with a very trendy lounge vibe, this place does everything from wood-fired pizzas to many Middle Eastern and Indian inspired delights. The food is delicious. Afterwards chill in an ultra-cool chair on the patio with a bottle of bubbly picked from the extensive wine list.

Barba's Café (☎ 051-430 2542; 16 2nd Ave; 🕑 breakfast, lunch & dinner Mon-Sat) Barba's is recommended by locals and rightly so: it's one of Bloem's hidden secrets. The Greek specialities are delicious. It has mezze (R140 for two), a large cocktail list and live music on Wednesday.

Jazz Time Café (☎ 051-430 5727; Waterfront; mains R20-50; 🕑 lunch & dinner) This hip eatery has an interesting menu featuring zippy *zivas* – Yemeni-style layered dough wrapped around a variety of fillings (such as Cajun chicken, feta and avocado), folded and toasted. There are cocktails and jazz recitals in the evenings – unusual in the rock-orientated Bloemfontein music scene.

Second Avenue (☎ 051-448 3088; 2nd Ave; mains R20-40; 🕑 lunch & dinner) It's kind of tacky looking, with galvanized steel-light fixtures and slate tiles, but this student diner-cum-bar gets rocking when university is in session and crowds pile in to socialise and tackle the 'tower of beer'.

Linda's Coffee House (☎ 051-430 6436; Park Rd; mains R17-32; 🕑 24hr) Near the information desk at the Tourist Centre, Linda's does good breakfasts (and coffee) for those early bus arrivals. If everywhere else is closed, it's a great option.

DRINKING & ENTERTAINMENT

As a university town, Bloemfontein has a good range of places to drink, party and, increasingly, listen to live music. The corners of 2nd Ave and Kellner St, and Zastron St and Nelson Mandela Ave bustle with revellers in the evening and compete for the nightlife scene with the Waterfront.

Mystic Boer (☎ 051-430 2206; 84 Kellner St) Bloem's most popular pub and live music venue provides an eccentric twist to Afrikaner culture, with psychedelic pictures of long-bearded Boers on the walls. One 'big' band plays per month, plus there are regular gigs by unsigned rock and (sometimes) hip-hop outfits. The bar specialises in tequila, while pizza and burgers provide the fuel.

Oolong Lounge (☎ 051-448 7244; 16a 2nd Ave; ☻ Tue-Sat) Bloem's latest hotspot, this ultra hip lounge attracts a trendy young crowd. The super-mod interior is slick and shiny with black leather chairs and space for dancing. Light meals are served.

Cool Runnings (☎ 051-430 7364; 163 Nelson Mandela Ave; admission R5-10) This is part of a nationwide chain of Caribbean-themed bar-restaurants, with DJs and live bands at weekends and karaoke on Sundays. Forget about reggae – the music on offer is the ubiquitous rock and blues.

Workshop Roadside Cafe (☎ 051-447 2761; cnr 2nd Ave & President Reitz St) A large, raucous pub with loud music, a big-screen TV and a reputation as a bit of a bikers' hangout, it's a good place to sink a few beers.

Sand du Plessis Theatre (☎ 051-552 4071; cnr Markgraaff & St Andrews Sts) The local paper lists music, ballet, drama and opera performances held at this striking modern building in the town centre.

There are cinemas in the Mimosa Mall and at the Waterfront.

GETTING THERE & AWAY
Air
Bloemfontein airport is 10km from the city centre and there is no transport to/from the airport, except private taxi.

SAAirlink (☎ 051-433 3225) and **Nationwide Airlines** (☎ 011 344 7200; www.flynationwide.co.za) connect Bloemfontein with Cape Town (R1200) and Jo'burg (R1000) among other destinations.

STA Travel (☎ 051-444 6062; laudep@statravel.co.za; Mimosa Mall) can organise flights.

Bus
Long-distance buses leave from the tourist centre in Park Rd. **Translux** (☎ 051-408 4888;

www.translux.co.za) runs daily buses to Durban (R150, nine hours), Jo'burg/Pretoria (R150, five hours), Port Elizabeth (R200, nine hours), East London (R180, seven hours), Knysna (R270, 12 hours) and Cape Town (R320, 10 hours).

Greyhound (☎ 051-447 1558; www.greyhound.co.za) runs daily buses to Durban (R230, 9½ hours), Pretoria (R200, seven hours), Cape Town (R360, 12 hours) and Port Elizabeth (R230, 10 hours).

A bus called **Interstate** (☎ 051-448 4951) runs from the information centre in Bloem to Thaba 'Nchu every hour (R10). There's also a shuttle bus to Bloem run by the hotels in Thaba 'Nchu daily except Tuesday and Thursday. The ticket price of R50 includes vouchers for drinks, food and a game on the casino tables. Book both at the tourist centre.

Big Sky Buses (www.bigskycoaches.co.za) run from the Central Park shopping centre in St Georges St to Maseru in Lesotho (R35, three hours) at 6.10am and 2.10pm Monday to Friday.

Minibus Taxi
Most minibus taxis leave from opposite the train station for Maseru, Lesotho (R45, three hours), Kimberley (R50, four hours) and Jo'burg (R80, six hours). There's usually at least one bus daily, but times vary.

Train
The **Shosholoza Meyl** (☎ 0860-008 888; www.spoornet.co.za) *Trans Oranje* runs weekly via Bloemfontein between Cape Town (1st/2nd/economy class R390/265/155) and Durban (R270/185/110). The *Algoa* runs five times weekly via Bloemfontein between Jo'burg (1st/2nd/economy R145/100/55, about seven hours) and Port Elizabeth (R235/160/95). The *Amatola* runs five times weekly via Bloemfontein on the run between Jo'burg (1st/2nd/economy R145/100/55) and East London (R210/145/85). The *Diamond Express* runs three times weekly between Bloemfontein and Jo'burg (1st/2nd/economy R145/100/90).

GETTING AROUND
Bloem's public-bus system, Interstate, provides infrequent services that finish early in the evening. The best place for schedules and information is the **Interstate office**

(☎ 051-448 4951) in the Central Park shopping centre in St Georges St. There is also a **bus information office** (Hoffman Sq).

If you're after a private taxi, try **President Taxis** (☎ 051-522 3399).

AROUND BLOEMFONTEIN
Thaba 'Nchu
☎ 051 / pop 38,693

Thaba 'Nchu (ta-*baan*-chu, meaning 'Black Mountain') is a small Tswana town east of Bloemfontein. The surrounding area was once a small piece of the scattered Bophuthatswana homeland, and this too was known as Thaba 'Nchu. As with most homelands, a Sun casino was built here.

Unless you're a compulsive gambler, it's hard to see any reason to stop here. If you'd like to try your luck, then hit the N8 to the **Protea Thaba 'Nchu** (☎ 051-871 4200; fax 051-873 2161; www.proteahotels.com; r R800; ✹ ▣).

About 10km from Thaba 'Nchu, it has well-appointed rooms, restaurants, lounges and the casino. There are often discounts.

There's a free shuttle that operates between town and the Protea Thaba 'Nchu hotel – call the hotel for a schedule.

Maria Moroka National Park
This small **national park** (☎ 051-873 2427) in a pretty, hilly location outside Thaba 'Nchu protects zebras, elands and red hartebeests among other species. You can hike through the park on a couple of different trails or stay the night in one of the self-catering chalets (R90 per person). The rangers offer guided wildlife drives. You'll need your own vehicle to get there. Enquire at the entrance about accommodation bookings.

NORTHERN FREE STATE

The towns sprinkled around this maize-farming region are decidedly untouristy, usually comprising little more than small rural enclaves in nowhere places. Unless you're really interested in mining or yearning to spend a few days on a farm, there's not much to attract travellers to the northern Free State.

Gold was discovered around here in April 1938 and a rush started immediately. Now the Free State goldfields produce more than a third of the country's output.

WINBURG & AROUND
It's difficult to imagine that the sleepy little town of Winburg, founded in 1842, was once the first capital of a Boer republic in the present-day Free State. It was in the dining room of Ford's Hotel (now a large shop on the town square) that the leaders of five Voortrekker groups finally agreed to form a government under the leadership of Piet Retief. Unless you're a serious South African history buff, however, there is little reason to visit Winburg.

Off the N1, about 20km north of Winburg and 70km south of Kroonstad, is the **Willem Pretorius Game Reserve** (☎ 057-651 4003; admission R20; ☒ 7am-6.30pm). Split in two by the Sand River and Allemanskraal Dam, the reserve encompasses two different ecosystems: grassy plains with large herds of eland, blesbok, springbok, black wildebeest and zebras; and, further north, the bushy mountain region with baboons, mountain reedbuck and duiker. White rhino and buffalo are equally at home on either side of the reserve.

A range of accommodation is available at **Aldam Resort** (☎ 057-652 2200; fax 057-652 0014; camp sites from R60; 2-bed chalets R380, 4-bed units R500), much of which has magnificent views over Allemanskraal Dam. Rates increase on weekends and in high season. The resort is near the dam and well sign-posted in the reserve. Fishing is popular here (you need to get a Free State angling licence from the resort) and there are hiking trails.

WELKOM
☎ 057 / pop 457,612

If you're interested in South Africa's gold mining industry (Welkom is at the centre of the Goldfields area) or you are a serious birder (there are more than 200 species present), Welkom is worth a stop. Otherwise don't bother going out of the way to visit this rather soulless, modern town. It is something of a showpiece, however, as it was completely planned – there are no traffic lights, which is touted as proof of a masterpiece of town planning.

Orientation
Stateway is Welkom's main street. Not far from Stateway is Mooi St, with most of the central shopping area in its horseshoe curve.

Information

First National Bank (Elizabeth St)

Main post office (Bok St)

Welkom information centre (☎ 057-352 9244; ☺ 8am-4.30pm Mon-Fri) In the clock tower at the Civic Centre on Stateway.

Sights & Activities

Tours of the **mines** in Welkom can be arranged by contacting the information centre in advance – they are informal affairs that go out when there's enough interest. Prices vary. The huge mine-evaporation pans are home to a wide variety of **birdlife**, including the greater and lesser flamingo and the grey-headed gull. More than 200 species of bird have been seen around the city, and this number accounts for 90% of all waterfowl species found in South Africa! Try Flamingo Pan, off the Rte 30 just west of the town, or Witpan at Oppenheimer Park, about 4km southeast of the town centre on the continuation of Stateway. Two other bird-watching spots are Theronia and Flamingo Lakes.

Sleeping & Eating

Stanville Inn (☎ 057-353 2452; 180 Tempest Rd; s/d R175/220; ❷) Stanville has spick-and-span budget rooms with TV and telephone. It's opposite Dagbreek Primary School.

Welkom Inn (☎ 057-357 3361; w-inn@global.co.za; cnr Stateway & Tempest Rd; s/d R300/345; ❷ ❷) This place is three-star rated and is a few blocks east of the centre. Neat rooms have TV and telephone. There's an attached O'Hagan's bar and restaurant. The food is decent and the bar can get lively.

Saddles Steak Ranch (☎ 057-353 4248; Stateway; mains R40-50) Opposite the Sanlam Plaza, Saddles is another southern African chain. The atmosphere is a bit cheesy Western, but the place does decent steaks among other hearty fare.

Getting There & Away

Several **Intercape** (☎ 0861-287 287; www.intercape .co.za) services stop daily in town on their way to destinations including Cape Town (R380, 15 hours), Bloemfontein (R120, two hours) and Jo'burg (R185, four hours).

The minibus taxis in the supermarket car park in town are mainly for the local area but you may find long-distance taxis here for Jo'burg (R55, four hours) or Cape Town (R130, 14 hours) in the early morning.

KROONSTAD

☎ 056 / pop 106,064

Kroonstad, on the N1, is a typical large, rural Free State town and makes a good base for exploring nearby Koppies Dam Nature Reserve, an anglers paradise. The town dates back to 1855, and the Voortrekker Sarel Celliers was one of the first settlers here. Kroonstad may have been named after the Voortrekker's horse, Kroon!

There's Internet access at **Compuwise** (☎ 056-213 4368; cnr Orange & President Sts; per hr R20; ☺ 7.30am-5pm Mon-Fri, 7.30am-1pm Sat) in the centre of town.

Sights & Activities

The **old market building** (cnr Mark & Murray Sts), opposite the pretty magistrate's building, is a national monument. You can see the **Celliers statue** in the grounds of the impressive **NG Moederkerk** (Mother Church; Cross St). Celliers is standing on a gun carriage making the Blood River vow.

Kroon Park (admission R20) offers swimming and other water activities (below).

The **national tournament of Jukskei** (an Afrikaner game in which clubs are tossed at a peg) is held annually in Kroonstad.

The 4000-hectare **Koppies Dam Nature Reserve** (☎ 056-72 2521; ☺ 7am-9pm), located about 70km northeast of Kroonstad on the Rhenoster River, is popular with anglers. Yellowfish, barbell, mudfish and carp are all abundantly available. Windsurfing, sailing, and water-skiing are also very popular here – although you'll have to have your own equipment and transport, or make friends.

Sleeping & Eating

Kroon Park (☎ 056-213 1942; fax 213 1941; camp sites R50, 2-/4-person chalets R200/250; ❷) With a couple of swimming pools, river tubing, boat rides and some beautiful camping spots on the river's edge, this place feels more like a resort than a municipal park. Book ahead during holiday seasons. It's well signposted from town.

Arcadia Guesthouse (☎ 056-212 8280; arcadia@gcs .co.za; s/d with breakfast R280/350) This smart guesthouse with classically-themed rooms is in the middle of a large garden scattered with faux-Greek statues. Dinner can be arranged (R60). It's well signposted in town.

Angelo's Trattoria (☎ 056-213 2833; 38 Reitz St; mains R30-65; ☺ lunch & dinner) Pizza with biltong (dried, salted meat), fettuccini with steak – the menu here is all about Italy merging with the African bush. The dining area is cosy. Look for it opposite the mosque.

Getting There & Away

There are daily **Translux** (☎ 408 4888; www.trans lux.co.za) services to Jo'burg/Pretoria (R150, four hours), East London (R220, 10 hours) and Paarl (R240, 14 hours). **Intercape** (☎ 0861-287 287; www.intercape.co.zaand) and **Greyhound** (☎ 477 1558; www.greyhound.co.za) also travel this route. All buses stop out on the highway at the Shell Ultra City.

The minibus taxi rank is opposite the train station. There are occasional buses to Jo'burg (R45, four hours) – ask around the taxi ranks to see if they're running. Otherwise minibus service is pretty much a local affair.

PARYS & VREDEFORT DOME

☎ 056 / pop 75,464

Parys, right on the border with the North-West Province, is handy for visiting Vredefort Dome, an area of hills created by the impact of a gigantic meteorite 2000 million years ago. Vredefort is the oldest and largest meteorite impact site on earth, measuring around 200km in diameter. In 2005 the dome was named a Unesco World Heritage Site, South Africa's sixth, which was more than a big deal for the little town.

The area around Parys is quite beautiful, consisting of valleys, ravines and cliffs, covered in lush flora and home to a variety of different plants, animals and birds. Activities on offer include abseiling and whitewater rafting. Although tourism is still in its infancy here, the place is slowly but surely taking off.

The **Parys Info Centre** (☎ 056-817 2986; www .parysinfo.co.za; 62b Bree St; ⏰ 8am-5pm Mon-Fri, 8am-1pm Sat) does bookings for the many adventure trails and camping sites in the Dome area.

This engaging area is best reached by private transport.

Sleeping & Eating

Suikerbos (☎ 018-294 3857; www.suikerbos.co.za; camp sites R60, dm R60, hut from R120, chalet from R400) Bookings are essential if you want to stay at this very popular farm-reserve where herds of impala graze peacefully between the

buildings. The chalets are airy and modern, with giant bathtubs and loads of light. You can also choose from simpler, and cheaper huts, or dorms in the main lodge. The reserve has a swimming hole and plenty of hiking and mountain biking trails.

Waterfront Guesthouse (☎ 083-452 6504; devills@ global.co.za; 22 Grewar Ave; s/d with breakfast R400/600; ✗ ⚫ ⚫ ⚫) The hospitality is warm at this upscale guesthouse that prides itself on being gay friendly. It's located down by the Vaal River, and rooms come with shiny bedspreads and mosquito netting. All sorts of activities can be arranged, including fishing and rafting trips, at the onsite info centre. Lunch and dinner are prepared upon request.

Mirro's (☎ 056-817 7191; 62 Bree St; mains R20-50; ⏰ lunch & dinner Tue-Sun) This little restaurant does half-decent pizza, along with steaks and burgers.

EASTERN HIGHLANDS

Bumped up against the wild and rugged mountains that guard Lesotho's border, this is the most beautiful portion of the Free State and well worth exploring. Long popular with weekenders from surrounding areas, the provincial government is now trying hard to get the word out to international visitors.

Encompassing an area roughly from Rte 26 and Rte 49 east of Bethlehem to Harrismith, the region boasts sandstone monoliths towering above undulating golden fields, hippy hideaways, fabulous country retreats and South Africa's newest art destination, trendy little Clarens.

HARRISMITH

☎ 058 / pop 35,178

The quiet rural centre of Harrismith features picturesque old buildings and a grassy square. It is well situated for exploring the northern Drakensberg range, and there are opportunities to partake in informal and untouristy township tours.

The **Harrismith Marketing Bureau** (☎ 058-622 3525; Pretoria St; ⏰ 9am-5pm Mon-Fri) in the back of the town hall can help with any local information.

There's Internet access at the **Koppie Shop** (Stuart St; per min R0.60; ⏰ 9am-5pm Mon-Fri).

FREE STATE

Sights & Activities

The marketing bureau arranges tours (R25) of Intabazwe, a township on a hill outside town. It can also arrange accommodation (around R150 with half board) there. It's inspiring to see a small, conservative town promoting this sort of thing, and the peaceful township is small enough for visitors to get a good feel for township life. Unusually for Free State, both Zulu and Sotho people live here.

The extensive **botanic gardens** (☎ 058-623 1078; admission R5; ⌚ 7am-7pm Sep-May, 7.30am-7pm Jun-Aug), about 5km south of town at the foot of the Platberg, have many plant species from the Drakensberg. Walking on the slopes of the Platberg you may see a few antelope species – there was once a nature reserve here.

Sleeping & Eating

Harrismith International Backpackers (☎ 058-623 0007; jmantz@oldmutualpfa.com; 44 Piet Retief St; camp sites/dm R30/55) There is a garden and braai (barbecue) facilities in this comfy B&B-cum-backpackers. The staff are able to arrange pick-ups from major bus stops in the area.

Sahara Lodge (☎ 058-622 2151; fax 058-622 2152; 100 McKechnie St; s/d from R225/320;) Under renovation (and new management) when we stopped by, this place is a lot more charming inside than it looks from the exterior. Rooms are in self-contained chalet-like structures. The executive suites are very plush, with sleek African furnishings. Look for it behind the BP petrol station at the N5 junction.

Pringles Country Inn & Restaurant (☎ 058-623 0255; louise@pringles-wimpy.co.za; Warden St; s/d R240/360;) There is nothing 'country' about this place, but it will do for a night. A newish motel right off the highway, it has smart rooms. Its restaurant (mains R25 to R50) is the best dining option in town, serving old-fashioned stodge such as bangers and mash, and lamb hotpot. Look for Pringles at the Bergview 1-stop petrol station.

Harrismith Inn (☎ 058-622 1011; harrismithinn@ dorea.co.za; McKechnie St; s/d R320/420;) Clean and modern, rooms are spacious with tile baths, TV and two double beds.

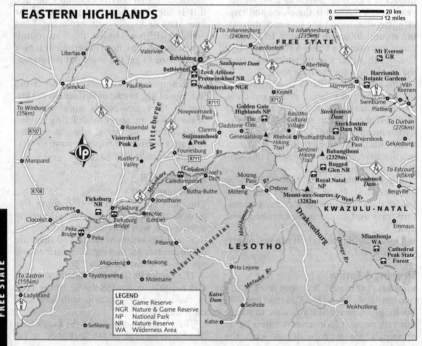

EASTERN HIGHLANDS

LEGEND
GR   Game Reserve
NGR Nature & Game Reserve
NP   National Park
NR   Nature Reserve
WA   Wilderness Area

The hotel has its own restaurant, which does a R45 breakfast buffet and à la carte choices (R20 to R40) at dinner. It's closed for lunch. Look for the hotel behind the Spur.

Getting There & Away

Translux (☎ 058-408 4888; www.translux.co.za) runs daily services to Durban (R150, four hours), Bloemfontein (R145, five hours), Jo'burg (R150, four hours) and Cape Town (R370, 17 hours), which stop at the Harrismith Country Lodge in McKechnie St.

The *Trans Oranje* train stops here daily between Durban (1st/2nd/economy class R135/95/55, eight hours) and Cape Town (R525/355/210, over 24 hours). See p380 for details.

AROUND HARRISMITH

The small **Sterkfontein Dam Nature Reserve** (☎ 058-622 3520; admission per vehicle R25; ⏰ 7.30am-10pm) is in a beautiful area of the Drakensberg foothills, 23km south of Harrismith on the Oliviershoek Pass road into KwaZulu-Natal. Looking out over this expansive dam with its backdrop of rugged peaks feels like gazing across an inland sea. At one of the many viewpoints there's a vulture 'restaurant', but there's no set day or time for feeding. Sunset cruises on the dam's lake are available.

Camp sites (R40) and rustic four-bed chalets (R200) are both available.

GOLDEN GATE HIGHLANDS NATIONAL PARK

Right before the darkness erases the remaining flecks of colour from the sky, something magical happens in **Golden Gate Highlands National Park** (☎ 058-255 0012; fax 058-255 0022; admission per vehicle R60). The jagged sandstone outcroppings fronting the foothills of the wild maroon-hued Maluti Mountains glow golden in the dying light; lemon yellow rays silhouette a lone kudu standing still in a sea of mint green grasses before the sky explodes in a fiery collision of purple and red.

The park might not boast any of the Big Five, but don't miss spending a sunset here if you're in the area. We'd suggest arriving around an hour before the sun is due to set (ask the locals when this happens as it changes throughout the year), this way

you'll have plenty of time to find the perfect spot. The scenery from the western approach is pretty tempting – loads of blazing sandstone and rusting old cars – but only stop here for a few moments, then head out into the open and take the turn-off for the Basatho Cultural Village. You'll now be off the main road and in the middle of the grasslands. Pull out a picnic basket, a bottle of good South African red and a bit of biltong (beef jerky) and toast the end of another perfect African day. You can pick up great picnic supplies at Mezzlauna Deli (p388) in Clarens.

There are quite a few animals in the park, including grey rheboks, blesboks, elands, oribis, Burchell's zebras, jackals, baboons and numerous bird species, including the rare bearded and Cape vulture as well as the endangered bald ibis. The park is popular with hikers on long treks, but there are also shorter walking trails. Winters (June to August) in the park can be very cold, with frost and snow; summers (January to March) are mild but rain falls at this time and cold snaps are possible: if you're out hiking, take warm clothing. Buy entry permits at the park reception.

Sights & Activities
RHEBOK HIKING TRAIL

This well-maintained, circular, 33km trail (R70 per person) is a two-day trek and offers a great way to see the park. The trail takes its name from the grey rhebok, a species of antelope that prefers exposed mountain plateaus, and you will probably see them while you're hiking. The trail starts at the Glen Reenen Rest Camp, located next to the park reception, and on the second day the track climbs up to a viewpoint on the side of Generaalskop (2732m), the highest point in the park, from where Mont-aux-Sources and the Malutis can be seen. The return trail to Glen Reenen passes Langtoon Dam.

There are some steep sections so hikers need to be reasonably fit. The trail is limited to 18 people and must be booked through the **South African National (SAN) Parks Board** (☎ 012-428 9111; www.sanparks.org).

There are also shorter hiking trails in the foothills, ranging from 45 minutes to half a day. Ask at the park reception for details.

FREE STATE

BASOTHO CULTURAL VILLAGE

Within the park you'll find the small **Basotho Cultural Village** (☎ 058-721 0300; basotho@dorea.co .za; tours R20; ☯ 8am-4.30pm Mon-Fri, 8am-5pm Sat & Sun). It's essentially an open-air museum, peopled by actors depicting various aspects of traditional Sotho life. There's a curio shop and an outdoor restaurant, open for lunch and dinner, serving a few Sotho dishes. Try the homemade ginger beer.

A two-hour guided hiking trail (R25 per person) explores medicinal and other plants, and a rock-art site. You can stay in two-person self-catering rondavels (R400), but bring your own food.

Although this is a friendly place, with a lot of good information on traditional customs and culture, it is also essentially artificial and idealised. To see how most Sotho live, take a township tour in nearby Harrismith (p384), or cross the border into Lesotho (p550).

Sleeping

Glen Reenen Rest Camp (☎ 011-428 9111; 2-person camp sites R95, d chalets R380) Popular with South Africans on holiday, this place has well-maintained chalets and campsites by the river. A shop sells basic supplies.

Protea Hotel Golden Gate (☎ 058-255 1000; www.proteahotels.com/goldengate; s/d around R360/500, d chalets R470, buffet dinner R80; ☐) The park's only 'proper' hotel is in a fabulous locale (up against red sandstone cliffs), even if it looks a bit outdated from the exterior. It boasts wonderful terrace views and has a snug coffee shop made for relaxing.

Clarens (opposite) is another sleeping option, located just 17km away.

Getting There & Away

Rte 712 is a sealed road that runs into the park from Clarens, south of Bethlehem. Minibus taxis run between Bethlehem and Harrismith, via Clarens and Phuthaditjhaba, and go right through the park. Alternatively, with your own vehicle you can approach from Harrismith on Rte 74 and then Rte 712.

PHUTHADITJHABA & AROUND

☎ 058 / pop 88,906

Phuthaditjhaba, about 50km southwest of Harrismith, was the capital of the apartheid homeland of QwaQwa (master the 'click'

pronunciation and you'll win friends). QwaQwa (meaning 'Whiter than White') was named after the sandstone hill that dominates the area. It was created in the early 1980s as a homeland for southern Sotho people. The dumping of 200,000 people on a tiny patch of agriculturally unviable land, remote from employment centres, was one of the more obscene acts of apartheid. Today, the highlands around Phuthaditjhaba are great hiking country.

The **QwaQwa information centre** (☎ 058-713 0012; fax 713 4342; ☯ 8am-4.30pm Mon-Fri, 8am-9pm Sat & Sun), on the road through town, has hiking information.

The most famous of the hiking trails in the area is the 10km **Sentinel Hiking Trail**, which commences in Free State and ends in KwaZulu-Natal. The trail starts at the Sentinel car park, on the way up to Witie-shoek Mountain Resort Hotel at an altitude of 2540m, and runs for 4km to the top of the Drakensberg plateau, where the average height is 3000m. It's about a two-hour ascent for those of medium fitness. At one point you have to use a chain ladder that runs up over a set of sheer rocks. Those who find the ladder frightening can take the route up The Gully, which emerges at Beacon Buttress (although some hikers argue this route is even more hair-raising!). The reward for the steep ascent is majestic mountain scenery and the opportunity to climb Mont-aux-Sources (3282m).

There are several rudimentary cafés and hotels in Phuthaditjhaba – ask the information centre for recommendations as they are constantly changing.

Witsieshoek Mountain Resort Hotel (☎ 058-713 6361; fax 058 713 5274; s/d R200/300, dinner R65) about 15km south of Phuthaditjhaba, is reputedly South Africa's highest-altitude hotel and is a good source for local hiking information. The accommodation, however, is pretty basic.

Minibus taxis from Phuthaditjhaba to Harrismith (R10) and Bethlehem (R35), usually via Clarens, run daily.

If you're driving into Phuthaditjhaba from the north, you'll eventually get through the urban sprawl to the tourist information centre (look for a cluster of tall thatched roofs on the left). If you're heading for the Witsieshoek Mountain Resort Hotel or the Sentinel Hiking Trail, turn left at the traffic lights at the information centre and keep going.

CLARENS

☎ 058

The jewel of the Free State, Clarens is one of those places you stumble upon expecting little then find yourself talking about long after you depart. Set to a backdrop of craggy limestone rocks, hunter green hills, spun gold fields and the magnificent Maluti Mountains, this town of whitewashed buildings and quite shady streets is the perfect bucolic country retreat.

Surprisingly sophisticated, it's a bit of an art destination – with 18 galleries focusing on quality works by well-known South African artists. Also home to charming guesthouses (ranging from very simple to extraordinarily posh), gourmet restaurants, eclectic cafés and a myriad of adventure activities, it's easy to see why international celebrities like Prince Harry and Brad Pitt have chosen Clarens to shack up in.

Orientation & Information

Clarens sits at the junction of Rte 712 and Rte 711 (a back road between Bethlehem and Fouriesburg) and is 17km west of Golden Gate Highlands National Park. Main St is the main road through town, and most businesses are clustered around the big grassy town square. The place is small and easily negotiated by foot.

The **Clarens Tourism Centre** (☎ 058-256 1542; www.clarenstourism.co.za; ☽ 8am-5pm Mon-Thu, 8am-6pm Fri, 8am-4pm Sat & Sun) has info on the area.

Mountain Odyssey Tourism (☎ 058-256 1173; www.infoclarens.com; Main St; per min R1.50) offers pricey Internet access.

Sights & Activities

With tidy tree-lined streets and a myriad of boutiques and galleries to peruse, Clarens is made for aimless wandering. The quality of the art varies from gallery to gallery, but there are plenty of them to choose from, so if you don't like what you see at the first place, try the shop down the street. Keep an eye out for pieces by Pieter van der Westhuizen or Hannetjie de Clerq, two well-respected South African artists. Favourite shops include the **Art & Wine Gallery on Main** (☎ 058-256 1298; 279 Main St; ☽ 9am-5pm), offering a fantastic selection of regional wines

and paintings and the **Bibliophile** (☎ 058-256 1692; 313 Church St; ☽ 9am-4.30pm), a quaint bookshop with a huge range of titles and jazz CDs.

When you tire of browsing, head over to **Mountain Odyssey Tourism** (☎ 058-256 1173; www .infoclarens.com; Main St; ☽ 8am-6pm), a one-stop shop for all things outdoors. Popular excursions include quad-biking (R250, one hour) through Golden Gate Highlands National Park, white-water rafting (R380, three hours) on the dam-fed Ash River (some rapids rate as high as Class IV) and horse riding (R175, two hours) through the mountains. Tell them if you're an experienced rider and you'll have a chance to gallop.

There are also plenty of opportunities for fly-fishing on dams and rivers around here, with rainbow and brown trout usually on offer. **Paul Ellis** (☎ 072-174 4380) is a recommended local guide who knows the area well. Call to arrange a trip or for info on obtaining permits and renting rods. Prices vary.

Sleeping

Clarens boasts 120 different guesthouses, so if none of these options sound appealing stop by the tourism centre for a list of plenty more.

Clarens Inn (☎ 058-256 1119; schwim@netactive.co .za; 93 Van Reenan St; r per person R100) Run by the same friendly folks that operate Mountain Odyssey Tourism, this is the town's best budget option. Open-fire pits and a tranquil locale against the mountain at the bottom of Van Reenen St (look for it after the Le Roux turn-off) are bonuses.

Bokpoort Holiday Farm & Game Ranch (☎ 058-256 1181; www.bokpoort.co.za; s/d with breakfast R190/380) This farmstay is backpacker-friendly and another great spot between Clarens and Golden Gate. Horse riding is available and there are mountain-bike trails (but you must have your own bike). To get here, travel 5km from Clarens on the Golden Gate road, then turn off at the big Bokpoort Holiday Farm sign and drive another 3km along the dirt road.

Lake Clarens Guesthouse (☎ 058-256 1436; weyer@intercom.co.za; r per person with breakfast from R220) Run by the enigmatic 'Big, Bad Bruce' (a real man about town), this impeccably maintained guesthouse offers buckets of intimate country charm. Fresh flowers, giant bathtubs, heated floors and silky soft linens are all highlights of luxuriously appointed bedrooms. There are fabulous views from the terrace, where you can enjoy a hearty morning breakfast or a cup of late afternoon tea.

If you've always dreamed of sleeping in the same bed as Brad Pitt (as our friend Shari had), ask to stay in 'his' room that he uses when he's in town – an experience Shari highly recommends. Jane Seymour's cottage is also an option, as is Prince Harry's light and airy corner nook.

Patcham Place (☎ 058-256 1017; patcham@net active.co.za; 262 Church St; r per person with breakfast R225) A good central option, this B&B has airy rooms with giant windows and fab views from the balconies. The bathrooms are spotless, the beds firm and there is even a small kitchen. A friendly host and a welcome tumbler of port are nice touches.

Castle in Clarens (☎ 082-468 0642; www.castlein clarens.com; r per person from R350) This place has the romantic fairy-tale market cornered – you get to sleep in an old picture-book castle. The tower rooms are self-catering affairs done up with thick curtains and frescos on the walls. To reach the castle from Clarens head towards Golden Gate Highlands National Park and take the Bokpoort turn-off then follow the signs.

Eating

Clarens has great places to indulge your stomach.

Clementines Restaurant (☎ 058-256 1616; 315 Church St; mains R45-60; ❤ lunch & dinner Tue-Sun) The food at this souped-up country kitchen tastes just as good as it looks on the gourmet international menu, featuring everything from creamy pastas to tender ostrich fillets. Professional service, intimate ambiance, a lengthy wine list and veggie options are more perks. Make sure to check out the daily specials on the wall.

Café Moulin (☎ 082-690 1382; Main St; mains R15-45; ❤ breakfast & lunch) A quaint local haunt, the outdoor patio is lovely and rustic and overlooks the square. The menu is creative and healthy – including everything from crepes with tender steak and asparagus, to regional specialities varying by season.

Mezzaluna Deli (☎ 058-256 1692; 313 Church St; dishes from R5; ❤ breakfast & lunch) Next to the

Bibliophile bookstore (p387), this tiny take-away sells the most delicious cheeses and olives. It also does coffee and pasta salads.

Getting There & Away

Clarens is best reached by private transport. There are a few minibus taxis to Bethlehem and Harrismith from Clarens – although frequencies and costs weren't exactly clear. There is no set departure point, head towards the suburbs on the outskirts of town and ask around.

BETHLEHEM

☎ 058 / pop 86,905

The main commercial centre of the eastern Free State, Bethlehem has little to interest travellers beyond a night's rest. The Voortrekkers established the town on a farmsite called Pretoriuskloof in 1864. Not content with the biblical name they chose for their town, the devout newcomers also gave the name Jordaan to the river that flows through it.

The **tourist information office** (☎ 058-303 5732; info@bethlehem.org.za; cnr Muller & Roux Sts; ❤ 7.30am-1pm & 2-4pm Mon-Fri) is in the civic centre.

Just outside of town is the **Wolhuterskop Game & Nature Reserve** (☎ 058-303 5732), which has several species of antelope. There are horse trails and a one-night hiking route here. Book through the tourist information office in town.

The best accommodation option in town is the acclaimed **Fisant & Bokmakierie Guesthouse** (☎ 058-303 7144; fisant@isat.co.za; 8-10 Thoi Oosthuyse St; s/d with breakfast R290/370; 🖳). The owners are very friendly and each room is tastefully furnished. Dinner (R70) can be arranged.

The rooms are far from flash at the **Park Hotel** (☎ 058-303 5191; 23 Muller St; r from R240; ❄), but everything is clean and bathrooms are spacious. The place has a quaint polished-wood bar that's a good spot to watch a rugby match with the Afrikaner locals. The restaurant is the best-value place to eat in Bethlehem – a three-course meal goes for R65.

African themes are prevalent at classy **La Croché** (☎ 058-303 9229; www.lacroche.co.za; cnr Kerk & Theron Sts; s/d R290/380). Rooms have an eclectic air with a mix of modern furniture and traditional wooden pieces; ask for one with a Jacuzzi. La Croché is next door to

O'Hagans, which is handy for breakfast or evening drinks.

Linger over a few pints at **Nix Pub** (☎ 058-303 0722; Kerk St), an old-fashioned joint with a divey country vibe. You'll find hearty dishes like chicken livers, bangers and mash, and lasagne on the small menu.

Getting There & Away

Translux (☎ 058-408 4888; www.translux.co.za) runs daily to Durban (R160, five hours) and Cape Town (R360, 16 hours), as does **Greyhound** (☎ 058-477 1558; www.greyhound.co.za) at similar fares. Translux buses stop at Top Grill in Church St, and Greyhound stops at Wimpy on the corner of Muller and Hospital Sts.

The minibus-taxi ranks are around the corner of Cambridge and Gholf Sts, north of the town centre on the way to the train station. There are minibus taxis to Harrismith via Clarens. These usually cost somewhere in the vicinity of R20, although prices vary as much as frequencies – you'll have to ask around.

The *Trans Oranje* train stops here on its weekly run between Durban (1st/2nd/economy class R180/120/70, 10 hours) and Cape Town (R500/340/210). See p380 for details.

FOURIESBURG
☎ 058

Entirely surrounded by wild, craggy mountains, Fouriesburg occupies a magnificent spot just 12km north of the Caledonspoort border post to Lesotho. Two nearby peaks, Snijmanshoek and Visierskerf, are the highest in Free State; and you'll also find the largest sandstone overhang in the southern hemisphere, **Salpeterkrans**, around here – look for the signs off Rte 26, it's just northwest of town. An eerie example of wind erosion, the place is still sacred and used by local tribes for ancestral worship.

Fouriesburg was a stronghold in the Anglo-Boer War and was pronounced the capital of Free State after the British occupied Bethlehem. There are a number of fine old **sandstone buildings** in the town including President Steyn's house.

About 11km outside Fouriesburg, and just 800m from the Lesotho border, **Camelroc Guest Farm** (☎ 058-223 0368; www.camelroc.co.za; dm R60, r per person R190, chalets from R390) sits in a spectacular location against a camel-shaped

sandstone outcropping with fine views over the Maluti Mountains. It's a great rustic retreat, offering a variety of sleeping options. Dorms are in a simple hikers hut, while chalets are fully equipped and range in size and style. Good hiking and 4WD trails are nearby.

RUSTLER'S VALLEY
☎ 051

To journey into the wildly beautiful heart of nowhere, ditch the pavement and let your subconscious guide you down rich brown dusty byways to random oases scattered amid this rough-and-ready countryside. The remote valley, located off Rte 26 between Fouriesburg and Ficksburg, is the vanguard of the 'dare to be different' movement in the new South Africa.

Although famous **Rustler's Valley Retreat** (☎ 051-933 3939; www.rustlers.co.za; dm R65, r from R250; 🖳), the country's original hippy hangout, was closed (and looking rather spooky) when we stopped by, a caretaker told us this was only a temporary break caused by the chaos of the long New Years celebration. When it's open, the place attracts a diverse crowd: yuppies from Jo'burg, remnant hippies from all parts of the continent and 'ideas' people from all over the globe. The signs clearly state the retreat is an 'experimental area', meaning you'll find people in various states of altered mental status (a Clarens resident once described the resort as 'the kind of place you go to have a special mushroom omelette. You know?')

If you grow tired of contemplating your navel, you can swim or fish in the many dams, walk up onto sandstone escarpments, climb imposing Nyakalesoba (Witchdoctor's Eye) or ride a horse into the labyrinthine *dongas* (see p569) all around. There's an onsite restaurant and digs in either dorms or individually painted cottages with private bathrooms. The once-legendary music festival no longer happens here, but it's been replaced with a calendar of smaller events, most notably the **One World** festival at Easter. There are also a variety of workshops on offer, from drumming to permaculture or creativity. Children are very welcome.

Rustler's Valley Retreat does pick-ups (R20) from Ficksburg. If you have your own vehicle, the main turn-off is about 25km south of Fouriesburg on Rte 26 to Ficks-burg. Follow the signposts down a dirt road that crosses a train line. From the turn-off it is about 12km to Rustler's, 13km to Franshoek.

In the same area, just a few kilometres in the other direction, is the **Franshoek Mountain Lodge** (☎ 051-933 2828; www.franshoek.co.za; r per person R255; 🖳 🏊), which is perfect if you're looking for a completely opposite experi-ence. A working farm with comfortable sandstone cottages in its garden, a terrific round swimming pool, Zulu steam room and great views of the valley, it emits a lovely country charm. The place has a Thai chef, who doubles as a masseuse, so there's lots of Thai cuisine at dinner and you can sign up for a Thai cooking course or try a traditional massage. Ask for the honey-moon suite with its open fire. Not only is it huge (sleeping four in two separate rooms), it doesn't cost any extra. A polo package, with full board, thoroughbred ponies and instruction from a pro, costs R1500 per day.

FICKSBURG
☎ 051

Nestled against the purple majesty of the Maluti Mountains on the banks of the Caledon River, Ficksburg is particularly spectacular in winter when the mountains are topped with whipped-cream dollops of snow. The village sports some fine **sandstone buildings**; keep an eye out for the town hall and the post office.

The mild summers and cold winters make this area perfect for growing stone fruits, and Ficksburg is the centre of the Free State's cherry industry. There's a **Cherry Festival** (www.cherryfestival.co.za) in November but September and October are the best times to see the trees in bloom. The **Cherry Trail** is a tourist route around the district; there are several orchards to visit, various art and craft shops and guest farms. Get a map from the **tourist office** (☎ 051-933 2130; 🕑 9am-4.30pm Mon-Fri) in the Caltex office on the main road, or visit the Cherry Festival website.

The African-themed rooms at the **High-lands Hotel Hoogland** (☎ 051-933 2214; fax 051-933 2750; 37 Voortrekker St; s/d R180/300) are another option, offering all the creature comforts and the movie channel on TV. There's an

onsite restaurant and secure parking. Look for it next to the town hall.

The **Bella Rosa Guesthouse** (☎ 051-933 2623; bellarosa@telkomsa.net; 21 Bloem St; r per person R250; 🖳) is in a charming, Victorian sandstone building. The 12 guest rooms are decked out with fine antiques and modern artwork. Dinner can be arranged, and there's a cosy pub with a well-stocked wine cellar.

Bottling Co Pub & Restaurant (☎ 051-933 2404; 57 Piet Retief St; mains R35-50; 🕑 lunch & dinner Mon-Sat) has an imaginative menu with a couple of veggie options and is a top little spot for an evening beer.

SOUTHERN FREE STATE

Southern Free State typifies much of the province: it's dusty, harsh and dry. It's pretty much an area that you'll just tran-sit through, although some of the small old towns such as Philippolis are worth a look.

LADYBRAND
☎ 051 / pop 17,263

Archaeologists and anthropologists should pay Ladybrand a visit. The small town on Rte 26, around 16km from Lesotho's capital, Maseru, has handsome **sandstone buildings** (check out the town hall and the old magistrate's court). Archaeological dis-plays, including local rock paintings, instru-ments and tools dating back to the Stone Age are on display at the rather fascinat-ing little **Catharina Brand Museum** (☎ 051-924 5131; malotiinfo@xsinet.co.za; 17 Church St; 🕑 8am-5pm Mon-Fri). You will find the tourist office here too. The museum also explains how ashes taken from an ancient hearth in the **Rose Cottage Cave**, not far from Ladybrand, prove humans first inhabited the area more than 55,000 years ago!

The helpful tourism staff can assist with info about visiting the 300-plus San rock-art sites in caves in the area around the town – they can also help organise guides. While you're at the museum grab a per-mit to visit one of the quaintest churches you are ever likely to see. **Modderpoort Cave Church**, built in 1869, is nestled under a huge boulder in scenic surroundings about 12km from Ladybrand, and well worth the short drive.

Sleeping & Eating

Fort Amity (☎ 051-924 3131; 18 van Riebeeck St; s/d with breakfast from R300/450; ☐ ☒) Ask for a room with a private balcony at this very smart B&B. The manicured garden is a nice place to relax, or take in a game of tennis on the resident court.

Casa Romana B&B (☎ 051-924 1627; casaromana@xsinet.co.za; 34 Piet Retief St; s/d with breakfast R300/510; ☐) The rooms in this smart pink-painted B&B have TV, minibar and a safe.

Cranberry Cottage (☎ 051-924 2290; www.cranberrycottage.co.za; 37 Beeton St; s/d from R310/500; ☐ ☒) Perhaps the most interesting B&B in town, Cranberry offers luxury accommodation in a main guesthouse, as well as good-value self-catering rooms in the disused train station 800m away. The three-course fusion-style dinner (R95) is recommended. There's a grapevine-covered patio for summer teatime and a log fireplace in the cosy dining room for winter meals.

Impero Romana restaurant (11 Church St; mains R20-60; ⏱ lunch & dinner Mon-Sat) This place, run by Casa Romana, offers sophisticated food and good service.

Getting There & Away

Minibus taxis can be found near the church on Piet Retief St. Most run to nearby areas, including Ficksburg (R20, one hour). For a wider choice of destinations, take a minibus taxi to Maseru Bridge (R5), at the Lesotho border, and find a long-distance taxi in the big minibus-taxi rank there.

ZASTRON

☎ 051 / 12,464

Zastron, on Rte 726, is a quiet little town set in the hills. The distant Aasvoëlberg (Vulture Mountain) and Maluti Mountains form a splendid backdrop. With Lesotho forming an arc around this section of Free State, Zastron has long-established trading links with the mountain kingdom. There are some **San paintings** in the area; the best are in the Seekoei and Hoffman Caves.

The three-star **Maluti Hotel** (☎ 051-673 2112; 22 Hoofe St; s/d with breakfast R185/320) has the Horse & Hound pub on site. The nearest town in Lesotho is Mohale's Hoek, 55km away on a dirt road.

TUSSEN DIE RIVIERE GAME FARM

☎ 051

This 23,000-hectare **reserve** (☎ 051-754 0026; admission per vehicle R20; ⏱ dawn-dusk Sep-Apr) has more animals than any other reserve in Free State. These are mostly small mammals and various species of antelope, but if you look hard enough you may also see white rhinos and hippos. The country' is varied, with plains and ridges and a long frontage on the Senqu (Orange) River. For keen hikers, there are the 7km Middelpunt, the 12km Klipstapel and the 16km Senqu (Orange) River hiking trails; water must be carried on all of them.

There are camp sites (R50), and inexpensive two-person chalets (R150), which feature shared bathrooms. You pay for both at the entrance gate to the reserve. No food is available, but there is a communal sitting- and dining-room complex with a bar, kitchen and a large braai (barbecue) area. The entrance gate is located on the road between Bethulie and Smithfield (Rte 701), about 15km from Bethulie, or 65km east of the N1. There is no public transport.

GARIEP DAM NATURE RESERVE

☎ 051

West of Tussen Die Riviere, on the Senqu (Orange) River, this 13,000-hectare **reserve** (☎ 051-754 0026; admission per vehicle R20) surrounds one of the largest dams in South Africa (it used to be called the Hendrik Verwoerd Dam). Be warned, the dam is described in brochures as 'a mecca for motorboats'. During February each year the world's longest **inland rubber-duck race** takes place on the Gariep Dam. The event, which runs over a distance of 500km, is completed in one day.

Choose from three chalets (R250) or a variety of camp sites (R45) in the reserve. There's quite a lot of accommodation in the town of Gariep Dam, near the dam wall at the western end. The **Gariep Aventura** (☎ 051-754 0045; www.aventura.co.za/gariep/gariep.htm; camp sites/2-person chalets R100/550) is well laid-out and has loads of water-sport activities available. The **Gariep Dam Hotel** (☎ 051-754 0060; r R400) offers comfortable, but ordinary universal motel-style digs.

PHILIPPOLIS

☎ 051

Founded in 1823 as a mission station, Philippolis, on Rte 717, is a beautiful place, and the oldest town in the Free State. Seventy-five buildings within the town have been declared national monuments, including the library and many places built in Karoo style (made with thick walls to keep the heat at bay).

If you've ever fancied spending a night in jail, the **Old Jail** (☎ 082-550 4421; s/d R120/220) is your big chance. The town's former jail has been converted into basic but comfortable self-catering accommodation. The prison also has a honeymoon suite!

Gauteng

If Africa, as the cliché goes, is the mother of all life, then Gauteng is a province born of the Western love for her gold-bearing ore. Fast, bustling and a cabaret of contradictions, Gauteng covers just 1.5% of the country's land surface, yet accounts for 34% of its GDP and, perhaps more extraordinarily, 10% of the GDP of the whole of Africa.

The laid-back, friendly atmosphere of Pretoria, the country's administrative capital, belies a turbulent past. Founded in 1855, it has been the seat of four governments; these days the grandiose Union Buildings look over a city at the centre of the world's most unexpected democracy. Fifty or so kilometres away is Johannesburg, or Jo'burg, or Egoli, or Jozi (depending on your mood), the provincial capital and third-largest city on the continent. Sprawling and booming, it's a strange conurbation of opulent suburbs, corporate headquarters, six-lane freeways and Tuscan-themed shopping malls set alongside some of the country's starkest urban poverty. While positive change is sweeping through parts of Soweto, particularly in its growing tourist industry, other sections of this famous township remain destitute. The province's perennial crime problem is perhaps the inevitable consequence of its palpable polarities.

Not all of Gauteng is caught in the feverish grip of growth; the province is chock-a-block with the history of mankind itself. The Cradle of Humankind, within an hour's drive of Jo'burg and Pretoria, is one of the world's most important palaeontological sites. It seems appropriate to find it here, for after a few days spent soaking up its sunshine and thunderstorms, its beauty and ugliness, all its idiosyncrasies, you'll get the feeling that things really do start and finish in Gauteng.

HIGHLIGHTS

- Experiencing the Johannesburg revival in the **Newtown Cultural Precinct** (p401)

- Keeping pace with the cheetahs of the **De Wildt Cheetah Research Centre** (p442)

- Checking out Pretoria's party scene in **Hatfield** (p439)

- Exploring the world's best-known township, **Soweto** (p420), and catching the Orlando Pirates and Kaizer Chiefs playing in the local **soccer derby** (p415)

- Escaping Jo'burg's shopping centres at the roadside cafés of **Old Melville** (p410) and **Norwood** (p411)

- Discovering more about where you come from at the **Cradle of Humankind** (p425)

De Wildt Cheetah Research Centre ★
★ Pretoria
★ Cradle of Humankind
Soweto ★ ★ Johannesburg

■ POPULATION: 10. 5 MILLION | ■ AREA: 17,010 SQ KM

GAUTENG

HISTORY

Gauteng's history reaches as far back as humankind itself. Dubbed the Cradle of Humankind (see p425), the northwestern corner of Gauteng (pronounced how-teng) is thought to have played a key role in human evolution, with sites across the region yielding as many as 850 sets of hominid remains. In 1947 Dr Robert Broom made one of the most famous discoveries, in Sterkfontein Caves, when he uncovered the 2.5-million-year-old fossilised skull of the affectionately named Mrs Ples.

Despite the massive disruption caused by the Zulu wars, when many local blacks left the region, the area now called Gauteng remained a relatively quiet and chiefly rural place right through until the end of the 19th century. A number of different tribes lived in the region and there is evidence of mining activities dating as far back as the Iron Age, but it was only in 1886, when gold was discovered, that the area was catapulted into the modern age.

Boers, escaping British rule in the Cape Colony, had been here since the mid-19th century, founding the independent Zuid-Afrikaansche Republiek (ZAR) and establishing its capital in the then frontier village of Pretoria. But as the British turned their attentions to the colossal profits being made in the gold mines, it was only a matter of time before the events that led to the 1899–1902 Anglo-Boer War were set in motion.

After suffering severe losses, particularly in British concentration camps, the Boers conceded defeat, leading to the Treaty of Vereeniging and ultimately to the Union of South Africa in 1910. The fledgling city of Jo'burg exploded into life, but little changed for the thousands of black miners. It was a theme that would persist throughout the coming century. Apartheid would be managed out of Pretoria, and the townships surrounding Jo'burg – not least of them Soweto – would become the hub of both the system's worst abuses and its most energetic opponents. Consequently Gauteng, then known as Transvaal, was at centre stage in South Africa's all-too-familiar 20th-century drama.

Post-transformative South Africa is all about change. Transvaal has been renamed Gauteng, a black president now rules out of Pretoria (itself subject to name-changing; see the boxed text, p431) and the country's new Constitutional Court has been built on the site of Jo'burg's most infamous apartheid-era jail, the Old Fort. However, it remains to be seen whether the new century will finally bring Gauteng's poor their slice of the pie.

CLIMATE

Largely on the highveld, the big cities of Gauteng benefit from the cooling effects of altitude. Both Jo'burg and Pretoria can become baking hot in summer, but a fresh breeze can often be relied upon to take the sting out of a Jo'burg January. At this time of year, cloudless days and plenty of sunshine are common, though most afternoons produce the famous highveld thunderstorm; Jo'burg is the most lightning-clattered city on earth.

Winters can get chilly, and frosts and freezing temperatures are experienced in the mornings and evenings. Early summer (September and October) and autumn (March and April) offer the best weather for a visit.

NATIONAL PARKS & RESERVES

Concrete streets, rather than open spaces, predominate in largely metropolitan Gauteng, but there are still a few decent day-trip escapes to be had. Suikerbosrand Nature Reserve (p426), Krugersdorp Game Reserve (p426) and the Rhino & Lion Nature Reserve (p426) all offer a reasonable spread of wildlife and a sense of the great outdoors, while the De Wildt Cheetah Research Centre (p442), near Pretoria, remains one of Gauteng's great attractions.

LANGUAGE

English is widely spoken in Gauteng, although Afrikaans is predominant in Pretoria. Sotho, Pedi, Tswana and Zulu are the main languages spoken among blacks, although many will communicate using *tsotsitaal* (gangster-speak) or *isicamtho*, the hybrid melange of South African languages that developed in the townships.

DANGERS & ANNOYANCES

Crime is a daily reality in Gauteng, and Jo'burg in particular, but the risks should always be kept in perspective. The worst crime is often limited to individual suburbs and so there is absolutely no need to feel trapped in your hotel room. Local advice is gold dust when it comes to having a good, safe time in the big cities: ask for it, listen to it and then go out there and enjoy yourself. See p608 for more information.

GETTING THERE & AROUND

As South Africa's major national and international transport hubs, there aren't many places you can't get to from Jo'burg and Pretoria. **Johannesburg International Airport** (JIA; ☎ 011-921 6262; www.acsa.co.za), easily accessible from Pretoria and Jo'burg, has flights to regional centres across the country, with airlines covering many of the smaller towns as well. Durban, Cape Town and Port Elizabeth are also connected to Jo'burg via a network of no-frills budget airlines – by far the best way of getting between the big cities.

South Africa's long-distance bus companies, **Translux** (☎ 0861-589 282; www.translux.co.za), **SA Roadlink** (☎ 011-333 2223; www.saroadlink.co.za), **Greyhound** (☎ 012-323 1154; www.greyhound.co.za) and **Intercape Mainliner** (☎ 0861-287 287; www .intercape.co.za), also link Jo'burg and Pretoria with just about anywhere you would want to go. Both cities are often served by the same buses, with buses heading north starting at Jo'burg's Park Station before passing through Pretoria, and services heading south commencing in Pretoria before stopping in Jo'burg. Prices are reasonable, with fares to destinations as far as Cape Town rarely exceeding R400. If you are backpacking, the **Baz Bus** (☎ 021-439 2323; www.bazbus.com) links up with most of Gauteng's hostels. See p633 for details.

Trains, although slower, are also an option and several named services pass through both Jo'burg and Pretoria en route to destinations including Musina, near the Zimbabwe border, Cape Town, Bloemfontein, Durban and Kimberley. If you have hired a car, you can even put your vehicle on the train and ship it all the way across to the Cape.

Hiring a car is easy in both cities and prices are competitive. If you are staying in Gauteng, there are few sights you can't reach as part of a tour, or via public bus, but Jo'burg remains a city of car owners and having one will make getting around easier. Despite its size, it isn't too much of a headache getting out of Jo'burg and onto regional and provincial highways.

If you are strapped for cash, minibus taxis also depart from Jo'burg for destinations across the country and fares tend to be considerably lower than those charged by the main bus companies. Just take a good look at the condition of the driver and the taxi you choose; some are hopelessly unfit for long-distance travel and their operators can be reckless.

See individual Getting There & Away sections for more details. See the Transport chapter for details of connections between Gauteng's major cities and neighbouring countries.

JOHANNESBURG

☎ 011 / pop 5.7 million

Few fateful moments in colonial history can compare with Australian prospector George Harrison's somewhat apocryphal 'stumble' over a piece of gold on the Langlaagte Farm (present-day Fordsburg) in 1886. One could argue that this single event led to a gold rush, a war, a series of wretched imperialist and nationalist policies, and ultimately to the most cosmopolitan city in Africa.

Jo'burg, or Jozi as it's commonly known, is without a doubt the great big beating heart of South Africa and has long played a Jekyll-and-Hyde role in the global consciousness. Often the stage on which the epic of this extraordinary nation has been played out, the colossus of Jo'burg – with all its thrills and foibles – is today a fascinating, multitudinous city, where all the ups and downs of 21st-century South Africa can be witnessed in three, multicolour, dimensions.

In the past, the city's darker personality proved the most enduring. The Jo'burg of the newsflash was a city where fear and loathing reigned supreme; a city where spiralling gun crime and poverty had manifested itself in a society where one half of the population stagnated, while the other looked on impassively through coils of razor wire.

As ever, there is an element of truth to the stereotypes. Jo'burg does bear the scars of South Africa's turbulent 20th century, and many will take time to heal. Stark inequalities persist: wealthy northern suburbs like Sandton and Melville bristle with glossy shopping precincts, chic restaurants and electric fences, while the worst slums of the townships are only down the road, yet a world apart.

But armed with a new self-confidence – ironically most pronounced in the infamous township of Soweto – Africa's giant hub is fast introducing itself to a healthy new diet of urban renewal and social regeneration. A black middle class is on the rise, tourists and investors are flooding into Soweto, and developments in the central Newtown district are providing the city with a communal hub where Jo'burg's many faces can come together as one. From the recently erected Mandela Bridge, which symbolically connects previously divided sections of the city, to the new Constitutional Court, built on the site of one of the country's most infamous apartheid-era prisons, Jo'burg's 21st-century monuments herald a new era of optimism.

Perhaps more than in any other big city (and at more than 2500 sq km, Jo'burg is *big*), it pays to keep your wits about you. Advances in the battle against crime have yet to win the war, and local advice is often the surest way of avoiding a costly run-in with its more sinister elements. Aware of its shortcomings and determined to make a difference, Jo'burg is an extraordinarily friendly and informal city, and not one to hide away in – get out there and live the big time.

HISTORY

Within a matter of months of Harrison's discovery, thousands of diggers descended on the small collection of farms on the Witwatersrand. Because the gold was deep – in reef form, not the more easily accessible alluvial form – mining was quickly concentrated in the hands of men who had the capital to finance large underground mines. Mining magnates, who had made their money at the Kimberley diamond field, bought up the small claims and soon came to be known as the Randlords.

By 1889 Jo'burg was the largest town in Southern Africa, a rowdy city of bars and brothels. The multicultural fortune-seekers – blacks and whites – were regarded with deep distrust by the Boers, the Transvaal government and especially by the president, Paul Kruger. Kruger introduced electoral laws that effectively restricted voting rights to the Boers, while laws aimed at controlling the movement of blacks also were passed. The tensions between the Randlords and *uitlanders* (foreigners) on one side, and the Transvaal government on the other, were crucial factors in the events that led to the 1899–1902 Anglo-Boer War. Jo'burg, which already had a population in excess of 100,000, became a ghost town during the war. It recovered quickly when the British took control and massive new mines were developed to the east and west.

Although gold-mining remained the backbone of the city's economy, manufacturing industries soon sprang up, gaining fresh impetus during WWII. Under increasing pressure in the countryside, thousands of blacks moved to the city in search of jobs. Racial segregation had become entrenched during the interwar years, and from the 1930s onwards vast squatter camps had sprung up around Jo'burg.

Under black leadership these camps eventually became well-organised cities, despite their gross overcrowding and negligible services. But in the late 1940s many were destroyed by the authorities, and the people were moved to new suburbs known as the South-Western Townships, or Soweto.

The official development of apartheid during the 1960s did nothing to slow the expansion of the city or the arrival of black squatters. Large-scale violence finally broke out in 1976, when the Soweto Students' Representative Council organised protests against the use of Afrikaans (regarded as the language of the oppressor) in black schools. Police opened fire on a student march and over the next 12 months more than 1000 would die fighting the apartheid system.

The regulations of apartheid were finally abandoned in February 1990 and since the 1994 elections the city has, in theory, been free of discriminatory laws. The black townships have been integrated into the municipal government system, the city centre is vibrant with black hawkers and street stalls, and inner suburbs have become multiracial.

Gold-mining is no longer undertaken in the city area, and the old pale-yellow mine dumps that created such a surreal landscape on the edge of the city are being reprocessed. Modern recovery methods allow the mining companies to extract as much gold from these waste tailings today as was found in the raw ore 100 years ago. The classic view of Jo'burg – a mine dump in the foreground and skyscrapers in the background – will be retained, however, as some dumps are being preserved as historical monuments.

ORIENTATION

Despite its size, it's not difficult to find your way around Jo'burg. However, cars are king here, so getting around with one is surprisingly easy and getting around without one can be extremely time-consuming. Johannesburg International Airport (JIA) is 25km northeast of the city and easily accessible (Rte 24 runs out of the CBD and becomes the N12 freeway), but if you need to get there during the weekday rush hour (5pm to 7pm) allow up to an extra hour's travelling time. Regular buses connect the airport with the main train station, Park Station, on the northern edge of the city centre (see p419).

The large city centre, which is laid out on a straightforward grid, is dominated by office blocks – in particular the 50-storey Carlton Centre on Commissioner St. There's no reason to stay in the city centre; after the shops close, the centre becomes a virtual ghost town. However, redevelopment

GAUTENG

JOHANNESBURG

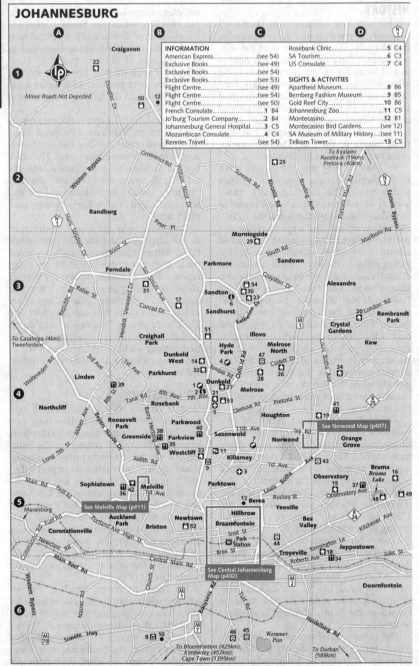

INFORMATION

American Express	(see 54)
Exclusive Books	(see 49)
Exclusive Books	(see 54)
Exclusive Books	(see 54)
Exclusive Books	(see 53)
Flight Centre	(see 49)
Flight Centre	(see 54)
Flight Centre	(see 50)
French Consulate	1 B4
Jo'burg Tourism Company	2 B4
Johannesburg General Hospital	3 C5
Mozambican Consulate	4 C4
Rennies Travel	(see 54)

Rosebank Clinic	5 C4
SA Tourism	6 C3
US Consulate	7 C4

SIGHTS & ACTIVITIES

Apartheid Museum	8 B6
Bernberg Fashion Museum	9 B5
Gold Reef City	10 B6
Johannesburg Zoo	11 C5
Montecasino	12 B1
Montecasino Bird Gardens	(see 12)
SA Museum of Military History	(see 11)
Telkom Tower	13 C5

GAUTENG

of the Newtown cultural precinct, at the northwestern edge of the city, is at the core of an effort to clean up central Jo'burg. North of the city centre, a steep ridge runs west–east from Braamfontein across to the dangerous suburb of Hillbrow. To the north-east of the centre is the equally dangerous Yeoville.

The northern suburbs are predominantly white middle- and upper-class areas, within an arc formed by the N1 and N3 freeways. These suburbs of big houses, big trees and big fences are where most travellers stay. Sterile shopping malls form the centre of most social life, although there are a few pockets of resistance. The inner-suburban restaurant enclaves of Melville, Greenside, Parkhurst and Norwood make a refreshing change.

The black townships ring the city and present a stark contrast to the northern suburbs. Conditions within the townships range from the stereotypically suburban to the appalling. The main township is Soweto, but there are also big townships at Alexandra (inside the N3 freeway to the northeast of the city centre) and fur-ther out at Thokoza (south of Alberton), Kwa-Thema and Tsakane (southeast and south of Brakpan, respectively), Davey-ton (east of Benoni) and Tembisa (to the northeast).

Maps

For maps try the **Map Office** (Map p402; ☎ 011-339 4941; Ground fl, Standard House, 40 De Korte St, Braamfontein; ۞ 8am-4pm Mon-Fri). This place sells government maps of all South African provinces for R40 a sheet.

INFORMATION
Bookshops

Book Dealers of Melville (Map p411; ☎ 011-726 4054; 12 7th St, Melville; ۞ 10am-9pm) Has a good antiquarian selection and buys second-hand books (from 2.30pm to 5.30pm Tuesday and Thursday).

Exclusive Books Eastgate Mall (Map pp398-9; ☎ 011-622 4870; upper fl; ۞ 9am-10pm); Rosebank Mall (Map pp398-9; ☎ 011-447 3028; level 3, the Zone; ۞ 9am-9pm); Sandton City Mall (Map pp398-9; ☎ 011-883 1010; lower level; ۞ 9am-9pm Mon-Sat, 9am-7pm Sun) This chain is the best in town, with the widest range of local press, travel guides and international newspapers. You'll have to fork out for international bestsellers, most of which are imported.

GAUTENG

Emergency
AIDS line (☎ 0800-012 322)
Cellphone emergency (☎ MTN 112; Vodacom 147)
Fire (☎ 10111)
Lifeline (☎ 011-728 1347)
Metro Emergency Rescue Service (☎ 10177)
Police (Map p402; ☎ 10111; Headquarters, Main Rd)
Rape Crisis Line (☎ 011-806 1888)

Internet Access
Most hostels and hotels have Internet facilities, charging anything from R20 to R60 per hour. Alternatively, most Jo'burg malls and suburbs have an Internet café and wi-fi hotspots are popping up everywhere. **Out of Print Books** (Map p411; ☎ 011-482 6026; 78 4th Ave, Melville; per min R1; ☺ 10am-9pm), in the centre of Melville, is pricey but open later than most.

Medical Services
Medical services are of a high standard but they are expensive, so make sure you're insured.
Johannesburg General Hospital (Map pp398-9; ☎ 011-488 4911; M1/Jubilee Rd, Parktown) Jo'burg's main public hospital.
Rosebank Clinic (Map pp398-9; ☎ 011-328 0500; 14 Sturdee Ave, Rosebank; ☺ 7am-10pm) A private hospital in the northern suburbs, with casualty, GP and specialist services.

Money
There are banks with ATMs and change facilities at every commercial centre. American Express and Rennies Travel (an agent for Thomas Cook) have branches at the airport and in major malls.
American Express Jo'burg International Airport (☎ 011-390 1233; ☺ 5am-9pm); Sandton City Mall (Map pp398-9; ☎ 011-883 9009; Shop B36c, level 5; ☺ 9am-6pm Mon-Sat, 10am-5pm Sun)
Rennies Travel Jo'burg International Airport (☎ 011-390 1040; ☺ 5.30am-9pm); Sandton City Mall (Map pp398-9; ☎ 011-884 4035; ☺ 9am-6pm Mon-Fri, 9am-3pm Sat, 10am-1pm Sun)

Post
There's a poste restante service at the **main post office** (Map p402; ☎ 0800 110 226; Jeppe St; ☺ 8.30am-4.30pm Mon-Fri, 8.30am-noon Sat), but be careful about having valuables sent here.

Tourist Information
Different offices provide information depending on whether you are interested in Jo'burg, Gauteng or South Africa as a whole. The following organisations have a monopoly on most of the best information available.
Gauteng Tourism Authority (Map p402; ☎ 011-639 1600; www.gauteng.net; 1 Central Pl, cnr Jeppe & Henry Nxumalo Sts, Newtown; ☺ 8am-5pm Mon-Fri) The tourist body's glistening new headquarters is in the middle of the Newtown Cultural Precinct, with ample parking. Staff members are eager but woefully undertrained, so check details with locals or your accommodation.
Jo'burg Tourism Company (Map pp398-9; ☎ 011-214 0700; deon@joburgtourism.com; ground fl, Grosvenor Cnr, 195 Jan Smuts Ave, Parktown North; ☺ 8am-5pm Mon-Fri) A private endeavour; covers the city of Jo'burg.
SA Tourism (Map pp398-9; ☎ 011-895 3000; fax 895 3001; 90 Protea Rd, Sandton; ☺ 8am-5pm Mon-Fri) Can be contacted for general South Africa information.

Travel Agencies
There are dozens of agencies in Jo'burg, and many hotels and hostels also arrange bookings. For flight bargains, check the *Saturday Star* newspaper's travel supplement.
Flight Centre (☎ Central Bookings 0860 400 747); Eastgate Mall (Map pp398-9; ☎ 011-616 7008; Shop L3; ☺ 9am-5.30pm Mon-Fri, 9am-3pm Sat); Fourways Mall (Map pp398-9; ☎ 011-467 0050; Shop G43; ☺ 9am-5.30pm Mon-Fri, 9am-2.30pm Sat); Sandton City Mall (Map pp398-9; ☎ 011-784 1571; Shop L80; ☺ 9am-5.30pm Mon-Fri, 9am-3pm Sat) Specialises in discounted flights and has branches in most major malls. It promises to beat any genuine quote from another agency.

DANGERS & ANNOYANCES
Crime is a big problem in Jo'burg, but it is important to put things in perspective. Remember that most travellers come and go without incident and that much of the crime afflicts suburbs you would have little reason to stray into. The secret to success is quite simple: seek local advice, listen to it and remain aware of what's going on around you.

You are really very unlikely to become the victim of a violent crime (even criminals understand that assault and murder attract far more attention from the authorities than robbery alone), but it's when using ATMs that you're most vulnerable. See p614 for advice on avoiding scams and safely using ATMs.

SIGHTS & ACTIVITIES
City Centre & Newtown
CITY CENTRE
The city centre choked and largely died in the mid-1990s, with many white businesses fleeing to the northern suburbs, leaving the district to vanish under a mountain of none-too-promising crime statistics and buildings to turn 'bad'. The area retains its edgy atmosphere today, but regeneration projects in Newtown to the south and university-oriented Braamfontein to the north are gradually helping to boost confidence once more in the heart of the city.

Jo'burg was once an Art Deco showpiece, but few good examples remain. There are plenty of colonial-era buildings that are worth a look: the defunct **Rissik St Post Office** (Map p402; Rissik St) and **City Hall** (Map p402; cnr Rissik & Market Sts), now a sometime concert venue, are among the finest. Sights aside, the thousands of hawkers and the smells of corn and beef being cooked at street-side stalls give the centre an urban atmosphere that you won't find in the northern suburbs, and that alone makes it worth a well-planned visit.

You might also like to pass by the building that housed the former **Mandela & Tambo Law Offices** (Map p402; Chancellor House, 25 Fox St) where, in the 1950s, these two famous men set up this pioneering law firm. There's not much in the way of tourist facilities here, but moves are being made to set something up. Contact the Gauteng Tourism Authority for the latest.

On the Noord St side of Joubert Park (itself a no-go area) is the **Johannesburg Art Gallery** (Map p402; ☎ 011-725 3130; Joubert Park; admission free; ⊙ 10am-5pm Tue-Sun). This place has a reputable collection of European and South African landscape and figurative paintings, and several exhibitions featuring more-adventurous contemporary work and long-overdue retrospectives of black artists.

To get an overview of the hub of Jo'burg, take the lift to the **Top of Africa** (Map p402; ☎ 011-308 1331; 50th fl, Carlton Centre, 152 Commissioner St; adult/child R10/8; ⊙ 9am-7pm). From the quiet remoteness of the observation deck, the sprawling city seems positively serene. The entrance is via a special lift one floor below street level and you can admire the views over lunch at the Marung restaurant.

BRAAMFONTEIN
The suburb of Braamfontein's focus is the **University of Witwatersrand** (Map p402; ☎ 011-717 1000; Jan Smuts Ave), more commonly known as Wits (pronounced vits) University, and there are plans to transform this currently quiet area into a lively student ghetto. Wits University is the largest English-language university in the country, with more than 20,000 students. It's an attractive campus and you can visit the worthwhile **Gertrude Posel Gallery** (Map p402; ☎ 011-717 1365; gallery@atlas.wits.ac.za; ground fl, Senate House; admission free; ⊙ 10am-4pm Tue-Fri); the **Standard Bank Foundation Collection of African Tribal Art**, which includes masks, Ndebele fertility dolls and beadwork; **Jan Smuts House** (Map p402) to see Smuts' study; the **Planetarium** (Map p402; ☎ 011-717 1390; Yale Rd; shows adult/concession R25/10; ⊙ 8.30am-4pm), which you can look around for free, or attend shows on Friday (8pm), Saturday (3pm) and Sunday (4pm). You can get a cheap café meal at the **Student Union Building**.

NEWTOWN
Known as Brickfields at the turn of the 20th century, Newtown was once the centre of a thriving brick-making industry, booming on the back of the area's rich clay deposits. In April 1904, the fire brigade unceremoniously torched most of the buildings to combat an outbreak of bubonic plague and it was subsequently renamed Newtown. Today, Newtown is at the centre of efforts to rejuvenate the downtown area. In recognition of this, in 2005 the new headquarters of the Gauteng Tourism Authority was opened here.

Surrounded by museums and cafés, Newtown's cultural precinct, which occupies the brushed-up **Mary Fitzgerald Sq** (named after South Africa's first female trade unionist), is a good place to start a tour of central Jo'burg. As well as being the staging ground for a number of annual events – check Jo'burg City's website (www.joburg.org.za for details) – it's also simply a good place to watch the city drift past. The square is decorated with an array of heads carved by Newtown artists from old railway sleepers.

Situated at the heart of the cultural precinct, **Museum Africa** (Map p402; ☎ 011-833 5624; museumafrica@joburg.org.za; 121 Bree St; adult/child R8/4;

CENTRAL JOHANNESBURG

0 — 500 m
0 — 0.3 miles

INFORMATION
Botswana Consulate.....................1 B4
Department of Home Affairs.........2 B5
Gauteng Tourism Authority...........3 A6
Main Post Office............................4 C5
Map Office....................................5 A4
SA Police Headquarters.................6 A6
Swaziland Consulate.....................7 A4
Zimbabwe Consulate.....................8 B6

SIGHTS & ACTIVITIES
Bus Factory...................................9 A6
City Hall.......................................10 C6
Constitution Hill...........................11 C3
Drum Café.................................(see 9)
Getrude Posel Gallery..................12 A4
Johannesburg Art Gallery.............13 D4
Mandela & Tambo Law Offices.....14 C6
Mary Fitzgerald Sq.......................15 A5
Museum Africa.............................16 A5
Nelson Mandela Bridge.................17 B5
Planetarium.............................(see 12)
Rissik St Post Office (closed).........18 A6
SAB Centenary Centre..................19 A6
St Mary's Anglican Cathedral.......20 C5

Sci-Bono Discovery Centre...........21 A6
Soweto Art Gallery......................22 B6
Standard Bank Foundation Collection
    of African Tribal Art..............(see 12)
Top of Africa...............................23 D6
Turbine Hall................................24 A5
University of the Witwatersrand....25 A3
Workers' Museum.........................26 A6

SLEEPING
Formule 1 Hotel Park Station.......27 C4
Orion Devonshire Hotel................28 B4
Protea Hotel Parktonian...............29 B4

EATING
Gramadoela's...........................(see 37)
Guildhall Bar & Restaurant..........30 B6
Kapitan's.....................................31 B6
Moyo's.....................................(see 37)

DRINKING
Horror Café.................................32 A6

ENTERTAINMENT
Civic Theatre...............................33 B3
Kaizer Chiefs Store.......................34 C6

Kippie's Jazz International.............35 A5
Laboratory...................................36 A5
Market Theatre............................37 A5
Windybrow Centre for the Arts.....38 D4
Wits Theatre Complex...............(see 12)

SHOPPING
Beautiful Things........................(see 9)
Kohinoor.....................................39 B6
Market Square Market..................40 A5

TRANSPORT
Long-Distance Buses Booking
    Offices....................................41 C4
Metrobus Terminal.......................42 C6
Minibus Taxis to Bulawayo,
    Zimbabwe...............................43 C4
Minibus Taxis to Durban...............44 C5
Minibus Taxis to Lesotho,
    Bloemfontein, Kroonstad &
    Ficksburg................................45 D5
Minibus Taxis to Pretoria.............46 C5
Minibus Taxis to Soweto..............47 D5
Minibus Taxis to Upington,
    Kimberley & Cape Town...........48 C4
Taxis to Rosebank & Sandton.......49 C5

To Northern
Suburbs &
M1 (750m)

To M1 (2km);
Norwood (4km);
Orange Grove (6km)

Pretoria St

Entrance

Hoofd St

Kotze St

To Berea (2.5km);
Yeoville (2.5km)

Esselen St

Hillbrow

Ameshoff St

Stiemens St

South African
Institute
for Medical
Research

Kapteijn St

Jorissen St

Braamfontein

Pieterson St

De Korte St

Juta St

Smit St

Smit St

Wolmarans St

Joubert
Park

Leyds St

Queen Elizabeth Dr

Leyds St

Bok St

Koch St

Park
Station

Hancock St

Noord St

De Villiers St

Plein St

Bree St

De Villiers St

Jeppe St

To Carfax
(100m)

Pim St

Kerk St

Bree St

Bree St

Pritchard St

Jeppe St

Jeppe St

Market

Newtown

To Oriental
Plaza & Fordsburg
(500m)

President St

President St

Library
Square

Market St

Commissioner St

Carlton
Centre

To Troyeville (1km)

Main Rd

Fox St

Gandhi
Square

Main St

Marshall St

Marshall St

Anderson

To Faraday
Market (200m)

9am-5pm Tue-Sun) is housed in the impressive old Bree St fruit market, next to the Market Theatre complex. The superb exhibition on the Treason Trials (1956–61), which featured most of the important figures in the 'new' South Africa, is a must-see for anyone looking for a better understanding of the country's more recent history. The Transformations exhibition details the evolution of Jo'burg and includes a simulated descent into one of the gold mines. The Sophiatown display is outstanding. There's also a large collection of rock art, a geological museum, a display on Gandhi's time in Jo'burg and the Bensusan Museum of Photography, which charts the history of photography and has regular exhibitions by famous South African snappers.

The nearby **Market Theatre** complex (p415), with its shows, bars and restaurants, is an excellent place to while away a few hours between museum visits.

Looming over Newtown is the **Nelson Mandela Bridge** (Map p402; www.blueiq.co.za). Officially opened by Nelson Mandela on 20 July 2003 (two days after his 85th birthday), the 295m, cable-stayed bridge is the longest of its kind in Southern Africa. It isn't the most impressive structure in Jo'burg, but it is an enduring symbol of efforts to resurrect long-forgotten sections of the city and an ongoing source of pride.

The **SAB Centenary Centre** (Map p402; ☎ 011-836 4900; 15 President St; admission R10; ☻ 10am-6pm Tue-Sat) delves into that other great South African pursuit: beer drinking. It unlocks the secrets of the country's brewing industries and there is a re-creation of a 1965 Soweto *shebeen* (unlicensed bar), which is all heavenly for appreciators of liquid amber.

The small but significant **Soweto Art Gallery** (Map p402; ☎ 011-492 1109; Suite 34, 2nd fl, Victory House, cnr Commissioner & Harrison Sts; admission free; ☻ 8am-6pm Mon-Fri, 8am-1pm Sat) is directed by well-known Sowetan artist Peter Sibeko and is one of the few places contemporary black artists from the townships can exhibit their paintings and sculptures. All works are for sale and offer a worthwhile insight into life in the townships.

Much of the area around Mary Fitzgerald Sq was once taken up by a giant power station – builders keep running into the foundations of the colossal cooling towers. The huge **Turbine Hall** (Map p402; cnr Jeppe & Bezuidenhout

Sts), next to the SAB World of Beer, is one of the city's more impressive buildings – a kind of Battersea Power Station for Jo'burg. Although derelict, the fantastic interior was used to launch the New Mini and there are several, tentative plans in the pipeline to transform the space into something more user-friendly. If you hear of an event being hosted here, scramble to get a ticket.

In the Electric Workshop building, you'll find the **Sci-Bono Discovery Centre** (Map p402; ☎ 082-575 6688; www.sci-bono.co.za; Bezuidenhout St; ☻ 9am-5pm Mon-Fri). The space includes a science museum and an interactive learning experience, and is an excellent way to keep the kids occupied for a couple of hours.

In the restored Electricity Department's compound you'll find the **Workers' Museum** (Map p402; ☎ 011-832 2447; 52 Jeppe St; admission free; ☻ 9am-5pm Mon-Sat). It was built in 1910 for 300-plus municipal workers and has been declared a national monument, but is not particularly inspiring. There is a Workers' Library, a resource centre and a display of the living conditions of migrant workers.

South of the cultural precinct, you will find the refurbished **Bus Factory** (Map p402; 2 President St), which includes Beautiful Things (p415), a new initiative exhibiting and selling crafts from across South Africa, and the **Drum Café** (Map p402; ☎ 011-834 4464; www.drumcafé.com; ☻ 9am-4pm), which has a free drum museum and stages regular drumming events.

HILLBROW & CONSTITUTION HILL
Crowned by the looming, 269m **Telkom Tower** (Map pp398-9; Goldreich St), Hillbrow was once among the liveliest and most interesting suburbs in the city, becoming one of the first districts in Jo'burg to witness the cracks opening in the shell of apartheid when it was designated the nation's first 'Grey Area' – a zone where blacks and whites could live side by side. These days, however, it also has a reputation for very real lawlessness and a trip into its guts, without an extremely savvy guide (see p405), is not recommended.

At a time when high-profile developments are being erected in washed-out areas throughout the city, however, it is no accident that the ever-egalitarian Rainbow Nation chose to build its new Constitutional Court on the very edge of Hillbrow. With any luck the court and the surrounding Constitutional Hill development – and the investment they will attract – will improve this suburb's fortunes.

Inspiring, impressive **Constitution Hill** (Map p402; ☎ 011-381 3100; www.constitutionhill.co.za; Kotze St; adult/child R20/10; ⏱ 9am-5pm Wed-Mon) is slowly becoming one of the city's – if not the country's – chief tourist attractions. Built within the ramparts of the **Old Fort**, which dates from 1892 and was once a notorious prison, the development focuses on South Africa's new **Constitutional Court**. Ruling on constitutional and human-rights matters, the court itself is a very real symbol of the changing South Africa: a *lekgotla* (place of gathering) rising from the ashes of one of the city's most poignant apartheid-system monuments, with cases heard in all 11 official languages. The modern structure incorporates sections of the old prison walls, plus large windows that allow visitors to watch proceedings. Not unlike the symbolism of Sir Norman Foster's glass Reichstag dome in Berlin, it underlines the sense of transparency at the heart of the country's political ethos.

As well as gaining access to the court, visitors will also be able to take tours of the Old Fort's various sections, including the Awaiting Trial Block, which held the 156 treason triallists – led by Nelson Mandela – of 1956; the notorious Number Four section, which held black male prisoners; and the Women's Gaol, where female offenders (their offence was often simply failing to produce an identity card) were incarcerated.

Northern Suburbs

Montecasino (Map pp398-9; ☎ 011-510 7777; www .montecasino.co.za; William Nicol Dr, Fourways) consistently draws more visitors than perhaps any other attraction in Jo'burg. Based around a large casino, this spectacularly cheesy development features an entire 'Tuscan village under one roof', with a menagerie of concrete doves, restaurants, shops, bars, the **Pieter Toerien Theatre** (p415) and the pleasant **Montecasino Bird Gardens** (Map pp398-9; ☎ 011-511 1864; adult/child R10/5; ⏱ 9am-5pm), where you can get a blast of country air in the heart of the city. The designers of the 'Tuscan village' left authenticity at the door (even the wall cracks are painted on), but it makes a

unique change from the sparkling floors and muzak of many of the city's shopping malls.

Perhaps it's South Africa's fascination with guns, or maybe it's the country's bloody history, but every year the **South African National Museum of Military History** (Map pp398-9; ☎ 011-646 5513; www.militarymuseum.co.za; 22 Erlswold Way, Saxonwold; adult/child R10/5; ⏱ 9am-4.30pm) is one of Jo'burg's most popular museums. If warfare is your thing you'll find this museum fascinating. You can see artefacts and implements of destruction from the 1899–1902 Anglo-Boer War through to WWII. The museum is at the eastern end of the grounds of the Jo'burg Zoo.

The **Johannesburg Zoo** (Map pp398-9; ☎ 011-646 2000; www.jhbzoo.org.za; Jan Smuts Ave, Westcliff; adult/ child R24/16; ⏱ 8.30am-5.30pm) has a reasonable array of the fierce and the furry. It seems rather bizarre going to a zoo in Africa but it has a particularly interesting wild-dog enclosure and kids love it. There are also night tours (R60) three times a week (no children); book through the zoo.

Also worth checking out are the **Bernberg Fashion Museum** (Map pp398-9; ☎ 011-646 0716; cnr Duncombe Rd & Jan Smuts Ave, Forest Town; admission free; ⏱ 9am-5pm Tue-Sat), which has a variety of fashions from yesteryear on display; and the **AECI Dynamite Factory Museum** (☎ 011-309 4700; 2 Main St, Modderfontein; ⏱ 10am-2pm Mon & Fri, 2-4.30pm Wed), which is housed in an original 1895 homestead 16km northeast of the city centre, and charts the development of South Africa's explosives industry (a crucial factor in Jo'burg's development as a mining centre).

Southern Suburbs

In stark contrast to the nearby Gold Reef City theme park, the **Apartheid Museum** (Map pp398-9; ☎ 011-309 4700; www.apartheidmuseum.org; cnr Gold Reef Rd & Northern Parkway; adult/child R25/12; ⏱ 10am-5pm Tue-Sun) details South Africa's era of segregation with chilling accuracy. With plenty of attention to detail and an unsparing emphasis on the inhuman philosophy of apartheid – visitors are handed a card stating their race when they arrive and are required to enter the exhibit through their allotted gate – this remains one of South Africa's most evocative museums. Charting the course of several South Africans through the apartheid era, the museum uses film, text, audio and live accounts to provide a colourful insight into the architecture, implementation and eventual unravelling of the apartheid system. It's an overwhelming experience; sensibly there's a garden at the exit for you to feel the value of freedom. If you are on your way to Soweto, where the excellent Hector Pieterson Museum pads out the story, this is an absolute must. It is 8km south of the city centre, just off the M1 freeway.

Nearby, **Gold Reef City** (Map pp398-9; ☎ 011-248 6800; www.goldreefcity.co.za; Gold Reef Rd; admission R70, children under 120cm free; ☺ 9.30am-5pm Tue-Sun) also has one foot in the past, but this time provides a light-hearted and reasonably riproaring take on gold-rush Jo'burg. Ninety per cent Disneyland clone, this theme park only offers a token nod to historical authenticity, but provides ample means for filling a spare afternoon, especially if you have kids in tow.

It features scary rides, a Victorian fun fair and various reconstructions, including a bank, brewery, pub and newspaper office. Visitors can go 220m down a shaft to see a gold mine from the inside (an extra R50), watch a gold pour and see an entertaining programme of 'gumboot' dancing, a traditional miners' choreographed dance.

There are numerous places to eat and drink, plus the Gold Reef City Arts & Crafts Centre and an expensive craft/souvenir shop. There are often special programmes on the weekend, sometimes with live music performed in an open-sided amphitheatre, and fireworks. Check the entertainment section in the *Star*.

If you want to stay over, there's the rocksolid Protea Hotel Gold Reef City and a **casino** (☎ 011-248 5000; ☺ 24hr). The attached Gold Reef City Casino Hotel also has rooms.

TOURS

All Jo'burg budget hostels should have information on cheap packages to Kruger National Park and on the best (and cheapest) travel links to Cape Town, Durban, Swaziland, Lesotho, Namibia, Botswana, Zimbabwe and Mozambique. Almost all can book Soweto tours as well. If you phone ahead, the following tour companies will arrange a pick-up or tell you how to get to the rendezvous.

Imbizo Tours (☎ 011-838 2667) Specialises in tours to Jo'burg's gritty townships, including half-day tours to Alexandra (R300 per person), perhaps the city's grimmest township, and Soweto (R310 per person). Also evening Soweto *shebeen* tours (R600 per person), where you get to eat and drink it up with the locals.

KDR Sports & Adventure Travel (☎ 011-326 1700; www.soweto.co.za) A well-connected outfit that can book accommodation in Soweto.

Parktown and Westcliff Heritage Trust (☎ 011-482 3349; per person from R150) Leads several tours through the more salubrious sections of town.

Queer Johannesburg Tours (☎ bookings 011-717 1963; anthonym@library.wits.ac.za) Run on the first Sunday of the month by the Gay & Lesbian Archives of South Africa (☎ 011-717 4239; www.gala.wits.ac.za) at Wits University. Gay or straight, the tours offer a fascinating insight into gay Jo'burg, taking you deep into the heart of Hillbrow and Soweto, and providing plenty of background on the role homosexuality played in the gold mines and the struggle against apartheid. Tours start at 9am, last four hours and cost R300 per person.

Take-A-Tour (☎ 011-624 1676; www.takeatour.info) Tours of Soweto (R280 per person), as well as trips through Jo'burg's city centre and heritage sites (R280 per person).

Taste of Africa (☎ 082-565 2520) Offers something different from the zoolike township tours, with a cheap shuttle (R60) from Melville to Soweto. There you can hire a guide (R50) or just cruise around using minibuses. It also offers tours where you can meet locals, drink in a *shebeen*, watch backyard theatre, milk a cow, listen to jazz and even visit a local healer. There is also shack accommodation (R100 per night).

Walks Tours (☎ 011-444 1639; www.walktours.co.za; per person from R120) Offers regular weekend walking tours around parts of Jo'burg as diverse as the city centre, Sandton, Troyeville, Parktown and Alexandra township. The walks go for between three and six hours and are led by well-informed guides. The only downside is that unless you can get enough people together for a private tour, you might have to wait weeks for the walk you want.

FESTIVALS & EVENTS

Chinese New Year At Wemmer Pan, south of the centre.
Rand Easter Show During April at the National Exhibition Centre.
Joy of Jazz Festival (☎ 011-832 1641; www.joyofjazz .co.za) Staged in venues across Newtown in late August.
Arts Alive Festival (☎ 011-549 2315; www.artsalive. co.za) Held in September. A strong element in the festival is the workshops that reveal the continent's rich cultures, denigrated for so long by the Eurocentrism of the apartheid years. The festival is a particularly good time to hear excellent music, on and off the official programme. Most events are staged in Newtown.

GAUTENG

Gay Pride March (☎ 082-547 2486; www.sapride.org) Held on the last Saturday every September.

SLEEPING

Hotels and hostels are scattered across Jo'burg with the only pattern being a steady drift north. The range of quality is broad, from the bare basics of some hostels to the opulence and perma-smile service of the many five-star hotels. Some Jo'burg hostels will allow you to pitch a tent, but it's wise to check before you arrive. (If backyards are not to your liking, the best caravan parks that permit camping are in the far south of the province.)

The agency **Portfolio** (☎ 011-880 3414; www .portfoliocollection.com) lists a number of top B&Bs, mainly in the northern suburbs; they're upmarket and reasonably expensive, with singles from R250 to R450, and doubles from R400 to anything approaching R1000.

If you're looking to party, a bed near Melville or Norwood would be handy if you can find one. Otherwise the Rosebank and, increasingly, Fourways areas have decent after-hours entertainment. Places in the northern suburbs tend to be quite spread out, with few obvious accommodation ghettoes. In fact, many suburbs are served by a single hotel in each range, meaning that visiting a number of places before you settle on your favourite is the privilege of those with a car.

There are a few sleeping options in the city centre and prices can be very reasonable, but standards tend to be lower and the streets considerably less secure.

Yeoville was for years a backpacker favourite but is no longer. All hostels have either closed or relocated to safer areas.

When you arrive in Jo'burg most hostels offer free pick-up from the airport or Park Station. If a car doesn't show up, call the hostel or get a taxi. Nearly all of the hostels are on the route of the Baz Bus (see p633). Internet and satellite TV facilities are standard and most hotels will organise tours to Soweto, Kruger National Park and elsewhere.

City Centre & Newtown

In terms of accommodation, central Jo'burg can't touch the smarter suburbs. That said, if you are keen on hanging around New-

town and the Market Theatre complex, these places will save you in taxi fares.

Most of the budget hotels in the city centre, Berea and Hillbrow are run-down and depressing. You can't really go out at night on foot and you can get a backpackers double somewhere safer for the same price as a double room here, so there's not much argument for staying. Some of the better hotels in this area are good value, as the crime rate has chased away custom.

Formule 1 Hotel Park Station (Map p402; ☎ 011-720 2111; Park Station, Berea; r R189) This place offers anodyne rooms for a standard price. It is near the northeast corner of the huge Park Station complex and might appeal if you arrive late. It's a short walk from the main bus and train arrivals hall, and you can sleep up to three people in the room for the same price.

Orion Hotel Devonshire (Map p402; ☎ 011-339 5611; www.oriongroup.co.za; cnr Melle & Jorissen Sts, Braamfontein; s/d incl breakfast R360/545; P) On the doorstep of Wits University (p401), this midranger in a former office building has all the mod cons and clean rooms.

Protea Hotel Parktonian (Map p402; ☎ 011-403 5741; www.proteahotels.com; 120 De Korte St, Braamfontein; s/d incl breakfast R750/910; P ☒) The Parktonian is the best hotel in the central Jo'burg area and draws visiting business types.

Melville

Pension Idube (Map p411; ☎ 011-482 4055; idube@ mail.com; 11 Walton Ave, Auckland Park; d with/without bathroom incl breakfast R330/270; ☒ P) This positively unpretentious place – bedecked in zebra motifs, to which its name refers – can't be beaten for its combination of comfort, price and location: walking distance to Melville and only 5km from the city centre. It serves inexpensive meals and has a patio that is the launch pad for some excellent braais (open-fire barbecue).

Thulani Lodge (Map p411; ☎ 011-482 1106; www .thulanilodge.co.za; 85 3rd Ave; s/d incl breakfast R400/500; P ☒) Despite its top location just metres from Melville's nightlife, Thulani lives up to its name, offering 'peace and quiet' in a series of small, neat rooms clustered intimately around a sparkling swimming pool.

Die Agterplaas (Map p411; ☎ 011-726 8452; agter plaas@icon.co.za; 66 Sixth Ave; s/d incl breakfast R420/530; ☒) Oozing with 'old' Melville grace, this colonial-era villa has lashings of comfy class, with Oregon pine flooring, a sun terrace and plenty of old-school bric-a-brac for décor.

Norwood

Garden Place (Map pp398-9; ☎ 011-485 3800; 53 Garden Rd, Orchards; s/d incl breakfast R445/750; P 🗙 🖳 🖭) It's slightly away from Grant Ave, but offers clean and comfortable rooms, superior service and facilities for overnighters, longer stayers, business people and newlyweds – a remarkably versatile and relaxing place to stay.

Northern Suburbs

BUDGET

Inchanga Ranch Resort (Map pp398-9; ☎ 011-708 2505; www.inchangaresort.co.za; 51 Inchanga Rd, Craigavon; camp sites R40, dm/s/d R75/200/250, cabins from R160; P 🖳 🖭) A wonderful country retreat just minutes from the shops and casino of Montecasino. Accommodation is in cute private A-frame huts with animal-print linens, and there are enough activities and privacy here for backpackers and families alike.

Gemini Backpackers (Map pp398-9; ☎ 011-882 6845; www.geminibackpackers.com; 1 Van Gelder Rd, Crystal Gardens; camp sites R50, dm/s/d with shared bathroom R65/150/190; P 🖳 🖭) Readers are divided about the merits of this place, but we think it's okay. Certainly there are many amenities, including a pizza oven, travel desk, volleyball and tennis courts, a gym and a video library for film buffs. It's a bit out of the way, but staff will pick you up from the airport and there's a daily shuttle to the shops. Ask about tours of nearby township Alexandra.

Sleek Backpackers (Map pp398-9; ☎ 011-787 8070; www.sleekhostel.150m.com; 477 Jan Smuts Ave, Randburg; dm/s/d with shared bathroom R85/100/200; P 🖳 🖭) A converted house is now a small hostel run with a personal touch. Dorms and doubles are basic but clean. It's in a handy location about halfway between the city centre and Fourways.

Backpackers Ritz (Map pp398-9; ☎ 011-325 7125; www.backpackers-ritz.co.za; 1A North Rd, Dunkeld West; dm/s/d with shared bathroom R85/175/260; P 🖳 🖭) Some readers love the 'Ritz', but we're not convinced. Certainly, you'll be sacrificing luxury, cleanliness and quiet for a great location (it's a safe hop-and-a-skip from Hyde Park Mall, and plenty of bars and restaurants), but it's lots of fun: there's a crypt-like bar and sunset braais with stunning views. It's in a characterful old mansion, yet curiously the dorm rooms are very large and the doubles a bit cramped. A real curate's egg: judge for yourself.

MIDRANGE

Craighall House (Map pp398-9; ☎ 011-326 0326; craighallhouse@mweb.co.za; 10 Alexandra Ave, Craighall; s/d incl breakfast R300/500; P 🖭) A purpose-built guesthouse with neatly designed rooms each with private entrance and patio, a beautiful garden, pergola and swimming pool. It's also in a good, secure location more or less halfway between Rosebank and Sandton.

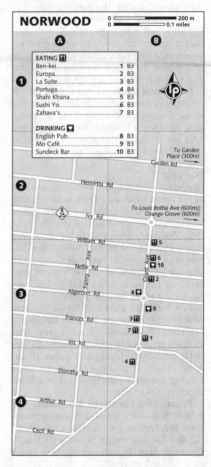

NORWOOD   0 ——— 200 m   0 ——— 0.1 miles

	A	B
EATING 🍴		
Ben-kei...............................1		B3
Europa................................2		B3
La Suite.............................3		B3
Portuga.............................4		B4
Shahi Khana.....................5		B3
Sushi Yo............................6		B3
Zahava's............................7		B3
DRINKING 🍷		
English Pub.....................8		B3
Mo Café............................9		B3
Sundeck Bar...................10		B3

To Garden Place (300m)

Garden Rd

Henrietta Rd

To Louis Botha Ave (600m); Orange Grove (600m)

Ivy Rd

William Rd

Nellie Rd

Algernon Rd

Frances Rd

Iris Rd

Dorothy Rd

Arthur Rd

Cecil Rd

GAUTENG

Don Suites Apartments at Rosebank (Map pp398-9; ☎ 011-880 1666; fax 880 3366; 10 Tyrwhitt Ave, Rosebank; s/d incl breakfast R530/655; P ꙮ) This is the only black-owned hotel chain in the land and it offers excellent rooms. This place is no exception.

Kosher B&B (Map pp398-9; ☎ 011-485 5006; www .kosherbandb.co.za; 124 3rd Ave, Fairmount; s/d incl breakfast from R550/750; P ꙮ) The only B&B under the supervision of the Johannesburg Beth Din, it offers clean, good-sized if uninspiring rooms and an onsite restaurant that's open to the public (but closed on Saturdays). Ask for the kosher sushi.

Quatermain Hotel (Map pp398-9; ☎ 011-290 0900; www.quatermain.co.za; 137 West Rd South, Morningside; s/d incl breakfast R765/1055; P ꙮ ꙮ) Named for the colonial Ryder Haggard creation but much more politically correct, this is one of Jo'burg's best midrange options, with stylish fittings, excellent service and a great location near (but not consumed by) the glitz of Sandton. Its award-winning restaurant, The Courier, is another huge bonus.

Protea Hotel Wanderers (Map pp398-9; ☎ 011-770 5500; www.proteahotels.com; cnr Rudd Rd & Corlett Dr, Melrose; s/d incl breakfast R915/1050; P ꙮ ꙮ) Being near Wanderers Stadium, this is the perfect spot for cricket aficionados, and straddles the midrange and top-end divide.

TOP END

Liliesleaf (Map pp398-9; ☎ 011-803 3787; liliesleaf@llt .co.za; 8 Winston Ave, Rivonia; s/d incl breakfast R600/1200; P ꙮ ꙮ) This stylishly appointed guesthouse may be a tad out of the way and therefore overpriced, but its history makes it priceless. It was here that Nelson Mandela met with the African National Congress to plot the overthrow of the Nationalist government before a police raid in 1963 led ultimately to his long incarceration.

Park Hyatt (Map pp398-9; ☎ 011-280 1234; www .johannesburg.hyatt.com; 191 Oxford Rd, Rosebank; s/d R1250/1450; P ꙮ ꙮ ꙮ) With a great spot in the heart of the northern suburbs, this reliable place offers plenty of five-star, chain-hotel luxury. It is the staple of the city's visiting business travellers and boasts an excellent wine cellar.

Palazzo Inter-Continental Montecasino (Map pp398-9; ☎ 011-510 3000; www.southernsun.com; Montecasino Blvd, Fourways; r incl breakfast R1600; P ꙮ ꙮ ꙮ) Another victim of Jo'burg's much-favoured faux Tuscan styling, this glossy

number mixes Mediterranean charm with superslick service and all the usual five-star trimmings. The adjacent Montecasino development provides plenty to do without having to jump in a car.

Melrose Arch Hotel (Map pp398-9; ☎ 011-214 6666; 1 Melrose Sq, Melrose Arch; s/d incl breakfast from R1750/2900; P ꙮ ꙮ ꙮ) While it has none of the old Jo'burg charm of suburban B&Bs, nor the homespun urban African chic of Soweto's guesthouses, this spare, slick, ultramodern masterpiece is as good a symbol of Jo'burg's confidence as you're likely to find. Charming features include a restaurant whose layout encourages you to engage with fellow diners, a soundproof room fitted with top-of-the-range audiovisual equipment, and a heated swimming pool where you can dine in the water. Its tasteful, unconventional styling and thoroughly mixed staff and clientele hint at a future South Africa of integration and prosperity. Dare to dream…

Intercontinental Sandton Sun & Towers (Map pp398-9; ☎ 011-780 5000; www.southernsun.com; cnr Fifth & Alice Sts, Sandton; r incl breakfast from R2200; P ꙮ ꙮ ꙮ) Just across the road from the Sandton City and Nelson Mandela Sq malls, this place is the pride of the Southern Sun Group. The Sandton Sun caters for the wealthy, while the Towers pampers the megarich.

Michelangelo (Map pp398-9; ☎ 011-282 7000; www .michelangelo.co.za; Nelson Mandela Sq, 135 West St; s/d incl breakfast from R2200/2450; P ꙮ ꙮ ꙮ) A six-storey hotel housing every imaginable amenity, including a spa and gym. All 242 rooms overlook a large atrium, and are tastefully designed in a muted version of the painted-on shutters and flamingo-pink porticoes of the surrounding building.

Grace in Rosebank (Map pp398-9; ☎ 011-280 7200; www.thegrace.co.za; 54 Bath Ave, Rosebank; d incl breakfast from R2400; P ꙮ ꙮ ꙮ) Offering a distinctly personal big-city experience, this stylish boutique hotel places an emphasis on service and keeps a galaxy of stars, honeymooners and well-heeled business travellers coming back for more.

Ten Bompas (Map pp398-9; ☎ 011-341 0282; www .tenbompas.com; 10 Bompas Rd, Dunkeld West; r incl breakfast R2400; P ꙮ ꙮ) A true original, with 10 individually styled, five-star suites, a restaurant with an excellent wine list and floor-mounted televisions in its unisex lobby toilet.

Westcliff (Map pp398-9; ☎ 011-481 6000; www.orient -expresshotels.com; 67 Jan Smuts Ave, Westcliff; d from R2470; P ❌ ⛉ 🏊) A favourite among visiting celebrities, this is a sprawling, stylish and very pink hotel with apartment block–style privacy and a majestic setting above the zoo. Luxuries are laid on with a trowel, including instant hot water and impeccable service.

Saxon (Map pp398-9; ☎ 011-292 6000; www.the saxon.com; 36 Saxon Rd, Sandhurst; r incl breakfast from R4250; P ❌ ⛉ 🏊) The *ne plus ultra* of impossibly opulent Jo'burg, this gorgeous, all-suite boutique hotel offers no-holds-barred luxury. In the 1990s, Nelson Mandela spent six months in the peace and comfort here as he finished off his autobiography; it's not difficult to see why. Now, there is a series of images on the corridor walls of the great man in various real and imagined settings.

Eastern Suburbs
BUDGET
Brown Sugar Backpackers (Map pp398-9; ☎ 011-648 7397; www.brownsugar.web.za; 75 Observatory Ave, Observatory East; camp sites R45, dm/d with shared bathroom R70/170; P ⛉ 🏊) In a large, somewhat grotty old mansion is this lively backpackers with enthusiastic staff and excellent views from its sunny braai deck.

Airport Backpackers (☎ 011-394 0485; airportback packer@hotmail.com; 3 Mohawk St, Rhodesfield; camp sites R60, dm/s/d with shared bathroom R80/190/240; P ⛉ 🏊) Just 2km from the airport (free pick-ups and drop-offs), this so-so place is best used for coming off the jet lag, but not really for long stays. There's a pleasant *lapa* bar (a low-walled building with a thatched roof) and decent pool.

Bruma Backpackers (Map pp398-9; ☎ 011-616 2741; egatebp@netactive.co.za; 41 Hans Pirow Rd, Bruma; dm R60, s/d with shared bathroom R140/160; P ⛉ 🏊) Within walking distance of Chinatown and Bruma Lake Market World (p415), this two-storey house feels more like a cheap B&B than a hostel, which means it's low on atmosphere but high on comfort.

Diamond Digger's Lodge (Map pp398-9; ☎ 011-624 1676; www.oneandonly.co.za; 36 Doris St, Kensington; dm/d with shared bathroom R70/180; P ⛉ 🏊) An excellent backpackers, with every imaginable amenity, including a Jacuzzi, sauna, a big-screen home cinema and a pub for post-tour frolics. It's set on a rambling conglomeration of properties so privacy is

also possible, and there are a few en suite doubles (R250).

Purple Palms (☎ 011-393 4393; info@purplepalms .co.za; 1 Boompeiper Ave, Kempton Park; d with/with out shared bathroom R260/220 tr R330; P ⛉ 🏊) Twinned with Pretoria's North South Backpackers, and in a quiet suburb 2km from the airport, this is a friendly, well-run way station for backpackers passing through Gauteng.

MIDRANGE
Emerald Guest House (☎ 011-394 1198; 19 Halifax St, Rhodesfield, Kempton Park; s/d R275/400; P ❌ ⛉ 🏊) We've been getting very good reports about this guesthouse, which boasts a good location within easy striking distance of the airport and plenty of home comforts and decent rooms. It makes a convenient stopover if you have an early flight; airport transfers are offered.

Duneden Hotel (☎/fax 011-453 2002; 46 Van Riebeeck Ave, Edenvale; s/d R340/450; P ❌ 🏊) Another option close to the airport, this passable midranger has a bar, tennis courts and a gym. Again, it's worth considering if you are flying in or out in the early hours.

Southern Suburbs
Gold Reef City Casino Hotel (Map pp398-9; ☎ 011-248 5025; www.threecities.co.za; cnr Northern Parkway & Data Cres, Ormonde; s/d R780/1050; P ❌) You are likely to spend as much again in the casino, but the opulent rooms are quite good value at this place, 8km south of the city centre by Gold Reef City.

Protea Hotel Gold Reef City (Map pp398-9; ☎ 011-248 5700; www.proteahotels.com; Northern Parkway, Ormonde; s/d incl breakfast R900/1010; P ❌) Cleverly designed in old Jo'burg memorabilia, this excellent place has charming rooms and bags of upmarket Wild West character. Eight kilometres south of the city centre, and actually inside the theme-park gates, it is also probably the most secure hotel in Jo'burg.

EATING
Jo'burg is stacked with places to eat, satisfying every whim, craving, occasion and budget. Unfortunately for visitors, especially those without cars, most of the best places are scattered around the northern suburbs and they can be difficult to find. The big hotels have restaurants and in

GAUTENG

shopping centres you'll find franchised steakhouses such as Spur Ranch and Italian places such as Panarotti's.

For self-caterers, head to the glitzy supermarkets in the bowels of every shopping mall for the widest range of produce.

City Centre & Newtown

There is a clutch of excellent restaurants around the cultural precinct in Newtown; alternatively, for a cheap meal of mealie pap (maize stew) and braaied meat, try the stalls on and nearby Diagonal St – just follow your nose.

Kapitan's (Map p402; ☎ 011-834 8048; 11A Kort St; mains R30-60; ⏰ lunch & dinner) Jo'burg is awash with award-winning restaurants offering just about every world cuisine, but for a taste of the new city in surroundings that reflect its past, there's nothing quite like Kapitan's. Don't let the grubby stairwell put you off – this is a Jo'burg institution, with authentic Indian food and eccentric décor that's been attracting luminaries for years (Nelson Mandela and Oliver Tambo used to eat here in the 1950s). It is positively unpretentious and one of the few places in town where you'll see young lions black and white drinking with hepcats and grizzly city stalwarts groaning about how it's all gone to the dogs.

Guildhall Bar & Restaurant (Map p402; ☎ 011-833 1770; 88 Market St, Marshalltown; mains R35-50; ⏰ lunch & dinner) Established way back in 1888, this was one of the city's first bars and makes you wish the nicotine-stained, wood-panelled walls could talk. You can while away the day in the dark English-style pub below, or sit out on the upstairs balcony and watch the City of Gold pass you by over a pie and chips.

Gramadoela's (Map p402; ☎ 011-838 6960; Bree St, Newtown; mains R40-90; ⏰ lunch & dinner; ⊠) Full of curios and character, this gay-friendly Newtown classic in the Market Theatre complex whips up a mean mix of African and Asian cuisine, blending recipes that range from the Cape to Cairo and adding a distinctly Malay twist. Diners include Hillary Clinton, Denzel Washington and Nelson Mandela.

Moyo's (www.moyo.co.za; mains R50-100; ⊠) Newtown (Map p402; ☎ 011-838 1715; Bree St; ⏰ lunch & dinner); Melrose Arch (Map pp398-9; ☎ 011-684 1477; 5 Melrose Sq; ⏰ lunch & dinner); Parkview (Map pp398-9;

☎ 011-646 0058; Zoo Lake; ⏰ breakfast & lunch) Oozing chi-chi African charm, this busy chain offers a wide range of contemporary African eats. Each has a stylish cigar bar and fresh, herb-packed cooking forms the backbone of the innovative menu. There's also a top-notch wine list for vinophiles. Thanks to its waterside setting, our favourite is the Zoo Lake branch (though it's not open for dinner).

Melville

Northwest of Braamfontein, Melville has become the trendiest eating strip in Jo'burg. Restaurants and cafés have sprung up in the area around 7th St, known as 'Old Melville', and around the busier Main Rd about 1km away, known as 'New Melville'.

The best food is in Old Melville, where a Bohemian, youthful atmosphere prevails. Most of the cafés have outdoor seating – a rarity in Jo'burg – and in the warmer months 7th St takes on a Parisian ambience, with patrons sipping drinks and watching the world go by from pavement tables.

RESTAURANTS
Ant Café (Map p411; ☎ 011-726 2614; 11 7th St; mains R30-45; ⏰ breakfast, lunch & dinner) This hole-in-the-wall Italian eatery has a distinctly Bohemian edge and whips up tasty pizzas in snug surrounds. Note that only cash is accepted.

Soulsa (Map p411; ☎ 011-482 5572; 16 7th St; mains R35-90; ⏰ lunch & dinner; ⊠) Funky décor, differing day and night menus featuring fusion South African cooking, and outdoor sofas have made Soulsa a Melville favourite among media types. Breakfast is served on weekends.

Paros Taverna (Map p411; ☎ 011-482 4781; cnr 7th St & 3rd Ave; mains R40-75; ⏰ lunch & dinner; ⊠) With fresh, white-and-blue taverna décor and tasty Greek eats, this little piece of the Mediterranean gets lively on the weekends. On Saturday morning, they're still sweeping up the smashed plates from the night before.

Soi (Map p411; ☎ 011-726 5775; cnr 7th St & 3rd Ave; mains R45-90; ⏰ lunch & dinner; ⊠) Flash, oh-so-trendy Asian décor gives this place a hip, stylish edge. The Thai and Vietnamese food is fresh and zesty, and there's a bar full of beautiful people attached.

Melville Grill (Map p411; ☎ 011-727 2890; cnr 7th St & 3rd Ave; mains R50-120; 🕑 lunch & dinner; 🗷) The only place for a hardcore meat feast, this upmarket steakhouse serves sublime aged cuts in modern surrounds. It also claims to cater for vegetarians.

Chaplin's (Map p411; ☎ 011-482 4657; 85 4th Ave; mains R80-110; 🕑 lunch & dinner; 🗷) This twee little bistro whips up some legendary food and, in an area where new places come and go in a flash, remains a true veteran. European meat and fish dishes predominate.

Eateries in New Melville are generally not as good as those around 7th St – this is where you will find the usual chain eateries – but they are generally easier on the pocket. The **Catz Pyjamas** (Map pp398-9; ☎ 011-726 8596; cnr Main Rd & 3rd Ave) can be a little sterile, but it is open 24 hours and the cheap food is welcome if you've had a long night out.

CAFÉS & QUICK EATS

Ish Caffé (Map p411; ☎ 011-482 4320; cnr 7th St & 4th Ave; light meals R25; 🕑 breakfast, lunch & dinner) Chic design, scrumptious breakfasts, great cappuccinos and gorgeous staff – what more could you ask for?

De La Creme (Map p411; ☎ 011-726 7716; cnr 7th St & 4th Ave; mains R40-55; 🕑 breakfast, lunch & dinner) One of Jo'burg's best patisseries, with a daily selection of freshly baked delicious sweet treats such as homemade gateaux, and a full meal menu. It's closed on Monday nights.

Spiro's Cafe (Map p411; ☎ 011-482 1162; cnr 7th St & 2nd Ave; mains R40-70; 🕑 breakfast, lunch & dinner) With terrace seating outside and huge, comfy sofas inside, this place heaves at breakfast time. Come nightfall, it serves up some tasty restaurant tucker before slowly transforming into a bar.

Norwood

This enclave of restaurants has grown and matured into an east Jo'burg version of Melville's 7th St. There are more than 20 bars, restaurants and cafés along Grant Ave, most of which are open every day.

RESTAURANTS

Portuga (Map p407; ☎ 011-728 0451; 37 Grant Ave; mains R25-45 🕑 lunch & dinner) This place brings all the flavours of Mozambique to its seafood menu. The setting is quite basic, but the food's good value.

Shahi Khana (Map p407; ☎ 011-728 8157; 80 Grant Ave; mains R30-60; 🕑 lunch & dinner; 🗷) Promising the 'top 40 curries of India', this is the place to try a hot dish and weep over your naan bread for the respite of a sweet lassi.

Sushi Yo (Map p407; ☎ 011-483 0293; 74 Grant Ave; mains R35-55; 🕑 lunch & dinner) This on-the-hop Japanese place has a rotating sushi counter and does deliveries.

Ben-kei (Map p407; ☎ 011-483 3296; 48 Grant Ave; mains R40-70; 🕑 lunch & dinner; 🗷) This jazzy Japanese place attracts Norwood's young trendies with its fashionable styling and authentic cooking. If you have had enough red meat, the sushi offers welcome reprieve from the braai, and it's the best in town at these prices. Try the all-you-can-eat sushi platter (R110).

La Suite (Map p407; ☎ 011-728 9262; cnr Grant Ave & Francis Rd; mains R40-80; 🕑 lunch & dinner; 🗷) This is one of Norwood's plusher eateries, with wicker chairs on the pavement and coffee-and-cream décor inside. There's a wide range of local and European dishes on the menu, or you can dig into the lunchtime buffet.

MELVILLE 0 ——— 600 m / 0 ——— 0.4 miles

INFORMATION	
ATM	1 B2
Book Dealers of Melville	2 B2
Out of Print Books	3 B2

SLEEPING 🛏	
Die Agterplaas	4 B1
Pension Idube	5 B3
Thulani Lodge	6 B2

EATING 🍴	
Ant Café	7 B2
Chaplin's	8 B2
De La Creme	9 B2
Ish Caffé	10 B2
Melville Grill	11 B2
Paros Taverna	12 B2
Soi	13 B2
Soulsa	14 B2
Spiro's Cafe	15 B2

DRINKING 🍷	
Berlin Bar	16 B2
Ratz Bar	17 B2
Six	18 B2
Tokyo Star	19 B2
Trance Sky	20 B2

To Main Rd; 'New' Melville (100m)

GAUTENG

CAFÉS & QUICK EATS

Zahava's (Map p407; ☎ 011-728 6511; 47A Grant Ave; snacks R15-30; ☺ breakfast & lunch; ✖) A cute coffee shop and hookah bar specialising in Middle Eastern snacks, including *zivas* (Yemenite flatbread) and *latkes* (Yiddish potato fritters).

Europa (Map p407; ☎ 011-483 0799; 66 Grant Ave; mains R20-50; ☺ breakfast & lunch) This open-fronted café heaves on the weekend, when the Norwood set congregates here to tuck into their weekly omelette.

Northern Suburbs

The many eating options in these affluent suburbs are centred on the huge shopping malls that form the core of northern-suburbs society; these are completely lacking in atmosphere once the shops have closed.

Not far from Melville, the suburb of Greenside also boasts a clutch of decent eateries. The area is rather more middle-aged – this is not a party zone – but a few of the restaurants draw punters from across the city. The restaurants are in a little cluster on Gleneagles Rd and Greenway, just off Barry Hertzog Ave.

Vida e Caffé (Map pp398-9; ☎ 011-646 1340; 24 Gleneagles Rd, Greenside; light meals R15-25; ☺ breakfast & lunch; ✖) Considered by many the best coffee fix in town, with tasty snacks and beautiful people moving in and out all day. Come just *after* closing time (5pm) and score a free leftover muffin; they're huge.

Cranks (Map pp398-9; ☎ 011-880 3442; Shop 52, Rosebank Mall; mains R35-55; ☺ lunch & dinner; ✖) Still going after almost 20 years, Cranks was one of the first Thai-Vietnamese places in Jo'burg. Among the tried-and-tested favourites is fish fillet with lemongrass (R45).

Gaia (Map pp398-9; ☎ 011-912 7879; cnr 4th Ave & 7th St, Linden; mains R35-70; ☺ lunch & dinner; ✖) The basement level of the former Linden Hotel is now an Afro-Mediterranean restaurant designed in earthy tones and with a suitably health-oriented menu to match. It's a bit out of the way, but worth the trip.

Ove Flo (Map pp398-9; ☎ 011-486 4576; 116 Greenway, Greenside; mains R40-60; ☺ lunch & dinner; ✖) This Continental-style bistro is a good spot for romantic dining, with an atmospheric, womb-red interior, plenty of gold-edged mirrors for checking your hair, and a menu offering everything from snail pizza to freshly ground coffee.

Karma (Map pp398-9; ☎ 011-646 8555; cnr Barry Hertzog Ave & Gleneagles Rd, Greenside; mains R40-70; ☺ lunch & dinner) Bringing traditional Indian cooking into the 21st century, this stylish place puts a contemporary spin on the old favourites and offers a smorgasbord of tasty vegetarian dishes for those sick of the South African meat obsession.

Yum (Map pp398-9; ☎ 011-486 1645; www.yum.co.za; 26 Gleneagles Rd, Greenside; mains R40-200; ☺ lunch & dinner; ✖) A small restaurant with a big reputation. One of the city's most celebrated dining rooms – it has even published its own cookbook – Yum specialises in innovative fusion cooking, with an emphasis on top-notch ingredients and lashings of culinary flair. It closes for most of the month of January.

Bite (Map pp398-9; ☎ 011-486 0449; 137 Greenway, Greenside; mains R50-80; ☺ lunch & dinner; ✖) Asian food is served in this slick eatery, whose clean lines and muted tones recall a Japanese Zen garden. Try the fresh line fish steamed in banana leaves.

Circle (Map pp398-9; ☎ 011-646 3744; 141 Greenway, Greenside; mains R90-120; ☺ lunch & dinner; ✖) With an emphasis on real ingredients, this informal, popular place is a restaurant for all seasons, with something on the menu to suit every fancy and appetite.

Eastern Suburbs

Near Bruma Lake is Derrick Ave, Cyrildene, off Observatory Rd, and there's an established Chinatown (Map pp398–9) with a number of cheap restaurants. Represented are Taiwanese, Korean, Sichuan, Shanghai and Hong Kong styles served in those lifeless places with Formica-top tables and plastic chairs; most close at about 9.30pm.

Radium Beerhall (Map pp398-9; ☎ 011-728 3866; 282 Louis Botha Ave, Orange Grove; mains R40-60; ☺ lunch & dinner) It's a tad crummy and the food (filling Portuguese fare) is nothing to write home about. But the draught beer is always cold, the crowd always festive and, as this was Jo'burg first ever-licensed pub, it has an atmosphere of the city's gold-rush days rich enough to have theme parks green with envy.

Adega do Monge (Map pp398-9; ☎ 011-614 3041; 32 Roberts Ave, Kensington; mains R60-80; ☺ lunch & dinner) A heaving, tastefully designed Luso–South African joint close to Diamond Digger's Lodge that draws in Eastern Suburbs locals and folks from further afield – bookings are highly advised. Portions are huge and waitrons are Portuguese-speaking. The real thing.

DRINKING

Party-loving Jo'burg has a constantly changing mix of bars, pubs and clubs, ranging from the outrageous to the downright conservative; whatever you prefer, you'll find somewhere to feel comfortable. Much of the nightlife is in the northern suburbs, particularly around Melville, Norwood and Rosebank – just ask around. The area around the cultural precinct in Newtown also has a few decent places for a tipple.

For a listing of live music venues and nightclubs, see (p414).

City Centre & Newtown

Horror Café (Map p402; ☎ 011-838 6735; 5 Becker St, Newtown) The neon-green décor is indeed a horror, but big crowds, and its proximity to the SAB World of Beer, ensure that this venue is never short of action. It's reggae on Thursdays, while Saturday is gay and lesbian night.

Guildhall Bar & Restaurant (Map p402; ☎ 011-833 1770; 88 Market St) A great place to soak up some history while stoking the fires with a pint or two of lager. There's an upstairs terrace for city-centre people-watching and food available.

Melville

Berlin Bar (Map p411; ☎ 011-482 9345; 6 7th St) With an ultracool design recalling the Black Forest and Jo'burg's most tortured artists lounging on its retro furniture, this was definitely Melville's hippest hangout when we swung through town.

Six (Map p411; ☎ 011-482 8306; 7th St) They haven't pulled out many stops decorating this place – the generous might call it 'industrial chic' – but it stays open later than most during the week, there are some decent cocktails on show, and punters come for the vibrant, unpretentious atmosphere.

Ratz Bar (Map p411; ☎ 011-726 2019; 9B 7th St) This cosy place has rats daubed on the walls rather than running across the floors and is only for over-24s. Try one of its tasty and well-priced cocktails (R18).

Trance Sky (Map p411; ☎ 011-726 2241; 7 7th St) The pun itself deserves a few brownie

points, but the whirly décor and trance-style tunes set the pace at this lively, late-night joint.

Tokyo Star (Map p411; ☎ 011-834 9187; 78 4th Ave) Anime chic and loads of plastic characterise this trendy, noisy Tokyo-style bar where young people nightly learn the rules of seduction and break the laws of attraction. Asian snacks such as tempura (R22) are served.

Cool Runnings (Map pp398-9; ☎ 011-482 4786; 27A 4th Ave) Reggae is a perennial favourite in Jo'burg, so it is no surprise that this franchise of Jamaican-style bars is popular. A relaxed atmosphere, thumping bass-lines and late, lively nights are a sure thing.

Norwood

Sundeck Bar (Map p407; ☎ 011-728 2279; 72 Grant Ave) Popular with pathological people-watchers, the upstairs terrace bar at this place is the perfect spot to sip a cocktail and watch Norwood drift by.

Mo Café (Map p407; ☎ 011-728 8256; Grant Ave) This camp, retro-style affair offers beautiful people, stacks of irony and lashings of orange décor. Fashionable facial hair is a must. There's a full food menu for late-night munchies.

English Pub (Map p407; ☎ 011-483 1101; cnr Algernon Rd & Grant Ave) Offering plenty of rough-and-tumble action and an English pub–style ambience, this is a good spot on the weekends for determined drinking and lively banter.

ENTERTAINMENT

The best entertainment guide is in Friday's *Mail & Guardian*. 'Tonight' in the daily *Star* is also good. For entertainment bookings by credit card, contact **Computicket** (☎ 011-915 8000; www.computicket.com), which can arrange seats for almost every theatre, cinema and sports venue. For parties and get-togethers, check out the following: www.jhblive.co.za or www.joburg.org.za.

Cinemas

Huge cinema centres can be found across Jo'burg, with almost every shopping centre boasting one. **Ster-Kinekor** (☎ central bookings 082 16789; www.sterkinekor.co.za) has the widest distribution of multiplexes, with screens in the Fourways, Westgate, Eastgate, Sandton and Rosebank malls.

If it's a large screen that you're seeking, the grandest addition to Jo'burg's entertainment scene is the **Imax Theatre** (Map pp398-9; ☎ 011-325 6182; Hyde Park Mall, Jan Smuts Ave, Hyde Park).

Live Music & Nightclubs

Jo'burg is home to a thriving live-music scene, and on any given night you can see rock, pop, kwaito, jungle, jazz and hip-hop acts, and all manner of house and techno (see p62 for more on kwaito and other local sounds). On weekends Jo'burgers really come out to play and regularly hold enormous raves. There's little pattern to the spread of venues, but you'd be safe to assume that in most cases the further north you go the tamer they become.

If you want to get a sense of what central Jo'burg has to offer, the area around the Newtown cultural precinct (Map p402), with its bars, eateries, theatres and music venues, is the best place to kick off an evening.

CLASSICAL

Johannesburg Philharmonic Orchestra (☎ 011-789 2733; www.jpo.co.za) The city's budding orchestra stages a regular circuit of concerts, utilising venues from Wits University to City Hall. Call or check its website for the latest programme.

CONTEMPORARY

The suburban venues tend to cater to a wealthier crowd, so prices also tend to be a little higher – and watch what you wear as dress codes apply.

Carfax (Map p402; ☎ 011-834 9187; 39 Pim St, Newtown; admission R70) This industrial space symbolises integrated Jo'burg and is one of the hottest club tickets in town, with weekend DJs and a house-oriented music scene. It's big, loud and a tons of fun – just watch out for pickpockets.

Kippie's Jazz International (Map p402; ☎ 011-833 3316; www.kippies.co.za; Bree St, Newtown; admission R50) Kippie's, named after the great Kippie 'Morolong' Moeketsi, is a 'must do' in Jo'burg as it's one of the best places to see South African jazz talent, which happens to be exceptional. Gigs and events kick off on Friday and Saturday nights at around 9.30pm.

Mix (Map pp398-9; ☎ 011-214 4300; 17 High St, Melrose Arch, Melrose; admission R80) Extremely slick (there's a 'smart-casual' policy and the bouncers mean it) and packed with the beautiful set, this glossy suburban number plays everything from African tribal rhythms to hardcore techno. Cocktails (from R26) are the drink of choice.

206 Live (Map pp398-9; ☎ 011-728 5333; 206 Louis Botha Ave, Orange Grove) Garage, ragga, drum 'n' bass and rock tracks keep the feet tapping here. Next door, 208 keeps the flag flying over the local hip-hop crowd.

Sport

South Africans love their sport. Their inability to prove themselves against the world's best (thanks to international boycotts) arguably contributed to the dismantling of apartheid.

CRICKET

The most important cricket venue is the impressive **Wanderers Cricket Ground** (Map pp398-9; ☎ 011-788 1008; Corlett Dr, Illovo), just off the M1 freeway to Pretoria. Either watch from the stands or head to the grassy banks and braai yourself a steak while you watch a local limited-overs match or see South Africa's best take on an international team.

GAY & LESBIAN GAUTENG

Gauteng has a thriving gay scene and, since the liberalisation of the constitution in 1994, the twin metropoles have become a centre for gays and lesbians from across Africa. Gays are well organised and increasingly accepted – a far cry from the puritanical attitudes of the past.

The annual **Gay Pride March** (☎ 011-717 4239; www.gala.wits.ac.za), held in Johannesburg on the last weekend of September, is the focal point, but by no means the only organised activity. In fact, one of the highlights is taking a Queer Johannesburg Tour (p405).

A number of websites provide information on the province's gay scene: www.togs.co.za, www .mask.org.za and www.heavensgate.co.za are all packed with useful material. Also check out the monthly *Gay Times* magazine.

For more information you can also contact **Out in Pretoria** (☎ 012-344 5108).

SOCCER

The Rand Stadium (Map pp398–9), near Turffontein; FNB Stadium (Map p422), also known as Soccer City, further east on Baragwanath Rd near Soweto; and Ellis Park (pp398–9) are the major venues for soccer, the country's most-supported sport (no, rugby is not the most popular; see the boxed text, p423). The most popular teams are also the greatest rivals: Soweto teams the Orlando Pirates (known as the 'Bucs') and the 'mighty, all conquering' Kaizer Chiefs, or 'Amakhosi'. The annual league derby between the two teams is a highlight, simultaneously dividing and uniting communities across the city. Dates change every year depending on league fixtures. Following in the footsteps of marketing-savvy European superclubs, there's now a **Kaizer Chiefs store** (Map p402; ☎ 011-838 6477; Gandhi Sq; ⌚ 8.30am-4.30pm Mon-Fri).

RUGBY

The spiritual home of Jo'burg – some would argue South African – rugby is **Ellis Park** (Map pp398-9; ☎ 011-402 8644; www.sarugby.net; Doornfontein), just east of the city centre. It's the headquarters of SA Rugby and was the scene of one of the new nation's proudest moments – victory in the 1995 World Cup. Rugby supporters are fanatical, and Ellis Park can hold 70,000: a Saturday afternoon at the rugby can be an almost religious experience. During the winter months, the stadium hosts some of the well-supported Super 14 matches.

OTHER SPORTS

Kyalami (☎ 011-466 2800), off the M1 between Jo'burg and Pretoria, is the venue for motor sports.

There are several horse-racing tracks, but the best known is **Turffontein Race Course** (Map pp398-9; ☎ 011-681 1500), 3km south of the city. There are race meetings most weeks.

Theatres

Market Theatre (Map p402; ☎ 011-832 1641; www .markettheatre.co.za; Bree St) The Market Theatre is the most important venue for live theatre. There are three live-theatre spaces – the Main, Laager and Barney Simon Theatres – as well as galleries, a café and the excellent Kippie's Jazz International (opposite). There is always some interesting theatre, ranging from sharply critical contemporary plays to musicals and stand-up comedy – check the programme in the *Mail & Guardian* entertainment section. Other theatres:

Civic Theatre (Map p402; ☎ 011-877 6800; www.showbusiness.co.za; Loveday St, Braamfontein)

Laboratory (Map p402; ☎ 011-836 0516; Bezuidenhout St) An offshoot of the Market Theatre that acts as a showcase for community talent, with free local-theatre shows every Saturday at 1pm.

Pieter Toerien Theatre (Map pp398-9; ☎ 011-511 1818; Montecasino, William Nicol Dr, Fourways)

Windybrow Centre for the Arts (Map p402; ☎ 011-720 7009; cnr Nugget & Pietersen Sts, Hillbrow) A good testing ground for emerging black playwrights.

Wits Theatre Complex (Map p402; ☎ 011-717 1381; Jorissen St, Braamfontein)

SHOPPING
Arts & Crafts

For decent-quality African curios, you can head just over the border into North-West Province for the Welwitischia Country Market at Hartbeespoort Dam. See the boxed text, p514 for details.

Rosebank Rooftop Market (Map pp398-9; ☎ 011-788 5530) One of the most convenient places to shop for traditional carvings, beadwork, jewellery, books and fertility dolls. Held every Sunday in Rosebank Mall's multilevel car park.

Beautiful Things (Map p402; ☎ 011-492 3696; Bus Factory, 2 President St, Newtown; ⌚ 10am-4pm) A community-run initiative selling arts and crafts from across the country.

Bruma Lake Market World (Map pp398-9; ☎ 011-622 9648; Observatory Rd) By Bruma Lake, this place sells a wide range of crafts and lots of kitsch.

Faraday Market (Map p402; cnr Eloff St & N2) This is an interesting place to wander around, with plenty of *muti* (traditional medicine) stalls.

Market Sq Market (Map p402; Bree St) Held on Saturday mornings in the car park opposite the Market Theatre, there's a lively, cheerful atmosphere (with buskers), and although most of the stalls sell flea-market rubbish, there are also some reasonable crafts amid the dross.

Malls

Jo'burg prides itself on its shops, and the city's malls are up there with the best. Jammed with Western consumer goods of every description, it sometimes seems like they are as much a wealthy white habitat as a place to go shopping.

A short walk from Newtown, you'll find **Oriental Plaza** (Map pp398-9; ☎ 011-838 6752; Bree St, Fordsburg; ⏰ 9am-5pm Mon-Fri, 8.30am-3pm Sat). This is our favourite mall in the city. It's unmissable for a look at the real Jo'burg in all its diversity, and the surrounding area of Fordsburg is historically and culturally fascinating. The centre itself is the place to come for cheap shoes, by-the-metre haberdashery and fresh samosas. Other malls:

Eastgate (Map pp398-9; ☎ 011-616 2209) Off the N12 just east of Bruma Lake. Boasts of being Africa's largest mall.

Fourways Mall (Map pp398-9; ☎ 011-465 6095; William Nicol Dr)

Hyde Park Mall (Map pp398-9; William Nicol Dr)

Nelson Mandela Square (Map pp398-9; ☎ 011-784 2750; Rivonia Rd) Adjoining and similar to Sandton City Mall, it's designed like an Italian piazza, with a large (and rather unflattering) statue of Nelson Mandela.

Rosebank Mall (Map pp398-9; ☎ 011-788 5530; Cradock Ave) If you're after serious retail therapy, head to this interlocking series of malls, with central parking on the corner of Cradock Ave and Baker St.

Sandton City Mall (Map pp398-9; ☎ 011-883 2011; Rivonia Rd) Very plush.

Music

You can get most titles in chain stores in the big malls. **Kohinoor** (Map p402; ☎ 011-834 1361; 54 Market St) is one of the best sources of ethnic/African music, and sells everything from kwaito to jazz.

GETTING THERE & AWAY
Air

South Africa's major international and domestic airport is **Johannesburg International Airport** (JIA; ☎ 011-921 6262; www.acsa.co.za). For more information, including international flight connections, see p622.

Be warned that you may be bombarded by several offers of travel, accommodation or even ATM help as you emerge from customs. If the person you deal with is not properly accredited as an Airports Company employee, odds-on he's a tout, dodgy porter or crook. A polite 'no, thank you' should be your response.

Distances in South Africa are large, so if you're in a hurry, some domestic flights

are definitely worth considering. For regular flights to national and regional destinations try **South African Airways** (SAA; ☎ 0861 359 722; www.flysaa.com), **South African Airlink** (SAAirlink; ☎ 011-961 1700; www.saairlink.co.za) and **South African Express** (☎ 011-978 5577; www.saexpress.co.za). All flights can be booked through SAA, which also has offices in the domestic and international terminals of JIA. It's worth checking and potentially booking fares online, but often prices don't differ tremendously.

Services include the following (prices are the average, one-way, one-week advance purchase fares). Note that fares tend to be determined more by route popularity rather that destination distance, so sometimes it might be cheaper and easier to go by bus.

Destination	One-way fare incl airport taxes (R)
Cape Town	790
Durban	650
East London	710
Kimberley	550
Manzini (Swaziland)	820
Maseru (Lesotho)	765
Nelspruit	750
Polokwane (Pietersburg)	805
Port Elizabeth	740
Upington	1300

Smaller budget airlines, including Comair, Kulula, 1time and Nationwide, also link Jo'burg with major destinations and often offer much cheapest fares. For contact details and details of other airline offices in Jo'burg, see p632.

Bus

There are a number of international bus services that leave Jo'burg from the Park Station complex (Map p402) for Mozambique (p629), Lesotho (p629), Botswana (p629), Namibia (p630), Swaziland (p630) and Zimbabwe (p631).

The main long-distance bus lines (national and international) also depart from and arrive at the Park Station transit centre, in the northwest corner of the site, where you will also find their respective booking offices. There is also a **Jo'burg information desk** (☎ 011-337 6650).

BAZ BUS

Backpackers can now be connected from Jo'burg to the most popular parts of the region (Swaziland, Durban, Garden Route and Cape Town) by **Baz Bus** (☎ 021-439 2323; www.bazbus.com), which picks up at hostels in Jo'burg and Pretoria, saving you the hassle of going into the city to arrange transport. All hostels have current timetables and prices. For more, see p633.

OTHER BUS COMPANIES

The most comprehensive range of services to/from Jo'burg is provided by government-owned lines **Translux** (☎ 0861-589 282; www.translux.co.za) and **City to City** (☎ 0861-589 282). For more information on these, plus the other major bus lines – **Greyhound** (☎ 012-323 1154; www.greyhound.co.za), **SA Roadlink** (☎ 011-333 2223; www.saroadlink.co.za) and **Intercape** (☎ 0861-287 287; www.intercape.co.za) – see p633.

With the exception of City to City buses, which commence in Jo'burg, all services that are not heading north commence in Pretoria at the Pretoria station.

TO CAPE TOWN

Translux has at least one bus running daily to Cape Town (R380, 19 hours) via Bloemfontein (R180, five hours). There are also less frequent services via Kimberley (R185, seven hours).

Greyhound has daily buses to Cape Town (R470, 18½ hours) via Bloemfontein (R200, six hours) and Kimberley (R210, seven hours).

Intercape also runs to Cape Town (R440, 19 hours) via Upington (R260, 10 hours). From Upington, you can also get an Intercape bus to Windhoek, Namibia (R250, 12 hours), but there isn't a direct connection.

SA Roadlink, the newest bus company, offers highly competitive rates from Jo'burg to Cape Town (R250, 19 hours). Buses depart daily.

TO DURBAN & KWAZULU-NATAL

Greyhound has four daily buses to Durban (R205, eight hours), including slower services via Newcastle (R195, five hours), Ladysmith (R175, 6½ hours) and Estcourt (R180, 7½ hours), and then to Richard's Bay (R220, eight hours). Translux has at least one bus a day to Durban (R170, eight hours), as does Intercape (R125, eight hours).

TO MPUMALANGA & KRUGER NATIONAL PARK

The nearest large town to Kruger National Park is Nelspruit. Greyhound runs there daily (R185, five hours). Note that this service starts in Jo'burg and picks up in Pretoria an hour later. Translux runs to Maputo, Mozambique, daily (R160, nine hours) via Nelspruit (R100, five hours).

City to City has some slow, cheap services from Jo'burg to Nelspruit (R80, seven hours) and Hazyview (R75, eight hours). Hazyview is closer to Kruger than Nelspruit, and has backpacker hostels that can arrange trips into the park.

Translux also has daily buses running to Phalaborwa (R150, 7½ hours), which is a good option if you're staying at a more northerly Kruger National Park camp such as Olifants.

TO THE NORTH

Several bus services run north up the N1. However, at the time of writing, no bus companies were offering services to Zimbabwe, largely because of the fuel shortages. Call to find out the current state of play. Most now only go as far as Polokwane (Pietersburg). From there you will have to catch a local bus or minibus taxi to get to the border.

Translux does has a daily service as far as Makhado (Louis Trichardt; R130, 6½ hours), but this strangely arrives at 2am! It goes via Mokopane (Potgietersrus; R125, four hours) and Polokwane (Pietersburg; R130, 4½ hours). It also has services that head east through Limpopo, stopping in Tzaneen (R125, 6½ hours) and Phalaborwa (R150, 7½ hours).

Greyhound has daily services to Polokwane (Pietersburg; R145, five hours). Intercape also heads north to Gaborone, Botswana (R150, seven hours).

There are daily City to City services to Sibasa, in Limpopo's Venda region (R100, 8½ hours). These services, which wind north through townships and ex-homelands, also stop in major towns on the N1.

North Link Tours (☎ 015-291 1867) runs buses between Jo'burg and Polokwane (Pietersburg; R120, 4½ hours) via Pretoria, and the smaller towns en route. From Polokwane, there are connections to Tzaneen and Phalaborwa.

TO THE SOUTH
Translux operates a daily service to East London (R320, 15 hours) via Bloemfontein (R150, seven hours). Translux also has five services a week (not on Sunday and Tuesday) from Jo'burg to Port Elizabeth (R350, 14½ hours) via Bloemfontein (R220, 10 hours) and Graaff-Reinet (R295, 14½ hours), and a Tuesday and Sunday service via Cradock (R300, 14½ hours).

Intercape has daily services to Port Elizabeth via Cradock (R300, 15 hours) and on to Plettenberg Bay (R385, 18 hours).

Greyhound has daily buses that travel overnight from Jo'burg to Port Elizabeth (R310, 15 hours) and East London (R270, 13 hours).

Translux runs to Knysna (R270) via Kimberley three times weekly or Bloemfontein four times weekly, then Oudtshoorn, Mossel Bay and George (all R285 from Jo'burg); the trip takes 17 hours. Intercape also operates to Knysna for the same price.

City to City runs to Mthatha (R115), the closest large town to Port St Johns and Coffee Bay, daily at 7pm. There are daily City to City services to Lusikisiki via Pietermaritzburg (R110) and to Dutywa via Queenstown (R95); call for times as they can vary substantially. Translux and Greyhound both run to Mthatha (R200, 12½ hours); Translux runs on Sunday, Tuesday, Thursday and Friday, and Greyhound runs daily except Saturday.

Car
All the major rental operators have counters at JIA and at various locations around the city. It is well worth calculating the length of your planned journey before you settle for a deal though. With many of the main operators offering a limited number of free kilometres, and distances in South Africa piling on the miles, you may end up with a nasty bill when it comes to returning the car.

Note that if you are paying with an international credit card, you may be asked for your passport and/or flight details. You will also need to produce a valid driver's licence (in English) or an International Driving Permit. Whichever you have, by law you must have it on your person at all times when at the wheel. For more about renting and listings of major rental agencies, see p636.

Hitching
We say don't hitch – especially here – but people do. Rather than hitching, ask about share-drives. These are often advertised in the weekly newspaper *Junk Mail,* and most hostels have notice boards with details of free or shared-cost lifts. But don't expect the hostel to take responsibility – remember it's up to you to check out the lift-giver and to decide whether or not you wish to travel with that person.

Minibus Taxi
The majority of minibuses taxis already use the new road-transport interchange in Park Station over the train tracks between the Metro Concourse and Wanderers St, but taxi ranks are still being chopped and changed. The best bet is to head to the Park Station concourse first, where taxi marshals can point you in the right direction. Because of the risk of mugging, it isn't a good idea to go searching for a taxi while carrying your luggage. Go down and collect information, then return in a taxi, luggage and all.

You can also find minibus taxis going in the direction of Kimberley, Cape Town and Upington on Wanderers St near Leyds St; Bulawayo taxis at the northern end of King George St; Pretoria taxis on Noord St; Lesotho, Bloemfontein (and other Free State destinations) on Noord St, east of Joubert Park; and Durban taxis near the corner of Wanderers and Noord Sts. Fares tend to fluctuate in line with petrol prices, but rates for trips from Jo'burg include:

Destination	Fare (R)
Bulawayo (Zimbabwe)	280
Cape Town	350
Durban	190
Gaborone (Botswana)	140
Harrismith	95
Kimberley	170
Komatipoort	160
Manzini (Swaziland)	135
Maputo (Mozambique)	220
Nelspruit	170
Polokwane (Pietersburg)	105
Pretoria	30
Thohoyandou (Venda)	130
Tzaneen	130

As well as these taxis, which only leave when they're full, there are a few door-to-door services you can book through hostels.

Train

For information on train services to/from Jo'burg and elsewhere in the country, see p641. Tickets can be booked at the **Spoornet** (☎ 0860-008 888) kiosk on the main concourse at Jo'burg's Park Station.

GETTING AROUND
To/From the Airport

JIA is about 25km east of central Johannesburg in Kempton Park. Between 5am and 10pm, buses run every half-hour between JIA and Park Station (R80, 45 minutes); contact **Metropolitan Bus Services** (Metrobus; ☎ 011-375 5555; www.mbus.co.za) for details. The area immediately around Park Station is confusing and known for muggings, so heading straight here is not to be advised if you are carrying your bags.

The **Airport Link** (☎ 011-884 3957) is another reputable airport shuttle.

Taxis are expensive at around R320 one way to the northern suburbs. Meters will generally be used, otherwise agree on a price before you get into the cab. Most hostels will collect you from the airport, and some still 'tout' there.

Bus

Metropolitan Bus Services (Metrobus; Map p402; ☎ 011-375 5555; www.mbus.co.za; Gandhi Sq) runs services covering 108 routes in the Greater Jo'burg area, though waiting for a bus in the car-dominated Northern Suburbs can be a bit like waiting for Godot. The main

bus terminal is at Gandhi Sq, two blocks west of the Carlton Centre, and fares work on a zonal system ranging from zone one (R3.60) to zone eight (R10). Metrobus prefers you to use their tag (starter tag R42) system. Travellers buy tags from the bus terminal or **Computicket** (☎ 011-915 8000; www .computicket.com), and the cost of the journey is automatically deducted each time you travel, as with a prepaid phonecard. Normal, adult tags are green and come in denominations of 52 trips monthly, 44 trips monthly, 14 trips weekly, 12 trips weekly and 10 trips weekly. The monthly tags must be used within 35 days, while the other tags have an expiry date of 10 days. You can still pay for journeys with cash, but Metrobus does its best to discourage this.

The following routes are useful (and there is a handy, interactive route-finder map at www.mbus.co.za).

Rte No	Destinations
5	Parktown, Houghton, Rosebank & Illovo
22	Yeoville & Bruma Lake
75	Braamfontein, Auckland Park & Melville
80	Rosebank & Dunkeld via Jan Smuts Ave

Minibus Taxi

Fares differ depending on routes, but Rte 5 will get you around the inner suburbs and the city centre and Rte 9 will get you almost anywhere (try to make sure you have small change before boarding).

It's easy enough to catch a minibus taxi into the city and, if you're waiting at a bus stop, the chances are a taxi will show up before the bus does. If you do take a minibus taxi into central Jo'burg, be sure to get

---

THE GAUTRAIN

One of the first things you might notice when driving on the M1 highway connecting Johannesburg and Pretoria is that you're not moving very fast. The tremendous growth of the province, along with South Africans' ongoing love affair with the car, have meant finding alternative transport has become a matter of urgency. The largest-scale solution is the Gautrain commuter train, a massive R120 billion project slated for completion in time for the 2010 Soccer World Cup. The proposed route is from Johannesburg International Airport to Park Station, through Rosebank and Sandton, then up to Pretoria before terminating in Hatfield, a trip of approximately 95km that this zippy piece of high-tech clickety-clack should be able to eat up in under an hour. At the time of writing, construction of the line had begun in earnest, but, thanks to legal wrangling and bitter fighting between consortia over tender awards, if you're planning to use it come footy time, be prepared for delays to your service.

GAUTENG

off before it reaches the end of the route and avoid the taxi rank – it's a mugging zone. Getting a minibus taxi home from the city is a more difficult proposition. Even locals often give up and take the bus. Minibus taxis do not generally run at night – if you do see one it's probably better not to take it.

There's a complex system of hand/finger signals to tell a passing taxi where you want to go, so it's best to look like you know where you're going and raise a confident index finger (drivers will stop if they are going the same way). You'll probably squeeze into an improbably small space, and money is passed forward row by row; change returned the same way. Shout out your desired stop when you get in, or just say 'Short left' or 'Short right' when you see your stop approaching. It's polite to thank the driver upon disembarking.

Taxi

Taxis are an expensive but necessary evil in this city. They all operate meters, which unfortunately seem to vary markedly in their assessment, if they work at all. Consequently, it's wise to ask a local the likely price and agree on a fare at the outset. From Park Station to Rosebank should cost around R75, and significantly more to Sandton. **International taxi** (☎ 011-390 1502), **Maxi Taxi Cabs** (☎ 011-648 1212) and **Rose's Radio Taxis** (☎ 011-403 9625) are three reputable firms.

Train

For inquiries about **Metro** (☎ 011-773 5878) train services call, or visit the helpful information office in the Park Station concourse. There has been a very serious problem with violent crime on the Metro system, mostly on those lines connecting with black townships. The Jo'burg–Pretoria Metro line should also be avoided.

SOWETO
☎ 011 / pop 2.3 million

No township in South Africa, even the world, has as much political and historical meaning as Soweto, born of a idea as simple and soulless as the acronym devised for its name – South-Western Townships. This sprawling conurbation of the country's migrant labour force and their descendants

is the biggest, most political, troubled and dynamic township too, and has of late embarked on a journey of self-discovery that is as much about the future as the past.

Tourists now flood into the area, attracted by some of the most poignant landmarks in South Africa's narrative and, after an initial exodus, local blacks are also returning, intent on forging a new identity for their community.

And so the face of this sprawling community – anything from 2.3 million (the latest official figure) to 4 million (local estimates) people live in Soweto – is changing. Large sections of the township are still characterised by desperate poverty, while others, such as Diepkloof Extension and Orlando West, are indicative of the growth of a new moneyed class. Against the Western media's beloved image of Soweto as a crime-ridden wasteland, the sprinkler-fed lawns of these middle-class suburbs are pleasant stereotype squashers.

The best place to start your visit is Vilakazi St, which may be the only street in the world to boast two Nobel peace laureates (Nelson Mandela and Desmond Tutu), both struggle heroes. Now that apartheid has been dismantled, new heroes will have to emerge in the battle against poverty, HIV/AIDS and crime. A resolution will be a long time coming, but Soweto remains a fascinating, living example of all that is good and bad in South Africa, suffering from the nation's devastating social problems, but also riding high on a community's determination to put them right.

History

Soweto's role in South Africa's recent history is unrivalled. As African National Congress (ANC) stalwart and long-time Soweto resident Walter Sisulu once said, the history of South Africa cannot be understood outside the history of Soweto.

Using the outbreak of bubonic plague in 1904 as an excuse, the Jo'burg City Council (JCC) moved 1358 Indians and 600 Africans from a Jo'burg slum to Klipspruit, 18km by road from the city centre (Klipspruit was, and still is, a long way from sources of employment).

It was a slow beginning, and by 1919 fewer than 4000 people called Klipspruit home. It wasn't until the late 1930s, after the suburb of Orlando had been built and cynically marketed by the JCC as 'Somewhat of a paradise', that the population began its astonishing growth.

By the end of WWII, Jo'burg's black population had risen by more than 400,000, and by 1958 more than 20 new suburbs had appeared around Orlando, each filled with row upon row of identical houses.

During the 1950s, organisations such as the ANC took a bigger role in opposing apartheid and before long Soweto (as it was officially named in 1961) would be recognised as the centre of resistance. Confirmation of this came in 1955 when 3000 delegates from around the country gathered in Kliptown Sq (known today as Freedom Sq) at the Congress of the People. The result was the Freedom Charter, which is the pillar of ANC philosophy and integral to the new constitution.

The demands of the charter were not unreasonable, but the response was less than sympathetic and the movement was forced underground in 1960 after the Sharpeville Massacre (see p41). Sowetans spent the next 15 years in a state of definite uncertainty – definite they wanted change but uncertain as to how and when it would come.

While the struggle continued at a slower pace, it was not the only change taking place here. The demographics of the townships were changing, and as second-generation Sowetans matured, so did Soweto style. New forms of music (see p59) emerged and the youth led the developments of a unique urban culture. Football also offered an escape, and massive support for teams such as Moroka Swallows, Orlando Pirates and (after they split from Pirates) Kaizer Chiefs, reflected the development of an urban black identity.

The development of this new identity only served to strengthen the desire to be treated as equals. Resistance eventually spilled over on 16 June 1976, when students organised a peaceful protest against the introduction of Afrikaans as a language of instruction in secondary schools. The students marched to the Orlando West Secondary School on Vilakazi St. When they arrived and refused to disburse, police fired tear gas into the crowd.

The chain of events that followed would eventually be seen as the turning point in the liberation struggle. In the resulting chaos police opened fire and a 13-year-old boy, Hector Pieterson, was shot dead. The ensuing hours and days saw students fight running battles with the security forces in what would become known as the Soweto Uprising. Dozens of government buildings were torched, but the euphoria of fighting the oppressor was tempered by the frightening human cost. On the first day alone, the official toll put two white policemen and 23 students as dead, but in reality closer to 200 teenage protesters had perished.

Many of the dead were buried as martyrs in Soweto's vast Avalon Cemetery, and the Hector Pieterson Memorial was built to commemorate all those who died in the struggle.

Within days, world opinion had turned irreversibly against the apartheid regime and Soweto became the most potent symbol of resistance to a racist South Africa.

Scenes of burning cars, 'necklaced' people and mass funerals flowed out of Soweto throughout the 1980s, as the death throes of apartheid could be felt. Mandela was released in 1990 and returned to live in his tiny home in Vilakazi St, just 200m from Archbishop Desmond Tutu. Tutu still lives here, while Mandela's old home has been converted into a museum.

However, Mandela's release was no panacea. Encouraged by the government, supporters of rival political parties murdered each other by the hundreds in the run up to the 1994 free elections.

More recently life has been stable, and since 1994 Sowetans have had ownership rights over their properties. The relative calm has been further compounded by a number of redevelopment projects, including the transformation of Hector Pieterson Sq into a memorial and major visitor attraction, along with growing tourist traffic and the return of many middle-class blacks. Indeed, many parts of Soweto are safer and more laid-back than Johannesburg's wealthy, high-security northern suburbs.

For a fabulous insight into Soweto's history, pick up a copy of Peter Magubane's photographic record *Soweto*.

Information

The new, impressive **Soweto Tourism and Information Centre** (☎ 011-945 3111; Walter Sisulu Sq,

Kliptown; ⏲ 8am-5pm Mon-Fri) is testament to a growing tourism policy here and a first for any township. It provides information and an accommodation and tour booking service, and there's an onsite Internet café (per hr R40) that also serves light meals (R25).

Sights & Activities

Soweto is by far the most visited township in the country, so don't feel that coming here as a tourist is either unsafe or inappropriate. Most visitors still come on a tour, but moves are being made to improve signposting (a perennial problem), and the infrastructure is now such that a self-guided tour is not out of the question – although heed local advice carefully. If you choose

to do this, stick to the area surrounding Vilakazi St and Hector Pieterson Sq.

If you are on a tour and want extra flexibility while avoiding the aloofness, take a tour as far as Vilakazi St (the greatest danger is getting hopelessly lost on the way into Soweto) and then rely on your guesthouse owner to get you safely between the various attractions, or contact Taste of Africa (p405). However you choose to see Soweto, the following attractions appear on most tour itineraries, or they can be visited on their own.

The first stop on most tours is the **Mandela Museum** (☎ 083-530 1521; 8115 Ngakane St; adult/child R20/10; ⏲ 9.30am-5pm), just off Vilakazi St. Nelson Mandela shared this tiny

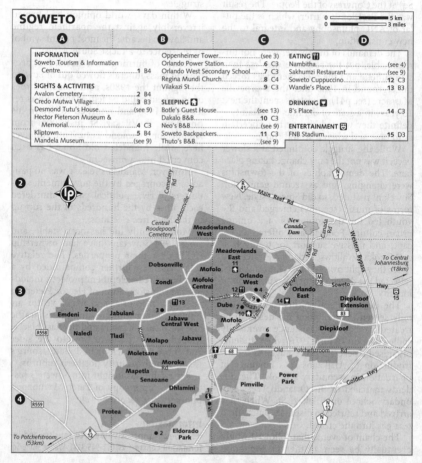

SOWETO

0 — 5 km
0 — 3 miles

INFORMATION
Soweto Tourism & Information Centre..................................1 B4

SIGHTS & ACTIVITIES
Avalon Cemetery............................2 B4
Credo Mutwa Village.....................3 B3
Desmond Tutu's House............(see 9)
Hector Pieterson Museum & Memorial....................................4 C3
Kliptown......................................5 B4
Mandela Museum....................(see 9)

Oppenheimer Tower...................(see 3)
Orlando Power Station...................6 C3
Orlando West Secondary School....7 C3
Regina Mundi Church....................8 C4
Vilakazi St....................................9 C3

SLEEPING 🏠
Botle's Guest House...................(see 13)
Dakalo B&B.................................10 C3
Neo's B&B..................................(see 9)
Soweto Backpackers...................11 C3
Thuto's B&B...............................(see 9)

EATING 🍽
Nambitha...................................(see 4)
Sakhumzi Restaurant..................(see 9)
Soweto Cuppuccino.....................12 C3
Wandie's Place...........................13 B3

DRINKING 🍷
B's Place....................................14 C3

ENTERTAINMENT 🎭
FNB Stadium...............................15 D3

IBOLA LETHU: OUR GAME

In 2004 world football governing body FIFA awarded the hosting of the 2010 World Cup to South Africa. This was not merely a proud moment for the African continent; it also marked the remarkable culmination of a journey of survival against the odds for the national game. Soccer has more than any other sport come to symbolise the insanity of apartheid.

In 1892 the whites-only Football Association of South Africa, or FASA, was formed. Similar associations for 'Indians', 'Bantus' and 'coloured' followed. Some games, under the auspices of the cheerily titled Inter Race Soccer Board, did take place during the 1940s, but once apartheid kicked in these were swiftly outlawed. Whites played in their own club competition, while non-whites played separately in underfunded leagues. After FIFA suspended South Africa in 1962, to curry favour FASA sanctioned a landmark inter-racial match between the 'white' Germiston Callies and the 'black' African Pirates. The trick worked and FASA was unbanned, but things turned silly when it released plans to send a white side to the 1966 World Cup in England, and a black team to Mexico in 1970!

After the then Minister of the Interior threatened to deny passports to anyone who attended a mixed-race game, South Africa was expelled from FIFA. The white game petered out at once, but the black game thrived in the townships, as fans poured into venues such as Orlando Stadium in Soweto to watch ball wizards such as Jomo Sono and Kaizer Motaung, now living legends. Soccer, as on so many continents, became the weekly escape from daily drudgery for the masses.

After Mandela's release, everything changed. On 8 December 1991, all separate soccer associations formed the South African Football Association on nonracial, democratic principles. The body was welcomed back into the African and world governing bodies in 1992. South Africa hosted the African Cup of Nations in 1996, and the national team was triumphant.

The 'people's game' is still the number-one sport in South Africa – it has the highest number of registered players (1.8 million), and the highest stadium and TV audiences. While it remains largely a 'black sport' (other races tend to support foreign leagues, particularly the English Premier League), interest is growing as 2010 approaches. If you're in town during the staging of the world-famous **Soweto Derby** (p415) – between local rivals Kaizer Chiefs (black/gold strip) and Orlando Pirates (black/white strip) – when the entire country splits in two and declares 'Up the Bucs!' (Pirates) or 'Amakhosi for life' (Chiefs), become part of South Africa's soccer revolution and head to the match.

Quick glossary of South African soccer terms

- Vuvuzela – long plastic trumpet-like horn blown at matches.
- Shibobo – getting past an opponent by kicking the ball between his legs (called a nutmeg in the UK).
- Bafana Bafana – the national team; means 'the boys'.
- Amaglug-glug – the under-23 side, named after a petrol-company sponsor.
- Laduuuuuuuma! – meaning 'it's in there'; the cry upon a team scoring, made famous by legendary commentator Zebulon 'Zama' Masondo.

home with his first wife, Evelyn, and it is filled with fascinating photographs and clutter. Among the exhibits is a letter from the State of Michigan asking George Bush Senior to apologise for the role the CIA played in Mandela's 1962 arrest. Needless to say, it never did. Just down Vilakazi St, by Sakhumzi Restaurant, is the home of **Archbishop Desmond Tutu**.

North of Vilakazi St is Soweto's showcase, Hector Pieterson Sq. Named after the 13-year-old who was shot dead in the run-up to the Soweto uprising (see p421), the square now features the poignant **Hector Pieterson Memorial** and the excellent **Hector Pieterson Museum** (☎ 011-536 0611; cnr Khumalo & Pela Sts; adult/child R10/5; ⏰ 10am-5pm), which offers an insight into Sowetan life and the history of the independence struggle. From the square, a line of shrubs leads up Moema St to the site where he was shot outside the school.

South of here, down Klipspruit Valley Rd, is the **Regina Mundi Church** (Mkhize St; admission by donation), which, as a community meeting place, was central to the struggle against apartheid. The police often retaliated and you can still see bullet holes in the ceiling to the right of the main altar. The right-hand 'community' altar rail is also chipped from where the butt of a police rifle smashed it. In recognition of the church's role in the struggle, several hearings of the Truth & Reconciliation Committee were heard here.

Other sights include the **Credo Mutwa Village** (Bolani Rd; admission free), which was largely destroyed after the artist who built it made controversial comments about the 1976 uprising; and the **Oppenheimer Tower** (Bolani Rd; admission free), erected in gratitude to the Chairman of the Anglo-American Corporation, Sir Ernest Oppenheimer, who in 1956 organised a loan from the Chamber of Mines to build 14,000 homes, improving living standards for thousands of Sowetans. You can also visit **Avalon Cemetery**, where you will find the graves of Hector Pieterson (Plot EC462) and Joe Slovo (Plot B35311), former leader of the South African Communist Party.

Kliptown, to the southwest of Orlando West, was established in 1904 and is the oldest settlement in Johannesburg to accommodate all races. It was also the site of the adoption of the Freedom Charter on 26 June 1955.

Tours

Dozens of companies offer tours of Soweto (see p405 for details); your accommodation should be able to put you in touch with them or offer an inhouse service.

Sleeping

Staying over in Soweto is the most rewarding way of getting a sense of the place. At last count there were more than 30 functional B&Bs in the township, most in the immediate vicinity of Vilakazi St. Either book through your tour or contact the **Soweto Accommodation Association** (☎ 011-936 8123; nrwaxa@hotmail.com), a community-run enter-

prise operated out of Thuto's B&B that can help find you a room or advise on safety issues.

Most of the following places offer comfortable rooms with private bathrooms in a small, middle-class home. In general, accommodation in Soweto does not come cheap, but remember that tourism has become a major source of income for this area.

Soweto Backpackers (☎ 011-326 1700; www.sowetobackpackers.co.za; 10823 A Powe St, Meadowlands East; dm/s/d with shared bathroom R70/85/170) Soweto's first backpackers, this is much recommended by readers. Standards are basic and the location is not ideal, but the beds are cheap and the friendly owner is a great source of information on the township.

Neo's B&B (☎ 011-536 0413, 082-629 2284; www.sowetobedandbreakfast.com; 8041 Bocela St, Orlando West; s/d incl breakfast R190/380) In a vintage Sowetan home, this tiny place offers cosy comforts on the doorstep of the township's major attractions. There is a thatched deck outside for evening eating.

Botle's Guest House (☎ 011-982 1872, 082-838 1886; 648 Monyane St; d with/without bathroom R350/250; ﹡) A good example of Soweto's growing prosperity, the owner of this place demolished her breeze-block bungalow to build a guesthouse. With typically Sowetan, mock-Versace décor, it offers a cash bar, a small restaurant space for breakfast and a TV in every room. It is near Wandie's Place nightspot.

Dakalo B&B (☎ 011-936 9328; www.sowetobedandbreakfast.com; 6963 Inhlathi St, Orlando West; s/d R350/500) Oriental rugs compete with chintzy stone walls, and both with rococo collectibles in this eccentric family home that's a superb example of African urban chic. Breakfasts are full English, Soweto-style: mango atchar (pickled), snoek (fish) and soft porridge to go with the expected eggs and toast.

Thuto's B&B (☎ 011-936 8123, 072-376 9205; www.sowetobedandbreakfast.com; 8123 Ngakane St, Orlando West; s/d incl breakfast R350/500) Very close to the Mandela Museum, this is Soweto's second-oldest B&B. It's wonderfully kitschy (we love the huge ceramic tigers), and Anastacia – an expert on local accommodation and attractions – is a great host.

Eating & Drinking

In Soweto you'll find you're never more than a short stagger from a drinking establishment, usually an informal *shebeen* (unlicensed tavern). With a growing number of tourists and wealthier locals looking for a slicker place to eat and drink, several decent bars and restaurants have sprung up around the township. Some even have a reputation that has spread into the northern suburbs of Jo'burg.

Wandie's Place (☎ 011-982 2796; www.wandies place.co.za; 618 Makhalemele St, Dube; buffet R45; ☑ lunch & dinner) Soweto's original and most-famous nightspot remains in pole position in the eating and drinking stakes. Fast expanding, it now has several different spaces, each packed to bursting point by 9pm. Cape wineries have even been known to come here to host tastings. The buffet is fabulous.

Sakhumzi Restaurant (☎ 011-939 4427; www.sak humzi.co.za; 6980 Vilakazi St, Orlando West; mains R40; ☑ lunch & dinner) In the very heart of the Vilakazi St area, this excellent little eatery draws a steady stream of tourists and locals alike. The food is tasty, there are sometimes jazz bands playing in the evening, and tours of the area can be arranged.

Nambitha (☎ 082-785 7190; 6877 Vilakazi St, Orlando West; mains R40-55; ☑ breakfast, lunch & dinner) Nambitha means 'to taste – expensively' in Zulu and this place represents the township's changing face. Stylish and open-fronted, it serves a delicious combination of contemporary and traditional African fare and a decent selection of drinks.

Soweto Cuppuccino (☎ 011-936 1998; 11787 Mtipa St, Orlando West Ext; mains R30; ☑ breakfast & lunch) It had to happen, and it has: a fresh brew in the townships. It's close to Winnie Madikizela Mandela's house, and the breakfasts are becoming a local favourite.

B's Place (☎ 011-935 4015; 5541 Shuenane St, Orlando East; mains R40; ☑ lunch & dinner) Local types meet up and cook together at this licensed bar and *shebeen* that's already winning the heart of international guests. There's West and South African food on offer, plus a selection of homemade pastries.

Getting There & Away

Most transport in and out of Soweto is by motor vehicle, usually by one of the minibus taxis (R12 one way) that arrive in Diepkloof or Orlando from the taxi rank (see p402) near Joubert Park in the Jo'burg city centre.

AROUND JOHANNESBURG

WESTERN GAUTENG

You wouldn't know to look at it, but this rolling highveld landscape is considered one of the world's most important palaeontological zones, and is a Unesco World Heritage Site, focused around the Sterkfontein hominid fossil fields. The whole area forms part of the **Cradle of Humankind** (www.cradleofhumankind.co.za), but its size (47,000 hectares) and number of facilities (280 businesses and counting) can make navigation a little daunting.

So it is perhaps best to start your exploration at **Maropeng** (Map p394; ☎ 014-577 9000; www .discover-yourself.co.za; off Rte 563 to Hekpoort; adult/child R65/35; ☑ 9am-5pm). Housed in a new building cleverly designed to reflect the progression of man (its façade is covered in grass, its rear modern steel and glass), it's an all-in-one information centre, visitor attraction, entertainment complex and **boutique hotel** (s/d incl breakfast R900/1370; P ⊠ ⬛ ⬛ ⬛). Its name is Tswana for 'returning to your origin', an appropriate description of its series of exhibits detailing humanity's progression from those swampy back-in-the-beginning days. There are market stalls, active fossil sites, restaurants, a curio shop and a 5000-seat amphitheatre for outdoor events. Children will love the somewhat cheesy but undeniably impressive boat ride through the four elements, and kids of all ages will love the interactive exhibits that follow.

Your next stop should be the new visitor centre at the **Sterkfontein Caves** (Map p394; ☎ 011-668 3200; Sterkfontein Caves Rd; adult/child R35/20; ☑ 9am-4pm), that includes a permanent hominid exhibit and from where you can book tours of one of the most significant archaeological sites in the world (see the boxed text, p427). Unfortunately, the caves' limestone interiors have been mined out so are not attractive. You can get a tasty light meal at its **restaurant** (mains R18-70; ☑ breakfast & lunch).

Not far away is the **Old Kromdraai Gold Mine** (Map p394; ☎ 011-957 0211; Ibis Ridge Farm, Kromdraai Rd; adult/child R25/10; ☑ 9am-5pm Sat & Sun, Tue-Fri by appointment), the first gold mine on the

GAUTENG

Witwatersrand. Guided tours leave the converted shed every hour.

Near the Swartkop Mountains is the **Rhino & Lion Nature Reserve** (Map p394; ☎ 011-957 0106; Kromdraai Rd; adult/child R70/40; ☒ 8am-5pm Mon-Fri, 8am-6pm Sat & Sun). It's not exactly the Kruger National Park, but is a good option for those who don't have time to get there. You can see cheetahs, wild dogs (painted wolf), buffaloes, Siberian tigers (!), lions and rhinos close up. There is a vulture hide for keen bird-watchers and huge animal creche and reptile centre for the kiddies. There is a comfortable **chalet** (four people R570) in a camp within the reserve, and **wildlife drives** (R180) are offered. Within the reserve is **Wonder Cave** (adult/child R45/25), nothing more than a commercial tourist cave but some compensation for those that came to Sterkfontein expecting a pristine interior. Tours run on the hour. If you're planning to do both the reserve and the cave, ask at the gate about the combined ticket that gives a 20% discount.

Krugersdorp Game Reserve (Map p394; ☎ 011-665 1735; adult/child R20/10; ☒ 8am-6pm) is a small grassland reserve 7km west of Krugersdorp on Rte 24 in the direction of Magaliesberg – it has four of the Big Five (no elephant). Within the reserve, **Ngonyama Lion Lodge** (☎ 011-665 4342; Rustenberg Rd; d R350) has a range of accommodation and is a good bet for those wishing to stay out of town.

Near Lanseria airport is a **Lion Park** (Map p394; ☎ 011-460 1814; Old Pretoria Rd/Rte 55; admission R75; ☒ 8.30am-5pm). This place is notable for its 'tree-climbing lions', terrible takeaways and heavy drinkers. If you do go, avoid Sundays at all costs when the crowds descend in legions.

Nearby, the **Lesedi Cultural Village** (Map p394; ☎ 012-205 1394; www.lesedi.com; off Rte 512; ☒ tours 11.30am & 4.30pm) offers a bit of culture-in-a-can. It's *very* touristy but gets a lot of good reports from readers. Lesedi means 'Place of Light' and there's much dancing and singing, particularly during the traditional African feasts; Xhosa, Ndebele, Pedi, Zulu and Sotho cultures are all represented. The full 'African Experience' costs R230, or you can opt for lunch or dinner only (R120) or just the show (R155). Kids under 12 eat/watch for half price. It's a good idea to book, especially if you're going for the full meal and show.

About halfway between Pretoria and Johannesburg is the **Cradle Nature Reserve** (Map p394; ☎ 011-659 1622; Kromdraai Rd; admission free; ☒ 8am-10pm), a more upmarket take on the wildlife experience, with wildlife walks/drives and palaeontological tours. Home base here is the **Cradle Restaurant** (mains R50-80; ☒ breakfast, lunch & dinner), offering international cuisine, a cocktail bar, a log fire in winter and one of the best restaurant views in the country. Accommodation is offered in charming self-catering thatched cottages at the **Forest Camp** (cottages per person R220; ℗).

Just outside the reserve is **Tweefontein Stables & Horse Trails** (☎ 011-957 0263; www.tweefontein .co.za; r R350; ℗ ☒), offering terrific horse riding and good quality self-catering accommodation.

SOUTHERN GAUTENG

This area, with the cities of Vereeniging, Sebokeng and Vanderbijlpark, is bisected by the Vaal River and is very rich in history. The natural barrier of the Vaal River – the *gij!garib* (tawny) to the San, *lekoa* (erratic) to the Sotho and *vaal* (dirty) to the Afrikaners – has been an important dividing line in Southern African history, separating the 'Transvaal' from the south.

The Treaty of Vereeniging was negotiated near the Vaal, effectively ending the 1899–1902 Anglo-Boer War, and in more recent times southern Gauteng has been an important place in the struggle for freedom. It was at Sharpeville and Evaton, on 21 March 1960, that black civilians protested against the pass laws by publicly burning their passbooks. The police opened fire on the protestors at Sharpeville, killing 69 and wounding about 180; most were shot in the back. Today, 21 March is commemorated in South Africa as Human Rights Day (a public holiday), but there's nothing specific for visitors to do at either township.

In 1984 in Sebokeng, the security forces violently reacted to a black boycott of rent and service tariffs, tearing apart townships looking for activists. About 95 people were killed. These slaughters galvanised the black population into a more unified force, and ultimately hastened the fall of apartheid.

Named after the sugar bush *Protea caffra*, the **Suikerbosrand Nature Reserve** (Map p394; ☎ 011-904 3930; Klip River Rd; adult/child R20/10, vehicle R10; ☒ 7.15am-6pm Mon-Fri, 7am-6pm Sat & Sun)

THE STERKFONTEIN CAVES

The Sterkfontein Caves were formed by the solution of dolomite beneath the water table, a process that began about 2.5 billion years ago. But it is that which was washed in much later (3.5 million years ago) that has spurred latter-day interest: deposits rich with bones.

In August 1936, Dr Robert Broom visited the caves after learning that extinct baboon fossils had been found in the dumps left from crude lime quarrying. A week after arriving in the area he had found the first adult skull of an 'ape-man', believed to be 2.6 to three million years old – he named it *Australopithecus africanus*. In 1947 the cranium of 'Mrs Ples' was blasted out of the debris and almost 10 years later, in 1956, Dr CK Brain discovered much younger stone tools. In 1997 the significance of the articulating foot bones of 'Little Foot' was revealed – their relationship to an ankle bone indicated that this 'ape-man', our ancestor, walked upright. In all, Sterkfontein has so far given up more than 600 hominid fossils, making it one of the world's most bountiful palaeontological sites.

Sterkfontein is significant as it indicates that erect walking creatures (hominids) roamed and hunted across this landscape more than three million years ago, side by side with several other now-extinct species (eg giant leaf-eating monkeys, hunting hyena and sabre-toothed cats).

is between the N3 freeway and Rte 59, and can be reached by either. There are 66km of walking trails, several drives and the historic **Diepkloof Farm Museum** (☎ 011-904 3964; admission R5), originally built in 1850 by Voortrekker Gabriel Marais, and renovated in the 1970s after being burnt during the Anglo-Boer War. Its opening hours are the same as for the reserve.

About the best accommodation in the area is at **Protea Hotel Suikerbosrand** (☎ 016-365 5334; www.proteahotels.com/suikerbosrand; camp sites only R95, per person R35, 4-/6-/8-person chalet R840/1150/1400; P ♨). Located 15km from Meyerton, it covers a large area and is ideal for families, as kids can occupy themselves with the putt-putt (miniature golf) course, play park or horse riding (R30). Look for signs from Meyerton or call for directions before setting off.

PRETORIA

☎ 012 / pop 1.65 million

At once the 'Afrikaner Jerusalem', former headquarters of the apartheid state and site of the presidential inauguration of Nelson Mandela, the pretty, laid-back city of Pretoria – the administrative capital – carries a remarkable amount of history for its age.

Built with great care on an extinct volcanic bed in the Apies River Valley as a Boer capital free from both British domination and clashes with indigenous tribes, it is now home to a growing number of black civil servants, importing the multiculturalism that had previously been resisted by rule of law. Against many other parts of the country, stately Pretoria is also proof positive that affluence is no longer an entirely white state of being.

It's just 50km from Jo'burg, and is expected within 15 years to form part of a megalopolis of 20 million people. Yet it is very different from Jo'burg in look, character and feel.

Pretoria remains Afrikaans culturally, and the bump-and-grind of downtown Jo'burg here gives way to a slower-paced, more reserved way of life. Jacarandas bring colour to the streets in October and November, and the city retains a faint whiff of the old school, with fewer skyscrapers and a flush of latter-day buildings.

Majority rule has brought scores of embassies back to the leafy suburbs of Arcadia and Hatfield, but not everything has changed – the military and educational institutions associated with the capital are still here. The universities are huge and tens of thousands of students drive Pretoria's vibrant nightlife.

There are several sights that must be visited. The looming Voortrekker Monument and Herbert Baker–designed Union Buildings are impressive, while the charm of Church Sq is best appreciated from the benches of Café Riche. Burgers Park, an English garden, is a midcity oasis and a relaxing spot for lunch. After dark, the music and cuisine centres of Hatfield and Brooklyn

PRETORIA

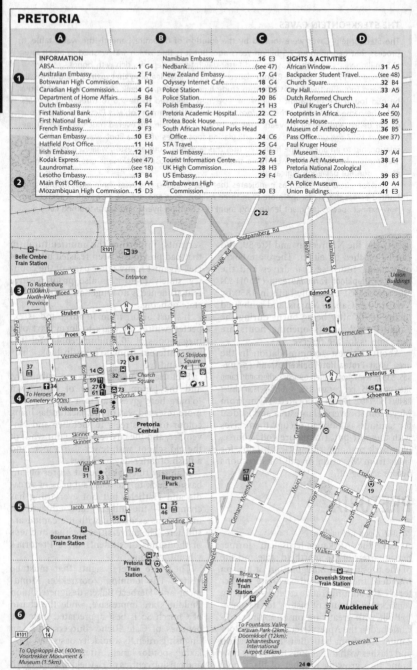

INFORMATION

ABSA	**1** G4
Australian Embassy	**2** F4
Botswanan High Commission	**3** H3
Canadian High Commission	**4** G4
Department of Home Affairs	**5** B4
Dutch Embassy	**6** F4
First National Bank	**7** G4
First National Bank	**8** B4
French Embassy	**9** F3
German Embassy	**10** E3
Hatfield Post Office	**11** H4
Irish Embassy	**12** H3
Kodak Express	(see 47)
Laundromat	(see 18)
Lesotho Embassy	**13** B4
Main Post Office	**14** A4
Mozambiquan High Commission	**15** D3

Namibian Embassy	**16** E3
Nedbank	(see 47)
New Zealand Embassy	**17** G4
Odyssey Internet Cafe	**18** G4
Police Station	**19** D5
Police Station	**20** B6
Polish Embassy	**21** H3
Pretoria Academic Hospital	**22** C2
Protea Book House	**23** G4
South African National Parks Head	
Office	**24** C6
STA Travel	**25** G4
Swazi Embassy	**26** E3
Tourist Information Centre	**27** A4
UK High Commission	**28** H3
US Embassy	**29** F4
Zimbabwean High	
Commission	**30** E3

SIGHTS & ACTIVITIES

African Window	**31** A5
Backpacker Student Travel	(see 48)
Church Square	**32** B4
City Hall	**33** A5
Dutch Reformed Church	
(Paul Kruger's Church)	**34** A4
Footprints in Africa	(see 50)
Melrose House	**35** B5
Museum of Anthropology	**36** B5
Pass Office	(see 37)
Paul Kruger House	
Museum	**37** A4
Pretoria Art Museum	**38** E4
Pretoria National Zoological	
Gardens	**39** B3
SA Police Museum	**40** A4
Union Buildings	**41** E3

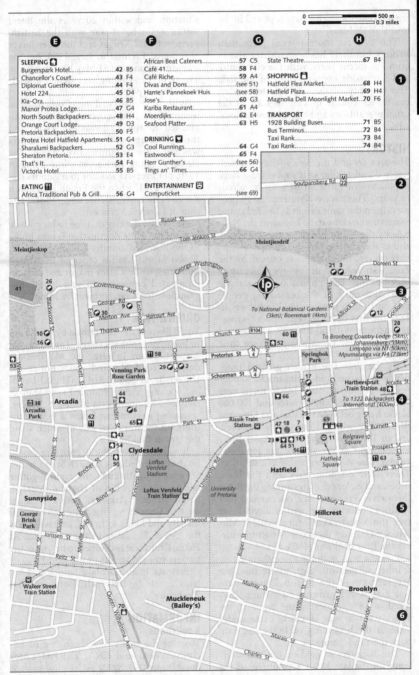

0 — 500 m
0 — 0.3 miles

SLEEPING
Burgerspark Hotel.....................42 B5
Chancellor's Court....................43 F4
Diplomat Guesthouse................44 F4
Hotel 224...............................45 D4
Kia-Ora..................................46 B5
Manor Protea Lodge.................47 G4
North South Backpackers..........48 H4
Orange Court Lodge.................49 D3
Pretoria Backpackers................50 F5
Protea Hotel Hatfield Apartments.51 G4
Sharalumi Backpackers.............52 G3
Sheraton Pretoria....................53 E4
That's It.................................54 F4
Victoria Hotel.........................55 B5

EATING
Africa Traditional Pub & Grill.......56 G4

African Beat Caterers..................57 C5
Café 41..................................58 F4
Café Riche..............................59 A4
Divas and Dons....................(see 51)
Harrie's Pannekoek Huis.......(see 58)
Jose's...................................60 G3
Kariba Restaurant.....................61 A4
Moerdijks...............................62 E4
Seafood Platter.......................63 H5

DRINKING
Cool Runnings..........................64 G4
Eastwood's.............................65 F4
Herr Gunther's.....................(see 56)
Tings an' Times........................66 G4

ENTERTAINMENT
Computicket..........................(see 69)

State Theatre...........................67 B4

SHOPPING
Hatfield Flea Market..................68 H4
Hatfield Plaza..........................69 H4
Magnolia Dell Moonlight Market..70 F6

TRANSPORT
1928 Building Buses..................71 B5
Bus Terminus..........................72 B4
Taxi Rank...............................73 B4
Taxi Rank...............................74 B4

are buzzing; meanwhile jazz is played in the township *shebeens*.

This is a far more relaxed place than Jo'burg, but there has been a sharp rise in crime in recent years, with the city centre and Sunnyside copping most of the flak. The majority of the city is safe by day, but things change quickly so take all the usual precautions and a large dose of local advice.

HISTORY

The area around the Apies River was well watered and fertile, so it supported a large population of cattle farmers for hundreds of years. These were Nguni-speaking peoples (from the same origin as the Zulus and Swazis), who came to be known as the Ndebele by the Sotho people of the Transvaal, and as the Matabele by the Europeans.

However, the disruption caused by the Zulu wars resulted in massive dislocation. Much of the black population was slaughtered and most of the remaining people fled north into present-day Zimbabwe. In 1841 the first Boers trekked into a temporary vacuum. With no-one around, they laid claim to the land that would become their capital.

By the time the British granted independence to the Zuid-Afrikaansche Republiek (ZAR) in the early 1850s, there were estimated to be 15,000 whites and 100,000 blacks living between the Vaal and Limpopo Rivers. The whites were widely scattered, and in 1853 two farms on the Apies River were bought as the site for the republic's capital. The ZAR was a shaky institution. There were ongoing wars with the black tribes, and violent disputes among the Boers themselves. Pretoria, which was named after Andries Pretorius, the hero of Blood River (see the Voortrekker Monument & Museum, p432), was the scene of fighting during the Boer civil war (1863–69).

Pretoria was nothing more than a tiny frontier village with a grandiose title, but the servants of the British Empire were watching it with growing misgivings. They acted in 1877, annexing the republic; the Boers went to war (Pretoria came under siege at the beginning of 1881) and won back their independence.

The discovery of gold on the Witwatersrand in the late 1880s revolutionised the situation and within 20 years the Boers would again be at war with the British. President Paul Kruger and the Boer forces abandoned Pretoria in June 1900, but the war ground on until 31 May 1902, when the Treaty of Vereeniging was signed at Melrose House (p433).

With the British making efforts towards reconciliation, self-government was again granted to the Transvaal in 1906, and through an unwieldy compromise Pretoria was made the administrative capital. The Union of South Africa came into being in 1910, but Pretoria was not to regain its status until 1961, when the Republic of South Africa came into existence under the leadership of Hendrik Verwoerd.

Ironically, the city that for so long was a byword for white domination is now home to the liberated country's black president. Thabo Mbeki has his office in the Union Buildings, while a black mayor and a black-dominated council hold seat in the less grandiose local-government buildings.

ORIENTATION

You'll likely arrive in Pretoria by road from Jo'burg or Johannesburg International Airport. From Jo'burg, the M1 freeway quietens suddenly, and you'll notice the University of South Africa (Unisa) building, looking like a grounded spaceship. A couple of kilometres on is the city proper, spreading west to east below a long kopje (hill), on the northern side of which stand the Union Buildings.

If you come from the airport, you should hit the eastern edge of Church St or Charles St, which run through the main nightlife and restaurant zones of Hatfield, Menlyn, Brooklyn and Arcadia, before heading west to Church Sq, the historic centre of the city and home to hotels, embassies and the Union Buildings to the northeast. At 26km, Church St is claimed to be one of the longest straight streets in the world.

Pretoria is also a good launch-pad for trips north to Nelspruit, Botswana and Zimbabwe.

INFORMATION
Bookshops

Most of the malls have branches of Exclusive Books and CNA. The **Protea Book House** (Map pp428-9; ☎ 012-362 5683; 1067 Burnett St;

9am-4.30pm Mon-Fri, 9am-noon Sat) also sells second-hand titles.

Emergency
Fire (☎ 10111)
Metro Emergency Rescue Service (☎ 10177)
Police (☎ 10111) There are police stations on Railway St (Map pp428-9) and on the corner of Leyds and Esselen Sts (Map pp428-9).

Internet Access
Most hostels and hotels offer Internet facilities, but cheaper alternatives are also available. **Odyssey Internet Cafe** (Map pp428-9; ☎ 012-362 2467; Hatfield Galleries, Burnett St; per 30min R15; ⏰ 9am-11pm) is a good bet.

Laundry
If you aren't staying in a hostel, **Laundromat** (Map pp428-9; ☎ 072-329 8222; Hatfield Galleries, Burnett St; ⏰ 7am-9pm) will clean your kit for a decent price.

Medical services
Hatfield Clinic (Map pp428-9; ☎ 012-362 7180; 454 Hilda St) A well-known suburban clinic.
Pretoria Academic Hospital (Map pp428-9; ☎ 011-354 1000; Dr Savage Rd) The place to head for in a medical emergency.

Money
There are banks with ATMs and change facilities across town.
ABSA (Map pp428-9; Hilda St)
American Express (Map p438; ☎ 012-346 2599; Brooklyn Mall; ⏰ 9am-5pm)
First National Bank Church Sq (Map pp428-9); Burnett St (Map pp428-9)

Nedbank (Map pp428-9; cnr Burnett & Festival Sts) Next to Hatfield Galleries.

Photography
Kodak Express (Map pp428-9; ☎ 012-362 0678; cnr Burnett & Festival Sts; ⏰ 8am-6pm Mon-Fri, 8am-1pm Sat) Offers a one-hour developing service and full digital studio.

Post
Hatfield post office (Map pp428-9; Hatfield Sq; ⏰ 8am-4.30pm Mon-Fri, 8am-noon Sat) Most commonly used post office, particularly by backpackers.
Main post office (Map pp428-9; cnr Church St & Church Sq; ⏰ 8am-4.30pm Mon-Fri, 8am-noon Sat) In a historic building on the main square.

Tourist Information
The **Tourist Information Centre** (Map pp428-9; ☎ 012-358 1430; www.tshwane.gov.za; Old Nederlandsche Bank Bldg, Church Sq; ⏰ 7.30am-4pm Mon-Fri) is pretty useless and, astonishingly for a city this size, closes on weekends. You can still get maps and brochures when it's closed, but you're better off asking your hotel or locals for advice.

Also in Pretoria is the national head office of **South African National Parks** (Map pp428-9; ☎ 012-428 9111; www.sanparks.org; 643 Leyds St, New Muckleneuk; ⏰ offices 8am-4pm Mon-Fri, 8am-noon Sat, call centre 7.30am-5pm Mon-Fri, 8am-2pm Sat) for all your wildlife-reserve bookings and inquiries. You can also purchase a Wild Card (see p85) here.

Travel Agencies
STA Travel (Map pp428-9; ☎ 012-342 5292; Hilda St; ⏰ 9am-5pm Mon-Fri, 9am-noon Sat)

WHAT'S IN A NAME: PRETORIA

If you're in Pretoria and finding yourself a little perplexed by what seems like several names for the area, or road signs that contradict your atlas, you've become the latest victim of a name change policy that's been confusing locals for years. Initially, the government sought to get rid of names deemed offensive or racially insensitive. Now, there's a clear policy of name change geared principally to meet two ends: the conglomeration of urban administrations for commercial reasons, and to make city names 'more African'. It's a policy that has faced fierce criticism from all races and classes, largely because of the phenomenal costs involved: many feel the money could be better spent on fixing the country's ills. Given its political significance, one of the most contentious actions has been Pretoria's name change to Tshwane. To be accurate, 'Pretoria' still exists, but merely as the central zone of the City of Tshwane (pronounced tswah-neh and named for the son of Chief Mushi, who settled here in the early 1800s), an area covering the entire conurbation. Still confused? Don't fret, most people have at least the memory of what names used to be, so try your best.

Student Flights (Map p438; ☎ 012-460 9889; Brooklyn Mall; ☯ 9am-5pm Mon-Fri, 9am-noon Sat)

Visa Extensions

Apply for visa extensions at the **Department of Home Affairs** (Map pp428-9; ☎ 012-324 1860; Sentrakor Bldg; Pretorius St; ☯ 8am-3pm Mon-Fri).

DANGERS & ANNOYANCES

Rated South Africa's 'happiest city' in a recent poll, with the best quality of life in the country, Pretoria is certainly safer and more relaxed than Jo'burg. That said, crime is a problem, particularly in the city centre and Sunnyside, with restaurants and other businesses moving to the safer Hatfield and Brooklyn areas. The square roughly formed by Vermeulen, Du Toit, Boom and Schubart Sts has a bad reputation.

It's important to remember that people in Pretoria live regular lives, so don't be scared into never leaving your lodgings. At the same time, things change quickly in South Africa, and Pretoria is no exception – always seek local advice before venturing into the unknown, and take all the usual precautions; see p608 for further information.

SIGHTS & ACTIVITIES
Freedom Park

One of the most exciting undertakings in Gauteng is **Freedom Park** (Map p441; ☎ 012-470 7400, 012-361 0021; Koch St, Salvokop; admission free; ☯ tours 8am-4.30pm Mon-Fri). The site chosen for this massive project, on a kopje (hill) facing the Vootrekker Monument, provoked an outcry from those who saw this as politically motivated, but this is hardly a self-important ode to nationalism. Rather, it's a sombre memorial to those people, local and international, who have sacrificed their lives in the name of freedom. It's earmarked for completion only in 2009, but you can still visit Hlapho, where the names of heroes have been inscribed, and the peaceful Isivivane Garden of Remembrance, which has a small kiosk and great views. Visitor numbers are strictly controlled, so calling beforehand is essential as you will not gain access if you merely turn up.

Voortrekker Monument & Museum

The looming **Voortrekker Monument & Museum** (Map p441; ☎ 012-323 0682; Eeufees Rd; adult/child R25/10, vehicle R10; ☯ 8am-6pm) is hallowed turf for many Afrikaners. Built between 1938 and 1949 to commemorate the achievements of the Voortrekkers, who trekked north over the coastal mountains of the Cape into the heart of the African veld, the structure remains a testament to the Boers' pioneering and independent spirit. In particular, it commemorates the Battle of Blood River on 16 December 1838, during which 470 Boers, under the command of Andries Pretorius, defeated approximately 12,000 Zulus.

The 'trekkers went on to found independent republics that in many ways form the genesis of modern South Africa. In terms of drama, determination, courage, vision and tragedy, their story surpasses the history of European colonists. Some Afrikaners go one step further, saying that the trek parallels the biblical Exodus, and that the Battle of Blood River was divine intervention: proof that the 'trekkers were a chosen people.

The monument was built at the time of great Afrikaner nationalism, with the scars of defeat in the Anglo-Boer War still fresh. The building's inauguration in 1949 was attended by 250,000 people and remains a powerful symbol of the 'white tribe of Africa' and its historical relationship to South Africa.

The edifice is surrounded by a stone wall carved with 64 wagons in a traditional defensive *laager* (circle). The building itself is a huge stone cube inspired by the ruins of Great Zimbabwe. Inside, a highly impressive bas-relief tells the story of the trek (not exactly the whole story – everyone appears to be white) and of the Battle of Blood River. On 16 December a shaft of light falls on the words *Ons vir jou, Suid Afrika* (We for thee, South Africa). A staircase and elevator lead to the roof and a great panoramic view of Pretoria and the highveld.

In the basement there is an small museum that reconstructs the lives of the 'trekkers, and a magnificent tapestry of naive artistry and tub-thumping chauvinism.

The monument is 3km south of the city and is clearly signposted from the N1 freeway. It is possible to catch the Voortrekkerhoogte or Valhalla bus from Kruger St near the corner of Church Sq. Ask the driver to let you off at the entrance road to the monument, from where it's a 10-minute walk uphill.

Church Square

At the heart of Pretoria, imposing public buildings surround Church Sq (Map pp428–9). These include the **Ou Raadsaal (Old Government) building** on the southern side; the **Old Capitol Theatre** in the northwestern corner; **First National Bank** in the northeast; the **Palace of Justice**, where the Rivonia Trial that sentenced Nelson Mandela to life imprisonment was held, on the northern side; the **Old Nederlandsche Bank building**, which adjoins the Café Riche and houses the Tourist Information Centre; and the **main post office** at the western side. Look for the **clock**, surrounded by nude figures by Anton van Wouw, above the Church Sq entrance to the post office.

In the centre, the **'Old Lion'**, Paul Kruger, looks disapprovingly at office workers lounging on the grass. The bronze figures of Kruger and the sentries, also by Van Wouw, were cast in Italy at the turn of the century, but lay in storage until 1954. In the early days, Boers from the surrounding countryside would gather in the square every three months for *nagmaal* (communion).

Paul Kruger House Museum

A short walk west from Church Sq, the former residence of Paul Kruger is now the **Paul Kruger House Museum** (Map pp428–9; ☎ 012-326 9172; 60 Church St; adult/child R10/5; ⏰ 8am-4.30pm Mon-Fri). It's interesting but, partly due to its setting right on a busy street, it's difficult to get a feeling for the man (unlike at Smuts' House Museum; see p441), despite the fact that he was undoubtedly an extraordinary human being. There are clues, however. The house is unpretentious, although there would have been few grander homes when it was built in 1883. Among all sorts of bric-a-brac there's the knife that Kruger used to amputate his thumb after a shooting accident. The **Dutch Reformed Church**, where he worshipped and preached, is just across the road.

Immediately left of the house is the neo-Georgian 1932 **Pass Office**. Hated by blacks for its function of economic and racial segregation, the building was nevertheless known to them as GaMothle, 'Beautiful Place', because the friezes and tableaux

decorating it represented black African peoples. Sadly it's now falling into disrepair and is not open to the public, but there are interesting explanations of its history outside.

Melrose House

Opposite Burgers Park is **Melrose House** (Map pp428–9; ☎ 012-322 2805; 275 Jacob Maré St; adult/child R5/3; ⏰ 10am-5pm Tue-Sun). This neobaroque mansion, a national monument, was built in 1886 for George Heys, and it's a somewhat fanciful cross between English Victorian and Cape Dutch styles.

During the 1899–1902 Anglo-Boer War, Lords Roberts and Kitchener (both British commanders) lived here. On 31 May 1902 the Treaty of Vereeniging, which marked the end of the war, was signed in the dining room.

Museum of Anthropology

Opposite City Hall, this **museum** (Map pp428–9; ☎ 012-322 7632; Paul Kruger St; adult/child R10/6; ⏰ 9am-5pm Mon-Sat, 11am-5pm Sun) has dioramas of various indigenous animals and birds. It's not exactly the Kruger, but you can't get malaria either. The most dramatic exhibit is the enormous whale skeleton outside the building.

South African Police Museum

The **police museum** (Map pp428–9; 021-321 1678; cnr Pretorius & Volkstem Sts; adult/child R10/6; ⏰ 9am-5pm Mon-Sat, 11am-5pm Sun) is one of the city's better museums, with scores of exhibits covering the turbulent history of the nation's police force. Many of the items date back to the apartheid era, when South Africa was a de facto police state.

African Window

Concentrating on the archaeological and anthropological records of Southern Africa, **African Window** (Map pp428–9; ☎ 012-324 6082; 102 Visagie St; adult/child R8/5; ⏰ 8am-4pm) focuses on the tribes of Gauteng, incorporating some San engravings, a traditional restaurant and regular dance and art exhibitions.

Pretoria Art Museum

Off Schoeman St, this **art museum** (Map pp428–9; ☎ 012-344 1807; Arcadia Park; adult/child R5/3; ⏰ 10am-5pm Tue & Thu-Sat, 10am-8pm Wed, noon-5pm Sun) has displays of South African art from

---

THE FABULOUS BAKER BUILDINGS

The day after a mob of rail commuters vented their frustration by burning down Pretoria station in February 2001, the gutted shell of the building seemed destined to be pulled down. It's a measure of the respect that South Africans have for its architect Sir Herbert Baker that by the following day money had been found to rebuild the station, and talk of demolition was a distant memory.

Born in Kent, Baker arrived in South Africa in 1891 and formed a friendship with the colony's richest and most powerful man, Cecil John Rhodes, who commissioned Baker to redesign his home. The young architect took the radical step of using the vernacular Cape gable on a double-storey building. The result was the timeless magnificence that is Groote Schuur in Cape Town (see p122); Rhodes was delighted.

Baker was prolific and designed an eclectic mix of homes and public buildings for the colony's wealthiest citizens, many of whom made their fortunes on the Witwatersrand goldfields. His credits include a raft of mansions in Johannesburg's Parktown district, the South African Institute for Medical Research in Braamfontein, St George's Cathedral in Cape Town, the Sunnyside and Arcadia cathedrals in Pretoria and the work for which he is best remembered, the classical lines of the imposing Union Buildings (below).

Baker left for India in 1913, eventually returning to England where he worked on South Africa House in London's Trafalgar Sq. He died in 1946 and is buried in Westminster Cathedral.

---

many periods of the country's history. It's a good place to get a feel for the contrasting influences that make up modern South Africa.

Pretoria National Zoological Gardens

About 1km north of the city centre are the **zoological gardens** (Map pp428–9; ☎ 012-328 3265; cnr Paul Kruger & Boom Sts; adult/child R35/22; ☼ 8am-6pm). The national zoo is an impressive and pleasant enough spot to while away an afternoon. There is an aquarium here, as well as a decent cafeteria and some areas of lawn. The highlight is probably the cable car that runs up to the top of a hill that overlooks the city. There are regular guided evening trips (R30 per person).

Heroes' Acre Cemetery

Around 1.5km west of Church Sq you'll find this **cemetery** (Map p441; Church St; ☼ 8am-6pm), the burial place of a number of historical figures including Andries Pretorius, Paul Kruger and Hendrik Verwoerd. Henry H 'Breaker' Morant, the Australian Boer War antihero executed by the British for war crimes, is also buried here – look for the low sign pointing to the grave stone from one of the north–south avenues. If you miss this, you'll never find it.

To get here by bus, take the West Park No 2 or Danville service from Church Sq.

Union Buildings

These buildings (Map pp428–9) are the headquarters of government. The impressive red sandstone structures (with a self-conscious imperial grandeur) are surrounded by expansive gardens and are home to the presidential offices.

The buildings, designed by Sir Herbert Baker (see the boxed text, above), are quite a long walk from the city centre; alternatively catch just about any bus heading east on Church St, and walk up through the gardens. There are no tours here, but access to the expansive grounds and public areas of the building is free and self-guided seven days a week.

TOURS

Backpacker Student Travel (Map pp428–9; ☎ 012-362 0989; info@northsouthbackpackers.com), at North South Backpackers hostel, runs a large range of tours to destinations including a local diamond mine (R250 per person), Pretoria city (R200), Soweto (R350) and to the popular Apartheid Museum (R330) in Johannesburg.

Footprints in Africa (Map pp428–9; ☎ 083-302 1976; info@footprintsinafrica.com), at Pretoria Backpackers, organises airport shuttles and township tours, among its many services. Ask about the excellent-value trips to Victoria Falls in Zimbabwe (two-day fly-ins from R2900 per person).

FESTIVALS & EVENTS

Oppikoppi Music Festival (www.oppikoppi.co.za)
A Woodstock-type bash, where local and international
rock bands congregate in a celebration of peace, love and
music. It is staged once or twice a year – visit the website
for the latest programme details.

Pretoria Show This immensely popular event is held
during the third week of August at the showgrounds.

SLEEPING

Pretoria has plenty of hostels and hotels
of every description. Hatfield, with its bars
and restaurants, has developed into something of a backpacker's ghetto and some of
the best cheap places to stay are in this area.
The well-to-do streets of Hatfield, Brooklyn
and New Muckleneuk are the best places to
start looking for midrange B&B options.

The city also has its fair share of upmarket business and boutique hotels. Again,
these tend to be east of the centre, out towards the wealthier suburbs.

If you want to explore a Gauteng city
centre, it makes more sense to do it here
than in crime-ridden (and much bigger),
inner-city Jo'burg. But Pretoria Central can
have similar criminal dangers, particularly
after dark. There are some decent places
to stay in town, particularly those near
centrally located museums, but if you do
choose to stay here always ask your accommodation before wandering around.

Budget

Sharalumi Backpackers (Map pp428-9; ☎ 012-342
8196; www.sharalumi.com; 1064 Pretorius St, Hatfield;
camp sites/dm R40/60, s/d with shared bathroom R120/140;
P 🖳 🕿) It's on a busy road, but no mat-
ter: the very large garden and pool will keep
you occupied at this decent backpackers in
a small house. It's also cracking good value
at these prices.

1322 Backpackers International (Map p441;
☎ 012-362 3905; www.1322backpackers.com; 1322 Arcadia St, Hatfield; camp sites/dm/s/d R45/65/95/150; P
🕿) A friendly hostel cleverly designed to
mimic log-cabin accommodation despite
its suburban setting. Dorm beds are made
of chunky wood and have their own night
lights, while the neat thatched outbuildings
are very good value.

North South Backpackers (Map pp428-9; ☎ 012-
362 0989; info@northsouthbackpackers.com; 355 Glyn St,
Hatfield; camp sites/dm R45/80, s/d with shared bathroom
R135/180; P 🖳 🕿) This hostel is within easy

walking distance of the high life of Burnett
St, but has a tirelessly convivial buzz of its
own. Trimmings include tasty dinners and
a savvy travel agency. There's a pleasant
garden for summer lounging and a cosy sitting room with a real fire for winter warming. There are also private en suite garden
cottages that sleep two (R260).

Fountains Valley Caravan Park (Map p441; ☎ 012-
440 7131; camp sites with/without electricity R58/48; P
🕿) Just off the M18, south of Pretoria, this
is a good facility, with plenty of sites, a pool,
a restaurant and tennis courts.

Bronberg Country Lodge (Map p441; ☎ 012-811
0496; www.bronbergbackpackers.co.za; Plot 207, Lynwood
Rd, Tiegerpoort; camp sites/dm/d R55/70/210; P) On
the eastern reaches of Pretoria, this rustic
place offers a breath of fresh, country air.
After a busy day's sightseeing, this is the
perfect spot to escape back into the bush,
or reinvigorate weary feet with a soak in
the Jacuzzi.

Kia-Ora (Map pp428-9; ☎ 012-322 4803; kia-ora@
vakaneo.co.za; 257 Jacob Maré St, Pretoria Central; dm R65,
s/d with shared bathroom R170/180) An exceedingly
scruffy joint, but it's the best bet if you want
to be based in the city centre.

Pretoria Backpackers (Map pp428-9; ☎ 012-343
9754; www.pretoriabackpackers.net; 425 Farenden St,
Clydesdale; dm R80, s/d with shared bathroom R150/220;
P 🖳 🕿) This is a large converted home
with a pleasant garden and fish pond, open-
plan chilling area and spacious, wood-
floored rooms. It's close to the Hatfield
good-time zone (and very close to the rugby
stadium). There's also a salon offering massages, aromatherapy and other invigorating
treatments.

Midrange

If you are looking for homey, B&B-style
accommodation, it is well worth contacting the **Bed & Breakfast Association of Pretoria**
(☎ 083-212 1989; www.accommodationinpretoria.co.za).

Hotel 224 (Map pp428-9; ☎ 012-440 5281; www
.hotel224.com; cnr Schoeman & Leyds Sts, Arcadia; s/d
R295/380; P 🔀) This high-rise hotel sells
itself as Pretoria's premier budget location
but is really just a faded remnant of the
hotelier age. The amenities just about slip
it into the midrange category, and while
things are now looking a little worn, it remains pretty good value for money.

That's It (Map pp428-9; ☎ 012-344 3404; www.thats
it.co.za; 5 Brecher St, Clydesdale; s/d incl breakfast R310/410;

P ⊠ ⊠) Near the corner of Farenden St, this is a guesthouse in a leafy suburb, not far from Loftus Versfeld Stadium. It's a pleasant house with good-sized rooms, if not a tremendous amount of atmosphere.

Chancellor's Court (Map pp428-9; ☎ 012-344 1404; www.chancellorscourt.co.za; 797 Park St, Clydesdale; s/d R350/400; P ⊠ ⊠) A well-located, reader-recommended guesthouse with spacious (if somewhat old-fashioned) rooms. It's a very good option for groups or families, who might like to stay in the four-sleeper, self-catering family unit (R500).

Crane's Nest Guesthouse (Map p438; ☎ 012-460 7223; cranesnest@absamail.co.za; 212 Boshoff St, New Muckleneuk; s/d R400/650; P ⊠ ⊠) This salubriously suburban B&B sits in the chi-chi section of New Muckleneuk, right next to the bird sanctuary – a big bonus in itself. It is a flick overpriced, but the rooms, overlooking a pleasant garden (with bunnies), are very comfortable.

Orange Court Lodge (Map pp428-9; ☎ 012-326 6346; orangecourt@absamail.co.za; 540 Vermeulen St, Arcadia; 1-/2-/3-bedroom apt R400/800/1200; P ⊠) On the corner of Hamilton St and not far from the Union Buildings, this oasis among concrete blocks is an excellent option. It offers serviced apartments, with phone, TV, kitchen and linen.

Top End

Victoria Hotel (Map pp428-9; ☎ 012-323 6054; fax 012-324 2426; 200 Scheiding St, Pretoria Central; s/d incl breakfast R450/615; P ⊠) Built in 1894, this gracious, historic place has 10 Victorian-style rooms with all the creature comforts. It is a great place to stay if you want a whiff of old Pretoria and offers a more idiosyncratic brand of top-end experience.

Burgerspark Hotel (Map pp428-9; ☎ 012-322 7500; hotel@burgerspark.co.za; cnr Van der Walt & Minnaar Sts; s/d R480/550; P ⊠) Opposite the well-manicured Burgers Park, this place is big, efficient and central.

Manor Protea Hotel (Map pp428-9; ☎ 012-362 7077; mphotel@satis.co.za; cnr Burnett & Festival Sts, Hatfield; s/d R557/616; P ⊠) Up an escalator from Burnett St, this hotel beats the Sheraton on location, but for the price fails to compete on any other level. It's plain, but perennially reliable.

Diplomat Guesthouse (Map pp428-9; ☎ 012-344 3131; www.thediplomat.co.za; 822 Arcadia St, Arcadia; s/d incl breakfast R580/760; P ⊠ □ ⊠) An early-

20th-century home and its beautiful garden are the setting for this immaculately designed four-star guesthouse filled with important-looking furniture. It's very much part of this century, however, with wireless Internet onsite and, for those arriving by GPS, provides exact coordinates (25°44'54"S, 28°13'16"E).

Protea Hotel Hatfield Apartments (Map pp428-9; ☎ 012-362 6105; www.proteahotels.com/hatfieldapartments; 1080 Prospect St, Hatfield; r R662/736; P ⊠ ⊠) One of the few self-catering options in the eastern suburbs, it's a tad overpriced, but it's secure, clean and well-serviced. If you don't feel like cooking, it's within walking distance of dozens of restaurants.

Sheraton Pretoria (Map pp428-9; ☎ 012-429 9999; www.sheraton.com; cnr Church & Wessels Sts, Arcadia; r from R759; P ⊠ □ ⊠) Pretoria's glitziest offering, this classy place saw Britain's Queen Liz shun the official guest residence in favour of one (or a whole floor) of the sparkling rooms. It offers all the reliable, spic-and-span Sheraton trimmings and top-notch service.

EATING

Food in Pretoria is generally of a high standard and prices are lower than Jo'burg's. There are a few places in the city centre but most people head to Hatfield, Brooklyn and New Muckleneuk. Most eateries seem to be concentrated along a few streets, so if there's nothing that appeals to you here, just choose a street and cruise. There are few eating recommendations in the city centre because of safety considerations.

City Centre

Kariba Restaurant (Map pp428-9; ☎ 012-326 5654; 1 Parliament St; mains R20-40; ☺ breakfast & lunch Mon-Sat) Based improbably in the beautiful former Capitol Theatre next door to the Tshwane Cultural Centre, this efficient restaurant is a lunchtime favourite with local business types, thanks largely to its selection of hearty West and South African dishes.

Café Riche (Map pp428-9; ☎ 012-328 3173; 2 Church St; mains R30-60; ☺ lunch & dinner) This is one of Pretoria's more historic eateries, enjoying a choice spot right in the heart of the city's Church Sq. The passing action, which you can view over a beer from the terrace outside, is the chief selling point, but the food isn't bad either. Don't be surprised if you bump into other travellers planning their Pretoria visit from here.

Hatfield & Arcadia

Hatfield and Arcadia are full of restaurants, cafés and bars, and are safe at any hour. If you're out for a drink and a feed, bustling Hatfield Sq on Burnett St is a good a place as any to start.

Seafood Platter (☎ 012-362 1144; Duncan Walk, Duncan St; mains R25-80; ☽ lunch Mon-Fri, dinner Mon-Sat; ☒) You guessed it: heaps of garlic-laden seafood is served up in convivial surroundings designed to make you forget you're in a landlocked province. Live musicians do their thing on Friday and Saturday nights.

Harrie's Pannekoek Huis (Harry's Pancake House; Map pp428-9; ☎ 012-342 3613; Eastwood Sq, Eastwood Rd; mains R30-40; ☽ breakfast, lunch & dinner) A slick outfit offering something different for the palate – savoury and sweet pancakes with extremely imaginative fillings. We tried the pickled fish and sultana chutney variant, but that's just the tip of the iceberg. Work off your selection at the adjacent curio shop, one of Pretoria's best.

Divas and Dons (Map pp428-9; ☎ 012-362 1674; Hatfield Sq, Burnett St; mains R30-50; ☽ lunch & dinner; ☒) Good solid fare is served in this plush eatery, with dark wood panelling and built-in leather sofas giving it an upmarket hotel-lounge feel.

Café 41 (Map pp428-9; ☎ 012-342 8914; Eastwood Sq, Eastwood St; mains R35-95; ☽ breakfast, lunch & dinner) A beautifully designed bistro-style restaurant meant to appeal to casual and business diners alike, with a massive menu and swift service. There's a large outdoor deck, and hidden section that makes you forget you're in a shopping village.

Africa Traditional Pub & Grill (Map pp428-9; ☎ 012-362 1604; cnr Prospect & Hilda Sts; mains R40; ☽ lunch & dinner) An outdoor deck, good vibes and traditional African beats make this one of the more upbeat, laid-back options in distinctly bourgeois Hatfield. The food's good, too.

Jose's (Map pp428-9; ☎ 012-430 7778; 235 Hilda St; mains R60; ☽ lunch & dinner) Platters of delicious Mediterranean foods mean you'll understand why this quality eatery is a local favourite. When it's plate-breaking nights (Fridays and Saturdays), you'll understand why there's so much outdoor seating. It's all great fun.

Brooklyn & New Muckleneuk

As the dining and nightlife has moved eastwards, the area around Middle and Fehrsen Sts has become home to a host of good restaurants. The food is generally better and more expensive than in Hatfield. Apart from the following places, you will find all of the staple, cheap-and-cheerful takeaways in the adjoining shopping malls.

Crawdaddy's (Map p438; ☎ 012-460 0589; Shop 3, Brooklyn Piazza, cnr Middle & Dey Sts; mains R40-60; ☽ lunch & dinner; ☒) With faux-Louisiana-swamp styling, this surf-and-turf place has a jumping, bar-style atmosphere and no-nonsense steak and seafood tucker.

Blue Crane (Map p438; ☎ 012-460 7615; Melk St; mains R40-80; ☽ lunch & dinner; ☒) The Blue Crane is part of the Austin Roberts Bird Sanctuary – the Roberts of the famous bird books. The restaurant overlooks a lake that is the breeding site for the endangered blue crane, South Africa's national bird. It does Afrikaner *potjiekos* (meat and vegetables stewed in an iron pot) and the pub is great at sundown. The entrance to the restaurant is off Melk St, which is a right turn off Middle St as you head west.

Taste Emporium (Map p438; ☎ 012-460 7181; 279 Dey St; mains R40-220; ☽ lunch & dinner; ☒) With a menu divided into sections, including 'From the Garden', 'Out of the Sea' and 'From the Farm', this place believes eating is about good ingredients, cooked simply. Piles of fresh wood and an open front add a rustic twist to the simple, neutral décor. No wonder readers love it.

Wangthai (Map p438; ☎ 012-346 6230; 281 Middle St; mains R50-100; ☽ lunch & dinner; ☒) Offering 'Royal Thai Cuisine', this upmarket eatery is decorated with an array of upper-echelon bric-a-brac, seemingly purchased from an expensive Bangkok souvenir shop. Standards are high, the food is good and it is a favourite of the Thai ambassador.

Cynthia's Indigo Moon (Map p438; ☎ 012-346 8926; 283 Dey St; mains R50-150; ☽ lunch & dinner; ☒) Accolades and glowing press reviews galore decorate the entrance hall, while the restaurant itself is surrounded by the colossal wine cellar. A lot of cows laid down their lives to make this menu possible, but the steak is fabulous, the seafood sublime and the atmosphere cosy and stylish.

Meat Company (Map p438; ☎ 012-460 2515; 273 Middle St; mains R65-120; ☽ lunch & dinner; ☒) The name doesn't lie: heat of every temperature is applied to flesh of every description in this cavernous paean to the carnivorous. The house burger (R42) is becoming a local legend, but vegetarians don't despair: there's an impressive platter of greens (R50), too.

Sunnyside

A shadow has fallen across Esselen St, Sunnyside, and it's not the eating experience it once was. There's a depressing field of takeaway chains scattered among the pawn and porn shops, with the odd café and restaurant thrown in. However, there are a few places still worth visiting in Sunnyside and the suburban streets of Arcadia to the east.

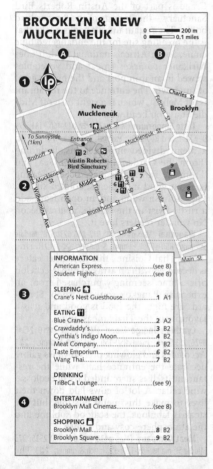

BROOKLYN & NEW MUCKLENEUK

0 —— 200 m
0 —— 0.1 miles

INFORMATION
American Express...........................(see 8)
Student Flights................................(see 8)

SLEEPING
Crane's Nest Guesthouse...................1 A1

EATING
Blue Crane......................................2 A2
Crawdaddy's....................................3 B2
Cynthia's Indigo Moon.......................4 B2
Meat Company.................................5 B2
Taste Emporium................................6 B2
Wang Thai.......................................7 B2

DRINKING
TriBeCa Lounge..............................(see 9)

ENTERTAINMENT
Brooklyn Mall Cinemas.....................(see 8)

SHOPPING
Brooklyn Mall...................................8 B2
Brooklyn Square...............................9 B2

Africa Beat Caterers (Map pp428–9; ☎ 072-276 7357; 115 Gerhard Moerdyk St; mains R15-30; ☽ lunch & dinner) This area is packed with cutesy, historic villas, and this vibey little place – popular with *amakwêre-kwêre* (foreign Africans) – is in one of them. There's a sun terrace out front and it serves up a regular mix of cheap, tasty food and live music.

Moerdijks (Map pp428–9; ☎ 012-344 4856; cnr Park & Beckett St; mains R45-100; ☽ lunch & dinner; ⊠) This upmarket place has pride of place in a graceful Dutch villa, with old-school styling, pleasant gardens and the type of food empires were built on.

DRINKING

There are several bars and nightspots in trendy Hatfield, catering for all types. Yet again, Hatfield Sq is a good place to start, but remember that 'guns, fireworks and motorbikes are strictly prohibited'. Unusually for South Africa, Burnett St offers a high density of bars, eateries and clubs, all cut through with lashings of backpacker bravado and student shenanigans. You can wander between venues easily and safely, saving the endless taxi journeys that usually punctuate a night in a big South African city. It's the easiest pub crawl in the country.

Cool Runnings (Map pp428–9; ☎ 012-362 0100; 1075 Burnett St) Reggae rules the roost at this perennially popular drinking haunt, but anyone's welcome at the party. Days start slow and lazy, while nights get hot, steamy and really quite drunken after 10pm.

Herr Gunther's (Map pp428–9; ☎ 012-362 6975; Hatfield Sq, Burnett St) A Germanic answer to the Irish bar, this raucous place serves 2L jugs of beer and sausages to soak them up.

Maloney's (Map pp428–9; ☎ 012-362 2883; Duncan Walk, Duncan St) As if to prove the old corporate adage that you can never have enough Irish pubs, here's another. And it's worth another night's drinking all to itself.

Tings an' Times (Map pp428–9; ☎ 012-430 3176; 1065 Arcadia St) This laid-back place calls itself a pita bar, but is much more about drinking than eating. It offers great ambience for late-night philosophising or just chilling. If you get the drunken hunger, pizzas are laid on till late.

TriBeCa Lounge (Map p438; ☎ 012-460 3068; Brooklyn Sq, Veale St) Coffees and cocktails create the mood at this trendy café-bar named after the New York City neighbourhood. On weekends, it fills up with the beautiful people, who stop in for a quick loosener, after a hard afternoon at the mall.

Eastwood's (Map pp428-9; ☎ 012-344 0243; cnr Eastwood & Park Sts) This Arcadia institution is packed before, during and after any rugby encounter. It's won the 'best pub in Pretoria' award three years in a row, though clearly not in the integration stakes. Speaking of steaks, try the T-bone with *pap en sous* (maize meal and sauce); it's terrific value (R36). In the summer, a fine mist is sprayed over the beer garden to keep the boozers standing.

Oppikoppi Bar (Map p441; ☎ 082-499 7668) On Magasyn Hill (opposite the Voortrekker Monument), this is one of the best-located pubs in Pretoria. The views over the city are great, particularly at sunset, and they offer DIY braais.

ENTERTAINMENT
Cinemas
There are several large cinema complexes in Pretoria. The *Pretoria News* lists screenings daily.

The **Brooklyn Mall Cinemas** (Map p438; ☎ 0860 300 222; tickets R38; Brooklyn Mall, Fehrson St, Brooklyn) are among the most popular in Pretoria, but to save yourself time, it might be best to call **Ster-Kinekor** (central bookings ☎ 082 16789; www.sterkinekor.co.za) for listings and bookings. For other movie-going experiences, grab your car and go to the **Menlyn Park Drive-In** (Map p441; ☎ 012-348 8766; Menlyn Park Shopping Centre) or visit the **Imax Theatre** (Map p441; ☎ 012-368 1168; Menlyn Park Shopping Centre) for big-screen oohs-and-aahs.

Live Music & Nightclubs
Despite being home to a large student population, Pretoria's live-music scene can be a bit of a damp squib at worst and as fickle as young love at best, with places opening and closing regularly. Check out the *Pretoria News* for the latest listings. If there's nothing that tickles your fancy, ask at your hostel or head to Burnett St in Hatfield and join the nearest queue.

The surrounding townships, especially Mamelodi and Atteridgeville, have plenty of *shebeens*; these are best visited with a black friend or as part of a tour. It's estimated that Gauteng has more than 36,000 *shebeens*.

Theatres
Most shows can be booked through **Computicket** (☎ 011-915 8000; www.computicket.com; Hatfield Plaza, Burnett St; ⏰ 8.30am-4.30pm Mon-Sat).

State Theatre (Map pp428-9; ☎ 012-392 4000; www.statetheatre.co.za; cnr Prinsloo & Church Sts) Designed by Hans and Roelf Botha, this huge theatre complex hosts a range of productions – including opera, music, ballet and theatre – in its five theatres: the Arena, Studio, Opera, Drama and Momentum. You can take guided tours of the building (R20).

Barnyard Theatre (Map p441; ☎ 012-368 1555; top fl, Menlyn Park Shopping Centre) It's out of town in Menlyn Park Shopping Centre, and also stages shows.

SHOPPING
Apart from the big Brooklyn Mall (Map p438), Brooklyn Sq (Map p438) and Menlyn Park (Map pp428-9) shopping centres, where you will find all the usual air-conditioned chain stores, Pretoria is best known for its markets.

Boeremark (Map p441; ☎ 082-416 3900; Meiring Naude Rd; ⏰ 6-9am Sat) East of the centre, and opposite the CSIR complex, this market is run by the Transvaal Agricultural Union and is the place to find fresh produce and old-style Boers, with traditional food and music.

Hatfield Flea Market (Map pp428-9; ☎ 012-362 5941; Hatfield Plaza car park, Burnett St, Hatfield; ⏰ 9.30am-5.30pm Sun) Peddles the usual flea-market paraphernalia, as well as some African stuff you can't import from China.

Magnolia Dell Moonlight Market (Map pp428-9; ☎ 012-308 8820; Magnolia Dell, Queen Wilhelmina Ave, New Muckleneuk; ⏰ 5.30-9.30pm Fri) Staged on the last Friday evening of the month, this is an excellent event and the place to pick up local crafts.

For decent-quality African curios, you can head just over the border into North-West Province for the Welwitischia Country Market at Hartbeespoort Dam. See the boxed text, p514 for details.

GETTING THERE & AWAY
Air
JIA is South Africa's international hub, accepting flights from across the globe. See p622 for details of airlines and flight options, and p440 for information on getting into town from JIA.

GAUTENG

Bus

Most national and international bus services commence in Pretoria before picking up in Jo'burg, unless the general direction is north. Most long-distance buses leave from the **1928 Building** (Map pp428-9; Railway St) in the Pretoria train-station forecourt. You will also find their booking and information offices here.

Most **Translux** (☎ 0861-589 282; www.translux.co.za), **City to City** (☎ 0861-589 282; www.translux.co.za), **Intercape** (☎ 0861 287 287; www.intercape.co.za), **Greyhound** (☎ 012-323 1154; www.greyhound.co.za) and **SA Roadlink** (☎ 012-323 5105; www.saroadlink.co.za) services running from Jo'burg to Durban, the south coast and Cape Town originate in Pretoria. Services running north up the N1 also stop here – see p417 for full details of these services.

Translux, Greyhound and Intercape fares from Pretoria are identical to those from Jo'burg regardless of the one-hour difference in time. If you only want to go between the two cities, it will cost about R45.

Baz Bus (Cape Town ☎ 021-439 2323; www.bazbus.com) will pick up and drop off at Pretoria hostels.

North Link Tours (☎ 012-323 0379) also runs from the 1928 Building and heads north to Polokwane (Pietersburg; R100, 3½ hours), Tzaneen (R160, five hours) and Phalaborwa (R195, 6½ hours).

Car

Having your own car makes getting around substantially easier, and local car rental agencies can offer good deals. Many larger local and international companies are represented in Pretoria; see p636 for details.

If you're staying for a long time, it might be worth your while to check out the weekly *Junk Mail* newspaper or monthly *Auto Trader* magazine for second-hand car sales.

Minibus Taxis

Minibus taxis go from the main terminal by the train station and travel to a host of destinations including Jo'burg (R30), but this is not the place to be wandering around with lots of luggage or after dark. Indeed, many locals would discourage you from using minibus taxis at all; it's worth asking around. See p640 for more information regarding minibus taxi travel.

Train

The historic Pretoria train station was rebuilt at a cost of R35 million after it was burned down by angry commuters in February 2001, and things are now back to normal. Despite commuter frustrations, most long-distance trains run on time, which is just as well as they seem to take forever.

Main Line (☎ 0860-008 888; www.spoornet.co.za) trains running through Pretoria are the *Trans Karoo* (daily from Pretoria to Cape Town) and the *Komati* (daily from Jo'burg to Komatipoort via Nelspruit). The *Bosvelder* runs north via Polokwane (Pietersburg) to Musina, near the Zimbabwe border. The luxury *Blue Train*, which links Pretoria, Jo'burg and Cape Town originates here (see p641 for details of the 'name' train services).

Pretoria train station (Map pp428–9) is about a 20-minute walk from the city centre. Buses run along Paul Kruger St to Church Sq, the main local bus terminal.

METRO

Because of a high incidence of crime, we don't recommend travelling between Pretoria and Jo'burg by Metro. For more info about the proposed Gautrain, see the boxed text, p419.

GETTING AROUND
To/From the Airport

If you call ahead, most hostels, and many hotels, offer free pick-up.

Get You There (☎ 012-346 3175) operates shuttle buses between JIA and Pretoria. The company does not have a set timetable but runs day and night about every hour, charging R95 to/from hostels and hotels.

Bus & Minibus Taxi

There's an extensive network of local buses. A booklet of timetables and route maps is available from the inquiry office in the main **bus terminus** (Map pp428-9; ☎ 012-308 0839; Church Sq) or from pharmacies. Fares range from R5 to R7, depending on the distance. Some services, including bus 3 to Sunnyside, run until about 10.30pm – unusually late for South Africa. Other handy buses include the 5 and 8, which run between Church Sq and Brooklyn via Burnett St in Hatfield.

Minibus taxis run just about everywhere and the standard fare is about R4. You won't see many white faces on these buses, but that doesn't mean they're unsafe. Seek local advice before you ride.

Taxi

There are taxi ranks on the corner of Church and Van der Walt Sts, and on the corner of Pretorius and Paul Kruger Sts. Or you can get a metered taxi from **Rixi Taxis** (☎ 0800 325 807; per km R8.50).

AROUND PRETORIA

Gauteng is perhaps better known for its cities than its countryside, but there are more than a few gems out in the sticks, if you have had enough urban living. The De

Wildt Cheetah Research Centre is a particular treat.

SMUTS' HOUSE MUSEUM

General JC Smuts was a brilliant scholar, Boer general, politician and international statesman. An architect of the Union of South Africa, he was the country's prime minister from 1919 to 1924 and 1939 to 1948.

Smuts' home was once known as Doorn-kloof and has been turned into an excellent **museum** (Map p441; ☎ 012-667 1941; smuts house@worldonline.co.za; Nelmapius Rd, Irene; adult/child R5/3, picnic garden per car R5; ⏲ 9.30am-4.30pm Mon-Fri, 9.30am-5pm Sat & Sun). It is worth visiting if you have private transport and are travelling to/from Pretoria. The wood-and-iron building

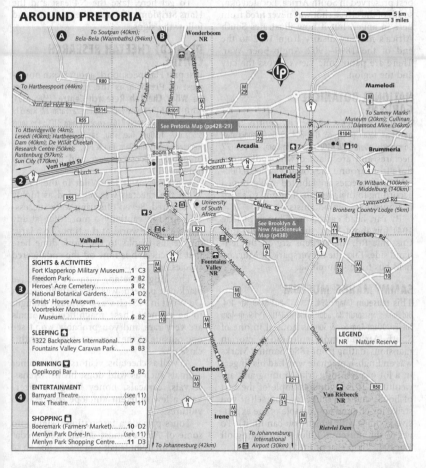

AROUND PRETORIA

0 —— 5 km
0 —— 3 miles

SIGHTS & ACTIVITIES
Fort Klapperkop Military Museum	**1** C3
Freedom Park	**2** B2
Heroes' Acre Cemetery	**3** B2
National Botanical Gardens	**4** D2
Smuts' House Museum	**5** C4
Voortrekker Monument & Museum	**6** B2

SLEEPING
1322 Backpackers International	**7** C2
Fountains Valley Caravan Park	**8** B3

DRINKING
Oppikoppi Bar	**9** B2

ENTERTAINMENT
Barnyard Theatre	(see 11)
Imax Theatre	(see 11)

SHOPPING
Boeremark (Farmers' Market)	**10** D2
Menlyn Park Drive-In	(see 11)
Menlyn Park Shopping Centre	**11** D3

LEGEND
NR   Nature Reserve

GAUTENG

was a British officers' mess at Middelburg but Smuts bought it and re-erected it on his 1600-hectare property at Irene, 16km south of Pretoria. Surrounded by a wide veranda and shaded by trees, it has a family atmosphere, and gives a vivid insight into Smuts' amazing life.

Unfortunately, there is no access by public transport. The house is signposted from both the N14 freeway (Rte 28) and Rte 21. The most direct route from Pretoria is along Louis Botha Ave to Irene.

FORT KLAPPERKOP MILITARY MUSEUM

This **fort** (Map p441; ☎ 082-807 5278; Johann Rissik Dr; adult/child R10/5; ☺ 10am-3.30pm) is one of the best preserved in South Africa. Located 6km south of the city, a shot was never fired from here in anger, but it now illustrates South Africa's military history from 1852 to the end of the 1899–1902 Anglo-Boer War. There are panoramic views across the city and the region.

NATIONAL BOTANICAL GARDENS

Around 9km east of the city centre, these **gardens** (Map p441; ☎ 012-804 3200; Cussonia Ave, Brummeria; adult/child R10/5; ☺ 6am-6pm) cover 77 hectares and are planted with indigenous flora from around the country. The 20,000-odd plant species are labelled and grouped according to their region of origin, so a visit is a must for keen botanists.

By car, head east along Church St (Rte 104) for about 8km, then turn right into Cussonia Rd; the gardens are on the left-hand side. Take the Meyerspark or Murrayfield bus from Church Sq.

SAMMY MARKS' MUSEUM

This **museum** (Map p394; ☎ 012-803 6158; Rte 104, Old Bronkhorstspruit Rd; adult/child R20/10; ☺ 9am-4pm Tue-Fri, 10am-4pm Sat & Sun) is housed in one of South Africa's most splendid Victorian mansions, dating from 1884. Sammy Marks was an English magnate who had his fingers in a lot of pies: industrial, mining and agricultural. It is a good example of the sort of house you can build for yourself if you strike it rich (and an example of the expensive goodies with which you can fill it). To get to the museum, follow signposting off Rte 104, 20km east of Pretoria.

CULLINAN DIAMOND MINE

After visiting Sammy Marks' Museum, go north to historic Cullinan (Map p394), a pretty 100-year-old village full of quaint Herbert Baker architecture. It is best explored on a sluggish, Sunday afternoon stroll. The village is home to Cullinan Diamond Mine one of the biggest and most productive diamond-bearing kimberlite pipes in the world. It has produced three of the largest diamonds ever found. The largest, the 3106-carat Cullinan, as it was called, was 11cm by 6cm in rough form and was presented to King Edward VII. You can don a tin hat and organise a tour of the mine through **Premier Diamond Tours** (☎ 012-734 0081, 083-261 3550; tours from R30).

To get here, take the N4 east and the Hans Strijdom off-ramp, then turn left and follow the signs.

DE WILDT CHEETAH RESEARCH CENTRE

Just past Hartbeespoort, about 50km northwest of Pretoria, is the highly impressive **De Wildt Cheetah Research Centre** (Map p394; ☎ 012-504 1921; www.dewildt.org.za; Farm 22, Rte 513 Pretoria North Rd; tours R165, cheetah runs R100; ☺ tours 8.30am & 1.30pm Tue, Thu, Sat & Sun, cheetah runs summer/winter 7am/8am Tue & Fri), famous for its breeding success of rare and endangered animals.

Work began at De Wildt in the 1960s, when the cheetah was regarded as highly endangered. Seven offspring were successfully bred in captivity – more than at any reserve in the world at the time. To a large degree it's thanks to the work done here that the cheetah is now off the endangered species list.

The king cheetah, with its distinctive black pelt pattern, was successfully bred at De Wildt in 1981; it was previously thought to be extinct. These magnificent animals are very rare and you probably won't see one outside of the reserve, at least not this close up.

As well as cheetahs, visitors can see other animals such as wild dogs, brown hyenas, servals, caracals, honey badgers, meerkats, a few different antelope species, and vultures.

Tours provide a fascinating insight into some of Africa's most endangered predators. In an open truck you'll see cheetah of different age groups being fed, and learn about their precarious existence in the wild. You can also go on a thrilling cheetah run, but only if you're fit! Professional wildlife photographers can also book special sessions with the cats (R2500). Bookings for all activities are essential and you should call at least a week in advance.

To get to De Wildt from Pretoria (via Hartbeespoort), take Rte 5131 northwest for 34km – the centre is on the left, about half a kilometre off the main road.

Mpumalanga

From the sluggish flow of the Crocodile River to the relaxed rhythm of its old mining towns and peaceful silence of its nature reserves, unassuming Mpumalanga (Place of the Rising Sun; pronounced M-poo-ma-lan-ga) adheres to a quieter pace of life.

This inland province, South Africa's smallest, is where the plateaus of the highveld begin their spectacular tumble onto the lowveld plains at the Drakensberg Escarpment. Tucked into the escarpment are historic towns, roaring waterfalls and some of the best hiking trails in South Africa. Many travellers zip through on their way to Kruger National Park, but it's worth setting aside a few days to explore the Blyde River Canyon, especially if you crave adventure sports like mountain biking, rafting and canyoning (known in these parts as 'kloofing').

The N4 splits Mpumalanga in two as it shoots toward Swaziland, Kruger and Mozambique. You can ignore the agricultural plains of the west as the scenery doesn't really pick up until you've hit Dullstroom, which is trying to make a name for itself as a fisherman's weekend getaway. Nearby Waterval Boven is justified in its claim to be South Africa's rock climbing capital.

The provincial capital Nelspruit is set among pretty hills and close to laid-back country towns like White River and Barberton. To the north, Sabie has emerged as a serious destination for adventure enthusiasts while quiet Graskop and Pilgrim's Rest offer unparalleled rural charm.

From Nelspruit, Kruger National Park's Numbi and Malelane gates are both an easy drive away, as is the Mozambique border at Komatipoort. Alternatively, head south to the charming old gold-mining town of Barberton and on into Swaziland. In Mpumalanga's far south is Piet Retief, a convenient transit junction if you're en route to Swaziland or KwaZulu-Natal.

Towns in this chapter are organised roughly clockwise west to east, and north to south.

HIGHLIGHTS

- Hiking, cycling or rafting around **Sabie** (p449), taking in the cool mountain air and beautiful views

- Dining on pancakes in **Graskop** (p452) or **Pilgrim's Rest** (p451)

- Exploring the **Blyde River Canyon** (p453) on foot

- Getting a taste of Shangaan life at **Shangana Cultural Village** (p455) near Hazyview

- Relaxing in historic **Barberton** (p462) while taking in the nearby Atlas gold mine and the intriguing labyrinth at **Boondocks** (p464)

Blyde River ★ Canyon
Pilgrim's Rest ★
Graskop ★
Sabie ★ ★ Shangana Cultural Village
Barberton ★

■ POPULATION: 3.1 MILLION | ■ AREA: 79,490 SQ KM

HISTORY

It's not too much of a stretch to say that *terra firma* got its first foothold in Mpumalanga. It was near Barberton, scientists allege, that the first stones cooled on the earth's surface 4.5 billion years ago, when the planet was still a half-baked ball of gases and molten lava.

Fast forward a few billion years to proto-man, who inhabited caves on the escarpment and in Blyde River Canyon. Tribal groups that today inhabit the province are descended from the Venda people and the Pedi, who broke away from the main migration route that headed south from Zimbabwe.

During the *difaqane* (forced migration), groups of Shangaan, Swazi and Ndebele entered the area in the wake of turbulence in Zululand. The Ndebele also threw their weight around, terrorizing rival tribes and taking young men and women hostage.

The first Voortrekkers moseyed onto the scene in the late 1830s and within 10 years established the Transvaal as a republic. This did not go down well with the British, especially after gold was discovered near Sabie. The entire Transvaal was annexed by the British in 1877.

The gold rush attracted miners from all over the globe. The strike, however, was not as large as everyone had hoped and soon the large mining camps near Sabie and Pilgrim's Rest packed up and moved elsewhere.

It was in the Transvaal that the first Anglo-Boer War erupted. The Boers were victorious, took back the Transvaal and made Paul Kruger their first President. This independence lasted only a few years, until the end of the war, when the Transvaal (and the Orange Free State) was returned to British hands.

When the gold rush ended the Transvaal diversified its economy to include modest tree farms and fruit plantations. Nowadays, the economy is kept afloat with the help of tourists attracted to nearby Kruger National Park. In the early 2000s, the province dropped the old Afrikaner name 'Transvaal' in favour of the more progressive 'Mpumalanga'.

CLIMATE

Winter temperatures in Mpumalanga can plummet to close to 0°C on the escarpment and frost is common. In the steamy lowveld, you can leave your jackets at home; bring a mosquito net and plenty of repellent instead. Summer temperatures here often exceed 35°C, with frequent rainstorms.

NATIONAL PARKS & RESERVES

The southern part of Kruger National Park lies in Mpumalanga, and is by far the province's biggest draw card. Other conservation areas include the many private wildlife reserves on Kruger's southwestern edge (p485), and the Blyde River Canyon Nature Reserve (p453).

LANGUAGE

Swati, Zulu and Ndebele are the main languages spoken in Mpumalanga, but it's easy to get by with English. In and around Nelspruit, you'll also hear a lot of Afrikaans.

GETTING THERE & AROUND

There are good domestic and regional air connections via Mpumalanga Kruger International Airport (MKIA), about 28km northeast of Nelspruit off Rte 40.

Mpumalanga is crossed by an extensive network of good tarmac roads. While there are frequent bus and minibus connections to/from Nelspruit, public transport is scarce away from major routes, and a hire car is definitely the best way of exploring.

A passenger train line cuts through the middle of the province, connecting Johannesburg (Jo'burg) with Komatipoort and Maputo (Mozambique), via Nelspruit.

For details on air, road and train connections to/from Jo'burg, see p460. For details on connections between Nelspruit and Kruger National Park, see p484. For information on crossing between Nelspruit and Swaziland and Mozambique, see p630 and p629, respectively.

DRAKENSBERG ESCARPMENT

The Drakensberg Escarpment (the section here is known as the Klein Drakensberg or the Transvaal Drakensberg) marks the point where the highveld plunges down over 1000m, before spilling out onto the eastern lowveld. It's one of South Africa's most scenic areas, marked by stunning views and an abundance of adventure activities. It's

MPUMALANGA

MPUMALANGA

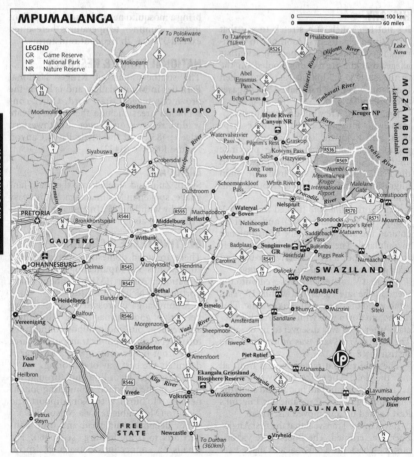

MPUMALANGA

| 0 | | 100 km |
| 0 | | 60 miles |

LEGEND
GR   Game Reserve
NP   National Park
NR   Nature Reserve

also prime holiday territory, which means that accommodation is pricier than in some other parts of the country, and invariably fills up during high season. While it's possible to get around via minibus taxi, the going is slow; car hire is the best option for really exploring the area.

DULLSTROOM
☎ 013 / pop 6000
If trout fishing is your thing, Dullstroom makes for a reasonable stopover on the route to Kruger National Park. The town, located 260km west of Jo'burg, only consists of a few quiet streets lined with pine trees and wood structures, but the surrounding area boasts more than 40 lodges and B&Bs where fishing

is the main activity. Even if angling is not your angle, it's still a great place for walking or horse riding among the lakes and forests. Sitting at an altitude of 2053m, Dullstroom enjoys a cool climate in summer and can receive frost and snow in wintertime.

If you happen to be in South Africa during the winter months, you can visit the **Dullstroom Derby**, an annual dog-sled race in early July. At the opposite end of the year, try catching the **Dullstroom Arts Festival** in mid-December.

Information
First National Bank At the main junction, with an ATM.
Tourist information centre (☎ 013-254 0020; www .dullstroom.co.za; Hugenote St; ⏰ 8.30am-5pm Mon-Fri,

9am-3pm Sat) Along the main road (Rte 540) at the southern end of town, near a collection of bait and tackle shops.

Video Shop & Internet Café (☎ 013-254 0454; Dullstroom Centre; per min R1; ☻ 11am-6.30pm) Internet access.

Sleeping & Eating

Caravan Park (☎ 083-528 5596; camp sites per person R25, caravans R60) Campers can put up at this park located on the edge of town by Groot Suikerbos Dam, 1.2km north of Rte 540.

Old Transvaal Inn (☎ 013-254 0222; Hugenote St; s/d with bathroom R125/200) If you prefer a roof over your head, try this good-value inn which offers 18 pleasant rooms behind a candy shop on the main road. Try to keep your sweet tooth in check.

Dullstroom Inn (☎ 013-254 0071; dullstroominn@ dullstroom.net; Teding van Berkhout St; s/d with breakfast R375/675) This is an unassuming place with cosy rooms and the Old English Pub restaurant (mains from R40), open lunch and dinner. It's on the northwestern edge of town.

Critchley Hackle (☎ 013-253 7000; www.critchley hackle.co.za; Teding van Berkhout St; s/d with breakfast from R690/1380; ⌨ ☎) This is an elegant mansion with its own trout pond and beautiful grounds planted with rose bushes. It's at the northeastern edge of town, signposted from the main road.

Pickles & Things (☎ 013-254 0115; Hugenote St; meals from R30; ☻ 7am-5pm Sun-Thu, 7am-5pm & 6.30pm-11pm Fri & Sat) For something substantial, try this pastel-painted place specialising in trout and continental dishes.

Casa Portuguesa (☎ 013-254 0977; 84 Hugenote St; mains R35-55; ☻ breakfast, lunch & dinner) This place offers some ethnic variety with good Portuguese dishes.

Scones, pancakes and tea are Dullstroom's culinary specialities. Places to sample these include **Rose Cottage** (☎ 013-254 0218; 60 Hugenote St; light meals from R25; ☻ 7am-5pm), which also offers cappuccino and light meals, and **Country Corner** (☎ 013-254 0812; Critchley Corner Complex, Hugenote St; light meals from R25; ☻ 8am-5pm), both on Rte 540, two blocks east of the Information Centre.

Getting There & Away

Minibus taxis pass Dullstroom en route to/ from Belfast, stopping along the main road, but the main way to get here and around is with your own vehicle.

WATERVAL BOVEN
☎ 013 / pop 2500

This tiny town is in scenic countryside just off the N4, and is known mainly as a base for some superb rock climbing and mountain biking. For details, contact Roc 'n Rope through **Climbers Lodge** (☎ 013-257 0363, 082-753 3695; www.rocrope.com). There's also the chance to abseil at the Elands River Waterfall (from which the town takes its name). A word of caution: don't let the sublime setting lead you into a false sense of security – several climbers have reported being robbed in the area. Take the usual precautions and if you plan on camping, first consult with the tourist info office or Roc 'n Rope.

Info Works (☎ 013-257 0444; www.linx.co.za/water val-boven; ☻ 8am-4pm Mon-Fri, 8am-1pm Sat) is a tourist info office located on the left as you enter the town from the N4.

Horse riding is available at **Blaaubosch Kraal Horse Trails** (☎ 013-257 0247, 082-853 3993; www.bbk trails.co.za) which offers two-hour horse trips for R120. They are located 8km from town on the road to Lydenburg.

Climbers' Lodge (☎ 013-257 0363, 082-753 3695; www.rocrope.com; dm/d R70/160) caters almost exclusively for rock climbers and mountain bikers. It's a spacious, clean and chilled out place, with several dorm rooms, a self-catering kitchen, lounge room and sun deck. Guesthouse owner Gustav Janse van

---

MPUMALANGA...

■ has the third largest canyon in the world (the Blyde River Canyon);

■ produces 80% of South Africa's coal;

■ is the country's second largest citrus-growing area;

■ encompasses all or part of the former homelands of KaNgwane, KwaNdebele, Gazankulu, Lebowa and Bophuthatswana;

■ has the world's largest artificial forests;

■ has South Africa's second-lowest adult literacy rate (75.5%);

■ is the fifth most densely populated province (38 people per sq km), with about 7% of the total population, of whom about 89% are African and 9% white.

MPUMALANGA

MPUMALANGA

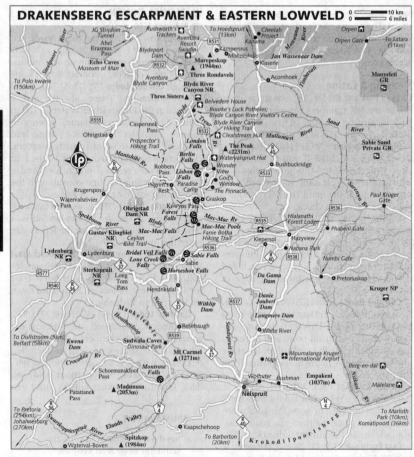

DRAKENSBERG ESCARPMENT & EASTERN LOWVELD

Rensburg also runs Roc 'n Rope and can organise all manner of outdoor activities. A half day of climbing (with equipment and instruction included) costs R300 per person. They can put you on a mountain bike for R30 per hour.

Aloes (☎ 013-257 7037; www.sa-venues.com/mpl/the aloesbp.htm; d/tr/q R300/375/400) is a self-catering lodge with spacious, well-appointed rooms and a porch that overlooks a trout-filled stream. It's a 10-minute drive out of Waterval Boven on the N4 towards Nelspruit.

The home-style **Shamrock Arms** (☎ 013-257 0888; www.linx.co.za/shamrockarms; 68 Third Ave; ☾ breakfast, lunch & dinner Tue-Sun) restaurant serves large portions of country English food. It's kitty-corner to Roc 'n Rope.

The restaurant also has a few rooms (s/d R230/430) with attached bathrooms.

Minibus taxis to Nelspruit cost R25 (two hours).

LYDENBURG
☎ 013 / pop 25,000

Lydenburg (Town of Suffering) was established by Voortrekkers in 1849 and was once the capital of the Republic of Lydenburg. Carrying on Boer traditions, it's still one of the most conservative towns in Mpumalanga. It's also where the famous Lydenburg Heads were found. These seven terracotta masks date to the 6th century AD, when they may have been used in initiation rituals, and are among the earliest

African sculpture forms known in Southern Africa.

Today Lydenburg is a quiet service centre for the farming district and one of Mpumalanga's more modest touristic offerings, unless you're interested in history. East of town along Rte 37 is the beautiful **Long Tom Pass** (2150m), one of Mpumalanga's more scenic drives.

There are ATMs at **First National Bank** (Voortrekker St) and **ABSA** (Voortrekker St), opposite each other near Kantoor St. **4U Computers** (☎ 013-235 1486; 55 Kantoor St; per hr R30; ⏰ 8am-5pm Mon-Fri, 8am-1pm Sat), one block north of Voortrekker St, has Internet access.

Sights

About 3km east of town along Rte 37 is the **Gustav Klingbiel Nature Reserve** (☎ 013-235 2213; admission R10; ⏰ 7.30am-4pm Mon-Fri, 8am-5pm Sat & Sun), with lots of birds, a small population of antelopes and short hiking trails, plus Iron-Age sites and Anglo-Boer War trenches. Also at the reserve is the very worthwhile **Lydenburg Museum** (☎ 013-235 2213; Long Tom Pass Rd; admission free; ⏰ 8am-1pm & 2-4pm Mon-Fri, 8am-5pm Sat & Sun), with a fascinating collection of animal and human terracotta masks, and replicas of the Lydenburg Heads. (The originals are in the South African Museum in Cape Town.)

Sleeping & Eating

Uitspan Caravan Park (☎ 013-235 2914; uitspanlyd@lantic.net; Viljoen St; camp sites from R75, s/d rondavels R155/275, s/d chalets R195/330; ⛽) This well-maintained place is on the road to Jo'burg. The chalets come with bathroom and kitchenette, while the rondavels have bedding and fridge only.

Manor Guest House (☎ 013-235 2099; cnr Viljoen & Potgier Sts; s/d with breakfast R280/460; ⛽) An indulgent, four-star B&B with a nice garden. If you are stuck in Lydenburg you can drink your sorrows away at the 'Jolly Roger' pub downstairs.

Misty Mountain Chalets (☎ 013-764 3377; www.mistymountain.co.za; s/d with breakfast R410/680, extra person R250) With great views, country cuisine and a log-cabin atmosphere, this place is a hard-to-beat rural retreat. Located along Rte 37 at the Long Tom Pass, it's an ideal base for mountain biking (you can rent them here for R50 per half-day), bird-watching or relaxing. Accommodation is

in fully equipped two-, four- or six-person self-catering cottages with fireplaces, and there's a restaurant (meals R40-R65) open for breakfast, lunch and dinner.

Lemon Tree Cafe & Take Away (☎ 013-235 3383; 31 Voortrekker St; ⏰ 7.45am-5pm Mon-Fri, 7.45am-1pm Sat), diagonally opposite the post office, and the cosy **Vroutjies Coffee Shop** (☎ 013-235 3016; 13 Voortrekker St; ⏰ 8.30am-4.30pm Mon-Fri, 8am-2pm Sat) have light meals.

Getting There & Away

The minibus taxi stop is in the town centre off Voortrekker St, with daily vehicles to Sabie (R25, one hour) and Belfast (R35, 1½ hours).

SABIE

☎ 013 / pop 12,000 / elevation 1100m

Perhaps the most inviting town on Drakensberg Escarpment, Sabie offers a good range of accommodation and activities to keep your pioneer spirit occupied for several days. Its attractions include a cool climate, trout fishing, extensive pine and eucalypt plantations in the surrounding area, almost unlimited possibilities for outdoor activities, and easy access to Kruger National Park.

Information

Bookcase (☎ 013-764 2014; cnr Main & Mac-Mac Sts; ⏰ 8am-5pm) Sells second-hand books.

First National Bank (Market Sq) Has an ATM.

Mobile Gateway (☎ 013-764 2400; per hr R35; Market Sq; ⏰ 8am-5pm Mon-Fri, 8am-1pm Sat) Internet access.

Tourist Information Office (☎ 013-764 1125; www.panoramainfo.co.za; Market Sq; ⏰ 8am-5pm Mon-Fri, 8am-1pm Sat)

Trips SA (☎ 764 1177; www.sabie.co.za; Main St) Information centre and booking agent for tours and accommodation.

Sights & Activities

The area around Sabie is dotted with beautiful **waterfalls** (admission to each R5-10). These include **Sabie Falls**, just north of town on Rte 532 to Graskop; the 70m **Bridal Veil Falls**, northwest of Sabie off Old Lydenburg Rd; the 68m **Lone Creek Falls**, also off Old Lydenburg Rd, and with wheelchair access on the right-hand path; and the nearby **Horseshoe Falls**, about 5km southwest of Lone Creek Falls. The popular **Mac-Mac Falls**, about 12km north of Sabie off Rte 532 to Graskop, take

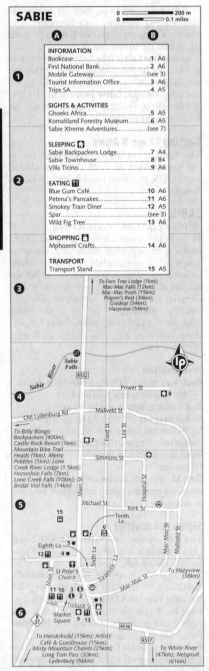

SABIE

0   200 m
0   0.1 miles

Ⓐ   **Ⓑ**

INFORMATION
Bookcase.................................**1** A6
First National Bank....................**2** A6
Mobile Gateway.....................(see **3**)
Tourist Information Office............**3** A6
Trips SA...................................**4** A5

SIGHTS & ACTIVITIES
Ghoeks Africa..........................**5** A5
Komatiland Forestry Museum........**6** A5
Sabie Xtreme Adventures.........(see **7**)

SLEEPING 🏠
Sabie Backpackers Lodge............**7** A4
Sabie Townhouse......................**8** B4
Villa Ticino..............................**9** A6

EATING 🍴
Blue Gum Café........................**10** A6
Petena's Pancakes....................**11** A6
Smokey Train Diner..................**12** A6
Spar...................................(see **3**)
Wild Fig Tree..........................**13** A6

SHOPPING 🛍
Mphozeni Crafts......................**14** A6

TRANSPORT
Transport Stand.......................**15** A5

To Fern Tree Lodge (1km);
Mac-Mac Falls (12km);
Mac-Mac Pools (15km);
Pilgrim's Rest (30km);
Graskop (34km);
Hazyview (54km)

Sabie River
Sabie Falls
R532
Power St
Maliveld St
Old Lydenburg Rd
To Billy Bongo
Backpackers (400m);
Castle Rock Resort (1km);
Mountain Bike Trail
Heads (1km); Merry
Pebbles (1km); Lone
Creek River Lodge (1.5km);
Horseshoe Falls (7km);
Lone Creek Falls (10km);
Bridal Veil Falls (14km)
Ford St
Lea St
Simmons St
Michael St
Kerk St
Hospital St
Tenth La
Eighth La
Sixth La
Mac-Mac St
Maliveld St
Main St
St Peter's Church
Seventh La
To Hazyview
(38km)
Mac-Mac St
Trichard St
Louis
Market Square
R37
R536
R537
To Hendriksdal (15km); Artists'
Café & Guesthouse (15km);
Misty Mountain Chalets (25km);
Long Tom Pass (30km);
Lydenburg (56km)
To White River
(47km); Nelspruit
(61km)

their name from the many Scottish names on the local mining register. About 3km southeast of the falls are the **Mac-Mac Pools**, where you can swim.

Komatiland Forestry Museum (☎ 013-764 1058; cnr Ford St & Tenth Lane; adult/child R5/2; 🕙 8am-4.30pm Mon-Fri, 8.30am-noon Sat) has displays on local forests and the timber industry. The tracts of artificial forest in these parts are the largest in the world. The museum has wheelchair access.

For horse riding contact **Creepers Creek** (☎ 013-764 2215; yurram@telkomsa.net) at Fern Tree Lodge, located 1km from town on the road to Graskop, or try **Sabie Horse Trails** (☎ 013-764 1011, 082-938 2060).

There are several excellent mountainbike trails, ranging from 13km to 45km and starting at Castle Rock Resort, near Merry Pebbles (below). Permits, which you'll need to ride on the trails, cost R20 and can be arranged at **Ghoeks Africa** (☎ 013-764 2123, 083-600 9863; bikedoc@lantic.net; cnr Main St & Tenth Lane), which also has bike rental (R30/180 including helmet per hour/day) and can help with repairs.

Hardy Ventures (☎ 013-751 1693; www.hardyventure.com) and **Sabie Xtreme Adventures** (☎ 013-764 2118; www.sabiextreme.co.za) can help organise abseiling, rafting and bungee jumping.

Sleeping

Sabie Backpackers Lodge (☎ 013-764 2118; www .sabiextreme.co.za; Main St; camp sites per person R40, dm R65, d with shared bathroom R160; 🖥 🏊) This popular establishment has a busy backpacker vibe with lots of activities and all the usual amenities, including cooking facilities and a pub. It's also the base for Sabie Xtreme Adventures (above).

Billy Bongo Backpackers (☎ 072-370 7219, 072-720 2130; www.billybongo.co.za; Old Lydenburg Rd; camp sites per person R45, dm R70, s/d R80/160) This place has a definite party atmosphere and owner Garth Lambert is an enthusiastic host who will lead you on adventure tours by day and long bongo drumming sessions by night. There are a handful of clean doubles and dorm rooms, plus self-catering facilities.

Merry Pebbles (☎ 013-764 2266; www.merrypebbles.co.za; camp sites per person R80, cabins s/d R160/380, 4-/8-person chalets R800/1200) Just north of town off Old Lydenburg Rd, Merry Pebbles is a large camping ground in shaded, spacious grounds on the banks of the Sabie River.

MPUMALANGA

Prices for the cabins rise on weekends and some holidays.

Sabie Townhouse (☎ 013-764 2292; www.sabie townhouse.co.za; Power St; s/d R325/650; ☒) This upscale B&B is a good choice for a treat, with arched windows, plush rooms with private entrances, and a quiet location.

Artists' Café & Guest House (☎ 013-764 2309; www.wheretostay.co.za/artistscafe; s/d with breakfast R330/620) This charming place is in Hendriksdal, about 15km south of Sabie along Rte 37. Accommodation is in old train station buildings that have been converted into rooms, and there's a very good Italian restaurant (meals R50) open for lunch and dinner.

Villa Ticino (☎ 013-764 2598; www.villaticino.co.za; cnr Louis Trichardt & Second Lane; s/d with breakfast R395/500; ☒) Readers highly recommend Villa Ticino, a comfortable Swiss-run B&B in the town centre with an old-world atmosphere and good breakfasts.

Lone Creek River Lodge (☎ 013-764 2611; www.lonecreek.co.za; Old Lydenburg Rd; s/d R900/1300, cabins from R700/920; ☐ ☒) Sabie's most upscale accommodation, with plush rooms in the main building backing onto the Sabie River, and comfortable two-storey self-catering cabins across the road. It's about 1.5km southwest of town.

Eating

Sabie has an excellent assortment of restaurants, only a small sampling of which are listed here.

Petena's Pancakes (☎ 013-764 1541; Main St; pancakes R20; ⊙ 9am-5.30pm) Dine on your choice of sweet or savoury pancakes in a cosy setting.

Wild Fig Tree (☎ 013-764 3098, 013-764 2239; mark uren@soft.co.za; 6 Third Lane; meals R35-90; ⊙ breakfast, lunch & dinner) This place features local specialities such as biltong pâté, ostrich fillet, grilled crocodile, warthog stew and home-made apple pie, all filling and, um, exotic. They also have Internet access and a guesthouse (singles/doubles with breakfast R200/370).

Smokey Train Diner (☎ 013-764 3445; Main St; mains about R40; ⊙ lunch & dinner) An Afrikaner diner, with some seating at booths in a refurbished train car and more on a large patio. The menu features *potjiekos* (stew cooked in a three-legged pot) and other Afrikaner dishes, plus a range of burgers and other standards.

Blue Gum Café (☎ 013-764 2209; 65a Main Rd; breakfast from R25, lunch R35; ⊙ 8am-5pm Tue-Fri, 9am-1pm Sat) This pleasant eatery right in the town centre features coffee, cakes, salads and light meals.

There's a Spar supermarket (Main St) north of Market Sq.

Shopping

There are several craft shops in the town centre, including **Mphozeni Crafts** (☎ 013-764 1541; thewoodsman.co.za; 94 Main St; ⊙ 9am-5pm) next door to Woodsman restaurant. Market Sq in the town centre has a small collection of shops.

Getting There & Away

There are daily buses from Jo'burg to Nelspruit, from where you can get minibus taxis to Sabie (R20, one hour between Nelspruit and Sabie). Minibus taxis also run frequently to and from Hazyview (R20, one hour). The transport stand (Main St) is behind Spar supermarket. At the stand is an office that dispenses timetable information.

PILGRIM'S REST

☎ 013 / pop 600

Tourist shops, craft stalls and historic buildings are the fabric of tiny Pilgrim's Rest, located a short detour off the main route between Sabie and Graskop.

The reason for the existence of Pilgrim's Rest dates all the way back to 1873 when gold was discovered nearby. For 10 years the area buzzed with diggers working small-scale alluvial claims. When the big operators arrived in the 1880s, Pilgrim's Rest became a company town, and when the gold finally fizzled out in 1972 the town was sold to the government as a ready-made historical village (it is now a national monument).

Tourism has replaced gold as the local cash cow and it can get very busy on weekends. Visitor activity centres on Uptown. Downtown – about 1.2km down the road – is quieter, with a few restaurants and craft outlets.

There's an **information centre** (☎ 013-768 1060; Main St, Uptown; ⊙ 9am-12.45pm & 1.15-4.30pm) at the museums building, and an ATM just down the road. Just up from Royal Hotel is a stand selling colourful batiks.

Sights & Activities

The town's three main **museums** (☎ 013-768 1060; total admission R10) feature a printing shop, a restored home and a general store. More interesting is historic **Alanglade** (☎ 013-768 1060; admission R20; ☽ tours 11am & 2pm Mon-Sat), a former mine-manager's residence at the northern edge of town furnished with period objects from the 1920s. Tours need to be booked 30 minutes in advance. Just east of town along the Graskop road is the open-air **Diggings Museum** (guided tours adult/child R10/5) where you can see how gold was panned. You need to visit on a tour, arranged through the information centre.

Sleeping & Eating

Pilgrims Rest Caravan Park (☎ 013-768 1427; pilgrims camp@mweb.co.za; camp sites per person R40, 2-person tents R140, d with shared bathroom R145; ▣) The cheapest place in town, with fixed tents, basic rooms and large grounds. It's just past Downtown on the Blyde River.

Royal Hotel (☎ 013-768 1100; s/d with breakfast R280/460; ▨) This is the historic centrepiece of Uptown and a fine example of wooden Victorian architecture. The rooms are elegantly furnished in period style and include brass four-poster beds. Church Bar, adjoining, is a good spot for a drink.

Scott's Cafe (☎ 013-768 1061; Uptown; meals from R25) A busy eatery with a large menu selection and a craft shop.

The Stables Deli & Café (☎ 083-454 4763; meals R22-40; ☽ 8.30am-5pm) This pleasant café serves light meals, sandwiches and cake, plus locally produced jams and sauces.

Getting There & Away

Sporadic minibus taxis run between Pilgrim's Rest and Graskop (R10, 30 minutes), but most traffic along this road is in private vehicles.

GRASKOP

☎ 013 / pop 2000 / elevation 1450m

A useful base to explore the dramatic Blyde River Canyon, the quiet town of Graskop is slowly emerging as a tourist destination. The town lacks the woodsy ambience of Sabie or Pilgrims Rest, but the nearby views over the edge of the Drakensberg Escarpment are hard to beat. A walking trail that includes places described in the popular South African classic *Jock of the Bushveld*

starts at the Graskop Municipal Holiday Resort, where you can get a map. The surrounding area is also good for mountain biking.

The best places for information are the **tourist information office** (☎ 013-767 1833; www .wildadventures.co.za; Pilgrim St; ☽ 8.30am-5pm Mon-Sat), inside Spar supermarket and Green Castle Backpackers (below). There's an ATM at **First National Bank** (Kerk St), just north of Louis Trichardt St, and Internet access at **Mobile Gateway** (☎ 072-333 3252; Pilgrim St; per hr R35; ☽ 8am-5pm Mon-Fri, 8am-1pm Sat).

Sleeping

Koka Moya (☎ 013-767 1761; www.krugertours.co.za; 63 Eeufees St; camp sites per person R40, dm R60, s/d with shared bathroom R120/160, with bathroom R150/200) Located in an atmospheric old house west of the centre across the train line, Koka Moya has a very communal feel and backpacker vibe. Andre the owner, a champion storyteller and *potjiekos* chef, arranges excellent day trips in the area and great-value safaris to Kruger National Park.

Graskop Valley View Backpackers (☎ 013-767 1112; www.yebo-afrika.nl; 47 de Lange St; camp sites R45, dm R70, s/d from R155/190, self-catering rondavel R275; ▨ ▣) This Dutch-run backpackers has a variety of rooms, plus rondavels, tent sites and a self-catering flat. The owners can organise adventure tours and they rent out mountain bikes for private use. Take the road to Sabie, turn left at the first four-way stop and another left on de Lange St.

Autumn Breath (☎ 013-767 1866, 082-877 2811; autumnbreath@cfmail.co.za; Louis Trichardt St; s/d with breakfast from R210/360) This quaint B&B has three modern rooms and a restaurant downstairs that is open to the public (so don't wander down in your bathrobe).

Log Cabin Village (☎ 013-767 1974; www.logcabin .co.za; Louis Trichardt St; s/d chalets R250/330; ▨ ▣) A fenced-in compound in a central location close to the pancake eateries, with pleasant self-contained chalets with TVs and fireplaces.

Graskop Hotel (☎ 013-767 1244; www.graskophotel .co.za; cnr Main & Louis Trichardt Sts; s/d with breakfast R280/500) This is a surprisingly charming hotel, with efficient staff and 34 spacious rooms. Avoid those facing the street as timber trucks roll by in the night. There is a cosy bar, a restaurant and a lounge area with lots of tasteful, modern-art sculptures and paintings.

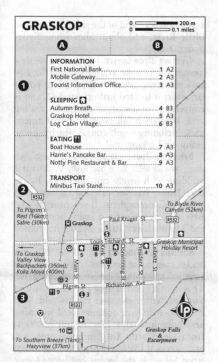

GRASKOP

0 ——————— 200 m
0 ——————— 0.1 miles

INFORMATION
First National Bank............................1 A2
Mobile Gateway.................................2 A3
Tourist Information Office..................3 A3

SLEEPING
Autumn Breath...................................4 B3
Graskop Hotel....................................5 A3
Log Cabin Village...............................6 B3

EATING
Boat House...7 A3
Harrie's Pancake Bar.........................8 A3
Notty Pine Restaurant & Bar.............9 A3

TRANSPORT
Minibus Taxi Stand...........................10 A3

R532
To Pilgrim's Rest (16km); Sabie (30km)
To Blyde River Canyon (52km)
Paul Kruger St
Graskop
R532
Louis Trichardt St
To Graskop Valley View Backpackers (350m); Koka Moya (400m)
Kerk St
Oxawinning St
President St
Leibnitz St
Graskop Municipal Holiday Resort
Pilgrim St
Richardson Ave
R533
To Southern Breeze (1km); Hazyview (37km)
Graskop Falls & Escarpment

MPUMALANGA

Eating & Drinking
Graskop is a gourmet's delight, and pancakes are the highlight.

Harrie's Pancake Bar (☎ 013-767 1273; Louis Trichardt St; pancakes R12-30; ☧ 8am-5.30pm) A classic pancake eatery with a cosy atmosphere. Don't expect a stack of buttermilk pancakes with butter and maple syrup – these pancakes are done up gourmet style; mostly stuffed with a choice of tasty meats or vegetables.

Southern Breeze (☎ 082-890 2587; dishes R30-50; ☧ dinner) Located in the Magodi Lodge about 1km out of town on the road to Hazyview, this local favourite serves up traditional South African dishes with a Malay influence.

Boat House (☎ 013-767 1980; 7 Main St; meals R40-60; ☧ 8am-9pm Tue-Sun) Designed like the interior of a ship, this newcomer offers English breakfasts and excellent seafood.

Notty Pine Restaurant & Bar (☎ 013-767 1030; Pilgrim St; meals R35-50; ☧ lunch & dinner Sat-Thu, dinner Fri) Specializes in trout dishes.

Getting There & Away
The minibus taxi stand (Main St) is at the southern end of town, with daily morning departures to Pilgrim's Rest (R10, 30 minutes), Sabie (R15, 40 minutes) and Hazyview (R18, one hour).

BLYDE RIVER CANYON
The Blyde River's spectacular canyon is nearly 30km long and one of South Africa's most impressive natural features. Much of it is rimmed by the 26,000-hectare **Blyde River Canyon Nature Reserve** (admission per person R20), which snakes north from Graskop, following the escarpment and meeting the Blyde River as it carves its way down to the lowveld. Most visitors drive along the edge of the canyon, with stops at the many wonderful viewpoints, but if you have the time, it's well worth exploring on foot.

Heading north from Graskop, look first for the **Pinnacle**, an impressive rock formation jutting out from the escarpment. (Lock up your vehicle here as there have been break-ins.) Just to the north along Rte 534 (a loop off Rte 532) are **God's Window** and **Wonder View** – two viewpoints with amazing vistas and batteries of souvenir sellers. At God's Window take the trail up to the rain forest (300 steps) where you might spot rare birds, including the elusive loeire.

When you return to Rte 532, take a short detour 2km south to the impressive **Lisbon Falls** (or if you are coming back to Graskop, catch it in the afternoon).

The Blyde River canyon starts north of here, near **Bourke's Luck Potholes**. These bizarre cylindrical holes were carved into the rock by whirlpools near the confluence of the Blyde and Treuer rivers. There's a **visitor's centre** (☎ 013-769 6019) where you can pay the reserve entry fee and get information on the canyon's geology, flora and fauna.

Continuing north past Bourke's Luck Potholes and into the heart of the nature reserve, you'll reach a viewpoint overlooking the **Three Rondavels** – huge cylinders of rock with hut-like pointed 'roofs' rising out of the far wall of the canyon. There are a number of short walks in the surrounding area to points where you can look down to the Blydepoort Dam at the reserve's far north.

West of here, outside the reserve and off Rte 36, are **Echo Caves** (admission R25) where Stone-Age relics have been found. The caves get their name from dripstone formations that echo when tapped. Be wary of the volunteer guides that attach themselves to you. Only pay them R5 even if they demand R50 (they will show you a doctored record showing that others paid R50 – they didn't). Nearby, and reached via the same turnoff from Rte 36, the open-air **Museum of Man** (adult/child R10/5; 8am-5pm), an archaeological site with rock paintings and other finds, is hardly worth your time or money.

Hiking

The main route is the popular and very scenic **Blyde River Canyon Hiking Trail** (R60; 2½ days), which begins at Paradise Camp and finishes at Bourke's Luck Potholes. The first night is spent at Watervalspruit Hut, and the second at Clearstream Hut. Bookings should be made through the **Mpumalanga Parks Board** (☎ 013-759 5432; mpbinfo@cis.co.za), or at the booking office at Bourke's Luck Potholes. As it's a one-way route, you'll need to sort out onward transport from the end of the trail.

The short but reasonably strenuous **Belevedere Day Walk** (admission R5; 5hr) takes you in a circular route to the Belvedere hydroelectric power station at Bourke's Luck Potholes. The station was built in 1911 and was once the largest of its kind in the southern hemisphere. Bookings should be made at Potholes. When walking here, don't go to the river bottom, instead turn left at the guesthouse down a path to some beautiful waterfalls and rock pools.

For more walks in the area, visit the Aventura Resort Blyde Canyon where you can mix and match a series of six hiking routes. Entry is R40 but this can be put towards credit at the restaurant.

Sleeping

It's easy to explore the canyon by car as a day jaunt from Graskop, Sabie or Pilgrim's Rest. If you're continuing further north, a good alternative is to stay in or around the nature reserve, or in Hoedspruit (p510). Ask about low-season (May to September) and midweek discounts.

Aventura Resort Swadini (☎ 015-795 5141; www .aventura.co.za; camp sites R60, plus per person R30, 6-person self-catering chalet R550;) Accommodation here is made more appealing by the good location and impressive views. In addition to hiking, the resort can organise white-water rafting, abseiling and more. It's

at the northern end of the reserve along the Blyde River, and about 5km from Blydepoort Dam.

Aventura Blyde Canyon (☎ 013-769 8005; www .aventura.co.za; camp sites R110 plus per person R22; 2-/4-person self-catering chalets R505/685;) This popular resort is located just off Rte 532, and is convenient for discovering the surrounding area. It offers a full range of resort amenities, including a golf course nearby, horse riding and hiking trails.

Belvedere House (☎ 013-759 5432; mpbinfo@cis .co.za; Mon-Fri R550, Sat & Sun R700) A historic building with lovely canyon views, Belvedere House has self-catering facilities and a peaceful atmosphere. It sits near the old Belvedere power station and is operated by the Mpumalanga Parks Board. It's rented out in its entirety (up to nine people).

Rushworth's Trackers (☎ 015-795 5033; www .trackers.truepath.com; camp sites per person R45, r per person with half board R290, r per person self-catering R160) This is in a good setting just northwest of Swadini, with views over the lowveld. Staff can also help you organise bird-watching and botanical trips. The easiest access is from Hoedspruit (in Limpopo province, and accessed from Nelspruit via Rte 40, or from Sabie via the longer but more scenic Rte 532 and Rte 527). Once in Hoedspruit, take Rte 527 west, turning south after about 20km onto the small Driehoek road (just after crossing the Blyde River). Continue for 6.5km, and watch for the signs.

EASTERN LOWVELD

It's in Mpumalanga's hot, dry eastern lowveld that you'll get a taste for bygone days, when vast bush-covered expanses were the playing fields for the ancestors of the animals that now roam Kruger National Park. While the area lacks the drama and scenic splendour of the Drakensberg Escarpment, it has numerous attractions. These include its location at Kruger National Park's doorstep and a laid-back, untouristy pace away from major towns.

HAZYVIEW

☎ 013 / pop 20,000

Strung out along Rte 40, the town of Hazyview acts as a service centre and gateway for nearby Kruger National Park. There

HOLLYWOOD IN MPUMALANGA

Mpumalanga may be one of the most famous places you've never heard of. While most visitors would have trouble trying to find it on a map, the province has attracted movie stars, cultural icons, royal families and billionaire business tycoons from all over the world.

What they are interested in is the wildlife and the luxury accommodation located on the eastern edge of Mpumalanga in Kruger National Park. Michael Jackson has made cameo appearances, and so have Brad Pitt, Wesley Snipes, former German Chancellor Helmut Kohl and others.

The star attraction is Ulusaba Safari Lodge, the luxurious hideaway owned by Sir Richard Branson. Ulusaba (technically in Limpopo province but accessible from Mpumalanga) is so exclusive that it has its own private landing strip for ultra-rich jet setters. The lodge itself is a sort of Hollywood-in-Africa, complete with hanging rope bridges that connect wood huts set upon stilts. The highlight is the Rock Lodge, carved out of the rock face of a cliff overlooking the Sabi Sand game reserve. Bill Gates was apparently left speechless.

This new-found fame has been good for tourism but also helps when Mpumalanga is looking for financial support to combat problems like HIV/AIDS and poverty. Richard Branson has taken the lead in charitable contributions, funding local business ventures, supporting health initiatives and providing scholarships to underprivileged kids.

are reasonable facilities, but consider it little more than an overnight stop before the early morning dash to the Phabeni (12km), Numbi (15km) or Paul Kruger (47km) Gates.

Information

Simunye Shopping Centre has an ATM and a Checkers supermarket.

Big 5 Country Tourist Office (☎ 013-737 7414; Perry's Bridge ☎ 013-737 8191; www.big5country.com; ✆ 8am-5pm Mon-Sat, 9am-1pm Sun) This helpful office is in the Rendezvous Tourism Centre. Big 5 Country operates a second branch at Perry's Bridge, on the right as you're coming in from the north.

Fx Africa (Perry's Bridge; ✆ 9am-noon & 1-5pm Mon-Fri, 9am-1pm Sat) Currency exchange.

Paper Chain (☎ 013-737 6537; Perry's Bridge; ✆ 8am-5pm Mon-Fri, 9am-1pm Sat) Internet access.

Rendezvous Tourism Centre (www.rendez.co.za) On the main road as you are coming into Hazyview from the south.

Sights

About 5km north of town along Rte 535, is **Shangana Cultural Village** (☎ 013-737 7000; www.shangana.co.za; ✆ 9am-5pm) a made-for-tourists re-creation of a traditional Shangaan community. At various times of day it features a market, farming activity, house building, displays of uniforms and weaponry of the *masocho* (warriors), the relation of customs and history by a *sangoma* (witch doctor or herbalist), cooking, dancing and the imbibing of *byala* (traditional beer).

Day tours cost R60, midday visits with a traditional meal cost from R120, and the evening program with a good dinner costs R190. The Marula Crafts Market is also located here.

Sleeping & Eating

Kruger Park Backpackers (☎ 013-737 7224; www.krugerparkbackpackers.com; camp sites per person R40, dm R75, d huts with shared bathroom R130; 🏊) Another spacious, somewhat rustic place, with trips to Kruger and accommodation in dorms or Zulu huts. It's about 2km south of the four-way stop, and about 500m along the road to Kruger's Numbi Gate.

Gecko Bushpackers & Campsite (☎ 013-737 8140; www.gecko-bushpackers.co.za; dm R70, d with/without bathroom R190/170; 🏊) Perhaps the most welcoming and cosy backpackers in the area, Gecko has a friendly staff and a laid-back atmosphere. It's about 2.5km from Hazyview just off Rte 536 to Sabie. It has bright dorm rooms, some doubles, shaded camping, a self-catering area and a pool table. Meals can also be arranged.

Big 5 Backpackers (☎ 013-737 7534, 083-524 6615; www.big5backpackers.co.za; dm/d R75/180; 🏊 🖥) This popular backpackers is in a wooded setting with a 'contemplation area', cooking facilities and safaris to Kruger. It's 3km up from the junction of Rte 40 and Rte 538; watch for the large, purple sign.

Hotel Numbi (☎ 013-737 7301; www.hotelnumbi.co.za; s/d with breakfast R460/720; 🏊) Hotel Numbi, just south of the four-way stop, has a colonial-era ambience, spacious grounds, the good Pioneer Grill (mains from R40) with views over the lawn, and a less expensive pub menu inside.

Thulamela (☎ 013-737 7171; www.thulamela.co.za; s/d cottages R500/840) Another upscale, comfortable place. It's set in the bush about 13km from Kruger, with majestic views and free-roaming wildlife in the area. Children under 16 aren't permitted. To get here, take the Umbhaba turn-off from Rte 40.

Hippo Hollow (☎ 013-737 7752; www.hippohollow .co.za; s/d chalet R570/850; 🏊) This is a large, sprawling resort-style complex on the Sabie River about 2.5km from Hazyview. Accommodation is in two- and four-bed chalets with a braai (barbecue) area and small kitchenette, or in hotel rooms overlooking the river. True to its name, hippos sometimes wade onto shore by the restaurant.

Rissington Inn (☎ 013-737 7700; www.rissington .co.za; d from R680; 🍴 🏊) An upscale retreat, with comfortable rooms in thatched, white cottages and views over Kruger in the distance. The inn is located a couple of kilometres south of Hazyview. It is 1km north of the Rte 40 and Rte 538 junction, and well signposted.

For meals head to Perry's Bridge, which has several restaurants including the Italian-styled **Pappas Pizzeria** (☎ 013-737 7428; 🕙 breakfast, lunch & dinner) and the slightly more upscale African-themed **Digby's Restaurant** (☎ 013-737 6957; dishes R50-70; 🕙 lunch & dinner Mon-Sat, lunch Sun). For something more intimate, head to **Tree Tops Restaurant** (☎ 013-737 8294; meals R60-80; 🕙 dinner Mon-Sat), which features a mix of continental and local cuisine. It's 10km from Hazyview along Rte 36 to Sabie.

Getting There & Away

City to City's daily Jo'burg–Acornhoek bus stops at the Shell petrol station in Hazyview (R95 from Jo'burg). The backpackers places do pick-ups from Nelspruit from about R15 (and some will do pick-ups at no charge if you book a Kruger safari with them).

Minibus taxis go daily to Nelspruit (R20, one hour) and Sabie (R20, one hour).

WHITE RIVER

☎ 013 / pop 10,000 / elevation 950m

White River (Witrivier) is a green, pleasant little town dating back to the days of the Anglo-Boer Wars. It's a bit higher and less humid than nearby Nelspruit, and worth a short stop. The town is the self-styled 'nut capital of South Africa', and just south of White River off Rte 40, you can visit some nut plantations.

The **tourist office** (☎ 013-750 1073; info@lowveld .info; 🕙 9am-4.30pm) is at the Casterbridge Centre about 2km north of town off Rte 40. There's an ATM at **First National Bank** (Tom Lawrence St) and Internet access at **Post Net** (☎ 013-750 0225; per hr R30; 🕙 8am-6pm Mon-Fri, 8am-3pm Sat, 10am-2pm Sun) in the White River Shopping Centre.

Hardy Ventures (☎ 013-751 1693; www.hardyven ture.com) organises various adrenalin activities in the area, including rafting trips on the Sabie, Olifants and Blyde Rivers and hiking.

Sleeping

Gypsies Traveller's Inn (☎ 013-750 0075; gypseytours@ iafrica.com; dm R70, s/d with shared bathroom R85/160; 🖳 🏊) Gypsies is a new place located 5km from the airport and 7km from White River. It offers accommodation in small wood cabins with a separate ablution block. There's a pleasant dining area, plus a pimped out converted campervan that sleeps up to four people. To get there, drive 5km east along Rte 538, and then 2km down Jatinga Rd.

Karula Hotel (☎ 013-751 2277; www.karulahotel .co.za; Old Plaston Rd; s R255-280, d R380-420; 🍴 🏊) This colonial-style hotel is the best midrange choice. Its award-winning rooms are pleasant, especially those in the 'luxury' wing, and the grounds – rimmed by jacaranda and bougainvillea – are relaxing. It's on a quiet, winding section of Rte 538.

Outside town there are several comfortable places which are good if you want to spend a few days relaxing in the countryside.

Igwala Gwala Country Lodge (☎ 013-750 1723; www.igwalagwala.co.za; d with breakfast from R550; 🏊) This place is about 3km south of White River off Rte 40 (signposted), with nice gardens and accommodation in plush attached suites (no children allowed).

Hulala Lakeside Lodge (☎ 013-764 1893; www .hulala.co.za; s/d with half board from R750/1100; 🏊) A large resort with a waterside setting, canoeing and row boats, and rooms with fireplaces. It's north of White River, signposted along Rte 40.

Greenway Woods Resort (☎ 013-751 1094; www
.greenway.co.za; 6-person chalets R1075; ✕ ⚍) A large
resort about 6km from White River near the
golf course. The self-catering chalets have
fireplaces, and there's a restaurant.

Eating

Fez at Baghdad (☎ 013-750 1250; meals from R30, set
menu R85; ✆ 9am-midnight Tue-Sat) This is a delightful bar and restaurant attached to a
craft shop. It's about 2km from the town
centre along Rte 40 to Hazyview, and opposite the Casterbridge Centre.

Green Bottles (☎ 013-750 1097; dishes R25-50;
✆ 9am-9pm Mon-Thu, 9am-10pm Fri & Sat, 9am-4pm
Sun) This chic, arty restaurant, located at the
Casterbridge Centre, serves up fine meat
and seafood dishes. It's also a good place to
relax with a fruit shake or glass of wine.

Getting There & Around

Minibus taxis go throughout the day to/
from Nelspruit (R5, 20 minutes) and Hazyview (R15, one hour).

NELSPRUIT

☎ 013 / pop 235,000

Nelspruit, Mpumalanga's largest town and
provincial capital, sprawls along the Crocodile River Valley in the steamy, subtropical
lowveld. There are some good, affordable
accommodation options and plenty of restaurants, making it a good place to sort out
your stuff while you consider the next direction of your plunge.

Orientation

At the centre of things, or at least trying
to be, is the Promenade Centre, with a
modest selection of shops and restaurants.
Opposite are the ticket offices for Translux
and other long-distance buses. About 5km
north of town off the White River road is
the large Riverside Mall, which has taken
much of Promenade Centre's business, and
is the best place to shop.

Information

EMERGENCY

Police station (☎ 013-759 1000; 15 Bester St) Opposite
Nelspruit Plaza.

INTERNET ACCESS

Alpha Internet (☎ 013-755 5015; Crossing Centre; per hr
R25; ✆ 8am-8pm Mon-Sat, 9am-4pm Sun) Internet access.

Mugg & Bean (☎ 013-757 1036; Riverside Mall; per hr
R50) There is a wi-fi hotspot here, although the charge is
borderline outrageous.

Nexus Internet Café (☎ 013-741 2303; Sonpark
Centre; per hr R30; ✆ 8am-7pm Mon-Fri, 9am-8pm Sat,
11am-5pm Sun) Internet access, opposite Town Lodge.

MEDICAL SERVICES

Nelmed Forum (☎ 013-755 1541; cnr Nel & Rothery
Sts) Offers 24-hour emergency medical care.

MONEY

ABSA (Brown St) With an ATM.
First National Bank (Bester St) Does foreign exchange.
Nelspruit Crossing Mall (cnr General Dan Pienaar &
Louis Trichardt Sts) With an ATM.

TOURIST INFORMATION

Dana Travel (☎ 013-753 3571; www.danaagency.co.za;
shop 12, Crossings Centre) This long-standing agent can
help with air tickets and other travel arrangements.

Lowveld Tourism (☎ 013-755 1988/9; www.lowveld
.info; cnr General Dan Pienaar & Louis Trichardt Sts;
✆ 8am-5pm Mon-Fri, 8am-1pm Sat) This helpful office
at Nelspruit Crossing Mall takes bookings for all national
parks, including Kruger, and can help arrange accommodation and tours.

Mozambique consulate (☎ 013-752 7396; moz
conns@mweb.co.za; 32 Bell St; ✆ 8am-2pm Mon-Fri)
Does same-day visa processing for R80 – half the price of a
visa at the border.

Sights & Activities

Pick up some fresh apples, mangos and
melons at Nelspruit's lively produce **market**
(cnr Brown & Currie Sts). If you're after something
quieter, take a stroll among manicured
stands of flowers, gnarled baobabs and
patches of indigenous forest in the 150-
hectare **National Lowveld Botanic Gardens**
(☎ 013-752 5531; adult/child R10/4; ✆ 8am-6pm). It's
on Rte 40 about 2km north of the junction
with the N4.

The small **Sonheuwel Nature Reserve** (☎ 013-
759 9111; admission free) features antelope species, vervet monkeys and rock paintings.
It's on the southern edge of Nelspruit, off
Van Wijk St.

Just northwest of Nelspruit and signposted from Rte 40 is the **Croc River Reptile
Park** (☎ 013-752 5511; adult/child R30/15; ✆ 8am-
5pm), where you can meet the original inhabitants of Crocodile River Valley.

The area around Nelspruit is good for
bird-watching; contact **Lawson's Bird Safaris**

MPUMALANGA

(☎ 013-741 2458; www.lawsons.co.za) to organise tours. There's also some challenging hiking, notably along the **Kaapschehoop trail** (per night R57; 2, 3 or 4 days) and the **Uitsoek trail** (per night R57; 1 or 2 days). For bookings, contact **Komatiland Forests Ecotourism** (☎ 013-754 2724; www.komati ecotourism.co.za; 10 Streak St).

There's an excellent 50m **swimming pool** (☎ 013-759 9411; Drysdale St; adult/child R6/5; ⊙ 10am-5.30pm Tue-Sat, 1-5.30pm Sun & public holidays) at Van Riebeeck Park sporting complex.

Festivals & Events

Held in the summer months (either June or July), **InniBos** (www.innibos.co.za) is Nelspruit's biggest festival. Basically a cultural fair, Inni-Bos brings together artists, musicians and

theatre groups for five days of events. Entry is around R20 per day.

If you are around in August, try to catch the **Nelspruit Jazz Festival** held at the Rugby Stadium behind Crossing Mall.

Sleeping

BUDGET

Nelspruit Backpackers (☎ 013-741 2237; nelback@hot mail.com; 9 Andries Pretorius St; camp sites per person R40, dm R70, s/d with shared bathroom R130/180; 🖳) Among Nelspruit's backpackers, this one best combines service, comfort and location. Rooms have recently been upgraded. It's a Baz Bus stop and its travel wing, Mbombela safaris, can organise itineraries in the area. Look for the red, yellow and green gate.

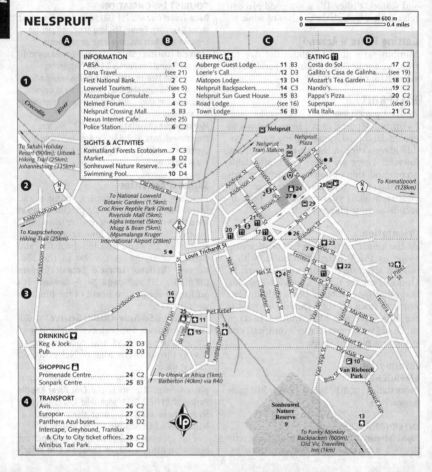

NELSPRUIT							0 ———— 600 m / 0 ———— 0.4 miles

INFORMATION		SLEEPING 🛏		EATING 🍴	
ABSA	1 C2	Auberge Guest Lodge	11 B3	Costa do Sol	17 C2
Dana Travel	(see 21)	Loerie's Call	12 D3	Gallito's Casa de Galinha	(see 19)
First National Bank	2 C2	Matopos Lodge	13 D4	Mozart's Tea Garden	18 D3
Lowveld Tourism	(see 5)	Nelspruit Backpackers	14 C3	Nando's	19 C2
Mozambique Consulate	3 C2	Nelspruit Sun Guest House	15 B3	Pappa's Pizza	20 C2
Nelmed Forum	4 C3	Road Lodge	(see 16)	Superspar	(see 5)
Nelspruit Crossing Mall	5 B3	Town Lodge	16 B3	Villa Italia	21 C2
Nexus Internet Cafe	(see 25)				
Police Station	6 C2				

SIGHTS & ACTIVITIES	
Komatiland Forests Ecotourism	7 C3
Market	8 D2
Sonheuwel Nature Reserve	9 C4
Swimming Pool	10 D4

DRINKING 🍷	
Keg & Jock	22 D3
Pub	23 D3

SHOPPING 🛍	
Promenade Centre	24 C2
Sonpark Centre	25 B3

TRANSPORT	
Avis	26 C2
Europcar	27 C2
Panthera Azul buses	28 D2
Intercape, Greyhound, Translux & City to City ticket offices	29 C2
Minibus Taxi Park	30 C2

Funky Monkey Backpackers (☎ 083-310 4755; www.funkymonkeys.co.za; 102 Van Wijk St; camp sites per person R40, dm R70, s/d with shared bathroom R130/180; 🖳 🍴) A popular, well-run place in a spacious house, with a pool table, braai area and friendly staff. It's a little far from town, but it is a Baz Bus stop, and pick-ups from the bus terminal can be arranged.

Nelspruit Sun Guest House (☎ 013-741 2253; sunlodge@absamail.co.za; 7 De Villiers St; dm R65, d with/without bathroom R200/180; 🖸 🖳 🍴) This quirky place has accommodation in tasteful wood buildings set in a lush garden. It's not as welcoming and 'backpacker friendly' as the previous two entries. The Baz Bus stops here.

Old Vic Travellers Inn (☎ 013-744 0993; www.krugerandmore.co.za; 12 Impala St; dm R90, d with/without bathroom R300/250, 4-person self-catering cottages R420; 🖳 🍴) A friendly, somewhat upscale backpackers, with self-catering facilities or meals on request, tents for rent and lots of information on the area. It's about 3km south of the centre, near an extension of Sonheuwel Nature Reserve, and a Baz Bus stop.

Safubi Holiday Resort (☎ 013-741 3253; 45 Graniet St; camp sites R120; .2-/4-/6-bed chalets R395/495/595; 🍴) Safubi is a well-kept, self-catering resort about 2.5km from the town centre in pleasant grounds backing on to a nature reserve. There's a coffee shop and a large swimming pool. Take the N4 west, and turn left at Graniet St (at the Caltex petrol station); it's 1km further on.

MIDRANGE & TOP END

Road Lodge (☎ 013-741 .1805; www.citylodge.co.za; tr R285; 🖸) In the same complex, but a step down from Town Lodge, with straightforward rooms.

Auberge Guest Lodge (☎ 013-741 2866; www.aubergeguestlodge.com; 3 de Villiers St; s/d with breakfast R285/385; 🍴) A quiet, well-maintained guesthouse with comfortable rooms in the main house, and a small yard. It's just down from Town Lodge.

Matopos Lodge (☎ 013-753 3549; www.matopos.co.za; 14 Sheppard Ave; s/d with breakfast R350/450; 🍴) Rooms at this comfortable place have ceiling fans, and some have balconies. It's in a quiet setting about 15 minutes on foot from the centre near Van Riebeeck Park.

Town Lodge (☎ 013-741 1444; www.citylodge.co.za; cnr General Dan Pienaar & Koorsboom Sts; s/d R415/500;

🖸 🖳 🍴) Town Lodge is downmarket from its sister chain, City Lodge, but good value.

Utopia in Africa (☎ 013-745 7714; www.utopiainafrica.com; 6 Daleen St; s/d with breakfast R425/720; 🖸 🍴) An exquisite guest villa with thoughtful décor and friendly service. This one overlooks the Sonheuwel Nature Reserve. To get there, head south on General Dan Pienaar St, turn left on John Vorster St, right on Halssnoer St (which becomes Augusta), and then right on Daleen.

Loerie's Call (☎ 013-744 1251; www.loeriescall.co.za; 2 du Preez St; s/d with breakfast from R450/590; 🍴 🖳) One of Nelspruit's classiest guesthouses. The rooms are set apart from the main house, each with their own entrance.

Eating & Drinking

Villa Italia (☎ 013-752 5780; cnr Louis Trichardt & Paul Kruger Sts; mains R35-60; ⏰ lunch & dinner) This longtime local favourite serves a wide range of good pastas, pizzas and other Italian fare.

Costa do Sol (☎ 013-752 6382; cnr Louis Trichardt & Paul Kruger Sts; meals R40-50; ⏰ lunch & dinner Mon-Sat) A quaint little Portuguese place opposite Villa Italia featuring seafood, good soups and classic Portuguese cuisine.

Keg & Jock (☎ 013-755 4969; Ferriera St; mains from R30; ⏰ lunch & dinner) Probably the best late-night hang-out in Nelspruit, the Keg & Jock is a lively place with good pub food and a streetside patio. There's live music on Wednesday and Friday nights.

Pub (☎ 755 4861; 10 Jones St; mains from R30; ⏰ 10am-midnight Mon-Sat) The Pub specialises in large platters of meat and big glasses of grog. It's pub crawling distance from the Keg & Jock.

Mozart's Tea Garden (☎ 013-755 2287; cnr Ferriera & Van der Merwe; light meals R25-35; ⏰ breakfast & lunch Mon-Sat) Offering a wide variety of healthy foods, Mozart's is a good place to go if you are on a diet. Of course, they also offer a few fattening items if you are not. It's tucked off the street behind a children's play park; enter from Van der Merwe.

Weisenhof Coffees (☎ 013-755 2853; cnr Louis Trichardt & Paul Kruger Sts; light meals from R20; ⏰ breakfast & lunch) This centrally located café is a good place to grab a snack or get your caffeine fix. It's next to Costa do Sol.

Superspar (cnr General Dan Pienaar & Louis Trichardt Sts) For self-caterers, there's a huge supermarket at Nelspruit Crossings Mall.

For fast food, head to Brown St, where you'll find **Nando's** (Brown St) and the similar **Gallito's Casa de Galinha** (☎ 013-52 5371; Brown St; ☺ breakfast, lunch & dinner). Opposite is **Pappa's Pizza** (☎ 013-755 1660; ☺ breakfast, lunch & dinner), which draws a good crowd with its tasty pizzas and open porch seating.

Shopping

The biggest shopping centres are the glitzy Riverside Mall (about 5km north of town off Rte 40, with a wide range of stores), and **Nelspruit Crossing Mall** (cnr General Dan Pienaar & Louis Trichardt Sts) with various shops and ATM facilities. Promenade Centre has a reasonable array of eateries and shops, while **Sonpark Centre** (Piet Retief St, between General Dan and de Villiers Sts) has an Internet café and a few restaurants.

Getting There & Around

AIR

Mpumalanga Kruger International Airport (MKIA; code MQP; ☎ 013-753 7500; www.kmiairport.co.za) is the closest commercial airport. There are daily flights with **South African Airways** (SAA; ☎ 013-750 2531; www.flysaa.com) and **SAAirlink** (☎ 013-750 2531; www.saairlink.co.za) to Jo'burg (R1200; one hour), Cape Town (R2040; 2¼ hours) and Durban (R1540; 1½ hours). You can usually score a big discount when booking online.

Nationwide Airlines (☎ 086-173 7737; www.nationwideair.co.za) flights also connect Nelspruit several times weekly with Jo'burg and Cape Town.

BUS

Baz Bus (☎ 021-439 2323; www.bazbus.com) connects Nelspruit with Jo'burg/Pretoria and Manzini (Swaziland), and stops at all the backpackers in town.

Intercape (☎ 086-1287 287; www.intercape.co.za), **Greyhound** (☎ 013-753 2100; www.greyhound.co.za) and **Translux** (☎ 013-755 1453; www.translux.co.za) all go daily between Jo'burg (and Pretoria) and Maputo (Mozambique) via Nelspruit. Among these, Greyhound offers the best service and charges R160-175 for Jo'burg or R140 to Maputo, they offers a 10% discount to foreign tourists. Their **ticket offices** (Louis Trichardt St) are together, just up from Henshall St, and opposite Promenade Mall. **Panthera Azul** (☎ 011-618 8811) also stops in Nelspruit – at the Excel petrol station (cor-

ner Bell and Louis Trichardt Sts) – on its run between Jo'burg and Maputo.

CAR RENTAL

Avis airport (☎ 013-741 1029); downtown (☎ 013-755 1567; 29 Bell St)
Budget (☎ 013-750 1774) At the airport.
Europcar (☎ 013-750 0965) At the airport.
Imperial (airport; ☎ 013-750 2871) Also has a desk at Hotel Promenade.

MINIBUS TAXI

The local bus and minibus taxi park is behind Nelspruit Plaza near the corner of Bester and Henshall Sts. Minibus taxi destinations and fares include White River (R6.50, 20 minutes), Barberton (R14, 40 minutes), Sabie (R15, one hour), Hazyview (R17, one hour), Graskop (R25, 1½ hours), Komatipoort (R45, two hours) and Jo'burg (R100, five hours).

City Bug (☎ 013-741 4114; www.citybug.co.za) operates a convenient shuttle service in town for R20 per person door-to-door. They also have a chauffeur service to/from Kruger Mpumalanga International Airport, a weekly shuttle to Durban (R380 per person one-way) and a three-times-daily shuttle between Nelspruit and Johannesburg International Airport (R180 per person).

TRAIN

The *Komati* (see p630) runs daily between Jo'burg and Komatipoort via Nelspruit.

MALELANE

☎ 013 / pop 6500

Spending a night at one of the guest lodges in Malelane makes for a good primer before entering Kruger National Park. Most of the lodges back up to the Crocodile River, where you'll be able to spot plenty of hippos, crocodiles and other wildlife. The town itself is a small, unattractive service centre, just off the N4.

An **information desk** (☎ 013-790 1193; ☺ 8am-6pm Mon-Fri, 8am-noon Sat & Sun) at the Spar supermarket can arrange tours.

If you are heading towards Swaziland, don't miss the **Matsamo Cultural Village** (☎ 013-781 0578, 082-457 8964, www.matsamo.com; ☺ 7am-6pm) located in no man's land between South Africa and Swaziland at the Jeppe's Reef border crossing. Matsamo is a sort of 'living museum' where you can sleep in a luxurious hut (room with half board R655, including show) decked out with animal skins and wood furnishings. Day visitors can go on a guided tour of the village and watch a cheerful song and dance performance for R100. Buffet breakfast (R65) and lunch (R85) are also available. It's all quite staged and targeted toward package tours, but still a fun introduction to Swazi culture, and certainly not your typical border crossing experience.

Sleeping & Eating

River House Lodge (☎ 013-790 1333; www.icon.co.za /~gardner; 22 Visarend St; camp site R45; cottage per person R300) This is an elegant five-star thatched estate with B&B-style accommodation. All rooms have their own small terraces, and there are attractive gardens bordering the river. It's west of River Cottage and signposted from the main road.

Lino's Lodge & Deck Restaurant (☎ 013-790 0793; s/d with breakfast R285/455; ⊗ restaurant breakfast & lunch Tue-Sun, dinner Tue-Sat) This place offers good dining, especially seafood, on a nice open deck. There's also accommodation in pleasant white-and-green cottages on the banks of the river. It's just west of River Cottage, and reached via a long, frangipani-lined driveway.

River Cottage (☎ 013-790 0825; s/d with breakfast R300/500, 6-person cottage R1200; ⊠ ⊡) This is a well-tended place sitting on the Crocodile River just west of town. The smaller cottages are set back on a clipped lawn, while the six-person one is close to the river; all are self-catering, with their own braai areas.

Casa Portuguesa (☎ 013-790 3314; dishes R45-70; ⊗ noon-9pm Mon-Sat, noon-2pm Sun) This unique restaurant is located about 2km south of Kruger National Park's Malelane Gate. Surrounded by a lagoon inhabited by crocodiles, the restaurant offers a tranquil setting and good Portuguese meals.

KOMATIPOORT

☎ 013 / pop 4700

This border town is at the foot of the Lebombo Mountains, near the confluence of the Komati and Crocodile Rivers and only 10km away from Kruger National Park's Crocodile Bridge Gate. It's a convenient stop if you're travelling to/from Mozambique or Swaziland.

At the time of writing, there were plans to set up an information desk inside the Spar supermarket. Close to Spar is a petrol station and ABSA bank with exchange facilities.

If you happen to be in Komatipoort in late June, ask around for the **Prawn Festival**, which celebrates the modest crayfish in all its glory.

Sleeping & Eating

Spice of Life (☎ 013-793 7373; www.spiceoflife.co.za; camping R40; dm R65; s/d R100/150; ⊡) This small, scruffy backpackers is on the N4 near the border with Mozambique. They have cooking and laundry facilities, and it's one of the only places around with Internet access. It's about 300m east of the Komati River Chalets.

Komati River Chalets (☎ 013-793 7623, 082-347 4669; www.komatiriverchalets.co.za; s/d with breakfast R260/460, 5-/7-person self-catering chalets R900/1050; ⊠ ⊡) This good-value place has plain stucco-and-thatch chalets set around large clipped grounds, a popular pub, and tiger fishing in season. It's signposted from the N4, and just over the railroad tracks, with a second access route signposted from town.

Trees Too (☎ 013-793 8262; www.treestoo.com; s/d with breakfast R290/380, 4-person f R675; ⊡) A small, nice private home with B&B accommodation around a small garden. The management also has plans to open up dormitory accommodation for R65 per person. It's on a leafy side street about 500m in from Rissik St and signposted.

Hippo's Restaurant & Lodge (☎ 013-793 8155; hipposrestaurant@telkomsa.net; 80 Rissik St; ⊗ breakfast, lunch & dinner Mon-Sat) Hippo's has a large menu selection featuring filling portions of meat and fish. Adjoining is **Pioneers Guest Lodge** (☎ 013-793 8028; s/d R220/280).

Restaurante Tambarina (☎ 013-790 7057; Rissik St; mains R40-55; ⊗ lunch & dinner) Tambarina is a good place to sample prawns and Portuguese fare before heading over the border into Mozambique. It's opposite Hippo's Restaurant & Lodge.

Getting There & Away

Minibus taxis leave from just off Rissik St near the Score supermarket, and regularly do the run between Komatipoort and Maputo (Mozambique; R65, 1½ to two hours). If you're driving, there are two tolls along the N4 on the Mozambique side. Exit procedures are fairly swift and on the Mozambique side you can buy a visa for R180 (you can get one for half the price at the Mozambique consulate in Nelspruit, p457).

BARBERTON

☎ 013 / pop 29,500

The splendid town of Barberton dates to the gold rush days of the late 19th century, when it was a boom town and home to South Africa's first stock exchange. However, most miners soon moved on to the newly discovered Rand fields near Jo'burg, and Barberton's prominence declined. All working gold mines in the region are now over 100 years old and the town itself plods along in a relaxed country manner.

The helpful **Tourist Information Centre** (☎ 013-712 2121; www.barberton.co.za; Market Sq, Crown St; ☾ 7.30am-4.30pm Mon-Fri, 9am-4pm Sat & Sun) in the town centre can assist with accommodation, tours of historic sites, and day hikes in the area. If you call in, ask for tourist info. There are ATMs at **First National Bank** (Crown St) and in **Shoprite** (Crown St). You can access the Internet at **NJR Computer Services** (☎ 013-712 4739; shop 2, Eureka Centre; per 30 min R10; ☾ 8.30am-5pm Mon-Fri, 8.30am-1pm Sat).

Sights & Activities

Barberton boasts several restored houses dating to the late-19th and early-20th centuries. All are open for touring (contact the Barberton Museum for more details) and give a glimpse into the town's early history. They include **Belhaven House** (Lee St; adult/child R10/5; ☾ 8.30am-4pm Mon-Fri), and **Stopforth House** (Bowness St; ☾ 8.30-4pm Mon-Fri) and **Fernlea House** (Lee St; ☾ 8.30am-4pm Mon-Fri), whose admissions are both included in the Belhaven ticket.

Barberton Museum (☎ 013-712 4208; 36 Pilgrim St; admission free; ☾ 10am-4pm) is also worth a look. Next door is **Umjindi Gallery** (☎ 013-712 5807; Pilgrim St; ☾ 8am-5pm Mon-Fri, 9am-4pm Sat), with various crafts and a jewellery workshop where you can watch the artists at work.

Located just off the eastern end of Judge St is an iron and wood **blockhouse** from the Anglo-Boer War, part of the chain built by the British when the war entered its guerrilla phase. On the southwestern edge of town is an abandoned 20.3km **aerial cable-way**. When it operated, it was the longest industrial cableway in the world, bringing asbestos down from a mine in Swaziland. Coal was carried in the other direction to provide counterweight.

Origins (☎ 013-712 5055, 083-266 9329; www.origins .co.za; 20 Sheba Rd) runs various tours, including a good Eureka City Ghost Town tour of the old Barberton gold mines.

Sleeping

Barberton Chalets & Caravan Park (☎ 013-712 3323; www.barbertonchalets.co.za; General St; camp sites per person R60, caravan sites R80, s/d/tr cottages 170/250/320; ☒) This caravan park is conveniently close to the town centre, with lots of shade and grassy areas, camping and self-catering chalets.

Cockney Liz (De Villiers St; s/d R150/200) The Chill Inn management runs Cockney Liz, opposite, with good functional rooms that include TV, and private bath.

Makhonjwa Nursery & Guest House (☎ 013-712 2584; 10 Duncan St; per person R150; ☒) Another good value guesthouse, this one is a self-catering place run by the folks who own Co-co Pan restaurant.

Chill Inn (☎ 013-712 3477, 082-733 6755; cnr De Villiers & Tate Sts; d R160-250) This welcoming hotel has a braai area and double rooms with TV.

Phoenix Hotel (☎ 013-712 4211; phoenix@soft .co.za; 20 Pilgrim St; s/d R180/320; ☒) This is an old-style country hotel with a staid pub, a tea room and comfortable, clean rooms.

Fountain Baths Holiday Guest Cottages (☎ 013-712 2707; www.fountainbaths.co.za; 48 Pilgrim St; cottages per person R200) This pleasant place with self-catering cottages is at the southern end of the street, where it resumes after merging into Sheba Rd (Crown St). It was built in 1885 and used to be Barberton's public pool.

Kloof House (☎ 013-712 4268; www.kloofhuis.co.za; 1 Kloof St; s/d with breakfast R200/360; ☐) A cosy B&B up a steep hill just southeast of Market Sq, with pleasant rooms, including some with private bathroom and good views.

Old Coach Road Guest House (☎ 013-719 9755; www.oldcoachroad.co.za; s/d R265/490; ☒) This very nice getaway has cosy rooms, all with their own entrance away from the main house. Some have wheelchair access. It's set in large grounds about 9km north of Barberton, and signposted from Rte 38.

Barberton Mountain Lodge (☎ 013-712 5055; 4-bed lodge R800; ☒) Up in the hills behind town (advance bookings only) is a pleasant, self-catering lodge operated by Origins tour agency.

Eating

Co-co Pan (☎ 013-712 2653; Crown St; mains R25-35; ⏰ 5.30-9pm Mon-Sat, 5.30-8pm Sun) This casual eatery opposite the museum is a good budget choice, with burgers, salads and other basics. Entry is through a small general shop.

Bye Apart Ate (☎ 013-712 2846; 27 De Villiers St; meals from R25; ⏰ 9am-9pm Wed-Mon, 9am-5pm Tue) Don't be put off by the portraits of the apartheid-era prime ministers; the owners of the restaurant don't take apartheid that seriously. As the name suggests, the theme is a tongue-in-cheek send off to the old system and what you'll find is a very relaxed, welcoming atmosphere. The menu here is simple but the food is fresh and tasty. Choose from pasta, steak or lamb chops.

Victorian Tea Garden & Restaurant (☎ 013-712 4985; light meals from R25; ⏰ 8am-5pm Mon-Fri, 8am-2pm Sat) The gazebo here is a great spot to relax and watch the passing parade. It's between Pilgrim and Crown Sts, next to

the tourist information office. The menu features sandwiches and fast food.

Globe Café (☎ 082-883 3105; 18 Pilgrim St; mains R50-60; ⏰ noon-8pm Mon-Fri, 5-8pm Sat) Globe is in a historic building with an agreeable ambience and excellent meals featuring some adventurous dishes, including lamb shanks and Thai chicken.

Getting There & Away

From Barberton to Badplaas, a winding tarmac road goes over the Nelshoogte Pass. The road to Swaziland has been upgraded.

A few minibus taxis stop in town near Shoprite, but it's better to go to the minibus taxi park near Emjindini (3km from town on the Nelspruit road). The fare to Nelspruit is R15 (40 minutes), to Badplaas it is R20 (one hour). Most departures are in the early morning, by 8am.

AROUND BARBERTON
Lone Tree Hill

Just southwest of town past the prison is **Lone Tree Hill** (admission R20 plus key deposit R50), a prime paragliding launch site. To get here,

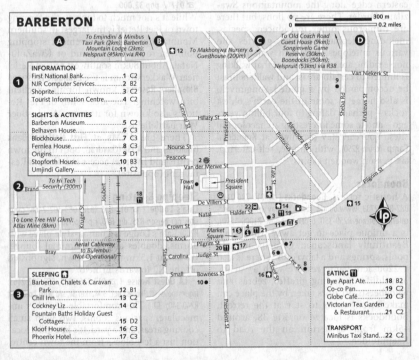

follow De Villiers St west from town, and turn left about 500m past the prison. **Hi Tech Security** (☎ 013-712 3256; McPherson St), just off Kruger St, can assist with keys and access.

Atlas Mine

Barberton has ridden the fortunes of its gold mines for more than a century. To see one in action, head 8km west of Barberton to the **Atlas Mine** (☎ 013-712 8026, 072-128 0604; andreab@soft.co.za; 2½-hr tour R150) where visitors don helmets, lights, gumboots and overalls before crawling through the caverns. If you're claustrophobic, you can stay above ground and pan for what the mine describes as the 'world's oldest gold'. This is no idle boast, scientists have proven that rocks and minerals in the area are indeed the oldest on Earth.

Songimvelo Game Reserve

This beautiful 56,000-hectare **reserve** (☎ 017-883 0964; mpbinfo@cis.co.za; admission adult/child R15/7) sits in lowveld country south of Barberton, with high-altitude grassland areas on its eastern edge along the mountainous Swaziland border. There are no lions, but there are numerous other introduced species, including elephants, zebras, giraffes and various antelopes, and both walking and horse riding are popular. (Note that walking is limited to certain areas, and walkers must be accompanied by a guide.) Songimvelo is also home to some of the earth's oldest rocks – perhaps dating to four billion years ago – and to some interesting archaeological sites. You can stay overnight at **Kromdraai Camp** (cabin R250), with simple, self-catering, six-person wooden cabins.

Boondocks

A holistic retreat, **Boondocks** (☎ 013-726 0140, 082-808 2733; www.boondocks.co.za; day visit R50; self-catering cottage R250-350, 6-person house R1000-1500), is a unique place to get away from it all. Beautifully landscaped gardens include pools, springs and a labyrinth. There is also a 2200-acre game reserve with a variety of wildlife, including giraffes, zebras and wildebeests. Visitors taken by the place can make arrangments to stay at the retreat. Boondocks is located on Rte 38, around 45km from Barberton on the road to Kaapmuiden.

BADPLAAS

☎ 017 / pop 8000

If relaxing in **thermal springs** (☎ 017-844 1000; admission per person/vehicle per day R50/30) appeals, Badplaas is worth a short stop. Rising up on the horizon are the dramatic Hlumuhlumu Mountains.

Aventura Badplaas (☎ 017-844 1000; www.aventura.co.za; camp sites R75, plus per person R30, s/d R265/530, 2-/4-bed self-catering chalets R420/R750; 🔲 🖳 🏊) is the best place to stay if you want a resort atmosphere, complete with beauty treatments and a choice of chalets or double rooms. There's also a caravan park. If you stay, admission to the hot springs is R10. It's well signposted – you can't miss it.

Baluli Lodge (☎ 017-844 1040; www.baluli.com; d/tr R300/330; 🏊) is smaller, simpler and quieter than the Aventura next door. In addition to nice rooms, it offers a bar, restaurant and TV room.

Minibus taxis run between Badplaas and Machadodorp, via the N4 (R18, one hour), and Barberton (R20, one hour).

PIET RETIEF

☎ 017 / pop 32,000

While it's not much to look at, the farming town of Piet Retief is the largest in southern Mpumalanga and a convenient stopping point en route to Swaziland or KwaZulu-Natal. About 80km southwest of Piet Retief near Wakkerstroom is the **Ekangala Grassland Biosphere Reserve**, known for its excellent bird-watching. The area south of Piet Retief is also known for its many Anglo-Boer War battlefields.

There are ATMs at **First National Bank** (Church St) and **ABSA** (Church St), both in the town centre, and Internet access at Böhmers Restaurant (opposite).

Sleeping & Eating

Lala's Lodge (☎ 017-826 1838, 083-302 2466; camp sites per person R35, dm R70, r per person with breakfast R200) Lala's Lodge is a nanna-style place with dorms, doubles and a communal lounge. It's about 1.5km north of town, signposted off the N2 towards Ermelo.

LA Guest House (☎ 017-826 2837, 082-292 2163; laguesthouse@telkomsa.net; 3 Market St; s/d with breakfast R240/340; 🔲) This comfortable B&B has immaculate, spacious rooms, two with small cooking areas, and a yard. It's in a quiet location just a few blocks from the town centre.

Weaver's Nest Country Village (☎ 017-730 0115; www.weavers.co.za; s/d with half board R575/850, 4-person self-catering cottages R600) Located near Wakkerstroom is this much larger place, signposted off Rte 543, with rooms and self-catering cottages.

Wetlands Lodge (☎ 017-730 0101; d with half board R600) Also near Wakkerstroom (about 90km southwest of Piet Retief), try this place just off Rte 543 with a fireplace and a well-stocked library.

Böhmers Restaurant (☎ 017-826 4178; 15A Church St; ☽ lunch & dinner Mon-Sat) Steak and chicken dishes abound at this low-key eatery on the main road through town.

Böhmers coffee shop (☎ 017-826 2236; ☽ 7am-9pm Mon-Sat, 10am-5pm Sun) Right next door is this cafe, which has light meals, snacks and Internet access for R20 per 30 minutes.

Getting There & Away

Greyhound (www.greyhound.co.za) stops in town at Waterside Lodge on the southern end of Church St on its daily Pretoria–Durban run. The fare from Piet Retief to Pretoria is R140; to Durban it's R180.

The minibus taxi stand is at the back of SuperMac (cnr Kerk & Brand Sts). From here to the Swaziland border post at Mahamba costs R15 (30 minutes).

MPUMALANGA

Kruger National Park

Try to imagine a national park the size of Israel, with huge tracts of acacia, sycamore figs and bushwillow interrupted by open savanna, rushing rivers and the occasional rocky bluff. Now fill it with lion, leopard, elephant, Cape buffalo and black rhino (the Big Five), plus cheetahs, giraffes, hippos and many species of smaller animals, and you'll start to have some notion of what it's like to visit Kruger National Park.

Kruger is one of the world's most famed protected areas – known for its size, history of conservation, diversity of wildlife and ease of access. It's a place where the drama of life and death is played out on a daily basis. One morning you may spot a pride of lions feasting on a recent kill and the next day you might spot a newborn impala struggling to take its first steps.

The park has an extensive network of sealed roads and comfortable camps, but if you prefer to keep it rough, there are also 4WD tracks, and mountain bike and hiking trails. Even when you stick to the tarmac, the sounds and scents of the bush are never more than a few metres away. Additionally, as long as you avoid weekends and school holidays, or stick to areas north of Phalaborwa Gate and along gravel roads, it's easy to travel for an hour or more without seeing another vehicle.

Southern Kruger is the most popular section of the park, with the highest animal concentrations and the easiest access. Further north, mopani takes over as the dominant vegetation. This is a favoured food of elephants, and you'll see these giant creatures in abundance here. Kruger is at its best in the far north, around Punda Maria and Pafuri. Here, although animal concentrations are somewhat lower, the bush setting and wilderness atmosphere are all-enveloping.

HIGHLIGHTS

- Exploring Kruger's hidden corners on one of its excellent **wilderness trails** (p471)
- Staying in a remote **bushveld camp** (p483) and falling asleep to the sounds of hippos grunting in a nearby river
- Taking a **night drive** (p472) and spotting the shining yellow eyes of one of the big cats gleaming from the roadside
- Sitting at a **water hole** (p470) at dawn, watching creation come alive
- Pampering yourself with a few nights at a luxurious **private wildlife reserve** (p485) bordering the park

■ AREA: 20,000 SQ KM

KRUGER NATIONAL PARK

HISTORY

The San were the first people to see Kruger's animals, and they have left their mark in rock paintings at numerous sites throughout the park. Prior to the San, various hominid species wandered the lowveld as much as 500,000 years ago. From around AD 500, Nguni peoples had settled in.

The area that is now Kruger first came under protection in 1898, when Paul Kruger (president of the Transvaal Republic and an avid hunter) established the Sabie Game Reserve, between the Sabie and Crocodile Rivers, as a controlled hunting area. In 1902, following the second Anglo-Boer War, James Stevenson Hamilton became the reserve's first warden. Hamilton was also the first to see the tourism potential of wildlife, and to bring a true conservation

KRUGER NATIONAL PARK

vision to the area. In 1926, Sabie Game Reserve was joined with neighbouring Shingwedzi Game Reserve and various private farms to become Kruger National Park, and in 1927 the park was opened to the public.

Since then, Kruger has become a major research and conservation centre and one of Africa's premier wildlife-watching destinations. In the early '90s, most of the fences came down between Kruger and the private wildlife reserves lining the park's western edge. In 2002, together with Zimbabwe's Gonarezhou National Park and Limpopo National Park in Mozambique, Kruger became part of the giant **Great Limpopo Transfrontier Park** (www.greatlimpopopark.com). The park is still in its earliest stages and has just one border crossing at Giriyondo, but once better infrastructure is in place, Kruger's wildlife will ultimately have a 35,000-sq-km area in which to roam.

ORIENTATION

Kruger is a long, narrow wedge bordered by Mozambique to the east, Limpopo province to the west and Mpumalanga to the west and south. It averages about 65km across, and is about 350km long. Rimming the park to the west, and sharing the same unfenced terrain, is a chain of private wildlife reserves.

Terrain ranging from the flat to the gently undulating covers the majority of the park, with the Lebombo Mountains rising up to the east along the Mozambique border. Major rivers flowing across Kruger from west to east include the Limpopo, Luvuvhu, Shingwedzi, Letaba, Olifants, Timbavati and Sabie.

There are 10 entry gates (*heks* in Afrikaans). On the park's southern edge are **Malelane** (☎ 013-735 6152) and **Crocodile Bridge** (☎ 013-735 6012). Both are readily accessible from the N4 from Johannesburg (Jo'burg), but if it has been raining then check road conditions as Crocodile Bridge occasionally floods and closes. The **Numbi** (☎ 013-735 5133), **Phabeni** (☎ 013-735 5890) and **Paul Kruger** (☎ 013-735 5107) gates are easily accessed from Hazyview (turn off the N4 at Nelspruit); Paul Kruger Gate is the closest to Skukuza (p482), Kruger's main rest camp. **Orpen** (☎ 013-735 6355), to the west, is convenient if you're coming from the Blyde River area. **Phalaborwa** (☎ 013-735 6509) is nearest

to Polokwane; **Punda Maria** (☎ 013-735 6870) is reached via Makhado (Louis Trichardt); and **Pafuri** (☎ 013-735 6888), in the far north, is accessed from Thohoyandou in the Venda region.

In addition, it is now possible to enter Kruger from Mozambique at the Giriyondo Gate, which doubles as an international border crossing (visas are available on both sides). Giriyondo, however, is only accessible with a 4WD vehicle as roads on the Mozambique side have not been upgraded. It is 95km from the Phalaborwa Gate to Giriyondo and 75km from Giriyondo to Massingir (Mozambique). When you enter Limpopo National Park (on the Mozambique side) you'll need to pay R50 per vehicle, R50 per adult and R25 per child.

The park is laced with a network of sealed roads (about 700km in total), one of which runs along its entire spine. These, together with more lightly travelled gravel side roads, form a road network of about 1900km.

INFORMATION
Bookings

Accommodation can be booked through **South African National (SAN) Parks central reservations office** (Map pp428-9; ☎ 012-428 9111; www .parks-sa.co.za; 643 Leyds St, Muckleneuk, Pretoria). It's also possible to book directly through Lowveld Tourism (p457) in Nelspruit, Cape Town Tourism (p106) and Tourist Junction (p305) in Durban. All of these local tourism offices have Kruger maps and publications, and they are also sold in the park in the larger rest camps.

Phone bookings are possible with credit card. Written applications for rest camps and wilderness trails can be made up to 13 months in advance. Except in the high season (school holidays, Christmas and Easter) and weekends, bookings are advisable but not essential.

Entry

Day or overnight entry to the park costs R120/60 for adults/children, with significant discounts available for South African citizens and residents, and for South African Development Community (SADC) nationals. The SAN Parks Wild Card (p85) also applies to Kruger.

Bicycles and motorcycles are not permitted to enter the park. During school holidays

JOCK OF THE BUSHVELD

After travelling around the eastern part of South Africa for a while you may start to wonder who was Jock of the Bushveld? His name is often attached to hotels, restaurants, tourist guidebooks and maps. Jock, actually, is South Africa's best-loved canine. He was immortalised in Percy Fitzpatrick's book, *Jock of the Bushveld* (published in 1907) and is still a popular marketing tool. This children's book, which paints a lively picture of the veld, is great to bring along to Kruger National Park if you have kids. In Kruger, you may spot the occasional tribute to the famed pooch – Jock Safari Lodge is named after him and there is a statue commemorating his famous duel with a sable antelope. You can also walk in Jock's paw prints along an 8km trail near Graskop (see p452). Jock's last resting place is something of a mystery. But contrary to what your safari guide might tell you, it is not at Kruger's 'dog graveyard'.

you can stay in the park for a maximum of 10 days, and at any one rest camp for five days (10 days if you're camping). Throughout the year, park authorities restrict the total number of visitors within the park, so in the high season it pays to arrive early if you don't have a booking.

Entry gate opening times vary slightly with the season, and are currently as follows.

Month	Gates/camps open (am)	Gates/camps close (pm)
Jan	4.30/5	6.30
Feb	5.30	6.30
Mar	5.30	6
Apr	6	6
May-Aug	6.30	5.30
Sep	6	6
Oct	6/5.30	6
Nov & Dec	5.30/4.30	6.30

It's an offence to arrive late at a camp and you can be fined for doing so (the camps are fenced). With speed limits of 50km/h on sealed roads and 40km/h on dirt roads (monitored by rangers with radars), it can take a while to travel from camp to camp, especially if you encounter a traffic jam near an interesting animal.

PLANT & ANIMAL DISTRIBUTION
Kruger encompasses a variety of landscapes and ecosystems, with each ecosystem favoured by particular species. Most mammals are distributed throughout the park, but some show a distinct preference for particular regions. The excellent *Find It* booklet, available from the park shops located at some of the bigger camps and at the National Parks office in Pretoria, points out

the most likely places to see all the major animals.

Impalas, buffaloes, Burchell's zebras, blue wildebeests, kudus, waterbucks, baboons, vervet monkeys, cheetahs, leopards and other smaller predators are all widespread. Birdlife is prolific along the rivers and north of the Luvuvhu River.

Rainfall is highest (700mm a year) in the southwestern corner between the Olifants and Crocodile Rivers. The area is thickly wooded and has a variety of trees including acacias, bushwillows and sycamore figs, plus flowering species such as the red-and-orange coral tree. This terrain is particularly favoured by white rhinos and buffaloes, but is less favoured by antelope and, therefore, by predators.

The eastern section of the park, to the south of the Olifants River on the plains around Satara rest camp and south to the Crocodile River, experiences reasonable rainfall (600mm) and has fertile soils. There are expanses of good grazing, with buffalo grass and red grass interspersed with acacia thorn trees (especially knobthorn), leadwood and marula trees. In this region there are large populations of impalas, zebras, wildebeests, giraffes and black rhinos. Joining them are predators, particularly lions, who prey on impalas, zebras and blue wildebeests.

North of the Olifants River the rainfall drops below 500mm and the dominant tree is mopani. This grows widely in the west, among red bushwillow, but has a tougher time on the basalt plains of the northeast, where it tends to be more stunted. The mopani is a favoured food of elephants, which are most common north of Olifants River, and is also eaten by tsessebes, elands, roans and sables.

BY THE NUMBERS

Kruger National Park's population is made up of:

- 34 amphibian species
- 49 fish species
- 116 reptile species
- 147 mammal species
- 380 indigenous tree species
- 507 bird species
- one million human visitors per year

Of the animal species, Kruger registered the following numbers in 2003:

- 200 cheetah
- 1000 leopard
- 1500 lion
- 3800 warthog
- 5000 kudu
- 5000 white rhino
- 9000 giraffe
- 10,500 elephant
- 25,150 buffalo
- 32,000 zebra
- 150,000 impala

Perhaps the most interesting area is in the far north around Punda Maria and Pafuri, which has a higher rainfall (close to 700mm at Punda Maria) than the mopani country. This enables it to support a wider variety of plants (baobabs are particularly noticeable) and greater wildlife concentrations. There is woodland, bushveld, grass plains and, between the Luvuvhu and Limpopo Rivers, a tropical riverine forest.

All of Kruger's rivers have riverine forest along their banks (often with enormous fig trees), which supports populations of bushbucks and nyalas.

Note that even outside the park borders there are still areas that support wildlife. The most prominent among these areas is along the Crocodile River on the southern border. On the banks of the Crocodile in Malelane and Komatipoort you can spot plenty of wildlife, including hippos, elephants and, you guessed it, crocodiles.

ACTIVITIES

Kruger is exceptionally well organised, with a plethora of activities to enhance your wildlife-watching. When planning an itinerary, keep in mind that the closer you can get to the bush, and the more time you can devote to becoming acquainted with its sounds, smells and rhythms, the more rewarding your experience will be. Although it's possible to get a sense for Kruger in a day, the park merits at least four to five days, and ideally at least a week. If the bush really gets into your blood, there's enough here to keep you coming back for a lifetime.

Interspersed with whatever activities you do, allow plenty of time for simply sitting still – preferably by a water hole, river or lake. The silence will soon become filled with nature's symphony, and you'll be able to watch Kruger come to life before you. Even without seeing a single animal, it's an incomparable experience to stand on a rise with Kruger stretching out before you, and savour the indescribable, primeval majesty of having such vast tracts set aside solely to protect earth's natural splendour.

Bush walks and drives can be booked from the gate and camps.

4WD Trails

The longest and most established of Kruger's 4WD trails is the **Lebombo Motorised Eco Trail**, a rough, rugged 500km 4WD route along the eastern boundary of the park, departing from Crocodile Bridge and ending at Pafuri. The trail lasts five days and costs R4940 per vehicle (maximum of four people per vehicle). You'll need to provide your own vehicle, food and drink (it's completely self-catering). Only five vehicles are permitted at a time on the trail (plus the vehicle of the ranger who accompanies you). Book well in advance through central reservations (p468).

There are also four shorter trails, all averaging about four hours, and costing R460 per vehicle plus a R100 refundable deposit. They (and the points where you can reserve them) are: **Northern Plains Adventure Trail** (Shingwedzi camp, p483); **Nonokani Adventure Trail** (Phalaborwa Gate); **Mananga Adventure Trail** (Satara camp, p483); **Madlabantu Adventure Trail** (Pretoriuskop camp, p482). All are closed after rains, and can only be booked on the morning of the day that you want to drive, with a maximum of six vehicles per trail per day. There are no facilities (including ablutions) along any of the trails, so bring whatever you'll need, plus ideally a global positioning system (GPS) handset.

Bird-Watching

There is excellent bird-watching throughout Kruger, with the far north (from Punda Maria Gate up past Pafuri Gate) arguably one of the best birding areas on the continent. There are a handful of hides scattered throughout the park; see the birding pages on the website for **SAN Parks** (www.parks-sa.co.za) for a listing of their locations. Several of the bushveld camps (p483) also have their own hides, and some of the larger camps run bird-watching excursions on request. There is also an annual 24-hour **Birding Big Day** in January. For information on this, and other birding activities in the park, contact **SAN Parks Honorary Rangers** (☎ 012-426 5026).

Bush Walks

Better than the drives are guided morning and afternoon **bush walks** (morning/afternoon per person R220/175), which are possible at all the larger camps, including Satara, Skukuza, Lower Sabie and Pretoriuskop. These are highly popular, and are an excellent way to experience Kruger at close range. All walks are accompanied by armed rangers. The morning walk – when you'll have a better chance of seeing wildlife on the move – is particularly recommended.

Golf

There's a nine-hole **golf course** (☎ 013-735 5611; skukuzagolf@parks-sa.co.za; R75) at Skukuza; bring your own clubs. Tee off times are between 7am and 9.30am Sunday to Friday. Tee times must be booked in advance.

Mountain Biking

There are currently three **mountain-bike trails** (morning/afternoon R315/175) in Kruger, ranging from 12km to 24km. Full-day trails can also be arranged for R650. All are based out of **Olifants** (☎ 013-735 6606) in central Kruger, and should be booked at least several days in advance directly through the camp, or through central reservations (p468).

Tours

At the budget level, the best places to contact are the backpacker lodges in Hazyview (p455), Nelspruit (p458) and Graskop (p452) all of which can organise tours into Kruger from about R450 per day, plus entry fees and meals. Another good budget option is **African Routes** (p641; ☎ 031-563 5080; www.africanroutes.co.za), which also includes Swaziland and the Drakensberg in its Kruger itineraries.

If you're on a tight schedule, and want to connect directly from Jo'burg or Cape Town, **SA Airlink Tours** (www.airlinktours.com) runs various flight-accommodation packages between Jo'burg and central Kruger.

Other operators include: **Wildlife Safaris** (www.wildlifesaf.co.za), which has four-day panorama tours taking in the Blyde River and Kruger for R4214 per person, including half board; **Bundu Safari Company** (☎ 011-675 0767; www.bundusafaris.co.za), which offers four-day Kruger tours for a minimum of R2900 per person (see p641); and many of the other tour operators listed in the Transport chapter (p641), most of which organise Kruger itineraries.

Wilderness Trails

Kruger's wilderness walking trails are one of the park's highlights, and a major attraction of the Southern African safari experience. They're done in small groups (maximum eight people), guided by knowledgeable armed guides and offer a superb opportunity to get a more intimate sense of the bush than would ever be possible in a vehicle. The walks are not overly strenuous, covering about 20km per day at a modest pace, and are appropriate for anyone who is reasonably fit. The itinerary is determined by the interests of the group, the time of year and the disposition of the wildlife.

Most wilderness trail walks last two days and three nights, with departures on Wednesday and Sunday afternoon. They cost R2240 per person, including accommodation in rustic, pleasant huts, plus food and equipment. Bring your own beer and wine if you'd like a drink. The walks are extremely popular, and should be booked well in advance. No children under 12 are allowed. Make bookings through Central Reservations (p468).

Brief descriptions of Kruger's seven wilderness trails:

Bushman Trail Near the Berg-en-dal rest camp in the southwestern corner of the park, this trail features treks to San rock paintings, plus the chance to see white rhinos, lions and large herds of antelope.

Metsimetsi Trail Midway between Lower Sabie and Satara rest camps on the eastern border of the park, the terrain consists of undulating savanna, ravines and the rocky gorge of the N'waswitsontso River. Because the river flows year-round, the surrounding area is noted for its abundant wildlife, including elephants and black rhinos.

Napi Trail Running through mixed bushveld, midway between Skukuza and Pretoriuskop rest camps, this area is home to white and black rhinos, lions, leopards, cheetahs, wild dogs, buffaloes and elephants. The trail is known for the opportunities it offers for seeing the Big Five, plus its excellent birding.

Nyalaland Trail In the far north of the park near the Luvuvhu River, in a region of strikingly diverse ecosystems, this trail is most memorable for its beauty and its wilderness ambience, rather than for opportunities to witness the Big Five. Birdlife is prolific and the area is a paradise for ornithologists.

Olifants Trail Based in the eastern part of the park on the Olifants River, its superb riverine setting offers the chance to get close to elephants, hippos, crocodiles and more, and is also known for its birding. Species you may see include fish eagles and the rare Pels fishing owl.

Sweni Trail A highly rewarding trail near Satara rest camp, many lions are attracted to the herds of wildebeests, zebras and buffaloes here – all against a highly evocative backdrop of vast grassy plains.

Wolhuter Trail Based in southern Kruger near the Bushman Trail, in an area inhabited by lions and white rhinos, the name commemorates legendary father and son rangers, Harry and Henry Wolhuter. You can find out more about Harry's exploits, including the time when he wrestled a lion, at the Stevenson-Hamilton Museum in Skukuza rest camp.

Wildlife Drives

Dawn (three hours), midmorning (two hours), sunset (three hours) and night (two hours) wildlife drives are available at most rest camps, and offer good chances to maximise your safari experience, especially as you'll have a ranger to point out interesting features. The drives are scheduled to take advantage of the natural rhythms of the wildlife, as many animals – including lions, leopards and rhinos – are at their most active from first light to around 10am, and then again later in the day. The drives are done in 10- or 20-seat vehicles and cost between R100 and R200 per person, depending on the time and vehicle size.

SLEEPING & EATING

Kruger boasts various types of accommodation, all of a high standard. Bookings can be made through central reservations, or at one of the local tourist offices that take Kruger bookings (see p468 for all contacts).

Most visitors stay in one of the park's 12 rest camps. These offer camping, plus a range of huts, bungalows and cottages and several other styles of accommodation, as well as shops, restaurants and other facilities. Several of the rest camps have satellite camps, which are set some distance away, and are much more rustic, without any facilities.

There are also five bushveld camps in the park (smaller, more remote clusters of self-catering cottages without shops or restaurants) and two bush lodges, which are set in the middle of the wilderness, and must be booked in their entirety by a single group. Finally, there are several private concessions within Kruger offering five-star comfort.

Another possibility is to stay outside the park. For budget travellers, the best places for this are Hazyview (p454), Nelspruit (p457) and Phalaborwa (p508). At the opposite end of the spectrum, there's very luxurious accommodation in many of the private reserves bordering Kruger to the west (p485).

Rest Camps

The larger rest camps are like small towns in the middle of the bush, though they're remarkably unobtrusive considering the facilities they offer and the volume of visitors they host. All rest camps are fenced, attractively laid out and immaculately maintained, and all have electricity. Most also have shops and reasonable restaurants with reasonable prices (meals about R40 to R55), plus shared cooking facilities (sinks, hotplates and braais), public telephones and fuel supplies (petrol and diesel). There are swimming pools at Berg-en-dal, Pretoriuskop (a converted natural rock pool), Lower Sabie, Skukuza, Mopani and Shingwedzi; banks at Skukuza and Letaba; and an ATM at Skukuza. Wildlife drives and bush walks can be arranged at all of the rest camps.

Accommodation in the rest camps varies but usually comprises huts, bungalows and cottages. All are supplied with bedding and towels, and most have air-con or fans. If a kitchen is not part of the accommodation (ie if there is a communal kitchen only), visitors must bring their own cooking and eating utensils.

(Continued on page 481)

ADRIAN BAILEY

Kingfisher in flight, Kruger National Park

ANDREW PARKINSON

Nile crocodile, Kruger National Park

Steenbok, Kruger National Park

CAROL POLICH

African sunset, Kruger National Park

CAROL POLICH

Veld fire, Kruger National Park

Lion, Kruger National Park

Male collared sunbird, Kruger National Park

Blesbok, Kruger National Park

475

Witsand Nature Reserve (p537), Northern Cape

Kalahari San woman, Northern Cape (p523)

Cheetahs, Kgalagadi Transfrontier Park (p537),
Northern Cape

Kgalagadi Transfrontier Park (p537), Northern Cape

476

Rock paintings (p349)

Children outside Nama hut, Riemvasmaak
(p526), Northern Cape

Sheep farmer, Kalahari (p533), Northern Cape

Meerkats, Kgalagadi Transfrontier Park (p537), Northern Cape

Pony trekking (p568), Lesotho

Woman in traditional dress, Malealea
(p568), Lesotho

Basotho boy, Lesotho (p550)

Sunrise over Katse Dam (p567), Lesotho

Fields of cosmos daisies, Malealea (p568), Lesotho

Basotho boys, Lesotho (p550)

Villagers from Malealea (p568), Lesotho

Shepherding sheep, Lesotho (p550)

Swazi woman

Tribal dancer, Swazi Cultural Village
(p583), Swaziland

Brown-hooded kingfisher, Mlilwane Wildlife
Sanctuary (p586), Swaziland

Wooden masks, Manzini (p588), Swaziland

Sunset over Mkhaya Game Reserve (p594), Swaziland

RICHARD I'ANSON

Woman preparing food, Swaziland (p574)

ARIADNE VAN ZAND

Sangoma (traditional healer), Swazi Cultural Village (p583), Swaziland

ARIADNE VAN ZANDBERGEN

Eland, Mkhaya Game Reserve (p594), Swaziland

ARIADNE VAN ZAND

(Continued from page 472)

Huts (two people around R240 to R285) are rustic and the cheapest option, with shared ablutions and communal cooking facilities. They sleep between two and six people, depending on the camp, and some have fridges.

Bungalows (two people around R475 to R535) are almost always en suite, and range from simple units with communal cooking facilities to more luxurious versions with kitchenettes.

Cottages (up to four people about R895) are the next step up in both comfort and price. They usually have a living room area,

WILDLIFE-WATCHING

It's a game of chance, but thanks to the variety and sheer numbers of animals in Kruger, you have a better probability of spotting wildlife here than anywhere else in the region. Viewing is best in the cooler, drier winter season, when trees lose their leaves and plant growth is sparser, improving visibility. Also at this time animals tend to be concentrated around the dwindling water sources, and there are fewer mosquitoes. However, the landscape is more attractive in summer, with fresh green growth and a plethora of newborn animals.

Whatever time of year you visit, patience and perseverance are vital prerequisites for rewarding wildlife-watching. Drive slowly, stop frequently and disengage the motor. It's amazing how often you first notice one animal, and only after stopping the car realise that there are many others in the vicinity. Even elephants can be well camouflaged when not in motion. Sitting still and staking out a water hole is always rewarding. Rest camps provide maps that have a 'coloured pin system' showing where animals have been spotted in the area that day and on the previous day – a good place to start.

Thanks to Kruger's excellent road system, you can get off the main roads quite easily, and won't need a 4WD for most secondary gravel roads. (If it has been raining heavily, check with rangers at your rest camp for routes that should be avoided.) Sunglasses and binoculars are essential.

Though different animals display varying behaviour at different times of the day (and tend to be more active in the morning and again in the late afternoon and evening), they don't follow rules, so there is always something to be seen. The more you know about the animals (especially their distribution and behaviour) the better your chance of finding them, so it's worth buying one of the detailed books available at the rest camp shops. Some tips:

- Watch for big cats enjoying the breezes from rocky knolls; leopards will often rest high off the ground in tree branches
- Circling vultures and parked cars are two obvious signs of something interesting, as are excited motorists attempting to flag you down
- Warthogs, baboons, zebras, giraffes and many antelope species will happily graze together, so if you see one species, there will often be more close by
- The presence of feeding herbivores does not preclude the possibility of a predator in the vicinity. Look carefully, as predators are expert stalkers and may not be obvious. Many animals do, however, seem to know whether a predator is actually hunting; if it isn't they will be quite relaxed in its presence.
- Antelopes will be nervous and alert if they are aware of a predator on the hunt, but may not immediately flee. They know they can nearly always outrun a predator if they have a sufficient head start, so they maintain a 'flight distance' between themselves and the threat. If the hunter encroaches, the antelope will move, but will try to keep the hunter in sight. If the hunter charges, the antelope will flee, though may not go far.
- Avoid driving too close to the animals, so as not to disturb their natural behaviour. If you do approach, be slow and steady, without sudden movements.
- Avoid frequent stopping and starting of the car engine – if you stop, it's best to stay put for a while. However, bear in mind that engine vibrations may create a problem with camera shake. There are a few designated spots in Kruger where you are permitted to get out of your car.

KRUGER NATIONAL PARK

as well as kitchen and bathroom, and come in several sizes, including multibedroom 'family cottages'.

Some camps also offer the option of staying in safari tents (two people about R240), all of which are furnished, take from two to four people, and have a refrigerator and fan. Most have shared kitchen and ablutions facilities. Several camps – notably Lower Sabie rest camp and Tamboti satellite camp (near Orpen) – also have safari tents with private bathroom and cooking facilities (from R395 to R425 for two people).

For those with tents or caravans, camping (camp sites for one to two people R105) is available at many rest camps; exceptions are in the reviews. The charge per extra person is R36, with a maximum of six extras; booking is not generally necessary. Many tent sites are not equipped with power points.

Facilities for disabled persons are available at Berg-en-dal, Crocodile Bridge, Pretoriuskop, Lower Sabie, Skukuza, Satara, Olifants, Letaba, Mopani, Shingwedzi and Tamboti. The website for **SAN Parks** (www .parks-sa.co.za) has an excellent overview of conditions at each camp for disabled travellers, and is well worth browsing when planning your travels.

Note that bookings for all rest camps should be made through central reservations, or at one of the local tourist offices that take Kruger bookings (see p468); the numbers listed in this section are for specific rest camp information and emergencies only. The camps are listed from south to north – the direction that most visitors travel.

Berg-en-dal (☎ 013-735 6106) A medium-sized camp 12km from Malelane Gate, and one of the most modern, with bungalows and family cottages sleeping up to six people. It's laid out in attractive bush landscape by the Matjulu River, about 5km from a water hole popular with rhinos. There's a visitors centre and nature trails. About 9km away on the southern border of Kruger, is the small and (except for its size) not particularly appealing **Malelane satellite camp**. Other than camping and a few bungalows, there are no facilities. If you want to stay here, you'll need to register at Malelane Gate.

Crocodile Bridge (☎ 013-735 6012) This small camp is near the Crocodile River just in

from Crocodile Bridge Gate, and is a good choice if you've arrived in Kruger too late to drive further into the park. There are crocodile and hippo pools a few kilometres away, and zebras, buffaloes and wildebeests in the surrounding acacia. Accommodation is in bungalows or a safari tent. There is no restaurant, and diesel fuel is not available.

Pretoriuskop (☎ 013-735 5128) This is Kruger's oldest camp, and one of its largest. It's located near Numbi Gate, in higher country than other places in the park, and is thus a bit cooler in summer. Accommodation is in huts, bungalows and several large cottages sleeping between six and nine people. The surrounding country is attractive, with granite outcrops, and is frequented by white rhinos. Hippos can be spotted at nearby Mestel Dam. The camp includes a natural rock swimming pool that is popular with kids.

Lower Sabie (☎ 013-735 6056) This medium-sized camp, about one hour (35km) from Crocodile Bridge Gate, overlooks a dam on the Sabie River that attracts many animals. For sleeping, there's a good selection of huts, safari tents, bungalows and cottages. Camp sites here have individual water taps.

Skukuza (☎ 013-735 4152) On the Sabie River, Skukuza is the main camp in Kruger, with facilities similar to those in a small town. There's a bank with an ATM, an Automobile Association (AA) workshop petrol station, a doctor, a library, the police, a post office, a small museum and a helpful information centre. There's also an extensive range of accommodation, including luxury bungalows and various cottages. Apart from its size, the main drawbacks are the slightly sanitised feel and the camp sites, which are distinctly average.

Orpen (☎ 013-735 6355) Near Orpen Gate, this is a small, attractive camp with a nearby water hole that attracts wildlife. There's no restaurant; cooking facilities are shared and no utensils are provided. Some accommodation doesn't have electricity, so bring a torch (flashlight). There are two satellite camps near Orpen. **Maroela**, 4km northeast, has basic camp sites with power points. The appealing **Tamboti**, 4km east, has nice safari tents, complete with wildlife wandering around outside. Some of the tents have private bathrooms and kitchens, and two have wheelchair access ramps. For both

Maroela and Tamboti, you'll need to check in at Orpen.

Satara (☎ 013-735 6306) East of Orpen Gate, Satara is situated in an area of flat and fertile plains that attracts large numbers of grazing animals. While its setting isn't that appealing (mainly because of the lack of any raised viewpoints), it has the highest lion population in the entire park. About 45km north of Satara near the Olifants River is **Balule satellite camp**, with camping and several rustic three-person huts. There's no electricity (kerosene lanterns are available at the camp, but bring a torch). There's a large freezer and a stove, but otherwise, you'll need to bring everything in with you, including cooking utensils. Although Balule is much closer to Olifants camp (11km further north), check-in must be done through Satara.

Olifants (☎ 013-735 6606) This camp has a fantastic position on the bluff high above the Olifants River and offers spectacular views. From the camp you can see elephants, hippos and many other animals as they come down to the river 100m below. There are no camp sites at Olifants, but it is possible to camp at nearby Balule satellite camp.

Letaba (☎ 013-735 6636) About 20km to the north, Letaba has excellent views over a wide bend of the Letaba River. It's an attractive camp with lots of shade, grassy camp sites and a restaurant. The Elephant Hall museum here focuses on the elephant and includes mounted tusks of the big bulls (Mafunyane, Dzombo, Shingwedzi and Shawu) that have died in the park. There are sections on poaching, the illegal ivory trade, geomorphology and biology, plus descriptions of elephant habits.

Mopani (☎ 013-735 6536) This modern rest camp is on the edge of the Pioneer Dam, 45km north of Letaba. The buildings are all of natural materials and thatch, and the overall impression is highly aesthetic. There are no camp sites, but about 3km away is **Shipandani** – a 'sleepover' hide with mattresses, bed linens, a modest collection of cooking utensils and toilet facilities. It can take up to six people.

Shingwedzi (☎ 013-735 6806) The large Shingwedzi is an old-style place in the northern section of the park, with many huts and cottages arranged in circles and shaded by tall mopani trees and palms. A restaurant overlooks the Shingwedzi River and there's a swimming pool. There are excellent drives in the vicinity.

Punda Maria (☎ 013-735 6873) The northernmost rest camp, Punda Maria is in sandveld (dry, sandy belt) country by Dimbo Mountain. The camp is a long-established place with an agreeable wilderness ambience. The area's ecology is fascinating and supports a wide range of animals, including lions and elephants.

Bushveld Camps

Bushveld camps are an excellent option if you want more of a wilderness experience than is possible at the rest camps, and are equipped for self-catering. Most are reasonably close to a rest camp where supplies can be bought. All have solar power, so electrical appliances other than lights, fans and fridges cannot be used. Bookings (made through central reservations or at one of the local tourist offices that take Kruger bookings; see p468) are essential. At most of the bushveld camps, it's possible to arrange night drives and bush walks. Accommodation is in cottages, all with private bathroom, most of which sleep up to six people. Prices range from R785 to R855 for four people, plus R185 per additional person. If you are just one person you still pay the unit price for the entire cottage (R785 to R855).

BIYAMITI

On the southern border of Kruger, between Malelane and Crocodile Bridge Gates, Biyamiti is in an easily accessed area known for its lions and other representatives of the Big Five. It accommodates up to 70 people in thatched cottages with a pleasant, semi-pampered feel.

TALAMATI

This lies about 30km southeast of Orpen Gate on the N'waswitsontso River in an exceptionally wildlife-rich area. It has two- and four-person cottages with basic kitchen facilities, plus a more luxurious four-person cottage, and several hides overlooking the nearby water hole.

SHIMUWINI

This camp is on the Letaba River, 50km northeast of Phalaborwa Gate in a riverine

KRUGER NATIONAL PARK

setting that's ideal for bird-watching. It has a bird hide overlooking the dam, and accommodation in two- to six-person cottages.

BATELEUR

If you make it to northern Kruger, it's well-worth staying a few nights here. It's the smallest and nicest of the bushveld camps – rustic but comfortable, with a good setting, a wilderness ambience and a small pan on the edge of the camp, plus two dams nearby that offer some excellent bird-watching. It's in northern Kruger, about 35km southwest of Shingwedzi.

SIRHENI

In a lightly wooded area about 40km northwest of Shingwedzi in Kruger's far north, Sirheni, like Shimuwini, is on a dam. It's an excellent spot for birding, with the added appeal of more of a wilderness atmosphere.

Bush Lodges

Kruger's two bush lodges are set off on their own and must be reserved in their entirety. The idea is to have as remote a bush experience as possible, in the privacy of your own group. There are no facilities other than equipped kitchens, braai areas and bedding; you'll need to bring all supplies in with you. For both lodges, you need to make reservations before arrival, either through central reservations (p468), or at any Kruger gate or rest camp. Neither lodge has electricity, other than solar power for lights and fans.

Boulders (up to 4 people R1665, per additional person R310) About 23km southwest of Mopani rest camp, Boulders takes up to 12 people in six rooms.

Roodewal (up to 4 people R1575, per additional person R310) About 28km northeast of Orpen Gate, Roodewal takes up to 19 people in a cottage and several bungalows.

Private Concessions

Kruger's private concessions are all located in wildlife-rich areas of the park and offer the chance to go on safari while enjoying all the amenities. Accommodation (in luxury tents or lodges) should be booked directly with the relevant concession operator. (There are also links from the SAN Parks website.) Prices start around R4500 per person. They include the following:

Jock Safari Lodge (☎ 013-735 5200; www.jocksafari lodge.com) In southern Kruger, about halfway between Berg-en-dal and Skukuza rest camps.

Lukimbi Safari Lodge (☎ 011-888 3713; www .lukimbi.com) Near the southern border of the park, and just southwest of Biyamiti bushveld camp.

Rhino Post Camp (☎ 011-467 1886; www.zulunet .co.za) Near Skukuza rest camp on the Mutlumuvi River.

Singita Lebombo Lodge (☎ 021-683 3424; www .singita.co.za) Part of a world-renowned resort; see p486.

GETTING THERE & AROUND
Air

SAAirlink (☎ 011-978 1111; www.saairlink.co.za) has daily flights linking both Jo'burg and Cape Town with Mpumalanga Kruger International Airport (MKIA) near Nelspruit (for Numbi, Malelane and Crocodile Bridge Gates), and with Kruger Park Gateway Airport in Phalaborwa (2km from Phalaborwa Gate). Sample one-way fares and flight times: Jo'burg to Phalaborwa (R1300, one hour); Jo'burg to MKIA (R1200, one hour); Cape Town to MKIA (R2200, 2¼ hours). SAAirlink also has daily flights connecting Cape Town with Hoedspruit (for Orpen Gate) via Sun City (R2400, 3¼ hours).

South African Airways (☎ 086-035 9722, 011-978 1111; www.flysaa.com) flies six times weekly between Durban and MKIA (R1400, 1½ hours), while **South African Express** (☎ 011-978 5577; www.saexpress.co.za) flies daily between Jo'burg and Hoedspruit Eastgate Airport (R1300, 1½ hours), with connections to Cape Town. **Nationwide Airlines** (☎ 086-173 7737, 011-327 3000; www.nationwideair.co.za) is another airline to check, with several flights weekly connecting both Cape Town and Jo'burg with MKIA.

Bus & Minibus Taxi

For most visitors, Nelspruit is the most convenient large town near Kruger, and is well served by buses and minibus taxis to and from Jo'burg (see p460). Numbi Gate is about 50km away, and Malelane Gate about 65km away. Phalaborwa, in the north on the edge of Kruger, is being increasingly promoted as a gateway for northern Kruger. It is served by regular bus services to/from Jo'burg and elsewhere in South Africa (see p509). Hoedspruit is another possible hub, with reasonable bus connections to elsewhere in South Africa (see p510). It's also the most convenient gateway for many of the private reserves bordering Kruger, and an easy 70km drive from the park's Orpen Gate. From the Venda region in Limpopo province, minibus taxis run close to the Punda Maria Gate.

Car

Skukuza is 500km from Jo'burg (six hours) and Punda Maria about 620km (eight hours). **Avis** (☎ 013-735 5651; www.avis.co.za) has a branch at Skukuza, and there is car rental from the Nelspruit, Hoedspruit and Phalaborwa airports.

Most visitors drive themselves around the park, and this is the best way to experience Kruger. If you're running low on funds, hiring a car between three or four people for a few days is relatively cheap (see p636).

Driving on the paved roads in Kruger is easy. There is little traffic and everyone drives slowly. But keep an eye out for sudden stops and distracted drivers. There are petrol stations at the biggest camps, but you'll save a little money by filling up before entering the park.

Train

The *Komati* (p643) runs from Jo'burg via Nelspruit to Komatipoort (1st/2nd/economy class R185/130/70), which is about 12km from Kruger's Crocodile Bridge Gate.

PRIVATE WILDLIFE RESERVES

Spreading over a vast lowveld area just west of Kruger is a string of private reserves that offer comparable wildlife-watching to what you'll experience in the park. The main reserves – Sabie Sand, Manyeleti and Timbavati – directly border Kruger (with no fences), and the same Big Five populations that roam the park are also at home here.

There are around 200 lodges and camps in the private reserves and most are pricey – from around R2000 to over R6000 per person sharing, all-inclusive. (Prices listed here are based on the high season rate.)

However, together with the handful of new private concessions operating within the park's boundaries (see opposite), the private reserves offer among Africa's best opportunities for safari connoisseurs, and are the place to go for those who want to experience the bush in the lap of luxury. Prices tend to be seasonal so it's best to have a look at their websites for the most accurate costs. Note that many of these places like to call themselves 'game reserves'. They're not. They are simply lodges inside of a designated wildlife reserve.

If your budget permits, it's also worth considering the private reserves as a complement to spending a few nights in the park. The rangers have a wealth of knowledge and, because of the personalised safari attention, can train you in the art of wildlife-watching before you head to Kruger for a self-guided trip. The major reserves and a few of their camps are described here. There are many more lodges and dozens of operators handling tours in this area. Hoedspruit has emerged as the gateway to the private lodges.

Note that even if you arrive with your own vehicle, self-drive safaris aren't permitted in any of the private reserves, and most can only be visited with advance booking. In addition to the reserves described here, there are numerous other smaller ones further north and west, including Klaserie, Makalali (which doesn't share any borders with Kruger) and Balule (also no borders with Kruger).

SABIE SAND GAME RESERVE

Within the borders of the large **Sabie Sand Game Reserve** (http://sabi.krugerpark.co.za) are some of Southern Africa's most luxurious safari lodges and best wildlife-watching on the continent. The area is routinely selected by safari connoisseurs as their destination of choice. As there's no fencing between the various private lodges within the greater Sabie Sand area, all share the same wealth of birds and animals. There's a R50 vehicle fee to enter Sabie Sand.

Nkorho Bush Lodge (☎ 013-735 5367; www.nkorho .com; all-inclusive s/d R2075/3200; 🏊) In the northern part of Sabie Sand, this is one of the more moderately priced lodges, with comfortable thatched chalets set around grassy grounds, and a low-key ambience.

Chitwa Chitwa Private Game Lodges (☎ 011-883 1354; www.chitwa.co.za; all-inclusive s/d R2400/3900; 🏊🏊) Chitwa Chitwa suffers a bit in the shadows of Londolozi and Singita, but offers good value, especially at its beautiful water-side Game Lodge.

Djuma Game Reserve (☎ 013-735 5118; www.djuma.co.za; all-inclusive r from R4200; 🔊) Djuma is notable for its straightforward, good-value accommodation. The most intriguing option here is Vuyatela Lodge, where local culture has been incorporated into every aspect of the building. It's an ideal choice if you're interested in learning about local people as well as the local wildlife.

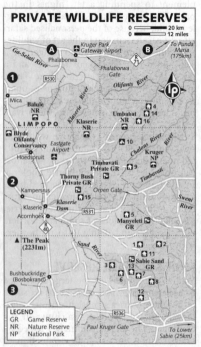

good value, especially at its beautiful waterside Game Lodge.

Mala Mala Game Reserve (☎ 011-442 2267; www.malamala.com; all-inclusive r from R6000; 🔊 🔊) Mala Mala competes with Londolozi and Singita for distinction as one of the region's most luxurious reserves, though it's not quite as polished as its two neighbours. Excellent wildlife-viewing compensates, and staff make every effort to ensure you spot the Big Five.

Singita Private Game Reserve (☎ 021-683 3424; www.singita.co.za; all-inclusive r from R7140; 🔊 🖥 🔊) Singita has been distinguished by the top-end travel industry as one of the best resorts in Africa, and one of the world's top travel destinations. Its Lebombo Lodge draws most of the attention, with a superb riverine location, an excess of amenities and impeccable service. It's operated as a private concession within Kruger's boundaries, on the park's western edge, southeast of Satara rest camp.

Londolozi Private Game Reserve (☎ 011-809 4300; www.londolozi.com; all-inclusive r from R8000; 🔊 🔊) This exclusive private lodge is operated by CC Africa, and is renowned for its luxury and its leopards. For sleeping, you have your choice of accommodation in one of several camps (most notable is the intimate Tree Camp) or in an equally comfortable lodge – all with excellent settings along the Sand River. Londolozi describes itself as 'unashamedly exclusive' and is the place to go if you want a five-star-plus experience in the bush, combined with excellent wildlife-watching.

Other places to check out include the following:

Idube Private Game Reserve (☎ 011-888 3713; www.idube.com; s/d R3980/5900; 🔊) Nice and comfortable, without the finesse of some of the other places, but with a more manageable price tag.

Exeter Private Game Lodges (☎ 013-735 5140; www.exeter-lodges.com; all-inclusive r from R5600; 🔊 🔊) An upmarket entity managing several lodges in western and southern Sabie Sand, notably the exclusive Leadwood and Dulini lodges.

Sabi Sabi Private Game Reserve (☎ 011-483 3939; www.sabisabi.com; all-inclusive r from R8800; 🔊 🔊) Known especially for its lions and for its subterranean and ultraluxurious Earth Lodge.

MANYELETI GAME RESERVE

During the apartheid era, the 23,000-hectare **Manyeleti** (http://manyeleti.krugerpark.co.za) was the only wildlife reserve that blacks were permitted to use. Today, it's the least crowded of the private wildlife reserves, with only a few camps. It is possible to see all the Big Five here, although with somewhat more effort than in Sabie Sands, its neighbour to the south. As compensation, accommodation here is significantly less expensive than in Sabie Sands.

Honeyguide (Khoka Moya; ☎ 015-793 1729; www .honeyguidecamp.com; all-inclusive per person R2300; ☒) A small place, taking a maximum of 16 people. It's one of the better-value private reserves, with accommodation in rustic cabins raised a bit off the ground on stilts.

TIMBAVATI PRIVATE GAME RESERVE

Timbavati (http://timbavati.krugerpark.co.za) was originally known for its white lion population, although it's the yellow versions you'll see today. It's less crowded than Sabie Sand, and its accommodation – while lacking the sumptuous settings of the lodges in Sabie Sand – tends to be more reasonably priced, without forgoing too many amenities. There's a R90 per person conservation fee and R75 vehicle entry fee to pay when entering the reserve.

Gomo Gomo (☎ 012-752 3954; www.gomogomo .co.za; s/d R1290/2580) A more moderately priced place, with rustic chalets and tents.

Umlani Bushcamp (☎ 012-346 4028; www.umlani .co.za; s/d R2950/4500; ☒) A good place if you want to immerse yourself in the bush, with no electricity and accommodation in simple but comfortable reed bungalows.

Tanda Tula (☎ 021-794 6500; www.tandatula.co.za; all-inclusive s/d from R4200/7800; ☒) Timbavati's most luxurious option, with cosy safari tents and a water hole practically at your doorstep. Children under 12 aren't permitted.

Ngala (☎ 011-809 4300; www.ccafrica.com; all-inclusive tent per person sharing R4800, lodge per person sharing R2600-6800; ☒ ☒) A subdued but luxurious place in a superb location on the border of Kruger, and managed by CC Africa. Accommodation is in your choice of a safari tent or lodge (prices for the lodge vary depending on the season), and comes with all the amenities.

THORNYBUSH PRIVATE GAME RESERVE

Thornybush (http://thornybush.krugerpark.co.za) opened in 1977 on 4000 acres of land. It has since expanded to 25,000 acres and is one of the few reserves in the area that is still enclosed by fences. There are 11 lodges on the reserve. It has no gate entrance fees.

Tangala (☎ 015-793 0488; www.tangala.co.za; all-inclusive s/d from R1495/2990; ☒) This electricity-free camp is beautifully designed and well maintained. Cost-wise it's one of the best deals in the area.

KRUGER NATIONAL PARK

Limpopo

The name Limpopo carries with it the mark of legends, lore and mystery. It is the infamous Crook's Corner where ivory traders and gunrunners hid from the law. And it was here, in the 'Valley of the Olifants', that 19th-century big game hunters spun yarns about enormous elephant herds. This is also a royal land, the scene of the vanished kingdom at Mapungubwe and the Rain Queen who still rules in the Venda area.

Modern Limpopo sits at a key crossroads between Botswana, Zimbabwe, Kruger National Park and Gauteng, and is oft considered a doormat into more exotic destinations. But driving along the busy N1 highway that connects these places gives little impression of what gems lie off the beaten path.

Heading north from Johannesburg (Jo'burg), southwest Limpopo (the Bushveld) undulates into scrubby hills that are home to several wildlife parks, lodges and resorts, including the hot springs at Bela-Bela. Big Five spotters will be better off heading north to the spectacular Mapungubwe National Park, a World Heritage Site that gives Kruger a run for its money.

East of the N1, the dry landscape gives way to the tropical fruit farms of the Letaba Valley, the cycad forests that surround the realm of the mystical Rain Queen, and the intriguing traditional homeland of the Venda people.

The area south of here, the Valley of the Olifants, is perhaps the most inviting of all. Plantations, relaxed country towns and some pretty valleys peppered with waterfalls make for great exploring, especially for DIY travellers with their own bike or car. Just east of here, at Phalaborwa, you can play golf on a spectacular course inhabited by giraffes, monkeys, elephants and the like, before heading into glorious Kruger National Park.

HIGHLIGHTS

- Soaking up the prehistory in **Mapungubwe National Park** (p500)
- Hiking through the lush green peaks of the **Soutpansberg Range** (p498)
- Saddling up the horses for a ride through the hills of **Haenertsburg** (p504)
- Munching through the mangoes in the fruit-growing centre of **Tzaneen** (p505)
- Skirting around the sacred sites of the mysterious **Venda Region** (p503)
- Getting drenched with the Rain Queen in **GaModjadji** (p507)

- POPULATION: 5.5 MILLION
- AREA: 123,910 SQ KM

HISTORY

After the battlefields of KwaZulu-Natal and the anti-apartheid struggle of Soweto, it is easy to overlook Limpopo's history. But the province has a rich past that spans millions of years. Makapan's Caves, near Mokopane, has offered up an archaeological record stretching back to protohuman times (including human tools from more than 500,000 years ago), while the area that is now Mapungubwe National Park was once the heart of one of Africa's most technologically advanced civilisations, holding sway over an area of 30,000 sq km and enjoying its heyday in the 8th and 9th centuries.

The Voortrekkers made this region home in the mid-19th century, establishing their base in Pietersburg (now Polokwane) in 1886. Conflict with the local Ndebele people marked a period of resistance against the settlers.

Around the turn of the 20th century, eastern Limpopo, near the borders with Mozambique and Zimbabwe, earned a reputation as a haven for ivory hunters, gunrunners and other outlaws – so much so that it was dubbed 'Crook's Corner'.

In recognition of its distinctly African origins, many of the region's towns have been renamed in recent years and the name of the province itself was changed to Limpopo at the turn of the 21st century.

Limpopo's economy is fuelled by mining and agriculture, with tourism making slow inroads around Hoedspruit. While this may sound familiar, Limpopo does face unique challenges in South Africa, not the least of which is its porous border through which illegal migrants head across from Botswana, Zimbabwe and Mozambique. Limpopo, which has one of the highest poverty rates in the country, is also a hot spot of racial tension: in 2005 alone some 35 farms were attacked, leading to the deaths of 13 white farmers.

CLIMATE

In general, Limpopo is hot and dry and gets steadily hotter as you head north. The high peaks of the Soutpansberg Range provide cooler, damper conditions and the rolling hills of the Letaba Valley and Venda regions also get more than their fair share of mist and drizzle.

NATIONAL PARKS & RESERVES

The **Limpopo Tourism and Parks Board** (☎ 015-290 7300; www.limpopotourism.org.za; cnr Kerk & Grobler Sts; ☯ 8am-4.30pm Mon-Fri), in Polokwane, provides information on most of the region's parks and reserves. The highlight is Mapungubwe National Park (p500), close to the Zimbabwe border. However, Limpopo is also home to numerous private wildlife reserves, the best of which are contiguous with Kruger National Park and covered in that chapter (see p485).

LANGUAGE

English and Afrikaans are widely spoken, but Afrikaans remains the language of choice in most areas.

GETTING THERE & AROUND

Limpopo is bisected by the excellent N1 highway (a toll road as far as Polokwane), which runs from Jo'burg and Pretoria to the Zimbabwe border at Beitbridge. Many of the province's large towns are on this artery and most are connected to Jo'burg and Pretoria via the **Translux** (www.translux.co.za) and **Greyhound** (www.greyhound.co.za) buses that run this way en route to Bulawayo and Harare. The *Bosevelder* train runs an almost identical route, but more slowly. Long-distance buses also link the regional capital, Polokwane, with destinations along Rte 71, including Tzaneen and Phalaborwa, on the edge of the Kruger National Park. Other destinations can be hard to access without a car, but minibus taxis do link most parts of the province.

Hiring a car is the best way to see Limpopo (most roads are good), but if you want to save some miles, you can also fly from Jo'burg to Polokwane, Phalaborwa or Hoedspruit (near Kruger's Orpen Gate) and hire a car there.

See p632 and individual Getting There & Away sections for more details.

CAPRICORN

The Capricorn region includes little more than Polokwane (Pietersburg), the provincial capital. The tropic of Capricorn crosses the N1 halfway between Polokwane and Makhado (Louis Trichardt), although the monument marking the spot is a little neglected.

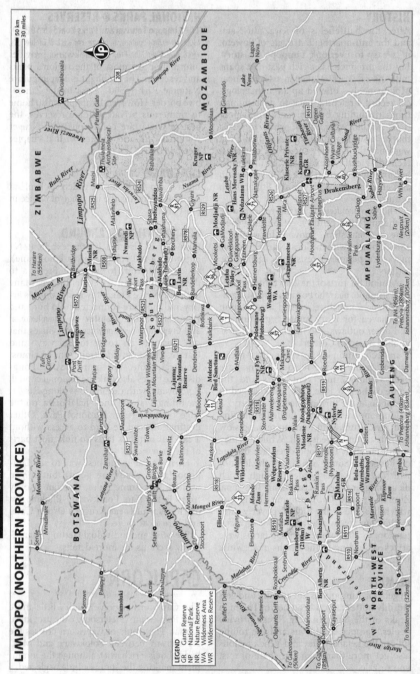

LIMPOPO (NORTHERN PROVINCE)

POLOKWANE (PIETERSBURG)

☎ 015 / pop 140,000

A rather agreeably sedate cluster of suburban streets surrounding a bustling commercial centre, Polokwane was founded in 1886 by Voortrekkers seeking to escape the usual cocktail of tropical disease and 'hostile natives'. Much of this conflict now seems to have dissipated and if you are wandering through the backstreets of South Africa's safest provincial capital these days, the biggest risk seems to be getting soaked by an over-zealous garden sprinkler.

Information

EMERGENCY
Police station (☎ 015-290 6000; cnr Schoeman & Bodenstein Sts)

INTERNET
Atlantic Internet (☎ 015-295 9203; Shop 13, Standard Bank Bldg, Hans van Rensburg St; per hr R35; ⏲ 8.30am-6pm Mon-Fri, 8.30am-2pm Sat)

MEDICAL SERVICES
Pietersburg Hospital (☎ 015-287 5000; cnr Hospital & Dorp Sts) For medical attention.

MONEY
There are plenty of banks throughout the town.
ABSA (☎ 015-290 2166; 70 Hans van Rensburg St) Has an ATM and change facilities.

POST
Main post office (☎ 015-291 3200; cnr Bodenstein & Landdros Mare Sts; ⏲ 8am-4.30pm Mon-Fri, 8am-noon Sat)

TOURIST INFORMATION
Limpopo Tourism & Parks Board (☎ 015-290 7300; www.golimpopo.com; cnr Kerk & Grobler Sts; ⏲ 8am-4.30pm Mon-Fri) Covers the whole province and offers the useful *Limpopo Explorer* map and the *Know Limpopo Guide*.
Polokwane Municipality Local Development Office (☎ 015-290 2010; www.polokwane.org.za; Civic Sq, Landdros Mare St; ⏲ 8am-4pm Mon-Fri) Has limited town information.

WARNING

Both malaria and bilharzia are prevalent in Limpopo, mainly in the east near Kruger National Park. For more information, see p647.

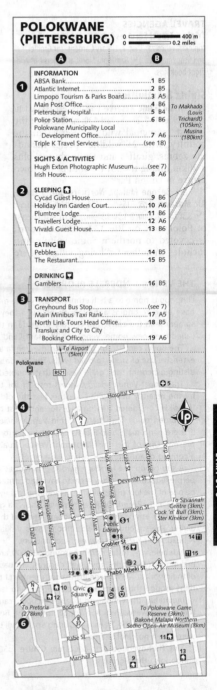

POLOKWANE (PIETERSBURG)

0 —— 400 m
0 —— 0.2 miles

INFORMATION
ABSA Bank...............................1 B5
Atlantic Internet.......................2 B5
Limpopo Tourism & Parks Board...........3 A5
Main Post Office........................4 B6
Pietersburg Hospital....................5 B4
Police Station..........................6 B6
Polokwane Municipality Local
  Development Office..................7 A6
Triple K Travel Services.............(see 18)

SIGHTS & ACTIVITIES
Hugh Exton Photographic Museum.......(see 7)
Irish House.............................8 A6

SLEEPING
Cycad Guest House.......................9 B6
Holiday Inn Garden Court................10 A6
Plumtree Lodge..........................11 B6
Travellers Lodge........................12 A6
Vivaldi Guest House.....................13 B6

EATING
Pebbles................................14 B5
The Restaurant.........................15 B5

DRINKING
Gamblers...............................16 B5

TRANSPORT
Greyhound Bus Stop...................(see 7)
Main Minibus Taxi Rank.................17 A5
North Link Tours Head Office...........18 B5
Translux and City to City
  Booking Office......................19 A6

To Makhado (Louis Trichardt) (105km); Musina (180km)

To Airport (5km)

Polokwane

R521

Hospital St

Excelsior St

Rissik St

Devenish St

Biccard St

Voortrekker St

Dorp St

To Savannah Centre (3km); Cock 'n' Bull (3km); Ster Kinekor (3km)

Jorrisen St

Market St

Kerk St

Joubert St

Schoeman St

Bok St

President Kruger St

Dahl St

Hans van Rensburg St

Landdros Mare St

Grobler St

Public Library

Thabo Mbeki St

Civic Square

To Pretoria (278km)

Bodenstein St

Rabe St

To Polokwane Game Reserve (3km); Bakone Malapa Northern Sotho Open-Air Museum (8km)

Marshall St

Suid St

LIMPOPO

TRAVEL AGENCIES

Triple K Travel Services (☎ 015-291 5748; info@ triplektravel.co.za; Shop 7, Library Gardens, cnr Grobler and Schoeman Sts; ☻ 8am-5pm Mon-Sat) Offers bus and flight bookings.

Sights & Activities

Polokwane Game Reserve (☎ 015-290 2331; adult/ child/vehicle R12/8/20; ☻ 7am-4.30pm) is one of the largest municipal wildlife reserves in the country, with 21 wildlife species including zebras, giraffes and white rhinos, plus a 20km hiking trail. It is south of the town centre in Union Park.

The **Bakone Malapa Northern Sotho Open-Air Museum** (☎ 015-295 2432; adult/child R3/1.50; ☻ 8.30am-12.30pm & 1.30-3.30pm), 9km southeast of Polokwane on Rte 37 to Chuniespoort, is devoted to northern Sotho culture and includes an authentic 'living' village where locals produce handicrafts. There are archaeological remains and paintings dating back to AD 1000, plus evidence of Ndebele iron and copper smelting.

The **Hugh Exton Photographic Museum** (☎ 015-290 2186; Civic Sq; admission free; ☻ 9am-3.30pm Mon-Fri) documents the first 50 years of the city's history with 23,000 glass slides. Nearby is the beautiful Victorian-era **Irish House** (cnr Thabo Mbeki & Market Sts).

Sleeping

As is the case in much of Limpopo, accommodation options are concentrated mainly in the midrange bracket. Those wanting some luxury will be better off at an up-market guesthouse, while budget travellers will struggle.

Travellers Lodge (☎ 015-291 5511; incatrav@world online.co.za; 43 Bok St; s/d R275/295; 🅿) Despite the

---

THE VENDA & NDEBELE PEOPLES

Limpopo is home to a rich ethnic tapestry. The main ethnic group in the area, the Venda people, have obscure origins although it's believed they they migrated across the Limpopo River sometime in the early 18th century to settle in the Soutpansberg area. When they arrived they called their new home 'Venda' or 'Pleasant Land'.

The Boers came into contact with the Venda at the end of the 18th century and noted their extensive use of stone to build walls. The Venda were skilled in leather and beadwork, and were distinguished for their grain vessels that doubled as artwork hung from their huts.

Traditional Venda society shows respect for the very young and the very old – the young having recently been with ancestors and the old about to join their ancestors. The Venda king (*kgosi*) is considered a living ancestor and must be approached on hands and knees.

Women enjoy high status within Venda society and can inherit property from their father if there is no male heir. Rituals cannot be performed unless the oldest daughter of a family is present. One of the most important Venda rituals is the snake (*domba*) dance, which serves as a coming of age ritual for young women.

A sub-group, the Lemba regard themselves as the nobility of the Venda. The Lemba have long perplexed scholars as they seem to have had contact with Islam. However, they themselves claim to be one of the lost tribes of Israel. Traditionally they keep kosher, wear head coverings and observe the Sabbath. Recent DNA testing even shows a genetic quality similar to Jews elsewhere.

Another ethnic group, the Ndebele, entered the region from KwaZulu-Natal at least 100 years earlier. The structure of their authority was similar to the Zulu, with several tiers of governance. A headman (*ikozi*) oversaw each community.

Ndebele, who today number around 600,000, are renowned for their beadwork, which goes into making rich tapestries, toys, wall decorations, baskets, bags and clothing. You can see examples of their work at www.thebeadsite.com/ub-nbart.htm. Traditionally, women wear copper and brass rings around their arms and neck, symbolising faithfulness to their husband.

Inevitably, the Venda and Ndebele peoples came into violent contact with their neighbours – the Boers, Swazis, Pedi and Tonga. It was the Boers who emerged victorious and annexed the Venda land into the Transvaal. During apartheid, both groups were forced onto 'homelands' that were given nominal self-rule.

The Thohoyandou Arts & Culture Centre (p502) is a good place to acquaint yourself with Limpopo's ethnic groups.

name, this smart, self-catering place doesn't cater to the backpacker market. If you want to whip up your own meals, however, this peaceful place is an excellent choice.

Vivaldi Guest House (☎ 015-295 6162; vivaldi1@ mweb.co.za; 2 Voortrekker St; s/d with breakfast R300/390; ✱) Surrounded by a garden filled with rare cycads and with a soundtrack provided by a brace of talking parrots, this tip-top hideaway offers friendly welcomes and oodles of home comforts.

Cycad Guest House (☎ 015-291 2181; www.bbgroup .co.za/cycad/index.html; cnr Schoeman & Suid Sts; s/d with breakfast R330/420; ✱ 🖳) Best filed in the drawer marked 'motel-style', this glossy, modern place falls on the practical side of the functional/cosy divide, earning its gold stars for cleanliness and slick service.

Plumtree Lodge (☎ 015-295 6153; www.plumtree .co.za; 138 Marshall St; s/d with breakfast R425/535; ✱ 🖳 🛋) The crowds vote with their feet at this busy little place, where rooms are in twee bungalows and all the couch potato creature comforts come as standard. They also have free wi-fi access for laptop users.

Polokwane Game Reserve (☎ 015-290 2331) South of town, the reserve (opposite) has camping (R100 per site) and two-bed chalets (R220).

Holiday Inn Garden Court (☎ 015-291 2030; hic polokwane@southernsun.com; Thabo Mbeki St; s/d with breakfast R500/760; ✱ 🖳 🛋) For the smartest, business-style beds in town.

Eating & Drinking

You can find all the usual takeaways in Library Gardens, but the Savannah Centre on Grobler St offers the widest selection of steak-based eats.

The Restaurant (☎ 015-291 1918; 50 Dorp St; mains R40-60; ☖ lunch & dinner Mon-Sat) It's not the most complex name, but The Restaurant does have a nice variety of dishes, including beef and chicken curries, salads and seafood. The African art adds colour to the historic house.

Pebbles (☎ 015-295 6999; 39 Grobler St; mains R40-60; ☖ 8am-10pm Mon-Sat, 8am-2.15pm Sun) Set inside a beautiful historical house, Pebbles has a nice patio where you can enjoy a salad, steak or a veggie dish. There's also an attached pub.

Cock 'n' Bull (☎ 015-296 0961; Savannah Centre, Rte 71; mains R30-70; ☖ lunch & dinner; ✱) This pub-style offering serves up steaks the size

> **WHAT'S IN A NAME?**
>
> Many town names in Limpopo, including the name of the province itself, have been changed in recent years. Throughout the chapter we use the new name then give the old name in brackets. Unfortunately, while all names have been changed on the official record, some road signs and many local residents have yet to catch up. As a result, travel can be confusing at times.

of a springbok's thighs in yee-har surrounds. There's big-screen sport and ice-cold beer to wash away the indigestion, and outdoor seating for those who prefer their meat alfresco.

Gamblers (☎ 015-291 1890; 1st fl, Palm Centre, Grobler St) This saloon-style drinking den keeps the beer flowing until the last person's standing. At weekends, there's plenty of action involving booze, singing and banter.

Entertainment

Ster Kinekor (☎ 086-300 222; Savannah Centre, Rte 71) Catch all the latest Hollywood flicks at this cinema.

Getting There & Away

AIR

SAAirlink (☎ 015-288 0166; www.saairlink.co.za), with offices at the airport, flies daily to/from Jo'burg (R820 to R1160 one way). **Polokwane airport** (☎ 015-288 0122) is 5km north of town.

BUS

Translux (☎ 015-295 5548; www.translux.co.za; cnr Joubert & Thabo Mbeki Sts) runs services to Pretoria (R140, 3½ hours), Jo'burg (R140, 4½ hours) and Lusaka (R350, 24 hours). It also runs the cheaper City to City buses, which serve a number of smaller towns.

Greyhound (☎ 011-276 8500; www.greyhound.co .za) links Polokwane with Jo'burg (R165, five hours) and Harare (R280, 12 hours). There isn't an office in town, but you can book through Triple K Travel Services (opposite). Buses stop on Civic Sq.

North Link Tours (☎ 015-291 1867; 13 Library Gardens, Hans Van Rensburg St) runs daily (10am) buses between Polokwane and Jo'burg. They stop at Mokopane (R45, 40 minutes), Mookgophong (R40, 1¼ hours), Pretoria (R100,

3½ hours) and Jo'burg (R120, 4½ hours). Buses depart from outside Library Gardens.

MINIBUS TAXI
The main minibus taxi rank is on the corner of President Kruger and Devenish Sts. Destinations and fares from Polokwane include Thohoyandou (R30, 2½ hours), Makhado (R20, 1¼ hours) and Jo'burg (R105, five hours).

TRAIN
The **Bosvelder** (☎ 086-000 8888) passes through Polokwane daily (except Saturday) en route between Jo'burg and Musina. Fares include: Jo'burg (1st/2nd class R110/75, eight hours), Makhado (1st/2nd class R70/40, four hours) and Musina (1st/2nd class R100/70, 7¼ hours).

BUSHVELD

The Bushveld region occupies the southwestern section of the province and is flat, dry and the most typical of South African savanna. It includes a string of towns along the N1, including Mokopane (Potgietersrus), Mookgophong (Naboomspruit) and Modimolle (Nylstroom), as well as the holiday resort of Bela-Bela (Warmbaths). West of the N1, the bushveld turns into the rolling mountains and scenic valleys of the Waterberg Range.

MOKOPANE (POTGIETERSRUS) & AROUND
☎ 015 / pop 120,000
This conservative town (they all seem to be up this way), 227km north of Pretoria, was settled early by Voortrekkers, not without resistance from the people already living there. Things are quieter now, and the town is an important base of operations for platinum and diamond mining. Fruit farms are another part of the economy – the largest citrus farm in the southern hemisphere, the Zedebiela Citrus estate, is nearby

The **Mokopane Tourism Association** (☎ 015-491 8458; www.mogalakwena.org.za; 97 Thabo Mbeki Dr; 7.30am-4.30pm Mon-Fri, 9am-noon Sat) is on Rte 101 and has plenty of local information.

You can get online at **Post Net** (☎ 015-491 1317; Crossing Mall, Thabo Mbeki Dr; per 15 min R10; 8.30am-5pm Mon-Fri, 8am-1pm Sat).

Sights
The **Arend Dieperink Museum** (☎ 015-491 9735; adult/student/child R3/1/1; 7.30am-4.30pm Mon-Fri), at the back of the Publicity Association, tells the story of the local people's resistance to the Voortrekkers.

Makapan's Caves (☎ 015-491 8458; adult/student R25/15), 23km northeast of town, is a palaeontological site of world significance, and has yielded bones of an early human, known as *Australopithecus africanus*, radiocarbon-dated to be three million years old. The Cave of Hearths records human development from the early Stone Age through to the Iron Age. In 1854, the caves were also the site of chief Makapan's resistance to the advancing Voortrekkers. You must pre-book visits at the Mokopane Tourism Association.

The **Game Breeding Centre** (☎ 015-491 4314; Thabo Mbeki Dr; adult/child R15/8; 8am-4pm Mon-Fri, 8am-6pm Sat & Sun), on Rte 101, is a breeding centre for the National Zoo in Pretoria and has a wide variety of native and exotic animals. You can drive through the reserve.

Sleeping & Eating
Thabaphaswa (☎ 015-491 4882, 012-346 3550; thabaphaswa@absamail.co.za; camp sites per person R40; hut per person bare/furnished R85/110;) If you don't mind roughing it a little, this unique property offers accommodation in climber's huts. The huts are small, but there are nearby patios with braai pits, plus open-air showers. If this sounds a little basic, there is also a furnished chalet for two people (R300). The area offers good rock-climbing routes, but you'll need all your own equipment. To get there, take the Percy Fyfe Rd from Mokopane. After 12km, turn at the 'Thabaphaswa Hiking and Mountains Bike Trail' sign. It's 2.1km to the gate and then another 1.3km to the homestead.

Game Breeding Centre (☎ 015-491 4314; Thabo Mbeki Dr; per person R120;) Possibly the best deal in town, the Game Breeding Centre has four large rooms in it's guesthouse, each with private bathroom. You also have the pleasure of watching breeding pairs of monkeys go about their daily affairs.

Koos Se Tonteldoos (☎ 015-491 4317, 082-979 0833; kobusmeyer@hotmail.com; 31 Thabo Mbeki Dr; s/d R180/250;) Certainly not your usual guesthouse, this place has rooms wedged into the back of an antique shop. Just be sure to keep your door closed lest the customers pop in and start buying up the bric-a-brac in your room. On the plus side, there's a kitchen for self-caterers and a braai in the yard out the back.

Protea Hotel – The Park (☎ 015-491 3101; www .proteahotels.com; Thabo Mbeki Dr; s/d with breakfast R400/550; ✷ ▯ ☒) This business-style option is part of a chain of hotels scattered all over this part of the country. This branch offers the plushest digs in town.

Oaks Pub & Grill (☎ 015-491 4355; Hooge St; mains R25-65; ✸ lunch & dinner) Adjoining Lonely Oak Hotel, this dark diner offers lively, bar-style eats (read: steaks and seafood) until midnight.

Getting There & Away

Translux (☎ 015-491 8457; www.translux.co.za; Thabo Mbeki Dr), next to the Wimpy restaurant, has buses to Polokwane (R45, one hour) and Jo'burg (R125, three hours).

Northern Link (☎ 015-491 4124; Thabo Mbeki Dr) buses run to Polokwane (R45, one hour) and Jo'burg (R105, three hours). You can buy tickets from Oasis Lodge Hotel on the main road through town – they stop here too.

Polokwane to Mokopane costs about R20 in a minibus taxi.

MOOKGOPHONG (NABOOMSPRUIT) & AROUND
☎ 014 / pop 12,000

Still plain old 'Naboom' to its Afrikaner residents, this innocuous little town sits at the hub of a rich agricultural area. Conservative, small-town attitudes prevail, but the local, home-distilled brandy (*mampoer*) injects a little life come the weekend.

The 3000-hectare **Nylsvley Nature Reserve** (☎ 014-743 1074; adult/child/vehicle R10/5/20; ✸ 6am-6pm), 20km south of Naboom, is one of the country's best places to see birds (there are a listed 426 species) and has a basic **camp site** (☎ 014-743 1074; camp sites R50). For the reserve, head 13km south on the N1 and turn east on to the road to Boekenhout for 8km.

Giraffes, kudus and zebras stroll through the grounds of **Inyathi Game Lodge** (☎ 014-743 2762; www.inyathigamelodge.co.za; tented camp sites/cottages per person R120/150; ☒). There are four-bed cottages and tented camps (without bedding) at this well-equipped lodge. Oh, and a pub too. It's 10km from Mookgophong.

For accomodation, try **Die Frei Gastehuis** (☎ 014-743 2981; guesthouse@mjvn.co.za; 80 Vierde St;

r per person with breakfast R200). It has a tropical garden and a big terrace for cocktail sipping. Head up Louis Trichardt St, turn right at the post office, keep going and it's on the left.

Getting There & Away

Translux (☎ 015-491 8457; www.translux.co.za) and **North Link Tours** (☎ 015-291 1867) buses stop in town; the fare to Polokwane is R80/40 (1¼ hours) respectively. Minibus taxis run to Mokopane (R15, 30 minutes).

MODIMOLLE (NYLSTROOM)
☎ 014 / pop 20,000

Modimolle (Place of the Spirits), a small town in cattle country, was named Nylstroom by Voortrekkers who thought they'd found the source of the Nile. After all, the river here seemed to fit the biblical description of the Nile: it was a river, it was in Africa and it had papyrus reeds growing along the banks.

Modimolle Info & Tourism (☎ 014-717 1818; www .modimolletourism.net; 31 Nelson Mandela Dr; ✸ 8am-4pm Mon-Fri) provides information and arranges tours. It's 1.3km east of Rte 101, along Nelson Mandela Dr.

Avuxeni Motel & Caravan Park (☎ 014-717 4005; www.avuxeni.com; camp sites R80, s/d R420/620; ✷ ☒), 3km north of Modimolle on Rte 101 to Mookgophong, has everything for the weary Voortrekker wishing to rest, water the horses, oil the wagon wheels and play putt-putt. You can camp, or stay in the attached motel.

Shangri-La (☎ 014-718 1600; www.shangri-la.co.za; s/d R450/620; ✷ ☒), 10km from the Kranskop tollgate, has thatched rondavels in a magnificent bush setting – it's perfect for escaping the hustle and bustle of the cities for a few days. This lodge is off Rte 33 on the Eersbewoond road.

BELA-BELA (WARMBATHS)
☎ 014 / pop 37,200

The small, soporific town of Bela-Bela (Warmbaths) has grown on the back of the hot springs discovered by the Tswana in the early 19th century. Around 22,000L of the warm stuff bubbles out of the earth every hour and there's no shortage of folk from the big cities to soak it up.

Bela-Bela Community Tourism Association (☎ 014-736 3694; www.belabelatourism.co.za; the Waterfront, Old Pretoria Rd; ✸ 8am-5pm Mon-Fri, 9am-2pm Sat)

LIMPOPO

is in the Waterfront development, on the main road into town.

The **hydro spa** (☎ 014-736 2200; www.aventura .co.za; Voortrekker St; adult/child R60/50, 5-10pm adult & child R40; ☉ 7am-4pm & 5-10pm) at the Aventura Resort is said to be the second biggest of its kind in the world and certainly sits at the centre of the Bela-Bela universe. Admission is cheaper in the evening.

Thaba Kwena Crocodile Farm (☎ 014-736 5059; tkwena@lantic.net; ☉ 9am-4pm Mon-Sat) is home to more than 10,000 crocodiles. These beasts are bred for their meat, which is served in restaurants worldwide. It's located about 8km north of Bela-Bela.

Sleeping & Eating

Aventura Spa Warmbaths (☎ 014-736 2200; www .aventura.co.za; Voortrekker St; camp sites per person R50, plus per tent R80, r with breakfast R800, 2-/4-bed chalet R590/900; ☒ ☒) Swimming-pool smells pervade every nook and cranny, but the town's headline resort offers comfortable rooms, camping, and self-contained chalets. Watersports are also on offer.

De Draai Gastehuis (☎ 014-736 4379, 082-820 0673; per person with breakfast R200) Located 10km north of town, this place offers comfortable, private rooms. It's not a very exciting place but there aren't many options around in this range. If you are coming from the south, turn right at the first set of traffic lights after the bridge (opposite the cinema) and keep going.

Elephant Springs Hotel (☎ 014-736 2101; www .avuxeni.com; 31 Sutter Rd; s/d with breakfast R455/670; ☒ ☒ ☒) A quick stroll from the spa, this is a typical resort-style hotel with plenty of colour, but not a whole lot of atmosphere.

O'Hagans (☎ 014-736 5068; Old Pretoria Rd; mains R30-60; ☉ 10am-10pm; ☒) Bring on the green paint and the Dublin car-boot-sale bric-a-brac. This Irish theme pub offers tasty food and decent beer. It's at the Waterfront, near the Tourism Association.

Dros (☎ 014-736 5223; cnr Marx & Potgieter Sts; mains R40-70; ☉ breakfast, lunch & dinner; ☒) One of the most popular restaurants in town, Dros offers your standard steak and seafood menu in stone and wrought iron surrounds. In summer, chill out on the patio where a lovely mist keeps things cool.

Getting There & Away

Translux (☎ 015-295 5548; www.translux.co.za) buses run through Bela-Bela en route between Jo'burg (R100, two hours) and Polokwane (R95, 2½ hours).

Minibus taxis run from behind the cinema on the corner of Marx and Potgeiter Sts to towns in the area, including Modimolle (R15, 20 minutes).

THE WATERBERG

The 150km-long Waterberg range, which makes up part of the Bushveld region, stretches from Thabazimbi in Limpopo's southwest up to the Lapalala River. It is a wild and inspirational place, with *sourveld* (a type of grassland) and bushveld etched by rivers.

Horse Riding Tours

The rolling terrain of the Waterberg Range is ideal for exploring on horseback, and several operators and lodges that can set you up with a steed. Each one charges around R180 to R250 for a two- to three-hour ride. Each of the following is located close to Vaalwater:

Equus Horse Safaris (☎ 014-721 0063; www.equus .co.za) Day rides only and no accommodation. Accepts cash payment only.

Horizon Horseback Adventures (☎ 014-755 4003; www.ridinginafrica.com) Offers the greatest variety of options, including an eight-day horse safari in the Dinaka Wildlife Reserve.

M'Solosolo (☎ 014-755 4106; msolosolo@telkomsa.net) A hunting lodge that also has horse riding.

Thabazimbi

☎ 014 / pop 10,300

Thabazimbi (Mountain of Iron) is 129km north of Rustenburg on Rte 510. Nearby is the imposing Kransberg (2100m), the highest peak of the Waterberg.

Ben Alberts Nature Reserve (☎ 014-777 1670; admission R15; ☉ 6am-6pm), about 7km south of town, has an abundance of wildlife and good wildlife-viewing vantage points. Accommodation in the reserve is in chalets (R170 for two people).

Marakele National Park

This rather isolated **national park** (☎ 014-777 1745; www.sanparks.org/parks/marakele; adult/child R60/30; ☉ 7.30am-6pm) is in the heart of the Waterberg's spectacular mountain country. Elephants, rhinos and many other large wildlife species, apart from lions, are now resident, with many having been relocated from Kruger National Park. The birdlife is prolific and includes the largest colony of the endangered Cape vulture *(Gyps coprotheres)* in the world (currently 800 breeding pairs).

The park can be reached from Thabazimbi by sealed road, but in the park itself, the roads deteriorate markedly and a 4WD is needed to access some of the best trails. From the north, there is a rough access road 6km past Vaalwater, over the spectacular Bakkers Pass.

The **booking office** (🕓 from 8am) is on the Thabazimbi–Alma road, 3km (on a limestone road) from where this road intersects with the Matlabas–Rooiberg road; entry is on the left and is signposted.

There is four-bed tented accommodation in the **Tlopi Tent Camp** (d R565, extras per person R104), located 17km from reception. These furnished tents, on the banks of the Matlabas River, have a bathroom, and kitchen with refrigerator and stove. There are communal barbecue facilities.

The park also offers some **tent sites** (2-person site R110, extras per person R38) at Bontle camping site.

Vaalwater

☎ 014 / pop 1100

A reasonable place to base yourself for exploration trips into the Waterberg, tiny Vaalwater is strung along Rte 33, around 60km northwest of Modimolle.

The Black Momba Centre has a Spar supermarket and the **Waterberg Tourism office** (☎ 014-755 3535; 🕓 9am-5pm Mon-Fri, 9am-1pm Sat), which can arrange tours and has Internet access (R40 per hour).

The only backpackers in this area, friendly **Zeederberg Cottage & Backpackers** (☎ 082-332 7088; www.zeederbergs.co.za; camp sites R30, dm/s/d R60/200/300; 🖥), is just off Rte 33, about 2km past Vaalwater (coming from Modimolle), behind the Spar supermarket. It is conveniently situated halfway between Lapalala and Marakele.

Big Five Restaurant (☎ 014-755 3567; 🕓 breakfast, lunch & dinner), on the highway in Vaalwater, is a good bet for pizza, pasta and burgers. In the evening it will be the only eating place open.

The refreshing **Bush Stop Café** (☎ 014-755 3508; Black Momba Centre; 🕓 breakfast & lunch) serves organic products, vegetarian dishes, salads and sandwiches. They also have a second-hand bookshop.

Lapalala Wilderness

The grunting hippos, sweaty blue wildebeests and tank-like rhinos of **Lapalala Wilderness** (☎ 014-755 4395; lapalala@parksgroup.co.za; 🕓 7am-6pm) can keep visitors enthralled for several days. This 25,600-hectare wilderness area also sports zebra and twenty species of antelope, not to mention more than 270 species of birds. Unfortunately, unless you stay here, you can only come as a day visitor.

Ask the rangers to point out the unusual termite mounds built under layers in the sandstone. It appears that ants have managed to lift the sandstone slabs and build beneath them, earning them the name 'Arnold Schwarzenegger ants'. Lapalala is famed for its history of conservation: thousands of children, often the disadvantaged, have gone through wilderness conservation courses.

Small self-catering bush camps are scattered through the wilderness; accommodation ranges from R180 to R220 per person. There are cooking facilities but you must bring your own supplies. There are midweek specials; book in advance as Lapalala is popular.

The **Rhino Cultural Museum** (☎ 014-755 4428; adult/child R5/2; 🕓 9am-5pm Tue-Sun), by the Melkrivier school, offers a detailed insight into all things rhinoceros. The lone black rhino kept here is fed daily at 4pm (admission adult/child R20/10).

Lapalala Wilderness is north of Modimolle, in the heart of the Waterberg. From Modimolle take Rte 33 to Vaalwater and from there head in the direction of Melkrivier. Take the turn-off to Melkrivier school 40km from Vaalwater, and continue for 25km to Lapalala.

SOUTPANSBERG

The Soutpansberg region incorporates the most northern part of South Africa, scraping southern Zimbabwe. The rainforest of the Soutpansberg is strikingly lush compared with the hot, dry lowveld to the north. The N1 towns of Makhado (Louis Trichardt) and Musina are here, as is the ancient Venda region to the east.

LIMPOPO

MAKHADO (LOUIS TRICHARDT)
☎ 015 / pop 90,000
Scruffy Makhado is a little hard on the eyes – a stark contrast to the verdant countryside that surrounds it. Treat the town as a springboard to some worthwhile country lodges, nature reserves and hiking trails in the nearby mountains.

Information
ABSA (cnr Songozwi Rd & Krogh Sts) Has an ATM and exchange facilities.

PCS Computers (☎ 015-516 4122; 84 Krogh St; per 30min R12; 8am-5pm Mon-Fri, 9am-2pm Sat) Internet access.

Police station (☎ 015-519 4300; Krogh St)

Soutpansberg Tourist Office (☎ 015-516 0040; www.tourismsoutpansberg.co.za; Songozwi Rd 8am-4.30pm Mon-Fri, 8am-noon Sat)

Activities
The spectacular mountains are the major drawcard here, boasting an extraordinary diversity of flora and fauna, including 615 of South Africa's 900 bird species. For a reliable tour operator, contact **Face Africa** (☎ 015-516 2076; faceafrika@mweb.co.za; per day R1200, maximum 4 people) or **Travel Africa Trails** (☎ 082-959 0102; africa@lantic.net; per day R1400, maximum 4 people).

Sleeping
There are several options in Makhado itself, but the best way to soak up the Soutpansberg is to stay in the hills above town – ask the tourist office for a map.

Makhado Municipal Caravan Park (☎ 015-519 3025; www.caravanparks.co.za/makhado; Grobler St; camp sites per person R45) A central camping option.

Louis Trichardt Lodge (☎ 015-516 2222; www.ltt lodge.co.za; Hlanganani St; s/d R200/270; ☐ ☒) This welcoming place on the main road has some basic rooms, kitchenettes and a braai area.

Mountain View Hotel (☎ 015-5177031; www.moun tainviewhotel.co.za; s/d with breakfast R275/385) This resort-style place, on the road to Musina, has clipped gardens, charming staff and the (often empty) Merry Monk pub. The rooms, however, are a little dowdy.

Ultimate Guest House (☎ 015-517 7005; ultimate gh@lantic.net; s/d with breakfast R310/410; ☒) With buckets of quirky character and colourful, individually styled rooms, this beautifully remote place prides itself on its convivial at-

mosphere and good nature. It's 10km from the centre – turn left 100m after Mountain View, head 1.6km along the dirt track and it'll be on your right.

Eating
Cafe d'Art (☎ 015-516 5760; 129 Krogh St; mains R20-50; breakfast, lunch & dinner) Whether kicking back in the garden listening to the chirruping crickets or sitting inside among the African paintings and pottery, this is a top spot for lazy breakfasts, lunches and light dinners.

Ricky's Takeaway (☎ 015-516 0414; 36 Boabab St; 8am-8pm Mon-Sat) This place gets absolutely packed with people trying to get hold of locally famous sausages, burgers and sandwiches.

Elephant & Castle (☎ 072-895 6541; mains R20-35; lunch & dinner; ☒) If you're heading south, save your appetite for this cosy inn, 13km out of town on the N1.

Getting There & Away
The **Louis Trichardt Travel Agency** (☎ 015-516 5042; 8am-1pm & 2-4pm Mon-Fri, 9-11am Sat), down an alley off Burger St (opposite Bradlows), is the local agent for Greyhound and Translux buses. Most buses linking Makhado with Jo'burg (R180, 5½ hours) and Harare (R375, 11 hours) stop by the Caltex petrol station on the corner of the N1 and Baobab St.

The train station is at the southwestern end of Kruger St. The **Bosvelder** (☎ 086-000 8888) stops here and links Makhado with Jo'burg (1st/2nd class R150/105, 11 hours) and Musina (1st/2nd class R70/40, 3½ hours).

The minibus taxi rank is in the Shoprite supermarket car park off Burger St, a block northeast of Songozwi Rd. Destinations and fares from Makhado include Thohoyandou (R20, 1½ hours), Polokwane (R20, 1¼ hours) and Musina (R30, 1½ hours).

AROUND MAKHADO
Soutpansberg Hiking Trails
The two-day 20.5km **Hanglip Trail** includes a climb up a 1719m peak; it begins at Hanglip forest station. Take precautions against malaria, bilharzia and ticks. Overnight accommodation is in huts and there's a trail fee of R40 per person per day, which includes a good walking map. Contact the **Soutpansberg**

Tourist Office (opposite) for more information and details of how to make reservations.

Perched in the clouds, **Lesheba Wilderness** (☎ 015-593 0076; www.lesheba.co.za; rondavel R250, r with full-board per person R850; 🖳 🖳) is an excellent hideaway based on a Venda-style village, recreated with the help of acclaimed Venda artist, Noria Mabasa. Surrounded by wildlife, including rare brown hyenas and leopards, and with greenery supplied by 340 tree species, the resort offers self-catering accommodation in rondavels, or a full-board option in bedrooms with cosy fireplaces and outdoor showers. It's 36km west of Makhado on Rte 522.

Lajuma Mountain Retreat (☎ 015-593 0352; www .lajuma.com; bungalow/lodge per person R130/150) is 7km off Rte 522 between Makhado and Vivo on the flanks of Letjuma (Soutpansberg's highest peak). This beautiful region is a hiker's paradise and there are archaeological sites, rare animals and a host of outdoor activities. A number of sites have self-catering accommodation, from basic bungalows to a more opulent lodge. Call ahead to check road conditions.

Ben Lavin Nature Reserve

Although somewhat neglected, this **reserve** (☎ 015-516 4534; www.satis.co.za/benlavin; adult/child R30/10; ⌚ 6am-6pm) is still worth visiting for its walking and mountain bike trails. The reserve contains 240 bird species, as well as giraffes, zebras and jackals. A range of **accommodation** (camp sites per person R40; d hut R215, per extra person R68; d lodge R265, per extra person R80) is available.

Take the N1 south from Makhado for about 10km, then take the Fort Edward turn-off to the left. After about 3km, you'll see the entrance gate on your left.

MUSINA

☎ 015 / pop 20,000

The closest town to the Zimbabwe border, Musina is a hot, dusty settlement with a frontier feel to it. The town grew around the copper mines, which operated from 1905 until the early 1990s. Just as important is the still-active DeBeers Venetia diamond mine, the second largest in the southern hemisphere. Away from the mines the town centre is a sleepy place, but there are moves

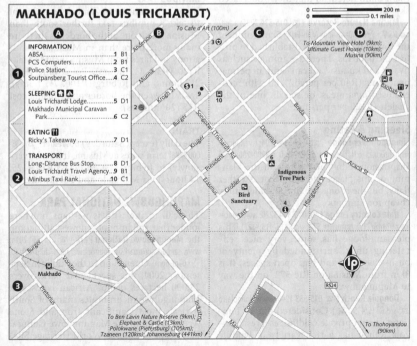

MAKHADO (LOUIS TRICHARDT)

0 ——————— 200 m
0 ——————— 0.1 miles

INFORMATION
ABSA....................................1 B1
PCS Computers.......................2 B1
Police Station.......................3 C1
Soutpansberg Tourist Office....4 C2

SLEEPING 🏠 🛈
Louis Trichardt Lodge..............5 D1
Makhado Municipal Caravan
  Park....................................6 C2

EATING 🍴
Ricky's Takeaway 7 D1

TRANSPORT
Long-Distance Bus Stop...........8 D1
Louis Trichardt Travel Agency..9 B1
Minibus Taxi Rank..................10 C1

To Café d'Art (100m)

To Mountain View Hotel (9km);
Ultimate Guest House (10km);
Musina (90km)

Indigenous
Tree Park

Bird
Sanctuary

Makhado

To Ben Lavin Nature Reserve (9km);
Elephant & Castle (13km);
Polokwane (Pietersburg) (105km);
Tzaneen (120km); Johannesburg (441km)

To Thohoyandou
(90km)

R524

LIMPOPO

to promote Musina as a regional centre in its own right, along with nearby tourist attractions such as the excellent Mapungubwe National Park.

Information

ABSA (☎ 015-534 0746; 6 National Rd) Has change facilities and an ATM. It is on the N1 as it passes through the centre of town.

Computer Shop Internet Café (☎ 015-534 1206; Palm Centre; per hr R20; ☼ 8.15am-5.30pm Mon-Fri, 9am-1pm Sat)

Limpopo Travel (☎ 015-534 2220; limpopotrav@lantic .net; National Rd; ☼ 8.30am-4.30pm Mon-Fri) Can help with all travel bookings. It's near the KFC.

Musina Tourism (☎ 015-534 3500; www.golimpopo .com; National Rd; ☼ 8.30am-4pm Mon-Fri) In a thatched hut on the way into town on the N1 from Polokwane.

Sights

Giant baobab (*Adansonia digitata*) trees characterise the region and it is on the road south of here that you will see some of the grandest – the largest in the country, near Sagole, is 3000 years old! Legend has it that the gods inverted the trees, which used to roam unhindered, so that their roots faced skywards.

Musina Nature Reserve (☎ 015-534 3235; adult/car R5/7; ☼ 8.30am-4pm Mon-Fri), 5km south of the town off the N1, was established to protect the baobabs. There are animals such as nyalas and kudus. You can camp in permanent tents (R40 per person), all with reed-enclosed *lapa* areas, or stay in one of the chalets (R120 per person).

Sleeping & Eating

Limpopo River Lodge (☎ 015-534 0204; riverlodge@ limpopo.co.za; 6 National Rd; s R125-160, d R200-280; ☒) Inspiration didn't play a role in the planning of this place, and the décor is rather flaky, but the rooms are fine and mercifully cheap for Limpopo.

Ilala Country Lodge (☎ 015-534 3220; www.places .co.za/html/2175.html; Rte 572; s/d R315/415; ☒) This pleasant lodge has some very nice self-catering units, surrounded by plenty of bush-style hush and big, open spaces. It is 8km from Musina on Rte 572, on the way to Mapungubwe.

Dongola Ranch (☎ 015-533 1948; www.dongola.co .za; s/d R315/415; ☒) Considered one of Limpopo's better private wildlife reserves, Dongola Ranch has a rich variety of wildlife species, including white rhinos, giraffes, leopards and hyenas. It's on the road to Mapungubwe, about 45km out of Musina.

Buffalo Ridge Spur (☎ 015-534 1127; National Rd; mains R30-60; ☼ breakfast, lunch & dinner; ☒) Corporate cowboy attitude and large platters of steak and ribs feature prominently at this chain restaurant, located near the tourist office.

Getting There & Away

The Zimbabwean border at Beitbridge, 14km north of Musina, is open 24 hours. If you are coming from Zimbabwe, there is a large taxi rank on the South African side of the border, 1km from the crossing itself. For detailed information on crossing the border into Zimbabwe, see p628.

BUS

Translux (☎ 015-295 5548; www.translux.co.za) buses on the Jo'burg-Harare route stop at the Limpopo River Lodge (left). Jo'burg costs R190 (7½ hours) and Harare costs R250 (10 hours).

MINIBUS TAXI

If you're coming from Zimbabwe and want to take a minibus taxi further south than Musina, catch one at the border as there are many more there than in Musina. Destinations and fares from Musina include Makhado (R30, 1½ hours), Polokwane (R40, 2½ hours) and Jo'burg (R100, 7½ hours). Taxis between the border and Musina cost R15 (20 minutes).

TRAIN

The daily (except Saturday) **Bosvelder** (☎ 086-000 8888) terminates at Musina. It travels (very slowly) to Jo'burg (1st/2nd class R185/125, 14 hours) via Makhado and Polokwane.

MAPUNGUBWE NATIONAL PARK

The call of the wild is perhaps nowhere louder than in Limpopo's newest attraction, the **Mapungubwe National Park** (☎ 015-534 2014; www.sanparks.org/parks/mapungubwe; adult/child R60/30; ☼ 6am-6pm). Opened up to the public in September 2004, this spectacular park covers 28,000 hectares of hot African landscape. Mapungubwe incorporates many of South Africa's most significant Iron and Stone Age sites within the Mapungubwe Cultural Landscape (a Unesco World Heritage Site)

LIMPOPO

and boasts populations of all of the Big Five, with almost unparalleled opportunities for wildlife-spotting. Mapungubwe will only improve if plans to incorporate it into an 800,000-hectare Trans-Frontier Conservation Area that will stretch into Botswana and Zimbabwe come to fruition.

The park is as much about history as wildlife. In April 1933, while digging on Mapungubwe Hill, researchers uncovered an 11th-century grave site containing ornaments, jewellery, bowls and amulets, much of it covered in gold. The most spectacular of these Iron Age pieces was a small gold plated rhino. Apartheid, however, kept this discovery under wraps, as the old government attempted to suppress any historical information that would have proven cultural sophistication.

The hill offers an excellent insight into Zimbabwe civilisation and many of the artefacts can be seen in an on-site museum. Short walks (R30) and fully-catered, three-day trails (R1800) to the major sites are already available.

At the Leokwe Rest Camp you can camp (R70), or stay in opulent, two-bed **chalets** (R400; ☒ ☒).

The park is at the confluence of the Shashe and Limpopo rivers, north of the Musina to Pontdrift road. It's a 60km drive from Musina on Rte 572.

VENDA REGION

Perhaps the most enigmatic section of the Soutpansberg region, this is the traditional homeland of the Venda people, who moved to the area from modern-day Zimbabwe at the start of the 18th century. Long neglected under the apartheid regime, the Venda region is a world away from the South Africa of uptown Jo'burg; here even a short diversion from the freeway takes you through an Africa of mist-clad hilltops, dusty streets and mud huts. A land where myth and legend continue to play a major role in everyday life, Venda is peppered with lakes and forests that are of great religious significance, and the region continues to support a thriving artistic heritage.

Thohoyandou & Sibasa

☎ 015 / pop 50,000

Created as the capital of the apartheid-era Venda Homeland, the city of Thohoyan-

dou (Elephant Head) blends some impressively functional town-planning with a healthy dose of African chaos – matching a looming shopping centre and adjacent casino resort with all the push-and-shove of the busy backstreet marketplace. The adjacent town of Sibasa is a few kilometres north. Most public transport leaves from Sibasa.

Thohoyandou is an easy 65km drive to Kruger's Punda Maria Gate, and a good entry/exit point if you plan to explore the park's far north.

Standard Bank (Mphephu St), on the main road through Thohoyandou, has ATMs. Tours to nearby sights, including Lake Fundudzi, can be arranged by a local guide, **Beth Mashawana**

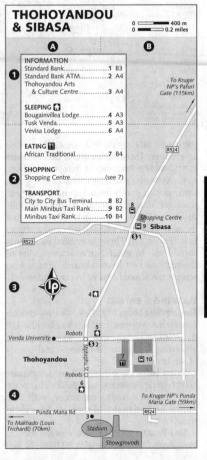

THOHOYANDOU & SIBASA

0 —— 400 m
0 —— 0.2 miles

INFORMATION
Standard Bank..........................1 B3
Standard Bank ATM..................2 A4
Thohoyandou Arts
& Culture Centre...................3 A4

SLEEPING
Bougainvillea Lodge.................4 A3
Tusk Venda............................5 A3
Vevisa Lodge..........................6 A4

EATING
African Traditional...................7 B4

SHOPPING
Shopping Centre...................(see 7)

TRANSPORT
City to City Bus Terminal.........8 B2
Main Minibus Taxi Rank..........9 B2
Minibus Taxi Rank..................10 B4

To Kruger
NP's Pafuri
Gate (115km)

R524

Shopping Centre
9 Sibasa
1
R523

Venda University

Robots
Thohoyandou
Robots

To Kruger NP's Punda
Maria Gate (59km)

Punda Maria Rd
To Makhado (Louis
Trichardt) (70km)
Stadium
Showgrounds

LIMPOPO

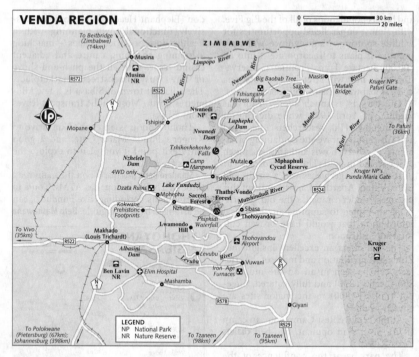

VENDA REGION

(☎ 072-401 1832; day trip for 4 from R350), as well as through **Thohoyandou Arts & Culture Centre** (☎ 082-401 9756; Punda Maria Rd, Thohoyandou; ❧ 6am-6pm). As well as selling crafts (some good, some not so good) from around the region, manager Mashudu Dima also organises full-day tours (R350, minimum three people) that include transport, village visits and a trip to Lake Fundudzi. Those interested in the arts should ask to meet Noria Mabasa, one of the region's best-known female artists, who sculpts traditional figures in clay and wood.

SLEEPING & EATING

Bougainvillea Lodge (☎ 015-962 4064; www.bougain villalodge.com; Mphephu St; s/d with breakfast R250/330) As promised by the name, there is plenty of blooming bougainvillea here – and plenty of smiles too.

   Vevisa Lodge (☎ 015-962 5252; vevisa@iafrica.com; 758 Mphephu St; s/d with breakfast R295/330) This place opts for mock-traditional décor, with fake mud walls and thatched roofs, and has clean rooms.

   Tusk Venda (☎ 015-962 4600; www.tusk-resorts.co .za; Mphephu St; s/d with breakfast R515/710; ❧ ⚊)

A little slice of Vegas in the heart of Venda, this casino resort looks rather incongruous among the local hustle and bustle. It offers plenty of trimmings and plenty of ways to fritter away a penny or two.

   All the usual fast-food establishments are represented in the shopping centre. **African Traditional** (buffet R30; ❧ breakfast, lunch & dinner), in the heart of the centre, offers something a little different, including a good selection of local favourites: chicken heart, chicken gizzard and lamb stew.

GETTING THERE & AWAY

City to City (☎ 015-295 5548; www.translux.co.za) buses run from a terminal just up Rte 524 from the centre of Sibasa. They leave every morning at 8.30am for Jo'burg (R100, 8½ hours) and Pretoria (R100, 7½ hours).

   The main minibus taxi rank is in Sibasa, on the corner of the road from Thohoyandou. Destinations and fares include Makhado (R20, 1½ hours) and Jo'burg (R100, nine hours).

   In Thohoyandou, minibus taxis congregate in the car park of the shopping centre near the Tusk Venda. The fare to Sibasa is R3.50.

Nwanedi National Park

The dry northern side of the Soutpansberg provides an extremely scenic backdrop to **Nwanedi National Park** (☎ 015-539 0723; adult/vehicle R10/15; ⏰ 6am-6pm), although it's a contrast to the Venda's lush landscapes. The vegetation is mainly mopani and mixed woodland and the major walk in the park is to the scenic **Tshihovhohovho Falls**. You can hire canoes for R50.

The park has **camp sites** (per person R20, plus per tent R50), and four-person **rondavels** (R350). Basic supplies are available and there's a fully licensed restaurant.

You can reach Nwanedi park from Thohoyandou, entering at the Nwanedi gate, though the road is scenic there is a good chance of getting lost, and there are several kilometres of rough dirt road. It is simpler to come via Tshipise and enter from the west. Tshipise is the nearest place you're able to buy fuel.

Nwanedi also makes a good combination with northern Kruger National Park. A possible itinerary is to head from Thohoyandou to Kruger's Punda Maria Gate, exit Kruger via the park's northernmost Pafuri Gate, then continue on to Nwanedi and Tshipise.

Lake Fundudzi & Around

This lake is a sacred site, as its water is believed to have come from the great sea that covered the earth before land was created. The python god, who holds an important place in the rites of the Venda's matriarchal culture, lives here.

The lake is 35km northwest of Thohoyandou, but you can't visit it without permission from the lake's custodians, the Netshiavha tribe. The easiest way to get permission is to have a tour organised from Thohoyandou or Makhado. Remember that when you approach the lake you must do so with proper respect; turn your back to it, bend over, and view it from between your legs. And try not to look silly doing it.

Near the lake is **Thathe-Vondo Forest** (admission free; ⏰ 8am-4pm Mon-Fri, 8am-5pm Sat & Sun), with a (usually) drivable dirt track leading to a section of Holy Forest (13km) and a pleasant viewpoint (17km), with vistas over Lake Fundudzi.

SLEEPING

Camp Mangwele (☎ 072-631 6670; camp sites per person R40) North of Lake Fundudzi, this camping ground is situated within the rugged country of the Soutpansberg, and is accessible only by a 4WD with high ground clearance. There are hot showers, braai facilities and firewood; many activities, including

---

SAVING LAKE FUNDUDZI

The importance of Lake Fundudzi cannot be underestimated. The traditional custodians of the lake, the Netshiavha (People of the Pool), consider it a holy place for the burial of their dead.

For scientists, the lake is also special as it's one of South Africa's few natural freshwater lakes. Its creation, they believe, came 20,000 years ago when a rock slide blocked the path of a river, causing the lake to rise behind it.

Recent years, however, have seen quite an unholy degradation of the lake. By the late 1990s, almost half of the catchment land around the lake – virgin forest and grassland – had been cut down to make way for tree and fruit plantations. This led to erosion, deterioration in water quality and loss of plant and animal species.

Access to the lake has long been a privilege granted by the Netshiavha. This was undermined in the mid-1990s when a road was constructed right down to the edge of the lake, giving open access to anyone with a vehicle. Soon picnickers arrived and rubbish began piling up on the lake shore. The current chief of the Netshiavha suggests that the loss of traditional tribal values has contributed to the degradation of the lake.

In recent years the chief launched a campaign to protect the lake. The Netshiavha, as well as neighbouring tribes, have implemented new laws to limit land use around the lake and mitigate the effects of tourism. Long-term management strategies are being hashed out with government bodies, the Mondi Wetlands Project (www.wetland.org.za) and the World Wide Fund for Nature (WWF).

LIMPOPO

rock climbing and mountain biking, are within range of the camp. There is also an on-site **tour guide** (☎ 082-768 8801).

To get to Camp Mangwele, head first to Makhado (not the former Louis Trichardt, but the smaller town to the north). Some 2km northeast of Makhado, turn north towards Musekwa. Follow this road for 21.7km, then turn right (east) and follow the road towards Tshixwadza. After 9km there is a sign indicating Mangwele Pothole (slightly worrying in itself); follow this road south for 1km until you reach the camp.

VALLEY OF THE OLIFANTS

These days, the Valley of the Olifants is devoid of any pachyderms, though it can still lend a feeling of the exotic. The region is culturally very rich, being the traditional home of the Tsonga-Shangaan and Lobedu peoples. It is also popular for a north–south traverse through Kruger National Park or a visit to one of the many private wildlife reserves in the Hoedspruit area (p485). The main town of Tzaneen, and the pretty village of Haenertsburg, in the Letaba Valley, make pleasant bases for trips into the scenic Modjadji and Magoebaskloof areas.

LETABA VALLEY

The Letaba Valley is east of Polokwane, between two chunks of the former Lebowa Homeland. The valley is subtropical and lush, with tea plantations and crops of tropical fruits below, and forested hills above.

At Haenertsburg the road splits in two, with the Rte 71 reaching Tzaneen via the steep Magoebaskloof Pass, while the Rte 528 runs along the more gentle George's Valley. Rte 71 is arguably the better drive, and there are plenty of places where you can get out and go for short hikes signposted from the road (see Magoebaskloof Pass, opposite).

Haenertsburg

☎ 015 / pop 300

Tucked into green peaks reminiscent of the Scottish Highlands, sedate little Haenertsburg offers an oasis of rural hush for those wanting to escape from it all. Established during the 1887 gold rush, the vil-

lage appears to have kept a little aside for a rainy day, retaining an affluent, suburban atmosphere.

INFORMATION

Magoebaskloof Tourist Association (☎ 015-276 4972; www.magoebaskloof.com; Rissik St; ☼ 8am-5pm Mon-Fri, 9am-noon Sat & Sun) has plenty of information and offers **Internet access** (per min R1). At the time of research there were no ATMs in town. Doubtless this will change but be prepared anyway.

ACTIVITIES

There are several good hiking trails near Haenertsburg, including the 11km **Louis Changuion Trail**, which has spectacular views.

Haenertsburg is also well endowed with operators offering outdoorsy activities.

Filly's Way (☎ 082-294 8349; michelle@slm.co.za), 2km west of town on Rte 71, offers one-hour (R110), half-day (R380) and two-day (R1950) horse trail rides.

Thaba-Metsi (☎ 083-866 1546; thabmetsi@mweb .co.za) runs adventure trips in the area, including quad biking, kloofing (canyoning), rafting and mountain biking.

The **Growth Centre** (☎ 015-276 2712, 072-277 4809), 6km east of town on Rte 71 towards Tzaneen, offers holistic health remedies, reflexology and meditation. It is signposted on the road as Stanford Lake Lodge.

SLEEPING & EATING

Bali Will Will (☎ 015-276 2212; glmccomb@absamail .co.za; camp sites per person R40, s/d with breakfast R200/370; ▯ ▧) This pleasant farmhouse offers several beautifully furnished guestrooms. There is also an adjacent cottage (per person R130) with more space. It's 2.4km out of town (follow the signs from Rte 71), but staff will pick you up from the village if you phone ahead.

Livingstone Place (☎ 015-276 5020, 082-892 5326; www.livingstoneplace.co.za; per person R150) These fairytale twee, Swiss-style chalets, 1km from town on Rte 71, are great value for keen self-caterers.

Magoebaskloof Hotel (☎ 015-276 5400; www.mag oebaskloof.co.za; Rte 71; s/d with breakfast R495/690; ▧ ▯ ▧) This business-standard place boasts monkeys, top views, plenty of trimmings and a Dutch-style pub for post-activity rehydration. It is 10km out of town, on Rte 71 towards Tzaneen.

Red Plate (☎ 083-305 2852; light meals R20-50; ⊙ breakfast, lunch & dinner) Next to the Tourist Association, this café has a zen quality about it, though its menu veers more towards the run-of-the-mill sandwich and pasta crowd.

GETTING THERE & AWAY
Beyer's Bus Service (☎ 015-307 5959, 082-434 3449) stops at Picasso's restaurant on Rte 71 on Friday and Sunday en route between Pretoria and Tzaneen. Fares from Haenertsburg include Tzaneen (R80, 30 minutes), Polokwane (R80, 40 minutes) and Pretoria (R180, 5½ hours).

Magoebaskloof Pass
The Magoebaskloof is the escarpment on the edge of the highveld, and the road here drops quickly down to Tzaneen and the lowveld, passing through plantations and large tracts of thick indigenous forest.

The high summer rainfall means there are a number of waterfalls in the area, including **Debengeni Falls** in the De Hoek State Forest. To get here, turn west off Rte 71 at Bruphy Sawmills.

Two recommended walking trails are the two-day, 21km **Debengeni Falls Trail** and the three-day, 40km **Dokolewa Waterfall Trail**. Overnight stays for the Dokolewa Waterfall Trail are in huts near waterfalls and streams. To book huts on these trails, contact **Komatiland Forestry Association** (☎ 012-481 3615; ecotour@safcol.co.za).

The Wheelbarrow (☎ 015-305-3039; www.tzaneen .com/thewheelbarrow; meals R30-60; ⊙ 9am-4.30pm) is a great place to break up the road trip between Haenertsburg and Tzaneen. You can get good country breakfasts plus locally produced jams and juices. An avocado festival is held here in July. It's on the bottom stretch of Rte 71, near the junction with Rte 36.

TZANEEN & AROUND
☎ 015 / pop 81,000
At the hub of a rich fruit-growing area, Tzaneen, the largest town near the Letaba Valley and the second-largest in Limpopo, is perhaps best known for its avocados and mangoes – be sure to try some. Surrounded by lush, subtropical hills, this is a pleasant spot with plenty of quiet corners. At the heart of this region, it also makes a convenient base for exploring the Valley of the Olifants.

Information
ABSA (Danie Joubert St) Has an ATM and exchange facilities.
First National Bank (Danie Joubert St) ATM and exchange facilities.
Limpopo Parks & Tourism Board (☎ 015-307 3582; www.tzaneeninfo.com; Rte 71; ⊙ 8am-4.30pm Mon-Fri) On the Rte 71 towards Phalaborwa, it has plenty of useful information on the region. A craft centre is also located here.
Post Net (☎ 083-639 9685; Ground fl, Tzaneen Crossing Mall; ⊙ 8am-5pm Mon-Fri, 8.30am-12.30pm Sat; per hr R20) Offers Internet access.
Post office (Lannie Lane) Behind Danie Joubert St.
Tzaneen Hospital (☎ 015-307 4475; Hospital St) Southeast of the centre.

Sights & Activities
Tzaneen Museum (☎ 015-307 5258; Agatha St; donation welcome; ⊙ 9am-4pm Mon-Fri, 9am-noon Sat) has an interesting collection of Tsonga cultural artefacts including a Rain Queen ceremonial drum, and looks back at 2000 years of tribal pottery and art.

There are plenty of chances to bike, climb or hike in the nearby mountains. For adventure trips, call Thaba-Metsi (opposite).

Sleeping
Satvik Backpackers Village (☎ 015-307 3920; satvik@ pixie.co.za; George's Valley Rd; camp sites R40, dm/d R70/180) Less technicolour tacky than many backpackers, Satvik offers a more rustic blend of budget accommodation, with a farm setting and beds in old workers' cottages.

Half Human Backpackers (☎ 015-304 3230; half humanback@telkomsa.co.za; George's Valley Rd; camp sites R40, dm/s/d R70/120/180) Out in the bush, this backpackers was just getting underway when we visited. They have a bar and accommodation in small rondavels that circle a braai area. It's 20km east of Tzaneen on the road to Phalaborwa.

Arborpark Lodge (☎ 015-307 1831; arborpark@ mweb.co.za; cnr Soetdoring & Geelhout Sts; s/d with breakfast R220/250; ⊠) This motel-style offering has a laundromat, a pub, a good restaurant and functional rooms. It's quite a way from the centre, but staff will collect you if you call ahead.

Fairview River Lodge (☎ 015-307 2679; www.fair viewlodge.co.za; s/d with breakfast R350/510; ⊠ ▢ ▣) One of the town's swankiest options, this thatched, four-star place has some very comfortable self-catering chalets and a leafy tropical garden. If you ask, there are also some basic rooms for R200.

LIMPOPO

Eating

The dining scene is painfully ordinary.

Casa Blanca (☎ 015-307 2792; 9 Danie Joubert St; mains R30-60; ☽ lunch & dinner; ☒) Casa Blanca is a popular restaurant with a mishmash of Italian food, grill and seafood. It also offers a few vegetarian dishes.

High Grove Lodge (☎ 015-307 7242; highgrove@ tzaneen.co.za; Agatha Rd; mains R40-60; ☽ breakfast, lunch & dinner) Probably the classiest place in town, it serves decent steaks, salads and a continental breakfast. It's also an upmarket hotel (single/double rooms R370/450) with 18 rooms and a pub.

Butterfield Bread (Danie Joubert St; ☽ breakfast & lunch) This reliable bakery chain is a good spot for fresh bread and tasty treats.

Tino's Pizzeria (☎ 015-307 1893; Agatha St; mains R25-45; ☽ lunch & dinner; ☒) This place has been around for a while now and the pizzas are still good.

Addison's (☎ 015-307 6261; cnr Soetdoring & Geelhout Sts; mains R25-60; ☽ lunch & dinner; ☒) In Arborpark Lodge, this is a lively little eatery, with a decent pub in which to wash your food down afterwards.

Getting There & Away

North Link Tours buses stop at the rear of the Letaba Boulevard shopping centre. They run to Jo'burg (R160, six hours) four days a week. You can book tickets at the **Caltex petrol station** (☎ 015-305 2424; Danie Joubert St).

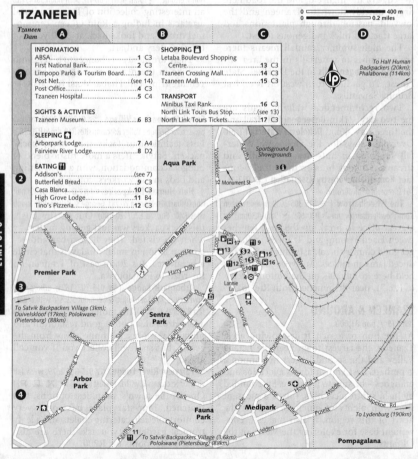

TZANEEN

INFORMATION
ABSA..1 C3
First National Bank.........................2 C3
Limpopo Parks & Tourism Board.......3 C2
Post Net....................................(see 14)
Post Office.....................................4 C3
Tzaneen Hospital............................5 C4

SIGHTS & ACTIVITIES
Tzaneen Museum............................6 B3

SLEEPING
Arborpark Lodge.............................7 A4
Fairview River Lodge.......................8 D2

EATING
Addison's...................................(see 7)
Butterfield Bread............................9 C3
Casa Blanca.................................10 C3
High Grove Lodge.........................11 B4
Tino's Pizzeria..............................12 C3

SHOPPING
Letaba Boulevard Shopping
Centre.......................................13 C3
Tzaneen Crossing Mall..................14 C3
Tzaneen Mall...............................15 C3

TRANSPORT
Minibus Taxi Rank........................16 C3
North Link Tours Bus Stop.........(see 13)
North Link Tours Tickets...............17 C3

Translux buses run to Pretoria (R140, 4½ hours), Jo'burg (R140, 5½ hours) and Phalaborwa (R100, one hour). Book tickets at the Limpopo Parks & Tourism Board (p505).

Most minibus taxis depart from a rank behind the Tzaneen Mall. Destinations and fares from Tzaneen include Duivelskloof (R7, 15 minutes) and Haenertsburg (R20, 30 minutes).

Duivelskloof
☎ 015 / pop 25,000

This small town is in the wooded hills north of Tzaneen. The name refers to the devilishly hard time the early European settlers had getting their wagons up and down the hills. Nearby is the large, black community of GaKgapane. On the road to GaKgapane, look out for the **Giant Baobab Tree** (☎ 015-309-9030; Sunland Nursery), which is probably the only tree in the world to have a bar inside of it. Tea, scones and beer are served to a maximum of 15 people at a time.

Tourist information is available from the **municipality** (☎ 015-309 9246; Botha St; 8.30am-4.30pm Mon-Fri).

Hotel Imp Inn (☎ 015-309 9253; Botha St; s/d R240/390) is a colonial-style villa housing a rather spartan hotel. It's a decent central option, though you'll find better-value in Tzaneen.

Minibus taxis depart from near the Spar on Botha St. The fare to Tzaneen is R6 (15 minutes).

Ndzalama Wildlife Reserve
Based on Ndzalama, a spectacular, phallic rock formation, this **reserve** (☎ 015-307 3065; ndzalama@pixie.co.za; 8.30am-6pm), near Letsitele, is host to four of the Big Five (everything but buffalo is represented). No day visitors are allowed into the reserve (you have to stay at least one night).

Self-catering **accommodation** (2-bed chalet from R400) is available. You must book in advance.

To get to the reserve from Tzaneen or Phalaborwa, take Rte 71. The southern turn-off is 9km north of Gravelotte; turn right and follow the dirt road for 12km to the reserve. The northern turn-off is 28km east of Tzaneen; at this turn-off, go left. After 16km, turn right. The reserve is 4km further on.

Modjadji Nature Reserve
Covering just 305 hectares, **Modjadji Nature Reserve** (☎ 082-393 5551; adult/vehicle R10/20; 7.30am-6pm) protects forests of the ancient Modjadji cycad. In the summer mists, this place and the surrounding Vulovedu Mountains take on an ethereal atmosphere. The reserve has accommodation in **rondavels** (per person R125).

MODJADJI, THE RAIN QUEEN

In Africa it is unusual for a woman to be sovereign of a tribe, but the Rain Queen is an exception. The queen resides in the town of GaModjadji in the Bolebodu district near Duivelskloof. Every year, around November, the queen presides over a festival held to celebrate the coming of the rains. The *indunas* (tribal headmen) select people to dance, to call for rain, and to perform traditional rituals, including male and female initiation ceremonies. After the ceremony, the rain falls. The absence of rain is usually attributed to some event such as the destruction of a sacred place – a situation resolved only with further ritual.

Henry Rider Haggard's novel, *She*, is based on the story of the original Modjadji, a 16th-century refugee princess.

In June 2001, Rain Queen, Modjadji V, died in Polokwane (Pietersburg). However, in an unfortunate turn of events, her immediate heir, Princess Makheala, had died three days earlier and it wasn't until April 2003 that the 25-year-old Princess Mmakobo Modjadji was crowned Modjadji VI. It was raining on the day of the ceremony, which was taken to be a good omen. She now lives the same secluded lifestyle practiced by her predecessors – her older brother conducts administrative duties. According to custom, she will never marry, but will bear children by members of the royal family.

The road to Modjadji is pretty rough and even if you make it you won't be allowed to visit the Rain Queen. She is confined to her royal kraal and only has contact with her attendants. However, you are allowed to visit the village and can enjoy the Modjadji cycad forest, which has braai facilities and a picnic area.

LIMPOPO

Take the GaKgapane turn-off from Rte 36 about 10km north of Duivelskloof; the turn-off to the reserve is a further 18km.

PHALABORWA

☎ 015 / pop 109,000

Phalaborwa is a neatly tended stretch of well-watered suburbia – the 'Beware Hippos' signs seem rather out of place – with a group of guesthouses and hotels thriving on the back of the town's proximity to the Kruger National Park. Phalaborwa means 'Better than the South', and was so called because Nguni tribes returned here after a foray to the south.

Phalaborwa makes an ideal starting point if you're intending to explore central and northern Kruger. For people with limited time in South Africa, it is possible to visit Kruger by flying from Jo'burg to Phalaborwa, hiring a car for touring the park and then returning the car at Phalaborwa airport before returning by air to Jo'burg.

Phalaborwa is also a new gateway to Mozambique as it's now possible to drive across Kruger and into Mozambique at the **Giriyondo border gate** (p627; ☎ 013-735 8919). This route is only for 4WD vehicles.

Information

Bollanoto Tourism Centre (☎ 015-781 5987; www .phalaborwa.co.za; cnr Hendrick van Eck & Pres Steyn Sts; ☺ 7am-4pm Mon-Fri) Has a community art shop and a tourist desk.

Net-o-Mania (☎ 015-781 7812; Shop 2, Phalaborwa Mall, Nelson Mandela St; per hr R25; ☺ 8.50am-5pm Mon-Fri, 9am-1pm Sat) Internet access.

Sights & Activities

You can tour the nearby **copper mine** (☎ 015-780 2911; admission free), said to boast the largest man-made hole in Africa, at 9am on Friday, but you must phone in advance.

The **Leka Gape organisation** (☎ 015-783 0770; www.lekagape.de) is an NGO working on community development projects in Lulekani, a township around 13km north of Phalaborwa. A tour of the township includes a visit to a workshop where handcrafts are produced. Tours are organised through Basambilu Lodge (see right).

The **Hans Merensky Estate** (☎ 015-781 3931; www .hansmerensky.com; Club Rd; 9/18-hole round R150/250), just south of Phalaborwa, has an 18-hole championship golf course with a difference:

here you have to hold your shot while wildlife, elephants included, crosses the fairways. Be careful – the wildlife is 'wild'.

Mad Safari Tours (☎ 072-536 0667; www.madsafari .com; Airport) runs trips into Kruger, Limpopo and Mpumalanga.

Sleeping

There are scores of places to stay in Phalaborwa; many of the best are just out of town in the bush.

BUDGET

Daan & Zena's (☎ 015-781 6049; www.daanzena.co.za; 15 Birkenhead St; camp sites per person R45, dm/s/d from R80/125/200; ✷ ☐ ☎) Bridging the gap between backpackers and B&B, this place is brought to life by lashings of colourful paint and a friendly atmosphere. It's a tad crumbly, but it's a good spot if you're looking for a comfy bed and a youthful vibe.

Elephant Walk (☎ 015-781 5860; www.elewalk.com; 30 Anna Scheepers Ave; camp sites R50, dm/s/d with shared bathroom R75/140/200, d with private bathroom R300) Close enough to Kruger to hear the lions roar, this is a great spot to plan your foray into the park. The owners will pick you up from the centre of town and offer an excellent range of reasonably priced tours and activities. The en-suite doubles are glossier.

Basambilu Lodge (☎ 015-783 0467; www.basambilu .com; 348 Akanani St, Lulekani; dm/d from R70/250; ✷ ☎) Located in the township of Lulekani (13km north of Phalaborwa), this backpackers includes a swimming pool, rondavels and open-air kitchen. There is also a lapa where locals and tourists get acquainted over beers. The management can organise tours around the area and in the township itself.

MIDRANGE & TOP END

African Lily Lodge (☎ 015-781 3805; www.africanlily .co.za; 35 Palm Ave; s/d/q/tr R250/350/460/500, s/d unit R100/150; ✷ ☎) Smack in the centre of town, the African Lily (owned by the same folks who run Daan & Zena's) is a functional sort of place good for families. Out back, there is the option of staying inside portable units that are cheap but baking hot in summer and generally unappealing year-round.

Masorini Lodge (☎ 015-781 3579; www.masorini .co.za; s/d R295/450) Out in the sticks, this atmospheric place has self-catering accommodation in thatched A-frames. As you enter town from Tzaneen, turn left (north) on Spekboom St and keep going for 8km.

Sefapane Lodge (☎ 015-780 6700; www.sefapane .co.za; cnr Koper & Essenhout Sts; s/d with breakfast R400/700; ▨ ▩) Sefapane has plenty of safari-park styling, a sunken bar, one of the town's best eateries and a whiff of genuine exclusivity. Accommodation is in rondavels. The restaurant here has a good mix of ethnic dishes, including some Moroccan food and *potjiekos*.

Phuza Moya (☎ 015-793 1971; www.phuzamoya.co .za; s/d with full-board & wildlife drives R1825/2500; ▩) This seriously stylish place only takes 24 guests at a time – and they are soon swallowed up by the surrounding 2800 hectares of private wildlife reserve. It is about an hour out of town on the S30 between Mica and Rte 36. Head south from Phalaborwa on the Lydenburg road.

Eating

The Phalaborwa Mall, on Nelson Mandela St, has the usual food chains. For posh eats, the restaurant at Sefapane Lodge is excellent.

La Grotto (☎ 015-781 7241; 38 Palm Ave; mains R25-50; ◷ breakfast, lunch & dinner Mon-Sat; ▨) This place keeps locals happy with a good-value menu of salads, seafood, burgers and beer. It's close to the African Lily Lodge.

Buffalo Pub & Grill (☎ 015-781 0829; 1 Lekkerbreek St; mains R30-70; ◷ lunch & dinner; ▨) This place is more tourist-orientated than La Grotto,

with a nice terrace for alfresco dining and African trimmings aplenty.

Getting There & Away

AIR

SAAirlink (☎ 015-781 5823; www.saairlink.co.za), with an office at the airport, flies daily to Jo'burg (R1300). The **airport** (☎ 015-781 5823) is 2km north of town.

BUS

Sure Turn Key Travel (☎ 015-781 7761; Shop 42, Phalaborwa Mall, Nelson Mandela St; ◷ 8.30am-4.30pm Mon-Fri, 9am-noon Sat) is the local agent for Translux and City to City buses. Translux services travel via Polokwane and connect Phalaborwa with Tzaneen (R100, one hour), Polokwane (R100, 2½ hours), Makhado (R170, four hours), Pretoria (R165, six hours) and Jo'burg (R170, seven hours). City to City buses travel to Jo'burg (R135, 9½ hours) via Middleburg, and are cheaper but slower. Sure Turn Key also has an office at the airport (☎ 015-781 2498).

CAR

Hiring a car is often the cheapest way of seeing Kruger Park. **Avis** (☎ 015-781 3169; ◷ 8am-6pm Mon-Fri, 10.30am-1pm Sat, 4-6pm Sun), **Imperial** (☎ 015-781 0376; ◷ 8am-6pm Mon-Fri, 10.30am-1pm Sat, 4-6pm Sun) and **Budget** (☎ 015-781 5404; ◷ 8am-6pm Mon-Fri, 10.30am-1pm Sat, 4-6pm Sun) all have offices at the airport.

THE MIGHTY MARULA

The silhouette of a Marula tree at dusk is one of the more evocative images of the African bush, but the real value of this mighty tree is what comes out of it.

In summer, the female marula sags under the weight of its pale yellow fruit. Chacna baboons love the stuff and you can see them by the road chomping on this vitamin-rich delicacy. Elephants, also big marula fans, spend their days ramming into the trunk of the tree to knock to the fruit to the ground. Their somewhat obsessive behaviour has led to the marula being dubbed the 'Elephant Tree'.

The marula fruit is considered an aphrodisiac by local custom, but recently it has grown in value as an alcoholic beverage. Amarula cream liqueur debuted in 1989 and is now available in 70 countries worldwide.

To produce this beverage, the fruit is fermented, distilled and then matured in oak casks for around two years. It is then blended with cream and bottled. Harvesting of the fruit is done between January and March. During the rest of the year, Amarula keeps fruit pickers busy with community-based work projects, such as brick making and fence mending.

The best way to enjoy a glass of Amarula cream is to visit the company lapa located next to its factory. You can make a booking at the lapa by ringing ☎ 015-781-7766 or checking their website (www.amarula.com). The lapa and the processing plant are 10km south of Phalaborwa on the road to Hoedspruit.

LIMPOPO

MINIBUS TAXI

There aren't many minibus taxis in this area, and most run from the township of Namakgale (R5, 20 minutes). From here, you can catch connections to Tzaneen (R35, 1½ hours).

HOEDSPRUIT & AROUND

☎ 015 / pop 11,000

There's not a whole lot in Hoedspruit but 250 neat houses and a large Air Force base – which is scaling down. It is, however, within striking distance of Kruger's Orpen Gate (67km), and makes a convenient launching point for exploring the central and northern sections of the park. It's also one of the main access towns for Timbavati and several of the other private wildlife reserves bordering western Kruger (see p485), with good air connections to/from Jo'burg.

Information & Tours

The **Tourist Information Centre** (☎ 015-793 1110; www.1africasafaris.com; Kamogelo Centre, Main Rd; ☽ 8am-5pm Mon-Fri) is on Rte 527, next to the Wimpy fast-food outlet. There is an **ABSA** (Main Rd) ATM nearby, plus Internet access at **MJ's Photographic** (☎ 015-793 3700; per hr R40; ☽ 8am-4.30 Mon-Fri, 8am-noon Sat).

McFarlane Safaris (☎ 015-793 3000; www.mcfarlane safaris.co.za; ☽ 8am-5pm Mon-Fri, 8am-noon Sat), by the Total petrol station on Rte 40, runs upmarket safaris in and around Kruger. **Off Beat Safaris** (☎ 015-793 2422; www.offbeatsafaris.co.za) runs horse safaris (R150 for two hours) from a nearby farm.

Sleeping & Eating

Loerie Guesthouse (☎ 015-793 3990; www.loerie guesthouse.com; 85 Jakkals St; s/d R265/395; 🖵 🐾) Specialises in warm welcomes and home cooking (breakfast R45, dinner R70). It is signposted off Main Rd.

Otters Den (☎ 015-795 5488; www.ottersden.co.za; full board per person R570; 🐾) Located around 20km west of Hoedspruit, this small, rustic camp contains four chalets built on stilts, overlooking the Blyde River. The hosts can organise all manner of tours, including hot-air ballooning and white-water rafting.

Ngena Deli (☎ 015-793 0452; Kamogelo Tourist Centre; ☽ 8am-5pm Mon-Wed, 8am-8pm Thu-Fri, 8am-2.30pm Sat) Homemade bread, local jams and hot and cold sandwiches are available at this deli near the Tourist Information Centre.

Getting There & Away

SA Express (☎ 015-793 3681) flies daily out of **Hoedspruit Eastgate airport** (☎ 015-793 3681) to Jo'burg (R1200 one-way). The airport is 7km from Hoedspruit.

You can hire a car with **Avis** (☎ 015-793 2014) at the airport.

There is a minibus taxi rank near the train station, with services to Phalaborwa (R25, 1½ hours). **Translux** (www.translux.com) runs daily bus to Jo'burg (R160).

Acornhoek

The township of Acornhoek, located near Kruger National Park's Orpen Gate, is a worthwhile detour to visit the successful **Mapusha Weavers Cooperative** (☎ 072-469-7060; www.mapusha.org).

The co-op, founded in 1972, produces excellent quality carpets and tapestries in its workshop next to a Catholic Mission. You can watch the women work, take home some of their products or go on a tour of the township with one of the co-op members. The standard tour (R100) includes lunch plus a visit to the *shebeen* (where you can sample some of the local brew), and a meeting with the village *sangoma* (traditional healer).

To get there, travel south on Rte 40 from Hoedspruit. After 26km take a left at the junction for Acornhoek. After 4.3km, turn right onto a dirt road marked 'Dingleydale'. After 1.8km you will see the Catholic Mission on your right.

Nyani Cultural Village

Home of the descendants of former local chief Kapama, **Nyani Cultural Village** (☎ 083-512 4865; Guernsey Rd; admission R50; ☽ 10am-5pm Mon-Fri) offers an interesting insight into how traditional Shangaan families live. The village recreates all aspects of tribal culture, and chief Axon Khosa is happy to explain traditional medicines and aspects of Tsonga life. Admission includes a one-hour tour and lunch (R35) is available. There's also evening tours (including dinner and dancing) for R150. If you want to eat, book ahead.

To reach the village, travel south on Rte 40 for 28km and turn onto Rte 531, which is the same road that leads to Kruger Park's Orpen Gate. After 12km you will see the signposted turnoff to the village.

North-West Province

With some of its most revered attractions just two hours from Johannesburg (Jo'burg), the North-West Province provides the perfect antidote for escaping big-city clutter. Home to some of the country's best-kept secrets, the region offers something for anyone – from music lovers to safari addicts to gamblers.

The Disney-esque Sun City and Lost City casino resorts are South Africa's most opulent theme parks. Once an exclusive sanctuary for the white elite, today the apartheid-era's most famous retreat is a multicultural place. Popular with South Africans of all colours (along with plenty of tourists), it's packed with all sorts of entertainment, from jet skiing to wave pools to slot machines. The complex is shamelessly gaudy and almost ridiculously kitsch, but it's also alluring enough to make for an ostentatiously fabulous place to pass an afternoon.

When you tire of artificial beaches, head into the wild. Nearby Pilanesberg National Park is our pick for a quick safari. Whether you drive yourself or join a tour, the wide-open spaces and numerous water-hole hides in this extinct volcano mean there's a decent chance of spotting something big, be it a lion, rhino or lumbering elephant.

Further afield, Madikwe Game Reserve is one of South Africa's best-kept secrets. Even though it's closer to Jo'burg than Kruger, and teeming with the same animals, it sees far fewer visitors. Translation? You get to search for herds of wild mammals in their natural habitat without herds of slobbering, gasping camera-clicking humans in tow.

This chapter concentrates on the eastern half of the province. It's not that we don't like the west, there is just little of interest there for travellers.

HIGHLIGHTS

- Listening to the melody of the bush from your camp under the stars in wild and wonderful **Madikwe Game Reserve** (p518)

- Searching for lions, rhinos and leopards amid rocky valleys and extinct volcanoes while on safari in super accessible **Pilanesberg National Park** (p516)

- Riding the waves, tanning on the beach or braving a fake earthquake in **Sun City** (p514), once a glittering icon of apartheid, now a playground for all South Africans

- Dancing to live music at the funky **Revel Inn** (p513), where chilling out is the religion of the house

- Shopping for handicrafts and enjoying the shimmering blue vistas at **Hartbeespoort Dam** (p514)

▪ POPULATION: 4 MILLION   ▪ AREA: 116,320 SQ KM

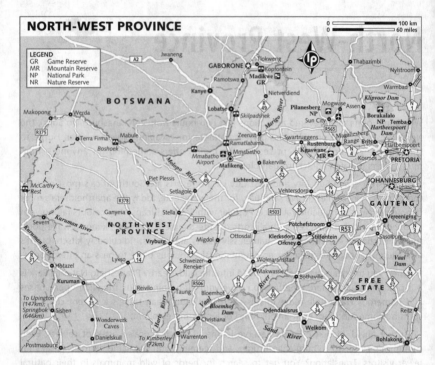

HISTORY

The North-West Province takes in much of the area once covered by the fragmented apartheid homeland of Bophuthatswana (often shortened to 'Bop'), dumping ground for thousands of 'relocated' Tswana people. The nominally independent homeland became famous for the excesses of the white South African men who visited its casinos and pleasure resorts for interracial encounters with prostitutes, which would have been illegal in South Africa itself.

The North-West Province was the site of a complex and sophisticated Iron-Age civilisation centred on the 'lost city' of Kaditshwene, about 30km north of modern-day Zeerust. The people who lived here had an economy so developed they traded copper and iron jewellery with China. By 1820, when European missionaries first visited the city, it was bigger than Cape Town. In the end, the peace-loving inhabitants of Kaditshwene proved no match for the aggression of the Sotho, displaced by Zulu incursions into the Free State. The city was sacked by a horde of 40,000 people and fell into ruins.

Diamonds were discovered in the province in the 1870s, resulting in an enormous rush to the fields around Lichtenburg. Mining is still important here and there are extensive platinum mines near Rustenburg.

CLIMATE

Summer temperatures range between 22°C and 34°C and winter brings with it dry, sunny days and chilly nights. The average winter (May-July) temperature is 15.5°C but can range from an average of 2°C to 20°C in a single day. The summer months (August-March) bring brief, refreshing afternoon thunderstorms.

LANGUAGE

Setswana is the principal language; most whites speak Afrikaans, with a minority having English as their first language.

GETTING THERE & AROUND

The principal towns in the province, Mafikeng and Rustenburg, are well connected by bus with Jo'burg and Pretoria. Potchefstroom is also a transport hub. Buses run regularly to Gaborone in Botswana via Zeerust. The main border crossing is Ramatlabama, north of Mafikeng.

Elsewhere in the province, especially the sparsely populated west, public transport is sporadic and you'll most likely need your own vehicle to get around. Car hire is available through **Avis** (www.avis.co.za) Pilanesberg Airport (☎ 014-552 1501); Mafikeng (☎ 018-385 1114); Potchefstroom (☎ 018-290 8535) and **Imperial Car Hire** (www.imperialcarrental.co.za) Pilanesberg Airport (☎ 014-552 1767); Mafikeng (☎ 018-381 7447).

RUSTENBURG

☎ 014 / pop 123,000

Sitting at the edge of the Magaliesberg Range, Rustenburg is a large and prosperous mining town about 115km northwest of Jo'burg. There's no particular reason to visit, other than it makes a handy base if you're visiting nearby Sun City or Pilanesberg National Park and want to stay elsewhere (budget travellers will find this option particularly appealing).

On the way into town, you will find the well stocked **tourist information centre** (☎ 014-597 0904; Main Rd; 🕒 7.30am-5pm Mon-Fri, 8am-1pm Sat) between Plein and Van Staden Sts. There is also an art gallery here, and an arts and crafts shop. There is Internet access at **Copy Express** (☎ 014-592 1970; Biblio Plaza; per hr R30).

Sleeping

The information centre has information on other accommodation options if these places are full.

Bushwillows B&B (☎ 014-537 2333; wjmcgill@lantic .net; s/d R150/300) This is a lovely option about 12km outside town off Rte 24. Set in natural bush, it's a tranquil B&B where the friendly owner (an artist) knows a lot about South African wildlife.

Joan's B&B (☎ 014-533 3086; joan@joansbnb.co.za; 61 Wildevy Ave, Protea Park; s/d with breakfast R150/250) Joan's is a good old-fashioned B&B with simple but tidy rooms; the owners serve a hearty breakfast with a smile. Just don't get them onto politics…

Cashane Hotel (☎ 014-592 8541; fax 592 3016; 66 Steen St; s/d R250/370; 🖭) A convenient, cheap and central option if you want to stay in a proper hotel. Rooms are clean, but ask for one towards the back, as the front can be noisy.

Traveller's Inn (☎ 014-592 7658; travinn@mweb .co.za; 99 Leyds St; s/d with half board R300/550) This guesthouse is quite a good bargain, considering rates include breakfast and dinner. Our top choice in town; rooms are comfy and well appointed, the staff friendly and the bar convivial.

Eating

In the Waterfall Mall, off Rte 30 around 3km south of town, you'll find most of the fast-food chains and a couple of decent coffee shops.

Royal Dutchman (☎ 014-537 3626; 58 Nelson Mandela; mains R60-80; 🕒 lunch & dinner Mon-Fri, dinner Sat) This dark and cosy restaurant has dining booths and a decent menu that features loads of seafood.

Karl's Bauernstube (☎ 014-537 2128; Rte 24; mains R20-50; 🕒 lunch & dinner Tue-Fri, dinner Sat, lunch Sun) An Austrian restaurant offering delights such as smoked warthog and sauerkraut (R40), and crocodile ragout (R35).

Getting There & Away

Intercape (☎ 0861-287 287; www.intercape.co.za) stops in Rustenburg daily on its run between Pretoria (R110, four hours) and Gaborone, Botswana (R150, five hours). The bus stops at the **BP petrol station** (cnr Van Staden & Smit Sts), from where you can catch a minibus taxi into town (about R5).

The main minibus taxi rank is west of the corner of Van Staden and Malan Sts, on the Sun City side of town.

AROUND RUSTENBURG

About 50km outside Rustenberg, at Bokfontein on the N4 towards Swartruggens, lies one of the province's best-kept secrets. Nestled in a green valley next to a small stream deep in the rural heart of Afrikanerdom, you'll find the **Revel Inn** (☎ 072-225 7182; www.revelin.co.za; camp sites R40, dm/d R50/130, bungalows R240; dinner R45; 🍴). A liberal bastion in a conservative wilderness, it's the perfect old-school hippy backpacker joint, where chilling out is the house creed. Psychedelic paintings (and maybe even a different kind of mushroom omelette) encourage you to get in the groove and join the crowd of eccentric regulars who like to party hard. Constantly. At sporadic intervals Revel Inn hosts mini music festivals with live drumming, DJs, or such esoteric events as the

Magic Carpet Carnival and the Spring Love Party. When there's no party on, you could well have the place to yourself, so simply recline in a hammock, chill out in a tree house, or float in the perfectly circular pool and contemplate the sky, man…

MAGALIESBERG RANGE

The 120km-long Magaliesberg Range, north of the N4, swings in a half moon from Rustenburg to Hartbeespoort Dam (below). The region has attractive mountain scenery and some good walks. You'll need your own car to get here.

South of Rustenburg, at the western end of the range is **Kgaswane Mountain Reserve** (☎ 014-533 2050; admission R20; ☽ 8am-4pm). Here you can look for hyenas, black-backed jackals and small antelopes amid a wild terrain dominated by rocky ridges and wooded ravines.

The **Hunter's Rest Hotel** (☎ 014-537 2140; www .huntersrest.co.za; s/d with half board R530/900; ☒) is an attractive resort with a big swimming pool and a golf course, in the Magaliesberg Range, 14km south of Rustenburg; follow the signs.

SUN CITY

☎ 014

Welcome to Sin City, South African style. At **Sun City** (☎ 014-557 1000; www.suncity.co.za; admission R60), the legendary creation of entrepreneur Sol Kerzer, Disneyland collides with ancient Egypt in a demented attempt to look like Vegas. Filled with gilded statues of lions and monkeys, acres of artificial

beaches, exploding volcanos and hundreds upon hundreds of clinking slot machines, it serves no other purpose than to entertain. Yet even though there's no question this gambling-centric resort is almost grotesquely gaudy, a visit here can also be pretty damn fun.

The complex is dominated by the spectacular Lost City, an extraordinary piece of kitsch claiming to symbolise African heritage. In fact it has less to do with African heritage than Disneyland Paris has to do with French heritage, but it's still entertaining. A sort of mega amusement park in high-glitz style, it teems with all sorts of attractions, from a wave pool to water slides to simulated earthquakes.

Started as an apartheid-era exclusive haven for wealthy whites, these days one of Sun City's best features is the mix of black, white and especially Asian people who flock here at weekends. Losers at the tables can console themselves with the thought that they are helping to pay over 3500 salaries.

If you're travelling with the kids (there's tons to keep them busy) or on a budget and tired of just hanging around the hostel, Sun City is a pretty good bargain. The admission fee covers all the main attractions, and you'll also be given R30 in 'Sunbucks', which can be spent at the various restaurants, shops or slot machines. Of course if you've got the cash to splash out, this place also boasts one of the world's most luxurious hotels – a shrine to all things glittery and golden.

HEADING HOME? NEED AFRICAN GIFTS QUICK? HEAD TO HARTBEESPOORT

Hartbeespoort Dam is a favourite weekend retreat for South Africans living around Jo'burg and Pretoria, but it also makes a great day trip for travellers hoping to escape the urban jungle for at least a little while. Less than an hour's drive from either city, it feels worlds apart. Gone is the hustle, replaced instead by rolling hills, winding country roads and the green-blue waters of the dam. And while there's no doubt the surrounding countryside is bucolic, the real reason to visit is to check out the fantastic **Welwitischia Country Market** (☽ 9am-5pm Tue-Sun). With more than 40 open-air stands full of African curios to choose from, it's a great place to stock up on all those gifts you meant to buy, but somehow didn't, before the plane takes off. Prices are reasonable, quality is fair to excellent (you can find some really nice pieces) and you can bargain.

If all your shopping has left you famished, head across the street to the **Upperdeck Restaurant** (mains from R15). There is a varied menu, including vegetarian dishes, and live music on weekends.

You'll need your own transport to reach the dam.

SUN CITY FOR KIDS

When the kids are good and sick of your idea of the great African adventure, cheer them up with a day at Sun City. Not only is this kid-friendly entertainment complex safe, it also offers plenty to keep the little ones amused. **Adventure Mountain** (admission included), in the Valley of the Waves, is kiddie paradise with child-sized pools and waterslides. Older kids will dig tubing down the Lazy River or flying through the twisty waterslides in the main park.

The **Kwena Gardens Crocodile Sanctuary** (admission R40), near the front entrance, is another favourite. It's home to the world's biggest captive crocs. Feeding time is 4.30pm.

Back inside the main entertainment centre, you'll find a children's arcade with loads of games.

If mum and dad need a little space themselves, a number of babysitting options are available, including the weekend **Kamp Kwena** activity centre where kids get to indulge in activities like face painting, limbo and castle jumping. Check at the welcome desk about rates and availability.

Orientation & Information

The car park for day visitors is at the entrance, about 2km from the entertainment centre. An elevated 'sky' train shuttles from the car park to the Cascades hotel and the entertainment centre.

The **welcome centre** (☎ 014-557 1544; ⏰ 9am-8pm Sun-Thu, 8am-1am Fri & Sat) at the entrance to the entertainment centre has maps and just about any information you could possibly need.

Sights & Activities

The best part of Sun City is undeniably **Lost City**, which is entered over a bridge flanked by life-sized fake elephants, and basically consists of **Valley of the Waves**, a pool with a large-scale wave-making machine, a sandy beach, numerous water slides and other amusement park rides. Every hour or so a voice booms out some nonsense about lost civilisations and earthquakes from a hidden mike, and the bridge shakes while dry ice pours out of either side. It's cheesy, but fun.

You'll find separate smoking and non-smoking casinos in the **entertainment centre**. Done up in a jungle theme with animal murals painted on the dome ceiling, it also houses food courts, shops and movie theatres.

In the heart of Lost City is **Palace of the Lost City**, a hotel that could inspire hallucinations, but to which access is prohibited to all but its lucky – and wealthy – guests.

Eighteen holes at the superb **Gary Player Country Club** or the **Lost City Golf Course** cost R500 (R350 for hotel guests).

Near the main entrance is **Waterworld**, on the shores of a large artificial lake, which has facilities for parasailing (R375), jet skiing (R235) and water-skiing (R240).

Sleeping

If the Sun City hotels are too expensive (and you have your own transport), consider staying at Pilanesberg National Park (p516) and making the complex a day trip only. The town of Rustenburg (p513) is also close enough to use as a base.

All the following hotels can be booked through **Sun City** (☎ 014-557 1000; www.suncity .co.za) or **Sun International central reservations** (☎ 011-780 7800; www.suninternational.com). The following places can often be found for less over an Internet hotel consolidator such as **Orbitz** (www.orbitz.com).

Sun City Cabanas (r from R1200; ✖ ☎) The cheapest option in the complex is laid-back and aimed at family groups. Rooms are modern with all the typical upmarket conveniences.

Sun City Hotel (r from R2000; ✖ ☎) The most lively of the hotels, with gambling facilities on the premises, as well as a number of restaurants, a nightclub and an entertainment centre.

Cascades (r from 2400; ✖ ☎) The Cascades has been displaced by the Palace of the Lost City as the most luxurious hotel in the complex, but the rooms are still easily described as palatial.

Palace of the Lost City (r from R3500; ✖ ☎) It's no wonder *Condé Nast Traveller* named it one of the best hotels in the world for 2006 as this over-the-top property redefines the fantasy of luxury. The rooms are done up with bold-coloured carpets and duvets and hand-painted ceilings, but seem a bit unimaginative when compared with the awesome public spaces. Set in a 25-hectare botanical garden, the grounds are filled with cascading waterfalls and pools, meandering paths and a watery rides to get your adrenalin rushing.

Eating

All the hotels have a selection of restaurants. There are plenty of fast-food joints in the entertainment centre. Your 30 Sunbucks will just about get you a burger and a soft drink.

Getting There & Away

Tiny Pilanesberg Airport once gloried in the name 'Pilanesberg International Airport', when it was the home of Bop Air, the airline of the former 'independent' homeland of Bophuthatswana. It's about 9km east of the Sun City complex. **SAAirlink** (☎ 011-978 1111; www.saairlink.co.za) operates flights six times a week from Jo'burg (R500) and three times a week from Cape Town (R1000). From the airport, you'll need to hire a car or arrange for your hotel to pick you up.

Surprisingly, the Sun City complex is poorly signposted, so navigators will really need to concentrate or you'll miss it. From Jo'burg it's a two-hour drive. The most straightforward route is via Rustenburg and Boshoek on the Rte 565.

PILANESBERG NATIONAL PARK

Don't be fooled into thinking this **national park** (☎ 014-555 5356; adult/child R20/10, per vehicle R15; ☒ dawn-dusk) is some kind of tacky superannuated zoo just because it's nearly on top of Sun City. In reality, it protects over 500 sq km of an unusual complex of extinct volcanoes, and is the fourth-largest national park in South Africa. The scenery is impressive, with towering rocky outcrops in the centre of the park, particularly in the area around Mankwe Lake, the centre of an extinct 1200-million-year-old volcano. It's near enough to Sun City to make it easy to visit both in one day (something many Jo'burg tour operators do), and it's close enough to the big city to be considered for a last quick safari before it's time to head home.

Since 1979, when Operation Genesis brought dozens of translocated animal species to the park, Pilanesberg has been home to extensive populations of many of Africa's most impressive animals. All the big cats are here, and along with the lions and leopards and cheetahs, you'll also find jackals, hyenas, white and black rhinos, elephants, giraffes, hippos, buffalos, zebras and a wide variety of antelopes (including sables, elands, kudus and gemsboks). Since early 2000, African wild dogs can be seen here too. The region also has a diverse population of birds – over 300 species have been recorded.

There is an excellent 100km network of gravel roads, hides and picnic spots, and some good-value accommodation. Since it is no more than 25km from one end of the park to the other, it is easy to cover the range of different environments in the park and to see a wide variety of animals. To do any real justice to it, however, you need a full day. On no account should you miss the viewpoints over the crater from Lenong Lookout.

You'll either need to join an organised tour from Jo'burg (p405) or Pretoria (p434) or have your own transport to visit the park. We liked **Footprints in Africa** (☎ 083-302 1976; www.footprintsinafrica.com; 425 Farenden St, Pretoria) based at the Pretoria Backpackers. They offer two-day Pilanesberg safaris, that also visit Sun City, starting at R1200 per person.

Orientation & Information

There are four gates into Pilanesberg. Enter from the direction of Sun City using either Bakubung Gate to the west (via Rte 556) or Manyane Gate to the northeast (via Rte 556 and Rte 510 if you're coming from Pretoria and Jo'burg).

A useful information booklet and map (R10) is available at the main park gates, where overnight visitors must enter and report to the **reception office** (☎ 014-555 5355; ☒ 24hr).

There is an **information centre** (☎ 014-555 7931; www.parksnorthwest.co.za/pilanesberg) with an interpretative display and shop in an old magistrates court in the centre of the park.

Activities

Gametrackers Outdoor Adventures (☎ 014-552 5020; www.gametrac.co.za) runs a dizzying variety of

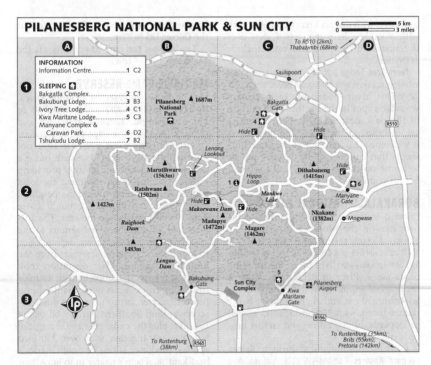

PILANESBERG NATIONAL PARK & SUN CITY

INFORMATION
Information Centre.....................1 C2

SLEEPING
Bakgatla Complex.....................2 C1
Bakubung Lodge.......................3 B3
Ivory Tree Lodge........................4 C1
Kwa Maritane Lodge................5 C3
Manyane Complex &
   Caravan Park..........................6 D2
Tshukudu Lodge.......................7 B2

activities within the park. Book at its offices at the Manyane or Bakgatla Complexes (below), or at the Sun City welcome centre (p515). There are early-morning, late-afternoon and night wildlife drives (2½ hours, R250). For something a bit more adventurous try tracking rhinos on foot with a guide (R300) or an elephant-back safari (R400).

Mankwe Safaris (☎ 014-555 7056; www.mankwe safaris.co.za) also runs a variety of activities; enquire at its office next to the Manyane Gate reception office. Wildlife drives with a bush braai (barbecue) cost R350, walking trails are R250 and the company can also organise museum trips and cultural tourism activities.

Sleeping & Eating

Manyane Complex & Caravan Park (☎ 014-555 5351; www.goldenleopard.co.za; camp sites R145, 2-person safari tent R350, d/tr chalet with breakfast from R730/1125; ❄ ☎) Near Manyane Gate, this complex is thoughtfully designed and laid out, with high-quality facilities, including a shop with a reasonable range of food items and a decent restaurant. The chalets are pretty posh, with good linens on firm mattresses, a grassy braai area, full kitchen and sitting room with TV. Rates include a hearty breakfast buffet.

Bakgatla Complex (☎ 014-555 5351; www.golden leopard.co.za; camp sites R165, d safari tent R880, d/tr chalet with breakfast R920/975; ❄ ☎) A smaller camp, but with the same quality digs, Bakgatla is northwest of Manyayne gate. The luxury safari tents come with full bathrooms and covered porches. Rates include a buffet breakfast, and half-board (lunch and dinner) options are available starting at R1100 for two people.

Kwa Maritane Lodge (s/d with breakfast & dinner R1600/2200; ❄ ⬛ ☎), **Bakubung Lodge** (s/d with breakfast & dinner R1600/2200; ❄ ⬛ ☎) and **Tshukudu Lodge** (s/d with full board R3500/5000; ❄ ☎), all run by **Legacy hotels** (☎ 011-806 6806; www .legacyhotels.co.za), are the park's three main luxury options. Kwa Maritane and Bakubong are essentially similar, with high standard accommodation. Both hotels have still managed to retain a bit of taste and character, though neither exactly represents a wild bush experience. Tshukudu is more exclusive, with just six luxury cottages, each with a sunken bath that has a view over the surrounding hills, and rates include activities.

Ivory Tree Lodge (☎ 011-706 8781; www.african anthology.co.za; s/d with full board R2800/3800; ✖ ▢ ▣) This luxury lodge sits in a tranquil woodland spot in the northeastern portion of the park near Bakgatla gate; activities are included in the rates. The resort says it welcomes children, but at the same time warns that children under 12 may not be welcome on the game drives. It's a better bet for couples.

BORAKALALO NATIONAL PARK

Located in the northeastern corner of the province on the Moratele River and the Klipvoor Dam, this **national park** (☎ 012-729 3337; admission R15, plus per car R10; ✆ 5am-8pm Dec-Apr, 6am-7pm May-Nov) lives up to the meaning of its name: Place of Relaxation. Most of the original animal inhabitants were relentlessly hunted out and are now slowly being reintroduced, with 350 bird species as well as leopards, otters, zebras and jackals now resident.

Book accommodation through **Golden Leopard Resorts** (☎ 014-555 6135; goldres@iafrica .com); camps in the reserve include **Pitjane Fishing Camp** (camp sites per person R60), **Phuduphudu** (4-person safari tents R425) and **Moretele** (camp sites R60, 4-bed safari tents R325).

To get here from Pretoria and Jo'burg, head to Brits, then take Rte 511 to Assen and follow the signs to Klipvoor Dam and the park. There is no public transport.

ZEERUST

☎ 018 / pop 17,600
As a major jumping-off point for Gaborone (Botswana), Zeerust sees a lot of in-and-out traffic and as a result has a certain vibrant bustle to it. The town is quite large; there are plenty of shops strung along Church St, including a couple of banks and 24-hour petrol stations. There are also a couple of basic hotels on the main street.

The **tourist information office** (☎ 018-642 1081; Church St; ✆ 7.30am-4pm Mon-Fri) is in the municipal building and has info on area attractions.

Intercape (☎ 0861-287 287; www.intercape.co.za) passes through Zeerust on its daily run between Pretoria (R130, two hours) and Ga-

borone (R75, three hours). The bus stops at the **Chicken Licken** (Church St).

The **minibus taxi rank** (Church St) is on the Mafikeng side of town.

MADIKWE GAME RESERVE

One of the largest reserves in South Africa, **Madikwe** (☎ 083-629 8282) comprises 760 sq km of bushveld, savanna grassland and riverine forest on the edge of the Kalahari Desert. The reserve was created in 1991, not only to protect endangered wildlife, but as a job-creation scheme and a way of providing a more sustainable environment for local people. A massive translocation operation, called Operation Phoenix, brought more than 10,000 animals into the area. The animals had all once been indigenous to the area, but their numbers were depleted due to hunting and farming pressures from the human inhabitants. The operation took over seven years to complete, with animals (including entire herds of elephants) being flown or driven in from various other reserves around Southern Africa. All of the Big Five, plus the endangered wild dog, are now present, together with over 350 bird species. Madikwe is one of South Africa's best-kept secrets: it's nearer to Jo'burg than the Kruger Park but has far less visitors. It's also malaria-free, making it a good option for children.

Sleeping & Eating

Madikwe is not open to day visitors, so to visit you'll have to book into one of the 24 lodges and camps within the park, all of which do guided wildlife drives in open vehicles.

Mosethla Bush Camp (☎ 011-444 9345; www.the bushcamp.com; s/d with full board & shared bathroom R1600/2500) There's nothing fancy about this rustic and intimate camp with abodes in open-fronted log cabins within an unfenced bush area. The place prides itself on being au naturale and there's no electricity or running water. But canvas bucket showers and hot water boilers ensure it's still very comfortable. Rates include bush walks, wildlife drives and all meals.

Jaci's Lodges (☎ 083-00 2071; www.madikwe.com; s/d with full board around R6500/8000, children R1500; ✖ ▢ ▣) For sheer luxury, panache and design flair, Jaci's two lodges – Safari Lodge and Tree Lodge – can compete with anywhere else in Africa. Activities are included and the quality of guiding is excellent, ensuring guests have the best chance of seeing great wildlife during their stay. Unusually for such an upmarket place, Jaci's welcomes children and has babysitters and various kids' activities for when parents need a break.

Getting There & Away

It takes about four hours to drive from Gauteng to the reserve gates via the N4 and the Rte 510 from Rustenburg, or Rte 49 from Zeerust. Buses on their way from Gaborone can be prevailed upon to stop in the reserve, while at the other end of the scale there is also a regular scheduled flight from Jo'burg airport. Ask about either of these options when booking your accommodation.

MAFIKENG

☎ 018 / pop 50,900

Mafikeng and Mmabatho were originally twin towns about 3km apart, but are now combined and Mmabatho is part of Mafikeng. Mmabatho was built as the capital of the 'independent' homeland of Bophuthatswana, and became famous for the monumental and absurd buildings erected by corrupt Bophuthatswana president, Lucas Mangope.

Today Mafikeng is a friendly and relaxed town with a large middle-class black population. The main reason to visit is the excellent Mafikeng Museum, one of the best in the country.

History

Mafeking (as the Europeans called it) was established as the administrative capital of the British Protectorate of Bechuanaland (present-day Botswana). The small frontier town, led by British colonel Lord Baden-Powell, was besieged by Boer forces from October 1899 to May 1900. The siege was in many ways a civilised affair, with the besieging Boers coming into town on Sundays to attend church. However, it was seized upon by the heroics-hungry Victorian press as a symbol of British courage and steadfastness. During the siege Baden-Powell created a cadet corps for the town's boys, which was the forerunner to his boy-scout movement.

In reality, the British officers dined on oyster patties and roast suckling pig in their mess while the Baralong and Mfengu people, who sustained equal casualties in the service of the colonialists, lived on dogs and locusts. The Baralong military hero Mathakong Kodumela, who saw his troops massacred by the Boers several times while raiding for cattle to feed the town, was dismissed by Baden-Powell as 'uncooperative' when he asked for arms to defend them.

Orientation

It's easy to get around Mafikeng on foot. Most shops and banks are around the central local bus station. It's 5km from the centre of Mafikeng to the Megacity shopping mall in Mmabatho; catch one of the many local buses. Megacity is a useful starting point if you're heading further north or west; you'll find banks, a post office and a supermarket.

Information

MONEY

All banks have ATMs and can change travellers cheques or cash at a pinch.
ABSA (cnr Warren & Main Sts)
First National Bank (Robinson St) Between Main and Shippard Sts.
Standard Bank (cnr Main & Robinson Sts)

POST & COMMUNICATIONS

Internet café (☎ 018-384 9071; per hr R20; ☼ 8.30am-5.30pm Mon-Thu; 8.30am-4.30pm Fri, 9am-2pm Sat) In the Megacity shopping mall.
Main post office Next to Megacity.
Post office (Carrington St) Between Main and Martin Sts.

TOURIST INFORMATION

Mafikeng Tourism Info & Development Centre (☎ 018-381 3155; www.tourismnorthwest.co.za; cnr Lichtenburg Rd & Nelson Mandela Dr; ☼ 8am-6pm Mon-Fri, 8am-noon Sat)

Sights

There is reams of interesting and quirky regional information, dating from prehistoric times onward, to be gleaned at the excellent **Mafikeng Museum** (☎ 018-381 6102; cnr Carrington & Martin Sts; admission by donation; ☼ 8am-4pm Mon-Fri, 10am-1pm Sat). Among the many displays in the museum is an exhibit charting the rise of the boy-scout movement, and an entire room dedicated to the famous siege, with original photographs and letters, and good information about the forgotten role played by the town's black population. There's also some

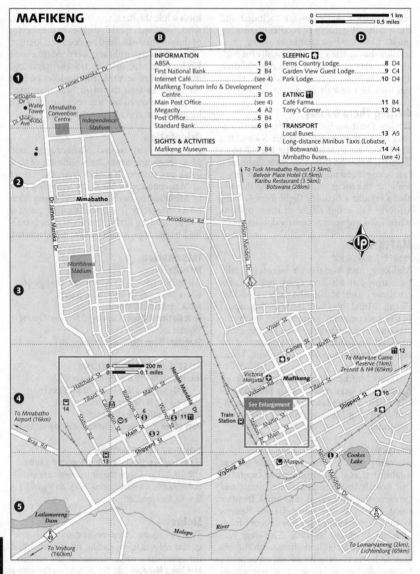

MAFIKENG

0		1 km
0		0.5 miles

INFORMATION
ABSA......................................1 B4
First National Bank....................2 B4
Internet Café.........................(see 4)
Mafikeng Tourism Info & Development
Centre................................3 D5
Main Post Office......................(see 4)
Megacity...............................4 A2
Post Office............................5 B4
Standard Bank.........................6 B4

SIGHTS & ACTIVITIES
Mafikeng Museum........................7 B4

SLEEPING
Ferns Country Lodge....................8 D4
Garden View Guest Lodge................9 C4
Park Lodge............................10 D4

EATING
Café Farma............................11 B4
Tony's Corner.........................12 D4

TRANSPORT
Local Buses...........................13 A5
Long-distance Minibus Taxis (Lobatse,
Botswana)............................14 A4
Mmbatho Buses........................(see 4)

To Tusk Mmabatho Resort (3.5km);
Belvoir Place Hotel (3.5km);
Karibu Restaurant (3.5km);
Botswana (28km)

information about the 'lost city' of Kaditshwene (p512), and a small coffee shop.

Sleeping

There are a few small B&Bs in town – mostly
just rooms in someone's house – starting at
around R150 per person. Ask at the tourist
centre for a complete list.

Garden View Guest Lodge (☎ 018-381 3110;
cnr North & Havenga Sts; s/d with shared bathroom from
R150/220; ☒) This is Mafikeng's best option
in this price bracket. The cheapest rooms
share bathrooms, but pay around R100 and
you'll get an en-suite. All the spick-and-span
rooms have a TV, fridge and kitchenette,
and there's a very convivial restaurant-bar.

NO HOME, NO LANDS

During the 1970s the Batloung inhabitants of Botshabelo, near Mafikeng, were forcibly removed from their well-established villages, farms and towns and 'resettled' in areas of arid, unfertile bush as part of the homelands policy. White farmers were given the plots left behind at 40% of their market value, while the original landowners received no compensation. In many cases, the dispossessed Batloung had watched their homes and possessions being bulldozed before they were removed.

After the reversal of the homelands policy in the 1990s, the displaced community began taking action to get their land back. In 1991, a group of white extremists led by Eugene Terreblanche attacked the families who had returned to Botshabelo. The final steps in the return of the Batloung to their rightful lands were only completed in 2001. In a final act of defiance, one departing farmer even poisoned the fruit trees in his orchard before he left.

Visit the excellent Mafikeng Museum (p519) to learn more about the machinations of the apartheid government in this part of South Africa.

Park Lodge (☎ 381 6753; 70 Shippard St; r with breakfast R250) The small but uncluttered rooms here all have TVs. Dinner is available for R45.

Belvoir Place Hotel (☎ 018-386 2222; ihtm@iafrica .co.za; Nelson Mandela Dr; s/d with breakfast R340/550; 🐾 🖥) If you can take the horrid 1980s décor, this is a fairly luxurious place that forms part of a hotel training school. Each of the enormous rooms has a TV, safe, fridge and telephone. The hotel is 3.5km from the town centre.

Ferns Country Lodge (☎ 018-381 5971; ferns@ worldonline.co.za; 12 Cook St; r R600; 🐾 🖥 🖥) Ferns is stylish and elegant with ultramodern furnishings and a beautiful garden. It's well signposted off Shippard St.

Tusk Mmabatho Resort (☎ 018-389 1111; mma bat ho@tusk-resorts.co.za; Nelson Mandela Dr; r R900; 🐾 🖥 🖥) Mafikeng's luxury option, this opulent resort and casino, 3.5km from the town centre, is a legacy of the old Bophuthatswana homeland.

Eating

Café Farma (☎ 018-381 4906; 17 Nelson Mandela Dr; mains R20; ☉ breakfast & lunch Mon-Sat) In Era's Pharmacy, this is *the* place for breakfast, light meals and heavy cakes. The atmosphere is buzzing.

Karibu Restaurant (☎ 018-386 2222; Nelson Mandela Dr; mains R45-80; ☉ lunch & dinner) This grand restaurant in the Belvoir Place Hotel does good meals (try the veggie curry). It also has delightfully old-fashioned service: the plates come covered with silver domes, which the tuxedoed waiters remove with a flourish.

Tony's Corner (☎ 018-381 0700; 12 Gemsbok St; mains R30-60; ☉ lunch & dinner Mon-Sat) This upmarket pub-restaurant has an interesting menu, including duck, stir-fry and plenty of seafood dishes.

Getting There & Around

Many people come through Mafikeng on their way to/from Botswana. Ramatlabama, 24km to the north, is the busiest border post and lies on the main route to/from Gaborone (Botswana).

SAAirlink (☎ 011-978 1111; www.saairlink.co.za) has flights four days a week to Jo'burg (R900) with connections to other cities. The airport is 16km northwest of Mafikeng. The Tusk Mmabatho Resort can arrange airport pick-ups for guests.

Mmbatho Buses (☎ 018-381 2680; Megacity) run daily from Megacity to Jo'burg (R100, six hours).

Long-distance minibus taxis leave from the forecourt of the Mafikeng train station, headed for the Botswana border (R5, running all day); Zeerust (R15); Lobatse (Botswana; R20); Gaborone (R35); and Rustenburg (R30). As usual, most leave early in the morning.

Numerous city buses ply the route between the **Mafikeng stop** (cnr Main St & Station Rd) and Megacity for a few rand.

POTCHEFSTROOM

☎ 018 / pop 122,100

The first European town to be established in the former Transvaal, Potchefstroom, known locally as 'Potch', remains staunchly conservative to this day. It's a large place, off the N12 about 115km southwest of Jo'burg, almost verging on a city, which looks rather unappealing from the main road. While there are some pleasant leafy suburbs around the university, the only real reason to stay is to check out the Vredefort Dome (p383) in the neighbouring Free State.

Maps of Potch and the Vredefort Dome are available at the **Tourist information office** (☎ 018-293 1611; cnr Potgieter & Church Sts; ☯ 9am-5pm Mon-Fri).

The whole of Potch can be found at the **Lake Holiday Resort** (☎ 018-299 5473; fax 018-299 5475; camp sites R75, rondavels with shared bathroom from R135; ☒) on a sunny weekend. The resort's facilities include fairground attractions, boats, a café and plenty of braais. The simple rondavels come in various sizes.

Smart and modern, the **Willows Garden Hotel** (☎ 018-297 6285; willowsgch@mweb.co.za; cnr N12 & Mooiriver St; s/d with breakfast R395/500; ☒ ☐ ☒) is a business-style hotel with all the mod cons you'd expect. Dros restaurant next door provides room service.

Intercape (☎ 0861-287 287; www.intercape.co.za) buses stop in Potch on their daily run between Pretoria (R85, 3½ hours) and Upington in the Northern Cape (R225, eight hours). **Greyhound** (☎ 012-323 1154; www.greyhound.co.za) buses run from Potch to Cape Town (R420, 16 hours) and Jo'burg (R110, two hours).

The *Trans Karoo* train also stops here on the way between Pretoria (1st/2nd class R80/60, five hours) and Cape Town (R450/305, 24 hours).

Northern Cape

Covering nearly a third of the country, the vast and sparsely populated Northern Cape surely is South Africa's last great frontier. With a restless air of untamed energy, this is a place where the Africa of storybooks comes alive – the kind of spot you'd expect to find the Marlboro Man and Indiana Jones swapping yarns with Lara Croft over pints of ale in some rough-and-ready old saloon. In this land of stark contrasts the red sands of the Kalahari tumble into the churning, inky waters of the desolate Atlantic Coast; while the Karoo's umber grasses and strange-shaped kopjes (hills) – home to grazing sheep, ramshackle windmills and tiny dorps (villages) – collide with the sun-scorched lunar landscape of Namaqualand, where roads dissolve into an oblivion of endless space. Lions stalk their prey across crimson plains in remote Kgalagadi Transfrontier Park at dawn, while in the evening big, orange-ball sunsets made for Hollywood movies steal the show. Days are best spent playing cowboy in the desert – building a fire in the middle of nowhere, listening for the hyena's call and dreaming under a twinkling velvet blanket made from a million stars.

The Northern Cape is a captivating magician with more than a few tricks up its sleeve. In its favourite, it appears as an inhospitable desert, so hot and dry you'd never believe anything could grow. But just when you're ready to fall for it, the Cape pulls a rabbit from the hat – turning dust to diamonds, rocks to flowers. Believe it or not, the hills around Kimberley have yielded enough of the world's favourite stone to fill a bathtub or two; in spring Namaqua gives birth to a miraculous sea of technicolour wildflowers.

HIGHLIGHTS

- Tracking lion through red, searing sands in remote and beautiful **Kgalagadi Transfrontier Park** (p537)
- Photographing the explosion of colourful wildflowers blanketing **Namaqua National Park** (p548) each spring
- Digging for diamonds and a dose of Wild West culture in the old mining town of **Kimberley** (p526)
- Hiking through stunning mountainous desert in **Richtersveld National Park** (p547), South Africa's wildest park
- Marvelling at pearly white dunes rising from a blanket of crimson sand in magnificent **Witsand Nature Reserve** (p537), a place where the desert roars

★ Kgalagadi Transfrontier Park

★ Richtersveld National Park

Witsand Nature Reserve ★

★ Kimberley

★ Namaqua National Park

- POPULATION: 816,976
- AREA: 361,830 SQ KM

NORTHERN CAPE

HISTORY

The Northern Cape's first residents were the San: skilled hunter-gatherers who gradually became settled pastoralists known as the Khoekhoen (men of men) – see p32 and p33 for more on the history of these people.

In northwest Namaqua is another well-known Khoekhoen tribe, the Nama (also known as Namaqua or Namakwa, which means 'Nama people'), famous for their copper metalworking skills. Not surprisingly, this attracted the attention of Dutch explorers, who came into contact with the tribe in 1661. Because of the region's isolation, however, the Namaqualand copper rush did not properly begin until the 1850s. The first

commercial mine (now a national monument) was established just outside Springbok in 1852, and there are still a number of working mines including one at Nababeep.

Diamonds were first discovered in the Kimberley area in 1866, when a young man by the name of Erasmus Jacobs stumbled upon a pretty white pebble, picked it up and altered the course of South African history. In his hand he held a 21.25-carat yellow diamond called Eureka. Five years later, the source, a small hill that came to be known as Colesberg Koppie (later Kimberley), was identified and the excavation of the mine known as the Big Hole commenced. By 1872 there were an estimated 50,000 miners in the vicinity and Cecil John Rhodes

NORTHERN CAPE

LEGEND
DR Desert Reserve
GR Game Reserve
NP National Park
NR Nature Reserve

(see the boxed text, p527) had arrived on the scene (he would later buy out all claims and found one of the world's most powerful diamond conglomerates, De Beers Consolidated Mines Company).

Namaqua is also an important source for alluvial diamonds. Prospectors converged on the area in 1925, after a young soldier named Jack Carstens found a glittering stone near Port Nolloth and it soon became clear that another enormously rich source of diamonds had been discovered.

CLIMATE

The Northern Cape is a land of extremes. The province is semidesert and summer temperatures in the Kalahari and the Karoo often soar above 40°C during the day and drop below freezing at night.

Rainfall in the region is scant, with annual precipitation between 50mm and 400mm, most of which falls in the western areas of the province. This rain leads to magnificent spring (July–November) wildflowers in Namaqualand. The Senqu (Orange) River runs through the Northern Cape and the river valleys are so fertile the area is called the Green Kalahari.

NATIONAL PARKS & RESERVES

The Northern Cape has the country's most spectacular and remote national parks. In the far north of the province, bordering Botswana and Namibia, is the outstanding Kgalagadi Transfrontier Park (p537), one of Africa's newer parks.

The wildest of all of South Africa's national parks is Richtersveld National Park, in a very remote location on the Namibian border in the northwest corner of the province. The park is mostly only accessible by 4WD, and due to the amount of time it takes to reach it, day visitors are discouraged. It's best to visit the park on an organised tour (see p547).

Two other major parks in the region are easily accessible: Augrabies Falls National Park (p541), where the Senqu (Orange) River plunges over a series of waterfalls; and newly established Namaqua National Park (p548), which offers some of the best wildflower-season views in the region.

Excellent nature reserves include the Witsand Nature Reserve (p537), 200km east of Upington, where you can feast your eyes on giant red-and-white dunes.

LANGUAGE

The Northern Cape is one of only two provinces in South Africa (the other is Western Cape) where coloureds, and not blacks, make up the majority of the population. Afrikaans is the most widely spoken language with about 66% of the province speaking it. The indigenous population is varied and includes the San, who can still be seen around the Kalahari (small numbers of San lead semitraditional lifestyles in isolated parts of neighbouring Botswana), the Tswana and some Khoekhoen groups. Tswana (19%) and Xhosa (6%) are the other main languages. English is spoken everywhere.

GETTING THERE & AROUND

The Northern Cape is easily accessible by car, bus, train and plane. With the exception of the Kgalagadi Transfrontier and Richtersveld National Parks, where private vehicle hire is a necessity, with a little patience most places can be reached by bus. There is daily bus service between the transportation hubs of Kimberley and Colesberg from both Cape Town and Johannesburg (Jo'burg). Buses to and from Cape Town, Jo'burg and Windhoek (Namibia) also pass through Upington and Springbok at least three times a week. **South African Airlink** (SAAirlink; ☎ 054-838 3337; www.saairlink.co.za) has flights from Jo'burg and Cape Town to Kimberley and Upington.

Public transport within the province is generally straightforward, and you won't be kept waiting anywhere for too long. If you're on a tight budget, but still want to experience the Kgalagadi on your own, it's possible to pick up a rental car in Upington for a couple of days, although prices are generally higher than if you rent in one of the country's major cities.

KIMBERLEY & UPPER KAROO

Kimberley is the epicentre of the region. An old diamond town with a chequered past, it's also the capital of the Northern Cape and definitely worth a few days' pause. The north–south N12, an alternative route between Jo'burg and Cape Town, passes through Kimberley and crosses the

TOP FIVE NORTHERN CAPE DRIVES

Although driving through much of the Northern Cape is a magnificent experience, there are some drives that take this province's unspoilt appeal entirely to another level. Whether you are an experienced back-roads driver, or simply looking for a beautiful spot to snap some pictures, we're sure these roads won't disappoint.

- Just outside Kakamas (p541) on the N14 heading towards Keimos is the turn-off for the **Riemvasmaak 4WD Trails** (☎ 054-431 0945). Here you can challenge your skills on three trails ranging from beginner to expert. The existence of this area is proof of the triumph over apartheid. In 1973 the government forcibly removed the local inhabitants – Xhosa, Nama and coloured – to the Eastern Cape and Namibia. Following the transition to democracy in 1994, efforts began to bring back the local population, and Riemvasmaak became one of the first land restitution projects in South Africa. In 2002, the formerly displaced residents were given the deeds to the plots they live on and a community-driven tourism initiative began. This now includes the 4WD trails as well as a mountain-bike route, hiking paths, a natural hot spring and accommodation in chalets.

- Rte 364 between Calvinia (p548) and Clanwilliam in the Western Cape runs through empty countryside and over several magnificent passes. There are excellent displays of wildflowers in early spring. There's a great view from the top of **Botterkloof Pass**, and a couple of nice flat rocks overlooking the gorge that are perfect for a picnic. You hit irrigation country around Doringbos, where you'll find dramatic views of the Cederberg Range. The **Pakhuis Pass** takes you through an amazing jumble of multicoloured rocks. Allow at least two hours for the journey – more if you have a picnic or are tempted to take the road to **Wuppertal**. This is an old Rhenish mission station and little has changed since it was established in 1830. It has whitewashed, thatched cottages, as well as cypresses and donkeys.

- There is a stunning stretch of Rte 27 between Calvinia and Vanrhynsdorp in the Western Cape with magnificent views over the Knersvlakte Plain from **Vanrhyns Pass**. In spring there can be a breathtaking contrast between the green and fertile wheat fields, the flowers at the top of the pass and the desert far below.

- The dirt roads around **Hondeklip Bay** on the Northern Cape's coastline are spectacular. After climbing through rocky hills you drop onto the desert-like coastal plain, which is dotted with enormous diamond mines. The flora is fascinating – make sure to take time to walk around, even if it's just off the side of the road. A 2WD is OK for this area.

- The **Namaqua 4WD Route** traverses some of South Africa's most remote and rugged territory east and south of Richtersveld National Park (p547). The route has been divided into two parts: Pella Mission Station to Viooolsdrif and Viooolsdrif to Alexander Bay. To drive either route you must first obtain a permit from the **tourism information office** (☎ 027-712 2011) in Springbok. Permits cost R150 per vehicle per route and include a detailed map and information on designated camping sites along the way. The first route, designed for novice drivers, traverses 328km and takes between two and four days to drive. The second route, designed for more experienced drivers, is 284km long and is usually completed in six hours.

east–west N10 at Britstown in the Upper Karoo.

The Upper Karoo, which is part of the Great Karoo (see p264 and p227), is sprinkled with small towns, scrub brush and little else; it's probably the least-enticing portion of the expansive Karoo. However, nearly everyone driving the N1 between Cape Town and Jo'burg stops for the night in Colesberg, as it's about halfway between the two cities.

KIMBERLEY

☎ 053 / pop 166,000

Like all good mining towns, Kimberley is pockmarked with legends and ghost stories. Step inside one of the atmospheric old pubs with their dark smoky interiors, scarred wooden tables and last century's Castle Lager posters, and you'll feel you've been transported back to the rough-and-ready diamond heyday. Spend a night in one of the old-world hotels, the slightly shabby air only adding to its charm, and you'll wake up thinking it's the late 1800s.

This is the city where De Beers Consolidated Mines began; where Cecil John Rhodes (see boxed text, below) and Ernest Oppenheimer (mining magnate and mayor of Kimberley) made their fortunes. It's been more than a century now, and yet Kimberley is still synonymous with diamonds and mining.

After a long slog across the Karoo the relatively bright lights of Kimberley are a welcome sight. The Big Hole is amazing, there are some excellent galleries around and the Galeshewe Township is inextricably linked with the history of the struggle against apartheid – although unfortunately at the time of research the once highly regarded tours were no longer running.

Orientation

The town centre is a tangle of streets, a legacy of the days when Kimberley was a rowdy shantytown, sprawling across flat and open veld. If you're trying to find the train station, look for the red-and-white communications tower. The tourist tram, which departs from the town hall, is a good means of getting your bearings.

The satellite township of Galeshewe is northwest of the city centre.

Information

Diamantveld Visitors Centre (☎ 053-832 7298; tourism@kbymun.org.za; 121 Bultfontein Rd; ☯ 8am-5pm Mon-Fri, 8am-noon Sat) Good maps and brochures of Kimberley and the Northern Cape; can arrange tours of the area.
Small World Net Café (☎ 053-831 3484; 42 Sidney St; per hr R30; ☯ 8am-5.30pm Mon-Fri, 9am-2pm Sat) Internet access.

Sights
THE BIG HOLE

The area surrounding the largest manually dug hole in the world was undergoing renovations worth R30 million when we stopped by. When completed, the touristy complex, dubbed the **Big Hole Project** (☎ 053-833 1557; West Circular Rd; phone for admission prices & opening hr), will combine the best of history and entertainment and include space for six hotels, numerous restaurants, shops, a cinema and a giant diamond display. As for the Big Hole itself, you'll be able to view it through a glass-enclosed complex with interactive displays and underground experiences. At 800m deep, water now fills it to within 150m

---

CECIL RHODES

The sickly son of an English parson, Cecil John Rhodes (1853–1906) was sent to South Africa in 1870 to improve his health. Shortly after arriving, he jumped on the diamond-prospecting bandwagon, and in 1887, after working feverishly, founded the De Beers Consolidated Mines Company and bought Barney Barnato's Kimberley Mine for UK£5 million. By 1891 De Beers owned 90% of the world's diamonds and a stake in the fabulous reef of gold on the Witwatersrand (near Johannesburg).

But personal wealth and power alone did not satisfy Rhodes. He believed in the concept of the empire, and dreamed of 'painting the map red' and building a railway from Cape to Cairo, running entirely through British territory. Rhodes was successful in establishing British control in Bechuanaland (later Botswana) and the area that was to become Rhodesia (later Zimbabwe).

In 1890 Rhodes was elected prime minister of the Cape Colony, but was forced to resign five years later after encouraging a raid on the Witwatersrand, in Paul Kruger's Transvaal Republic (see p37). The British government was publicly embarrassed by these actions, and along with forcing Rhodes' resignation, took control of his personal fiefdoms of Bechuanaland and Rhodesia.

Rhodes' health deteriorated after these disasters. Following his death in South Africa in 1906, though, Rhodes' reputation was largely rehabilitated by his will, which devoted most of his fortune to the Rhodes Scholarship that still sends winners from the Commonwealth and other countries to study at Oxford University.

If you're interested in learning more, *Rhodes* by Antony Thomas has received good reviews. Thomas, a native South African best known for his movie-production work, was exiled from the country in 1977 after creating an anti-apartheid documentary. His biography on Cecil John Rhodes, which spurred a six-part Masterpiece Theatre TV show, presents a thorough picture of the man without trying to force too many personal opinions on the reader.

NORTHERN CAPE

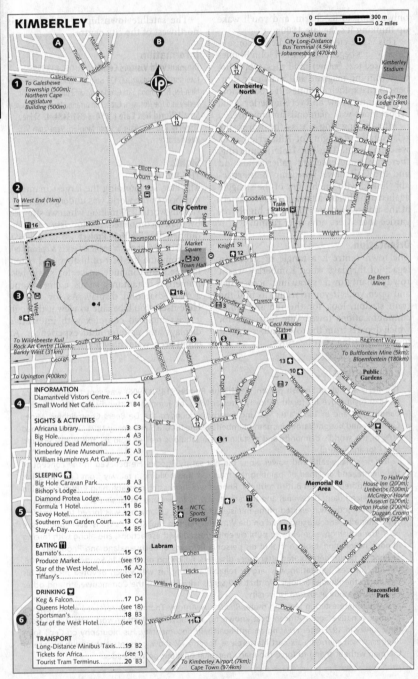

KIMBERLEY

INFORMATION	
Diamantveld Vistors Centre	1 C4
Small World Net Café	2 B4

SIGHTS & ACTIVITIES	
Africana Library	3 C3
Big Hole	4 A3
Honoured Dead Memorial	5 C5
Kimberley Mine Museum	6 A3
William Humphreys Art Gallery	7 C4

SLEEPING	
Big Hole Caravan Park	8 A3
Bishop's Lodge	9 C5
Diamond Protea Lodge	10 C4
Formula 1 Hotel	11 B6
Savoy Hotel	12 C3
Southern Sun Garden Court	13 C4
Stay-A-Day	14 B5

EATING	
Barnato's	15 C5
Produce Market	(see 19)
Star of the West Hotel	16 A2
Tiffany's	(see 12)

DRINKING	
Keg & Falcon	17 D4
Queens Hotel	(see 18)
Sportsman's	18 B3
Star of the West Hotel	(see 16)

TRANSPORT	
Long-Distance Minibus Taxis	19 B2
Tickets for Africa	(see 1)
Tourist Tram Terminus	20 B3

of the surface, which still leaves an impressive void, but don't forget that there is over four times as much hole below the water's surface. Diamond mining stopped here in 1914, but not before 14.5 million carats of diamonds were carted away.

The complex will also incorporate the already excellent **Kimberley Mine Museum**, set up as a reconstruction of Kimberley in the 1880s, where you can browse for ladies shoes, bottled water or petticoats amid the dusty shops and dance halls. It also includes a diamond-digging area perfect for the kids.

The renovations were scheduled to conclude in May 2006.

GALESHEWE TOWNSHIP

The satellite township of Galeshewe rates with Soweto as an important source of activists in the struggle against apartheid. The township is home to the house and grave of Sol Plaatje, a founding member of the African National Congress (ANC), noted journalist and one of the first black South Africans to have a novel published in English. It is also home to Robert Sobukwe, founder and first president of the then-Pan African Congress (PAC). Galeshewe was where the Self Help Scheme was implemented by Helen Joseph, an organiser of the 1956 mass demonstration in Pretoria against the extension of regulations governing the carrying of passes.

A visit to Galeshewe may well be one of the highlights of your stay in South Africa. Unfortunately, at the time of research organised township tours were no longer operating. Check with the visitors centre, however, as this could easily change (the guy who used to run them went off to college, so we really can't feel anything but happy for him). The township is not particularly dangerous, however, and if you have transport and go during the day you'll likely be met more with smiles than trouble, especially if you show interest in the area and its history. If you choose to visit, show respect. Galeshewe provides a chance to glimpse how the ANC's commitment to provide housing is progressing, but desperate conditions still exist and the reality is that there are simply too many people and too little money for drastic change to really occur.

The outskirts of the township are also home to the **Northern Cape Legislature Building** (☎ 053-830 0600; Nobengula Rd; ☿ hr vary),

where the provincial government meets. Creatively designed, it features hardly any hard lines, instead opting for underemphasised angles and inviting curves. Numerous sculptures, depicting the varied faces of the people of the province, grace both interior and exterior surfaces of this building, which resembles a fine work of art. The location, in a low-income area, was no coincidence. Government officials built it here in the hope of creating new employment opportunities for township residents.

ANGLO-BOER WAR BATTLEFIELDS

The Brits and Boers really had it out in the land surrounding Kimberley between 1899 and 1902. The siege of Kimberley lasted for 124 days before the British army of Lords Roberts and Kitchener relieved the town on 15 February 1900. The **Honoured Dead Memorial**, to those who lost their lives in the siege, is at the intersection of Memorial and Dalham Rds, 2km south of the city centre. The large gun is Long Cecil, built and used in Kimberley during the siege.

Several major battles were fought in the vicinity of Kimberley, both during the siege and after. The most important was Magersfontein on 11 December 1899, when entrenched Boers decimated the famous Highland Brigade. The visitors centre has details on the Diamond Fields N12 Battlefields Route southeast of Kimberley.

Rhodes sat out the Kimberley siege in two downstairs rooms of the building now home to the **McGregor House Museum** (☎ 053-442 0099; Atlas St; adult/child R8/4; ☿ 9am-5pm Mon-Sat, 2-5pm Sun). The museum has exhibits on the Anglo-Boer War and runs daily **Magersfontein battlefield tours** (tour R10), when there's enough interest.

WILDEBEEST KUIL ROCK ART TOURISM CENTRE

There's not a lot going on at this government-funded **tourism initiative** (☎ 053-833 7069; www.museumsnc.co.za/wildebeestkuil.htm; Barkly West Rd; adult/child R10/5; ☿ 9am-5pm) right now, but it has the potential to be a culturally fascinating excursion if enough folks visit to sustain it. Built with a grant from the department of environmental affairs and tourism to help create jobs for poor local communities and a renewed understanding of the Khoesaan past, this place is worth visiting for this cause alone. There are 10 rock-art displays on the property. Each is marked and you will be given headphones and a cassette player before you start out on the self-guided walking tours. Also check out the 20-minute film on the Xun and Khwe peoples. The gift shop is free to browse and has a very reasonably priced, although limited, selection of traditional regional crafts. The centre is 10km west of town.

OTHER MUSEUMS

A unique collection of photographs of tribes taken in the 1920s and 1930s before many aspects of traditional life were lost can be found at the **Duggan Cronin Gallery** (☎ 053-842 0099; Egerton Rd; admission by donation; ☒ 10am-5pm Mon-Sat, 2-5pm Sun).

An excellent collection of contemporary works by black artists, in addition to pieces by Dutch, Flemish, English and French artists can be found at the **William Humphreys Art Gallery** (☎ 053-831 1724; admission R2; ☒ 10am-5pm Mon-Sat, 2-5pm Sun). Some argue it's the best gallery in South Africa.

The **Africana Library** (☎ 053-830 6247; 63-65 Du Toitspan Rd; admission free; ☒ 10am-5pm Mon-Fri) collection covers the first period of contact between the Tswana and the missionaries. Included in its holdings is missionary Robert Moffat's copy of his translation of the Old Testament into Tswana.

Tours

De Beers Tours (☎ 053-842 1321; tours R15; ☒ 9am & 11am Mon-Fri) offers group visits to the diamond treatment and recovery plants at Bultfontein Mine, located 5km east of the centre on the city's outskirts. Tours depart from the visitors centre at the Bultfontein Mine gate.

Diamond Tours Unlimited (☎ 053-861 4983; www .diamondtours.co.za; tours from R150) offers a variety of tours including battlefield trips, diamond digs and city-sightseeing trips. They also organise personalised yellowfish fly-fishing trips. Call for departure times and to arrange pick-up.

To tap into Kimberley's wild past from a different angle, take a haunting hike down memory lane by joining a ghost tour. Both **Jaco Powell** (☎ 093-256 4795) and **Dirk Potgieter** (☎ 053-861 4983; www.diamondtours.co.za) offer 3½-hour trips for R150 (book in advance). Tours depart from the Honoured Dead Memorial (p529) at 6pm – just in time for the sky to darken and your guide to inform you

that the vault here is supposedly haunted with the souls of 27 British soldiers who perished during the siege of Kimberley. From the monument, tours continue to Kimberley's most haunted sights, dishing up an entertaining and educational introduction to town legends.

Underground tours (☎ 053-842 1321; tours R80; ☒ 9.30am Mon, 8am Tue-Fri), also run by De Beers, is the more adventurous of the mine tours. Descend deep under the earth and get a feel for the life of a miner. You can't wear contact lenses because of the pressure at the depths you'll descend to, and you have to be over 16 to go on one of these 3½-hour tours. The tours depart from the visitors centre at the mine gate.

Sleeping

BUDGET

Kimberley doesn't have any traditional backpacking options, but its budget places, while a little sterile, are perfectly adequate for a few nights.

Big Hole Caravan Park (☎ 053-053-830 6322; West Circular Rd; camp sites R25, plus per person R15; ☒) Cool off in the swimming pool on a hot day or lounge in the grass under the shady trees and read a novel; either way this centrally located camp site is an appealing spot.

Gum Tree Lodge (☎ 053-832 8577; fax 831 5409; cnr Hull St & Bloemfontein Rd; dm R50, s/d R110/180; ☒) This former jail is a good place to bring the family – there's a playground and lots of grass. Accommodation is in basic flats with a stove and fridge and shared ablution facilities. It's about 3km east of the town centre.

Stay-A-Day (☎ 053-832 7239; 72 Lawson St; s/d from R110/180) It doesn't have much atmosphere and the rooms are tiny, but it's also sparkling clean and you'll feel good knowing profits go towards an orphaned children's home. Most rooms share bathrooms, but a few en suites are available for R250.

Halfway House Inn (☎ 053-831 6324; 229 Du Toitspan Rd; s/d R160/190) If you're hoping to literally stumble into bed this is a good option – the place is attached to a lively pub. Those seeking quiet, look elsewhere. Rooms are large and come with TV.

MIDRANGE

If none of these options sound appealing head to the Diamantveld Visitors Centre, which has details on more guesthouses.

Formula 1 Hotel (☎ 053-831 2552; www.formula1 hotels.co.za; cnr Memorial & Welgevonden Aves; r R200; 🅿) Rooms are tiny, but they are also spotless, come with TV and air-con and are great value (they can sleep up to three). It's a little way out of town, but perfect for odd-numbered groups just wanting a place to crash.

Savoy Hotel (☎ 053-832 6211; 15 Old De Beers Rd; r from R300) An old-fashioned hotel that charms with cosy well-loved rooms and the soft-spoken gracious ambience of a time long past, this good-value place appeals to those interested more in attitude than amenities.

Bishop's Lodge (☎ 053-831 7876; www.bishops lodge.co.za; 9 Bishops Ave; r from R300; 🅿 🖭) Modern and spotless inside, the self-contained flats come with sitting rooms, TV and full kitchenettes. Chill by the inviting pool and throw together your own private braai (barbecue). There are cheaper doubles in the main house.

Diamond Protea Lodge (☎ 053-831 1281; dplkim@ global.co.za; 124 Du Toitspan Rd; r from R400; 🅿) Rooms are decked out with the standard chain-hotel schlock, but they are larger than usual with firm beds, nicer than expected linens and extra-cool air-con for those unbearably hot days. Not bad value and there are often specials.

TOP END

Southern Sun Garden Court (☎ 053-833 1751; fax 053-832 1814; 120 Du Toitspan Rd; r R600; 🅿 🖭) Under new ownership this place has a giant, quite posh, lobby. Rooms are all clones of each other but come with all the amenities including wi-fi access. The attached Spur restaurant means you don't have to wander far for sustenance. Children stay free.

Edgerton House (☎ 053-831 1150; 5 Edgerton Rd; r R1000; 🅿 🖭) Exquisite furniture, African hospitality and a tea garden make this charming guesthouse the best luxury option in Kimberley. It has the honour of having had Nelson Mandela stay on more than one occasion.

Eating

Tiffany's (☎ 053-832 6211; Old De Beers Rd; mains R25-50; 🕑 breakfast, lunch & dinner) This is a lovely, if very pink, old-style restaurant in the Savoy Hotel with good service and a varied menu – including a few vegetarian options. The leather-and-wood bar adjoining Tiffany's is good for a quiet drink before dinner.

Umbertos (☎ 053-832 5741; 229 Du Toitspan Rd; mains R35-80; 🕑 lunch & dinner) Big hearty portions of Italian food are served along with loads of ambience. For dining choose either the rooftop patio with its pretty sunset views or the more intimate downstairs area, with a red-and-white theme. There are loads of pizza and pasta options and lots of dishes for vegetarians.

Star of the West Hotel (☎ 053-832 6463; North Circular Rd; mains R35; 🕑 breakfast, lunch & dinner) Walk through the thick wooden door and step back into Kimberley's mining heyday at this atmospheric city staple. Tables are scarred, and old posters and newspaper clippings grace the walls (this was a men-only pub until the late 1980s). Food is pub grub, the clientele mostly local. Despite its past, women won't feel uncomfortable eating or drinking here.

Barnato's (☎ 053-833 4110; 6 Dalham Rd; mains R60-90; 🕑 lunch & dinner Mon-Fri, dinner Sat, lunch Sun) Posh and always popular, Barnato's is a favourite with locals and tourists alike. It's known for its creative gourmet menu, elegant atmosphere and professional service.

There's a produce market and takeaway food at the Indian shopping centre on Duncan St.

Drinking

Kimberley is one of the few towns in South Africa with a range of decent pubs, some of which have been around from the time diamonds were the town's lifeblood. In fact at one time the number of bars in the city apparently twice outnumbered its churches.

Halfway House Inn (☎ 053-831 6324; 229 Du Toitspan Rd) It's easy to resurrect the bad old days at this ultimate dive. Once a ride-in bar (a concept invented by Rhodes, who was afraid to dismount from his horse and reveal his true height), today it's a drive-in kind of place – yes, believe it or not you can pull up front, toot your horn and someone will come out and deliver you a beer. We'd suggest wandering inside, however, and having a whisky at the scarred old bar amid the ancient beer posters, dusty mirrors and floor-side spittoons. The Half has pool tables downstairs and live music on Friday and Saturday nights in the pleasant rooftop beer garden.

Star of the West Hotel (☎ 053-832 6463; North Circular Rd) There are often live bands in the big beer garden. Pool tables and a cocktail bar upstairs add to the ambience.

Queens Hotel (☎ 053-831 3704; 12 Stockdale St) In the centre of town this large pub in the hotel gets rowdy on weekends and has gambling. Sportsman's is the attached disco.

Keg & Falcon (☎ 053-833 2075; 187 Du Toitspan Rd; mains R35-60) Head here if you're looking for a slightly older crowd. You have to be over 23 to get in and the dress code is smart casual. It also serves food.

Getting There & Away

AIR

SA Express (☎ 011-978 5315; www.saexpress.co.za) has regular direct services from Jo'burg (R1000, 1½ hours). **SAAirlink** (☎ 054-838 3337; www.saairlink.co.za) has a direct service to Cape Town (R1600, two hours).

BUS

Translux (☎ 011-774 3333; www.translux.co.za) stops in Kimberley on its run between Jo'burg/Pretoria (R140, seven hours, daily) and Cape Town (R230, 10 hours, daily). **Greyhound** (☎ 012-323 1154; www.greyhound.co.za) and **Intercape** (☎ 086-128 7287; www.intercape.co.za) have similar fares and routes.

Book tickets for all three companies through **Tickets for Africa** (☎ 053-832 6043), at the Diamantveld Visitors Centre. Buses stop at the Shell Ultra City long-distance bus terminal on the N12.

MINIBUS TAXI

The main minibus taxi area in Duncan St is around the Indian shopping centre in the city centre. Destinations from Kimberley include Bloemfontein (R50, 2½ hours), Kuruman (R75, two hours), Jo'burg (R120, seven hours), Upington (R75, four hours) and Cape Town (R135, 10 hours).

TRAIN

For information on trains call **Spoornet** (☎ 053-838 2111; www.spoornet.co.za). The *Trans Karoo* runs daily between Cape Town (R150, 18 hours) and Jo'burg/Pretoria (R80, nine hours) via Kimberley; the *Diamond Express* runs overnight between Jo'burg/Pretoria and Bloemfontein via Kimberley (R80, nine hours, three times weekly); and the *Trans Oranje* between Cape Town and Durban (R120, 18 hours, weekly) takes a slow and circuitous route via Kimberley.

Getting Around

The Kimberley airport is about 7km south of the city centre. A taxi costs about R150.

Kimberley has one surviving antique tram (one-way/return R7/14) that departs from the terminus near the town hall every hour on the hour (9am to 4pm daily) and runs to the Big Hole complex.

A minibus taxi around town costs about R1.50. Try **AA Taxi** (☎ 053-861 4015) or **Rikki's Taxi** (☎ 083-342 2533) for a private taxi from the pubs.

VAALBOS NATIONAL PARK

This is the only **national park** (☎ 053-561 0088; adult/child R60/30) in South Africa where three distinct ecosystems are present: the Karoo, *grassveld* (grasslands) and the Kalahari. Proclaimed in 1986 and divided in two by a belt of private land, the park is 61km northwest of Kimberley on Rte 31. There are **camping sites** (camp sites R75) and **self-catering cottages** (up to 4 people R350), but you must bring all your supplies with you, as the park does not have restaurant or shopping facilities.

DE AAR

☎ 053 / pop 26,000

Too big to be called a one-horse town, but not quite justifying a two-horse title, De Aar is a major service centre for the Karoo and one of those places you'll likely forget as soon as you pass through. If you need a break from driving, however, it's a good lunch stop.

The **De Aar Hotel** (☎ 053-631 2181; Friedlander St; s/d R180/260; 🖭) is a large, well-maintained place with a pleasant feel. It's not luxurious, but the bathrooms are spotless and the rooms have TV. There is an attached restaurant and bar.

The **Upstairs Restaurant** (☎ 053-631 1000; cnr Hoof & Voortrekker Sts; mains R25-50; 🕑 breakfast, lunch & dinner) has a rather extensive menu of seafood, pasta, pizza and various meats. Eat on the upstairs patio and catch all the town's action on the main drag below.

The *Trans Karoo* and *Blue Train* (Jo'burg/Pretoria–Cape Town), and the *Trans Oranje* (Durban–Bloemfontein–Kimberley–Cape Town) stop here; see p641.

BRITSTOWN

☎ 053

At the centre of a prosperous sheep-grazing area in the Upper Karoo, tiny Britstown is a pleasant and orderly place at the crossroads of the N10 and the N12. If you find yourself here at dusk and want to stay, try the long-established **Transkaroo Country Lodge** (☎ 053-672 0027; fax 053-672 0363; s/d R200/380; ✵ ☻). It has a provincial French feel with a cosy lounge, friendly staff and quaintly furnished, immaculate rooms. The attached restaurant and bar does a dinner buffet for R75 and light lunches. It also runs activities such as bird-watching trips, and excursions to San rock-art sites.

Minibuses pass through Britstown; ask at the Transkaroo Country Lodge.

COLESBERG

☎ 051 / pop 12,000

A classic Karoo town, Colesberg's only real attraction is that it's an ideal halfway stopping point on the N1 between Cape Town and Jo'burg. It's big enough to offer a choice of sleeping and eating options, but not too big to get lost trying to find your way around.

Founded in 1829, many of the old buildings are still intact, including a beautiful **Dutch Reformed church** built in 1866.

Colesberg's friendly **information centre** (☎ 051-753 0678; belinda@mjvn.co.za; Murray St; ✵ 8am-4.30pm Mon-Fri) is in the town museum. If you're yearning to surf the Web, try the **Colesberg Apteek** (☎ 051-753 0618; 18 Church St; per hr R60; ✵ 9am-5pm Mon-Sat).

Sleeping

Most of the town's accommodation options are on Church St, which is sometimes spelled the Afrikaans way – Kerk St.

Colesberg Backpackers (☎ 051-753 0582; 39 Church St; dm/d R50/120) A homely place right on the main drag, this backpackers doesn't have tonnes of atmosphere but it's quiet and is good value. Often empty, you'll probably have the dorm to yourself. All rooms share bathrooms.

Light House (☎ 051-753 0043; 40A Church St; r R250) The best option in town, the Light House is in a large rambling home with stately, well-appointed and airy rooms.

Colesberg Lodge (☎ 051-753 0734; fax 753 0667; Church St; r R280-360; ✵ ☻) A solid choice for quality service, Colesberg Lodge offers three classes of rooms – budget, regular and luxury. The budget digs have fans only, while the luxury abodes come with air-con and TV. There's a bar and restaurant attached.

Eating

Bordeaux Coffee Shop & Restaurant (☎ 051-753 1582; 7A Church St; mains R20-50; ✵ breakfast, lunch & dinner) With a cosy atmosphere, decent wine list and flavoursome, if nothing fancy, country cooking this is Colesberg's best eating option. Vegetarians might be happier elsewhere.

JC's Pizzeria (☎ 051-753 1170; 29 Church St; mains R30-55; ✵ lunch & dinner) The menu at Colesberg's best veggie option focuses on pizzas, pastas and steaks, with pizzas coming out best. Sit outside under the vines or inside among the twinkling candles.

Getting There & Around

Translux (☎ 011-774 3333; www.translux.co.za) and **Intercape** (☎ 086-128 7287; www.intercape.co.za) both pass through Colesberg on their daily Jo'burg (R220, 7½ hours) to Cape Town (R300, 9½ hours) run and stop at the Shell Ultra to the north of town on the N1. Intercape also has services to Bloemfontein (R110, 2½ hours, daily).

THE KALAHARI

A voyage to the Kalahari is akin to catapulting into a parallel universe – a surreal Alice-through-the-looking-glass experience where you'll feel really small and everything around you looms larger than life. Timeless and magical, solitary stretches of space spin on into infinity; shapes distort under a blanket of scorching desert heat. A mystifying collage of fiery sunsets and shifting crimson sands, of lush green fields and gushing waterfalls, magnificent wildlife preserves and tidy vineyards, this region will enchant long after you depart. Laurens Van der Post brought the world of the Kalahari alive in many of his books including *Lost World of the Kalahari* and *A Far Off Place,* but even if you know these tomes by heart be ready to be swept away again after tasting the real thing.

The Kalahari is not limited to South Africa. It actually covers much of Botswana and its fingers extend into Angola and Namibia as well. In South Africa it's divided into two distinct areas – the arid, semidesert and desert regions on its periphery and the 'green' Kalahari, the irrigated, fertile region along the banks of the Senqu (Orange) River. Most visitors to South

Africa miss the Kalahari. Don't. Even the extra driving it takes to reach the Kgalagadi Transfrontier Park is well worth it.

KURUMAN

☎ 053 / pop 9000

An oasis in the desert – thanks to a permanent water supply in the shape of an amazing natural spring – Kuruman has the rough-and-tumble vitality of a feisty little frontier town set deep in the heart of wild country. Its name derives from a San word, but the Batlhaping, a Batswana tribe, also settled in the area c1800.

The main road is called simply that, and most businesses are concentrated around the intersection of this and Voortrekker/Tsening Sts. Adjacent to the Eye of Kuruman is a useful **tourist office** (☎ 053-712 1095; Main Rd; ☼ 8am-4.30pm Mon-Fri, 8am-12.30pm Sat).

Sights & Activities

Kuruman is worth an out-of-the-way stop if birds of prey fascinate you. The **Raptor Rehabilitation Centre** (☎ 053-712 0620; Tsening St; admission free; ☼ 8am-4.30pm Mon-Fri) provides a map of the best routes to follow when searching for these creatures. The Kalahari is home to 40 of South Africa's 67 raptor and vulture species.

The **Eye of Kuruman** (Main Rd; adult/child R1/0.50) is the natural spring that produces 18 to 20 million litres of water per day, every day. It has never faltered. The surrounding area has been developed into a pleasant-enough picnic spot, and is a good place to break your journey – note the masked weaver-birds and their nests over the pond.

Sleeping & Eating

Kuruman Caravan Park (☎ 053-712 1479; Voortrekker St; camp sites R50, chalets R200) Another decent option, it offers well-equipped and comfortable chalets. Camping spots are mostly shady, and the place is just a short walk from the town centre.

Riverfield Guesthouse (☎ 053-712 0003; www.riverfield.co.za; 12 Seodin Rd; s/d R210/330; ☒ ☒) Rooms are good value and quite comfortable with modern conveniences. The grounds are shady. The on-site bar is a great meeting place, dinners can be arranged during the week and the included breakfasts are mighty.

Over-de-Voor (☎ 053-712 3224; Hoof St; mains from R25; ☼ lunch & dinner) Over-de-Voor, which

serves 'Kalahari cuisine', is the town's best eating option. Vegetarians beware – the menu is meat plus meat.

Getting There & Around

Intercape (☎ 086-128 7287; www.intercape.co.za) stops daily in Kuruman on its way between Jo'burg (R250, seven hours) and Upington (R170, three hours).

The taxi rank is next to the Shop Rite supermarket on Voortrekker St.

MOFFAT MISSION

The first white settlement in the area, the London Missionary Society, established the **Moffat mission** (☎ 053-732 1352; adult/child R5/2; ☼ 8am-5pm Mon-Sat, 3-5pm Sun) in 1816 to work with the local Batlhaping people. It was named after Robert and Mary Moffat, two Scots who worked at the mission from 1817 to 1870. They converted the Batlhaping to Christianity, started a school and translated the Bible into Tswana. The mission became a famous staging point for explorers and missionaries heading further into Africa. The Moffats' daughter, Mary, married David Livingstone in the mission church, which is a stone and thatch building with 800 seats.

The mission is a quiet and atmospheric spot shaded by large trees that provide a perfect escape from the desert heat. It is along Rte 31 to Hotazel, about 4km from the N14.

UPINGTON

☎ 054 / pop 53,000

On the banks of the Senqu (Orange) River, orderly and prosperous Upington is a good place to catch your breath on either end of a long Kalahari slog. The area is intensively cultivated, thanks to limitless sunlight and irrigation water. Wide boulevards slightly cluttered with supermarkets and chain stores line the centre of town, but step onto one of the side streets and you'll enter a world where lazy river views and endless rows of trees create a calm and quiet atmosphere perfect for an afternoon stroll (if the heat is not too stifling).

Information

Café de Net (☎ 054-331 2252; Pick 'n Pay Centre; per half hr R20; ☼ 8.30am-5pm Mon-Fri) Has Internet access; look for it behind the Dros pub. You pay in half-hour blocks, so don't go over or you'll be paying another R20.

First National Bank (cnr Schröder & Hill Sts) On the northwestern corner.

Standard Bank (cnr Hill & Scott Sts)

Tourist office (☎ 054-332 6046; greenkal@mweb.co.za; ⏱ 8am-5pm Mon-Fri, 9am-noon Sat) This helpful office is in the Kalahari Oranje Museum.

Tours

Readers highly recommend **Kalahari Safaris** (☎ 054-332 5653; www.kalaharisafaris.co.za; 3 Oranje St) who run a variety of safaris to Kgalagadi, Augrabies Falls, Witsand Nature Reserve and Kruger. The three-day Kgalagadi starts at R3500 and includes entrance fees, equipment and meals. If you'd rather just hire a guide to help you explore on your own, it costs R1000 per day for a guide and R2500 for a guide, vehicle and trailer. It's best to book through the website or by phone, as the office doesn't seem to regularly open.

Sleeping

BUDGET

All backpackers in Upington have shut their doors, so budget options tend to be on the higher end of the price scale.

Eiland Holiday Resort (☎ 054-334 0286; tourism@ kharahais.gov.za; camp sites R60, r from R150;) The town's cheapest option offers a range of huts and bungalows and shaded camping spots on tranquil and expansive grounds adjacent to the eastern bank of the river.

River City Inn (☎ 054-331 1971; cnr Park & Scott Sts; s/d R225/285;) The rooms are the standard aging provincial hotel variety – bland but affordable with perks like TV and air-con. It's smack in the middle of town, so if you're coming through late at night it makes a good crash pad. There's no off-street parking.

MIDRANGE & TOP END

Budler St has some gorgeous guesthouses with grassed areas overlooking the river.

Affinity Guesthouse (☎ 054-331 2101; www.affinity guesthouse.co.za; 4 Budler St; s/d R280/380;) Right on the river, this place is great value for money. The rooms are small, but comfortable with firm mattresses and a movie channel. The air-con is cold enough to take the edge off the city's mind-numbing heat. Ask for a river-view room – they come with giant windows looking out on the gardens.

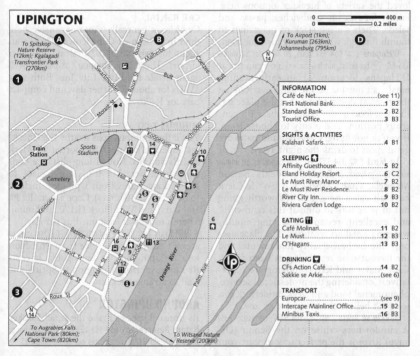

UPINGTON

0 — 400 m
0 — 0.2 miles

To Spitskop
Nature Reserve
(12km); Kgalagadi
Transfrontier Park
(270km)

To Airport (1km);
Kuruman (263km);
Johannesburg (795km)

INFORMATION
Café de Net............................(see 11)
First National Bank.......................**1** B2
Standard Bank..............................**2** B2
Tourist Office...............................**3** B3

SIGHTS & ACTIVITIES
Kalahari Safaris...........................**4** B1

SLEEPING 🏠
Affinity Guesthouse......................**5** B2
Eiland Holiday Resort....................**6** C2
Le Must River Manor.....................**7** B2
Le Must River Residence................**8** B2
River City Inn..............................**9** B3
Riviera Garden Lodge..................**10** B2

EATING 🍴
Café Molinari..............................**11** B2
Le Must.....................................**12** B3
O'Hagans...................................**13** B3

DRINKING 🍷
CFs Action Café..........................**14** B2
Sakkie se Arkie..........................(see 6)

TRANSPORT
Europcar..................................(see 9)
Intercape Mainliner Office............**15** B2
Minibus Taxis............................**16** B3

Train
Station

Sports
Stadium

Cemetery

Orange River

To Augrabies Falls
National Park (80km);
Cape Town (820km)

To Witsand Nature
Reserve (200km)

Le Must River Manor (☎ 054-332 3971; www.le mustupington.com; 12 Murray Ave; s/d from R390/580; 🆒 🆒) For those on a tighter budget, the quality at River Manor is only slightly less luxurious than the River Residence and also well worth a stay.

Riviera Garden Lodge (☎ 054-332 6554; 16 Budler St; d incl breakfast R400; 🆒) The gardens here are a fairy-tale creation, all sweetly scented flowers, leafy trees and fountains cascading down to the river. The friendly lodge has two cosy rooms with flowery bedspreads.

Le Must River Residence (☎ 054-432 3971; www.le mustupington.com; 14 Budler St; s/d from R590/700; 🆒 🆒) The classiest of the Le Must franchises, this place was awarded five stars by the South African Tourism Grading Council. Service and facilities are impeccable. Rooms are luxuriously decorated with antique furniture and African themes and come with satellite TV; the grounds are a work of art.

Eating & Drinking

The town has a few good spots to indulge.

Café Molinari (☎ 054-331 2928; Pick 'n Pay Centre; mains R20-40; 🕑 breakfast, lunch & dinner; 🆒) We loved the variety of breakfast options here. Lunch focuses on sandwiches, pastas and salads. There's a big stack of magazines to thumb through while waiting for your food.

O'Hagans (☎ 054-331 2005; 20 Schröder St; mains R35-60; 🕑 breakfast, lunch & dinner) You can't beat O'Hagans' location for an early evening meal – sit outside on the patio overlooking the river. It doesn't hurt that the place has the best food of the 'chain' pubs, with generous portions and plenty to choose from. If you're not hungry, the bar and patio are good spots to drink the night away.

Le Must (☎ 054-332 3971; 11 Schröder St; mains R65-90; 🕑 lunch & dinner) Presidents Nelson Mandela, Thabo Mbeki and FW de Clerk have all eaten here, and it's worth going out of your way to dine at this renowned, and excellent, restaurant serving mouthwatering Kalahari creations. The place uses only the highest-quality ingredients, and the flavoursome results it gets from fusing Cape Malay and Karoo cooking are superlative. Considering the professional service, phenomenal food and sleek modern décor, we can't believe the prices are so low.

Sakkie se Arkie (☎ 082-564 5447; admission R35) A sundowners cruise on the Senqu (Orange) River is the perfect way to start your evening. Admission covers the cruise; drinks are extra. The company picks up from many of the riverfront guesthouses.

CFs Action Café (☎ 054-332 1414; 65 Mark St) A dance floor and pool tables draw a young rowdy crowd.

Getting There & Away

AIR

If you're short on time and want to see the Kgalagadi, it may be worth flying into Upington and then renting a car. **SAAirlink** (☎ 054-838 3337; www.saairlink.co.za) flies to/from Jo'burg (R1660, daily) and to/from Cape Town (R1660, Sunday to Friday). Upington hotels usually provide a free taxi from the airport.

BUS

Two Intercape services provide links to the rest of the country. For tickets visit **Intercape Mainliner office** (☎ 054-332 6091; Lutz St). Buses go to Jo'burg and Pretoria (R260, 10 hours, daily), Windhoek, Namibia (R250, 12 hours, four times weekly), Cape Town (R220, 10½ hours, four times weekly) and Calvinia (R145, five hours, four times weekly).

CAR RENTAL

Car hire is generally more expensive here than in Jo'burg or Cape Town. There's an agent for **Avis** (☎ 054-332 4746) at Upington airport. There is a **Europcar** (☎ 082-426 8489) agent inside the River City Inn. Both rent 4WDs for about R950 per day, and compact cars for R400.

MINIBUS TAXI

You'll find minibus taxis nearby the Checkers supermarket near the corner of Mark and Basson Sts. Not all long-distance taxis leave from here but it's a good place to start asking. Fares from Upington include Jo'burg (R170, 10 hours), Cape Town (R180, 10 hours) and Windhoek (R170, 10 hours). There's usually at least one bus per day.

VIP Taxis (☎ in Port Nolloth 027-851 8780) operates a weekday taxi service from Port Nolloth to Upington, via Springbok. It costs R80 to travel from Upington to Springbok. Call to arrange pick-up.

AROUND UPINGTON

Its unusual species make the small **Spitskop Nature Reserve** (☎ 054-332 1336; teuns@intekom.co .za; adult/child R12/6; camp sites per adult/child R25/12, huts/chalets per person R60/80), about 13km north of Upington, so interesting. Most intriguing are the black springbok (there are six), whose colour results from genetic mutations that are seldom seen. The all 'black' zebra you see dominating a group of female zebra is a runt of a pony who decided to take over the herd – just look at the intensity on his face when he rounds up a female who breaks away. The camels are remnants of those that the German cameleers left in the region after skirmishes during WWI.

The reserve also has gemsboks, springboks, wildebeests, bonteboks, zebra and elands among other smaller animals.

There are 37km of gravel roads through the reserve as well as three short hiking trails and a novice 4WD trail. You can view wildlife through a telescope from the top of the prominent Spitskop.

Accommodation includes sandy, shady camp sites, a four-bed chalet and, most fascinating of all, a rustic, isolated 'veld hut' in the middle of the reserve (bring your own bedding). There is no electricity in the hut, which sleeps five.

WITSAND NATURE RESERVE
As if a **reserve** (☎ 053-313 1062; www.witsandkalahari .co.za; adult/child R20/10; ☺ 8am-6pm) based on a 9km-wide by 2km-long by 100m-high white sand dune standing out in stark contrast to the typical red Kalahari sands surrounding it weren't enough, this one also comes with a soundtrack. When the wind blows here the sand sings. Known as 'roaring sands' the effect is created by the movement of air across the dunes and creates a bass, organlike sound; walking on the sands produces a muted groan.

The reserve is approximately 200km east of Upington (or 200km southwest of Kuruman). You can walk anywhere in the park, but 4WDs are restricted to the roads. A bird hide, and mountain bike (R50 per day) and dune board (R70 per day) hire are added entertainment.

There's a delightful bush camp with two swimming pools and 10 thatch-roofed, open-plan, tastefully decorated **self-catering lodges** (per adult/child R200/100; ☒). The lodges have three bedrooms and can sleep up to six people. On weekends there is a minimum charge of R660 per lodge. The reserve does not have a restaurant or bar, but for R725 per person a chef will prepare you dinner and breakfast in your lodge. The fee also includes your accommodation, park entrance fee and a guided walk. Advance booking is essential. **Camping** (camp sites per person R50) is also an option.

KGALAGADI TRANSFRONTIER PARK
If you have the means (namely a vehicle), a visit to the other-worldly **Kgalagadi Transfrontier Park** (☎ 054-561 0021; www.sanparks.org; adult/ child R120/60) is more than worth the effort it takes to get there. The scenery in this magical place is phenomenal. Even the drive in, a seemingly endless jostle down dusty crimson roads, is an invigorating trip, evoking images of the grand African safaris of lore. Once inside, the sight of a giant blackmaned lion napping under the shade of a camel thorn tree in a land of shifting red-and-white sands is an awesome experience. Herds of gentle-looking gemsbok picking their way through sparse vegetation, those massive yellow-pink sunsets the continent is famous for and the chance to watch wildlife without the crowds all heighten this remote park's delicious appeal.

Proclaimed a national park in April 1999, Kgalagadi is the result of a merger between the former Kalahari-Gemsbok National Park in South Africa and the Mabuasehube-Gemsbok National Park in Botswana.

The accessible section of the park lies in the triangular segment of South African territory between Namibia and Botswana. This region covers 9591 sq km. The protected area continues on the Botswana side of the border (there are no fences) for a further 28,400 sq km. South Africa's side of the park was proclaimed in 1931 and Botswana's in 1938. Kgalagadi is one of the largest protected wilderness areas in Africa, allowing the unhindered migration of antelopes, which are forced to travel great distances in times of drought to reach water and food.

Although the countryside is described as semidesert (with around 200mm of rainfall a year) it is richer than it appears and supports large populations of birds, reptiles, rodents, small mammals and antelopes. These in turn support a large population of predators. Most of the animals are remarkably tolerant of cars. This allows you to get extraordinarily close to animals that are otherwise wild – it's as if you are invisible.

NORTHERN CAPE

The landscape is hauntingly beautiful – at times it feels you've reached the ends of the earth. The Nossob and Auob Rivers (usually dry) run through the park and meet each other a few kilometres north of the entrance at Twee Rivieren rest camp. Between the two rivers, the Kalahari dunes are characteristically red due to iron oxide. In other areas the sand varies from pink and yellowish to grey.

Orientation & Information

Visitors are restricted to four gravel/sand roads – one running up the bed of the Nossob River, one running up the bed of the Auob River (there are also some small loop roads) and two linking these. Make sure to take one of the roads linking the rivers for unobstructed views of the empty expanses of the Kalahari. Visitors must remain in their cars, except at a small number of designated picnic spots.

The best time to visit is in June and July when the days are coolest (below freezing at night) and the animals have been drawn to the bores along the dry river beds. September to October is the wet season and if it does rain, many of the animals scatter out across the plain to take advantage of the fresh pastures. Despite the fact that temperatures frequently reach 45°C in December and January, the chalets in the park are fully booked during the school holidays.

All the rest camps have shops where basic groceries, soft drinks and alcohol can be purchased (fresh vegetables are hard to come by); these are open from 7am until 30 minutes after the gates close. Petrol and diesel are available at each camp. There are public phones, a pub, a swimming pool and an information centre detailing the history of the park and giving details of the flora and fauna (there are also slide shows four nights a week) at Twee Rivieren rest camp (see opposite).

The gate opening hours change based on month, but generally follow the rising and setting sun. Gates open between 5.30am and 7.30am and shut between 6pm and 7pm.

The speed limit is 50km/h. The minimum travelling time from the entrance gate at Twee Rivieren to Nossob rest camp is 3½ hours; to Mata Mata rest camp it's 2½ hours. Allow plenty of time to get to the camps as no driving is permitted after dark.

If you want to venture into the Botswana side of the park, this is only possible via a 4WD trail. You need to make arrangements with the **Botswana Department of Wildlife & National Parks** (☎ 09-267 580774) in Gaborone.

Wildlife

PLANTS

Only hardy plants survive the periodic droughts that afflict the Kalahari. Many have adapted so that they germinate and produce seed within four weeks of a shower of rain.

The river beds have the widest variety of flora and are dominated by a variety of camel thorn trees. Various grasses and woody shrubs survive on the dunes. There are occasional shepherd's trees (*Boscia albitrunca*),

KGALAGADI TRANSFRONTIER PARK

0 —— 40 km
0 —— 20 miles

To Aranos (95km)

Xchoi Pan
Dimpho Pan
Gate Closed (No border crossing)
Union's End
Grootkolk
Polentswe Pan
Langklass
Lijersdraai
Kgalagadi Transfrontier Park
Kwang Kwang Pan
Lekkerwater
Sewe Panne
Marie se Draai
NORTHERN CAPE (SOUTH AFRICA)
NAMIBIA
BOTSWANA
To Gochas (144km)
Bitterpan Dikbaardskolk
Gate Closed (No border crossing)
Eland
Craig Lockhart Vloorskop (959m)
Dalkeith Kameelsleep
14th Bore Hole
13th Bore Hole
Vaalpan
Pula Urikaruus
Kamqua
Montrose Kransbrak
Kielie
Gemsbok Plain Krankie
Auchterlonie Tier
Kop Kij Kij
Rooiputs To Rooiduin (25km); Kalahari Trails Nature Reserve (35km); Andriesvale (53km); Molopo Lodge (60km); Upington (270km); Kuruman (385km)
Houmoed
Samevloeiing
Twee Rivieren Gate

SLEEPING
Bitterpan Camp.....................................1 A2
Gharagab Camp...................................2 A1
Grootkolk Camp..................................3 A1
Kalahari Tent Camp.............................4 A3
Kieliekrankie Camp..............................5 A3
Mata Mata Rest Camp.........................6 A2
Nossob Rest Camp..............................7 B2
Twee Rivieren Rest Camp.....................8 B3
Urikaruus Camp...................................9 B3

EATING
Lion's Den Restaurant.....................(see 8)

which have white bark and a dense thicket of short low branches where many animals take refuge in the heat of the day. The dried-oring shrub (Rhigozum trichotomum), with fine leaves and forked branches, is the most common shrub in the park.

Many of the animals depend on plants as their source of moisture. In particular, the tsamma (Citrillus lanatus), a creeper with melon-like fruit, is an important source of water. There are several prickly cucumbers that are important for the survival of animals, especially the gemsbok.

ANIMALS

Finding fauna requires luck, patience and a little intelligence. There is no guarantee that you will see one of the big predators, but you are more likely to here than in many other places. Most of the region's wildlife, with the exception of elephants, rhinos and zebras, are found in the park.

There are 19 species of predator here, including the dark-maned Kalahari lion, cheetah, leopard, wild dog, spotted hyena, black-backed jackal, bat-eared fox, Cape fox, honey badger and meerkat. The most numerous antelope is the springbok but there are also large numbers of gemsbok, eland, red hartebeest and blue wildebeest.

Spend an hour or so in the morning and the afternoon by a water hole. Watch for signs of agitation among herds of antelope – they don't automatically flee at the sight of a predator but wait until the predator commits itself to a charge before they run. Be sure to keep an eye on the top of the ridges overlooking the river beds, especially near herds of grazers, as these are good places to spot predators surveying their next meal. The lions like to walk along the side of the road because the soft dust is kind to their paws. Look for recent prints, as the lion may have moved off the road at the sound of your vehicle. Binoculars are essential.

Some 215 species of bird have been recorded here. Sighting birds of prey is a real treat and they are incredibly numerous; the Mata Mata road is especially good. Some of the most impressive species are the bateleur eagle, martial eagle, red-necked falcon, pygmy falcon, pale chanting goshawk and tawny eagle.

Two common birds are the secretary bird, seen strutting self-importantly over the claypans, and the kori bustard, the largest flying bird in Southern Africa.

A distinctive sight is the huge thatched nests of the weaverbird. These birds live in many-chambered nests that can last for more than a century and are inhabited by as many as 200 birds at a time. They weave twigs and straw in the crowns of acacias, on quiver trees and atop telephone poles.

Tours

Park rangers offer early morning, sunset and night **wildlife drives** (adult/child R110/55) from the rest camps at Twee Rivieren and Nossob. These can be booked at the ranger stations. Trips run when at least four people sign up.

Sleeping & Eating

There is accommodation both inside and outside the park. The park's only restaurant is at Twee Rivieren. Park fees are based on a daily rate, so if you arrive late in the afternoon you may want to spend the night outside the park to avoid paying that day's fees and head in early the next morning.

INSIDE THE PARK

There are three rest camps and six luxury wilderness camps. All can be booked through the **South African National (SAN) Parks Board** (☎ 012-428 9111; www.sanparks.org; 643 Leyds St, Muckleneuk, Pretoria). Advanced bookings are recommended.

Traditional Rest Camps

All rest camps have **camp sites** (per 2 people R110, extra person R38) without electricity and with shared ablutions facilities. The camps also have a range of huts, bungalows and cottages equipped with bedding, towels, cooking and eating utensils, kitchens and bathrooms.

Twee Rivieren (6-bed cottage per 2 people R520, extra adult/child R110/54; 🍴 🛒) The closest camp to the park's entrance, and the one with the most facilities, it's also the only rest camp with a swimming pool and air-con.

Mata Mata (d R275, 6-person chalets per 4 people R660, per extra adult/child R110/54) This camp, 2½ hours' from Twee Rivieren, is on the park's western boundary with Namibia. Surrounded by thorny Kalahari dune bushveld it's a good place to spot giraffe. There are a limited number of park homes and chalets so booking is advised through SAN (above).

Nossob (2-person chalets R400, 4-person guesthouse R785) Situated within the dry river bed of the Nossob, this camp is a good place to spot predators; it even has a predator information centre. The camp is a 3½-hour drive from Twee Rivieren.

Lion's Den Restaurant (breakfast/dinner from R30/60; 7.30-9am & 6.30-9pm) At Twee Rivieren, this restaurant offers a menu of mostly meat and seafood, with only one vegetarian option. The food is not bad. There's also a snack bar selling burgers and other takeaways.

Wilderness Camps

A few years back the park built three luxury wilderness camps, which were a big-enough hit for authorities to go ahead and construct three more. These remote sleeping options give you the opportunity to really get off-the-beaten path. The camps are not fenced, which means animals can wander in at will, although a ranger is on duty at all times. Make sure to stock up on petrol and drinking water before visiting, as neither is available on-site. All six camps have been designed to accommodate disabled people. The camps fill quickly, so book ahead.

Bitterpan Camp (2-person cabins R600) Constructed from reed and canvas, this stilted camp blends beautifully into the environment. The camp is on a one-way 4WD route starting from Nossob and will allow you to access a very remote portion of the park. It takes about 2½ hours to drive from Nossob to Bitterpan, so either start early in the day or first spend the night at Nossob. From Bitterpan it's about three hours' drive back to Twee Rivieren.

Gharagab Camp (2-person cabins R660) In a camel-thorn veld in the northern reaches of the park, the log cabins at this new camp are built on stilts above the hot sand. Outdoor showers and a private deck with water-hole views are perks at this remote spot.

Grootkolk Camp (2-person cabins R660) Nestled amid red sand dunes, and only 20km from Union's End where South Africa, Botswana and Namibia meet, this camp is a six-hour drive from Twee Rivieren rest camp. The camp has desert cabins made from sand bags and canvas – definitely a different sleeping experience. At night the silence and the stars will overwhelm you.

Kieliekrankie Camp (2-person cabins R660) One of the newest camps, about 44km north of

Twee Rivieren, the entrance is pretty spectacular – a tunnel through a dune. The four cabins built into the red sand environs have private balconies with views over the conveniently located water hole.

Urikaruus Camp (2-person cabins R660) On the banks of the Auob River, the four units at this new place are nestled amid gnarled old camel thorn trees. Perched over the dry river bed, they are connected with wooden walkways. The camp is easy to access, about halfway down the road between Twee Rivieren and Mata Mata.

Kalahari Tent Camp (2-person desert tents R690, 3-person tents R800, honeymoon tents R820;) The most accessible of the wilderness camps is also the most luxurious. Only 3km from Mata Mata rest camp, accommodation is in 15 desert tents created from wood, sand and canvas and decorated with rustic furnishings.

OUTSIDE THE PARK

There are a few options near the road to the Twee Rivieren gate.

Rooiduin (☎ 082-589 6659; camp sites per person R25) Rooiduin is about 32km from the Twee Rivieren gate on the road into the park, and offers camping sites under wooden structures (to keep the blowing sand out). Rooiduin rents sandboards for R25 per day, including a short lesson. It also does horse riding on the dunes for R50 per half-hour.

Kalahari Trails Nature Reserve (☎ 054902 ask for 91634; www.kalahari-trails.co.za; camp sites R60, s/d from R170/340) Run by a former professor of animal behaviour and desert ecology, this 3500-hectare reserve is 35km from the Twee Rivieren gate on Rte 360 towards Andriesvale. The reserve is home to all the wildlife found inside the park, with the exception of the big cats, and offers visitors a Kalahari experience they will not see from a car. Morning and evening dune walks (R35 per person) and wildlife drives (R45, three hours) teach basic tracking skills and provide geology lessons. Responsible tourism is emphasised heavily here – the host hopes visitors leave with a deeper respect for the Kalahari and all that lives in it. There are a variety of sleeping options from tented bush chalets 2km into the reserve to a guesthouse sleeping four. Meals can be arranged. For a different look at the magnificent world of the Kalahari we highly recommend stopping by.

Molopo Kalahari Lodge (☎ 054-511 0008; www .molopo.co.za; s/d R200/400; ☒ ☐ ☒) This lodge is about 60km before the Twee Rivieren gate on Rte 360. It is an attractive place built in traditional African safari-lodge style. Accommodation is in thatched roof huts, and the lounge area is covered in animal skins. It makes a good stop either before or after a park visit. Children aged 12 and under stay half-price. There is also a restaurant.

Getting There & Away

It's a solid, 385km, six-hour drive from Kuruman to Twee Rivieren. The drive from Upington to Twee Rivieren gate is 250km, made up of about 190km on bitumen and 60km on dirt roads.

Be very careful driving on the dirt roads as we've had several letters from travellers who wrecked their cars on this trip. If you stop, don't pull too far off the road or you might become bogged in the sand. Beware of patches of deep sand and loose gravel, which makes corners treacherous. Petrol is not available between Upington and Twee Rivieren, so start out with a full tank.

It's important to carry water, as you may have to wait a while for help if you break down.

KEIMOS & KAKAMAS
☎ 054

The N14 southwest of Upington follows the course of the Senqu (Orange) River and passes through oases of vineyards (still irrigated with the aid of wooden water wheels) and the quaint and quiet little towns of Keimos and Kakamas. Keimos is particularly lush, with palm tree–lined streets and plenty of green grass. The turn-off to Augrabies Falls National Park is just west of Kakamas.

With big grassy lawns where springbok graze between self-contained cottages, **Die Werf** (☎ 054-461 1634; s/d R215/308; ☒ ☒) is the best sleeping option in Keimos. The on-site **café** (mains R15-60; ☾ breakfast, lunch & dinner) and bar is a good place to grab a quick meal, especially if you're on the run. At night it serves more substantial fare. It stays open all day too, so it just might save you from having to lunch on crisps from the petrol station if you arrive in these parts during an off-hour. Die Werf is on the N14; if you're coming from Upington it will be on your right side just before Keimos.

In Kakamas, the **Kalahari Gateway Hotel** (☎ 054-431 0838; www.kalaharigateway.co.za; Main Rd; s/d R275/385; ☒ ☒) has massive rooms with coffee tables, couches and TVs. The zebra-themed restaurant (mains from R50, pizzas R30; open for dinner) and bar inside the hotel serve an assortment of steak and sea-food dishes, as well as pasta, burgers and pizzas. There is a large wine list focusing on regional wines. The Kalahari Gateway also provides information on the area and can arrange 4WD hire.

AUGRABIES FALLS NATIONAL PARK
☎ 054

The Khoesaan people called it 'Aukoerbis', meaning place of great noise. And when the waterfall for which this **park** (☎ 054-452 9200; www.sanparks.org; adult/child R60/30; ☾ dawn-dusk) is named is fat with rainy season run-off, its thunderous roar is nothing short of spectacular. You won't find any big animals here, but the place doesn't suffer for it. Set in a rocky mosaic around an 18km ravine through which the Senqu (Orange) River flows, the most interesting facet of Augrabies Falls is the fascinating desert/riverine ecosystems on either side of the river. The ravine was created around 500 million years ago when a scar in the underlying granite caused the river to chisel a deep abyss with several impressive cataracts. The main falls drop 56m, while the Bridal Veil Falls on the northern side drop 75m.

The park has a harsh climate, with an average rainfall of only 107mm and daytime summer temperatures that often reach 40°C. The flora includes kokerboom aloes, the Namaqua fig, several varieties of thorn trees and succulents. The park has 47 species of mammal (most of which are small) including klipspringer and other antelope species, rock dassie and ground squirrel.

Activities

The three-hour, 9km **Dassie Trail** is well-worth doing, particularly if your time is short. It involves clambering over rocks through some magical landscape – if you haven't seen any of the cute little rock daisies yet, this is your big chance.

The popular three-day, 40km **Klipspringer Hiking Trail** (R125) runs along the southern bank of the Senqu (Orange) River. Two nights are spent in huts built from local

SENQU (ORANGE) RIVER WINE ROUTE

Although not as well known as its Western Cape counterparts, the wine region along the banks of the Senqu (Orange) River is starting to take off. Tastings here are a much less pretentious affair, and meandering between the five vineyards run by the **Orange River Wine Cellars Cooperative** (☎ 054-337 8800; www.owk.co.za) is a pleasant way to pass an afternoon.

Wine making in the region dates back to the early 1900s when vineyards were planted in the fertile river valley for raisin production. However, it was discovered that the sultana grape was much more suitable for wine than raisins and in 1965 the Orange River Wine Cellars was born. The first grapes were harvested in Upington in 1968, and since then the co-op has grown to be the largest in South Africa with about 750 members and five cellars concentrated along the N10 and N14. The cellars produce about 30 different products, including grape juice concentrates. They are best known for their desert wines. Try the earthy Jerepigo with a taste of pineapple and plum or the sweet Muscadel with flowery undertones and an essence of peach and apricot.

All five cellars are well signposted – just keep an eye out for the Orange River Wine Trail signs. Keimos and Kakamas make good bases from which to explore the region, and each features a cellar. The **Keimos Winery** (☎ 054-461 1006; admission free; ⊗ 8am-5pm Mon-Fri, 8.30am-noon Sat) is just off the N14 slightly north of the intersection with Rte 2. The **Kakamas Winery** (☎ 054-431 0830; admission free; ⊗ 8am-5pm Mon-Fri, 8.30am-noon Sat) is just off the N14, in Kakamas. Both cellars offer tastings, and during harvest time (mid-January to mid-March) tours of the vineyards and a chance to chat with the wine maker.

---

stone (these can sleep 12 people). Camping is not allowed. Hikers must supply their own sleeping bags and food. Advance booking is advised. The trail is closed from mid-October to the end of March because of the heat. The **Gariep 3-in-1 Route** includes canoeing, walking and mountain biking; book and check out prices at the visitors centre when you enter the park.

The **Kalahari Adventure Centre** (☎ 054-451 0177; www.kalahari.co.za) runs canoeing and rafting trips on the Senqu (Orange) River. Try its very popular 'Augrabies Rush'. You will raft an exciting grade 2 to 3, 8km section of the river in an inflatable kayak; it costs R275 per person. It also runs a 60km five-day/four-night canoe trail for R1695. If you want to explore the desert in depth, join its safari trip. Guides are super-knowledgeable and you'll get to look for animals in the Kgalagadi Transfrontier Park (p537). The five-day/four-night trip costs around R5250 per person, although prices are based on fuel prices and likely to fluctuate. The office is 10km outside the park on the road from Kakamas. Follow the signs.

Sleeping & Eating

Accommodation in the park can be booked through the **SAN Parks Board** (☎ 012-428 9111; www.sanparks.org; 643 Leyds St, Muckleneuk, Pretoria), or you can take your chance and just show

up as there's often space. Options include **camp sites** (per 2 people R110, extra person R38) and a variety of **self-contained chalets** (from R420). Many of the chalets have outstanding views and are within earshot of the falls.

There's a cafeteria where you can buy sandwiches and cold drinks, and a **restaurant** (mains around R65; ⊗ lunch & dinner) with meals such as fillet steak or chicken. Cold water is free from the dispenser – you'll probably drink it dry if you are here in summer.

The friendly **Augrabies Falls Backpackers** (☎ 054-451 0177; www.kalahari.co.za; camp sites per person R30, s/d R75/150) has a great reed bar for watching the distant thunderclouds build, a chilled-out atmosphere and clean, comfortable rooms with animal-print-patterned bedding. Run by the **Kalahari Adventure Centre** (☎ 054-451 0177; www.kalahari.co.za), it's perfect for chilling out after a day on the river. The hostel is about 10km before Augrabies Falls National Park on the road from Kakamas. Follow the signs.

Getting There & Away

Private transport is recommended. The park is 38km northwest of Kakamas and 120km from Upington. The Kalahari Adventure Centre will pick you up from Upington (and other towns in the area). The shuttle fare is R150 per person (minimum of four).

NAMAQUA

In the Northern Cape's rugged northwestern corner the roads stretch on forever, traversing the unspoilt expanses of ever-shifting scenery that is Namaqualand and the Hantam Karoo. The region is immense – a wild void stretching from the Namibian border in the north to the west coast's bleak beaches, then south towards Vanrhynsdorp in the Western Cape before merging with the area known as Bushmanland in the east.

The region has a noticeable 'frontier atmosphere', due largely to its bleak and beautiful landscape and the presence of diamond miners. This is a land of immense sky and stark country. At night the sky is bright with stars, and it's easy to drive for ages without seeing another car.

SPRINGBOK

☎ 027 / pop 10,400

Springbok lounges in a valley surrounded by harsh rocky hills that explode with colour in flower season. Outside of flower season there's little to see or do, although the town's remoteness is alluring. The air always feels fresh, the desolate landscape is

endearing and step outside at night and it will be thoroughly still and quiet.

The first European-run copper mine, the Blue Mine, was established on the town's outskirts in 1852. From an edgy frontier town, Springbok has been transformed into a busy service centre for the copper and diamond mines in the region.

In the 1920s, Springbok had a large population of Jews who traded in the region. Most have moved away and their synagogue (built in 1929) has been converted into a small but good **museum** (☎ 027-712 2011; admission free; ☉ 9am-4pm Mon-Fri). Look for it behind the Springbok Hotel, west of Kowie Cloete Street.

Orientation & Information

The town is quite spread-out but most places are within walking distance of the small kopje (hill) in the elbow of the main street's right-angled bend.

Tourism information office (☎ 027-718 2985; Voortrekker St; ☉ 7.30am-4.15pm Mon-Fri, 9am-noon Sat & Sun) Has loads of information about flowers, attractions and drives in the area.

Sleeping

During flower season accommodation in Springbok can fill up. The tourist office can

---

WILDFLOWERS OF NAMAQUALAND

For the majority of the year Namaqualand appears a barren wasteland where seemingly nothing but the hardiest shrubs can survive. But with the winter rains comes the revelation of a secret: the dry lands are transformed into a kaleidoscope of colour as daisies, perennial herbs, aloes, lilies and a host of other species blanket the ground creating a sight that will enchant and mesmerise the eye, the artist's pallet and the photographer's lens. At this time visitors are drawn from all over the world to this often-forgotten corner of the country. All in all about 4000 species of plant grow in the region.

The optimum time to visit varies from year to year, but you have the best chance of catching the flowers at their peak between mid-August and mid-September (sometimes the season can begin early in August and extend to mid-October). The best flower areas also vary from year to year, so it is essential to get local advice on where to go. Bear in mind most varieties of wildflower are protected by law, and you can incur heavy fines if you pick them.

The flowers depend on rainfall, which is variable, and the blooms can shrivel quickly in hot winds. Many of the flowers are light-sensitive and only open during bright sunshine. Overcast conditions, which generally only last a day or two, will significantly reduce the display, and even on sunny days the flowers only open properly from around 10am to 4pm. They also face the sun (basically northwards), so it is best to travel with the sun behind you.

There are generally good flowers east of the N7 between Garies and Springbok. Other reliable flower-viewing routes are between Springbok and Port Nolloth, and through Kamiesberg, which is southeast of Kamieskroon in the direction of Garies. The Goegap Nature Reserve (p545), east of Springbok, and the hills around Nababeep are also good.

tell you about private, overflow accommodation. There is a big difference between low-season prices (given here) and flower-season prices.

Cat Nap Accommodation (☎ 027-718 1905; Voortrekker St; dm R80, r from R300; ☒) One of the best-value options in town. The walls of the spacious old house are adorned with nature photos and original art, and rooms are cosy African-themed affairs. There's a self-catering kitchen and backpackers can shack up in dorm beds in the barn.

Annie's Cottage (☎ 027-712 1451; annie@springbok info.com; 4 King St; s/d from R185/370; ☒) Each of the 10 rooms is decorated differently, but all are lovely. The pool and garden area is quaint with fountains, trees, flowers and benches. Room rates vary depending on amenities. This is an excellent choice.

Springbok Lodge (☎ 027-712 1321; fax 712 2718; 37 Voortrekker St; s/d from R190/310) This place is actually a collection of old houses scattered around town that have been steadily upgraded over the years; rooms range in size from the small Matchbox to the sizable Die Gewelhuis and Die Ark.

Springbok Hotel (☎ 027-712 1161; fax 712 1932; 87 Van Riebeeck St; s/d R200/325; ☒) It's your typical South African tourist-class hotel – nothing special, but the clean and acceptable rooms have TVs. There is an attached restaurant (mains R35 to R70) that serves buffet breakfasts and a variety of lunch options.

Blue Diamond Lodge (☎ 027-718 2624; 19 Union St; s/d incl breakfast R270/400; ☒) An attractive place north of the centre with neat units set around a swimming pool, with a resident macaw and a trail up the mountain behind the lodge with good views.

Old Mill Lodge (☎ 027-718 1705; 69 Van Riebeeck St; d/tr incl breakfast R400/500) Pleasantly situated in a peaceful garden up against the rocks on a quiet side street, the rooms here are plush and done up with modern art. Bathrooms are larger than average, with lovely touches like candles by the tub. Beds come with firm mattresses and luxurious, fluffy white duvets.

Eating

Springbok Restaurant (☎ 027-712 1321; 37 Voortrekker St; mains R20-50; ☒ breakfast, lunch & dinner; ☒) Pictures and animal heads clutter the

SPRINGBOK

0 — 300 m
0 — 0.2 miles

To Annie's Cottage (500m)
Luckhoff St
To Nababeep (21km)
To Blue Diamond Lodge (1km)
To Port Nolloth (145km); Windhoek (Namibia) (945km)

Van der Stel St
Hospital St
Lodge St
River St
Uitgan St
President St

Kowie Cloete St
Kopje
Voortrekker St

Pieter Malan St
Eerste Laan

Pastorie St
Eerste Laan
Wolkom St
Voortrekker St
To Upington (395km); Johannesburg (1270km)

Showgrounds

Appie Visser St
To Namastat (2km)

To Goegap Nature Reserve (15km); Garies (112km); Cape Town (555km)

walls and seating is at plastic dinner tables. There is a good breakfast selection. Lunch and dinner include steaks, chicken and schnitzel as well as pizza and burgers.

Titbits Restaurant (☎ 027-718 1455; cnr Namaqua & Voortrekker Sts; mains R25-50; ☯ breakfast, lunch & dinner) Despite the name and the mural of the big-breasted woman on the pink wall, this place does have a certain titillating atmosphere. There are loads of tasty options, including sandwiches, steak, pasta, pizzas and breakfast choices. There's also an outdoor balcony and kiddie's menu.

Godfather Restaurant (☎ 022-518 1877; Voortrekker St; mains R25-50; ☯ lunch & dinner) This simple, small place has a large menu, featuring everything from meat to pasta to sandwiches, all served to a very peppy soundtrack. There's a fun bar out the back.

BJ's (☎ 027-718 2270; cnr Van der Stel & Hospital Sts; mains R35-50; ☯ lunch & dinner; ✖) This classy basement joint with a cellar vibe serves tasty, and very reasonably priced, steak cooked exactly how you like it. White archways, wooden beams and leopard-skin print make up the décor. Classical music adds to the ambience, and the food does not disappoint. Vegetarians will be happier elsewhere.

Getting There & Away
BUS
Intercape (☎ 086-128 7287; www.intercape.co.za) has buses to Cape Town (R210, 7½ hours, twice weekly) that leave from opposite the Springbok Lodge. Buses leave for Windhoek, Namibia (R330, 12 hours, four times weekly) at 6.45pm from the same spot.

CAR RENTAL
Springbok is a popular jumping-off point for Richtersveld National Park and Namibia. For 4WD hire, stop by **Cat Nap Accommodation** (☎ 027-718 1905; Voortrekker St); it rents vehicles for R750 per day, or R900 per day including camping equipment. These prices include unlimited kilometres and insurance. Ask at the **Springbok Lodge** (☎ 027-712 1321; 37 Voortrekker St) or the **tourism information office** (☎ 027-718 2985; Voortrekker St) for other rental options.

MINIBUS TAXI
Van Wyk's Busdiens (☎ 021-559 1601) runs a daily door-to-door taxi to Cape Town (R160, five hours) and Kamieskroon (R45, one hour). You'll find ordinary minibus taxis at the taxi rank opposite the First National Bank near the kopje. Destinations include Cape Town (R160, five hours, daily) and Port Nolloth (R40, 2½ hours, five times weekly).

VIP Taxis (☎ 027-851 8780) operates a taxi from Springbok to Upington (R80, four hours, Monday to Friday) that departs from the Masonic Hotel (across the street from Springbok Hotel).

AROUND SPRINGBOK
Nababeep
☎ 027
The hills surrounding Nababeep are fantastic during flower season, when they turn a rainbow of colours. The town is on the site of a large copper mine, and mining enthusiasts will find a visit to the **Nababeep Mine Museum** (☎ 027-713 8121; admission free; ☯ 9am-5pm) worthwhile. **Nababeep Hotel** (☎ 027-713 8151; s/d R110/190) is a simple country hotel on the town's main street that also serves meals. Breakfasts are about R40 and dinners from R65. Prices go up considerably here in flower season.

Nababeep is 16km northwest of Springbok on the N7. Public transport options are sporadic. Ask at the minibus stop in Springbok if there are any minibuses heading in this direction.

Goegap Nature Reserve
Don't miss this semidesert **nature reserve** (☎ 027-712 1880; admission R10; ☯ 7.45am-4.15pm), famous for its extraordinary display of spring flowers and a nursery of 200 amazing Karoo and Namaqualand succulents at the **Hester Malan Wildflower Garden**.

There are a few driving routes around the reserve, but you'll see more on one of the circular walks (4km, 5.5km and 7km). There are two **mountain-biking routes** (14km and 20km), which are particularly memorable during flower season; bring your own bike (R7 bike permit per person).

PORT NOLLOTH
☎ 027 / pop 5000
The drive in to Port Nolloth could be worthy of a visit alone. One minute you're engulfed in nothingness, covered in a layer of red Kalahari sand. The next you're cresting a hill, watching the ground lighten and the icy blue vastness of the Atlantic appear on the horizon. Way off-the-beaten path, the place

NORTHERN CAPE

exudes a certain kind of raw, last frontier at the end-of-the-earth vitality. An exposed and sandy little nowhere town, where the bracing air smells of fish and salt, it's home to a motley, multicultural group of fortune-seekers.

First developed as the shipping point for the region's copper, Port Nolloth is now dependent on the fishing boats that catch diamonds and crayfish. The boats are fitted with pumps, and divers vacuum up the diamond-bearing gravel from the ocean floor.

Bedrock (☎ 027-851 8865; www.bedrocklodge.co.za; s/d/tr/q from R225/300/380/460), an extremely funky place crammed with all sorts of eccentric knick-knacks and antique collectables, occupies a number of old wooden cottages lining the seafront. The shabby nautical-chic self-catering cottages are spacious with sea views. Turn right onto the beachfront road from the main road through town and the Bedrock is the second building along.

The other sleeping option, the **Scotia Inn Hotel & Restaurant** (☎ 027-851 8353; s/d R195/225) is also on the beachfront road, in a large, white building to the left. It's a modern place with comfortable rooms and big windows.

Across from the Scotia, **Anita's Tavern Seafood & Grill** (☎ 084-726 7090; mains R25-40; ☽ dinner) is a rustic, reed, beach shack. Full of fishing junk and nonchalant character, it's not a bad place to pop in for a drink and dinner. The menu is seafood oriented (of course).

Mare Sole (☎ 082-821 2083; Main Rd; mains R20-40; ☽ breakfast, lunch & dinner) is another option. It's a lovely little spot with cheery yellow walls and bright environs. A range of breakfasts, sandwiches, light meals and a variety of coffee and tea drinks are on the menu.

There's little public transport, and hitching from the N7 turn-off at Steinkopf is slow.

VIP Taxis (☎ 027-851 8780) runs a taxi to Springbok (R40, 2½ hours, five times a week).

ALEXANDER BAY
☎ 027
The archetypal remote seaside community of Alexander Bay is a government-controlled diamond mine on the southern bank of the mouth of the Senqu (Orange) River (Namibia is on the north side). Basically it looks like a smaller, even more remote version of Port Nolloth and there is not much going on. The road from Port Nolloth is open to the public, but stopping anywhere along it is illegal. North of Alexander Bay, the road to the Namibian border is entirely off limits.

Activities in town include **mine tours** (☎ 027-331 1330; ☽ 8am Thu), which should be booked one day in advance. Bird-watchers come here looking for Barlow's lark, which is found nowhere else in the world.

Brandkaros (☎ 027-831 1856; fax 831 1390; camp sites per person R50, d R150; ☒) is a citrus farm by the river, about 30km northeast of Alexander Bay. It has a great swimming pool. The farm is en route to Richtersveld National Park and is a good base from which to tour this area. Accommodation is in self-catering rondavels. Bring your own food.

VIOOLSDRIF
This town is at the border post with Namibia on the N7, 677km north of Cape Town. The short drive from Steinkopf, with its views of the Senqu (Orange) River carving its way through desolate mountains, is spectacular. The border is open from 7am to 7pm.

Peace of Paradise (☎ 027-761 8968; camp sites R150, s/d R200/300) is 22km west of Vioolsdrif on the banks of the Senqu (Orange) River.

ILLEGAL DIAMOND BUYING

In South Africa it is illegal to sell diamonds to any person or company other than the De Beers Consolidated Mines Company. The diamond mines are thus hives of security. The independent divers who work Port Nolloth and other submarine diamond fields on the west coast, however, have more opportunity to get away with extracting diamonds from their catch and selling them on the black market. Diamond diving is hard work and it isn't lucrative – the divers can only work about 10 days per month because of the weather.

Illegal diamond buying (known as IDB) is a subcurrent of life in the Port Nolloth area and chances are that a few of your fellow patrons in a diamond town bar are undercover members of the police IDB branch. You may meet locals who offer to sell you cheap diamonds – don't do it! Not only is this highly illegal, you are also likely to end up with what is known as a *slenter*, or fake diamond. These are cut from lead crystal and only an expert can pick them.

It's very pleasant with hot showers, clean toilets and electricity for campers, as well as canoes for hire. There are San engravings 100m from the camp, and you can cool off with a swim in the river.

RICHTERSVELD NATIONAL PARK

Within a mountainous desert – a spectacular wilderness of jagged peaks, grotesque rock formations, deep ravines and gorges – is this enormous (185,000 hectares) **national park** (☎ 027-831 1506; www.sanparks.org; adult/child R80/40; ☺ 7am-6pm). It's especially spectacular during the spring flower season, when the park turns into a technicolour wonderland.

In the northern loop of the Senqu (Orange) River, northwest of Vioolsdrif and the N7, the park is the property of the local Nama people who continue to lead a semitraditional, seminomadic pastoral existence; hopefully they will benefit from increased job opportunities from tourism and the rent paid by the park authorities.

The hiking possibilities in this surreal, almost lunar-like landscape, are excellent (though demanding). Despite its apparent barrenness, the region has a prolific variety of succulents – 30% of South Africa's known succulent species grow here.

Fill up your petrol tank and cooler in Alexander Bay before entering the park; there are no shops in the parks, and only one petrol station and a small general store, both at Sendelingsdrift (see right). Neither is open on weekends.

Hiking Trails

Three hiking trails have been established in the park. The **Ventersvalle Trail** (42km, four days) encompasses the southwest wilderness; the **Lelieshoek-Oemsberg Trail** (23km, three days) takes in a huge amphitheatre and waterfall; and the **Kodaspiek Trail** (15km, two days) allows the average walker to view mountain desert scenery. Accommodation is in *matjieshuis* (woven Nama 'mat' huts) and there are field toilets. The trails are open from April to September and you must take a guide. For information about prices contact the **SAN Parks Board** (☎ 012-428 9111; www.sanparks.co.za; 643 Leyds St, Muckleneuk, Pretoria).

Tours

An organised tour could be the easiest way to visit this remote park. The **Richtersveld**

Challenge (☎ 027-718 1905; www.adventureaddicts .com) is run by Springbok photographer Rey van Rensburg, and operates between April and October. Rey is enthusiastic, experienced and very knowledgeable about the area. A five-day vehicle tour costs R650 per person per day including camping equipment and meals (minimum eight people). Try to book a few months in advance.

Sleeping & Eating

To make accommodation bookings, contact the **national park** (☎ 027-831 1506; www.san parks.org).

There is a brand-new rest camp at **Sendelingsdrift** (2-person camp sites R110, chalets from R415; ✖ ✺), which is surprisingly luxurious for such a remote area. The self-catering chalets have porches with river views, and campers can cool off in the sparkling pool.

Tatasberg (chalets R420) and **Ganakouriep** (cabins R420) are the park's wilderness camps. Both provide remote, and simple, digs in rustic self-catering cabins or chalets. Bring your own drinking water.

There are four other **camping areas** (per 2 people R110) around the park. All accommodation should be booked in advance.

Getting There & Around

Most of the park is virtually inaccessible without a fully-equipped 4WD and maybe a local guide, although it is slowly becoming easier to access. Two-wheel drive vehicles with high clearance, such as a *bakkie* (pickup truck) can usually negotiate the southern section of the park without problems.

KAMIESKROON & AROUND
☎ 027

Out amid the tumbleweed and scrub brush, forgotten-looking Kamieskroon sits in the heart of wild country. Craggy mountains and boulder-strewn hills surround the little place. The feel is desolate and remote, and many of the roads in town are still not paved. The name Kamieskroon means 'Jumble' or 'Huddles Together' in Nama. It's a great spot to get away from it all and to explore the area, especially in flower season.

The **town clerk** (☎ 027-672 1627; Voortrekker St; ☺ 9am-5pm Mon-Fri) serves as the tourist information office.

About 18km southwest of Kamieskroon is the newly established **Namaqua National**

Park (☎ 027-672 1948; www.sanparks.org; admission R60; ☼ 8am-5pm Jul-Oct), which incorporates the old Skilkop Nature Reserve. The shrubland and old wheat fields burst into flower in spring, and their clarity and prevalence often surpass all other areas in the region, making this one of the best places to photograph the flowers (visit between 10am and 4.30pm when the flowers look their best). Note that the park is only open during flower season and that it has no sleeping or eating facilities – pack a picnic before you head out.

Just off the N7 (follow the signs), you'll find the **Kamieskroon Hotel & Caravan Park** (☎ 027-672 1614; www.kamieskroonhotel.com; camp sites per person R45, s/d R150/250; ▣). It's quite comfortable and deservedly popular, especially from July to September (when bookings are essential and prices rise). It serves a set price dinner every night for R80 and breakfast for R35. During flower season it runs photographic workshops.

Kamieskroon is 80km south of Springbok on the N7. **Van Wyk's Busdiens** (☎ 021-559 1601) runs a bus service to Springbok (R45, one hour, daily). From here, if you're looking for a little scenic adventure, head west to Hondeklip Bay. While the town itself is just a smaller, less interesting version of Port Nolloth, the local dirt roads are spectacular.

CALVINIA
☎ 027 / pop 8100

Engulfed in a sea of 'Wild West' countryside, Calvinia is the main centre of the Hantam Karoo. As the church clock tolls the hours, it's easy to imagine that decades, if not centuries, have slipped away. The nearby township is friendly, with several convivial eateries and *shebeens* (unlicensed bars).

The **tourist information office** (☎ 027-341 1712; 44 Church St; ☼ 8am-1pm & 2-5pm Mon-Fri, 8am-noon Sat), adjoining the museum, is well organised. Staff can provide a walking-tour map of town and will help arrange accommodation; bookings are advisable in flower season.

Sights
For a small town, the **Calvinia Museum** (☎ 027-341 1712; 44 Church St; admission R2; ☼ 8am-5pm Mon-Fri, 8am-noon Sat) is of a surprisingly high standard. The main building was a synagogue – it's incongruous but not unusual to find disused Jewish buildings in tiny, remote South

African towns. The museum concentrates on the white settlement of the region, including sheep and farming activities, and there are some great oddities such as a four-legged ostrich chick (a fake used by a travelling con artist), and a room devoted to the lives of a local set of quadruplets.

Sleeping & Eating
Die Tuishuis, Die Dorphuis & Die Hantamhuis (☎ 027-341 1606; www.calvinia.co.za; 44 Hoop St; s/d from R225/370; mains R100) These are a complex of antique guesthouses that are some of the oldest buildings in town. Die Tuishuis and Die Dorphuis are your lodging options: both are furnished with antiques and offer a variety of elegant rooms. Candles and romantic music set the atmosphere for traditional three-course dinners served in Die Hantamhuis; meals include old favourites such as mutton on a stick.

Pionierslot (☎ 027-341 1263; 35 Water St; s/d incl breakfast R180/320) One of the nicest B&Bs in town, the owners here are hospitable without being overwhelming.

Cobusegat (☎ 027-341 2326; caves per person R70, stone houses per person R90) Definitely a unique experience, this place is 116km south of Calvinia on Rte 355. Accommodation is in self-catering caves – OK, they are really more like over-hanging rocks enclosed three-quarters of the way around and come complete with electricity, fridges and a stove. Each cave can accommodate up to eight people. The place also has two thatched-roof stone houses. The area boasts glacier scrapings from the last ice age.

Die Blou Nartjie Restaurant (☎ 027-341 1484; Pionierslot St; mains R35-75; ☼ lunch & dinner Mon-Sat) The range of dishes at this excellent restaurant is limited, but very good quality for such a small town. We love an open kitchen! Traditional *bobotie* (curried mincemeat topped with beaten egg, and served with turmeric rice and chutney) is delicious.

Getting There & Away
Intercape (☎ 086-128 7287; www.intercape.co.za) has buses to Cape Town (R170, six hours, four times weekly) and Upington (R145, five hours, four times weekly). Book at the **travel agency** (☎ 027-344 1373) incongruously situated in the *slaghuis* (butcher). Buses stop at the *trokkie* (truck) stop on the western side of town.

Lesotho

DI JONES

Lesotho

Lesotho (le-*soo*-too) is called Southern Africa's 'kingdom in the sky' for good reason. This stunningly beautiful, mountainous country is nestled island-like in the middle of South Africa. It came into being during the tumultuous years of the early 19th century, when both the *difaqane* (forced migration) and Boer incursions into the hinterlands were at their height. Under the leadership of the legendary king Moshoeshoe the Great, the Basotho people sought sanctuary and strategic advantage amid the forbidding terrain of the Drakensberg and Maluti ranges. The small nation they forged has managed to resist more recent pressures as well, and continues to be an intriguing anomaly in a sea of modernity.

The only way to reach Lesotho is via South Africa, and it is a fascinating travel detour from its larger neighbour. The country offers superb mountain scenery, the opportunity to meet and stay with people living traditional lifestyles, endless hiking trails and the chance to explore remote areas on Basotho ponies. Throughout, you'll find Lesotho refreshingly free of the after-effects of apartheid, with proud, friendly people and a laid-back pace.

While infrastructure may not be on par with South Africa, Lesotho has adequate and enjoyable amenities, including a handful of comfortable hotels and lodges. With an ordinary rental car you can reach most areas. Adventure-seekers can use the good (albeit slow) public transport around much of the country, or can just head off on foot.

The 'lowland' areas (all of which are still above 1000m) offer some cultural fun: there's craft shopping around Teyateyaneng or you can follow in the footsteps of dinosaurs around Quthing and Leribe (Hlotse). Yet, it's in the highlands in the northeast and centre that Lesotho is at its most beautiful. Here, towering peaks climb over 3000m, riven by verdant valleys and tumbling streams, and hiking or pony trekking from village to village are the best ways of exploring.

HIGHLIGHTS

- Trekking on ponies around **Malealea** (p568) and **Semonkong** (p567)
- Heading up to **Sani Top** (p565) and absorbing the awesome vistas from Sani Pass
- Revelling in the splendid isolation of **Sehlabathebe National Park** (p572), **Ts'ehlanyane National Park** (p563) or **Bokong Nature Reserve** (p567)
- Hiking in the **northeastern** and **central highlands** (p563)
- Shopping for crafts in **Teyateyaneng** (p560), **Leribe** (p561) or **Maseru** (p558)

■ POPULATION: 2.1 MILLION   ■ AREA: 30,355 SQ KM

HISTORY
The Early Days
Lesotho is the homeland of the Basotho – Sotho-Tswana peoples who originally lived in small chiefdoms scattered around the highveld in present-day Free State. Cattle and cultivation were their economic mainstays, and trading was at the heart of daily life.

As the 19th century moved into full swing, this comparatively tranquil existence came under threat. The Voortrekkers and various white entrepreneurs began to encroach on Basotho grazing lands, which the Basotho themselves had already pushed to capacity. On top of this came the *difaqane* (see p35), which was just beginning to unleash its wave of destruction.

Yet, unlike neighbouring groups, many of whom were dispersed or decimated, the Basotho emerged from this period more united. This was largely due to the leadership of the brilliant Moshoeshoe the Great, a village chief who rallied his people and forged a powerful kingdom. To do this, Moshoeshoe first led his own villagers to the mountain stronghold of Butha-Buthe, where he established a base from which he was able to resist the early incursions of the *difaqane*. In 1824, to enhance his position, Moshoeshoe began a policy of assisting refugees of the *difaqane* in return for their help with his own defence. He moved his headquarters to the more easily defended hilltop perch of Thaba-Bosiu, from where he repulsed wave after wave of invaders.

By 1840 Moshoeshoe's rule was firmly entrenched. His people numbered about 40,000 and his power base was protected by groups who had settled on outlying lands and were partially under his authority. Ultimately, Moshoeshoe was able to bring these various peoples together as part of the loosely federated Basotho state, which, by the time of his death in 1870, had a population exceeding 150,000.

Moshoeshoe had also welcomed Christian missionaries into his territory. The first to arrive, in 1833, were from the Paris Evangelical Missionary Society. Moshoeshoe made one of them his adviser, and the sophisticated diplomacy that had marked his dealings with local chiefs now extended to his dealings with the Europeans. The missions, often situated in remote parts of the kingdom, served as tangible symbols of his authority. In return for some Christianisation of Basotho customs, the missionaries were disposed to defend the rights of 'their' Basotho against a rising new threat: Boer and British expansion.

Defending the Territory
The Basotho spent much of the early and mid-19th century fending off Boer forays into their areas. In 1843 – in response to continuing Boer incursions – Moshoeshoe allied himself with the British Cape Colony government. While the resulting treaties defined his borders, they did little to stop squabbles with the Boers, who had established themselves in the fertile lowveld west of the Mohokare (Caledon) River. In 1858 tensions peaked with the outbreak of the Orange Free State-Basotho War. This was followed in 1865 by a second war between the Boers and the Basotho. After gaining an early victory, Moshoeshoe began to suffer setbacks, and was ultimately forced to sign away much of his western lowlands.

In 1868 Moshoeshoe again called on the British, this time bypassing the Cape Colony administration and heading straight to the imperial government in London. It had become obvious that no treaty between the Boers and the Basotho would hold for long, and the British viewed continual war between the Orange Free State and Basotholand as bad for their own interests. To resolve the situation, the British annexed Basotholand.

The decade after Moshoeshoe's death was marked by ongoing squabbles over succession, and increasing colonial infringements on Basotho autonomy. After briefly changing hands between the British imperial government and the Cape Colony, Basotholand again came under direct British control in 1884. One unexpected benefit of this was that, when the Union of South Africa was created in 1910, Basotholand was a British protectorate and was not included; had Cape Colony retained control, Lesotho would have become part of South Africa, and later a homeland under the apartheid regime.

Independence at Last
During the early 20th century, migrant labour to South Africa increased, and the Basotho gained greater autonomy under

LESOTHO

LEGEND
NP National Park
NR National Reserve
GR Game Reserve
FR Forest Reserve
WA Wilderness Area

the British administration. The main local governing entity during this period was the Basotholand National Council, an advisory body to the colonial government. In the mid-1950s the council requested internal self-government, with elections to determine its members. Meanwhile, political parties were being formed, led by the Basotholand Congress Party (BCP; similar to South Africa's African National Congress) and the Basotholand National Party (BNP), a conservative group headed by Chief Leabua Jonathan.

Lesotho's first elections in 1960 were won by the BCP, which made full independence from Britain the first item on its agenda. Agreement was reached, with independence to come into effect in 1966. At the next elections, in 1965, the BCP lost to the BNP. Chief Jonathan became the first prime minister of the newly independent Kingdom of Lesotho, with King Moshoeshoe II as nominal head of state.

Chief Jonathan's rule was unpopular, and in the 1970 election, the BCP regained power. Chief Jonathan responded by suspending the constitution, arresting and then expelling the king, and banning opposition parties. Lesotho effectively became a one-party state.

Chief Jonathan was deposed in a military coup in 1986, and Moshoeshoe II restored as head of state. Yet following ongoing power disputes between the king and the coup leader, Moshoeshoe II was deposed in favour of his son, Prince Mohato Bereng Seeisa (Letsie III). Elections in 1993 returned the BCP to government. In 1995 Letsie III abdicated in favour of his father, who again managed to bring some semblance of order to Lesotho. Less than a year after being reinstated, Moshoeshoe II was killed when his 4WD plunged over a cliff in the Maluti Mountains. Letsie III was again made king. (As head of state, Letsie III does not exercise executive power. Under traditional law, he can be deposed by a majority vote of the College of Chiefs. The real power lies with the cabinet, headed by the prime minister, and with parliament. Parliament is bicameral, consisting of a 120-member elected national assembly and a non-elected senate, comprised of 22 chiefs and 11 nominated members.)

The BCP was split between those who wanted the then-prime minister, Ntsu Mokhehle, to remain as leader and those who opposed him. In response, Mokhehle formed the breakaway Lesotho Congress for Democracy (LCD) and continued to govern, with the BCP now in the opposition. Mokhehle died in 1998, and Pakalitha Mosisili took over the leadership of the LCD. Later that year, the LCD won a landslide victory in elections that were declared reasonably fair by international observers, but were widely protested within Lesotho. Tensions between the public service and the government became acute, and the military was also split. In September 1998 the government called on its Southern African Development Community (SADC) treaty partners – Botswana, South Africa and Zimbabwe – to help it restore order in the country. Rebel elements of the Lesotho army resisted, which resulted in heavy fighting and widespread looting in Maseru. Elections – initially scheduled for 2000 – were finally held in May 2002. The LCD won, and Mosisili began his second five-year term as prime minister.

Current Events

Since 2002 Lesotho has enjoyed a period of peace, and parliamentary reform has progressed reasonably well, as has the general political process. Lesotho's literacy rate is comparatively high (about 85%), but nonetheless it ranks among the poorer countries in the region and it has few natural resources other than water and diamonds. For most of the 20th century, Lesotho's main export was labour, with approximately 60% of males working in South Africa, primarily in the mining industry. Since the early 1990s, these numbers have dropped by almost half with the restructuring of the South African gold-mining industry, increasing mechanisation and the closure of marginal mines. While male migrant workers were being retrenched in large numbers, the Lesotho economy was being transformed through the rapid growth of the textile industry. Since then, thousands have lost their jobs due to stiff competition from China and changes to international agreements (see the boxed text, p562). Unemployment is now estimated at about 45%, with the domestic economy unable to take up the slack. Yet it is hoped that economic initiatives will soon inject some energy into the revival of the local business sector.

Overshadowing the political and economic issues is the spectre of HIV/AIDS. The infection rate (adult prevalence) is estimated at about 30% – one of the highest in the region and the world. Government, business, NGOs (Nongovernment Organisations) and community organisations are working to combat the situation, but scarce resources, lack of capacity and a continued high level of social stigma attached to the disease hinder their efforts.

The elections of 2007 may bring challenges of another kind. Questions being considered are whether to back the current prime minister for a third term, whether corruption is being tackled vigorously enough and whether the 'grass roots' is being neglected in favour of a more 'gentrified' party.

CLIMATE

Clear, cold winters, with frosts and snow in the highlands, await you in Lesotho, so pack warm clothing. In summer (late November to March), dramatic thunderstorms are common, as are all-enveloping clouds of thick mist. Temperatures at this time can rise to over 30°C in the valleys, though it's usually much cooler in the mountains, even dropping below freezing. Nearly all of Lesotho's rain falls between October and

April. Throughout the year, the weather is notoriously changeable.

Visits are possible at any time, with spring and autumn optimal. For more information about when to go, see p20.

NATIONAL PARKS & RESERVES

Sehlabathebe is Lesotho's most famous national park. While you won't encounter the Big Five (lion, leopard, buffalo, elephant and rhino) here, its high-altitude grasslands, lakes, bogs and otherworldly rock formations offer a wonderful wilderness experience and are ideal for hiking or just getting away from it all. Sehlabathebe is under the jurisdiction of the **Parks Office** (☎ 2232 3600) of the Ministry of Forestry & Land Reclamation, just off Raboshabane Rd in Maseru.

The country's other main conservation areas – Ts'ehlanyane National Park (p563), Bokong Nature Reserve (p567) and the Liphofung Cave Cultural Historical Site (p564) – are under the jurisdiction of the **Lesotho Highlands Development Authority Nature Reserves** (LHDA; ☎ 2246 0723, 2291 3206; www .lesothoparks.com), which handles all accommodation bookings. All have simple accommodation, established trails, helpful staff, are relatively easy to access and well worth visiting.

LANGUAGE

The official languages are South Sotho (Sesotho) and English. For some useful words and phrases in South Sotho, see the Language chapter (p651). For more on Sotho language and culture, see www.sesotho.web.za.

DANGERS & ANNOYANCES

Several years ago, high unemployment rates and a weak economy resulted in a pronounced increase in crime – carjackings and muggings – mostly in Maseru. While such incidents have declined, travellers should not flaunt valuables and should be especially vigilant in Maseru, particularly at night.

If you're hiking without a guide, you might be hassled for money or 'gifts' by shepherds in remote areas, and there's a very slight risk of robbery.

Several lives are lost each year from lightning strikes; keep off high ground during an electrical storm and avoid camping in the open. Waterproof clothing is essential for hiking and pony trekking.

GETTING THERE & AROUND

It's possible to fly to Lesotho from South Africa, but most travellers enter by bus or private vehicle. For details, see p622. Once in Lesotho, there are good bus and minibus taxi networks that cover the country. See p634 for bus information and p640 for minibus taxi information. Note that minibus taxis do not normally operate to a schedule; they wait until the bus is full before departing.

For charter flights within Lesotho, the best contact is **Mission Aviation** (☎ 2232 5699).

MASERU
pop 175,000 / elevation 1600m

Maseru is the kind of place that grows on you. It sprawls across Lesotho's lower-lying western edge, rimmed by the Berea and

---

LESOTHO SAMPLER

Lesotho is an adventure traveller's destination *par excellence*. Hire a car, or brush up on your pony- or public transport-riding skills, and set off into the country's more remote corners. Some possible routes:

- Enter Lesotho at Tele Bridge by Quthing, and make your way east via Mt Moorosi, Mphaki and Qacha's Nek to Sehlabathebe National Park.

- Get a taste of the mountainous 'lowlands' by entering at Qacha's Nek and heading west via Quthing and Mohale's Hoek to Malealea, then to Morija, Roma and up to Semonkong.

- Take in some of Southern Africa's most impressive scenery on a circuit from Butha-Buthe to Oxbow and Mokhotlong (with a possible detour to Sani Top), then back either via Thaba-Tseka and the Katse Dam, or to Maseru via Likalaneng and Mohale Dam.

- Travel in a loop from Maseru via Morija to Malealea, continue on pony to Semonkong and then make your way back to Maseru via Roma.

Qeme Plateaus. Occupied by the British in 1869 as an administrative post, the city was a relative backwater for some time, and those coming from Johannesburg (Jo'burg) today might think it still is. However, Maseru has rapidly expanded over the past few decades, and boasts a modest array of modern amenities. A major city rebuilding program has hidden many of the once-visible scars of the 1998 political unrest (see p551).

The city boasts a temperate climate, well-stocked shops, a decent selection of restaurants and accommodation, and personable, peppy people. Maseru is the perfect place to get one's bearings, sort out logistics and stock up on supplies before heading into the highlands.

Orientation

Maseru's main street is Kingsway, which was paved in 1947 for a visit by the British royals and long remained the capital's only tarmac road. It runs from the Maseru Bridge border crossing southeast through the centre of town to the Circle – a major traffic roundabout best identified by the cathedral spires on its eastern edge. At the Circle, Kingsway splits into Lesotho's two major traffic arteries: Main North Rd (for Teyateyaneng and points north) and Main South Rd (for Mohale's Hoek and points south). A bypass road rims the city to the south. About midway along on Kingsway is the conical Basotho Hat building, a good landmark.

Although Maseru has few sights, just walking around the town and getting a feel for Lesotho life can be enjoyable. If you're feeling more adventurous, head into the urban villages surrounding Maseru for a taste of local life.

MAPS
The **Department of Land, Surveys & Physical Planning** (Lerotholi Rd; ☼ 9am-3pm Mon-Fri) sells a good 1:50,000 map of Maseru (M50), a 1:250,000 map of Lesotho (M50), plus 1:50,000 hiking maps covering the country (M35). Look for the brown building marked 'LSPP'. The tourist information office (right), on Kingsway, also sells a Lesotho map (M5).

Information
BOOKSHOPS
Basotho Hat (☎ 2232 2523; Kingsway; ☼ 8am-5pm Mon-Sat) This craft shop has books on Lesotho.

Maseru Book Centre (Kingsway; ☼ 8am-4.30pm Mon-Fri, 9am-noon Sat) Near Nedbank.

EMERGENCY
Ambulance (☎ 2231 2501)
Fire Department (☎ 115)
Police (☎ 2231 9900)

INTERNET ACCESS
Data Kare (LNDC Centre, Kingsway; per hr M10; ☼ 8am-9pm) The best and cheapest place for Internet access.
Leo (Orpen Rd; per min M0.50; ☼ 8am-5pm Mon-Fri) Behind the Basotho Hat building.

MEDICAL SERVICES
For anything serious, you'll need to go to South Africa. In an emergency, also try contacting your embassy (p610), as most keep lists of recommended practitioners.
Maseru Private Hospital (☎ 2231 3260) In Ha Thetsane, about 7km south of Maseru.
Queen Elizabeth Ii Hospital (☎ 2231 2501; Kingsway) Opposite Husters Pharmacy.

MONEY
The top-end hotels will do foreign exchange transactions (at poor rates). Otherwise try the following:
International Business Centre (Ground fl, Lesotho Bank Tower, Kingsway; ☼ 8.30am-3.30pm Mon-Fri, 8.30am-noon Sat)
Nedbank (Kingsway) Does foreign exchange transactions Monday to Friday.
Standard Bank (Kingsway) Has an ATM.

POST
Post office (cnr Kingsway & Palace Rd) Has unreliable poste restante.

TELEPHONE
International phone calls are expensive; if possible, wait until you are in South Africa. Note: no telephone networks function in the highlands. Cellphone signals are extremely rare and can be picked up on a few mountain passes only. They should not be relied upon.

Public telephones can be found at the **public phone shop** (LNDC Centre, Kingsway).

TOURIST INFORMATION & TRAVEL AGENCIES
City Centre Maseru Travel (☎ 2231 4536; Kingsway), located in the Book Centre building next to

MASERU

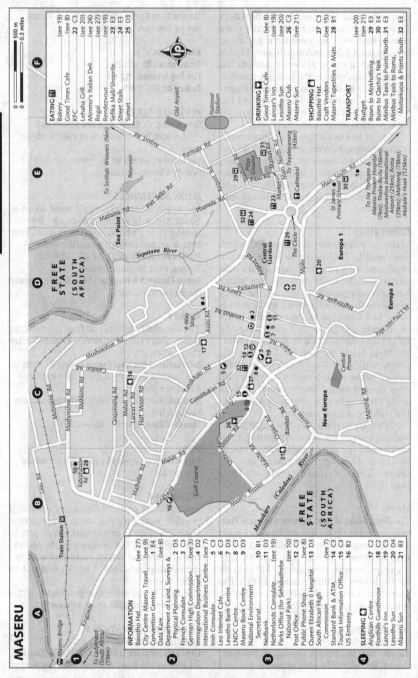

INFORMATION

Basotho Hat................................	(see 27)
City Centre Maseru Travel..........	(see 9)
Convention Centre....................1	E4
Data Kare...................................	(see 8)
Department of Land, Surveys &	
Physical Planning....................2	D3
French Consulate.......................3	C3
German High Commission.........4	D2
Immigration Department.............4	D2
International Business Centre.....	(see 7)
Irish Consulate...........................5	C3
Leo Internet Cafe.......................6	C3
Lesotho Bank Centre..................7	C3
LNDC Centre..............................8	C3
Maseru Book Centre..................9	D3
National Environment	
Secretariat............................10	B1
Nedbank.................................11	D3
Netherlands Consulate............	(see 19)
Parks Office (for Sehlabathebe	
National Park).......................12	D3
Post Office..............................13	D3
Public Phone Shop...................	(see 8)
Queen Elizabeth II Hospital.....13	D3
South African High	
Commission.........................	(see 7)
Standard Bank & ATM..............14	C3
Tourist Information Office.........15	C3
US Embassy.............................16	B2

SLEEPING

Anglican Centre........................17	C2
Foothills Guesthouse................18	C2
Lancer's Inn.............................19	C3
Lesotho Sun............................20	D4
Maseru Sun.............................21	B3

EATING

Bakery.....................................	(see 19)
Good Times Cafe......................	(see 8)
KFC...22	C3
Lehaha Grill..............................	(see 20)
Mimmo's Italian Deli.................	(see 26)
Regal.......................................	(see 27)
Rendezvous..............................	(see 19)
Sefika Mall/Shoprite.................23	E3
Street Stalls.............................24	E3
Sunset.....................................25	D3

DRINKING

Good Times Cafe......................	(see 8)
Lancer's Inn.............................	(see 19)
Lesotho Sun............................	(see 20)
Maseru Club............................26	C3
Maseru Sun.............................	(see 21)

SHOPPING

Basotho Hat.............................27	C3
Craft Vendors..........................	(see 15)
Maseru Tapestries & Mats........28	B1

TRANSPORT

Avis...	(see 20)
Budget....................................	(see 21)
Buses to Mokhotlong...............29	E3
Buses to Qacha's Nek..............30	E4
Minibus Taxis to Points North..31	E3
Minibus Taxis to Roma,	
Mafeteng (78km)..................31	E3
Motsekuoa & Points South..32	E3

LESOTHO

A GOOD BREAKFAST & A HOT SHOWER

Despite calling themselves 'bed & breakfasts', many B&Bs in Lesotho don't include breakfast in their prices. In this chapter, we've noted those places – hotels, lodges, B&Bs – that do. Otherwise, expect to pay about M35 to M55 per person for breakfast.

Also on the topic of amenities: a shower is a rare luxury in Lesotho. Many places – even some of the nicer hotels – only have baths, and the water (when available) is piping hot.

Nedbank, does regional and international flight bookings. They can also arrange tickets for Intercape and other long-distance buses. (Also visit Shoprite's 'Money Market' kiosk in LNDC Mall for Greyhound and Intercape bus tickets.)

The **tourist information office** (☎ 2231 2427; Kingsway; ◷ 8am-4.30pm Mon-Fri, 8.30am-5pm Sat), managed by the Lesotho Tourism Development Corporation, is a helpful office that has lots of brochures, lists of tour guides, information on public transport and free Maseru city maps (if you're lucky).

Dangers & Annoyances
Maseru is reasonably safe, but walking around at night, especially off the main street, is not recommended. Bag-snatching and pickpocketing are the main risks during the day.

Tours
The **tourist information office** (☎ 2231 2427; Kingsway) keeps an updated list of tour operators, and many of the main lodges listed in this chapter arrange tours and activities.

A few South African operators run tours up Sani Pass and over the border into Lesotho; see p356 and p641.

Sleeping
Maseru has a decidedly modest range of accommodation, though you should be able to find something that will suit for a night or two. Alternatively, it is also possible to overnight in Thaba-Bosiu or Roma, both of which are nice and easy drives from the capital.

BUDGET
Anglican Centre (☎ 2232 2046; dm/tw with shared bathroom M50/100) This offers austere but clean rooms, and meals are available with advance notice. It's about 500m north of Kingsway on the bend where Assisi Rd becomes Lancer's Rd. If you get lost, ask for St James Church, which is next door.

MIDRANGE & TOP END
Foothills Guesthouse (☎ 5870 6566; melvin@xsinet.co.za; 121 Maluti Rd; s/d with breakfast M295/450) A welcome addition to Maseru's sleeping options, this converted sandstone house has large and airy rooms with décor c 1960s, and a pleasant enclosed veranda for breakfasts. It's in a peaceful part of town, but may be a bit far on foot.

Lancer's Inn (☎ 2231 2114; lancers-inn@ilesotho .com; cnr Kingsway & Pioneer Rd; s/d/tr with breakfast M475/ 575/695; ⚄) Business travellers flock to this central option for its pleasant colonial-era ambience and excellent restaurant, but the price is overinflated for what you get. It's behind the French consulate in the town centre.

Maseru Sun (☎ 2231 2434; maseru@sunint.co.za; 12 Orpen Rd; r M945; ⚄ ⚘) You're on a safe bet in these comfortable, modern rooms with a grassy outlook, although the slot machines might eat any extra pennies you have. Maseru Sun is just southwest of the junction of Kingsway and Pioneer Rd, and signposted. Often has weekend specials.

Lesotho Sun (☎ 2231 3111; lesoresv@sunint.co.za; r M970; ⚄ ⚏ ⚘) A predictable gamble is Lesotho's other Sun – perched on a quiet hillside with a great setting overlooking town. It boasts the ubiquitous casino, two restaurants and offers a typical modern motel experience. There are plans to upgrade. Ask about specials.

Eating
Happily, Maseru offers more variety for dining out than for accommodation, with several good restaurants.

Rendezvous (☎ 2231 2114; Lancer's Inn, Kingsway; mains M37-70; ◷ lunch & dinner) A fave among the expats and locals who goss in the garden café or have a tipple in the traditional chandeliered restaurant, complete with gingham napkins and large menu.

Mimmo's Italian Deli (☎ 2232 4979; Maseru Club, United Nations Rd; mains from M28; ◷ lunch & dinner)

Mimmo's setting in an old building with outdoor terrace is as pleasant as its pasta and pizza dishes.

Lehaha Grill (☎ 2231 3111; Lesotho Sun; meals from M55; ☺ dinner) This upscale place features crisp tablecloths, a three-course menu and à la carte selections. If nothing suits, Chinese food is usually served during the evening in the Sun's second restaurant next door. The luncheon buffet costs M92.

Regal (☎ 2231 3930; Level 1, Basotho Hat; mains M22-49; ☺ lunch & dinner Mon-Sat) Dripping with photographs, bright cushions, silk-covered bar stools and an Asian theme, this stylish place dishes up everything from Indian curries to Chinese noodles, as well as excellent vegetarian options.

Good Times Cafe (☎ 2231 7705; Level 1, LNDC Mall; ☺ breakfast, lunch & dinner M18-50) The funky red and blue suede sofas, stylish lights (with saxophone motif) and oh-so-shiny chrome trimmings make this 'it' for the local cool crowd. Friendly staff, TV screens and regular live music (including jazz) are an added bonus.

Sunset (☎ 6276 0030; Kingsway; mains M15-28; ☺ lunch & dinner) Popular among local business people, this pleasant, corporate-looking place, with its cream and brown tablecloths and piped music, offers the best-value and most authentic 'à la carte' dining experience in Maseru. It's above Fruit & Veg City.

On the eastern end of Kingsway, towards the minibus stations are Shoprite, are **street stalls** (meals about M8; ☺ lunch) selling grilled meat, curry and rice. For Western fast food, KFC is on Kingsway. Shoprite is the best option for self-caterers.

Next to Lancer's Inn is a good **bakery** (☺ 7am-8.30pm) with pies, cakes and other delicacies.

Drinking

Popular meeting spots include **Lancer's Inn** (☎ 2231 2114; lancers-inn@ilesotho.com; cnr Kingsway & Pioneer Rd), **Maseru Club** (☎ 2232 6008; United Nations Rd) and the bar/slot-machine lounges at **Maseru Sun** (☎ 2231 2434; 12 Orpen Rd) and **Lesotho Sun** (☎ 2231 3111; lesoresv@sunint.co.za). It's worth checking out the recently opened **Good Times Cafe** (☎ 2231 7705; Level 1, LNDC Mall).

Shopping

Basotho Hat (☎ 2232 2523; Kingsway; ☺ 8am-5pm Mon-Sat) This government-run craft shop is the best place to start, although prices are generally higher than elsewhere in the country. If you plan on walking or pony trekking, the horsehair fly whisks sold here make good investments.

The **craft vendors** (Kingsway) in front of the tourist information office have a supply of woven Basotho hats and other souvenirs. For tapestries, try **Maseru Tapestries & Mats** (☎ 2231 1773; Raboshabane Rd), near the train station, and **Seithati Weavers** (☎ 2231 3975), about 7km from town along the airport road.

Getting There & Away

For getting to Maseru from South Africa, see p629.

There are three main transport stands to the northeast of the Circle: behind Shoprite/Sefika Mall for minibus taxis to Roma (M8), Motsekuoa (M13, for Malealea) and other points south; just off Main North Rd near Pitso Ground (take the turn-off by the KFC sign) for minibus taxis to points north; and, about a block away from here, reached via the same turn-off, for large buses to points south and north. Buses to Mokhotlong (M35) depart from next to Feida supermarket on Stadium Rd behind Pitso Ground, while those to Qacha's Nek (M96) depart from next to St James Primary and High Schools on Main Rd South.

For car rental agencies, **Avis** (☎ 2232 0087) is at Lesotho Sun and **Budget** (☎ 2231 6344) at Maseru Sun. Avis has a kiosk at the airport.

Getting Around

TO/FROM THE AIRPORT

Moshoeshoe International Airport is 21km from town, off Main South Rd. Minibus taxis (from the transport stand at Shoprite/Sefika Mall) cost M5. A private taxi company charges around M50.

MINIBUS TAXI & TAXI

The standard minibus taxi fare around town is M2.50. Taxi companies include **Moonlite** (☎ 2231 2605), **Planet** (☎ 2231 7777) and **Luxury** (☎ 2232 6211). These can also be chartered for long-distance transport elsewhere in the country.

AROUND MASERU

Maseru's surrounding areas hold several attractions, all of which make easy day or overnight excursions from the capital.

They're covered here clockwise, from north to south.

Thaba-Bosiu

About 25km east of Maseru is the famed and flat-topped Thaba-Bosiu (Mountain at Night), where King Moshoeshoe the Great established his mountain stronghold in 1824 (see p551). It's regarded as the birthplace of the Basotho nation, and, although quite an unassuming spot, is Lesotho's most important historical site.

The origins of its name are unclear. Some people say it may have been bestowed because the site was first occupied at night, while others believe that to intimidate the enemies, rumours were spread that Thaba-Bosiu, a hill in daylight, grew into an unconquerable mountain at night-time.

At the mountain's base is a **visitors information centre** (admission M5; ☷ 8am-5pm Mon-Fri, 9am-1pm Sat) with maps and an information pamphlet. An official guide will accompany you on the short walk to the top of the mountain, for which you should pay a tip.

From the summit, there are good views over the surrounding area, including to **Qiloane Hill**, which allegedly provided the inspiration for the Basotho hat. Also fascinating to see are the remains of fortifications, Moshoeshoe's grave and parts of his original settlement.

Mmelesi Lodge (☎ 5250 0006; s/d M220/250) offers well-organised flowery rondavels (round huts with conical roofs), about 2km before the visitors information centre, and is the only accommodation available. It does a brisk local business with government workshops, and has a dining room.

GETTING THERE & AWAY

Minibuses to Thaba-Bosiu (M8, 30 minutes) depart from Maseru at the transport stand at Shoprite/Sefika Mall. If you're driving, take the Mafeteng Rd for about 13km and turn left at the Roma turn-off; after about 6km take the signposted road left. Thaba-Bosiu is 10km further along.

Ha Baroana

Ha Baroana is one of Lesotho's more important and publicised rock-art sites. It's worth a visit if you have extra time, although neglect and vandalism have taken their toll.

To get here, take the Roma turn-off from the Mafeteng Rd; continue for about 8km to the Thaba-Tseka junction. Follow the northern fork (to Thaba-Tseka) about 12km to Nazareth village. Just before Nazareth, there's a signposted gravel track to the paintings. Follow this 3km to Ha Khotso village, turn right at a football field and continue 2.5km to a hilltop overlooking a gorge. A footpath zigzags down the hillside to the rock shelter with the paintings. Minibus taxis go as far as Nazareth.

Roma

Nestled amid sandstone cliffs about 35km southeast of Maseru, Roma was established as a mission town in the 1860s. Today it's Lesotho's centre of learning, with the country's only university, as well as several seminaries and secondary schools. The southern entry/exit to Roma takes you through a striking gorge landscape, and is best travelled during the morning or late afternoon when the lower sun lights the cliffs to full advantage.

The attractive **Trading Post Guest House** (☎ 2234 0202/67; www.tradingpost.co.za; camp sites per person M50, dm M80, rondavels per person M175, s/d with shared bathroom M150/300; 🖳) is a legacy of Lesotho colonial history: it's a trading post that has been operated since 1903 by the Thorn family (locals still bring their grain daily to the mill), who also run the guesthouse. There's a choice of accommodation, including rondavels and the original sandstone homestead, with shared kitchen, set in a lush garden. A self-contained cottage sleeps six (minimum two) for M300. Breakfasts and dinners are available (M35/65). Pony trekking, hiking, 4WD trails and other action adventures can be arranged. There are even *minwane* (dinosaur footprints) nearby. Head to the western end of town and follow the signposts off the main (Semonkong) road from Maseru.

About 35km southeast along the same road is Ramabanta village, where the same owners run **Trading Post Adventures Guest House** (camp sites per person M50, rondavels per person M200, r per person M175) with self-catering facilities, and the chance to link up Roma, Ramabanta and other places in the area on overnight hikes and pony treks. Bookings are taken for Trading Post Adventures Guest House through the Trading Post Guest House.

The humble **Speakeasy Restaurant** and **Kaycees** (meals M30) serve basic fare.

Minibus taxis run throughout the day to/from Maseru (M8, 30 minutes). They depart Maseru from the stand next to Sefika Mall/Shoprite.

Morija

Morija is a tiny town with a big history, and the site of the first European mission in Lesotho. It is easy to get to, and a 'must see' for those interested in Lesotho's history and culture. Before coming to Morija, hunt out a copy of Tim Couzens' *Murder at Morija*, which attempts to get behind the 1920 poisoning of one of the country's early missionaries.

SIGHTS & ACTIVITIES

Morija Museum & Archives (☎ 2236 0308; www.morijafest.com; admission M6; ☒ 8am-5pm Mon-Sat, noon-5pm Sun) The best museum in Lesotho, this impressive place holds well-presented ethnographical exhibits, archives from the early mission and scientific artefacts. Staff are knowledgeable and there's an excellent collection of books for sale, including those by the curator himself. The museum staff will guide you to nearby dinosaur footprints (for a small fee) and direct you to accommodation. There's even a small courtyard tea room.

Other places of interest include the good **Maeder House Crafts Centre** (☎ 2236 0487; ☒ by appointment Sun), near the museum, and Lesotho's first **printing press**, on the same grounds. **Pony trekking** (M50 per hour and less for longer trips) and overnight **hikes** (M200 incl meals, with cost of guide negotiable) can be organised through the Morija Guest Houses – you must reserve one day in advance.

FESTIVALS & EVENTS

The popular **Morija Arts & Cultural Festival** (www.morijafest.com) is an annual event held in early October which showcases the diversity of Sotho culture through dance, music and theatre, and includes horse racing and *moraba-raba* (the African equivalent of chess) competitions. The festival began in 1999 as a means of reuniting the people of Lesotho after the turmoil created by the 1998 political upheaval, and to revive aspects of culture and boost tourism.

SLEEPING & EATING

Mophato Oa Morija (☎ 2236 0219; mophatooamo@leo.co.ls; dm M60) This ecumenical conference centre is sometimes willing to accommodate travellers, but it's best to book in advance. Meals can be arranged. Take the first right after the museum and wind your way back about 700m – ask locals to point the way.

Morija Guest House (☎ 6306 5093; mgh@leo.co.ls; r per person M180) It's hard to move from the deck of this comfortable and very private stone-and-thatch cottage – the views are as pleasant as the accommodation itself. There's a kitchen or meals can be arranged. Take the road up from the museum about 1.5km, turning right at the signpost.

Other smaller guesthouses managed together with this main guesthouse are also available. Backpackers arriving by public transport may be charged a lower fee.

GETTING THERE & AWAY

Minibus taxis run throughout the day between Maseru and Morija (M10, 45 minutes, 40km).

NORTHERN LESOTHO

Northern Lesotho – the area from Maseru up to Butha-Buthe – is relatively densely populated, and dotted with a series of bustling lowland towns. The towns themselves offer little of 'typical tourist' interest to visitors, except for Teyateyaneng and Leribe (Hlotse), both of which have some good craft shopping. But the region shouldn't be ignored. It's an important entry or exit to/from South Africa and the main gateway to the spectacular northeastern highlands. If you're driving, it's worth allowing at least half a day or more to absorb the region's local flavours: the markets, welcoming locals and the unique geographical backdrop. If you're travelling on public transport, Teyateyaneng and Leribe are the best overnight stops.

Teyateyaneng

Teyateyaneng (Place of Quick Sands; usually known simply as 'TY') is the craft centre of Lesotho, and is worth a stop to buy tapestries or watch them being made.

Some of the best come from **Helang Basali Crafts** (☎ 2250 0382; ☒ 8am-5pm) at St Agnes Mission, about 2km before Teyateyaneng and signposted to the east of the Maseru road. Other good places (both open similar

BLANKET COVERAGE

The Basotho blanket is an important part of public, social and private life, not only as a practical article of clothing, but also as a symbol and status. So common is the blanket you'd be forgiven for thinking it's a centuries-old tradition. In fact, as recently as 1860 European traders presented King Moshoeshoe I with a blanket. The Basotho people were so taken with it that they chose to disregard their animal hides in its favour and by the 1880s traders were overwhelmed with demands. The original blankets were manufactured from high-quality woven cloth in England and sold in Fraser's Stores (few stores survive today) and the manufacturers experimented with the designs and improved the quality. The blanket's popularity fluctuated throughout the 1900s, mainly influenced by the European's and missionaries' preferences. (It is said that when the Prince of Wales visited Lesotho in 1925, those with blankets were ordered to the back of the crowd.)

Today, however, the woollen blanket is an important practical and symbolic item for the Basotho (not to be confused with plain or synthetic blankets worn by those who can't afford the real article). A blanket provides insulation in the heat and the cold, is fireproof and a status symbol – each costs a hefty M500. Look out for maize cob (a symbol of fertility), a crown or military markings (a legacy of British imperialism) and a cabbage leaf (meaning prosperity). Young married women wear a blanket around their hips until their first child is conceived and young boys are presented with a blanket upon circumcision, symbolising their emergence from boyhood to manhood.

The solid lines on a blanket's edges are worn vertically – the Basotho believe that worn horizontally the blanket can stunt growth, wealth and development.

Less common, but still used in rural areas, is the Basotho hat, or *mokorotlo* or *molianyeo*, with its distinctive conical shape and curious top adornment. The style of the hat is supposedly modelled on the shape of Qiloane Hill (p559), near Thaba-Bosiu.

hours) include Setsoto Design, near Blue Mountain Inn, and Hatooa Mose Mosali, just west of the main road at the town entrance. Elelloang Basali Weavers is about 4km to the north of TY. At most places you can watch the weavers at work.

Blue Mountain Inn (☎ 2250 0362; s/d M230/280) offers truly blue rooms with motel-like trimmings set in a shady compound. New rooms are being constructed – and will be the outlook for some unfortunate guests. It has a restaurant and is about 1km off the main road and signposted.

Minibus taxis run throughout the day between Teyateyaneng and Maseru (M12, 45 minutes, 35km). Chartering a taxi from Maseru costs about M130 one-way.

Maputsoe

This chaotic border town, 86km north of Maseru, is across the Mohokare (Caledon) River from the Free State town of Ficksburg, and has no appeal other than as a transit point.

The banging at **Sekekete Hotel** (☎ 2243 0789; s/d about M220/280) ain't the sound of bottles being slammed down on the hotel's bar; it's best to stay across the border at Ficksburg (see p390).

Maputsoe is a major transport junction, and for northbound transport from Maseru, you'll usually need to change vehicles here. Minibus taxis to both Maseru (M17, one hour), Butha-Buthe (M13, 45 minutes) and Leribe (M7, 30 minutes) run throughout the day from the Total petrol station.

Leribe (Hlotse)

Leribe (also known as Hlotse) is a busy regional market hub. It served as an administrative centre under the British, as witnessed by a few old buildings slowly decaying in the leafy streets. The main sight is the crumbling **Major Bell's Tower** near the market. It was built in 1879, and spent most of its career as a storehouse for government records.

The good **Leribe Craft Centre** (☎ 2240 0323; ☻ 8am-4.30pm Mon-Fri, 9.30am-1pm Sat), just off the main road at the northern end of town, sells a range of high-quality woollen goods (and excellent books on Lesotho) at reasonable prices.

Dinosaur footprints abound around Leribe. The most accessible set is a few kilometres south of town at Tsikoane village. Immediately after the Tsikoane Primary School, take the small dirt road to the right towards some rocky outcrops. Follow it up to the church. Many children will vie to lead you the 1km slog up the mountainside to the *minwane*, in a series of caves. The prints are clearly visible on the rock ceiling.

About 7km north of Leribe are the Subeng River dinosaur footprints. At the signpost indicating the river, walk down about 250m to a concrete causeway. The worn footprints of at least three species of dinosaur are about 15m downstream on the right bank.

If you're heading into the highlands, Leribe is the last good place to stock up. A new Shoprite was due to open in February 2006.

SLEEPING & EATING

Leribe Hotel (☎ 2240 0559; Main St; s/d M180/250; meals from M25) The dining room's décor may be out of a *Fawlty Towers* set, but this 1970s-style place offers clean accommodation in the main building or in private rondavels. It has an invitingly green and leafy tea garden and serves meals. One of the country's best hotel options, it's located 100m uphill from the central junction.

Pelican Steakhouse & Bar (Main St; mains M15-20) As authentic a local hang-out as you can get, this place dishes out the daily dose of hearty mutton, pork and chicken curries from massive pots. It's opposite the Golden Rule Funeral House before the Leribe Hotel.

GETTING THERE & AWAY

Minibus taxis run throughout the day between Leribe and Maseru (M26, 1½ hours), usually with a change of vehicles at Maputsoe. There are also several vehicles daily between Leribe and Katse (M36, three hours), and between Leribe and Butha-Buthe (M8, 35 minutes), many originating further south.

Butha-Buthe

Lesotho's second-largest town, Butha-Buthe (Place of Lying Down) was named by King Moshoeshoe the Great because it was here that his people first retreated during the chaos of the *difaqane*. Its frontier-town scrappiness is redeemed by an attractive setting alongside the Hlotse River, with the beautiful Maluti Mountains as a backdrop.

SLEEPING & EATING

Ha Thabo Ramakatane Hostel (dm M30) Comments in the guestbook – 'magical', 'most favourite place' – urge a stay here as a must-do experience. The abode of the Ramakatane family (Mr Ramakatane is now 95) has few amenities and guests are treated to a true dip into a rural lifestyle: water from a well, gas cooking and candlelight (bring your own supplies). Access is best via 4WD or walking. It's 3.5km from Butha-Buthe in Ha Sechele village. Turn off the main road at the sign for St Paul's High School in central Butha-Buthe, go left up the lane immediately after the school, then take the

---

LESOTHO UNRAVELLED

In 1999 employment opportunities for Basotho people in Lesotho were looking good. Chinese and Taiwanese investors had flooded into the country to set up textile factories and take advantage of the cheap labour and hassle-free access that followed the creation of a US incentive, the African Growth and Opportunity Act (AGOA). This gave textile exports from approved African countries duty-free access to the US market.

The textile industry soon became Lesotho's economic mainstay. By 2003, Lesotho was a major textile manufacturer, producing some 31% of the textiles exported to the US under the AGOA scheme. The textile industry employed 20,000 in 2002 and up to 56,000 by 2004 as investors took advantage of the scheme, and exports grew from US$140 million to US$456 million in 2004; that is, around 90% of Lesotho's export earnings.

However, things unravelled at the end of 2004. A falling US dollar and the end of WTO restrictions on Chinese imports to the US killed Lesotho's US market. Six factories closed overnight (many were rumoured to have left without paying wages) and thousands were left unemployed. Since then, the majority of remaining factories have closed, despite government efforts, including export incentives, to sustain them. Although Lesotho still has duty-free access to the US market, it is said that advanced technology in China limits Lesotho's opportunities.

CULTURE BASOTHO-STYLE

Traditional Basotho culture is flourishing, and colourful celebrations marking milestones, such as birth, puberty, marriage and death, are a central part of village life. While hiking you may see the *lekolulo*, a flute-like instrument played by herd boys; the *thomo*, a stringed instrument played by women; and the *setolo-tolo*, a stringed instrument played with the mouth by men. Cattle hold an important position in daily life, both as sacrificial animals and as important symbols of wealth. Crop cultivation and weather are also central, and form the heart of many traditions.

The Basotho believe in a Supreme Being and place a great deal of emphasis on *balimo* (ancestors), who act as intermediaries between people and the capricious forces of nature and the spirit world. Evil is a constant danger, caused by *boloi* (witchcraft; witches can be either male or female) and *thkolosi* (small, maliciously playful beings, similar to the Xhosa's tokoloshe). If you're being bothered by these forces, head to the nearest *ngaka* – a learned man, part sorcerer and part doctor – who can combat them. Basotho are traditionally buried in a sitting position, facing the rising sun and ready to leap up when called.

next right. Ask for directions once you're on this road.

Crocodile Inn (☎ 2246 0223; Reserve Rd; s/d/tr from M198/231/335) This one can be a bit of a 'croc'. The simple but clean rooms often don't have water. The newer, nicer rondavels are out the back and are frequented for night kips or day rests (note, the latter is advertised). The restaurant here is Butha-Buthe's main dining establishment. The white hotel is about 500m off the main road (signposted to Butha-Buthe Hospital), at the southern end of town.

GETTING THERE & AWAY
Many minibus taxis travel between Maseru and Butha-Buthe via Maputsoe (1½ hours), where you'll usually need to change vehicles. From Maputsoe to Butha-Buthe costs M13 and takes about 20 minutes. Both minibus taxis and a bus go to Mokhotlong. The minibus taxis costs M50, and the bus costs M35. Butha-Buthe is the last reliable place to buy petrol if you're heading north.

Ts'ehlanyane National Park
This LHDA-administered **national park** (admission per person/vehicle M15/5) protects a beautiful 5600-hectare patch of rugged wilderness, including one of Lesotho's only stands of indigenous forest. This underrated and underused place is about as far away from it all as you can get and is perfect for hiking.

For accommodation, there's a **guesthouse** (6-person M350), a **conference centre** (d & tr per person M60) at the park entrance and various **camp sites** (per person from M20). Unfortunately, the pleasant stone rondavels have been depleted

of their amenities but check on their status. Bookings can be made through **LHDA** (☎ 2246 0723, 2291 3206; www.lesothoparks.com). Bring your own food and cooking equipment.

In addition to day walks, there's a challenging 39km hiking trail from Ts'ehlanyane southwest to Bokong Nature Reserve (p567) through some of Lesotho's most dramatic terrain. Guides fees are M30 per day. **Pony trekking** (per half/full day M50/75) can be arranged through LHDA with advance notice.

If you're driving, take the signposted turn-off from the main road about 8km south of Butha-Buthe, from where it's 31km further on a gravel access road (easily negotiable in a 2WD). Occasional taxis run from Butha-Buthe to the park entrance, but mainly towards Khabo, on the access road, from where you'll need to walk or hitch.

NORTHEASTERN & CENTRAL HIGHLANDS
Northeast of Butha-Buthe, the road weaves up dramatically through spectacular mountains – part of the Ukhahlamba-Drakensberg range – with rocky cliffs and rolling hills. South Africa does a good job of marketing its portion of the Drakensberg escarpment, but for raw beauty, it can't compare with the part in Lesotho, where the combination of snow (in winter), low population density and stunning highland panoramas is hard to beat. All the areas covered in this section are excellent for hiking, but you'll need to be fully equipped with a four-season sleeping bag, waterproof gear, topographical maps and a compass. Trout fishing is reputed to be topnotch.

Liphofung Cave Cultural Historical Site

Just beyond the village of 'Muela is the signposted turn-off for this small LHDA-administered site, which includes a cave with some San paintings and Stone-Age artefacts. King Moshoeshoe the Great is rumoured to have stopped here on his travels around Lesotho.

There is a **visitors centre** (adult/child M15/5; ⊗ 8.30am-4.30pm Mon-Fri, 9am-4.30pm Sat & Sun), with unhelpful staff and a small shop selling local crafts. Accommodation is two simple stone four-person **rondavels** (per person M50, minimum 2) with kitchen facilities. Not that the latter gets used much (the sign says 'Day rest and overnight accommodation available'). **Camping** (M20) may also be permitted – check at the visitors centre. You'll need to bring your own food. Day hikes are possible and you can arrange **pony trekking** (M2 per hour) with advance notice.

Liphofung is an easy 1.5km walk down from the main road along a tarmac access ramp. Via public transport, take a taxi heading from Butha-Buthe towards Moteng, and get off at the Liphofung turn-off (M8, 25 minutes). If you stay overnight at Liphofung, the bus to Mokhotlong passes in the morning (ask for times).

Oxbow

Reached after crossing the dramatic Moteng Pass (2820m), Oxbow consists of a few huts and a couple of lodges nestled amid some wonderful mountain scenery, and is an ideal place to get away from the bustle while still enjoying amenities. The area regularly receives snow in winter, and

boasts a 1.5km ski slope. It's also popular with South African trout anglers and birdwatchers. Except for a small supply of basics at the shop at New Oxbow Lodge, there's nowhere to stock up.

Skiing is available through **Afri-Ski** (www.afriski.co.za), about 10km past Oxbow.

New Oxbow Lodge (☎ in South Africa 051-933 2247; www.oxbow.co.za; s/d with breakfast M310/545) is an incongruous chalet more at home in alpine Austria than on the banks of the Malibamat'so River. But the resort atmosphere, cosy bar and good restaurant draw the holiday-makers. Ski-hire, half-board arrangements and triples and quads are all available.

The bus between Maseru and Mokhotlong will drop you at Oxbow (M50, 4½ hours). Several minibus taxis run daily between Butha-Buthe and Oxbow (M25, 1½ hours). The route follows a series of hairpin turns up the pass, and can be treacherous in snow and ice.

Mokhotlong

From Oxbow, a good tarmac road winds its way over a series of 3200m-plus passes and through some superb high-altitude scenery before dropping down to Mokhotlong (Place of the Bald Ibis). The route was the original **Roof of Africa Rally** (www.roofofafrica.org.ls) course.

Mokhotlong is the main town in eastern Lesotho, but it is still very much an outpost, and has something of a Wild West feel to it. There's not much to do other than watch life go by, with the locals on their horses, sporting Basotho blankets. However, the Senqu (Orange) River – Lesotho's main waterway – has its source near Mokhotlong, and the town makes a good base for walks. There are a number of reasonably well-stocked shops; petrol and diesel are sometimes available.

SLEEPING & EATING

Molumong Guesthouse & Backpackers (☎ in South Africa 033-394 3072; molumong@worldonline.co.za; camp sites per person M45, dm/d M70/180) Most travellers head out of town to Molumong (pronounced 'moodoomong'), signposted about 15km southwest of Mokhotlong off the road to Thaba-Tseka. This rustic lodge, a former colonial trading post, is an integral part of the village and offers a basic (electricity-free) self-catering experience. Bring what-

---

CAMPING CAPERS

If you choose to camp in Lesotho, it is advisable to always ask permission from the local chief of the nearby village. This is not only an important courtesy, but with a chief's permission you are less likely to have problems (remember that all land is accounted for, so you are on someone's 'property' at all times). It is possible that the chief will invite you to pitch your tent near his or her home, or in a safe area. You should offer or expect to pay a small fee for the camping privilege.

ever food you'll need from Mokhotlong. The rooms are bright, as are the stars at this studded height. Pony trekking is available.

Grow (☎ 2292 0205; dm R50) This Lesotho-registered development program has an office just off the main road into Mokhotlong. It offers clean and basic dorms and a simple kitchen. It's happy to accept travellers if training groups aren't staying.

St James Lodge (☎ in South Africa 033-326 1601; stjamesguestlodge@yahoo.com; dm/d M75/95) This is the most recent lodge option in the area, housed in an old stone building on a working mission. It's self-catering so bring your own supplies, and offers pony trekking and scenic walks. It's 12km south of Mokhotlong on the road to Thaba-Tseka.

Senqu Hotel (☎ 2292 0330; s/d with shared bathroom M180/240, s/d M200/280) This place has lifted its standards since the recent construction of a new wing. Despite the older shabby rooms, the new rooms make it the pick of the motels (complete with mod cons and restaurant). It's at the western end of town along the main road.

A good shop in the town centre, next to the library, is Thia-Lala Butchery & Cafe, with takeaway sandwiches and a range of basics, including chilled juices.

GETTING THERE & AWAY

There are a few minibus taxis daily to/from Butha-Buthe (M55, six hours). A bus goes daily to/from Maseru, departing in each direction by about 8am (M70, eight hours) except on Sunday (one-way, Mokhotlong to Maseru only) and Saturday (one-way, Maseru to Mokhotlong only). There's also a daily minibus taxi from Mokhotlong to Sani Top, which continues on to Underberg (South Africa) via the Sani Pass. It departs from Mokhotlong daily at 6am (M65, five hours to Underberg). Minibus taxis to Linakaneng (on the Thaba-Tseka road) will drop you by Molumong Lodge. For transport from Molumong to Sani Pass, wait on the road that runs past the lodge, and change minibus taxis.

Sani Top

Sani Top sits atop the steep Sani Pass, the only dependable road into Lesotho through the Drakensberg range in KwaZulu-Natal. It offers stupendous views on clear days and unlimited hiking possibilities.

Thabana-Ntlenyana (3482m), Africa's highest peak south of Mt Kilimanjaro, is a popular, but long and arduous hike. The mountain's height was only calculated in 1955 and not confirmed by satellite technology until 30 years later. There's a path, but a guide would be handy. It's also possible to do the ascent on horseback.

Hodgson's Peaks (3258m) is a much easier hike 6km south, from where you can see into Sehlabathebe National Park and KwaZulu-Natal.

Sehlabathebe National Park offers a rugged three-day hike from Sani Top Chalet (below) south along the remote escarpment edge to Sehlabathebe National Park; only try this if you're well prepared, experienced and in a group of at least three people.

Other hikes in this area are outlined in the excellent booklet *A Backpackers' Guide to Lesotho* by Russell Suchet, available through the **Morija Museum** (☎ 2236 0308; www .morijafest.com) or **Sani Lodge** (☎ in South Africa 033-702 0330; www.sani-lodge.co.za) at Sani Pass.

SLEEPING & EATING

Sani Top Chalet (☎ in South Africa 033-702 1158; www .sanitopchalet.co.za; camp sites per person M50, dm M85, r with shared bathroom M300) On the edge of the escarpment at a lofty 2874m, this popular (monopolistic) place resembles an old-fashioned ski chalet and boasts the highest pub in Africa, with simple, cosy rooms and excellent meals. There's no lofty praise for the backpackers dorm – its condition has plummeted in recent years and although it features a wonderful fireplace, its draughty, stained room detracts from experiencing a real high. New rondavels are being constructed (let's hope for the budget traveller). In winter the snow is sometimes deep enough for skiing; pony trekking can be arranged with advance notice.

There are also several good hostels on the KwaZulu-Natal side of the pass; see p356.

GETTING THERE & AWAY

A minibus taxi runs daily from Mokhotlong via Sani Top down to Underberg (South Africa) and back (M65, five hours). Coming from the north, taxis from Butha-Buthe cost M53.

If you're driving, you'll need a 4WD to go up the pass; 2WD with clearance can make it down, though with difficulty. The

South African border crossing is open 8am to 4pm daily; the Lesotho side stays open until 5pm to let the last vehicles through. Hitching is best on weekends.

Hostels on the KwaZulu-Natal side arrange transport up the pass, and various agencies in Himeville and Underberg (the nearest South African towns) arrange tours – see p355 and p354.

Thaba-Tseka

Thaba-Tseka is a remote town on the western edge of the Central Range, over the sometimes-tricky Mokhoabong Pass. It was established in 1980 as a centre for the mountain district, and is a scrappy place serving mostly as a convenient transport junction for travel north to Katse or west to Maseru.

The **Farmer Training Centre** (☎ 2290 0294; dm/r M100/50) has the usual: a basic room with few trimmings, as well as a shared guesthouse. It's on the street behind the tower. The most colourful thing about Thaba-Tseka's main hotel, **Mountain Star Hotel** (☎ 2290 0415; s/d M140/170), is the public lounge's bright red sofa and the 'Adam' and 'Eve' public loo signs. Otherwise, you're in for a dull, if adequate stay. The Lilala Butchery and General Cafe is a clean place with a good selection of sandwiches, drinks and frozen foods.

Three buses run daily between Maseru and Thaba-Tseka (M34, seven hours), departing from Maseru between about 8am and 9.30am. Minibuses also go as far as Sehonghong (M22, two hours); from here you'd need to try your luck for a lift. From Thaba-Tseka to Mokhotlong, get a minibus taxi to Linakaneng (M22, two hours), and from there another to Mokhotlong (M14, two hours). Several minibus taxis travel daily along the unsealed, but good, road from Thaba-Tseka via Katse (M16), and on to Leribe (M32) and Maseru (M50, five hours).

Mohale Dam

Built across the Senqunyane River, the impressive 145m-high rock-fill Mohale Dam was completed in 2004 as the second phase of the Lesotho Highlands Water Project. There are commanding views of the lake and massive mountains beyond. You can drive as far as the Mohale Tunnel through which water can flow for 32km between Mohale and Katse Dams.

Basotho Pony Trekking Centre

About 85km west of Thaba-Tseka, on the top of God Help Me Pass, is the **Basotho Pony Trekking Centre** (☎ 2231 2318). It's a fairly no-frills and DIY experience compared to other pony-trekking places, but it is one of the most easily accessible from Maseru. Reports are that it's foundered a little of late; it's managed by the Ministry of Agriculture and, at the time of research, was up for privatisation. Visit the **Maseru Tourist Information Office** (☎ 2231 2427; Kingsway; ☺ 8am-4.30pm Mon-Fri, 8.30am-5pm Sat) for an update before booking.

Katse

Tiny Katse's main claim to fame is as the former purpose-built base for the Lesotho

---

LESOTHO HIGHLANDS WATER PROJECT

The Lesotho Highlands Water Project (LHWP) is an ambitious scheme developed jointly by Lesotho and South Africa to harness Lesotho's abundant water resources to provide water to a large tract of Southern Africa and hydropower to Lesotho. The project, being implemented in stages until 2020, will result in five major dams (two of which are completed – the Katse and Mohale), many smaller ones and approximately 200km of tunnels.

Immediate effects of this development include vastly improved roads and telecommunications in the interior of the country, benefiting the residents of many remote villages.

However, there are detrimental effects as well. These include flooding of significant portions of Lesotho's already scarce arable land and potential silting problems. Relocation difficulties occur as locals settle into other villages. Billboards in each village warning of AIDS hint at other risks caused by easier contact with the outside world now that the road network has been improved. Also disturbing is that several multinational companies involved in the project's construction have been prosecuted for corruption. For more background on the water project see www.lhwp.org.ls.

Highlands Water Project and the site of Africa's highest dam (185m). Katse Dam's lake is serene, ringed by steep, green hillsides; even if you're not impressed by the engineering feats, the area makes for a relaxing pause. Fishing is allowed from the sides; permits (M10) are on sale at the Bokong Nature Reserve or the information office.

There's a **visitors centre** (admission M6), with a video about the dam, tours of the dam (9am and 2pm) and a dam viewpoint. Exposed and windy camping is also on offer here. The centre is about 2km east of the Katse village junction, along the main road.

Katse Lodge (☎ 2291 0202; dm M145, s/d incl breakfast M240/430), at the far end of the suburban-like Katse village beyond the barrier gate, resembles a hospital – in looks but not nature. You're better off sleeping in the 'dorm' accommodation with clean twin rooms and massive shared bathrooms (ask about this as it's not always offered, dammit). To get here, follow the signs to Katse village.

Signposted off the main road in Pitseng village, **Aloes Guest House** (☎ 2700 5626; s/d M150/180) provides a local 'cushy' base for exploring Katse or Bokong Nature Reserve. Situated in front of an old sandstone trading post, the rooms and rondavels have a stylish African touch and look out over a lush garden to the mountains. Perfect for catching up on the postcards.

GETTING THERE & AWAY

The 122km road between Leribe and Katse is excellent, although steep and winding, and slick in the rain. Allow at least two hours for driving, longer if going by public transport.

Minibus taxis go daily from Leribe to Katse (M37, three to five hours), with some continuing on to Thaba-Tseka (M51). In Katse, public transport stops near the Katse village junction.

Hikers may be interested in the 'stick boat' (rowing boat) that ferries locals across the dam to three villages – Ha Sepinare, Ha Theko and Ha Lihalahaleng (M5).

Bokong Nature Reserve

Bokong has perhaps the most dramatic setting of the three LHDA reserves, with stunning vistas over the Lepaqoa Valley from the **visitors centre** (adult/child M5/3; ☼ 8am-5pm), various short walks and a good, rugged two-

to three-day hike to Ts'ehlanyane National Park (p563). Bearded vultures, rock shelters and valleyhead fens (wetland areas) are features here. You can gush about the impressive waterfall, located near both the visitors centre and where you can **camp** (per person M20). You can also stay overnight in a very basic four-person **hut** (per person M40) – bring your own food, sleeping bag, mattress and stove. **Guides** (per person M20) are available, and **pony trekking** (per half/full day M50/75) can be arranged. The reserve sits at just over 3000m and gets cold at night, so come prepared. Bookings must be made through **LHDA** (☎ 2246 0723, 2291 3206; www.lesothoparks.com).

Bokong lies roughly midway between Katse and Leribe at the top of Mafika-Lisiu Pass (3090m). Minibus taxis from Leribe will drop you at the visitors centre (M22, 1½ hours); when leaving, you may need to wait a while before one with space passes by.

Semonkong

Semonkong (Place of Smoke) is a one-horse town in the serene and lofty Thaba Putsoa range. It's the perfect base to hit the pony trails, hike or abseil; **Maletsunyane Falls** (204m) are a 1½-hour walk or a minute's abseil away. The falls are at their most awesome in summer – especially from the bottom of the gorge – where there are **camp sites** (per person M20). **Ketane Falls** (122m) are an exciting day's ride (30km) from Semonkong by a spectacular gorge.

The peaceful and recommended **Semonkong Lodge** (☎ in South Africa 051-933 3106; www.placeofsmoke.co.ls; camp sites per person M40, dm/s/d M80/230/380), near the Maletsunyane River, is one of *the* places to stay; its good range of accommodation includes camping and rondavels. For those who aren't content just soaking up the atmosphere or the excellent food and refreshments at the restaurant and bar, a hike or pony trek are always on offer, and (as you'll hear) the world's longest commercially operated single-drop abseil (204m) down the Maletsunyane Falls. The lodge is signposted from the town centre.

GETTING THERE & AWAY

Semonkong is about 120km southeast of Maseru, past Roma. The final 70km are gravel, though in reasonable condition (negotiable with 2WD). Allow three to four hours from Maseru. Buses between Maseru and Semonkong (M25) leave from either town in the morning, arriving in late afternoon. The road dead-ends at Semonkong; an excellent alternative to retracing your steps is to hike south to Christ the King Mission (see p571) on the Quthing-Qacha's Nek road.

SOUTHERN LESOTHO

Southern Lesotho – from Mafeteng and Malealea southwards, across to Sehlabathebe National Park in the southeast – is less developed than the northwest between Maseru and Butha-Buthe and equally (if not more) spectacular. The massive mountain ranges, awesome valleys, rivers (including the Senqu River) and villages have an enticing off-the-beaten-track feel. The tarmac roads cease east of Qacha's Nek, and public transport connections take more time than in the north, but the rewards are all the greater.

Malealea

Shortly before reaching Malealea is the Gates of Paradise Pass. A plaque announces 'Wayfarer – Pause and look upon a gateway of Paradise'. This says it all. The breathtaking mountainous surrounds and this tiny village is many travellers' introduction to Lesotho life, and is the ideal place to learn about local customs, gather information and start exploring the country.

The area has been occupied for centuries, as shown by the many **San rock paintings** in the vicinity. Today, the heart of the village is Malealea Lodge (see opposite), which offers a smorgasbord of cultural and outdoor activities, fittingly promoted as 'Lesotho in a nutshell'. 'Don't leave Lesotho without…' would also be appropriate.

SIGHTS & ACTIVITIES
Pony Trekking

Most of the treasures of this area are reachable by **pony treks** (per person per trek M160-750, overnight M260-330). Particular gems include: Ribaneng Waterfall (two days, one night); Ribaneng and Ketane Waterfalls (four days, three nights); and Semonkong (five to six days). Bring food, a sleeping bag, rainwear, sunscreen, warm clothing, a flashlight and water purification tablets. Accommodation is in **Basotho village huts** (per person M50).

PONY TREKKING & HIKING

Pony trekking is one of Lesotho's top drawcards. It's done on sure-footed Basotho ponies, the result of crossbreeding between short Javanese horses and European full mounts. King Moshoeshoe the Great is recorded as having ridden a Basotho pony in 1830. Since that time, these animals have become an integral part of life in the highlands, and the preferred mode of transport for many villagers.

Advance booking is recommended, and no prior riding experience is necessary. Whatever your experience level, expect to be sore after a day in the saddle. For overnight treks, you'll need to bring food (stock up in Maseru), a sleeping bag and warm, waterproof clothing. The following places can organise treks:

- Malealea Lodge (opposite)
- Semonkong Lodge (p567)
- LHDA conservation areas: Ts'ehlanyane National Park (p563), Bokong Nature Reserve (p567) and the Liphofung Cave Cultural Historical Site (p564).

Hiking rivals pony trekking as the best way to explore Lesotho. Plan a day in Maseru to buy topographical maps and stock up on food and supplies. Any specialist hiking supplies, including a compass, should be brought from South Africa. Once on the trail, respect the cairns that mark graves. However, a mound of stones near a trail, especially between two hills, should be added to by passing travellers, who ensure their good luck by spitting on a stone and throwing it onto the pile.

Several lodges have worked out trail networks in their areas, including Malealea and Semonkong. The owner of Fuleng Guest House (p571) is also helpful with hikes. For more hiking possibilities, see the Sani Top section (p565).

Hiking
Malealea Lodge (below) has maps for hikes and can arrange pack ponies for your gear. Stunning destinations include: Botso'ela Waterfall (two hours return); Pitseng Gorge (six hours return, bring swimwear); Pitseng Plateau (one hour return); and along the Makhaleng River. The walks include visits to surrounding villages and **San art** sites. Overnight and longer jaunts are also possible.

Other Activities
Village visits provide a stimulating insight into the local people and their customs. The tiny museum, housed in a traditional Basotho hut, is as interesting for the owner/guide as it is for its exhibits. You can visit a **sangoma** (only for the genuinely interested) and visit Mr Musi's reclaimed donga (see right). Malealea Lodge can also point you to some good, scenic drives suitable for both 2WD and 4WD vehicles.

SLEEPING & EATING
Malealea Lodge (☎ in South Africa 051-436 6766, 082-552 4215; www.malealea.co.ls, www.malealea.com; camp sites per person M50, backpacker huts with shared bathroom per person M80, r per person M100-200) The hub of local life, Malealea Lodge provides an extraordinary entrée into the 'Kingdom in the Sky' and its cultural riches. The lodge began life in 1905 as a trading post, established by teacher, diamond miner and soldier Mervyn Smith. From 1986 the hospitable and highly respected Mick and Di Jones (aka 'Mrs Malealea') ran the store, before transforming it into accommodation and impressively integrating it with the surrounding community. In 2003 it was the overall winner in the prestigious Imvelo responsible tourism awards for Southern Africa; a proportion of tourist revenue and donations goes directly to supporting projects in the area. Almost every night the local choir performs at the lodge.

The wealth of accommodation options range from camp sites and two-person 'forest', or backpacker, huts (those with linen M100) in a pretty wooded setting away from the lodge, to simple, cosy rooms and rondavels.

The lodge also offers a bar, hearty meals (breakfast/lunch/dinner M40/50/70) and self-catering facilities. A village shop stocks basic goods.

DEALING WITH DONGAS
Throughout Lesotho you may spot massive gullies or ravines stemming from the tops of hills and snaking all the way to the bottom of a valley. Known as dongas, these eroded areas developed primarily from the use of steel ploughs and an increase in arable farming during the latter part of the 19th century. The unstable duplex soils were quickly disturbed by the heavy summer storms. Increasingly, local people are reclaiming the dongas by building rock dams (or terraces) to capture silt and detritus. As the area above the dam wall or terrace fills, another dam is built lower down, until the gully is refilled with fertile soils, grasses or stabilising tree species. You can visit a successful donga reclamation at the Musi family farm at Malealea (see left).

There's no phone at the lodge (just a two-way radio) so enquiries must be made through South Africa. September to November are the busy months.

GETTING THERE & AWAY
Two Sprinter minibus taxis connect Maseru and Malealea, departing Maseru at around 11.30am and 4.30pm, and Malealea at 6am and 2pm (M40, 2½ hours, 83km). Otherwise, catch a minibus taxi from near Shoprite/Sefika Mall to the junction town of Motsekuoa (M13, two hours), from where there are frequent connections to Malealea (M10, 30 minutes).

If you're driving, head south from Maseru on Mafeteng Rd (Main Rd South) for 52km to Motsekuoa. Here, look for the Malealea Lodge sign and the collection of minibus taxis. Turn left (east) onto a tarmac road. Ten kilometres further on take the right fork and continue another 15km. When you reach the signposted turn-off to Malealea, head 7km along an unsealed road to the lodge.

It's also possible to approach Malealea from the south, via Mpharane and Masemouse, but the road is rough and most drivers travel via Motsekuoa.

Mafeteng
Mafeteng (Place of Lefeta's People) is named after an early magistrate, Emile Rolland,

who was known to the local Basotho as Lefeta (One Who Passes By). Little has changed; you're best to move on. That said, the town is an important bus and minibus taxi interchange, a border junction (it's 22km to Wepener in Free State) and a possible stocking-up point before heading south. The town centre has a small statue commemorating soldiers of the Cape Mounted Rifles who fell in the Gun War of 1880.

Golden Hotel (☎ 2270 0566; s/d M175/240) is a small brick establishment with as much personality as a robot, but with adequate rooms and meals. It's at the northern edge of town along the main road.

Straight out of the '60s TV sitcom *Lost in Space*, polygon-shaped **Mafeteng Hotel** (☎ 2270 0236; s/d from M200/250) is a blast from the past. Its features include bedheads with radio control knobs, peach interiors and the funkiest-shaped pool this side of the Drakensbergs. It's signposted from the main road at the southern end of town. There's a garden, restaurant and disco to bring you back to earth.

Frequent minibus taxis connect Mafeteng with Maseru (M15, 1½ hours) and Mohale's Hoek (M9, 30 minutes). For Quthing, change at Mohale's Hoek.

Mohale's Hoek

Mohale's Hoek takes its name from the younger brother of King Moshoeshoe the Great, Mohale, who in 1884 gave this land to the British for administrative purposes. The town's brush with royalty continued more recently when Britain's Prince Harry spent time helping in an orphanage in a nearby village. The town centre is agreeable enough, and a better spot to overnight than Mafeteng.

Monateng Lodge (☎ 2278 5337; s/d M170/200) lacks something – security and the 'it' factor. The rowdy male-frequented bar offers meals. **Hotel Mount Maluti** (☎ 2278 5224; mmh@leo .co.ls; s/d with breakfast M257/380), built in 1950, is an appealing place that has established gardens and lawns, comfortable rooms and a good restaurant. It was due to change management in January 2006. It's signposted off the main road.

Regular minibus taxis depart for Quthing (M12, 45 minutes) and throughout the day to Mafeteng (M9, 30 minutes). There are also several minibus taxis daily to Maseru (M25, 2½ hours) and a bus (M20).

Quthing

Quthing, the southernmost major town in Lesotho, is also known as Moyeni (Place of the Wind). It was established in 1877, abandoned during the Gun War of 1880 and then rebuilt at the present site.

Activity centres around Lower Quthing spread out along the main road. Up on the hill, overlooking the Senqu (Orange) River gorge, is Upper Quthing, the former colonial administrative centre, with a post office, hospital, police station, hotel and some good views. There are minibus taxis between Lower and Upper Quthing.

SIGHTS & ACTIVITIES

Five kilometres west of Quthing is the intriguing **Masitise Cave House Museum** (☎ 5879 4167; admission free, donation appreciated), part of an old mission that was built directly into a San rock shelter in 1866 by Reverend David-Frédéric Ellenberger, a Swiss who was among the first missionaries to Lesotho. With the help of Morija Museum, the cave house was converted into a small museum, with interesting displays on local culture and history. There's a cast of a dinosaur footprint in the ceiling and San paintings nearby. To get here, take the signposted turn-off for Masitise Primary School and follow the road about 1.5km back past the small church. The caretaker's house (for the key to the cave house) is just behind, and the museum about five minutes further on foot. Accommodation is available on a B&B basis in the house of the caretaker (herself a pastor at the church) or the very rustic (read unrenovated) rondavels. Ring in advance to arrange local meals (breakfast/lunch/dinner M25/40/40).

Quthing's other claim to fame is a proliferation of **dinosaur footprints** in the surrounding area. The most easily accessible are just off the main road to Mt Moorosi; watch for the small, pink building to your left. These are believed to be 180 million years old.

Between Quthing and Masitise, and visible from the main road, is **Villa Maria Mission**, with a striking, twin-spired sandstone church. About 10km southeast of town near Qomoqomong is a collection of **San paintings**. Several minibus taxis ply this route daily; once in Qomoqomong, ask at the General Dealer's store to arrange a guide for the 20-minute walk to the paintings.

The road from Quthing to Qacha's Nek is one of Lesotho's most stunning drives, taking you along the winding Senqu (Orange) River gorge and through some striking canyon scenery before climbing up onto the escarpment. If you're equipped, the whole area is ideal for hiking.

En route is the village of **Mt Moorosi**, named after a Basotho chieftain who, in 1879, stuck it out for eight months against the British on his fortified mountain until he was killed; the pretty **Mphaki** village, a possible base for hiking; and **Christ the King Mission**, with wide views over the Senqu (Orange) River valley. From the mission, it's a good two- to three-day hike north to Semonkong (p567).

SLEEPING & EATING

Fuleng Guest House (☎ 2275 0260; r per person from M80) Perched on a hill, this is the place for excellent-value rooms and rondavels-with-a-view plus a friendly local experience. Keen to promote tourism, the owner arranges activities and excursions. It's signposted from the main road just before the bend to Upper Quthing.

Mountain Side Hotel (☎ 2275 0257; s/d M210/285) This faded place has dark (if spacious) rooms and a decent restaurant. Ask for a room in the main building; those at the back are very cramped. It's about 100m down the dirt lane leading off the main road to the left, where the hill begins to climb to Upper Quthing.

For an inexpensive meal, head to the well-stocked, no-name shop selling grilled chicken, omelettes and other fast food in Lower Quthing, just before Fuleng Guest House.

In Mphaki, there's the attractive bluestone **Farmers' Training Centre** (dm M50) with clean rondavels and dorms and a kitchen (meals per day M50), and a few small shops nearby.

Moorosi Chalets (☎ in South Africa 051-436 6766; chalet per person from M80, with bath per person from M100) The folks from Malealea (in partnership with the Quthing Wildlife Development Trust) offer a new initiative – basic rondavel accommodation, trout fishing, visits to 'unseen' Bushman paintings and other activities. Incorporated into your visit, you can experience a Basotho village stay in one of two villages where local hosts have constructed basic, but very comfortable, guest rondavels (per person M50). The fee goes directly to the village for equipment and supplies. The chalets are 6km from Mt Moorosi village; take the turn-off to Ha Moqalo 2km out of the village in the direction of Qacha's Nek.

GETTING THERE & AWAY

Minibuses ply the route between Quthing and Qacha's Nek (M51, three hours) or a bus does the same trip, leaving Quthing at about 9am (M35, five hours). Several minibus taxis go to Maseru (M96, 3½ hours). The transport stand is situated in Lower Quthing. The Quthing–Qacha's Nek road is tarmac the entire way despite what many maps indicate.

Qacha's Nek

Originally a mission station, Qacha's Nek was founded in 1888 near the pass (1980m) of the same name. Its more recent claim to fame was as host of King Letsie III's 42nd birthday in 2005. This pleasant place has an attractive church and a variety of colonial-era sandstone buildings. Nearby are stands of California redwood trees, some over 25m high.

SLEEPING & EATING

Anna's B&B (☎ 2295 0374; annasb&b@leo.col.ls; s M100-150, d M180-280) On the main road, diagonally opposite the Farmers' Training Centre, it has clean, pleasant rooms in the new wing, and some less appealing ones with a shared bathroom in the old wing.

Letloepe Lodge (☎ 2295 0383; www.letloepelodge.co.ls; dm/s/d with breakfast M125/280/400) Letloepe means 'palace just below the clouds' and this is certainly the bastion of well-equipped rondavels with all the frills (including the frilliest, fanciest toilet seat covers and bed covers in Southern Africa) and a serene outlook. It's at the top of town on the hill. To enter, turn into the cream gate (the lodge's back wall faces the road).

Hotel Nthatuoa (☎ 2295 0260; s/d with breakfast M250/300) The most happenin' thing about this place is the plush red carpeted 'dining' room; the simple rooms' prices are classified by 'blocks' depending on their status (probably to cater for the government workshops). It's signposted along the main road at the northern edge of town.

GETTING THERE & AWAY

Regular minibus taxis go from Qacha's Nek and Maseru via Quthing (M96, six hours). There's also a daily bus between Maseru and Qacha's Nek departing from Maseru between 5am and 6am (M66, nine hours), and a bus from Qacha's Nek to Sehlabathebe National Park departing from Qacha's Nek around noon (M30, five hours).

Sehlabathebe National Park

Lesotho's first national park, proclaimed in 1970, is remote, rugged and beautiful, and getting there is always a worthwhile adventure, especially if you're into wilderness, seclusion and fishing. The rolling grasslands, wildflowers and silence provide a sense of complete isolation, which is the case, apart from the prolific birdlife (including the bearded vulture) and the odd rhebok. Hiking (and horse riding from Sani Top or the Drakensbergs) is the main way to explore the waterfalls and surrounds, and angling is possible in the park's dams and rivers.

You'll need to bring all your food, and be well prepared for the elements. This is a summer-rainfall area, and thick mist, potentially hazardous to hikers, is common. Winters are clear but cold at night, with occasional light snowfalls.

SLEEPING & EATING

Camping is permitted throughout the park, though there are no facilities besides plenty of water.

Sehlabathebe Park Lodge (☎ bookings 2232 3600; camp sites per person M30, r per person M80) This is the only option to stay in the park with facilities, and is an excellent (albeit secluded) one. Built in the 1970s for the prime minister of the time (it's been suggested he loved trout fishing, which may explain the park's existence), this time-warped lodge makes for a groovy stay. It's set on a remote flat grassland, and looks onto hills and ponds. Bring all your own food, plus extra petrol or diesel – there's none available at the park. The lodge takes up to 12 people, and has bedding and a fully equipped kitchen. It is 12km into the park, and 4WD vehicles are required if driving. Due to its isolation, it's not recommended for lone travellers. Sehlabathebe is currently under the jurisdiction

of the **National Environment Secretariat** (☎ 2231 1767 or 2232 6075; New Postal Office Building, 6th Floor, Kingsway, Maseru), but management seems to change regularly.

If you're travelling by public transport, the buses reach Sehlabathebe in the evening, which means you'll need to overnight in Mavuka village near the park gate. The clean and modern **Range Management Education Centre** (dm M35), 2km down the road to the left after the Mavuka Primary School, has dorm beds, but at the time of research had no water or gas. Alternatively, a last resort (but by no means a luxury one) is the **Mabotle Hotel** (d M70) in Mavuka itself. Despite the dusty and shabby setting, the rondavels have clean linoleum floors, 'new' bedheads (the plastic covering hasn't been removed) and spotless bathrooms. There is a reason: few people stay and there is no water.

GETTING THERE & AWAY

There's an airstrip at Paolosi, about 3km south of Mavuka, for charter flights.

A daily bus connects Qacha's Nek and Sehlabathebe, departing from Qacha's Nek at around noon and Sehlabathebe at 5.30am (M30, five hours). The bus terminates in Mavuka village, near the park gate. From here, it's about 12km further on foot to the lodge. If you're driving, the main route into the park is via Quthing and Qacha's Nek. The road from Qacha's Nek is unpaved but in reasonable condition, and negotiable at most times of the year in 2WD. You can arrange to leave your vehicle at the police station in Paolosi village while you're in the park.

Probably the simplest way into the park is to hike the 10km up the escarpment from Bushman's Nek in KwaZulu-Natal. From Bushman's Nek to the Nkonkoana Gate border crossing takes about six hours. Horses can also be arranged through **Khotso Trails** (☎ in South Africa 033-701 1502; www.khotsotrails .co.za) in Underberg.

The road between Sehlabathebe and Sehonghong is for 4WDs only. Even then, these roads can be affected by storms and landslides. Always ask locals if the roads are passable – signs are seldom erected; they rely on the 'bush telegraph'.

Swaziland

RICHARD I'ANSON

Swaziland

Embedded between Mozambique and South Africa, the kingdom of Swaziland is one of the smallest countries in Africa. What the country lacks in size, it makes up for in its rich culture and heritage, and relaxed ambience. With its laid-back, friendly people and relative lack of racial animosities, it's a complete change of pace from its larger neighbours.

During apartheid, Swaziland was known primarily for its casinos and nightclubs – forbidden pleasures in apartheid-era South Africa. Since the dismantling of apartheid this reputation has faded fast and the country's true attractions have come to the fore. Visitors can enjoy rewarding and delightfully low-key wildlife-watching, adrenaline-boosting activities such as rafting, taking in stunning mountain panoramas and a lively traditional culture. Swaziland also boasts superb walking and an excellent selection of high-quality handicrafts.

Overseeing all this is King Mswati III, one of three remaining monarchs in Africa. The monarchy has its critics, but combined with the Swazis' history of resistance to the Boers, the British and the Zulus, it has fostered a sense of national pride, and local culture is flourishing.

The excellent road system makes Swaziland easy to access and navigate. There's accommodation to suit every taste, ranging from a decent network of hostels to family-friendly hotels and upscale retreats. Many travellers make a flying visit on their way to Kruger National Park, but it's well worth lingering at least a week. If you come during one of the national festivals, notably the Incwala ceremony or the Umhlanga (Reed) dance (see the boxed text, p583), you can have a tantalising taste of the culture for which Swaziland is so renowned.

HIGHLIGHTS

- Watching wildlife, including rare black rhinos in the wild, at the excellent **Mkhaya Game Reserve** (p594)
- Hiking in **Malolotja Nature Reserve** (p590) or **Ngwempisi Gorge** (p595), two of Swaziland's most enchanting wilderness areas
- Browsing the craft shops and royal heartland of the **Ezulwini Valley** (p582) and the **Malkerns Valley** (p587)
- Shooting white-water rapids on the **Usutu River** (see the boxed text, p595)
- Walking around **Mlilwane Wildlife Sanctuary** (p586) and relaxing in its comfortable bargain lodges
- Exploring the ghost town of **Bulembu** (p592) in the country's northwest

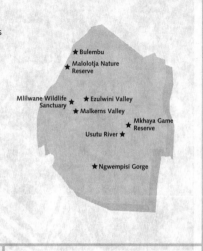

★ Bulembu
★ Malolotja Nature Reserve
Mlilwane Wildlife Sanctuary ★ ★ Ezulwini Valley
★ Malkerns Valley
Mkhaya Game Reserve ★
Usutu River ★
★ Ngwempisi Gorge

■ POPULATION: 1.1 MILLION   ■ AREA: 17,364 SQ KM

HISTORY
The Beginnings of a Nation

The area that is now Swaziland has been inhabited for millennia, and human-like remains possibly dating back as far as 100,000 years have been discovered around the Lebombo Mountains in eastern Swaziland. However, today's Swazis trace their ancestors to much more recent arrivals. By around AD 500, various Nguni groups had made their way to the region as part of the great Bantu migrations (p32). One of these groups settled in the area around present-day Maputo (Mozambique), eventually founding the Dlamini dynasty. In the mid-18th century, in response to increasing pressure from other clans in the area, the Dlamini king, Ngwane III, led his people southwest to the Pongola River, in present-day southern Swaziland and northern KwaZulu-Natal. This became the first Swazi heartland, and today, Swazis consider Ngwane III to have been their first king.

It was Ngwane's successor, Sobhuza I, who established a base in the Ezulwini Valley, which still remains the centre of Swazi royalty and ritual. Following Sobhuza I on the throne was the renowned King Mswazi (or Mswati), after whom the Swazi take their name. Despite considerable pressure from the neighbouring Zulu, Mswazi succeeded in unifying the whole kingdom. He also extended Swazi territory northwards as far as Hhohho, in what is now northwestern Swaziland, largely in response to continued Zulu incursions on Swazi territory to the south. By the time he died in 1868, the foundations of the young Swazi nation were secure.

From the mid-19th century, Swaziland began to attract increasing numbers of European farmers in search of land for their cattle, as well as hunters, traders and missionaries. Mswazi's successor, Mbandzeni, inherited a kingdom rife with European carpetbaggers, and proved much weaker at reining them in than Mswazi. Under Mbandzeni, increasing amounts of the kingdom's land were alienated through leases granted to Europeans, with bribes for the king featuring heavily in some of the deals.

Over the next decades, the Swazis saw their territory whittled away as the British and Boers jostled for power in the area.

In 1902, following the second Anglo-Boer War (p37), the Boers withdrew and the British took control of Swaziland as a protectorate.

Struggle for Independence

Swazi history in the early 20th century centred around the ongoing struggle for independence. Under the leadership of King Sobhuza II (guided by the capable hands of his mother acting as regent while Sobhuza was a child), the Swazis succeeded in regaining much of their original territory. This was done in part by direct purchase and in part by British government decree. By the time of independence in 1968, about two-thirds of the kingdom was again under Swazi control. This was a major development, as Swazi kings are considered to hold the kingdom in trust for their subjects, and land ownership is thus more than just a political and economic issue. Having a large proportion of the country owned by foreigners threatened the credibility of the monarchy and the viability of Swazi culture. It was also during this time that many Swazis began seeking work as migrant labourers in the Witwatersrand mines of South Africa, in part to raise money to buy back their lands.

In 1960 King Sobhuza II proposed the creation of a Legislative Council, to be composed of Europeans elected along European lines, and a National Council formed in accordance with Swazi culture. One of the Swazi political parties formed at this time was the Mbokodvo (Grindstone) National Movement, which pledged to maintain traditional Swazi culture while eschewing racial discrimination. When the British finally agreed to elections in 1964, Mbokodvo won a majority. At the next elections, in 1967, it won all the seats. Independence was finally achieved – the culmination of a long and remarkably nonviolent path – on 6 September 1968, 66 years after the start of the British protectorate.

The first Swazi constitution was largely a British creation, and in 1973 the king suspended it on the grounds that it did not accord with Swazi culture. Four years later parliament reconvened under a new constitution vesting all power in the king.

Sobhuza II died in 1982, at that time the world's longest-reigning monarch. Most

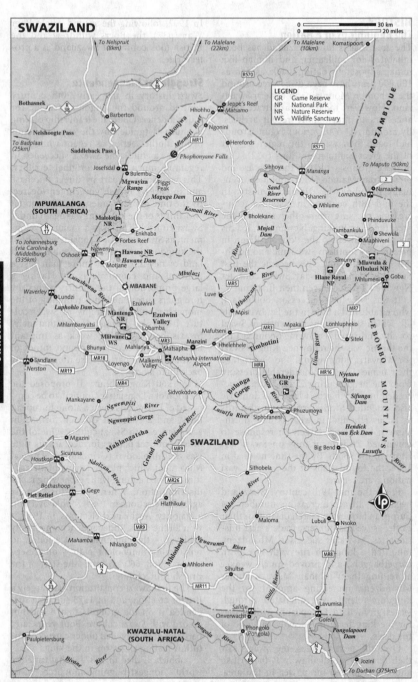

SWAZILAND

0 ——————— 30 km
0 ——————— 20 miles

LEGEND
GR Game Reserve
NP National Park
NR Nature Reserve
WS Wildlife Sanctuary

THE PILLAR OF POLYGAMY

When King Sobhuza II died, at age 83, he left about 120 official wives, with unofficial estimates putting the number of his wives and mistresses at more than double this number. The current King Mswati III has 13 wives. The king was the centre of controversy in 2001 when he married a 17 year old, two months after imposing a five-year sex ban on the kingdom's teenage females. The 'forced' chastity was imposed to fight the spread of HIV/AIDS. He ended the ban a year early.

Despite this proliferation of spouses among prominent figures, formal polygamy is declining in Swaziland. One of the main reasons for this is that it has become too expensive: each time a man marries, he must pay *lobola* (bride price – usually cattle) to the family of his fiancé. This has led to an increase in the number of 'informal' affairs.

---

significant among his accomplishments was his success in ensuring the continued existence of his country and culture, under threat since his father's reign. He is still referred to as 'the late king'. In 1986 the young Mswati III ascended the throne, where he continues today to represent and maintain the traditional Swazi way of life, and to assert his pre-eminence, for better and often worse, as absolute monarch.

Current Events

Swaziland is run by King Mswati III and a small core of advisers (Council of Ministers). Most Swazis seem happy with (or perhaps apathetic to) their political system, and focus instead on ensuring that their culture survives in the face of modernisation. However, there is an undercurrent of political dissent, and the movement for democratic change has slowly gained momentum over the past decade. In 1996 the king appointed a constitutional review commission, and in 2003 a new constitution was finally unveiled – though it was promptly dismissed by reform-minded Swazis as doing little more than preserving the status quo.

Opposition parties are officially banned, but several exist. The main ones are People's United Democratic Movement (Pudemo) and Swaziland Youth Congress (Swayoco), both of which enjoy only limited support. In addition, the trade union movement has long been agitating for change, though there is a royal ban on its meetings. Yet, despite these political tensions and increasing popular dissatisfaction with recent abuses of royal privilege, it's likely that the king and his advisers will continue to hold the upper hand in Swazi politics for the foreseeable future. Even reformers call only for

modification of the monarchy (demanding a constitutional instead of an absolute monarchy), rather than its complete abandonment.

Putting these constitutional wranglings into sharp perspective is the scourge of AIDS: Swaziland has now surpassed Botswana as the country with the world's highest HIV infection rate in the world (see boxed text, p578).

CLIMATE

Most of Swaziland enjoys a climate similar to that of South Africa's eastern lowveld, with rainy, steamy summers and agreeably cooler winters. Between December and February, temperatures occasionally exceed 40°C and torrential thunderstorms are common. May to August are the coolest months. In the higher-lying areas of the west, winters bring cool, crisp nights and sometimes even frost.

NATIONAL PARKS & RESERVES

Swaziland has five main reserves, reflecting the tiny country's impressively diverse topography. Easiest to get to is Mlilwane Wildlife Sanctuary (p586) in the Ezulwini Valley, which is privately run by **Big Game Parks** (☎ 528 3944; www.biggameparks.org), based at Mlilwane. Also under the same jurisdiction, and both well worth visiting, are the excellent Mkhaya Game Reserve (p594), with black rhinos and many other animals, and Hlane Royal National Park (p593).

In the northwestern highlands is the beautiful Malolotja Nature Reserve (p590), known for its hiking trails. It, together with Mlawula Nature Reserve (p593) in the eastern lowveld and tiny Mantenga Nature Reserve (p583) in the Ezulwini Valley, is run by the **National Trust Commission** (☎ 416 1151,

SWAZILAND

HIV/AIDS

Swaziland has now surpassed Botswana as the country with the world's highest HIV infection rate in the world – around 39% of the adult population in Swaziland is HIV positive (compared to 3.9% in 1992). According to a survey by the national health ministry, one-quarter of Swaziland's population is predicted to be dead from the disease by 2010, and already over 60,000 children have lost either one or both parents to the disease.

There are many possible reasons for this: more Swazis work in South Africa (primarily in the mining, sugar and timber industries) than in Swaziland, and these populations – including the wives or girlfriends they have left behind – are particularly at risk. Other reasons include cultural practices such as widow inheritance (where a widow has been entrusted to her brother-in-law in her husband's absence). In some cases, the decline in polygamy has led to more 'informal' relations outside the marriage. Other contributing factors include the legal lack of equality for women, the accessibility of the country and good road system (useful trucking routes), and the stigma attached to AIDS, which hinders the flow of communication and hampers prevention efforts.

---

416 1178; www.sntc.org.sz), with its head office at the National Museum in Lobamba (Ezulwini Valley) and a bookings representative at the Ezulwini Valley **tourist information office** (☎ 404 2531; www.welcometoswaziland.com).

LANGUAGE

The official languages are Swati and English, and English is the official written language. For information on Swati, see the Language chapter (p651).

DANGERS & ANNOYANCES

Street crime in Mbabane is rising, so take common-sense precautions, especially at night. There has been an increase in attacks on tourists and locals in Manzini – do not flaunt valuables and be vigilant at all times.

Schistosomiasis (bilharzia) and malaria are both present in Swaziland; see p648 and p647 for information on avoiding these diseases.

GETTING THERE & AROUND

There are flights into Swaziland (Matasapha International Airport) from Johannesburg (Jo'burg) and Durban in South Africa and from Maputo in Mozambique; see p625.

Swazi Express Airways (☎ 518 6840; www.swazi express.com), together with its sister company, Steffen Air Charters, operates charter flights within the kingdom and around the region.

Most travellers enter Swaziland overland. For details of border posts, see p628. For bus connections, see p630 and for information on driving around Swaziland, including car hire, see p635.

Once in Swaziland, there is a good network of minibuses covering the country. There are private taxis in Mbabane, the Ezulwini Valley and Manzini. See the Getting Around sections of these areas for details.

MBABANE

pop 60,000

Swaziland's capital and second-largest city, Mbabane (pronounced mm-bah-bahn), may sound grand, but it's not. However, though plain, it's a relaxed and functional place in a lovely setting in the Dlangeni Hills, and is a good place to get things done. There's a handful of OK restaurants, accommodation options and a busy market, but the adjacent Ezulwini Valley has most of the attractions. Mbabane is growing fast and has recently seen a surge in commercial development, making it a sharp contrast to the surrounding rural areas.

During the colonial era, the British originally had their base in Manzini, but moved it in 1902 to Mbabane to take advantage of the cooler climate in the hills.

Orientation

Street names in Mbabane have been changed over recent years and seem to have finally been captured on official maps. Occasionally, people will still refer to the old name (or both).

The main street is Gwamile St, which runs roughly north–south through the town centre. Just off its southern end is Swazi

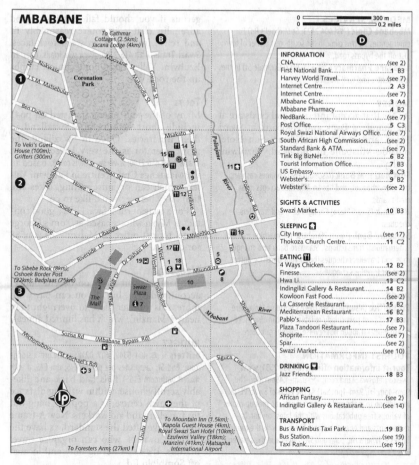

MBABANE

INFORMATION
CNA	(see 2)
First National Bank	1 B3
Harvey World Travel	(see 7)
Internet Centre	2 A3
Internet Centre	(see 7)
Mbabane Clinic	3 A4
Mbabane Pharmacy	4 B2
NedBank	(see 7)
Post Office	5 C3
Royal Swazi National Airways Office	(see 7)
South African High Commission	(see 7)
Standard Bank & ATM	(see 7)
Tink Big BizNet	6 B2
Tourist Information Office	7 B3
US Embassy	8 C3
Webster's	9 B2
Webster's	(see 2)

SIGHTS & ACTIVITIES
Swazi Market	10 B3

SLEEPING
City Inn	(see 17)
Thokoza Church Centre	11 C2

EATING
4 Ways Chicken	12 B2
Finesse	(see 2)
Hwa Li	13 C2
Indingilizi Gallery & Restaurant	14 B2
Kowloon Fast Food	(see 2)
La Casserole Restaurant	15 B2
Mediterranean Restaurant	16 B2
Pablo's	17 B2
Plaza Tandoori Restaurant	(see 7)
Shoprite	(see 7)
Spar	(see 2)
Swazi Market	(see 10)

DRINKING
Jazz Friends	18 B3

SHOPPING
African Fantasy	(see 2)
Indingilizi Gallery & Restaurant	(see 14)

TRANSPORT
Bus & Minibus Taxi Park	19 B3
Bus Station	(see 19)
Taxi Rank	(see 19)

SWAZILAND

Plaza, a large shopping mall with the tourist information office, banks and ATMs, an Internet centre and a good range of shops. Just across the street is Mbabane's other main shopping centre, the Mall.

The city's central commercial area is easily negotiated on foot. Away from here, the streets become green and residential as they wind over the hills, and a car is handy if you'll be staying in any outlying B&Bs.

MAPS

The **tourist information office** (☎ 404 2531; www .welcometoswaziland.com; ⏰ 9am-4.45pm Mon-Thu, 9am-4pm Fri, 9am-1pm Sat) has a free map with Mbabane, Manzini and Swaziland on one side, and information on the reverse.

Information
BOOKSHOPS
CNA (Swazi Plaza) A good option.
Webster's (120 Dzeliwe St) The best-stocked bookshop in Mbabane.

EMERGENCY
Fire (☎ 404 3333)
Police (☎ 404 2221, 999)

INTERNET ACCESS
There are Internet centres at Swazi Post, located upstairs at Swazi Plaza, and in the Mall, near Spar. Internet acces starts from E25 per hour.
Tink Big BizNet (109 Dzeliwe St) The most cutting-edge Internet joint in Swaziland.

MEDICAL SERVICES

Mbabane Clinic (☎ 404 2423; St Michael's Rd) For emergencies try this clinic in the southwest corner of town just off the bypass road.

Mbabane Pharmacy (☎ 404 2817; Gwamile St) In the town centre and well stocked.

MONEY

ATMs that accept international cards are at the Standard Bank and Nedbank in Swazi Plaza, and at the Royal Swazi Sun Hotel outside Mbabane in the nearby Ezulwini Valley.

First National Bank (Msunduza St) Changes cash and travellers cheques, and has an ATM that accepts most credit cards.

Nedbank (Swazi Plaza) Changes cash and travellers cheques.

Standard Bank (Swazi Plaza) Use the machine marked 'international transactions'. Standard Bank also changes cash and travellers cheques (bring your purchase agreement for travellers cheques).

POST

Post office (Msunduza St) There's poste restante here, though it's not particularly reliable. You can also make international (though not reverse-charge) calls here.

TOURIST INFORMATION

Tourist information office (☎ 404 2531; www .welcometoswaziland.com; ⏰ 9am-4.45pm Mon-Thu, 9am-4pm Fri, 9am-1pm Sat) At the edge of Swazi Plaza. In addition to maps and brochures, you can pick up copies of various free publications with the latest on hotels, restaurants and entertainment. These include the tourist Bibles – *What's Happening in Swaziland* and the smaller *What's on in Swaziland*.

TRAVEL AGENCIES

Harvey World Travel (☎ 404 1538; www.harvey world.co.za; Swazi Plaza) Can assist with flight bookings and other travel arrangements.

Royal Swazi National Airways Office (Swazi Plaza) Helpful with booking regional flights.

Sights & Activities

Walking around the town centre, shopping and taking care of errands is the main activity in Mbabane for most travellers. The **Swazi Market** is sometimes worth a browse, with good but pricey crafts and fresh produce.

About 8km northeast of Mbabane is **Sibebe Rock**, a massive granite dome hulking over the surrounding countryside. Much of the rock is completely sheer, and dan-

gerous if you should fall, but it's a good adrenalin charge if you're reasonably fit and relish looking down steep rock-faces. **Swazi Trails** (☎ 416 2180; www.swazitrails.co.sz) in Ezulwini Valley takes nontechnical climbs up the rock.

Tours

Many of the tour operators listed on p641 include short detours into Swaziland in their itineraries. Once in Swaziland, the main operator is the very keyed-in **Swazi Trails** (☎ 416 2180; www.swazitrails.co.sz), based in the Mantenga Craft Centre in Ezulwini Valley, which can organise rafting, hikes and tours to wherever you'd like to go.

For a taste of rural Swazi life, a good contact is Myxo who is based at Tum's George Hotel tourist office in Manzini – see p588 for details.

Sleeping

Mbabane is a bit short on decent budget accommodation, but if you can pay a bit more, it is a better place to overnight than nearby Manzini, which has limited appeal.

BUDGET

Grifters (☎ 404 5342, 617 0218; www.grifterslodge .com; End St; camp sites per person E45, dm E75, d with shared bathroom E165) This laid-back and likeably scruffy house, within walking distance of the town centre, is a popular hang-out for travellers and aid workers. New A-frame dorms have lifted the standard, as have the friendly owners, who can organise travel matters. It's self-catering only and located off Somhlolo Rd.

Thokoza Church Centre (☎ 404 6681; Polinjane Rd; s/d with shared bathroom E125/160, s/d E190/210) Fittingly monastic in nature, these small clean rooms might be just the thing to convert you to Mbabane. Inexpensive meals can be arranged. To get here from Gwamile St on foot, turn onto Mhlonhlo St, cross the bridge at the bottom of the hill, turn left at the police station and head up Polinjane Rd for about 10 minutes. Take a taxi at night (E20 from Swazi Plaza).

Veki's Guest House (☎ 404 8485; www.swazilodg ings.com/cathmar; 233 Gilfillan St; s/d E220/300) Fairly overpriced and nondescript house with a slightly hippy feel, this place comes recommended by expat Swazis. There are seven rooms with DSTV and meals on request.

MIDRANGE & TOP END

Cathmar Cottages (☎ 404 3387; www.swazilodgings
.com/cathmar; 167 Lukhalo St; r from E200-320; ☒) Various self-catering cottages and dolls-house–
style cabins dotted around a quiet residential
garden on a hill overlooking Sibebe Rock,
about 3.5km north of the town centre (off
Pine Valley Rd). All have TV and minifridge,
and range from OK to pleasant. Meals are
also available.

City Inn (☎ 404 2406; cityinn@realnet.co.sz; Gwamile
St; s/d incl breakfast E300/390) The red carpet and
olive green bathrooms in the city's most
central hotel – and Mbabane institution –
are the most colourful part of a rather
shabby stay. Ask for a room in the newer
west wing.

Jacana Lodge (☎ 405 0277; www.jacanalodge.co.sz;
s/d incl breakfast from E350/490; ☒) Another good-
value B&B (under new management since
March 2005), this bright, spotless place is
in a quiet hilltop location about 5km from
the centre. There's a family room with its
own balcony and massive bathroom, and a
tiny pool. Staff can also organise reasonably
priced tours of Swaziland.

Kapola Guest House (☎ 404 0906; www.kapola
_eden.co.sz; s/d incl breakfast E390/650) Lay back like
a local lizard and overlook the greenery
from the massive porch of this comfortable
abode. The rooms – complete with shells,
plants and paraphernalia – are busier than
the chef who prepares à la carte meals (E26
to E65). It's about 5km from Mbabane just
off the MR3; watch for the wall painted
with flags.

Foresters Arms (☎ 467 4177; www.forestersarms.co
.za; s & d with half board from E445) Penelope Keith
(from BBC-TV's *To the Manor Born*) would
be right at home here. But it's not just the
cream teas and British-style interiors that
make this Swaziland's 'Country Estate'.
Situated 27km southwest of Mbabane in
the hills around Mhlambanyatsi (Watering
Place of the Buffaloes), it makes an excellent alternative to sleeping in the city. There
are cosy rooms and attractive gardens plus
a smorgasbord of activities (trout fishing,
horse riding and water sports on the nearby
Luphohlo Dam). Gourmands can gracefully
gorge at the large and popular Sunday lunch
buffet (reservations are recommended). To
top it all off, the owner knows all there is
to know about Swaziland. Follow the MR19
from Mbabane. If you're leaving Swaziland

from here, you can continue southwest
along the MR19 and exit via the Nerston
border post near Sandlane.

Mountain Inn (☎ 404 2781; www.mountaininn.sz;
s/d incl breakfast from E525/670; ☒ ☐ ☒) This inn
is a throwback to the colonial era, complete
with stains here and there. The rooms are
supplemented by its luxurious genteel ambience, pool, library, lawn and panoramas
looking over the valley from the inviting
restaurant (mains from E45), open for
breakfast, lunch and dinner.

Eating

Pablo's (☎ 404 2406; Gwamile St; burgers from E12, breakfast from E20; ☽ breakfast, lunch & dinner) Smell that
grease – just the place for the beefy burger
and fatty fries.

4 Ways Chicken (Gwamile St; mains E13; ☽ 7am-6pm)
It ain't nothin' fancy, but at these prices this
is the tastiest hen quarter in Swaziland.

Plaza Tandoori Restaurant (☎ 404 7599; Swazi
Plaza; mains E32-85; ☽ lunch & dinner) It's not the
size of the Taj Mahal, but it's certainly got
the atmosphere. As well as great-value curries, the usual grills and burgers add a touch
of the international.

eDladleni (☎ 404 5743; Manzini/Mbabane Hwy; mains
E40-80; ☽ lunch & dinner) Out there on its own,
this self-proclaimed 'Queen of Swazi food fit
for a King' lives up to its name. It's got the
best vegetarian options around. It's about
6km from Mbabane off the main highway.

Indingilizi Gallery & Restaurant (☎ 404 6213;
indingi@realnet.co.sz; 112 Dzeliwe St; snacks from E22, light
meals from E22-45; ☽ 8am-5pm Mon-Fri, 8.30am-2pm
Sat) This small outdoor café offers quiches,
salads and similar fare, plus decadent desserts and craft shopping at the adjoining
gallery.

Hwa Li (☎ 404 5986; Dhlan'ubeka House, Mhlonhlo
St; mains from E35; ☽ lunch & dinner Mon-Sat) A good
spot for spring rolls, chow mein and spicy
soups.

La Casserole Restaurant (☎ 404 6426; Gwamile St;
mains E49-80; ☽ lunch & dinner) It's got a French
name, but this long-standing friendly place
serves German and international cuisine,
including pizzas. It also offers a few vegetarian dishes, plus a good wine selection.

Mediterranean Restaurant (☎ 404 3212, Gwamile St; mains E49-100; ☽ lunch & dinner) The bland
atmosphere is forgotten thanks to the spicy
Indian curries and tasty Portuguese morsels
on offer.

Finesse (☎ 404 5936; the Mall; mains E69-100; ☽ lunch & dinner Mon-Sat) This French-owned place offers a fancier setting under a covered terrace, and serves a good range of seafood and meat dishes, many with an Indian Ocean flavour.

There's a Shoprite at Swazi Plaza and a Spar at the Mall. For fast food, try the street food vendors at **Swazi Market** (Msunduza St); or Kowloon Fast Food in the Mall.

Drinking

Most people head to the Ezulwini Valley for nightlife (see p585). In Mbabane, try **Plaza Bar** (Swazi Plaza), a popular local boozy haunt. **Jazz Friends** (Gwamile St) is another local hang-out.

Shopping

Indingilizi Gallery & Restaurant (☎ 404 6213; indin gi@realnet.co.sz; 112 Dzeliwe St; ☽ 8am-5pm Mon-Fri, 8.30am-2pm Sat) This gallery has an idiosyncratic collection that's pricey but well worth a look. There is traditional craft, including some interesting old pieces, and excellent art and craftwork by contemporary Swazi artists.

African Fantasy (☎ 404 0205; Shop 11, the Mall) African Fantasy offers a great selection of locally made T-shirts and cards; it also has a branch at Mantenga Craft Centre (p585) and the Gables Shopping Centre (p585).

Getting There & Around

The main bus and minibus taxi park is just behind Swazi Plaza. Minibus taxis leave for Jo'burg early in the morning; otherwise your best bet is to catch one from Manzini. See p622 for more information on connections to/from South Africa and Mozambique.

There are several minibus taxis daily to Piggs Peak (E12.50, one hour), Ngwenya and the Oshoek border post (E5, 50 minutes), and Malkerns Valley (E7, 45 minutes). All vehicles heading towards Manzini (E7, 35 minutes) and points east pass through the Ezulwini Valley, although most take the bypass road.

Nonshared taxis congregate just outside the transport park behind Swazi Plaza. At night, you can also usually find a taxi near the City Inn. Nonshared taxis to the Ezulwini Valley cost from E50, more to the far end of the valley (from E100), and still more

if hired at night. To Matsapha International Airport, expect to pay from E140.

EZULWINI VALLEY

The Ezulwini Valley, or Valley of Heaven as the region is called, is Swaziland's royal heartland and tourism centre. It begins just outside Mbabane and extends down past Lobamba, 18km away. For most of Swazi history, it has been home to the Swazi royal family. It's possible to whiz through on the MR3 bypass road, but to see the sights and lush countryside, you'll need to take the old MR103. Don't let the tacky-hotel-strip atmosphere along some sections deter you: just in from the road is some beautiful woodland scenery, with brilliant orange flame trees, flowering jacarandas and views over the surrounding mountains. There's a good selection of places to stay here and some of the best craft shopping in Southern Africa.

Information

There are ATMs at the Gables Shopping Centre.

Big Game Parks (☎ 528 3943; www.biggameparks .org) Accessed through the Mlilwane Wildlife Sanctuary. Contact it for accommodation in Mlilwane Wildlife Sanctuary, Mkhaya Game Reserve and Hlane Royal National Park.

Friendly Whistle Internet Cafe (per half hr E38; ☽ 8.30am-6.30pm) In the Gables Shopping Centre, opposite the Happy Valley Motel.

National Trust Commission (☎ 416 1151, 416 1178; www.sntc.org.sz) Headquarters of the Mlawula, Malolotja and Mantenga Nature Reserves, it's based at the National Museum in Lobamba.

Swazi Trails (☎ 416 2180; www.swazitrails.co.sz) Tourist information is available here, based at the Mantenga Craft Centre. It also takes bookings for Malolotja, Mlawula and Mantenga Nature Reserves and organises a plethora of activities, trails and tours all over the kingdom.

Lobamba

Lobamba is the heart of Swaziland's Royal Valley – a position it has held since the early days of the Swazi monarchy. The royal Embo State Palace was built by the British – in grand proportions, as it had to house the entire royal clan (Sobhuza II had 600 children). It isn't open to visitors, and photos aren't allowed. Swazi kings now live in **Lozitha State House**, about 10km from Lobamba.

To see the monarchy in action, head to the **Royal Kraal** (Eludzidzini Royal Residence) during the Incwala ceremony or the

SWAZI CEREMONIES

Incwala

Incwala (also known as Ncwala) is the most sacred ceremony of the Swazi people. It is a 'first fruits' ceremony, where the king gives permission for his people to eat the first crops of the new year. Preparation for the Incwala begins some weeks in advance, according to the cycle of the moon. *Bemanti* (learned men) journey to the Lebombo Mountains to gather plants; other *bemanti* collect water from Swaziland's rivers and some travel across the mountains to the Indian Ocean to skim foam from the waves. Meanwhile, the king goes into retreat.

On the night of the full moon, young men all over the kingdom harvest branches of the *lusekwane*, a small tree, and begin a long hike to the Royal Kraal at Lobamba. They arrive at dawn, and use their branches to build a kraal. If a branch has wilted, it is seen as a sign that the young man bearing it has had illicit sex. Songs prohibited during the rest of the year are sung, and the *bemanti* arrive with their plants, water and foam.

On the third day of the ceremony a bull is sacrificed. On the fourth day, to the pleadings of all the regiments of Swaziland, the king comes out of his retreat and dances before his people. He eats a pumpkin, the sign that Swazis can eat the new year's crops. Two days later there's a ritual burning of all the items used in the ceremony, after which the rains are expected to fall.

Umhlanga (Reed) Dance

Though not as sacred as the Incwala, the Umhlanga (Reed) dance serves a similar function in drawing the nation together and reminding the people of their relationship to the king. It is something like a weeklong debutante ball for marriageable young Swazi women, who journey from all over the kingdom to help repair the queen mother's home at Lobamba.

After arriving at Lobamba, they spend a day resting, then set off in search of reeds, some not returning until the fourth night. On the sixth day the reed dance is performed as they carry their reeds to the queen mother. The dance is repeated the next day. Those carrying torches (flashlights) have searched for reeds by night; those with red feathers in their hair are princesses.

As the Swazi queen mother must not be of the royal clan, the reed dance is also a showcase of potential wives for the king. As with the Incwala, there are signs that identify the unchaste – an incentive to avoid premarital sex.

Umhlanga (Reed) dance (see the boxed text, above). It's next to Lozitha State House. Just north of here, towards the main road, is **Somhlolo National Stadium**, which hosts sports events (mainly soccer) and important state occasions, such as coronations.

The nearby **National Museum** (adult/child E20/10; 8am-4pm Mon-Fri, 10am-4pm Sat & Sun) has some interesting displays of Swazi culture, as well as a traditional beehive village and cattle enclosure.

Next to the museum is the **parliament**, which is sometimes open to visitors; if you want to visit, wear neat clothes and use the side entrance. Across the road from the museum is a **memorial** to King Sobhuza II, the most revered of Swazi kings. A ticket to both the museum and memorial costs adult/child E25/15.

About 3km from Mantenga Lodge is **Mantenga Nature Reserve** (adult/child E45/11; 7am-6pm). The ticket cost covers entrance to the

reserve's **Swazi Cultural Village**. This 'living' cultural village has authentic beehive huts and cultural displays, and it's possible to take guided tours and watch the **sibhaca dance** (11.15am & 3.15pm). Next door, the pleasant restaurant, set in a lush rainforest (watch out for thieving monkeys), provides relief from the heat. Nearby, and part of the reserve, are **Mantenga Falls**, which you can visit on guided walks.

For personal pampering, head to the Royal Valley's own **hot mineral springs** (416 1164; adult/child E5/2; 6am-10pm), also known as the Cuddle Puddle. In the same complex is the **Swazi Spa Health & Beauty Studio** (416 1164; 10am-6pm), with an aromatherapy steam tube, oxygen multistep and a Jacuzzi.

SLEEPING

There's no accommodation in Lobamba village itself, but there are plenty of options in the immediate vicinity.

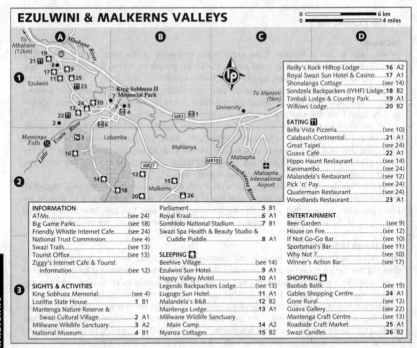

EZULWINI & MALKERNS VALLEYS

0 — 6 km
0 — 4 miles

Reilly's Rock Hilltop Lodge	16 A2
Royal Swazi Sun Hotel & Casino	17 A1
Shonalanga Cottage	(see 14)
Sondzela Backpackers (IYHF) Lodge	18 B2
Timbali Lodge & Country Park	19 A1
Willows Lodge	20 B2

EATING

Bella Vista Pizzeria	(see 10)
Calabash Continental	21 A1
Great Taipei	(see 24)
Guava Café	22 A1
Hippo Haunt Restaurant	(see 14)
Kanimambo	(see 24)
Malandela's Restaurant	(see 12)
Pick 'n' Pay	(see 24)
Quatermain Restaurant	(see 24)
Woodlands Restaurant	23 A1

INFORMATION

ATMs	(see 24)
Big Game Parks	(see 18)
Friendly Whistle Internet Cafe	(see 24)
National Trust Commission	(see 4)
Swazi Trails	(see 13)
Tourist Office	(see 13)
Ziggy's Internet Cafe & Tourist Information	(see 12)

SIGHTS & ACTIVITIES

King Sobhuza Memorial	(see 4)
Lozitha State House	1 B1
Mantenga Nature Reserve & Swazi Cultural Village	2 A1
Mlilwane Wildlife Sanctuary	3 A2
National Museum	4 B1

Parliament	5 B1
Royal Kraal	6 A1
Somhlolo National Stadium	7 B1
Swazi Spa Health & Beauty Studio & Cuddle Puddle	8 A1

SLEEPING

Beehive Village	(see 14)
Ezulwini Sun Hotel	9 A1
Happy Valley Motel	10 A1
Legends Backpackers Lodge	(see 13)
Lugogo Sun Hotel	11 A1
Malandela's B&B	12 B2
Mantenga Lodge	13 A1
Mlilwane Wildlife Sanctuary Main Camp	14 A2
Nyanza Cottages	15 B2

ENTERTAINMENT

Beer Garden	(see 9)
House on Fire	(see 12)
If Not Go-Go Bar	(see 10)
Sportsman's Bar	(see 11)
Why Not ?	(see 10)
Winner's Action Bar	(see 17)

SHOPPING

Baobab Batik	(see 15)
Gables Shopping Centre	24 A1
Gone Rural	(see 12)
Guava Gallery	(see 22)
Mantenga Craft Centre	(see 13)
Roadside Craft Market	25 A1
Swazi Candles	26 B2

Budget

For more budget options in the Lobamba area, see Mlilwane Wildlife Sanctuary (p586).

Legends Backpackers Lodge (☎ 416 1870; leg ends@mailfly.com; camp sites per person E50, dm E75, d with shared bathroom E190; 🖳) This place is now legendary for the wrong reasons: it looks as shabby and worn-out as the adventurers who've just spun out on an activity organised by Swazi Trails, the lodge's sister-company. And, like those who've overindulged at the lodge's inhouse *shebeen* (drinking establishment), it's in need of a good pick-me-up. But hey, it's a bed.

Midrange

There are several good midrange accommodation options available.

Mantenga Nature Reserve (☎ 416 1151, 416 1178; mnr@africaonline.co.sz; beehive huts per person E60, s/d tented chalets incl breakfast E305/460) Soft 'safari' adventure in tented style and canvas comfort: these delightful shelters, set in lush bushland, have small porches and creative separate outdoor showers. You can also stay in traditional beehive huts at the Cultural

Village, and there is a restaurant serving a good selection of luncheon dishes from noodles to steaks.

Happy Valley Motel (☎ 416 1061; happyvalley@ africaonline.co.sz; r incl breakfast E370; 🏊 🖭) This place boasts multipersonalities: the bland-looking outer hides a fun side (pizzeria, steakhouse and bar); generous side (mid-week discounts are available, and children under 12 stay for free); and an outright raunchy aspect – the If Not Go-Go Bar and Why Not Disco (entries are free for guests). It's along the MR103, opposite the turn-off for Mantenga Lodge.

Mantenga Lodge (☎ 416 1049; reservations@man tengalodge.com; s/d incl breakfast from E380/500; 🏊 🖭) A safe, peaceful and predictable option, the unassuming rooms are set in a lush wooded area about 1.5km off the main road. The restaurant's dining patio overlooks the hills and stands of flame and jacaranda trees. Take the signposted turn-off for the Mantenga Craft Centre; the hotel is 500m further along this road.

Timbali Lodge & Country Park (☎ 416 2632; www .visitswazi.com; s/d incl breakfast from E400/500; 🏊 🖭)

This moderately upscale place, at the western end of the valley, has modern, self-catering white-coloured cottages set in pleasant, grassy and secluded grounds.

Top End

Top-end lodging is dominated by the Sun chain, which has three properties here, all clustered along the MR3 about 6km northwest of Lobamba and about 3km from Mbabane. Rates are always changing, so inquire in advance. All offer weekend specials at some times of the year for about half-price and all have restaurants.

Lugogo Sun Hotel (☎ 416 4500; www.suninternational.com; s/d E1205/1300; 🏊 🅿 🍴) The largest and slightly more low-key of the Swazi Suns, it's bright and light and popular with ankle-biters – there's Kamp Kwena for children. It is on the same grounds as the Royal Swazi Sun.

Ezulwini Sun Hotel (☎ 416 6500; www.suninternational.com; s/d E1330/1425; 🏊 🍴) This two-storey pink palace is less ostentatious than its sister hotels directly across the road. It has a more apartment-like feel, with the usual international hotel features, including pools and tennis courts.

Royal Swazi Sun (☎ 416 5000; www.suninternational.com; s/d E1910/2025; 🏊 🖥 🍴) As fancy as its name suggests, and the most luxurious of the three Sun hotels, this OTT place flaunts a golf course, tennis courts, Internet café, a casino and the necessary ATM.

EATING

Guava Café (☎ 416 1343; light meals from E30; ⏰ 9am-5pm Tue-Sat, 10am-5pm Sun) A chic eatery at Guava Gallery, just before Swazi Cultural Village, with salads, soups and lunch fare.

Bella Vista Pizzeria (☎ 416 1061; pizza from E32; ⏰ lunch & dinner) Bella Vista is at Happy Valley Motel along the MR103, and does a brisk local business.

Diagonally opposite Bella Vista is the Gables Shopping Centre, with a Pick 'n' Pay and several good restaurants. **Kanimambo** (☎ 416 3549; mains E57-100; ⏰ lunch & dinner Tue-Sat) has Mozambican chefs and specialises in Mozambican seafood and *piri-piri* (hot pepper) meat dishes, and **Great Taipei** (☎ 416 2300; mains from E45; ⏰ lunch & dinner) is the place to go for chop suey and other Chinese dishes.

Quatermain's (☎ 416 3023; mains E58-80; ⏰ lunch & dinner Tue-Sun) Based on the name of the author of *King Solomon's Mines*, this eatery's dishes represent a journey through Africa – the menu features an interpretation of places relating to the source of the food. It offers everything from savoury pancakes to massive steaks.

Calabash Continental (☎ 416 1187; mains E60-100; ⏰ lunch & dinner) German and Austrian-Swiss cuisine are the incongruous highlights at this popular and long-standing place. It's at the upper end of Ezulwini Valley, and is easily accessible from Mbabane.

Woodlands Restaurant (☎ 416 3466; ⏰ lunch & dinner) After you've shopped till you've dropped at the Ezulwini craft market, head next door to the lovely outside setting and shady veranda of this recently opened eatery. There are good vegetarian options as well as international cuisine, including *eisbein* (pork knuckles).

ENTERTAINMENT

Why Not? (☎ 416 1061; Happy Valley Hotel; admission E30) The name says it all. If you want to let it all hang out (or see others doing so) head here for a big night. Also here is the dimly lit and somewhat tawdry If Not Go-Go Bar (entry to Why Not? includes If Not). Bands play regularly (E40).

There are also several nightspots at the Sun hotels, including **Beer Garden** (☎ 416 6500; Ezulwini Sun Hotel), with live music and meals; **Sportsman's Bar** (☎ 416 1550; Lugogo Sun Hotel), with a pub night on Wednesday; and **Winner's Action Bar** (Royal Swazi Sun Hotel), with live music on Friday.

Also check out what's playing at **House on Fire** (☎ 528 2001; houseonfire@africaonline.co.sz), in Malkerns Valley.

SHOPPING

The Ezulwini Valley, together with the nearby Malkerns Valley, offers some of the best craft shopping in the region, with a wide selection, high quality and reasonable prices.

Mantenga Craft Centre (☎ 416 1136) This rather tired-looking craft centre is on the access road leading to Mantenga Lodge, with numerous shops featuring everything from weaving and tapestries to candles, woodcarvings and T-shirts.

Guava Gallery (☎ 416 1343; ⏰ 9am-5pm Tue-Sat, 10am-5pm Sun) A chic boutique with various local crafts.

SWAZILAND

The well-stocked roadside craft market along the M103 just south of the Ezulwini Sun Hotel sells a large range of local carvings, weavings and artefacts.

GETTING THERE & AWAY

Nonshared taxis from Mbabane cost E60 to E100, depending on how far down the valley you go. For a pick-up from the Ezulwini Valley, you'll have to call a Mbabane-based taxi service.

During the day you could get on a minibus bound for Manzini, but make sure the driver knows that you want to alight in the valley, as many aren't keen on stopping.

If you're driving from either Mbabane or Manzini, take the Ezulwini Valley/Lobamba exit off the bypass road. This puts you on the MR103, from where everything is well signposted.

Mlilwane Wildlife Sanctuary

This beautiful and tranquil **private reserve** (☎ 528 3943; www.biggameparks.org; admission E25; ☻6am-5pm) near Lobamba was Swaziland's first protected area, created by conservationist Ted Reilly on his family farm in the 1950s. Reilly later opened Mkhaya Game Reserve and supervised the establishment of Hlane Royal National Park. Mlilwane means 'Little Fire', named after the many fires started by lightning strikes in the region.

While it doesn't have the drama or vastness of some of the bigger South African parks, the reserve is easily accessible and well worth a visit. Its terrain is dominated by the precipitous Nyonyane (Little Bird) peak, with several fine walks in the area. Animals to be seen include zebras, giraffes, warthogs, many antelope species, crocodiles, hippos and a variety of birds. In summer, you may also spot black eagles near Nyonyane.

Activities on offer in the reserve include **walking** (per person per hr with guide E25), two-hour **vehicle safaris** (per person E130), **cycling** (per person per hr E40) and day and overnight **horse-riding trips** (per person from E100).

Mlilwane gets very busy during South African school holidays (see p612). The entrance is 2km southeast of the Happy Valley Motel on the old Mbabane–Manzini road, and signposted from the turn-off. Night access is via an alternative gate.

SLEEPING & EATING

All accommodation in the sanctuary can be booked in advance at **Big Game Parks** (☎ 528 3943; www.biggameparks.org), behind Sondzela Backpackers Lodge. It can be reached either through the wildlife sanctuary, or via Malkerns, though there's no real reason to go there as you can make bookings via telephone or email. Bookings need to be paid in advance, either via post or credit card.

Sondzela Backpackers (IYHF) Lodge (☎ 528 3117; www.biggameparks.org; camp sites per person E40, dm E55, s/d with shared bathroom E100/160, s/d rondavels E150/200) Sondzela is in the southern part of the reserve, around 1.5km beyond the main camp, and about 2km from both Malandela's B&B and Gone Rural in Malkerns Valley. This self-proclaimed 'Africa's Rolls Royce of Backpacker Hostels' is in need of a slight fine-tuning (at least, a couple of the dorm bathrooms are) but it is a superior model all the same. It has large gardens, a central living area including the Hog & Wart Bar (which can be a bit noisy), and a hilltop perch that gives it one of the best backpackers' settings in Southern Africa. The pick-up point is at Malandela's in Malkerns Valley (see opposite), where the **Baz Bus** (☎ in Durban 031-304 9099; www.bazbus.com) stops. If you're driving, you'll need to use the main Mlilwane Wildlife Sanctuary entrance, pay the entry fee and drive through the park to reach Sondzela.

Mlilwane Wildlife Sanctuary Main Camp (camp sites per person E45, dm E80, s/d 2-person huts E240/340) This homely camp is set in a scenic wooded location about 3.5km from the entry gate, complete with simple thatched huts – including traditional beehive huts (s/d per person E225/320, with shared bathroom E150/240) – and the occasional warthog snuffling around. There's a small shop, the Hippo Haunt restaurant (buffet E90), and an area for braais (barbecues). If there are groups staying there are often dance performances in the evenings.

Shonalanga Cottage (s/d E290/380, per additional person E110) This spacious self-catering cottage is near the main camp, and a good choice for families.

Reilly's Rock Hilltop Lodge (s/d from E855/1450) Rock on in to this luxurious and tranquil accommodation, promoted as 'quaintly colonial'. Indeed it has a colourful history: it was the first dwelling in Swaziland to have

---

SWAZI SNIPPETS

At the centre of Swazi culture is the monarchy, which rests with both the king (*ngwenyama*, the lion) and his mother (*ndlovukazi*, the she-elephant). In addition to loyalty to the monarchy, Swazi identity is supported by a long-standing tradition of age-related royal military regiments. During the *difaqane* (forced migration), these regiments provided the military clout to hold off invaders, while in more recent years they have helped to minimise potentially divisive differences between clans and to solidify the nation behind the king.

The Swazi deity is known as Mkhulumnchanti, and respect for both the aged and ancestors plays an important role. Unlike in many other postcolonial countries, the wearing of traditional clothing is as common among people in the Westernised middle classes as it is among rural labourers. It's not unusual to see a man on his way to work wearing an *amahiya* (traditional Swazi robe), with a spear in one hand and a briefcase in the other.

---

electric lighting, and the original structure was built in exchange for a UK£80 ox wagon. Surrounded by aloes and cycads, 'the Rock' has striking views of the valley and Mdzimba Mountains from the veranda.

MALKERNS VALLEY

About 7km south of Lobamba on the MR103 is the turn-off to the fertile Malkerns Valley, known for its arts and crafts outlets, and together with the Ezulwini Valley, offering a scenic and fun drive.

There's Internet access and tourist information at **Ziggy's Internet Cafe & Tourist Information** (☎ 528 3423; per hr E45; ☒ 9am-6pm Mon-Sat) at Malandela's complex.

Sleeping & Eating

For budget accommodation, also check out Sondzela Backpackers (IYHF) Lodge (opposite), which is readily accessible from Malkerns Valley.

Nyanza Cottages (Nyanza Horse Trails; ☎ 528 3090; nyanza@africaonline.co.sz; dm E65, caravan s/d E160/220, d E190, cottages per adult E220) A working farm with stables, the cottages here sleep four, have a galley-style kitchen, are secluded and overlook pastureland. The kids can help out on the farm and there's as much horse riding as you'd like (around E80/370 per hour/day). There's also a small backpackers dorm and a well-equipped caravan that takes up to six people. Bring your own towels for the backpackers, caravan and camping. Nyanza is just off the main road, signposted next to Baobab Batik.

Malandela's B&B (☎ 605 2598, 528 3448; r per person with breakfast E180; ☒) Offers creative and stylish rooms with a touch of ethnic Africa, a pool and a sculpture garden. Malandela's is

along the MR27, about 1km from the junction with the MR103.

Malandela's Restaurant (☎ 528 3115; entrées from E15, mains E30-60; ☒ lunch & dinner Mon-Sat, lunch Sun) Next door and part of the Malandela complex, this is one of the best restaurants in the region, with good old-fashioned meals and serving an array of meat and seafood dishes under a thatched shelter.

Willows Lodge (☎ 602 1284; www.swaziwillows .com; s/d E270/395) The small private bar overlooking the sugar-cane fields indicates the tranquil scene of these nine pleasant self-catering cottages (sleeping four or five people). This place is set off the MR27 in Malkerns Valley, near Malandela's B&B.

Entertainment

House on Fire (☎ 528 2001; houseonfire@africaonline .co.sz) A cultural-site-cum-living-gallery or experimental-performance space? Whatever it is, this mosaic- and sculpture-filled site is the hot place for cool locals and is popular among travellers as well. Part of the Malandela complex, the well-known venue hosts everything from African theatre, music and films, raves and other forms of entertainment. Some nights are sizzlers (but even during daytime it's worth a look). Phone to see what's on.

Shopping

There's some excellent shopping in the Malkerns Valley.

Gone Rural (☎ 528 3436; www.goneruralswazi.com; ☒ 8am-5pm Mon-Sat, 9am-5pm Sun) The place to go for baskets, mats and traditional clay pots made by groups of local women. It's based at Malandela's B&B. Also here are Baobab Too, offering colourful African batiks;

and Southern Country, selling handmade leather goods.

Swazi Candles (☎ 528 3219; www.swazicandles .com; ☺ 8.30am-5pm) Wax lyrical about these creative pigment-coloured candles – in every African-animal shape and hue. This signposted shop is 7km south of the MR103/Malkerns turn-off. Umgololo Gallery sells art and craft on the same premises. Shop till you melt and enjoy a snack at the coffee shop.

Baobab Batik (☎ 528 3242; www.baobab-batik.com; ☺ 8am-5pm) Next to Nyanza Cottages, 1km on from Swazi Candles, it's a small place that's worth a poke around, particularly if you're dye-ing for a wall hanging. You can also pop into the on-site workshop.

Getting There & Away

The **Baz Bus** (☎ in Durban 031-304 9099; www.bazbus .com) stops outside Malandela's. This is the pick-up point for Sondzela Backpackers Lodge in Mlilwane Wildlife Sanctuary. You can also get minibus taxis between here and the Ezulwini Valley for around E2 to E5 depending on the trip. As the craft shops and places to stay are spread out, you'll really need a car to get around.

MANZINI
pop 80,000

Manzini started out as the combined administrative centre for the squabbling British and Boers between 1890 and 1902. So adversarial was their relationship that during the Anglo-Boer War a renegade Boer *kommando* (militia unit) burned the town down. Today Manzini, Swaziland's largest town, is an active commercial and industrial hub whose small centre is dominated by office blocks and a couple of shopping malls. Manzini is also Swaziland's main transport hub, so you're likely to pass through here if you're getting around on public transport. Otherwise, it's of minimal appeal – it's much better to base yourself in the Ezulwini Valley. Be extra careful at night, and watch for pickpockets; the city's crime rate is rising – muggings (some violent) are common.

Manzini's main drawcard is its colourful **market** (cnr Mhlakuvane & Mancishane Sts; ☺ closed Sun). The upper section of the market is packed with handicrafts from around the country and elsewhere in Africa. Thursday morning is a good time to see the rural vendors bringing in their handicrafts to sell to the retailers. Many Mozambican traders sell wooden carvings and the market also has a wide selection of African textiles.

Orientation

Central Manzini is set out in a grid pattern, with most of the activity on or around Ngwane and Nkoseluhlaza Sts, the main east–west thoroughfares. The large Bhunu Mall, with a good range of shops, is on Ngwane St between Sandlane and Louw Sts.

Information

Internet café (1st fl, Bhunu Mall; per hr E25) Opposite Milady's.

Standard Bank (cnr Nkoseluhlaza & Louw Sts) Does foreign exchange (Monday to Friday only).

Tours

At the time of research, Myxo, a local guide and former owner of (now-defunct) Myxo's Backpackers, was in the process of opening another backpackers. Myxo himself can be found at the **tourist office** (☎ 604 4102) next to Tum's George Hotel. He organises highly recommended **village visits** and overnight stays (E420), including transport, meals and guide.

Sleeping

Swaziland Backpackers (☎ 518 7225; www.swaziland backpackers.com; camp sites per person E45, dm E75, d with shared bathroom E180; ☐ ☒) Formerly a doctor's house, this place operates as efficiently as a surgery but with much more fun. Activities centre around the happening 'jungle' bar and pool, as well as in the local area. It offers laundry service, email, kitchen (it also serves breakfast and dinner) and has a small pool in a lush garden with mango trees beyond. Head 8km west of town along the M103 towards Ezulwini Valley, opposite the Taiwanese Agricultural Mission compound. It's a Baz Bus stop.

Park Hotel (☎ 505 7423; 9 Mancishane St; s/d incl breakfast E200/250; ☒) The most interesting thing about this hotel is its name. But the rooms are decent, with balconies, air-con, TV and phones. It's at the eastern end of town, a block up from the police station.

Matsapha Inn (☎ 518 6893; MR103; s/d E210/280) It's near the airport and ironically, resembles an airport corridor. It has clean, spartan rooms and a restaurant.

Gibela Getaway (☎ 505 3024; www.visitswazi.com /gibela; d E250, cottages from E450) Situated 10km northeast of Manzini off the main road, these tasteful, self-contained stone cottages (named 'Leopard', 'Lion' and 'Cub' with the inevitable animal-print theme) are near the Salugazi River in private garden settings. They save you from a clinical hotel experience, but arrive in daylight. Ring for directions.

Tum's George Hotel (☎ 505 8991; www.tgh.sz; cnr Ngwane & du Toit Sts; s/d incl breakfast from E600/800; 🖭) The newest and fanciest hotel in Manzini, this smart place attempts an international-hotel atmosphere and caters for the conference crowd. It has a gym, pool bar and several stylish restaurants with extensive menus.

Eating

Currie House Halal (☎ 505 6144; cnr Mancishane & Louw Sts; mains from E10) This is your 'cheap and cheerful' takeaway, serving a good range of curries.

Egg Yolk Coffee Shop/Sports Bar (cnr Ngwane & du Toit Sts; snacks from E15, pizza E30; 🕑 breakfast, lunch & dinner) Not a bad place for a breather and serves a selection of snacks. It's run by Tum's George Hotel next door.

Fontana di Trevi Pizzeria (☎ 505 3608; the Hub, Villiers St; breakfast/pizza from E23/30; 🕑 breakfast, lunch & dinner) In an African *piazza* – a shopping mall – this place is the best spot to head for a decent coffee, plus pizza, pasta, salads and burgers at good prices.

Mozambique Hotel & Restaurant (☎ 505 2489; Mahleka St; mains E30-55; 🕑 breakfast, lunch & dinner) A good place to get a taste of life across the border, with delicious prawns and seafood, various Portuguese dishes, and a generous selection of Portuguese and South African wines.

Gil Vincente Restaurant (☎ 505 3874; Ilanga Centre, Martin St; mains E40-60; 🕑 breakfast, lunch & dinner Tue-Sun) Another good spot for Portuguese and Mozambican dishes.

On Louw St in town there are a few basic food outlets that are open during the day. Bhunu Mall houses various fast-food places, including Nando's. There are two KFCs, Debonaire's Pizza and Kowloon Fast Foods on Ngwane St.

MANZINI

	0 —— 400 m
	0 —— 0.2 miles

INFORMATION
Internet Cafe .... (see 12)
Standard Bank 1 C2

SIGHTS & ACTIVITIES
Market 2 B2

SLEEPING 🛏
Park Hotel 3 D2
Tum's George Hotel 4 D1

EATING 🍴
Currie House Halal 5 C2
Debonaire's Pizza .... (see 10)
Egg Yolk Coffee Shop/Sports Bar ... (see 4)
Fontana di Trevi Pizzeria 6 C2
Gil Vincente Restaurant 7 C1

KFC 8 C1
KFC 9 C1
Kowloon Fast Foods 10 C1
Mozambique Hotel & Restaurant 11 C1
Nando's .... (see 12)

SHOPPING 🛍
Bhunu Mall 12 C2
Shoprite .... (see 12)
Super Spa 13 B2

TRANSPORT
Bus & Minibus Taxi Park 14 C1
Minibus Taxis to Mozambique .... (see 9)

SWAZILAND

Shopping

Bhunu Mall (Ngwane St) is the main shopping centre, with fast food, an array of stores and a Shoprite. The Hub shopping centre is on Mhlakuvane St and has a Super Spa supermarket.

Getting There & Away

The main bus and minibus taxi park is at the northern end of Louw St, where you can also find some nonshared taxis. A minibus taxi trip up the Ezulwini Valley to Mbabane costs E8 (35 minutes). A nonshared taxi to Matsapha International Airport costs around E50. Minibus taxis to Mozambique leave from the car park next to KFC up the hill.

For information about transport to/from South Africa, see p632.

NORTHERN SWAZILAND

Lush hills, plantations and woodlands, streams and waterfalls, and plunging ravines are the main features of Swaziland's beautiful north. As well as boasting the best scenery in Swaziland, the northern region offers some excellent hiking and accommodation options. Away from the MR1, which runs from near the Oshoek border post northeast to the Jeppe's Reef border post, all roads are unpaved, though easily negotiable with a 2WD during most of the year. Especially in the summer months, heavy mists roll in that can limit visibility to almost zero.

Ngwenya

Tiny Ngwenya (the Crocodile), 5km east of the border with Mpumalanga, is the first town you'll reach if you're arriving in Swaziland via Oshoek. If you can't wait until you reach the Ezulwini Valley to do your shopping, there are several craft outlets here, including **Ngwenya Glass Factory** (☎ 442 4142; ☷ 7am-5pm Mon-Fri, 8am-4.30pm Sat & Sun), which creates beautiful African animal and bird figures from recycled glass, and **Endlotane Studios/Phumulanga Swaziland Tapestries** (☎ 442 4196; ☷ 8am-5pm), which features beautiful tapestries and lets you watch the weavers at work. Both are within 1km of each other and signposted from the main road.

Also here is the **Ngwenya iron ore mine** (admission E25; ☷ 8am-4pm), dating from around 40,000 BC and one of the world's oldest known mines. The mine is part of Malol-

otja Nature Reserve (below) and has a new **Ngwenya Mines & Visitors Centre** with an interesting display of photographs and information about the mine, including the original excavation tools. There's also a picnic area overlooking the mine. The entrance is signposted near the Ngwenya Glass Factory, although you can't continue on into the rest of Malolotja from here. To visit the mine, including visits made by vehicle, you'll need to be accompanied by a ranger.

Nearby, on the opposite side of the MR1, is **Hawane Dam** and the small **Hawane Nature Reserve** (no facilities).

SLEEPING & EATING

Hawane Resort (☎ 627 6714, 442 4744; www.hawane .co.sz; dm E86, d chalets incl breakfast E524, beehives per person E120) A touch of country luxury, and framed by the Malolotja peaks, these stylish chalets are a blend of traditional Swazi materials and glass, with ethnic African interiors. Backpackers are stabled in a converted barn, one of the most inventive dormitory accommodations around. It's a great base for visiting Malolotja Nature Reserve and horse riding is on the premises, after which you can devour delicious African fusion cuisine in the resort restaurant. It's about 8km up the Piggs Peak road from the junction of the MR1 and MR3, and 1.5km off the main road.

Malolotja Nature Reserve

This beautiful middleveld/highveld **reserve** (☎ 416 1151, 442 4241; www.sntc.org.sz; adult/child E20/12; ☷ 6am-6pm) is a true wilderness area, rugged and in the most part unspoiled. It's also an excellent walking destination, with around 200km of hiking trails, and an ornithologist's paradise, with over 280 species of birds, including several rare species. Wildflowers and rare plants are added attractions, with several – including the Woolly, Barberton and Kaapschehoop cycads – found only in this part of Africa.

Various antelope species make Malolotja their home, as do herds of zebras, elands and wildebeest. The terrain ranges from mountainous and high-altitude grassland to forest and lower-lying bushveld. The reserve is laced by streams and cut by three rivers, including the Komati River, which flows east through a gorge in a series of falls and rapids until it meets the lowveld.

Hiking trails range from short walks to a weeklong jaunt that extends from Ngwenya in the south to the Mgwayiza Range in the north. For all longer walks, you'll need to bring whatever food you'll need, as well as a camp stove, as fires are not permitted outside the base camp. You'll also need to arrange a permit (E5) with the reserve office at the entrance gate. Wildlife drives can be arranged with advance notice.

In addition to the Ngwenya mine, it's also possible to visit **Forbes Reef gold mine** in Forbes Reef Forest towards the centre of the reserve.

Accommodation consists of **camping** (per person at main camp/on trails E60/40), either at the well-equipped (but infrequently used) main site, with ablutions and braai area, or along the overnight trails (no facilities). There are also pleasant, fully equipped self-catering wooden **cabins** (per person E230, children half-price), each of which sleeps a maximum of six persons. Book through **Swazi Trails** (☎ 416 2180; www.swazitrails.co.sz) or directly with the **National Trust Commission** (☎ 416 1151, 416 1178; www.sntc.org.sz), both in Ezulwini Valley.

The entrance gate for Malolotja is about 35km northwest of Mbabane, along the Piggs Peak road (MR1); minibus taxis will drop you here.

Piggs Peak & Around

This small town reached its pinnacle during the late 19th and early 20th centuries, when gold was discovered here by William Pigg in 1884. The last mine closed in 1954. Nowadays, this gritty frontier town is the small centre of Swaziland's logging industry, which is based on the huge pine plantations in the area. It has a couple of petrol stations, a bank or two (though no foreign-exchange facilities) and a supermarket.

Piggs Peak is in a highly scenic, hilly and forested section of the country, with one of the highlights, **Phophonyane Falls**, about 8km north of town.

In addition to the scenery, the Piggs Peak area is known for its handicrafts. A good place to check these out is at the Peak Craft Centre just north of Orion Piggs Peak Hotel & Casino, where you'll find **Ethnic Bound** (☎ 437 3099; ethnicbound@africaonline.co.sz), which specialises in African fabrics, and **Likhweti Kraft** (☎ 437 3127), a branch of **Tintsaba Crafts** (☎ 437 1260; www.tintsaba.com), which sells sisal

baskets, jewellery and many other Swazi crafts. There are also numerous craft vendors along the road up from Mbabane.

SLEEPING & EATING

Highlands Inn (☎ 437 1144; s/d incl breakfast E160/300) This inn, 1km south of the town centre on the main road, is the only place to stay in town itself and only worth considering if you're on a tight budget. Khulilie Craft Shop, and Woodcutter's Restaurant (mains from E25, open for breakfast, lunch and dinner) are both attached to the inn.

Jabula Guest House (☎ 437 1052; www.swaziplace .com/jabulaguesthouse; s/d E225/375; ☒) Turn right at the Piggs Peak Clinic sign and then take the first right again. Even its promo-speak is right: 'With so many rights you can't go wrong' is this place's catch-cry. The best B&B in Piggs Peak with small, neat rooms in a residential setting.

Phophonyane Lodge & Nature Reserve (☎ 437 1319; www.phophonyane.co.sz; tents E490-700, s/d cottages incl breakfast from E700/980) This stunning hideaway lies northeast of Piggs Peak on a river in its own nature reserve of lush indigenous forest. It has a network of walking trails around the river and waterfall, and you can swim in the rock pools. Accommodation is in comfortable cottages (with a self-catering option) or East African–style luxury safari tents overlooking cascades. Excellent meals are available at the Dining Hut (mains from E50, open for breakfast, lunch and dinner). Entry to the reserve and therefore the lodge is an additional E20/10 per adult/child. Day visitors are charged E30/20 per adult/child to enter the surrounding reserve. The lodge is about 14km from Piggs Peak: head northeast (towards the casino), and the signposted turn-off (minibus taxis will drop you here) is about 1.5km before the casino. Continue down this road until you cross a bridge over a waterfall; the turn-off to the lodge is about 500m further, on the right. You can arrange with the lodge to be picked up from Piggs Peak; a taxi costs about E60.

Orion Piggs Peak Hotel & Casino (☎ 437 1104; www.oriongroup.co.za; d with half board E1200) South Africans flock to this safe bet: a massive sanitised upscale-resort-and-casino-in-one, complete with amenities. It's about 10km northeast of Piggs Peak, on the road to the Jeppe's Reef border post. Midweek specials are often available.

SWAZILAND

Bulembu

A fascinating detour from Piggs Peak is to wind your way 20km through scenic plantation country to the historic town of Bulembu. The town was built in 1936 for the Havelock Mine, which became the fifth-largest chrysotile (asbestos) mine in the world. At its peak it supported 10,000 mine workers, but the mines started to scale down and then eventually closed; by 2003 Bulembu was a ghost town with around 100 residents and no amenities. To visit it today is to enter a true-life time warp; thousands of deserted corrugated iron houses and many Art Deco buildings nestle on a pretty hilly landscape. There are churches, an **Art Deco cinema**, a **hospital** (complete with equipment from the 1930s), a golf course and the longest **cableway** in the world, extending from the old mine to Barberton, 20km away. The town has seen much adversity – from litigation over the mine to major environmental and ecological issues (the mine dumps have not been rehabilitated). Today, however, two passionate investors (who also run the village's saw mill and charcoal kilns) have started to rehabilitate the village and have major plans for its future.

Stunning hikes include the highest mountain in Swaziland, Emlembe Peak (1863m), plus there's excellent off-road cycling around streams, and waterfalls in the natural riverine forest amid the plantations. Afterwards, you can cool off in the village pool. The region's features include the oldest mountains in the world – claimed to contain some of the oldest life forms.

Accommodation is in the main **Bulembu Lodge** (☎ 437 3888, 602 4577; bulembulodge@realnet.co.sz; per person from E150) in the former General Manager's residence or stylish Directors' cottages, all renovated. If you care less about status and more about novelty, choose the spacious and delightfully converted backpackers cottage (E80). Family suites are available, as are all meals (breakfast/lunch/dinner E40/35/65).

GETTING THERE & AWAY

If you're heading east towards Hlane National Park, the roads are mainly dirt and they're in reasonably rough condition, although a 2WD can handle them if you take it slowly.

The stretch of dirt road running west from Piggs Peak to Bulembu can be boggy in wet conditions. The road can be rough further to Barberton (Mpumalanga).

The minibus taxi stand is next to the market at the top end of the main street, with several vehicles daily to Mbabane (E14, one hour).

EASTERN SWAZILAND

The eastern Swaziland lowveld nestles in the shadow of the Lebombo Mountains, within an easy drive to the Mozambique border. The area is known for its sugar-cane plantations, as well as for the Lubombo Conservancy, a conservation area comprising Hlane Royal National Park, Mkhaya Game Reserve, and Mlawula, Shewula and Mbuluzi Nature Reserves. Together these provide excellent wildlife-viewing and cultural experiences.

Simunye

Simunye is a manicured sugar-company town with little of interest for travellers, except as a possible stocking-up point for visiting the nearby Hlane Royal National Park, or Mlawula and Mbuluzi Nature Reserves.

For a more cultural and rural experience away from the crowds, head to **Shewula Mountain Camp** (☎ 605 1160, 603 1931; shewula@realnet.co.sz; dm/r E75/220), a community-owned camp northeast of Simunye in the Lebombo Mountains, 36km by dirt road (15km as the crow flies). As well as amazing views, on offer are guided cultural walks to nearby villages, plus nature and bird-watching walks (guided walks per person E10). You can camp or stay in basic rondavels, with shared ablutions and self-catering facilities. Local meals can also be arranged (breakfast/lunch/dinner E25/40/40; must be booked in advance). You can organise a visit through **Swazi Trails** (☎ 416 2180; www.swazitrails.co.sz) or, if you're arriving via public transport, get a minibus taxi from Simunye to the camp (E9, one hour).

Tambankulu Country Club B&B (☎ 373 7111; tam@realnet.co.sz; s/d E244/352; 🏊 🎾) has comfortable if slightly jaded rooms, plus green lawns, a restaurant, swimming pool and tennis court. The club is north of Simunye – head 6km west of the junction at Maphiveni, and another 3km off the Tshaneni road.

Simunye Country Club (☎ 313 4792; www.visitswa zi.com; s/d from E244/352, cottages E347/580; ✶ ✷) is a friendly and tranquil spot with small single rooms, modern self-catering cottages and a bar/restaurant. Although it's a club, visitors are welcome and you can use the club facilities (swimming pool, golf course, tennis and squash courts).

Several minibus taxis run daily to Simunye (and further north to the junction for Mlawula and Mbuluzi) from Manzini (E18, one hour). There's also at least one minibus taxi daily to/from Piggs Peak (E30, 2½ hours).

Hlane Royal National Park

This **park** (☎ 528 3943; www.biggameparks.org; admission E25; ◷ 6am-6pm) is near the former royal hunting grounds. Hlane (the name means 'wilderness') is Swaziland's largest protected area, home to elephants, lions, cheetahs, leopards, white rhinos and many antelope species, and offers wonderfully low-key wildlife-watching.

There are guided walking trails (E30 per person), which afford the opportunity to see elephants and rhinos, as well as two-hour wildlife day drives (E130 per person, minimum two), a cultural village tour with dance performances (E40 per person, minimum four) and mountain-bike rentals (R55 per hour).

Hlane has two good camps. Both can be booked through **Big Game Parks** (☎ 528 3944; www.biggameparks.org) in Mlilwane Wildlife Sanctuary.

Ndlovu Camp (camp sites per person E40, s/d rondavels from E225/320, 8-person cottage per person E190) is pleasant and rustic, with no electricity, a gas-cooking area and a restaurant. Accommodation is in self-catering rondavels and cottages. It's just inside the main gate, and near a water hole (fenced off, although you can see the odd antelope). Bring your own food and supplies.

Bhubesi Camp (s/d cottages E290/380) is the pick of the spots: it overlooks a river about 10km from Ndlovu Camp. Accommodation is in tasteful, stone, four-person, self-catering cottages, and electricity is available.

Minibus taxis to Simunye will drop you at the entrance to Hlane (E5; the gate is about 7km south of Simunye). Once at the park, you can explore most of it with a 2WD, with the notable exception of the

special lion compound. For this you'll need to hire a guide (E30 per hour). The main road in the park branches off right just before Ndlovu Camp.

Mlawula Nature Reserve

This tranquil **reserve** (☎ 416 1151; www.sntc.org .sz; adult/child E25/12; ◷ 6am-6pm), where the lowveld plains meet the Lebombo Mountains, boasts antelope species and hyenas, among others, plus rewarding bird-watching. You can hire fishing rods for E20 and bring your own mountain bike.

For accommodation, there's **Sara Camp** (s/d E150/300), with self-catering double safari-style tents, about 3km from the main gate, and **Siphiso camping ground** (camp sites per person E60), where you can pitch your own tent. The self-catering **Mapelepele Cottage** (accommodates 4 people E500) has a gas stove and fridge. Twenty new chalets are being built in the southern part of the reserve, with plans to open access from Siteki. Accommodation can be booked through the **National Trust Commission** (☎ 416 1151, 416 1178; www.sntc.org.sz).

The turn-off for the entrance gates to the reserve is about 10km north of Simunye, from where it's another 4km from the main road. Minibus taxis will drop you at the junction (E17, 1¼ hours from Manzini). There is no transport from the junction to the reserve but if you call in advance a lift may be possible if there's a reserve vehicle available. Ask for the *Trails and Day Walks* flier.

Mbuluzi Game Reserve

The small and privately owned **Mbuluzi Game Reserve** (☎ 383 8861; mbuluzi@swazi.net; adult/child E20/10) boasts a range of animals, including giraffes, zebras, hippos, antelope species and wildebeests. There have also been over 300 bird species recorded here.

Accommodation here, in a choice of lovely five- or eight-person self-catering **lodges** (s/d E375/530; ✶), is more luxurious than at neighbouring Mlawula Nature Reserve. Some lodges have spacious verandas and wooden viewing decks and are set on the Mlawula River. **Camp sites** (per person E30) are also available near the Mbuluzi river.

The turn-off for Mbuluzi is the same as for Mlawula; the reserve entrance is about 600m from the turn-off on the left.

SWAZILAND

Siteki

Siteki (Marrying Place) is a trading town in the foothills of the Lebombo Mountains about 8km from Lonhlupheko off the MR16. It got its name when Mbandzeni (great-grandfather of the present king) gave his frontier troops permission to marry. Siteki is the fastest route to Mozambique from Manzini through the Mhlumeni/Goba border. It lies above the surrounding lowveld, with wide views, cooler temperatures and a bustling market. There's an ATM on the main street.

Siteki (Stegi) Hotel (☎ 343 4126; s/d with half board E195/280) harks back to colonial days with cane chairs and a smoking area and modest, no-frills rooms and meals. The friendly Marie has worked there for over 30 years and is the one in the know.

History buffs will admire the colonial relics that decorate the pleasant self-catering cottage, **Mabuda Farm** (☎ 343 4124; www.geocities.com /mabudafarm; s/d incl breakfast E200/400), on a working farm just outside Siteki town; others will love the green outlook. Highly recommended.

Minibus taxis from Manzini run twice daily (E13, one hour). There are also one or two minibus taxis daily connecting Siteki with Big Bend (E10, one hour) and Simunye (E7, 30 minutes).

Mkhaya Game Reserve

This topnotch **private reserve** (☎ 528 3943; www.biggameparks.org) was established in 1979 to save the pure Nguni breed of cattle from extinction. Its focus expanded to include other animals including roan and sable antelopes, tsessebe, elephants, and white and black rhinos (it boasts that you're more likely to meet rhinos here than anywhere else in Africa). It's near the hamlet of Phuzumoya, off the Manzini–Big Bend road. The reserve takes its name from the *mkhaya* (or knobthorn) tree, which abounds here. *Mkhaya*s are valued not only for their fruit, from which Swazis brew beer, but for the insect and birdlife they support.

Note that you can't visit the reserve without booking in advance, and even then you can't drive in alone; you'll be met at Phuzumoya at a specified pick-up time, usually 10am or 4pm. While day tours can be arranged, it's ideal to stay for at least one night.

Stone Camp (all-inclusive s/d with full board E1035/ 1780) is reminiscent of a 19th-century hunting camp, with accommodation in rustically luxurious stone and thatch cottages surrounded by bush. The price includes wildlife drives, walking safaris, park entry and meals, and is good value compared to many of the private reserves near Kruger National Park in South Africa.

SOUTHERN SWAZILAND

In former years, because of its easy access to KwaZulu-Natal, southern Swaziland was frequently visited for its roulette tables, rather than its surroundings. Nowadays many tourists don't gamble on a visit; they think it lacks the north's dramatic scenery. While the entire area is quiet and rural, it's a good place to set off on a bike or on foot to discover the 'real' Swaziland, especially around the Ngwempisi Gorge, and is the base for some good horse-riding (near Nsoko).

Big Bend

The picturesque panoramas from the edge of town set off this sleepy sugar town, appropriately set on a big bend in the Lusutfu River just before it joins the Usutu. If you're here during summer, you can cool off in the pool at the Bend Inn Hotel.

There's an ATM at the First National Bank booth next to the BP petrol station on the main street just before the Bend Inn Hotel.

SLEEPING & EATING

Riverside Motel (☎ 363 6910; s/d with breakfast E171/262; 🖳) Friendly with decent rooms and a good restaurant (mains E40 to E70; open breakfast, lunch & dinner). It's nearly 2km further south past Lismore Lodge on the MR8.

Bend Inn Hotel (☎ 363 6855; s/d E189/280; 🖳) The faded foyer in this classic place features a massive faux 'window' framed by lime-green curtains depicting a forest 'outlook'. Its own views are quite pleasant enough: it faces out over the river from a hilltop position south of town. It also has a restaurant and an outdoor bar.

Lismore Lodge (☎ 363 6613; d from E200) Has small, comfortable, good-value doubles. It's about 4km south of Big Bend on the MR8.

LL Restaurant Bar (☎ 363 6380; mains E40-80; 🕒 lunch & dinner). Located next door to Lismore Lodge, you can get great seafood dishes, including calamari, seafood kebabs and seafood curry.

WHITE-WATER RAFTING

One of the highlights of Swaziland is rafting the Usutu River (which becomes the Lusutfu River). The river is usually sluggish and quite tame, but near Mkhaya Game Reserve it passes through the narrow Bulungu Gorge, which separates the Mabukabuka and Bulunga Mountains, generating rapids.

Swazi Trails (☎ 416 2180; www.swazitrails.co.sz) is the best contact to organise a rafting trip. It offers a full-day trip (E610 per person, minimum two, including lunch and equipment) involving portaging a 10m waterfall, followed by a sedate trip through scenic country with glimpses of the 'flat dogs' (crocodiles) sunning on the river bank. The crocs haven't devoured anyone recently, hence the claim that rafting here is '...safer than driving through Jo'burg'. In sections, you'll encounter Grade-IV rapids, which aren't for the faint-hearted, although even first-timers with a sense of adventure should handle the day easily.

GETTING THERE & AWAY

Big Bend makes a convenient stop en route to/from KwaZulu-Natal in South Africa. Minibus taxis go daily to Manzini (E15, one hour) and to Lavumisa border post (E16, one hour).

Nsoko

Nsoko, halfway between Big Bend and the border post of Lavumisa, lies in the heart of sugar-cane country, with the Lebombo Mountains as a backdrop.

Nisela Safaris (☎ 303 0318; www.niselasafaris.co .za; camp sites per person E65, beehive huts E100, lodge incl breakfast per person from E250) is a small touristy private reserve, and is convenient if you're coming from the south. It has accommodation options galore, including creative chalets-cum-safari-lodge (note the internal trees and basins) and simple beehive huts. Also on offer are wildlife drives (E65 per person, minimum two) and guided walks (E30 per person). There's a restaurant with craft shop and traditional Swazi dancing.

Nhlangano

Nhlangano is the closest town to the border post at Mahamba, but unless you want to visit the casino, there's no real reason to stop here. There's a well-stocked Spar supermarket in the shopping mall in the town centre.

The pleasant **Phumula Farm Guest House** (☎ 207 9099; s/d incl breakfast E230/460) is about 3km from the border gate and about 1km off the main road. It's a private house with a manicured lawn and garden setting, pleasant rooms and a braai area. Dinner can also be arranged.

On offer at the **Nhlangano Sun Hotel & Casino** (☎ 207 8211; s/d E597/665; ⊠) is a grandiose setting and somewhat faded tiny rooms, together with a popular casino. It's 4km southeast of town along the Lavumisa road (MR11).

Several minibus taxis run daily between Nhlangano and Manzini (E16, 1½ hours), from where you can get another vehicle on to Mbabane. There are also frequent connections to the Mahamba border post (E4), where you must change for Piet Retief in South Africa (E20, one hour). Large minibus taxis go direct to Jo'burg (E110, 4½ hours).

Ngwempisi Gorge

The **Ngwempisi Gorge** (☎ 625 6004), 30km south of the Malkerns Valley, is one of the country's few remaining untouched environments, with beautiful natural forests and the Ngwempisi River. Adventure-seekers will be thrilled by the **Ngwempisi Hiking Trail**, a community-run 33km trail in the Ntfungula Hills on the Mankayane–Vlelzizweni road. You can spend two to three days exploring the area and sleep en route in two different huts. The atmospheric double-storey **Khopho Hut** (dm E90) is built around massive boulders and Mhlabeni Hut is by a waterfall. It's compulsory to take a local guide (E50 per day plus E10 for each hiker; you can park your transport in a secure location near reception). You must also take your own food and bedding, although porters are available (E15 per day). Another accommodation option, **Horseshoe Estate B&B** (☎ 606 1512), is near the trail entrance and can arrange hikes.

Directory

CONTENTS

ACCOMMODATION

South Africa offers a wide selection of good-value accommodation. Whatever your budget, you'll generally find high standards, often for significantly less than you would pay for the equivalent in Europe, Australasia or North America.

At the budget level, the main options are camping grounds, backpackers hostels and self-catering cottages. With just a few exceptions, you can expect clean surroundings and good facilities. The main caveat with places in this price category is that

there aren't enough of them; away from tourist areas sometimes the only budget option is camping.

Midrange accommodation is particularly good value, especially for B&Bs. Expect a private or semi-private bathroom and a clean, comfortable room. Self-catering accommodation at national parks – usually priced in the budget to midrange category – also tends to be very good value.

At the top end, South Africa boasts some of the best wildlife lodges in the region, as well as classic guesthouses and several superb hotels. Places at this level offer all the amenities you would expect for prices that are similar to, or slightly less than, those you would pay in Europe or North America. There are also some not-so-superb hotels which can be expensive disappointments, so be selective.

Accommodation in Swaziland is priced similarly to that in South Africa. At the

PRACTICALITIES

- All three countries use the metric system for weights and measures (see the conversion chart inside the front cover).

- Access electricity (220-250V AC, 50Hz) with a three-pin adaptor (round pins, though South Africa has its own unique version); they're easy enough to find – check in camping supply stores.

- Best weekly: *Mail & Guardian*. Best daily: the *Sowetan*. Others to look for: the *Sunday Independent*; the *Sunday Times*; the Johannesburg *Star*; and *Business Day*. Check out *Getaway* magazine for travel news.

- Tune the TV to SABC for the news (SABC3 is mostly English). e-TV has a more independent viewpoint. M-Net has movies and sports.

- SABC radio comes in 11 languages. BBC's World Service is available on short wave, medium wave and (in and near Lesotho) FM.

budget level, there are a handful of backpacker hostels, and free-camping is possible in most areas of the country. Lesotho is not known for its high-class hotel accommodation. However, there are several notable exceptions, and camping opportunities abound away from major towns.

Accommodation listings in this book are ordered from budget to midrange to top end. Expect to pay somewhat more in major tourist areas such as Cape Town (which is one of the most expensive places in the region), and somewhat less in Lesotho.

There are significant seasonal price variations, with rates rising steeply during the December-January school break, and again around Easter, when room prices often double, and minimum stays are imposed. Advance bookings are essential during these times. The other school holidays are also often classified as high season, although it's more common to have 'midseason' pricing. Conversely, you can get some excellent deals during the winter low season, which is also the best time for wildlife-watching. Many places offer discounted midweek rates, so always ask. To save money during peak holiday periods, the best bets are camping, backpacker hostels or self-catering places.

Online Booking

Many regions have B&B organisations and tourist offices that take bookings (see listings in the regional chapters, and on p618). Another option, if you can't be bothered contacting places individually, is to use one of the many online booking services that cover South Africa. Because most charge listings fees, the cheapest places usually aren't included. Camping grounds (including those with self-catering accommodation) are also not listed, and pickings are slim outside major tourist centres.

www.bookabed.co.za Covers most provinces.
www.bookaholiday.co.za For Cape Town and the Garden Route.
www.farmstay.co.za For farm stays.
www.hostelafrica.com Hostels across Africa; also takes Baz Bus bookings.
www.portfoliocollection.com For upscale B&Bs, private game reserve lodges and boutique hotels, also in Swaziland.
www.sabreakaway.co.za Mostly upmarket listings; covers most provinces, plus Swaziland's Ezulwini Valley.
www.seastay.co.za For coastal areas.
www.wheretostay.co.za Covers most of the country, and also includes disabled-friendly listings.

B&Bs & Guesthouses

B&Bs and guesthouses (the line between them is often indistinguishable) are two of South Africa's accommodation treats. They're found throughout the country, in cities as well as small towns, and in rural areas you can often stay on farms. Some of the cheapest places aren't much to write home about, but on the whole standards are high, and rooms are generally excellent value.

Unlike British B&Bs, many South African establishments offer much more than someone's spare room, and unlike motels they are individual and often luxurious. Antique furniture, a private veranda, big gardens and a pool are common. In the Winelands north of Cape Town, and in other rural areas, wonderful settings are also part of the deal. Many have separate guest entrances and private bathrooms. Breakfasts are usually large and delectable. Prices start around R400 per double, including breakfast and private bathroom.

In Soweto (p424), Khayelitsha (p165) and several other areas, you can also stay in township B&Bs, which are an excellent way to get insights into township life. Many owners offer tours of the township, and unparalleled African hospitality. Expect to pay from about R200 per person.

Camping

Camping grounds and caravan parks have long been the accommodation of choice for many South African families. Most towns have an inexpensive municipal camping ground and caravan park, ranging from nice to unappealing. Those near larger towns are often not safe. Privately run camping grounds, and those in national parks are much better. These are invariably well equipped and pleasant, with ablution blocks, power points, cooking areas and water supply.

In tourist areas, there are often fancy resorts, complete with swimming pool, restaurant and mini-market. Camping prices are either per person (averaging R80) or per site (averaging R100 for two people, plus R10 per additional person). Camping grounds in popular areas are often booked out during school holidays.

Many caravan parks ban nonporous groundsheets (which are sewn in to most small tents) to protect the grass. If you're only staying a night or two, you can usually convince the manager that your tent won't do any harm. Some caravan parks don't allow tents at all, though if you explain that you're a foreigner without a caravan, it's usually possible to get a site.

In Lesotho and Swaziland, apart from sites in national parks and nature reserves, there are few official camping grounds. However, it's usually possible to free-camp (ie camp anywhere). Always ask permission from elders in the nearest village before setting up, both out of respect for the local community and to minimise any security risks. As a local courtesy, you may be offered a hut for the night; expect to pay about R5 for this. Free-camping isn't recommended in South Africa.

Hostels

South Africa is backpacker-friendly, with a profusion of hostels. However, most of these are clustered in popular areas such as Cape Town and along the Garden Route, so there are still large areas of the country where camping is the only option for shoestringers. Most hostels are of a high standard, with Internet access, self-catering facilities and a travellers bulletin board. Many offer meals, and all can dispense information on the area and on the best transport connections. Many are also on the Baz Bus route (p417), or staff may be willing to collect you at the nearest stop. In addition to dorm beds (which average R80 per night), hostels often also offer private rooms from about R180 per double, and some are willing to let doubles as singles for a bit less. Some hostels will also allow you to pitch a tent on their grounds.

> ### ACCOMMODATION PRICES
>
> Watch out for advertising that boasts room rates that look too good to be true. If a hotel touts rooms costing R200, this usually means R200 per person in a twin or double room, with a single room priced, for example, at R300. Prices for double rooms in this book are quoted per room, not per person. Except as noted, prices in this book refer to rooms with bathroom, excluding breakfast and for high season weekends. However, note that Cape Town accomodation prices include breakfast. Prices quoted with half board include breakfast and dinner; those quoted with full board include all meals. 'All-inclusive' prices – mainly found in listings for wildlife lodges – generally cover all meals, wildlife drives and sometimes also park entry fees.

In Swaziland, there are backpacker hostels in Mbabane, the Ezulwini Valley and Manzini; in Lesotho, you'll find them in or near Malealea, Semonkong, Mokhotlong and Sani Pass. Prices and facilities are similar to those in South Africa. Many towns in Lesotho also have Agricultural Training Centres or Farmers' Training Centres that accommodate travellers on a space-available basis. Rooms are simple but adequate, with shared bathroom, and rates (R50 per person throughout the country) make it a good deal. Most have a communal kitchen.

While hostels affiliated with the international Youth Hostel Association (YHA) are thin on the ground in South Africa, it's worth carrying a YHA (or alternatively, Hostelling International) card if you happen to have one already, as it may entitle you to discounts with some bus lines, tour operators, surf shops and more. See www.hihostels.com for links to national YHAs and membership information.

Hotels

There are a few decent old-style country hotels, where you can get a double room from R250, have a meal and catch up on gossip in the pub. However, most in the budget category are too run-down for comfort. The selection is better for midrange, where you can expect good value and atmospheric surroundings from about R350 per double.

ABUSING RIGHTS OF ADMISSION *Simon Richmond*

Because of its recent history of apartheid, racial discrimination remains a prominent issue in South Africa, one that nearly everyone is sensitive about. When a Cape Town newspaper, the *Cape Argus*, recently ran an investigation into whether backpacker lodges were using race-based criteria when they accepted guests, what they found was disturbing. Two undercover reporters – one young black man, one young white woman – were sent to six of the city's lodges; at three the black reporter was told the lodge was full, while his white counterpart was offered a room.

The lodges that had refused entry to the black reporter defended their rights to decide whom to grant admission to. Such rights of admission policies are common – not just in backpacker lodges, and not just in South Africa. The security and comfort of existing guests has to be respected, and we acknowledge the necessity for establishments to make split-second decisions on whether a potential customer should be allowed entry or not – and how difficult it is to get this right all the time.

From the *Cape Argus's* investigation and other reports sent to Lonely Planet it would seem that rights of admission policies are occasionally abused. In particular, if you're a black or coloured South African male, the chances of you being refused entry are likely to be higher than if you're a black or coloured South African female, a white South African or an overseas visitor. This could happen whether you just turn up at a hostel or make an advance booking.

Establishments rated by the South African Grading Council can be stripped of their stars if found to be racially discriminating against guests. We urge all travellers who experience racial discrimination to share their stories with both local tourism authorities and us – such information is taken into account for upcoming guides.

More common are chain hotels, which are found in all major cities and tourist areas. The main ones include the following:

Formula 1 (☎ 011-807 0750; www.hotelformula1 .co.za) The cheapest, with functional but cramped three-person rooms from R229 without breakfast.

City Lodge (☎ 011-884 5327; www.citylodge.co.za) Decent value, with Road Lodges (slightly superior standards to Formula 1, for about R285 per tr); Town Lodges (around R520 per double); City Lodges (quite pleasant, with good buffet breakfasts from about R700 per double); and Courtyard Hotels (about R940 per double).

Holiday Inn (☎ 0861-447 744, 011-461 9744; www .southernsun.com) No-frills rooms in 'Express by Holiday Inn' hotels; better rooms with minimal service at 'Garden Court' hotels; and more comforts at 'Holiday Inn' hotels. Ask about special weekend deals.

Southern Sun Group (☎ 0861-447 744, 011-461 9744; www.southernsun.com) In addition to running South Africa's Holiday Inn chain, it also operates various more-expensive hotels, including those under the InterContinental name.

Protea (☎ 0861-119 000, 021-430 5000; www.protea hotels.com) A network of three- to five-star hotels; Protea's Prokard Club gives a 20% discount to members.

Sun International (☎ 011-780 7800; www.sun-inter national.co.za) Runs top-end, resort-style hotels in Swaziland and the former homelands, with casinos attached (left over from the apartheid era, when gambling was illegal in South Africa but legal in the homelands). Standards are generally high and package deals are available.

Lodges

In and around national parks, especially Kruger National Park, you can relax comfortably in bush settings. Accommodation is usually in a safari-style tent, or in a luxurious lodge. Expect all the amenities that you would find in a top-end hotel (including en-suite bathroom with running hot and cold water, comfortable bedding, delicious cuisine etc), although many of these places don't have telephones and televisions. Most luxury lodges charge 'all-inclusive' rates, which include wildlife drives and meals.

Self-Catering Accommodation

This can be excellent value, from around R500 per four-person cottage (also called chalets, cabins and rondavels). Farm cottages are usually the least expensive. Small town information centres are the best places to find out about these, and in a small community there's a chance that you'll get a ride to the cottage if you don't have transport.

Self-catering chalets or cottages are also often available in caravan parks and camping grounds, both municipal and private, and are common in coastal and tourist areas.

Apart from the occasional run-down place with just a mattress and basin, most self-catering accommodation comes with bedding, towels and a fully equipped kitchen, though confirm what is included in advance. In some farm cottages you'll have to do without electricity, and you might even have to pump water.

The **South African National (SAN) Parks Board** (☎ 012-428 9111; www.sanparks.org) has good-value, fully equipped bungalows and cottages. These are aimed at family groups and start at around R550/935 for two/four people. Many parks also have simpler huts, with shared bathrooms and kitchens from around R200 per double.

ACTIVITIES

Thanks to South Africa's diverse terrain and favourable climate, almost anything is possible – from ostrich riding to the world's highest bungee jump. Good facilities and instruction mean that most activities are accessible to anyone, whatever their experience level.

There are dozens of operators. In addition to the ones listed here, ask other travellers and at hostels. Try to book day or overnight trips as close to your destination as possible. For example, if you're in Durban and want to visit a reserve further north, it's better (and usually cheaper) to travel to a hostel closer to the reserve and take a day trip from there, rather than booking a longer trip from Durban.

Aerial Pursuits

Ideal weather conditions and an abundance of high points from which to launch yourself make South Africa a fine destination for aerial pursuits. Added attractions of taking to the South African skies are that it is relatively inexpensive, compared with elsewhere in the world, and conditions are generally favourable year-round. A helpful contact for getting started is the **Aero Club of South Africa** (☎ 0861-018 018; www.aeroclub.org.za).

South Africa is one of the world's top destinations for paragliding, particularly Cape Town's Table Mountain. Although the flying is good year-round, the strongest thermals are from November to April. For experienced pilots, airspace restrictions are minimal and there's great potential for long-distance, cross-country flying. **South African Hang Gliding and Paragliding Association** (☎ 012-668 1219; www.sahpa.co.za) can provide names of operators, and numerous schools

offer courses for beginners. In Cape Town, try **Paragliding Cape Town** (☎ 021-554 0592). In Swaziland, **Emoyeni Paragliding School** (☎ 505 7405; airsports@realnet.co.sz) in Manzini has paragliding courses.

Good places to float over the countryside in a hot air balloon include Sabie (p449) and the surrounding Mpumalanga area. Microlight flying is another way to get a bird's eye view on things. Check out www.otto.co.za /micro/for an overview and a list of airfields.

South Africa boasts the world's highest bungee jump (p242) at Bloukrans River Bridge, between Plettenberg Bay and Storms River. There are several other popular jumps as well, including one at Gouritz Bridge, near Mossel Bay (p211).

Bird-Watching

With its enormous diversity of habitats, South Africa is a paradise for bird-watchers. Top spots include the following:

Cape Peninsula & West Coast Cape of Good Hope, within Table Mountain National Park (p164), is excellent for seabird-watching, as is West Coast National Park (p232), about 120km to the north.

Kruger National Park (p466) One of the continent's best areas for birding; the south and the far north are considered the prime areas, and the park is known particularly for its raptors and migrants.

Northern KwaZulu-Natal Mkhuze Game Reserve (p345) hosts over 400 species within its 36,000 hectares, and the Greater St Lucia Wetland Park (p339) protects one of the most significant water-bird breeding grounds in Southern Africa.

Eyries in Lesotho's Maluti Mountains near the eastern Drakensberg escarpment, and Swaziland's Malolotja Nature Reserve (p590) are also favourable destinations.

There are bird-watching clubs in all major South African cities, and most parks and reserves can provide you with birding lists. Other useful contacts include **Southern Africa Birding** (www.sabirding.co.za), which also covers Lesotho and Swaziland; **Birdlife South Africa** (www.birdlife.org.za) and **Cape Birding Route** (www.capebirdingroute.org).

Many parks and reserves have field guides on hand, but it's still worth bringing your own.

Canoeing, Kayaking & Rafting

South Africa has few major rivers, but the ones that do flow year-round offer reward-

---

SAFE DIVING

In popular diving areas, including Sodwana Bay, we've had some reports about slipshod diving operations. When choosing an operator, make quality, rather than cost, the priority. Factors to consider include an operator's experience and qualifications; knowledgeableness and seriousness of staff; whether it's a fly-by-night operation or well established; and the type and condition of equipment and frequency of maintenance. Assess whether the overall attitude is professional, and ask about safety considerations – radios, oxygen, emergency evacuation procedures, boat reliability and back-up engines, first-aid kits, safety flares and life jackets. On longer dives, do you get an energising meal, or just tea and biscuits?

An advantage of using operators offering PADI- or NAUI-certified courses is that you'll have the flexibility to go elsewhere in the world and have your certification recognised at other PADI or NAUI dive centres. To check an operator's credentials, contact the **South Africa Underwater Federation** (☎ 021-930 6549; www.sa-underwater.org.za).

---

ing canoeing and rafting. Popular ones include the Blyde and Sabie Rivers, both in Mpumalanga province; the waterways around Wilderness (p218) and Wilderness National Park (p219) in the Western Cape; the Senqu (Orange) River, especially through Augrabies Falls National Park (p541); and the Tugela (p312). There's some serene canoeing at the Greater St Lucia Wetland Park (p339). In Swaziland, the classic rafting destination is the Great Usutu River (p595).

Rafting is highly rain-dependent, with the best months in most areas from December/January to April. Good contacts include **Felix Unite** (☎ 021-425 5181; www.felixunite.com), **Hardy Ventures** (☎ 013-751 1693; www.hardyventure .com) and **Intrapid Rafting** (☎ 021-461 4918). In Swaziland, the main operator is **Swazi Trails** (☎ 416 2180; www.swazitrails.co.sz).

For sea kayaking, try the Cape Town-based **Coastal Kayak** (☎ 021-439 1134; www.kayak.co .za) and the **Sea Kayaking Association of South Africa** (☎ 021-790 5611; www.doorway.co.za/kayak /recskasa/).

Diving

Take the plunge off the southernmost end of the African continent into your choice of oceans. To the west, the main dive sites are around the Cape Peninsula, known for its many wrecks and giant kelp forests. To the east, the main area is the KwaZulu-Natal north coast where – particularly around Sodwana Bay – there's some excellent warm-water diving with beautiful coral reefs and the chance to see dolphins and sometimes whale sharks. There are several sites off the Eastern Cape coast near Port

Elizabeth, and many resort towns along the Garden Route have diving schools.

Conditions vary widely. The best time to dive the KwaZulu-Natal shoreline is from May to September, when visibility tends to be highest. In the west, along the Atlantic seaboard, the water is cold year-round, but at its most diveable, with many days of high visibility, between November and January/February.

All coastal towns where diving is possible have dive outfitters, and costs are generally lower here than elsewhere in the region. Expect to pay from around R2000 for a four-day open-water certification course, and from about R200 for full equipment rental. With the exception of Sodwana Bay during the warmer months (when a 3mm wetsuit will suffice), you'll need at least a 5mm wetsuit for many sites, and a drysuit for some sites to the south and west. Strong currents and often windy conditions mean that advanced divers can find challenges all along the coast. Sodwana Bay is probably the best all-round choice for beginners.

A variant on all this is shark diving, which involves being lowered in a cage and seeing sharks up close without having to worry that you'll become their next meal. The main place for this is Gansbaai near Hermanus (p189). Some operators allow snorkellers in the cage, too, if you're not a qualified diver. While shark diving offers an introduction to these shadows of the deep, there are some ecological downsides. The most obvious problem is that the sharks are baited to draw them close, and so come to associate humans with food.

Fishing

Sea fishing is popular, with a wide range of species in the warm and cold currents that flow past the east and west coasts, respectively. River fishing, especially for introduced trout, is popular in parks and reserves, with some particularly good highland streams in the Drakensberg. Licences are available for a few rand at park offices, and some places rent equipment. Useful websites include **South African Fishing** (www.safishing.co.za), **South African Bass Fishing** (www.bassfishing.co.za) and **Fly Fishing South Africa** (www.flyfisher.co.za).

Lesotho is an insider's tip among trout anglers. The season runs from September to May (same in South Africa), and there is a small licence fee, a size limit and a bag limit of 12 fish. Only rod and line and artificial nonspinning flies may be used. For more information, contact the **Ministry of Agriculture Livestock Division** (☎ 2232 3986; Private Bag A82, Maseru 100). The nearest fishing area to Maseru is the Makhaleng River, 2km downstream from Molimo-Nthuse Lodge (a two-hour drive from Maseru). Other places to fish are the Malibamat'so River near Oxbow; the Mokhotlong River near Mokhotlong in the northeast; and the Thaba-Tseka main dam.

Hiking

SOUTH AFRICA

South Africa is wonderful for hiking, with an excellent system of well-marked trails varied enough to suit every ability. Some trails have accommodation – from camping to simple huts with electricity and running water – and all must be booked well in advance. Many have limits as to how many hikers can be on them at any one time. Most longer trails and wilderness areas require hikers to be in a group of at least three.

Designated wilderness areas, such as Cederberg Wilderness Area (p235), have off-trail hiking only. Little information is available on suggested routes, and it's up to you to survive on your own.

KwaZulu-Natal Nature Conservation (KZN Wildlife; ☎ 033-845 1000; www.kznwildlife.com) controls most trails in KwaZulu-Natal. Elsewhere, most trails are administered by the **SAN Parks Board** (☎ 012-428 9111; www.sanparks.org) or the various Forest Region authorities. To find out about local hiking clubs, contact **Hiking South Africa** (☎ 083-535 4538; www.hiking-south-africa.info).

Shorter hikes, from an hour up to a full day, are possible almost everywhere and require no advance arrangements. Prime areas include the Cape Peninsula near Cape Point and the Drakensberg.

It's also possible to take guided walks in national parks, accompanied by armed rangers. You won't cover much distance, but they offer the chance to experience the wild with nothing between you and nature; see p86.

Safety is not a major issue on most trails, although on a few longer trails there have been muggings. Check with the local hiking club when booking your hike. On longer trails, hike in a group, and limit the valuables you carry.

Hiking is possible year-round, although you'll need to be prepared in summer for extremes of wet and heat. The best time is March to October.

Some useful books include *Drakensberg Walks* and *Western Cape Walks* by David Bristow, and *Hiking Trails of Southern Africa* by Willie and Sandra Olivier. Jaynee Levy's *Complete Guide to Walks & Trails in Southern Africa* is too heavy to carry, but good for an overview.

LESOTHO

The entire country is ideal for hiking, away from major towns. In particular, the eastern highlands and the Drakensberg crown attract serious hikers, with Sehlabathebe (p572) and Ts'ehlenyane (p563) parks, Bokong Nature Reserve (p567) and the area around Sani Top (p565) among the highlights. Malealea (p568) and Semonkong (p567) also make ideal bases. Wherever you are, there are few organised hiking trails as in South Africa (just footpaths) and you can walk almost everywhere, accompanied by a compass, and the relevant topographical maps (p555).

In all areas, especially the remote eastern highlands, rugged conditions can make walking dangerous if you aren't experienced and prepared. Temperatures can plummet to near-zero even in summer, and thunderstorms and thick fog are common. Waterproof gear and warm clothes are essential. In summer many rivers flood and fords can become dangerous. Be prepared to change your route or wait until the river subsides. By the end of the dry season, good water can be scarce, especially in higher

SOUTH AFRICA'S TOP HIKES

Following are some of South Africa's top hiking trails and their booking contacts; more details are given in the relevant chapters.

Cape Peninsula & Western Cape

Hoerikwaggo Hiking Trails (p107; Table Mountain National Park; ☎ 021-465 8515; www.hoerikwagotrails .co.za) A series of three trails (one now open, the other two to open soon) that take you from City Bowl over the mountain, and ultimately along the stunningly beautiful Atlantic Coast to Cape Point.

Boesmanskloof Trail (p201; Cape Nature Conservation; ☎ 028-425 5020; www.capenature.org.za) Two days of hiking from Greyton to McGregor through the majestic *fynbos*-clad Riviersonderend Mountains.

Whale Hiking Trail (p193; De Hoop Nature Reserve; ☎ 028-425 5020) Five days of hiking along the coastline in De Hoop Nature Reserve, with the added bonus of whale-watching opportunities in season.

Eastern Cape

Otter Trail (p242; SAN Parks Board; ☎ 012- 428 9111; www.sanparks.org) Five days on the coast along the Garden Route (note that this trail is nearly always booked out).

Tsitsikamma Trail (p242; Forestry Department; ☎ 042-281 1712) A five-day hike running inland through the forests, parallel to the Otter Trail but hiked in the opposite direction (this trail is rarely booked out).

Amathole Trail (p273; Department of Water Affairs & Forestry; ☎ 043-642 2571; www.amatola.co.za) Up to six days in the former Ciskei homelands, ending at the Tyumie River near Hogsback.

Free State

Rhebok Hiking Trail (p385; SAN Parks Board; ☎ 012-428 9111; www.sanparks.org) Two days in Golden Gate Highlands National Park.

KwaZulu-Natal

Giant's Cup (p356; KZN Wildlife; ☎ 033-845 1000) Up to five days in the southern Drakensberg. There are also wilderness trails and guided walks in Hluhluwe-Imfolozi, Mkhuze and Lake St Lucia parks and reserves.

Limpopo

Hanglip Trail (p498; Komatiland Eco-Tourism; ☎ 013-754 2724; www.komatiecotourism.co.za) Up to two days in the verdant Soutpansberg Range.

Mpumalanga

Blyde River Canyon Hiking Trail (p454; Mpumalanga Parks Board; ☎ 013-759 5432; mpbinfo@cis.co.za) Up to 2½ days in the Blyde River Canyon area.

Kruger National Park (p471; SAN Parks Board; ☎ 012-428 9111; www.sanparks.org) Wilderness trails and guided walks.

Northern Cape

Klipspringer Hiking Trail (p541; Augrabies Falls National Park; ☎ 054-452 9200) Three days of stunning scenery along the banks of the Senqu (Orange) River.

Kodaspiek Trail (p547; Richtersveld National Park; ☎ 027-831 1506) Two days wandering amid incredible mountain desert landscapes.

areas. For more information see the boxed text on p568.

SWAZILAND
The best place for hiking is Malolotja Nature Reserve (p590). Mlawula Nature Reserve (p593) also has good trails. In almost any rural area, you can set out on foot, following the generations-old tracks that crisscross the countryside. Weather conditions aren't as extreme as in Lesotho, but if you're hiking during the summer, be prepared for torrential downpours and hail storms.

Horse Riding & Pony Trekking
In South Africa and Swaziland it's easy to find rides ranging from several hours to several days, and for all experience levels. Particularly good areas in South Africa include the KwaZulu-Natal Drakensberg (p346), Limpopo's Waterberg range (p496), and the Wild Coast (p283). Riding is also offered in several national parks, including Addo Elephant (p255) and Golden Gate (p385) National Parks. In Swaziland, you can ride at Mlilwane Wildlife Sanctuary (p586), among other places.

Some contacts:

Equus Horse Safaris (www.equus.co.za) Waterberg.
Fynbos Horse Trails (www.fynbostrails.com) Western Cape.
Horizon Horseback Adventures (www.ridinginafrica.com) Waterberg.
Khotso Horse Trails (www.khotsotrails.co.za) Drakensberg.
Nyanza Horse Trails (nyanza@africaonline.co.sz) Swaziland.
Wild Coast Trails (www.wildcoast.org.za) Wild Coast.

In Lesotho, pony trekking on tough Basotho ponies is a popular way of seeing the highlands; see p568.

Kloofing (Canyoning)
Kloofing (called canyoning elsewhere), is a mix of climbing, hiking, swimming and some serious jumping. It has a small but rapidly growing following in South Africa. You can give this a try in Cape Town (with several nearby possibilities, see p122) and along the Drakensberg Escarpment (p445) in Mpumalanga. Operators who can sort you out include **Adventure World** (www.adventurevillage.co.za), **Day Trippers** (www.daytrippers.co.za) and **Abseil Africa** (www.abseilafrica.co.za). There's

a definite element of risk in the sport, so when hunting for operators, check their credentials carefully before signing up.

Mountain Biking
There are trails almost everywhere in South Africa. Some suggestions to get you started: the De Hoop Nature Reserve (p193), with overnight and day trails; the ride up (and down) Sani Pass, on the border between South Africa and Lesotho (p565); Citrusdal (p236), with a network of trails; the area around Cederberg Wilderness area (p235); Mountain Zebra National Park (p266); Knysna (p219) and surrounding area, with a good selection of trails; Sabie (p449), with several excellent trails; and Swaziland's Mlilwane Wildlife Sanctuary (p586). Cape Town is something of an unofficial national hub.

Useful sources of information include **Mountain Bike South Africa** (www.mtbsa.co.za); **Mountain Bike South Africa e-zine** (www.mtb.org.za); the **Linx Africa trail listing** (www.linx.co.za/trails/lists/bikelist.html); and Paul Leger's *Guide to Mountain Bike Trails in the Western Cape*. The bimonthly *Ride* is the main South African mountain-biking magazine.

Rock Climbing
Some of the most challenging climbing is on the close-to-sheer faces of the KwaZulu-Natal Drakensberg. Another of South Africa's top sites is in Mpumalanga at Waterval Boven. The **South African Climbing Info Network** (www.saclimb.co.za) has listings and photos of many other climbing and bouldering sites. For information on regional clubs, contact the **Mountain Club of South Africa** (MCSA; ☎ 021-465 3412; www.mcsa.org.za). **Roc'n Rope** (☎ 013-257 0363; www.rocrope.com) is another useful contact.

Surfing
Most surfers will have heard of Jeffrey's Bay, but South Africa offers myriad alternatives, particularly along the Eastern Cape coast from Port Alfred northwards. The best time of the year for surfing the southern and eastern coasts is autumn and early winter (from about April to July).

Boards and gear can be bought in most of the big coastal cities. New boards cost around US$185 and good-quality second-hand boards around US$100. If you plan to surf Jeffrey's Bay, you'll need a decent-sized board, as it's a fast wave.

For more information see the boxed texts on p215 and p245. Also check out www .wavescape.co.za, and **Zig Zag** (www.zigzag.co.za), South Africa's main surf magazine.

Whale-Watching

South Africa is considered one of the world's best spots to sight these graceful giants from land, without needing to go out in a boat. Southern right and humpback whales are regularly seen offshore between June/July and November, with occasional spottings also of Bryde's and killer whales. Hermanus (p188) – where southern right whales come to calve – is the unofficial whale-watching capital, complete with a whale crier and an annual Whale Festival.

At nearby Walker Bay, whales approach to within 50m of the shoreline. Other favoured spots include the False Bay shoreline, especially between Cape Point and Muizenberg, and from Gordon's Bay southeast; and Mossel (p211) and Plettenberg (p225) Bays. The whales continue on around the Cape and up the KwaZulu-Natal coast, although by the time they reach Durban, they're often considerably further out to sea. See the boxed text on p187 for more information.

Wildlife-Watching

South Africa's populations of large animals are one of the country's biggest attractions. In comparison with other countries in the region (Botswana and Zambia, for example), wildlife-watching in South Africa tends to be very accessible, with good roads and excellent accommodation for all categories of traveller. It is also comparatively inexpensive, although there are plenty of pricier choices for those seeking a luxury experience in the bush. For more, see the Environment chapter (p85) and Kruger National Park chapter (p470).

Swaziland also offers some excellent wildlife-watching, in generally low-key surroundings. Among the highlights: Mlilwane Wildlife Sanctuary (p586), Mkhaya Game Reserve (p594) and Hlane Royal National Park (p593).

BOOKS

Following is a listing of some books – a mix of fiction and nonfiction – to begin immersing yourself in regional life and culture. Also see p22.

A Short History of Lesotho from the Late Stone Age to the 1993 Elections by Stephen J Gill. A concise and readable history of the Mountain Kingdom.

Basali: Stories by and about Women in Lesotho by K Limakatso. Good insights into Lesotho's rural life as seen through the eyes of local women.

Country of my Skull by Antjie Krog. A wrenching recounting of the hearings of the Truth & Reconciliation Commission by a prominent Afrikaaner journalist.

Indaba, My Children by Credo Mutwa. An excellent compendium of traditional mythology and folktales.

No Future Without Forgiveness by Desmond Tutu. Another, somewhat more hope-filled, chronicling of the work of the Truth and Reconciliation Commission by its chairman.

Strikes Have Followed Me All My Life by Emma Mashinini. A powerful recounting of one woman's struggle against domination and injustice.

The Heart of the Hunter: Customs & Myths of the African Bushman by Laurens van der Post. An intriguing accounting of southern Africa's San people and their culture.

The Wild Almond Line by Larry Schwartz. A memoir of growing up in a segregated country and being a conscript in the apartheid-era army.

BUSINESS HOURS

Usual business hours are listed inside the front cover. Exceptions to this have been noted in individual listings in this book. In addition to regular banking hours, many foreign exchange bureaus remain open until 5pm Monday through Friday, and until noon on Saturday. In urban areas, many supermarkets stay open until 6pm or 8pm and are also open 9am to noon on Sundays.

CHILDREN
South Africa

South Africa is an eminently suitable destination if you're travelling with children. With its abundance of national parks, beaches, swimming pools and hiking trails, plus a good collection of museums and a handful of amusement parks, it offers plenty to do for travellers of all ages in a generally hazard-free setting. Most South Africans are welcoming to children, and you should have no shortage of offers for assistance. For some help sorting things out, and for equipment rental or purchase, try the Cape Town–based **Tiny Tourists** (www.tinytourists.com).

PRACTICALITIES

Baby-changing rooms are not common, though clean restrooms abound, and in most you should be able to find a make-shift spot to change a nappy (diaper). Nappies, powdered milk and baby food are widely available, except in very rural areas. It's difficult to find brands of proc-essed baby food without added sugar. These are available at supermarkets in all major towns; always check the security seal on jars, and the expiry date. Short-term day-care is becoming more common, and many upscale hotels and resorts in tourist areas can arrange childcare.

Many wildlife lodges have restrictions on children under 12, so in most national parks and reserves the main accommodation options will be camping or self-catering. Otherwise, family-oriented accommoda-tion, such as triple-bed hotel rooms and four- to six-person self-catering cottages, are common throughout South Africa, and most hotels can provide cots. Many hotels offer children's discounts, averaging 50%. Children under 12 are also usually admitted at discounted rates to parks (free for chil-dren under two years of age, discounted for those aged under 16), museums and other places where entry fees are charged.

Most car-rental agencies will provide safety seats, but you'll need to book them in advance, and usually pay extra. When planning your itinerary, try to minimise long distances between stops.

Breast-feeding in public won't raise an eyebrow among Africans, but in other cir-cles it's best to be discreet.

Seek medical advice on malaria prophy-lactics for children if you'll be in malarial areas (anywhere in the lowveld, includ-ing Kruger National Park). Swimming in streams should generally be avoided, due to the risk of bilharzia infection. Otherwise, there are few health risks. Should your child become ill, good-quality medical care is available in all major cities.

Lonely Planet's *Travel with Children* by Cathy Lanigan is full of tips for keeping children and parents happy on the road.

SIGHTS & ACTIVITIES
Botanical gardens, an aquarium, the cable car to Table Mountain, swimming pools, good facilities, and a low-key ambience make Cape Town the best urban desti-nation if you're travelling with children. Among smaller towns, Oudtshoorn (p207)

deserves mention because of its ostriches and the nearby Cango Caves.

For seaside relaxation, some of the beaches near Cape Town and along the Garden Route are ideal for families. One to try, because of its calmer waters and shel-tered setting, is at Arniston (p193).

For older children, hiking in the Drakens-berg is another option.

Wildlife-watching is suitable for older children who have the patience to sit for long periods in a car, but less suitable for younger ones. Addo Elephant National Park is one of the better destinations, in part because it's malaria-free, and in part because of the likelihood of sighting ele-phants. Kruger National Park is tempting because of its easy accessibility and family-friendly rest camps. However think twice before going, as it's in a malaria area. If pos-sible, try to visit in the winter when the risk of malaria is lower, and come prepared with nets, repellent and suitable clothing.

Lesotho & Swaziland
Lesotho and Swaziland are also welcoming destinations for children. Swaziland in partic-ular is a good family destination, with a very child-friendly attitude and a relaxed pace. The main caveat is the presence of malaria, which is a real risk in lower-lying areas of the country. There's no malaria in Lesotho, but because of its more rugged terrain and condi-tions, it's better suited for older children who would enjoy hiking or pony trekking (note that most pony trekking centres only arrange treks for those over 12 years old).

Many hotels in Swaziland offer family-friendly accommodation, and there are amusements such as mini golf to keep chil-dren occupied. In Lesotho, everything is a bit rougher around the edges, though if you (and your children) are of an adventurous bent, you'll likely find travel here straight-forward and enjoyable. Informal childcare arrangements can be made in both coun-tries; ask at your hotel. Major hotels have Western-style bathrooms, but in rural areas often the only choice is a long-drop. Nap-pies, powdered milk and baby food are avail-able in Mbabane, Manzini and Maseru, with only a limited selection in smaller towns.

There are reasonable medical facilities in Mbabane and Maseru, but for anything ser-ious, you'll need to head to South Africa.

CLIMATE CHARTS

South Africa has been favoured by nature with one of the most temperate climates on the African continent, and plenty of sunny, dry days. The main factors influencing conditions are altitude and the surrounding oceans (see p20 for more on when to visit).

COURSES
Language

There are numerous language schools for learning Xhosa, Zulu and Afrikaans, including the following:

Inlingua Cape Town (☎ 021-419 0494; www.inlingua .co.za) Afrikaans.

Interlink Cape Town (☎ 021-439 9834; www.inter link.co.za) Afrikaans, Xhosa.

Language Teaching Centre Cape Town (☎ 021-425 3585; www.languageteachingcentre.co.za) Afrikaans, Xhosa.

University of Natal (☎ 031-260 2510; www.nu.ac .za/department/default.asp?dept=zuludund; Durban) Zulu.

University of the Witwatersrand (☎ 011-717 4245; http://slls.uiplay.co.za/index.aspx?Action=AFL) Zulu.

A good contact for getting below South Africa's surface is **TALK** (Transfer of African Language Knowledge; ☎ 011-487 1798; www.phaphama.org). They organise 'immersion visits' in which you live in a homestay arrangement in either a township or rural area while receiving an hour or so daily of instruction in an African language and getting introduced to local culture. Costs vary, but average about R600 per person for a three-night stay. The main focus is Soweto, but they can also sort out visits in other parts of the country.

Wine Tasting

For the ultimate in fine living, ensconce yourself in an atmospheric B&B in the Winelands and enrol in a wine-tasting course. Some useful contacts:

Cape Wine Academy (☎ 021-889 8844; www.cape wineacademy.co.za) Based in Stellenbosch, and runs courses in both Stellenbosch and Cape Town.

Nose Wine Bar (Map pp116-17; ☎ 021-425 2200; www .thenose.co.za; Cape Quarter, Dixon St, Waterkant) Runs wine-tasting courses.

CUSTOMS

You're permitted to bring 1L of spirits, 2L of wine, 400 cigarettes and up to R1250 worth of souvenirs into South Africa without

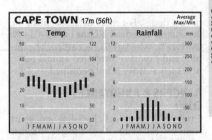

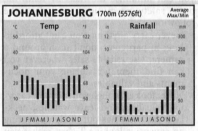

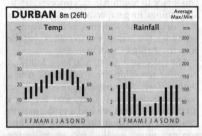

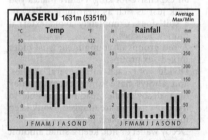

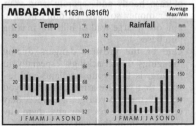

paying duties. For more details, contact the **Department of Customs & Excise** (☎ 012-422 4000, 0800 002 870; Private Bag X923, Pretoria 0001). The import and export of protected animal products such as ivory is not permitted.

DANGERS & ANNOYANCES
Crime

Crime is the national obsession and, apart from car accidents, it's the major risk that you'll face in South Africa. However, try to keep things in perspective, and remember that despite the statistics and newspaper headlines, the majority of travellers visit the country without incident.

The risks are highest in Jo'burg, followed by some township areas and other urban centres. Daylight muggings are common in certain sections of Jo'burg, and the city's metro train system has had a problem with violent crime. No matter where you are, you can minimise the risks by following basic safety precautions, including the following:

■ Never carry anything you can't afford to lose; in particular, don't flash around a camera. Use reliable safes wherever you can find them for storing your documents and valuables.
■ Never look as though you might be carrying valuables, and leave watches, necklaces and earrings out of sight; wearing an expensive-looking T-shirt makes you look just as rich as wearing jewellery or a suit does. Completely avoid external money pouches.
■ Avoid groups of young men; trust older mixed-sex groups.
■ Divide your cash into several stashes, and always have some 'decoy' money or a 'decoy' wallet readily accessible to hand over if you are mugged. Don't keep money in your back pocket.
■ Decoy wallet or not, keep a small amount of cash handy and separate from your other money so that you don't need to pull out a large wad of bills for making purchases.
■ One of the greatest dangers during muggings or carjackings, especially in Jo'burg, is that your assailants will assume that you are armed, and that you will kill them if you get a chance. Stay calm, and don't resist or give them any reason to think that you will fight back.

■ Listen to local advice on unsafe areas.
■ Avoid deserted areas day and night, and especially avoid the commercial business district areas of larger cities at night and weekends.
■ If you're going to visit a township – and it will certainly be one of the highlights of your visit to South Africa – go with a trusted guide or as part of a tour.
■ Try not to look apprehensive or lost.
■ Avoid driving at night and, day or night, keep your doors locked and windows up. Especially if you'll be driving alone, it's worth hiring a mobile phone. Leave your car in secure parking at night, and don't leave anything valuable inside.

Crime rates are nowhere near as high in Lesotho and Swaziland as they are in South Africa. Maseru has seen an increase in armed robberies, break-ins and carjackings targeting expatriates (though it's still small-scale compared with South Africa), and street crime is rising in Mbabane and Manzini. As long as you follow the basic precautions, you should be fine. Elsewhere in Lesotho and Swaziland, crime is negligible.

Drugs

Dagga or *zol* (marijuana) was an important commodity in the Xhosa's trade with the San. Today it is illegal but widely available. There are heavy penalties for use and possession but many people still use the drug – often quite openly, as you'll discover in some of the backpacker hostels and bars you might frequent. The legal system does not distinguish between soft and hard drugs.

Ecstasy is just as much a part of rave and clubbing culture in South Africa as it is elsewhere. South Africa is also reputed

---

TRAVEL ADVISORIES

Government travel advisories are good sources of updated security information, and are well worth perusing before heading to South Africa:

Australia (www.dfat.gov.au)
Canada (www.voyage.gc.ca/dest/ctry/report page-en.asp)
UK (www.fco.gov.uk)
US (http://travel.state.gov)

to be the world's major market for the barbiturate Mandrax, which is now banned in many countries (including South Africa) because of its devastating effects. Drugs such as cocaine and heroin are becoming widely available and their use accounts for much property crime.

DISCOUNT CARDS

A membership card for **Hostelling International** (www.hihostels.com) or the affiliated international Youth Hostel Association entitles you to occasional discounts on bus lines, tour operators, surf shops and more. A valid student ID will also get you discounts for some bus lines, museums etc.

EMBASSIES & CONSULATES
South African Embassies & Consulates

Diplomatic representations abroad include the following. For a full listing see www.dfa .gov.za/foreign/sa_abroad/index.htm.

Australia (☎ 02-6273 2424; www.sahc.org.au; Rhodes Pl, Yarralumla, Canberra ACT 2600)

Botswana (☎ 390 4800; sahcgabs@botsnet.bw; 29 Queens Rd, Gaborone)

Canada (☎ 613-744 0330; www.southafrica-canada .com; 15 Sussex Dr, Ottawa, Ontario K1M 1M8)

France (☎ 01 53 59 23 23; www.afriquesud.net; 59 Quai d'Orsay, 75343 Paris, Cedex 07)

Germany (☎ 030-22 0730; www.suedafrika.org; Tiergartenstrasse 18, Berlin 10785)

Ireland (☎ 01-661 5553; information@saedublin.com; 2nd fl, Alexandra House, Earlsfort Centre, Earlsfort Tce, Dublin 2)

Israel (☎ 03-525 2566; www.safis.co.il; 16th fl, Top Tower, 50 Dizengoff St, 64332, Tel Aviv)

Kenya (☎ 020-282 7100; sahc@africaonline.co.ke; Roshanmaer Place, Lenana Rd, Nairobi)

Malawi (☎ 01-773 722; sahc@malawi.net; 3rd fl, Kang'ombe House, Robert Mugabe Crescent, Lilongwe)

Mozambique (☎ 01-490059, 491614; sahc@tropical .co.mz; Avenida Eduardo Mondlane 41, Maputo)

Namibia (☎ 061-205 7111; sahcwin@iafrica.com.na; RSA House, cnr Jan Jonker St & Nelson Mandela Ave, Windhoek 9000)

Netherlands (☎ 70-392 4501; www.southafrica.nl; Wassenaarseweg 40, the Hague 2596 CJ)

New Zealand Representation accredited from Australia, see above.

UK (☎ 020-7451 7299; www.southafricahouse.com; South Africa House, Trafalgar Sq, London WC2N 5DP)

USA (☎ 202-232 4400; www.saembassy.org; 3051 Massachusetts Ave NW, Washington DC 20008) Also consulates in New York, Chicago and Los Angeles.

Zimbabwe (☎ 04-753147; dhacon@mweb.co.zw; 7 Elcombe St, Belgravia, Harare)

Lesotho Embassies & Consulates

In countries without Lesotho representation, contact the UK representative. Lesotho's diplomatic representations abroad include the following:

Belgium (☎ 02-705 3976; lesothobruemb@skynet.be; Blvd General Wahis 45, 1030 Brussels)

Germany (☎ 030-257 5720; embleso@yahoo.com; Kurfürstenstrasse 84, 10787 Berlin)

Italy (☎ 06-854 2419; les.rome@flashnet.it; Via Serchio 8, 00198 Rome)

UK (☎ 020-7235 5686; www.lesotholondon.org.uk; 7 Chesham Pl, Belgravia, London SW1 8HN)

USA (☎ 202-797 5533/4; www.lesothoemb-usa.gov.ls; 2511 Massachusetts Ave, NW, Washington DC 20008)

Swazi Embassies & Consulates

In countries without Swazi representation, contact the UK representative.

Mozambique (☎ 021-493846, 021-491721; Avenida Kwame Nkrumah, Maputo)

UK (☎ 020-7630 6611; www.swaziland.org.uk; 20 Buckingham Gate, London SW1E 6LB)

USA (☎ 202-234 5002; 1712 New Hampshire Ave, NW, Washington DC 20009)

Embassies & Consulates in South Africa

Most countries have their main embassy in Pretoria, with an office or consulate in Cape Town (which becomes the official embassy during Cape Town's parliamentary sessions). Some countries also maintain consulates in Jo'burg and in Durban.

South Africa is a gold mine for travellers hunting for visas for other African countries. As some of these can be difficult to collect as you travel around, it makes sense to get as many as you can here.

The following list includes some of the more important embassies and consulates; most are open in the mornings only for visa services, usually between 9am and noon. For more listings, check www.dfa.gov.za /foreign/forrep/index.htm.

Australia (Map pp428–9; ☎ 012-342 3740; www .australia.co.za; 292 Orient St, Arcadia, Pretoria)

Botswana High Commission in Pretoria (Map pp428–9; ☎ 012-430 9640; 24 Amos St, Colbyn); Consulate in Cape Town (Map pp110–11; ☎ 021-421 1045; 4th fl, Southern Life Centre, 8 Riebeeck St, City Bowl); Consulate in Jo'burg (Map p402; ☎ 011-403 3748; 2nd fl, Future Bank Bldg, 122 De Korte St, Braamfontein)

Canada High Commission in Pretoria (Map pp428–9; ☎ 012- 422 3000; www.dfait-maeci.gc.ca/southafrica/; 1103 Arcadia St, Hatfield); Consulate in Cape Town (Map pp110–11; ☎ 021-423 5240; 19th fl, Reserve Bank Bldg, 60 St George's Mall, City Bowl)

France Embassy in Pretoria (Map pp428–9; ☎ 012-425 1600; france@ambafrance-rsa.org; 250 Melk St, New Muckleneuk); Consulate in Cape Town (Map p114; ☎ 021-423 1575; 2 Dean St); Consulate in Jo'burg (Map pp398-9; ☎ 011-778 5600; 3rd fl, Standard Bank Bldg, 191 Jan Smuts Ave, Rosebank)

Germany Embassy in Pretoria (Map pp428–9; ☎ 012-427 8977; germanembassypretoria@gonet.co.za; 180 Blackwood St); Consulate in Cape Town (Map pp110–11; ☎ 021-405 3000; 19th fl, Safmarine House, 22 Riebeeck St)

Ireland Embassy in Pretoria (Map pp428–9; ☎ 012-342 5062; 1st fl, Southern Life Plaza, 1059 Schoeman St); Consulate in Cape Town (Map pp110–11; ☎ 021-423 0431; 54 Keerom St, City Bowl)

Lesotho High Commission in Pretoria (Map pp428–9; ☎ 012-460 7648; 391 Anderson St, Menlo Park); Consulate in Jo'burg (Map p402; ☎ 011-339 3653; 76 Juta St, Indent House, Braamfontein); Consulate in Durban (Map p306–7; ☎ 031-307 2168; 2nd fl, Westguard House, cnr West & Gardiner Sts)

Mozambique High Commission in Pretoria (Map pp428–9; ☎ 012-401 0300; 529 Edmond St, Arcadia); Consulate in Jo'burg (Map pp398-9; ☎ 011-327 2938, 327 2944; 252 Jeppe St); Consulate in Cape Town (Map pp110–11; ☎ 021-426 2944; 3rd fl, Castle Bldg, 45 Castle St); Consulate in Durban (Map pp306-7; ☎ 031-304 0200; Room 520, 320 West St); Consulate in Nelspruit (Map p458; ☎ 013-753 2089; 43 Brown St)

Namibia (Map pp428–9; ☎ 012-481 9100; secretary@ namibia.org.za; 197 Blackwood St, Arcadia, Pretoria)

Netherlands Embassy in Pretoria (Map pp428–9; ☎ 012-344 3910; www.dutchembassy.co.za; 825 Arcadia St); Consulate in Cape Town (Map pp110–11; ☎ 021-421 5660; 100 Strand St, City Bowl)

New Zealand (Map pp428–9; ☎ 012-342 8656; Block C, Hatfield Gardens, Arcadia, Pretoria)

Swaziland High Commission in Pretoria (Map pp428–9; ☎ 012-344 1910; 715 Government Ave, Arcadia); Consulate in Jo'burg (Map p402; ☎ 403 7372, 403 2036; 6th fl, Braamfontein Centre, 23 Jorissen St)

UK High Commission in Pretoria (Map pp428–9; ☎ 012-421 7500; bhc@icon.co.za; 255 Hill St, Arcadia); Consulate in Cape Town (Map pp110–11; ☎ 021-425 3670; Southern Life Centre, 8 Riebeeck St, City Bowl); Consulate in Durban (Map pp306-7; ☎ 031-305 3041; 22 Gardner St)

USA Embassy in Pretoria (Map pp428–9; ☎ 012-431 4000; http://pretoria.usembassy.gov; 877 Pretorius St, Arcadia); Consulate in Cape Town (Map pp110–11; ☎ 021-421 4280; 4th fl, Broadway Industries Centre, Foreshore); Consulate in Jo'burg (Map pp398-9; ☎ 011-646 6900; 1 River St, Killarney); Consulate in Durban (Map pp306-7; ☎ 031-304 4737; 29th fl, Durban Bay House, 333 Smith St)

Zimbabwe High Commission in Pretoria (Map pp428–9; ☎ 012-342 5125; 798 Merton Ave, Arcadia); Consulate in Cape Town (Map pp110–11; ☎ 021-461 4710; 55 Kuyper St, Zonnebloem); Consulate in Jo'burg (Map p402; ☎ 011-838 2156; 17th fl, 20 Anderson St)

Embassies & Consulates in Lesotho

Canada (Map p556; ☎ 2231 4187, 2231 6435; www .dfait-maeci.gc.ca/southafrica/; 5th fl, LNDC, Block D, Kingsway, Maseru)

France (Map p556; ☎ 2232 5722; alliancefrancaise@ ilesotho.com; Alliance Française Bldg, cnr Kingsway & Pioneer Rd, Maseru)

Germany (Map p556; ☎ 2233 2292; germanembassy pretoria@gonet.co.za; 70C Maluti Rd, Maseru West)

Ireland (Map p556; ☎ 2231 4068; lesotho@dfa.ie; Tonakholo Rd, Maseru West)

Netherlands (Map p556; ☎ 2231 2114; lancers -inn@ilesotho.com; c/o Lancer's Inn, Maseru)

South Africa (Map p556; ☎ 2231 5758; sahcmas@leo .co.ls; 10th fl, Lesotho Bank Towers, Kingsway, Maseru)

USA (Map p556; ☎ 2231 2666; http://maseru.usembassy .gov; 254 Kingsway, Maseru)

Embassies & Consulates in Swaziland

Mozambique (Map p579; ☎ 404 3700; Mountain Inn Rd, Mbabane)

South Africa (Map p579; ☎ 404 4651; sahc@africa online.co.sz; 2nd fl, the Mall, Plasmall St, Mbabane)

USA (Map p579; ☎ 404 6441/2; http://mbabane.us embassy.gov; 7th fl, Central Bank Bldg, Warner St, Mbabane)

FESTIVALS & EVENTS

South Africa hosts dozens of festivals, and there's always something going on somewhere in the country. A small sampling is listed here, including a few highlights from Lesotho and Swaziland. For other events, see the destination chapters. Good places to check on what's happening include www .safrica.info/plan_trip/holiday/culture_her itage/festivals.htm and www.festivals.co.za.

JANUARY

Cape Town New Year Karnaval (Cape Town Minstrel Carnival) Cape Town's longest-running street party is held 1–2 January, with ribald song and dance parades, colourful costumes and general revelry. It's followed by a Jazzathon at the Waterfront.

FEBRUARY

Kavadi Festival The major Hindu festival, held twice annually (January–February and April–May) in Durban, in honour of the Hindu god Muruga. It's accompanied by the piercing of the body with skewers as a sign of devotion.

MARCH
Cape Argus Cycle Tour (www.cycletour.co.za) Held in the second week of March, this spin around the Cape Peninsula is the largest bicycle race in the world, with over 30,000 entries.

Absa Klein Karoo National Arts Festival (☎ 044-203 8600; info@kknk.co.za) Enjoy all things Afrikaans at this festival that aims to seek unity between Afrikaans speakers of all races; held in Oudtshoorn (Western Cape) in late March/early April.

APRIL
Old Mutual Two Oceans Marathon (www.twooceans marathon.org.za) One of the world's most beautiful marathon routes, held around the Cape Peninsula on Easter Saturday.

Rustler's Valley One World Unity Party (www .rustlers.co.za) An off-beat music-centred party held around Easter weekend that's an annual highlight for alternative lifestyle lovers of every sort. Rustler's Valley, Free State.

Splashy Fen Music Festival (www.splashyfen.co.za) Rock, pop and jazz with a fringe; held in late April at Splashy Fen Farm, about 20km north of Underberg in the foothills of the southern Drakensberg.

JUNE
Comrades Marathon (www.comrades.com) Held in mid-June, this 89km road race (queen of marathons) is run between Durban and Pietermaritzburg, alternating directions each year.

Durban International Film Festival (diff@ukzn.ac.za) A cinematic showcase for films from around the country and the continent; held in Durban.

JULY
National Arts Festival (www.nafest.co.za) Get in touch with South Africa's creative pulse at the country's largest arts festival, held annually in early July at Grahamstown (Eastern Cape).

AUGUST/SEPTEMBER
Umhlanga (Reed) Dance Swaziland's week-long debutante ball in August/September; young Swazi women journey to Lobamba to help repair the queen mother's home and then dance before the king.

OCTOBER
Morija Arts & Cultural Festival (www.morijafest.com) A celebration of Basotho culture; held in early October in Morija (Lesotho).

Standard Bank Awesome Africa Music Festival (www.awesomeafricafestival.co.za) Highlighting music and theatre groups from across the continent; held in Durban in early October.

NOVEMBER
Diwali The Durban Indian community's three-day Festival of Lights.

DECEMBER
Soweto Arts Festival (☎ 011 487 2818; www.joburg .org.za) A week-long festival to promote the arts, unity and culture. Held annually in mid- to late-December at various locales in Soweto.

Incwala The sacred rain and harvest festival of the Swazi, held in December/January, depending on the moon.

FOOD
Dining in South Africa is generally pleasurable and good value. Sit-down meals in restaurants (without getting into *haute cuisine*) average between R60 and R80 per person (less in pubs), and fresh produce everywhere is good value.

Restaurants are generally open daily from around 11.30am until 2.30pm or 3pm for lunch, and from about 6.30pm or 7pm until about 10pm for dinner. Cafés generally open from about 7.30am or 8am until about 5pm or 6pm. If there's a closing day, it's usually Sunday or Monday. Variations have been noted in individual listings.

For more on eating well in South Africa (and in Lesotho and Swaziland), see the Food & Drink chapter (p92).

GAY & LESBIAN TRAVELLERS
South Africa's constitution is one of the few in the world that explicitly prohibits discrimination on the grounds of sexual orientation, and there are active gay and lesbian communities and scenes in Cape Town, Jo'burg, Pretoria and Durban. Cape Town is without doubt the focal point, and the most openly gay city on the continent.

Things have come a long way since 1990, when Jo'burg hosted a gay pride parade, with many supporters wearing brown paper bags over their heads to conceal their identity. The parade, which is held annually in late September, is still going strong. There's also a separate annual gay and lesbian film festival, **Out in Africa** (www.oia.co.za), with a good selection of international and local films in Jo'burg, Pretoria and Cape Town. In December everyone fights for tickets for the popular **Mother City Queer Project party** (www.mcqp.co.za) in Cape Town.

Despite the liberality of the new constitution, it will be a while before the more

DIRECTORY

conservative sections of society begin to accept it. Outside the cities, in both black and white communities, homosexuality remains frowned upon, if not taboo.

The country's longest-running gay newspaper is the monthly *Exit* (www.exit.co.za). The glossy monthly *OUTright* is for gay males; *Womyn* is its lesbian equivalent. Both are available at CNA and other chain bookstores nationwide. The Gauteng-based magazine *Rush* is also worth looking out for; it's often available at gay venues. There's a gay and lesbian link on the South Africa tourism website (www.southafrica.net). Another good contact is Cape Town's **Triangle Project** (☎ 021-448 3812; www.triangle.org.za), which offers professional counselling, legal advice and education programmes, and is also a leading AIDS support organisation. Also see www.mask.org.za; and the boxed texts on p153 and p414.

Swaziland is much more conservative than South Africa. Both male homosexual and lesbian activities are officially illegal, and gay sexual relationships are culturally taboo. In Lesotho, there is no official prohibition of homosexual activity, though gay sexual relationships are taboo and open displays of affection – whatever your orientation – are frowned upon.

HOLIDAYS
Public Holidays
After the 1994 elections, public holidays underwent a dramatic shake-up. For example, the Day of the Vow, which celebrated the Boers' victory in the Battle of Blood River, has become the Day of Reconciliation. The officially ignored but widely observed Soweto Day, marking the Soweto uprisings, is now celebrated as Youth Day. Human Rights Day is held on the anniversary of the Sharpeville massacre (p41).

Current public holidays follow:

SOUTH AFRICA
New Year's Day 1 January
Human Rights Day 21 March
Good Friday March/April
Easter Sunday March/April
Easter Monday March/April
Family Day 17 April
Constitution or Freedom Day 27 April
Workers' Day 1 May
Youth Day 16 June

Women's Day 9 August
Heritage Day 24 September
Day of Reconciliation 16 December
Christmas Day 25 December
Day of Goodwill 26 December

LESOTHO
New Year's Day 1 January
Moshoeshoe Day 11 March
Good Friday March/April
Easter Monday March/April
Hero's Day 4 April
Workers' Day 1 May
Ascension Day May
King's Birthday 17 July
Independence Day 4 October
Christmas Day 25 December
Boxing Day 26 December

SWAZILAND
New Year's Day 1 January
Good Friday March/April
Easter Monday March/April
King Mswati III's Birthday 19 April
National Flag Day 25 April
King Sobhuza II's Birthday 22 July
Umhlanga (Reed) Dance August/September
Somhlolo Day 6 September (Independence)
Christmas Day 25 December
Boxing Day 26 December
Incwala Ceremony December/January (dates vary yearly)

School Holidays
South Africa's major holiday periods are the December–January school holidays as well as the Easter break. Many shops and businesses close, accommodation in national parks and tourist areas is fully booked and peak-season prices are in effect. At the beginning and end of these holiday periods, public transport fills up, as do seats on domestic and international flights, and you'll likely encounter long queues at popular border posts.

The situation is similar during other school holidays, but not as intense. During these times, accommodation prices are often increased, but not by as much.

The provinces stagger their school holidays. They are approximately late March to early April (varying, depending when Easter is); late June to mid-July; late September to early October; and early December to mid-January. For exact dates, see www.saschools.co.za/sas/calendar.htm. The main school holiday periods in Lesotho and Swaziland parallel those in South Africa.

INSURANCE

Travel insurance covering theft, loss and medical problems is highly recommended. Before choosing a policy spend time shopping around, as those designed for short package tours in Europe may not be suitable for the South African veld. Also be sure to read the fine print, as some policies specifically exclude 'dangerous activities', which can mean scuba diving, motorcycling, bungee jumping and more. At a minimum, check that the policy covers emergency evacuation at least to Jo'burg and/or an emergency flight home. If you'll be in Lesotho and Swaziland, check to see whether the evacuation plan extends to these countries.

If your policy requires you to pay first and claim later for medical treatment, be sure to keep all documentation. Some policies ask you to call back (reverse charges) to a centre in your home country where an immediate assessment of your problem is made.

For information about vehicle insurance, see p637; for health insurance see p644.

Worldwide cover to travellers from over 44 countries is available online at www.lonelyplanet.com/travel_services.

INTERNET ACCESS

Internet access is widely available in South Africa. Many hostels offer email facilities, and there are Internet cafés in every major town. Costs average R10 to R30 per hour. If you're travelling with your own computer, hooking up in hotel rooms is straightforward, requiring only the phone connection jack for your modem. Most top hotels have wireless access and/or broadband (for which they should be able to provide the cable).

In Swaziland, there's Internet access in Mbabane, Manzini and in a few places in the Ezulwini and Malkerns Valleys; elsewhere in the country, connections are few and far between. In Lesotho, you can log on in Maseru.

LEGAL MATTERS

If you have the misfortune to be arrested in South Africa, you have the right to keep silent; the right to be released on bail or warning, unless there's a good reason to keep you in jail; the right to a lawyer; and the right to food and decent conditions.

Apart from traffic offences such as speeding and drunk driving, the main area to watch out for is drug use and possession. Despite a relatively open drug culture, use and possession are illegal: arrests happen and penalties are stiff.

MAPS

Good country maps are widely available for all three countries, and a recommended investment if you'll be driving. Some to look for are Map Studio's *Tourist Map* (1:2,500,000) and the Automobile Association of South Africa (AASA) series of maps covering the country. Michelin maps also cover South Africa, Lesotho and Swaziland. Lonely Planet's *Cape Town City Map* is useful whether you're visiting the city by car or on foot. All of these are readily available in map stores and bookstores in major cities in South Africa. A good place to look is **Map Studio** (www.mapstudio.co.za), with branches in Cape Town, Durban and Jo'burg. Many bookstores in the CNA chain also usually stock a good selection of road atlases.

For any hiking done away from established trails, a topographical map is highly recommended. Government maps are available from **Maps Unlimited** (☎ 011-882 1741; www.mapoffice.co.za; 10 Rembrandt Park Plaza, cnr Lister & Heine Rds, Rembrandt Park, Jo'burg). Drakensberg maps – essential if you plan on hiking there – are available from KwaZulu-Natal Nature Conservation (p85).

In Lesotho, 1:50,000 topographical maps are available from the Department of Land, Surveys & Physical Planning (p555). It also sells a good 1:250,000 country map (1994). The AASA puts out the helpful *Motoring in Lesotho*, available at the tourist information office and bookstores in Maseru.

In Swaziland, the tourist office hands out a free country map, with city plans for Mbabane and Manzini on the reverse, though none are particularly accurate. Better is the AASA's *Motoring in the Kingdom of Swaziland* map, which is on sale at the tourist information office in Mbabane, and at bookstores. Topographical maps (1:50,000) are available from the **Ministry of Public Works & Transport Surveyor General's office** (☎ 404 2321; Mhlambanyatsi Rd, Mbabane).

DIRECTORY

MONEY

South Africa's currency is the rand (R), which is divided into 100 cents. There is no black market. The coins are one, two, five, 10, 20 and 50 cents, and R1, R2 and R5. The notes are R10, R20, R50, R100 and R200. There have been forgeries of the R200 note and some businesses are reluctant to accept them.

In Lesotho, the currency is the loti (plural maloti, M), which is divided into 100 lisente. In Swaziland, it's the lilangeni (plural emalangeni, E). Both the loti and the lilangeni are fixed at a value equal to the South African rand. Rand are accepted everywhere in both Lesotho and Swaziland, though you will invariably be given maloti or emalangeni in change.

The value of the rand has fluctuated wildly in recent years, and is currently on the upswing, although South Africa is still less expensive than Europe and North America. For exchange rates, see the table inside the front cover. For information on costs, see p21.

The best currencies to bring are US dollars, euros or British pounds in a mixture of travellers cheques and cash, plus a Visa

or MasterCard for withdrawing money from ATMs.

ATMs

There are ATMs in all cities in South Africa, most of which give cash advances against cards belonging to the Cirrus network. For safety precautions, see below.

In Lesotho there is an ATM in Maseru that accepts international cards. All other ATMs in Lesotho only work if you have a local bank account.

In Swaziland, there are ATMs that accept international cards in Mbabane, the Ezulwini Valley and a few other locations around the country.

Credit Cards

These are widely accepted in South Africa, especially MasterCard and Visa, and can also be used at many ATMs for cash advances. Nedbank is an official Visa agent and Standard Bank is a MasterCard agent – both have branches across the country.

In Lesotho and Swaziland, credit cards are only accepted by the major tourist establishments.

BEATING THE ATM SCAMS

If you are a victim of crime in South Africa, it's most likely to occur at an ATM. There are dozens of scams that involve stealing your cash, your card or your personal identification number (PIN) – usually all three. Thieves are just as likely to operate in Stellenbosch as in downtown Jo'burg and they are almost always well-dressed and well-mannered men.

The ATM scam you're most likely to encounter involves the thief tampering with the machine so your card becomes jammed. By the time you realise this you've entered your PIN. The thief will have seen this, and when you go inside to report that your card has been swallowed, he will take the card and leave you several thousand rand shorter. We make no guarantees, but if you follow the rules listed here you stand a better chance of avoiding this and other scams.

- Avoid ATMs at night and in secluded places. Rows of machines in shopping malls are usually the safest.
- Most ATMs have security guards. If there's no guard around when you're withdrawing cash, watch your back, or get someone else to watch it for you.
- Watch the people using the ATM ahead of you carefully. If they look suspicious, go to another machine.
- Use ATMs during banking hours and if possible take a friend. If your card is jammed in a machine, one person can stay at the ATM while the other seeks assistance from the bank.
- When you put your card into the ATM press cancel immediately. If the card is returned then you know there is no blockage in the machine and it should be safe to proceed.
- Don't hesitate to be rude in refusing any offers of help to complete your transaction.
- If someone does offer, end your transaction immediately and find another machine.
- Carry your bank's emergency phone number and if you do lose your card report it immediately.

Moneychangers

SOUTH AFRICA

Cash is readily exchanged at banks (First National, Nedbank and Standard Bank are usually the best) and foreign exchange bureaus in all major cities.

Most banks change travellers cheques in major currencies with varying commissions. Nedbank is associated with American Express, and First National Bank and Nedbank are associated with Visa. Thomas Cook has travellers cheques in rand, though it works out best in the end to buy US dollar cheques. If you do buy some rand cheques, do so just before departure to minimise the effects of devaluation.

The Thomas Cook agent in South Africa is Rennies Travel, a large chain of travel agencies, and there are American Express offices in major cities. Neither charges a commission for its own travellers cheques, though you'll usually get a higher rate of exchange from a bank. Rennies also changes other travellers cheques without fees.

Keep at least some of your exchange receipts as you'll need these to reconvert leftover rand when you leave.

LESOTHO

The only place where you can reliably exchange foreign cash and travellers cheques is in Maseru. Commissions average 2.5% on travellers cheques (minimum M25), and 1.25% on cash (minimum M40). Rand notes are usually available on request.

SWAZILAND

First National and Nedbank change cash and travellers cheques. Rates are similar at both, but commissions vary. Most banks ask to see the purchase receipt when cashing travellers cheques.

Standard Bank has branches in Mbabane, Manzini, Nhlangano, Piggs Peak, Simunye, Tshaneni, Matsapha and Big Bend. First National also has branches around the country, while Nedbank is in Mbabane, Manzini and Matsapha.

Taxes & Refunds

SOUTH AFRICA

South Africa has a value-added tax (VAT) of 14%, but departing foreign visitors can reclaim much of this on goods being taken out of the country. To make a claim, the goods must have been bought at a shop participating in the VAT foreign tourist sales scheme, their total value must exceed R250, and you will need a tax invoice for each item. This is usually the receipt, but must include the following:

- the words 'tax invoice'
- the seller's VAT registration number
- the seller's name and address
- a description of the goods purchased
- the cost of the goods and the amount of VAT charged, or a statement that VAT is included in the total cost of the goods
- a tax invoice number
- the date of the transaction.

For purchases over R500, your name and address and the quantity of goods must also appear on the invoice. All invoices must be originals – no photocopies.

At your point of departure, you'll need to fill in a form or two and show the goods to a customs inspector. At airports, make sure you have goods checked by the inspector before you check in your luggage. After going through immigration, make the claim and pick up your refund cheque; at some airports you can cash it immediately at a bank (in any major currency). If your claim comes to more than R3000, a cheque will be mailed to your home address. There's an efficient system in place in the Cape Town Tourism offices, and those of other major cities, enabling you to process the paperwork beforehand. It's also possible to arrange for a refund to your credit card.

You can claim at the international airports in Jo'burg, Cape Town and Durban, and at the following local airports: Bloemfontein, Gateway, Lanseria, Mmabatho, Mpumalanga Kruger (Nelspruit), Port Elizabeth and Upington. It's also possible to claim at the Beitbridge (Zimbabwe) and Komatipoort (Mozambique) border crossings and at major harbours.

LESOTHO & SWAZILAND

Both Lesotho and Swaziland have a VAT of 14%, applied similarly to that in South Africa although there are not yet any systems for refunds in place. In both countries, many hotels omit the tax when quoting rates, although we've included it in the listings in this book.

Tipping

Wages are low, and tipping is expected; around 10% to 15% is usual in tourist areas. The main exceptions are in rural parts of Lesotho and Swaziland, where it's generally the custom to simply round up the bill.

PHOTOGRAPHY & VIDEO

In South Africa, film (slide and print), cameras and accessories are readily available in large towns, and processing, including slide processing, is generally of a high standard. Blank video tapes are available in major cities, although they won't work on North American machines. Film selection is much more limited in Lesotho and Swaziland, with a modest selection of print film available in major towns.

For wildlife photos, a good lightweight 35mm single lens reflex (SLR) automatic camera with a lens between 210mm and 300mm should do the trick. Video cameras with zoom facility may be able to get closer and digital cameras will perform all sorts of magic. An early start to the day is advisable as most wildlife is active during the cooler hours.

When photographing animals, take light readings on the subject to avoid underexposure. The first two hours after sunrise and the last two before sunset are the best times of day to take photos on sunny days. In Lesotho and Swaziland, you can often capture some excellent special effects with the sunlight just after a summer storm.

In all three countries, be careful about taking photos of soldiers, police, airports, defence installations and government buildings. It goes without saying that you should always ask permission before taking a photo of anyone, but particularly so if you're in a tribal village.

Lonely Planet's *Travel Photography: A Guide to Taking Better Pictures* by Richard I'Anson will help you do exactly what the title says.

POST

Post offices are open from 8.30am to 4.30pm Monday to Friday, and 8am to noon Saturday. In South Africa and Swaziland, both domestic and international deliveries are generally reliable, but can be slow. In Lesotho, delivery is slow and unreliable. For mailing anything of value consider using one of the private mail services, such as Postnet. Poste restante is available in all major cities in South Africa, in Maseru in Lesotho, and in Manzini and Mbabane in Swaziland.

SHOPPING
South Africa

Handicrafts of varying quality are sold everywhere – though more expensively here than in Lesotho and Swaziland. Most carvings of animals and people are not traditional, although some are still quite attractive. Items to watch for include Venda pottery and woodcarvings, and Zulu beadwork and basketry. Township-produced crafts, such as wirework, also make great gifts, and are inexpensive and light to carry.

Western consumer goods are readily available in major towns and cities, where you'll invariably find department stores and shopping malls.

Lesotho

The famous Lesotho blanket – the country's all-purpose garment – is usually made outside Lesotho. However some local production remains, and these colourful wool and mohair textiles have been transformed into an art form in the internationally acclaimed wall hangings produced by Moteng weavers.

Other handicrafts include mohair tapestry, and woven-grass products such as mats, baskets and the ubiquitous Basotho hat. Trekking sticks come plain or decorated and can be found everywhere.

Swaziland

Because of the strength of Swaziland's traditional culture, many items here are made for the local market as much as for tourists. Popular items include woven grassware such as *liqhaga* ('bottles' that are so tightly woven that they are used for carrying water) and mats; and wooden items, ranging from bowls to *knobkerries* (traditional Southern African weapons/sticks). Swazi candles – works of art in wax – are also well worth seeking out. Good places to look for crafts include Malkerns, Mbabane and the Ezulwini Valley.

Bargaining

With the exception of the occasional curio stand, bargaining isn't expected in South

Africa. In Lesotho and Swaziland, you'll find a mix of fixed-price shops, and curio stands where the vendors are willing to bargain.

SOLO TRAVELLERS

Solo travel in South Africa, Lesotho and Swaziland – whether you're male or female – is straightforward. While you may be a minor curiosity in rural areas, especially solo women travellers, it's likely that in most places nobody will even bat an eye.

Times when you'd likely want to find a group to join up with would be for a safari (to cut costs), on hiking trails (many in South Africa have a three-person minimum for safety reasons), and at night. Especially in urban areas and at night, women travelling alone should use caution, and avoid isolating situations. See also p620.

TELEPHONE
South Africa

South Africa has good telephone facilities, which will likely become better and more competitively priced once an already-approved second national operator (SNO Telecommunications) becomes operational and breaks up Telkom SA's long-held monopoly.

Local calls are relatively inexpensive (about R1 for three minutes), whereas domestic long-distance calls (from about R2 per minute) and international calls (from R7 per minute to Europe) can be pricey. Phonecards are widely available. There are also private phone centres where you can pay cash for your call, but at double the rate of public phones. International calls are cheaper after 8pm on weekdays, and between 8pm Friday and 8am Monday. For reverse-charge calls, dial ☎ 0900.

A good way to avoid high charges when calling home, or to make reverse-charge calls, is to dial your 'Country Direct' number, which puts you through to an operator in your country. Some major Country Direct numbers:

Australia Direct (☎ 0800 990 061)
Belgium Direct (☎ 0800 990 032)
Canada Direct (☎ 0800 990 014)
Denmark Direct (☎ 0800 990 045)
Ireland Direct (☎ 0800 990 353)
Japan Direct (☎ 0800 990 081)
Netherlands Direct (☎ 0800 990 031)

New Zealand Direct (☎ 0800 990 064)
UK Direct – BT (☎ 0800 990 044)
UK Direct – Call UK (☎ 0800 990 544)
USA Direct – AT&T (☎ 0800 990 123)
USA Direct – MCI Call US (☎ 0800 990 011)
USA Direct – Sprint Express (☎ 0800 990 001)

PHONE CODES

South Africa's country code is ☎ 27. To make an international call from South Africa (including to Lesotho and Swaziland), dial ☎ 09, followed by the country code, local area code (without the initial zero) and telephone number.

Telephone numbers in South Africa are 10 digits, including the local area code, which must always be dialled, unless you are in the same town. South African area codes are given at the start of each section, or with the telephone number. There are also several four-digit nationwide prefixes (for use within South Africa only) followed by six-digit numbers. These prefixes include: ☎ 0800 (toll free), ☎ 0860 (charged as a local call), and ☎ 0861 (flat-rate calls).

MOBILE PHONES

The mobile-phone network covers most of the country, and mobile-phone ownership is widespread. The network operates on the GSM digital system, which you'll need to know if you're thinking of bringing your phone from home.

The three major mobile networks are **Vodacom** (www.vodacom.co.za), **MTN** (www.mtn.co.za) and **Cell C** (www.cellc.co.za). Hiring a mobile phone is relatively inexpensive, but call charges average about R3 per minute. Some car-rental firms offer deals on mobile phones. An easy alternative is to use your own phone (check ahead that it's compatible), and insert a local prepaid or pay-as-you-go SIM card from one of the three mobile networks. These cards are available almost everywhere at shopping malls and shops in all larger cities and towns.

The main codes for mobile phones are: ☎ 082 (Vodacom), ☎ 083 (MTN) and ☎ 084 (Cell C).

Lesotho

Lesotho's telephone system works reasonably well, although you don't have to go far off the beaten track to be away from the telephone system altogether.

The country code is ☎ 266; there are no area codes. To make international calls, including to South Africa, dial ☎ 00, followed by the country code, area code (minus the initial zero) and telephone number. For international reverse charge calls dial ☎ 109.

The main mobile phone service is provided by **Vodacom Lesotho** (www.vodacom.co.ls), based in Maseru. The coverage area extends north to Butha-Buthe, south to Quthing (Moyeni) and east to Mohale Dam. Charges are similar to those in South Africa.

Swaziland

Swaziland also has a reasonably good telephone network. The country code is ☎ 268; there are no area codes. To make international calls, including to South Africa, dial ☎ 00 for international, then the country code and city code. Dial ☎ 94 to make a reverse-charge call.

International calls are expensive, and most easily made using phonecards. You can also make international calls (but not reverse-charge calls) at the Mbabane post office. Outside of major towns, it's necessary to book international calls through an operator (☎ 94).

Mobile-phone services are provided by both **MTN** (www.mtn.co.sz) and **Vodacom** (www.vodacom.co.za).

TIME

South African Standard Time is two hours ahead of GMT/UTC, seven hours ahead of USA Eastern Standard Time, and eight hours behind Australian Eastern Standard Time. At noon in Jo'burg, it's 10am in London, 5am in New York, and 8pm in Sydney. There is no daylight-saving time. Lesotho and Swaziland are in the same time zone as South Africa.

This is a wide region to be covered by one time zone and the sun rises and sets noticeably earlier in Durban than it does in Cape Town. Most timetables and businesses use the 24-hour clock.

TOILETS

Finding a clean, Western-style toilet in South Africa is usually not a problem. There are few public toilets, but tourist information offices and restaurants are often willing to give you a key to their facilities.

In rural areas, and anywhere outside of major towns in Swaziland and Lesotho, long-drops (holes in the ground, sometimes with footrests or makeshift seats) are the norm.

TOURIST INFORMATION
South Africa

The main government tourism organisation is **South African Tourism** (☎ 011-895 3000, 083-123 6789; www.southafrica.net), which has a helpful website with news of upcoming events and various links.

For more details on individual provinces, there are provincial tourism organisations, of varying quality. In addition to these, almost every town in the country has at least one tourist office. These are private entities, and rely on commissions (5% is usually built into their hotel rates) for their existence. Also, be aware that many tourist offices will only recommend the services of member organisations (ie those that have paid up). You may well have to push to find out about all the possible options, especially cheaper accommodation.

Provincial tourist offices include the following:

Eastern Cape Tourism Board (☎ 043-701 9600; www.ectb.co.za)

Free State Tourism Board (☎ 051-447 1362; www.dteea.fs.gov.za)

Gauteng Tourism Authority (☎ 011-832 2780; www.gauteng.net)

KwaZulu-Natal Tourism Authority (☎ 031-366 7500; www.kzn.org.za)

Limpopo Tourism Board (☎ 015-295 8262, 0860-730 730; www.golimpopo.com)

Mpumalanga Tourism Authority (☎ 013-752 7001; www.mpumalanga.com)

North-West Province Parks & Tourism Board (☎ 018-397 1500, 293 1611; www.tourismnorthwest.co.za)

Northern Cape Tourism Authority (☎ 053-832 2657; www.northerncape.org.za)

Western Cape Tourism Board (☎ 021-426 5639; www.tourismcapetown.co.za)

TOURIST OFFICES ABROAD

South African Tourism offices abroad include the following:

Australia (☎ 02-9261 5000; info@southafrica.net; Level 1, 117 York St, Sydney, NSW 2000)

France (☎ 01 45 61 01 97; info.fr@southafrica.net; 61 Rue La Boëtie, 75008 Paris)

Germany (☎ 069-280 950; info.de@southafrica.net; Friedenstrasse 6-10, D-60311 Frankfurt)
Japan (☎ 03-3478 7601; info@southafricantourism.or.jp; Akasaka Lions Bldg, 1-1-2 Moto Akasaka, Minato-ku, Tokyo 107-0051)
UK (☎ 020-8971 9350; info.uk@southafrica.net; 6 Alt Grove, Wimbledon, London SW19 4DZ)
USA (☎ 212-730 2929; newyork@southafrica.net; 20th fl, 500 Fifth Ave, New York, NY 10110)

Lesotho & Swaziland

The helpful **Tourist Information Office** (☎ 2231 2427; Kingsway) in Maseru (see p555) has information on all major tourist areas, plus maps and transport tips. For more general information, check the tourism page on the **Lesotho government website** (www.lesotho.gov.ls).

Swaziland's main **tourist information office** (☎ 404 2531; www.welcometoswaziland.com; Swazi Plaza) is in Mbabane. Also check www.min tour.gov.sz.

TRAVELLERS WITH DISABILITIES

South Africa is one of the best destinations on the continent for disabled travellers, with an ever-expanding network of facilities catering to those who are mobility impaired or blind. **SAN Parks** (☎ 012-428 9111; www.sanparks.org) has an excellent and inspirational overview of accommodation and trail accessibility for the mobility impaired at all its parks, with particular detail on Kruger, and is the best travel website we have seen anywhere in terms of incorporating disabled access information throughout its pages.

Wheelchairs are sometimes available for visitors at several botanical gardens, including Kirstenbosch (Cape Town), though you should call in advance to confirm. Kirstenbosch and several nature reserves also have Braille or guided trails for the visually impaired. Also of note are the wonderful penguin boardwalk at Table Mountain National Park (p107), and the discovery trail and horse riding possibilities at Addo Elephant National Park (p255). Other destinations with facilities for the disabled have been noted throughout the book.

Hand-controlled vehicles can be hired at Avis (p636) and other major car rental agencies (see p636) in major cities, and (through Avis) at Kruger Park's Skukuza Camp.

A helpful initial contact is the **National Council for Persons with Physical Disabilities in**

South Africa (☎ 011-726 8040; www.ncppdsa.co.za). Other useful sources of information:
Access-Able Travel Source (www.access-able.com) Has lists of operators offering tours for travellers with disabilities.
Carpe Diem Tours (☎ /fax 027-217 1125) Specialises in tours for the physically challenged and the elderly in Western and Northern Capes.
Central Reservations (www.centralres.co.za/disabled .html) A small listing of disabled-friendly accommodation.
Eco-Access (www.eco-access.org) An overview of disabled-related initiatives in South Africa.
Epic-Enabled (www.epic-enabled.com) Can help arrange tours, plus Kruger safaris.
Flamingo Tours (www.flamingotours.co.za) Tours for the disabled in Western and Eastern Cape, Kruger and elsewhere in South Africa.
Linx Africa (www.linx.co.za/trails/lists/disalist.html) For province-by-province listings of disabled-friendly trails.
Rolling SA (www.rollingsa.co.za) Tours and Kruger safaris.

VISAS
South Africa

Visitors on holiday from most Commonwealth countries (including Australia and the UK), most Western European countries, Japan and the USA don't require visas. Instead, you'll be issued with a free entry permit on arrival. These are valid for a stay of up to 90 days. However, if the date of your flight out is sooner than this, the immigration officer will use it as the date of your permit expiry unless you specifically request otherwise.

If you aren't entitled to an entry permit, you'll need to get a visa (also free) before you arrive. These aren't issued at the borders, and must be obtained at a South African embassy or consulate. Allow up to several weeks for processing. South Africa has consular representation in most countries, with a partial listing given on p609. The website of the South African High Commission in London (www.southafricahouse.com) has an overview of visa requirements, and lists the nationalities that require visas.

If you do need a visa (rather than an entry permit), get a multiple-entry visa if you plan to make a foray into Lesotho, Swaziland or any other neighbouring country. This avoids the hassle of applying for another South African visa in a small town such as Maseru or Mbabane.

For any entry – whether you require a visa or not – you need to have at least two completely blank pages in your passport, excluding the last two pages.

VISA EXTENSIONS

Applications for visa or entry-permit extensions, and for re-entry visas, should be made at the **Department of Home Affairs** (http://home-affairs.pwv.gov.za). There are branches in Cape Town (p106), Durban, Jo'burg and Pretoria.

Lesotho

Citizens of most Western European countries, Japan, Israel, the USA and most Commonwealth countries are granted a free entry permit at the border. The standard permitted stay is two weeks, although if you ask for longer it's often granted. For a lengthier stay, you'll need to apply in advance to the **Director of Immigration & Passport Services** (☎ 2232 3771, 2232 1110; PO Box 363, Maseru 100).

Travellers who require visas can get these in South Africa (see Embassies & Consulates, p609). You'll need one passport photo and about R30/50 for single/multiple entry; processing takes 24 hours. If you arrive at the Maseru Bridge border crossing without a visa, with some luck you'll be issued a temporary entry permit to allow you to get into Maseru, where you can apply for a visa at the Ministry of Immigration. However, don't count on this, as it depends completely on the whim of the border officials.

Swaziland

Most people don't need a visa to visit Swaziland. For those who do (including citizens of Austria and Switzerland), they are available free of charge at border posts and at the airport. In South Africa, you can get them in Pretoria and Jo'burg (see p609). In countries without Swazi diplomatic representation, contact the UK representative.

Anyone staying for more than 60 days must apply for a temporary residence permit from the **Chief Immigration Officer** (☎ 404 2941; PO Box 372, Mbabane).

Visas for Neighbouring Countries

Visas for Namibia are not issued at the border, though many nationalities don't require one. Visas for Zimbabwe and Mozambique are available at the borders. (South African nationals don't need a visa

for Mozambique.) For Mozambique it's cheaper to arrange your visa in advance at the Mozambican High Commission in Mbabane, or in Nelspruit. Both issue express visas in 24 hours.

If you'll be arranging your visa in advance: Zimbabwean visas take at least a week to issue in South Africa; those for Namibia take two to three days; and those for Botswana take between four and 14 days. Non-express Mozambique visas take one week.

VOLUNTEERING

Volunteer work is possible, especially if you're interested in teaching or wildlife conservation. A good initial contact is **Volunteer Abroad** (www.volunteerabroad.com), with extensive listings of volunteer opportunities in the country.

Unless you have a UK passport, anyone coming to South Africa to do volunteer work needs to get a work permit. Applications for these should be made through the South African embassy or consulate in your home country; processing usually takes one month.

WOMEN TRAVELLERS
Attitudes Towards Women

Sexism is a common attitude among South African men, regardless of colour. Modern ideas such as equality of the sexes have not filtered through to many people, especially away from the cities. Women are usually called 'ladies' unless they play sport, in which case they are called 'girls'.

Fortunately times are changing and nowadays there are plenty of women who don't

---

COMING OF AGE

- The legal age for voting in South Africa (and in Lesotho and Swaziland) is 18.
- Driving is legal once you're 18.
- The legal drinking age is 18.
- Heterosexual sex is legal when you turn 16 (18 in Swaziland). In Lesotho the age of consent is 14 for boys and 16 for girls.
- The homosexual age of consent is 19 in South Africa, and undefined in Lesotho and Swaziland.

put up with this, but South African society as a whole is still decades behind most developed countries. Also, ironically, there has been something of an antifeminist backlash without there having been many feminist gains in the first place. The fact that black women were at the forefront in the liberation struggle and that many of these women have entered politics may change this, however.

Not surprisingly, there are big differences between the lives of women in the region's various cultures. In traditional black cultures, women often have a very tough time, but this is changing to some extent because a surprising number of young girls have the opportunity to stay at school while the boys are sent away to work. In South Africa's white communities, however, the number of girls finishing secondary school is significantly lower than the number of boys, which goes against international trends.

The practice of female genital mutilation (female circumcision) is not part of the traditional cultures of South Africa (or Lesotho or Swaziland).

There's a very high level of sexual assault and other violence against women in South Africa, the majority of which occurs in townships and rural areas. Given the extremely high levels of HIV/AIDS in the country, the problem is compounded through the transfer of infection.

A large part of the problem in South Africa is the leniency of the judicial system that repeatedly lets perpetrators of sex offences off with short sentences. This, particularly in recent times, has had women's groups around the country voicing their concerns and demanding that the government step in and take tougher action.

There have been incidents of travellers being raped, but these cases are isolated, and cause outrage in local communities. For most female visitors, paternalistic attitudes are the main problem rather than physical assault.

Safety Precautions

Single female travellers have a curiosity value that makes them conspicuous, but it may also bring forth generous offers of assistance and hospitality. It is always difficult to quantify the risk of assault – and there is such a risk – but plenty of women do travel alone safely in South Africa.

Obviously the risk varies depending on where you go and what you do. Hitching alone is extremely foolhardy. What risks there are, however, are significantly reduced if two women travel together or, even better, if a woman travels as part of a mixed-sex couple or group. But while the days of apartheid have long gone, a mixed-race couple will almost certainly attract attention and receive some antagonistic reactions – old attitudes die hard.

However you travel, especially inland and in the more traditional black communities, it's best to behave conservatively. On the coast, casual dress is the norm, but elsewhere dress modestly (full-length clothes that aren't too tight) if you do not wish to draw attention to yourself. Don't go out alone in the evenings on foot – always take a taxi; avoid isolated areas, roadways and beaches during both day and evening hours; avoid hiking alone; and carry a mobile phone if you'll be driving alone.

Although urban attitudes are more liberal, common sense and caution, particularly at night, are essential.

WORK

Unempoyment is high in South Africa, and finding work is difficult. There are tough penalties for employers taking on foreigners without work permits, although this doesn't seem to have stopped foreigners getting jobs in restaurants or bars in tourist areas. If you do line something up, you can usually earn from around R25 per hour plus tips (which can be good). The best time to look for work is from October to November, before the high season starts, and before university students begin holidays.

Transport

CONTENTS

GETTING THERE & AWAY

Flights, tours and rail tickets can be booked online through www.lonelyplanet.com/travel _services.

ENTRY REQUIREMENTS
Passports

As long as you have complied with visa and entry-permit requirements (see p619), there are no restrictions on any nationalities for entering South Africa, Lesotho or Swaziland.

Entering South Africa

Once you have an entry permit or visa, South Africa is straightforward and hassle-free to enter. Travellers arriving by air are often required to show an onward ticket – preferably an air ticket, though an overland ticket also seems to be acceptable. On arrival you may have to satisfy immigration officials that you have sufficient funds for your stay, so it pays to be neat, clean and polite.

If you're coming to South Africa after travelling through the yellow-fever zone in Africa (which includes most of East, West

and Central Africa) or South America, you must have an international vaccination certificate against yellow fever. No other vaccinations are mandatory, although there are some you should consider (see p644).

Entering Lesotho

Almost everyone enters Lesotho overland from South Africa, although it's also possible to fly from Johannesburg (Jo'burg). Entry permits are easy to get at any of Lesotho's borders and at the airport. If you are a citizen of a country for which a visa is required (see p620), it's best to arrange this in advance. Vaccination certificate requirements are the same as those for South Africa.

Entering Swaziland

Most travellers enter Swaziland overland, although it's also possible to fly in from South Africa and Mozambique. Entry is usually hassle-free. Visas are readily available at the border for those nationalities that require one (see p620), although you'll save yourself queuing time by arranging the visa in advance. Vaccination-certificate requirements are the same as for South Africa.

AIR
Airports & Airlines

The major air hub for South Africa, and for the entire surrounding region, is **Johannesburg International Airport** (JIA or JNB; ☎ 011-921 6262; www.worldairportguides.com/johannesburg-jnb). It has a full range of shops, restaurants,

---

THINGS CHANGE

The information in this chapter is particularly vulnerable to change. Check directly with the airline or a travel agent to make sure you understand how a fare (and ticket you may buy) works, and be aware of the security requirements for international travel. Shop carefully. The details given in this chapter should be regarded as pointers and are not a substitute for your own careful, up-to-date research.

Internet access, ATMs, foreign-exchange bureaus and mobile-phone and car rental outlets.

Cape Town International Airport (CPT; ☎ 021-937 1200; www.airports.co.za) receives numerous direct flights from Europe, and is becoming an increasingly important gateway. It has a forex bureau, and mobile-phone rental and car-rental outlets.

The smaller **Durban International Airport** (DUR; ☎ 031-451 6758; www.airports.co.za) handles several regional flights, as does **Mpumalanga Kruger International Airport** (MQP; ☎ 013-753 7500; www.kmiairport.co.za) near Nelspruit and Kruger National Park.

Lesotho's **Moshoeshoe International Airport** (MSU; ☎ 2235 0777), 21km southeast of Maseru, and Swaziland's **Matsapha International Airport** (MTS; ☎ 518 6840), 8km west of Manzini, handle regional flights only.

South African Airways (SAA; airline code SA; ☎ 0861-359 722, 011-978 5313; www.flysaa.com; hub JIA) is the national airline, with an excellent route network and safety record. In addition to its international routes, it operates regional flights together with its subsidiaries **South African Airlink** (SAAirlink; ☎ 011-978 5313; www.saairlink.co.za) and **South African Express** (☎ 011-978 5577; www.saexpress.co.za).

Some other international carriers flying to/from Jo'burg (except as noted):

Air France (AF; ☎ 0860-340 340; www.airfrance.fr) Hub: Charles de Gaulle Airport, Paris.

Air Mauritius (MK; www.airmauritius.com) Jo'burg (☎ 011-444 4600); Cape Town (☎ 021-671 5225) Hub: SSR Airport, Mauritius. Also serves Cape Town.

Air Namibia (SW; www.airnamibia.com.na) Jo'burg (☎ 011-390 2876); Cape Town (☎ 021-936 2755) Hub: Chief Hosea Kutako Airport, Windhoek. Also serves Cape Town.

British Airways (BA; www.britishairways.com) Jo'burg (☎ 011-441 8600); Cape Town (☎ 021-936 9000) Hub: Heathrow Airport, London. Also serves Cape Town.

Cathay Pacific (CX; ☎ 011-700 8900; www.cathaypacific.com) Hub: Hong Kong International Airport.

Comair (MN; ☎ 0860-435 922, 011-921 0222; www.comair.co.za) Hub: JIA. Operates British Airways flights within Africa.

Egyptair (MS; ☎ 011-390 2202, 011-880 4126/9; www.egyptair.com.eg) Hub: Cairo International Airport.

Emirates Airlines (EK; ☎ 011-883 8420; www.emirates.com) Hub: Dubai International Airport.

Kenya Airways (KQ; ☎ 011-881 9795, 011-571 8817; www.kenya-airways.com) Hub: Jomo Kenyatta International Airport, Nairobi.

> **DEPARTURE TAX**
>
> Airport departure tax is included in ticket prices in South Africa. Departure tax in Lesotho is M20, and in Swaziland it's E20. On flights from Swaziland into South Africa, there is an additional tax of R120.

KLM (KL; ☎ 0860-247 474, 011-881 9696; www.klm.com) Hub: Schiphol Airport, Amsterdam. Also serves Cape Town.

LTU International Airways (LT; ☎ 021-936 1190; www.ltu.de) Hub: Düsseldorf Airport. Flights to Cape Town only.

Lufthansa (LH; ☎ 0861-842 538, 021-415 3506; www.lufthansa.com) Hub: Frankfurt International Airport. Also serves Cape Town.

Malaysia Airlines (MH; www.malaysiaairlines.com) Jo'burg (☎ 011-880 9614); Cape Town (☎ 021-419 8010) Hub: Kuala Lumpur. Also flies to Cape Town.

Qantas (QF; ☎ 011-441 8550; www.qantas.com.au) Hub: Kingsford Smith Airport, Sydney.

Singapore Airlines (SQ; www.singaporeair.com) Jo'burg (☎ 011-880 8560); Cape Town (☎ 021-674 0601) Hub: Singapore Changi Airport. Also serves Cape Town.

Swiss International Airlines (LX; ☎ 0860 040 506; www.swiss.com) Hub: Kloten Airport, Zurich.

Virgin Atlantic (VS; ☎ 011-340 3400; www.virgin-atlantic.com) Hub: London. Also serves Cape Town.

SAAirlink is the only commercial carrier currently flying into Lesotho. **Swazi Express Airways** (☎ 518 6840; www.swaziexpress.com) and **Swaziland Airlink** (☎ 518 6155; www.saairlink.co.za), both based at Matsapha International Airport, are the main regional carriers servicing Swaziland. Swaziland Airlink – a joint venture between the Swazi government and SAAirlink in South Africa – has replaced Royal Swazi Airways as the national carrier.

Tickets

South Africa is served by various European carriers, as well as by direct flights from Australasia and North America. Fares from Europe and North America are usually highest in December and January, and again between July and September. They're lowest in April and May (except for the Easter holiday period) and in November. The rest of the year falls into the shoulder-season category, although it's worth hunting for special deals at any time. London is the main hub for discounted fares. It's often

CLIMATE CHANGE & TRAVEL

Climate change is a serious threat to the ecosystems that humans rely upon, and air travel is the fastest-growing contributor to the problem. Lonely Planet regards travel, overall, as a global benefit, but believes we all have a responsibility to limit our personal impact on global warming.

Flying & Climate Change

Pretty much every form of motorised travel generates CO_2 (the main cause of human-induced climate change) but planes are far and away the worst offenders, not just because of the sheer distances they allow us to travel, but because they release greenhouse gases high into the atmosphere. The statistics are frightening: two people taking a return flight between Europe and the USA will contribute as much to climate change as an average household's gas and electricity consumption over a whole year.

Carbon-Offset Schemes

Climatecare.org and other websites use 'carbon calculators' that allow travellers to offset the level of greenhouse gases they are responsible for with financial contributions to sustainable-travel schemes that reduce global warming – including projects in India, Honduras, Kazakhstan and Uganda.

Lonely Planet, together with Rough Guides and other concerned partners in the travel industry, support the carbon-offset scheme run by climatecare.org. Lonely Planet offsets all of its staff and author travel.

For more information check out our website: www.lonelyplanet.com.

---

slightly cheaper to fly into Jo'burg, than directly to Cape Town. Note that fares quoted in this book for international and domestic flights are full-fare economy. Always ask about seasonal and advance-purchase discounts, and other special rates, and always check the airline websites for online deals. Useful online ticket sellers include the following:

Cheap Tickets (www.cheaptickets.com)
Cheapflights (www.cheapflights.co.uk)
Expedia (www.expedia.co.uk, www.expedia.ca)
Flight Centre (www.flightcentre.com)
Flights.com (www.flights.com)
LowestFare.com (www.lowestfare.com)
OneTravel.com (www.onetravel.com)
Orbitz (www.orbitz.com)
STA Travel (www.statravel.com)
Travel.com.au (www.travel.com.au) Bookings from Australia.
Travel Jungle (www.traveljungle.co.uk)
Travelocity (www.travelocity.com)

COURIER FLIGHTS

Courier fares can be an inexpensive way of getting to South Africa, although you may have to surrender all your baggage allowance, take only carry-on luggage, and have limited or no flexibility with flight dates and times. Most courier flights are

into Jo'burg, with some into Cape Town. The **Air Courier Association** (www.aircourier.org) is a good place to start looking; you'll need to pay a modest membership fee to access its fares. Be aware that many of the advertised courier fares are for one way only.

INTERCONTINENTAL (ROUND-THE-WORLD) TICKETS

Round-the-world (RTW) tickets give you a limited period (usually a year) to circumnavigate the globe. You can go anywhere that the carrying airline and its partners go, as long as you stay within the set mileage or number of stops, and don't backtrack. RTW tickets that include Jo'burg or Cape Town start at around UK£1500 from the UK (about A$3000 from Australia). While it's possible to include both Jo'burg and Cape Town on a RTW itinerary, this usually means flying into one city and out of the other. In between the two cities you'll need to travel overland or arrange a domestic flight.

Travel agents can also put together 'alternative' RTW tickets, which are more expensive, but more flexible, than standard RTW itineraries. If you want a multiple-stop itinerary without the cost of a RTW ticket, consider combining tickets from two low-cost airlines.

Some online RTW ticket sellers:

Airbrokers (www.airbrokers.com) For travel originating in North America.

Airtreks (www.airtreks.com) For travel originating in Canada or the USA.

Oneworld (www.oneworld.com) An airline alliance offering RTW packages.

Roundtheworldflights.com (www.roundtheworld flights.com) For travel originating in the UK.

Star Alliance (www.staralliance.com) An airline alliance offering RTW packages.

From Africa

There are good connections between Jo'burg and most major African cities on SAA and on regional airlines.

Antananarivo, Madagascar Air Madagascar (www .airmadagascar.mg) Connections to Mauritius and Réunion.

Bulawayo, Zimbabwe Air Zimbabwe (www.airzim.co.zw)

Dar es Salaam, Tanzania SAA (www.flysaa.com); Kenya Airways (www.kenya-airways.com)

Gaborone, Botswana Air Botswana (www.airbotswana .co.bw)

Harare, Zimbabwe Air Zimbabwe; Comair (www.comair .co.za); Kulula.com (www.kulula.com)

Lagos, Nigeria SAA

Lusaka, Zambia Kulula.com; SAA

Maputo, Mozambique SAA; Linhas Aéreas de Moçam-bique (www.lam.co.mz)

Mauritius Air Mauritius (www.airmauritius.com)

Nairobi, Kenya SAA; Kenya Airways

Victoria Falls, Zimbabwe side Air Zimbabwe; Comair

Vilankulo, Mozambique Pelican Air Services (www .pelicanair.co.za) Some flights via Mpumalanga Kruger International Airport, and all with connections to Mozam-bique's Bazaruto Archipelago.

Windhoek, Namibia Comair; Kulula.com; Air Namibia (www.airnamibia.com.na) Air Namibia also has direct flights between Windhoek and Cape Town.

Also check with **1time** (www.1time.co.za), which is planning to start some regional flights. Most intra-African flights have set pric-ing, with little of the competition-driven discounting that you'll find in other parts of the world. However, there are sometimes good deals available. For round-trip fares, always ask about excursion rates and stu-dent discounts. Discounters include **Rennies Travel** (www.renniestravel.com) and **STA Travel** (www .statravel.co.za). Both have offices throughout Southern Africa. **Flight Centre** (☎ 0860 400 727, 011-778 1720; www.flightcentre.co.za) has offices in Jo'burg, Cape Town and several other cities.

The only commercial flight to/from Le-sotho is SAAirlink's three-times daily run between Jo'burg and Moshoeshoe airport (one hour).

Swaziland Airlink, a division of SAAir-link, flies three times daily between Mat-sapha and Jo'burg (one hour). Swazi Express flights link Swaziland's Matsapha airport with Durban (one hour), with con-nections on to Maputo and Vilankulo in Mozambique.

From Asia

You can fly to Jo'burg direct from Singa-pore (10½ hours, Singapore Airlines), Hong Kong (13 hours, Cathay Pacific) and Kuala Lumpur (10½ hours, Malaysia Airlines. It's also possible to connect from Asia (Singapore, Hong Kong and Mumbai) to Mauritius on Air Mauritius, and then from there to Jo'burg (four hours between Mauritius and Jo'burg). Singapore, Hong Kong and Bangkok are the best places to shop for discount tickets. Some useful ticket discounters:

Four Seas Tours (☎ 2200 7760; www.fourseastravel .com/English) Hong Kong.

No 1 Travel (☎ 03 3205 6073; www.no1-travel.com) Japan.

STA Travel Bangkok (☎ 02-236 0262; www.statravel .co.th); Singapore (☎ 6737 7188; www.statravel.com.sg); Hong Kong (☎ 2736 1618; www.statravel.com.hk); Japan (☎ 03 5391 2922; www.statravel.co.jp)

STIC Travels (www.stictravel.com) Delhi (☎ 11-233 57 468); Mumbai (☎ 22-221 81 431). Also has offices in dozens of other Indian cities.

From Australia & New Zealand

There are direct flights from Sydney on Qan-tas, and from Perth on Qantas and SAA, to Jo'burg and Cape Town (flying time about 14 hours from Sydney, 10½ hours from Perth). Air Mauritius has a few direct flights from Perth to Mauritius with a stopover, fol-lowed by a direct flight to Jo'burg. Alterna-tively, you can connect on Air Mauritius via Singapore, Hong Kong or Mumbai (Bom-bay). Ticket discounters include **Flight Centre** (☎ Australia-wide 131 600; www.flightcentre.com.au) and **STA Travel** (☎ 1300-733 035; www.statravel.com .au), both with branches around the country. Singapore Airlines and Malaysia Airlines are both worth checking for special deals, and return tickets to/from the UK via Jo'burg and Asia are also worth looking into.

TRANSPORT

There are no direct flights from New Zealand; the best options are going via Australia, Singapore or Malaysia. **Flight Centre** (☎ 0800-243 544; www.flightcentre.co.nz) and **STA Travel** (☎ 0508-782 872; www.statravel.co.nz) both have branches throughout the country. The site www.travel.co.nz is recommended for online bookings.

Also check with some of the operators listed on p631.

From Canada & the USA

SAA flies direct from New York and Atlanta to Jo'burg (17½ hours), and this is generally one of the least expensive routings. Otherwise, the cheapest routing is generally to London on a discounted transatlantic ticket, where you can then purchase a separate ticket on to Johannesburg or Cape Town. Most of the airlines mentioned under Continental Europe also offer through-fares from North America. From the US west coast, you can sometimes get good deals via Asia. Malaysia Airlines flies from Los Angeles to Kuala Lumpur, from where you can connect to Jo'burg and Cape Town.

Discount travel agents in the USA are known as consolidators (although you won't see a sign on the door saying 'Consolidator'). San Francisco is the ticket-consolidator capital of America, although some good deals can be found in Los Angeles, New York and other big cities. See p624 for recommended online booking agencies. Other discounters:

Flight Centre (☎ 888-967 5355; www.flightcentre.ca) Canada.

STA Travel (☎ 800-781 4040; www.statravel.com) USA; for travellers under 26.

Travel Cuts (☎ 800-667 2887; www.travelcuts.com) Canada.

Some of the operators listed, p632, also sell flight-only packages.

From Continental Europe

You can fly to South Africa from any European capital, with the major hubs being Paris, Amsterdam, Frankfurt and, to a lesser extent, Zurich. All are within an approximately nine-hour flight of Jo'burg. All the European airlines listed on p622 fly into Jo'burg, with several, including British Airways and KLM, also flying into Cape Town. Some will allow you to fly into one city and out of the other for no extra charge. The following agencies offer discounted fares:

Airfair (☎ 020 620 5121; www.airfair.nl) Netherlands.

Anyway (☎ 0892 893 892; www.anyway.fr) France.

Barcelo Viajes (☎ 902 116 226; www.barceloviajes .com) Spain.

CTS Viaggi (☎ 06 462 0431; www.cts.it) Italy; specialising in student and youth travel.

Just Travel (☎ 089 747 3330; www.justtravel.de) Germany.

Lastminute (www.lastminute.fr; www.lastminute.de) France; Germany.

Nouvelles Frontières (www.nouvelles-frontieres.fr, www.nouvelles-frontieres.es) France and Spain.

OTU Voyages (www.otu.fr) France.

STA Travel (☎ 01805-456 422; www.statravel.de) Germany; for travellers under the age of 26.

Voyageurs du Monde (☎ 01 40 15 11 15; www.vdm .com) France.

From the Middle East

The best connections are to Jo'burg from Cairo (Air Kenya via Nairobi), and from Dubai (Emirates). Agencies to try in the region include the following:

Al-Rais Travels (www.alrais.com) Dubai.

Egypt Panorama Tours (☎ 02-359 0200; www .eptours.com) Cairo.

Orion-Tour (www.oriontour.com) Istanbul.

The Israel Student Travel Association (ISTA; ☎ 02-625 7257) Jerusalem.

From South America

SAA and **Varig** (www.varig.com.br) link São Paulo and Jo'burg (about nine hours), with connections in South America to Rio de Janeiro, Brasília and various other cities. Malaysia Airlines flies between Buenos Aires, Cape Town and Jo'burg. Discounters include the following:

ASATEJ (☎ 54-011 4114-7595; www.asatej.com) Argentina.

IVI Tours (☎ 0212-993 6082; www.ividiomas.com) Venezuela.

The Student Travel Bureau (☎ 3038 1555; www.stb .com.br) Brazil.

From the UK & Ireland

Airlines flying between London and South Africa include British Airways, Virgin Atlantic and SAA. Flying time is about 13½ hours, and fares are very competitive. There are no direct flights between Ireland and South Africa. You'll need to connect via London or a Continental European capital.

Most British travel agents are registered with the **Association of British Travel Agents** (ABTA; www.abta.com), which will give you some protection if the agent you buy your ticket from goes out of business. Tickets from unregistered bucket shops are riskier but sometimes cheaper. London is the best place to buy a ticket, but specialist agencies elsewhere in the UK can provide comparable value. Recommended travel agencies include the following:

Bridge the World (☎ 0870 444 7474; www.b-t-w.co.uk)

Flight Centre (☎ 0870 890 8099; flightcentre.co.uk)

Flightbookers (☎ 0870 814 4001; www.ebookers.com)

North-South Travel (☎ 01245 608 291; www.north southtravel.co.uk) North-South Travel donates part of its profit to projects in the developing world.

Quest Travel (☎ 0870 442 3542; www.questtravel .com)

STA Travel (☎ 0870 160 0599; www.statravel.co.uk) For travellers under the age of 26

Trailfinders (www.trailfinders.co.uk)

Travel Bag (☎ 0870 890 1456; www.travelbag.co.uk)

Also check ads in the travel pages of the weekend broadsheet newspapers, in *Time Out,* the *Evening Standard,* in the free online magazine **TNT** (www.tntmagazine .com) and in the free *SA Times,* which is aimed at South Africans in the UK.

LAND
Bicycle

There are no restrictions on bringing your own bicycle into South Africa, Lesotho or Swaziland. Two helpful sources of background information are the **International Bicycle Fund** (☎ in the USA 206-767 0848; www.ibike .org) and **SA-Cycling** (www.sa-cycling.com).

Border Crossings
BOTSWANA

There are 18 official South Africa/Botswana border posts. All are open between 8am and 4pm, and many have longer hours.

Grobler's Bridge (☯ 8am-6pm) Northwest of Polokwane/ Pietersburg.

Kapfontein/Tlokweng Gate (☯ 6am-10pm) North of Zeerust; a main border post.

McCarthy's Rest (☯ 8am-4.30pm) Near Kgalagadi Transfrontier Park.

Ramatlhabama (☯ 6am-8pm) North of Mafikeng; a main border post.

Skilpadshek/Pioneer Gate (☯ 6am-10pm) North-west of Zeerust; a main border post.

Some of the more remote crossings are impassable to 2WD vehicles, and may be closed completely during periods of high water. Otherwise, the crossings are hassle-free.

LESOTHO

All of landlocked Lesotho's borders (listed next) are with South Africa and are straightforward to cross. The main crossing is at Maseru Bridge, east of Bloemfontein; queues here are often very long exiting Lesotho and, on some weekend evenings, coming into Lesotho, so use other posts if possible.

LESOTHO BORDERS

Border crossing	Opening hours	Nearest Lesotho/ South Africa town
Caledonspoort	6am-10pm	Butha-Buthe/ Fouriesburg
Ficksburg Bridge	24hr	Maputsoe/Ficksburg
Makhaleng Bridge	8am-4pm	Mohale's Hoek/ Zastron
Maseru Bridge	24hr	Maseru/Ladybrand
Nkonkoana Gate	8am-4pm	Sehlabathebe/ Bushman's Nek
Ongeluksnek	8am-4pm	Mphaki/Matatiele
Peka Bridge	8am-4pm	Peka/Clocolan
Qacha's Nek	7am-8pm	Qacha's Nek/ Matatiele
Ramatseliso's Gate	8am-4pm	Tsoelike/Matatiele
Sani Pass	8am-4pm	Mokhotlong/ Himeville
Sephapo's Gate	8am-4pm	Mafeteng/ Boesmanskop
Tele Bridge	8am-10pm	Quthing/Sterkspruit
Van Rooyen's Gate	6am-10pm	Mafeteng/Wepener

MOZAMBIQUE

The South Africa/Mozambique border posts are:

Giriyondo (☯ 8am-4pm Oct-Mar, 8am-3pm Apr-Sep) West of Massingir (Mozambique).

Komatipoort/Ressano Garcia (☯ 6am-10pm) East of Nelspruit and heavily travelled.

Kosi Bay/Ponta d'Ouro (☯ 8am-4pm) On the coast, well north of Durban.

Pafuri (☯ 8am-4pm) In Kruger National Park's north-eastern corner.

TRANSPORT

NAMIBIA

South Africa/Namibia border posts include those at Nakop/Ariamsvlei (24 hours) west of Upington; at Vioolsdrif/Noordoewer (24 hours) north of Springbok and en route to/from Cape Town; and at Rietfontein/Aroab (8am to 4.30pm) just south of Kgalagadi Transfrontier Park. It's not possible to cross the border at Kgalagadi Transfrontier Park itself; Rietfontein is the closest crossing. There's also a border post at Alexander Bay/Oranjemund (6am to 10pm) on the coast, but public access is usually not permitted. Note that Namibian visas are not available at any of these border posts.

SWAZILAND

There are 11 South Africa/Swaziland border posts, all of which are hassle-free. Note that small posts close at 4pm. The busiest crossing (and a good place to pick up lifts) is at Oshoek/Ngwenya (7am to 10pm) about 360km southeast of Pretoria. Some others include the following:

Golela/Lavumisa (☼ 7am-10pm) En route between Durban and Swaziland's Ezulwini Valley.

Josefsdal/Bulembu (☼ 8am-4pm) Along the unpaved road from Piggs Peak to Barberton (Mpumalanga) and tricky in wet weather.

Mahamba (☼ 7am-10pm) The best crossing to use from Piet Retief in Mpumalanga.

Mananga (☼ 7am-6pm) Southwest of Komatipoort.

Matsamo/Jeppe's Reef (☼ 7am-8pm) Southwest of Malelane and a possible route to Kruger National Park.

Onverwacht/Salitje (☼ 8am-6pm) North of Pongola in KwaZulu-Natal.

The main Swaziland/Mozambique border is at busy Lomahasha/Namaacha (7am to 5pm) in the extreme northeast of the country, with another, quieter border post at Goba/Mhlumeni. Visas for Mozambique (which are no longer required for South African nationals) are currently being issued at the border, but it's better and cheaper to get them in Mbabane.

There's an E5 road tax for vehicles entering Swaziland. If you're continuing from Swaziland into Mozambique, your car must have two red hazard triangles in the boot in case of a breakdown. All of Swaziland's borders can be comfortably crossed in a 2WD, except for Josefsdal/Bulembu, which is possible in a 2WD but smoother with a 4WD.

ZIMBABWE

The only border post between Zimbabwe and South Africa is at Beitbridge (24 hours) on the Limpopo River. There's lots of smuggling, so searches are thorough and queues often long. The closest South African town to the border is Musina (15km south), where you can change money.

When entering or leaving South Africa, vehicles pay a toll at the border to use the Limpopo Bridge. South Africans need a visa (free) to get into Zimbabwe but can obtain it at the border. Most other nationalities, including Commonwealth and US passport holders, require visas, which are available at the border and payable in US dollars only.

Ignore the touts on the Zimbabwe side trying to 'help' you through Zimbabwe immigration and customs. Despite their insistence, there's no charge for the government forms needed for immigration.

Bus

Numerous buses cross the borders between South Africa and all of its neighbours. These are the most efficient way to travel overland, unless you have your own vehicle. Other than sometimes lengthy queues, there are usually no hassles. At the border, you'll need to disembark to take care of visa formalities, then reboard your same bus and continue on. Visa prices are not included in the ticket price for transborder routes. Many bus lines offer student discounts, upon presentation of a student ID.

It's also possible to travel to/from all of South Africa's neighbours by local minibus taxi. A few routes go direct, though sometimes it's necessary to walk across the border and change vehicles on the other side.

Car & Motorcycle

If you're arriving in South Africa via car or motorcycle, you'll need the vehicle's registration papers, liability insurance and your driving licence (see p635). You'll also need a *carnet de passage en douane,* which acts as a temporary waiver of import duty. The carnet – which should be arranged through your local automobile association – should specify any expensive spare parts that you're planning to carry with you, such as a gearbox. South African–registered vehicles don't need a carnet to visit any of South Africa's neighbouring countries.

The requirements for entering Swaziland and Lesotho are the same as for South Africa. If you're driving a car rented in South Africa and plan to take it across international borders, including into Lesotho or Swaziland, you'll need to get a permission form from your rental company.

For information on road rules, see p639.

Border posts generally don't have petrol stations or repair shops; you'll need to go to the nearest large town.

From Botswana

BUS

From Jo'burg/Pretoria, **Intercape Mainliner** (☎ 0861 287 287, 021-380 4400; www.intercape.co.za) runs daily buses to Gaborone (R150, six hours). A cheaper but less safe and less comfortable alternative is one of the minibuses that run throughout the day between Jo'burg and Gaborone (about R100, six hours) via Mafikeng (North-West Province). In Gaborone, these leave from the northwest corner of the main bus terminal, starting at 6am. In Jo'burg, departures are from Park Station. To do the trip in stages, take a City Link bus from Jo'burg to Mafikeng, from where there are direct minibuses over the border to Lobatse (1½ hours). There are also direct minibuses between Jo'burg and Palapye (Botswana) via Martin's Drift (eight hours).

TRAIN

There are no cross-border trains, but it's possible to travel the Botswana leg of the journey between Francistown, near the border with Zimbabwe, and Lobatse, near the border with South Africa, via Gaborone.

From Lesotho

BUS

Big Sky Coaches (www.bigskycoaches.co.za) runs two buses daily in each direction between Bloemfontein and Maseru Bridge (R35, three hours), with express services from Bloemfontein (two hours) on Friday and on Saturday morning, and from Maseru Bridge on Friday and on Sunday afternoon. Tickets are sold at the Big Sky booths at Bloemfontein's Central Park, and on the bus at Maseru Bridge.

Via minibus taxi, the quickest connections are from Bloemfontein to Botshabelo (Mtabelo; R30, one hour), and then from there to Maseru (R15, 1½ hours). There

are also at least three buses weekly between Jo'burg and Maseru (six to seven hours), and daily minibus taxis between both Jo'burg and Ladybrand (16km from the Maseru Bridge border crossing) and Maseru. All these routes will bring you into Maseru coming from South Africa; leaving Maseru, you'll need to go to the South Africa side of Maseru Bridge.

Other useful connections include a daily minibus taxi between Mokhotlong (Lesotho) and Underberg (South Africa) via Sani Pass (see p565); and several taxis daily between Qacha's Nek (Lesotho) and Matatiele (South Africa; about R15, 45 minutes). If you're travelling between Jo'burg and northern Lesotho, take a minibus taxi to Ficksburg, cross the border, and then get a minibus taxi on to Butha-Buthe and points north. There are sometimes direct taxis between Jo'burg and Butha-Buthe via Caledonspoort border (about R125, five hours).

CAR

The easiest entry points for car and motorcycle are on the northern and western sides of the country. Most of the entry points to the south and east are unpaved, though all are possible in a 2WD except Sani Pass. You'll need a 4WD to enter Lesotho via Sani Pass; it's possible to exit via this route with a 2WD with sufficient clearance, but a 4WD is recommended.

It's more economical to rent a car in South Africa than in Lesotho (you'll need the necessary permission papers, see p636). There's a road tax of M5 (M4 at smaller border posts) payable on entering Lesotho.

From Mozambique

BUS

Several large 'luxury' buses go daily between Jo'burg/Pretoria and Maputo via Nelspruit and Komatipoort (R160 to R220, eight to nine hours). These include the following:

Greyhound (☎ 012-323 1154; www.greyhound.co.za)

Intercape Mainliner (☎ 0861 287 287, 021-380 4400; www.intercape.co.za)

Panthera Azul (☎ 011-618 8811, in Maputo 021-302 077, 302 083; www.pantherazul.com)

Translux (☎ 011-774 3333; www.translux.co.za)

You can also travel in each direction on these lines between Nelspruit and Maputo, but not between Nelspruit and Jo'burg.

Alternatively, the **Baz Bus** (☎ 021-439 2323; www.bazbus.com) links Jo'burg/Pretoria, Nelspruit and Durban with Manzini (Swaziland), from where you can get a minibus taxi to Maputo. See p417 for more on the Baz Bus.

Panthera Azul has buses three times weekly between Durban and Maputo (R230, 8½ hours) via Big Bend (Swaziland) and Namaacha.

Minibuses depart from Maputo daily in the morning for the Namaacha/Lomahasha border post (US$2, 1½ hours) with some continuing on until Manzini (US$4.50, 3½ hours).

CAR

For travel to/from Mozambique via the Kosi Bay border, you'll need your own vehicle (4WD is necessary on the Mozambique side). Alternatively, most places to stay in Ponta d'Ouro (Mozambique) do transfers for about US$20. Hitching between the border and Ponta d'Ouro is easy on weekends and during South African school holidays.

There's a good sealed toll road connecting Jo'burg with Maputo via Ressano Garcia, with tolls on the South African side between Middelburg and Witbank, at Machadodorp and 45km east of Nelspruit.

From Mozambique to Swaziland via either Namaacha or Goba, the road is good tarmac, and easily negotiated with 2WD.

TRAIN

The daily (except Saturday) *Komati* train operated by Shosholoza Meyl (see p641) links Jo'burg and Komatipoort via Pretoria and Nelspruit (1st//2nd/economy class from R185/130/70, 13 to 14 hours). Once at Komatipoort, you can change to the Mozambican train to Maputo (Mtc15,000, economy class only, five hours), but as service on the Mozambique side is so slow, it is better to take a minibus (US$3.50, 1½ hours). Even if you take the train the whole way, you'll need to buy the ticket for the Mozambique section at the border.

From Namibia
BUS

The **Intercape Mainliner** (www.intercape.co.za) runs four times weekly between Cape Town and Windhoek via Upington (R485, 20 hours). It's also possible to travel between Jo'burg

and Windhoek with Intercape Mainliner (R615, 25 hours) on these same days, with a change of buses in Upington.

TRAIN

The **Trans-Namib** (☎ Namibia 061-298 2175; www.trans namib.com.na) 'StarLine' runs twice weekly between Windhoek and Upington (25 hours).

From Swaziland
BUS

The best connections are on the **Baz Bus** (☎ 021-439 2323; www.bazbus.com), which runs from Jo'burg/Pretoria to Manzini via Nelspruit, and between Durban and Manzini via the KwaZulu-Natal coast.

Minibus taxis run daily between Jo'burg (Park Station), Mbabane and Manzini (R7, four hours), between Manzini and Durban (R120, eight hours), and between Manzini and Maputo (Mozambique; US$4.50, 2½ hours). For many routes, you'll need to change minibuses at the border. Most long-distance taxis leave early in the morning.

HITCHING

If you're hitching into Swaziland, most South Africans enter through the Oshoek/Ngwenya border post. The casinos in the north (near the Matsamo/Jeppe's Reef border post) and southwest (near the Mahamba border post) attract traffic, especially on weekends, and are also good places to look for lifts into/out of the country.

CROSS-BORDER RAIL LINKS

Other than the *Trans-Namib* (above) and the Komati cross-border connection (left), there are no regularly scheduled passenger rail services between South Africa and neighbouring countries. However, some of the special trains listed on p642 do cross-border routes. *Shongololo Express* has a 16-day South Africa routing that also takes in Mbabane (Swaziland), Bulawayo, Great Zimbabwe and Victoria Falls (all Zimbabwe) and Maputo (Mozambique), and another linking Cape Town with various points in Namibia. *Rovos Rail* has a route linking Pretoria with Swapkomund (Namibia), and another that passes through Victoria Falls and Bulawayo en route between Cape Town and Dar es Salaam (Tanzania).

See p640 for general information on hitching.

From Zimbabwe

BUS

At the time of research, bus services between Jo'burg and Zimbabwe were suspended, due in part to fuel shortages. For connections between Jo'burg and the border, see p417.

SEA

South Africa is an important stop on world shipping routes. Cape Town in particular is a major port of call for cruise ships. Many cruise ships also stop at Durban, and several freighter lines sailing from Europe have passenger cabins. It's also possible to find both cruise and freighter lines linking South African ports with various points in Mozambique (including the Bazaruto Archipelago), Madagascar and Mauritius.

The thrill of approaching the tip of the continent by sea doesn't come cheap. Even on the freighters, passenger accommodation is usually comfortable (sometimes even plush) cabins. Expect to pay from about US$2500 per person one way for a 23- to 27-day journey from a UK port to Cape Town, often via the Canary Islands. Fares from South Africa tend to be lower than fares to South Africa. Some useful contacts:

Freighter World Cruises Inc (☎ 800-531 7774, 626-449 3106; www.freighterworld.com) Based in the USA.

Royal Mail Ship St Helena (☎ 020-7575 6480; www.rms-st-helena.com) Based in the UK.

Safmarine (☎ 021-408 6911; www.safmarine.com) This company actively seeks passengers for its container ships, which sail to many of the world's major ports; fares are often negotiable.

Starlight Lines (www.starlight.co.za) A good contact for connections to Mozambique, Madagascar and Mauritius; based in South Africa.

Strand Voyages (☎ 020-7766 8220; www.strandtravel.co.uk) Based in the UK.

Tall Ships (www.tallships.co.za) Has cargo ships between Durban and various Mozambican ports that sometimes take passengers; based in South Africa.

The Cruise People (☎ 020-7723 2450, 0800 526 313; www.cruisepeople.co.uk) Based in the UK.

Another good source of information about routes and the shipping lines plying them is the *OAG Cruise & Ferry Guide*, published quarterly by the **Reed Travel Group** (☎ 01582-600 111) in the UK. Durban is one of the better places to look for a lift on private yachts sailing up the East African coast.

TOURS

Dozens of tour and safari companies organise package tours to South Africa. As an alternative, if you prefer a more independent approach, you can prebook flights and hotels for the first few nights, then join tours locally (see p641). Almost all operators include Kruger National Park and Cape Town and the Peninsula in their itineraries. For special interests (bird-watching, flower-watching etc), check the advertisements in specialist magazines. Following is a list of tour companies:

Australia

Adventure World (☎ 02-8913 0755; www.adventureworld.com.au) Offers a wide range of tours, safaris, car hire and hotel packages in South and Southern Africa.

African Wildlife Safaris (☎ 03-9696 2899; www.africanwildlifesafaris.com.au) Customised wildlife safaris in South Africa and neighbouring countries.

Peregrine Travel (☎ 03-8601 4444; www.peregrine.net.au) Caters to all budgets, from overland truck tours to upscale wildlife safaris, and including a South Africa and Swaziland cycling itinerary.

France

Makila Voyages (☎ 01 42 96 80 00; www.makila.fr) Upper-end tailored tours in South Africa and Swaziland, plus safaris.

UK

Dragoman (☎ 0870-499 4475; www.dragoman.co.uk) Overland tours.

Exodus Travels (☎ 0870-240 5550; www.exodustravels.co.uk) Organises a variety of tours, including overland trips, and walking and cycling itineraries, covering South Africa, Lesotho and Swaziland.

Guerba (☎ 01373-826 611; www.guerba.com) Overland tours.

In the Saddle (☎ 01299-272 997; www.inthesaddle.com) Strictly for horse aficionados, with various rides in South Africa, including in the Western Cape and in the Greater St Lucia Wetlands Park.

Naturetrek (☎ 01962-733 051; www.naturetrek.co.uk) Specialist nature tours, including springtime wildflower itineraries in Namaqualand and a botanically oriented tour in the Drakensberg and Lesotho.

Temple World (☎ 020-8940 4114; www.templeworld.co.uk) Upper-end luxury 'educational' tours in South

TRANSPORT

632 GETTING AROUND •• Air

Africa, Swaziland and elsewhere in the region focusing on history, ecology and wildlife.

Wildlife Encounters (☎ 01737-214 214; www.wild life-encounters.co.uk) Train-based safaris in South Africa, including Kruger National Park.

USA

Adventure Centre (☎ 510-654 1879, 800-228 2747; www.adventurecenter.com) Budget to midrange tours including a 22-day South Africa circuit that takes in bits of Swaziland and Lesotho; it's also the US agent for several overland operators.

Africa Adventure Company (☎ 954-491 8877, 800-882 9453; www.africa-adventure.com) Upper-end wildlife safaris, including the private reserves around Kruger National Park, plus other itineraries in Cape Town and along the Garden Route.

Born Free Safaris (☎ 800-472 3274; www.born freesafaris.com) Offers a good range of Cape to Kruger itineraries.

Bushtracks (☎ 707-433 4492, 800-995 8689; www .bushtracks.com) Private air luxury safaris.

International Expeditions(☎ 205-428 1700, 800-633 4734; www.ietravel.com) Upper-end, wildlife-oriented safaris that sometimes take in Cape Town and other South Africa destinations.

Wilderness Travel (☎ 510-558 2488, 800-368 2794; www.wildernesstravel.com) Offers various southern Africa packages, including a two-week Cape Town and Garden Route itinerary.

GETTING AROUND

AIR
Airlines in South Africa, Lesotho & Swaziland

In addition to being the international flag carrier, **South African Airways** (SAA; ☎ 0861-359 722, 011-978 5313; www.flysaa.com) is the main domestic carrier, with an extensive and efficient route network to major cities. Its subsidiaries, **SAAirlink** (☎ 011-978 5313; www.saairlink .co.za) and **SA Express** (☎ 011-978 5577; www.sa express.co.za), also service domestic routes and share SAA's excellent safety record.

Domestic fares aren't cheap. If you plan to take some internal flights, check with a travel agent before you leave home for special deals on tickets and air passes. If these are available, it may be worth booking your domestic flights from home. It can also sometimes be cheaper to book domestic connections from home if these can be tied into your international flight

ticket. Another way to save significantly – whether you're at home or already in South Africa – is to book online rather than going into a travel agent or ticket office, which can sometimes save you up to 50% of the standard quoted ticket price. General fare and route information is given in the regional chapters, and local travel agencies are listed under the Information sections for major cities.

In addition to SAA and its affiliates, airlines flying domestically include those following:

1time (☎ 0861-345345; www.1time.co.za) No-frills flights linking Jo'burg with Cape Town, Durban and East London, George and Port Elizabeth, and between Cape Town and East London. Also offers car rentals.

Comair (☎ 0860-435 922, 011-921 0222; www.comair .co.za) Operates British Airways flights within Africa, and has flights linking Cape Town, Durban, Jo'burg and Port Elizabeth.

Kulula.com (☎ 0861-585 852; www.kulula.com) Operates no-frills flights linking Jo'burg, Cape Town, Durban, George, Port Elizabeth and Mpumalanga Kruger. Also offers airport transfer services and car rentals.

Nationwide Airlines (☎ 0861 -737 737, 011-344 7200; www.nationwideair.co.za) Operates in partnership with Virgin Atlantic, and has flights linking Jo'burg, Cape Town, Durban, George, Port Elizabeth, Sun City and Nelspruit.

Swazi Express Airways (☎ 518 6840, 031-408 1115; www.swaziexpress.com) Several flights weekly connecting Manzini with Durban, and with Maputo and Vilankulo (Mozambique); charter service in Swaziland and surrounding region.

Swaziland Airlink (☎ 518 6155; www.saairlink.co.za) Daily flights between Jo'burg and Manzini/Matsapha.

BICYCLE
South Africa

As long as you're fit enough to handle the many hills, South Africa offers some rewarding cycling. It has scenic and diverse terrain, an abundance of camping places, and many good roads, most of which don't carry much traffic (although most don't have any sort of shoulder). The Cape Peninsula and the Winelands of the Western Cape are excellent biking areas. The Wild Coast in the Eastern Cape is beautiful and challenging, while the northern lowveld offers wide plains.

When planning, keep in mind that much of the country (except for Western Cape and the west coast) gets most of its rain in summer (late November to March), in the form of violent thunderstorms. When it isn't raining, summer days can be unpleasantly hot, especially in the steamy lowveld. Distances between major towns are often long but, except in isolated areas such as the Karoo or Limpopo Province, you're rarely very far from a village or a farmhouse.

Safety is another consideration. Before heading off anywhere, contact other cyclists through local cycling clubs or bicycle shops to get the most recent information on the routes you're considering. **SA-Cycling** (www .sa-cycling.com) posts cyclists' diaries, suggests several routes, and has listings of cycling clubs. Other things to remember are that it's illegal to cycle on highways, and that roads near urban areas are too busy for comfort.

Mixing cycling with public transport doesn't work well, as most bus lines don't want bicycles in their luggage holds, and minibuses don't carry luggage on the roof. In some cases, the only alternative may be to arrange transporting your bicycle with a carrier company.

Mountain bikes and their spare parts are widely available. However, it's often difficult to find specialised parts for touring bikes, especially away from Cape Town and Jo'burg. It's worth establishing a relationship with a good bike shop in a city before you head off into the veld, in case you need something couriered to you. Bring a good lock to counter the ever-present risk of theft, leave the bicycle inside your accommodation (preferably inside your room) and chain it to something solid.

Lesotho & Swaziland

Both Lesotho and Swaziland are excellent cycling destinations, especially Lesotho, although the country's mountainous terrain means that it's only for the fit. You'll need a mountain bike for both countries; stock up on spares in South Africa. The main weather constraints are icy roads in winter in Lesotho, and thunderstorms and flooding in both countries during the summer.

The classic mountain-bike route in Lesotho is over the Sani Pass, but there are almost unlimited other options as well. It's sometimes possible to rent bicycles through some of the lodges on the South Africa side of the Sani Pass.

Swaziland is also ideally suited for cycling, except for main towns and the heavily travelled Ezulwini Valley. Other options include the shorter mountain-bike trails in Hlane Royal National Park and in Mlilwane Wildlife Sanctuary, both of which rent bicycles.

It's not common to transport bicycles on public transport in Lesotho and Swaziland, but you can usually arrange something with the driver.

Hire & Purchase

If you'll be doing extensive cycling, it's best to bring your own bicycle. For day rides, some hostels in South Africa have short-term mountain bike rental. Rentals can also sometimes be arranged through bike shops in Cape Town and other cities, though you'll usually be required to leave a credit-card deposit.

There's a good selection of mountain bikes for sale in all larger South African cities, with Cape Town probably the best place to look. For touring bikes, the main markets are Cape Town and Jo'burg. To resell your bicycle at the end of your trip, hostel bulletin boards are good places to advertise.

BOAT

Despite South Africa's long coastline, there are few opportunities to travel by boat. The most likely possibilities are taking a ship between Cape Town and Durban, and between Port Elizabeth and Durban. Useful contacts include the local offices of **Safmarine** (☎ 021-4086911; www.safmarine.com) and **Tall Ships** (www.tallships.co.za), as well as local yacht clubs. Also check out the informative www.cruiser.co.za, which posts a bulletin board matching up crews with ships.

BUS
South Africa

Buses in South Africa aren't the deal that they are in many other countries. However, together with the less-appealing minibus taxis (see p640), they're the main form of public transport, with a reliable and reasonably comfortable network linking all major cities. Note that many long-distance services run through the night.

A good alternative to the standard bus lines is **Baz Bus** (☎ 021-439 2323; www.bazbus.com), catering almost exclusively to backpackers and travellers. It offers hop-on, hop-off

TRANSPORT

fares and door-to-door service between Cape Town and Jo'burg via the Northern Drakensberg, Durban and the Garden Route. It also has a loop from Durban via Zululand and Swaziland to Jo'burg, passing near Kruger National Park. Point-to-point fares are more expensive than on the other major lines, but can work out more economically if you take advantage of the hop-on/hop-off feature. It's also worth checking out its one- and two-week travel passes.

The Baz Bus drops off and picks up at many hostels along the way, and has transfer arrangements with those off the main routes for a nominal extra charge. You can book directly with Baz Bus, as well as with most hostels.

In partnership with Translux, **City to City** (☎ 011-774 3333, 0861-589 282; www.translux.co.za) has taken over the routes that once carried people from the homelands to and from the big cities during the apartheid regime. Services are less expensive than on the other lines, and go to many off-the-beaten-track places, including townships and mining towns. Destinations from Jo'burg include Mthatha, Nelspruit, Hazyview, Beitbridge (for Zimbabwe), Piet Retief and various towns in KwaZulu-Natal. Many services originate at Jo'burg's Park Station transit centre, where there are booking counters and an information desk.

Offering an extensive network, with routes and pricing similar to those for Translux, **Greyhound** (☎ 083-915 9000; www.greyhound.co.za) also has a Jo'burg to Durban route via Zululand and Richards Bay, and offers frequent special deals.

Servicing primarily the western half of the country, plus Nelspruit (en route to Mozambique), **Intercape Mainliner** (☎ 0861 287 287, 021-380 4400; www.intercape.co.za) prices are somewhat less than Translux and Greyhound. For longer hauls, it's worth paying more (about 8% above regular fares) for a reclining seat on one of Intercape's new Sleepliner buses.

SA Roadlink (☎ 011-333 2223; www.saroadlink.co.za) is a new line linking Pretoria and Johannesburg with Bloemfontein, Port Elizabeth, East London, Mthatha, Durban and points in between. Though routes are still limited, prices are very reasonable – generally just above City to City's fares.

The main long-distance bus operator, **Translux** (☎ 011-774 3333, 0861-589 282; www.translux.co.za), has services connecting Cape Town, Knysna, Plettenberg Bay, Durban, Bloemfontein, Port Elizabeth, East London, Mthatha, Nelspruit (en route to Mozambique) and various towns along the Garden Route.

There are no class tiers on any of the bus lines, although Translux, Intercape and Greyhound, as well as SA Roadlink's newer buses would be the equivalent of 'luxury' lines, with air-con and often video and a toilet. City to City's service is no-frills.

Except for Baz Bus, which has it's own pricing structure, fares are roughly calculated by distance, though short runs are disproportionately expensive. Some sample approximate one-way fares/durations: Jo'burg to Cape Town (R440, 19 hours); Jo'burg to Durban (R85 to R150, eight hours); and Cape Town to Knysna (R170, eight hours). Baz Bus one-way fares for hop-on, hop-off service are: Cape Town to Durban via the Garden Route (R1600); Jo'burg–Swaziland–Durban–Drakensberg–Jo'burg loop (R1010).

Prices rise during school holidays; all lines offer student and senior-citizen discounts, and Intercape has backpacker discounts. Also inquire about travel passes, if you'll be taking several bus journeys, and always check with the bus companies to see if they are running any specials, which can sometimes save you up to 40%.

For the main lines, reservations should be made at least 24 hours in advance (or 72 hours in advance for Intercape Mainliner, and as much in advance as possible for travel during peak periods). It's sometimes possible to get a seat at the last minute, but this shouldn't be counted on.

Lesotho

Lesotho has a good network of buses and minibuses (known locally as 'minibus taxis' or – more commonly – just 'taxis') covering most parts of the country. Buses are slightly cheaper than minibus taxis, and somewhat slower, and service all major towns. Minibus taxis also service the major towns, as well as many smaller towns.

For the larger buses, although you'll be quoted long-distance fares, it's best to just buy a ticket to the next major town. Most of the passengers will get off there anyway, which means you'll likely be stuck waiting for the bus to fill up again while other buses leave first. Buying tickets in stages is only slightly more expensive than buying a direct ticket. Heading northeast from Maseru, you usually need to change at Maputsoe, although this also sometimes happens en route into Maputsoe if your bus meets another coming the other way.

There are no classes, and service is very much no-frills. It's not necessary (or possible) to reserve a seat in advance. Most departures are in the morning (generally, the longer the journey, the earlier the departure).

Swaziland

In Swaziland, there are only a few domestic buses, most of which start and terminate at the main stop in the centre of Mbabane. The main form of public transport is minibus. These run almost everywhere, with frequent stops en route, and cost slightly more than buses. Minibuses leave when full; no reservations are necessary. Sample fares include: Mbabane to Manzini (E7, 35 minutes); Mbabane to Piggs Peak (E13, one hour); Manzini to Big Bend (E7, one hour).

CAR & MOTORCYCLE

South Africa is ideal for driving, and away from the main bus and train routes, having your own wheels is the best way to get around. If you're in a group, it's also often the most economical. Most major roads are in excellent condition, and off the main routes there are interesting back roads to explore.

The country is crossed by many national routes (eg N1). On some sections a toll is payable, based on distance. There's always plenty of warning that you're about to enter a toll section (marked by a black 'T' in a yellow circle), and there's always an alternative route (marked by a black 'A' in a yellow circle). On alternative routes, signposting is sparse, generally only directing you to smaller towns or giving route numbers, rather than the direction of the next large city. Smaller roads are numbered (eg R44 – shown in this book as Rte 44), and when you ask directions most people will refer to these numbers rather than destinations, so it pays to have a good road map.

Lesotho and Swaziland are also well-suited to driving, though you'll find more gravel and dirt away from major routes. Main routes in Lesotho are numbered beginning with A1 (Main North Rd), and side routes branching off from these are given 'B' route numbers. Ice is a major hazard in winter.

Swaziland is crossed roughly from west to east by the MR3, which is a major highway as far east as Manzini. Good tarmac roads also connect other major towns; elsewhere you'll find mostly unpaved roads, most in reasonably good condition, except after heavy rains. For more on road conditions, see (p638).

For information on road maps, which are readily available in all three countries, see p613.

Automobile Associations

The **Automobile Association of South Africa** (AASA) ☎ membership 083-843 22, emergencies 083-843 22; www.aasa.co.za) has a limited vehicle breakdown service that can be useful if you'll be driving in the areas it covers. It also has a good supply of maps, available free to members and for sale in many tourist offices and bookstores. For breakdown service, hold onto the window stickers that you get with membership. The initial joining fee is waived for members of many foreign motoring associations, so it's worth bringing your membership details.

In theory, the AASA covers Lesotho and Swaziland, although its towing and breakdown service doesn't extend to these countries. In South Africa, the emergency breakdown service covers Gauteng, Cape Town, Durban, Pietermaritzburg, East London and Port Elizabeth. In Lesotho and Swaziland, you'll need to rely on local repair facilities in the major towns.

Bringing Your Own Vehicle

For requirements on bringing your own vehicle, see p628.

Driving Licence

In South Africa, you can use your driving licence from your home country if it is in

---

PARKING

In Johannesburg and other areas where secure parking is an issue, information is included on parking availability (**P**) in Sleeping listings. In rural areas, and in Lesotho and Swaziland, hotels generally have guarded lots.

TRANSPORT

ROAD DISTANCES (KM)

	Bloemfontein	Cape Town	Durban	East London	George	Graaff-Reinet	Johannesburg	Kimberley	Maseru	Mbabane	Nelspruit	Polokwane (Pietersburg)	Port Elizabeth	Pretoria	Springbok	Upington
Bloemfontein	---															
Cape Town	998	---														
Durban	628	1660	---													
East London	546	1042	667	---												
George	764	436	1240	630	---											
Graaff-Reinet	422	672	945	388	342	---										
Johannesburg	396	1405	598	992	1168	826	---									
Kimberley	175	960	842	722	734	501	467	---								
Maseru	157	1160	590	630	913	519	438	334	---							
Mbabane	677	1680	562	1238	1450	1097	361	833	633	---						
Nelspruit	754	1779	689	1214	1509	1167	358	832	713	173	---					
Polokwane (Pietersburg)	727	1736	929	1323	1499	1595	331	798	769	488	315	---				
Port Elizabeth	676	756	927	300	330	251	1062	763	822	1548	1373	1398	---			
Pretoria	454	1463	656	1050	1226	859	58	525	488	372	328	273	1119	---		
Springbok	975	554	1642	1365	846	911	1274	800	1252	1678	1543	1474	1289	1200	---	
Upington	576	821	1243	958	857	667	875	401	731	1157	1144	1075	902	813	387	---

English (or if you have a certified translation), and if it carries your photo; otherwise you'll need an international driving permit, obtainable from a motoring organisation in your home country. In Lesotho and Swaziland, licences from most other countries are accepted for stays of less than six months, as long as they are in English, or you have a certified translation.

Fuel & Spare Parts
Petrol costs about R5.40 per litre for leaded or unleaded in all three countries, and must be paid for in cash. There's no self-service. An attendant will always fill up your tank for you, clean your windows and ask if the oil or water needs checking, and should be tipped between R2 and R5. In addition to unleaded petrol (suitable for newer cars with catalytic converters), lead-replacement petrol (LRP) is also available for older cars that used to run on 97 octane leaded petrol.

Along main routes in South Africa and Swaziland, there are plenty of petrol stations, many open 24 hours. In rural areas, and in Lesotho, fill up whenever you can,

and in Lesotho, carry a jerry can with extra fuel. Unleaded fuel is readily available, except in the more remote areas of Lesotho. There are service stations in all major South African towns. In Lesotho, the main service stations are in Maseru, with limited facilities in other major towns. In Swaziland, Mbabane and Manzini have the best facilities; Manzini is the best place for sourcing spare parts.

Hire
Car rental is relatively inexpensive in South Africa. Most companies have a minimum age requirement of 21 years (23 years in Swaziland). All accept major credit cards. Car-rental rates in Swaziland are similar to those in South Africa. For Lesotho, it usually works out less expensive to rent the vehicle in South Africa and drive it over the border.

Major international car-rental companies are listed below. All the South Africa listings have offices in major cities; in Swaziland, the only agents are in Manzini; in Lesotho, they are in Maseru.

Rates start at about US$40 per day including, insurance and 200km free per day. Rental of a 4WD starts at about US$60, though better deals are often available. For cheaper rates and unlimited mileage deals, it's best to book and prepay through your agent at home before coming to South Africa. If a non-nominated driver has an accident, you will not be covered by insurance.

Around About Cars (☎ 0860 422 0422; www.around aboutcars.com)

Avis South Africa (☎ 0861-113 748, 011-923 3660; www.avis.co.za); Swaziland (Matsapha Airport ☎ 518 6226); Lesotho (Moshoeshoe Airport ☎ 2235 0328, Lesotho Sun Hotel ☎ 2232 0087)

Budget South Africa (☎ 0861-016 622, 011-398 0123; www.budget.co.za); Lesotho (☎ 2231 6344)

Europcar (☎ 0800 011 344, 011-574 4457; www .europcar.co.za) South Africa.

Hertz (☎ 021-935 4800, 011-390 9700; www.hertz .co.za) South Africa.

It's also worth checking with **Travelocity** (www.travelocity.com) and the no-frills airline **Kulula.com** (www.kulula.com), both of which often have good car-rental deals.

Local car-rental companies are usually less expensive, though they tend to come and go, and some have limits on how far you can take the car from the rental point. Several are listed below, all with agents in major cities. Also check with backpacker hostels; many can arrange better deals, from around US$25 per day or less.

Affordable Car Hire (☎ 404 9136; affordable@posix .co.sz) Swaziland.

Imperial South Africa (☎ 0861 131 000, 011-574 1000; www.imperialcarrental.co.za); Swaziland (☎ 404 0459, 518 4396); Lesotho (☎ 2235 0292)

Tempest (☎ 0860-031 666, 011-396 1080; www .tempestcarhire.co.za) South Africa.

Renting a camper van is another option, although one-way rentals are often not possible, or attract large fees. Some camper-van rentals include camping gear. 'Bakkie' campers, which sleep two in the back of a canopied pick-up, are cheaper. Two places to try, both in Jo'burg, are **African Leisure Travel** (☎ 011-792 1884; www.africanleisure.co.za) and **Britz 4x4 Rentals** (☎ 011-396 1860; www.britz.co.za).

For motorcycle rental, good contacts include **Motozulu** (www.motozu.lu.ms) in Port Shepstone (KwaZulu-Natal), and **Le Cap**

Motorcycle Hire (☎ 021-423 0823; www.lecap.co.za) in Cape Town; see also p158. Mopeds and scooters are available for hire in Cape Town and several other tourist areas.

Insurance

Insurance for third-party damage and damage to or loss of your vehicle is highly recommended, though not legally required for private-vehicle owners. It can be difficult to arrange by the month. The AASA is a good contact, and may be willing to negotiate payment for a year's worth of insurance with a pro-rata refund when you sell the car. Insurance agencies include **African Independent Brokers** (☎ 086-100 1002), **Lions Head Insurance Brokers** (☎ 021-761 8332) and **First Bowring** (☎ 021-425 1460), all based in Cape Town.

Purchase

South Africa is the best place in the region to purchase a vehicle for use on a long South Africa itinerary or on a larger sub-Saharan itinerary. Although prices tend to be cheaper in Jo'burg, most people do their buying in Cape Town – a much nicer place to spend the week or two that it will likely take for the process. Cape Town is also not a bad place to sell, as prices tend to be higher, although the market is small.

Cape Town's main congregation of used-car dealers is on Voortrekker Rd between Maitland and Belleville Sts, where you may also find a dealer willing to agree to a buy-back deal.

Buying privately, you won't have any dealer warranties, but prices will be cheaper. The weekly **Cape Ads** (www.capeads.com) is the best place to look. Also try **Auto Trader** (www .autotrader.co.za), which advertises thousands of cars around the country.

No matter who you buy from, make sure that the car details correspond accurately with the ownership (registration) papers, that there is a current licence disc on the windscreen and that the vehicle has been checked by the **police clearance department** (☎ in Cape Town 021-945 3891; ⏱ 7.30am-3.30pm Mon-Fri). Check the owner's name against their identity document, and check the car's engine and chassis numbers. Consider getting the car tested – in Cape Town, try **Same Garage** (Map pp120-1; ☎ 434 1058; 309 Main Rd, Sea Point). A full test can cost up to R300; less detailed tests are around R150.

CHOOSING A DEAL

South Africa is a big country, but unless you're on a tight schedule you probably don't need to pay higher rates for unlimited kilometres. For meandering around, 400km a day should be more than enough, and if you plan to stop for a day here and there 200km a day might be sufficient.

However, if you're renting with an international company and you book through the branch in your home country, you'll probably get unlimited kilometres at no extra cost, except at peak times such as December–January. When getting quotes, be sure that they include the 14% value-added tax (VAT).

One-way rentals are usually possible with larger companies if you are driving between major cities, although there's sometimes a drop-off charge.

Choose a car powerful enough to do the job. The smallest cars are OK for one person but with any more they'll be straining on the hills, which, even on major highways, are steep. Really steep hills may also make automatics unpleasant to drive. If you'll be going into Lesotho, consider a 4WD.

During the summer months, hail damage is a distinct and costly possibility, so see if it's covered before signing the rental agreement. Many contracts used to stipulate that you couldn't enter townships. While this usually isn't the case now, check anyway. If you plan to visit Swaziland, Lesotho or any other country, check that the rental agreement permits this, and make sure you get the standard letter from the rental company granting permission.

Finally, pay attention to the amount of 'excess' (the amount for which you're liable before insurance covers the rest) built into the insurance arrangement. Sometimes you'll have the choice of paying a higher insurance premium to lower or cancel the excess. A few companies offer 100% damage and theft insurance at a higher rate.

Cheap cars will often be sold without a roadworthy certificate. This certificate is required when you register the change-of-ownership form and pay tax for a licence disc. A roadworthy used to be difficult to obtain but some private garages are now allowed to issue them (R220), and some will overlook minor faults.

For something decent, plan on spending at least R25,000. For a 4WD, Series 1, 2 and 3 Land Rovers will cost from R15,000 to R40,000, depending on the condition. A recommended contact in Cape Town is **Graham Duncan Smith** (☎ 021-797 3048), who's a Land Rover expert and has helped people buy 4WDs in the past; he charges a R120 consultation fee and R165 per hour for engineering work.

To register your car, present yourself along with the roadworthy, a current licence, an accurate ownership certificate, a completed change-of-ownership form (signed by the seller), a clear photocopy of your ID (passport) along with the original, and your money to the **City Treasurer's Department, Motor Vehicle Registration Division** (Map pp120-1; ☎ 021-400 4900; ⏲ 8am-2pm Mon-Fri) in the Civic Centre on the foreshore in Cape Town. Call ahead to check how much

cash you'll need, but it will be under R500. Blank change-of-ownership forms are also available here.

Road Conditions
SOUTH AFRICA
Main roads are generally in excellent condition. Outside large cities and towns, you may encounter dirt roads, most of which are regularly graded and reasonably smooth. In the former homeland areas, beware of dangerous potholes, washed-out roads, unannounced hairpin bends and the like.

LESOTHO
Driving in Lesotho is more challenging, although it's getting easier as new roads are built in conjunction with the Highlands Water Project. The sealed roads in the highlands are good, but very steep in places. Rain will slow you down and ice and snow in winter can make things dangerous. If you're driving an automatic car, you'll be relying heavily on your brakes to get around steep downhill corners. Away from main roads, there are still many places where even a 4WD will get into trouble. Apart from rough roads, river floodings after summer storms present the biggest

problem. People and animals on the road can also be a hazard.

There are sometimes army roadblocks, usually searching for stolen cars. If you're driving a car hired from South Africa and get stopped, you'll need to present the letter from the rental agency giving you permission to take the car into Lesotho.

SWAZILAND

Swaziland's road network is quite good, and most major routes are tarred. There are also some satisfyingly rough back roads through the bush. The road between Tshaneni (northwest of Hlane Royal National Park) and Piggs Peak is gravel for most of the way, and slippery when wet.

Malagwane Hill, from Mbabane into the Ezulwini Valley, was once listed in the *Guinness Book of Records* as the most dangerous stretch of road in the world. Although conditions are greatly improved, driving down the Ezulwini Valley in heavy traffic and bad conditions can still be dangerous. Away from the population centres and border-crossing areas there is very little traffic.

Road Hazards

South Africa has a horrific road-accident record, with the annual death toll around 10,000 (although some estimates place it at more than 15,000). The N1 between Cape Town and Beaufort West is considered to be the most dangerous stretch of road in the country.

The main hazards are your fellow drivers, with overtaking blind and overtaking with insufficient passing room the major dangers. Drivers of cars coming up behind you will expect you to move into the emergency lane to let them pass, though the emergency lane may already be occupied. Drivers on little-used rural roads often speed and assume that there is no other traffic. Watch out especially for oncoming cars at blind corners on these roads. There is alcohol breath-testing in South Africa and in Swaziland, but given the high blood-alcohol level permitted (over 0.08% in South Africa, and 0.15% in Swaziland) drunk drivers remain a danger.

Animals and pedestrians on the roads are another hazard, especially in rural areas. Standard advice is that if you hit an animal

in an area in which you're uncertain of your safety, it's best to continue to the nearest police station and report it there. During the rainy season, and especially in higher areas of steamy KwaZulu-Natal, thick fog can slow you to a crawl. In the lowveld, summer hailstorms can damage your car.

In Lesotho, watch out for the steep terrain, hairpin turns, and ice and other inclement weather conditions.

In Swaziland, apart from drunk drivers and wandering cattle, the main danger is speeding minibuses, especially on gravel roads.

CARJACKING

In Jo'burg, and to a lesser extent in the other big cities, carjacking is a problem, though it's more likely if you're driving something flash rather than a standard rental car. The carjackers are almost always armed, and people have been killed for their cars. Stay alert, keep windows wound up and doors locked at night, and keep your taste in cars modest. If you're stopped at a red light and notice anything suspicious, it's standard practice to check that the junction is clear, and run the light. If you do get carjacked, don't resist, just hand over the keys immediately.

Road Rules

In South Africa, Lesotho and Swaziland, driving is on the left-hand side of the road, as in the UK, Japan and Australia. Seatbelts are mandatory for the driver and front-seat passenger in all three countries.

There are a few local variations on road rules. The main one is the 'four-way stop' (crossroad), which can occur even on major roads. All vehicles are required to stop, with those arriving first the first to go (even if they're on a minor cross street). On freeways, faster drivers will expect you to move into the emergency lane to let them pass, and will probably flash their hazard lights as thanks. At roundabouts, vehicles already in the roundabout, and those approaching it from the right, have the right of way.

In Swaziland, if an official or royal motorcade approaches, you're required to pull over and stop.

In Johannesburg and other urban areas, you'll encounter car guards – usually otherwise unemployed Africans from elsewhere

TRANSPORT

on the continent who will (most usefully) keep an eye on your parked car while you do your shopping or other errands. Be nice to them (they don't bite) and tip them between R2 and R5 for their services.

SPEED LIMITS

In South Africa, the speed limit is 100km/h on open roads, and 120km/h on most major highways, though it's widely ignored. The usual limit in towns is 60km/h.

In Lesotho, the speed limit is 80km/h on main roads, and 50km/h in villages. In Swaziland, it's 80km/h on open roads, and 60km/h in towns.

HITCHING

Hitching is never entirely safe in any country. This is especially true in South Africa, particularly in and near urban areas, and it's not a form of travel we can recommend. However, sometimes in rural areas it may be the only way to get somewhere. If you do decide to hitch, do so in pairs, avoid hitching at night, and let someone know where you are going. It's also advisable to catch public transport well beyond city limits before starting to hitch. Women should never hitch alone.

Hitching is easier and arguably safer in Swaziland and Lesotho, although you should still follow the same precautions. Be prepared to wait a long time for a car on back roads, and for lots of competition from locals.

LOCAL TRANSPORT

For getting around within a city or town (as opposed to intercity travel, which is covered under Buses, p633), the main options are city buses, minibus taxis and regular taxis –

either shared or private hire. In a few places, such as Cape Town and Durban, you'll have other options such as the Rikki (small open vans) and tuk-tuk (motorised tricycle), and Cape Town, Jo'burg and Pretoria have metro commuter trains (see p643).

Bus

Cape Town, Jo'burg, Pretoria and several other urban areas have city bus systems. Fares are cheap and routes, which are signboarded, are extensive. However, services usually stop running early in the evening, and there aren't many buses on weekends.

Minibus Taxi

Minibus taxis run almost everywhere – within cities, to the suburbs and to neighbouring towns. They leave when full and, happily – especially if you've travelled elsewhere in sub-Saharan Africa – 'full' in South Africa isn't as full as it is in many neighbouring countries. Most accommodate 14 to 16 people, with the slightly larger 'Sprinters' taking about 20.

Minibus taxis have the advantages of an extensive route network and cheap prices. These are outweighed, however, by the fact that driving standards and vehicle conditions often leave a lot to be desired, and there are many accidents. The reputation of minibus taxis has also been tarnished by isolated outbreaks of gangster-style shoot-outs between the various companies competing for business, including incidents where crowded taxis were machine-gunned. Although things have settled down in recent years, minibuses in some areas and on some routes are still considered highly unsafe, and reports of muggings and other incidents remain a regular feature. In other

---

MINIBUS TAXI ETIQUETTE

Before using minibus taxis, always check out the local situation, and get local advice on the lines and areas where you want to travel. If you do use them, here are some tips on etiquette:

- Passengers with lots of luggage should sit in the first row behind the driver.
- Pay the fare with coins, not notes. Pass the money forward (your fare and those of the people around you) when the taxi is full. Give it to one of the front-seat passengers, not the driver. If you're sitting in the front seat you might have to collect the fares and provide change.
- If you sit on the folding seat by the door it's your job to open and close the door when other people get out. You'll have to get out of the taxi each time.
- Say 'Thank you, driver!' when you want to get out, not 'Stop!'

areas – notably central Cape Town, where they're a handy and popular way to get around – they are fine.

Away from train and main bus routes, minibus taxis may be the only choice of public transport. They're also a good way to get insights into local life. If you want to try one, read the newspapers, don't ride at night, and always ask for local advice on lines and areas to avoid before using minibus taxis as transport. As most minibus taxis don't carry luggage on the roof, stowing backpacks can be a hassle.

Although minibus taxis in Lesotho and Swaziland don't have stellar road safety records either, they have none of the violence that's associated with their South African counterparts, and are widely used, both for short and longer routes.

Private Taxi

Larger cities in all three countries have a private taxi service. (In Lesotho, you'll only find taxis in Maseru.) Occasionally, you'll find a taxi stand, but usually you'll need to telephone for a cab. Numbers are given in the Getting Around sections of the individual cities. Prices average about R8 per kilometre.

Shared Taxi

In some towns (and on some longer routes), the only transport option is a shared taxi, basically a smaller version of the minibus taxi. They are slightly more expensive than minibus taxis, and comparable in safety.

TOURS

There are dozens of tours available, ranging from budget-oriented overland truck tours to exclusive luxury safaris. The best way to get information on tours geared to budget travellers is from the network of backpacker hostels around the country. Many have travellers bulletin boards, and some are directly affiliated with budget-tour operators.

Some tour operators to try include the following:

African Routes (☎ 031-563 5080; www.africanroutes .co.za) Offers camping and overland itineraries for younger travellers, including a whirlwind one-week trip taking in Kruger National Park, Swaziland and the Drakensberg, plus various bus options for seniors.

BirdWatch Cape (☎ 021-762 5059; www.birdwatch .co.za) A small outfit for twitchers, focusing on Cape Town and surrounding areas.

Bok Bus (☎ 082-320 1979; www.bokbus.com) Budget-oriented tours along the Garden Route.

Bundu Safari Company (☎ 011-675 0767; www .bundusafaris.co.za) Budget-oriented tours ranging from one to several days, focusing on Kruger National Park and the surrounding area.

Cape Town Gourmet Adventure Tours (☎ 083-693 1151; http://gourmet.cape-town.info) Wining and dining in Cape Town, plus 'wellness' tours and lots of other options in and around Cape Town and the Western Cape.

Connex (☎ 011-274 41; www.connex.co.za) Similar to Springbok-Atlas.

Eco-Ist (☎ 021-559 2420; www.eco-tourisminvest ments.co.za) Outdoor-oriented 'biodiversity' tours around Cape Town, plus longer itineraries taking in Kruger National Park, the Garden Route and other areas. Especially recommended for their West Coast spring flower tour.

Encompass Africa (☎ 021-434 9932; encompass africa@yebo.co.za) A backpacker-oriented outfit offering various itineraries based out of Cape Town.

Malealea Lodge (☎ 051-436 6766; www.malealea .co.ls) The main operator for tours in Lesotho, offering everything from cross-country horse treks to 4WD excursions; can also arrange pick-ups from Bloemfontein in South Africa.

Springbok-Atlas (☎ 021-460 4700; www.springbok atlas.com) One of the major coach-tour operators, offering midrange tours along popular routes, including day tours. Aimed at older tourists.

Swazi Trails (☎ 416 2180 in Swaziland; www.swazi trails.co.sz) Specialises in day or half-day tours around Swaziland, including white-water rafting, cultural tours and hiking.

Thaba Tours (☎ 033-701 2888; www.thabatours.co.za) 4WD-based tours of Lesotho and the Drakensberg.

Thompsons South Africa (☎ 031-201 3100; www .thompsonssa.com) Midrange and top-end package tours and safaris, including a two-week tour taking in South Africa's main tourist spots.

Wilderness Safaris (www.wilderness-safaris.com) Upscale specialist operator offering high-end luxury safaris and special-interest trips, including bird-watching, botanical and short cycling itineraries; also operates several luxury bush camps.

Wildlife Safaris (☎ 011-791 4238; www.wildlifesaf.co .za) Midrange safaris from Jo'burg and Pretoria to Kruger and Pilanesberg National Parks for individuals and small groups.

TRAIN

South Africa's Shosholoza Meyl passenger trains are run by **Spoornet** (☎ 011-773 2944; www.spoornet.co.za, click on 'Passengers'), and offer

TRANSPORT

RIDING THE RAILS

Train travel in South Africa has a place of its own, with an eclectic band of devotees. In addition to the routes mentioned in this section – where the emphasis is on functionality and getting from one place to another – there are numerous special lines.

Blue Train

South Africa's most famous train, the **Blue Train** (☎ 012-334 8459, 021-449 2672; www.bluetrain .co.za) has such a reputation among train aficionados that some people come to South Africa just to ride it. Schedules vary, and are now much curtailed from what they once were, but the train usually runs about once or twice weekly between Pretoria and Cape Town. For 27 hours of luxury, one-way fares (per person sharing) are R9695/10,470 for deluxe/luxury, including all meals and drinks.

In addition to the contacts listed here, some travel agents, both in South Africa and in other countries, also take bookings. It's worth inquiring about special packages, including one-way flights from Pretoria/Jo'burg to Cape Town and a night's accommodation. Also inquire about low-season fares if you are thinking about travelling between January and August, or between mid-November and late December.

Rovos Rail

Rivalling the *Blue Train* as the most luxurious and expensive service in Africa, **Rovos Rail** (☎ 012-315 8242; www.rovos.co.za) has regular trips including Pretoria–Cape Town over two nights/three days (as opposed to the *Blue Train*'s one night/two days), with stops at Matjiesfontein and Kimberley; Pretoria–Durban; and Cape Town–George.

Shongololo Express

Not as luxurious as the other classic trains (though it's still quite acceptable) is the **Shongololo Express** (☎ 011-781 4616; www.shongololo.com); you travel by night and then disembark for a day's sightseeing. Among other trips, it offers a 16-day tour taking in South Africa's major sights.

Tulbagh.com

Tulbagh.com (☎ /fax 023-230 1348; http://tulbagh.com/Visitor's%20Information/attractions.htm) organises a range of package trips by train from Cape Town to Tulbagh, the Klein Cederberg Nature Reserve and Matjiesfontein.

Union Ltd Steam Rail Tours

The *Union Limited* was the pre–*Blue Train* king of the line in South Africa, running to Cape Town with passengers who were meeting liners to Europe. The train was luxurious in its time and has been meticulously restored. **Union Ltd Steam Rail Tours** (☎ 021-449 4391; http://home.intekom.com /bluegrass/sites/steamsa) runs several tours, including the six-day 'Golden Thread' from Cape Town along the coast to Oudtshoorn and back again. Passengers have more room than they once did, with two people now sharing a four-berth compartment and singles in a two-berth compartment.

There are also many less-ritzy steam train trips, including the *Apple Express* from Port Elizabeth (p251), the *Outeniqua Choo-Tjoe* between Knysna and George (p216), and the *Banana Express* along the KwaZulu-Natal south coast from Port Shepstone (p324).

regular services connecting major cities on 'name trains' (some of the main routes are listed, opposite). These are a good and safe, albeit slow, way to get around, and more comfortable than taking the bus. The trains are also relatively affordable and, unlike the long-distance buses, fares on short sectors are not inflated.

On overnight journeys, 1st- and 2nd-class fares include a sleeping berth, but there's an additional charge for bedding hire. Alternatively, you can hire a private compartment (which sleeps four in 1st class and six in 2nd class) or a coupe (which sleeps two in 1st class and three in 2nd class) – these are a good way of travelling more securely.

Meals are available in the dining car, or in the comfort of your compartment.

Tickets must be booked at least 24 hours in advance (you can book up to three months in advance). Bookings for anywhere in the country can be done at any individual station, or through the **Shosholoza Meyl Reservations Centre** (☎ 0860-008 888, 011-774 4555). For an overview of what awaits you on the South African rails, check out **The Man in Seat 61** (www.seat61.com/South%20Africa.htm).

Routes
Main routes include the following:
Algoa Jo'burg–Port Elizabeth via Bloemfontein; daily; 20 hours.
Amatola Jo'burg–East London via Bloemfontein; Sunday to Friday; 20 hours.
Bosvelder Jo'burg–Musina via Makhado; daily; 17 hours.
Diamond Express Jo'burg-Bloemfontein; three times weekly; nine hours.
Komati Jo'burg–Komatipoort via Pretoria, Middleburg and Nelspruit; daily; 13 hours; connects to the Komatipoort-Maputo train.

Trans Karoo Pretoria/Jo'burg–Cape Town via Kimberly; daily; 28 hours.
Trans Natal Jo'burg–Durban via Ladysmith and Pietermaritzburg; five times weekly; 13½ hours.
Trans Oranje Cape Town–Durban via Kimberley, Bloemfontein and Kroonstad; weekly; 31 hours.

Some 1st-/2nd-/economy-class sample fares are: Jo'burg–Durban R250/165/100; Cape Town–Pretoria R550/350/230; Jo'burg–Port Elizabeth R365/245/145. Return fares are double the one-way fares. It's possible to put a vehicle on board the *Trans Karoo* for an extra R1345.

There are no passenger trains in Lesotho or Swaziland.

Metro Trains
There are metro services in Jo'burg (p420), Cape Town (p159) and Pretoria (p440), though most lines aren't recommended for security reasons. The new **Gautrain** (www.gautrain.co.za) may soon connect Jo'burg and Pretoria.

Health

CONTENTS

As long as you stay up to date with your vaccinations and take basic preventive measures, you're unlikely to succumb to most of the health hazards covered in this chapter. While South Africa, Lesotho and Swaziland have an impressive selection of tropical diseases on offer, it's more likely you'll get a bout of diarrhoea or a cold than a more exotic malady. The main exception to this is malaria, which is a real risk in lower-lying areas of Swaziland, and in eastern South Africa.

BEFORE YOU GO

A little predeparture planning will save you trouble later. Get a check-up from your dentist and from your doctor if you have any regular medication or chronic illness, eg high blood pressure and asthma. You should also organise spare contact lenses and glasses (and take your optical prescription with you); get a first-aid and medical kit together; and arrange necessary vaccinations.

Travellers can register with the **International Association for Medical Advice to Travellers** (IAMAT; www.iamat.org), which provides directories of certified doctors. If you'll be spending much time in more remote areas, such as parts of Lesotho, consider doing a first-aid course (contact the Red Cross or St John's Ambulance), or attending a remote medicine first-aid course, such as that offered by **Wilderness Medical Training** (WMT; www.wildernessmedicaltraining.co.uk).

If you are bringing medications with you, carry them in their original containers, clearly labelled. A signed and dated letter from your physician describing all medical conditions and medications, including generic names, is also a good idea. If carrying syringes or needles, be sure to have a physician's letter documenting their medical necessity.

INSURANCE

Find out in advance whether your insurance plan will make payments directly to providers, or will reimburse you later for overseas health expenditures. In South Africa, Lesotho and Swaziland, most doctors expect payment in cash. It's vital to ensure that your travel insurance will cover any emergency transport required to get you to a hospital in a major city, or all the way home, by air and with a medical attendant if necessary. Not all insurance covers this, so check the contract carefully. If you need medical assistance, your insurance company might be able to help locate the nearest hospital or clinic, or you can ask at your hotel. In an emergency, contact your embassy or consulate.

RECOMMENDED VACCINATIONS

The **World Health Organisation** (WHO; www.who.int/en/) recommends that all travellers be covered for diphtheria, tetanus, measles, mumps, rubella and polio, as well as for hepatitis B, regardless of their destination. The consequences of these diseases can be severe, and outbreaks do occur.

According to the **Centers for Disease Control & Prevention** (www.cdc.gov), the following vaccinations are recommended for South Africa, Lesotho and Swaziland: hepatitis A, hepatitis B, rabies and typhoid, and boosters for tetanus, diphtheria and measles. Yellow fever is not a risk in the region, but the certificate is an entry requirement if you're travelling from an infected region (see p648).

MEDICAL CHECKLIST

It's a good idea to carry a medical and first-aid kit with you, to help yourself in the case of minor illness or injury. Following is a list of items to consider packing.

- antibiotics (prescription only), eg ciprofloxacin (Ciproxin) or norfloxacin (Utinor)
- antidiarrhoeal drugs (eg loperamide)
- acetaminophen (paracetamol) or aspirin
- anti-inflammatory drugs (eg ibuprofen)
- antihistamines (for hay fever and allergic reactions)
- antibacterial ointment (eg Bactroban) for cuts and abrasions (prescription only)
- antimalaria pills, if you'll be in malarial areas
- bandages, gauze
- scissors, safety pins, tweezers, pocket knife
- DEET-containing insect repellent for the skin
- permethrin-containing insect spray for clothing, tents and bed nets
- sun block
- oral rehydration salts
- iodine tablets (for water purification)
- sterile needles, syringes and fluids if travelling to remote areas

INTERNET RESOURCES

There is a wealth of travel health advice on the Internet. The Lonely Planet website at www.lonelyplanet.com is a good place to start. The World Health Organisation (WHO) publishes the helpful *International Travel and Health,* available free at www .who.int/ith/. Other useful websites include **MD Travel Health** (www.mdtravelhealth.com) and **Fit for Travel** (www.fitfortravel.scot.nhs.uk).

Official government travel health websites include:

Australia www.smartraveller.gov.au/tips/travelwell.html
Canada www.hc-sc.gc.ca/index_e.html
UK www.dh.gov.uk/PolicyAndGuidance/HealthAdviceFor Travellers/fs/en
USA www.cdc.gov/travel/

FURTHER READING

- *A Comprehensive Guide to Wilderness and Travel Medicine* (1998) Eric A Weiss
- *Healthy Travel* (1999) Jane Wilson-Howarth
- *Healthy Travel Africa* (2000) Isabelle Young
- *How to Stay Healthy Abroad* (2002) Richard Dawood
- *Travel in Health* (1994) Graham Fry
- *Travel with Children* (2004) Cathy Lanigan

IN TRANSIT

DEEP VEIN THROMBOSIS

Prolonged immobility during flights can cause deep vein thrombosis (DVT) – the formation of blood clots in the legs. The longer the flight, the greater the risk. Although most blood clots are reabsorbed uneventfully, some might break off and travel through the blood vessels to the lungs, where they could cause life-threatening complications.

The chief symptom is swelling or pain of the foot, ankle or calf, usually but not always on just one side. When a blood clot travels to the lungs, it may cause chest pain and breathing difficulty. Travellers with any of these symptoms should immediately seek medical attention. To prevent DVT walk about the cabin, perform isometric compressions of the leg muscles (ie contract the leg muscles while sitting), drink plenty of fluids and avoid alcohol.

JET LAG

If you're crossing more than five time zones you could suffer jet lag, resulting in insomnia, fatigue, malaise or nausea. To avoid jet lag try drinking plenty of fluids (non-alcoholic) and eating light meals. Upon arrival, get exposure to natural sunlight and readjust your schedule (for meals, sleep, etc) as soon as possible.

IN SOUTH AFRICA, LESOTHO & SWAZILAND

AVAILABILITY & COST OF HEALTH CARE

Good quality health care is available in all of South Africa's major urban areas, and private hospitals are generally of excellent standard. Public hospitals by contrast are often underfunded and overcrowded, and in off-the-beaten-track areas, such as the former homelands; and in Lesotho and Swaziland, reliable medical facilities are rare.

Prescriptions are generally required in South Africa. Drugs for chronic diseases should be brought from home. There is a high risk of contracting HIV from infected blood transfusions. The **BloodCare Foundation** (www.bloodcare.org.uk) is a useful source of safe, screened blood, which can be transported to any part of the world within 24 hours.

INFECTIOUS DISEASES

Following are some of the diseases that are found in South Africa, Lesotho and Swaziland, though with a few basic preventative measures, it's unlikely that you'll succumb to any of these.

Cholera

Cholera is caused by a bacteria, and spread via contaminated drinking water. In South Africa, the risk to travellers is very low; you're only likely to encounter it in eastern rural areas, where you should avoid tap water and unpeeled or uncooked fruits and vegetables. The main symptom is profuse watery diarrhoea, which causes debilitation if fluids are not replaced quickly. An oral cholera vaccine is available in the USA, but it is not particularly effective. Most cases of cholera can be avoided by close attention to drinking water and by avoiding potentially contaminated food. Treatment is by fluid replacement (orally or via a drip), but sometimes antibiotics are needed. Self-treatment is not advised.

Dengue Fever (Break-bone Fever)

Dengue fever, spread through the bite of mosquitos, causes a feverish illness with headache and muscle pains similar to those experienced with a bad, prolonged attack of influenza. There might be a rash. Mosquito bites should be avoided whenever possible. This disease is present in southeastern coastal areas of South Africa, and in Lesotho and Swaziland. Self-treatment: paracetamol and rest.

Filariasis

Filariasis is caused by tiny worms migrating in the lymphatic system, and is spread by the bite from an infected mosquito. Symptoms include localised itching and swelling of the legs and/or genitalia. Treatment is available. Self-treatment: none.

Hepatitis A

Hepatitis A, which occurs in all three countries, is spread through contaminated food (particularly shellfish) and water. It causes jaundice and, although it is rarely fatal, it can cause prolonged lethargy and delayed recovery. If you've had hepatitis A, you shouldn't drink alcohol for up to six months afterwards, but once you've recovered, there won't be any long-term problems. The first symptoms include dark urine and a yellow colour to the whites of the eyes. Sometimes a fever and abdominal pain might be present. Hepatitis A vaccine (Avaxim, VAQTA, Havrix) is given as an injection: a single dose will give protection for up to a year, and a booster after a year gives 10-year protection. Hepatitis A and typhoid vaccines can also be given as a single dose vaccine, hepatyrix or viatim. Self-treatment: none.

Hepatitis B

Hepatitis B, found in all three countries, is spread through infected blood, contaminated needles and sexual intercourse. It can also be spread from an infected mother to the baby during childbirth. It affects the liver, causing jaundice and occasionally liver failure. Most people recover completely, but some people might be chronic carriers of the virus, which could lead eventually to cirrhosis or liver cancer. Those visiting high-risk areas for long periods or those with increased social or occupational risk should be immunised. Many countries now routinely give hepatitis B as part of the childhood vaccination programme. It is given singly or can be given at the same time as hepatitis A (hepatyrix).

A course will give protection for at least five years. It can be given over four weeks or six months. Self-treatment: none.

HIV

HIV, the virus that causes AIDS, is an enormous problem in South Africa, Lesotho and Swaziland, with a devastating impact on local health systems and community structures. KwaZulu-Natal has one of the highest rates of infection on the continent, with an HIV-positive incidence of close to 40% according to some surveys, and South Africa has more people living with HIV than any country in the world. The statistics are similarly sobering for Lesotho and Swaziland: Swaziland has the world's highest HIV prevalence, with Lesotho close behind. The virus is spread through infected blood and blood products, by sexual intercourse with an infected partner, and from an infected mother to her baby during childbirth and breastfeeding. It can be spread through 'blood to blood' contacts, such as with contaminated instruments during medical, dental, acupuncture and other body-piercing procedures, and through sharing used intravenous needles. At present there is no cure; medication that might keep the disease under control is available, but these drugs are too expensive, or unavailable, for the overwhelming majority of South Africans. If you think you might have been infected with HIV, a blood test is necessary; a three-month gap after exposure and before testing is required to allow antibodies to appear in the blood. Self-treatment: none.

Malaria

Malaria is mainly confined to the eastern half of South Africa (northern KwaZulu-Natal, Mpumalanga, Limpopo) and to Swaziland, although parts of North-West Province can also be malarial. Apart from road accidents, it's probably the only major health risk that you face travelling in this area, and precautions should be taken. The disease is caused by a parasite in the bloodstream spread via the bite of the female Anopheles mosquito. There are several types of malaria; falciparum malaria is the most dangerous type and the predominant form in South Africa. Infection rates vary with season and climate, so check out the situation before departure. Several different drugs are used to prevent malaria, and new ones are in the pipeline. Up-to-date advice from a travel health clinic is essential as some medication is more suitable for some travellers than others (eg people with epilepsy should avoid mefloquine, and doxycycline should not be taken by pregnant women or children aged under 12).

The early stages of malaria include headaches, fevers, generalised aches and pains, and malaise, which could be mistaken for flu. Other symptoms can include abdominal pain, diarrhoea and a cough. Anyone who develops a fever in a malarial area should assume malarial infection until a blood test proves negative, even if you have been taking antimalarial medication. If not treated, the next stage could develop within 24 hours, particularly if falciparum malaria is the parasite: jaundice, then reduced consciousness and coma (also known as cerebral malaria) followed by death. Treatment in hospital is essential, and the death rate might still be as high as 10% even in the best intensive-care facilities.

Many travellers think that malaria is a mild illness, and that taking antimalarial drugs causes more illness through side effects than actually getting malaria. This is unfortunately not true. If you decide against antimalarial drugs, you must understand the risks, and be obsessive about avoiding mosquito bites. Use nets and insect repellent, and report any fever or flulike symptoms to a doctor as soon as possible. Some people advocate homeopathic preparations against malaria, such as Demal200, but as yet there is no conclusive evidence that this is effective, and many homeopaths do not recommend their use.

Malaria in pregnancy frequently results in miscarriage or premature labour, and the risks to both mother and foetus during pregnancy are considerable. Travel throughout the region when pregnant should be carefully considered. Adults who have survived childhood malaria have developed immunity and usually only develop mild cases of malaria; most Western travellers have no immunity at all. Immunity wanes after 18 months of nonexposure, so even if you have had malaria in the past and used to live in a malaria-prone area, you might no longer be immune.

Rabies

Rabies is spread by receiving bites or licks from an infected animal on broken skin. Few human cases are reported in South Africa, with the risks highest in rural areas. It is always fatal once the clinical symptoms start (which might be up to several months after an infected bite), so postbite vaccination should be given as soon as possible. Postbite vaccination (whether or not you've been vaccinated before the bite) prevents the virus from spreading to the central nervous system. Animal handlers should be vaccinated, as should those travelling to remote areas where a reliable source of postbite vaccine is not available within 24 hours. Three preventive injections are needed over a month. If you have not been vaccinated you'll need a course of five injections starting 24 hours or as soon as possible after the injury. If you have been vaccinated, you'll need fewer postbite injections, and have more time to seek medical help. Self-treatment: none.

Schistosomiasis (Bilharzia)

This disease is a risk in eastern parts of South Africa, and in Swaziland. (Lesotho, happily, is considered schistosomiasis-free.) It's spread by flukes (minute worms) that are carried by a species of freshwater snail, which then sheds them into slow-moving or still water. The parasites penetrate human skin during swimming and then migrate to the bladder or bowel. They are excreted via stool or urine and could contaminate fresh water, where the cycle starts again. Swimming in suspect freshwater lakes or slow-running rivers should be avoided. Symptoms range from none, to transient fever and rash, and advanced cases might have blood in the stool or in the urine. A blood test can detect antibodies if you might have been exposed, and treatment is readily available. If not treated, the infection can cause kidney failure or permanent bowel damage. It is not possible for you to infect others. Self-treatment: none.

Tuberculosis

Tuberculosis (TB) is spread through close respiratory contact and occasionally through infected milk or milk products. BCG vaccination is recommended if you'll be mixing closely with the local population, especially on long-term stays, although it gives only moderate protection against the disease. TB can be asymptomatic, only being picked up on a routine chest X-ray. Alternatively, it can cause a cough, weight loss or fever, sometimes months or even years after exposure. Self-treatment: none.

Typhoid

This is spread through food or water contaminated by infected human faeces. The first symptom is usually a fever or a pink rash on the abdomen. Sometimes septicaemia (blood poisoning) can occur. A typhoid vaccine (typhim Vi, typherix) will give protection for three years. In some countries, the oral vaccine Vivotif is also available. Antibiotics are usually given as treatment, and death is rare unless septicaemia occurs. Self-treatment: none.

Yellow Fever

Although not a problem within South Africa, Lesotho or Swaziland, you'll need to carry a certificate of vaccination if you'll be arriving in South Africa from an infected country. Infected countries include most of South Africa's neighbours; for a full list see the websites of **WHO** (www.who.int/wer/) or the **Centers for Disease Control & Prevention** (www.cdc.gov/travel/blusheet.htm).

ANTIMALARIAL A TO D

■ **A** – Awareness of the risk. No medication is totally effective, but protection of up to 95% is achievable with most drugs, as long as other measures have been taken.

■ **B** – Bites, to be avoided at all costs. Sleep in a screened room, use a mosquito spray or coils, sleep under a permethrin-impregnated net at night. Cover up at night with long trousers and long sleeves, preferably with permethrin-treated clothing. Apply appropriate repellent to all areas of exposed skin in the evenings.

■ **C** – Chemical prevention (ie antimalarial drugs) is usually needed in malarial areas. Expert advice is needed as resistance patterns can change, and new drugs are in development. Not all antimalarial drugs are suitable for everyone. Most antimalarial drugs need to be started at least a week before and continued for four weeks after the last possible exposure to malaria.

■ **D** – Diagnosis. If you have a fever or flulike illness within a year of travel to a malarial area, malaria is a possibility, and immediate medical attention is necessary.

TRAVELLERS' DIARRHOEA

While less likely in South Africa than elsewhere on the continent, this is a common travel-related illness, sometimes simply due to dietary changes. It is possible that you will succumb, especially if you are spending a lot of time in rural areas or eating at inexpensive local food stalls. To avoid diarrhoea, only eat fresh fruits or vegetables that have been cooked or peeled, and be wary of dairy products that might contain unpasteurised milk. Although freshly cooked food can often be a safe option, plates or serving utensils might be dirty, so be selective when eating food from street vendors (make sure that cooked food is piping hot all the way through).

If you develop diarrhoea, be sure to drink plenty of fluids, preferably an oral rehydration solution containing lots of water and some salt and sugar. A few loose stools don't require treatment but, if you start having more than four or five stools a day, you should start taking an antibiotic (usually a quinoline drug, such as ciprofloxacin or norfloxacin) and an antidiarrhoeal agent (such as loperamide) if you're not within easy reach of a toilet. If diarrhoea is bloody, persists for more than 72 hours or is accompanied by fever, shaking chills or severe abdominal pain, you should seek medical attention.

Amoebic Dysentery

Contracted by eating contaminated food and water, amoebic dysentery causes blood and mucus in the faeces. It can be relatively mild and tends to come on gradually, but seek medical advice if you think you have the illness as it won't clear up without treatment (which is with specific antibiotics).

Giardiasis

This, like amoebic dysentery, is also caused by ingesting contaminated food or water. The illness usually appears a week or more after you have been exposed to the offending parasite. Giardiasis might cause only a short-lived bout of typical travellers' diarrhoea, but it can also cause persistent diarrhoea. Ideally, seek medical advice if you suspect you have giardiasis, but if you are in a remote area you could start a course of antibiotics.

ENVIRONMENTAL HAZARDS
Heat Exhaustion

This condition occurs following heavy sweating and excessive fluid loss with inadequate replacement of fluids and salt, and is primarily a risk in hot climates when taking unaccustomed exercise before full acclimatisation. Symptoms include headache, dizziness and tiredness. Dehydration is already happening by the time you feel thirsty – aim to drink sufficient water to produce pale, diluted urine. Self-treatment: fluid replacement with water and/or fruit juice, and cooling by cold water and fans. The treatment of the salt-loss component consists of consuming salty fluids as in soup, and adding a little more table salt to foods than usual.

Heatstroke

Heat exhaustion is a precursor to the much more serious condition of heatstroke. In this case there is damage to the sweating mechanism, with an excessive rise in body temperature, irrational and hyperactive behaviour, and eventually loss of consciousness and death. Rapid cooling by spraying the body with water and fanning is ideal. Emergency fluid and electrolyte replacement is usually also required by intravenous drip.

Insect Bites & Stings

Mosquitoes might not always carry malaria or dengue fever, but they (and other insects) can cause irritation and infected bites. To avoid these, take the same precautions as you would for avoiding malaria (see p647). Bee and wasp stings cause real problems only to those who have a severe allergy to the stings (anaphylaxis), in which case, carry an adrenaline (epinephrine) injection.

Scorpions are found in arid areas. They can cause a painful bite that is sometimes life-threatening. If bitten by a scorpion, take a painkiller. Medical treatment should be sought if collapse occurs.

Ticks are always a risk away from urban areas. If you get bitten, press down around the tick's head with tweezers, grab the head and gently pull upwards. Avoid pulling the rear of the body as this may squeeze the tick's gut contents through the attached mouth parts into the skin, increasing the

HEALTH

risk of infection and disease. Smearing chemicals on the tick will not make it let go and is not recommended.

Snake Bites

Basically, avoid getting bitten! Don't walk barefoot, or stick your hand into holes or cracks. However, 50% of those bitten by venomous snakes are not actually injected with poison (envenomed). If bitten by a snake, do not panic. Immobilise the bitten limb with a splint (such as a stick) and apply a bandage over the site with firm pressure, similar to bandaging a sprain. Do not apply a tourniquet, or cut or suck the bite. Get medical help as soon as possible.

Water

High-quality water is widely available in South Africa and drinking from taps is fine, except in rural areas. In Lesotho and Swaziland, stick to bottled water, and purify stream water before drinking it.

TRADITIONAL MEDICINE

According to some estimates, as many as 85% of residents of South Africa, Lesotho and Swaziland rely in part, or wholly, on traditional medicine. It's believed that there are more than 200,000 traditional healers in South Africa alone (in comparison with some 20,000 Western medical practitioners). Given the comparatively high costs, and the unavailability of Western medicine in many rural areas, these traditional healers are the first contact for much of the population when they fall ill. The *sangoma* (traditional healer) and *inyanga* (herbalist) hold revered positions in many communities, and traditional medicinal products are widely available in local markets. On the darker side of things, *muti* killings (in which human body parts are sought for traditional medicinal purposes) are also common – reported approximately monthly – as are abuses in which false claims are made for cures, or in which diseases spread by unsanitary practices.

While there is still no national legislation regulating traditional medicinal practitioners, there are several umbrella groups, including the Traditional Healers' Association of South Africa, and the African Herbal Medicine Association. These aim to raise awareness and curb abuses in the practice of traditional medicine, but there is a long way to go.

Language

CONTENTS

WHO SPEAKS WHAT WHERE?
South Africa

South Africa's official languages were once only English and Afrikaans, but nine others have since been added to the list. The following list shows all 11 official languages and their number of first language speakers as a percentage of total population. Names in brackets show the correct spelling of the languages when used within the language itself. Figures are from the most recent census (2001):

Zulu (isiZulu)	23.8%
Xhosa (isiXhosa)	17.6%
Afrikaans	13.3%
Northern Sotho (Sepedi)	9.4%
English, Tswana (Setswana)	8.2%
Southern Sotho (Sesotho)	7.9%
Tsonga (Xitsonga)	4.4%
Swati (siSwati)	2.7%
Venda (Tshivenda)	2.3%
Ndebele (isiNdebele)	1.6%

Forms, brochures and timetables are usually bilingual (English and Afrikaans) but road signs alternate. Most Afrikaans speakers also speak good English, but this is not always the case in small rural towns and among older people. However, it's not uncommon for blacks in cities to speak at least six languages; whites can usually speak two.

In and around Cape Town only three languages are prominent: Afrikaans (spoken by many whites and coloureds), English (spoken by nearly everyone) and Xhosa (spoken mainly by blacks).

Lesotho & Swaziland

The official languages of Lesotho are Southern Sotho (Sesotho) and English.

The official languages of Swaziland are Swati (Siswati) – also known as Swazi – and English. English is the medium of instruction in all schools and is widely understood. Parliamentary proceedings and debates are held in both languages.

AFRIKAANS

Although Afrikaans is closely associated with Afrikaners, it is also the first language of many coloureds. Ironically, it was probably first used as a common language by the polyglot coloured community of the Cape, and passed back to whites by nannies and servants. Around six million people speak the language, roughly half of whom are Afrikaners and half of whom are coloured.

Afrikaans developed from the High Dutch of the 17th century. It has abandoned the complicated grammar of Dutch and incorporated vocabulary from French, English, other indigenous African languages and even Asian languages (as a result of the influence of East Asian slaves). It's inventive, powerful and expressive, but it wasn't recognised as one of the country's official languages until 1925, before which it was officially termed a dialect of Dutch.

Pronunciation

a	as the 'u' in 'pup'
e	when word stress falls on **e**, it's as in 'net'; when unstressed, it's as the 'a' in 'ago'
i	when word stress falls on **i**, it's as in 'hit'; when unstressed, it's as the 'a' in 'ago'
o	as the 'o' in 'fort', but very short
u	as the 'e' in 'angel' with lips pouted
r	a rolled 'rr' sound
aai	as the 'y' sound in 'why'
ae	as 'ah'
ee	as in 'deer'

LANGUAGE

SOUTH AFRICAN ENGLISH

English has undergone some changes during its life in South Africa. Quite a few words have changed meaning, new words have been appropriated and, thanks to the influence of Afrikaans, a distinctive accent has developed. Vocab tends to lean more towards British rather than US English (eg 'lift' not 'elevator', 'petrol' not 'gas'), as does grammar and spelling, but there are influences from other indigenous languages like Zulu and Xhosa as well. Repetition for emphasis is common: something that burns you is 'hot hot'; fields after the rains are 'green green'; a crowded minibus with no more room is 'full full', and so on. Here's just a smattering of the local lingo you're likely to hear:

babalaas (from Zulu) – a monster hangover
bakkie – pick-up truck (US); ute/utility (Aus)
bonnet – car hood (US)
boot – car trunk (US)
cool drink – soda (US)
Howzit? – Hello/Greetings; How are you?
Izzit? – Is that so? Really?
just now – soon
lekker – nice, delicious
naartjie – tangerine
petrol – gasoline (US)
robot – traffic light
rubbish – garbage (US)
(Og) shame! – Ohh, how cute! (in response to something like a new baby or a little puppy); Really! Oh no! (said with a sympathetic tone)
soda – soda water; club soda (US)
sweeties – lollies; candy
tekkies – runners; joggers

ei	as the 'ay' in 'play'
oe	as the 'u' in 'put'
oë	as the 'oe' in 'doer'
ooi/oei	as the 'ooey' in 'phooey'
tj	as the 'ch' in 'chunk'

Greetings & Conversation

Hello.	Hallo.
Good morning.	Goeiemôre.
Good afternoon.	Goeiemiddag.
Good evening.	Goeienaand.
Good night.	Goeienag.
Please.	Asseblief.
Thank you (very much).	(Baie) Dankie.
How are you?	Hoe gaan dit?
Good, thank you.	Goed dankie.
Pardon.	Ekskuus.
Yes.	Ja.
No.	Nee.
What?	Wat?
How?	Hoe?
How many/much?	Hoeveel?
Where?	Waar?
Do you speak English?	Praat U Engels?
Do you speak Afrikaans?	Praat U Afrikaans?
I only understand a little Afrikaans.	Ek verstaan net 'n bietjie Afrikaans.
Where are you from?	Waarvandaan kom U?
from ...	van ...
son/boy	seun
daughter/girl	dogter
wife	vrou
husband	eggenoot
mother	ma
father	pa
sister	suster
brother	broer
nice/good/pleasant	lekker
bad	sleg
cheap	goedkoop
expensive	duur
party/rage	jol

Shopping & Services

art gallery	kunsgalery
bank	bank
building	gebou
church	kerk
city	stad
city centre	middestad
emergency	nood
enquiries	navrae
exit	uitgang
information	inligting
office	kantoor
pharmacy/chemist	apteek
police	polisie
police station	polisiestasie
post office	poskantoor
rooms	kamers
tourist bureau	toeristeburo
town	dorp

Transport

avenue	laan
car	kar
freeway	vrymaak

highway	snelweg	6		ses
road	pad, weg	7		sewe
station	stasie	8		ag
street	straat	9		nege
track	spoor	10		tien
traffic light	verkeerslig	11		elf
utility/pick-up	bakkie	12		twaalf
		13		dertien
arrival	aankoms	14		veertien
departure	vertrek	15		vyftien
one way ticket	enkel kaartjie	16		sestien
return ticket	retoer kaartjie	17		sewentien
to	na	18		agtien
from	van	19		negentien
left	links	20		twintig
right	regs	21		een en twintig
at the corner	op die hoek	30		dertig
travel	reis	40		veertig
		50		vyftig
		60		sestig

In the Country

bay	baai	70	sewentig
beach	strand	80	tagtig
caravan park	woonwapark	90	negentig
field/plain	veld	100	honderd
ford	drif	1000	duisend
game reserve	wildtuin		
hiking trail	wandelpad		
lake	meer		
marsh	vlei		
mountain	berg		
river	rivier		

NDEBELE

Ndebele (isiNdebele) is spoken as a first language in relatively small numbers in South Africa's northern provinces.

Time & Days

When?	Wanneer?	**Hello.**	Lotsha.
am/pm	vm/nm	**Goodbye.**	Khamaba kuhle/Sala kuhle.
soon	nou-nou	**Yes.**	I-ye.
today	vandag	**No.**	Awa.
tomorrow	môre	**Please.**	Ngibawa.
yesterday	gister	**Thank you.**	Ngiyathokaza.
daily/weekly	daagliks/weekblad	**What's your name?**	Ungubani ibizo lakho?
public holiday	openbare vakansiedag	**My name is ...**	Ibizo lami ngu ...
		I come from ...	Ngibuya e ...

NORTHERN SOTHO

Monday	Maandag (Ma)
Tuesday	Dinsdag (Di)
Wednesday	Woensdag (Wo)
Thursday	Donderdag (Do)
Friday	Vrydag (Vr)
Saturday	Saterdag (Sa)
Sunday	Sondag (So)

Most mother-tongue speakers of Northern Sotho (Sepedi) inhabit South Africa's north-eastern provinces, with the vast majority to be found in Limpopo.

Numbers

1	een	**Hello.**	Thobela.
2	twee	**Goodbye.**	Sala gabotse.
3	drie	**Yes.**	Ee.
4	vier	**No.**	Aowa.
5	vyf	**Please.**	Ke kgopela.
		Thank you.	Ke ya leboga.
		What's your name?	Ke mang lebitso la gago?
		My name is ...	Lebitso laka ke ...
		I come from ...	Ke bowa kwa ...

SOUTHERN SOTHO

Southern Sotho (Sesotho) is one of two official languages in Lesotho (English being the other). It is also spoken by the Basotho people in the Free State, North-West Province and Gauteng in South Africa. It's useful to know some words and phrases if you're planning to visit Lesotho, especially if you want to trek in remote areas.

Hello.	*Dumela.*
Greetings father.	*Lumela ntate.*
Peace father.	*Khotso ntate.*
Greetings mother.	*Lumela 'me.*
Peace mother.	*Khotso 'me.*
Greetings brother.	*Lumela abuti.*
Peace brother.	*Khotso abuti.*
Greetings sister.	*Lumela ausi.*
Peace sister.	*Khotso ausi.*

There are three commonly used ways of saying 'How are you?':

How are you?	*O kae?* (sg)
	Le kae? (pl)
How do you live?	*O phela joang?* (sg)
	Le phela joang? (pl)
How did you get up?	*O tsohile joang?* (sg)
	Le tsohile joang? (pl)

The responses are:

I'm here.	*Ke teng.* (sg)
	Re teng. (pl)
I live well.	*Ke phela hantle.* (sg)
	Re phela hantle. (pl)
I got up well.	*Ke tsohile hantle.* (sg)
	Re tsohile hantle. (pl)

These questions and answers are quite interchangeable. Someone could ask you *O phela joang?* and you could answer *Ke teng.*

When trekking, people always ask *Lea kae?* (Where are you going?) and *O tsoa kae?* or the plural *Le tsoa kae?* (Where have you come from?). When parting, use the following expressions:

Stay well.	*Sala hantle.* (sg)
	Salang hantle. (pl)
Go well.	*Tsamaea hantle.* (sg)
	Tsamaeang hantle. (pl)

'Thank you' is *kea leboha*, pronounced 'ke·ya le·bo·wa'. The herd boys often ask for *chelete* (money) or *lipompong* (sweets), pronounced 'dee·pom·pong'. If you want to say 'I don't have any', the answer is *ha dio*, pronounced 'ha dee·o'.

SWATI

Swati (siSwati) is one of two official languages in Swaziland (the other is English) and is also widely spoken as a first language in South Africa's Mpumalanga province. It's very similar to Zulu, and the two languages are mutually intelligible.

Hello. (to one person)	*Sawubona.* (lit: 'I see you')
Hello. (to more than one person)	*Sanibonani.*
How are you?	*Kunjani?*
I'm fine.	*Kulungile.*
We're very well.	*Natsi sikhona.*
Goodbye. (if leaving)	*Salakahle.* (lit: 'stay well')
Goodbye. (if staying)	*Hambakahle.* (lit: 'go well')
Please.	*Ngicela.*
I thank you.	*Ngiyabonga.*
We thank you.	*Siyabonga.*
Yes.	*Yebo.* (this is also a common all-purpose greeting)
No.	*Cha.* (pronounced as a click)
Sorry.	*Lucolo.*
What's your name?	*Ngubani libito lakho?*
My name is ...	*Libitolami ngingu ...*
I'm from ...	*Ngingewekubuya e ...*
Do you have?	*Une yini?*
How much?	*Malini?*
Is there a bus to ...?	*Kukhona ibhasi yini leya?*
When does it leave?	*Isuka nini?*
Where is the tourist office?	*Likuphi lihovisi leti vakashi?*

today	*lamuhla*
tomorrow	*kusasa*
yesterday	*itolo*
morning	*ekuseni*
afternoon	*entsambaba*
evening	*kusihlwa*
night	*ebusuku*

TSONGA

Tsonga (Xitsonga) is spoken as a first language in South Africa's north, predominantly in the provinces of Limpopo and Gauteng, and to a lesser extent in Mpumalanga and North-West Province.

Hello.	*Avusheni.* (morning)
	Inhelekani. (afternoon)
	Riperile. (evening)
Goodbye.	*Salani kahle.*

Yes.	Hi swona.
No.	A hi swona.
Please.	Nakombela.
Thank you.	I nkomu.
What's your name?	U mani vito ra wena?
My name is ...	Vito ra mina i ...
I come from ...	Ndzihuma e ...

TSWANA

Tswana (Setswana) is spoken in South Africa as a first language mainly in North-West Province and Gauteng, with lesser numbers of first language speakers in the eastern areas of Northern Cape and the western parts of the Free State.

Hello.	Dumela.
Goodbye.	Sala sentle.
Yes.	Ee.
No.	Nnya.
Please.	Ke a kopa.
Thank you.	Ke a leboga.
What's your name?	Leina la gago ke mang?
My name is ...	Leina la me ke ...
I come from ...	Ke tswa ...

VENDA

Venda (Tshivenda) is spoken mainly in the northeastern border region of South Africa's Limpopo province.

Hello.	Ndi matseloni. (morning)
	Ndi masiari. (afternoon)
	Ndi madekwana. (evening)
Goodbye.	Kha vha sale zwavhudi.
Yes.	Ndi zwone.
No.	A si zwone.
Please.	Ndikho u humbela.
Thank you.	Ndo livhuwa.
What's your name?	Zina lavho ndi nnyi?
My name is ...	Zina langa ndi ...
I come from ...	Ndi bva ...

XHOSA

Xhosa (isiXhosa) is the language of the Xhosa people. It's the dominant indigenous language in South Africa's Eastern Cape province, although you'll meet Xhosa speakers throughout the region.

It's worth noting that bawo is a term of respect used when addressing an older man.

Good morning.	Molo.
Goodnight.	Rhonanai.
Do you speak English?	Uyakwazi ukuthetha siNgesi?

Are you well?	Uphilile na namhlanje?
Yes, I'm well.	Ewe, ndiphilile kanye.
Where are you from?	Uvela phi na okanye ngaphi na?
I'm from ...	Ndivela ...
When will we arrive?	Siya kufika nini na?
The road is good.	Indlela ilungile.
The road is bad.	Indlela imbi.
I'm lost.	Ndilahlekile.
Is this the road to ...?	Yindlela eya ... yini le?
Would you show me the way to ...?	Ungandibonisa na indlela eye ...?
Is it possible to cross the river?	Kunokwenzeka ukuwela umlambo?
How much is it?	Idla ntoni na?

day	usuku
week	iveki
month (moon)	inyanga
east	empumalanga
west	entshonalanga

ZULU

Zulu (isiZulu) is the language of the people of the same name. In terms of numbers, it is South Africa's predominant first language, with most mother-tongue speakers residing in KwaZulu-Natal.

As with several other Nguni languages, Zulu uses a variety of 'clicks' that take some dedicated practice to master to any degree. Many people don't try, although it's worth the effort, if just to provide amusement for your listeners. To ask a question, add na to the end of a sentence.

Hello.	Sawubona.
Goodbye.	Sala kahle.
Please.	Jabulisa.
Thank you.	Ngiyabonga.
Yes.	Yebo.
No.	Cha.
Excuse me.	Uxolo.
Where does this road go?	Iqondaphi lendlela na?
Which is the road to ...?	Iphi indlela yokuya ku ...?
Is it far?	Kukude yini?
north	inyakatho
south	iningizimu
east	impumalanga
west	intshonalanga
water	amanzi
food	ukudla
lion	ibhubesi
rhino (black)	ubhejane
rhino (white)	umkhombe

Glossary

For more food and drink terms, see the Menu Decoder (p96) and Food & Drinks Glossary (p97); for general terms see the Language chapter (p651).

amahiya – traditional Swazi robe
ANC – African National Congress; national democratic organisation formed in 1912 to represent blacks
AWB – Afrikaner Weerstandsbeweging, Afrikaner Resistance Movement; an Afrikaner extremist right-wing group

bakkie – pick-up truck
balimo – ancestors (Sotho)
Bantu – literally 'people'; during the apartheid era, used derogatorily to refer to blacks; today, used only in reference to ethnolinguistics – ie Bantu languages, Bantu-speaking peoples
Bantustans – see homelands
BCP – Basotholand Congress Party
Big Five (the) – lion, leopard, elephant, Cape buffalo and black rhino
bilharzia – another name for schistosomiasis, a disease caused by blood flukes, passed on by freshwater snails
biltong – dried meat
bittereinders – 'bitter enders' in Afrikaans; Boer resistors in the 1899–1902 South African War who fought until the 'bitter end'
BNP – Basotholand National Party
bobotie – curried mince with a topping of savoury egg custard
Boers – see Trekboers
braai – short for braaivleis, a barbecue at which meat is cooked over an open fire (Afrikaans)
Broederbond – secret society open only to Protestant Afrikaner men; was highly influential under National Party rule
bubblegum – a form of township music influenced by Western pop
byala – traditional beer

coloureds – apartheid-era term used to refer to those of mixed-race descent

dagga – marijuana, also known as *zol*
diamantveld – diamond fields
difaqane – 'forced migration' of many of Southern Africa's Nguni peoples; known as *mfecane* in Zulu
dorp – small village or rural settlement
drostdy – residence of a Landdrost

free-camp – camping where you want, away from a formal campsite; permission should be sought and money offered
fynbos – literally 'fine-leafed bush', primarily proteas, heaths and ericas

gogo – grandmother (Zulu)

highveld – high-altitude grassland region
homelands – areas established for blacks under apartheid and considered independent countries by South Africa (never accepted by UN); reabsorbed into South Africa after 1994

IFP – Inkatha Freedom Party; black political movement, founded around 1975 and lead by Chief Mangosouthu Buthelezi, working against apartheid
igogogo – musical instrument made from an oil can
iGqirha – Xhosa spiritual healer
impi – Zulu warrior
indunas – tribal headmen
inyanga – medicine man and herbalist who also studies patterns of thrown bones
isicathamiya – a soft-shoe-shuffle style of vocal music from KwaZulu-Natal
iXhwele – Xhosa herbalist

jol – party, good time

karamat – tomb of a Muslim saint
Khoekhoen – pastoralist San
Khoesaan – collective term referring to the closely related San and Khoekhoen peoples
kloof – ravine
kloofing – canyoning
knobkerry – traditional African weapon; a stick with a round knob at the end, used as a club or missile
kommando – Boer militia unit
kopje – small hill
kraal – a hut village, often with an enclosure for livestock; also a Zulu fortified village
kroeg – bar
kwaito – form of township music; a mix of mbaqanga, jive, hip-hop, house, ragga and other dance styles
kwela – township interpretation of American swing music

Landdrost – an official acting as local administrator, tax collector and magistrate
lapa – a circular building with low walls and a thatched roof, used for cooking, partying etc

LCD – Lesotho Congress for Democracy

lekgotla – place of gathering

lekker – very good, enjoyable or tasty

lekolulo – a flute-like instrument played by herd boys (Sotho)

lesokoana – wooden stick or spoon, traditionally used for stirring mealie pap

liqhaga – 'bottles' that are so tightly woven that they are used for carrying water

lowveld – low-altitude area, having scrub vegetation

maskanda – Zulu form of guitar playing

matjieshuis – Afrikaans term for traditional woven Nama 'mat' huts

mbaqanga – form of township music; literally 'dumpling' in Zulu, combining church choirs, doo-wop and sax jive

mdube – vocal style mixing European and African church choirs

mfecane – see *difaqane*

minwane – dinosaur footprints

Mkhulumnchanti – Swazi deity

mokorotlo – conical hat worn by the Basotho

molianyeoe – see *mokorotlo*

moraba-raba – popular board game played with wooden beads and four rows of hollows; known elsewhere in Africa as *mancala* and *bao*

moroka-pula – rainmaker

mqashiyo – similar vocal style to mbaqanga

muti – traditional medicine

Ncwala – Swazi first-fruits ceremony

ndlovukazi – she-elephant, and traditional title of the Swazi royal mother

ngaca – (also *ngaka*) learned man

ngwenyama – lion, and traditional title of the Swazi king

PAC – Pan African Congress; political organisation of blacks founded in 1959 to work for majority rule and equal rights

piri-piri – hot pepper

pinotage – a type of wine, a cross between Pinot Noir and Hermitage or Shiraz

pont – river ferry

Poqo – armed wing of the PAC

rikki – an open, small van used as public transport in Cape Town

robot – traffic light

rondavel – a round hut with a conical roof

San – nomadic hunter-gatherers who were South Africa's earliest inhabitants

sangoma – traditional healer

sandveld – dry, sandy belt

setolo-tolo – stringed instrument played with the mouth by men (Sotho)

shebeen – drinking establishment in black township; once illegal, now merely unlicensed

slaghuis – butchery

slenter – fake diamond

snoek – firm-fleshed migratory fish that appears off the Cape in June and July; served smoked, salted or curried

sourveld – a type of grassland

swart gevaar – 'black threat'; term coined by Afrikaner nationalists during the 1920s

Telkom – government telecommunications company

thkolosi – small, maliciously playful beings (Sotho)

thomo – stringed instrument played by women (Sotho)

thornveld – a vegetation belt dominated by acacia thorn trees and related species

tokoloshe – evil spirits, similar to the Sotho *thkolosi* (Xhosa)

township – planned urban settlement of blacks and coloureds; legacy of the apartheid era

Trekboers – the first Dutch who trekked off into the interior of what is now largely Western Cape; later shortened to Boers

trokkie – truck stop

tronk – jail (Afrikaans)

tuk-tuk – motorised tricycle

uitlanders – 'foreigners'; originally the name given by Afrikaners to the immigrants who poured into the Transvaal after the discovery of gold

Umkhonto we Sizwe – armed wing of the ANC

veld – elevated open grassland (pronounced 'felt')

velskoene – handmade leather shoes

VOC – Vereenigde Oost-Indische Compagnie (Dutch East India Company)

volk – collective Afrikaans term for Afrikaners

volkstaal – people's language (Afrikaans)

volkstaat – an independent, racially pure Boer state (Afrikaans)

Voortrekkers – original Afrikaner settlers of Orange Free State and Transvaal who migrated from the Cape Colony in the 1830s in search of greater independence

Behind the Scenes

THIS BOOK

This is the 7th edition of *South Africa, Lesotho & Swaziland*. The 1st edition of this book was researched and written by Richard Everist and Jon Murray. The 2nd, 3rd and 4th editions were updated by Jon Murray and Jeff Williams. The 5th edition was updated by Simon Richmond, Alan Murphy, Kim Wildman and Andrew Burke. The 6th edition was updated by Mary Fitzpatrick, Becca Blond, Gemma Pitcher, Matt Warren and Simon Richmond. This 7th edition was updated by Mary Fitzpatrick, Kate Armstrong, Becca Blond, Michael Kohn, Simon Richmond and Al Simmonds. Also contributing were Jane Cornwell (Music); Dr Caroline Evans (Health); and Chester Mackley, David Malherbe, Patrick Moroney and Nic Vorster (surfing boxed texts).

This guidebook was commissioned in Lonely Planet's Melbourne office, and produced by the following:

Commissioning Editors Will Gourlay; Lucy Monie; Marg Toohey; Tasmin McNaughtan; Janine Eberle
Coordinating Editors Dianne Schallmeiner; Trent Holden
Coordinating Cartographer Erin McManus
Coordinating Layout Designer Vicki Beale
Managing Editor Suzannah Shwer
Managing Cartographer Shahara Ahmed
Assisting Editors Elizabeth Anglin; Yvonne Byron; Monique Choy; Pete Cruttenden; Brooke Lyons; Anne Mulvaney
Assisting Cartographers James Ellis; Matthew Kelly; Valentina Kremenchutskaya; Simon Tillema
Cover Designer Annika Roojun

Language Content Coordinator Quentin Frayne
Project Manager Chris Love

Thanks to Sally Darmody; Jennifer Garrett; Kate McDonald; Raphael Richards; Celia Wood

THANKS
KATE ARMSTRONG

Many thanks to Will Gourlay and Mary Fitzpatrick for this great African adventure. Also to navigator extraordinaire Tom, for his hilarity and wit – and the meander. In KZN: Pat, Keith, Donnée, Linda, Molly Barkes, Russell Suchet, Roland Vorwerk, Jeff Gaisford, Liz Spiret, Andy and Sheila. For the best of African hospitality, thank you Camilla, Carlos and Rose. In Lesotho: three cheers to the warmth and humour of the Spontaneous Club – Di Jones, Tony Hocking and Elmar Neethling, and thanks to Stephen Gill, Colin Pedlar, Sponky Rakhetla and the staff at the Tourism Information Centre in Maseru. In Swaziland: Millen family, thanks for a wild new year. A massive *ngiyabonga* to Elmar, whose passion, enthusiasm and 4am starts never cease to amaze me.

BECCA BLOND

Aaron and Shari, you guys are the best! Thanks for putting up with travelling through the Free State. I owe you a cold Castle. Big thanks to my co-authors at Lonely Planet and also to Will Gourlay for giving me the chance to return to my favourite country. On the road, I owe a lot of people some big thanks including John Martin at North-South Backpackers

---

THE LONELY PLANET STORY

The story begins with a classic travel adventure: Tony and Maureen Wheeler's 1972 journey across Europe and Asia to Australia. There was no useful information about the overland trail then, so Tony and Maureen published the first Lonely Planet guidebook to meet a growing need.

From a kitchen table, Lonely Planet has grown to become the largest independent travel publisher in the world, with offices in Melbourne (Australia), Oakland (USA) and London (UK). Today Lonely Planet guidebooks cover the globe. There is an ever-growing list of books and information in a variety of media. Some things haven't changed. The main aim is still to make it possible for adventurous travellers to get out there – to explore and better understand the world.

At Lonely Planet we believe travellers can make a positive contribution to the countries they visit – if they respect their host communities and spend their money wisely. Every year 5% of company profit is donated to charities around the world.

(Pretoria), Ilsa Roberts at Amphitheatre Backpackers (the Drakensberg), Bruce Weyer in Clarens, Yurietta at the Kloof Lodge (Bloem), Elly and Garth at Wildside Backpackers, and Pieter and Magda King in Upington. As always, thanks to my family, David, Patricia, Jessica, Vera, Jennie and John for their constant support. To Aaron, thanks not only for hitting the road for me, but also for always being there when I need you most.

MICHAEL KOHN

First off, thanks to the great team of editors and cartographers at the Lonely Planet office in Melbourne, especially Will Gourlay and Shahara Ahmed. Thanks also to my fellow authors and Mary Fitzpatrick for bringing it all together. In South Africa, thanks to Garth in Sabie, Andre in Graskop, Gustav in Waterval Boven, Paul in Nelspruit, Sean in Cintsa and the helpful crew at Amapondo. Cheers to the many anonymous people who helped me find my way while getting lost on the South African back roads. Back home, thanks to friends and family, especially Baigalmaa for her patience and support.

SIMON RICHMOND

As always it's been a pleasure working with Cape Town's clued up tourism professionals and enjoying the company of the fun people who live there. Many thanks then to Mmatsatsi Ramasodi and her team at Cape Routes Unlimited; Mariëtte du Toit and the guys at Cape Town Tourism; and Fiona Kalk and all at Table Mountain National Park (especially the great guides on the Hoerikwaggo Trail). As always the wonderful Sheryl Ozinsky was on hand for insider advice and recommendations as were my Capetonian guardian angels Lee and Toni. Thanks to both Brent Meersman and Lucy Jameson for their various insights and lovely company, and to fellow author Al Simmonds for his advice. Thope Lekau and Faizal Gangat were a great help out in the Cape Flats, as were Fiona Hinds, Sally Grierson, Trish Wood, Allan Wellburn and Jenny Trikoven in the deep south of the peninsula. Thanks to Natasha for the apartment and last, but not least, to Tonny for all his love and support.

AL SIMMONDS

A big thanks, of course, to Gabi who put up with my grumpiness, my continual travelling and, upon my return, coming to bed at 3am right up until deadline. And thanks to her and Jean for making sure I wasn't stuck on my own in the Sandveld sand on New Year's Eve. Anastacia, from Soweto Accommodation Association, you're a gracious host, and Geoff Higgo, from Around About Cars, you're a star. Thanks to Pretoria Backpackers and Highfield Backpackers in Knysna. Thanks to my dad for trusting me with his car in the Winelands, and to my mum for putting me up (and putting up with me) in Jozi. And, of course, many thanks to all the people on my travels who made me feel I had a home away from home. And finally, thanks to all the Lonely Planet staff who supported me and gave me useful advice.

OUR READERS
Many thanks to the travellers who used the last edition and wrote to us with helpful hints, useful advice and interesting anecdotes:

A Helen Abbott, Gillian Ackroyd, Brett Adamson, Liz Agostino, Vanessa Alberts, Zoe Alexander, Maja Arnold, Junjun Arpon, Britt Ashton, Claire Atkins **B** Frits Bakker, Jonathon & Claire Barnes, Trudie Barry, Hans Beckers, Bart Bender, Jan Bennink, Rob Bianchi, Klaus Blex, Damian Blogg, Cynthia Bothma, Carol Bouchard, John & Jill Bowden, Andrew Branch, Clare Brennan, Catherine Brinkley, Ian Brown, Christian Burtchen, John Butler, Christian Byhahn **C** Eleanor Callen, Fabienne Callens, Marco Cardillo, Marina Carmona, Faurie Caroline, Christophe Charier, Caroline Charlton, Odette Claassen, Mary Clay, Robin Coates, Alarmi Coetzee, Brian Coughlan, Allan Couthard **D** Laura Dalton, John Daniel, Gerald Davie, A J de Jesus Pinto, Floor de Vink, Karin Degenaar, Suzanne

---

SEND US YOUR FEEDBACK

We love to hear from travellers – your comments keep us on our toes and help make our books better. Our well-travelled team reads every word on what you loved or loathed about this book. Although we cannot reply individually to postal submissions, we always guarantee that your feedback goes straight to the appropriate authors, in time for the next edition. Each person who sends us information is thanked in the next edition – and the most useful submissions are rewarded with a free book.

To send us your updates – and find out about Lonely Planet events, newsletters and travel news – visit our award-winning website: **www.lonelyplanet.com/feedback**.

Note: We may edit, reproduce and incorporate your comments in Lonely Planet products such as guidebooks, websites and digital products, so let us know if you don't want your comments reproduced or your name acknowledged. For a copy of our privacy policy visit www.lonelyplanet.com/privacy.

Deuleer, Alison Dieguez, Laura Dimopolus Madronal, Luc & Erna Doesburg, Laura Dominguez, Anouk Donker, Heike Doppstaedt, Robyn Doyle, Kornelia Drinhausen, Carien du Plessis **E** Steve Edwards, Markus Eichinger **F** Terri Festa, Arne Fleissner, Tuula Forsskåhl, Susan Freese **G** Rob Gabriel, Fabiana Gamberini, Marco Gandini, Simon George, Edwin Greyling, Peggy Gumede **H** Theo Hafmans, Marlene Haines, Paul Hand, Felix Hardach, James Harding, Haley Harvey, Wolfgang Haslinger, Brendan Haworth, Toby Hayes, Karin Heemskerk, Vincent Heemskerk, Sabine Heiland, Ken Henley, Chris Hillidge, Andrew Hindmarch, Tom Hollington, Corne de Hoon, Peter Hopley, David Howes, Anne Hughes, Niki Hurst, Julie-Ann Hurwood **J** Victoria Jacobsson, Johnathon Jacoby, Florence Jegoux, Sascha Jillich, Rob & Michael Joosten, Karen Julyan **K** Julia Karbaum, Raphael Keller, Marion Kelly, Phil Kenealy, Karen Kenny, Miriam Kersten, David Kezilas, David Knieter, Wilma Koeppen, Cheryl Kovarskis, Michal Kyselica **L** Jodi Lancaster, Susanne Laven, Ashley Leigh, Keith LeMieux, Rochelle Lester, Kaung-Chiau Lew, Jessy Lipperts, Ruth Lucas, Antje Ludewig, Renee Lustman, Lisa Lyons **M** Alexis Marchand, Claudia Marti, Horst Marz, Kirsty Mcadam, Alistair & Solveig McCleery, Mxolisi Mdluli, Amy Melsaether, John Mileham, Andrew Millar, Alan Mitzner, Charles Mondahl, Amanda Moore, John Moratelli, Arnd Morgenroth **N** Tessa Nagels, Amy Nahabedian, Tinie & Elly Need, Leni Neoptolemos, Amanda Nicholl, Kristopher Nichols, Eva Nott, Simon Nutt **O** Thea Oeschger, Amanda Oostendorp, Carsten Ottesen, Keith Otto **P** Tim Parker, Yogi Patel, Giorgio Perversi, Dale Pesmen, Monique Philipse, Sara Phillips,

Peter Phillp, Gareth Pike, Thomas Preimesberger, Anne Pyke **R** Howard Radley, Markus Radner, Michael Read, Meloney Retallack, Christy Robinson, Egbert Ruschitzka, Joshua Russell **S** Sally & Robert Sale, Melanie Schneider, Perry Schneiderman, Michael & Juanita Schofiled, Alette Schoon, Mariska Schrever, Thorste Schröder, Hans Schuppert, Katie Sewell, Barbara Sheridan, Kerry & Tony Shilling, Raymond Short, Göran Simonsson, Maja Sjöskog, Pieter Slager, Helen Smith, Julia Smith, Lynda Smith, Paul Smith, Michelle Solomon, Martin Spierings, Lynne Stephenson, Henk Stockmans, Simone Strothers Jack, Richard Stubbs **T** Ben Taylor, Donny Thieme, Ger Thijsen, William & Debra Thomson, Christopher Tilbury, James Tomlinson, John Towler, Linda Treviño **U** Shaun Unger, Wynand Uys **V** Sjoerd van de Steene, Marije van der Kooi, Jaap van der Meer, Thimo van Riet, Johan van Splunter, Jeffrey van Wylick, Jeremy Vera **W** Ian Walker, Chris Walton, Kate Walton, Vic Warren, Natalie Weber, Harald Wegele, Brad & Karin Weller, Rachel West, Mike Whillis, Jeff Widdup, Robert Wienand, Monica Wiese, Ro Wietecha, Susan Wilburn, Thomas Wiser, Debbie Wolfe, Jenny Woodford **Y** Brian Young **Z** Jeffrey Zoet, Pablo Zorzoli

ACKNOWLEDGMENTS

Many thanks to the following for the use of their content:

Globe on back cover ©Mountain High Maps 1993 Digital Wisdom, Inc.

Index

INDEX

INDEX

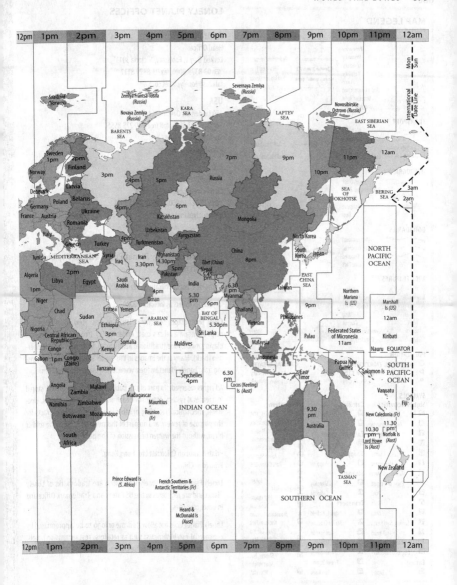

MAP LEGEND

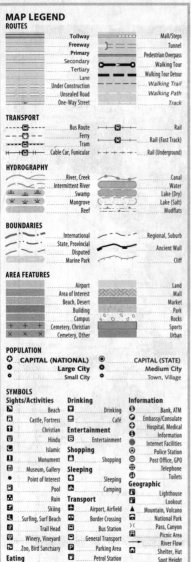

ROUTES

Tollway	Mall/Steps
Freeway	Tunnel
Primary	Pedestrian Overpass
Secondary	Walking Tour
Tertiary	Walking Tour Detour
Lane	Walking Trail
Under Construction	Walking Path
Unsealed Road	Track
One-Way Street	

TRANSPORT

Bus Route	Rail
Ferry	Rail (Fast Track)
Tram	
Cable Car, Funicular	Rail (Underground)

HYDROGRAPHY

River, Creek	Canal
Intermittent River	Water
Swamp	Lake (Dry)
Mangrove	Lake (Salt)
Reef	Mudflats

BOUNDARIES

International	Regional, Suburb
State, Provincial	Ancient Wall
Disputed	Cliff
Marine Park	

AREA FEATURES

Airport	Land
Area of Interest	Mall
Beach, Desert	Market
Building	Park
Campus	Rocks
Cemetery, Christian	Sports
Cemetery, Other	Urban

POPULATION

CAPITAL (NATIONAL)	CAPITAL (STATE)
Large City	Medium City
Small City	Town, Village

SYMBOLS

Sights/Activities	Drinking	Information
Beach	Drinking	Bank, ATM
Castle, Fortress	Café	Embassy/Consulate
Christian	**Entertainment**	Hospital, Medical
Hindu	Entertainment	Information
Islamic	**Shopping**	Internet Facilities
Monument	Shopping	Police Station
Museum, Gallery	**Sleeping**	Post Office, GPO
Point of Interest	Sleeping	Telephone
Pool	Camping	Toilets
Ruin	**Transport**	**Geographic**
Skiing	Airport, Airfield	Lighthouse
Surfing, Surf Beach	Border Crossing	Lookout
Trail Head	Bus Station	Mountain, Volcano
Winery, Vineyard	General Transport	National Park
Zoo, Bird Sanctuary	Parking Area	Pass, Canyon
Eating	Petrol Station	Picnic Area
Eating	Taxi Rank	River Flow
		Shelter, Hut
		Spot Height
		Waterfall

LONELY PLANET OFFICES

Australia
Head Office
Locked Bag 1, Footscray, Victoria 3011
☎ 03 8379 8000, fax 03 8379 8111
talk2us@lonelyplanet.com.au

USA
150 Linden St, Oakland, CA 94607
☎ 510 893 8555, toll free 800 275 8555
fax 510 893 8572
info@lonelyplanet.com

UK
72–82 Rosebery Ave,
Clerkenwell, London EC1R 4RW
☎ 020 7841 9000, fax 020 7841 9001
go@lonelyplanet.co.uk

Published by Lonely Planet Publications Pty Ltd
ABN 36 005 607 983

© Lonely Planet Publications Pty Ltd 2006

© photographers as indicated 2006

Cover photographs by Lonely Planet Images: Red-billed oxpecker helps maintain a zebra's coat, Adrian Bailey (front); Swazi woman playing *makhoyane* (traditional instrument), Ariadne Van Zandbergen (back). Many of the images in this guide are available for licensing from Lonely Planet Images: www.lonelyplanetimages.com.

Printed through Colorcraft Ltd, Hong Kong.
Printed in China